Dana Facaros and
Michael Pauls

# TUSCANY

'the enduring charm of Tuscany is
in that dreamy glass of wine, in those hills
that look exactly as they did when Piero
painted them, in the bartender who's a
dead ringer for Lorenzo de' Medici...'

**CADOGAN**guides

# About the authors

**Dana Facaros and Michael Pauls** are professional travel writers. They spent three years in a tiny Italian village, where they suffered massive overdoses of food, art and wine, and enjoyed every minute of it. They reckon they could whip 98 per cent of the world's non-Italian population at Trivial Pursuit (except for the sport questions). They now live in southwest France. They have written over 30 guides for Cadogan.

# About the updater

**Gabriella Giganti** is a keen and curious traveller in and outside Italy. Her background in history and the arts supports and nourishes her interest in different places, people and cultures. She lives in London and has worked as a researcher, librarian and translator.

Cadogan Guides
165 The Broadway,
Wimbledon, London. SW19 1NE
info.cadogan@virgin.net
www.cadoganguides.com

The Globe Pequot Press
246 Goose Lane, PO Box 480, Guilford,
Connecticut 06437–0480

Cover and photo essay design by Kicca Tommasi
Book design by Andrew Barker
Cover photographs: John Ferro Sims
Maps © Cadogan Guides,
    drawn by Map Creation Ltd
Editorial Director: Vicki Ingle
Series Editor: Linda McQueen
Editor: Matthew Tanner
Art direction: Sarah Rianhard-Gardner
Indexing: Isobel McLean
Production: Book Production Services

Printed in Italy by Legoprint
A catalogue record for this book is available
    from the British Library
ISBN 1-86011-860-7

# Tuscany
## a photo essay

by John Ferro Sims

01

autumn mist at twilight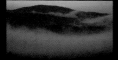

 Palio, Siena

landscape with cypress
trees near Volterra

 Castello Aldo, Certaldo

Il Campo, Siena

Duomo, Florence

cypress trees

landscape with clover
near Volterra

Brunello di Montalcino
vineyard

 Duomo, Sovana

mural, Massa Marittima

Piazza Pio II, Pienza

trees and vineyard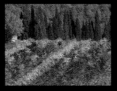

 Leaning Tower, Pisa

landscape with farm
spring near Volterra

Campanio grapes

Chianti barrels

 view through the
Campanile, Florence

pecorino cheese
with herbs

panforte

market, Grosseto

salami-curing room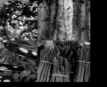

 San Miniato al Monte,
Florence

Lucca

## About the photographer
John Ferro Sims was born of Anglo-Italian parents in
Udine, Italy. He worked successfully for five years as an
investment analyst before quitting the world of money
for a career as a professional photographer which has
taken him around the world. He has published 9 books.

# Introduction

02

A glass of wine before dinner on the garden terrace, the olives glinting in the last flash of the setting sun as the geometric vineyards lose their rigid order in the melting darkness, and only the black daggers of the cypresses stand out against the first stars of the evening – where could you be but Tuscany? It needs no introduction, this famous twilit land, where Titans of art five hundred years ago copied and then outdid nature, and where nature gets her gentle revenge by rivalling art.

Travellers have been coming to central Italy ever since the Middle Ages, to learn, to see and to understand. Most have come with their Baedekers or Ruskins or Berensons in hand, and even today it isn't easy to escape the weight of generations of worthy opinions or to avoid treading on those same old grapes of purple prose. After all, most of what we call Western civilization was either rediscovered or invented here, leaving behind works that have lost none of their power; at times it seems as if the artists of the early 1400s descended from outer space with their secret messages for the imagination. Anyway, to the mass of accumulated opinion we now add ours, for better or worse, but mostly in the hope of provoking some of your own.

But at the end of the day – or, as we are, at the dawn of the 21st century, when times seem to be changing faster than we can or care to – the enduring charm of Tuscany is in that dreamy glass of wine, in those hills that look exactly as they did when Piero painted them, in the bartender who's a dead ringer for Lorenzo de' Medici, in those bewitching Etruscan smiles that seem to have been smiled only yesterday. Things have stayed the same way for centuries not by any accident, or economic reason, or by divine decree of some Tuscan National Trust, but because that's the way people like them. People here make as few concessions to the new millennium as possible, and their Brigadoon may not be for everyone. They're not catching up with the world; the world's catching up with them.

# A Guide to the Guide

After a photo essay to inspire and delight you, the begining of this guide gives you the background information you need to understand Tuscany. The chapter on **History and Art** provides a detailed background to the development and culture of the region, one of the most artistically rich in the world, and includes a directory of some of the artists you are most likely to encounter. **Topics**, a series of short essays, gives more insights into the people of Tuscany and their customs, while **Food and Drink** provides an overview of regional specialities as well as an Italian menu vocabulary.

The comprehensive **Travel** section covers how to get to and around Tuscany, and includes details of specialist tour operators. **Practical A–Z** supplies all the information you are likely to need, on subjects ranging from the climate to official holidays, dealing with the police and even buying a house.

The gazetteer section starts in the treasure-house of **Florence**, and then moves out to the delights of the surrounding countryside with its villages and hill towns, and other major art centres including **Pisa**, **Siena** and **Arezzo**. The gazetteer is divided into sections which focus on a key city or town and the area around it, or on a journey between two featured places.

## Chapter Divisions

EMILIA-ROMAGNA

Pontremoli

**11
LUCCA,
THE GARFAGNANA
& LUNIGIANA**

Abetone

**09
CHIANTI & THE
MUGELLO**

Pistoia

Prato

**12
THE
TUSCAN
COAST**

Lucca

**o8
FLORENCE**

Florence

**10
THE
VALDARNO,
PRATO & PISTOIA**

THE
MARCHES

Pisa

Livorno

Casciana Terme

**09
CHIANTI & THE
MUGELLO**

**16
AREZZO &
ITS PROVINCE**

Sestino

Gorgona

S. Gimignano

Castellina in Chianti

Volterra

Arezzo

T U S C A N Y

Siena

**13
SIENA**

**14
HILL TOWNS
WEST OF SIENA**

Massa
Marittima

Montepulciano

Capraia

Piombino

UMBRIA

*Elba*

**12
THE
TUSCAN
COAST**

**15
SOUTHERN
TUSCANY**

*Pianosa*

Orbetello

LAZIO

*Montecristo*

*Giglio*

N

*Giannutri*

20 km

10 miles

*T y r r h e n i a n   S e a*

The book concludes with a glossary of **Architectural, Artistic and Historical Terms**. A chapter on **Language** supplies essential vocabulary for travelling around and booking hotels etc. There are also suggestions for **Further Reading**.

# Itineraries

## A Week of Roman and Etruscan Sites
1 **Florence** (Archaeology Museum; Etruscan tombs at Sesto Fiorentino) and **Fiesole** (Etruscan Walls, Roman theatre, and museum).
2 **Volterra** (museum, Etruscan arch and Roman theatre).
3–4 The Etruscan cities of the coast: **Populonia**, **Vetulonia**, **Roselle** and **Ansedonia**, with stops at the Archaeology Museum in **Grosseto** and 'Frontone' (temple pediment) in **Orbetello**.
5 **Chiusi** (fine museum and only painted Etruscan tombs in Tuscany).
6 **Arezzo** (Roman amphitheatre and museum).
7 **Cortona** (Etruscan walls, gate, tombs and museum).

## Early Medieval Art and Architecture, in 10 Days
The best in Tuscany before 1200:
1 **Florence** (Baptistry, San Miniato).
2 **Pistoia** (Sant'Andrea, San Giovanni Fuorcivitas).
3 The bizarre **Pieve di Castelvecchio**, near **Pescia**, and **Barga** cathedral.
4 **Lucca** (Cathedral and San Michele).
5 **Pisa** (Piazza of Miracles, Museums and San Piero a Grado).
6 **Rosia**, **Sovicille** and the other churches just west of **Siena**.
7 **Sant'Antimo**, outside **Montalcino** and **Abbadia San Salvatore** (town and abbey).
8 The well-preserved medieval town of **Sovana**, near **Pitigliano**.
9 **Grópina**, near Loro Ciuffenna in the Valdarno, and **Poppi** (Castle).
10 **Stia** (San Pietro and Castello di Romena).

## 8-Day Tour of High Medieval Art and Architecture
1–2 **Florence**: Orsanmichele, Bargello, Cathedral, Palazzo Vecchio, Palazzo Davanzati.
2 **Empoli** (Collegiata and museum) and **Certaldo** (Boccaccio's well-preserved home town).
3 **San Gimignano**: Collegiata frescoes and the city itself – a genuine, extraordinary, medieval monument.
4 **Volterra**: civic buildings and art in Cathedral, San Francesco.
5 **Massa Marittima** and **San Galgano**.
6–8 **Siena**: Palazzo Pubblico, Cathedral – and nearly everything else!

## 11 Days Shooting a Renaissance Loop Outside Florence
Renaissance art somehow seems especially rarefied out in the provinces. Once you've paid your respects to Great Aunt Florence, visit:

1 **Impruneta** (Collegiata), **Certosa di Galluzzo, Lastra a Signa** (Alberti's church) and **Poggio a Caiano**, the archetypal Renaissance villa.

2 **Prato** (Santa Maria delle Carceri, Filippo Lippi's fresco cycle in the Cathedral, Donatello and Michelozzo's pulpit).

3 **Lucca**, for the sculpture of Matteo Civitali and Jacopo della Quercia.

4 **San Gimignano**, which has much of the best painting outside Florence, by Gozzoli, Ghirlandaio, Sodoma, and more.

5 **Siena**, for the Sienese side of the Renaissance (Cathedral, especially pavements, tombs, and Piccolomini Library, and the Pinacoteca).

6–7 The exquisite monastic complex and frescoes at **Monte Oliveto Maggiore**, on the way to Pius II's planned city of **Pienza**; nearby **Montepulciano** for the best of classic Renaissance temples, Sangallo's San Biagio, as well as other churches and palaces.

8 **Cortona** (Renaissance temples, Signorelli and Fra Angelico) and **Monte San Savino**.

9 **Arezzo** (Piero della Francesco's frescoes and S. Maria delle Grazie).

10 More Pieros in **Monterchi** and **Sansepolcro**.

11 **La Verna** (Andrea della Robbia) and over the Passo di Consuma to Florence.

## Villas and Gardens, in a Week or So

This would be a 'Two-Centre Holiday' as all the villas and gardens mentioned are located near Florence and Lucca. Do check the opening hours and do the necessary telephoning before setting out. In **Florence** itself there are beautiful walks around the Boboli Gardens, the villas and gardens of **Arcetri**, the **Villa Stibbert and Garden**, and the villas and gardens in and around **Fiesole**. Then:

1 Medici villas and gardens of **La Petraia, Castello** and **Careggi**.

2 Into the Mugello: Gardens of **Pratolino**, and Medici Villas at **Cafaggiolo** and **Trebbio**.

3 More Medici villas and gardens: **Poggio a Caiano, Villa Artimino** and **Cerreto Guidi**.

4–5 Villas in Chianti: although only the **Castello di Brolio** and **Badia a Coltibuono** are open to the public; other striking estates include: Villa Tattali, Palazzo al Bosco, Villa Le Corti, Poggio Torselli, Vignamaggio, and several around Castellina.

6–7 From **Lucca, Castello Garzoni**, with fabulous gardens, near Collodi, and the three villas northeast of Lucca itself: **Villa Mansi, Villa Torrigiani**, and **Villa Pecci-Blunt**.

## Nature and Scenery

For Tuscany at its least civilized: starting with southern Tuscany's **Monte Amiata**, an isolated patch of lovely mountain forests. **Mediterranean Coastal Scenery**: maquis and pine forests, on **Monte Argentario**, with side trips to **Giglio** and the surrounding marshlands with wildlife reserves and exotic birds, like the **Monti dell'Uccellina**. Further north, there are ancient coastal forests around **Pietrasanta** and **San Rossore**.

**Coastal Mountains**: the **Apuan Alps**, lush, streaked with marble, are located along the coast from Carrara down, while a bit further inland are the dense forests of the **Garfagnana**. Serious **Apennines**: the ridge between Tuscany and Emilia-Romagna, around **Abetone, Firenzuola, Camaldoli** (with its ancient forest), **Pratomagno** (Monte Secchieta, and its panoramic roads), and the enchanting **Casentino**.

## Two Weeks of Wine

For the best of Tuscan DOC wines, and some of the most ravishing scenery:

1 **Florence** to **Carmignano, Cerreto Guidi** and **Vinci** (wines: Carmignano and Chianti).

2 **Montecatini Alta, Collodi** and **Montecarlo** (wines: Bianco della Valdinievole and Montecarlo).

3 South of the Arno to **San Miniato** and environs, and **Certaldo** (wines: Bianco Pisano di S. Torpè and Chianti).

4 **San Gimignano** and **Colle di Val d'Elsa** (wines: Vernaccia di San Gimignano and Chianti Colli Senesi).

5 **Barberino Val d'Elsa** and **San Casciano** to the Florence–Siena wine route, the Chiantigiana and **Greve in Chianti** (wines: Chianti, Chianti Colli Fiorentini and Chianti Classico).

6 **Panzano** and **Radda in Chianti** (wine: Chianti Classico).

7 **Gaiole in Chianti, Castello di Brolio** and **Siena**, with a stop at the Enoteca Nazionale (wines: Chianti Classico and Chianti Colli Senesi).

8 **Montalcino** (wine: Brunello).

9 **Montepulciano** (wine: Vino Nobile).

10 **Cortona** (wine: Bianco Vergine della Valdichiana).

11 **Sovana, Pitigliano, Saturnia** (wines: Morellino di Scansano and Bianco di Pitigliano).

12 Check in at the spa at **Chianciano Terme** for liver repairs!

## One Week of Curiosities

The unexpected, unique side of Tuscany doesn't jump out at you; you'll have to look for it. In **Florence** you spend

1–3 seeing **Galileo's Forefinger** at the Museum of the History of Science; gruesomely realistic **wax anatomical models** at La Specola museum; a **151kg topaz** at the Museum of Mineralogy; a **16th-century Mexican bishop's mitre** made out of feathers, in the Museo degli Argenti; **Islamic and Japanese armour** in the Villa Stibbert; or an ornate **Mozarabic Synagogue** or onion-domed **Russian Orthodox Church**. From there, head to Tuscany's northernmost town, **Pontrémoli**...

4 to see the mysterious **Neolithic statue-steles**, and then down to **Carrara** for the eerie, almost black whiteness of the **marble quarries**.

5 **Pisa**: the **Leaning Tower** is only one of a score of oddities in the Piazza of Miracles; also take a look at the **Turkish war pennants** in Santo Stefano.

6 **Volterra**, to see the *balze* and the unusual **Etruscan sculpture** in the Guarnacci Museum, on your way to the geothermal carnival of the **Metal Hills – geysers and sulphur lakes** around Larderello and Monterotondo.

7 Detour to Elba for **Napoleon's Death Mask**, or even better, inland to **San Galgano**, with its ruined Gothic abbey and genuine **Sword-in-the-stone**.

8 If it's Saturday or Sunday, try the **Giardino dei Tarocchi** (at Capalbio, east of Orbetello), a bizarre collection of colossal modern sculptures, covered in bright ceramics and mirrors, dedicated to the 22 major arcana of the Tarot deck.

# History and Art

# Historical Outline

At times, the history of Tuscany has been a small part of a bigger story – Rome's, or modern Italy's. However, the crucial eras of the Middle Ages and the Renaissance provided a tremendous chronicle of contending city states, each with a complex history of its own. For that reason, we have included detailed histories of the most important towns – Florence, Siena and Pisa – and covered the rest to a lesser extent. Here is a brief historical outline for the region as a whole.

## The Etruscans

Neolithic cultures seem to have occupied this region of Italy since about 4500 BC without distinguishing themselves artistically or politically. The dawn of history in these parts comes with the arrival of the **Etruscans**, though where they came from and precisely when they arrived remains one of the major mysteries of early Mediterranean history. According to their traditions, the Etruscans migrated from western Anatolia, *c.*900 BC. Classical authors were divided on this point; some believed the migration theory, while others saw the Etruscans as the indigenous inhabitants of west-central Italy. Their language remains murky to modern scholars, but the discovery of Etruscan inscriptions on the Greek island of Lemnos, along with other clues, tends to support the Etruscan story.

Whatever it was, they were a talented people, and the great wealth they derived from intensive agriculture, manufacturing, and above all mining (Elba and the Metal Hills) allowed these talents to blossom into opulence by the 7th century BC. Though they gave their name to modern Tuscany, the real centre of Etruscan civilization lay to the south; roughly the coast from Orbetello to Cervéteri (Caere) in Lazio and around Lakes Bolsena and Trasimeno. Never a unified nation, the Etruscans preferred the general Mediterranean model of the independent city state; the 12 greatest dominated central Italy in a federation called the **Dodecapolis**. Which cities were members is uncertain, but the 14 possible cities include *Veii, Cervéteri, Tarquinia* and *Vulci* (in Lazio), *Roselle, Vetulonia* and *Populonia* (on or near the Tuscan coast), *Volterra, Fiesole, Arezzo, Chiusi, Orvieto, Cortona* and *Perugia*.

The Etruscans always maintained extremely close trade and cultural ties with classical Greece. They sold Elban iron and bought Greek culture wholesale; the artistic thieving magpies of antiquity, they adapted every style of Greek art, from the Minoan-style frescoes at Tarquinia to the classical bronzes now in the Florence Museum, and created something of their very own. In expressive portrait sculpture, though, they surpassed even the Greeks.

A considerable mythology has grown up around the Etruscans. Some historians and poets celebrate them as a nation of free peoples, devoted to art, good food and easy living. A less sentimental views shows a slave society run for the benefit of a military, aristocratic élite. Whichever, the art they left behind gives them a place as the most enigmatic, vivid and fascinating people of early Italy. It isn't difficult to see echoes of their culture in everything that has happened in this part of Italy for the last 2,000 years.

## Romans

Etruscan kings once ruled in Rome, but after the establishment of the Republic, this precocious city was to prove the end of the Etruscan world. All of southern Etruria was swallowed up by 358 BC, and internal divisions between the Etruscan cities allowed the Romans to push their conquest inevitably northwards. After the conquest of an Etruscan city, Roman policy was often diabolically clever; by establishing veterans' colonies in new towns nearby to draw off trade, Rome was able to ensure the withering of Etruscan culture and the slow extinction of many of Etruria's greatest cities.

Most of the Etruscan cities joined with neighbouring peoples, the Unbrii of Umbria and Piceni of the Marches, in the Social Wars of 92–89 BC, the last doomed attempt of the Italians to fight free of Roman imperialism. Two distinct cultures occupied the northern fringes. The wandering **Celts**, who occupied all northern Italy, often made themselves at home in the Apennines and northern Etruria; their influence on the region's culture is slight. Finally there was the unnamed culture of the rugged **Lunigiana**, around Pontrémoli, a people who carried their Neolithic customs and religion (see the statue-steles in the Pontrémoli museum) well into the modern era.

Under the empire, Etruria was relatively quiet, though the region experienced a north–south economic split to mirror the bigger one beginning across Italy. Southern Etruria, the old Etruscan heartland, shrivelled and died under Roman misrule, never to recover. The north became more prosperous, and important new cities appeared: Lucca, Pisa, Florence and, to a lesser extent, Gubbio and Siena.

## The Dark Ages

Later Italians' willingness to create fanciful stories about the 'barbarian invasions' makes it hard to define what did happen in this troubled time. The first (5th-century) campaigns of the **Goths** in Italy did not seem to cause too much damage, but the curtain finally came down on Roman civilization with the Greek-Gothic wars of 536–563, when Eastern Emperor Justinian and his generals Belisarius and Narsus attempted to recapture Italy for Byzantium. The chronicles of many cities record the devastation of the Gothic King, Totila (the sack of Florence), though the Imperial aggressors were undoubtedly just as bad. In any case, the damage to an already weakened society was fatal, and the wars opened the way for the conquest of much of Italy by the terrible **Lombards** (568), who established the Duchy of Spoleto, with loose control over much of central Italy. Lucca, the late Roman and Gothic capital of Etruria, alone managed to keep the Lombards out. By this time, low-lying cities like Florence had practically disappeared, while the remnants of the other towns survived under the control of local barons, or occasionally under their bishops. Feudal warfare and marauding became endemic. In the 800s even a band of Arabs came looting and pillaging up the Valnerina, almost in the centre of the peninsula.

By the 10th century, things were looking up. Florence had re-established itself, and built its famous baptistry. The old counts of Lucca extended their power to become counts of Tuscany, under the Attoni family, lords of Canossa. As the leading power in the region, they made themselves a force in European affairs. In 1077, the great

Countess Matilda, allied with the Pope, humbled Emperor Henry IV at Canossa – the famous 'penance in the snow' during the struggles over investiture. Perhaps most important of all was the growth of the maritime city of **Pisa** which gave Tuscany a window on the world, building wealth through trade and inviting cultural influences from France, Byzantium and the Muslim world.

## Medieval Tuscany

By 1000, with the new millennium, all of northern Italy was poised to rebuild the civilization that had been lost centuries before. In Tuscany, as elsewhere, increasing trade had created a rebirth of towns, each doing its best to establish its independence from local nobles or bishops, and to increase its influence at the expense of its neighbours. Thus a thousand minor squabbles were played out against the background of the major issues of the day; first the conflict over investiture in the 11th century, evolving into the endless factional struggles of **Guelphs** and **Ghibellines** after 1215 (*see* pp.135–7). Throughout, the cities were forced to choose sides between the partisans of the popes and those of the emperors. The Ghibellines' brightest hours came with the reigns of strong Hohenstaufen emperors **Frederick I Barbarossa** (1152–90) and his grandson **Frederick II** (1212–46), both of whom spent much time in Tuscany. An early Guelph wave came with the papacy of **Innocent III** (1198–1216), most powerful of the medieval pontiffs, and the Guelphs would come back to dominate Tuscany after the invasion of Charles of Anjou in 1261. Florence, Arezzo and Lucca were the mainstays of the Guelphs, while Pisa, Pistoia and Siena usually supported the Ghibellines.

In truth, it was every city for itself. By 1200, most towns had become free *comuni*; their imposing public buildings can be seen in almost every corner of Tuscany. All the trouble they caused fighting each other (at first with citizen militias, later increasingly with the use of hired *condottieri*) never troubled the booming economy. Florence and Siena became bankers to all Europe, great building programmes went up, beginning with the Pisa cathedral complex in the 1100s, and the now tamed and urbanized nobles built fantastical skyscraper skylines of tower-fortresses in the towns. Above all, it was a great age for culture, the age of Dante (b. 1265) and Giotto (b. 1266). Another feature of the time was the 13th-century religious revival, dominated by the figure of St Francis of Assisi.

## Background of the Renaissance

Florence, biggest and richest of the Tuscan cities, increased its influence all through the 1300s, gaining Prato and Pistoia, and finally winning a seaport with the capture of declining Pisa in 1406. This set the stage for the relative political equilibrium of Tuscany during the early Renaissance, the height of the region's wealth and artistic achievement. The popes, newly established in Rome, sent Cardinal Albornoz across the territory in the 1360s with the aim of binding the region more closely to the Papal State; he built a score of fortresses across Umbria.

The **Wars of Italy**, beginning in 1494, put an end to Renaissance tranquillity. Florence was once more lost in its internal convolutions, twice expelling the **Medici**, while French and Imperial armies marched over the two regions. When the dust had cleared, the last of the free cities (with the exception of Lucca) had been extinguished, and most of Tuscany came under the rule of the Grand Duke **Cosimo I** (1537–74), the Medici propped on a newly made throne by Emperor Charles V. Tuscany's economic and artistic decline was gentle until 1600. After that, it was precipitate; the old banking and textile businesses collapsed, and serious artistic production practically ceased.

## The Modern Era

Though maintaining a relative independence, Tuscany had little to say in Italian affairs. After the Treaty of Câteau-Cambrésis in 1559, the Spaniards established a military enclave, called the Presidio, around Orbetello, precisely to keep an eye on central Italy. Cosimo I proved a vigorous ruler, though his successors gradually declined in ability. By 1600 it didn't matter. The total exhaustion of the Florentine economy kept pace with that of the Florentine imagination. By 1737, when the Medici dynasty became extinct, Tuscany was one of the torpid backwaters of Europe. It had no chance to decide its own destiny; the European powers agreed to bestow Tuscany on the House of Lorraine, cousins to the Austrian Habsburgs. Surprisingly enough, the Lorraines proved able and popular rulers, especially during the rule of the enlightened, progressive Peter Leopold (1765–90).

The languor of Lorraine and Papal rule was interrupted by Napoleon, who invaded central Italy twice and established a Kingdom of Etruria from 1801 to 1807. Austrian rule returned after 1815, continuing the series of well-meaning, intelligent Grand Dukes. By now, however, the Tuscans and the rest of the Italians wanted something better. In the tumults of the Risorgimento, one of the greatest and kindest of the Lorraines, Leopold II, saw the writing on the wall and allowed himself to be overthrown in 1859. Tuscany was almost immediately annexed to the new Italian kingdom.

Since then, the two regions have followed the history of modern Italy. The head start Tuscany gained under the Lorraine dukes allowed it to keep up economically with northern Italy. Florence had a brief moment of glory (1865–70) as capital of Italy, awaiting the capture of Rome. More recently, the biggest affair was the Second World War, with a long, tortuous campaign dragging across Tuscany. The Germans based their Gothic Line on the Arno, blowing up all but one of Florence's bridges.

# Art and Architecture

## Etruscans

Although we have no way of knowing what life was like for the average man in Camars or Velathrii, their tomb sculptures and paintings convince us that they were a talented, likeable people. Almost all their art derives from the Greek; the Etruscans built classical temples (unfortunately of wood, with terracotta embellishments, so little survives), carved themselves sarcophagi decorated with scenes from Homer, and painted their pottery in red and black after the latest styles from Athens or Corinth.

They excelled at portrait sculpture, and had a remarkable gift for capturing personality, sometimes seriously, though never heroically, often with an entirely intentional humour, and the serene smiles of people who truly enjoyed life.

Etruscan art in museums is often maddening; some of the works are among the finest productions of antiquity, while others – from the same time and city – are awkward and childish. Their talent for portraiture, among much else, was carried on by the Romans, and they bequeathed their love of fresco painting to the artists of the Middle Ages and Renaissance, who of course weren't even aware of the debt. After introducing yourself to the art of the Etruscans, it will be interesting to reconsider all that came later – in Tuscany, and indeed all Italy, you will find subtle reminders of this enigmatic people.

## Romans and Dark Ages

After destroying the Etruscan nation, the Romans also began the extinction of its artistic tradition; by the time of the Empire, there was almost nothing left that could be called distinctively Etruscan. Tuscany contributed little under the Empire. In the chaos that followed, there was little room for art. What painting survived followed styles current in Byzantium.

## The Middle Ages

In both architecture and sculpture, the first influence came from the north. Lombard masons filled Tuscany with simple Romanesque churches; the first (Spoleto, Bevagna, Grópina, Abbadia S. Salvatore and in the Garfagnana, to name a few) follow the northern style, although it wasn't long before two distinctive Tuscan forms emerged: the Pisan style, characterized by blind rows of colonnades, black and white zebra stripes, and lozenge-shaped designs; and the 'Tuscan Romanesque' which developed around Florence, notable for its use of dark and light marble patterns and simple geometric patterns, often with intricate mosaic floors to match (the Baptistry and San Miniato in Florence are the chief examples). In the cities in between – Lucca, Arezzo and Pistoia – there are interesting variations on the two different styles, often carrying an element like stripes or arcades to remarkable extremes. The only real example of French Gothic in Tuscany is San Galgano built by Cistercians in the 1200s, although the style never caught on here or anywhere else in Italy.

From the large pool of talent working on Pisa's great cathedral complex in the 13th century emerged Italy's first great sculptor, **Nicola Pisano**, whose Baptistry pulpit, with its realistic figures, derived from ancient reliefs. His even more remarkable son, **Giovanni Pisano**, prefigures Donatello in the expressiveness of his statues and the vigour of his pulpits; his façade of Siena cathedral, though altered, is a unique work of art. **Arnolfo di Cambio**, a student of Nicola Pisano, became chief sculptor-architect of Florence during its building boom in the 1290s, designing its cathedral and Palazzo Vecchio with a hitherto unheard-of scale and grandeur, before moving on to embellish Orvieto with statues and tombs. Orvieto, however, hired the more imaginative **Lorenzo Maitani** in the early 1300s to create a remarkable cathedral façade as individualistic as Siena's, a unique combination of reliefs and mosaics.

Painting at first lagged behind the new realism and more complex composition of sculpture. The first to depart from Byzantine stylization, at least according to the account in Vasari's *Lives of the Artists* (*see* **Topics**, pp.57–8), was **Cimabue**, in the late 1200s, who forsook Greek forms for a more 'Latin' or 'natural' way of painting. Cimabue found his greatest pupil, **Giotto**, as a young shepherd, chalk-sketching sheep on a piece of slate. Brought to Florence, Giotto soon eclipsed his master's fame (artistic celebrity being a recent Florentine invention) and achieved the greatest advances on the road to the new painting with a plain, rather severe approach that shunned Gothic prettiness while exploring new ideas in composition and expressing psychological depth in his subjects. Even more importantly, Giotto through his intuitive grasp of perspective was able to go further than any previous artist in representing his subjects as actual figures in space. In a sense Giotto actually invented space; it was this, despite his often awkward and graceless draughtsmanship, that so astounded his contemporaries. His followers, **Taddeo and Agnolo Gaddi** (father and son), **Giovanni da Milano**, and **Maso di Banco** filled Florence's churches with their own interpretations of the master's style. In the latter half of the 1300s, however, there also appeared the key figure of **Andrea Orcagna**, the most important Florentine sculptor, painter and architect of his day. Inspired by the more elegant style of **Andrea Pisano**'s Baptistry doors, Orcagna broke away from the simple Giottesque forms for a more elaborate, detailed style in his sculpture, while the fragments of his frescoes that survive have a vivid dramatic power, which undoubtedly owes something to the time of the Black Death and social upheavals in which they were painted.

Siena never produced a Vasari to chronicle its accomplishments, though they were considerable; in the 13th and 14th centuries, Siena's Golden Age, the city's artists, like its soldiers, rivalled and often surpassed those of Florence. For whatever reason, it seemed purposefully to seek inspiration in different directions from Florence; at first from central Italian styles around Spoleto, then, with prosperity and the advent of **Guido da Siena** in the early 1200s to the more elegant line and colour of Byzantium. Guido's work paved the way for the pivotal figure of **Duccio di Buoninsegna**, the catalyst who founded the essentials of Sienese art by uniting the beauty of Byzantine line and colour with the sweet finesse of western Gothic art. With Duccio's great followers **Pietro and Ambrogio Lorenzetti** and **Simone Martini**, the Sienese produced an increasingly elegant and rarefied art, almost oriental in its refined stylization. They were less innovative than the Florentines, though they brought the 'International Gothic' style – flowery and ornate, with all the bright tones of May – to its highest form in Italy. Simone Martini introduced the Sienese manner to Florence in the early 1400s, where it influenced most notably the work of **Lorenzo Monaco**, **Masolino**, and the young goldsmith and sculptor, **Ghiberti**.

## The Renaissance

Under the assaults of historians and critics over the last two centuries, the term 'Renaissance' has become a vague and controversial word. Nevertheless, however you choose to interpret this rebirth of the arts, and whatever dates you assign to it, Florence inescapably takes the credit for it. This is no small claim. Combining art,

# Masters and Students: the Progress of the Renaissance

*The purpose of this chart is to show who learned from whom: an insight into some 300 years of artistic continuity.*

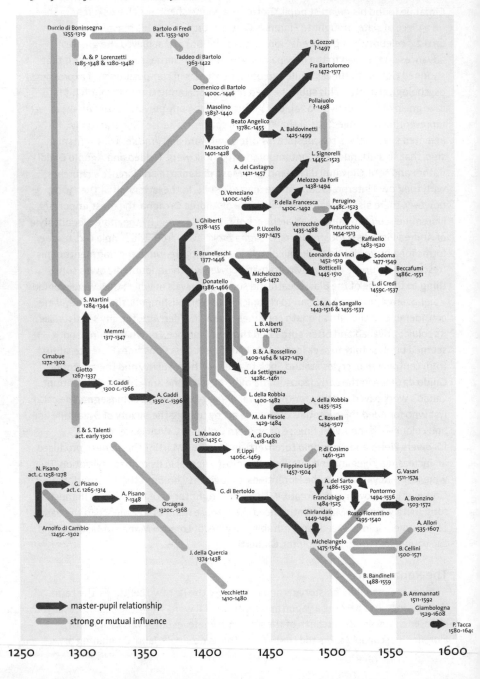

Duccio di Boninsegna
1255-1319

Bartolo di Fredi
act. 1353-1410

A. & P. Lorenzetti
1285-1348 & 1280-1348?

Taddeo di Bartolo
1363-1422

Domenico di Bartolo
1400c.-1446

Masolino
1383?-1440

Beato Angelico
1378c.-1455

B. Gozzoli
?-1497

Fra Bartolomeo
1472-1517

Pollaiuolo
?-1498

A. Baldovinetti
1425-1499

Masaccio
1401-1428

A. del Castagno
1421-1457

L. Signorelli
1445c.-1523

Melozzo da Forlì
1438-1494

D. Veneziano
1400c.-1461

P. della Francesca
1410c.-1492

Perugino
1448c.-1523

L. Ghiberti
1378-1455

P. Uccello
1397-1475

Verrocchio
1435-1488

Pinturicchio
1454-1513

Raffaello
1483-1520

F. Brunelleschi
1377-1446

Michelozzo
1396-1472

Leonardo da Vinci
1452-1519

Botticelli
1445-1510

Sodoma
1477-1549

Beccafumi
1486c.-1551

Donatello
1386-1466

L. di Credi
1459c.-1537

S. Martini
1284-1344

G. & A. da Sangallo
1443-1516 & 1455-1537

L. B. Alberti
1404-1472

Memmi
1317-1347

B. & A. Rossellino
1409-1464 & 1427-1479

Cimabue
1272-1302

Giotto
1267-1337

D. da Settignano
1428c.-1461

T. Gaddi
1300 c.-1366

A. Gaddi
1350 c.-1396

L. della Robbia
1400-1482

A. della Robbia
1435-1525

M. da Fiesole
1429-1484

C. Rosselli
1434-1507

F. & S. Talenti
act. early 1300

L. Monaco
1370-1425 c.

A. di Duccio
1418-1481

P. di Cosimo
1461-1521

F. Lippi
1406c.-1469

Filippino Lippi
1457-1504

G. Vasari
1511-1574

N. Pisano
act. c. 1258-1278

G. Pisano
act. c. 1265-1314

A. Pisano
?-1348

G. di Bertoldo
?

A. del Sarto
1486-1530

Pontormo
1494-1556

A. Bronzino
1503-1572

Orcagna
1320c.-1368

Franciabigio
1484-1525

Ghirlandaio
1449-1494

Rosso Fiorentino
1495-1540

A. Allori
1535-1607

Arnolfo di Cambio
1245c.-1302

Michelangelo
1475-1564

B. Cellini
1500-1571

J. della Quercia
1374-1438

B. Bandinelli
1488-1559

Vecchietta
1410-1480

B. Ammannati
1511-1592

Giambologna
1529-1608

P. Tacca
1580-1640

→ master-pupil relationship

→ strong or mutual influence

1250    1300    1350    1400    1450    1500    1550    1600

science and humanist scholarship into a visual revolution that often seemed pure sorcery to their contemporaries, a handful of Florentine geniuses taught the Western eye a new way of seeing. Perspective seems a simple enough trick to us now, but its discovery determined everything that followed, not only in art, but in science and philosophy as well.

Leading what scholars used self-assuredly to call the 'Early Renaissance' is a triumvi-rate of three geniuses: Brunelleschi, Donatello and Masaccio. **Brunelleschi**, neglecting his considerable talents in sculpture for architecture and science, not only built the majestic dome of Florence cathedral, but threw the Pandora's box of perspective wide open by mathematically codifying the principles of foreshortening. His good friend **Donatello**, the greatest sculptor since the ancient Greeks, inspired a new generation of both sculptors and painters to explore new horizons in portraiture and three-dimensional representation. The first painter to incorporate Brunelleschi and Donatello's lessons of spatiality, perspective and expressiveness was the young prodigy **Masaccio**, who along with his master Masolino painted the famous Brancacci Chapel in the Carmine, studied by nearly every Florentine artist down to Michelangelo.

The new science of architecture, sculpture and painting introduced by this triumvi-rate ignited an explosion of talent unequalled before or since – a score of masters, most of them Tuscan, each following the dictates of his own genius to create a remarkable range of themes and styles. To mention only the most prominent: **Lorenzo Ghiberti**, who followed Donatello's advice on his second set of Baptistry doors to cause a Renaissance revolution; **Leon Battista Alberti**, who took Brunelleschi's ideas to their most classical extreme in architecture, creating new forms in the process; **Paolo Uccello**, one of the most provocative of artists, who according to Vasari drove himself bats with the study of perspective and the possibilities of illusionism; **Piero della Francesca** of Sansepolcro, who explored the limits of perspective and geometrical forms to create the most compelling, haunting images of the quattrocento; **Fra** (now Beato) **Angelico**, who combined Masaccio's innovations and International Gothic colours and his own deep faith to create the most purely spiritual art of his time; **Andrea del Castagno**, who made use of perspective to create monumental, if often restless figures.

Some of Donatello's gifted followers were **Agostino di Duccio, Benedetto da Maiano, Desiderio da Settignano, Antonio and Bernardo Rossellino, Mino da Fiesole** and perhaps most famously, **Luca della Robbia**, who invented the coloured terracottas his family spread throughout Tuscany. And still more: **Benozzo Gozzoli**, whose enchanting springtime colours and delight in detail are a throwback to the International Gothic; **Antonio and Piero Pollaiuolo**, sons of a poultryman, whose new, dramatic use of line and form, often violent and writhing, would be echoed in Florentine Mannerism; **Fra Filippo Lippi**, a monk like Fra Angelico but far more earthly, the master of lovely Madonnas, teacher of his talented son **Filippino Lippi; Domenico Ghirlandaio**, whose gift of easy charm and flawless technique made him society's fresco painter; **Andrea del Verrocchio**, who could cast in bronze, paint, or carve with perfect detail; **Luca Signorelli**, who achieved apocalyptic grandeur in Orvieto

Cathedral; **Perugino** (Pietro Vannucci) of Umbria, who painted the stillness of his native region into his landscapes and taught the young **Raphael** of Urbino; and finally **Sandro Botticelli**, whose highly intellectual but lovely and melancholy, mythological paintings are in a class of their own.

The 'Early Renaissance' came to a close near the end of the 1400s with the advent of **Leonardo da Vinci**, whose unique talent in painting, only one of his hundred interests, challenged the certainty of naturalism with a subtlety and chiaroscuro that approaches magic. One passion, however, obsessed the other great figure of the 'High Renaissance', **Michelangelo Buonarroti**: his consummate interest was the human body, at first graceful and serene as in most of his Florentine works, later contorted and anguished after he left for Rome.

## Mannerism

Michelangelo left in Florence the seeds for the bold, neurotic avant-garde art that has come to be known as Mannerism. The first conscious 'movement' in Western art can be seen as a last fling amidst the growing intellectual and spiritual exhaustion of 1530s Florence, conquered once and for all by the Medici. The Mannerists' calculated exoticism and exaggerated, tortured poses, together with the brooding self-absorption of Michelangelo, are a prelude to Florentine art's remarkably abrupt turn into decadence, and prophesy its final extinction. Foremost among the Mannerist painters are two surpassingly strange characters, **Jacopo Pontormo** and **Rosso Fiorentino**, who were not in such great demand as the coldly classical **Andrea del Sarto** and **Bronzino**, consummate perfectionists of the brush, both much less intense and demanding. There were also charming reactionaries working at the time, especially **Il Sodoma** and **Pinturicchio**, both of whom left their best works in Siena. In sculpture **Giambologna** and to a lesser extent **Bartolommeo Ammanati** specialized in virtuoso *contrapposto* figures, each one more impossible than the last. With their contemporary, **Giorgio Vasari**, Florentine art lost almost all imaginative and intellectual content, and became a virtuoso style of interior decoration perfectly adaptable to saccharine holy pictures, portraits of newly enthroned dukes, or absurd mythological fountains and ballroom ceilings. In the cinquecento, with plenty of money to spend and a long Medici tradition of patronage to uphold, this tendency soon got out of hand. Under the reign of Cosimo I, indefatigable collector of *pietra dura* tables, silver and gold gimcracks, and exotic stuffed animals, Florence gave birth to the artistic phenomenon modern critics call 'kitsch'.

## The Rest Compressed

In the long, dark night of later Tuscan art a few artists stand out – the often whimsical architect and engineer, **Buontalenti**; **Pietro Tacca**, Giambologna's pupil with a taste for the grotesque; the charming Baroque fresco master **Pietro da Cortona**. Most of Tuscany, and particularly Florence, chose to sit out the Baroque – almost by choice, it seems, and we can race up to the 19th century for the often delightful 'Tuscan Impressionists' or *Macchiaioli* ('Splatterers'; best collection in Modern Art section of

Pitti Palace); and in the 20th century, **Modigliani** of the oval faces (from Livorno); the Futurist **Gino Severini** (from Cortona); and **Alberto Burri**, one of the first to use junk as a medium (from Città di Castello, where there's a museum). There is an exceptionally good collection of contemporary Italian art at Macerata in the Marches; others include a museum dedicated to sculptor **Marino Marini** in Florence, and another to **Manzù**, in Orvieto, although newest and most entertaining of all is French artist Niki de Saint-Phalle's Giardino dei Tarrochi south of Orbetello.

# Artists' Directory

This includes the principal architects, painters and sculptors of Tuscany and its nearby regions. The works listed are far from exhaustive, bound to exasperate partisans of some artists and do scant justice to the rest, but we have tried to include only the best and most representative works to be found locally.

**Agostino di Duccio** (Florentine, 1418–81). A precocious and talented sculptor, his best work is in the Malatesta Temple at **Rimini** – he was exiled from Florence after being accused of theft (**Florence**, Bargello; **Pontrémoli**, S. Francesco).

**Alberti, Leon Battista** (Florentine, b. Genoa 1404–72). Architect, theorist, and writer, also a sculptor and painter. His greatest contribution was recycling the classical orders and the principles of Vitruvius into Renaissance architecture; he was a consultant to the architecture loving Duke of Urbino. (**Florence**, Palazzo Rucellai, façade of S. Maria Novella, SS. Annunziata; **Lastra a Signa**, S. Martino).

**Allori, Alessandro** (1535–1607). Florentine Mannerist painter, prolific follower of Michelangelo and Bronzino (**Florence**, SS. Annunziata, S. Spirito, Spedale degli Innocenti).

**Ammanati, Bartolomeo** (1511–92). Florentine architect and sculptor. Restrained, elegant architect (**Florence**, S. Trínita bridge, courtyard of Pitti Palace); neurotic, twisted Mannerist sculptor (**Florence**, Fountain of Neptune, Villa di Castello).

**Andrea del Castagno** (c. 1423–57). Precise, dry Florentine painter, one of the first and greatest slaves of perspective. Died of the plague (**Florence**, Uffizi, S. Apollonia, SS. Annunziata).

**Angelico, Fra** (or **Beato**) (Giovanni da Fiesole, c. 1387–1455). Monk first and painter second, but still one of the great visionary artists of the Renaissance (**Florence**, S. Marco – spectacular Annunciation and many more; **Cortona**, Cathedral Museum; **Fiesole**, S. Domenico).

**Arnolfo di Cambio** (born in Colle di Val d'Elsa; c. 1245–1302). Architect and sculptor, pupil of Nicola Pisano and a key figure in his own right. Much of his best sculpture is in Rome, but he changed the face of Florence as main architect to the city's greatest building programme of the 1290s (**Florence**, cathedral and Palazzo Vecchio).

**Baldovinetti, Alesso** (Florentine, 1425–99). A delightful student of Fra Angelico who left few tracks; most famous for fresco work in **Florence** (SS. Annunziata, Uffizi, S. Niccolò sopr'Arno, S. Miniato).

**Bandinelli, Baccio** (1488–1559). Florence's comic relief of the late Renaissance; supremely serious, vain, and so awful it hurts – of course he was court sculptor to Cosimo I (**Florence**, Piazza della Signoria and SS. Annunziata).

**Barna da Siena** (active mid–late 1300s), one of the chief followers of Simone Martini, more dramatic and vigorous than the usual ethereal Sienese (**San Gimignano**, Collegiata).

**Bartolo di Fredi** (Sienese, active *c*. 1353–1410). Student of Ambrogio Lorenzetti, a genuine pre-Raphaelite soul, entirely at home in the Sienese trecento; employs colours never before seen on this planet (**Montepulciano**, Duomo; **San Gimignano**, Collegiata).

**Bartolommeo, Fra** (*c*.1472–1517) Florentine painter, master of the High Renaissance style (**Florence**, San Marco, Pitti Palace).

**Beccafumi, Domenico** (*c*. 1486–1551). Sienese painter; odd mixture of Sienese conservatism and Florentine Mannerism (**Siena**, Pinacoteca, Palazzo Pubblico, cathedral pavement).

**Benedetto da Maiano** (Florentine, 1442–97). Sculptor, specialist in narrative reliefs (**Florence**, S. Croce, Strozzi Palace, Bargello; he also designed the loggia of S. Maria delle Grazie, **Arezzo**).

**Bigarelli, Guido** (13th century). Talented travelling sculptor from Como, who excelled in elaborate and sometimes bizarre pulpits (**Barga**, **Pistoia**, S. Bartolomeo, and **Pisa Baptistry**).

**Bonfigli, Benedetto** (Perugia, *c*. 1420–96). Meticulous Umbrian painter, known for his painted banners in many Perugia churches; best works, especially the Cappella dei Priori frescoes, are in that city's National Gallery.

**Botticelli, Sandro** (Florentine, 1445–1510). Though technically excellent in every respect, and a master of both line and colour, there is more to Botticelli than this. Above every other quattrocento artist, his works reveal the imaginative soul of the Florentine Renaissance, particularly the great series of mythological paintings (**Florence**, Uffizi). Later, a little deranged and under the spell of Savonarola, he reverted to intense, though conventional religious paintings. He was almost forgotten in the philistine 1500s and not rediscovered until the 19th century, and thus many of his best works are probably lost (**Florence**, Accademia; **Montelupo**, S. Giovanni Evangelista).

**Bronzino, Agnolo** (1503–72). Virtuoso Florentine Mannerist with a cool, glossy hyperelegant style, at his best in portraiture; a close friend of Pontormo (**Florence**, Palazzo Vecchio, Uffizi, S. Lorenzo, SS. Annunziata).

**Brunelleschi, Filippo** (1377–1446). Florentine architect, credited in his own time with restoring the ancient Roman manner of building – but really deserves more credit for developing a brilliant new approach of his own (**Florence**, Duomo cupola, Spedale degli Innocenti, S. Spirito, S. Croce's Pazzi Chapel, S. Lorenzo). Also a sculptor (he lost the competition for the Baptistry doors to Ghiberti), and one of the first theorists on perspective.

**Buontalenti, Bernardo** (1536–1608). Late Florentine Mannerist architect and planner of the new city of **Livorno**, better known for his Medici villas (**Artimino**, also the fascinating grotto in **Florence**'s Boboli Gardens, and Belvedere Fort, Uffizi Tribuna).

**Cellini, Benvenuto** (1500–71). Goldsmith and sculptor. Though a native of Florence, Cellini spent much of his time in Rome. In 1545 he came to work for Cosimo I and to torment Bandinelli (*Perseus*, Loggia dei Lanzi; also works in the Bargello). As famed for his catty *Autobiography* as for his sculpture.

**Cimabue** (*c.* 1240–1302). Florentine painter credited by Vasari with initiating the 'rebirth of the arts'; one of the first painters to depart from the stylization of the Byzantine style (**Florence**, mosaics in Baptistry, Crucifix in Santa Croce; **Pisa**, cathedral mosaic).

**Civitali, Matteo** (Lucchese, *c.* 1435–1501). Sweet yet imaginative sculptor, apparently self-taught. He would be much better known if all of his works weren't in Lucca (**Lucca**, cathedral, Guinigi Museum).

**Coppo di Marcovaldo** (Florentine, active *c.* 1261–75). Another very early painter, as good as Cimabue if not as well known (**San Gimignano**; **Pistoia**, cathedral).

**Daddi, Bernardo** (active 1290–*c.* 1349). Florentine master of delicate altarpieces (**Florence**, Orsanmichele, S. Maria Novella's Spanish chapel).

**Desiderio da Settignano** (Florentine, 1428/31–61). Sculptor, follower of Donatello (**Florence**, S. Croce, Bargello, S. Lorenzo).

**Dolci, Carlo** (Florentine, 1616–86). Unsurpassed Baroque master of the 'whites of their eyes' school of religious art (**Florence**, Palazzo Corsini; **Prato**, Museo del Duomo).

**Domenico di Bartolo** (Sienese, *c.* 1400–46). An interesting painter, well out of the Sienese mainstream; the unique naturalism of his art is a Florentine influence. (Spedale di Santa Maria della Scala, Pinacoteca in **Siena**).

**Domenico Veneziano** (Florentine 1404–61). Painter, teacher of Piero della Francesca; master of perspective with few surviving works (**Florence**, Uffizi).

**Donatello** (Florentine, 1386–1466). The greatest Renaissance sculptor appeared as suddenly as a comet at the beginning of Florence's quattrocento. Never equalled in technical ability, expressiveness, or imaginative content, his works influenced Renaissance painters as much as sculptors. A prolific worker, the favourite of Old Cosimo de' Medici, and a quiet fellow who lived with his mum, Donatello was the perfect model of the early Renaissance artist – passionate about art, self-effacing, and a little eccentric (**Florence**, Bargello – the greatest works including the original *St George* from Orsanmichele, *David* and *Cupid-Atys*, also the great pulpits, the masterpiece of his old age in San Lorenzo; other works in Palazzo Vecchio, and the Cathedral Museum; **Siena**, cathedral, baptistry).

**Duccio di Buoninsegna** (d. 1319). One of the first and greatest Sienese painters, Duccio was to Sienese art what Giotto was to Florence; ignored by Vasari, though his contributions to the new visual language of the Renaissance are comparable to Giotto's (**Siena**, parts of the great Maestà in the Cathedral Museum, also Pinacoteca; **Florence**, altarpiece in the Uffizi; **Massa Marittima**, Cathedral; **Castelfiorentino**, Pinacoteca).

**Francesco di Giorgio Martini** (Sienese, 1439–1502). Architect – mostly of fortresses – sculptor and painter, his works are scattered all over Italy (**Siena**, Cathedral, Pinacoteca; **Cortona**, S. Maria di Calcinaio).

**Franciabigio** (Florentine, 1482–1525). Most temperamental of Andrea del Sarto's pupils but only mildly Mannerist (**Florence**, Poggio a Caiano and SS. Annunziata).

**Gaddi, Taddeo** (c. 1300–c. 1366). Florentine; most important of the followers of Giotto. He and his son **Agnolo** (d. 1396) contributed some of the finest trecento fresco cycles (notably at S. Croce, and S. Ambrogio, **Florence**).

**Gentile da Fabriano** (c. 1360–1427). Master nonpareil of the International Gothic style, from Fabriano in the Marches. Most of his work is lost (Uffizi, **Florence**).

**Ghiberti, Lorenzo** (1378–1455). Goldsmith and sculptor. The first artist to write an autobiography was naturally a Florentine. He would probably be better known had he not spent most of his career working on the doors for the Florence Baptistry after winning the famous competition of 1401 (also **Florence**, statues at Orsanmichele; **Siena** Baptistry).

**Ghirlandaio, Domenico** (Florentine, c. 1448–94). The painter of the quattrocento establishment, master of colourful, lively fresco cycles (with the help of a big workshop) in which he painted all the Medici and Florence's banking élite. A great portraitist with a distinctive, dry, restrained style (**Florence**, Ognissanti, S. Maria Novella, S. Trinita, Spedale degli Innocenti; **San Gimignano**, Collegiata).

**Giambologna** (1529–1608). A Fleming, born Jean Boulogne; court sculptor to the Medici after 1567 and one of the masters of Mannerist virtuosity – also a man with a taste for the outlandish (**Florence**, Loggia dei Lanzi, Bargello, Villa della Petraia; **Pratolino**, the *Appennino*).

**Giotto** (c. 1266–1337). Shepherd boy of the Mugello, discovered by Cimabue, who became the first great Florentine painter – and recognized as such in his own time. Invented an essential and direct approach to portraying narrative fresco cycles, but is even more important for his revolutionary treatment of space and of the human figure. (**Florence**, S. Croce, cathedral campanile, Horne Museum, S. Maria Novella).

**Giovanni da Milano** (14th century). An innovative Lombard inspired by Giotto (**Florence**, S. Croce; **Prato**, Cathedral Museum).

**Giovanni di Paolo** (d. 1483). One of the best of the quattrocento Sienese painters; like most of them, a colourful, often eccentric reactionary who continued the traditions of the Sienese trecento (**Siena**, Pinacoteca).

**Giovanni di San Giovanni** (1592–1633). One of Tuscany's more prolific, but likeable Baroque fresco painters (**Florence**, Pitti Palace, Villa della Petraia).

**Gozzoli, Benozzo** (Florentine, d. 1497). Learned his trade from Fra Angelico, but few artists could have less in common. The most light-hearted and colourful of quattrocento artists, Gozzoli created enchanting frescoes at **Florence**, Medici chapel; **San Gimignano**, S. Agostino; **Pisa**, Camposanto.

**Guido da Siena** (13th century). One of the founders of Sienese painting, still heavily Byzantine in style; little is known about his life (**Siena**, Palazzo Pubblico, Pinacoteca; **Grosseto** museum).

**Leonardo da Vinci** (1452–1519). We could grieve that Florence's 'universal genius' spent so much time on his scientific interests and building fortifications, and that his meagre artistic output was largely unfinished or lost. All that is left in Tuscany is the *Annunciation* (**Florence**, Uffizi) and also models of all his gadgets at his birthplace, **Vinci**. As the pinnacle of the Renaissance marriage of science and art, Leonardo requires endless volumes of interpretation. As for his personal life, Vasari records him buying up caged birds in the market-place just to set them free.

**Lippi, Filippino** (Florentine, 1457–1504). Son and artistic heir of Fra Filippo. Often seems a neurotic Gozzoli, or at least one of the most thoughtful and serious artists of the quattrocento (**Florence**, S. Maria Novella, S. Maria del Carmine, Badia, Uffizi).

**Lippi, Fra Filippo** (Florentine, 1406–69). Never should have been a monk in the first place. A painter of exquisite, ethereal Madonnas, with one of whom he ran off (the model, at least, a brown-eyed nun named Lucrezia). The pope forgave them both. Lippi was a key figure in the increasingly complex, detailed painting of the middle 1400s (**Florence**, Uffizi; **Prato**, cathedral and Civic Museum).

**Lorenzetti, Ambrogio** (Sienese, d. 1348). He could crank out golden Madonnas as well as any Sienese painter, but was also a great innovator in subject matter and the treatment of landscapes. Created the first and greatest of secular frescoes, the *Allegories of Good and Bad Government* in **Siena**'s Palazzo Pubblico, while his last known work, the 1344 *Annunciation* in Siena's Pinacoteca is one of the 14th century's most revolutionary treatments of perspective (also **Massa Marittima**, museum).

**Lorenzetti, Pietro** (Sienese, d. 1348). Ambrogio's big brother, and also an innovator, standing square between Duccio di Buoninsegna and Giotto; one of the precursors of the Renaissance's new treatment of space (**Siena**, S. Spirlto; **Arezzo**, Pieve di S. Maria; **Cortona**, Cathedral Museum). Both Lorenzettis seem to have died in Siena during the Black Death.

**Lorenzo di Credi** (1439–1537). One of the most important followers of Leonardo da Vinci, always technically perfect if occasionally vacuous (**Florence**, Uffizi).

**Lorenzo Monaco** (b. Siena 1370–1425). A monk at S. Maria degli Angeli in Florence and a brilliant colourist, Lorenzo forms an uncommon connection between the Gothic style of Sienese painting and the new developments in early Renaissance Florence (**Florence**, Uffizi, S. Trínita).

**Manetti, Rutilio** (1571–1639). Quirky but somehow likeable Baroque painter, the last artist of any standing produced by Siena (**Massa Marittima**, cathedral).

**Margarito d'Arezzo** (Arezzo, 13th century). Also called Margaritone. A near contemporary of Giotto who stuck firmly to his Byzantine guns (**Arezzo**, museum).

**Martini, Simone** (Sienese, d. 1344). Possibly a pupil of Giotto, Martini took the Sienese version of International Gothic to an almost metaphysical perfection, creating luminous, lyrical, and exquisitely drawn altarpieces and frescoes perhaps unsurpassed in the trecento (**Siena**, Palazzo Pubblico; **Pisa**, Museo S. Matteo; **Florence**, Uffizi).

**Masaccio** (Florentine, 1401–c. 1428). Though he died young and left few works behind, this precocious 'shabby Tom' gets credit for inaugurating the Renaissance in painting by translating Donatello and Brunelleschi's perspective on to a flat surface. Also revolutionary in his use of light and shadow, and in expressing emotion in his subjects' faces (**Florence**, S. Maria del Carmine, S. Maria Novella; **Pisa**, Museo S. Matteo).

**Maso di Banco** (Florentine, active 1340s). One of the more colourful and original followers of Giotto (**Florence**, S. Croce).

**Masolino** (Florentine, d. 1447). Perhaps 'little Tom' also deserves much of the credit, along with Masaccio, for the new advances in art at the Carmine in **Florence**; art historians dispute endlessly how to attribute the frescoes. It's hard to tell, for this brilliant painter left little other work behind to prove his case (**Empoli**, civic museum; also attributed Tau chapel, **Pistoia**).

**Matteo di Giovanni** (Sienese, 1435–95). One Sienese quattrocento painter who could keep up with the Florentines; a contemporary described him as 'Simone Martini come to life again' (**Siena**, Pinacoteca, Cathedral pavement, S. Agostino, S. Maria delle Neve; **Grosseto**, Museum).

**Memmi, Lippo** (Sienese, 1317–47). Brother-in-law and assistant of Simone Martini (**Siena**, S. Spirito; **San Gimignano**, museum).

**Michelangelo Buonarroti** (Florentine, 1475–1564). Born in Caprese (now Caprese Michelangelo) into a Florentine family of the minor nobility come down in the world, Michelangelo's early years and artistic training are obscure; he was apprenticed to Ghirlandaio, but showing a preference for sculpture was sent to the court of Lorenzo de' Medici. Nicknamed Il Divino in his lifetime, he was a complex, difficult character, who seldom got along with mere mortals, popes, or patrons. What he couldn't express by means of the male nude in paint or marble, he did in his beautiful but difficult sonnets. In many ways he was the first modern artist, unsurpassed in technique but also the first genius to go over the top (**Florence**, Medici tombs and library in San Lorenzo, three works in the Bargello, the *Pietà* in the Museo del Duomo, the *David* in the Accademia, Casa Buonarroti, and his only oil painting, in the Uffizi).

**Michelozzo di Bartolomeo** (Florentine, 1396–1472). Sculptor who worked with Donatello (**Prato**, pulpit of the Holy Girdle, and the tomb in **Florence**'s Baptistry), he is better known as the classicizing architect favoured by the elder Cosimo de' Medici (**Florence**, Medici Palace, Chiostro of SS. Annunziata, library of San Marco; Villas at **Trebbio** and **Cafaggiolo**, **Montepulciano**, S. Agostino; **Impruneta**, Tempietto).

**Mino da Fiesole** (Florentine, 1429–84). Sculptor of portrait busts and tombs; like the della Robbias a representative of the Florentine 'sweet style' (**Fiesole**, cathedral; **Empoli**, museum; **Volterra**, cathedral; **Florence**, Badia, Sant'Ambrogio; **Prato**, cathedral).

**Nanni di Banco** (Florentine, 1384–1421). Florentine sculptor at the dawn of the Renaissance (**Florence**, Orsanmichele, Porta della Mandorla).

**Orcagna, Andrea** (Florence, d. 1368). Sculptor, painter and architect who dominated the middle 1300s in Florence, though greatly disparaged by Vasari, who destroyed much of his work. Some believe he is the 'Master of the Triumph of Death' of Pisa's Camposanto (**Florence**, Orsanmichele, S. Croce, S. Maria Novella, *Crucifixion* in refectory of S. Spirito, also often given credit for the Loggia dei Lanzi).

**Perugino** (Pietro Vannucci, Perugia, *c.* 1450–1523). Perhaps the most distinctive of the Umbrian painters; created some works of genius, along with countless idyllic nativity scenes, each with its impeccably sweet Madonna and characteristic blue-green tinted background. Some of his later works are awful, although he may not always be responsible: in his cynical old age he let his workshop sign his name to anything (**Florence**, Uffizi, S. Maddalena dei Pazzi, Cenacolo di Foligno).

**Piero della Francesca** (*c.* 1415–1492). Painter, born at Sansepolcro, and one of the really unique quattrocento artists. Piero, a leading light in the famous court of Urbino, wrote two of the most important theoretical works on perspective, then illustrated them with a lifetime's work reducing painting to the bare essentials: geometry, light and colour. In his best work his reduction creates nothing dry or academic, but dreamlike, almost eerie scenes similar to those of Uccello. And like Uccello or Botticelli, his subjects are often archetypes of immense psychological depth, not to be fully explained now or ever (**Arezzo**, S. Francesco and the cathedral; **Sansepolcro**, civic museum; **Monterchi**, cemetery church; **Florence**, Uffizi).

**Piero di Cosimo** (Florentine, 1462–1521). Painter better known for his personal eccentricities than his art, which in itself is pretty odd. Lived on hard-boiled eggs which he boiled with his glue (**Florence**, Uffizi; **Fiesole**, S. Francesco).

**Pietro da Cortona** (Cortona, 1596–1699). The most charming of Tuscan Baroque painters; his best is in Rome, but there are some florid ceilings in the Pitti Palace (**Florence**; also works in **Cortona**).

**Pinturicchio** (Perugia, 1454–1513). This painter got his name for his use of gold and rich colours. Never an innovator, but as an absolute virtuoso in colour, style and grace no one could beat him. Another establishment artist, especially favoured by the popes, and, like Perugino, he was slandered most vilely by Vasari (**Siena**, Piccolomini Library).

**Pisano, Andrea** (b. Pontedera, *c.* 1290–1348). Artistic heir of Giovanni and Nicola Pisano and teacher of Orcagna; probably a key figure in introducing new artistic ideas to **Florence** (Baptistry, south doors). Not related to the other Pisani.

**Pisano, Nicola** (active *c.* 1258–78). The first great medieval Tuscan sculptor really came from down south in Apulia, which was then enjoying a flowering of classically orientated art under Emperor Frederick II. He created a little Renaissance all his own, when he adapted the figures and composition of ancient reliefs to make his wonderful pulpit reliefs in **Siena** and **Pisa**'s Baptistry. His son **Giovanni Pisano** (active *c.* 1265–1314) carried on the tradition, notably in the façade sculptures at **Siena** cathedral (also **Perugia**, S. Domenico, Fontana Maggiore; great relief pulpits in **Pisa** cathedral, Sant'Andrea, **Pistoia**).

**Pollaiuolo, Antonio** (Florentine, d. 1498). A sculptor, painter and goldsmith whose fame rests on his brilliant, unmistakable line; he occasionally worked with his less gifted brother **Piero** (**Florence**, Uffizi and Bargello).

**Pontormo, Jacopo** (Florentine, b. Pontormo, 1494–1556). You haven't seen pink and orange until you've seen the work of this determined Mannerist eccentric. After the initial shock, though, you'll meet an artist of real genius, one whose use of the human body as sole means for communicating ideas is equal to Michelangelo's (**Florence**, S. Felicità – his *Deposition* – and Uffizi; **Carmignano**; **Poggio a Caiano**).

**Quercia, Jacopo della** (Sienese, 1374–1438). Sculptor who learned his style from Pisano's cathedral pulpit; one of the unsuccessful contestants for the Florence baptistry doors. Maybe Siena's greatest sculptor, though his most celebrated work, that city's Fonte Gaia, is now ruined (**Lucca**, cathedral *tomb of Ilaria del Carretto*; **San Gimignano**, Collegiata; **Siena**, Baptistry; **Volterra**, cathedral).

**Raphael** (Raffaello Sanzio, 1483–1520). Born in Urbino, Raphael spent time in Città di Castello, Perugia, and Florence before establishing himself in Rome. Only a few of the best works of this High Renaissance master remain in the region; those are in the Pitti Palace and Uffizi, **Florence**.

**Robbia, Luca della** (Florentine, 1400–82). Greatest of the famous family of sculptors; he invented the coloured glaze for terracottas that we associate with the della Robbias, but was also a first-rate relief sculptor (the *cantorie* in **Florence**'s cathedral museum; **Impruneta**, Collegiata). His nephew **Andrea della Robbia** (1435–1525; best works in convent of **La Verna** and the Tempietto at **Montevarchi**) and Andrea's son **Giovanni** (1469–1529; best work, **Pistoia**, Ospedale del Ceppo) carried on the blue and white terracotta sweet style in innumerable buildings across Tuscany.

**Rosselli, Cosimo** (Florentine, 1434–1507). Competent middle of the road Renaissance painter who occasionally excelled (**Florence**, S. Ambrogio).

**Rossellino, Bernardo** (1409–64). Florentine architect and sculptor best known as the planner and architect of the new town of **Pienza**. Also a sculptor (**Florence**, S. Croce, S. Miniato; **Empoli**, Pinacoteca). His brother **Antonio Rossellino** (1427–79) was also a talented sculptor (**Florence**, S. Croce).

**Rossi, Vicenzo de'** (1525–87). Florentine Mannerist sculptor of chunky male nudes (**Florence**, Palazzo Vecchio).

**Rosso Fiorentino** (Giovanni Battista di Jacopo, 1494–1540). Florentine Mannerist painter, he makes a fitting complement to Pontormo, both for his tortured soul and for the exaggerations of form and colour he used to create gripping, dramatic effects. Fled Italy after the Sack of Rome and worked for Francis I at Fontainebleau. (**Volterra** Pinacoteca has his masterpiece, the *Deposition*; **Florence**, Uffizi and S. Lorenzo; **Città di Castello**, Duomo).

**Salviati, Francesco** (Florentine, 1510–63). Friend of Vasari and a similar sort of painter – though much more talented. Odd perspectives and decoration, often bizarre imagery (**Florence**, Palazzo Vecchio and Uffizi).

**Sangallo, Antonio da** (brother of Giuliano, 1455–1537). Architect at his best in palaces and churches in the monumental style – notably at the great temple of S. Biagio, **Montepulciano**; the son, **Antonio da Sangallo the Younger**, also an architect, and the family's best, practised mainly in Rome.

**Sangallo, Giuliano da** (Florentine, 1443–1516). Architect of humble origins who became the favourite of Lorenzo de' Medici. Often tripped up by an obsession, inherited from Alberti, with making architecture conform to philosophical principles (**Poggio a Caiano; Florence**, S. Maddalena dei Pazzi; **Prato**, S. Maria delle Carceri).

**Il Sassetta** (Stefano di Giovanni; active *c.* 1390–1450). One of the great Sienese quattrocento painters, though still working in a style the Florentines would have found
hopelessly reactionary; an artist who studied Masaccio but preferred the Gothic
elegance of Masolino. His masterpiece, the Borgo Sansepolcro polyptych, is
dispersed through half the museums of Europe.

**Signorelli, Luca** (Cortona, d. 1523). A rarefied Umbrian painter and an important influence on Michelangelo. Imaginative, forceful compositions, combining geometrical
rigour with a touch of unreality, much like his master Piero della Francesca (**Cortona**,
civic and cathedral museums; **Monte Oliveto Maggiore**; **Sansepolcro**, museum).

**Il Sodoma** (Giovanni Antonio Bazzi, 1477–1549). Born in Piedmont, but a Sienese by
choice, he was probably not the libertine his nickname and Vasari's biography
suggest. An endearing, serene artist, who usually eschewed Mannerist distortion,
he got rich through his work, then blew it all feeding his exotic menagerie and died
in the poorhouse (**Monte Oliveto Maggiore**; **Siena**, Pinacoteca and S. Domenico).

**Spinello Aretino** (Arezzo, late 14th century–1410). A link between Giotto and the
International Gothic style; imaginative and colourful in his compositions (**Florence**,
S. Miniato; **Siena**, Palazzo Pubblico; **Arezzo**, museum). His son **Parri di Spinello** did
many fine works, all around **Arezzo** (S. Maria delle Grazie).

**Tacca, Pietro** (1580–1640). Born in Carrara, pupil of Giambologna and one of the best
early Baroque sculptors (**Livorno**, *Quattro Mori*; **Florence**, Piazza SS. Annunziata fountains; **Prato**, Piazza del Comune).

**Taddeo di Bartolo** (Volterra, 1363–1422). The greatest Sienese painter of the late 1300s
– also the least conventional; never a consummate stylist, he often shows a remarkable imagination in composition and treatment of subject matter (**Siena**, Palazzo
Pubblico, S. Spirito; **Perugia**, Pinacoteca; **Colle di Val d'Elsa** museum and Collegiata;
**Volterra**, Pinacoteca; **San Gimignano**, Museo Civico).

**Talenti, Francesco** (early 14th century). Chief architect of **Florence** cathedral and
campanile after Arnolfo di Cambio and Giotto; his son **Simone** made the beautiful
windows in **Orsanmichele** (and perhaps the Loggia dei Lanzi) in **Florence**.

**Torrigiano, Pietro** (1472–1528). Florentine portrait sculptor, famous for his work in
Westminster Abbey and for breaking Michelangelo's nose (**Siena**, cathedral).

**Uccello, Paolo** (Florentine, 1397–1475). No artist has ever been more obsessed with the
possibilities of artificial perspective. Like Piero della Francesca, he used the new
technique to create a magic world of his own; contemplation of it made him
increasingly eccentric in his later years. Uccello's provocative, visionary subjects
(*Noah* fresco in S. Maria Novella, and *Battle of San Romano* in the Uffizi and cloister
of San Miniato, **Florence**) put him up with Piero della Francesca and Botticelli as the
most intellectually stimulating of quattrocento artists (also attributed frescoes,
**Prato** cathedral).

**Vasari, Giorgio** (Arezzo, 1511–74). Florentine sycophant, writer and artist. Also a pretty
good architect (**Florence**, Uffizi, Corridoio, and Fish Loggia, and the palace in **Città di
Castello**).

**Il Vecchietta** (Lorenzo di Pietro, 1412–80). Sienese painter and sculptor, dry and linear, part Sienese Pollaiuolo and part Donatello. One wonders what he did to acquire his nickname, 'Little Old Woman' (**Siena**, Loggia della Mercanzia, Baptistry).

**Verrocchio, Andrea del** (1435–88). Florentine sculptor who worked in bronze; spent his life trying to outdo Donatello. Also a painter, a mystic alchemist in his spare time, and interestingly enough the master of both Botticelli and Leonardo (Uffizi, S. Lorenzo, Orsanmichele, Palazzo Vecchio, and Bargello, **Florence**).

# Topics

04

# A Country Calendar

If there's a great sense of continuity in the land, it is the same with the rhythms of rural life in central Italy. Old traditions and seasonal changes are still of primary importance – Italians, for the most part, won't buy imported fruit or vegetables (although this is unfortunately changing); even in the cities it's difficult to find a decent tomato in January. Even chocolates disappear off the counter in July. Tuscany, like most of Italy, chooses to follow the calendar as a sort of sentimental journey through the rise and fall of the Year.

The traditional Florentine New Year began on Annunciation Day in March, the time when the countryside really did seem to awaken – until the Medici Grand Dukes finally aligned Tuscany to the papal calendar in the 1500s. **January** still hibernates; if the ground is soft farmers may put in peas and garlic; roast chestnuts, polenta, *bruschetta* and game dishes are the highlights of the table. **February** is the month of pruning and planting garden vegetables in frames. Sticky sweet carnival pastries are unavoidable. In **March** new fruit trees are planted and the vines are pruned; potatoes, fennel, spinach, carrots, parsley and lettuce are planted directly in the garden. Blood oranges (from Sicily) and artichokes appear in the shops. The fruit trees burst into blossom, and continue through **April**, the time to plant sunflowers and corn, the other garden vegetables and most flowers. Lambs are slaughtered for Easter; young turkeys and pigs are purchased. The hunt for wild asparagus and salad greens is in full swing.

Strawberries and medlars are the fruits of **May**, central Italy's most glorious month, when the irises and roses bloom in profusion. *Fave* (broad beans) are the big treat, and in the mountains, in most years, you can stop lighting fires to stay warm in the evening. The first garlic, French beans and potatoes are harvested in **June**, which is also the time to plant cabbage and cauliflowers. Cherries, apricots, plums, the first watermelons and fresh tomatoes appear; everyone's eating melon and prosciutto *antipasti* and dishes with courgette flowers (*fiori di zucca*).

**July** brings an avalanche of *zucchini* and peaches. Country folk begin staying up past 10pm, and scorpions come into your house to cool off. In **August** chickens meet their maker, while the end of the month brings masses upon masses of tomatoes, which country families join together to conserve – a messy operation of steaming kettles and grinders that puts up a year's supply of tomato sauce. Apples, pears and fresh figs are harvested in **September**, a golden, placid month when the village stationery shops begin stocking the schoolbooks for the new year.

**October** is the *vendemmia*, or grape harvest, the highlight of the year for everyone outside the Umbrian Apennines; to make *vinsanto* it's essential to pick out very mature bunches and hang them up to dry. The hunting season opens, and folks begin to poke around for wild mushrooms. **November** is a busy month, the time to hunt for truffles, harvest olives, pomegranates and chestnuts, and take care of wine business. In **December** the family pig is slaughtered for next year's *prosciutto* and sausages. Orange persimmons hang like ornaments on the trees and plague the table – no one likes them, but everyone has plenty to give away; if they are indeed the apples of the

Hesperides, as some scholars suggest, the afterlife must be a major disappointment. Stick to the tiny tangerines from the south that flood the market. Christmas turkeys realize their time has come; and cakes are everywhere: dense confections of walnuts, raisins, chocolates and pepper (*panforte* of Siena) or tall, airy *panettone* sold in cylindrical boxes.

# The First Professional Philistine

Many who have seen Vasari's work in Florence will be wondering how such a mediocre painter should rate so much attention. Ingratiating companion of the rich and famous, workmanlike over-achiever and tireless self-promoter, Vasari was the perfect man for his time. Born in Arezzo, in 1511, a fortunate introduction to Cardinal Silvio Passerini gave him the chance of an education in Florence with the young Medici heirs Ippolito and Alessandro. In his early years, he became a fast and reliable frescoist gaining a reputation for customer satisfaction – a real innovation in an age when artists were increasingly becoming eccentric prima donnas. In the 1530s, after travelling around Italy on various commissions, he returned to Florence just when Cosimo I was beginning his plans to remake the city in the image of the Medici. It was a marriage made in heaven. Vasari became Cosimo's court painter and architect, with a limitless budget and a large group of assistants, the most prolific fresco machine ever seen in Italy – painting over countless good frescoes of the 1300s.

But more than for his paintings, Vasari lives on through his book, the *Lives of the Painters, Sculptors and Architects*, a series of exhaustive, gossipy biographies of artists. Beginning with Cimabue, Vasari traces the rise of art out of Byzantine and Gothic barbarism, through Giotto and his followers, towards an ever-improving naturalism, finally culminating in the great age of Leonardo, Raphael and the divine Michelangelo, who not only mastered nature but outdid her. Leon Battista Alberti gets the credit for drafting the first principles of artistic criticism, but it was Vasari who first applied such ideas on a grand scale. His book, being the first of its kind, and containing a mine of valuable information on dozens of Renaissance artists, naturally has had a tremendous influence on all subsequent criticism. Art critics have never really been able to break out of the Vasarian straitjacket.

Much of Vasari's world seems quaint to us now: the idea of the artist as a kind of knight of the brush, striving for Virtue and Glory, the slavish worship of anything that survived from ancient Rome, artistic 'progress' and the conviction that art's purpose was to imitate nature. But many of Vasari's opinions have had a long and mischievous career in the world of ideas. His blind disparagement of everything medieval – really the prejudice of his entire generation – lived on until the 1800s. His dismissal of Sienese, Umbrian and northern artists – of anyone who was not a Florentine – has not been entirely corrected even today. Vasari was the sort who founded academies, a cheerful conformist who believed in a nice, tidy art that went by the book. With his interior decorator's concept of Beauty, he created a style of criticism in which virtuosity, not imagination, became the standard by which art was to be judged;

history offers few more instructive examples of the stamina and resilience of dubious ideas.

# Flora and Fauna

No one would come to this part of Italy expecting to find an unspoiled wilderness. Most of Tuscany, in particular, has been cultivated so long and so intensively that wildlife is completely pushed to the fringes. Nevertheless, there is a great variety of birds and beasts to complement the surprisingly wide range of landscapes. Cultivated Tuscany (*see* below, 'Landscapes') is another world, a land of vineyards and olive groves, cypresses, poplars and the occasional umbrella pine. The rest of the territory divides neatly into three parts: the coastal zone, with its beaches and wetlands, the central hills and the mountains.

For nature-lovers, the coast will be by far the most interesting region; the malaria mosquito kept much of the southern Maremma undeveloped for centuries, leaving vast stretches of pine forest, along with cork oak and holm oak, a thriving wildlife (including even some wild horses) and marshlands that host a marvellous array of birds, from eagles to woodpeckers. Its protected nesting grounds (*see* the Monti dell'Uccellina, pp.353–4, Orbetello lagoons, p.356, and Lago di Burano, p.359) are Italy's greatest stopover for migrating waterfowl – herons, cormorants, storks, kingfishers, osprey and the only flamingoes left on the mainland. Deforested land beyond the marshes is covered with the characteristic Mediterranean scrub, or maquis (*macchia*, in Italian); either *macchia alta* with shrub versions of pines (they harvest the pine nuts), oaks, beech, cypress and laurel; or the *macchia bassa* in drier regions, thick patches of broom, heather, lentisk and other fragrant plants.

As for the **animals**, there are pretty much the same characters throughout Tuscany starting with those two regional totems, the viper and the boar. The bad old viper, the only really unpleasant thing you may meet out in the woods and fields, proliferates especially where farmlands have been abandoned; he's brownish-grey, about a foot and half long (never more than a yard), and has a vaguely diamond-shaped head. Vipers are a nuisance only because there are so many of them, and because they object to being stepped on. If one bites you, you've got half an hour to find someone with the serum – or you can buy your own in any pharmacy and keep it in the fridge. The boar, a shy, well-mannered creature, flourishes everywhere despite the Italians' best efforts to turn him into salami or *prosciutto*. In summer, you may hear them nosing around the villages at night looking for water.

Beyond these, there are plenty of hares and rabbits, foxes and weasels, also polecats, badgers and porcupine in the wilder areas. Wolves, lynxes and deer were once common, and a few of each survive in the higher reaches of the Apennines; deer have been reintroduced in the Maremma coastal parks. There is a little isolated region in Tuscany, the Val di Farma north of Roccastrada, where you can find all of these, and even wildcats. The only mountain goats are found on the island of Montecristo.

Many writers on this part of Italy comment on the absence of **birdsong**. They're exaggerating. Italian hunters do shoot anything that flies, but there are still quite a few thrushes, starlings, wrens and such, along with the white doves that always make you think of Assisi and St Francis. Cuckoos unfailingly announce the spring, pheasants lie low during the hunting season, and an occasional owl can be heard in the country. Nightingales are rare, but there are supposed to be some around Lago di Massacuccioli and the northern coasts – in the evening you're far more likely to see bats.

The **insect** world is well represented, and if you spend time in the country, you'll meet many of them: lovely butterflies and moths, and delicate white creatures with wings apparently made of feathers; rather forbidding black bullet bees, and wasps that resemble vintage fighter planes. Beetles especially reach disproportionate sizes – if you're lucky you may see a *diavolo*, a large black or red beetle with long, gracefully curving antlers that sings when you trap it; Leonardo drew one in his notebooks. There are enough mosquitoes, midges and little biting flies to be a nuisance in the summer, and, perhaps most alarming at first sight, the shiny black scorpion, who may crawl inside through the window or up drains (you may want to keep the plugs in) or come in with the wood if you have a fire. Once inside they head for dark places like beds or shoes. One thwack with a shoe will do in even the largest scorpion (they're actually quite soft). If you happen to be stung, it may be painful but not deadly; the Italians recommend a trip to the doctor for treatment against an infection or allergic reaction. One of the most stunning insect spectacles is the fireflies in midsummer. In a cornfield it is a truly magical sight – and they are such dull little creatures in daylight.

As for the **forests**, oaks, chestnuts and beech predominate, along with tall, upright poplars ('Lombardy' type), pines, willows (not the weeping variety) and a few maples – with rounded leaves, not pointed as in northern Europe and America. Cypress trees are common. Incidentally the idea that there are erect, needle-like 'male' cypresses and blowsy 'female' ones is a misconception; the tidier ones have been planted, while shaggy cypresses are the wild variety. Parasol or umbrella pines (really the maritime pine), that most characteristic Italian tree, make a grand sight isolated on a hill crest, or in large groves along the Maremma coast. At higher altitudes, there are large beech forests, along with pines and firs – some beautiful groves of silver firs grow around Monte Amiata, while in the Casentino near Camaldoli is a vast stretch of old, protected beech and pine forest; another, primarily chestnut forest, is contained in the Garfagnana's *Parco Naturale dell'Orecchiella*.

Though at first **wild flowers** may seem unfamiliar, many of the most common Italian wild flowers are close cousins to those seen in northern Europe and America. There are a million varieties of buttercup, usually tiny ones like the *ranuncolo* and *bottoncini d'oro*, and of bluebell, often called *campanella* or *campunellina*. Many of the common five-petalled pink blossoms in spring fields are really small wild geraniums (*geranio*), with pointed leaves like the anemone, and you'll see quite a few varieties of violets (*violette*) with round or spade-shaped leaves (a few species are yellow). A daisy, in Italian, is a *margherita*, and they come in all sizes. Tiniest of all are the wild pink and blue forget-me-nots (*non ti scordar di me*); you'll have to look closely to see them in overgrown fields. Large swatches of lavender are one of the charms of the hills of Chianti.

The real star of Italian fields is the poppy, bright red and thriving everywhere. Dandelions and wild mustard are also plentiful, along with white, umbrella-like bunches of florets called *tragosellino* or *podragraria*, similar to what Americans call Queen Anne's Lace. More exotic flowers include wild orchids, some with small florets growing in spiky shoots, rhododendrons (in mountainous areas), five-petalled wild roses and water lilies in the coastal Maremma. The best wildflowers are found up in the Sibillini mountains; the Piano Grande blooming in early summer is an unforgettable sight.

There are other **plants** to look for; a dozen kinds of greens that go into somewhat bitter salads, anise, fennel, mint, rosemary and sage are common. The Italians beat the bushes with fervour every spring looking for wild asparagus and repeat the performance in autumn searching for truffles and *porcini* (boletus) mushrooms.

## A Florentine Puzzle

In a city as visually dry and restrained as Florence, every detail of decoration stands out. In the Middle Ages and Renaissance, Florentine builders combined their passion for geometry with their love of making a little go a long way; they evolved a habit of embellishing buildings with simple geometrical designs. Though nothing special in themselves – most are easily drawn with a compass and straight edge – in their context they stand out like mystic hieroglyphs, symbols upon which to meditate while contemplating old Florence's remarkable journey through the western mind.

The city is full of them, incorporated into façades, mosaics, windows and friezes. Here are eight of them, a little exercise for the eye while tramping the hard pavements of Florence. Your job is to find them. Some are really obvious, others obscure. For No.6 you should be able to find at least three examples (two across the street from each other) and if you're clever you'll find not only No.5, a rather late addition to the cityscape, but also the medieval work that inspired it. Don't worry too much about the last one. But if you're an art historian or a Florentinophile, it's only fair that you seek out this hard one too. For the answers, *see* the last page of the index, p.490.

 1
 2
 3
 4

 5
 6
7
8

# Landscapes

Other regions in Italy are lusher, have taller mountains and more fertile valleys, support a far greater variety of flora and enjoy a more temperate climate. Yet, when all is said and done, the landscapes of Tuscany exert the most lasting charm. In the painting of the Renaissance, the background of rolling hills, cypresses, poplars and parasol pines, the vineyards and winding lanes are often more beautiful than the nominally religious subject in the foreground. Very early on, beginning with Giotto, artists took care to relate the figures in their composition to the architecture and the landscape around them, epitomized in the paintings of Leonardo da Vinci, where each tree and rock takes on an almost mystic significance.

Every Italian is born with an obsessive instinct to put in order, or *sistemare* things; with a history of wars, earthquakes, foreign rulers, and an age-old tendency to extremes of all descriptions, the race has had a bellyful of disorder and unpre- dictability. The tidy, ordered geometry and clipped hedges of an Italian garden are a perfect example of the urge to sistemare nature, and you'll find good examples of these in the Boboli Gardens and the Medici villas at Castello; the Tuscans, in the vanguard of Italy in so many ways, were the first to sistemare their entire territory. The vicious wars of the Middle Ages between cities and the Guelphs and Ghibellines devastated the countryside and much of the forests (as is visible in the harsh, barren brown and grey hills of trecento painting); the Black Death in the 1300s depopulated the cultivated areas, giving the Tuscans the unique opportunity to arrange things just so. Not entirely by coincidence, the late 14th century was the time when the élite, weary of the strife in the city, were discovering the joys of the country and building villas, playing the country squire and gentleman farmer whenever possible – already, in the *Decameron*, the nobles had estates in the environs of Florence. And they planted everything in its place according to elegance and discipline, each tree with its own purpose, a boundary marker, for shade, or to support a vine. Often cypresses and parasol pines stand strikingly along the crest of hills, not for aesthetics or a study in perspective, but for a windbreak. Strongest of all is the feeling that nothing has changed for centuries, that in the quattrocento Gozzoli and Fra Angelico painted the same scene you see today. Few landscapes anywhere are more ancient, or civilized.

# Tuscany on Wheels

Tuscans have always loved a parade, and to the casual reader of Renaissance history, it seems they're forever proceeding somewhere or another, even to their own detri- ment – during outbreaks of plague, holy companies would parade through an inflicted area, invoking divine mercy, while in effect aiding the spread of the pesti- lence. They also had a great weakness for allegorical parade floats. During the centuries of endless war each Tuscan city rolled out its war chariot or battle wagon, called the *Carroccio*, invented by a Milanese bishop in the 11th century. A *Carroccio*, drawn by six white oxen, was a kind of holy ship of state in a hay cart; a mast held up a crucifix while a battle standard flew from the yard-arm, there was an altar for priests to say mass during the battle and a large bell to send signals over the din to the armies. The worst possible outcome of a battle was to lose one's Carroccio to the enemy, as Fiesole did to Florence. One is still in operation, in Siena, rumbling out twice a year for the Palio (*see* p.373).

Medieval clerical processions, by the time of Dante, became melded with the idea of the Roman 'triumph' (*trionfo*); in Purgatory, the poet finds Beatrice triumphing with a cast of characters from the Apocalypse. Savonarola wrote of a *Triumph of the Cross*; Petrarch and Boccaccio wrote allegorical triumphs of virtues, love and death. More interesting, however, are the secular Roman-style Triumphs staged by the Medici, especially at Carnival (the name of which, according to Burckhardt, comes from a cart, the pagan *carrus navalis*, the ship of Isis, launched every 5 March to symbolize the reopening of navigation). You can get a hint of their splendour from the frescoes at Poggio a Caiano; the best artists of the day would be commissioned to design the decorations – two particularly famous *trionfi* in Florence celebrated the election of the Medici Pope Leo X. The last relics of these parades are the huge satirical carnival floats at Viareggio.

Two lovely memories of Florence's processions remain. One is Gozzoli's fairy-tale frescoes in the chapel of the Medici palace, of the annual procession staged by the Compagnia de' Re Magi, the most splendid and aristocratic of pageants. The other comes from the Florentine Carnival, famous for its enormous floats, in which scenes from mythology were portrayed to songs and music. One year, for the masque of Bacchus and Ariadne, Lorenzo de' Medici composed the loveliest Italian poem to come out of the Renaissance, with the melancholy refrain:

*Quanto è bella giovinezza,*
*Che si fugge tuttavia!*
*Chi vuol esser lieto, sia:*
*Di doman non c'è certezza.*

# Florentines 2, Giants 1

*Sono vulgari, quei Fiorentini...* You won't spend much time in Italy (or especially in Tuscany) before you hear someone commenting on the vulgarity of the Florentines. Such a remark may be occasioned by a lad standing next to an Alfa with Florence number plates, leaning on the horn and waking up the babies, or by a couple with sunglasses in a dark restaurant who manage to get in three cigarettes after each course. As everyone knows, Florentines are also the most arrogant and conceited people in the universe, surpassing even the Romans and Milanese.

After some initial dismay, you may find it refreshing to encounter a people with so many peculiar facets to their personality. We know about the Florentines of old, their fascination with mathematics and technology, and their matchless talent for art, and we know about the foppish prancing Florentine courtiers of the decadent 1600s. But more up-to-date models are not entirely without interest. Florentines are famous for their dry wit, and their penny-pinching economy, a talent for making a little go a long way. Their tenaciously conservative *dov'era com'era* mentality towards their museum city-home is extreme even by Italian standards. And a redeeming share of their old Renaissance craftsmanship remains, an attention to detail that makes them skilled seamstresses and the best art restorers in the world.

The refinement, as well as the arrogance and conceit, are one side of the coin; on the other we find a surprising streak of down-to-earth hillbilly cussedness. Florentines and the rest of the Tuscans are after all dismissed as *mangiafagioli*, 'beaneaters', by other Italians. According to one perceptive observer, all the shortcomings of the Florentines are due to a diet of too much beans, tripe and cockscombs – the very mention of these conjures up the uneasy shade of the bloated, horrible Catherine de' Medici up in Paris, gorging herself on cockscombs and puking all over the Louvre.

For all these singular qualities, it is surprising that Florentines hardly ever make it into literature; it's hard to imagine a novel that could not be improved by giving a Florentine a small role. The only interesting one we have been able to find is the star of a fairy-tale heard in Pisa, one of those transcribed by Italo Calvino in his wonderful collection *Italian Folktales*. It seems there was this Florentine who had never in his entire life left Florence. Unable to talk knowledgeably about the comings and goings of the wide world, he felt at a loss in polite conversation, and finally he resolved to go out and do some travelling. He packed his bags and hit the road, in no particular direction, and along the way he met first a priest and then a farmer, both of whom felt the same way about their own lives and decided to join the Florentine as travelling companions. Eventually the three of them came to the house of a giant. The Florentine thought they should go and knock on the door, so that he could tell the folks back home about meeting a giant, and when they did they found the giant a rather courteous fellow who had need of a priest for his village church, and a farmer for his farm. He couldn't think of any particular use for a Florentine, but he took him in too.

Now, in fact this giant's courtesy was but a devious façade concealing a giant-size black-hearted stinker. He took the priest aside, supposedly to show him his duties, but once the door was closed he whacked off his head and kicked the corpse through a trap door. He did the same to the farmer – but the Florentine was watching through the keyhole this time, as Florentines will do, and while he was pretty excited about the story he would have to entertain folks back home, it dawned on him that he would most certainly be next. At this point the storyteller, for lack of something better, gives the tale a turn straight from Homer (remember Odysseus and the Cyclops?). The giant had a squinty eye, and the Florentine had the presence of mind to tell him that he could cure it with a decoction made from a certain herb, which he had noticed growing in those parts. The giant was delighted to let him try, and the Florentine tied him to a marble table and poured the boiling mess into both his eyes. Now comes the chase scene, but the blinded giant couldn't very well catch a Florentine with a marble table tied to his back, and he tried to trick him by offering him his gold ring to finish the cure for his eyes. This was a magic ring, unfortunately, and when the poor guy put it on, his finger became as heavy as stone and weighed him to the ground. The Florentine couldn't get it off again (because it was a magic ring, remember), but he saved himself by chopping off the finger with a penknife. He made it home to Florence, finally, but he never bothered to tell anyone about his wonderful adventures, and whenever anyone asked him about the finger he said he'd had an accident while cutting the grass.

## The First Tuscans

Up in Rome's Capitoline Museum you can see the famous bronze statue of the she-wolf suckling Romulus and Remus, the symbol of Rome since ancient times. Not many people know that this was actually not the work of a Roman artist, but an Etruscan. There are plenty of other things they never taught you in school about the Romans. Specifically, nearly every art or talent we usually give them credit for was bought or more likely stolen from somebody else. Roman painting, sculpture and architecture were seldom more than a grandiose pastiche of the Greek, and plenty of the other Roman trademarks – religion and superstition, gladiators, rectilinear surveying and town planning, portrait sculpture, sewers, togas and even concrete – were simply taken over whole from Rome's nearest neighbours and favourite victims, the Etruscans.

We often forget that, long before Brunelleschi and Donatello, Tuscany was home to another great civilization – Italy's first. But when Rome was still a collection of mud and timber huts among the miasmal swamps of the Tiber, the people of Etruria were collecting Greek urns, reclining on couches at their lavish banquets and dressing up for the races. Etruscan culture blossomed in the 8th century for the usual reasons – most importantly, a nice surplus of ready cash. Just as classical Athens's rise to prominence was financed by the silver mines at nearby Laurion, Etruria exploited the mineral wealth of the Colline Metallifere and Elba; there was plenty of iron, especially, for weapons and for exports. Cities grew opulent as trade boomed, and to protect their trade routes the cities developed powerful navies that dominated the Etruscan *mare nostrum*, the Tyrrhenian (so named because the Greeks called this people *Tyrrhenoi* ; to the Romans they were *Tuscii* or *Etruscii* , while in their own language they are properly called the *Rasena*).

The overwhelming impression given by painting and sculpture is of a people who, whatever their flaws, were wonderfully alive. Etruscan art is full of expressive faces that either wear a smile, or are blissfully caught on the verge of breaking into one. Some of the jolly sculptures in the museums of Volterra and Rome must rank among the first conscious caricatures in art. Everything about this art paints a picture, true or not, of a people cheerfully devoted to the joys of this world. Indeed, their contemporaries dropped plenty of gossip about Etruscan hedonism and licentiousness (much of this comes from the devoutly male-chauvinist Greeks and Romans, shocked at a society where women seem to have enjoyed considerable rights and respect).

In any case, it would be difficult to find anyone in antiquity more fashion-conscious. Elaborately carved mirrors and make-up cases constitute a large part of the Etruscan collection in any museum, and the evidence from tomb frescoes suggests the ladies also liked to dye their hair blonde. The jewellery is remarkable – as good as anything between the Minoans and Fabergé. Some of it goes completely over the top, filigree work and granulation so ornate and flashy it could be worn in Las Vegas. Or whatever was the Etrurian equivalent thereof – after considering the Etruscans closely you'll begin to suspect they must have had one somewhere (perhaps Tuscany's thermal spas; the Etruscans, celebrated for their medical skills, were the first to develop these, and passed the habit down to the Romans). Coiffures and clothes could be equally elaborate; in art you will hardly ever find two Etruscan ladies with the same hairdo. Then, as now, Tuscan shoemakers were famous around the known world; the fashions of the 5th century, as shown in frescoes, featured pointed, curling toes.

Another of their talents was music; Etruscans are often pictured dancing or playing the trumpet, the lyre, and, most commonly of all, a type of pan-pipes. According to a Hellenistic Greek account, they even used music in their hunting; pipers would play charmed melodies to draw the animals out of their lairs and towards the nets. Such a story is not surprising, considering another essential Etruscan trait, an attachment to magic and fortune-telling unsurpassed in the ancient world. Etruscan augurs, or *haruspices*, scrutinized the livers of sacrificed animals and scanned the skies for birds to fortell the future. Their skill was so great that *haruspices* were still employed around the Roman Empire in the 4th century AD, the last people on earth who understood the Etruscan language.

Nobody knows quite why, but after 500 BC everything started to fall apart for the Etruscans. Manufacture and art declined, slave revolts became common, and the archaeologists report that everything from tombs to pottery were being made less skilfully, more cheaply. The once-formidable Etruscan navy was getting regularly whipped by the Greeks, while the Celts destroyed the colonies in the north that had been built up with so much painstaking effort for so long. Most dire of all were the Romans. Rome's closest Etruscan neighbours, Fidenae and Veii, were captured and wiped out in 425 and 396. Veii suffered an epic siege of ten years, and, typically, during that time none of the other Etruscan cities did much to help. Chronic disunity among the members of the Dodecapolis allowed Rome to gobble up Etruria a bit at a time. The last important city, Volsinii, fell about 350, and from then on Etruria was nothing more than a Roman province – the first of many.

But the cultural heritage of these gifted people was too great to disappear completely. The Romans, as we have seen, swallowed Etruscan culture whole, and they passed quite a bit of it on to us. Hundreds of words in modern languages probably stem from the Etruscan, by way of Latin: *person*, for example, which originally meant an Etruscan theatre or ritual mask, or *temple* (this meant one of the 16 sections into which the Etruscan augurs divided the sky for divination by birdflight).

The Etruscan influence on the art of the Renaissance is a fascinating subject that has never been thoroughly explored. When medieval Tuscans revived the art of fresco painting, they probably had no idea they were simply following in the footsteps of their ancestors. Raymond Bloch, an authority on the Etruscans, noticed an eerily perfect resemblance between Donatello's famous *St George* , the very model of quattrocento *prontezza* , and an Etruscan head found long ago at Veii. In one of Michelangelo's sketchbooks we see an image of the Etruscan god Atia, undoubtedly copied from the frescoes in a tomb. And all those little faces we see staring out at us from Renaissance sculptural friezes, frescoes and book decorations are called 'grotesques', because Raphael found their originals in a painted 'grotto' in Rome. This was really a floor of buried rooms of Emperor Nero's palace, the famous Golden House, decorated in a style inherited from the Etruscans of old.

# Food and Drink

05

In Italy, the three Ms (the *Madonna*, *Mamma* and *Mangiare*) are still a force to be reckoned with, and in a country where millions of otherwise sane people spend much of their waking hours worrying about their digestion, standards both at home and in the restaurants are understandably high. Everybody is a gourmet, or at least thinks he or she is, and food is not only something to eat but a subject approaching the heights of philosophy – two Umbrian businessmen once overheard on a train heatedly discussed mushrooms for over *four* hours. Although ready-made pasta, tinned *minestrone* and frozen pizza in the *supermercato* tempt the virtue of the Italian cook, few give in (although many a working mother wishes she could at times).

For the visitor this national culinary obsession comes as an extra bonus to the senses – along with Italy's remarkable sights, music, and the warm sun on your back, you can enjoy some of the best tastes and smells the world can offer, prepared daily in Italy's kitchens and fermented in its countless wine cellars. Eating *all'Italiana* is not only delicious and wholesome, but now undeniably trendy. Foreigners flock here to learn the secrets of Italian cuisine and the even more elusive secret of how the Italians can live surrounded by such a plethora of delights and still fit into their sleek Armani trousers.

# Restaurant Generalities

**Breakfast** (*colazione*) in Italy is no lingering affair, but an early morning wake-up shot to the brain: a *cappuccino* (*espresso* with hot foamy milk, often sprinkled with chocolate – incidentally first thing in the morning is the only time of day at which any self-respecting Italian will touch the stuff), a *caffè latte* (white coffee) or a *caffè lungo* (a generous portion of *espresso*), accompanied by a croissant-type roll, called a *cornetto* or *briosca*, or a fancy pastry. This repast can be consumed in any bar and repeated during the morning as often as necessary. Breakfast in most Italian hotels seldom represents great value.

**Lunch** (*pranzo*), generally served around 1pm, is the most important meal of the day for the Italians, with a minimum of a first course (*primo piatto* – any kind of pasta dish, broth or soup, or rice dish or pizza), a second course (*secondo piatto* – a meat dish, accompanied by a *contorno* or side dish – a vegetable, salad, or potatoes usually), followed by fruit or dessert and coffee. You can, however, begin with a platter of *antipasti* – the appetizers Italians do so brilliantly, ranging from warm seafood delicacies, to raw ham (*prosciutto crudo*), salami in a hundred varieties, lovely vegetables, savoury toasts, olives, pâté and many many more. There are restaurants that specialise in *antipasti*, and they usually don't take it amiss if you decide to forget the pasta and meat and just nibble on these scrumptious hors-d'œuvres (though in the end it may well cost more than a full meal). Most Italians accompany their meal with wine and mineral water – *acqua minerale*, with or without bubbles (*con* or *senza gas*), which supposedly aids digestion – concluding their meals with a *digestivo* liqueur.

*Cena*, the **evening meal**, is usually eaten around 8pm – earlier in the north and later in the south. This is much the same as *pranzo* although lighter, without the pasta;

a *pizza* and beer, eggs or a fish dish. In restaurants, however, they offer all the courses whatever the time of day, so if you have only a sandwich for lunch you can have a full meal in the evening.

In Italy the various terms for types of **restaurants** – *ristorante, trattoria* or *osteria* – have been confused. A *trattoria* or *osteria* can be just as elaborate as a restaurant, though rarely is a *ristorante* as informal as a traditional *trattoria*. Unfortunately the old habit of posting menus and prices in the windows has fallen from fashion, so it's often difficult to judge variety or prices. Invariably the least expensive eating place is the *vino e cucina*, a simple establishment serving simple cuisine for simple everyday prices. It is essential to remember that the fancier the fittings, the fancier the **bill**, though neither of these points has anything at all to do with the quality of the food. If you're uncertain, do as you would at home – look for lots of locals.

People who haven't visited Italy for years and have fond memories of eating full meals for under a pound will be amazed at how much **prices** have risen; though in some respects eating out in Italy is still a bargain, especially when you figure out how much all that wine would have cost you at home. In many places you'll often find restaurants offering a *menu turistico* – full, set meals of usually meagre inspiration for a reasonable set price. More imaginative chefs often offer a *menu degustazione* – a set-price gourmet meal that allows you to taste their daily specialities and seasonal dishes. Both of these are cheaper than if you had ordered the same food *à la carte*.

As the pace of modern urban life militates against traditional lengthy home-cooked repasts with the family, followed by a siesta, alternatives to sit-down meals have mushroomed. Many office workers now behave much as their counterparts elsewhere in Europe and consume a rapid snack at lunchtime, returning home after a busy day to throw together some pasta and salad in the evenings.

The original Italian fast food alternative is known as the 'hot table' (*tavola calda*), a buffet serving hot and cold foods, where you can choose a simple prepared dish or a whole meal, depending on your appetite. The food in these can occasionally be truly impressive, though nowadays they are becoming harder to find among the growing number of international and made-in-Italy fast food franchises. However, bars often double as *paninotecas* (these make sandwiches to order), and if everywhere else is closed, you can always try the railway station bars – these will at least have sandwiches and drinks. Some of the station bars also prepare *cestini di viaggio*, full-course meals in a basket to help you survive long train trips.

Common snacks you'll encounter include *panini* of prosciutto, cheese and tomatoes, or other meats; *tramezzini*, little sandwiches on plain, square white bread that are always much better than they look; *pizza*, of course, or the traditional sandwich of Tuscany and Umbria, a hard roll filled with fat slices of warm *porchetta* (roast whole pig stuffed with fennel and garlic, complete with all the fat and gristle). Little shops that sell pizza by the slice (*al taglio*) are common in city centres; some, called *gastronomie*, offer other take-out delicacies as well. At any delicatessen (*pizzicheria*), or grocer's (*alimentari*) or market (*mercato*) you can buy the materials for countryside picnics; some places in smaller towns will make the sandwiches for you.

## Siena's Salami

There are hundreds of different types of salami in Tuscany, each made to an age-old, much treasured recipe, and tasting far better than some of the ingredients might suggest. Siena has several of its own. *Buristo* is a cooked salami made from the blood and fatty leftovers of sausages and heavily spiced; *finocchiona* is peppered sausage meat seasoned with fennel seeds and stuffed into the sausage skin; *soppressata* is a boiled salami made from a mixture of rind and gristle; the alternative version, *soppressata in cuffia*, is made in the same way and then stuffed into a boned pig's head. The *salsiccioli secchi* are perhaps the most appetising salami of all, made from the leanest cuts of pork or wild boar, enhanced with garlic and black or red pepper.

# Regional Specialities

Regional traditions are strong in Italy, not only in dialect but in the kitchen. Tuscany is no exception and firmly maintains its distinctive cuisine. Although Tuscany does not rank as one of the great culinary regions of Italy, it offers good, honest, traditional dishes, often humble, rarely elaborate. The Medici may have put on some legendary feedbags, but the modern Tuscan is known by his fellow Italians as a *mangiafagioli*, or bean-eater. Some observers hold it as part of the austere Tuscan character, others as another sign of their famous alleged miserliness.

The truth is, although beans and tripe often appear on the menu, that most people when dining out want to try something different, from other regions, perhaps, or the recent concoctions of Italian nouvelle cuisine, or *cucina nuova*, or perhaps a recipe from the Middle Ages or Renaissance. Some of the country's finest restaurants are in Tuscany; in practice, the diversity of dishes in the region, from traditional to bizarre, is almost endless.

# Food

The Tuscans will tell you the basic simplicity of their kitchen is calculated to bring out the glories of their wine, which may well be true, as it tends to be the perfect complement to a glass of Chianti or Vino Nobile. Nearly all Tuscan dishes, however, are born more of thrift than anything else, like **bruschetta**, a Tuscan favourite that takes sliced stale bread, roasted over the fire, covered with olive oil and rubbed with garlic. *Acqua cotta*, popular in southern Tuscany, is *bruschetta* with an egg; another version adds mashed tomatoes. Another traditional Tuscan *antipasto* is **crostini**, thin slices of toast with a piquant pâté spread of chicken livers, anchovies, capers and lemons, or other variations.

For **primo**, the traditional Tuscan relies mostly on **soups**. Perhaps most traditional is *ribollita* ('reboiled'), a thick, hearty soup made with chunks of yesterday's bread, beans, black cabbage and other vegetables. Similar is *pappa col pomodoro*, another bread-based soup flavoured with fresh tomatoes, basil and sludgy local olive oil. *Panzanella*, or Tuscan *gazpacho* (a cold soup of tomatoes, cucumbers, onions, basil, olive oil and bread) can be a godsend on a hot summer's day. The prince of Tuscan soups is Livorno's *cacciucco*, a heavenly fish soup that you have to go to Livorno to try. Other first courses you'll find are *fagioli al fiasco* (beans with oil and black pepper simmered in an earthenware pot) or *fagioli all'uccelletto* (beans with garlic and tomatoes); the most Tuscan of pasta dishes is *pappardelle alla lepre* (wide egg-noodles with a sauce of stewed hare); others are the simple but delicious *spaghetti con briciolata* (with olive oil, breadcrumbs and parsley); *nastri alla Borracina* (ribbons of pasta served with a 'moss' of freshly chopped spinach and marjoram, basil, rosemary, mint and sage); and, most splendid of all *turtui cu la cua* (tortellini with tails), filled with mascarpone, ricotta and spinach, with a butter and basil sauce.

One the whole, Tuscany does not offer exceptional **secondi**: grilled meats, salad, and fried potatoes are the typical *trattoria* standby. Tuscany has its famous steak, *bistecca alla fiorentina* (*see* 'Florence's Most Ephemeral Art', below); otherwise Tuscans are content with grilled chops – lamb, pork or veal. *Fritto misto* is an interesting alternative, where lamb chops, liver, sweetbreads, artichokes and courgettes (*zucchini*) are dipped in batter and deep fried. Otherwise look for *arista di maiale* (pork loin with rosemary and garlic), *francesina* (meat, onion and tomato stew in Vernaccia di San Gimignano wine), *anatra* (duck, often served with truffles in Umbria), *piccione* (stuffed wild pigeon), *cinghiale* (boar), either roasted, in sausages or *stufato* (stewed).

### Florence's Most Ephemeral Art

Florence in its loftier moods likes to call itself the 'birthplace of international haute cuisine', a claim that has very much to do with Catherine de' Medici, a renowned trencherwoman, who brought a brigade of Florentine chefs with her to Paris and taught the Frenchies how to eat artichokes, but has little to do with the city's contribution to the Italian kitchen. Florentine food is on the whole extremely simple, with the emphasis on the individual flavours and fresh ingredients. A typical *primo* could be *pappardelle* (*see* above), usually served with a meat sauce, or game such as wild boar, rabbit and duck. Soups are also popular: try the *ribollita*, unique to the region, or *pappa col pomodoro* (*see* opposite).

The most famous main course in Florence is the *bistecca alla fiorentina*, a large steak on the bone, two inches thick, cut from loin of beef and cooked over coals. It is served charred on the outside and pink on the inside and simply seasoned with salt and black pepper. As for the vegetables, you could try *piselli alla fiorentina*, peas cooked with oil, parsley and diced bacon; or *tortino di carciofi*, a delicious omelette with fried artichokes; *fagioli all' uccelletto*, cannellini beans stewed with tomatoes, garlic and sage; and *spinaci saltati* – fresh spinach sauteed with garlic and olive oil. Florentine desserts tend to be sweet and fattening: *bomboloni alla crema* are vanilla-filled doughnuts and *le fritelle di San Giuseppe* are bits of deep-fried batter covered in sugar. If you prefer cheese, try the sturdy *pecorino toscano*. For better or worse, real Florentine soul food rarely turns up on many restaurant menus, and unless you make an effort you'll never learn what a Florentine cook can do with cockscombs, intestines, calves' feet and tripe.

# Italian Menu Vocabulary

## Antipasti

These before-meal treats can include almost anything; these are among the most common.

*antipasto misto* mixed antipasto
*bruschetta* garlic toast (sometimes with tomatoes)
*carciofi (sott'olio)* artichokes (in oil)
*frutti di mare* seafood
*funghi (trifolati)* mushrooms (with anchovies, garlic and lemon)
*gamberi ai fagioli* prawns (shrimps) with white beans
*mozzarella (in carrozza)* cow/buffalo cheese (fried with bread in batter)
*olive* olives
*prosciutto (con melone)* raw ham (with melon)
*salami* cured pork
*salsicce* sausages

## Minestre (Soups) and Pasta

*agnolotti* ravioli with meat
*cacciucco* spiced fish soup
*cannelloni* meat/cheese rolled in pasta tubes
*cappelletti* small ravioli, often in broth
*crespelle* crêpes
*fettuccine* long strips of pasta
*frittata* omelette
*gnocchi* potato dumplings
*lasagne* sheets of pasta baked with meat and cheese sauce
*minestra di verdura* thick vegetable soup
*minestrone* soup with meat, vegetables and pasta
*orecchiette* ear-shaped pasta, served with turnip greens
*panzerotti* ravioli with mozzarella, anchovies and egg
*pappardelle alla lepre* pasta with hare sauce
*pasta e fagioli* soup with beans, bacon, and tomatoes
*pastina in brodo* tiny pasta in broth

*penne all'arrabbiata* quill-shaped pasta with tomatoes and hot peppers
*polenta* cake or pudding of corn semolina
*risotto (alla Milanese)* Italian rice (with stock, saffron and wine)
*spaghetti all'Amatriciana* with spicy pork, tomato, onion and chilli sauce
*spaghetti alla Bolognese* with ground meat, ham, mushrooms etc.
*spaghetti alla carbonara* with bacon, eggs and black pepper
*spaghetti al pomodoro* with tomato sauce
*spaghetti al sugo/ragú* with meat sauce
*spaghetti alle vongole* with clam sauce
*stracciatella* broth with eggs and cheese
*tagliatelle* flat egg noodles
*tortellini* pasta caps filled with
  *al pomodoro* meat and cheese, with tomato sauce
  *con panna* with cream
  *in brodo* in broth
*vermicelli* very thin spaghetti

## Carne (Meat)

*abbacchio* milk-fed lamb
*agnello* lamb
*animelle* sweetbreads
*anatra* duck
*arista* pork loin
*arrosto misto* mixed roast meats
*bistecca alla fiorentina* Florentine beef steak
*bocconcini* veal mixed wih ham and cheese and fried
*bollito misto* stew of boiled meats
*braciola* hop
*brasato di manzo* braised beef with veg
*bresaola* dried raw meat
*capretto* kid
*capriolo* roe-buck
*carne di castrato/suino* mutton/pork
*carpaccio* thinly sliced raw beef
*cassoeula* pork stew with cabbage
*cervello (al burro nero)* brains (in black butter sauce)

Both Tuscans and Umbrians are rather too fond of their *girarrosto*, a great spit of tiny birds and pork livers.

In Tuscany it's fairly easy to find **seafood** as far inland as Florence – one traditional dish is *seppie in zimino*, or cuttlefish simmered with beets. Hardy souls in Florence can try *cibreo* (cockscombs with chicken livers, beans and egg yolks).

*cervo* venison
*cinghiale* boar
*coniglio* rabbit
*cotoletta* veal cutlet
  *alla Milanese* fried in breadcrumbs
  *alla Bolognese* with ham and cheese
*fagiano* pheasant
*faraona* guinea fowl
  *alla creta* in earthenware pot
*fegato alla veneziana* liver with filling
*lepre (in salmi)* hare (marinated in wine)
*lombo di maiale* pork loin
*lumache* snails
*maiale (al latte)* pork (cooked in milk)
*manzo* beef
*osso buco* braised veal knuckle
*pancetta* rolled pork
*pernice* partridge
*petto di pollo* boned chicken breast
  *alla fiorentina* fried in butter
  *alla bolognese* with ham and cheese
  *alla sorpresa* stuffed and deep fried
*piccione* pigeon
*pizzaiola* beef steak in tomato and oregano
*pollo* chicken
  *alla cacciatora* with tomatoes and
  mushrooms, cooked in wine
  *alla diavola* grilled
  *alla Marengo* fried with tomatoes, garlic
  and wine
*polpette* meatballs
*quaglie* quails
*rane* frogs
*rognoni* kidneys
*saltimbocca* veal scallop with prosciutto and
  sage, cooked in wine and butter
*scaloppine* thin slices of veal sautéed in butter
*spezzatino* pieces of beef/veal, usually stewed
*spiedino* meat on a skewer/stick
*stufato* beef and vegetables braised in wine
*tacchino* turkey
*trippa* tripe
*uccelletti* small birds on a skewer
*vitello* veal

## *Pesce* (Fish)

*acciughe* or *alici* anchovies
*anguilla* eel
*aragosta* lobster
*aringa* herring
*baccalà* dried salt cod
*bonito* small tuna
*branzino* sea bass
*calamari* squid
*cappe sante* scallops
*cefalo* grey mullet
*coda di rospo* angler fish
*cozze* mussels
*datteri di mare* razor (or date) mussels
*dentice* dentex (perch-like fish)
*dorato* gilt head
*fritto misto* mixed fried delicacies, mainly fish
*gamberetto* shrimp
*gamberi (di fiume)* prawns (crayfish)
*granchio* crab
*insalata di mare* seafood salad
*lampreda* lamprey
*merluzzo* cod
*nasello* hake
*orata* bream
*ostriche* oysters
*pesce spada* swordfish
*polipi/polpi* octopus
*pesce azzurro* various small fish
*pesce di San Pietro* John Dory
*rombo* turbot
*sarde* sardines
*seppie* cuttlefish
*sgombro* mackerel
*sogliola* sole
*squadro* monkfish
*stoccafisso* wind-dried cod
*tonno* tuna
*triglia* red mullet (rouget)
*trota* trout
*trota salmonata* salmon trout
*vongole* small clams
*zuppa di pesce* mixed fish in sauce or stew

Tuscany's tastiest **cheese** is *pecorino*, made from ewe's milk; the best is from around Pienza. When aged it becomes quite sharp and is grated over pasta dishes.

Typical **desserts**, to be washed down with a glass of Vinsanto, include Siena's *panforte* (a rich, spicy dense cake full of nuts and candied fruit), *cenci*, a carnival sweet (deep-fried strips of dough), *castagnaccio* (chestnut cake, with pine nuts, raisins and

## Contorni  (Side Dishes, Vegetables)

*asparagi* asparagus
　*alla fiorentina* with fried eggs
*broccoli* broccoli
*carciofi (alla giudia)* artichokes (deep fried)
*cardi* cardoons/thistles
*carote* carrots
*cavolfiore* cauliflower
*cavolo* cabbage
*ceci* chickpeas
*cetriolo* cucumber
*cipolla* onion
*fagioli* white beans
*fagiolini* French (green) beans
*fave* broad beans
*finocchio* fennel
*funghi (porcini)* mushrooms (boletus)
*insalata (mista/verde)* salad (mixed/green)
*lattuga* lettuce
*lenticchie* lentils
*melanzane* aubergine/eggplant
*patate (fritte)* potatoes (fried)
*peperoncini* hot chilli peppers
*peperoni* sweet peppers
*peperonata* stewed peppers, onions, etc.
　(similar to ratatouille)
*piselli (al prosciutto)* peas (with ham)
*pomodoro(i)* tomato(es)
*porri* leeks
*radicchio* red chicory
*radice* radish
*rapa* turnip
*rucola* rocket
*sedano* celery
*spinaci* spinach
*verdure* greens
*zucca* pumpkin
*zucchini* courgettes

## Formaggio  (Cheese)

*bel paese* soft white cow's cheese
*cacio/caciocavallo* pale yellow, sharp cheese
*caprino* goat's cheese
*fontina* rich cow's milk cheese

*groviera* mild cheese (gruyère)
*gorgonzola* soft blue cheese
*parmigiano* parmesan cheese
*pecorino* sharp sheep's cheese
*provolone* sharp, tangy; *dolce* is less strong
*stracchino* soft white cheese

## Frutta  (Fruit, Nuts)

*albicocche* apricots
*ananas* pineapple
*arance* oranges
*banane* bananas
*cachi* persimmon
*ciliege* cherries
*cocomero* watermelon
*datteri* dates
*fichi* figs
*fragole (con panna)* strawberries (with cream)
*lamponi* raspberries
*limone* lemon
*macedonia di frutta* fruit salad
*mandarino* tangerine
*mandorle* almonds
*melagrana* pomegranate
*mele* apples
*mirtilli* bilberries
*more* blackberries
*nespola* medlar fruit
*nocciole* hazelnuts
*noci* walnuts
*pera* pear
*pesca* peach
*pesca noce* nectarine
*pinoli* pine nuts
*pompelmo* grapefruit
*prugna/susina* prune/plum
*uva* grapes

## Dolci  (Desserts)

*amaretti* macaroons
*cannoli* crisp pastry tubes filled with ricotta,
　cream, chocolate or fruit
*coppa gelato* assorted ice cream
*crema caramella* caramel-topped custard

rosemary), Florentine *zuccotto* (a cake of chocolate, nuts and candied fruits), *biscottini di Prato* (almond biscuits softened in wine), *crostate* (fruit tarts) or perhaps a *gelato ai Baci* (made with Perugia's famous hazelnut chocolates). In Assisi, the shops sell *rocciata*, a spicy strudel filled with a mixture of almonds, walnuts, prunes, figs, raisins and honey.

*crostata* fruit flan
*gelato (produzione propria)* ice cream (home-made)
*granita* flavoured ice, often lemon or coffee
*monte bianco* chestnut pudding with cream
*panettone* sponge cake with candied fruit and raisins
*panforte* dense cake of chocolate, almonds and preserved fruit
*saint honoré* meringue cake
*semifreddo* refrigerated cake
*sorbetto* sorbet/sherbet
*spumone* a soft ice cream
*tiramisù* layers of sponge, mascarpone, coffee and chocolate
*torrone* nougat
*torta* cake, tart
*torta millefoglie* layered pastry and custard cream
*zabaglione* eggs and Marsala wine, served hot
*zuppa inglese* trifle

**Bevande (Beverages)**
*acqua minerale* mineral water
  *con/senza gas* with/without fizz
*aranciata* orange soda
*birra (alla spina)* beer (draught)
*caffè (freddo)* coffee (iced)
*cioccolata* chocolate
*gassosa* lemon-flavoured soda
*latte (intero/scremato)* milk (whole/skimmed)
*limonata* lemon soda
*succo di frutta* fruit juice
*tè* tea
*vino* wine
  *rosso* red
  *bianco* white
  *rosato* rosé

**Cooking Terms (Miscellaneous)**
*aceto (balsamico)* vinegar (balsamic)
*affumicato* smoked
*aglio* garlic

*alla brace* on embers
*bicchiere* glass
*burro* butter
*cacciagione* game
*conto* bill
*costoletta/cotoletta* chop
*coltello* knife
*cucchiaio* spoon
*filetto* fillet
*forchetta* fork
*forno* oven
*fritto* fried
*ghiaccio* ice
*griglia* grill
*in bianco* without tomato
*magro* lean meat/pasta without meat
*marmellata* jam
*menta* mint
*miele* honey
*mostarda* candied mustard sauce
*olio* oil
*pane* bread
*pane tostato* toasted bread
*panini* sandwiches (in roll)
*panna* cream
*pepe* pepper
*piatto* plate
*prezzemolo* parsley
*ripieno* stuffed
*rosmarino* rosemary
*sale* salt
*salmi* wine marinade
*salsa* sauce
*salvia* sage
*senape* mustard
*tartufi* truffles
*tavola* table
*tazza* cup
*tovagliolo* napkin
*tramezzini* finger sandwiches
*umido* cooked in sauce
*uovo* egg
*zucchero* sugar

# Tuscan Wines

Quaffing glass after glass of Chianti inspired Elizabeth Barrett Browning to write her best poetry, and there's no reason why the wines of Tuscany shouldn't bring out the best in you as well. The first person to really celebrate Tuscan wines was a naturalist by the name of Francesco Redi in the 1600s, who, like many of us today, made a wine tour of the region, then composed a dithyrambic eulogy called 'Bacchus in Tuscany'. Modern Bacchuses in Tuscany will find quite a few treats, some of which are famous and some less so, along with plenty of cellars and *enoteche* (wine bars) where you can do your own survey – one particularly renowned place in Siena boasts a stock including not only every wine produced in Tuscany, but the rest of Italy as well.

Most Italian wines are named after the grape and the district they come from. If the label says DOC (*Denominazione di Origine Controllata*) it means that the wine comes from a specially defined area and was produced according to a certain traditional method; DOCG (the G stands for *Garantita*) means that a high quality is also guaranteed, a badge worn only by the noblest wines. *Classico* means that a wine comes from the oldest part of the zone of production; *Riserva*, or *Superiore*, means a wine has been aged longer. Most Tuscan farmers also make a cask of *Vinsanto*, a dessert wine that can be sweet or almost dry, and which according to tradition is holy only because priests are so fond of it.

Tuscany produces 19 DOC and DOCG wines, including some of Italy's noblest reds: the dry, ruby **Brunello di Montalcino** and the garnet **Vino Nobile di Montepulciano**, a lovely deep red with the fragrance of violets. The famous Chianti may be drunk either young or as a *Riserva*, especially the higher octane **Chianti Classico**. There are seven other DOC Chianti wines (**Montalbano, Rufina, Colli Fiorentini, Colli Senesi, Colli Aretini, Colline Pisa** and simple **Chianti**). The chief grape in the Chianti region is Sangiovese, shared by all the classified red wines of Tuscany.

Lesser known DOC reds include a dry, bright red named **Rosso delle Colline Lucchesi**, from the hills north of Lucca; the hearty **Pomino Rosso**, from a small area east of Rufina in the Mugello; **Carmignano**, a consistently fine ruby red that can take considerable ageing, produced just west of Florence; and **Morellino di Scansano**, from the hills south of Grosseto, a dry red to be drunk young or old. The three other DOC reds from the coast are **Parrina Rosso**, from Parrina near Orbetello, **Montescudaio Rosso**, and **Elba Rosso**, a happy island wine, little of which makes it to the mainland. All three have good white versions as well.

Of the Tuscan whites, the most notable is **Vernaccia di San Gimignano** (also a *Riserva*), dry and golden in colour, the perfect complement to seafood; delicious but more difficult to find are dry, straw-coloured **Montecarlo** from the hills east of Lucca and **Candia dei Colli Apuani**, a light wine from mountains of marble near Carrara.

From the coast comes **Bolgheri**, white or rosé, both fairly dry. Cortona and its valley produce **Bianco Vergine Valdichiana**, a fresh and lively wine; from the hills around Montecatini comes the golden, dry **Bianco della Valdinievole**. **Bianco di Pitigliano**, of a yellow straw colour, is a celebrated accompaniment to lobster.

# Travel

06

# Getting There

## By Air from the UK and Ireland

If you are arriving in Tuscany by plane, you will fly into one of three airports:

**Aeroporto Amerigo Vespucci, Florence, t** 055 373498, lies 5kms (3 miles) west of the city centre. It has grown from a dinky little place to a bustling airport handling as much, if not more, international traffic than Pisa. Due to the diminutive length of the runway, it only handles small planes. A special airport bus (the Volainbus) connects with the city centre.

**Pisa International Airport,** Galileo Galilei, **t** 050 500707, just outside the city and some 80kms (50 miles) west of Florence. It is connected to Florence by a dual carriageway (the 'Firenze-Pisa-Livorno') which runs into the airport. The airport handles flights from Italy and the rest of Europe. To get into Pisa city centre, either take the N5 bus from outside the arrivals building which runs every 15 mins into Pisa Centrale train station (tickets from the info desk) or take a taxi. Trains run from the airport to Florence and stations in between (Pisa Centrale, Pontederra and Empoli). For Siena, change at Empoli, for Livorno, Viareggio and Massa Carrara change at Pisa Centrale. For Arezzo change in Florence.

## Major Carriers

### UK and Ireland
**Aer Lingus,** Dublin, **t** (01) 886 8888; or Belfast, (0845) 737 747, *www.aerlingus.ie.*
**Alitalia,** London, **t** (08705) 448 259; Dublin, **t** (01) 677 5171, *www.alitalia.co.uk.*
**British Airways, t** 0845 77 333 77, *www.britishairways.com.*
**Lufthansa, t** (0345) 737 747, *www.lufthansa.com.*
**KLM Direct, t** (0870) 507 4074.
**Meridiana, t** (020) 7839 2222, *www.meridiana.it.*
**Sabena, t** (0845) 601 0933, *www.swissair.com.*

### USA and Canada
**Air Canada: t** (1 888) 247 2262, *www.aircanada.ca.*
**Alitalia:** (USA) **t** (800) 223 5730, *www.alitaliausa.com.*
**British Airways: t** 800 AIRWAYS, TTY **t** (1 877) 993 9997, *www.britishairways.com.*
**Continental, t** (800) 231 0856,or hearing impaired **t** (800) 343 9195 , Canada **t** (800) 525 0280, *www.continental.com.*
**Delta: t** (800) 241 4141, *www.delta.com.*
**Northwest Airlines, t** (800) 225 2525, *www.nwa.com.*
**TWA, t** (800) 892 4141, *www.twa.com.*
**United Airlines, t** (800) 241 6522, *www.ual.com.*

## Low-cost Carriers

### UK and Ireland
**Go, t** (0845) 605 4321, *www.go-fly.com,* operates flights between London Stansted and Bologna (7 times a week).
**Ryanair, t** (08701) 569 569, *www.ryanair.com.* Offers flights from Stansted to Pisa.
**Virgin Express, t** (01293) 747747, or **t** (020) 7744 0004, *www.virgin-express.com.* Flies to Rome via Brussels, where you must change planes and possibly wait for a few hours.

## Discounts, Students and Special Deals

### UK and Ireland
**Italy Sky Shuttle,** 227 Shepherd's Bush Road, London W6 7AS, **t** (020) 8748 1333.
**Italflights,** 125 High Holborn, London WC1V 6QA, **t** (020) 7405 6771.
**Trailfinders,** 215 Kensington High Street, London W8, **t** (020) 7937 1234.
**Budget Travel,** 134 Lower Baggot Street, Dublin 2, **t** (01) 661 1866.
**United Travel,** Stillorgan Bowl, Stillorgan, County Dublin, **t** (01) 288 4346/7.

Besides saving 25 per cent on regular flights, young people under 26 have the choice of flying on special discount charters.
**Europe Student Travel,** 6 Campden Street, London W8, **t** 020 7727 7647. Caters for non-students as well.

There is also an infrequent service which runs to Lucca. Trains to Florence do not always coincide with flight arrivals and departures; they run roughly every hour from 10am–5pm, but are much more infrequent before and after these times. Beware; the last train into Florence leaves Pisa airport 7:14 pm.

**Aeroporto G. Marconi, Bologna**, t 051 647 9615, handles more flights than either Pisa or Florence and has two terminals. BA flights from London Gatwick to Bologna can be cheaper than those to Pisa, and Go fly here, so it is worth bearing in mind as an arrival point. The airport lies 6kms north of central Bologna and is connected to the central station by a special bus service. From Bologna Centrale station, trains into Florence can take from 50 mins to 1½ hours depending on the type of train. If you hire a car, take the horrendous A1 motorway south to Florence; journey time is about 1 hour 20 mins.

From London Heathrow there are daily Alitalia and British Airways flights to airports at Pisa and Rome as well as to Genoa (near the Lunigiana) and Bologna. There are also daily flights from London Gatwick to Florence with Meridiana (three times daily and twice a day on Tuesdays). British Airways also have direct flights from Manchester to Rome and Milan.

From Ireland, there are direct flights most weeks from Dublin and Cork to Milan on either Alitalia or Aer Lingus, from where you

---

**STA**, 6 Wright's Lane, London W8 6TA, t (020) 7361 6161, www.statravel.com. With other branches around the UK.
**Trailfinders**, 215 Kensington High Street, London W8 6BD, t (020) 7937 5400, www.trailfinder.com. Additional branches in other major cities.
**Usit Campus Travel**, 52 Grosvenor Gardens, SW1W 0AG, t (0870) 240 1010 www.usit-campus.co.uk. Other branches at UK universities.
**USIT Now**, 19-21 Aston Quay, Dublin 2, t (01) 679 8833, www.usitnow.ie. With other branches in Ireland.

### USA and Canada
**Airhitch**, 2790 Broadway, Suite 100, New York, NY 10025, t (212) 864 2000, www.airhitch.org.
**Council Travel**, 205 E 42nd Street, New York, NY 10017, t (800) 743 1823. Major specialists in student and charter flights; branches all over the USA. Can also provide Eurail and Britrail passes.
**Last Minute Travel Club**, 132 Brookline Avenue, Boston, MA 02215, t 800 527 8646.
**Now Voyager**, 74 Varick St, Suite 307, New York, NY 10013, t (212) 431 1616. For courier flights.
**STA**, 10 Downing Street, New York, NY 10014, t 800 781 4040, t (212) 627 3111, www.sta travel.com; ASUC Building, 2nd Floor, University of California, Berkeley, CA 94720, t (510) 642 3000. Also with branches at universities.

**TFI**, 34 West 32nd Street, New York, NY 10001, t (212) 736 1140, toll free t 800 745 8000.
**Travel Cuts**, 187 College St, Toronto, Ontario M5T 1P7, t (416) 979 2406. Canada's largest student travel specialists; branches in most provinces.

## Websites
You can find some of the best last minute bargains of all, of course, on the **internet**.

### UK and Ireland
www.airtickets.co.uk
www.cheapflights.com
www.lastminute.com
www.skydeals.co.uk
www.sky-tours.co.uk
www.thomascook.co.uk
www.travelocity.com
www.travelselect.com

### USA and Canada
www.xfares.com (carry on luggage only)
www.smarterliving.com
www.air-fare.com
www.expedia.com
www.flights.com
www.orbitz.com
www.priceline.com
www.travellersweb.ws
www.travelocity.com

can pick up a connecting flight to Florence, Perugia, Rome, Ancona or Rimini. Keep your eye open for bargains and charters in the papers.

The carriers listed have a variety of **discounts** if booked in advance. APEX fares have fixed arrival and departure dates, and the stay in Italy must include at least one Saturday night. Children under the age of two usually travel free, and both British Airways and Alitalia offer cheaper tickets on some flights for students and those under 26. Alitalia in particular often has promotional perks like rental cars (Jetdrive), or discounts on domestic flights within Italy, on hotels, or on tours. British Airways do a fly-drive package to Pisa and Florence. At the time of writing, the lowest Apex return fare (booked at least two weeks in advance) between London and Pisa or Rome is around £200 off season; midsummer fares will be well over £250. British Airways occasionally have special World Offer fares to Italy which can work out as low as £135 not including tax.

# By Air from the USA and Canada

From the United States, the major carriers fly only to Rome or Milan, though British Airways has a New York–London–Pisa service. Your travel agent may find a much cheaper fare from your home airport to your Italian airport by way of London, Brussels, Paris, Frankfurt or Amsterdam. Alitalia flies direct to Italy from both the US and Canada.

To be eligible for low cost or APEX fares, you'll have to have fixed arrival and departure dates and spend at least a week in Italy, but no more than 90 days. SuperAPEX, the cheapest normal fares available, must be purchased at least 14 days (or sometimes 21 days) in advance and there are penalties to pay if you change your flight dates. At the time of writing the lowest mid-week SuperAPEX between New York and Rome in the off-season is around $508, rising to the $900 zone in summer.

To sweeten the deal, Alitalia in particular often has promotional perks like rental cars (Jetdrive), or discounts on domestic flights within Italy, on hotels, or on tours. Ask your travel agent. Children under the age of two

usually travel for free and both British Airways and Alitalia offer cheaper tickets on some flights for students and the under-25s.

# By Train

Note that the train costs a lot more than the cheapest air fares, and it takes a lot longer. It's about 17 hours by Eurostar from London's Waterloo Station to Florence (changing in Paris), and will set you back around £225 for a standard return fare, including your *couchette* and reservations throughout. Travelling by train and ferry takes about 22 hours and costs around £176 for a second-class return. These trains are, if you take along a good book, a fairly painless way of getting there. There are also Motorail links from Denderleeuw in Belgium to Bologna (contact Rail Europe, *see* below, for more details).

Discounts are available for senior citizens, families and for children, and anyone under 26. Get them from Rail Europe or Rail Choice (*see* below) and throughout Europe at student offices (CTS in Italy) in main railway stations. An **Interail Pass** (available to EU residents only) offers unlimited travel for all ages throughout Europe for up to a month. At the time of writing, a 22-day pass covering Zone G (Italy, Greece, Turkey, Slovenia) costs £129 for the under-26s and £185 if you're over 26; a month's pass covering Zone G and also Zone E (France, Belgium, Luxembourg and the Netherlands) costs £169 for under-26s and £239 for over-26s.

Various youth fares and inclusive rail passes are also available within Italy, and if you're planning on doing a lot of train travel solely in Italy you can organize these before leaving home at Rail Choice. The **Freedom/ EuroDomino Pass** allows between 3 and 8 days' unlimited travel in any month; travel need not be on consecutive days. Prices for those under 26 range from £67 for 3 days to £107 for 8 days; over 26s will pay from £89 for 3 days to £139 for 8 days 2nd class (£130/205 1st class). Rail Choice have further discounts for those students and under-26s using Eurostar.

**Rail Europe Travel Centre**, 179 Piccadilly, London W1V 0BA, **t** 08705 848 848, *www.raileurope.co.uk*.

**Eurostar**, EPS House, Waterloo Station, London SE1, **t** (08705) 186 186, *www.eurostar.com*.

Rail Choice, 15 Colman House, Empire Square, High Street, Penge, London SE20 7EX, t (020) 8659 7300, *www.railchoice.com* and *www.railchoice.co.uk.*

## From North America

*See* opposite, p.80, for notes on travelling to Italy by train from the UK.

For information on Italian rail passes and special deals, contact:

CIT, 15 West 44th Street, 10th Floor, New York, NY 10036, t (212) 730 2121, *www.cittours.com* or *www.fs-on-line.com*; (Canada) 80 Tiverton Court, Suite 401, Markham, Toronto L3R O94, t (905) 415 1060.

Rail Choice, 15 Colman House, Empire Square, High Street, Penge, London SE20 7EX, t (020) 8659 7300, *www.railchoice.com.* They can send rail passes and Motorail tickets to the USA by Fedex.

Rail Europe, 226 Westchester Ave, White Plains, NY 10064, t (914) 682 2999, or t (800) 438 7245, *www.raileurope.com.*

# By Coach

Usually more expensive than a charter flight, the coach is the last refuge of airplane-phobic bargain hunters. The journey time from London to Rome or Siena is around 32 hours, changing in Paris and/or Milan; the return fare is around £115. There are, again, discounts for under 26s, senior citizens and children.

Eurolines UK Ltd, 4 Cardiff Road, Luton, LU1 1PP, t 08705 143219, f (01582) 400694, *www.gobycoach.com. Open Mon–Fri 8am–8pm, Sun 10–2.*

# By Car

Driving to Italy from the UK is a rather lengthy and expensive proposition, and if you're only staying for a short period figure your costs against Alitalia's or other airlines' fly-drive scheme. No matter how you cross the Channel, it is a good two-day drive, about 1,600km from Calais to Rome.

Ferry information is available at any travel agent or direct from the ferry companies. You can cut many of the costly motorway tolls by going from Dover to Calais, through France, to Basle, Switzerland, and then through the Gotthard Tunnel over the Alps; in the summer you can save the steep tunnel tolls by taking one of the mountain passes (one-way tolls range from about 40–70SFr for a small car). You can avoid some of the driving by putting your car on the train (although again balance the sizeable expense against the price of hiring a car for the period of your stay). There are Motorail links from Denderleeuw, in Belgium, to Bologna and Rome (infrequently in winter: for further details contact Rail Choice, t (020) 8659 7300, *www. railchoice.co.uk*).

To bring your car into Italy, you need your car registration (log book), valid driving licence and valid insurance (a Green Card is not necessary, but you'll need one if you go through Switzerland). If your driving licence is of the old-fashioned sort without a photograph the AA strongly recommends that you apply for an international driving permit as well (available from the AA or RAC).

Make sure everything is in excellent working order or your slightly bald tyre may enrich the coffers of the Swiss or Italian police – it's not uncommon to be stopped for no reason and have your car searched until the police find something to stick a fine on. Also beware that spare parts for some non-Italian cars are difficult to come by, almost impossible for pre-1988 Japanese models.

Foreign-plated cars are no longer entitled to free breakdown service by the Italian Auto Club (ACI), but their prices are fair. Phone ACI on t 06 44 77 to find out the current rates. At the time of writing the motorway tunnel tolls are as follows: Fréjus Tunnel, *www.tunnel dufrejus.com*, from Modane (France) to Bardonècchia. Prices range from €15– €30. Gran San Bernardo, *www.grandsaint bernard. ch*, from Bourg St Pierre (Switzerland) to Aosta. Small car or motorcycle €17 single, €24 return.

For more information on driving in Italy, contact the AA, t 0870 600 0371, *www.theaa.com* or RAC, t (0800) 550 550 or 0906 470 1740 (travel services), *www.rac.co.uk*, in the UK, and AAA, t (407) 444 4000, *www.aaa.com*, in the USA.

# Courses for Foreigners

The **Italian Institute**, 39 Belgrave Square, London SW1X 8NX, t 020 7235 1461, or 686 Park Avenue, New York, NY 10021, t (212) 889 4057, is the main source of information on courses for foreigners in Italy. Graduate students should also contact their nearest Italian consulate to find out about scholarships – apparently many go unused each year because no one knows about them.

One obvious course to take, especially in this linguistically pure land of Dante, is **Italian language and culture**: there are special summer classes offered by the Scuola Lingua e Cultura per Stranieri of the University of **Siena**. Similar courses are held in **Cortona**, **Viareggio** (run by the University of Pisa), **Urbino** (at the University of Urbino, Via Saffi 2, Urbino), and, not surprisingly, **Florence** – sometimes there seem to be more American students than Florentines in the city. The following offer courses year-round:

**British Institute**, Piazza Strozzi 2, t 055 267 78200, f 055 267 7822, *www.british institute.it*. Runs courses on Florentine art and history. The school is located at Via Tornabuoni 2, t 055 284 033.

**Centro Fiorenza**, Via di Santo Spirito, t 055 287 148. Offers history, literature and art at both basic and advanced levels. Also offers cooking courses.

**Scuola Lorenzo de' Medici**, Via dell'Alloro 14r, t 055 287 143. Classes in language and art.

**Centro Linguistico Italiano Dante Alighieri**, Via de' Bardi 12, t 055 234 2984. Specializes in language courses.

**Music courses** complement the regions' numerous music festivals. Certaldo's medieval music society, Ars Nova, sponsors a seminar in July. Siena's Accademia Musicale Chigiana, Via di Città, offers master classes for instrumentalists and conductors. In July and August **Barga** holds an International Opera workshop, t 0583 723 250.

**Art-lovers** can take a course on medieval art at Florence's Università Internazionale dell'Arte, in the Villa Tornabuoni, Via Incontri 3; courses are offered from October to April in history of art, restoration and design, while the Istituto per l'Arte e il Restauro, in Palazzo Spinelli, Borgo Santa Croce 10, holds work-

shops in art restoration. In Spoleto, the Centro Italiano Studi di Alto Medioevo, in the Palazzo Ancaiani, offers classes on medieval art in April. Perugia's Accademia delle Belle Arti Pietro Vanucci, at Piazza San Francesco al Prato 5, has painting and sculpture courses.

**A Taste of Florence**, Via Taddea 31, t 055 292 578, *www.divinacucina.com*. American cook Judy Witts has lived in Florence for many years, and her knowledge of the local food and culture is extensive. Courses are run from her home near the central market in Florence, and the day starts with a shopping session, progressing to the kitchen. Groups are limited to six, and most courses run for a day or a week.

**Capezzana Wine and Culinary Centre**, Via Cappezana 100, 59011 Loc. Seano, Carmignano, t 055 870 6005. This estate some 30km from Florence, which produces wine and olive oil, hosts courses designed for food professionals, skilled cooks and those involved with food and wine. Accommodation is available in a wing of the villa.

# Specialist Tour Operators

## In the UK

**Abercrombie & Kent**, Sloane Square House, Holbein Place, London SW1W 8NS t (020) 7559 8686, f (020) 7730 9376, *info@ abercrombiekent.co.uk*. Exclusively tailored holidays in Tuscany.

**Ace Study Tours**, Babraham, Cambridge CB2 4AP, t (01223) 835055, f (01223) 837394, *www.study-tours.org*. Cultural tours through Tuscany.

**Alternative Travel (ATG)**, 69–71 Banbury Road, Oxford OX2 6PE, t (01865) 315678, f 315697, *www.atg-oxford.co.uk*, *info@atg-oxford.co.uk*. Offers walking, wild flower, art and cycling tours as well as truffle hunts and painting courses.

**Andante Travels**, The Old Telephone Exchange, Winterborne Dauntsey, Salisbury SP4 6EH, t (01980) 610555, *www.andantetravels.co.uk*. Owned and run by archeologists, offers 'Romantic ruins in rural Italy': a 5-day tour of Tuscany's most important Etruscan archaeological sites, art and architecture.

**Arblaster & Clarke Wine Tours**, Farnham Road, West Liss, Petersfield, Hants GU33 6JQ, t (01730) 893344, f (01730) 892888, *www. arblasterandclarke.com*. Wine tours, truffle hunts and gourmet cooking tours

**British Airways Holidays**, Astral Towers, Betts Way, Crawley, West Sussex, RH10 2XA, t (0870) 242 4243/(01293) 723 100, f (01293) 722702, *www.baholidays.co.uk*. Florentine city breaks.

**Brompton Travel**, Brompton House, 64 Richmond Road, Kingston-upon-Thames, Surrey KT2 5EH, *www.bromptontravel.co.uk*, t 020 8549 3334. Organizers of tailor-made trips, city breaks and opera tours.

**The Caravan Club**, East Grinstead House, West Sussex, RH19 1UA, t (01342) 326944, f (01342) 327989, *www.caravanclub.co.uk*. Arranges advance booking and pitch reservation.

**Citalia**, Marco Polo House, 3–5 Lansdowne Road, Croydon CR9 1LL, t (020) 8686 5533, or t 8681 0712, *www.citalia.co.uk*. Modest resort and self-catering holidays.

**Erna Low**, 9 Reece Mews, London, SW7 3HE, t (020) 7584 2841, f (020) 7589 9531, *www.bodyandsoulholidays.com*. Pamper yourself at their spa resort in Grosseto.

**Fine Art Travel**, 15 Savile Row, London W1X 1AE, t (020) 7437 8553, f (020) 7437 1733. Recreates the spirit of the Grand Tour, staying in private villas and palazzi.

**Inscape Fine Art Tours**, Austins Farm, High Street, Stonesfield, Witney, Oxfordshire OX8 8PU, t (01993) 891726, f (01993) 891718. Escorted art tours with guest lecturers.

**Italiatour**, 9 Whyteleafe Business Village, Whyteleafe Hill, Whyteleafe, Surrey CR3 0AT, t (01883) 621 900, f (01883) 625 255, *www.italiatour.com*. Resort holidays, city breaks, cookery courses and horse-riding.

**Kirker Holidays**, 3 New Concordia Wharf, Mill Street, London SE1 2BB, t 08700 270 480, f (020) 7231 4771, *http://kirker.ping.co.uk*. City breaks and tailor-made tours; also arranges internal rail travel and any length of stay.

**Magic of Italy**, 227 Shepherd's Bush Road, London W6 7AS, t (020) 8748 7575, f (020) 8748 3731, *www.magictravelgroup.co.uk*. City breaks and villa or farmhouse holidays.

**Magnum**, 7 Westleigh Park, Blaby, Leicester, t (01162) 777123. Organizes holidays for senior citizens in Florence.

**Martin Randall Travel**, 10 Barley Mow Passage, Chiswick, London W4 4PH, t (020) 8742 3355, f (020) 8742 7766, *www.martinrandall.com*. Imaginatively put together cultural tours with guest lecturers.

**Prospect Music and Art Tours**, 36 Manchester Street, London W1M 5PE, t (020) 7486 5704, f (020) 7486 5868, *sales@prospecttours.com*. Art tours in Florence; specialist holidays devoted to figures such as Dante and Piero della Francesca.

**Ramblers Holidays**, Box 43, Welwyn Garden City, Hertfordshire AL8 6PQ, t (01707) 331 133, f (01707) 333 276, *www.ramblersholidays .co.uk*. Walking holidays.

**Real Holidays**, 66–68 Essex Road, London N1 8LR, t (020) 7359 3938, f (020) 7226 5800, *www.realhols.co.uk*. Designers of quirky holidays for demanding folk.

**Rhodes School of Cuisine**, t (01428) 685140, f (01428) 683424, *www.rhodeschoolofcuisine .com*. Culinary holidays in a private villa in Vorno, near Lucca.

**Sherpa Expeditions**, 131a Heston Road, Hounslow, Middlesex, TWR ORD, t (020) 8577 2717, f (020) 8572 9788 *www.sherpa-walking-holidays.co.uk*. Walking and cycling holidays.

**Simply Tuscany and Umbria**, Kings House, Wood Street, Kingston-upon-Thames, Surrey KT1 1UG, t (020) 8541 2206, f (020) 8541 2280, *www.simply-travel.com*. Tailormade itineraries, also art, architecture and vegetarian cookery courses, balloon flights, spa resorts and painting holidays.

**Sovereign Tours**, 2nd Floor, Astral Towers, Betts Way, Crawley, West Sussex, t (0161) 742 2255, *www.sovereign.com*. Wide range of 7–14-day package tours in the Florence and Chianti areas: 3- and 4-star accommodation.

**Specialtours**, 81 Elizabeth St, London SW1W 9PG, t (020) 7730 2297, f (020) 7823 5035. Cultural tours of Tuscany.

**Tasting Places**, Unit 40, Buspace Studios, Conlan Street, London W10 5AP, t (020) 7460 0077, f (020) 7460 0029, *www.tasting-places.com*. Cookery courses.

**Travelsphere**, Compass House, Rockingham Road, Market Harborough, Leicestershire LE16 7QD, t (01858) 464818, f (01858) 434323, *www.travelsphere.co.uk*. Singles holidays and coach tours.

**Venice Simplon-Orient Express,** Suite 200, Hudson's Place, Victoria Station, London SW1V 1JL, t 020 7928 6000. London–Florence luxury rail tours.

**Voyages Jules Verne,** 21 Dorset Square, London NW1 6QG, t 020 7616 1000, *www.vjv.co.uk*. Tours from May to November, staying in 4-star accommodation with escorted excursions.

**Wallace Arnold,** Gelderd Road, Leeds LS12 6DH, t 01132 310 739. Based in a hotel in Montecatini Terme, with excursions to Florence, Pisa and Lucca.

**Waymark,** 44 Windsor Road, Slough, t (01753) 516 477, f (01753) 517 016. Walking tours.

## In the USA and Canada

The Italian Tourist Office in New York can provide an extensive list of specialist tour operators. Here is a selection:

**Abercrombie & Kent,** 1520 Kensington Rd., Oak Brook, IL 60523 2141, t (630) 954 2944 or toll free t (800) 323 7308, *www.abercrombie kent.com*. City breaks and walking holidays.

**Archaeological Tours Inc.,** Suite 904, 271 Madison Avenue, New York, NY 10016, t (212) 986 3054. Etruscan sites.

**Bike Riders' Tours,** PO Box 130254, Boston, MA 02113, t (617) 723 2354, f (617) 723 2355, *www.bikeriderstours.com*. Cycling tours, and a culinary 'Cucina Toscana' tour.

**Butterfield & Robinson,** 70 Bond Street, Suite 300, Toronto, Ontario M5B 1X3, t (416) 864 1354, or t 800 678 1147, f (416) 864 0541, *www.butterfield.com*. Cycling and walking holidays in areas of Tuscany.

**Certified Vacations,** 300 Pinnacle Way, Norcross, GA 30093, t (800) 241 1700. Prepackaged or tailor-made FIT tours.

**CIT Tours,** 15 West 44th St, New York, NY 10173, t (212) CIT-TOUR, *www.cit-tours.com*; also 9501 West Devon Ave, Rosemount, Il 60018, t (800) CIT-TOUR, and, in Canada, 80 Tiverton Court, Suite 401, Markham, Ontario L3R 0GA, t (800) 387 0711. Tailor-made tours for individuals and groups, plus cookery courses.

**Esplanade Tours,** 581 Boylston Street, Boston, MA 02116, t (617) 266 7465, or toll free t (800) 426 5492, *www.specialtytravel.com*. Art, architecture and FIT itineraries.

**Europe Train Tours,** 198 E. Boston Post Rd., Mamaroneck, NY 10543, t (914) 698 9426, or

toll free t (800) 551 2085, f (914) 698 9516. Escorted tours by train and car.

**Italian Connection,** 11 Fairway Drive, Suite 210, Edmonton, Alberta, T6J 2W4, t 1-800-462-7911, or t (780) 438 5712, f (780) 436 4085, *www.italian-connection.com*. Walking and culinary tours.

**Italiatour,** 666 5th Avenue, New York, NY 10103, t (800) 845 3365 (US) and (888) 515 5245 (Canada), *www.italiatour.com*. Fly-drive holidays and sightseeing tours organised by Alitalia.

**La Dolce Vita Wine Tours,** 576 Fifth Street, Brooklyn, NY 11215, toll free t (888) 746 0022, t (718) 788 6365, f (718) 499 2618, *www.dolcetours.com*. Wine tours with 'epicurean', walking or biking options.

**Maupintour,** 1421 Research Park Drive, Kansas 66049, t (785) 331 1000, or toll free t (800) 255 4266, *www.maupintour.com*. Sailing holidays along Tuscan waterways.

**Rhodes School of Cuisine,** t 1 888 254 1070, *www.rhodeschoolofcuisine.com*. Culinary holidays in a private villa in Vorno, near Lucca.

**Stay and Visit Italy,** 5506 Connecticut Avenue NW, Suite 23, Washington, DC 20015, t (202) 237 5220, t (800) 411 3728, f (202) 966 6972, *www.stayandvisit.com*. Tailor-made tours throughout Tuscany and Umbria.

**Trafalgar Tours,** 11 East 26th Street, New York, NY 10010, t (212) 689 8977, *www.trafalgar tours.com*. Ask about their 10-day tour 'Rome and the Tuscan Highlights'.

**Worldwide Classroom,** P.O. Box 1166, Milwaukee, WI 53201, t (414) 351 6311, or toll free (800) 276 8712, f (414) 224 3466, *www.worldwide.edu*. Database listing educational organizations around the world.

## In Italy

**Corymbus Viaggi,** Via Massetana Romana 56, 53100 Siena, t (+39 577) 271 654, f (+39 577) 271615, *corymbus@ntt.it*. For groups or individuals: tours focusing on the Etruscans, wine tours, art and cookery in Tuscany, painting and stencil classes, mountain bike tours of Chianti.

**Cook Italy,** t 0039 051 644 8612, f 0039 051 644 8612, *www.cookitaly.com, ccaruana@iol.it*. Culinary tours and cookery courses in the Lucca and Arezzo provinces of Tuscany.

# Entry Formalities

## Passports and Visas

To get into Italy you need a valid passport. EU citizens do not need visas in order to enter Italy. US, Canadian and Australian nationals do not need visas for stays of up to 90 days. If you mean to stay for longer than 90 days in Italy you will have to get a *permesso di soggiorno*. For this you will need to state your reason for staying, be able to prove a source of income and have medical insurance. After a couple of exasperating days at some provincial Questura office filling out forms you should walk out with your permit.

According to Italian law, you must register with the police within eight days of your arrival. If you check into a hotel this is done automatically. If you come to grief in the mesh of rules and forms, you can at least get someone to explain it to you in English by calling the Rome Police Office for visitors, t 06 4686, ext. 2987.

## Customs

EU nationals over the age of 17 can now import a limitless amount of goods for their personal use.

Arrivals from non-EU countries have to pass through Italian Customs which are usually benign, although how the frontier police manage to recruit such ugly, mean-looking characters to hold the submachine guns and drug-sniffing dogs from such a good-looking population is a mystery. However, they'll let you be if you don't look suspicious (sadly, not being caucasian is often 'suspicious' enough).

Duty-free allowances have now been abolished within the EU. For travellers entering the EU from outside, the duty-free limits are 1 litre of spirits or 2 litres of liquors (port, sherry or champagne), plus 2 litres of wine, 200 cigarettes and 50 grams of perfume. Much larger quantities – up to 10 litres of spirits, 90 litres of wine, 110 litres of beer and 800 cigarettes – bought locally and provided you are travelling between EU countries, can be taken through customs if you can prove that they are for private consumption only and taxes have been paid in the country of purchase. Under-17s are not allowed to bring tobacco or alcohol

into the EU. **Pets** must be accompanied by a bilingual Certificate of Health from your local Veterinary Inspector.

For residents of Britain and other EU countries, the usual regulations apply regarding what you can carry home. Note that you cannot bring fresh meat, vegetables or plants into the UK.

Residents of the USA may each take home US$400-worth of foreign goods without attracting duty, including the tobacco and alcohol allowance. Canadians can bring home $300-worth of goods in a year, plus their tobacco and alcohol allowances.

# Getting Around

The republic has an excellent network of airports, railways, highways and byways, and you'll find getting around fairly easy – unless one union or another goes on strike (to be fair, this rarely happens during the main holiday season). There's plenty of talk about passing a law to regulate strikes, but don't count on it happening soon. Instead learn to recognize the word in Italian: *sciopero* (SHO-per-o) and be prepared to do as the Romans do when you hear it – quiver with resignation. There's always a day or two's advance notice, and usually strikes last only 12 or 24 hours – but long enough to throw a spanner in the works if you have to catch a plane, so keep your ears open.

# By Train

*FS information from anywhere in Italy,*
*t 1478 88088, open 7am–9pm,*
*www.fs-on-line.com*

Italy's national railway, the FS (*Ferrovie dello Stato*) is well run and often a pleasure to ride. There are also several private rail lines around cities and in country districts. We have tried to list them all in this book. Some, you may find, won't accept Interail or EurRail passes.

Train **fares** have increased greatly over the last couple of years and only those without extra supplements can still be called cheap. Possible FS unpleasantnesses you may encounter, besides a strike, are delays and crowding (especially on Friday nights, weekends and in the summer). **Reserve a seat** in advance (*fare una prenotazione*). The fee is small and can save you hours standing. For the upper echelon trains and the *Eurostars*, reservations are mandatory. Do check when you purchase your ticket in advance that the date is correct; tickets are only valid the day they're purchased unless you specify otherwise.

**Tickets** may be purchased not only in the stations, but also at many travel agents, and it's wise to buy them in advance as the queues can be long. Be sure you ask which **platform** (*binario*) your train arrives at; the big permanent boards posted in the stations are not always correct.

Always remember to **stamp your ticket** (*convalidare*) in the not-very-obvious machine at the head of the platform before boarding the train. Failure to do so will result in a fine. If you get on a train without a ticket you can buy one from the conductor, with an added 20 per cent penalty. You can also pay a conductor to move up to first class as long as there are places available.

There is a strict hierarchy of **trains**. A *Regionale* travels shortish distances, and tends to stop at all the stations. There are only a few *Espressi* trains left in service, but they are in poor condition, and mostly service the long runs from the south of Italy. No supplement is required. *Intercity* trains link Italian cities, with minimum stops. Some carry an obligatory seat reservation requirement (free in this case), and all have a supplement. The true Kings of the Rails are the super-swish and super-fast *Eurostars* (Rome–Florence in 1½ hours). These make very few stops, have both first and second class carriages, and carry a supplement which includes an obligatory seat reservation. So, the faster the train, the more you pay.

The FS offers several **passes**. A flexible option is the **Flexi Card** (also available through CIT, *see* above) which allows unlimited travel for either 4 days within a month, 8 days within a month or 12 days within a month, plus supplements and seat reservations on *Eurostars* (all prices quoted are second class). Another ticket, the **Kilometrico**, gives you 3,000 kilometres of travel, made on a maximum of 20 journeys and is valid for two months; one advantage is that it can be used by up to five people at the

same time. However, supplements are payable on *Intercity* trains.

Other **discounts**, available only once you're in Italy, are 15 per cent on same-day return tickets and three-day returns (depending on the distance involved), and discounts for families of at least four travelling together. Senior citizens (men 65 and over, women 60) can also get a *Carta d'Argento* ('silver card') entitling them to a 20 per cent reduction in fares. A *Carta Verde* bestows a 20 per cent discount on people under 26 .

**Refreshments** on routes of any great distance are provided by buffet cars or trolleys; you can usually get sandwiches and coffee from vendors along the tracks at intermediary stops. Station bars often have a good variety of take-away travellers' fare; consider at least investing in a plastic bottle of mineral water, since there's no drinking water on the trains.

Besides trains and bars, Italy's stations offer other **facilities**. Most have a *deposito*, where you can leave your bags for hours or days for a small fee. The larger ones have porters (who charge around €5 per piece) and luggage trolleys; major stations have an *albergo diurno* ('day hotel', where you can take a shower, get a shave and haircut, etc.), information offices, currency exchanges open at weekends (not at the most advantageous rates, however), hotel-finding and reservation services, kiosks with foreign papers, restaurants, etc. You can also arrange to have a rental car awaiting you at your destination – Avis, Hertz and Maggiore are the firms that provide this service.

# By Coach and Bus

Intercity coach travel is often quicker than train travel, but also a bit more expensive. The Italians aren't dumb; you will find regular coach connections only where there is no train to offer competition. Coaches almost always depart from the vicinity of the train station, and tickets usually need to be purchased before you get on. In many regions they are the only means of public transport and are well used, with frequent departures. If you can't get a ticket before the coach leaves, get on anyway and pretend you can't speak a word of Italian; the worst that can happen is that someone will make you pay for a ticket. Bear in mind that the base for all country bus lines will be the provincial capitals; we've done our best to explain the connections even for the most out-of-the-way routes.

**City buses** are the traveller's friend. Most cities label routes well; all charge flat fees for rides within the city limits and immediate suburbs, at the time of writing around €2.50.

Bus tickets must always be purchased before you get on, either at a tobacconist's, a newspaper kiosk, many bars, or from ticket machines near the main stops.

Once you get on, you must 'obliterate' your ticket in the machines in the front or back of the bus; controllers stage random checks to make sure you've punched your ticket. Fines for cheats are about €25, and the odds are about 12 to 1 against a check, so you may decide that you can take your chances against how lucky you feel. If you're good-hearted, you'll buy a ticket and help some overburdened municipal transit line meet its annual deficit.

# By Taxi

Taxi meters start at around €2 plus extras, and add €0.75 per km. There is a minimum charge of €3.5. Each piece of baggage will cost extra, and there are surcharges for trips outside the city limits, trips between 10pm and 6am, and trips on Sundays and holidays.

# By Car

The advantages of driving in Tuscany generally outweigh the disadvantages. Before you bring your own car or hire one, consider the kind of holiday you're planning. If it's a tour of art cities, you'd be best off not driving at all: parking is impossible, traffic impossible, deciphering one-way streets, signals and signs impossible. In nearly every other case, however, a car gives you the freedom and possibility of making your way through Italy's lovely countryside.

Be prepared to encounter some of the highest fuel costs in Europe, to spend a very long time looking for a place to park in any

town bigger than a peanut, and to face drivers who look at motoring as if it were a video game. The Italians, whether 21-year-old madcaps or elderly nuns, turn into aggressive starfighters once behind the wheel, whose mission is to reach their destination in a certain allotted time (especially around lunch or dinner, if they think the pasta is already on the boil), regardless of minor nuisances such as other cars, road signs, traffic signals, solid no-passing lines, or blind curves on mountain roads. No matter how fast you trip along on the *autostrade* (Italy's toll motorways, official speed limit **130km/80 mph**) someone will pass you going twice as fast.

If you aren't intimidated, buy a good road map of Tuscany (the Italian Touring Club produces excellent ones). Many petrol stations close for lunch in the afternoon, and few stay open late at night, though you may find a 'self-service' where you feed a machine nice smooth €5 notes. *Autostrada* tolls are high – to drive on the A1 from Milan to Rome will cost you around €30 at the time of writing. Most exits now accept credit cards. The rest stops and petrol stations along the motorways are open 24 hours. Other roads – *superstrade* on down through the Italian grading system – are free of charge. The Italians are good about signposting, and roads are almost all excellently maintained – some highways seem to be built of sheer bravura, suspended on cliffs, crossing valleys on enormous piers – feats of engineering that will remind you, more than almost anything else, that this is the land of the ancient Romans. Beware that you may be fined on the spot for speeding, a burnt-out headlamp, etc.; if you're especially unlucky you may be slapped with a *super multa*, a superfine, of €75or more. You may even be fined for not having a portable triangle danger signal (these can be picked up at the border or from an ACI office for €1.25).

The **Automobile Club of Italy** (ACI) is a good friend to the foreign motorist. Besides having bushels of useful information and tips, they can be reached from anywhere by calling t 116 – also use this number if you have an accident, need an ambulance, or simply have to find the nearest service station. If you need major repairs, the ACI can make sure the prices charged are according to their guidelines.

## Specialist Organizations for Disabled Travellers

### In Italy

**Accessible Italy**, Promotur-Mondo Possibile, La Viaggeria, Via Lemonia 161, 00174 Roma, t 067 158 2945, f 067 158 3433, *www.tour-web.com/accessibleitaly/*. Travel agency which provides valuable, detailed help and information on access in Italy, including detailed coverage of accessible tourist spots, transport and accommodation in Tuscany.

**APT (Azienda Provinciale per Il Turismo di Roma)**, Via Parigi, 5, Roma, t 06 4889 9253, or t 06 4889 9255. The official tourist information office, which provides some information.

**Centro Studi Consulenza Invalidi**, Via Gozzadini 7, 20148 Milan. Publishes an annual guide, *Vacanze per Disabili*, with details of suitable accommodation in Italy.

**CO.IN (Consorzio Cooperative Integrate)**, Via Enrico Giglioli 54a, 00169 Rome, t (06) 232 67504, toll free in Italy t 800 271 027, f (06) 232 67505 . Their tourist information centre (*open Mon–Fri 9–5*) offers advice and information on accessibility. They also offer **COINtel**, t (06) 2326 7695, a 24-hour information line in English, and can assist with bookings for guided tours with suitable transport, t (06) 7128 9676.

**Vacanze Serene**, toll-free t 800 271 027. Gives information on accessibie travel throughout Italy (*open 9–5 Mon–Fri*).

### In the UK and Ireland

**Holiday Care Service**, 2nd Floor, Imperial Buildings, Victoria Road, Horley, Surrey RH6 9HW, t (01293) 774535, f 771500, *www.holidaycare.org.uk*. Holiday Care can give up-to-date information on destinations both in the UK and abroad, on transportation and on suitable tour operators.

**Irish Wheelchair Association**, Blackheath Drive, Clontarf, Dublin 3, t 01 833 8241, *www.iwa.ie/*. An organization with services for disabled travellers.

**RADAR (Royal Association for Disability and Rehabilitation)**, 12 City Forum, 250 City Road, London EC1V 8AF, t (020) 7250 3222, f 7250 0212, *www.radar.org.uk*. RADAR publish several useful books, including *Access to Air Travel*, as well as holiday fact-packs.

**Royal National Institute for the Blind (RNIB)**, 224 Great Portland Street, London W15 5TB, t (020) 7388 1266, *www.rnib.org.uk*. Its mobility unit offers 'Plane Easy', an audio cassette which advises blind or partially-sighted people on travelling by plane. They also advise on accommodation.

**Royal National Institute for the Deaf (RNID)**, 19-23 Featherstone Street, London EC1Y 8SL,

Hiring a car is fairly simple if not particularly cheap. Italian car rental firms are called *autonoleggi*. There are both large international firms through which you can reserve a car in advance, and local agencies, which often have lower prices. Air or train travellers should check out possible discount packages.

Most companies will require a deposit amounting to the estimated cost of the hire, and there is 19 per cent VAT added to the final cost. At the time of writing, a 5-seat Fiat Panda costs around €35 a day. Petrol is 50 per cent more expensive than in the UK. Rates become more advantageous if you take the car for a week with unlimited mileage. If you need a car for more than three weeks, leasing is a more economic alternative. The National Tourist Office has a list of firms in Italy that hire caravans (trailers) and campers.

## By Motorbike and Bicycle

The means of transport of choice for many Italians, motorbikes, mopeds and Vespas can be a delightful way to get between the cities and see the countryside. You should only consider it, however, if you've ridden them before – Italy's hills and aggravating traffic make it no place to learn. Helmets are compulsory. Hire costs for a *motorino* (moped) range from about €18 per day; Vespas (scooters) somewhat more (from about €22).

Italians are keen cyclists as well, racing drivers up the steepest hills; if you're not training for the Tour de France, consider the hillyness of the region well before planning a bicycling tour – especially in the hot summer months. Bikes can be transported by train in

Infoline **t** 0808 808 0123, textphone **t** 0808 808 9000, **f** (020) 7296 8199, *www.rnid .org.uk*, *informationline@rnid.org.uk*. Call their information line for help and advice.
**Tripscope**, Alexandra House, Albany Road, Brentford, Middlesex TW8 0NE, **t** 08457 585641, **f** (020) 8580 7022, *www.justmo-bility.co.uk/tripscope/*. Practical advice and information on aspects of travel and transport for elderly and disabled travellers. Information by letter or tape.

### In the USA and Canada
**Access America**, Washington DC, DC 20202, USA, *www.accessamerica.gov*. Provides information on facilities for disabled people at international airports. The US government website, *www.dot.gov/airconsumer/disabled.htm*, also has useful information.
**American Foundation for the Blind**, 15 West 16th Street, New York, NY 10011, **t** (212) 620 2000, toll free **t** 800 232 5463. The best source for information in the USA for visually impaired travellers.
**Federation of the Handicapped**, 211 West 14th Street, New York, NY 10011, **t** (212) 747 4262. Organizes summer tours for members; there is a nominal annual fee.
**Mobility International USA**, PO Box 10767, Eugene, Oregon 97440, **t** (541) 343 1284, **f** (541) 343 6812, *www.miusa.org*,

*info@miusa.org*. This international non-profit organization, based in the USA, provides information and a range of publications for the disabled traveller. There is a $35 annual membership fee.
**SATH (Society for Accessible Travel and Hospitality)**, 347 5th Avenue, Suite 610, New York NY 10016, **t** (212) 557 0027, **f** (212) 725 8253, *www.sath.org*. Advice on all aspects of travel for the disabled, for a $3 charge, or unlimited to members ($45, concessions $25). Their website ios a good resource.
**Travel Information Service**, MossRehab Hospital, 1200 West Tabor Road, Philadelphia PA 19141-3099, *www.mossresourcenet .org/travel.htm*. Telephone advice and information on all aspects of accessible travel.

### Useful Websites
**Access Tourism**, *www.accesstourism.com*. Pan-European website with information on hotels, guesthouses, travel agencies and specialist tour operators, etc.
**The Able Informer**, *www.sasquatch.com/ableinfo*. International on-line magazine with tips for travelling abroad.
**Emerging Horizons**, *www.emerginghorizons. com*. International on-line travel newsletter for people with disabilities.
**Global Access**, *www.geocities.com*. On-line network for disabled travellers, with links,

Italy, either with you or within a couple of days; you need to apply at the baggage office (*ufficio bagagli*). Hire prices range from about €10 per day; to buy one costs upwards of €125, either in a bike shop or through the local classified adverts. Alternatively, if you bring your own bike, do check with the airline to see what their policy is on transporting them.

# Travellers with Disabilities

Recent access-for-all laws in Italy have improved the once dire situation: the number of ramps and stair lifts has increased a hundredfold in the past few years, and nearly every hotel has one or two rooms with facilities for the disabled – although the older ones

don't have a lift, or one large enough for a chair. Although service stations on the *autostrade* have equipped restrooms, you could get very stuck in the middle of a city – Florence, visited by zillions of tourists, is notoriously lacking in accessible loos. Local tourist offices are helpful, and have been known to find someone to give you a hand on the spot, while the National Tourist Office can offer suggestions on hill towns that are particularly difficult to get around – some will tire out the fittest tourist. Italian churches are a problem unto themselves. Long flights of steps in front were designed to impress on would-be worshipper the feeling of going upwards to God – another raw deal for the disabled.

archives and information on travel guides for the disabled, etc.

# Tour Operators for Disabled Travellers

## UK
**Alternative Leisure Co.**, 165 Middlesex Turnpike, Suite 206, Bedford, MA 01730, t (718) 275 0023, *www.alctrips.com*. Organizes vacations abroad.

**Assistance Travel Service**, 1 Tank Lane, Purfleet, Essex RM19 1TA, t (01708) 863198, f (01708) 860514, www.assistedholidays.com. Organizes tailor-made trips all over the world, for people with any disability.

**Can Be Done**, 7–11 Kensington High Street, London W8 5NP, t (020) 8907 2400, f 8909 1854, *www.canbedone.co.uk*. Cruises, city-breaks, self-drive holidays .

**Chalfont Line Ltd**, 4 Medway Parade, Perivale, Middlesex UB6 8HR, t (020) 8997 3799, f 8991 2892, *www.chalfont-line.co.uk*. A large range of accessible international holidays, which can be tailored to suit. They also have adapted vehicles for hire.

**Rollaround Travel**, Unit 4, Phillips House, Chapel Lane, Emley, Huddersfield HD8 9ST, t (01924) 844600, f 844606,

*www.rollaround.org*. Specialist travel agency. They also have an office in the US.

**Travelability**, Avionics House, Naas Lane, Quedgeley, Gloucestershire GL2 4SN, t 0870 241 6127, f (01452) 740898, *www. travelability.co.uk*. International tailor-made holidays.

## USA and Canada
**Accessible Journeys**, 35 West Sellers Avenue, Ridley Park, PA 19078, t 1 800 846 4537, or t 610 521 0339, f 610 521 6959, *www. disabilitytravel.com*. Individual travel in Italy.

**Flying Wheels Travel**, 143 W Bridge Street, Owatonna, MN 55060, t (507) 451 5005, f (507) 451 1685, *www.flyingwheelstravel. com*. Escorted tours and custom itineraries.

**The Guided Tour Inc**, 7900 Old York Rd, Suite 114-B, Elkins Park, PA 19027-2339, *www. guidedtour.com*. Accompanied holidays.

**Nautilus Tours and Cruises**, 22567 Ventura Blvd, Woodland Hills, California 91364, t 1 800 797 6004, or t 818 591 3159, *www.nautilustours.com*. Accessible Italian tours.

**TASC Travel Adventures**, 99 Washington Street, Melrose, MA 02176, t (781) 979 0400, *www.tascnet.org*. Offering packages to Florence, plus customized vacations.

# Practical A–Z

# Children

Even though a declining birthrate and the legalization of abortion may hint otherwise, children are still the royalty of Italy, and are pampered, often obscenely spoiled, probably more fashionably dressed than you are, and never allowed to get dirty. Yet most of them somehow manage to be well-mannered little charmers. If you're bringing your own *bambini* to Italy, they'll receive a warm welcome everywhere. Many hotels offer advantageous rates for children and have play areas, and most of the larger cities have permanent **Luna Parks**, or fun fairs. Other activities young children enjoy (besides the endless quantities of pizza, spaghetti and ice cream) are the **Pinocchio Park** in Collodi, near Pisa, the **Pistoia Zoo** and the **Nature Park** in Cavriglia in the Valdarno. If a **circus** visits town, you're in for a treat; it will either be a sparkling showcase of daredevil skill or a poignant, family-run, modern version of Fellini's *La Strada*.

# Climate and When to Go

The climate in Tuscany is temperate along the coasts and in the valleys, and considerably cooler up in the mountains; the higher Apennines and Monte Amiata have enough snow to support skis until April. Summers are hot and humid; in August the Florentines, Sienese and Pisans abandon their cities to the tourists and head for the sea or the mountains. Spring, especially May, when it rains less, is pleasantly warm, as fields and gardens brim with flowers. Autumn, too, is a classic time to visit, in October and November; before the winter rains begin and the air is clear, the colours of the countryside are brilliant and rare. The hills of Tuscany are always beautiful, but in October, they're extraordinary.

Winter can be an agreeable time to visit the indoor attractions of the cities and avoid crowds, particularly in Florence, where it seldom snows but may rain for days at a time. The mountains, especially the Apuan Alps along the coast, also get a considerable amount of rain, with 80–120mm in a year.

# Electricity

Your electric appliances will work if you adapt them to run on 220 AC with two round prongs on the plug. American appliances need transformers as well.

# Embassies and Consulates

If you have a choice, use the consulate in Florence.
**Australia**: Via Alessandria 215, Rome,
t (06) 85 2721.
**Canada**: Via Zara 30, Rome, t (06) 440 3028.
**Ireland**: Largo Nazareno 3, Rome,
t (06) 697 9121.
**New Zealand** Via Zara 28, Rome,
t (06) 440 2928.
**UK**: Via XX Settembre 80a, Rome,
t (06) 482 5441.
Lungarno Corsini 2, Florence, t (055) 284 133.
**USA**: Via Vittorio Veneto 121/a, Rome,
t (06) 487 0235 or 4788 8629.
Lungarno Amerigo Vespucci 38, Florence,
t (055) 239 8276.

## Average Temperatures in °C (°F)

|  | January | April | July | October |
| --- | --- | --- | --- | --- |
| Florence | 6 (42) | 13 (55) | 25 (77) | 16 (60) |
| Livorno | 9 (47) | 15 (59) | 24 (75) | 15 (59) |
| Siena | 5 (40) | 12 (54) | 25 (77) | 15 (59) |

## Average monthly rainfall in millimetres (inches)

|  | January | April | July | October |
| --- | --- | --- | --- | --- |
| Florence | 61 (3) | 74 (3) | 23 (1) | 96 (4) |
| Livorno | 71 (3) | 62 (3) | 7 (0) | 110 (4) |
| Siena | 70 (3) | 61 (3) | 21 (1) | 112 (4) |

# Calendar of Events

## January
1 Feast of the Gift, the mayor's donation of gold, frankincense and myrrh at **Castiglione di Garfagnana**

## February
**Carnival** is celebrated in private parties nearly everywhere, and in **Viareggio** there's an enormous public one, with huge satirical floats, music and parades. In **Bibbiena**, the last day of Carnival is celebrated with a grand dance called the *Bello Ballo* and a huge bonfire, the *Bello Pomo*. The date of Carnival varies with Easter: the last day, with the most important festivities, is on Shrove Tuesday (Martedi Grasso), and other parties are thrown on preceding Sundays

## March
19 **Greve-in-Chianti** pancake festival; also in San Giuseppe, **Siena** (with rice fritters) and **Torrita di Siena**, with a donkey race and tournament

## April
**Good Friday** Way of the Cross candlelight procession, **Grássina**, near Florence
**Easter** Easter morning, *Scoppio del Carro*, expulsion of the cart in **Florence**
Mary's girdle displayed from Donatello's pulpit in **Prato**
10 Liberty Festival, **Lucca**, honouring the former Republic of Lucca with a special mass, costumes, etc.

**1st Sunday after Easter** National Kite Festival, San Miniato
**2nd Sunday after Easter** Donkey Palio, **Querceta**, near Lucca
**April–June** Music festival, **Lucca**

## May
**All month** Iris Festivals, Florence, **San Polo Robbiana** (Chianti)
**Third week** Historical parade and crossbow tournament, **Massa Marittima**
**Ascension Day** Cricket Festival, with floats, and crickets sold in little cages, **Florence**
**May and June** *Maggio Musicale Fiorentino* music festival, **Florence**

## June
**Early June** Procession on sawdust designs in the streets at **Camaiore** (Lucca)
**First Sunday**, garlic toast (*bruschetta*) festival, **Montecatini Terme**
**Mid June–August** *Estate Fiesolana* – music, cinema, ballet and theatre, **Fiesole**
**16–17** *Festa di San Ranieri* – lights festival and historic regatta in **Pisa**
**18** *Festa del Barbarossa*, celebrating the meeting of the pope and emperor, with ballet, archery, snails, beans and *pici* at **San Quirico d'Orcia**
**3 weekends** *Calcio in Costume*, Renaissance football game, in **Florence**
**3rd Sunday** *Palio di Rioni*, neighbourhood horse racing, in **Castiglion Fiorentino**
**24** St John the Baptist's Day, with fireworks, in **Florence**

# Festivals

Although festivals in Tuscany are often more show than spirit (though there are several exceptions to the rule), they can add a note of pageantry or culture to your holiday. Some are great costume affairs, with roots dating back to the Middle Ages, and there are quite a few music festivals, antique fairs, and most of all, festivals devoted to food and drink.

Above is a calendar of the major events and festivals throughout the region.

# Food and Drink

When you eat out, mentally add to the bill (*conto*) the bread and cover charge (*pane e coperto*, L1,500–4,000) and a 10 per cent

## Restaurant Price Categories
We have divided restaurants into the following categories (for full meal, per person, but not including wine):

*very expensive* over €45
*expensive* €30–45
*moderate* €20–30
*inexpensive* below €20

**25** *Giocco del Ponte*, a traditional tug-of-war game, held on a bridge with a cart in the middle, **Pisa**;
**Last Sunday** *La Bruscellata*, a week of dancing and singing old love songs around a flowering tree, **San Donato in Poggio** (Florence province)

## July
**1** Versilian Historical Trophy, with a flag-throwing contest, **Querceta** (Lucca)
**1–15** lyric season, **Camaiore** (Lucca)
**2** *Palio*, the world-famous horse race around Il Campo, **Siena**
**2nd Sunday** 16th-century archery contest in **Fivizzano** (Massa) between court and country archers
**3rd Sunday** Feast of San Paolino, **Lucca**, featuring a torchlight parade and crossbow contest
**25** Joust of the Bear, a tournament dating back to the 1300s, **Pistoia**
**July–August** concert and theatre festival, **San Gimignano**
**Late July–August** 10-day chamber music festival, *Inconti in Terra di Siena*, in fabulous settings near **Chianciano Terme**

## August
**All month** Outdoor Opera festival, **Torre del Lago Puccini**
**First weekend** Traditional thanksgiving festival in honour of San Sisto, **Pisa**
**2nd Sunday** Regatta, **Porto Santo Stefano**; *Bruscello* stories, food and wine, in **Montepulciano**;

Crossbow tournament, **Massa Marittima**
**15** Beefsteak Festival, **Cortona**
**16** *Palio*, dating from 1147, in **Siena**
**17** *Palio Marinaro*, neighbourhood boat races, in **Livorno**
**15–30** International choir contest, **Arezzo**

## September
**First Sunday** Joust of the Saracen, **Arezzo**; *Palio dei Cerri*, competition between neighbourhoods and Renaissance processions, **Cerreto Guidi**; **Florence**, lantern festival
**2nd Sunday** Crossbow contest with Gubbio in **Sansepolcro**; eating and dancing in **Greve in Chianti**
**13** Holy Procession in honour of the *Volto Santo*, by torchlight in **Lucca**
**3rd Sunday** Impruneta wine festival

## October
**All month** Wine festivals

## November
**22** Santa Cecilia, patroness of music, has concerts held in her honour in **Siena**

## December
**8** Fair of the Immaculate Conception, **Bagni di Lucca**
**13** Santa Lucia, celebrated with a pottery fair in **Siena**
**24** Evergreen bonfire, **Camporgiano** (Lucca)
**25–26** Display of the holy girdle and St Stephen's feast, **Prato**

service charge. This is often included in the bill (*servizio compreso*); if not, it will say *servizio non compreso*, and you'll have to do your own arithmetic. Additional tipping is at your own discretion, but never do it in family-owned and -run places. Prices quoted for meals in this book are for an average complete meal, Italian-style with wine, for one person.

## Insurance and Health

*Emergencies, t 113*

You can insure yourself against almost any mishap – cancelled flight, stolen or lost

baggage, and medical bills – for a price. While national health services in the UK and Australia have reciprocal health care agreements with Italy (pack an E111 form), others should check their current policies to see if they cover you while abroad, and under what circumstances, and judge whether you need a special traveller's insurance policy. Travel agencies, as well as insurance companies, sell policies, but they are not cheap.

Minor illnesses and problems that crop up in Italy can usually be handled free of charge in a public hospital clinic or *ambulatorio*. If you need minor aid, Italian pharmacists are highly trained and can probably diagnose your problem; look for a *farmacia* (they all have a list in the window with details of which ones are open during the night and on holidays). Extreme cases should head for the *Pronto Soccorso* (First Aid Service). Italian doctors are not always great linguists; contact your embassy or consulate for a list of English-speaking doctors.

# Internet

Florence is full of internet points; you will have no difficulty finding one in the centre of town. Cyber cafés haven't caught on in Italy big-time, so you will most likely find a shop offering anything from basic computer and internet services to those offering much more (proof-reading and correction, CD-burning, photocopying, international telephone lines, photo services, etc) plus, at most, a soft drinks machine.

**Internet train**: Via Zannoni 1r, t 055 211103. *www.internettrain.it*. Open daily 9.30am–10.30pm. Branches at Borgo San Jacopo 30r; Via dell'Oriuolo 40r; Via de' Benci 36r; Borgo la Croce 33r. Opening hours differ from branch to branch.

**Intotheweb**: Via de' Conti 23r, t 055 2645628. Open daily 10am-midnight. Uses Macs.

**Nettyweb**: Via Santo Spirito 42r, t 055 2654549. *www.nettyweb.com*. Open 10am–8pm Mon–Fri; Sat and Sun 12.30–10pm. Meeting and business room available for rent.

**The Netgate**: Via Sant'Egidio 10r, Tel 055 2347967. Open 11–9 daily, *www.thenetgate.it*. Branches: Via Nazionale 156r; Via de' Cimatori 17r; Via dei Serragli 76r; Stazione Santa Maria Novella. Opening hours differ from branch to branch.

# Lavatories

Italy's stakes in toilet cleanliness improve steadily; there are fewer holes in the ground, and paper is more common, though as ever they only exist in places like train and bus stations and bars. If you can't find one, try the nearest bar; they are legally obliged to let you use their *bagno*. In stations, motorway stops and smarter cafés, there are toilet attendants

who expect a small tip. Don't get confused by Italian plurals: *signori* (gents), *signore* (ladies).

# Maps and Publications

The maps in this guide are for orientation only and it is worth investing in a good, up-to-date regional map before you arrive from any of the following bookshops:

**Stanford's**, 12–14 Long Acre, London WC2 9LP, t (020) 7836 1321.

**The Travel Bookshop**, 13 Blenheim Crescent, London W11 2EE, t (020) 7229 5260.

**The Complete Traveller**, 199 Madison Ave, New York, NY 10016, t (212) 685 9007.

Excellent maps are produced by **Touring Club Italiano**, **Michelin** and the **Istituto Geografico de Agostini**. These are available at major bookshops in Italy or sometimes on news-stands. Italian tourist offices are helpful and can often supply good area maps and town plans.

Books are more expensive in Italy than in the UK, but some excellent shops stock English-language books. A few useful ones are listed below.

**The Paperback Exchange**, Via Fiesolana 31r, Florence.

**Feltrinelli**, Via Cavour 12–20r, Florence.

# Media

Many of the main news stands in Tuscan towns and cities sell English **newspapers**; in the summer months they arrive the same evening. They cost a fortune, though; a Sunday paper will cost nearly €4, and most of them don't come with the colour supplements.

The only American paper available is the *Herald Tribune* which has an 'Italy Daily' insert. The same insert also comes with the Italian language *Corriere della Sera*. Even smaller news stands stock *Time* and *Newsweek*. Most good '*giornalaii*' keep a good stock of both American and English glossy magazines – again at a price.

For Italian speakers, a look at the local press always provides insight into the country you are visiting. Tuscany's most popular daily is *La Nazione*, a right-wing rag with lots of gossipy items. Each province has its own insert and it is useful for 'what's on' listings and flats-for-rent searches (in the Sunday edition). *La Repubblica* is a more reliable centre-left bet and has some excellent journalism. It is based in Rome, but has a Florence insert. The Milan-based *Corriere della Sera* is another decent paper with an English-language insert (see above). *Panorama* and *L'Espresso* are both good weekly current affairs magazines with some excellent journalism (in Italian).

Italian **television** is pretty dire and even the more 'serious' state-owned RAI channels (1,2 and 3) are dominated by game and quiz shows and by appalling 'variety' shows featuring an amazing amount of almost bare bums and cleavage. All channels are dominated by ad breaks. Prime Minister Silvio Berlusconi's Mediaset network. Italia 1, Canale 5 and Rete 4 show endless versions of the above, lots of cheap soaps and the odd decent documentary. Films (the best are on Canale 5) are all dubbed as are such familiar sights as ER, Friends and other well-known US imports.

There are dozens of smaller TV stations; if you can manage to pick up Pistoia-based TVL, they show Sky news and CNN between about midnight and 8am.

There are endless **radio** stations available in Tuscany. The national networks RAI 1, 2 and 3 broadcast a mix of music and current affairs while there is plenty of choice in music staions. Among the best choices are Florence-based Radio Montebeni (108.5MHz) relays classical music (albeit of a very dated variety); Radio Montecarlo (104.4MHz) comes from...Montecarlo; Controradio (93.6MHz); Radio Diffuzione (MHz102.7). All are full of publicity spots.

# Money and Banks

It's a good idea to bring some local currency with you for when you arrive; you never know when unforeseen delays and/or unexpected public holidays might foul up your plans to find an open bank. **Traveller's cheques** or Eurocheques remain the most secure way of financing an Italian holiday; they are easy to change and an insurance against unpleasant surprises. **Credit cards** (American Express, Diner's Club, Mastercard, Access, Eurocard,

Barclaycard, Visa) are accepted in most hotels, restaurants, shops and most petrol stations (possibly not in single pump operations in the middle of the country). If you have a PIN number you can use the many **cashpoint machines**. Do not be surprised if you are asked to show identification when paying with a credit card.

You can have money transferred to you through an Italian bank but this process may take over a week, even if it's sent urgent – *espressissimo*. You will need your passport as identification when you collect it. Sending cheques by post is inadvisable.

Most British banks have an arrangement with the Italian banking authorities so you can (for a significant commission) use your bank card at Italian cash machines, but check with your bank first. Besides traveller's cheques, most banks will also give you cash on a recognized credit card or Eurocheque with a Eurocheque card (taking little or no commission), and in big cities you can find automatic tellers (ATMs) to spout cash on a Visa, American Express or Eurocheque card. You need a PIN number to use these. Read the instructions carefully, or your card may be retained by the machine.

**Credit cards** (American Express, Diner's Club, Eurocard, Barclaycard, Visa) are accepted in large hotels, resort-area restaurants, shops and most car-hire firms, but bear in mind that MasterCard (Access) is much less widely acceptable in Italy. From sad experience, Italians are wary of plastic – you can't even always use it at motorway petrol stops. Do not be surprised if you are asked for identification when paying by credit card.

## The Euro

From January 2002 the lire was be replaced by the euro; already all prices are quoted in both currencies. The exchange rate between the lire and the euro is fixed at L1,936.27 to €1. Or, as the ad campaign in Italy says, drop 3 zeros and divide by half.

ATMs in Italy will cough up €10, €20 and €50 notes; but how long it will take to convert all sorts of other money slots (take, for example, the light machines in churches!) is anyone's guess.

### Banking Hours

Banks are usually open 8.30am–1.20pm, and 3–4 or 4–5pm. They are closed on Saturdays, Sundays and national holidays. **American Express in Florence:** Via Dante Alighieri 22R, t 055 50981, just off Piazza della Repubblica and Via Guicciardini 49R, PO Box 617, t 055 288751. The Via Guicciardini office offers change facilities.

# Official Holidays

The Italians have cut down somewhat on their official national holidays, but note that every town has one or two local holidays of its own – usually the feast day of its patron saint. Official holidays, shown on transport timetables and museum opening hours, etc., are treated the same as Sundays. Most museums, as well as banks and shops, are closed.

# Opening Hours and Museums

Most of Tuscany closes down at 1pm until 3 or 4pm, to eat and properly digest the main meal of the day, although things are now beginning to change in the cities. Many more shops in the centre of town now stay open during lunch. Afternoon working hours are

from 4 to 7, often from 5 to 8 in the hot summer months. In any case, don't be surprised if you find anywhere in Italy unexpectedly closed (or open for that matter), whatever its official stated hours.

**Food shops** shut on Wednesday afternoons in the winter. They close on Saturday afternoons only from the end of June to the beginning of September. Sunday opening is becoming more usual, particularly for shops in the centre of town. Bars are often the only places open during the early afternoon and sometimes on a Sunday. (For **bank** opening hours, *see* p.96.)

**Churches** have always been a prime target for art thieves and as a consequence are usually locked when there isn't a sacristan or caretaker to keep an eye on things. All churches, except for the really important cathedrals and basilicas, close in the afternoon at the same hours as the shops, and the little ones tend to stay closed. Always have a pocketful of coins to feed the light machines in churches, or what you came to see is bound to be hidden in ecclesiastical gloom. Don't do your visiting during services, and don't come to see paintings and statues in churches the week preceding Easter – you will probably find them covered with mourning shrouds.

Most major **museums** are now open all day from 9am to 7pm and tend to close on a Monday and often Sunday afternoons as well. Many are magnificent, many are run with shameful neglect, and many have been closed for years for 'restoration', with slim prospects of reopening in the foreseeable future. With an estimated one work of art per inhabitant, Italy has a hard time financing the preservation of its national heritage; it would be as well to enquire at the tourist office to find out what is open and what is 'temporarily' closed before setting of on a wild-goose chase.

Entrance charges vary wildly; you should expect to pay between €2 and €4 for museum entrance; expensive ones run to €5–€6 (like the Uffizi). The good news is that state run museums and monuments are free if you're under 18 or over 60 (bring ID).

Art-lovers should consider visiting Florence during '**Museum Week**' (usually in April), when all the state-run museums are free for the week.

# Packing

You simply cannot overdress in Italy. Now, whether or not you want to try to keep up with the natives is your own affair and your own heavy suitcase – you may do well to compromise and just bring a couple of smart outfits for big nights out. It's not that the Italians are very formal; they simply like to dress up with a gorgeousness that adorns their cities just as much as those old Renaissance churches and palaces. The few places with dress codes are the major churches and basilicas (no shorts or sleeveless shirts), and the smarter restaurants.

After agonizing over fashion, remember to pack small and light: transatlantic airlines limit baggage by size (two pieces are free, up to 1.5m, in height and width; in second class you're allowed one of 1.5m and another up to 110cm). Within Europe limits are by weight: 20kg (44lbs) in second class, 30kg (66lbs) in first. You may well be penalized for anything bigger. If you're travelling mainly by train, you'll especially want to keep bags to a minimum: jamming big suitcases in overhead racks isn't much fun.

Never take more than you can carry, but do bring the following: any prescription medicine you need, an extra pair of glasses or contact lenses, a torch (for dark frescoed churches and hotel corridors), a travel alarm (for those early trains) and a pocket Italian-English dictionary (for flirting and other emergencies).

You may want to invest in earplugs if you're a light sleeper. European electric appliances will work in Italy; just change your plug to the two-prong variety or buy a travel plug. American appliances need transformers as well.

# Photography

Film and developing are much more expensive than they are in the USA or UK. You are not allowed to take pictures in most museums and in some churches. Most cities now offer one-hour processing if you need your pics in a hurry.

# Police Business

*Police/Emergency, t 113*

There is a fair amount of petty crime in the cities – purse snatchings, pickpocketing, white-collar thievery (always check your change) and car break-ins – but violent crime is rare. Nearly all mishaps can be avoided with adequate precautions. Stay on the inside of the pavement and keep a firm hold on your property; be aware of pickpockets in crowds; don't carry too much cash and don't keep all that you have in one place. Be extra careful around stations, don't leave valuables in hotel rooms, and park your car in garages, guarded car parks, or on well-lit streets, with any temptations out of sight. Purchasing small quantities of cannibis is legal, although what a small quantity might be exactly is unspecified, so if the police dislike you to begin with, it may be enough to get you into big trouble.

Once the scourge of Italy, political terrorism has declined drastically in recent years, mainly thanks to special squads of the *Carabinieri*, the black-uniformed national police, technically part of the Italian army. Local matters are usually in the hands of the *Polizia Urbana*; the nattily dressed *Vigili Urbani* concern themselves with directing traffic and handing out parking fines. You probably will not have anything to do with the *Guardia di Finanza*, the financial police, who spend their time chasing corrupt politicians and their friends (unless they catch you leaving a bar or restaurant without a receipt).

# Post Offices

*In cities usually open Mon–Sat 8–6 or 7.*

Dealing with *la posta italiana* has always been a risky, frustrating, time-consuming affair: it is expensive and slow. Even buying the right stamps requires dedicated research and saintly patience. One recent scandal that mesmerized Italy involved the Minister of the Post Office, who disposed of literally tons of backlog mail by tossing it in the Tiber. When the news broke, he was replaced – the new minister, having learned his lesson, burned all the mail the Post Office was incapable of delivering. Not surprisingly, the fax machine is seen as a gift from the Madonna.

To have your mail sent *poste restante* (general delivery), have it addressed to the central post office (*Fermo Posta*) and allow three to four weeks for it to arrive. Make sure your surname is very clearly written in block capitals. To pick up your mail you must present your passport and pay a nominal charge.

Stamps (*francoboli*) may be purchased in post offices or at tobacconists (*tabacchi*, identified by their blue signs with a white T). Prices fluctuate. The rates for letters and postcards (depending how many words you write!) vary according to the whim of the tobacconist or postal clerk. Packages have to be a certain size, under a certain weight to be sent in certain ways, and must have a flap open for inspection or be sealed with string and lead. You're best off taking it to a stationer's shop (*cartoleria*) and paying them to wrap it – they usually know what the postal demons require.

Express postal services are called *Espresso* (Swift Air Mail) or *Raccomandata* (Registered Delivery): both require supplements. If you want to make hotel reservations at short notice, faxing or telephoning ahead is best.

Money can be telegraphed to you via the post office; if all goes well, it might take three days, but a proportion goes into commission.

## Purchasing a House

Of all the regions in Italy Tuscany has the most foreigners with homes, so many, in fact, that prices have shot into the stratosphere in the most popular areas (especially around Florence and Siena, and in the Chianti). The more obscure areas of Tuscany still have a number of abandoned farmhouses just waiting for someone to renovate them. Rural real estate is one of Italy's great buys, and the recommended way to do it is to buy a run-down property and restore it to your own needs and taste. But beware the pitfalls.

One agent we know is amazed that all English clients invariably express two major concerns about a property: drainage, and the presence of a bidet in the bathroom, as if it were a tool of the devil. What they should be asking are questions about water supply (a major problem in Tuscany), electricity and road access – often big problems for that isolated, romantic farmhouse that has caught your eye. Another thing to remember before purchasing a home or land is that you need permission from the local *comune* to make any changes or improvements, so it's no good buying anything unless you're pretty sure the *comune* will consent (for a sizeable fee, of course) to let you convert that old cellar or stable into a spare bedroom. A further point to remember is that though there are no annual rates (property tax) to pay, there is a 10 per cent IVA tax (VAT) to be paid on the purchase price for a house and 19 per cent on land, as well as hefty Capital Gains Tax on selling price and profit to be paid by the seller. Italians tend to get around this by selling at one price and writing down another on the contract. But remember, if you sell you'll be in the same bind.

Once you've agreed to buy, you pay a deposit (usually 25–30 per cent) and sign a *compromesso*, a document that states that if you back out, you lose your deposit, and if the seller changes his mind, he forfeits double the deposit to you (be sure your *compromesso* includes this feature, called *caparra confermatoria*). Always transfer payment from home through a bank, taking care to get and save a certificate of the transaction so you can take the sum back out of Italy when you sell. After the *compromesso*, your affairs will be handled by a *notaio*, the public servant in charge of registering documents and taxes who works for both buyer and seller. If you want to make sure your interests are not overlooked, you can hire a *commercialista* (lawyer-accountant) who will handle your affairs with the notaio, including the final transfer deed (*rogito*), which completes the purchase at the local Land Registry. Upon signing, the balance of the purchase price generally becomes payable within a year.

The next stage for most buyers, restoration, can be a nightmare if you aren't careful. Make sure the crew you hire is experienced and that you're pleased with their work elsewhere – don't hesitate to ask as many other people in your area as possible for advice. Keep all receipts, and beware when builders and agents give you receipts for far less than their charges (or no receipts at all) to avoid taxes; you'll pay the difference in sales tax when you sell. Also expect to pay a lofty surcharge on electricity, water and telephone bills unless you become an Italian resident and your Italian house is your primary residence. One book that offers some clues on the ins and outs of taxes, inheritance law, residency, gardening, etc., is *Living in Italy*, published by Robert Hale, London 1991.

# Shopping

'Made in Italy' has long been a byword for style and quality, especially in fashion and leather, but also in home design, ceramics, kitchenware, jewellery, lace and linens, glass-ware and crystal, chocolates, hats, straw-work, art books, engravings, handmade stationery, gold and silverware, a hundred kinds of liqueurs, wine, aperitifs, coffee machines, gastronomic specialities and antique repro-ductions, as well as antiques themselves. If you are looking for the latter and are spending a lot of money, be sure to demand a certificate of authenticity – reproductions can be very, very good. Non-EU nationals should save their receipts for Customs on the way home.

Florence, which increasingly resembles a glittering medieval shopping mall, has the best variety of goods in the region. There are major monthly antique fairs in Arezzo (first Sunday), Pistoia (second Sunday), Lucca (third Sunday), and Florence (last Sunday). Ceramics are an old tradition in Montelupo, Deruta; porcelain in Sesto Fiorentino; glassware in Empoli. Volterra is famous for its alabaster and alabaster art; Castelfidardo for its accordions; in Elba you can buy semi-precious stones and minerals, in the Mugello and Casentino wrought-iron and copperware, straw goods in the lower Valdarno, and marble in Carrara, though taking it home may pose a bit of a problem. Wine and olive oil, bags of *porcini* mushrooms, jars of truffles and other 'gastro-nomic' specialities are available everywhere.

Italians don't like department stores, but there are a few chains – *COIN* stores often have good buys on almost the latest fashions. *Standa* and *UPIM* are more like Woolworth's, with a reasonable selection of clothes, house-ware, etc., and often supermarkets in their basements. Most stay open throughout the day, but some take the same break as other Italian shops – from 1pm to 3 or 4pm.

Non-EU nationals should save their receipts for Customs on the way home. Shipping goods is a risky business unless you do it through a very reputable shop. Note well that the attrac-tion of shopping in Italy is limited to luxury items; for less expensive clothes and house-hold items you'll always, always do better in Britain or America. Prices for clothes, even in street markets, are often ridiculous. Bargains of any kind are rare, and the cheaper goods are often very poor quality. Italian clothes are lovely, but if you have a large-boned Anglo-American build, you may find it hard to get a good fit, especially on trousers or skirts (Italians are a long-waisted, slim-hipped bunch). Shoes are often narrower than the sizes at home.

# Smoking

Tobacconists ('*Tabacchi*') display a blue and white 'T' sign outside the shop; they and some bars sell cigarettes which are cheaper than in the UK.

Italy is still a great nation of smokers although recent legislation has banned smoking in poublic offices (post offices, banks etc), on public transport (although trains have smoking compartments) and in any public places with inadequate air filtering. However these rules are frequently ignored, and you are unlikely to get much sympathy if you ask someone to stop blowing smoke in your face in a restaurant or in a non-smoking train carriage.

No-smoking rooms in hotels are rare as are non-smoking sections in bars and restaurants.

# Sports and Activities

### Birdwatching

The islands and coastal parks near Argentario are great places to go bird-watching; ecologically hyper-aware Giglio offers **nature appreciation** and **sketching** classes for Italian speakers, t 0564 809 034. The bird park at Lago Burano near Capalbio is another place for bird-watching, t 0564 898 829.

## Boats and Sailing

The **sailing** is beautiful among the coves of the Tuscan archipelago and around the Argentario; there's a good sailing school in Torre del Lago Puccini, t (0584) 342 084. You can bring your boat to Italy for six months without any paperwork if you bring it by car; if you arrive by sea you must report to the Port Authority of your first port to show passports and receive your '*Constituto*' which identifies you and allows you to purchase fuel tax-free. Boats with engines require a number plate, and if they're over 3 horsepower you need insurance. To leave your boat in Italy for an extended period, you must have a Navigation Licence; after a year you have to start paying taxes on it. All yachts must pay a daily berthing fee in Italian ports. The National Tourist office has a list of ports that charter yachts in Tuscan ports.

## Clubs

Sporting clubs are usually privately owned and are open only to members, who pay on a yearly basis. Do not expect to be able to use a swimming pool, gym or sailing club by paying a daily rate.

## Diving and Swimming

The **diving** is fabulous around the Argentario and its outlying islands, and very popular.

The best (cleanest) **swimming** is to be found on the islands, especially on the beaches that look away from the mainland.
**Elba Diving Centre**, Marciana Marina, t 0336 709 259.
**Giglio Diving Club**, Giglio Porto, t 0564 804 065.

## Fishing

Fishing in the sea is possible from the shore, boats, or under water (but not with an aqualung) without a permit, though it may not be especially fruitful; the Tyrrhenian has been so thoroughly fished commercially that the government has begun to declare two- and three-month moratoria on all fishing, to give the fish a break. Man-made lakes and streams are well stocked, however, and if you're more interested in the eating than the sport, there are trout farms where you can almost pick the fish out of the water with your hands. To fish in fresh water you need to purchase a year's membership card and you must be resident in Italy. The licence costs about L189,000 for a year and is available from the Federazione Italiana della Pesca Sportiva. At its offices (in every province) they can inform you on local conditions and restrictions. Bait and equipment are readily available.

## Golf

There are golf courses in Florence, Montecatini Terme, Punta Ala, Tirrenia, Orbetello, and Portoferraio on Elba.

## Horse-riding

**Horse-riding** is increasingly popular, and Agriturist (*see* 'Where to Stay', below) has a number of villa and riding holidays on offer in Tuscany. The National Association of Equestrian Tourism (ANTE) is probably more active here than anywhere in Italy. For more information, write directly to the local Agriturist office. There are **race and trotting courses** in Florence and Montecatini Terme.

## Hunting

The most controversial sport in Italy is hunting, pitting avid enthusiasts against a burgeoning number of environmentalists who stage protests. The Apennines are boar territory, and in autumn the woods are full of hunters. Pathetically tiny birds, as well as ducks and pigeons, are the other principal game.

## Medieval Sports

Some **ancient sports** like the annual horse races, or *palios* (two in Siena) are still popular, and not entirely as a tourist attraction; the rivalries between neighbourhoods and cities are intense. The Florentines play three games of Renaissance football a year (*calcio in costume*); Sansepolcro and Gubbio stage two annual crossbow matches a year against each other, while in Lucca the archers compete from different city quarters. Arezzo and Pistoia have annual jousts; in Pisa it's medieval tug-of-war.

## Potholing

Spelunkers can find caves to explore around Montecatini Alta, Monsummano and Sarteano.
**Centro Nazionale di Speleologia Monte Cucco,** Costacciaro, **t** 075 917 0236.

## Rowing

When there's enough water, you can try your skills in the Arno (*see* **Florence**, p.116). There is also the annual race between the four old maritime republics of Venice, Amalfi, Genoa and Pisa, which alternates between the cities.

## Skiing

Tuscany has major ski resorts at Abetone, north of Pistoia, and at Monte Amiata.

## Tennis

Tennis courts are nearly everywhere; each *comune* has at least one or two that you can hire by the hour.

## Walking

Hiking and signed trails are best developed in Tuscany; April–October is the best and safest time to go. There are several scenic routes through the mountains: the four-day High Trail of the Apuan Alps, beginning from the Rifugio Carrara, above Carrara (for information call **t** 0585 841 972, or the Italian Alpine Club (CAI) in Carrara, Via Giorgio, **t** 0585 776 782). A second trail, the Grand Apennine Excursion from Lake Scaffaiolo, goes along the mountain ridge that separates Tuscany from Emilia-Romagna, departing from Pracchia, **t** 0573 630 790 for information.

There's a circular trail through the Garfagnana, starting from Castelnuovo di Garfagnana; contact the Comunità Montana Garfagnana, **t** 0583 658 990. In southern Tuscany, trails cover Monte Amiata from Abbadia San Salvatore (Comunità Montana dell'Amiata, **t** 0564 967 064).

Other fine day trails are in the Casentino, from Badia Prataglia or Stia, or in the Nature Parks of Monti dell'Uccellina from Alberese or the Maremma. Maremmagica organizes trekking and walking tours with guides, **t** 0564 496 670 for information. In Florence, you can get information from CAI, Via dello Studio 5, **t** 055 211 731.

# Telephones

To **call Italy from abroad,** dial **t** 00 39 followed by the area prefix (e.g. for Florence **t** 00 39 55 etc.). For **calls inside Italy** you need to dial the complete regional or city code, including the zero, even from inside the region. So when in Florence you still need to use **t** 055. **International calls from Italy** may be made by dialling the international prefix (for the UK **t** 0044, Ireland **t** 00353, USA and Canada **t** 001, Australia **t** 0061, New Zealand **t** 0064).

**Public telephones** for international calls may be found in the offices of Telecom Italia, Italy's telephone company. They are the only places where you can make reverse-charge calls (*a erre*, collect calls) but be prepared for a wait, as all these calls go through the operator in Rome. **Rates** for long-distance calls are among the highest in Europe. (Calls within Italy are cheapest after 10pm; international calls after 11pm.) Most phone booths now take either coins (L100, 200, 500 or 1,000), *gettoni* (L200 tokens, often given to you in place of change) or **phone cards** (*schede telefoniche*) available in L5,000, L10,000 and sometimes L15,000 amounts at tobacconists and news-stands – you will have to snap off the small perforated corner in order to use them. Try to avoid telephoning from hotels, which often add 25% to the bill.

As with most countries, Italy has a constant need for new telephone numbers and, as with other countries, this has forced the Italian telephone authorites to change numbers, usually by adding a digit to the area code, in order to cope with demand. Also, as elsewhere, it is usually realized after a couple of years that this renumbering has been based on a severe underestimation of the potential demand and that the numbers will have to change again. In an attempt to stay one step ahead of the game, however, Telecom Italia has unveiled new plans which require people to dial the entire phone number including the area code when they make a call, even if they are calling from within that area code. We have included all former area codes with phone numbers in the guide.

Many places now have public fax machines, but the speed of transmission means that costs can be very high.

# Time

Italy is an hour ahead of the UK and clocks go forward and back in spring and autumn on the same day as in the UK.

# Tipping

Refreshingly, there is not a lot of pressure in Italy to leave major tips. It was customary until the end of 2001 to round restaurant bills up a few thousand lire to the nearest 10,000 or 5,000; less in modest places. It remains to be seen how this will work out with Euros...

Most Florentines feel that taxis are so expensive that drivers deserve no tip; they are right! Any tip should be minimal and drivers don't expect more. A few coins are sometimes expected in public loos for the caretaker (in motorway services or in stations.) In hotels, the usual kinds of 'rules' apply; 10–15%, but it should reflect your general satisfaction with the service offered.

# Tourist Offices

For more information before you go, write to the Italian National Tourist Office:

**Australia:** Level 26-44 Market Street, NSW 2000 Sydney, t (02) 92 621666, f (02) 92 621677, *lenitour@ihug.com.au*.

**Canada:** 175 Bloor Street East, Suite 907, South Tower, Toronto M4W 3R8 (ON), t (416) 9254882/9253725, f (416) 9254799, *www.italiantourism.com*.

**New Zealand:** c/o Italian Embassy, 34 Grant Road, Thorndon, Wellington, t (04) 736 065.

**UK:** Italian State Tourist Board, 1 Princes Street, London W1R 8AY, t (020) 7408 1254, f 7493 6695, *www.enit.it, www.italiantourism.com*; Italian Embassy, 14 Three Kings Yard, Davies Street, London W1Y 2EH, t (020) 7312 2200, f 7312 2230, *www.embitaly.org.uk*.

**USA:** 630 Fifth Avenue, Suite 1565, New York, NY 10111, t (212) 245 5095/4822, f (212) 586 9249;
500 N. Michigan Avenue, Suite 2240, Chicago, ILL 60611, t (312) 644 0996. f (312) 644 3019;
12400 Wilshire Boulevard, Suite 550, Los Angeles, CA 90025, t (310) 820 1898/9807, f (310) 820 6357, *www.italiantourism.com*.

Tourist and travel information may also be available from **Alitalia** (Italy's national airline) or **CIT** (Italy's state-run travel agency) offices in some countries.

You can pick up more detailed information by writing directly to any of the city or provincial tourist offices (addresses are in the text). These are usually helpful in sending out lists of flats, villas or farmhouses to hire, or at least lists of agents who handle the properties.

# Where to Stay

## Hotels

Tuscany is endowed with hotels (*alberghi*) of every description, from the spectacular to the humble. These are rated by the government's tourism bureaucracy, from five stars at the luxurious top to one star at the bottom. Ratings take into account such things as a restaurant on the premises, plumbing, air-conditioning, etc., but not character, style or charm. Use the stars, which we include in this book, as a quick reference only. Another thing to remember about government ratings is that a hotel can stay at a lower rating than it has earned, so you may find a three-star hotel as comfortable as a four.

Breakfast is not always optional and in *pensiones* it is mandatory. You might well have to face half- or full-board requirements, particularly during high season at hotels in seaside, lake or mountain resorts, spas or country villas. Otherwise, meal arrangements are optional. In the majority of cases hotel food is bland, just as it is anywhere else.

### Prices

Prices listed here are for double rooms only. For a single, count on paying two-thirds of a double; to add an extra bed in a double will add 35 per cent to the bill. Taxes and service charges are included in the given rate. Some establishments charge €5–12 for air-

> ### Accommodation Price Ranges
> *luxury* €225–400
> *very expensive* €150–225
> *expensive* €100–150
> *moderate* €60–100
> *cheap* up to €60

conditioning. If rooms are listed without bath, it simply means the shower and lavatory are in the corridor. For rooms without bath, subtract 20–30 per cent. Prices are by law listed on the door of each room and are printed in the hotel lists available from the local tourist office; any discrepancies should be reported to the tourist office. Rooms rates are seasonal: it could cost a third less if you travel in the low season. In resorts, hotels may close down for several months of the year.

Hotel prices rise by 6–8 per cent each year, and are often more expensive in northern Europe. Each province or region sets its own price guidelines for accommodation: a three-star hotel in Florence, for instance, will cost much more than a three-star hotel in the Umbrian countryside. In general, the further south you go, the cheaper the rates.

The National Tourist office has a complete list and booking information for motels and five- and four-star hotels and chains. If you want to stay in a different kind of accommodation, you'll have to book ahead, several months in advance and preferably by fax rather than by post. A booking is valid once a deposit has been paid. If you have to cancel your reservation, the hotel will keep the deposit unless another agreement has been reached. If you come in the summer without reservations, start calling around for a place in the morning or put yourself at the mercy of one of the tourist office hotel finding services.

Besides classic hotels, there are an increasing number of alternatives, nearly always in historic buildings, in Umbria classified as *residenza d'epoca* or country houses.

## Inexpensive Accommodation

Bargains are few and far between in Italy. The cheapest hotel is called an inn, or *Locanda*. Most cheaper places will always be around the railway station, though in the large cities you'll often find it worth your while to seek out some more pleasant location in the historic centre. You could find anything in a one-star Italian hotel; they might be almost perfect, and memorably bad experiences will be few, and largely limited to the major cities. Most tourist offices have a list of rooms to rent in private homes. Besides the youth hostels (*see* below), there are several city-run hostels, with dormitory-style rooms open to

all. Monasteries and convents in the country sometimes take guests as well; if you seek that kind of experience, bring a letter of introduction from your local priest, pastor, etc.

## Youth and Student Hostels

You'll find youth hostels in Florence, Lucca, Tavarnelle Val di Pesa, in Chianti, Abetone, Cortona, San Gimignano and Marina di Massa e Carrara. You can nearly always buy an IYHF card on the spot. There are no age limits, and senior citizens are often given added discounts.

Accommodation – a bunk bed in a single-sex room and breakfast – costs around €8 per day. There is often a curfew, and you usually can't check in before 5 or 6pm. Book in advance by sending your arrival and departure dates along with the number of guests (by sex) to the individual hostel, including international postal coupons for the return reply. Avoid the spring, when noisy Italian school groups use them for field trips.

The *Centro Turistico Studentesco e Giovanile* (CTS), which has offices in most Italian cities (and one in London), can also book cheap accommodation for students.

## Self-catering Holidays: Villas, Farmhouses and Flats

Renting a villa, farmhouse, cottage or flat has always been the choice way to visit Tuscany. If you're travelling with a family it is the most economic alternative – there are simple, inexpensive cottages as well as the fabulous Renaissance villas furnished with antiques, gourmet meals and swimming-pools. The internet has made finding a place easier than ever, with companies providing detailed listings and photos of their offerings online. Another place to look for holiday villas is in the Sunday paper; or, if you have your heart set on a particular area, write to its tourist office for a list of local rental agencies. These ought to provide photos of the accommodation to give you an idea of what to expect, and make sure all pertinent details are written down in your rental agreement to avoid misunderstandings later. In general minimum lets are for two weeks; rental prices usually include insurance, water and electricity, and sometimes linen and maid service. Don't be surprised if upon arrival the owner 'denounces' (*denunziare*) you to the police; according to Italian law, all visitors must be registered upon arrival. Common problems are water shortages, unruly insects (*see* Topics, 'Flora and Fauna'), and low kilowatts. Most companies offer all-inclusive packages, with flights and car-hire. Book as far in advance as possible for the summer season.

## Rural Self-catering

For a breath of rural seclusion, the gregarious Italians head for a spell on a **working farm**, in accommodation (usually self-catering) that often approximates to the French *gîte*. The real pull of the place may in fact be cooking by the hosts – a chance to sample home-grown produce. This branch of

# Self-catering Operators

## In the UK

Many of the major Italian firms are handled by **International Chapters** (*see* below), but there's no shortage of choice.

**Accommodation Line**, 46 Maddox Street, London W1R 9PB, **t** (020) 7499 4433, **f** (020) 7409 2606.

**Citalia**, 3–5 Lansdowne Road, Croydon CR9 1LL, **t** (020) 8686 5533, **f** (020) 8681 0712, *ciao@citalia.co.uk*, *www.citalia.co.uk*.

**Cuendet**, c/o **International Chapters** (*see* below). Has an extensive list of villas, farmhouses, castles and flats for most budgets.

**Inghams**, 10–18 Putney Hill, London SW15 6AX, **t** (020) 8780 4450/ 7700, **f** (020) 8780 7705, *www.inghams.co.uk*.

**Interhome**, 383 Richmond Road, Twickenham, Middx TW1 2EF, **t** (020) 8891 1294, **f** (020) 8891 5331, *www.interhome.co.uk*.

**International Chapters**, 47–51 St John's Wood High Street, London NW8 7NJ, **t** (020) 7722 0722, (*toll free from USA only*: **t** 1 866 493 8340), **f** (020) 7722 9140, *info@villa-rentals. com*, *www.villa-rentals.com*. One of the best.

**Italian Chapters**, c/o **International Chapters** (*see* above). Well established, with quality villas and farmhouses including maid service and catering if required, chiefly in Tuscany.

**Italianvillas.com** (website), *www.italianvillas .com/search.htm*.

**Magic of Italy**, 227 Shepherds Bush Road, London W6 7AS, **t** (020) 8748 7575, **f** (020) 8748 3731, *www.magictravelgroup.co.uk*.

**Simply Travel**, *www.simply-travel.co.uk*.

**Topflight**, D'Olier Chambers, D'Olier Street, Dublin 2, **t** (01) 679 9177, *www.topflight.ie*.

**Vacanze in Italia**, Manor Courtyard, Bignor, Pulborough, West Sussex RH20 1QD, **t** (01798) 869421 / (0870) 0772 772, **f** (0870) 0780 190, *www.indiv-travellers.com*.

## In the USA

**At Home Abroad**, 405 East 56th Street 6C, New York, NY 10022-2466, **t** (212) 421 9165, **f** (212) 752 1591, *www.athomeabroad.com*.

**CIT Tours**, **t** (800) CIT-TOUR, 15 West 44th St, New York, NY 10173, **t** (212) CIT-TOUR, *www.cit-tours.com*, and 9501 West Devon Ave, Rosemount, Il 60018, and, in Canada, 80 Tiverton Court, Suite 401, Markham, Ontario L3R 0GA, **t** (800) 387 0711.

**Hideaways International**, 767 Islington St., Portsmouth, NH 03802, **t** (603) 430 4433 or toll free (800) 843 4433, **f** (603) 430 4444, *www.hideaways.com*.

**Homebase Abroad**, *www.homebase-abroad. com*. Luxury villas.

**Rentals in Italy (and Elsewhere!)**, Suzanne T. Pidduck, 1742 Calle Corva, Camarillo, CA 93010, **t** (805) 987 5278 or toll free (800) 726 6702, **f** (805) 482 7976, *www.rentvillas.com*.

**RAVE**, Market Place Mall, Rochester, NY 14607, **t** (716) 427 0259.

**The Apartment Service**, 5–6 Francis Grove, London SW19 4DT, **t** (020) 8944 1444, **f** (020) 8944 6744, *www.apartmentservice.com*.

**Tuscan Enterprises**, c/o **International Chapters** (*see* p.xxx).

**Vacation Villas**, *www.vacationvillas.net*.

## In Italy

**The Best in Italy**, Via Ugo Foscolo 72, Firenze, **t** 055 223 064.

**Immobiliare Tirrenia**, Via XXIV Maggio 63, Marina di Grosseto (GR), **t** 0564 34 672.

**Toscana Vacanze**, Via XX Settembre 6, 52047 Marciano della Chiana, **t** 0575 845 348.

**Toscanamare Villas**, Via W della Gheradesca 5, Castagneto Carducci (LI), **t** 0565 744 012, **f** 0565 744 339 (villas on the Versilia coast).

**Vela**, Via Colombo 16, Castiglione della Pescaia, **t** 0564 933 495.

the Italian tourist industry is run by **Agriturist**. It has burgeoned in recent years, with several offices in each region. Prices, compared with the over-hyped 'Tuscan villa', are still reasonable. Local tourist offices will have information on this type of accommodation in their areas.

The APT publishes an annual listing, or contact:

**Associazione Regionale Agriturist**, Piazza S. Firenze 3, 50122 Firenze, t (055) 287 838

**Solemar**, Via Cavour 80, Firenze, t (055) 287 157.

**Turismo Verde**, c/o Confcoltivatori, Piazza Indipendenza 10, 50129 Firenze, t (055) 471 261.

Or write directly to the individual **provincial Agriturist offices** (UPA):

**Arezzo**: Via Guido Monaco, 52100 Arezzo, t (0575) 300 751.

**Grosseto**: Via della Chiesa 4, 58100 Grosseto, t (0564) 21 010.

**Livorno**: Via G. Marradi 14, 57126 Livorno, t (0586) 812 744.

**Lucca**: Viale. Barsanti e Matteucci, 55100 Lucca, t (0583) 332 044.

**Massa Carrara**: Via V.M. Giuliani 9, 54011 Massa Carrara, t (0187) 421 028.

**Pisa**: Via B. Croce 62, 56100 Pisa, t (050) 26 221.

**Pistoia**: Via F. Pacini 45, 51100 Pistoia, t (0573) 21 231.

**Siena**: Via della Sapienza 39, 53100 Siena, t (0577) 46 194.

## Alpine Refuges

The Club Alpino Italiano operates a large percentage of the *Rifugi Alpini*, or mountain

huts in the Apennines. Facilities range from the basic to the grand; some are exclusively for hikers and climbers, while others are reached by *funivie*, and are used by skiers in winter and holiday-makers in summer. Rates average L18–25,000 a night, but rise by 20 per cent between December and April.

**Club Alpino Italiano**, Via Fonseca Pimental 7, Milan, t 02 2614 1378. Write to the club for a list of huts, their opening dates, and booking information.

## Camping

Most of the official campsites are near the sea, the mountains or the lakes, and there is usually one within commuting distance of major tourist centres. A complete list with full details for all of Italy is published annually in the Italian Touring Club's *Campeggi e Villaggi Turistici*, available in Italian bookshops for L29,500, or you can obtain an abbreviated list free from the Centro Internazionale Prenotazioni Federcampeggio, Casella Postale 23, 50042, Calenzano (Firenze); request a booking form to reserve a space – in summer the tents and caravans are packed cheek to cheek. Fees vary according to the site facilities, but are roughly L6–8,000 per person (less for children); L8,000–15,000 per tent or caravan; and L4,000 per car. You may camp outside an official site if you ask the landowner's permission. Caravans are expensive to hire: the National Tourist Office and local tourist offices have lists of firms.

# Florence

08

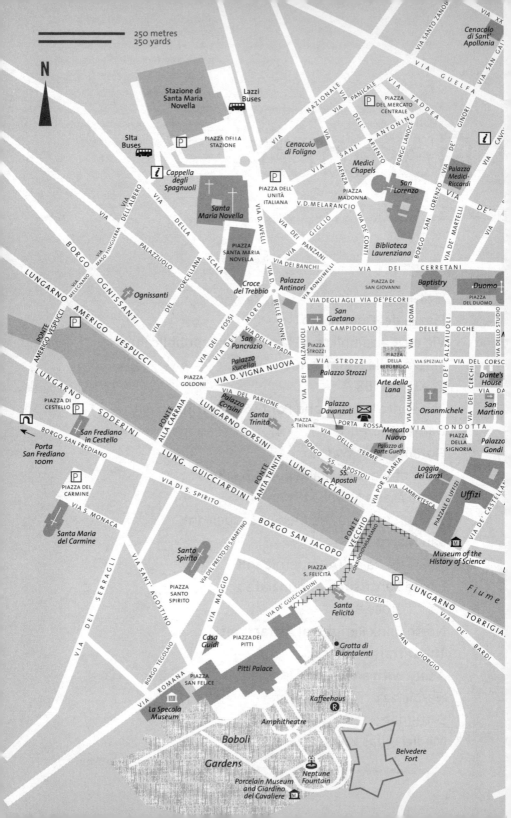

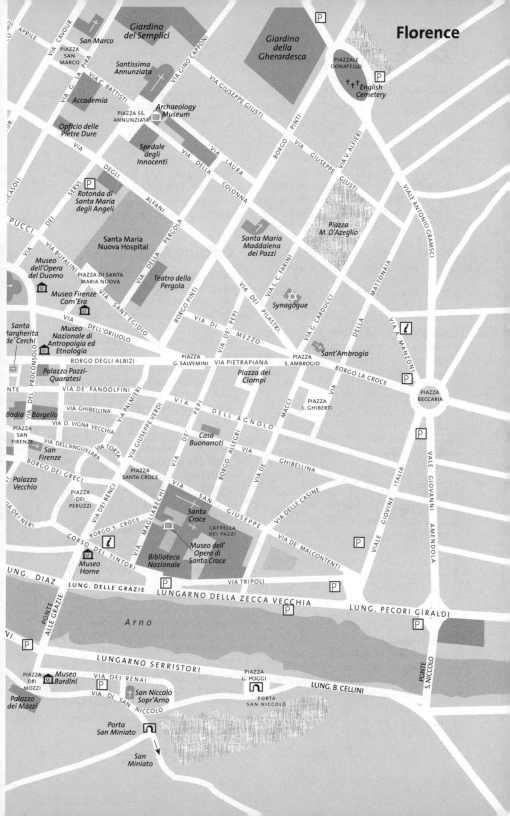

# Getting There

Florence is the central transport node for Tuscany and harder to avoid than to reach.

## By Air

Florence's Vespucci airport was lengthened in 1996, and it now bustles with more international traffic than Pisa. It is 6km out at Peretola, t 055 373 498, flight information t 055 306 1702 (recorded message in Italian and English), and is connected to the city by a regular bus service to Santa Maria Novella Station (15mins). A taxi to the centre will cost about €15.50.

**Alitalia**: Lungarno Acciaioli 10/12r, t 055 27888, or freephone/toll free t 1478 65643, f 055 278 8400, *www.alitalia.it*.

**British Airways**: freephone/toll free t 1478 12266, or contact Pisa office, t 050 40866, *www.britishairways.com*.

**Meridiana** (for London Gatwick): Lungarno Vespucci 28r, t 055 230 2314, f 055 230 2046.

**TWA**: Via dei Vecchietti 4, t 055 239 6856, f 055 214 634.

## By Train

The central station is **Santa Maria Novella**, call t 8488 88088 for information, *www.fs-online.com*. Many long-distance trains arriving at night use **Campo di Marte** station, bus nos.12 or 91.

## By Bus

It's possible to reach nearly every city, town and village in Tuscany from Florence, which is wonderfully convenient – once you know which of several bus companies to patronize. The tourist office has a complete list, but here are some of the most popular:

**SITA** (near station, Via S. Caterina da Siena 15, t 800 373 760 daily, Sat and Sun until 1pm): towns in the Val d'Elsa, Chianti, Val di Pesa, Mugello and Casentino; Arezzo, Bibbiena, Castelfiorentino, Certaldo, Consuma, Figline Valdarno, Firenzuola, Marina di Grosseto, Montevarchi, Poggibonsi (for San Gimignano and Volterra), Pontassieve, Poppi, Pratovecchio, Scarperia, Siena, Stia and Vallombrosa.

**LAZZI** (Piazza Stazione 47r, t 055 351 061 Mon–Fri): along the Arno to the coast, including Calenzano, Cerreto Guidi, Empoli, Forte dei Marmi, Livorno, Lucca, Marina di Carrara, Marina di Massa, Montecatini Terme, Montelupo, Montevarchi, Pescia, Pisa, Pistoia, Pontedera, Prato, Signa, Tirrenia, Torre del Lago, Viareggio.

**CAP** (Via Nazionale 13, t 055 214 637): Borgo S. Lorenzo, Impruneta, Incisa Valdarno, Montepiano, Prato.

**COPIT** (Piazza S. Maria Novella, t 0573 21170): Abetone, Cerreto Guidi, Pistoia, Poggio a Caiano, Vinci.

**RAMA** (Lazzi Station, t 055 215 155): Grosseto.

# Getting Around

Florence is now one of the best Italian cities to get around; best, because nearly everything you'll want to see is within easy walking distance and large areas in the centre are pedestrian zones. In addition, there are no hills to climb, and it's hard to lose your way for very long.

Just to make life difficult, Florence has two sets of **address numbers** on every street – red ones for business, blue or black for residences; your hotel might be either one. However, recent years have seen some improvement in the signage department: every major piazza, landmark or monument now has a plaque offering relevant background information, and helpful maps have been posted in strategic positions throughout the city.

## By Bus

**City buses** (ATAF; *www.ataf.net*) can whizz or inch you across Florence, and are an excellent means of reaching sights on the periphery. Most lines begin at Santa Maria Novella station, and pass by Piazza del Duomo or Piazza San Marco. ATAF supply an excellent and comprehensive booklet, including a clear map, with details of all bus routes. These are available at the information/ticket booth at the station, tourist offices, some bars, and at ATAF's central office in Piazza della Stazione, t 055 565 0222. Ticket prices: €1.03 for 60 mins, €1.81 for 3 hours, €4.13 for 24 hours. The most useful buses for visitors are listed below.

6   Via Rondinella–Piazza San Marco– Duomo–Station–Soffiano

7  Station–Duomo–San Domenico–Fiesole
10 Station–Duomo–S. Marco–Ponte a
   Mensola–Settignano
11 Viale Calatafimi–S.Marco–Piazza
   Indipendenza–Station–Porta Romana–
   Poggio Imperiale
11a Viale Calatafimi–Duomo–Porta Romana
   –Poggio Imperiale
13 Station–Ponte Rosso–Parterre (car park)–
   Piazza Libertà–Viale Mazzini–Campo di
   Marte–Piazzale Michelangelo–Porta
   Romana
14c Rovezzano–Duomo–Station–Careggi
   (hospital)
17 Cascine–station–Duomo–Via
   Lamarmora–Salviatino (for the youth
   hostel)
25 Station–S. Marco–Piazza Libertà–Via
   Bolognese–Pratolino
28 Station–Via R. Giuliani–Castello–Sesto
   Fiorentino
37 Station–Ponte alla Carraia–Porta
   Romana–Certosa del Galluzzo
38 Porta Romana–Pian del Giullari (you
   need to book this from the
   telephone near the bus stop at Porta
   Romana, t 0167 019 794)

As part of the continuing campaign against city smog, a fleet of Lilliputian electric buses, routes A, B and D, have recently been introduced in the city. These mainly serve the centre, often taking circuitous routes 'round the houses', and are a good way of seeing some of the sights if you've had enough walking. Details of routes can be found on the ATAF maps.

## By Taxi

Taxis in Florence don't cruise; you'll find them in ranks at the station and in the major *piazze*, or else ring for a radio taxi: t 055 4798 or 4390. Taxi metres will start at €2.21 plus extras, adding €.74 per km. There is a minimum charge of €3.65.

## By Car

Just a few years ago the traffic problem in Florence was one of the grimmest and most carcinogenic in Italy. But in 1988, with great fanfares and to howls of protest, Florence attempted to do something about the cars that were choking it to death by greatly

enlarging the limited access zone, the *zona di traffico limitato*, which the Florentines, with clenched teeth, somehow pronounce as ZTL. Within the ZTL only buses, taxis, and cars belonging to residents are permitted; otherwise, you are permitted to pay to park in one of the city's **car parks** (there's the underground car park at the station, or the cheaper, big park at the Parterre, near Piazza Libertà) or take your chances on a side street or on metred parking around the Fortezza. This new regulation was then followed by whole areas, especially around Piazza della Signoria and the Duomo, becoming totally trafficfree zones. The only danger is the odd ambulance or police car, the speeding mopeds (all of which you can easily hear) and the deadly silent bicycle.

## Bicycle, Scooter and Car Hire

Hiring a bike can save you tramping time and angst but it's not risk free. Watch out for cars and pedestrians. You can hire a motorbike at:

**Alinari**, Via Guelfa 85r, t 055 280 500 or Via dei Bardi 35, t 055 234 6436.
**Motorent**, Via S. Zanobi 9r, t 055 490 113.
**Florence by Bike**, Via S. Zanobi 120/122r, t 055 488 992.
**Promoturist**, Via Baccio Bandinelli 43, t 055 701 863. For mountain bikes only.

Between 8am and 7.30pm, visitors can now take advantage of one of the (almost) free bicycles supplied by the *comune* of Florence. There are various pick-up points around town, the most central being the Fortezza, the Parterre (for the car parks), Piazza Strozzi, Piazza Stazione, Piazza San Marco, the central market and Porta Romana. They cost about €.5 for the day.

When you can't take any more art, hire a car and escape into the ravishing countryside. Most rental firms are within easy walking distance of the station.

**Avis**, Borgo Ognissanti 128r, t 055 239 8826/ 055 213 629.
**Europcar**, Borgo Ognissanti 53r, t 055 290 438.
**Hertz**, Via M. Finiguerra 33, t 055 239 8205.
**Italy by Car**, B.go Ognissanti 134r, t 055 287 161.
**Maggiore-Budget**, Via M. Finiguerra 11r, t 055 210 238.
**Program**, Borgo Ognissanti 135, t 055 282 916.

# Tourist Information

APT tourist service: *www.firenze.turismo. toscana.it*, *info@firenze.turismo.toscana.it*

Florence becomes more tourist-friendly all the time and there is now a genuine effort on the part of the city administration to provide helpful tourist information. The *comune* publishes a leaflet listing bars and cafés which 'offer their clients a welcoming reception, politeness and, should they need it, bathroom facilities...'; believe it or not, finding a toilet you could use in a bar or café used to be no mean feat. In addition, there are two **guides for the disabled**, both of which can be picked up at the tourist office. The more comprehensive is only in Italian, but it covers access to sites and restaurants etc. in great detail and has a good map.

## Florence

The main tourist office is a bit out of the way, near Piazza Beccaria on **Via Manzoni 16**, **t** 055 23320 (*open Mon–Fri 8–6, Sat 8–2*).

There is a branch at Via Cavour 1r, **t** 055 290 832, *infoturismo@provincia.fi.it* (*open Mon–Sat 8.15–7.15, Sun 8.30–1.30*).

There is also an office at Borgo Santa Croce 29r, **t** 055 234 0444, **f** 055 226 4524 (*open Mon–Sat 9–7, Sun & hols 9–2*).

A new office has opened on the south side of the station in Piazza della Stazione, **t** 055 212 245, **f** 055 238 1226, *turismo3@comune.fi.it*, *www.comune.firenze.it* (*open Mon–Sat 8.30–7, Sun 8.30–1.30*).

During the summer, look out for the temporary mobile 'Tourist Help Points' run by the Vigili Urbani (the traffic police), set up in the centre of town.

## Fiesole

**Via Portigiani 3**, **t** 055 598 720/055 597 8373, **f** 055 598 822 (*open year round Mon–Sat 8.30–7.30, Sun 10–7*).

# Practical A–Z

**American Express**: Via Dante Alighieri 22r, **t** 055 50981, just off Piazza della Repubblica.

**Central post office**: Via Pellicceria, near Piazza della Repubblica (*open Mon–Sat 8.15–6;*

*telegram office open Mon–Sat 8.15–6; call* **t** *160 for information*).

**Consulates**: UK, Lungarno Corsini 2, **t** 055 284 133; US, Lung. Vespucci 38, **t** 055 239 8276.

**E-mail services**: you can send e-mail, use the Internet or fax from all over the city nowadays; one such service is **Internet Train**, Via Zannoni 1r, **t** 055 21113, *www.internettrain.it*, or Via Guelfa 24a, **t/f** 055 214 794 (*opening hours differ from branch to branch*); they are also agents for the Swiss Post International if you want to avoid the bureaucratic slowpokes in the Posta Italiana. Mac users might try **Intotheweb**, Via de' Conti 23r, **t** 055 264 5628 (*open daily 10am–midnight*).

**Libraries**: British Institute Library, Lungarno Guicciardini 9, **t** 055 2677 8270 (*open 9.45–1 and 3.15–6.30, closed Sat and Sun*). American Library, Via S. Gallo 10 (*open 9–12.30, closed Sat and Sun*). There are so many other libraries in Florence that one, the Biblioteca del Servizio Beni Librari, Via G. Modena 13, **t** 055 438 2655, does nothing but dispense information on all the others.

**Lost property** in Italian is *Oggetti smarriti* or *Oggetti ritrovati*. The office is in Via Circondaria 19, **t** 055 328 3942.

**Medical**: for an ambulance or first aid, Misericordia, Piazza del Duomo 20, **t** 055 212 222. Doctor's night service, **t** 055 477 891. For general medical **emergencies** call **t** 118. The general **hospital** Santa Maria Nuova, in Piazza S. M. Nuova, **t** 055 27581, is the most convenient. **Tourist Medical Service** (24hrs a day) is staffed by English- and French-speaking physicians at Via Lorenzo il Magnifico 59, ring first on **t** 055 475 411. If you find yourself hospitalized while in Florence, the **AVO** (Association of Hospital Volunteers) provides volunteer interpreters to deal with language problems, **t** 055 425 0126/055 234 4567.

**Pharmacies**: open 24 hours every day in **S. Maria Novella station**, also **Molteni**, Via Calzaiuoli 7r and **Taverna**, Piazza S. Giovanni 20r, by the baptistry.

**Police**: emergency **t** 113. The *Ufficio Stranieri*, in the *questura*, Via Zara 2, **t** 055 49771 (*open Mon–Fri 8.30–12.30*), handles most foreigners' problems, and usually has someone around who speaks English. Go here for residents' permits, etc.

Tourist Aid Police: Via Pietrapiana 50, t 055 203 911, (open Mon–Fri 8.30–7.30, Sat 8.30–1.30). Interpreters available to help you report thefts or resolve other problems.

Towed-away cars: there are three car pounds in the city, at Via del Olmatello (open 24hrs a day), Via Arcovata (bus 23, 33 to Viale Corsica) and Parchiggio Parterre (near Piazza Libertà); they have one central phone number, t 055 308 249, and will tell you where your car has been taken.

# Festivals and Events

Traditional festivals in Florence date back for centuries. The following are listed roughly in the order they take place in the year:

*Scoppio del Carro* (Explosion of the Cart), *Easter Sunday*. Commemorates Florentine participation in the First Crusade, which took place in 1096. The Florentines were led by Pazzino de' Pazzi, who was the first over the walls of Jerusalem and upon returning home, received the special custody of the flame of Holy Saturday, with which the Florentines traditionally relit their family hearths. To make the event more colourful, the Pazzi constructed a decorated wooden ox cart to carry the flame. They lost the job after the Pazzi conspiracy in 1478, and since then the city has taken over the responsibility. In the morning, a firework-filled wooden float is pulled by white oxen from Il Prato to the cathedral, where, at 11am, during the singing of the Gloria, it is ignited by an iron 'dove' that descends on a wire from the high altar.

*Maggio Musicale Fiorentino*, Teatro Comunale, Corso Italia 12 (off Lungarno Vespucci), t 055 211 158 for ticket information, *late April–early July*. The city's big music festival, bringing in big-name concert stars. Some performances may also be held at Teatro della Pergola, or other venues.

**Flower and Plant Show**, the Parterre, *late April*. A huge show near Piazza Libertà, a must for horticulture fans.

**International Iris festival**, Piazzale Michelangelo, *May*.

*Festa del Grillo* (cricket festival), Cascine, Ascension Day, *May*. Michelangelo was thinking of the festival's little wooden cricket cages when he mocked Ammannati's gallery on the cathedral dome.

*Calcio Storico in Costume*, Piazza Santa Croce, *June*. Each June, four matches of historical football are played, in 16th-century costume, by 27-man teams from Florence's four quarters, in memory of a defiant football match played there in 1530, during the siege by Charles V. It's great fun with flag-throwing and a parade in historical costume as part of the pre-game ceremonies. The only fixed date is 24 June; the dates for the other matches are pulled out of a hat on Easter Sunday.

*Festa di San Giovanni*, *24 June*. The festival of Florence's patron saint, marked by a big firework display near Piazzale Michelangelo at 10pm.

*Estate Fiesolana*, *late June–Aug*. This is one of the annual cultural events generally adored by Florentines, when the old Roman theatre is made the venue for concerts, dance, theatre and films, for reasonable prices.

**Summer concerts**, Piazza Signoria, *summer months*. The piazza occasionally plays host to concerts and other events during the summer. Countless smaller-scale concerts are given, often outdoors or in cloisters, churches and villas. Look out for posters or ask at the tourist office.

*Maggio Musicale* festival closing concert, *late June/early July*. A free-for-all heralding the end of the annual music festival.

*MaggioDanza* ballet company, *late June/early July*. An evening of dance, held annually, also a free-for-all.

**Florence Dance Festival**, t 055 289 276 for information, *July*. Presents an interesting combination of classical and contemporary dance performances.

*Teatro Comunale* summer opera and ballet season, *July*. This festival runs throughout the month with performances at the Comunale itself and sometimes in the Boboli Gardens.

*Festa delle Rificolona*, *7 Sept*. A children's festival: Florentine kids gather in the evening in Piazza SS. Annunziata and along the river armed with paper lanterns, and then, after dark, they parade singing around the streets.

# Shopping

## Fashion

Although central Florence sometimes seems like one solid boutique, the city is no longer the queen of Italian fashion – the long lack of a central airport, more than anything else, sent most of the big designers to Milan. Nevertheless, the big fashion names of the 1960s and 70s, and the international chain stores, are well represented in smart Via Tornabuoni, Via Calzaiuoli and around the Duomo, and the new overhaul of Gucci and the arrival of Prada has updated the city's slightly fusty image.

## Leather

**Via della Vigna Nuova.** Leather is something Florence is still known for, and you'll see plenty of it in this central street.

**Via del Parione.** Another central street where leather goods are readily available.

**The Leather School,** entrance at Piazza Santa Croce 16 or Via S. Giuseppe 5r. An unusual institution, occupying part of Santa Croce's cloister, with less expensive goods.

## Jewellery

**Ponte Vecchio.** Florence is also famous for its jewellery. The shops on and around the bridge are forced by the nature of their location into wide-open competition, and good prices for Florentine brushed gold (although much of it is made in Arezzo these days) and antique jewellery are more common than you may think. Elsewhere, there are two other stores worth seeking out.

**Il Gatto Bianco,** Borgo SS Apostoli 12r. Contemporary designs (earrings, rings, necklaces etc) are crafted on the premises in silver, gold and other metals with pearls and precious stones.

**Pepita Studio,** Borgo degli Albizi 23r. Fun, chunky, young designs in plexiglass, wood and glass. Prices are very reasonable.

## Marbled Paper

Florence is one of the few places in the world to make marbled paper, an art brought over from the Orient by Venice in the 12th century. Each sheet is hand-dipped in a bath of colours to create a delicate, lightly coloured clouded design; no two sheets are alike. Marbled-paper-covered stationery items or just sheets of marbled paper are available at:

**Giulio Giannini e Figlio,** Piazza Pitti 37r. The oldest manufacturer in Florence.

**Il Papiro,** with three shops at: Via Cavour 55r; Piazza del Duomo 24r; Lung. Acciaiuoli 42r.

**La Bottega Artigiana del Libro,** Lungarno Corsini 40r.

**Il Torchio,** Via de' Bardi 17. Here the workbench is in the shop so you can see the artisans in action. These shops (and many others) also carry Florentine paper with its colourful Gothic patterns.

## Books

Bookworms do better in Florence than most Italian cities, and prices of books in English seem to have come down in recent years, so there are a fair number of places to browse.

**The Paperback Exchange,** Via Fiesolana 31r. A wide selection in English, with many books about Florence.

**Seeber,** Via Tornabuoni 70r. An alternative to the Exchange, also has a good selection.

**Feltrinelli,** Via Cavour 12–20r. Books in English and an excellent range of art books.

**BM Bookshop,** Borgo Ognissanti 4r. Ditto here.

**Franco Maria Ricci,** Via delle Belle Donne 41r. A fabulous collection of art books.

**Il Viaggio,** Borgo degli Albizi 41r. Florence's best travel bookshop, stocking a wide selection of travel guides and maps, including walking maps, covering both Italy and the rest of the world, in English and Italian. The big English-stocking bookshops like Seeber and Feltrinelli also have a wide selection of books in Italian.

## Antiques and Art Galleries

Borgo Ognissanti and the various Lungarni are the place to look.

**P. Bazzanti e Figli,** Lungarno Corsini 44. Here you can pick up an exact replica of the bronze boar in the Mercato Nuovo.

**Atelier Alice,** Via Faenza 72r. Much easier to carry is an Italian carnival mask, available here, and for those who are keen to learn more about the art of the mask the shop runs five-lesson courses. Ring Prof. A. Dessi on t 055 215 961 for details.

**Via Maggio.** Full of upmarket antique shops.

Serious collectors may want to check Florence's busy auction houses:

**Casa d'Aste Pandolfini**, Borgo degli Albizi 26, **t** 055 234 0888.

**Casa d'Aste Pitti**, Via Maggio 15, **t** 055 239 6382.

**Sotheby's Italia**, Via G. Capponi 26, **t** 055 247 9021 (*call for appointment*).

## Cloth
**Casa dei Tessuti**, Via de' Pecori 20–24r, **t** 055 215 961. Keeps Florence's ancient cloth trade alive with lovely linens, silks and woollens. During the lunch break, you might catch a lecture on the history of Florence with special reference to the textile industry.

## Silver, Crystal and Porcelain
**A. Poggi**, Via Calzaiuoli 105r and 116r. One of the city's widest selections (including Florence's own Richard-Ginori).

## Children's Toys and Clothes
**Città del Sole**, Borgo Ognissanti 37. The best toy shop in Florence.

**Cirri**, Via Por S. Maria 38–40r. If you happen to have or know the kinds of little girls who can wear white, this has a fairy tale selection of dresses.

## Food
**Mercato Centrale.** Good for a number of speciality food shops.

**Allrientar Gastronomia**, Borgo SS. Apostoli. Pick up items such as truffle cream.

**La Porta del Tartufo**, Borgo Ognissanti 133r. Virtually confines itself to different types of truffles or 'truffled' foods ranging from *grappa* to salmon paste.

**Il Procacci**, Via Tornabuoni 64r. A high-quality *alimentari* (food shop) selling regional specialities as well as foreign foods. It's most famous as the venue for a lunchtime *Prosecco* and *panino tartufato*, a glass of sparkling white wine and a truffle-filled sandwich. Also a bar.

**Gola e Cantina**, Piazza Pitti 16. Offers a good selection of wines, oils and vinegars, and cookery books (in both English and Italian) to go with them.

**La Bottega del Brunello**, Via Ricasoli 81r. Divided in two parts, one for display and one for tasting the wine and specialities on sale.

**Casa del Vino**, Via dell' Ariento 16r. With wine tastings plus snacks in the San Lorenzo street market.

**Enoteca**, Via Giraldi. Specializes exclusively in Tuscan wines from lesser-known producers, with over 140 labels (you can also eat there).

**Le Volpi e L'Uva**, Piazza dei Rossi 1r. Situated behind the Ponte Vecchio on the square, this also stocks lesser-known labels.

**Enoteca Murgia**, Via dei Banchi 57, off Piazza S. Maria Novella. Good for wines and spirits in general.

**Marchesi de' Frescobaldi**, Via di S. Spirito 11. One of the largest wine suppliers in Italy; visit their ancient cellars.

**Farmaceutica di Santa Maria Novella**, Via della Scala 16b. Selling medieval cures and Dominican remedies, and little changed since 1612.

## Markets
Florence's lively street markets offer good bargains, fake designer glad rags and even some authentic labels.

**San Lorenzo market**. Easily the largest and most boisterous.

**Sant'Ambrogio.** A bustling food market.

**Mercato Nuovo** (Straw Market). The most touristic, but not flagrantly so.

**Piazza Santo Spirito.** Home to different markets on different days:
Food, clothes and shoes (small). *Open daily exc Sun*.
Craft and flea market (big). *Open every 2nd Sun of month*.
Organic food market. *Open every 3rd Sun*.

**Cascine**, along the river. A weekly market where many Florentines buy their clothes. Here you may easily find designer clothes off the back of a lorry, shoes and lots more besides. *Open Tues am*.

**Mercato delle Pulci** (Flea Market), Piazza dei Ciompi. Perhaps the most fun market, offering all kinds of desirable junk. *Open Sun*.

# Sports and Activities

## On the Water
The one activity most summertime visitors begin to crave after tramping through the sights is a dip in a pool.

**Piscina le Pavoniere**, Cascine. The prettiest in Florence. *Open June–Sept 10–6.30.*
**Bellariva**, up the Arno at Lungarno Colombo 2. *Open June–Sept 11–5.*
**Amici del Nuoto**, Via del Romito 38, t 055 483 951. *Open all year.*
**Costoli**, Via Paoli, near Campo di Marte, t 055 669 744. *Open all year.*

If there's enough water in the Arno, you can try rowing or canoeing:
**Società Canottieri Comunali**, Lungarno Ferrucci 6, t 055 681 2151.
**Società Canottieri Firenze**, Lungarno dei Medici 8, t 055 238 1010 (membership only).

### Horse-racing and Riding
**Ippodromo Le Cascine**, Cascine, t 055 360 598. Florence's race course.
**Ippodromo della Mulina**, Cascine, t 055 422 6076. Also at the Cascine, Florence's trotting course.
**Maneggio Mirinella**, Via di Macia 21, t/f 055 887 8066. The nearest place to go riding in the Tuscan hills.
**Centro Ippico Ugolino**, Via Oliveta 12, t 055 230 1289. You can also ride here, near the golf course.

### Golf
**Golf Club Ugolino**, on the Chiantigiana-Impruneta, t 055 230 1009. The nearest 18-hole golf course to Florence is in Gràssina, 7km southeast of the city; a lovely course.

### Squash and Tennis
**Centro Squash**, Viale Empoli 16, t 055 732 3055.
**Circolo Tennis**, Cascine, t 055 354 326.

# Where to Stay

### Florence ✉ 50100
Florence has some lovely hotels, and not all of them at Grand Ducal prices, although base rates are the highest in Tuscany. As in any city, the higher cost of living means you won't find much *cheap* accommodation. In fact, Florence, Venice and Rome are the most expensive places to stay in Italy, and you should count on having to pay around 25 per cent more for a room here than you would anywhere else.

Historic old palace-hotels are the rule rather than the exception; those listed below are some of the more atmospheric and charming, but to be honest, few are secrets, so reserve as far in advance as possible. Also note that nearly every hotel in Florence with a restaurant will require half-board, and many will also try to lay down a heavy breakfast charge as well that is supposed to be optional.

There are almost 400 hotels in Florence but not enough for anyone who arrives in June and September without a reservation (Easter is even more busy). But don't despair; there are several hotel consortia that can help you find a room in nearly any price range for a small commission. If you're arriving by car or train, the most useful will be ITA.

**ITA**: in Santa Maria Novella station, t 055 282 893, *open 9–9, in winter until 8*; or in the AGIP service station at Peretola, to the west of Florence on A11, t 055 421 1800. Between March and November there's an office in the Chianti-Est service plaza on the A1, t 055 621 349. No bookings can be made over the telephone and a booking fee of between L3,000 and L10,000 is charged, according to the category of hotel.
**Florence Promhotels**: Viale A. Volta 72, t 055 570 481, f 055 587 189. Free booking service.

For *agriturismo* or farmhouse accommodation in the surrounding countryside (self-catering or otherwise), contact: Agriturist Toscana, Piazza S. Firenze 3, t/f 055 287 838; or Turismo Verde Toscana, Via Verdi 5, t 055 234 4925.

### Luxury
★★★★**Calzaiuoli**, Via Calzaiuoli 6, t 055 212 456, f 055 268 310, *info@calzaiuoli.it, www.calzaiuoli.it*. Just a few steps from Piazza Signoria and on a traffic-free street is a comfortable hotel with modern, nicely decorated rooms and wonderful views from the top floor.
★★★★★**Excelsior**, Piazza Ognissanti 3, t 055 2715, f 055 210 278, *www. westin.com/excelsiorflorence*. In the city the luxury leader is former Florentine address of Napoleon's sister Caroline. Lots of marble, neoclassically plush, lush and green with plants, immaculately staffed, with decadently luxurious bedrooms, many of which have river views (for a price).

****Helvetia & Bristol**, Via dei Pescioni 2, **t** 055 287 814, **f** 055 281 336, *www. charminghotels.it*. If you prefer luxury on a smaller scale, this has 52 exquisitely furnished bedrooms, each one different, all with rich fabrics adorning windows, walls and beds; Stravinsky, Bertrand Russell and Pirandello stayed here; added pluses are the restaurant and the winter garden.

*****Regency**, Piazza d'Azeglio 3, **t** 055 245 247, **f** 055 234 6735, *info@regencyhotel.com*, *www.regency-hotel.com*. In Florence's plane-tree-shaded 'London Square', there's an even smaller gem, charming and intimate with only 33 air-conditioned rooms; between the two wings there's an elegant town garden. The public rooms are beautifully panelled, and the fare in the dining room superb; there's a private garage for your car.

**Relais Uffizi**, Chiasso de' Baroncelli/Chiasso del Buco 16, **t** 055 2676239, **f** 055 2657909; *info@relaisuffizi.it*, *www.relaisuffizi.it*. The only hotel which overlooks Piazza della Signoria, the Relais Uffizi is hidden down a series of narrow lanes. The 13 rooms of varying shapes and sizes are decorated and furnished with style while the atmosphere is informal. You can relax in the sitting room and watch the ever-changing piazza below.

****The Savoy**, Piazza Repubblica 7, **t** 055 283 313, **f** 055 284 840, *www.rfhotels.com*. The old, crumbling Savoy reopened in spring 2000 under the Forte Group, now striking a minimalist tone with décor in shades of cream, beige and grey; it has a bar and restaurant where you can sit out on the piazza.

****Lungarno**, Borgo San Jacopo 14, **t** 055 27261, **f** 055 268 437, *lungarnohotels@ lungarnohotels.com*, *www.lungarnohotels. com*. A discreet hotel enjoying a marvellous location on the river, only two minutes' walk from the Ponte Vecchio. The ground floor sitting/breakfast room and bar, and the new restaurant, which specializes in fish, take full advantage of this with picture windows looking on to the water. The building is modern, but incorporates a medieval tower, and has just been refurbished; the small-ish bedrooms are decorated in smart blue and cream. The best have balconies with 'The View'. Book ahead for these.

****Monna Lisa**, Borgo Pinti 27, **t** 055 247 9751, **f** 055 247 9755, *hotel@monnalisa.it*, *www.monnalisa.it*. A Renaissance palace, now owned by the descendants of sculptor Giovanni Dupre, which has a stern façade and, it is said, staff to match, but behind them hides one of the loveliest small hotels in Florence. The palazzo is well preserved and the furnishings are family heirlooms, as are the many works of art. Rooms vary wildly; try to reserve one of the tranquil rooms that overlook the garden; breakfast is available, and it has private parking.

****Grand Hotel Baglioni**, Piazza Unità Italiana 6, **t** 055 23580, **f** 055 235 8895, *www.hotelbaglioni.it*. A reliable and reasonably priced (for its category) choice right next to the train station, the Baglioni is popular with tour groups and business clients but has managed to retain a pleasant, old-fashioned feel to it. Rooms are comfortable, and all due to be updated over the next year or so, but its biggest plus is the top-floor restaurant, which offers close-up views of the Duomo and Medici chapels from huge picture windows. In the summer, the bar and restaurant move outside to the extensive terrace, beautifully set out with shrubs and flowers in terracotta pots. Combined with 360° views across the cityscape, this has to be one of Florence's most romantic spots to wine and dine.

**Gallery**, Vicolo del'Oro 2, **t** 055 27263, **f** 055 268 557, *galleryhotel@lungarnohotels.it*. Florence's most exciting hotel is a shrine to contemporary interior design. It is by no means stark, however, and the position (a mere two minutes from the Ponte Vecchio) is superb. It has a comfortable library, a smart bar and a restaurant serving trendy fusion food.

****Astoria**, Via del Giglio 9, **t** 055 239 8095, **f** 055 214 632. Recently refurbished, in a grand 16th-century palazzo near San Lorenzo market, this has more character than many of those located near the station. Public rooms are suitably impressive and some of the bedrooms likewise; avoid those on the lower floors by the street.

****Kraft**, Via Solferino 2, t 055 284 273, f 055 239 8267. Frequently used by upmarket tour groups, this is handy for the opera season (it is two minutes walk from the Teatro Comunale), and has the added advantage of a small rooftop pool. Bedrooms are light and sunny, and comfortably furnished with cheerful fabrics. The suites on the top floor have great views. There is a restaurant.

****Principe**, Lungarno Vespucci 34, t 055 284 848, f 055 283 458. This is one of the most pleasant among the many hotels along the Arno – a small, comfortable hotel, centrally air-conditioned and soundproofed, with a little garden at the back; the nicer rooms have terraces over the river.

****Villa Carlotta**, Via Michele di Lando 3, t 055 233 6134, f 055 233 6147, *villacarlotta@slashnet.it*, *www.venere.it/firenze/villacarlotta*. Located in a quiet residential district in the upper Oltrarno, close to the Porta Romana, this Tuscan-Edwardian building has 26 sophisticated rooms which have been tastefully refurnished and have every mod con. There's a garden and glassed-in veranda, where the large breakfasts are served; a private garage offers safe parking.

## Very Expensive

***Hermitage**,Vicolo Marzio 1, t 055 287 216, f 055 212 208, *florence@hermitagehotel.com*. You have to look hard to find this little hotel tucked away behind the Ponte Vecchio on the north side of the river. It is built upside down; the lift takes you to the fifth floor with its ravishing roof garden, reception and elegant blue and yellow sitting room. The bedrooms below are on the small side, but you will find them charmingly furnished with antiques and tasteful fabrics. Some have river views.

****Villa Belvedere**, Via Benedetto Castelli 3, t 055 222 501, f 055 223 163, *reception@villabelvedere.com*, *www.villabelvedere.com*. Not one of the more interesting buildings to be found in this part of peripheral Florence (a kilometre above Porta Romana), but a very pleasant alternative to central accommodation nevertheless, with a beautiful garden, tennis court, a nice little pool and good views. Rooms are modern and comfortable with lots of wood and plenty of space. For trips into town, you can leave your car and catch a nearby bus. Light meals are served in the restaurant.

***Beacci Tornabuoni**, Via Tornabuoni 3, t 055 212 645, f 055 283 594. Another excellent small hotel which puts you in the centre of fashionable Florence, on the top three floors of an elegant Renaissance palace. The rooms are comfortable, air-conditioned and equipped with minibars, though it's more fun to sit over your drink on the panoramic roof terrace.

***Loggiato dei Serviti**, Piazza SS Annunziata 3, t 055 289592, f 055 289595, *info@loggiatodeiservitihotel.it*. Located on Florence's most beautiful square (now traffic-free), the front rooms of this delightful hotel overlook Brunelleschi's famous portico. The 16th-century building was originally a convent, and many of the architectural features remain. Rooms are furnished with antiques and tasteful fabrics; each is very different from the next. Recommended.

***Morandi alla Crocetta**, Via Laura 50, t 055 234 4747, f 055 248 0954. Small but popular, with 10 rooms in the university area northeast of Piazza San Marco. Run by an Irishwoman and her family, the building was a convent in the 16th century, and some of the comfortable and pleasant rooms still have the odd fresco. Two have private terraces.

***Torre Guelfa**, Borgo SS. Apostoli 8, t 055 239 6338, f 055 239 8577. This boasts the tallest privately owned tower in Florence, bang in the middle of the *centro storico*. There's a grand double salon, a sunny breakfast room, and stylish bedrooms in pastel shades with wrought iron and hand-painted furniture, as well as the chance to sip an *aperitivo* while contemplating a 360° view.

## Expensive

***Mario's**, Via Faenza 89, t 055 216 801, f 055 212 039. A haven in a street with more than its fair share of hotels, many of them of dubious quality. Convenient for the station and a block or two from the central market, the atmosphere is friendly and the décor rustic Florentine. A generous breakfast is served and guests are pampered with fresh flowers and fruit on arrival. If you don't want to sleep with your windows closed, ask for a room at the back; the street can be noisy.

**★★★Aprile**, Via della Scala 6, **t** 055 211 509, **f** 055 280 947. Convenient for the station, this was once a Medici palace and appropriately has a bust of Cosimo I above the door. Vaulted ceilings and frescoes remain intact, and the bedrooms all have period furniture although some are on the gloomy side; there's a shady courtyard.

**★★★Orto de' Medici** , Via San Gallo 30, **t** 055 483 427, **f** 055 461 276, *hotel@ortodeimedici.it, www.ortodeimedici.it*. A little 19th-century palazzo near Piazza San Marco in the university district, this has grand public rooms with frescoed ceilings and chandeliers. The bedrooms, not all with private bath, are plain in comparison, but perfectly adequate. There is a pretty terrace.

**★★★Silla**, Via dei Renai 5, **t** 055 234 2888, **f** 055 234 1437, *hotelsilla@tin.it*. Ten minutes walk east of the Ponte Vecchio on the south bank of the river, this manages to be central, yet in a quiet and relatively green neighbourhood. The old-fashioned *pensione* is on the first floor of a 16th-century palazzo and the spacious breakfast terrace has great views over the Arno and beyond.

**★★★Delle Tele**, Via Panzani 10, **t** 055 290 797, **f** 055 238 2419. Recently renovated rooms with double-glazed windows, on the busy street which runs from the station to the Duomo.

**★★Alessandra**, Borgo SS. Apostoli 17, **t** 055 283 438, **f** 055 210 619. A modest hotel in a palazzo designed by Michelangelo's pupil, Baccio d'Agnolo, on a central but quiet back street; there are 25 rooms of varying standards. Not all have private baths; the best have waxed parquet floors and antiques.

**★★Casci**, Via Cavour 13, **t** 055 211 686, **f** 055 239 6461. The Lombardis, owners of this 15th-century palazzo (once home to Rossini), run a relaxed and cheerful ship. The reception area is full of helpful information, the breakfast room has a frescoed ceiling while the recently refurbished bedrooms are bright and modern. The choice few look on to a garden at the back.

**★★La Scaletta**, Via Guicciardini 13, **t** 055 283 028, **f** 055 289 562, *www.lascaletta.com*. Between the Ponte Vecchio and the Pitti Palace is a friendly *pensione* with a roof garden and great views into Boboli. The 12 bedrooms (not all with bathrooms and some of which sleep up to four) are decently furnished, the nicest with some antique pieces. Very moderately priced dinner available.

If you are travelling by car, staying in the centre is more trouble (and expense) than it's worth. There are some nice alternatives in this price range a little further out.

**★★★Classic Hotel**, Viale Machiavelli 25, **t** 055 229 351, **f** 055 229 353, *info@classichotel.it, www.classichotel.it*. A good alternative in a very pleasant location just above Porta Romana on the way to Piazzale Michelangelo, a five-minute walk to a bus stop for downtown. The pink-washed villa stands in a shady garden (a welcome respite from the heat of the city), and breakfast is served in the conservatory in summer.

## Moderate

**★Bellavista**, Largo Alinari 15, **t** 055 284528, **f** 055 284874, *bellavistahotel@iol.it*. A simple and clean choice. Situated in west Florence, it is convenient for both train and bus stations. A couple of the rooms have views of the Duomo; a few have private bathrooms.

**★★Belletini**, Via de' Conti 7, **t** 055 213 561, **f** 055 283 551. A friendly place near the Medici chapels, decorated in traditional Florentine style; a couple of rooms have stunning views of the nearby domes. There's a good, generous breakfast.

**★★Hotel Boboli**, Via Romana 63, **t** 055 2298645, **f** 055 2337169, *hotelboboli@hotelboboli.com*. As the name suggests, this modest hotel is located near the back entrance of the Boboli gardens. The brightest rooms are right at the top of the four-storey building, but there is no lift. Or if you want quiet (Via Romana is quite noisy), go for a room on the inner courtyard. Breakfast is served on a little terrace in summer.

**★Maxim**, Via dei Medici 4, **t** 055 217 474, **f** 055 283 729. Very central, though there are better bargains to be had. Rooms sleep from two to four, all have the same bright green linoleum, and the bathrooms are new.

**Residenza Johlea Uno**, Via San Gallo 80, **t** 055 4633292, **f** 055 4634552, *johlea@johanna.it*, *www.johanna.it*. A remarkable bargain in terms of what it offers for the price, the Johlea is under the same ownership as the Johannas above. Situated ten minutes walk north of the central market, the rooms are comfortable and well furnished with taste and style and all have excellent bathrooms. Breakfast is supplied on trays in the rooms. On the top floor is a small sitting room and a roof terrace affording 360° views of the city. If all the rooms here are full, there is a sister' residenza' (the Johlea Due) a few doors down.

**\*Sorelle Bandini**, Piazza Santo Spirito 9, **t** 055 215 308, **f** 055 282 761. Remains popular, in spite of its state of disrepair and relatively high prices. This is partly due to the romantic loggia along one side of the fourth-storey hotel, but also to its location on fascinating Piazza Santo Spirito, bustling by day and lively (and noisy) at night. Expect uncomfortable beds, cavernous rooms, heavy Florentine furniture and a certain shabby charm.

**\*Bavaria**, Borgo degli Albizi 26, **t/f** 055 234 0313, *www.eidnet.com/hotelbavaria*. The 16th-century façade is said to be frescoed by Vasari, but don't get your hopes up. The furniture is spartan minimalist formica, though the rooms (some of them vast) are clean and cheap. Some have splendid views of the city.

**\*Il Granduca**, Via Pier Capponi 13, **t** 055 572 230, **f** 055 579 252. Between Piazza Donatello and Piazza della Libertà is one of the nicest hotels in this category, with a garden and garage; not all rooms are en suite.

**\*Firenze**, Piazza dei Donati 4, **t** 055 268 301, **f** 055 212 370. Newly renovated in an excellent location, between Piazza Signoria and the Duomo; the rather unimaginative rooms now all have bathrooms.

**\*\*Residence Johanna Cinque Giornate**, Via Cinque Gionate 12, **t** 055 473 377, **f** 055 481 896, *www.johanna.it*. Good value for money in a city where bargains are few and far between, located some way from the centre (near the Fortezza da Basso). The villa stands in its own garden and there are six comfortable rooms, each equipped with a breakfast tray and kettle, as well as a sitting room with plenty of reading material. Guests are left to themselves, but other facilities are of a three-star standard; parking available nearby at extra cost.

**Residenza Johanna**, Via Bonifacio Lupi 14, **t** 055 481 896, **f** 055 482 721. Only a tiny brass plaque over the bell identifies this building, just north of Piazza San Marco. There are no TVs or phones in the rooms, no doorman, and not all rooms have private baths, but the furnishings are comfortable, the bedrooms are prettily decorated and there's lots of reading material to hand. Breakfast is on a do-it-yourself tray in each room, and there are kettles out in the corridor.

## Cheap

**\*Scoti**, Via Tournabuoni 7, **t/f** 055 292 128. A simple and cheap *pensione* with a surprisingly upmarket address, which could be ideal if you would rather splurge on the wonderful clothes in the surrounding shops. It has basic, large rooms of up to four beds and no private bathrooms, but bags of atmosphere, starting with the floor-to-ceiling frescoes in the sitting room. The owners are friendly.

**\*Orchidea**, Borgo degli Albizi 11, **t/f** 055 248 0346, *hotelorchidea@yahoo.it*. Run by an Anglo-Italian family in a 12th-century building where Dante's in-laws once lived. One of the seven cheerful rooms offered has a private shower, and the best look on to a garden at the back.

**Azzi**, Via Faenza 56, **t/f** 055 213 806. This friendly, clean, simple *pensione* is near the market, and has the added bonus of a terrace for summer.

**Istituto Gould**, Via dei Serragli 49, **t** 055 212 576, **f** 055 280 274. An excellent budget choice near Santo Spirito, the Isitituto Gould is run by the Valdese church. Rooms vary in size from singles (a couple) to quads and not all have their own bathrooms; book early to secure singles or doubles. The best rooms have access to a terrace and the noisiest are on Via dei Serragli. No smoking is allowed in the building and you have to check in during office hours.

## Rooms to Let

Besides hotels, a number of institutions and private homes let rooms – there's a complete list in the back of the annual provincial hotel book. Many take women only, and fill up with students in the spring.

## Youth Hostels

**Archi Rossi**, Via Faenza 94r, t 055 290 804, f 055 230 2601. Purpose-built and fully wheelchair-accessible, this is the nearest hostel to the station, spanking new and well equipped. You can book a place after 6am and occupy your room after 2.30. Phone bookings are accepted and there is a 12.30am curfew.

**Ostello Europa Villa Camerata**, Viale A. Righe 2/4 (bus 17B from the station), t 055 601 451, f 055 610 300. Has 500 beds for people with IYHF cards. Located in an old palazzo with gardens, it is a popular place, and you'd be wise to show up at 2pm to get a spot in the summer; maximum stay three days.

**Ostello Santa Monaca**, Via Santa Monaca 6, t 055 268 338, f 055 280 185. Has 111 beds near the Carmine church; sign up for a place in the morning.

## Camping

There are a few campsites within easy striking distance of Florence:

**Camping Panoramico Fiesole**, Via Peramonda 1, t 055 599 069, f 055 59186. Beautifully situated just above Fiesole on a hill with fabulous views over Florence, but packed and expensive in the summer. *Open all year.*

**Camping Internazionale**, Via S. Cristofano 2, t 055 237 4704. South of the city in Bottai Tavarnuzze, near the A1 exit Autostrada Firenze–Certosa. *Open end Mar to mid-Oct.*

**Camping Italiani e Stranieri**, Viale Michelangelo 80, t 055 681 1977. Fine views over the city and free hot showers; arrive early to get a spot. On the other hand, there's no shade and the disco goes on until 1am. Bus 13 will take you there from the station. *Open all year.*

**Mugello Verde International Camping**, Via Masso Rondinaio 2, in San Piero a Sieve, t 055 848 511, f 055 848 6910. 25km north of Florence on the road to Bologna, with a very pleasant setting among hills and forests,

and frequent buses down to Florence. *Closed Nov–Dec.*

## Fiesole ✉ 50014

Many frequent visitors to Florence wouldn't stay anywhere else: it's cooler, quieter, and at night the city far below twinkles as if made of fairy lights.

**\*\*\*\*\*Villa San Michele**, Via Doccia 4, t 055 5678 200, f 055 678 250, *reservation@ villasanmichel.net, www.villasanmichele_ orient_express.com (luxury)*. Built as a monastery in the 14th century, this hotel is the superb choice if money happens to be no object, set in a breathtaking location just below Fiesole with a façade and loggia reputedly designed by Michelangelo himself. After suffering bomb damage during the Second World War, it was carefully reconstructed to create one of the most beautiful hotels in Italy, set in a lovely Tuscan garden, complete with a pool. Each of its 29 rooms is richly and elegantly furnished and air-conditioned; the more plush suites have jacuzzis. The food is delicious, and the reasons to go down to Florence begin to seem insignificant; a stay here is complete in itself. Paradise, however, comes at a price.

**\*\*\*\*Villa Aurora**, Piazza Mino 38, t 055 59100, f 055 59587, *h.aurora@fi.flashnet.it, www.logicad.net/aurora (very expensive)*. An agreeable 19th-century villa, located right on Fiesole's famous piazza from where the no.7 bus will whisk you down to central Florence in 20 minutes. The 25 bedrooms have rustic antiques and splendid views over the city. Some of the bathrooms are poky. There is a restaurant – on a terrace overlooking Florence in the summer – and the bar next door (which can be noisy at times) is under the same ownership.

**\*\*\*Villa Fiesole**, Via Beato Angelico 35, t 055 597 252, f 055 599 133, *info@villafiesole.it, www.villafiesole.it (luxury)*. This new hotel was once part of the San Michele convent, and shares part of its driveway with the hotel of the same name. The smart, neoclassical-style interiors are variations on a fresh blue and yellow colour scheme. Light meals are served in a sunny dining room or on the adjacent terrace, and there is a pool. The whole is wheelchair-accessible. The facilities (and prices) here are decidedly four-star.

***Pensione Bencistà**, Via Benedetto di Maiano 4, t/f 055 59163, *pensionebencista@iol.it* (*expensive*). Another former monastery with views from its flower-decked terrace which are every bit as good as those at Villa San Michele (*see* p.122), and the welcome will be more friendly. Bedrooms, each one different from the next, are all comfortably furnished with solid antique pieces. The three little sitting rooms are particularly inviting in cooler weather when fires are lit. Half-board – breakfast and either lunch or dinner – is obligatory here, but prices are reasonable.

**Le Cannelle**, Via Gramsci 52, t 055 597 8336, f 055 597 8292, *info@lecannelle.com* (*moderate–expensive*). A new, friendly B&B run by two sisters on the main street. Rooms are comfortably rustic and there is a pretty breakfast room.

*****Villa Baccano**, Via Bosconi 4, t/f 055 59341 (*cheap*). In the hills 2km out of the centre of Fiesole, in a lovely garden setting.

*****Villa Sorriso**, Via Gramsci 21, t 055 59027, f 055 597 8075 (*cheap*). An unpretentious, comfortable hotel in the centre of Fiesole, with a terrace overlooking Florence.

## Villa Hotels in the Florentine Hills

If you're driving, you may consider lodging outside the city where parking is hassle-free and the summer heat is less intense.

### Luxury

*****Villa La Massa**, Via La Massa 6, t 055 62611, f 055 633 102, *villamassa@galactica.it*, *www. villamassa.com*. A lovely choice, located up the Arno some 6km from Florence at Candeli. This is the former 15th-century villa of Count Giraldi, and retains the old dungeon (now one of two restaurants), the family chapel (now a bar), and other early-Renaissance amenities, combined with 20th-century features like tennis courts, a pool and air-conditioning. The recently refurbished furnishings are fit for a Renaissance princeling, there's dining and dancing by the Arno in the summer, a shady garden, and a hotel bus to whizz you into the city. Excellent restaurant.

*****Grand Hotel Villa Cora**, Viale Machiavelli 18–20, t 055 229 8451, f 055 229 086, *reservations@villacora.it*, *www.villacora.com*. Near Piazzale Michelangelo is another luxury choice, an opulent 19th-century mansion set in a beautiful formal garden overlooking the Oltrarno. Built by the Baron Oppenheim, it later served as the residence of the wife of Napoleon III, Empress Eugénie. Its conversion to a hotel has dimmed little of its splendour; some of the bedrooms have frescoed ceilings and lavish 19th-century furnishings – all are air-conditioned and have frigo-bars, and there's a pretty pool. In the summer meals are served in the garden, and there's a fine view of Florence from the roof terrace.

****Torre di Bellosguardo**, Via Roti Michelozzi 2, t 055 229 8145, f 055 229 008, *torredibellosguardo@dada.it*, *www.torrebellosguardo.it*. In the 12th century a tower was built at Bellosguardo, enjoying one of the most breathtaking views over the city. It was later purchased by the Cavalcanti, friends of Dante, and a villa was added below the tower; after that, Cosimo I confiscated it, the Michelozzi purchased it from the Medici, Elizabeth Barrett Browning wrote about it, and finally, in 1988, it opened its doors as a small hotel. There are frescoes by Baroque master Poccetti in the entrance hall, and fine antiques adorn the rooms, each of which is unique and fitted out with modern bath. The large and beautiful terraced garden has a pool. For a splurge, reserve the two-level tower suite, with fabulous views in four directions. Superb formal gardens look down to the city below, and lunch is served around the pool.

### Very Expensive

***Villa Villoresi**, Via Campi 2, Colonnata di Sesto Fiorentino, t 055 443 212, f 055 442 063, *cvillor@tin.it*, *www.ila-chateau.com/villores*. Contessa Cristina Villoresi's family home is a lovely oasis in the middle of one of Florence's more un-lovely suburbs, which hasn't been too pristinely restored, retaining much of its slightly faded appeal as well as its frescoed ceilings, antiques and chandeliers. The villa

boasts the longest loggia in Tuscany, to which five of the best, and grandest, bedrooms have direct access. Other rooms are a good deal plainer and somewhat cheaper.
★★★**Villa le Rondini**, Via Vecchia Bolognese 224, **t** 055 400 081, **f** 055 268 212, *www.villalerondini.it*. Occupying several buildings in a pleasant setting about 7km north of Florence, surrounded by olives and cypress trees. The most interesting rooms are in the original 16th-century villa. There is a very pleasant pool.

### Expensive
**Villa Poggio San Felice**, Via S. Matteo ad Arcetri 24, **t** 055 220 016, **f** 055 233 5388. A delightful alternative to city hotels, this is a 15th-century villa perched on a hill just south of Porta Romana, near the observatory. It was once owned by a Swiss hotel magnate, whose descendants have recently restored the house and gardens (designed by Porcinaie) and opened them up to guests. There are five double bedrooms, all beautifully furnished with family antiques, and all sharing stunning views with the tranquil gardens. Bed and breakfast only.
★★★★**Paggeria Medicea**, Viale Papa Giovanni XXIII 3, Artimino, near Carmignano, **t** 055 871 8081, **f** 055 871 8080, *hotel@artimino.com*, *www.artimino.com*. You can play the Medici in the refurbished outbuildings of Grand Duke Ferdinand's villa, which has some unusual amenities – a hunting reserve and a lake stocked with fish, also a pool and tennis court, and pleasant modern rooms, many with balconies, all air-conditioned. A short walk across the gardens brings you to the restaurant Biagio Pignatta, which specializes in Medici dishes, in the former butcher's quarters.

### Moderate
★★★**Hermitage**, Via Gineparia 112, Bonistallo, **t** 055 877 040, **f** 055 879 7057. Near Poggio a Caiano is a fine, affordable choice for families; there's a pool in the grounds and air-conditioned rooms, not to mention gallons of fresh air and quiet.
★★**Villa Natalia**, Via Bolognese 106, **t** 055 490 773, **f** 055 470 773. A rather faded villa, with bedrooms filled with antiques; the

atmosphere downstairs in the public rooms is a little institutional, but it's convenient, with a bus stop nearby for the short journey into Florence. Book well ahead.

# Eating Out

Like any sophisticated city with many visitors, Florence has plenty of fine restaurants; even in the cheaper places standards are high, and if you don't care for anything fancier, there will be lots of good red Chianti to wash down your meal. By popular demand, the city centre is full of *tavole calde*, pizzerias and snack bars, where you can grab a sandwich or a salad instead of a full sit-down meal (one of the best pizza-by-the-slice places is just across from the Medici Chapels).

Please note that many of the best places are likely to close for all or part of August; you would also be wise to call ahead and reserve, even a day or two in advance.

### Very Expensive
**Enoteca Pinchiorri**, Via Ghibellina 87, near the Casa Buonarroti, **t** 055 242 777. One of the finest gourmet restaurants in Italy, boasting two Michelin stars. The owners inherited the wine shop and converted it into a beautifully appointed restaurant, with meals served in a garden court in the summer; the cellars contain some 80,000 bottles of the best Italy and France have to offer. The cooking, a mixture of *nouvelle cuisine* and traditional Tuscan recipes, wins prizes every year. Italians tend to complain about the minute portions. Prices are reckoned to be €100 excluding wine, but the sky's the limit if you go for a more interesting bottle. *Open Mon and Wed 7.30–10, Tue, Thurs–Sat 12.30–2 and 7.30–10, closed Aug.*
**Cibreo**, Via dei Macci 118r, **t** 055 234 1100. One of the most Florentine of Florentine restaurants is close to the market of Sant' Ambrogio. The décor is simple – food is the main concern, and all of it is market-fresh. You can go native and order tripe *antipasto*, cockscombs and kidneys, or play it safe with prosciutto from the Casentino, a fragrant soup (no pasta here) of tomatoes, mussels and bell-pepper, leg of lamb stuffed with

artichokes, topped off with a delicious lemon *crostata*, cheesecake, or a chocolate cake to answer every chocaholic's dream. Booking is essential. *Open 12.50–2.30 and 7.30–11.15, closed Mon and Aug.*

**Alle Murate**, Via Ghibellina 52r, **t** 055 240 618. By the Bargello, this 'creative traditional' restaurant is elegant but relaxed, serving two set menus, one Tuscan and one different – spaghetti with sea bass, or pigeon stuffed with peppers and potatoes, or duck's livers with ceps and rosemary. *Dinner only, closed Mon.*

**Da Stefano**, Via Senese 271, Galuzzo, **t** 055 204 9105. Generally acknowledged to be the best seafood restaurant in the town, this is worth the ten-minute drive it takes to get there: *solo pesce, solo fresco e solo la sera* (only fish, only fresh and only in the evening) is Stefano's rule. Try *spaghetti allo Stefano* – a mountain of steamy spaghetti overflowing with shellfish. Stefano's now has a sushi chef and is able to deliver more exotic dishes as well. *Eves only, closed Sun.*

**Don Chisciotte**, Via C. Ridolfi 4r, **t** 055 475 430. A small place between the Fortezza Basso and Piazza dell'Indipendenza, serving inventive Italian food with a particular emphasis on fish and vegetables. Let yourself be tempted by baked baby squid, delicate warm vegetable and fish salad, or green tagliatelle with scampi and courgettes. *Closed Sun and Mon lunch.*

### Expensive

**Buca Lapi**, Via del Trebbio 1r, **t** 055 213 768. Located since 1800 in the old wine cellar of the lovely Palazzo Antinori, serving traditional favourites, from *pappardelle al cinghiale* (wide pasta with boar) and a *bistecca fiorentina con fagioli* that is hard to beat, downed with many different Tuscan wines. *Closed Sun and Mon lunch.*

**Beccofino**, Piazza degli Scarlatti, **t** 055 290 076. On the river under the British Institute, you could almost be in London or New York once inside this new, trendy restaurant, but the food is decidedly Italian. Dishes are enhanced by a creative touch and are elegantly presented. Both fish and meat dishes are excellent and change with the seasons: octopus salad, pasta flavoured with courgettes and saffron, sea bass on a bed of truffle-flavoured mash, steak fillet with caramelized shallots, and a fabulous *bistecca alla Fiorentina*. You can also eat a light meal in the wine bar where prices are considerably lower. *Closed Mon.*

**Caffé Concerto**, Lungarno C. Colombo 7, **t** 055 677 377. This has a lovely setting on the north bank of the Arno east of the city centre, and a warm wood and glass interior with lots of greenery. Creative cuisine, where hearty portions of traditional ingredients are given a new twist. *Open Mon–Sat noon–2.30 and 8–11, closed three weeks in Aug.*

**Coco Lezzone**, Via del Parioncino 26r (off Lungarno Corsini), **t** 055 287 178. In old Florentine dialect, this means big, smelly cook, but this shouldn't put you off. The atmosphere is informal and the food – Tuscan classics using the highest quality ingredients – is excellent. *Open Mon–Sat 12.30–2 and 8–10.30.*

**Oliviero**, Via delle Terme 51r, **t** 055 212 421. Five minutes from the Piazza della Signoria, this has somewhat passé décor and a slightly bizarre clientele, but it also has excellent food, serving curiosities such as *gnudi di fiori di zucchina e ricotta* (ravioli stripped of its pasta coating with ricotta cheese and courgette flowers) and boned pigeon stuffed with chestnuts. *Eves only, closed Sun.*

**Pane e Vino**, Via San Niccolò 70r (in the Oltrarno, just in from Ponte alla Grazie), **t** 055 247 6956. This pleasant and informal place has a superb wine list, and very knowledgeable staff to go with it. The *menu degustazione* changes daily, and offers seven small courses; with any luck, the superb porcini mushroom flan will be available. *Mon–Sat 7.30–midnight.*

**Taverna del Bronzino**, Via delle Route 25–27r, **t** 055 495 220. An elegant, traditional restaurant north of the Duomo, featuring plenty of Tuscan dishes – the *bistecca alla fiorentina* is succulent and tender – and delights like truffle-flavoured tortellini; there are several seafood choices for each course. *Open Mon–Sat 12.30–2.30 and 7.30–10.30, closed three weeks in Aug.*

**Ristorante Ricchi**, Piazza S. Spirito 8r, **t** 055 215 864. Annexed to the popular Bar and Gelateria of the same name (*see* **Cafés and Gelaterie**, below), this is a new restaurant in the Oltrarno serving exclusively fish in elegant-rustic surroundings. The menu changes daily according to the market produce available, but you'll find the freshest ingredients prepared skilfully and without too much fuss. Generous mixed *antipasto* offers such goodies as *sarde al beccofino* (fried, breaded sardines rolled with pinenuts and a hint of orange), and a delicious tepid squid salad. Try the catch of the day, cooked in the oven on a bed of potatoes, tomatoes and black olives *al isolana*. In summer, tables are laid in the square. *Closed Sun.*

## Moderate

**Antico Fattore**, Via Lambertesca 1/3r, **t** 055 288975. This traditional Florentine *trattoria*, popular with locals and tourists alike, suffered serious damage in the 1993 Uffizi bomb, but it is back in business now and serving excellent and reasonably-priced local dishes. Try pasta with wild boar or deer sauce, *Il Fritto* (deep-fried rabbit, chicken and brains) and *involtini* with artichoke hearts. *Open Mon–Sat 12.15–2.45 and 7.15–10.30, closed Sun and 2 weeks in Aug.*

**Il Latini**, Via dei Palchetti 6r (by Palazzo Rucellai), **t** 055 210 916. Something of an institution in Florence, crowded (prepare to queue; they don't accept bookings) and noisy but fun, where you eat huge portions of Florentine classics at long tables. The *primi* aren't great; so go for the *bistecca* or, more unusual, the *gran pezzo* – a vast rib-roast of beef. The house wine is good; try a *riserva. Closed Mon and all of Aug.*

**Angiolino**, Via Santo Spirito 57r, **t** 055 239 8976. It has lost some of its genuinely 'characteristic' qualities after renovation, but it's still a reliable place to eat Tuscan standards. The vegetable *antipasti* are especially good, and the simple *pollastrina sulla griglia* (grilled spring chicken) is succulent and tasty. *Closed Mon.*

**Baldovino**, Via Giuseppe 22r (Piazza S. Croce), **t** 055 241 773. An excellent *trattoria*/pizzeria run by a young Scotsman, where you can

eat anything from a big salad, filled foccaccia or pizza (from a wood-burning oven) to a full menu of pasta, fish and steaks from the Val di Chiana. *Open Tues–Sun 11.30–2.30 and 7–11.30.*

**Buca Mario**, Piazza degli Ottaviani 16r, **t** 055 214179. A steep flight of stairs will take you down into one of Florence's traditional 'cellar restaurants'; a place full of Florentine atmosphere with a menu to match. The soups here are superb – *pappa al pomodoro* and *ribollita*, or you could try the tagliatelle with porcini. *Ossobuco* is also excellent (cooked in tomato sauce, Florentine-style), or the *bistecca* is of the best quality. *Open Thurs–Tues 12.30–2.30 and 7.30–10.30.*

**Cavolo Nero**, Via dell' Ardiglione 22, **t** 055 294744. This little restaurant, tucked away in a side street near Piazza del Carmine, has quite a following among Florentine trendies. The interior is white on yellow with tables crowded into the attractive room and there is a pretty garden at the back. The food is mainly Mediterranean with a twist (curried monk fish, rabbit with wild fennel), but there are also plenty of local standards such as spaghetti with clams. *Open Mon–Sat noon–2.30 and 8–11, closed 2 weeks mid Aug.*

**Coquinarius**, Via della Oche 15r, **t** 055 2302153. You can eat or drink just about anything at this café/wine bar/restaurant. It is a useful stop off for a light meal or snack in the centre of tourist land. Snacks include a series of hot *crostone* (toasted Tuscan bread with various toppings) and various salads, but you can also order a pasta dish or a *carpaccio*. Wines by the bottle or the glass. *Open Sept–April daily 9am–11pm; May–Aug Mon–Sat 9am–11pm.*

**The Fusion Bar**, Gallery Hotel Art, Vicolo dell'Oro 5, **t** 055 27263. Go for something completely different in the ultra-cool, East-meets-West atmosphere of the Gallery hotel's (*see* Where to Stay) bar and restaurant. Their version of 'Fusion Food' (rather strange sushi combinations such as those involving *foie gras* or ratatouille and mayonnaise) is not completely convincing, but the setting makes up for this. They also serve light lunches and brunch at the weekends. *Open Tues–Sun 7.30pm–10.30pm, Sat, Sun Brunch 11.30am–2.30pm.*

**Ristoro di Cambi**, Via Sant' Onofrio 1r, **t** 055 217 134. In the Oltrarno, some way to the west of the centre, is a place very popular with the Florentine *intellighenzia*. The food is genuinely Florentine, the classic soups – *ribollita* and *pappa al pomodoro* – are tasty and warming, and the *bistecca alla Fiorentina* impressive. *Open Mon–Sat noon–2.30 and 7.30–10.30.*

**La Vecchia Bettola**, Viale Ariosto 32–34r, **t** 055 224 158. A noisy *trattoria*, west of the Carmine, with great food; the menu changes daily, but you can nearly always find their classic *tagliolini con funghi porcini*. The grilled meats are tasty and succulent, and the ice cream comes from Vivoli. *Closed Sun and Mon.*

**Osteria Santo Spirito**, Piazza Santo Spirito 16r, **t** 055 238 2383. If there is no room at Borgo Antico, this is just a walk across the piazza, offering a choice of cold dishes, pastas (try the gnocchi with melted cheese infused with truffle oil), and more. Outside seating on a lovely piazza. *Open daily 12.30–2.30 and 7.30–11.30.*

**Ottorino**, Via delle Oche 12/16r, **t** 055 215151. An elegant restaurant just south of the Duomo which serves typically Tuscan food including a mixed platter of deep-fried brains, tiny lamb cutlets and vegetables. *Open Mon–Sat 12.15–2.30, 7.15–10.30. Closed the 2nd half of Aug.*

**Sostanza**, Via della Porcellana 25r, **t** 055 212 691. Just west of Santa Maria Novella is one of the last authentic Florentine trattorias, a good place to eat *bistecca*. One of their most famous dishes is the simple, but delectable *petto di pollo al burro*, chicken breast sauteed in butter. *Open 12.30–2 and 7.30–9.30.*

**Zibibbo**, Via di Terzollina 3r, **t** 055 433383. A wonderful restaurant serving traditional Tuscan fare but in a stylish, un-Tuscan setting (pink-varnished floorboards, contemporary furniture). Plenty of choice between meat and fish dishes; *pasta e fagioli*, delicious *spaghetti alle vongole*, *inzimino* (squid stew with Swiss chard), tripe 'alla fiorentina', *fricasée* of rabbit and pigeon wrapped in 'lardo' and cooked with prunes. Worth the trip up to the northern most extremes of town. *Open Mon–Sat 1–3 and 8–11.*

**Cheap**

**Aquacotta**, Via dei Pilastri 51r, **t** 055 242 907. This restaurant, north of Piazza S. Ambrogio, is named for the simple but delicious bread soup, one of the specialities; you could follow that by deep-fried rabbit accompanied by crisply fried courgette flowers. *Open Mon–Sat 12.30–2 and 7.30–10.*

**Borgo Antico**, Piazza Santo Spirito 6, **t** 055 210 437. Popular with a young trendy crowd, so you may have to wait for a table, especially in summer. Inside, the music can be unbearably loud, but the pizza is decent, and there are plenty of other choices – interesting pastas, big salads and more substantial meat and fish dishes. *Open daily 12.30–2.30 and 7.30–11.30.*

**La Casalinga**, Via Michelozzi 9r, **t** 055 218 624. A family-run *trattoria*, also near Piazza Santo Spirito, and always busy, which is not surprising given the quality of the simple home cooking and the low prices. The *ribollita* is excellent. *Open Mon–Sat noon–2.30 and 7–9.45.*

**Ristorante Ricchi**, Piazza Santo Spirito 8r, **t** 055 215864. This new fish restaurant has tables on magical Piazza Santo Spirito. Inside, the décor is contemporary and elegant, with tables lined up against the walls. The generous plate of *antipasto* is good and main courses include the catch of the day roasted on a bed of potatoes and tomatoes. There are a few meat dishes too. *Open Mon–Sat 8–10.30.*

**Trattoria Cibreo**, Via de' Macci 114, **t** 055 234 1100. A little annexe to smart Cibreo (*see* p.123), this is one of the best deals in town; the food is the same (excluding the odd more extravagant dish), but served in a rustic setting on cheaper porcelain; and your bill will be a third of that of those dining next door. *Open Tues–Sat 12.50–2.30 and 7.30–11.55.*

**Trattoria del Carmine**, Piazza del Carmine 185, **t** 055 218 601. A traditional, bustling *trattoria* in the San Frediano district, often full. The long menu includes such staples as *ribollita, pasta e fagioli* and roast pork, but also features seasonal dishes such as risotto with asparagus or mushrooms, pasta with wild boar sauce and *osso buco*. *Closed Sun.*

**Al Tranvai**, near the Carmine in Piazza Torquato Tasso 14r, **t** 055 225 197. The two rows of tables in this cheerful little place are always full, and you may not get much elbow room. The menu changes daily, but the *crostini misti* are always on offer, and there's lots of offal: tripe, *lampredotto* (intestines), chicken gizzards etc. *Open Mon–Fri noon–2.30 and 7.30–10.30*.

**Il Pizzaiuolo**, near the Sant'Ambrogio market at Via dei Macci 113r, **t** 055 241 171. One of the best, boasting a real Neapolitan pizza maker, whose creations are puffy and light. There's lots more to choose from, but long queues. *Open Mon–Sat 12.30–3.30 and 7.30–1am, closed Aug*.

**Da Mario**, Via delle Rosina 2r, **t** 055 218550. Marios' *trattoria*, located at the back of the central market, is always buzzing, and there is usually a queue for the few rather cramped tables; don't expect a table to yourself. The food is pure Tuscan, excellent and cheap; *ribollita*, *spezzatino con patate* (beef stew with potatoes) and mixed boiled meats with a deliciously pungent *salsa verde*. *Open Mon–Sat noon–2, closed Sun*.

**Da Ruggero**, Via Senese 89r, **t** 055 220 542. A tiny, family-run *trattoria* a little way from the centre of town; it's always full, so book. The traditional food is home cooked; try the excellent *pappardelle alla lepre* (with hare sauce) and good puddings. *Closed Tues and Wed*.

**Sabatino**, Via Pisana 2r, **t** 055 225 955. Just outside the old city gate of San Frediano, this simple, family-run *trattoria* feels as if it has always been this way. Cooking methods, too, are old-fashioned and suitably rustic, and prices are similarly retro. *Open Mon–Fri noon–2.30 and 7.30–10, closed Aug*.

**Santa Lucia**, Via Ponte alle Mosse 102r, **t** 055 353 255. North of the Cascine there is a genuine Neapolitan pizzeria. It's a noisy, steamy and unromantic place but it makes up for its lack of glamour by serving what is possibly the best pizza in Florence, topped with the sweetest tomatoes and the creamiest *mozzarella di buffala*. *Open 7.30–1am, closed Wed and Aug*.

There aren't many vegetarian restaurants as such in Florence, though non-meat eaters will find plenty of choice (pastas, risotto etc) to tempt them. Specifically **vegetarian** restaurants include:

**Ruth's**, Via Farini 2a, **t** 055 248 0888. A new, bright and modern kosher vegetarian restaurant next to the synagogue, serving fish and Middle Eastern dishes. Try a *brick*, a savoury pastry, filled with fish, potatoes or cheese that tastes better than it sounds. *Open 12.30–2.30 and 8–10.30, closed Fri dinner and Sat lunch*.

**Il Vegetariano**, Via delle Ruote 30r, **t** 055 475 030. Located to the west of San Marco; self-service with excellent fresh food including a wide choice of soups, salads and more substantial dishes. *Closed Sun lunch and Mon*.

## Restaurants Around Florence

**Biagio Pignatta**, Artimino, **t** 055 875 1406 *(expensive)*. Near the Medici villa in Artimino and named after a celebrated Medici chef, this serves Tuscan dishes with a Renaissance flavour – *crepes alla Catherina de' Medici* – on a terrace overlooking vines and olives. *Closed Wed, and Thurs lunch in winter*.

**Da Delfina**, Via della Chiesa, Artimino, near Carmignano, **t** 055 871 8074 *(expensive)*. In the same village, this is worth the drive out for its enchanting surroundings, lovely views, the charming atmosphere and sublime cooking – home-made tagliatelle with a sauce made from greens, risotto with garden vegetables, asparagus, succulent kid and lamb dishes. *Open 12.30–2.30 and 8–10.30, closed Sun and Mon evening*.

**Centanni**, Via di Centanni, Bagno a Ripoli, **t** 055 630 122 *(expensive)*. An elegant restaurant to the east of Florence, set in an olive grove with a lovely terrace for warm weather. Dishes are along traditional lines – home-made pasta with pigeon or wild boar sauce, *bistecca*, deep-fried chicken or brains – and there is an excellent wine list. *Closed Sat lunch and Sun*.

**Bibé**, Via delle Bagnese 1r, **t** 055 204 9085 *(moderate)*. A couple of kilometres south of Porta Romana, occupying an old farmhouse with a lovely garden (somewhat marred by its proximity to the road and mosquitoes). Try the *crespelle alla Fiorentina* – crêpes filled with ricotta and spinach – and the roast meats, fried chicken and rabbit. Desserts here are creative and divine. *Open 12.30–2 and 7.30–9.45, closed Wed and Thurs lunchtime.*

**Osteria al Ponte Rotto**, Via Certaldese 8, San Casciano, t 055 828 090 *(cheap)*. From San Casciano (a few kilometres down the Siena *superstrada*), follow the signs to Montespertoli-Certaldo to find this simple little *trattoria* at the back of the family-run grocery, serving home-cooked food. *Closed Tue; open for lunch only Mon–Fri, also dinner Sat and Sun.*

## Cafés and *Gelaterie*

**Gilli**, Piazza della Repubblica 13–14r. Many of Florence's grand old cafés were born in the last century, though this one, the oldest, dates back to 1733, when the Mercato Vecchio still occupied this area; its two panelled back rooms are especially pleasant in the winter.

**Giubbe Rosse**, Piazza della Repubblica. Famous as the rendezvous of Florence's literati at the turn of the century; the chandelier-lit interior has changed little since.

**Rivoire**, Piazza della Signoria 5r. The most classy watering hole, with a marble-detailed interior as lovely as the piazza itself.

**Dolce Vita**, Piazza del Carmine. The place where fashionable young Florentines strut their latest togs – a favourite pastime since the 14th century. *Closed Sun and 2 weeks in Aug.*

**Dolci e Dolcezze**, Piazza Cesare Beccaria 8r, t 055 234 5458. East of Sant' Ambrogio market, this has the most delicious cakes, pastries and marmalades in the city – the *crostate*, *torte* and *bavarese* are expensive but worth the price. *Closed Mon.*

**Hemingway**, near Piazza Carmine, t 055 284 781 *(booking advised)*. A lovely café serving, as well as cocktails, interesting light meals and an excellent brunch on Sundays. The owner is a chocaholic, so the hand-made chocs and puddings are a dream. Try the *sette veli* chocolate cake. *Open weekdays 4.30–late, Sun 11–8.*

**Caffè Italiano**, Via Condotta 56r, t 055 291 082. Right in the centre of town, a popular lunchtime stop for locals who crowd in for the excellent hot and cold dishes on offer. The atmosphere is old-fashioned, particularly in the tearoom upstairs. Newspapers are on offer for browsing. *Closed Sun.*

**Caffè Ricchi**, Piazza Santo Spirito. A local institution. It has just undergone a major refit, but continues to serve excellent and good-value light lunches and wonderful ice cream. The outside tables enjoy the benefit of one of the most beautiful piazzas in Florence.

**La Via del' Té**, Piazza Ghiberti 22r. Looking on to the Sant' Ambrogio food market, this offers a huge range of teas to choose from plus sweet and savoury snacks.

**Vivoli**, Via Isola delle Stinche 7r, between the Bargello and S. Croce. Florence lays some claim to being the ice cream capital of the world, a reputation that owes much to the decadently delicious confections and rich *semifreddi* served here. *Closed Mon.*

**Festival del Gelato**, Via del Corso 75r. Boasts over 100 variations.

**Perché no?**, Via Tavolini 19r. Arctic heaven near Via Calzaiuoli.

**Granduca**, Via dei Calzaiuoli 57r. Yet another option, with more sublime concoctions. *Closed Wed.*

**Ricchi**, Piazza S. Spirito. The Oltrarno champ, with a huge choice and a scrumptious *tiramisú*. *Closed Sun and early Aug.*

**Baby Yoghurt**, Via Michelozzo 13r. Nearby, this frozen yoghurt claims to be healthy, though it tastes so creamy that it's hard to believe. Apparently, the secret lies in whipping the yoghurt for hours, before serving it up topped with fresh fruit, hot chocolate or nuts.

**Gelateria de' Ciompi**, Via dell'Agnolo 121r. This traditional Florentine ice cream parlour, tucked around the corner from Santa Croce, prides itself on its authentic home-made recipes, some of which are over 50 years old.

## Wine Bars

Florence is full of wine bars, from new-generation places to simple 'holes in the wall'.

**Vini**, Via dei Cimatori 38r. One of the last of its kind in Florence, where you can join the locals standing on the street, glass and *crostino* in hand. *Closed Sun.*

**Le Volpi e L'Uva**, Piazza dei Rossi. Just south of the Ponte Vecchio, where the knowledgeable and helpful owners specialize in relatively unknown labels, and snacks include a marvellous selection of French and Italian cheeses.

**Fuori Porta**, San Niccolo. Possibly the most famous of all, where there are some 600 labels on the wine list and dozens of whiskeys and grappas. Among the snacks and hot dishes on offer, try one of the *crostoni*, a huge slab of local bread topped with something delicious and heated under the grill. *Closed Sun*.

**Enoteca dei Giraldi**, Via dei Giraldi. Near the Bargello, this hosts art exhibitions and runs wine-tasting courses as well as supplying excellent food and drink.

**Enoteca Baldovino**, Via San Giuseppe. A bright and cheerful wine bar down the northern side of Santa Croce with good snacks and pasta dishes.

**Pitti Gola e Cantina**, Piazza Pitti 16, t 055 212 704. A delightful little place situated bang opposite the Pitti palace, with a good choice of wines from Tuscany and beyond, snacks and other more substantial dishes, as well as a few outside tables. *Closed Mon*.

**Cantinetta dei Verazzano**, Via dei Tavolini 18–20r. Part bakery (selling delicious bread and cakes), part wine bar, this centrally located place belongs to the Verazzano wine estate and serves its own very good wine exclusively; sip it with a plate of mixed *crostini* at hand.

**The bar on the corner of Via de' Neri and Via de' Benci**, more traditional and full of office workers at lunchtime and locals in the early evenings, all of whom appreciate the range of tasty nibbles and hot dishes at reasonable prices. *Closed Sun*.

# Entertainment and Nightlife

Nightlife with Great Aunt Florence is still awaiting its Renaissance; according to the Florentines she's conservative, somewhat deaf and retires early – 1am is late in this city. However, there are plenty of people who wish

it weren't so, and slowly, slowly, Florence by night is beginning to mean more than the old *passeggiata* over the Ponte Vecchio and an ice cream, and perhaps a late trip up to Fiesole to contemplate the lights.

Look for listings of concerts and events in Florence's daily, *La Nazione*. The tourist office's free *Florence Today* contains bilingual monthly information and a calendar, as does a booklet called *Florence Concierge Information*, available in hotels and tourist offices. The monthly *Firenze Spettacolo*, sold at newsstands, contains a brief section on events in English, but the comprehensive listings (including anything from ecology and trekking events, film societies, clubs, live music, opera and concerts) are easy to understand even in Italian. The annual guide *Guida locali di Firenze* also gives listings. For all current films being shown in Florence, look in the local paper.

## Performance Arts

The opera and ballet season runs from September to Christmas and concerts from January to April at the **Teatro Comunale**, and the **Maggio Musicale** festival, which features all three, from mid-April until the end of June. There is usually more opera in July.

## Classical Concerts

Concerts are held mainly in the following venues:

**Teatro del Maggio Musicale Fiorentino**, Corso Italia 16, t 055 211 158, *www.maggiofiorentino.com*. Symphonic concerts, recitals, opera and ballet are all held at Florence's municipal opera house.

**Teatro della Pergola**, Via della Pergola 12–32, t 055 226 4316, *www.amicimusica.fi.it*. The excellent chamber music series held in the stunning 18th-century Teatro della Pergola is promoted by the Amici della Musica.

**Teatro Verdi**, Via Ghibellina 99–101, t 055 212 320, *www.teatroverdifirenze.it*. The red and gold Teatro Verdi is home to Tuscany's regional orchestra who perform there regularly from late Nov–May.

**Scuola di Musica di Fiesole**, Villa la Torraccia, San Domenico, Fiesole, t 055 59785, *www.scuolamusica.fiesole.fi.it*. One of Italy's best known music schools promotes a series of chamber music concerts.

Many smaller events take place year-round in churches, cloisters and villas, with plenty of outdoor concerts in summer. Look out for posters: they are not always well publicized.

## Rock and Jazz Concert Venues

**Auditorium Flog**, Via M. Mercatl 24b, **t** 055 490 437. One of the best places in Florence to hear live music year-round, often hosting ethnic music events. Look out for the Musica dei Popoli festival in November.

**Teatro Verdi**, Via Ghibellina 101, **t** 055 212 320.

**Teatro Puccini**, Via delle Cascine 41, **t** 055 362 067.

**Tenax**, Via Pratese 46, **t** 055 308 160, *www.tenax.org*. A spacious but always crowded venue on the outskirts of town, where there are lots of live rock concerts. Live bands range from international names to local groups. DJs take over after the live music stops. *Open 10.30pm–4am*.

**Palasport**, Viale Paoli, **t** 055 678 841. Big-name rock and jazz bands nearly always play at this venue in Campo di Marte, which seats several thousand.

**Saschall**, Lungarno Aldo Moro 3, **t** 055 6504112. Risen from the ashes (not literally) of the old Teatro Tenda, the brand new 3,000-seat venue plays host to all kinds of music (including musicals). See local press for details.

In the summer, there are lots of live music venues all over the city, many of them free, for when Florence moves outdoors to cool off.

**Musicus Concentus**, Piazza del Carmine 14, **t** 055 287 347. Brings in big-name jazz performers, classical artists and others to Florence.

**Box office**, Via Alamanni 39, **t** 055 210 804. A central ticket agency for all the major events in Tuscany and beyond, including classical, rock, jazz etc.

## Cinemas

Summer is a great time to catch the latest films. English-language films are shown throughout the summer two evenings a week at the Odeon in Piazza Strozzi and open-air screens are erected in several venues in Florence with two different films in Italian

each evening from mid-June until mid-Sept. Details appear in the local newspapers.

The following show original language (usually English) films:

**Odeon**, Piazza Strozzi, **t** 055 214 068. Shows latest releases on Mon and Tues.

**Fulgor**, Via Masi Finiguerra, **t** 055 238 1881. Showings in English on Thurs.

**Cinema Astro**, Piazza San Simone, opposite Vivoli's, no **t**. Films have usually been around for a while. *Closed Mon and July*.

**Spazio Uno**, Via del Sole 10, **t** 055 215 634. Occasionally has original language films.

## Clubs

Many clubs have themed evenings; keep an eye out for posters or handouts or buy the listings magazine *Firenze Spettacolo*. Places are somewhat seasonal as well.

**Universale**, Via Pisana 77r. A vast ex-cinema, newly opened with designer décor, a restaurant, several bars and a pizzeria, all accompanied by live music and a giant cinema screen. Fast becoming the hottest hang-out in town, these are chic, sleek surroundings for a sleek and chic crowd. *Open 8.30pm–2am, closed Mon*.

**Rex Café**, Via Fiesolana 23. The number one winter hotspot until Universale opened its doors, featuring an unusual décor, tapas, music and dancing.

**Central Park**, Parco delle Cascine. In summer, possibly the trendiest place in Florence, full of serious clubbers dancing to live music on three dance floors.

**Parterre**, Piazza della Libertà. Another outdoor club, which boasts two bars, concerts and video screens.

**Lido**, Lungarno Pecori Giraldi 1. A small place in a pretty setting on the Arno, playing mixed music to a mixed crowd. *Closed Mon*.

**Full-Up**, Via della Vigna Nuova 25r. Another possibility, with mirrored walls, disco lighting, and dated music. *Closed Sun and Mon and June–Sept*.

**Mago Merlino**, Via dei Pilastri 31r. A relaxed tearoom/bar with live music, theatre, shows and games.

**Du Monde**, Via San Niccolò 103r. End up at this cocktail bar offering food, drink and music for the elegant Florentine until 5 in the morning.

**Caffedecò**, Piazza della Libertà 45–46r. There's often live jazz here in elegant Art Deco surroundings, where Florence's swells put on the dog. *Closed Mon.*

**Jazz Café**, Via Nuova de' Caccini 3. A pleasant but smoky atmosphere with live jazz every Friday and Saturday night, and a free jam session on Tuesdays. *Closed Sun and Mon.*

**Caffè La Torre**, Lungarno Cellini 65r, t 055 680 643. A small club which hosts regular jazz concerts.

**Jazz Club**, Via Nuova de' Cacini 3, t 055 247 9700. Also small, also with regular jazz.

**Riflessi d'Epoca**, Via dei Renai 13r. Frequently has live jazz in a smoky ambience. It also stays open later than the average club (i.e. after 1am).

**Maracanà**, Via Faenza 4. Try this for live samba, mambo and bossanova.

**Maramao**, Via dei Macci 79r. Slick and cool; the music is often Latin-American. *Closed Mon.*

**Ex-Mood**, Corso dei Tintori 4. The old Mood club has been re-vamped and given an appropriate new name. Still a cool venue, it is located below ground in a cavernous basement with bar and decent dance space. *Open Wed–Sun 10pm–4am.*

**Yab**, Via Sassetti 5r. Yab has been around for a long time, and so have some of the punters who hang out there; it is favoured by a decidedly older crowd. It has recently been completely redesigned and has a vast dance space and a great sound system.

**Soulciety**, Via San Zanobi 114b, t 055 8303513. Popular with Florence's Senegalese community but otherwise a relatively little-known dance venue, A good alternative to the city's run-of-the-mill clubs and, with its Rococo décor, has an exotic feel to it. *Open Tues–Sun 11.30pm–4am, closed June–Sept.*

**Girasol**, Via del Ronito 1, t 055 474948. If its Latin sounds you are into, head north to Girasol for live bands and DJs who supply a good mix of Cuban, Flamenco, Brazilian, Caribbean and Salsa rhythms. The space is small, so arrive early if you want a table. *Open Tues–Sun 8pm–2.30am.*

## Pubs

Irish pubs are big in Florence, and there's also the odd English and Scottish version.

**The Fiddler's Elbow**, Piazza Santa Maria Novella. One of the original ones, with some live music and an ex-pat atmosphere. A handy place to wait for a train, but a bit grim.

**James Joyce**, Lungarno B Cellini 1r. An Irish pub with literary pretensions, the James Joyce enjoys a pleasant location with a big garden near the river. Books and magazines are on hand for browsing.

**Robin Hood**, Via dell'Oriuolo. Similar to the above.

**The Lion's Fountain**, Borgo degli Albizi 34r. A nice place which also serves food until late.

**Rifrullo**, Via S. Niccolò 55r. Year-round, an older pub/wine bar; probably the most popular of all and one of the first to attract people to the Oltrarno. There's no word for 'cosy' in Italian, but the Rifrullo does the best it can.

## Gay Clubs

There are a few gay clubs in Florence.

**Tabasco**, Piazza Santa Cecilia 3r. Italy's first gay bar, opened in the 1970s.

**Crisco**, Via Santí Egidio 43r. Another one to try. *Closed Tues.*

**Piccolo Café**, Borgo Santa Croce 23r. A tiny, friendly, arty bar. *Open daily from 5pm.*

**Flamingo**, Via Pandolfini 26r. Offers a cocktail bar and disco. *Closed Tues.*

## Discos

**Tenax**, Via Pratese 47, t 055 308 160. Lots of live music – the current place to go in Florence, out near the airport. *Closed Mon.*

**Space Electronic**, Via Palazzuolo 37, t 055 293 082. A high-tech noise box. *Open daily.*

**Meccanó**, Viale degli Olmi 1, t 055 331 371. Where the younger crowd get their kicks to different music each night.

**Rock Caffè**, Borgo degli Albizi 66r, t 055 244 662. A theme every night. *Closed Sun.*

**Andromeda**, Via dei Climatori 13, t 055 292 002. Particularly popular with young foreigners. *Closed Sun.*

**Auditorium Flog**, Via M. Mercantl 24b, t 055 490 437. A favourite and usually packed student venue.

**Jackie O**, Via Erta Canina 24. An old favourite for the 30ish crowd, which includes a piano bar. *Closed Mon, Tues, Wed.*

*Fine balm let Arno be;*
*The walls of Florence all of silver rear'd,*
*And crystal pavements in the public way...*
14th-century madrigal by Lapo Gianni

*Magari!* – if only! – the modern Florentine would add to this vision, to this city of art and birthplace of the Renaissance, built by bankers and merchants whose sole preoccupation was making more florins. The precocious capital of Tuscany began to slip into legend back in the 14th century, during the lifetime of Dante; it was noted as *different* even before the Renaissance, before Boccaccio, Masaccio, Brunelleschi, Donatello, Leonardo da Vinci, Botticelli, Michelangelo, Machiavelli, the Medici...

*This city of Florence is well populated, its good air a healthy tonic; its citizens are well dressed, and its women lovely and fashionable, its buildings are very beautiful, and every sort of useful craft is carried on in them, more so than any other Italian city. For this many come from distant lands to see her, not out of necessity, but for the quality of its manufactures and arts, and for the beauty and ornament of the city.*
Dino Compagni in his Chronicle of 1312

According to the tourist office, in 1997, 685 years after Dino, a grand total of over seven million tourists (Americans, Germans, French and Britons are still the top four groups) spent at least one night in a Florentine hotel. Some, perhaps, had orthodontist appointments. A large percentage of the others came to inhale the rarefied air of the cradle of Western civilization, to gaze at some of the loveliest things made by mortal hands and minds, to walk the streets of new Athens, the great humanist 'city built to the measure of man'. Calling Florence's visitors 'tourists', however, doesn't seem quite right; 'tourism' implies pleasure, a principle alien to this dour, intellectual, measured town. 'Pilgrims' is perhaps the better word, cultural pilgrims who throng the Uffizi, the Accademia, the Bargello to gaze upon the holy mysteries of our secular society, to buy postcards and replicas, the holy cards of our day.

Someone wrote a warning on a wall near Brunelleschi's Santo Spirito, in the Oltrarno: *'Turista con mappa/alla caccia del tesoro/per finire davanti ad un piatto/di spaghetti al pomodoro'* ('Tourist with a map, on a treasure hunt, only to end up in front of a plate of spaghetti with tomato sauce'). Unless you come with the right attitude, Florence can be as disenchanting as cold spaghetti. It only blossoms if you apply your mind as well as your vision, if you go slowly and do not let the art bedazzle until your eyes glaze over in dizzy excess (a common complaint, known in medical circles as the Stendhal syndrome). Realize that loving and hating Florence at the same time may be the only rational response. It is the capital of contradiction; you begin to like it because it goes out of its way to annoy.

## History

The identity of Florence's first inhabitants is a matter of dispute. There seems to have been some kind of settlement along the Arno long before the Roman era, perhaps as early as 1000 BC; the original founders may have been either native Italics

# Florentine Duality

Dante's *Vita Nuova*, the autobiography of his young soul, was only the beginning of Florentine analysis; Petrarch, the introspective 'first modern man', was a Florentine born in exile; Ghiberti was the first artist to write an autobiography, Cellini wrote one of the most readable; Alberti invented art criticism; Vasari invented art history; Michelangelo's personality, in his letters and sonnets, looms as large as his art. In many ways Florence broke away from the medieval idea of community and invented the modern concept of the individual, most famously expressed by Lorenzo de' Medici's friend, Pico della Mirandola, whose *Oration on the Dignity of Man* tells us what the God on the Sistine Chapel ceiling was saying when he created Adam: '...And I have created you neither celestial nor terrestrial, neither mortal nor immortal, so that, like a free and able sculptor and painter of yourself, you may mould yourself entirely in the form of your choice.'

To attempt to understand Florence, remember one historical constant: no matter what the issue, the city always takes both sides, vehemently and often violently, especially in the Punch and Judy days of Guelphs and Ghibellines. In the 1300s this was explained by the fact that the city was founded under the sign of Mars, the war god; but in medieval astronomy Mars is also connected with Aries, another Florentine symbol and the sign of the time of spring blossoms. (The Annunciation, at the beginning of spring, was Florence's most important festival.) One of the city's oldest symbols is the lily (or iris), flying on its oldest gonfalons. Perhaps even older is its *marzocco*, originally an equestrian statue of Mars on the Ponte Vecchio, later replaced by Donatello's grim lion.

Whatever dispute rocked the streets, Great Aunt Florence often expressed her schizophrenia in art, floral Florence versus stone Florence, epitomized by the irreconcilable differences between the two most famous works of art: Botticelli's graceful *Primavera* and Michelangelo's cold, perfect *David*. The 'city of flowers' seems a joke; it has nary a real flower, nor even a tree, in its stone streets; indeed, all effort has gone into keeping nature at bay, surpassing it with geometry and art. And yet the Florentines were perhaps the first since the Romans to discover the joys of the countryside. The rusticated stone palaces, like fortresses or prisons, hide charms as delightful as Gozzoli's frescoes in the Palazzo Medici-Riccardi. Luca della Robbia's dancing children and floral wreaths are contemporary with the naked, violent warriors of the Pollaiuolo brothers; the writhing, quarrelsome statuary in the Piazza della Signoria is sheltered by one of the most delicate *loggie* imaginable.

After 1500, all the good, bad and ugly symptoms of the Renaissance peaked in the mass fever of Mannerism. Then, drifting into a debilitating twilight, Florence gave birth to the artistic phenomenon known as kitsch – the Medici Princes' chapel is an early kitsch classic. Since then, worn out perhaps, or embarrassed, this city built by merchants has kept its own counsel, expressing its argumentative soul in overblown controversies about traffic, art restoration and the undesirability of fast-food counters and cheap *pensioni*. We who find her fascinating hope she some day comes to remember her proper role, bearing the torch of culture instead of merely collecting tickets for the culture torture.

or Etruscans. Throughout the period of Etruscan dominance, the village on the river lived in the shadow of *Faesulae* – Florence's present-day suburb of Fiesole was then an important city, the northernmost member of the Etruscan Dodecapolis. The Arno river cuts across central Italy like a wall. This narrow stretch of it, close to the mountain pass over to Emilia, was always the most logical place for a bridge.

Roman Florence can claim no less a figure than **Julius Caesar** for its founder. Like so many other Italian cities, the city began as a planned urban enterprise in an under-developed province; Caesar started it as a colony for his army veterans in 59 BC. The origin of the name – so suggestive of springtime and flowers – is another mystery. First it was *Florentia*, then *Fiorenza* in the Middle Ages, and finally *Firenze*. One guess is that its foundation took place in April, when the Romans were celebrating the games of the Floralia.

The original street plan of *Florentia* can be seen today in the neat rectangle of blocks between Via Tornabuoni and Via del Proconsolo, between the Duomo and Piazza della Signoria. Its Forum occupied roughly the site of the modern Piazza della Repubblica, and the outline of its amphitheatre can be traced in the oval of streets just west of Piazza Santa Croce. Roman *Florentia* never really imposed itself on the historian. One writer mentions it as a *municipia splendidissima*, a major town and river crossing along the Via Cassia, connected to Rome and the thriving new cities of northern Italy, such as Bononia and Mediolanum (Bologna and Milan). At the height of the Empire, the municipal boundaries had expanded out to Via de' Fossi, Via S. Egidio, and Via de' Benci. Nevertheless, Florentia did not play a significant role either in the Empire's heyday or in its decline.

After the fall of Rome, Florence weathered its troubles comparatively well. We hear of it withstanding sieges by the Goths around the year 400, when it was defended by the famous imperial general Stilicho, and again in 541, during the campaigns of Totila and Belisarius; all through the Greek–Gothic wars Florence seems to have taken the side of Constantinople. The Lombards arrived around 570; under their rule Florence was the seat of a duchy subject to the then Tuscan capital of Lucca. The next mention in the chronicles refers to Charlemagne spending Christmas with the Florentines in the year 786. Like the rest of Italy, Florence had undoubtedly declined; a new set of walls went up under Carolingian rule, about 800, enclosing an area scarcely larger than the original Roman settlement of 59 BC. In such times Florence was lucky to be around at all; most likely throughout the Dark Ages the city was gradually increasing its relative importance and strength at the expense of its neighbours. The famous baptistry, erected some time between the 6th and 9th centuries, is the only impor-tant building from that troubled age in all Tuscany.

By the 1100s, Florence was the leading city of the County of Tuscany. **Countess Matilda**, ally of Pope Gregory VII against the emperors, oversaw the construction of a new set of walls in 1078, this time coinciding with the widest Roman-era boundaries. Already the city had recovered all the ground lost during the Dark Ages, and the momentum of growth did not abate. New walls were needed again in the 1170s, to enclose what was becoming one of the largest cities in Europe. In this period, Florence owed its growth and prosperity largely to the textile industry – weaving and 'finishing' cloth not only from Tuscany but wool shipped from as far afield as Spain and England. The capital gain from this trade, managed by the *Calimala* and the *Arte della Lana*, Florence's richest guilds, led naturally to an even more profitable business – banking and finance.

## The Florentine Republic Battles with the Barons

In 1125, Florence once and for all conquered its ancient rival Fiesole. Wealth and influence brought with them increasing political responsibilities. Externally the city often found itself at war with one or other of its neighbours. Since Countess Matilda's death in 1115, Florence had become a self-governing *comune*, largely independent of the emperor and local barons. The new city republic's hardest problems, however, were closer to home. The nobles of the county, encouraged in their anachronistic feudal behaviour by representatives of the imperial government, proved irreconcilable enemies to the new merchant republic, and Florence spent most of the 12th century trying to keep them in line. Often the city actually declared war on a noble clan, as with the Alberti, or the Counts of Guidi, and razed their castles whenever they captured one. To complicate the situation, nobles attracted by the stimulation of urban life – not to mention the opportunities for making money – often moved their entire families into Florence itself.

They brought their country habits with them: a boyish eagerness to brawl with their neighbours on the slightest pretext, and a complete disregard for the laws of the *comune*. Naturally, they couldn't feel secure without a little urban castle of their own, and before long Florence, like any prosperous Italian city of the Middle Ages, featured a remarkable skyline of hundreds of tower-fortresses, built as much for status as for defence. Many were over 200ft in height. It wasn't uncommon for the honest citizen to come home from a hard day's work at the bank, hoping for a little peace and quiet, only to find siege engines parked in front of the house and a company of bowmen commandeering the children's bedroom.

But just as Florence was able to break the power of the rural nobles, those in the town also eventually had to succumb. The last tower-fortresses were chopped down to size in the early 1300s. But even without the nobles raising all manner of hell, the Florentines managed to find brand new ways to keep the pot boiling. The rich merchants who dominated the government, familiarly known as the *popolari grossi*, resorted to every sort of murder and mayhem to beat down the demands of the lesser guilds, the *popolari minuti*, for a fair share of the wealth; the two only managed to settle their differences when confronted by murmurs of discontent from what was then one of Europe's largest urban proletariats. But even beyond simple class issues, the city born under the fiery sign of Mars always found a way to make trouble for itself. Not only did Florentines pursue the Guelph–Ghibelline conflict with greater zest than almost any Tuscan city; according to the chronicles of the time, they actually started it. In 1215, men of the Amidei family murdered a prominent citizen named Buondelmonte dei Buondelmonti over a broken wedding engagement, the spark that touched off the factionalist struggles first in Florence, then quickly throughout Italy.

## Guelphs and Ghibellines

In the 13th century, there was never a dull moment in Florence. Guelphs and Ghibellines, often more involved with some feud between powerful families than with real political issues, cast each other into exile and confiscated each other's property with every change of the wind. Religious strife occasionally pushed politics off the front page. In the 1240s, a curious foreshadowing of the Reformation saw Florence wrapped up in the **Patarene heresy**. This sect, closely related to the Albigensians of southern France, was as obsessed with the presence of Evil in the world as John Calvin – or Florence's own future fire-and-brimstone preacher, Savonarola. Exploiting a streak of religious eccentricity that has always seemed to be present in the Florentine psyche, the Patarenes thrived in the city, even electing their own bishop. The established Church was up to the challenge; St Peter Martyr, a bloodthirsty Dominican, led his armies of axe-wielding monks to the assault in 1244, exterminating almost the entire Patarene community.

In 1248, with help from Emperor Frederick II, Florence's Ghibellines booted out the Guelphs – once and for all, they thought, but two years later the Guelphs were back, and it was the Ghibellines' turn to pack their bags. The new Guelph regime, called the *primo popolo*, was for the first time completely in the control of the bankers and merchants. It passed the first measures to control the privileges of the turbulent, largely Ghibelline nobles, and forced them all to chop the tops off their tower-fortresses. The next decades witnessed a series of wars with the Ghibelline cities of Tuscany – Siena, Pisa and Pistoia, not just by coincidence Florence's habitual enemies. Usually the Florentines were the aggressors, and more often than not fortune favoured them. In 1260, however, the Sienese, reinforced by Ghibelline exiles from Florence and a few imperial cavalry, destroyed an invading Florentine army at the **Battle of Monteaperti**. Florence was at the Ghibellines' mercy. Only the refusal of Farinata degli Uberti, the leader of the exiles, to allow the city's destruction kept the Sienese from putting it to the torch – a famous episode recounted by Dante in the *Inferno*. (In a typical Florentine gesture of gratitude, Dante found a home for Uberti in one of the lower circles of hell.)

In Florence, a Ghibelline regime under Count Guido Novello made life rough for the wealthy Guelph bourgeoisie. As luck would have it, though, only a few years later the Guelphs were back in power, and Florence was winning on the battlefield again. The new Guelph government, the *secondo popolo*, earned a brief respite from factional strife. In 1289, Florence won a great victory over another old rival, Arezzo. This was the **Battle of Campaldino**, where the Florentine citizen army included young Dante Alighieri. In 1282, and again in 1293, Florence tried to clean up an increasingly corrupt government with a series of reforms. The 1293 Ordinamenti della Giustizia once and for all excluded the nobles from the important political offices. By now, however, the real threat to the Guelph merchants' rule did not come so much from the nobility, which had been steadily falling behind in wealth and power over a period of two centuries, but from the lesser guilds, which had been completely excluded from a share of the power, and also from the growing working class who were employed in the textile mills and the foundries.

Despite all the troubles, the city's wealth and population grew tremendously throughout the 1200s. Its trade contacts spread across Europe, and crowned heads from London to Constantinople found Florentine bankers ready to float them a loan. About 1235 Florence minted modern Europe's first gold coin, the *florin*, which soon became a standard currency across the continent. By 1300 Florence counted over 100,000 souls – a little cramped, even inside the vast new circuit of walls built by the *comune* in the 1280s. It was not only one of the largest cities in Europe, but certainly one of the richest. Besides banking, the wool trade was also booming: by 1300 the wool guild, the Arte della Lana, had over 200 large workshops in the city alone. Naturally, this new opulence created new possibilities for culture and art. Florence's golden age began perhaps in the 1290s, when the *comune* started its tremendous programme of public buildings – including the Palazzo della Signoria and the cathedral; important religious structures, such as Santa Croce, were under way at the same time. Cimabue was the artist of the day; Giotto was just beginning, and his friend Dante was hard at work on the *Commedia*.

As in so many other Italian cities, Florence had been developing its republican institutions slowly and painfully. At the beginning of the *comune* in 1115, the leaders were a class called the *boni homines*, which was made up mostly of nobles. Only a few decades later, these were calling themselves *consules*, evoking a memory of the ancient Roman republic. When the Ghibellines took over, the leading official was a *podestà* appointed by the Emperor. Later, under the Guelphs, the *podestà* and a new officer called the *capitano del popolo* were both elected by the citizens. With the reforms of the 1290s Florence's republican constitution was perfected – if that is the proper word for an arrangement that satisfied only a few citizens and guaranteed lots of trouble for the future. Under the new dispensation, power was invested in the council of the richer guilds, the *Signoria*; the new Palazzo della Signoria was designed expressly as a symbol of their authority, replacing the old Bargello, which had been the seat of the *podestà*. The most novel feature of the government, designed to overcome Florence's past incapacity to avoid violent factionalism, was the selection of officials by lot from among the guild members. In effect, politics was to be abolished.

## Business as Usual: Riot, War, Plagues and Revolution

Despite the reforms of the Ordinamenti, Florence found little peace in the new century. As if following some strange and immutable law of city-state behaviour, no sooner had the Guelphs established total control than they themselves split into new factions. The radically anti-imperial **Blacks** and the more conciliatory **Whites** fought each other through the early 1300s with the same fervour that both had once exercised against the Ghibellines. The Whites, who included Dante among their partisans, came out losers when the Blacks conspired with the pope to bring Charles of Valois' French army into Florence; almost all the losing faction were forced into exile in 1302. Some of them must have sneaked back, for the chronicles of 1304 record the Blacks trying to burn them out of their houses with incendiary bombs, resulting in a fire that consumed a quarter of the city.

Beginning in 1313, Florence was involved in a constant series of inconclusive wars with Pisa, Lucca and Arezzo, among others. In 1325, the city was defeated and nearly destroyed by the great Lucchese general **Castruccio Castracani** (*see* p.287). Castruccio died of a common cold while the siege was already under way, another instance of Florence's famous good luck, but unfortunately one of the last. The factions may have been suppressed, but fate had found some more novel disasters for the city. One far-off monarch did more damage to Florence than its Italian enemies had ever managed – King Edward III of England, who in 1339 found it expedient to repudiate his foreign debts. Florence's two biggest banks, the Bardi and the Peruzzi, immediately went bust, and the city's standing as the centre of international finance was gravely damaged.

If anything was constant throughout the history of the republic, it was the oppression of the poor. The ruling bankers and merchants exploited the labour of the masses and gave them only the bare minimum in return. In the 14th century, overcrowding, undernourishment and plenty of rats made Florence's poorer neighbourhoods a perfect breeding ground for epidemics. Famine, plagues and riots became common in the 1340s, causing a severe political crisis. At one point, in 1342, the Florentines gave over their government to a foreign dictator, Walter de Brienne, the French-Greek 'Duke of Athens'. He lasted only for a year before a popular revolt ended the experiment. The **Black Death** of 1348, which was the background for Boccaccio's *Decameron*, carried off perhaps one half of the population. Coming on the heels of a serious depression, it was a blow from which Florence would never really recover.

In the next two centuries, during the whole period when the city was to stake its position as the great innovator in Western culture, it was already in relative decline, a politically decadent republic with a stagnant economy, barely holding its own among the turbulent changes in trade and diplomacy. For the time being, however, things didn't look too bad. Florence found enough ready cash to buy control of Prato, in 1350, and was successful in a defensive war against expansionist Milan in 1351. Warfare was almost continuous for the last half of the century, a strain on the exchequer but not usually a threat to the city's survival; this was the heyday of the mercenary companies, led by *condottieri* like **Sir John Hawkwood** (Giovanni Acuto), immortalized by the equestrian 'statue' in Florence's cathedral. Before the Florentines made him a better offer, Hawkwood was often in the employ of their enemies.

Throughout the century, the Guelph party had been steadily tightening its grip over the republic's affairs. Despite the selection of officials by lot, by the 1370s the party organization bore an uncanny resemblance to some of the big-city political machines common not so long ago in America. The merchants and the bankers who ran the party used it to turn the Florentine Republic into a profit-making business. With the increasingly limited opportunities for making money in trade and finance, the Guelph ruling class tried to make up the difference by soaking the poor. Wars and taxes stretched Florentine tolerance to breaking point, and finally, in 1378, came revolution. The **Ciompi Revolt** (*ciompi* – wage labourers in the textile industries) began in July, when a mob of workers seized the Bargello. Under the leadership of a wool-carder named Michele di Lando, they executed a few of the Guelph bosses and announced a new, reformed constitution. They were also foolish enough to believe the Guelph magnates when they promised to abide by the new arrangement if only the *ciompi* would go home. Before long di Lando was in exile, and the ruling class firmly back in the seat of power, more than ever determined to eliminate the last vestiges of democracy from the republic.

## The Rise of the Medici

In 1393, Florentines celebrated the 100th anniversary of the great reform of the Ordinamenti, while watching their republic descend irresistibly into oligarchy. In that year **Maso degli Albizzi** became *gonfaloniere* (the head of the Signoria) and served as virtual dictator for many years afterwards. The ruling class of merchants, more than a bit paranoid after the Ciompi Revolt, were generally relieved to see power concentrated in strong hands; the ascendancy of the Albizzi family was to set the pattern for the rest of the republic's existence. In a poisoned atmosphere of repression and conspiracy, the spies of the Signoria's new secret police hunted down malcontents while whole legions of Florentine exiles plotted against the republic in foreign courts. Florence was almost constantly at war. In 1398 she defeated an attempt at conquest by Giangaleazzo Visconti of Milan. The imperialist policy of the Albizzi and their allies resulted in important territorial gains, including the conquest of Pisa in 1406, and the purchase of Livorno from the Genoese in 1421. Unsuccessful wars against Lucca finally disenchanted the Florentines with Albizzi rule. An emergency *parlamento* (the in frequent popular assembly usually called when a coming change of rulers was obvious) in 1434 decreed the recall from exile of the head of the popular opposition, **Cosimo de' Medici**.

Perhaps it was something that could only have happened in Florence – the darling of the plebeians, the great hope for reform, happened to be the head of Florence's biggest bank. The Medici family had their roots in the Mugello region north of Florence. Their name seems to suggest that they once were pharmacists (later enemies would jibe at the balls on the family arms as 'the pills'). For two centuries they had been active in Florentine politics; many had acquired reputations as troublemakers; their names turned up often in the lists of exiles and records of lawsuits. None of the Medici had ever been particularly rich until **Giovanni di Bicci de' Medici** (1360–1429) parlayed his wife's dowry into the founding of a bank. Good fortune – and a temporary monopoly on the handling of the pope's finances – made the Medici Bank Florence's biggest.

Giovanni had been content to stay on the fringe of politics; his son, **Cosimo** (known in Florentine history as 'il Vecchio', the 'old man') took good care of the bank's affairs but aimed his sights much higher. His strategy was as old as Julius Caesar – the patrician reformer, cultivating the best men, winning the favour of the poor with largesse and gradually, carefully forming a party under a system specifically designed to prevent such things. In 1433 Rinaldo degli Albizzi had him exiled, but it was too late; continuing discontent forced his return only a year later, and for the next 35 years Cosimo would be the unchallenged ruler of Florence. Throughout this period, Cosimo

# Know your Medici

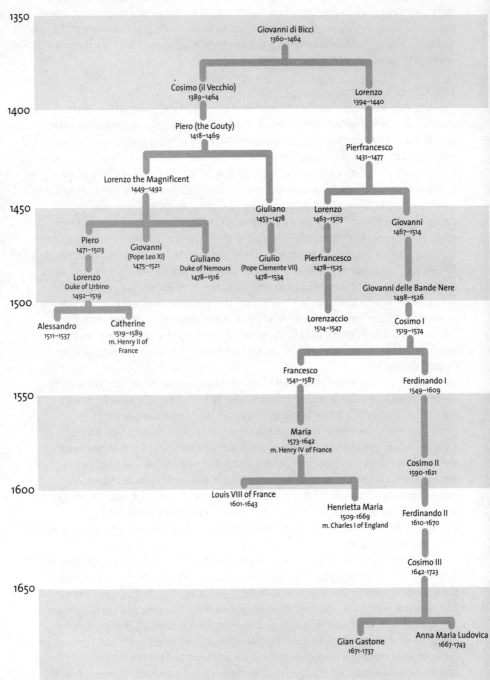

1350

Giovanni di Bicci
1360–1464

Cosimo (il Vecchio)
1389–1464

Lorenzo
1394–1440

1400

Piero (the Gouty)
1418–1469

Pierfrancesco
1431–1477

Lorenzo the Magnificent
1449–1492

1450

Giuliano
1453–1478

Lorenzo
1463–1503

Giovanni
1467–1514

Piero
1471–1503

Giovanni
(Pope Leo XI)
1475–1521

Giuliano
Duke of Nemours
1478–1516

Giulio
(Pope Clemente VII)
1478–1534

Pierfrancesco
1478–1525

Lorenzo
Duke of Urbino
1492–1519

Giovanni delle Bande Nere
1498–1526

1500

Alessandro
1511–1537

Catherine
1519–1589
m. Henry II of
France

Lorenzaccio
1514–1547

Cosimo I
1519–1574

Francesco
1541–1587

Ferdinando I
1549–1609

1550

Maria
1573-1642
m. Henry IV of France

Cosimo II
1590-1621

1600

Louis VIII of France
1601-1643

Henrietta Maria
1509-1669
m. Charles I of England

Ferdinando II
1610-1670

Cosimo III
1642-1723

1650

Gian Gastone
1671-1737

Anna Maria Ludovica
1667-1743

1700

occasionally held public office – this was done by lottery, with the electoral lists manipulated to ensure a majority of Medici supporters at all times. Nevertheless, he received ambassadors at the new family palace (built in 1444), entertained visiting popes and emperors, and made all the important decisions. A canny political godfather and usually a gentleman, Cosimo also proved a useful patron to the great figures of the early Renaissance – including Donatello and Brunelleschi. His father had served as one of the judges in the famous competition for the baptistry doors, and Cosimo was a member of the commission that picked Brunelleschi to design the cathedral dome.

Cosimo did oversee some genuine reforms; under his leadership Florence began Europe's first progressive income tax, and a few years later the state invented the modern concept of the national debt – endlessly rolling over bonds to keep the republic afloat and the creditors happy. The poor, with fewer taxes to pay, were also happy, and the ruling classes, after some initial distaste, were positively delighted; never in Florence's history had any government so successfully muted class conflict and the desire for a genuine democracy. Wars were few, and the internal friction negligible. Cosimo died in August 1464; his tomb in San Lorenzo bears the inscription *Pater patriae*, and no dissent was registered when his 40-year-old son **Piero** took up the boss's role.

## Lorenzo il Magnifico

Piero didn't quite have the touch of his masterful father, but he survived a stiff political crisis in 1466, when he proved able to outmanoeuvre a new faction led by wealthy banker Luca Pitti. In 1469 he succumbed to the Medici family disease, the gout, and his 20-year-old son **Lorenzo** succeeded him in an equally smooth transition. He was to last for 23 years. Not necessarily more 'magnificent' than other contemporary princes, or other Medici, Lorenzo's honorific reveals something of the myth that was to grow up around him in later centuries. His long reign corresponded to the height of the Florentine Renaissance. It was a relatively peaceful time, and in the light of the disasters that were to follow, Florentines could not help looking back on it as a golden age.

As a ruler, Lorenzo showed many virtues. Still keeping up the pretence of living as a private citizen, he lived relatively simply, always accessible to the voices and concerns of his fellow citizens, who would often see him walking the city streets. In the field of foreign policy he was indispensable to Florence and indeed all Italy; he did more than anyone to keep the precarious peninsular balance of power from disintegrating. The most dramatic affair of his reign was the **Pazzi conspiracy**, an attempt to assassinate Lorenzo plotted by Pope Sixtus IV and the wealthy Pazzi family, the pope's bankers and ancient rivals of the Medici. In 1478, two of the younger Pazzi attacked Lorenzo and his brother Giuliano during mass at the cathedral. Giuliano was killed, but Lorenzo managed to escape into the sacristy. The botched murder aborted the planned revolt; Florentines showed little interest in the Pazzis' call to arms, and before nightfall most of the conspirators were dangling from the cornice of the Palazzo Vecchio.

Apparently, Lorenzo had angered the pope by starting a syndicate to mine for alum in Volterra, threatening the papal monopoly. Since Sixtus failed to murder Lorenzo, he had to settle for excommunicating him, and declaring war in alliance with King Ferrante of Naples. As events turned out, the war went badly for Florence and, in the most memorable act of his career, Lorenzo walked into the lion's cage, travelling to negotiate with the terrible Neapolitan, who had already murdered more than one important guest. As it turned out, Ferrante was only too happy to dump his papal entanglements; Florence found itself at peace once more, and Lorenzo returned home to a hero's welcome.

In other affairs, both foreign and domestic, Lorenzo was more a lucky ruler than a skilled one. Florence's economy was entering a long, slow decline, but for the moment the banks and mills were churning out just enough profit to keep up the accustomed level of opulence. The Medici Bank was on the ropes. Partly because of Lorenzo's neglect, it came close to collapsing on several occasions – and it seems that Lorenzo blithely made up the losses with public funds. Culturally, he was fortunate to be nabob of Florence at its most artistically creative period; future historians and Medici propagandists gave him a reputation as an art patron that is entirely undeserved. His own tastes tended towards bric-a-brac, jewellery, antique statues and vases; there is little evidence that he really understood or could appreciate the scores of great artists around him. Perhaps because he was too nearsighted to see anything very clearly, he did not commission a single important canvas or fresco in Florence (except for Luca Signorelli's mysterious *Pan*, lost in Berlin during the last war). His favourite architect was the hack Giuliano da Sangallo.

The Medici had taken great care with Lorenzo's education: he was brought up with some of the leading humanist scholars of Tuscany for tutors and his real interests were literary. His well-formed lyrics and winsome pastorals have earned him a place among Italy's greatest 15th-century poets; they neatly reflect the private side of Lorenzo, the retiring, scholarly family man who enjoyed life better in one of the many rural Medici villas than in the busy city. In this, he was perfectly in tune with his class and his age. Plenty of Florentine bankers were learning the joys of country life, reading Horace or Catullus in their geometrical gardens and pestering their tenant farmers with well-meant advice.

Back in town, they had thick, new walls of rusticated sandstone between them and the bustle of the streets. The late 15th century was the great age of palace-building in Florence. Following the example of Cosimo de' Medici, the bankers and merchants erected dozens of palaces (some of the best can be seen around Via Tornabuoni). Each one turns blank walls and iron-barred windows to the street. Historians always note one very pronounced phenomenon of this period – a turning inward, a 'privatization' of Florentine life. In a city that had become a republic only in name, civic interest and public life ceased to matter so much. The very rich began to assume the airs of an aristocracy, and did everything they could to distance themselves from their fellow citizens. Ironically, just at the time when Florence's artists were creating their greatest achievements, the republican ethos, the civic soul that had made Florence great, began to disintegrate.

## Savonarola

Lorenzo's death, in 1492, was followed by another apparently smooth transition of power to his son **Piero**. But after 58 years of Medicean quiet and stability, the city was ready for a change. The opportunity for the malcontents came soon enough, when the timid and inept Piero allowed the invading King of France, **Charles VIII**, to occupy Pisa and the Tuscan coast. A spontaneous revolt chased Piero and the rest of the Medici into exile, while a mob sacked the family's palace. A new regime, hastily put together under **Piero Capponi**, dealt more sternly with the French and tried to pump some new life into the long-dormant republican constitution.

The Florence that threw out the Medici was a city in the mood for some radical reform. Already, the dominating figure on the political stage was an intense Dominican friar from Ferrara named **Girolamo Savonarola**. Perhaps not surprisingly, this oversophisticated and overstimulated city was also in the mood to be told how wicked and decadent it was, and Savonarola was happy to oblige. A spellbinding revival preacher with a touch of erudition, Savonarola packed as many as 10,000 into the Duomo to hear his weekly sermons, which were laced with political sarcasm and social criticism. Though an insufferable prig, he was also a sincere democrat. There is a story that the dying Lorenzo called Savonarola to his bedside for the last rites, and that the friar refused him absolution unless he 'restored the liberty of the Florentines', a proposal that only made the dying despot sneer with contempt.

Savonarola also talked Charles VIII into leaving Florence in peace. Pisa, however, took advantage of the confusion to revolt, and the restored republic's attempts to recapture it were in vain. Things were going badly. Piero Capponi's death in 1496 left Florence without an able leader, and Savonarolan extremists became ever more influential. The French invasion and the incessant wars that followed cost the city dearly in trade, while the Medici, now in Rome, intrigued to destroy the republic. Worst of all, Savonarola's attacks on clerical corruption made him another bitter enemy in Rome – none other than **Pope Alexander VI** himself, the most corrupt cleric who ever lived. The Borgia pope scraped together a league of allies to make war on Florence in 1497.

This war proceeded without serious reverses for either side, but Savonarola was able to exploit it brilliantly, convincing the Florentines that they were on a moral crusade against the hated and dissolute Borgias, Medici, French, Venetians and Milanese. The year 1497 was undoubtedly the high point of Savonarola's career. The good friar's spies – mostly children – kept a close eye on any Florentines who were suspected of enjoying themselves, and collected books, fancy clothes and works of art for the famous **Bonfire of Vanities**. It was a climactic moment in the history of Florence's delicate psyche. Somehow the spell had been broken; like the deranged old Michelangelo, taking a hammer to his own work, the Florentines gathered the objects that had once been their greatest pride and put them to the torch. The bonfire was held in the centre of the Piazza della Signoria; a visiting Venetian offered to buy the whole lot, but the Florentines had someone sketch his portrait and threw that on the flames, too.

One vanity the Florentines could not quite bring themselves to part with was their violent factionalism. On one side were the Piagnoni ('weepers') of Savonarola's party, on the other the party of the Arrabbiati ('the angry'), including the gangs of young delinquents who would demonstrate their opposition to piety and holiness by sneaking into the cathedral and filling Savonarola's pulpit with cow dung. A Medicean party was also gathering strength, a sort of fifth column sowing discontent within the city and undermining the war effort. Three times, unsuccessfully, the exiled Medici attempted to seize the city with bands of mercenaries. The Pisan revolt continued, and Pope Alexander had excommunicated Savonarola and was threatening to place all Florence under an interdict. In the long hangover after the Bonfire of Vanities, the Florentines were growing weary of their preacher. When the Arrabbiati won the elections of 1498, his doom was sealed. A kangaroo court found the new scapegoat guilty of heresy and treason. After some gratuitous torture and public mockery, the very spot where the Bonfire of Vanities had been held now witnessed a bonfire of Savonarola.

Pope Alexander still wasn't happy. He sent an army under his son, Cesare Borgia, to menace the city. Florence weathered this threat, and the relatively democratic 'Savonarolan' constitution of 1494 seemed to be working out well. Under an innovative idea, borrowed from Venice and designed to circumvent party strife, a public-spirited gentleman named **Piero Soderini** was elected *gonfaloniere* for life in 1502. With the help of his friend and adviser, **Niccolò Machiavelli**, Soderini kept the ship of state on an even keel. Pisa finally surrendered in 1509. Serious trouble returned in 1512, and once more the popes were behind it. As France's only ally in Italy, Florence ran foul of Julius II. Papal and Spanish armies invaded Florentine territory and, after their gruesome sack of Prato, designed specifically to overawe Florence, the frightened and politically apathetic city was ready to submit to the pope's conditions – the expulsion of Soderini, a change of alliance and the return of the Medici.

## The End of the Republic

At first, the understanding was that the Medici would live in Florence strictly as private citizens. But **Giuliano de' Medici**, son of Lorenzo and current leader, soon united the upper classes for a rolling back of Savonarolan democracy. With plenty of hired soldiers to intimidate the populace, a rigged *parlamento* in September 1512 restored Medici control. The democratic Grand Council was abolished; its new meeting hall in the Palazzo Vecchio (where Leonardo and Michelangelo were to have their 'Battle of the Frescoes') was broken up into apartments for soldiers. Soldiers were everywhere, and the Medicean restoration took on the aspect of a police state. Hundreds of political prisoners spent time undergoing torture in the Palazzo Vecchio's dungeons, among them Machiavelli.

Giuliano died in 1516, succeeded by his nephew **Lorenzo, Duke of Urbino**, a snotty young sport with a tyrant's bad manners. Nobody mourned much when syphilis carried him off in 1519, but the family paid Michelangelo to give both Lorenzo and Giuliano fancy tombs. Ever since Giuliano's death, however, the real Medici boss had been not Lorenzo, but his uncle Giovanni, who in that year became **Pope Leo X**. The Medici, original masters of nepotism, had been planning this for years. Back in the

1470s, Lorenzo il Magnifico realized that the surest way of maintaining the family fortunes would be to get a Medici on the papal throne. He had little Giovanni ordained at the age of eight, purchased him a cardinal's hat at 13, and used bribery and diplomacy to help him accumulate dozens of benefices all over France and Italy. For his easy-going civility (as exemplified in his famous quote: 'God has given us the papacy so let us enjoy it'), and his patronage of scholars and artists, Leo became one of the best-remembered Renaissance popes. On the other side of the coin was his criminal mismanagement of the Church; having learned the advantages of parasitism, the Medici were eager to pass it on to their friends. Upper-class Florentines descended on Rome like a plague of locusts, occupying all the important sinecures and rapidly emptying the papal treasury. Their rapacity, plus the tremendous expenses involved in building the new St Peter's, caused Leo to step up the sale of indulgences all over Europe – disgusting reformers like Luther and greatly hastening the onset of the Reformation.

Back in Florence, Lorenzo Duke of Urbino's successor Giulio, bastard son of Lorenzo il Magnifico's murdered brother Giuliano, was little more than a puppet; Leo always found enough time between banquets to manage the city's affairs. Giulio himself became pope in 1523, as **Clement VII**, thanks largely to the new financial interdependence between Florence and Rome, and now the Medici presence in their home city was reduced to two more unattractive young bastards, Ippolito and Alessandro, under the guardianship of Cardinal Silvio Passerini. As Leo had done, Clement attempted to run the city from Rome, but high taxes and the lack of a strong hand made the new Medici regime increasingly precarious; its end followed almost immediately upon the sack of Rome in 1527. With Clement a prisoner in the Vatican and unable to intervene, a delegation of Florentine notables discreetly informed Cardinal Passerini and the Medicis that it was time to go. They took the hint, and for the third time in less than a century Florence had succeeded in getting rid of the Medici.

The new republic, though initiated by the disillusioned wealthy classes, soon found radical Savonarolan democrats gaining the upper hand. The Grand Council met once more, and extended the franchise to include most of the citizens. Vanities were cursed again, books were banned and carnival parades forbidden; the Council officially pronounced Jesus Christ 'King of the Florentines', just as it had done in the heyday of the Savonarolan camp meetings. In an intense atmosphere of republican virtue and pious crusade, Florence rushed headlong into the apocalyptic climax of its history. This time it did not take the Medici long to recover. In order to get Florence back, the witless Clement became allied to his former enemy, **Emperor Charles V**, a sordid deal that would eventually betray all Italy to Spanish control. Imperial troops were to help subdue Florence, and Clement's illegitimate son Alessandro was to wed Charles' illegitimate daughter. The bastards were closing in. Charles' troops put Florence under siege in December 1529. The city had few resources for the struggle, and no friends, but a heroic resistance kept the imperialists at bay all through the winter and spring. Citizens gave up their gold and silver to be minted into the republic's last coins. The councillors debated seizing little Catherine de' Medici, future Queen of France, but then a prisoner of the republic, and dangling her from the walls to give the enemy a good target. Few artists were left in Florence, but Michelangelo stayed to help with his city's fortifications (by night he was working on the Medici tombs in San Lorenzo, surely one of the most astounding feats of fence-straddling in history; both sides gave him safe passage when he wanted to leave Florence).

In August of 1530, the Florentines' skilful commander, Francesco Ferruccio, was killed in a skirmish near Pistoia; at about the same time the republic realized that its mercenary captain within the walls, Malatesta Baglioni, had sold them out to the pope and emperor. When they tried to arrest him, Baglioni only laughed, and directed his men to turn their artillery on the city. The inevitable capitulation came on 12 August; after almost 400 years, the Florentine republic had breathed its last.

At first, this third Medici return seemed to be just another dreary round of history repeating itself. Again, a packed *parlamento* gutted the constitution and legitimized the Medici takeover. Again the family and its minions combed the city, confiscating back every penny's worth of property that had been confiscated from them. This time, however, was to be different. Florence had gone from being a large fish in a small Italian pond to a minuscule but hindersome nuisance in the pan-European world of papal and imperial politics. Charles V didn't much like republics, or disorderly politicking, or indeed anyone who might conceivably say no to him. The orders came down from the emperor in Brussels; it was to be Medici for ever.

## Cosimo I: the Medici as Grand Dukes

At first little was changed; the shell of the republican constitution was maintained, but with the 20-year-old illegitimate **Alessandro** as 'Duke of the Florentine Republic'; the harsh reality was under construction on the height above the city's west end – the Fortezza da Basso, with its Spanish garrison, demanded by Charles V as insurance that Florence would never again be able to assert its independence. If any further symbolism was necessary, Alessandro ordered the great bell to be removed from the tower of the Palazzo Vecchio – the bell that had always summoned the citizens to political assemblies and the mustering of the army. In 1537, Alessandro was treacherously murdered by his jealous cousin Lorenzaccio de' Medici. With no legitimate heirs in the direct line Florence was in danger of falling under direct imperial rule, as had happened to Milan two years earlier, upon the extinction of the Sforza dukes. The assassination was kept secret while the Medici and the diplomats angled for a solution. The only reasonable choice turned out to be 18-year-old **Cosimo de' Medici**, heir of the family's cadet branch. This son of a famous mercenary commander, Giovanni of the Black Bands, had grown up on a farm and had never been involved with Florentine affairs; both the elder statesmen of the family and the imperial representatives thought they would easily be able to manipulate him.

It soon became clear that they had picked the wrong boy. Right from the start, young Cosimo had a surprisingly complete idea of how he meant to rule Florence, and also the will and strength of personality to see his commands carried out. No one ever admitted liking him; his puritanical court dismayed even the old partisans of Savonarola, and Florentines always enjoyed grumbling over his high taxes, going to support 'colonels, spies, Spaniards, and women to serve Madame' (his Spanish consort

Eleanor of Toledo). More surprising, in this pathetic age when bowing and scraping Italians were everywhere else losing both their liberty and their dignity, Cosimo held his own against both pope and Spaniard. To back up his growing independence, Cosimo put his domains on an almost permanent war footing. New fortresses were built, a big fleet begun, and a paid standing army took the place of mercenaries and citizen levies. The skeleton of the old republic was revamped into a modern, bureaucratic state, governed as scientifically and rationally as any in Europe. The new regime, well prepared as it was, never had a severe test. Early in his reign Cosimo defeated the last-ditch effort of the republican exiles, unreconstructed oligarchs led by the banker Filippo Strozzi, at the **Battle of Montemurlo**, the last threat ever to Medici rule. Cosimo's masterstroke came in 1557, when with the help of an Imperial army he was able to gobble up the entire Republic of Siena. Now the Medicis controlled roughly the boundaries of modern Tuscany; Cosimo was able to cap off his reign in 1569 by purchasing from the Pope the title of Grand Duke of Tuscany.

## Knick-knacks and Tedium: the Later Medici

For all Cosimo's efforts, Florence was a city entering a very evident decline. Banking and trade did well throughout the late 16th century, a prosperous time for almost all of Italy, but there were very few opportunities for growth, and few Florentines interested in looking for it. More than ever, wealth was going into land, palaces and government bonds; the tradition of mercantile venture among the Florentine élite was rapidly becoming a thing of the past. For culture and art, Cosimo's reign turned out to be a disaster. It wasn't what he intended; indeed the Duke brought to the field his accustomed energy and compulsion to improve and organize. Academies were founded, and research underwritten. Cosimo's big purse and his emphasis on art as political propaganda helped change the Florentine artist from a slightly eccentric guild artisan to a flouncing courtier, ready to roll over at his master's command. The Florentines, if they were fooled, weren't the only ones: the city had as great an influence in its age of decay as in its age of greatness. The cute, well-educated Florentine pranced across Europe, finding himself praised as the paragon of culture and refinement. Even in England – though that honest nation soon found him out:

A little Apish hatte, couched fast to the Pate, like an Oyster,
French Camarick Ruffes, deepe with a witnesse, starched to the purpose,
Delicate in speach, queynte in arraye: conceited in all poyntes:
In Courtyly guyles, a passing singular odde man...
Mirror of Tuscanism, Gabriel Harvey, 1580

Michelangelo, despite frequent entreaties, always refused to work for Cosimo. Most of the other talented Florentines eventually found one excuse or another to bolt for Rome or even further afield, leaving lapdogs like **Giorgio Vasari** to carry on the grand traditions of Florentine art. Vasari, with help from such artists as Ammannati and Bandinelli, transformed much of the city – especially the interiors of its churches and public buildings. Florence began to fill up with equestrian statues of Medici, pageants and plaster triumphal arches displaying the triumphs of the Medici, sculptural allegories (like Cellini's *Perseus*) reminding us of the inevitability of the Medici and, best of all, portraits of semi-divine Medici floating up in the clouds with little Cupids and Virtues. It was all the same to Cosimo and his successors, whose personal tastes tended more to engraved jewels, exotic taxidermy and sculptures made of seashells. But it helped hasten the extinction of Florentine culture and the quiet transformation of the city into just another Mediterranean backwater. Cosimo himself grew ill in his later years, abdicating most responsibility to his son **Francesco** from 1564 to his death 10 years later. Francesco, the genuine oddball among the Medici, was a moody, melancholic sort who cared little for government, preferring to lock himself up in the family palaces to pursue his passion for alchemy, as well as occasional researches into such subjects as perpetual motion and poisons – his agents around the Mediterranean had to ship him crates of scorpions every now and then. Despite his lack of interest, Francesco was a capable ruler, best known for his founding of Livorno.

Later Medici followed the general course established by other great families, such as the Habsburgs and Bourbons – each one was worse than the last. Francesco's death in 1587 gave the throne to his brother, **Ferdinando I**, founder of the Medici Chapels at San Lorenzo and another indefatigable collector of bric-a-brac. Next came **Cosimo II** (1609–21), a sickly nonentity who eventually succumbed to tuberculosis, and **Ferdinando II** (1621–70), whose long and uneventful reign oversaw the impoverishment of Florence and most of Tuscany. For this the Medici do not deserve much blame. A long string of bad harvests, beginning in the 1590s, plagues that recurred with terrible frequency as late as the 1630s, and general trade patterns that redistributed wealth and power from the Mediterranean to northern Europe, all set the stage for the collapse of the Florentine economy. The fatal blow came in the 1630s, when the long-deteriorating wool trade collapsed with sudden finality. Banking was going too, partly a victim of the age's continuing inflation, partly of high taxes and lack of worthwhile investments. Florence, by the mid-century, found itself with no prospects at all, a pensioner city drawing a barely respectable income from its glorious past.

With **Cosimo III** (1670–1723), the line of the Medici crossed over into the realm of the ridiculous. A religious crank and anti-Semite, this Cosimo temporarily wiped out free thought in the universities, allowed Tuscany to fill up with nuns and Jesuits, and decreed fantastical laws like the one that forbade any man to enter a house where an unmarried woman lived. To support his lavish court and pay the big tributes demanded by Spain and Austria (something earlier Medici would have scorned) Cosimo taxed what was left of the Florentine economy into an early grave. His heir was the incredible **Gian Gastone** (1723–37). This last Medici, an obese drunkard, senile and slobbering at the age of 50, has been immortalized by the equally incredible bust in the Pitti Palace. Gian Gastone had to be carried up and down stairs on the rare occasions when he ever got out of bed (mainly to disprove rumours that he was dead); on the one occasion he appeared in public, the chronicles report him vomiting repeatedly out of the carriage window.

As a footnote on the Medici there is Gian Gastone's perfectly sensible sister, **Anna Maria Ludovica**. As the very last surviving Medici, it fell to her to dispose of the family's vast wealth and hoards of art. When she died, in 1743, her will revealed that the whole bundle was to become the property of the future rulers of Tuscany – whoever they should be – with the provision that not one bit of it should ever, ever, be moved outside Florence. Without her, the great collections of the Uffizi and the Bargello might long ago have been packed away to Vienna or to Paris.

## Post-Medici Florence

When Gian Gastone died in 1737, Tuscany's fate had already been decided by the great powers of Europe. The Grand Duchy would fall to **Francis Stephen**, Duke of Lorraine and husband-to-be of the Austrian Empress Maria Theresa; the new duke's troops were already installed in the Fortezza da Basso a year before Gian Gastone died. For most of the next century, Florence slumbered under a benign Austrian rule. Already the first Grand Tourists were arriving on their way to Rome and Naples, sons of the Enlightenment like Goethe, who never imagined anything in Florence could possibly interest him and didn't stop, or relics like the Pretender Charles Edward Stuart, 'Bonnie Prince Charlie', Duke of Albany, who stayed two years. Napoleon's men occupied the city for most of two decades without making much of an impression.

After the Napoleonic Wars, the Habsburg restoration brought back the Lorraine dynasty. From 1824 to 1859, Florence and Tuscany were ruled by **Leopold II**, that most useful and likeable of all Grand Dukes. This was the age when Florence first became popular among the northern Europeans and the time when the Brownings, Dostoevsky, Leigh Hunt and dozens of other artists and writers took up residence, rediscovering the glories of the city and of the early Renaissance. Grand Duke Leopold was decent enough to let himself be overthrown in 1859, during the tumults of the Risorgimento. In 1865, when only the Papal State remained to be incorporated into the Kingdom of Italy, Florence briefly became the new nation's capital. King Vittorio Emanuele moved into the Pitti Palace, and the Italian Parliament met in the great hall of the Palazzo Vecchio.

It was really not meant to last. When the Italian troops entered Rome in 1870, Florence's brief hour as a major capital was at an end. Not, however, without giving the staid old city a memorable jolt towards the modern world. In an unusual flurry of exertion, Florence finally threw up a façade for its cathedral, and levelled the pictur-esque though squalid market area and Jewish ghetto to build the dolorous Piazza della Repubblica. Fortunately, the city regained its senses before too much damage was done. Throughout the 20th century, Florence's role as a museum city has been confirmed with each passing year. The hiatus provided by the Second World War allowed the city to resume briefly its ancient delight in black-and-white political epic. In 1944–5, Florence offered some of the most outrageous spectacles of Fascist fanaticism, and also some of the most courageous stories of the Resistance – including that of the German consul Gerhard Wolf, who used his position to protect Florentines from the Nazi terror, often at great personal risk.

In August 1944, the Allied armies were poised to advance through northern Tuscany. For the Germans, the Arno made a convenient defensive line, requiring that all the bridges of Florence be demolished. They all were, except for the Ponte Vecchio, saved in a last-minute deal, though the buildings on either side of it were destroyed to provide piles of rubble around the bridge approaches. After the war, all were repaired; the city had the Ponte della Trinità rebuilt stone by stone exactly as it was. No sooner was the war damage redeemed, however, than a greater disaster attacked Florence's heritage. The flood of 1966, when water reached 21ft, did more damage than Nazis or Napoleons; an international effort was raised to preserve and restore the city's art and monuments. Since then the Arno has been deepened under the Ponte Vecchio and 18ft earthen walls have been erected around Ponte Amerigo Vespucci; video screens and computers monitor every fluctuation in the water level. Should another flood occur, Florence will have time to protect herself. Far more insoluble is terrorism, which touched the city in May 1993, when a bomb destroyed the Gregoriophilus library opposite the Uffizi, damaged the Vasari Corridor and killed a family. Florence, shocked by this intrusion from the outside world into its holy of holies, repaired most of the damage in record time with funds raised by a national subscription.

Careful planning has saved the best of Florence's immediate countryside from a different sort of flood – post-war suburbanization – but much of the other territory around the city has been coated by an atrocity of suburban sprawl, some of the most degraded landscapes in all Italy. The building of a new airport extension, which the Florentines hope will help make up some of the economic ground they've lost to Milan, includes the building of a whole new satellite city, a new Florence ('Firenze Nuova'), nothing less than 'the greatest urban planning operation of the century,' they say, with some of the old audacity of Brunelleschi. The buildings on the marshland (northwest of the city) have been demolished, the land flattened and the project for a new city to include housing, shops, leisure facilities, a new law court and a new Fiat factory (Fiat along with the insurance group, La Fondiaria, are the sponsors) is already under way, with some apartment blocks nearing completion. The law court building was actually started in 1999. But who knows when it will all be finished?

Meanwhile Florence works hard to preserve what it already has. Although new measures to control the city's bugbear – the traffic problems of a city of 500,000 that receives seven million visitors a year – have been enacted to protect the historic centre, pollution from nearby industry continues to eat away at monuments; Donatello's statue of St Mark at Orsanmichele, perfectly intact 50 years ago, is now a mutilated leper. Private companies, banks and even individuals finance 90 per cent of the art restoration in Florence, with techniques invented by the city's innovative Institute of Restoration. Increasingly, copies are made to replace original works. Naturally, half the city is for them, and the other half against.

# Piazza del Duomo

Tour groups circle around the three great spiritual monuments of medieval Florence like sharks around their prey. Postcard vendors prey, and sax players play to a human carnival from a hundred nations that mills about the cathedral good-naturedly while ambulances of a medieval brotherhood dedicated to first aid stand at the ready in case anyone swoons from ecstasy or art-glut.

# The Baptistry

*Open Mon–Sat 12–7, Sun 8.30–2; adm.*

In order to begin to understand what strange magic made the Renaissance first bloom by the Arno, then look here; this ancient, mysterious building is the egg from which Florence's golden age was hatched. By the quattrocento, Florentines firmly believed their baptistry was originally a Roman temple to Mars, a touchstone linking them to a legendary past. Scholarship sets its date of construction between the 6th and 9th centuries, in the darkest Dark Ages, which makes it even more remarkable; it may as well have dropped from heaven. Its distinctive dark green and white marble facing, the tidily classical pattern of arches and rectangles that deceived Brunelleschi and Alberti, was probably added around the 11th century. The masters who built it remain unknown, but their strikingly original exercise in geometry provided the model for all of Florence's great church façades. When it was new, there was nothing remotely like it in Europe; to visitors from outside the city it must have seemed almost miraculous.

Every 21 March, New Year's Day on the old Florentine calendar, all the children that had been born over the last 12 months would be brought here for a great communal baptism, a habit that helped make the baptistry not merely a religious monument but a civic symbol, in fact the oldest and fondest symbol of the republic. As such the Florentines never tired of embellishing it. Under the octagonal cupola, the glittering 13th- and 14th-century gold-ground mosaics show a strong Byzantine influence, perhaps laid by mosaicists from Venice. The decoration is divided into concentric strips: over the apse, dominated by a 28ft figure of Christ, is a *Last Judgement*, while the other bands, from the inside out, portray the *Hierarchy of Heaven*, *Story of Genesis*, *Life of Joseph*, *Life of Christ* and the *Life of St John the Baptist*, the last band believed to be the work of Cimabue. The equally beautiful mosaics over the altar and in the vault are the earliest, signed by a monk named Iacopo in the first decades of the 1200s. New lighting was installed in 1999 which has vastly improved the visitors' view of the ceiling.

To match the mosaics, there is an intricate tessellated marble floor, decorated with signs of the Zodiac; the blank, octagonal space in the centre was formerly occupied by the huge font. The green and white patterned walls of the interior, even more than the exterior, are remarkable, combining influences from the ancient world and modern inspiration for something entirely new, the perfect source that architects of the Middle Ages and Renaissance would strive to match. Much of the best design work is up in the **galleries**, not accessible, but partially visible from the floor.

The baptistry is hardly cluttered; besides a 13th-century Pisan style baptismal font, only the **Tomb of Anti-Pope John XXIII** by Donatello and Michelozzo stands out. This funerary monument, with scenographic marble draperies softening its classical lines, is one of the great prototypes of the early Renaissance. But how did this Anti-Pope John, deposed by the Council of Constance in 1415, earn the unique privilege of a fancy tomb in the baptistry? Why, it was thanks to him that Giovanni di Bicci de' Medici made the family fortune as head banker to the Curia.

## Highlights of Florence

Florence's museums, palaces and churches contain more good art than perhaps any city in Europe, and to see it all without hardship to your eyes, feet and sensibilities would take at least three weeks. If you have only a few days to spend, and if you might never come back again, the highlights will easily take up all of your time – the **Cathedral** and **Baptistry**, the paintings in the **Uffizi** (preferably not all in the same day) and the sculptures in the Bargello, which is more worthy of your brief time than the **Accademia**, where the rubbernecks pile in to see Michelangelo's *David*. Stop in for a look at the eccentric **Orsanmichele**, and see the Arno from the **Ponte Vecchio**, taking in some of the oldest streets in the city.

If your heart leans towards the graceful lyricism of the 1400s, don't miss the **Cathedral Museum** and the Fra Angelicos in **San Marco**; if the lush virtuosity of the 1500s is your cup of tea, visit the Pitti Palace's Galleria Palatina. Two churches on the edges of the centre, **Santa Maria Novella** and **Santa Croce**, are galleries in themselves, containing some of the greatest Florentine art; **Santa Maria del Carmine** has the restored frescoes of Masaccio and company. Devotees of the Michelangelo cult won't want to miss the Medici Chapels and library at **San Lorenzo**. When the stones begin to weary you, head for the oasis of the **Boboli Gardens**. Finally, climb up to **San Miniato**, for the beautiful medieval church and enchanting view over the city.

Florence's 'secondary' sights are just as interesting. You could spend a day walking around old **Fiesole**, or 15 minutes looking at Gozzoli's charming fresco in the **Palazzo Medici-Riccardi**. The **Palazzo Vecchio** has more, but less charming, Medici frescoes. You can see how a wealthy medieval Tuscan merchant lived at the **Palazzo Davanzati**, while the **Museum of the History of Science** will tell you about the scientific side of the Florentine Renaissance; **Santa Trinita**, **Santo Spirito**, **Ognissanti** and the **Annunziata** all contain famous works from the Renaissance. The **Casa Buonarroti** has some early sculptures of Michelangelo; the **Archaeology Museum** has even earlier ones by the Etruscans, Greeks and Egyptians; the Pitti Palace's **Museo degli Argenti** overflows with Medicean jewellery and trinkets. Take a bus or car out to Lorenzo il Magnifico's villa at **Poggio a Caiano**, or to the Medicis' other garden villas: **La Petraia** and **Castello**, or Villa Demidoff at **Pratolino**.

There are two museums with 19th- and 20th-century collections to bring you back to the present: the recently expanded **Galleria d'Arte Moderna** in the Pitti Palace, and the **Collezione della Ragione**. There are two museums founded by Englishmen: the **Horne Museum** with Renaissance art, and the eccentric **Stibbert Museum** with everything but the kitchen sink. Strangest of all are the museums in **La Specola**, featuring stuffed animals and wax figures.

Most of the important museums, excluding the Palazzo Vecchio, are state-run and can be pre-booked. Call **t** 055 294 883.

## The Gates of Paradise

Most historians used to pinpoint the beginning of the 'Renaissance' as the year 1401, when the merchants' guild, the Arte di Calimala, sponsored a competition for the baptistry's north doors. The **South Doors** (the main entrance into the baptistry) had already been completed by Andrea Pisano in 1330, and they give an excellent lesson on the style of the day. The doors are divided into 28 panels in quatrefoil frames and depict scenes from the life of St John the Baptist as well as the eight Cardinal and Theological Virtues; they are formal and elegant works in the best Gothic manner.

The celebrated competition of 1401 – perhaps the first ever held in the annals of art – pitted the seven greatest sculptors of the day against one another. Judgement was based on trial panels on the subject of the Sacrifice of Isaac, and in a dead heat at the end of the day were the two by Brunelleschi and Lorenzo Ghiberti. Both of these are now displayed in the Bargello. Ghiberti's more classical-style figures were eventually judged the better of the two, and it was a serendipitous choice; he devoted nearly the rest of his life to creating the most beautiful bronze doors in the world while Brunelleschi, disgusted by his defeat, went on to build the most perfect dome. Ghiberti's first efforts, the **North Doors** (1403–24), are contained, like Pisano's, in 28 quatrefoil frames. In their scenes on the Life of Christ, the Evangelists, and the Doctors of the Church, you can trace Ghiberti's progress over the 20 years he worked in the increased depth of his compositions, not only visually but dramatically; classical backgrounds begin to fill the frames, ready to break out of their Gothic confines. Ghiberti also designed the lovely floral frame of the doors; the three statues, of John the Baptist, the Levite and the Pharisee, by Francesco Rustici, were based on a design by Leonardo da Vinci and added in 1511.

Ghiberti's work pleased the Arte di Calimala, and they set him loose on another pair of portals, the **East Doors** (1425–52), his masterpiece and one of the most awesome achievements of the age. Here Ghiberti (perhaps under the guidance of Donatello) dispensed with the small Gothic frames and instead cast 10 large panels that depict the Old Testament in Renaissance high gear, reinterpreting the forms of antiquity with a depth and drama that have never been surpassed. Michelangelo declared them 'worthy to be the Gates of Paradise', and indeed it's hard to believe these are people, buildings and trees of bronze and not creatures frozen in time by some celestial alchemy. The doors (they're actually copies – some of the original panels, restored after flood damage, are on display in the Museo dell' Opera del Duomo) have been cleaned recently, and stand in gleaming contrast to the others. In 1996 copies of Andrea Sansovino's marble statues of Christ and John the Baptist (1502) and an 18th-century angel were installed over the doors. The originals had begun to fall to bits in 1974; they too are now in the Museo dell' Opera.

Ghiberti wasn't exactly slow to toot his own horn; according to himself, he personally planned and designed the Renaissance on his own. His unabashedly conceited *Commentarii* were the first attempt at art history and autobiography by an artist, and a work as revolutionary as his doors in its presentation of the creative God-like powers of the artist. It is also a typical exhibition of Florentine pride that he should put busts of his friends among the prophets and sibyls that adorn the frames of the East Doors. Near the centre, the balding figure with arched eyebrows and a little smile is Ghiberti himself.

## The Duomo

*Open Mon–Thurs and Sat 9.30–5, Fri and Sun 1–5.*

For all its importance and prosperity, Florence was one of the last cities to plan a great cathedral. Work began in the 1290s, with the sculptor Arnolfo di Cambio in charge, and from the beginning the Florentines attempted to make up for their delay with sheer audacity. 'It will be so magnificent in size and beauty,' according to a decree of 1296, 'as to surpass anything built by the Greeks and Romans.' In response Arnolfo planned what in its day was the largest church in Catholicism; he confidently laid the foundations for an enormous octagonal crossing 146ft in diameter, then died before working out a way to cover it, leaving future architects the job of designing the biggest dome in the world.

Beyond its presumptuous size, the cathedral of Santa Maria del Fiore shows little interest in contemporary innovations and styles; a visitor from France or England in the 1400s would certainly have found it somewhat drab and architecturally primitive. Visitors today often don't know what to make of it either; they circle confusedly around its grimy, ponderous bulk (this is one of the very few cathedrals in Italy that you can walk completely around). Instead of the striped bravura of Siena or the elegant colonnades of Pisa, they behold an astonishingly eccentric green, white and red pattern of marble rectangles and flowers – like Victorian wallpaper, or as one critic expressed it, 'a cathedral wearing pyjamas'. In the sun, the cathedral under its sublime dome sports festively above the dullish dun and ochre sea of Florence; in dismal weather it sprawls morosely across its piazza like a beached whale tarted up with a lace doily front.

The fondly foolish **façade** cannot be blamed on Arnolfo. His original design, only one-quarter completed, was taken down in a late 16th-century Medici rebuilding programme that never got off the ground. The Duomo turned a blank face to the world until the present neo-Gothic extravaganza was added in 1888. Walk around to the north side to see what many consider a more fitting door, the **Porta della Mandorla** crowned with an Assumption of the Virgin in an almond-shaped frame (hence 'Mandorla') made by Nanni di Banco in 1420.

## Brunelleschi's Dome

*Open Mon–Fri 8.30–7, Sat 8.30–5.40; closed Sun; adm.*

Yet if this behemoth of a cathedral, this St Mary of the Floral Wallpaper, was created for no other reason than to serve as a base for its dome, it would be more than enough. Brunelleschi's dome, more than any landmark, makes Florence Florence. Many have noted how the dome repeats the rhythm of the surrounding hills, echoing them with its height and beauty; from those city streets fortunate enough to have a clear view, it rises among the clouds with all the confident mastery, proportions, and perfect form that characterize the highest aspirations of the Renaissance. But if it seems miraculous, it certainly isn't divine; unlike the dome of the Hagia Sophia, suspended from heaven by a golden chain, Florence's was made by man – one man, to be precise.

Losing the competition for the baptistry doors was a bitter disappointment to Filippo Brunelleschi. His reaction was typically Florentine: not content with being the second-best sculptor, he turned his talents to a field where he thought no one could beat him, launching himself into an intense study of architecture and engineering, visiting Rome and probably Ravenna to snatch secrets from the ancients. When proposals were solicited for the cathedral's dome in 1418, he was ready with a brilliant *tour de force*. Not only would he build the biggest dome of the time, and the most beautiful, but he would do it without any need for expensive supports while work was in progress, making use of a cantilevered system of bricks that could support itself while it ascended.

Brunelleschi studied, then surpassed the technique of the ancients with a system more simple than that of the Pantheon or Hagia Sophia. To the Florentines, a people who could have invented the slogan 'form follows function' for their own tastes in building, it must have come as a revelation: the most logical way of covering the space turned out to be a work of perfect beauty. Brunelleschi, in building this dome, put a crown on the achievements of Florence. After 500 years it is still the city's pride and symbol.

The best way to appreciate Brunelleschi's genius is by touring inside the two concentric shells of the dome (*see* over), but before entering, note the eight marble ribs that define its octagonal shape; hidden inside are the three huge stone chains that bind them together. Work on the balcony around the base of the dome, designed by Giuliano da Sangallo, was halted in 1515 after Michelangelo commented that it resembled a cricket's cage. As for the lantern, the Florentines were famous for their fondness and admiration for Doubting Thomas, and here they showed why. Even though they marvelled at the dome, they still doubted that Brunelleschi could construct a proper lantern, and forced him to submit to yet another competition. He died before it was begun, and it was completed to his design by Michelozzo.

## The Interior

After the façade, the austerity of the Duomo interior is almost startling. There is plenty of room; contemporary writers mention 10,000 souls packed inside to hear the brimstone and hell-fire sermons of Savonarola. Even with that in mind, the Duomo hardly seems a religious building – more a *Florentine* building, with simple arches and counterpoint of grey stone and white plaster, full of old familiar Florentine things. Near the entrance, on the right-hand side, are busts of Brunelleschi and Giotto. On the left wall, posed inconspicuously, are the two most conspicuous monuments to private individuals ever erected by the Florentine Republic. The older one, on the right, is to **Sir John Hawkwood**, the famous English *condottiere* whose name the Italians mangled to Giovanni Acuto, a legendary commander who served Florence for many years and is perhaps best known to English speakers as the hero of *The White Company* by Sir Arthur Conan Doyle. All along, Hawkwood had the promise of the Florentines to build him an equestrian statue after his death; it was a typical Florentine trick to pinch pennies and cheat a dead man, but they hired the greatest master of perspective, Paolo Uccello, to make a fresco that looked like a statue (1436).

Twenty years later, they pulled the same trick again, commissioning another great illusionist, Andrea del Castagno, to paint the non-existent equestrian statue of another *condottiere*, Niccolò da Tolentino. A little further down, Florence commemorates its own secular scripture with Michelino's well-known fresco of Dante, a vision of the poet and his *Paradiso* outside the walls of Florence. Two singular icons of Florence's fascination with science stand at opposite ends of the building: behind the west front, a bizarre clock painted by Uccello, and in the pavement of the left apse, a gnomon fixed by the astronomer Toscanelli in 1475. A beam of sunlight strikes it every year on the day of the summer solstice.

For building the great dome, Brunelleschi was accorded a special honour – he is one of the few Florentines to be buried in the cathedral. His tomb may be seen in the **Excavations of Santa Reparata** (*the stairway descending on the right of the nave; open Mon–Sat 10–5.40; closed Sun; adm*). Arnolfo di Cambio's cathedral was constructed on the ruins of the ancient church of Santa Reparata, which lay forgotten until 1965. Excavations have revealed not only the palaeo-Christian church and its several reconstructions, but also the remains of its Roman predecessor – a rather confusing muddle of walls that have been tidied up in an ambience that resembles an archaeological shopping centre. A coloured model helps explain what is what, and glass cases display items found in the dig, including the spurs of Giovanni de' Medici, who was buried here in 1351. In the ancient crypt of Santa Reparata are 13th-century tomb slabs, and in another section there's a fine pre-Romanesque mosaic pavement.

There is surprisingly little religious art – the Florentines for reasons of their own have carted most of it off into the Cathedral Museum (*see* over). Under the dome are the entrances to the two sacristies, with terracotta lunettes over the doors by Luca della Robbia; the scene of the Resurrection over the north sacristy is one of his earliest and best works. He also did the bronze doors beneath it, with tiny portraits on the handles of Lorenzo il Magnifico and his brother Giuliano de' Medici, targets of the Pazzi conspiracy in 1478. In the middle apse, there is a beautiful bronze urn by Ghiberti containing relics of the Florentine St Zenobius. The only really conventional religious decorations are the hack but scarcely visible frescoes high in the dome (some 200ft up), mostly the work of Vasari. As you stand there squinting at them, try not to think that the cupola weighs an estimated 25,000 tons.

A door on the left aisle near the Dante fresco leads up into the **dome** (*open Mon–Fri 8.30–7 and 1st Sat of the month 8.30–4; adm*). The complicated network of stairs and walks between the inner and outer domes (not too difficult, if occasionally claustrophobic and vertiginous) was designed by Brunelleschi, and offers an insight on how thoroughly the architect thought out the problems of the dome's construction, even inserting hooks to hold up scaffolding for future cleaning or repairs; Brunelleschi installed restaurants to save workers the trouble of descending for meals. There is also no better place to get an idea of the dome's scale; the walls of the inner dome are 13ft thick, and those of the outer dome 6ft. These give the dome enough strength and support to preclude the need for further buttressing.

From the gallery of the dome you can get a good look at the lovely **stained glass** by Uccello, Donatello, Ghiberti and Castagno, in the seven circular windows, or *occhi*, made during the construction of the dome, which are being restored one by one. Further up, the views through the small windows offer tantalizing hints of the breathtaking panorama from the marble lantern at the top. The bronze ball at the very top was added by Verrocchio, and can hold almost a dozen people when open.

## Giotto's Campanile

There's no doubt about it: the dome steals the show on Piazza del Duomo, putting one of Italy's most beautiful bell towers in the shade both figuratively and literally. The dome's great size – 366ft to the bronze ball – makes the campanile look small, though 280ft is not exactly tiny. Giotto was made director of the cathedral works in 1334, and his basic design was completed after his death (1337) by Andrea Pisano and Francesco Talenti. It is difficult to say whether they were entirely faithful to the plan. Giotto was an artist, not an engineer. After he died, his successors realized the thing, then only 40ft high, was about to tumble over, a problem they overcame by doubling the thickness of the walls.

Besides its lovely form, the green, pink and white campanile's major fame rests with Pisano and Talenti's **sculptural reliefs** – a veritable encyclopaedia of the medieval world view with prophets, saints and sibyls, allegories of the planets, virtues and sacraments, the liberal arts and industries (the artist's craft is fittingly symbolized by a winged figure of Daedalus). All of these are copies of the originals now in the Cathedral Museum. If you can take another 400 steps or so, the **terrace** on top (*open summer daily 9–6.50; winter 9–4.20; adm*) offers a slightly different view of Florence and of the cathedral itself.

## Loggia del Bigallo

The most striking secular building on the Piazza del Duomo is the Loggia del Bigallo, south of the baptistry near the beginning of Via de' Calzaiuoli. This 14th-century porch was built for one of Florence's great charitable confraternities, the Misericordia which still has its headquarters across the street and operates the ambulances parked in front; in the 13th and 14th centuries members courageously nursed and buried victims of the plague. The Loggia itself originally served as a lost and found office, although instead of umbrellas it dealt in children; if unclaimed after three days they were sent to foster homes. In the 15th century the Misericordia merged with a similar charitable confraternity called the Bigallo, and works of art accumulated by both organizations over centuries are displayed in the diminutive but choice **Museo del Bigallo**, located next to the loggia at Piazza San Giovanni 1. The most famous picture here is the fresco of *Madonna della Misericordia*, featuring the earliest known view of Florence (1342); other 14th-century works (by Bernardo Daddi, Niccolò di Pietro Gerini and sculptor Alberto Arnoldi) portray the activities of the brotherhood, members of which may still be seen wearing the traditional black hoods that preserve their anonymity.

East of the Loggia del Bigallo is a stone bench labelled the 'Sasso di Dante' – **Dante's Stone** – where the poet would sit and take the air, observing his fellow citizens and watching the construction of the cathedral.

# Museo dell'Opera del Duomo

*Open Mon–Sat 9–7.30, Sun 9–1.40; adm. Please note that at the time of writing not all works are yet in their permanent positions, so some of the details below may change.*

The Cathedral Museum (Piazza del Duomo 9, near the central apse) is one of Florence's finest, and houses both relics from the actual construction of the cathedral and the masterpieces that once adorned it. It reopened in early 2000 after major restructuring to improve the layout and make it more visitor-friendly: there is now full disabled access, better information, a more logical layout, in a more or less chronological order, and greatly increased floor space. The courtyard has been covered by a glass roof and turned into an exhibition room; and there are long-term plans to incorporate two neighbouring buildings into the museum, doubling its size, over the next decade.

The entrance leads into the newly constructed ticket hall – pristine in marble and stone, the same materials as used in the Duomo's construction – and past the bookshop. Just after the entrance are several fragments of Roman reliefs, then two anterooms which contain restored statues or bits of statues that once adorned the façade of the Duomo.

The first hall is devoted to the cathedral's sculptor-architect Arnolfo di Cambio and contains the statues he made to adorn it: the unusual Madonna with the glass eyes, Florence's old patron saints, Reparata and Zenobius, and nasty old Boniface VIII, who sits stiffly on his throne like an Egyptian god. There are the four Evangelists, including a St John by Donatello, and a small collection of ancient works – Roman sarcophagi and an Etruscan cippus carved with dancers. Note the 16th-century 'Libretto', a fold-out display case of saintly odds and ends, all neatly labelled. The Florentines were never enthusiastic about the worship of relics, and long ago they shipped San Girolamo's jawbone, John the Baptist's index finger and St Philip's arm across the street to this museum.

A nearby room contains a collection of altarpieces, triptychs and paintings of saints including Giovanni del Biondo's *Saint Sebastian*. Also here are a series of marble relief panels by Baccio Bandinelli from the altarpiece of the cathedral. A small room adjacent to this contains a section (several fragments pieced together) of the door known as the 'Porta della Mandorla' on the north side of the Duomo. This is an intricately carved marble relief including a small figure of Hercules with his stick, significant in that it was the first representation of the adult male nude and a taste of things to come, more of a statue than a relief. Also in this room are two statues known as *The Profetini*, which once stood over the door and are attributed to the young Donatello.

On the landing of the stairs stands the *Pietà* that Michelangelo intended for his own tomb. The artist, increasingly cantankerous and full of *terribilità* in his old age, became exasperated with this complex work and took a hammer to the arm of the Christ – the first known instance of an artist vandalizing his own creation. His assistant repaired the damage and finished part of the figures of Mary Magdalene and Christ. According to Vasari, the hooded figure of Nicodemus is Michelangelo's self-portrait.

Upstairs, the first room is dominated by the two **Cantorie**, two marble choir balconies with exquisite bas-reliefs. These were made in the 1430s by Luca della Robbia and Donatello. Both works rank among some of the Renaissance's greatest productions. Della Robbia's delightful horde of laughing children dancing, singing and playing instruments is a truly angelic choir, Apollonian in its calm and beauty. It is perhaps the most charming work ever to have been inspired by the forms of antiquity. Donatello's *putti*, by contrast, dance, or rather race, through their quattrocento decorative motifs with fiendish Dionysian frenzy. Grey and weathered prophets by Donatello and others stand along the white walls surveying the proceedings. These originally adorned the façade of the campanile. According to Vasari, while carving the most famous of these, *Habbakuk* (better known as *lo Zuccone*, or 'baldy'), Donatello would mutter under his breath 'Speak, damn you. Speak!' The next room contains the original panels on the Spiritual Progress of Man from Giotto's campanile, made by Andrea Pisano.

The first thing you see as you enter the last room is Donatello's statue *Mary Magdalene*, surely one of the most jarring figures ever sculpted, ravaged by her own piety and penance, her sunken eyes fixed on a point beyond this vale of tears. This room is dedicated to works removed from the baptistry, especially the lavish silver altar (14th–15th-century), made by Florentine goldsmiths, portraying scenes from the life of the Baptist. Antonio Pollaiuolo used the same subject to design the 27 needlework panels that once were part of the priest's vestments. There are two 12th-century Byzantine mosaic miniatures, masterpieces of the intricate, and a St Sebastian triptych by Giovanni del Biondo that may well be the record for arrows; the poor saint looks like a hedgehog.

A ramp now leads into the new part of the museum from the room containing the panels from the campanile. Cases either side of this now display the fascinating collection of pulleys and other instruments that were used in the construction of the cathedral. At the bottom of the ramp on the left you can see Brunelleschi's death mask, facing a model of the lantern, which he was never to see. A window behind this model cleverly gives a close up view of the cupola itself, which is topped by that self-same lantern.

A series of rooms off a long corridor contain bits and pieces brought out of storage. These include the four carved façades, artists' models for the design of the cricket's-cage pattern round the base of the cupola. The corridor then leads into a room whose walls are filled with drawings of the Duomo from the 1875 competition to design the façade.

From here, a staircase leads down into the courtyard where eight of Ghiberti's panels from the *Gates of Paradise* are on display. The original plan was to reconstruct the doors in their entirety, including the surrounds, and then to display them on the huge marble wall which has been constructed in the courtyard. This was due to happen in March 2000. However there were a few inevitable hiccups and the restoration of the final panels is far from finished, and the doors won't be ready for another two years or so; meanwhile this blank marble wall sits there, rather bare but for the three statues at its foot.

# Via de' Calzaiuoli and Piazza della Repubblica

Of all the streets that radiate from the Piazza del Duomo, most people almost intuitively turn down the straight, pedestrian-only Via de' Calzaiuoli, the Roman street that became the main thoroughfare of medieval Florence, linking the city's religious centre with the Piazza della Signoria. Widening of this 'Street of the Shoemakers' in the 1840s has destroyed much of its medieval character, and the only shoe shops to be seen are designer-label. Its fate seems benign, though, compared with what happened to the Mercato Vecchio, in the fit of post-Risorgimento 'progress' that converted it into the **Piazza della Repubblica**, a block to the right along Via Speziali.

On the map, it's easy to pick out the small rectangle of narrow, straight streets around Piazza della Repubblica; these remain unchanged from the little *castrum* of Roman days. At its centre, the old forum deteriorated through the Dark Ages into a shabby market square and the Jewish ghetto, a piquant, densely populated quarter known as the Mercato Vecchio, the epitome of the picturesque for 19th-century tourists but an eyesore for the movers and shakers of the new Italy, who tore down its alleys and miniature *piazze* to create a fit symbol of Florence's reawakening. They erected a triumphal arch to themselves and proudly blazoned it with the inscription 'THE ANCIENT CITY CENTRE RESTORED TO NEW LIFE FROM THE SQUALOR OF CENTURIES'. The sad result of this well-intentioned urban renewal, the Piazza della Repubblica, is one of the most ghastly squares in Italy, a brash intrusion of ponderous 19th-century buildings. Just the same it is popular with locals and tourists alike, closed to traffic and full of outdoor cafés, something of an oasis among the narrow, stern streets of medieval Florence.

From Piazza della Repubblica the natural flow of street life will sweep you down to the **Mercato Nuovo**, the old Straw Market, bustling under a beautiful loggia built by Grand Duke Cosimo in the 1500s. Although you won't see more than a wisp of straw these days, vendors hawk purses, stationery, toys, clothes, umbrellas and knick-knacks. In medieval times this was the merchants' exchange, where any merchant who committed the crime of bankruptcy was publicly spanked before being carted off to prison; in times of peace it sheltered Florence's battle-stained *carroccio*. Florentines often call the market the 'Porcellino' (piglet) after the large bronze boar erected in 1612. The current boar was put in place in 1999, a copy of a copy of the ancient statue in the Uffizi. The drool spilling from the side of its mouth reminds us that, unlike Rome, Florence is no splashy city of springs and fountains. Rub the piglet's shiny snout, and supposedly destiny will one day bring you back to Florence. The pungent aroma of the tripe sandwiches sold nearby may give you second thoughts.

## Orsanmichele

*Open daily 9–12 and 4–6.*

There is a wonderfully eccentric church on Via de' Calzaiuoli that looks like no other church in the world: Orsanmichele rises up in a tall, neat three-storey rectangle. It was built on the site of ancient San Michele ad Hortum (popularly reduced to

'Orsanmichele'), a 9th-century church located near a vegetable garden, which the *comune* destroyed in 1240 to erect a grain market; after a fire in 1337 the current market building (by Francesco Talenti and others) was erected, with a loggia on the ground floor and emergency storehouses on top where grain was kept against a siege.

The original market had a pilaster with a painting of the Virgin that became increasingly celebrated for performing miracles. The area around the Virgin became known as the Oratory, and when Talenti reconstructed the market, his intention was to combine both its secular and religious functions; each pilaster of the loggia was assigned to a guild to adorn with an image of its patron saint. In 1380, when the market was relocated, the entire ground floor was given over to the functions of the church, and Francesco Talenti's talented son Simone was given the task of closing in the arcades with lovely Gothic windows, later bricked in.

The church, however, is most famous as a showcase of 15th-century Florentine sculpture; there is no better place to get an idea of the stylistic innovations that succeeded one another throughout the decades. Each guild sought to outdo the others by commissioning the finest artists of the day to carve their patron saints and create elaborate canopied niches to hold them. The first statue to the left of the door is one of the oldest; Ghiberti's bronze *St John the Baptist*, erected in 1416 for the Arte di Calimala, was the first life-sized Renaissance statue cast in bronze. Continuing to the left on Via de' Lamberti you can compare it with Donatello's *St Mark*, patron of the linen dealers and used-cloth merchants. Finished in 1411, it is considered the first free-standing marble statue of the Renaissance.

The niches continue around Via dell'Arte della Lana, named after the Wool Merchants' Guild, the richest after that of the Bankers. Their headquarters, the **Palazzo dell'Arte della Lana**, is linked by an overhead arch with Orsanmichele; built in 1308, it was restored in 1905 in a delightful William Morris style of medieval pictur-esque. The first statue on this façade of Orsanmichele is *St Eligio*, patron of smiths, by Nanni di Banco (1415), with a niche embellished with the guild's emblem (black pincers) and a bas-relief below showing one of this rather obscure saint's miracles – apparently he shod a horse the hard way, by cutting off its hoof, shoeing it, then sticking it back on the leg. The other two statues on this street are bronzes by Ghiberti, the Wool Guild's *St Stephen* (1426) and the Exchange Guild's *St Matthew* (1422), the latter an especially fine work in a classical niche.

On the Via Orsanmichele façade stands a copy of Donatello's famous *St George* (the original is now to be found in the Bargello) done in 1417 for the Armourers' Guild, with a dramatic predella of the saint slaying the dragon, also by Donatello, that is one of the first known works making use of perspective; next are the Stonecutters' and Carpenters' Guild's *Four Crowned Saints* (1415, by Nanni di Banco), inspired by Roman statues. Nanni also contributed the Shoemakers' *St Philip* (1415), while the next figure, *St Peter*, is commonly attributed to Donatello (1413). Around the corner on Via Calzaiuoli stands the bronze *St Luke*, patron of the Judges and Notaries, by Giambologna, a work of 1602 in a 15th-century niche, and the *Doubting of St Thomas* by Andrea del Verrocchio (1484), made not for a guild but the Tribunal of

Merchandise, who like St Thomas wanted to be certain before making a judgement. In the rondels above some of the niches are terracottas of the guilds' symbols by Luca della Robbia.

Orsanmichele's dark **interior** (*open Mon–Fri 9–12 and 4–6, Sat and Sun 9–1 and 4–6; closed first and last Mon of month*) is ornate and cosy, with more of the air of a guild-hall than a church. It makes a picturebook medieval setting for one of the masterpieces of the trecento: Andrea Orcagna's beautiful Gothic **Tabernacle** (*open 9–12 and 4–6*), a large, exquisite work in marble, bronze and coloured glass framing a contemporary painting of the Madonna (either by Bernardo Daddi or Orcagna himself), replacing the miraculous one, lost in a fire. The Tabernacle was commissioned by survivors of the 1348 Black Death. On the walls and pilasters are faded 14th-century frescoes of saints, placed as if members of the congregation; if you look at the pilasters on the left as you enter and along the right wall you can see the old chutes used to transfer grain.

# Piazza della Signoria

Italian city builders are renowned for effortlessly creating beautiful squares, but it's an art where the Florentines are generally all thumbs. Only here, in the city's civic stage do they achieve a grand, meaningful space, a much-needed antidote to the stone gullies of the ancient centre, dominated by the sombre fortress and tower of the Palazzo Vecchio and a lively gathering of some of the best and worst of Florentine sculpture.

Although the Piazza della Signoria currently serves as Great Aunt Florence's drawing-room-cum-tourist-overflow-tank, in the old days it saw the public assemblies of the republic, which in Florence meant that the square often degenerated into a battleground for impossibly inscrutable internecine quarrels. These could be stirred up to mythic levels of violence; in the 14th century a man was eaten by a crowd maddened by a political speech. Such speeches were given from the *arringhiera*, or oration terrace, in front of the Palazzo Vecchio, a word which gave us 'harangue'. It was in the Piazza della Signoria that Savonarola ignited his notorious Bonfire of Vanities in 1497, and here, too, the following year, the disillusioned Florentines ignited Savonarola himself. A small plaque in the pavement marks the exact spot, not far from Ammanati's fountain.

If, on the other hand, trouble came from without, the Florentines would toll the famous bell in the tower of the Palazzo Vecchio, and the square would rapidly fill with the gonfalons of the citizens' militia and the guilds. 'We will sound our trumpets!' threatened the French king Charles VIII, when the Florentines refused to shell out enough florins to make him and his army leave town. 'And we will ring our bell!' countered the courageous republican Piero Capponi – a threat that worked; Charles had to settle for a smaller sum. When Alessandro de' Medici was restored as duke of Tuscany three years later, one of his first acts was to smash the bell as a symbol of Florence's lost liberty.

Having a citizen's militia, as opposed to depending on foreign mercenaries, answered one of Machiavelli's requirements for a well-governed state. Training was taken fairly seriously; to build up their endurance, the republic's citizens played a ball game similar to rugby, believed to be descended from a Roman sport. Known these days as *Calcio in Costume*, it is played every June on a special ground of sand in the Piazza Santa Croce, and it's good fun to watch the usually immaculate Florentines in their Renaissance duds mixing it up in the dirt (fighting is more than permitted, as long as it's one to one).

In 1974, while searching for signs of the original paving stones of the Piazza, the *Soprintendenza ai Beni Archeologici* found, much to their surprise, an underground medieval casbah of narrow lanes, houses and wells – the ruins of 12th-century Ghibelline Florence, built over the baths and other portions of Roman and Etruscan *Florentia*. The *comune* ordered the excavations filled in; from the city's point of view, the piazza, essential to the essential tourist trade, was untouchable. In the 1980s, the communal government fell, and the excavations were reopened on the portion of the piazza near the loggia. There are proposals to excavate the rest of the square, much to the horror of the *comune*, and to create eventually an underground museum similar to the one in Assisi. Until the issue is decided, don't be surprised to find the piazza full of gaping holes.

## The Loggia dei Lanzi

Generally of a lower key than a political harangue was the *parlamento*, a meeting of eligible male citizens to vote on an important issue (usually already decided by the bosses). On these occasions, the Florentines heard speeches from the platform of the graceful three-arched Loggia dei Lanzi, also known as the Loggia della Signoria or the Loggia dell'Orcagna, after Andrea Orcagna, the probable architect. Completed in 1382, when pointed Gothic was still the rage, the Loggia with its lofty round arches looks back to classical antiquity and forward to the Renaissance; it is the germ of Brunelleschi's revolutionary architecture. If the impenetrable stone Palazzo Vecchio is a symbol of the republic's strength and authority, the Loggia dei Lanzi is a symbol of its capacity for beauty, a vote for the gentle, floral side of its personality.

The loggia received its name 'of the lances' after the hated Swiss lancers, the private bodyguard of Cosimo I. It was Cosimo who, in 1545, was responsible for the *Perseus*, not by commissioning it from the volatile Cellini, but by scoffing, saying a life-sized bronze statue was impossible. Cellini set out to prove him wrong, although it took ten years, and cost his health and the roof of his house which caught fire as he stoked the furnace to melt the bronze. The result, his masterpiece, is a Mannerist *tour de force* with its attention to detail and expressive composition, graceful and poised atop the gruesome bleeding trunk, eyes averted from the horrible head with its petrifying eyes. The subject was a hint to the Florentines, to inspire their gratitude for Grand Ducal rule which spared them from the monstrosity of their own unworkable republic. During his restoration *Perseus* was removed to a workshop near the Uffizi so that the restoration could be seen by the public. He returned to his rightful place in the loggia in 2000.

Another gamble was behind the *Rape of the Sabines* (1583). Giambologna took a rough block of marble all the other sculptors in Florence had rejected as impossible to work with, on the bet that he would be able to do something with it. Its curious shape 'liberated', as Michelangelo would say, became an old man, a young man and a woman spiraling upwards in a fluid *contrapposto* convulsion, one of the first sculptures designed to be seen from all sides: the title was stuck on after its completion. The loggia also shelters Giambologna's less successful *Hercules and Nessus*, a chorus line of six Roman vestal wallflowers, and several other works that contribute to the rather curious effect at night, of people at a wild party frozen into stone by Medusa's magical gaze.

The first two statues that were placed in the square were carried there by republican enthusiasm. Donatello's *Judith and Holofernes* was hauled from the Medici palace and placed here in 1494 as a symbol of the defeat of tyranny. Michelangelo's *David* was equally seen as the embodiment of republican triumph (when it was finished in 1504, the Medici were in exile), though it is doubtful whether Michelangelo himself had such symbolism in mind, as the statue was intended to stand next to the cathedral, only to be shanghaied to the Piazza della Signoria by eager republican partisans.

It was replaced by a copy in 1873 when the original was relocated with much pomp on a specially built train to the Accademia. Later Florentine sculptors attempted to rival the *David*, especially the awful Baccio Bandinelli, who managed to get the commission to create a pendant to the statue and boasted that he could surpass Il Divino himself. The pathetic result, *Hercules and Cacus*, was completed in 1534; as a reward for his efforts, Bandinelli had to listen to his arch-enemy Cellini insult the statue in front of their patron, Cosimo I. An 'old sack full of melons' he called it, bestowing what has since become, for all practical purposes, the sculpture's alternative title.

Another overgrown victim of the chisel stands at the corner of the Palazzo Vecchio. Ammanati's **Neptune Fountain** (1575) was dubbed *Il Biancone* ('Big Whitey') almost as soon as it was unveiled; Michelangelo felt sorry for the huge block of marble Ammanati 'ruined' to produce Neptune, a lumpy, bloated symbol of Cosimo I's naval victories, who stands arrogantly over a low basin and a few half-hearted spurts of water, pulled along by four struggling sea steeds, mere hobby-horses compared with Big Whitey himself.

The last colossus to be found in the Piazza della Signoria is the *Equestrian Monument to Cosimo I* by Giambologna (1595), the only large-scale equestrian bronze of the Late Renaissance. The scheme on the panels below the statue depicts scenes of Cosimo's brutal conquest of Siena, and of the 'Florentine Senate' and the Pope conferring the Grand Dukedom on Cosimo. Directly behind Cosimo stands the **Tribunale di Mercanzia**, built in the 14th century as a commercial court for merchants of the guilds and adorned with heraldic arms. To the left of this (No.7) is a fine, 16th-century contribution, the **Palazzo Uguccioni**, very much in the spirit of High Renaissance in Rome, and sometimes attributed to a design by Raphael.

## Palazzo Vecchio

*Open in summer Tues, Wed and Sat 9–7, Mon and Fri 9am–11pm,
Thurs and Sun 9–2; in winter Fri–Wed 9–7, Thurs 9–2; adm.*

When Goethe made his blitz-tour of Florence, the Palazzo Vecchio (also called the Palazzo della Signoria) helped pull the wool over his eyes. 'Obviously,' thought the great poet, 'the people...enjoyed a lucky succession of good governments' – a remark which, as Mary McCarthy wrote, could make the angels in heaven weep. But none of Florence's chronic factionalism mars Arnolfo di Cambio's temple of civic aspirations, part council hall and part fortress. In many ways, the Palazzo Vecchio is the ideal of stone Florence: rugged and imposing, with a rusticated façade that was to inspire so many of the city's private palaces, yet designed according to the proportions of the Golden Section of the ancient Greeks. Its dominant feature, the 308ft tower, is a typical piece of Florentine bravado, for long the highest point in the city.

The Palazzo Vecchio occupies the site of the old Roman theatre and the medieval Palazzo dei Priori. In the 13th century this earlier palace was flattened along with the Ghibelline quarter interred under the piazza, and in 1299 the now ascendant Guelphs called upon Arnolfo di Cambio, master builder of the cathedral, to design the most impressive 'Palazzo del Popolo' (as the building was originally called) possible, with an eye to upstaging rival cities. The palace's unusual trapezoidal shape is often, but rather dubiously, explained as Guelph care not to have any of the building touch land once owned by Ghibellines. One doubts that even in the 13th century property realities allowed such delicacy of sentiments; nor does the theory explain why the tower has swallowtail Ghibelline crenellations, as opposed to the square Guelph ones on the palace itself. Later additions to the rear of the palace have obscured its shape even more, though the façade is essentially as Arnolfo built it, except for the bet-hedging monogram over the door hailing Christ the king of Florence, put up in the nervous days of 1529, when the imperial army of Charles V was on its way to destroy the last Florentine republic; the inscription replaces an earlier one left by Savonarola. The room at the top of the tower was used as prison for celebrities and dubbed the *alberghetto*; inmates in 'the little hotel' included Cosimo il Vecchio before his brief exile, and Savonarola, who spent his last months, between torture sessions, enjoying a superb view of the city before his execution in the piazza below.

Palazzo Vecchio recently found a new claim to fame as the setting for some of the more gruesome scenes in the filming of *Hannibal*, the sequel to *The Silence of the Lambs*, when an Italian detective ends up hanging from the balcony under the tower with his entrails dangling!

## Inside the Palazzo Vecchio

*Open Mon–Wed, Fri and Sat 9–7, also in summer Mon and Fri
9am–11pm; Sun and hols 9–2; closed Thurs; adm.*

Today the Palazzo Vecchio serves as Florence's city hall, but nearly all its historical rooms are open to the public. With few exceptions, the interior decorations date from the time of Cosimo I, when he moved his Grand Ducal self from the Medici palace in

1540. To politically 'correct' its acres of walls and ceilings in the shortest amount of time, he turned to his court artist Giorgio Vasari, famed more for the speed at which he could execute a commission than for its quality. On the ground floor of the palazzo, before you buy your ticket, you can take a look at some of Vasari's more elaborate handiwork in the **Courtyard**, redone for the occasion of Francesco I's unhappy marriage to the plain and stupid Habsburg Joanna of Austria in 1565.

Vasari's suitably grand staircase ascends to the largest room in the palace, the vast **Salone dei Cinquecento**. The *salone* was added at the insistence of Savonarola for meetings of the 500-strong Consiglio Maggiore, the reformed republic's democratic assembly. Art's two reigning divinities, Leonardo da Vinci and Michelangelo, were commissioned in 1503 to paint the two long walls of the *salone* in a kind of Battle of the Brushes to which the city eagerly looked forward. Unfortunately, neither of the artists came near to completing the project; Leonardo managed to fresco a section of the wall, using the experimental techniques that were to prove the undoing of his *Last Supper* in Milan, while Michelangelo only completed the cartoons before being summoned to Rome by Julius II, who required the sculptor of the *David* to pander to his own personal megalomania.

In the 1560s Vasari removed what was left of Leonardo's efforts and refrescoed the room as a celebration of Cosimo's military triumphs over Pisa and Siena, complete with an apotheosis of the Grand Duke on the ceiling. These wall scenes are inane; big, busy, crowded with men and horses who appear to have all the substance of overcooked pasta. The sculptural groups lining the walls of this almost uncomfortably large room (the Italian parliament sat here from 1865 to 1870 when Florence was the capital) are only slightly more stimulating; even Michelangelo's *Victory*, on the wall opposite the entrance, is more virtuosity than vision: a vacuous young idiot posing with one knee atop a defeated old man still half-submerged in stone, said to be a self-portrait of the sculptor, which lends the work a certain bitter poignancy. The neighbouring work, a muscle-bound *Hercules and Diomedes* by Vicenzo de' Rossi, probably was inevitable in this city obsessed by the possibilities of the male nude.

Beyond the *salone*, behind a modern glass door, is a much more intriguing room the size of a closet. This is the **Studiolo of Francesco I**, designed by Vasari in 1572 for Cosimo's melancholic and reclusive son, where he would escape to brood over his real interests in natural curiosities and alchemy. The little study, windowless and more than a little claustrophobic, has been restored to its original appearance, lined with allegorical paintings by Vasari, Bronzino and Allori, and bronze statuettes by Giambologna and Ammannati, their refined, polished, and erotic mythological subjects part of a carefully thought-out 16th-century programme on Man and Nature. The lower row of paintings conceals Francesco's secret cupboards where he kept his most precious belongings, his pearls and crystals and gold.

After the *salone* a certain fuzziness begins to set in. Cosimo I's propaganda machine in league with Vasari's fresco factory produced room after room of self-glorifying Medicean puffery. The first series of rooms, known as the **Quartiere di Leone X**, carry ancestor-worship to extremes, each chamber dedicated to a different Medici: in the first Cosimo il Vecchio returns from exile amid tumultuous acclaim; in the second Lorenzo il Magnifico receives the ambassadors in the company of a dignified giraffe; the third and fourth are dedicated to the Medici popes, while the fifth, naturally, is for Cosimo I, who gets the most elaborate treatment of all.

Upstairs the next series of rooms is known as the **Quartiere degli Elementi**, with more works of Vasari and his studio, depicting allegories of the elements. In a small room, called **Terrazzo di Giunone**, is the original of Verrocchio's boy with the dolphin, from the courtyard fountain. A balcony across the Salone dei Cinquecento leads to the **Quartiere di Eleonora di Toledo**, Mrs Cosimo I's private apartments. Of special note here is her chapel, one of the masterpieces of Bronzino, who seemed to relish the opportunity to paint something besides Medici portraits. The **Sala dell' Udienza**, beyond the second chapel, has a magnificent quattrocento coffered ceiling by Benedetto and Giuliano da Maiano, and walls painted with rather fine pomp by Mannerist Francesco Salviati (1550–60).

The last room, the **Sala dei Gigli** ('of the lilies') boasts another fine ceiling by the da Maiano brothers; it contains Donatello's restored bronze *Judith and Holofernes*, a late and rather gruesome work of 1455; the warning to tyrants inscribed on its base was added when the statue was abducted from the Medici palace and placed in the Piazza della Signoria. Off the Sala dei Gigli are two small rooms of interest: the **Guardaroba**, or unique 'wardrobe' adorned with 57 maps painted by Fra Egnazio Danti in 1563, depicting all the world known at the time. The **Cancelleria** was Machiavelli's office from 1498 to 1512, when he served the republic as a secretary and diplomat. He is commemorated with a bust and a portrait. Poor Machiavelli died bitter and unaware of the notoriety that his works would one day bring him, and he would probably be amazed to learn that his very name had become synonymous with cunning, amoral intrigue. After losing his job upon the return of the Medici, and at one point being tortured and imprisoned on a false suspicion of conspiracy, Machiavelli was forced to live in idleness in the country, where he wrote his political works and two fine plays, feverishly trying to return to favour, even dedicating his most famous book, *The Prince*, to the incompetent Lorenzo, Duke of Urbino; his concern throughout was to advise realistically, without mincing words, the fractious and increasingly weak Italians on how to create a strong state. His evil reputation came from openly stating what rulers do, rather than what they would like other people to think they do.

The **Collezione Loeser**, a fine assortment of Renaissance art left to the city in 1928 by Charles Loeser, the Macy's department-store heir, is also housed in the Palazzo Vecchio, in the mezzanine before you exit the museum.

## Collezione A. Della Ragione

*Open Wed–Mon, entry at 9am, 10.30am and 12 noon; closed Tues; adm.*

After the pomposity of the Palazzo Vecchio and a Campari cure at the Piazza della Signoria's Café Rivoire, you may be in the mood to reconsider the 20th century. The best place to do this in Florence is at its only museum of modern art, located on the Piazza della Signoria, above the Cassa di Risparmio bank (*but about to move to the* renovated *Complesso delle Oblate* in Via Sant'Egidio 21, near the Museo di Firenze Com'Era, see p.181). There are typical still lifes by De Pisis; equally still landscapes by Carlo Carra; mysterious baths by De Chirico; Tuscan landscapes by Mario Mafai, Antonio Donghi and Ottone Rosai; a speedy Futurist horse by Fortunato Depero and a window with doves by Gino Severini; a number of richly coloured canvases by Renato Guttuso and paintings after Tintoretto by Emilio Vedova, and many others, surprises, perhaps, for those unfamiliar with living Italians as opposed to dead ones.

## The Uffizi

*Queues in the summer are very common; try to arrive early.*
*Open summer Tues–Fri 8.30–9, Sat 8.30–12 midnight, Sun 8.30–8;*
*winter Tues–Sun 8.15–6.50; adm exp. You can now pre-book by phone,*
*t 055 294 883: pay at the door when you pick up your ticket.*

Florence has the most fabulous art museum in Italy, and as usual we have the Medici to thank; for the building that holds these treasures, however, credit goes to Grand Duke Cosimo's much maligned court painter. Poor Giorgio Vasari! His roosterish boastfulness and the conviction that his was the best of all possible artistic worlds, set next to his very modest talents, have made him a comic figure in most art criticism. Even the Florentines don't like him. On one of the rare occasions when he tried his hand as an architect, though, he gave Florence something to be proud of. The Uffizi ('offices') were built as Cosimo's secretariat, incorporating the old mint (producer of the first gold florins in 1252), the archives and the large church of San Pier Scheraggio, with plenty of room for the bureaucrats needed to run Cosimo's efficient, modern state. The matched pair of arcaded buildings have coldly elegant façades that conceal Vasari's surprising innovation: iron reinforcements that make the huge amount of window area possible and keep the building stable on the soft sandy ground. It was a trick that would be almost forgotten until the Crystal Palace and the first American skyscrapers. Almost from the start the Medici began to store some of their huge collection in parts of the building. There are galleries in the world with more works of art – the Uffizi counts some 1,800 – but the Uffizi overwhelms by the fact that everything in it is worth looking at.

The Uffizi has undergone major **reorganization** in the last couple of years. Some of this involved the restoration of remaining damage after the bomb (all but a very few paintings are now back on display), but improvements have also been made on a practical level. The most significant changes involve the ground floor which housed the state archive. Major restoration of the vaulted rooms has resulted in a vastly improved space; there are now three entrances (for individuals, for groups and for pre-paid tickets), bookshops, cloakrooms, video and computer facilities and information desks.

If you are particularly keen on seeing a certain painting, note that rooms may be temporarily closed when you visit; this often seems to depend on staff availability. There is a list of these closures at the ticket counters. For the moment, some works are still hung out of chronological order, and the rooms containing work by Caravaggio and Rubens are closed until further notice (although two of the Caravaggios are presently hung in room 16 – *see* over).

From the ticket counter you can take the lift or sweeping grand stair up to the second floor, where the Medici once had a huge theatre, now home to the **Cabinet of Drawings and Prints**. Although the bulk of this extensive and renowned collection is only open to scholars with special permission, a roomful of tempting samples gives a hint at what they have a chance to see.

Nowadays one thinks of the Uffizi as primarily a gallery of paintings, but for some hundred years after its opening, visitors came almost exclusively for the fine collection of Hellenistic and Roman marbles. Most of these were collected in Rome by Medici cardinals, and not a few were sources of Renaissance inspiration. The **Vestibule** at the top of the stair contains some of the best, together with Flemish and Tuscan tapestries made for Cosimo I and his successors. **Room 1**, usually shut, contains excellent early Roman sculpture.

## Rooms 2–6: 13th and 14th centuries

The Uffizi's paintings are arranged in chronological order, the better to educate its visitors on trends in Italian art. The roots of the Early Renaissance are most strikingly revealed in **Room 2**, dedicated to the three great **Maestà** altarpieces by the masters of the 13th century. All portray the same subject of the Madonna and Child enthroned with angels. The one on the right, by Cimabue, was painted around the year 1285 and represents a breaking away from the flat, stylized Byzantine tradition. To the left is the so-called *Rucellai Madonna*, painted around the same period by the Sienese Duccio di Buoninsegna for Santa Maria Novella. It resembles Cimabue's in many ways, but with a more advanced technique for creating depth, and the bright colouring that characterizes the Sienese school. Giotto's altarpiece, painted some 25 years later, takes a great leap forward, not only in his use of perspective, but in the arrangement of the angels, standing naturally, and in the portrayal of the Virgin, gently smiling, with real fingers and breasts.

To the left, **Room 3** contains representative Sienese works of the 14th century, with a beautiful Gothic *Annunciation* (1333) by Simone Martini and the brothers Pietro and Ambrogio Lorenzetti. **Room 4** is dedicated to 14th-century Florentines: Bernardo Daddi, Nardo di Cione, and the delicately coloured *San Remigio Pietà* by Giottino. **Rooms 5 and 6** portray Italian contributions to the International Gothic school, most dazzlingly Gentile da Fabriano's *Adoration of the Magi* (1423), two good works by Lorenzo Monaco, and the *Thebaid* of Gherardo Starnina, depicting the rather unusual activities of the 4th-century monks of St Pancratius of Thebes, in Egypt; a composition strikingly like Chinese scroll scenes of hermits.

## Rooms 7–9: Early Renaissance

In the Uffizi, at least, it's but a few short steps from the superbly decorative International Gothic to the masters of the Early Renaissance. **Room 7** contains minor works by Fra Angelico, Masaccio and Masolino, and three masterpieces. Domenico

Veneziano's pastel *Madonna and Child with Saints* (1448) is one of the rare pictures by this Venetian master who died a pauper in Florence. It is a new departure not only for its soft colours but for the subject matter, unifying the enthroned Virgin and saints in one panel, in what is known as a *Sacra Conversazione*. Piero della Francesca's famous *Double Portrait of the Duke Federigo da Montefeltro and his Duchess Battista Sforza of Urbino* (1465) depicts one of Italy's noblest Renaissance princes – and surely the one with the most distinctive nose. Piero's ability to create perfectly still, timeless worlds is even more evident in the allegorical 'Triumphs' of the Duke and Duchess painted on the back of their portraits. A similar stillness and fascination floats over into the surreal in Uccello's *Rout of San Romano* (1456), or at least the third of it still present (the other two panels are in the Louvre and London's National Gallery; all three once decorated the bedroom of Lorenzo il Magnifico in the Medici palace). Both Piero and Uccello were deep students of perspective, but Uccello went half-crazy; applying his principles to a violent battle scene has left us one of the most provocative works of all time – a vision of warfare in suspended animation, with pink, white and blue toy horses, robot-like knights, and rabbits bouncing in the background.

**Room 8** is devoted to the works of the rascally romantic Fra Filippo Lippi, whose ethereally lovely Madonnas were modelled after his brown-eyed nun. In his *Coronation of the Virgin* (1447) she kneels in the foreground with two children, while the artist, dressed in a brown habit, looks dreamily towards her; in his celebrated *Madonna and Child with Two Angels* (1445) she plays the lead before the kind of mysterious landscape Leonardo would later perfect. Lippi taught the art of enchanting Madonnas to his student Botticelli, who has some lovely works in this room and the next; Alesso Baldovinetti, a pupil of the far more holy Fra Angelico, painted the room's beautiful *Annunciation* (1447).

**Room 9** has two small scenes from the *Labours of Hercules* (1470) by Antonio Pollaiuolo, whose interest in anatomy, muscular expressiveness and violence presages a strain in Florentine art that would culminate in the great Mannerists. He worked with his younger brother Piero on the refined, elegant *SS. Vincent, James and Eustace*, transferred here from San Miniato. This room also contains the Uffizi's best-known forgery: *The Young Man in a Red Hat* or self-portrait of Filippino Lippi, believed to have been the work of a clever 18th-century English art dealer who palmed it off on the Grand Dukes.

## Botticelli: Rooms 10–14

To accommodate the bewitching art of 'Little Barrels' and his throngs of 20th-century admirers, the Uffizi converted four small rooms into one great Botticellian shrine. Although his masterpieces displayed here have become almost synonymous with the Florentine Renaissance at its most spring-like and charming, they were not publicly displayed until the beginning of the 19th century, nor given much considera-tion outside Florence until the turn of the century. Botticelli's best works date from the days when he was a darling of the Medici – family members crop up most noticeably in the *Adoration of the Magi* (1476), where you can pick out Cosimo il Vecchio, Lorenzo il Magnifico and Botticelli himself (in the right foreground, in a yellow robe, gazing at the spectator). His *Annunciation* is a graceful, cosmic dance between the Virgin and the Angel Gabriel. In the *Tondo of the Virgin of the Pomegranate* the lovely melancholy goddess who was to become his Venus makes her first appearance.

Botticelli is best known for his sublime mythological allegories, nearly all painted for the Medici and inspired by the Neoplatonic, humanistic and hermetic currents that pervaded the intelligentsia of the late 15th century. Perhaps no painting has been debated so fervently as *La Primavera* (1478). This hung for years in the Medici Villa at Castello, and it is believed that the subject of the Allegory of Spring was suggested by Marsilio Ficino, one of the great natural magicians of the Renaissance, and that the figures represent the 'beneficial' planets able to dispel sadness. *Pallas and the Centaur* has been called another subtle allegory of Medici triumph – the rings of Athena's gown are supposedly a family symbol. Other interpretations see the taming of the sorrowful centaur as a melancholy comment on reason and civilization.

Botticelli's last great mythological painting, *The Birth of Venus*, was commissioned by Lorenzo di Pierfrancesco and inspired by a poem by Poliziano, Lorenzo il Magnifico's Latin and Greek scholar, who described how Zephyr and Chloris blew the newborn goddess to shore on a scallop shell, while Hora hastened to robe her, a scene Botticelli portrays once again with dance-like rhythm and delicacy of line. Yet the goddess of love floats towards the spectator with an expression of wistfulness – perhaps reflecting the artist's own feelings of regret. For artistically, the poetic, decorative style he perfected in this painting would be disdained and forgotten in his own life-time. Spiritually, Botticelli also turned a corner after creating this haunting, uncanny beauty – his and Florence's farewell to a road not taken. Although Vasari's biography of Botticelli portrays a prankster rather than a sensitive soul, the painter absorbed more than any other artist the *fin-de-siècle* neuroticism that beset the city with the rise of Savonarola. So thoroughly did he reject his Neoplatonism that he would only accept commissions of sacred subjects or supposedly edifying allegories like his *Calumny*, a small but rather disturbing work, and a fitting introduction to the dark side of the quattrocento psyche.

This large room also contains works by Botticelli's contemporaries. There are two paintings of the *Adoration of the Magi*, one by Ghirlandaio and one by Filippino Lippi, which show the influence of Leonardo's unfinished but radical work in pyramidal composition (in the next room); Leonardo himself got the idea from the large *Portinari Altarpiece* (1471), at the end of the room, a work by Hugo Van der Goes, brought back from Bruges by Medici agent Tommaso Portinari.

## Rooms 15–24: More Renaissance

**Room 15** is dedicated to the Florentine works of Leonardo da Vinci's early career. Here are works by his master Andrea Verrocchio, including the *Baptism of Christ*, in which the young Leonardo painted the angel on the left. Modern art critics believe the large *Annunciation* (1475) is almost entirely by Leonardo's hand – the soft faces, the botanical details, the misty, watery background would become the trademarks of his magical brush. Most influential, however, was his unfinished *Adoration of the*

*Magi* (1481), a highly unconventional composition that Leonardo abandoned when he left Florence for Milan. Although at first glance it's hard to make out much more than a mass of reddish chiaroscuro, the longer you stare, the better you'll see the serene Madonna and Child surrounded by a crowd of anxious, troubled humanity, with an exotic background of ruins, trees and horsemen, all charged with expressive energy.

Other artists in Room 15 include Leonardo's peers: Lorenzo di Credi, whose religious works have eerie garden-like backgrounds, and the nutty Piero di Cosimo, whose dreamy *Perseus Liberating Andromeda* includes an endearing mongrel of a dragon that gives even the most reserved Japanese tourist fits of giggles. Tuscan maps adorn **Room 16**, as well as scenes by Hans Memling. Temporarily housed here, away from their normal home in Room 43, are Caravaggio's *Bacchus* and *The Head of Medusa*, believed to be self-portraits. In its day the fleshy, heavy-eyed *Bacchus*, half portrait and half still life, but lacking the usual mythological appurtenances, was considered highly iconoclastic.

The octagonal **Tribuna** (Room 18) with its mother-of-pearl dome and *pietra dura* floor and table was built by Buontalenti in 1584 for Francesco I and, like the Studiolo in the Palazzo Vecchio, was designed to hold Medici treasures. For centuries the best-known of these was the *Venus de' Medici*, a 2nd-century BC Greek sculpture, farcically claimed as a copy of Praxiteles' celebrated *Aphrodite of Cnidos*, the most erotic statue in antiquity. In the 18th century, amazingly, this rather ordinary girl was considered the greatest sculpture in Florence; today most visitors walk right by without a second glance. Other antique works include the *Wrestlers* and the *Knife Grinder*, both copies of Pergamese originals, the *Dancing Faun*, the *Young Apollo*, and the *Sleeping Hermaphrodite* in the adjacent room, which is usually curtained off.

The real stars of the Tribuna are the Medici court portraits, many of them by Bronzino, who was not only able to catch the likeness of Cosimo I, Eleanor of Toledo and their children, but could also aptly portray the spirit of the day – these are people who took themselves very seriously indeed. They have for company Vasari's posthumous portrait of *Lorenzo il Magnifico* and Pontormo's *Cosimo il Vecchio*, Andrea del Sarto's *Girl with a Book by Petrarch*, and Rosso Fiorentino's *Angel Musician*, an enchanting work entirely out of place in this stodgy temple.

Two followers of Piero della Francesca, Perugino and Luca Signorelli, hold pride of place in **Room 19**; Perugino's *Portrait of a Young Man* is believed to be modelled on his pupil Raphael. Signorelli's *Tondo of the Holy Family* was to become the inspiration for Michelangelo's (*see* opposite). The room also contains Lorenzo di Credi's *Venus*, a charmer inspired by Botticelli. The Germans appear in **Room 20**, led by Dürer and his earliest known work, the *Portrait of his Father* (1490), done at age 19, and *The Adoration of the Magi* (1504), painted after his first trip to Italy. Also here are Lucas Cranach's Teutonic *Adam and Eve* and his *Portrait of Martin Luther* (1543), not someone you'd necessarily expect to see in Florence. **Room 21** is dedicated to the great Venetians, most famously Bellini and his uncanny *Sacred Allegory* (1490s), the meaning of which has never been satisfactorily explained. There are two minor works by the elusive Giorgione, and a typically weird *St Dominic* by Cosmè Tura.

Later Flemish and German artists appear in **Room 22**, works by Gerard David and proto-Romantic Albrecht Altdorfer, and a portrait attributed to Hans Holbein of *Sir Thomas More*. **Room 23** is dedicated to non-Tuscans Correggio of Parma and Mantegna of the Veneto, as well as Boltraffio's strange *Narcissus* with an eerie background reminiscent of Leonardo.

## Rooms 25–27: Mannerism

The window-filled South Corridor, with its views over the city and its fine display of antique sculpture, marks only the halfway point in the Uffizi but nearly the end of Florence's contribution. In the first three rooms, however, local talent rallies to produce a brilliantly coloured twilight in Florentine Mannerism. By most accounts, Michelangelo's only completed oil painting, the *Tondo Doni* (1506), was the spark that ignited Mannerism's flaming orange and turquoise hues. Michelangelo was 30 when he painted this unconventional work, in a medium he disliked (sculpture and fresco being the only fit occupations for a man, he believed). It's a typical Michelangelo story that when the purchaser complained the artist was asking too much for it, Michelangelo promptly doubled the price. As shocking as the colours are the spiralling poses of the Holy Family, sharply delineated against a background of five nude, slightly out-of-focus young men of uncertain purpose (are they pagans? angels? boyfriends? or just fillers?) – an ambiguity that was to become a hallmark of Mannerism; as the *Ignudi* they later appear on the Sistine Chapel ceiling. In itself, the *Tondo Doni* is more provocative than immediately appealing; the violent canvas in Room 27, Rosso Fiorentino's *Moses Defending the Children of Jethro*, was painted some 20 years later and at least in its intention to shock the viewer puts a cap on what Michelangelo began.

**Room 26** is dedicated mainly to Raphael, who was in and out of Florence in 1504–8. Never temperamental or eccentric like his contemporaries, Raphael was the sweetheart of the High Renaissance. His Madonnas, like *The Madonna of the Goldfinch*, a luminous work painted in Florence, have a tenderness that was soon to be overpopularized by others and turned into holy cards, a cloying sentimentality added like layers of varnish over the centuries. It's easier, perhaps, to see Raphael's genius in non-sacred subjects, like *Leo X with Two Cardinals*, a perceptive portrait study of the first Medici pope with his nephew Giulio de' Medici, later Clement VII.

The same room contains Andrea del Sarto's most original work, the fluorescent *Madonna of the Harpies* (1517), named after the figures on the Virgin's pedestal. Of the works by Pontormo, the best is in **Room 27**, *Supper at Emmaus* (1525), a strange canvas with peasant-faced monks emerging out of the darkness, brightly clad diners with dirty feet, and the Masonic symbol of the Eye of God hovering over Christ's head.

## Rooms 28–45

Although we now bid a fond farewell to the Florentines, the Uffizi fairly bristles with masterpieces from other parts of Italy and abroad. Titian's delicious nudes, especially the incomparably voluptuous *Venus of Urbino*, raise the temperature in **Room 28**; Parmigianino's hyper-elegant *Madonna with the Long Neck* (1536) in **Room 29** is a fascinating Mannerist evolutionary dead-end, possessing all the weird beauty of a foot-long dragonfly. **Room 31** holds Paolo Veronese's *Holy Family with St Barbara*, a late work bathed in a golden Venetian light, with a gorgeously opulent Barbara gazing on. Sebastiano del Piombo's recently restored *Death of Adonis*, in **Room 32**, is notable for its melancholy, lagoony, autumn atmosphere, and the annoyed look on Venus' face. His contemporary Tintoretto is represented by a shadowy *Leda* languidly pretending to restrain the lusty swan.

**Room 41** is Flemish domain, with brand-name art by Rubens and Van Dyck; the former's *Baccanale* may be the most grotesque canvas in Florence. **Room 42**, the *Sala della Niobe*, was reopened in December 1998 after the bomb damage was repaired. A series of statues, *Niobe and her Sons* (18th-century copies of Hellenic works), are housed in the high, arched-ceilinged room, which is covered in pristine plaster and gold leaf. **Room 43** houses some striking Caravaggios.

Struggle on gamely to **Room 44**, where there are three portraits by Rembrandt including two of himself, young and old, and landscapes by Ruysdael. **Room 45** is given over to some fine 18th-century works, including two portraits of children by Chardin, and others by Goya and Longhi, and Venetian landscapes by Guardi and Canaletto. Even more welcome by this time is the **bar** at the end of the corridor, with a summer terrace and in a superb position overlooking Piazza Signoria. It has been renovated and is now a smart (and expensive) place for a drink, snack or light meal.

The **Contini Bonacossi** collection, once housed in the Meridiana Pavilion at Palazzo Pitti, was moved to the Uffizi in 1999. Visits are by appointment only (**t** 055 265 4321), and there is a separate entrance in Via Lambertesca. The Uffizi ticket is also valid for this. This recent bequest includes works of Cimabue, Duccio and Giovanni Bellini, some sculpture and china, and also paintings by El Greco, Goya and Velazquez – the last represented by an exceptional work, *The Water Carrier of Seville*.

## Corridoio Vasariano

*Open for limited periods during the year. It is now open to individuals, not just groups. Hours are also very limited. Call **t** 055 2654 321 for info and bookings (obligatory); adm exp.*

In 1565, when Francesco I married Joanna of Austria, the Medici commissioned Vasari to link their new digs in the Pitti Palace with the Uffizi and the Palazzo Vecchio in such a manner that the Archdukes could make their rounds without rubbing elbows with their subjects. With a patina of 400 years, it seems that Florence wouldn't look quite right without this covered catwalk, leapfrogging on rounded arches from the back of the Uffizi, over the Ponte Vecchio, daintily skirting a medieval tower, and darting past the façade of Santa Felicità to the Pitti Palace.

The Corridoio does not only offer interesting views of Florence: it has been hung with a celebrated collection of artists' self-portraits, beginning, reasonably, with Vasari himself before continuing in chronological order, past the Gaddis and Raphael to Rembrandt, Van Dyck, Velazquez, Hogarth, Reynolds, Delacroix and Corot.

## The Museum of the History of Science (Museo di Storia della Scienza)

*Open summer 9.30–5, Tues and Sat 9.30–1, closed Sun; winter 9.30–5, Tues 9.30–1; adm exp.*

For all that Florence and Tuscany contributed to the birth of science, it is only fitting to have this museum in the centre of the city, behind the Uffizi in Piazza Giudici. Much of the ground floor is devoted to instruments measuring time and distance that are often works of art in themselves: Arabian astrolabes and pocket sundials, Tuscan sundials in the shape of Platonic solids, enormous elaborate armillary spheres and a small reliquary holding the bone of Galileo's finger, erect, like a final gesture to the city that until 1737 denied him a Christian burial. Here, too, are two of his original telescopes and the lens with which he discovered the four moons of Jupiter. Other scientific instruments come from the Accademia del Cimento (of 'trial' or 'experiment'), founded in 1657 by Cardinal Leopoldo de' Medici, the world's first scientific organization, dedicated to Galileo's principle of inquiry and proof by experimentation. 'Try and try again' was its motto.

Upstairs, there's a large room filled with machines used to demonstrate principles of physics, which the women who run the museum will operate if you ask. Two unusual ones are the 18th-century automatic writer and the instrument of perpetual motion. The rooms devoted to medicine contain a collection of 18th-century wax anatomical models, designed to teach budding obstetricians about unfortunate foetal positions, as well as a fine display of surgical instruments from the period.

## The Ponte Vecchio and Ponte Santa Trínita

*Bent bridges seeming to strain like bows*
*And tremble with arrowy undertide...*
Elizabeth Barrett Browning, 'Casa Guidi Windows'

Often at sunset the Arno becomes a stream of molten gold, confined in its walls of stone and laced into its bed with the curving arches of its spans. That is, during those months when it has a respectable flow of water. But even in the torrid days of August, when the Arno shrivels into muck and spittle, its two famous bridges retain their distinctive beauty. The most famous of these, the **Ponte Vecchio** or 'Old Bridge', crosses the Arno at its narrowest point; the present bridge, with its three stone arches, was built in 1345, and replaces a wooden construction from the 970s, which in turn was the successor to a span that may well have dated back to the Romans. On this wooden bridge, at the foot of the *Marzocco*, or statue of Mars, Buondelmonte dei Buondelmonti was murdered in 1215, setting off the wars of the Guelphs and Ghibellines. The original *Marzocco* was washed away in a 14th-century flood, and Donatello's later version has been carted off to the Bargello.

Like old London Bridge, the Ponte Vecchio is covered with shops and houses. By the 1500s, for hygienic reasons, it had become the street of hog butchers, though after

Vasari built Cosimo's secret passage on top, the Grand Duke, for personal hygienic reasons, evicted the butchers and replaced them with goldsmiths. They have been there ever since, and shoppers from around the world descend on it each year to scrutinize the traditional Florentine talent for jewellery – not a few of the city's great artists began their careers as goldsmiths, beginning with Ghiberti and Donatello, and ending with Cellini, who never gave up the craft, and whose bust adorns the middle of the bridge. In the 1966 flood the shops did not prove as resilient as the Ponte Vecchio itself, and a fortune of gold was washed down the Arno.

In the summer of 1944, the river briefly became a German defensive line during the slow painful retreat across Italy. Before leaving Florence, the Nazis blew up every one of the city's bridges, saving only, on Hitler's special orders, the Ponte Vecchio, though they blasted a large number of ancient buildings on each side of the span to create piles of rubble to block the approaches. Florence's most beautiful span, the **Ponte Santa Trínita**, was the most tragic victim. Immediately after the war the Florentines set about replacing the bridges exactly as they were: for Santa Trínita, old quarries had to be reopened to duplicate the stone, and old methods revived to cut it (modern power saws would have done it too cleanly). The graceful curve of the three arches was a problem; they could not be constructed geometrically, and considerable speculation went on over how the architect (Ammannati, in 1567) did it. Finally, recalling that Michelangelo had advised Ammannati on the project, someone noticed that the same form of arch could be seen on the decoration of the tombs in Michelangelo's Medici Chapel, constructed most likely by pure artistic imagination. Fortune lent a hand in the reconstruction; of the original statues of the 'Four Seasons', almost all the pieces were fished out of the Arno and rebuilt. Spring's head was eventually found by divers completely by accident in 1961.

# Dante's Florence

In 1265 Dante Alighieri was born in the quarter just to the north of the Piazza della Signoria; he was only nine 'when first the glorious Lady of my mind was made manifest to mine eyes; even she who was called Beatrice by many who know not wherefore'. Beatrice went on to wed another, and died suddenly in 1290; Dante tried to forget his disappointment and grief in battle, fighting in the wars against Arezzo and Pisa, then in writing his 'autopsychology' *La Vita Nuova*. In 1302, as a White Guelph, he was sent into exile. A friend just managed to rescue the manuscript of the *Inferno* from the crowds who came to sack and pillage his home. Dante died in Ravenna in 1321, and although he was never allowed to return home, the Florentines have belatedly tried to make amends to their poet. Yet the memorials fall curiously flat. His grand tomb in Santa Croce is empty and his huge statue in front of the church a glowering failure.

The best place to summon the shade of Italy's greatest poet is in the narrow medieval lanes of Florence, especially in his old haunts just to the north of Piazza della Signoria. Most scholars believe Dante was born on what is now Via Dante

Alighieri. A modern bas-relief on one of the buildings shows the sights that would have been familiar to Dante, one of which would have been the sturdy well-preserved **Torre del Castagno** on Piazza San Martino, used as the residence of the *priori* before the construction of the Palazzo Vecchio. Here, too, is the tiny **San Martino del Vescovo**, Dante's parish church (*open Mon–Sat 10–12 and 3–5; closed Sun*), founded in 986 but rebuilt in 1479 when it became the headquarters of the charitable Compagnia dei Buonuomini. The Compagnia commissioned a follower of Ghirlandaio to paint a series of colourful frescoes on the *Life of St Martin and the Works of Charity*, scenes acted out by quattrocento Florentines, in their own fashions on their own streets. The church also has a fine Byzantine Madonna, and one by Perugino, the latter by a *finestra a tromba*, a window used to distribute bread during the plague.

Opposite, from Via S. Margherita an alley leads north to the so-called **Casa di Dante** (*open daily 9.30–12.30 and 3.30–6.30, closed Wed and Sun afternoons; adm*). The house was actually built in 1911 over the ruins of an amputated tower house of Giuochi family, although scholars agree that the Alighieri lived somewhere close by. A museum since 1960, it makes a game attempt to evoke Dante's life and times, in spite of neglect and stingy Florentine low-watt light bulbs. There is a model of Florence as it was in the 13th century, and mock-ups of the battle of Campaldino, where Dante as a soldier fought Arezzo. Near the entrance is an edition of *The Divine Comedy*, printed in tiny letters on a poster by a mad Milanese; of the manuscript reproductions, the most interesting is an illumination of the infamous murder of Buondelmonte dei Buondelmonti, with the Ponte Vecchio and a statue of Mars, the original *Marzocco*, in place. Upstairs you can see copies of Botticelli's beautiful line illustrations for the *Commedia*.

From the house, Via S. Margherita continues to **Santa Margherita de' Cerchi** (*open daily 10–noon and 3–5*), built in 1032. Dante as a boy first espied the young Beatrice here in 1273 and later wed his second choice, Gemma Donati, whose family arms still emblazon the 13th-century porch. Both Beatrice and Gemma were buried here in their family tombs, now sunk without trace, although you can still see the tombstone of Monna Tessa, Beatrice's nurse.

## The Badia Fiorentina

*Entrance on Via Dante Alighieri; open Mon only 3–6, or during Mass, held Mon–Sat 6.15pm, Sun 11am.*

Dante would also recognize the two great towers in Piazza San Firenze, the looming Bargello and the beautiful Romanesque campanile of the ancient Benedictine abbey, or Badia, which he cited in the *Paradiso*. The abbey was founded at the end of the 10th century by the widow of Umberto, the Margrave of Tuscany, and further endowed by their son Ugo, 'the Good Margrave'. Dante would come here to gaze upon his Beatrice, and some 50 years after the poet's death, Dante's first biographer, Boccaccio, used the Badia as his forum for innovative public lectures on the text of *The Divine Comedy*. Curiously, Boccaccio's (and later the Renaissance's) principal criticism of the work is that Dante chose to write about lofty, sacred things in the vulgar tongue of Tuscany.

Except for the campanile, the Badia has become a hotchpotch from too many remodellings. Inside, however, are two beautiful things from the Renaissance: the *Tomb of Count Ugo* (1481) by Mino da Fiesole and the *Madonna Appearing to St Benedict* (1485), a large painting by Filippino Lippi.

Through an unmarked door to the right of the choir, you can reach the upper loggia of the **Chiostro degli Aranci**, where the Benedictines grew oranges. Built in the 1430s, it is embellished with a fine contemporary series of frescoes on the life of St Benedict, generally thought to be by Rossellino.

## Museo Nazionale del Bargello

*Open daily 8.15–1.50; closed 1st and 3rd Sun and 2nd and 4th Mon of month; adm.*

Across from the Badia Fiorentina looms the Bargello, a battlemented urban fortress, well proportioned yet of forbidding grace; for centuries it saw duty as Florence's prison. Today its only inmates are men of marble, gathered together to form Italy's finest collection of sculpture, a fitting complement to the paintings in the Uffizi. The Bargello is 'stone Florence' squared to the sixth degree, rugged and austere *pietra forte*, the model for the even grander Palazzo Vecchio. Even the treasures it houses are hard, definite, certain – and almost unremittingly masculine. The Bargello offers the best insight available into Florence's golden age, and it was a man's world indeed.

Completed in 1255, the Bargello was intended as Florence's Palazzo del Popolo, though by 1271 it served instead as the residence of the foreign *podestà*, or chief magistrate, installed by Guelph leader Charles of Anjou. The Medici made it the headquarters of the captain of police (the *Bargello*), the city jail and torture chamber, a function it served until 1859. In the Renaissance it was the peculiar custom to paint portraits of the condemned on the exterior walls of the fortress; Andrea del Castagno was so good at it that he was nicknamed Andrea of the Hanged Men. All of these ghoulish souvenirs have long since disappeared, as have the torture instruments – burned in 1786, when Grand Duke Peter Leopold abolished torture and the death sentence in Tuscany, only a few months after the Venetians led the way. Today the **Gothic courtyard**, former site of the gallows and chopping block, is a delightful place, owing much to an imaginative restoration in the 1860s. The encrustation of centuries of *podestà* armorial devices and plaques in a wild vocabulary of symbols, the shadowy arcades and stately stairs combine to create one of Florence's most romantic corners.

### The Michelangelo Room

The main ground-floor gallery is dedicated to Michelangelo and his century, although it must be said that the Michelangelo of the Bargello somewhat lacks the accustomed angst and ecstasy. Especially irritating is his *Bacchus* (1496), a youthful work inspired by bad Roman sculpture, with all the personality of a cocktail party bore. Better to invite his noble *Brutus* (1540), even if he's just a bust – the only one the sculptor ever made, in a fit of republican fervour after the assassination of Duke

Alessandro de' Medici. Also by Michelangelo is the lovely *Pitti Tondo* and the unfinished *Apollo/David*. From Michelangelo's followers there's another tippling *Bacchus* by Sansovino, and Ammannati's *Leda and the Swan* (a work inspired by a famous but lost erotic drawing by Michelangelo).

The real star of the room is **Benvenuto Cellini**, who was, besides many other things, 'an exquisite craftsman and daring innovator. His large bust of *Cosimo I* (1548), with its fabulously detailed armour, was his first work cast in bronze; the unidealized features did not at all curry favour with the boss that poor Cellini worked so avidly to please. Here, too, are two preliminary models of the *Perseus*, as well as four small statuettes and the relief panel from the original in the Loggia dei Lanzi.

The last great work in the room is by Medici court sculptor Giambologna, now again enjoying a measure of the fashionableness he possessed during his lifetime; art historians consider him the key Mannerist figure between Michelangelo and Bernini. Giambologna's most famous work, the bronze *Mercury* (1564), has certainly seeped into popular consciousness as the representation of the way the god should look. The stairway from the courtyard leads up to the shady **Loggia**, now converted into an aviary for Giambologna's charming bronze birds, made for the animal grotto at the Medici's Villa di Castello.

## Donatello: the Salone del Consiglio Generale

This magnificent hall, formerly the courtroom of the *podestà*, contains the greatest masterpieces of Early Renaissance sculpture. And when Michelangelo's maudlin self-absorption and the Mannerists' empty virtuosity begin to seem tiresome, a visit to this room, to the profound clarity of the greatest of Renaissance sculptors, will prove a welcome antidote. Donatello's originality and vision are strikingly modern – and mysterious. Unlike Michelangelo, who went so far as to commission his own biography when Vasari's didn't please him, Donatello left few traces, not only of his long life, but of what may have been the sources of inspiration behind his three celebrated works displayed here. The chivalric young *St George* (1416), from the façade of Orsanmichele, has an alert watchfulness, or *prontezza*, which created new possibilities in expressing movement, emotion and depth of character in stone. Note the accompanying bas-relief of the gallant saint slaying the dragon, a masterful work in perspective. Donatello's fascinatingly androgynous *David*, obviously from a different planet from Michelangelo's *David*, is young, cool and suave, and conquers his Goliath more by his charming enigmatic smile than muscles. Cast for Cosimo il Vecchio in 1430, this was the first free-standing nude figure since antiquity, and one of the most erotic, exploring depths of the Florentine psyche that the Florentines probably didn't know they had.

The same erotic energy and mystery surrounds the laughing, dangerous-looking, precocious boy Cupid, or *Atys Amor*; with its poppies, serpents and winged sandals, it could easily be the ancient idol people mistook it for in the 1700s. Like Botticelli's mythological paintings, Cupid is part of the intellectual undercurrents of the period, full of pagan philosophy, a possibility rooted out in the terror of the Counter-Reformation and quite forgotten soon after.

Other Donatellos in the *salone* further display the sculptor's amazing diversity. The small marble *David* (1408) was his earliest important work. In the centre of the hall, his *Marzocco*, the symbol of Florence, long stood on the Ponte Vecchio. Although the two versions of Florence's patron saint, John the Baptist, are no longer attributed to Donatello, they show his influence in that they strive to express the saint's spiritual character physically rather than by merely adding his usual holy accessories. The *Dancing Putto* and two busts are Donatello's; his workshop produced the gilded bas-relief of the Crucifixion.

On the wall hang the two famous trial reliefs for the second set of baptistry doors, by Ghiberti and Brunelleschi, both depicting the Sacrifice of Isaac. Between the panels, the vigorous relief of a tumultuous *Battle Scene* is by the little-known Bertoldo di Giovanni, Donatello's pupil and Michelangelo's teacher. There are a number of other excellent reliefs and busts along the walls, by Agostino di Duccio, Desiderio da Settignano, and some of Luca della Robbia's sweet Madonnas.

## Decorative Arts

The remainder of the first floor houses fascinating collections of decorative arts donated to the Bargello in the last century. The **Sala della Torre** is devoted to Islamic art. The **Sala Carrand**, named after the French donor of works in this room, contains Byzantine and Renaissance jewellery, watches and clocks, and a Venetian astrolabe. Off this room is the **Cappella del Podestà** where the condemned were given their last rites, eyes filled with a damaged fresco of the *Last Judgement* by the school of Giotto, discovered under the plaster in 1840s; note the scene of Paradise, with the earliest known portrait of Dante, with his piercing gaze and eagle's beak nose.

Some of the most interesting items are in the next rooms, especially the works in the **ivory collection** – Carolingian and Byzantine diptychs, an 8th-century whalebone coffer from Northumbria adorned with runes, medieval French miniatures chronicling 'The Assault on the Castle of Love', 11th-century chess pieces, and more.

A stairway from the ivory collection leads up to the **Second Floor**. It houses some of the finest enamelled terracottas of the della Robbia family workshop, a room of portrait busts, works by Antonio Pollaiuolo and Verrocchio, including his *David* and lovely *Young Lady with a Nosegay*. There is also a collection of armour, and the most important collection of small Renaissance bronzes in Italy.

## Piazza San Firenze to the Duomo

The strangely shaped square that both the Badia and the Bargello call home is named after the large church of **San Firenze**, an imposing ensemble, now partially used as Florence's law courts. At the corner of the square and Via Gondi, the **Palazzo Gondi** is a fine Renaissance palace built for a merchant by Giuliano da Sangallo in 1489 but completed only in 1884; it's not easy to pick out the discreet 19th-century additions. A block from the square on Via Ghibellina, the **Palazzo Borghese** (No.110) is one of the finest neoclassical buildings in the city, erected in 1822 – for a party in honour of Habsburg Grand Duke Ferdinand III. The host of this famous affair was one of the wealthiest men of his day, the Roman prince Camillo Borghese, husband of the fascinating Pauline Bonaparte and the man responsible for shipping many of Italy's artistic treasures off to the Louvre.

From Piazza San Firenze, Via del Proconsolo leads straight to the Piazza del Duomo, passing by way of the **Palazzo Pazzi-Quaratesi** (No.10), the 15th-century headquarters of the banking family that organized the conspiracy against Lorenzo and Giuliano de' Medici. No.12, the Palazzo Nonfinito – begun in 1593 but, as its name suggests, never completed – is now the home of the **Museo Nazionale di Antropologia ed Etnologia** (*open Wed–Mon 9–1; closed Tues; adm*), founded in 1869, the first ethnological museum in Italy, with an interesting collection of Peruvian mummies, musical instruments collected by Galileo Chini (who decorated the Liberty-style extravaganzas at Viareggio), some lovely and unusual items of Japan's Ainu and Pakistan's Kafiri, and a large number of skulls from all over the world.

# Florence As It Was

Borgo degli Albizi, the fine old street passing in front of the Palazzo Nonfinito, was in ancient times the Via Cassia, linking Rome with Bologna, and it deserves a leisurely stroll for its palaces (especially No.18, the cinquecento Palazzo Valori, nicknamed 'Funny Face Palace' for its surreal, semi-relief herm-busts of Florentine immortals on three floors of the façade). If Borgo degli Albizi, too, fails to answer to the Florence you've been seeking, take Via dell'Oriuolo (just to the left at Piazza G. Salvemini) for the **Museo di Firenze Com'Era** (Museum of Florence As It Was), located at the big garden at No.24 (*open Fri–Wed 9–2; closed Thurs; adm*). The jewel of this museum is right out in front, the nearly room-sized *Pianta della Catena*, most beautiful of the early views of Florence. It is a copy; the original, made in 1490 by an unknown artist – that handsome fellow pictured in the lower right-hand corner – was lost during the last war in a Berlin museum. This fascinating painting captures Florence at the height of the Renaissance, a city of buildings in bright white, pink and tan; the great churches are without their façades, the Uffizi and Medici chapels have not yet appeared, and the Medici and Pitti palaces are without their later extensions.

The museum is not large. At present it contains only a number of plans and maps, as well as a collection of amateurish watercolours of Florence's sights from the last century, and paintings of Florence's surroundings by Ottone Rosai, a local favourite who died in 1957. Today's Florentines seem much less interested in the Renaissance than in the city of their grandparents. For some further evidence, look around the corner of Via S. Egidio, where some recent remodelling has uncovered posters over the street from 1925, announcing plans for paying the war debt and a coming visit of the *Folies Bergère*. The Florentines have restored them and put them under glass.

From Via dell'Oriuolo, Via Folco Portinari takes you to Florence's main hospital, **Santa Maria Nuova**, founded in 1286 by the father of Dante's Beatrice, Folco Portinari. A tomb in the hospital's church, Sant'Egidio, is all that remains of the family. Readers of Iris Origo's *The Merchant of Prato* will recognize it as the workplace of the good notary, Ser Lapo Mazzei. The portico, by Buontalenti, was finished in 1612.

## Medieval Streets North of the Arno

Just west of Via Por S. Maria, the main street leading down to the Ponte Vecchio, you'll find some of the oldest and best-preserved lanes in Florence. Near the Mercato Nuovo at the top of the street (*see* p.160) stands the **Palazzo di Parte Guelfa**, the 13th-century headquarters of the Guelph party, and often the real seat of power in the city, paid for by property confiscated from the Ghibellines; in the 15th century Brunelleschi added a hall on the top floor and an extension. Next door is the guildhall of the silk-makers, the 14th-century **Palazzo dell' Arte della Seta** still bearing its bas-relief emblem, or *stemma*, of a closed door, the age-old guild symbol. It's worth continuing around the Guelph Palace to Via Pellicceria to see the fine ensemble of medieval buildings on the tiny square near Via delle Terme, named after the old Roman baths.

## Palazzo Davanzati

*The palazzo, closed for restoration since 1994, was due to reopen partially in July 2001, though timings have slipped. The ground floor and first floor rooms will open first, the rest who knows when... Until then, you can see an exhibition on the palace on the ground floor, 8.30–1.50; closed alternate Sundays and Mondays.*

To get an idea of what life was like inside these sombre palaces some 600 years ago, stroll over to nearby Via Porta Rossa, site of the elegant Palazzo Davanzati, now arranged as the **Museo della Casa Fiorentina Antica**, one of the city's most delightful museums, offering a chance to step back into domestic life of yore. Originally built in the mid-14th century for the Davizzi family, the house was purchased by merchant Bernardo Davanzati in 1578 and stayed in the family until the 1900s. Restored by an antique collector in 1904, it is the best-preserved medieval-Renaissance house in Florence.

The façade is basically as it was, except for a 16th-century addition of a fifth-floor loggia, replacing the battlements – in the rough-and-tumble 14th century, a man's home literally had to be a castle. But it was also a showroom for his prosperity, and by the standards of the day, the dwellers of this huge palace were multi-millionaires. From the grand loggia, used for sumptuous public entertainment, you enter the palace by way of a strikingly vertical **Courtyard**, which could be quickly cut off from the street in times of danger, as evidenced by the stout, iron-bolted door. Nor would any family feel safe without a year's store of grain and oil – against famine, siege, plagues or inflation. One storeroom is now used for an audio-visual history of the house. Note the medieval dumb waiter used to transport the shopping up to the kitchen on the top floor.

Upstairs, past a 14th-century fresco of St Christopher on the landing, the elegant **Sala Grande** was used for formal gatherings, and again, for defence, when boiling oil and such other ghoulish forms of defence could be dropped down through the four hatches in the floor. The room contains a beautiful 16th-century table and cupboard, and luxuries like an automatic bellows and flues at the fireplace, glass windows, and a prettily painted ceiling. The bright and cosy dining room next door, the **Sala dei Pappagalli**, was named after the parrots that adorn the frescoes, cleverly painted with pretend hooks to resemble far more costly tapestries. Off the **Sala Piccola**, a child's bedroom, is one of the palace's bathrooms, which must have seemed almost decadently luxurious in the medieval city, where, according to law, one had to shout three loud warnings before emptying a chamber pot into the street. An elegant bedroom called the **Sala dei Pavoni** has an almost Moorish-style pattern painted on the walls with coats of arms, topped by a frieze of peacocks and other exotic birds flitting among the trees. The bedspread is a rare 14th-century example from Sicily, portraying the story of Tristan and King Mark.

The pattern of rooms is repeated on the next floor. The **Salone** is adorned with 15th-century Flemish tapestries and a portrait of Giovanni di Bicci de' Medici. The dining room contains outlandish salt cellars and games chests. The **Sala Piccola** houses a fine collection of *cassoni*, the elaborate wedding chests in which a bride stored her dowry of household linens, nearly all decorated with the secular subjects in contemporary dress. The bedroom, the **Camera della Castellana di Vergi**, is decorated with a lovely fresco from a medieval French romance. The 14th-century shoes displayed here were found in Boccaccio's house. The **kitchen**, as is usual in a medieval house, is located on the top floor in the hope that in case of fire, only the roof would burn. Women would spend most of their day here, supervising the servants, sewing and gossiping; as no servants' quarters existed in the palace, it is believed that the help sacked out on the floor.

## Piazza Santa Trínita

Three old Roman roads – Via Porta Rossa, Via delle Terme and Borgo SS. Apostoli – lead into the irregularly shaped Piazza Santa Trínita. Borgo SS. Apostoli is named after one of Florence's oldest churches, the little Romanesque **Santi Apostoli** (11th century), which is located in the sunken Piazzetta del Limbo, former cemetery of unbaptized babies.

Piazza Santa Trínita itself boasts an exceptionally fine architectural ensemble, grouped around the 'Column of Justice' from the Roman Baths of Caracalla, given by Pius IV to Cosimo I, and later topped with a red statue of Justice by Francesco del Tadda. Its pale granite is set off by the palaces of the piazza: the High Renaissance-Roman **Palazzo Bartolini-Salimbeni** by Baccio d'Agnolo (1520) on the corner of Via Porta Rossa, formerly the fashionable Hôtel du Nord where Herman Melville stayed; the medieval **Palazzo Buondelmonti**, with a 1530 façade by Baccio d'Agnolo, once home to the reading room and favourite haunt of such literati in the 19th century as Dumas, Browning, Manzoni and Stendhal; and the magnificent curving **Palazzo Spini-Ferroni**, the largest medieval palace in Florence, built in 1289 and still retaining its original battlements. This is now home to the heirs of the Florentine designer Ferragamo and houses a retail outlet and a fascinating small **museum** of Ferragamo's life and work, including some of the most beautiful shoes in the world (*open Mon–Fri 9–1 and 2–6 by appt only*, t 055 336 0456; *adm*).

Around the corner on Lungarno Corsini, the British Consulate occupies the **Palazzo Masetti**, which, ironically, was once home to the flamboyant Countess of Albany, wife of Bonnie Prince Charlie, who found happiness by leaving the Pretender for Italian dramatist Vittorio Alfieri, but insisted to the end that she was England's rightful Queen Louise.

## Santa Trínita

*Open Mon–Sat 8–12 and 4–6; Sun 4–6 only.*

The church of Santa Trínita has stood here, in one form or another, since the 12th century; its unusual accent on the first syllable (from the Latin *Trinitas*) is considered proof of its ancient foundation. Although the pedestrian façade added by Buontalenti in 1593 isn't especially welcoming, step into its shadowy 14th-century interior for several artistic treats, beginning with the **Bartolini-Salimbeni Chapel** (fourth on the right), frescoed in 1422 by the Sienese Lorenzo Monaco; his marriage of the Virgin takes place in a Tuscan fantasy backdrop of pink towers. He also painted the chapel's graceful, ethereally coloured altarpiece, the *Annunciation*.

In the choir, the **Sassetti Chapel** is one of the masterpieces of Domenico Ghirlandaio, completed in 1495 for wealthy merchant Francesco Sassetti and dedicated to the Life of St Francis, but also to the life of Francesco Sassetti, the city and his Medici circle: the scene above the altar, of Francis receiving the Rule of the Order, is transferred to the Piazza della Signoria, watched by Sassetti (to the right, with the fat purse) and Lorenzo il Magnifico; on the steps stands the great Latinist Poliziano with Lorenzo's three sons. The *Death of St Francis* pays homage to Giotto's similar composition in Santa Croce. The altarpiece, the *Adoration of the Shepherds* (1485), is one of Ghirlandaio's best-known works, often described as the archetypal Renaissance painting, a contrived but charming classical treatment; the Magi arrive through a triumphal arch, a Roman sarcophagus is used as manger and a ruined temple for a stable – all matched by the sibyls on the vault; the sibyl on the outer arch is the one who supposedly announced the birth of Christ to Augustus.

Santa Trínita is a Vallombrosan church and the first chapel to the right of the altar holds the Order's holy of holies, a painted crucifix formerly located up in San Miniato. The story goes that on a Good Friday, a young noble named Giovanni Gualberto was on his way to Mass when he happened upon the man who had recently murdered his brother. But rather than take his revenge, Gualberto pardoned the assassin in honour of the holy day. When he arrived at church to pray, this crucifix nodded in approval of his mercy. Giovanni was so impressed that he went on to found the Vallombrosan order in the Casentino.

The **Sanctuary** was frescoed by Alesso Baldovinetti, though only four Old Testament figures survive. In the second chapel to the left the marble *Tomb of Bishop Benozzo Federighi* (1454) is by Luca, the first and greatest of the della Robbias. In the fourth chapel, a detached fresco by Neri di Bicci portrays San Giovanni Gualberto and his fellow Vallombrosan saints; over the arch you can (just about) see him forgiving the murderer of his brother.

# West of Piazza della Repubblica

The streets west of Piazza della Repubblica have always been the choicest district of Florence, and **Via de' Tornabuoni** the city's smartest shopping street. These days you won't find many innovations: Milan's current status as headquarters of Italy's fashion industry is a sore point with Florence, which used to be top dog and lost its position in the 1970s for lack of a large international airport. This changed in 1997, and Florence hopes to steal back as much of the trade that it can.

In the bright and ambitious 1400s, however, when Florence was the centre of European high finance, Via de' Tornabuoni and its environs was the area the new merchant élite chose for their palaces. Today's bankers build great skyscrapers for the firm and settle for modest mansions for themselves; in Florence's heyday, things were reversed. Bankers and wool tycoons really owned their businesses. While their places of work were quite simple, their homes were imposing city palaces, all built in the same conservative style and competing with each other in size like some Millionaires' Row in 19th-century America.

The champion was the **Palazzo Strozzi**, a long block up Via de' Tornabuoni from Piazza Trínita. This rusticated stone cube of fearful dimensions squats in its piazza like the inscrutable monolith in *2001: A Space Odyssey*, radiating almost visible waves of megalomania. The palazzo was begun by Benedetto da Maiano in 1489 for the extraordinarily wealthy Filippo Strozzi, head of one of Florence's greatest banking clans and adviser to Lorenzo il Magnifico. When he died in 1491, the cornice facing Piazza Strozzi was almost complete; future generations had neither the money nor the interest to finish the job. And one wonders whether his son, also called Filippo, ever took much pleasure in it; though at first a Medici ally like his father and wed to Piero de' Medici's daughter, Filippo attempted to lead a band of anti-Medici exiles against Florence; captured and imprisoned in the Fortezza da Basso, he stabbed himself, while many other Strozzi escaped to Paris to become bankers and advisers to the king of France.

There are few architectural innovations in the Palazzo Strozzi, but here the typical Florentine palace is blown up to the level of the absurd: although three storeys like other palaces, each floor is as tall as three or four normal ones, and the rings to tie up horses could hold elephants. Like Michelangelo's *David*, Florence's other beautiful monster, it emits the unpleasant sensation of what Mary McCarthy called the 'giganticism of the human ego', the will to surpass not only antiquity but nature herself. Nowadays, at least, the Strozzi palace is moderately useful as a space to hold temporary exhibitions.

## Palazzo Rucellai

There are two other exceptional palaces in the quarter. At the north end of Via de' Tornabuoni stands the beautiful golden **Palazzo Antinori** (1465, architect unknown), which has Florence's grandest Baroque façade, **San Gaetano** (1648, by Gherardo Silvani), as its equally golden companion, despite being decorated with statues that would look right at home in Rome but look like bad actors in Florence.

The second important palace, Florence's most celebrated example of domestic architecture, is the **Palazzo Rucellai**, in Via della Vigna Nuova. Its original owner, Giovanni Rucellai, was a quattrocento tycoon like Filippo Strozzi, but an intellectual as well, whose *Zibaldone*, or 'commonplace book' is one of the best sources available on the life and tastes of the educated Renaissance merchant. In 1446 Rucellai chose his favourite architect, Leon Battista Alberti, to design his palace. Actually built by Bernardo Rossellino, it follows Alberti's precepts and theories in its use of the three classical orders; instead of the usual rusticated stone, the façade has a far more delicate decoration of incised irregular blocks and a frieze, elements influential in subsequent Italian architecture – though far more noticeably in Rome than Florence itself. Originally the palace was only five bays wide, and when another two bays were added later the edge was left ragged, unfinished, a nice touch, as if the builders could return at any moment and pick up where they left off. The frieze, like that on Santa Maria Novella, portrays the devices of the Medici and the Rucellai families (Giovanni's son married a daughter of Piero de' Medici), a wedding fêted in the **Loggia dei Rucellai** across the street, also designed by Alberti.

Behind the Rucellai palace (on Via della Spada) stands the ancient church of **San Pancrazio**, with an antique-style porch by Alberti; at one point in its up-and-down career the church served as a tobacco factory. Now it's been given a new life as the **Museo Marino Marini**, (*open 10–5, Sun 10–1, plus Thurs 10–11pm in summer; closed Tues and Aug; adm*), containing 180 works by Marini, one of the greatest Italian sculptors of this century (1901–80). Marini also worked as a painter and lithographer, and his portraits and favourite subjects (especially the Horse and Rider) are known for their sensuous surfaces and uncanny psychological intensity. If you come on a Saturday at 5.30 (*also open Mon–Sat 10–noon except in July, Aug and Sept*) the **Rucellai Chapel** behind San Pancrazio at 18 Via della Spada should be open for Mass, providing an opportunity to see this minor Renaissance gem designed in 1467 by Alberti, housing a unique model of the Sanctuary of the Holy Sepulchre in Jerusalem that is Giovanni Rucellai's funerary monument.

## Piazza Goldoni and Ognissanti

Before taking leave of old Florence's west end, head back to the Arno and **Piazza Goldoni**, named after the great comic playwright from Venice. The bridge here, the **Ponte alla Carraia**, is new and nondescript, but its 1304 version played a leading role in that year's most memorable disaster: a company staging a water pageant of the *Inferno*, complete with monsters, devils and tortured souls, attracted such a large crowd that the bridge collapsed under the weight, and all were drowned. Later it was drily commented that all the Florentines who went to see Hell that day found what they were looking for.

The most important building on the piazza, the **Palazzo Ricasoli**, was built in the 15th century but bears the name of one of unified Italy's first Prime Ministers, Bettino 'Iron Baron' Ricasoli. Just to the east on Lungarno Corsini looms the enormous **Palazzo Corsini**, the city's most prominent piece of Roman Baroque extravagance, begun in 1650 and crowned with a bevy of statues. The Corsini, the most prominent family of

17th- and 18th-century Florence, were reputedly so wealthy that they could ride from Florence to Rome entirely on their own property. The **Galleria Corsini** (*adm by appt only, t 055 218 994; Mon, Wed and Fri between 9 and 12, enter from Via Parione*), houses paintings by Giovanni Bellini, Signorelli, Filippino Lippi and Pontormo, and *Muses* from the ducal palace of Urbino, painted by Raphael's first master, Timoteo Viti. It also has the rarest of Florentine amenities: a garden, a 17th-century oasis of box hedges, Roman statues, lemon trees and tortoises. Further east on Lungarno Corsini stood the Libreria Orioli, which caused a scandal when it published the first edition of *Lady Chatterley's Lover* in 1927.

To the west of Piazza Goldoni lies the old neighbourhood of the only Florentine to have a continent named after him. Amerigo Vespucci (1451–1512) was a Medici agent in Seville, and made two voyages from there to America on the heels of Columbus. His parish church, **Ognissanti** (All Saints) (*open 8–12.30 and 5–7 .30*), is set back from the river behind a Baroque façade, on property donated in 1256 by the Umiliati, a religious order that specialized in wool-working. The Vespucci family tomb is below the second altar to the right, and little Amerigo himself is said to be pictured next to the Madonna in the fresco of the Madonna della Misericordia – probably another Florentine tall tale. Also buried in Ognissanti was the Filipepi family, one of whom was Botticelli. In the church are two scholarly saints: Ghirlandaio's *St Jerome* and, on the right, young Botticelli's *St Augustine*.

The best art is to be found in the **Convent**, just to the left of the church at No.42 (*open Sat, Mon and Tues 9–12; you may have to ring*). Frescoed in the refectory is the great *Last Supper*, or *Cenacolo*, painted by Domenico Ghirlandaio in 1480. It's hard to think of a more serene and elegant Last Supper, alike to a garden party with its background of fruit trees and exotic birds; a peacock sits in the window, cherries and peaches litter the lovely tablecloth.

# Santa Maria Novella

*Open Mon–Thurs and Sat 9.30–5, Fri, Sun and hols 1–5; adm.*

As in so many other Italian cities, the two churches of the preaching orders – the Dominicans' Santa Maria Novella and the Franciscans' Santa Croce – became the largest and most prestigious in the city, where wealthy families vied to create the most beautiful chapels and tombs. In Florence, by some twitch of city planning, both of these sacred art galleries dominate broad, stale squares that do not invite you to linger; in the irregular **Piazza Santa Maria Novella** you may find yourself looking over your shoulder for the ghosts of the carriages that once raced madly around the two stout obelisks set on turtles, just as in a Roman circus, in the fashionable carriage races of the 1700s. The arcade on the south side, the **Loggia di San Paolo**, is very much like Brunelleschi's *Spedale degli Innocenti*, although it suffers somewhat from its use as a busy bus shelter; the lunette over the door, by Andrea della Robbia, is the *Meeting of SS. Francis and Dominic*. Santa Maria Novella redeems the anomie of its square with its stupendous black and white marble **façade**, the finest in Florence. The lower part,

# Santa Maria Novella

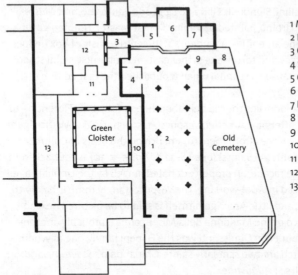

1 Masaccio's *Trinity*
2 Brunelleschi's Pulpit
3 Cappèlla Strozzi
4 Sacristy
5 Cappella Gondi
6 Sanctuary
7 Fillippo Strozzi Chapel
8 Rucellai Chapel
9 Gothic Tombs
10 *Universal Deluge*
11 Spanish Chapel
12 Chiostrino dei Morte
13 Refectory

with its looping arcades, is Romanesque work in the typical Tuscan mode, finished before 1360. In 1456 Giovanni Rucellai commissioned Alberti to complete it, a remarkably fortunate choice. Alberti's half not only perfectly harmonizes with the original, but perfects it with geometrical harmonies to create what appears to be a kind of Renaissance Sun Temple. The original builders started it off by orienting the church to the south instead of west, so that at noon the sun streams through the 14th-century rose window. The only symbol Alberti put on the façade is a blazing sun; the unusual sundials, over the arches on the extreme right and left, were added by Cosimo I's court astronomer Egnazio Danti. Note how the base of the façade is also the base of an equilateral triangle, with Alberti's sun at the apex. The beautiful frieze depicts the Rucellai emblem (a billowing sail), as on the Palazzo Rucellai. The wall of Gothic recesses to the right, enclosing the old cemetery, are *avelli*, or family tombs.

The **interior** is vast, lofty and more 'Gothic' in feel than any other church in Florence – no thanks to Vasari, who was set loose to remodel the church to 16th-century taste, painting over the original frescoes, removing the rood screen and Dominicans' choir from the nave, and remodelling the altars; in the 1800s restorers did their best to de-Vasari Santa Maria with neo-Gothic details. Neither party, however, could touch two of the interior's most distinctive features – the striking stone vaulting of the nave and the perspective created by the columns marching down the aisles, each pair placed a little closer together as they approach the altar.

Over the portal of the main south door is a fresco lunette by Botticelli that has recently been restored. One of Santa Maria Novella's best-known pictures has also been restored and is where the third altar on the left used to be: Masaccio's *Trinità*, painted around 1425, and one of the revolutionary works of the Renaissance. Masaccio's use of architectural elements and perspective gives his composition both physical and intellectual depth. The flat wall becomes a deeply recessed Brunelleschian chapel, calm and classical, enclosed in a coffered barrel vault; at the foot of the fresco a bleak skeleton decays in its tomb, bearing a favourite Tuscan reminder: 'I was that which you are, you will be that which I am.' Above this morbid suggestion of physical death kneel the two donors; within the celestially rational inner sanctum the Virgin and St John stand at the foot of the Cross, humanity's link with the mystery of the Trinity. In the nearby pulpit, designed by Brunelleschi, Galileo was first denounced by the Inquisition for presuming to believe that the earth went around the sun. There is little else to detain you in the aisles, but the first chapel in the left transept, the raised **Cappella Strozzi**, is one of the most evocative corners of 14th-century Florence, frescoed entirely by Nardo di Cione and his brother, Andrea Orcagna; on the vault pictures of St Thomas Aquinas and the Virtues are echoed in Andrea's lovely altarpiece *The Redeemer Donating the Keys to St Peter and the Book of Wisdom to St Thomas Aquinas*; on the left wall there's a crowded scene of Paradise, with the righteous lined up in a medieval school class photograph. On the right, Nardo painted a striking view of Dante's Inferno, with all of a Tuscan's special attention to precise map-like detail. Dramatically in the centre of the **Nave** hangs Giotto's *Crucifix* (*c.* 1300), one of the artist's first works. In the **Gondi Chapel** hangs another famous *Crucifix*, carved in wood by Brunelleschi, which, according to Vasari, so astonished his friend Donatello that he dropped the eggs he was carrying in his apron for their lunch when he first saw it.

   The charming fresco cycle in the **Sanctuary** (1485–90), painted by Domenico Ghirlandaio, is the *Lives of the Virgin, St John the Baptist and the Dominican Saints* portrayed in magnificent architectural settings; little Michelangelo was among the students who helped him complete it. Nearly all of the bystanders are portraits of Florentine quattrocento VIPs, including the artist himself (in the red hat, in the *Expulsion of St Joachim from the Temple*), but most prominent are the ladies and gents of the Tornabuoni house. More excellent frescoes adorn the **Filippo Strozzi Chapel**, the finest work ever to come from the brush of Filippino Lippi, painted in 1502 near the end of his life; the exaggerated, dark and violent scenes portray the lives of St Philip (his crucifixion and his subduing of the dragon before the Temple of Mars, which creates such a stench that it kills the heathen prince) and of St John the Evangelist (raising Drusiana from the dead and being martyred in boiling oil). The chapel's beautifully carved tomb of Filippo Strozzi is by Benedetto da Maiano. The **Rucellai Chapel** contains a marble statue of the Madonna and Bambino by Nino Pisano and a fine bronze tomb by Ghiberti, which makes an interesting comparison with the three Gothic tombs nearby in the right transept. One of these contains the remains of the Patriarch of Constantinople, who died in here after the failure of the Council of Florence in 1439 to reunite the Western and Eastern Churches.

## The Green Cloister and Spanish Chapel

More great frescoes, restored after the flood, await the visitor in Santa Maria Novella's Cloisters, open as a city museum (*entrance just to the left of the church; open Sat–Thurs 9–2; closed Fri; adm*). The first cloister, the so-called **Green Cloister**, one of the masterpieces of Paolo Uccello and his assistants, is named for the *terraverde* or green earth pigment used by the artist, which lends the scenes from Genesis their eerie, ghostly quality. Much damaged by time and neglect, they are nevertheless striking for their two Uccellian obsessions – perspective and animals, the latter especially on display in the scene of the Creation. Best known, and in better condition than the others, is Uccello's surreal *Universal Deluge*, a composition framed by the steep walls of two arks, before and after views, which have the uncanny effect of making the scene appear to come racing out of its own vanishing point, a vanishing point touched by divine wrath in a searing bolt of lightning. In between the claustrophobic walls the flood rises, tossing up a desperate ensemble of humanity, waterlogged bodies, naked men bearing clubs, crowded in a jam of flotsam and jetsam and islets rapidly receding in the dark waters. In the right foreground, amidst all the panic, stands a tall robed man, seemingly a visionary, perhaps even Noah himself, looking heavenward while a flood victim seizes him by the ankles. Some of Uccello's favourite perspective studies were of headgear, especially the wooden hoops called *mazzocchi* which he puts around the necks and on the heads of his figures.

The **Spanish Chapel** opens up at the far end of the cloisters, taking its name from the Spanish court followers of Eleonora di Toledo who worshipped here; the Inquisition had earlier made the chapel its headquarters in Florence. The chapel is, again, famous for its frescoes, the masterpiece of a little-known 14th-century artist named Andrea di Buonaiuto, whose subject was the Dominican cosmology, perhaps not something we have much empathy for these days, but here beautifully portrayed so that even the 'Hounds of the Lord' (a pun on the Order's name, the 'Domini canes') on the right wall seem more like pets than militant bloodhounds sniffing out unorthodox beliefs. The church behind the scene with the hounds is a fairy-pink confection of what Buonaiuto imagined the Duomo would look like when finished; it may well be Arnolfo di Cambio's original conception. A group of famous Florentines, including Giotto, Dante, Boccaccio and Petrarch, stand to the right of the dais supporting the pope, emperor and various sour-faced hierophants. Off to the right the artist has portrayed four rather urbane Vices with dancing girls, while the Dominicans lead stray sheep back to the fold. On the left wall, St Thomas Aquinas dominates the portrayal of the Contemplative Life, surrounded by Virtues and Doctors of the Church.

The oldest part of the monastery, the **Chiostrino dei Morti** (1270s), contains some 14th-century frescoes, while the **Great Cloister** beyond is now off limits, the property of the Carabinieri, the new men in black charged with keeping the Italians orthodox. Off the Green Cloister, the **Refectory** is a striking hall with cross vaulting and frescoes by Alessandro Allori, now serving as a museum.

## Around Santa Maria Novella

Just behind, but a world apart from Santa Maria Novella, another large, amorphous square detracts from one of Italy's finest modern buildings – the **Stazione Centrale**, designed by the architect Michelucci in 1935. Adorned by only a glass block canopy at the entrance (and an early model of that great Italian invention, the digital clock), the station is nevertheless remarkable for its clean lines and impeccable practicality; form following function in a way that even Brunelleschi would have appreciated.

One of the medieval lanes leading south from Piazza Santa Maria Novella, Via delle Belle Donne was once known for its excellent brothels. Today it is worth a short stroll to see one of the very few crossroads in Italy marked by a cross, a Celtic custom that never really caught on here – Italians are far more fond of corner shrines to the Madonna or some lucky saint. According to legend, **Croce del Trebbio** (from a corruption of 'trivium') marks the spot of a massacre of Patarene heretics in the 1240s, after the masses had been excited by a sermon given by the fire-eating Inquisitor St Peter Martyr from the pulpit of Santa Maria Novella.

# San Lorenzo and the Medici Chapels

The lively quarter just east of Santa Maria Novella has been associated with the Medici ever since Giovanni di Bicci de' Medici commissioned Brunelleschi to rebuild the ancient church of San Lorenzo in 1420; subsequent members of the dynasty lavished bushels of florins on its decoration and Medici pantheon, and on several projects commissioned from Michelangelo. The mixed result of all their efforts could be held up as an archetype of the Renaissance, and one which Walter Pater described as 'great rather by what it designed or aspired to do, than by what it actually achieved'. One can begin with San Lorenzo's façade of corrugated brick, the most *nonfinito* of all of Michelangelo's unfinished projects; commissioned by Medici Pope Leo X in 1516, the project never got further than Michelangelo's scale model, which may be seen in the Casa Buonarroti. To complete the church's dingy aspect, the piazza in front contains a universally detested 19th-century statue of Cosimo I's dashing father, Giovanni delle Bande Nere, who died at the age of 28 of wounds received fighting against Emperor Charles V.

The **interior**, although completed after Brunelleschi's death is true to his design, classically calm in good grey *pietra serena*. The artistic treasures it contains are few but choice, beginning with the second chapel on the right housing *The Marriage of the Virgin*, a 1523 work by the Mannerist Rosso Fiorentino. Joseph, usually portrayed as an old man, according to Rosso is a Greek god with golden curls in a flowing scene of hot reds and oranges – a powerful contrast to the chapel's haunting, hollow-eyed tomb slab of the Ray Charles of the Renaissance, Francesco Landini (d. 1397), the blind organist whose madrigals were immensely popular and influential in Italian music. At the end of the right aisle, there's a lovely delicately worked tabernacle by Desiderio da Settignano.

Most riveting of all, however, are **Donatello's pulpits**, the sculptor's last works, completed by his pupils after his death in 1466. Cast in bronze, the pulpits were commissioned by Donatello's friend and patron Cosimo il Vecchio, some think to keep the sculptor busy in his old age. Little in Donatello's previous work prepares the viewer for these scenes of Christ's passion and Resurrection with their rough and impressionistic details, their unbalanced, highly emotional and overcrowded compositions, more reminiscent of Rodin than anything Florentine; called by one critic 'the first style of old age in the history of art'.

Unfortunately they were set up on columns in the 17th century, just above eye level like so many things in Florence, a fault somewhat redeemed by a new lighting system. Nearby, directly beneath the dome, lies buried Donatello's patron and Florence's original godfather, Cosimo il Vecchio; the grille over his grave bears the Medici arms and the simple inscription, *Pater Patriae*.

It was the godfather's father, Giovanni di Bicci de' Medici, who in 1420 commissioned Brunelleschi to build the **Old Sacristy**, which is off the left transept. Often cited as one of the first and finest works of the early Renaissance, Brunelleschi designed this cube of a sacristy according to carefully calculated mathematical proportions, emphasized with a colour scheme of white walls, articulated in soft grey *pietra serena* pilasters and cornices. It is a dignified decoration that would become his trademark and something Florentine architects would borrow for centuries. For his own part, Donatello contributed the terracotta tondi and lunettes, as well as the bronze doors, embellished with lively Apostles. The Sacristy was built to hold the sarcophagi of Giovanni di Bicci de' Medici and his wife; in 1472 Lorenzo il Magnifico and his brother Giuliano had Verrocchio design the beautiful bronze and red porphyry wall tomb for their father Piero the Gouty and their uncle Giovanni. Unfortunately Verrocchio saw fit to place this in front of Brunelleschi's original door, upsetting the careful balance.

Don't miss the chapel across the transept from the entrance to the Old Sacristy, which houses a 19th-century monument to Donatello, who was buried here at his request near Cosimo il Vecchio. The lovely *Annunciation* is by Filippo Lippi; the large, colourful fresco of the *Martyrdom of St Lawrence* around the corner in the aisle is by Bronzino.

Just beyond the Bronzino a door leads into the 15th-century **Cloister**, and from there a stair leads up to Michelangelo's celebrated **Biblioteca Laurenziana** (*open Mon–Sat 8.30–1.30*). If Brunelleschi's Old Sacristy heralded the Renaissance, Michelangelo's library is Mannerism's prototype, or Brunelleschi gone completely haywire, no longer serene and mathematically perfect, but complicated and restless, the architectural elements stuck on with an eye for effect rather than for any structural purpose. The vestibule barely contains the remarkable stair, flowing down from the library like a stone cascade, built by Ammanati after a drawing by Michelangelo. This grand entrance leads into a fascinating collection that ranges from a very rare 5th-century Virgil and other Greek and Latin codices, to beautifully illuminated manuscripts, and the original manuscript of Cellini's autobiography; ask for a look around.

## The Medici Chapels

*Open daily (exc Sun and Mon as detailed) 8.15–5; closed 2nd and 4th Sun and 1st, 3rd and 5th Mon of month.*

San Lorenzo is most famous, however, for the Medici Chapels, which lie outside and behind the church . The entrance leads through the crypt, a dark and austere place where many of the Medici are actually buried.

Their main monument, the family obsession, is just up the steps, and has long been known as the **Chapel of the Princes**, a stupefying, fabulously costly octagon of death that, as much as the Grand Dukes fussed over it, lends their memory an unpleasant aftertaste of cancerous bric-a-brac that grew and grew. Perhaps only a genuine Medici could love its insane, trashy opulence; all of Grand Duke Cosimo's descendants, down to the last, Anna Maria Ludovica, worked like beavers to finish it according to the plans left by Cosimo's illegitimate son, dilettante architect Giovanni de' Medici. Yet even today it is only partially completed, the *pietre dure* extending only part of the way up the walls. The 19th-century frescoes in the cupola are a poor substitute for the originally planned 'Apotheosis of the Medici' in lapis lazuli, and the two statues in gilded bronze in the niches over the sarcophagi (each niche large enough to hold a hippopotamus) are nothing like the intended figures to be carved in semi-precious stone. The most interesting feature is the inlaid *pietra dura* arms of Tuscan towns and the large Medici arms above, with their familiar six red boluses blown up as big as beachballs. (The balls probably derive from the family's origins as pharmacists (*medici*), and opponents called them 'the pills'. Medici supporters, however, made them their battle cry in street fights: 'Balls! Balls!')

A passageway leads to Michelangelo's **New Sacristy**, commissioned by Leo X to occupy an unfinished room originally built to balance Brunelleschi's Old Sacristy. Michelangelo's first idea was to turn it into a new version of his unfinished, overly ambitious Pope Julius Tomb, an idea quickly quashed by his Medici patrons, who requested instead four wall tombs. Michelangelo only worked on two of the monuments, but managed to finish the New Sacristy itself, creating a silent and gloomy mausoleum, closed in and grey, a chilly introspective cocoon calculated to depress even the most chatty tour groups.

Nor are the famous tombs guaranteed to cheer. Both honour nonentities: that of *Night and Day* belongs to Lorenzo il Magnifico's son, the Duke of Nemours, and symbolizes the Active Life, while the *Dawn and Dusk* is of Guiliano's nephew, Lorenzo, Duke of Urbino (and dedicatee of *The Prince*), who symbolizes the Contemplative Life (true to life in one respect – Lorenzo was a disappointment to Machiavelli and everyone else, passively obeying the dictates of his uncle Pope Leo X). Idealized statues of the two men, in Roman patrician gear, represent these states of mind, while draped on their sarcophagi are Michelangelo's four allegorical figures of the Times of Day, so heavy with weariness and grief they seem ready to slide off on to the floor. The most finished figure, *Night*, has always impressed the critics; she is almost a personification of despair, the mouthpiece of Michelangelo's most bitter verse:

*Sweet to me is sleep, and even more to be like stone*
*While wrong and shame endure;*
*Not to see, nor to feel, is my good fortune.*
*Therefore, do not wake me; speak softly here.*

Both statues of the dukes look towards the back wall, where a large double tomb for Lorenzo il Magnifico and his brother Giuliano was originally planned, to be decorated with river gods. The only part of this tomb ever completed is the statue of the *Madonna and Child* now in place, accompanied by the Medici patron saints, the doctors Cosmas and Damian.

In 1975, a number of charcoal drawings were discovered on the walls of the little room off the altar (*ask at the cash desk for a permit, as only 12 people can enter at one time*). They were attributed to Michelangelo, who may have hidden here in 1530, when the Medici had regained Florence and apparently would only forgive the artist for aiding the republican defence if he would finish their tombs. But Michelangelo had had enough of their ducal pretences and went off to Rome, never to return to Florence.

## Mercato Centrale and Perugino

What makes the neighbourhood around San Lorenzo so lively is its street market, which the Florentines run with an almost Neapolitan flamboyance (*open daily exc Sun and Mon; but also open Mon in summer*). Stalls selling clothes and leather extend from the square up Via dell' Ariento and vicinity (nicknamed 'Shanghai') towards the **Mercato Centrale**, Florence's main food market (*open Mon–Sat 7–2*), a cast-iron and glass confection of the 1870s, brimful of fresh fruit and vegetables, leering boars' heads and mounds of tripe.

Beyond the market, at Via Faenza 42, is the entrance to Perugino's **Cenacolo di Foligno** fresco, housed in the ex-convent of the Tertiary Franciscans of Foligno (*open daily 9–12; ring the bell*). This 1490s Umbrian version of the Last Supper was discovered in the 1850s and has recently been restored.

## Palazzo Medici-Riccardi

A block from San Lorenzo and the Piazza del Duomo stands the palace that once held Florence's unofficial court, where ambassadors would call, kings would lodge, and important decisions would be made. Built in 1444 by Michelozzo for Cosimo il Vecchio, it was the principal address of the Medici for a hundred years, until Cosimo I abandoned it for larger quarters in the Palazzo Vecchio and the Pitti Palace. In 1659 the Riccardi purchased the palace, added to it and did everything to keep it glittering until Napoleon and his debts drove them to bankruptcy in 1809. The palace is now used as the city's prefecture.

In its day, though, it was the largest private address in the city, where the family lived with the likes of Donatello's *David* and *Judith and Holofernes*, Uccello's *Battle of San Romano* and other masterpieces now in the Uffizi and Bargello. Frescoes are much harder to move, however, and the Palazzo Medici is worth visiting to see the most charming one in Italy, Benozzo Gozzoli's 1459 *Procession of the Magi*, located in the **Cappella dei Magi** upstairs (*open Thurs–Tues 9–7; closed Wed; adm. Only a few people allowed in at a time; in summer you can reserve, t 055 276 0340*).

Painting in a delightful, decorative manner more reminiscent of International Gothic than the awakening Renaissance style of his contemporaries, Gozzoli took a religious subject and turned it into a merry, brilliantly coloured pageant of beautifully dressed kings, knights and pages, accompanied by greyhounds and a giraffe, who travel through a springtime landscape of jewel-like trees and castles. This is a largely secular painting, representing less the original Three Kings than the annual pageant of the *Compagnia dei Magi*, Florence's richest confraternity. The scene is wrapped around three walls of the small chapel – you feel as if you had walked straight into a glowing fairy tale world. Most of the faces are those of the Medici and other local celebrities; Gozzoli certainly had no qualms about putting himself among the crowd of figures on the right wall, with his name written on his red cap. In the foreground, note the black man carrying a bow. Blacks, as well as Turks, Circassians, Tartars and others, were common enough in Renaissance Florence, originally brought as slaves. By the 1400s, however, contemporary writers mention them as artisans, fencing masters, soldiers and one famous archery instructor, who may be the man pictured here.

The altarpiece is a copy of an ethereal *Madonna* by Filippo Lippi, the original being in Berlin. In the **Gallery**, up the second flight of stairs on the right, from the courtyard, is a different, but original Lippi *Madonna*. It's hard to imagine a more striking contrast than that between Gozzoli and the Neapolitan Luca Giordano (nicknamed 'Luca fa presto' or 'Luke Does-it-fast'), who painted this hilarious ceiling for the Riccardi in 1683, as a left-handed compliment to the Medici for selling them the palace. No longer mere players in a religious pageant, the Medici, or at least the overstuffed Grand Duke Cosimo III and his unspeakable heir Gian Gastone, take the leading roles, defying the laws of gravity and good taste in an apotheosis of marshmallow clouds.

# San Marco

*Convent open daily (exc Sun and Mon as detailed) 8.15–1.50, Sat 8.15–6.50; closed 1st and 3rd Sun of month and 2nd and 4th Mon of month; adm. Church open 7–12 and 4–7 daily.*

From the Medici palace, Via Cavour heads north for Piazza San Marco, a lively square full of art students from the nearby Accademia. The north side of the square is occupied by the **church and Dominican Convent of San Marco**. The Convent was Cosimo il Vecchio's favourite pious project; in 1437 he commissioned Michelozzo to enlarge and rebuild it, and to add to it Europe's first public library, where Florentine scholars invented humanism through the ancient classics collected by Cosimo's agents (now in the Laurenziana Library). A later prior of San Marco, Savonarola, had little use for the Medicis, though he owed his position to the influence of Lorenzo il Magnifico in 1491.

San Marco is best known for the works of the other-worldly Fra Angelico (1387–1455). His spiritual qualities were endorsed in 1982 when he was beatified by John Paul II; in 1984 the Pope declared him the patron saint of artists, taking over St Luke's old job. In residence here between 1436 and 1447, the now Blessed Angelico was put in charge of decorating the new convent constructed by Cosimo. His paintings and frescoes in San Marco, itself unchanged from the 1400s, offer a unique opportunity to see his works in the peaceful, contemplative environment in which they were meant to be seen.

Every painter in the 15th century earned his living painting sacred subjects, but none painted them with the deep conviction and faith of Angelico, who communicated his biblical visions in soft angelic pastels, bright playroom colours and an ethereal blondness, so clear and limpid that they just had to be true. 'Immured in his quiet convent,' wrote Henry James, 'he apparently never received an intelligible impression of evil; and his conception of human life was a perpetual sense of sacredly loving and being loved.' Yet the gentle friar was certainly not artistically naive, and adopted many of his contemporaries' innovations, especially artificial perspective, in his technique.

A visit to San Marco begins with Michelozzo's harmonious **Cloister of Sant' Antonio** in which Angelico painted the frescoes in the corners. Just off the cloister, the **Pilgrims' Hospice**, also by Michelozzo, has been arranged as a gallery of the blessed master's paintings, gathered from all over Florence. Here you'll find his great *Last Judgement* altarpiece (1430), a serenely confident work in which all the saved are well-dressed Italians holding hands, led by an angel in a celestial dance. They are allowed to keep their beautiful clothes in heaven, while the bad (mostly princes and prelates) are stripped to receive their interesting tortures.

One of the most charming works is the *Thirty-five Scenes from the Life of Christ*, acted out before strikingly bare, brown Tuscan backgrounds, painted as cupboard doors for Santissima Annunziata. Three of the scenes are by Angelico's talented apprentice, Alesso Baldovinetti. The noble, gracefully lamenting figures in the magnificent *Deposition* altarpiece from Santa Trínita stand before an elegant townscape dominated by Angelico's ziggurat-style concept of the Temple in Jerusalem. Other masterpieces include the *Tabernacle of the Linaioli* (the flax-workers), with a beautiful *predella*. The same holds true for the *Pala di San Marco*, the *predella* picturing SS. Cosmas and Damian, patrons of medicine and the Medici, in the act of performing history's first leg transplant. Other rooms off the cloister contain works by Fra Bartolomeo, another resident of the convent, whose portraits capture some of the most sincere spirituality of the late 15th century.

The **Chapter House** contains Angelico's over-restored fresco of *Crucifixion and Saints*, a painting that lacks his accustomed grace; in the smaller **Refectory** there's a more pleasing *Last Supper* by the down-to-earth Domenico Ghirlandaio.

Stairs lead up to Michelozzo's **Convent**, where at the top your eyes meet the Angelic Friar's masterpiece, a miraculous *Annunciation* that must have earned him his beatification. The subject was a favourite with Florentine artists, not only because it was a severe test – expressing a divine revelation with a composition of strict economy – but because the Annunciation, falling near the spring equinox, was New Year's Day for Florence until the Medici adopted the pope's calendar in the 1600s.

The monks of San Marco each had a small white cell with a window and a fresco to serve as a focal point for their meditations. Angelico and his assistants painted 44 of these; those believed to have been done by the master are along the outer wall (cells 1–9, the *Noli me Tangere*, another *Annunciation*, a *Transfiguration*, a *Harrowing of Hell*, a *Coronation of the Virgin*, and others). He also painted the scene in the large cell used occasionally by Cosimo il Vecchio and other visiting celebrities. One corridor is entirely painted with scenes of the Crucifixion, all the same but for some slight difference in the pose of the Dominican monk at the foot of the Cross; walking past and glancing in the cells successively gives the impression of an animated cartoon. In 1993, during restoration on the structure of the convent, fragments of paintings were found under the cells' floor. They are the incomplete 14th-century remains of the wall decoration in the original building and are only made visible by a series of mirrors in holes in the floor. Although it is hard to imagine the frescoes in their original glory, a comparison between them and the work of Beato Lippi underlines the artistic developments that occurred in Florence during the 14th and early 15th centuries.

The **Prior's cell** at the end belonged to Savonarola; it has simple furniture of the period and a portrait of Savonarola in the guise of St Peter Martyr (complete with an axe in his brain) by his friend Fra Bartolomeo. A copy of the anonymous painting in the Corsini Gallery, of Savonarola and two of his followers being burned at the stake in the Piazza della Signoria, also hangs here. The **Library**, entered off the corridor, is as light and airy as the cloisters below, and contains a collection of beautiful choir books. Architecturally the library was one of Michelozzo's greatest works, radiating a spirit of serenity, church-like with its vaulted nave and aisles.

The **church of San Marco** was rebuilt, along with the convent, in the 15th century, though the interior was rearranged by Giambologna and the Baroque façade added in 1780. The right aisle has an 8th-century mosaic from Constantinople, reminiscent of works from Ravenna. The fine *Madonna and Six Saints* is by Fra Bartolomeo, and in the left aisle, behind a statue of Savanarola, the tomb of the great linguist, humanist, and poet Poliziano, a member of Lorenzo il Magnfico's inner circle.

Near San Marco, at Via G. La Pira 4, the **University of Florence** runs several small museums; nearly all the collections were begun by the indefatigable Medici. The **Geology and Palaeontology Museum** (*open Tues–Sat and 2nd Sun of month 9–1; adm*) has one of Italy's best collections of fossils, many of which were uncovered in Tuscany. The **Mineralogy and Lithology Museum** (*open Tues–Sat and 2nd Sun of month 9–1; adm*) houses a collection of strange and beautiful rocks, especially from Elba. The **Botanical Museum** (*open on request only, t 055 275 7462 for details*) is of less interest to the casual visitor, though it houses one of the most extensive herbariums in the world; most impressive here are the exquisite wax models of plants made in the early 1800s.

Also on Via La Pira is the entrance to the University's **Giardino dei Semplici**, the botanical garden created for Cosimo I. The garden maintains its original layout, with medicinal herbs, Tuscan plants, flowers and tropical plants in its greenhouses (*open Mon–Fri 9–1; adm*).

## Sant'Apollonia and the Scalzo

*Cenacoli*, or frescoes of the Last Supper, became almost *de rigueur* in monastic refectories; in several of these the Last Supper is all that remains of a convent. Until 1860, the Renaissance convent of **Sant'Apollonia**, off Piazza S. Marco at Via XXVII Aprile 1 (*open daily 8.15–1.50; closed 2nd and 4th Mon and 1st, 3rd and 5th Sun of month*) was the abode of cloistered nuns, and the *cenacolo* in their refectory was a secret. When the convent was suppressed, and the painting discovered under the whitewash, the critics believed it to be the work of Paolo Uccello, but lately have unanimously attributed it to Andrea del Castagno, painted 1445–50. The other walls have sinopie of the Crucifixion, Entombment and Resurrection by Castagno; in the vestibule there are good works by Neri di Bicci and Paolo Schiavo.

Not far away you can enter a radically different artistic world in the **Chiostro dello Scalzo**, again off Piazza S. Marco at Via Cavour 69 (*open Mon, Thurs and Sat 9–1, ring the bell*). Formerly part of the Confraternity of San Giovanni Battista, all that has survived is this cloister, frescoed (1514–24) with scenes of the life of St John the Baptist by Andrea del Sarto and his pupil Franciabigio. Del Sarto, Browning's 'perfect painter', painted these in monochrome grisaille, and while the scene of the *Baptism of Christ* is a beautiful work, some of the other panels are the most unintentionally funny things in Florence – the scene of Herod's banquet is reduced to a meagre breakfast where the king and queen look up indignantly at the man bringing in the platter of the Baptist's head as if he were a waiter who had made a mistake with their order.

# The Galleria dell'Accademia

*Open Tues–Sun 8.15–6.50 and summer Sat 8.15–10pm; closed Mon; adm exp.*

From Piazza San Marco, Via Ricasoli makes a beeline for the Duomo, but on most days the view is obstructed by the crowds milling around No.60; in the summer the queues are as long as those at the Uffizi, everyone anxious to get a look at Michelangelo's *David*. Just over a hundred years ago Florence decided to take this precocious symbol of republican liberty out of the rain and install it, with much pomp, in a specially built classical exedra in this gallery.

Michelangelo completed the *David* for the city in 1504, when he was 29, and it was the work that established the overwhelming reputation he had in his own time. The monstrous block of marble – 16ft high but unusually shallow – had been quarried 40 years earlier by the Cathedral Works and spoiled by other hands. The block was offered around to other artists, including Leonardo da Vinci, before young Michelangelo decided to take up the challenge of carving the largest statue since Roman times. And it is the dimensions of the *David* that remain the biggest surprise in these days of endless reproductions. Certainly as a political symbol of the Republic, he is excessive – the irony of a David the size of a Goliath is disconcerting – but as a symbol of the artistic and intellectual aspirations of the Renaissance he is unsurpassed.

And it's hard to deny, after gazing at this enormous nude, that these same Renaissance aspirations by the 1500s began snuggling uncomfortably close to the frontiers of kitsch. Disproportionate size is one symptom; the calculated intention to excite a strong emotional response is another. In the *David*, virtuosity eclipses vision, and commits the even deadlier kitsch sin of seeking the sterile empyrean of perfect beauty – most would argue that Michelangelo here achieves it, perhaps capturing his own feelings about the work in the *David*'s chillingly vain, self-satisfied expression. This is also one of the few statues to have actually injured someone. During a political disturbance in the Piazza della Signoria, its arm broke off and fell on a farmer's toe. In 1991 it was David's toe that fell victim when a madman chopped it off. Since then, the rest of his anatomy has been shielded by glass.

In the Galleria next to the *David* are Michelangelo's famous *nonfiniti*, the four *Prisoners* or *Slaves*, worked on between 1519 and 1536, sculpted for Pope Julius' tomb and left in various stages of completion, although it is endlessly argued whether this is by design or through lack of time. Whatever the case, they illustrate Michelangelo's view of sculpture as a prisoner in stone just as the soul is a prisoner of the body. When Michelangelo left them, the Medici snapped them up to decorate Buontalenti's Grotta fountain in the Boboli gardens.

The Gallery was founded by Grand Duke Pietro Leopold in 1784 to provide Academy students with examples of art from every period. The big busy Mannerist paintings around the *David* are by Michelangelo's contemporaries, among them Pontormo's *Venus and Cupid*, with a Michelangelesque Venus among theatre masks. Other rooms contain a good selection of quattrocento painting, including the *Madonna del Mare* by Botticelli, a damaged Baldovinetti, the *Thebaid* by a follower of Uccello, and Perugino's *Deposition*. The painted frontal of the **Adimari chest** shows a delightful wedding scene of the 1450s with the baptistry in the background that has been reproduced in half the books ever written about the Renaissance.

The hall off to the left of the *David* was formerly the women's ward of a hospital, depicted in a greenish painting by Pontormo. Now it is used as a gallery of plaster models by 19th-century members of the Accademia.

The excellent **Collection of Old Musical Instruments** once housed in the Palazzo Vecchio has moved to the Accademia. The collection of some 150 exhibits, including several violins and cellos by Cremona greats like Stradivarius and Guarneri, has been on display in a room on the ground floor, properly organized and labelled since early spring 2001.

## Opificio delle Pietre Dure

*Open 8.15–2 (Thurs 8.15–7), closed Sun; adm.*

Around the corner from the Accademia, in Via degli Alfani 78, is the workshop of pietre dure, inlaid 'hard stones' or semi-precious stones. Cosimo I was the first to actively promote what was to become Florence's special craft, and it was Ferdinando I who founded the Opificio in 1588 as a centre for craftsmen.

Still on Via degli Alfani, across Via dei Servi, stands the **Rotonda di Santa Maria degli Angeli**, an octagonal building begun by Brunelleschi in 1434, one of his last works and one of the first centralized buildings of the Renaissance.

# Piazza Santissima Annunziata

This lovely square, really the only Renaissance attempt at a unified ensemble in Florence, is surrounded on three sides by arcades. In its centre, gazing down the splendid vista of Via dei Servi towards the Duomo, stands the equestrian statue of Ferdinand I (1607) by Giambologna and his pupil Pietro Tacca, made of bronze from Turkish cannons captured during the Battle of Lepanto. More fascinating than Ferdinand are the pair of bizarre Baroque fountains, also by Tacca, that share the square. Though of a nominally marine theme, they resemble tureens of bouillabaisse that any ogre would be proud to serve, topped by grinning winged monkeys.

In the 1420s Filippo Brunelleschi struck the first blow for classical calm in this piazza when he built the celebrated **Spedale degli Innocenti** (*open daily 8.30–2, closed Wed; adm*) and its famous portico – an architectural landmark, but also a monument to Renaissance Italy's long, hard and ultimately unsuccessful struggle towards some kind of social consciousness. Even in the best of times, Florence's poor were treated like dirt; if any enlightened soul had been so bold as to propose even a modern conservative 'trickle down' theory to the Medici and the banking élite, their first thought would have been how to stop the leaks. Babies, at least, were treated a little better. The Spedale degli Innocenti was the first hospital for foundlings in Italy and the world (at the left end of the loggia you can still see the original window-wheel where babies were anonymously abandoned until 1875). It still serves as an orphanage today, as well as a nursery school. The Spedale was Brunelleschi's first completed work and demonstrates his use of geometrical proportions adapted to traditional Tuscan Romanesque architecture. His lovely portico is adorned with the famous blue and white tondi of infants in swaddling clothes by Andrea della Robbia, added as an appeal to charity in the 1480s after several children died of malnutrition. Brunelleschi also designed the two beautiful cloisters of the convent; the **Chiostro delle Donne**, reserved for the hospital's nurses (located up the ramp on the right at No.13), is especially fine. Upstairs, the **Museo dello Spedale** (*open Thurs–Tues 8.30–2; closed Wed; adm*) contains a number of detached frescoes from Ognissanti and other churches, among them an unusual series of red and orange prophets by Alessandro Allori; other works include a *Madonna and Saints* by Piero di Cosimo, a *Madonna and Child* by Luca della Robbia, and the brilliant *Adoration of the Magi* (1488) painted by Domenico Ghirlandaio for the hospital's church, a crowded, colourful composition featuring portraits of members of the Arte della Lana, who funded the Spedale.

## Santissima Annunziata

*Open daily 7–12.30 and 4–6.30.*

The second portico on the piazza was built in 1600 in front of Florence's high society church, Santissima Annunziata. Founded in 1250, the church was rebuilt by Michelozzo beginning in 1444 and funded by the Medici, who saw the need for a grander edifice to contain the pilgrims attracted by a miraculous picture of the Virgin. As a shelter for the crowds, Michelozzo designed the **Chiostrino dei Voti**, an atrium in front of the church. Most of the Chiostrino's frescoes are by Andrea del Sarto and his students but the most enchanting work is Alesso Baldovinetti's *Nativity* (1462) – unfortunately faded, though you can make out the ghost of a transcendent landscape. Also present are two youthful works: Pontormo's *Visitation* and Rosso Fiorentino's more Mannerist *Assumption*.

The interior is the most gaudy, lush Baroque creation in the city, the only one the Florentines ever spent much money on during the Counter-Reformation. Michelozzo's design includes an unusual polygonal Tribune around the sanctuary, derived from antique buildings and entered by way of a triumphal arch designed by Alberti. Directly to the left as you enter is Michelozzo's marble **Tempietto**, hung with lamps and candles, built to house the miraculous *Annunciation*, painted by a monk with the help of an angel who painted the Virgin's face. Its construction was funded by the Medici, who couldn't resist adding an inscription on the floor that 'The marble alone cost 4,000 florins'. The ornate canopy over the *tempietto* was added in the 17th century.

The next two chapels on the left side contain frescoes by Andrea del Castagno, painted in the 1450s but whitewashed over by the Church when it read Vasari's phoney story that Castagno murdered his fellow painter Domenico Veneziano – a difficult feat, since Veneziano outlived his supposed murderer by several years. Rediscovered in 1864, Castagno's fresco of *St Julian and the Saviour* in the first chapel has some strange Baroque bedfellows by Giambattista Foggini; the next chapel contains his highly unusual *Holy Trinity with St Jerome*. The right aisle's fifth chapel contains a fine example of an early Renaissance tomb, that of the obscure Orlando de' Medici by Bernardo Rossellino. The neighbouring chapel in the transept contains a painted crucifix by Baldovinetti, while the next one has a *Pietà*, the funerary monument of Cosimo I's court sculptor and Cellini's arch-rival Baccio Bandinelli; in this *Pietà* he put his own features on Nicodemus, as Michelangelo did in the *Pietà* in the Museo del Duomo. Bandinelli's most lasting contribution (or piece of mischief) was his establishment of the first 'Accademia' of art in 1531, which eventually did away with the old artist-pupil relationship in favour of the more impersonal approach of the art school.

Nine semicircular chapels radiate from the Tribune. The one at the rear contains the sarcophagus of Giambologna, a far more successful follower of Michelangelo; his pupil Pietro Tacca is buried alongside him, in this chapel designed by Giambologna before his death. The next chapel to the left contains a *Resurrection* by Bronzino, one of his finest religious paintings. On the left side of Alberti's triumphal arch, under a statue of St Peter, is the grave of Andrea del Sarto; next to this can be found the tomb of bishop Angelo Marzi Medici (1546), one of Florence's loudest Counter-Reformation blasters.

A door from the left transept leads into the **Chiostro dei Morti**, most notable for Andrea del Sarto's highly original fresco, the *Madonna del Sacco* (1525), named after the sacks of grain on which St Joseph leans. The **Cappella di San Luca**, located off the cloister belongs to Florence's Academy of Design and contains the graves of Cellini, Pontormo, Franciabigio and other artists (*open on request from 7–12.30 and 4–6.30*).

# Archaeology Museum

*Open Mon 2–7, Tues and Thurs 8.30–7, Wed and Fri–Sun 8.30–2; adm.*

From Piazza SS. Annunziata, Via della Colonna leads to Florence's **Museo Archeologico**, housed in the 17th-century Palazzo della Crocetta, originally built for Grand Duchess Maria Maddalena of Austria. Like nearly every other museum in Florence, this impressive collection was begun by the Medici, beginning with Cosimo il Vecchio and accelerating with the insatiable Cosimo I and his heirs. The Medici were especially fond of Etruscan things, while the impressive Egyptian collection was begun by Leopold II in the 1830s.

The **Etruscan collection** is on the first floor, and includes the famous bronze *Chimera*, a remarkable beast with the three heads of a lion, goat and snake. This 5th-century BC work, which was dug up near Arezzo in 1555 and immediately snatched by Cosimo I, had a great influence on Mannerist artists. There is no Mannerist fancy about its origins, though; like all such composite monsters, it is a religious icon, a calendar beast symbolizing the three seasons of the ancient Mediterranean agricultural year. In the same corridor stands the *Arringatore*, or Orator, a monumental bronze of the Hellenistic period, a civic-minded and civilized-looking gentleman, dedicated to Aulus Metellus, and the statue of *Minerva*. Also to be found in this section are other Etruscan bronzes, big and small. The cases here are full of wonderful objects, anything from tiny animals to jewellery, carved mirrors and household objects such as plates – there's even a strainer. All these show just how skilled the Etruscans were in casting bronze.

The beautifully lit **Egyptian collection**, also on the first floor, has been expanded and modernized. It includes some interesting small statuettes, mummies, canopic vases, and a unique wood-and-bone chariot, nearly completely preserved, found in a 14th-century BC tomb in Thebes.

On the second floor there is plenty of Greek art; Etruscan noble families were wont to buy up all they could afford. The beautiful Hellenistic horse's head once adorned the Palazzo Medici-Riccardi. The *Idolino*, a bronze of a young athlete, is believed to be a Roman copy of a 5th-century BC Greek original. There is an excellent *Kouros*, a young man in the archaic style from 6th-century BC Sicily. An unusual, recent find, the silver *Baratti Amphora*, was made in the 4th century BC in Antioch and covered with scores of small medallions showing mythological figures. Scholars believe that the images and their arrangement may encode an entire system of belief, the secret teaching of one of the mystic-philosophical cults common in Hellenistic times, and they hope some day to decipher it. There's a vast collection of Greek pottery (including the massive *François vase* in Room 2), and large Greek, Roman and Renaissance bronzes, recently brought out of storage. There are also several fabulous Greek marble sculptures dating from *c.* 500 BC.

There is virtually nothing displayed on the ground floor now although temporary exhibitions are held there. Out in the garden are several reconstructed Etruscan tombs (*open to visitors on Sat at 9.30, 10.30, 11.30 and 12.30*).

The fabulous collection of precious stones, coins and, most notably, cameos (amassed by the Medici) is now permanently on display in the corridor which runs between the museum and the church of Santissima Annunziata.

## Santa Maria Maddalena dei Pazzi and the Synagogue

East of the Archaeological Museum, Via della Colonna becomes one of Florence's typical straight, boring Renaissance streets. It's well worth taking a detour down Borgo Pinti, to No.58, to visit one of the city's least known but most intriguing churches, **Santa Maria Maddalena dei Pazzi** (*open daily 9–12 and 5–7 ; voluntary donation*), a fine example of architectural syncretism. The church itself was founded in the 13th century, rebuilt in classically Renaissance style by Giuliano da Sangallo, then given a full dose of Baroque when the church was rededicated to the Counter-Reformation saint of the Pazzi family.

Inside it's all high theatre, with a gaudy trompe l'œil ceiling, paintings by Luca Giordano, florid chapels, and a wild marble chancel. From the Sacristy a door leads down into a crypt to the chapterhouse, which contains a frescoed *Crucifixion* (1496), one of Perugino's masterpieces. Despite the symmetry and quiet, contemplative grief of the five figures at the foot of the Cross and the stillness of the luminous Tuscan-Umbrian landscape, the fresco has a powerful impact, giving the viewer the uncanny sensation of being able to walk right into the scene. The fresco has never been restored; in the 1966 flood, the water came within four inches of the scenes, and stopped.

Florence's Jewish community, although today a mere 1,200 strong, has long been one of the most important in Italy, invited to Florence by the Republic in 1430, but repeatedly exiled and readmitted until Cosimo I founded Florence's Ghetto in 1551. When the Ghetto was opened up in 1848 and demolished soon after, a new **Synagogue** (1874–82) was built in Via L. C. Farini: a tall, charming, Mozarabic Pre-Raphaelite hybrid inspired by the Hagia Sophia and the Transito Synagogue of Toledo (*open April, May, Sept and Oct Sun–Thurs 10–5 and Fri 10–2; June–Aug Sun–Thurs 10–6 and Fri 10–3; Nov–Feb Sun–Thurs 10–2; adm*).

Although seriously damaged by the Nazis in August 1944, as well as by the Arno in 1966, it has since been lovingly restored. There's a small **Jewish Museum** upstairs (*opening hours as for Synagogue; call t 055 245 252/3 for info*), which has a documentary history of Florentine Jews as well as a collection of ritual and ceremonial items from the treasure.

From the synagogue it's a long two blocks north to **Piazzale Donatello** through pretty green Piazza d'Azeglio. Donatello's name has suffered terrible indignities of late (many people under the age of 25 only know him as a Teenage Mutant Ninja Turtle) but the Florentines, at least, could spare their greatest sculptor something more dignified than this swollen artery in the city's frenetic system of *viali* that take traffic around the centre. Pity, too, Elizabeth Barrett Browning (1809–61) and the other expatriates buried in the piazza's **English Cemetery** – now a traffic island choked in eternal exhaust fumes.

## Sant'Ambrogio and the Flea Market

The streets of Sant'Ambrogio are among the most dusty and piquant in the city centre, a neighbourhood where tourists seldom tread. Life revolves around **Sant'Ambrogio** and its neighbouring food market made of cast iron in 1873; the church (rebuilt in the 13th century, 19th-century façade) is of interest for its artwork: the second chapel on the right has a lovely fresco of the *Madonna Enthroned with Saints* by Orcagna (or his school) and the **Cappella del Miracolo**, just left of the high altar, contains Mino da Fiesole's celebrated marble *Tabernacle* (1481) and his own tomb. The chapel has a fresco of a procession by Cosimo Rosselli, especially interesting for its depiction of 15th-century celebrities, including Pico della Mirandola and Rosselli himself (in a black hat, in the group on the left). Andrea Verrocchio is buried in the fourth chapel on the left; on the wall by the second altar, there's a *Nativity* by Baldovinetti. The fresco of an atypical *St Sebastian* in the first chapel of the left is by Agnolo Gaddi.

From Sant'Ambrogio take Via Pietrapiana to the bustling **Piazza dei Ciompi**, named after the wool-workers' revolt of 1378. In the morning, Florence's flea market or **Mercatino** takes place here, the best place in town to buy that 1940s radio or outdated ball gown you've always wanted. One side of the square is graced with the **Loggia del Pesce**, built by Vasari in 1568 for the fishmongers of the Mercato Vecchio; when that was demolished the loggia was salvaged and re-erected here.

## Casa Buonarroti

*Open Wed–Mon 9.30–4; adm exp; look out for their temporary exhibitions.*

Michelangelo never lived in this house at Via Ghibellina 70, although he purchased it in 1508. That wasn't the point, especially to an artist who had no thought for his own personal comfort, or anyone else's – he never washed, and never took off his boots, even in bed. Real estate was an obsession of his, as he struggled to restore the status of the semi-noble but impoverished Buonarroti family. His nephew Leonardo inherited the house and several works of art in 1564; later he bought the two houses next door to create a memorial to his uncle, hiring artists to paint scenes from Michelangelo's life. In the mid-19th century, the house was opened to the public as a Michelangelo museum.

The ground floor is dedicated to mostly imaginary portraits of the artist, and works of art collected by his nephew's descendants, including an eclectic Etruscan and Roman collection. The main attractions, however, are upstairs, beginning with Michelangelo's earliest known work, the beautiful bas-relief *The Madonna of the Steps* (1490–1), the precocious work of a 16-year-old influenced by Donatello and studying in the household of Lorenzo il Magnifico; the relief of a battle scene, inspired by classical models, dates from the same period. Small models and drawings of potential projects line the walls; there's the wooden model for the façade of San Lorenzo, with designs for some of the statuary Michelangelo intended to fill in its austere blank spaces – as was often the case, his ideas were far too grand for his patron's purse and patience.

The next four rooms were painted in the 17th century to illustrate Michelangelo's life, virtues and apotheosis, depicting a polite, deferential and pleasant Michelangelo hobnobbing with popes. Those who know the artist best from *The Agony and the Ecstasy* may think they painted the wrong man by mistake. One of the best sections is a frieze of famous Florentines in the library. Other exhibits include a painted wooden *Crucifix* discovered in Santo Spirito in 1963 and believed by most scholars to be a documented one by Michelangelo, long thought to be lost; the contrapposto position of the slender body, and the fact that only Michelangelo would carve a nude Christ, weigh in favour of the attribution.

# Santa Croce

*Open summer Mon–Sat 9.30–5.30, Sun 3–5.30; winter Mon–Sat 9.30–12.30 and 3–5.30, Sun 3–5.30.*

No place in Florence so feeds the urge to dispute as the church of Santa Croce, Tuscany's 'Westminster Abbey', the largest Franciscan basilica in Italy, a must-see for every tour group. It was here that Stendhal gushed: 'I had attained to that supreme degree of sensibility where the divine intimations of art merge with the impassioned sensuality of emotion. As I emerged from the port of Santa Croce, I was seized with a fierce palpitation of the heart; I walked in constant fear of falling to the ground.' But don't be put off; most people manage to emerge without tripping over themselves.

The contradictions begin in the **Piazza Santa Croce**, which has its interesting points – the row of medieval houses with projecting upper storeys, supported by stone brackets; the faded bloom of dancing nymphs on the **Palazzo dell' Antella**; the curious 14th-century **Palazzo Serristori-Cocchi**, opposite the church; a grim 19th-century statue of Dante (if Dante really looked like that, it's no wonder Beatrice married someone else). Because this piazza is the lowest-lying in the city, it suffered the worst in the 1966 flood, when 20ft of oily water poured in; note the plaque marking the waterline on the corner of Via Verdi.

Dominant over all is Santa Croce's neo-Gothic façade, built in 1857–63 and financed by Sir Francis Sloane, whose Sloane Square in London has more admirers than this black and white design, derived from Orcagna's Tabernacle in Orsanmichele. Yet of all the modern façades built on Italy's churches to atone for the chronic Renaissance inability to finish anything, this is one of the least offensive.

### The Interior

Santa Croce was founded by St Francis himself; during repairs after the flood, vestiges of a small, early 13th-century church were discovered under the present structure. It went by the board in Florence's colossal building programme of the 1290s. The great size of the new church speaks for the immense popularity of Franciscan preaching. Arnolfo di Cambio planned it, and it was largely completed by the 1450s but, as in Santa Maria Novella, Giorgio Vasari and the blinding forces of High Renaissance mediocrity were unleashed upon the interior. Vasari never had

# Santa Croce

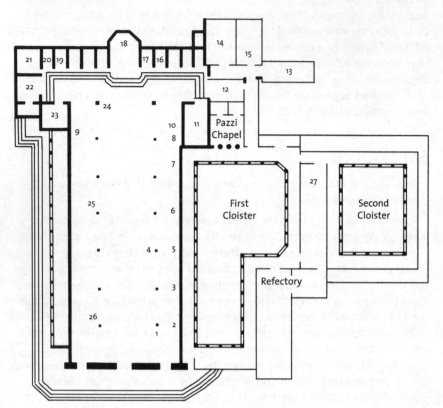

| | |
|---|---|
| 1 Madonna del Latte | 15 Rinuccini Chapel |
| 2 Tomb of Michaelangelo | 16 Peruzzi Chapel |
| 3 Monument to Dante | 17 Bardi Chapel |
| 4 Benedetto da Maiano's Pulpit | 18 Sanctuary |
| 5 Vittorio Alfieri's Tomb | 19 Bardi di Libertà Chapel |
| 6 Tomb of Machiavelli | 20 Bardi di Vernio Chapel |
| 7 Donatello's *Annuniciation* | 21 Niccolini Chapel |
| 8 Tomb of Leonardo Bruni | 22 Bardi Chapel |
| 9 Tomb of Carlo Malaspini | 23 Salviati Chapel |
| 10 Tomb of Rossini | 24 Monument to Alberti |
| 11 Castellani Chapel | 25 Tomb of Lorenzo Ghiberti |
| 12 Baroncelli Chapel | 26 Galileo's Tomb |
| 13 Medici Chapel | 27 Museo dell'Opera di S. Croce |
| 14 Sacristy | |

much use for the art of Andrea Orcagna – he not only left him out of his influential *Lives of the Artists* but in Santa Croce he destroyed Orcagna's great fresco cycle that once covered the nave, replacing it with uninspired side altars.

For centuries it was the custom to install monuments to illustrious men in Santa Croce and, as you enter, you can see them lining the long aisles. Like many Franciscan churches, Santa Croce's large size, its architectural austerity and open timber roof resemble a barn, but at the end there's a lovely polygonal sanctuary, which shimmers with light and colour streaming through 14th-century stained glass. The whole interior has recently been treated to an overhaul, completed in 2000, including restoration of the ceiling.

Perversely, the greater the person buried in Santa Croce, the uglier their memorial. A member of the Pazzi conspiracy, Francesco Nori, is buried by the first pillar in the right aisle, and graced by one of the loveliest works of art, the *Madonna del Latte* (1478), a bas-relief by Antonio Rossellino, while the **Tomb of Michelangelo** (1570, the first in the right aisle) by Vasari is one of the least attractive. Michelangelo died in Rome in 1564, refusing for 35 years to return to Florence while alive, but agreeing to give the city his corpse. Dante has fared even worse, with an 1829 neoclassical monument that's as disappointing as the fact (to the Florentines, anyway) that Dante is buried in Ravenna, where he died in exile in 1321.

Facing the nave, Benedetto da Maiano's **marble pulpit** (1476) is one of the most beautiful the Renaissance ever produced. Behind it, the **Vittorio Alfieri Monument** (1809) was sculpted by neoclassical master Antonio Canova and paid for by his lover, the Countess of Albany. Next is the nondescript 18th-century **Monument of Niccolò Machiavelli**, and then Donatello's *Annunciation* (1430s), a tabernacle in gilded lime-stone, the angel wearing a remarkably sweet expression as he gently breaks the news to a grave, thoughtful Madonna. Bernardo Rossellino's **Tomb of Leonardo Bruni** (1447), another masterpiece of the Renaissance, is perhaps the one monument that best fits the man it honours. Bruni was a Greek scholar, a humanist, and the author of the first major historical work of the period, *The History of Florence*, a copy of which his tran-quil effigy holds. The tomb, with its Brunelleschian architectural setting, proved a great inspiration to other artists, most obviously Desiderio da Settignano and his equally beautiful **Tomb of Carlo Marsuppini** (1453) directly across the nave, and the less inspired, more imitative **Monument to Rossini** crowded in to the left. The last tomb in the aisle belongs to poet and patriot Ugo Foscolo.

Santa Croce is especially rich in trecento frescoes, providing a unique opportunity to compare the work of Giotto with his followers. The south transept's **Castellani Chapel** has some of the later, more decorative compositions by Agnolo Gaddi (*Scenes from the Lives of Saints*, 1380s). The beautiful **Baroncelli Chapel** was painted with scenes from the Life of the Virgin by Agnolo's father Taddeo, Giotto's assistant in the 1330s and includes a bright, gilded altarpiece, the *Coronation of the Virgin* by Giotto and his workshop. The *Annunciation to the Shepherds* by Taddeo, seen to the left of the window, is important as it is thought to be the first nocturnal scene in the history of western art.

## The Legend of the True Cross

This popular medieval story begins with Noah's son, Seth, as an old man, asking for the essence of mercy. The Angel Gabriel replies by giving Seth a branch, saying that 5,000 years must pass before mankind may know true redemption. Seth plants the branch over Adam's grave on Mount Sinai, and it grows into a magnificent tree. King Solomon orders the tree cut, but as it is too large to move, the trunk stays where it is and is used as the main beam of a bridge. The Queen of Sheba is about to cross the bridge when she has a vision that the saviour of the world will be suspended from its wood, and that his death will mark the end of the Kingdom of the Jews. She refuses to cross the bridge, and writes of her dream to Solomon, who has the beam buried deep underground. Nevertheless, it is dug up and used to make the cross of Christ.

The cross next appears in the dream of Emperor Constantine before the Battle of Milvan Bridge, when he hears a voice saying that under this sign he will conquer. When it proves true, he sends his mother Helen to find the cross in Jerusalem. There she meets Judas Cyriacus, a pious Jew who knows where Golgotha is, but won't tell until Helen has him thrown in a well and nearly starved to death. When at last he agrees to dig, a sweet scent fills the air, and Judas Cyriacus is immediately converted. To discover which of the three crosses they find is Christ's, each is held over the coffin of a youth; the True Cross brings him back to life. After all this trouble in finding it, Helen leaves the cross in Jerusalem, where it is stolen by the Persians. Their King Chosroes thinks its power will bring him a great victory, but instead he loses the battle, and Persia, to Emperor Heraclius, who decides to return the holy relic to Jerusalem. But the gate is blocked by the Angel Gabriel, who reminds the proud Heraclius that Jesus entered the city humbly, on the back of an ass. And so, in a similar manner, the emperor returns the cross to Jerusalem.

The next portal gives on to a **Corridor** and the **Medici Chapel** (*open for Mass at 6pm*), both designed by Michelozzo, containing one of Andrea della Robbia's finest altar-pieces and a 19th-century fake Donatello, a relief of the *Madonna and Child* that fooled the experts for decades. From the corridor a door leads to the **Sacristy**, its walls frescoed by Taddeo Gaddi (*The Crucifixion*), Spinello Aretino and Niccolò di Pietro Gerini. Behind the 14th-century grille, the **Rinuccini Chapel** was frescoed by one of Giotto's most talented followers, the Lombard Giovanni da Milano, in the 1360s.

## Giotto's Chapels

The frescoes in the two chapels to the right of the sanctuary, the **Peruzzi Chapel** and the **Bardi Chapel**, were painted by the legendary Giotto in the 1330s, towards the end of his life when the artist returned from Padua and his work in the Arena chapel. The frescoes have not fared well during the subsequent 660 years. Firstly Giotto painted large parts of the walls *a secco* (on dry plaster) instead of *affresco* (on wet plaster), presenting the same kind of preservation problems that bedevil Leonardo's *Last Supper*; secondly, the 18th century thought so little of the frescoes that they were whitewashed over as eyesores. Rediscovered some 150 years later and finally restored in 1959, the frescoes now, even though fragmentary, may be seen more or less as

Giotto painted them. The Peruzzi Chapel contains scenes from the Lives of St John the Evangelist and the Baptist. In the Bardi Chapel is the *Life of St Francis*, which makes an interesting comparison with the frescoes in Assisi. The contrast between Giotto's frescoes and the chapel's 13th-century altarpiece, also showing the *Life of St Francis*, is a fair yardstick for measuring the breadth of the Giottesque revolution.

Agnolo Gaddi designed the stained glass around the **Sanctuary**, as well as the fascinating series of frescoes on the *Legend of the True Cross*.

Further to the left are two more chapels frescoed by followers of Giotto: the fourth, the **Bardi di Libertà Chapel**, by Bernardo Daddi, and the last, the **Bardi di Vernio Chapel**, by Maso di Banco, one of the most innovative and mysterious artists of the trecento. The frescoes illustrate the little-known *Life of St Sylvester* – his baptism of Emperor Constantine, the resurrection of the bull, the closing of the dragon's mouth and resurrection of two sorcerers; on the other wall of the chapel are a *Dream of Constantine* and *Vision of SS. Peter and Paul*. In the corner of the transept, the richly marbled **Niccolini Chapel** offers a Mannerist-Baroque change of pace, built by Antonio Dossi in 1584 and decorated with paintings by Allori (*under restoration*). Next, the second **Bardi Chapel** houses the famous crucifix by Donatello that Brunelleschi disdainfully called 'a peasant on the Cross'. The last funeral monuments, near the door, are those of Lorenzo Ghiberti and Galileo, the latter an 18th-century work. For running foul of the Inquisition, Galileo was not permitted a Christian burial until 1737.

## The Pazzi Chapel

*Open Thurs–Tues 10–5, later opening hours in summer; closed Wed; adm.*

This chapel carries an entrance fee, but it's well worth it. Brunelleschi, who could excel on the monumental scale of the cathedral dome, saved some of his best work for small places. Without knowing the architect, and something about the austere religious tendencies of the Florentines, the Pazzi Chapel is inexplicable, a Protestant reformation in architecture unlike anything ever built before. The 'vocabulary' is essential Brunelleschi, the geometric forms emphasized by the simplicity of the decoration: *pietra serena* pilasters and rosettes on white walls, arches, 12 terracotta tondi of the Apostles by Luca della Robbia, coloured rondels of the Evangelists in the pendentives by Donatello, and a small, stained-glass window by Baldovinetti. Even so, that is enough. The contemplative repetition of elements makes for an aesthetic that posed a direct challenge to the International Gothic of the time.

Leaving the Pazzi Chapel (notice Luca della Robbia's terracotta decorations on the portico), a doorway on the left of the cloister leads to another work of Brunelleschi, the **Second Cloister**, designed with the same subtlety and one of the quietest spots in Florence.

The old monastic buildings off the first cloister now house the **Museo dell'Opera di Santa Croce** (*open 10–5, until 6 in summer; closed Wed; adm*), where you can see Cimabue's celebrated *Crucifix*, devastated by the flood, and partly restored after one of Florence's perennial restoration controversies. The refectory wall has another fine fresco by Taddeo Gaddi, of the *Tree of the Cross and the Last Supper*; fragments of

Orcagna's frescoes salvaged from Vasari's obliteration squads offer powerful, nightmarish vignettes of The Triumph of Death and Hell. Donatello's huge, gilded bronze statue *St Louis of Toulouse* (1423) – a flawed work representing a flawed character, according to Donatello – was made for the façade of Orsanmichele. The museum also contains works by Andrea della Robbia, and a painting of Mayor Bargellini with a melancholy Santa Croce submerged in the 1966 flood for a backdrop; under the colonnade there's a statue of Florence Nightingale, born in and named after the city in 1820.

### Around Santa Croce: the Horne Museum

The east end of Florence, a rambling district packed with artisans and small manufacturers, traditionally served as the artists' quarter in Renaissance times. It's still one of the livelier neighbourhoods today, with a few lingering artists lodged in the upper storeys, hoping to breathe inspiration from the very stones where Michelangelo walked. It is a good place to observe the workaday Florence behind the glossy façade. Just west of Piazza Santa Croce is a series of streets – Via Bentaccordi (where a plaque marks Michelangelo's boyhood home), Via Torta and Piazza dei Peruzzi – which makes an almost complete ellipse. These mark the course of the inner arcade of the Roman amphitheatre, some stones of which can still be seen among the foundations of the old palaces.

From Santa Croce, the pretty Borgo Santa Croce leads towards the Arno and the delightful **Horne Museum**, housed in a Renaissance palace, at Via de' Benci 6 (*open Mon–Sat 9–1; closed Sun and hols; adm*). Herbert Percy Horne (1844–1916) was an English art historian, biographer of Botticelli, and Florentinophile, who bequeathed his collection to the nation. A large *Deposition*, the last work of Gozzoli, sadly darkened with age, a painting by the great Sienese Pietro Lorenzetti, and a *tondo* by Piero di Cosimo hang on the first floor. The next room contains Horne's prize, Giotto's golden painting of young *St Stephen*, also Signorelli's *Redeemer*, a beardless, girlish youth, Beccafumi's *Decalione e Pirra*, and a saccharine *St Sebastian* by Carlo Dolci. Room 3 has a rousing quattrocento battle scene, taken from a marriage chest, good 15th-century wood inlays, and a relief of the head of *St John the Baptist* by Desiderio da Settignano. Upstairs a diptych attributed to Barna da Siena holds pride of place, together with an impressive array of Renaissance furniture and household objects.

# North Bank Peripheral Attractions

## The Cascine

The newer sections of the city are, by and large, irredeemably dull. Much of Florence's traffic problem is channelled through its ring of avenues, or *viali*, laid out in the 1860s by Giuseppe Poggi to replace the demolished walls. On and along them are scattered points of interest, including some of the old city gates; the distances involved and danger of carbon monoxide poisoning on the *viali* make the idea of walking insane.

Bus 17C from the station or Duomo will take you through the congestion to the **Cascine**, the long (3.5km), narrow public park lining this bank of the Arno, originally used as the Medici's dairy farm, or *cascina*, and later as a Grand Ducal hunting park and theatre for public spectacles. A windy autumn day here in 1819 inspired Shelley to compose the 'Ode to the West Wind'. Three years later Shelley's drowned body was burnt on a pyre in Viareggio, by his friend Trelawny; curiously, a similar incineration took place in the Cascine in 1870 when the Maharaja of Kohlapur died in Florence. According to ritual his body had to be burned near the confluence of two rivers, in this case, the Arno and Mugnone at the far end of the park, on a spot now marked by the Maharaja's equestrian statue. Florentines come to the Cascine by day to play; it contains a riding school, race tracks, a small amusement park and zoo for the children, tennis courts, and a swimming pool. At night they come to ogle the transvestites strutting their stuff on the *viale*.

Beyond the train station, cars and buses hurtle around and around the **Fortezza da Basso**, an enormous bulk built by Antonio da Sangallo on orders from Alessandro de' Medici in 1534. It immediately became the most hated symbol of Medici tyranny. Ironically, the duke who built the Fortezza da Basso was one of very few to meet his end within its ramparts – stabbed by his relative and bosom companion 'Lorenzaccio' de' Medici. As a fortress, the place never saw any action as thrilling or vicious as the Pitti fashion shows that take place behind the walls in its 1978 aluminium exhibition hall.

Just east of the Fortezza, at the corner of Via Leone X and Viale Milton, there's an unexpected sight rising above the sleepy residential neighbourhood – the five graceful onion domes of the **Russian Church**, made even more exotic by the palm tree tickling its side. In the 19th century, Florence was a popular winter retreat for Russians who could afford it, among them Dostoevsky and Maxim Gorky. Completed by Russian architects in 1904, it is a pretty jewel box of brick and majolica decoration, open on the third Sunday of the month, when the priest comes from Nice to hold a morning service in Russian.

## The Stibbert Museum

*Open in summer Mon–Wed 10–2, Fri–Sun 10–6; in winter Mon–Wed 10–2, Fri–Sun 10–6; closed Thurs; adm.*

From Piazza della Libertà, dull Via Vittorio Emanuele heads a kilometre north to Via Stibbert and the Stibbert Museum (alternatively, take bus 31 or 32 from the station). Those who make the journey to see the lifetime's accumulations of Frederick Stibbert (1838–1906), who fought with Garibaldi and hobnobbed with Queen Victoria, can savour Florence's most bizarre museum, and one of the city's most pleasant small parks, laid out by Stibbert with a mouldering Egyptian temple sinking in a pond; and just try to obey the sign on the door: 'Comply with the Forbidden Admittances!'.

Stibbert's Italian mother left him a 14th-century house, which he enlarged, joining it to another house to create a sumptuous Victorian's version of what a medieval Florentine house should have looked like – 64 rooms to contain a pack-rat's treasure hoard of all things brilliant and useless, from an attributed Botticelli, to snuff boxes, to what a local guide intriguingly describes as 'brass and silver basins, used daily by Stibbert'.

Stibbert's serious passion, however, was armour, and he managed to amass a magnificent collection from all times and places. The best pieces are not arranged in dusty cases, but with a touch of Hollywood, on grim knightly mannequins ranked ready for battle.

# The Oltrarno

Once over the Ponte Vecchio, a different Florence reveals itself: greener, quieter, and less burdened with traffic. The Oltrarno is not a large district: a chain of hills squeezes it against the river, and their summits afford some of the best views over the city.

Once across the Arno, the Medici's catwalk becomes part of the upper façade of **Santa Felicità**, one of Florence's most ancient churches, believed to have been founded by the Syrian Greek traders who introduced Christianity to the city, and established the first Christian cemetery in the small square in front of the church.

Rebuilt in the 18th century, there is one compelling reason to enter, for here, in the first chapel on the right, is the *ne plus ultra* of Mannerism: Pontormo's weirdly luminous *Deposition* (1528), painted in jarring pinks, oranges and blues that cut through the darkness of the little chapel. The composition itself is highly unconventional, with an effect that derives entirely from the use of figures in unusual, exaggerated poses; there is no sign of a cross, the only background is a single cloud. Sharing the chapel is Pontormo's *Annunciation* fresco, a less idiosyncratic work, as well as four tondi of the Evangelists in the cupola, partly the work of Pontormo's pupil and adopted son, Bronzino.

## The Pitti Palace

As the Medici consolidated their power in Florence, they made a point of buying up the most important properties of their former rivals, especially their proud family palaces. The most spectacular example of this was Cosimo I's acquisition of the Pitti Palace, built in 1457 by a powerful banker named Luca Pitti who seems to have had vague ambitions of toppling the Medici and becoming the big boss himself. The palace, with its extensive grounds, now the Boboli Gardens, was much more pleasant than the medieval Palazzo Vecchio, and in the 1540s Cosimo I and his wife Eleanor of Toledo moved in for good.

The palace remained the residence of the Medici, and later the House of Lorraine, until 1868. The original building, said to have been designed by Brunelleschi, was only as wide as the seven central windows of the façade. Succeeding generations found it too small for their burgeoning hoards of bric-a-brac, and added several stages of symmetrical additions, resulting in a long, bulky profile, resembling a rusticated Stalinist ministry, but a landscaped one, ever since the 1996 European Summit.

There are eight separate **museums** in the Pitti – a tribute to Medici acquisitiveness in the centuries of decadence, a period from which, in the words of Mary McCarthy, 'flowed a torrent of bad taste that has not yet dried up...if there had been Toby jugs and Swiss weather clocks available, the Grand Dukes would certainly have collected them.' For the diligent visitor who wants to see everything, the Pitti is pitiless; it is impossible to see all in one day.

## Galleria Palatina

*Open Tues–Sun 8.15–6.50 (until 10pm on Sat in summer); adm.*

The Pitti museum most people see is the Galleria Palatina, containing the Grand Dukes' famous collection of 16th–18th-century paintings, stacked on the walls in enormous gilt frames under the berserk opulence of frescoed ceilings celebrating planets, mythology and, of course, the ubiquitous Medici. The gallery is on the first floor of the right half of the palace; the ticket office is on the ground floor, off Ammannati's exaggerated rustic courtyard, a Mannerist masterpiece.

After the entrance to the Galleria is the neoclassical **Sala Castagnoli**, with the *Tavola delle Muse* in its centre, itself an excellent introduction to the Florentine 'decorative arts'; the table, a paragon of the intricate art of *pietra dura*, was made in the 1870s. The Galleria's best paintings are in the five former reception rooms off to the left, with colourful ceilings painted in the 1640s by Pietro da Cortona, one of the most interesting Italian Baroque artists.

However, the set route takes you through the other part of the palace first, starting with the adjacent **Sala di Prometeo** containing Filippo Lippi's lovely *Tondo of the Madonna and Child* and Baldassare Peruzzi's unusual *Dance of Apollo*. Next you can peek into the **Sala di Bagni**, the Empire bathroom of Elisa Baciocchi, Napoleon's sister, who ruled the Département de l'Arno between 1809 and 1814, and seemingly spent much of those years redecorating the Pitti. Caravaggio's *Sleeping Cupid* is a couple of rooms up, in the **Sala dell'Educazione di Giove**. The next room to this is the pretty **Sala della Stufa**, frescoed with the *Four Ages of the World* by Pietro da Cortona.

The first of the reception rooms, the **Sala dell'Iliade** (frescoed in the 19th century), has some fine portraits by the Medici court painter and Rubens' friend, Justus Sustermans. Two *Assumptions* by Andrea del Sarto, *Philip II* by Titian and a Velazquez equestrian portrait of Philip IV share the room with one of the most unusual residents of the gallery, *Queen Elizabeth*, who seems uncomfortable in such company.

The **Sala di Giove**, used as the Medici throne room, contains one of Raphael's best-known portraits, the lovely and serene *Donna Velata* (1516). The small painting *The Three Ages of Man* is usually attributed to Giorgione. Salviati, Perugino, Fra Bartolomeo and Andrea del Sarto are also represented. (While there, take a look at the ceiling frescoes which have been restored.) The **Sala di Marte** has two works by Rubens, *The Four Philosophers* and the *Consequences of War*, as well as some excellent portraits by Tintoretto and Van Dyck (*Cardinal Bentivoglio*). The newly restored *Annunciation of San Godenzo*, by Andrea del Sarto, is now back in place after a long absence, and there is also Titian's rather dashing *Cardinal Ippolito de' Medici* in

Hungarian costume. Ippolito, despite being destined for the Church, was one of the more high-spirited Medici and helped defend Vienna from the Ottomans before being poisoned at the age of 24.

In the **Sala di Apollo** there's more Titian – his *Portrait of a Grey-eyed Gentleman*, evoking the perfect 16th-century English gentleman, and his more sensuous than penitent *Mary Magdalene* – as well as works by Andrea del Sarto and Van Dyck. The last reception room is the **Sala di Venere**, with several works by Titian, including his early *Concert*, believed to have been partly painted by Giorgione and a powerful *Portrait of Pietro Aretino*, Titian's close and caustic friend, who complained to the artist that it was all too accurate and gave it to Cosimo I. There are two beautiful landscapes by Rubens, painted at the end of his life, and an uncanny self-portrait, *La Menzogna* ('The Falsehood') by Neapolitan Salvator Rosa. The centrepiece statue, the *Venus Italica*, was commissioned by Napoleon from neoclassical master Antonio Canova in 1812 to replace the *Venus de' Medici* which he 'centralized' off to Paris – a rare case of the itchy-fingered Corsican trying to pay for something he took.

Next to the Sala di Venere is the **Sala delle Nicchie**, currently home to several paintings from Raphael's Florence days as long as work continues on the frescoes in the **Sala di Saturno**. These include the *Maddalena and Agnolo Doni* (1506) and the *Madonna 'del Granduca'*, influenced by the paintings of Leonardo. Some 10 years later, Raphael had found his own style, beautifully evident in his famous *Madonna della Seggiola* ('of the chair'), perhaps the most popular work he ever painted, and one that is far more complex and subtle than it appears. The rounded, intertwining figures of the Madonna and Child are seen as if through a slightly convex mirror, bulging out – one of the first examples of conscious illusionism in the Renaissance.

Some of the more interesting paintings to ferret out in the remainder of the gallery include Filippino Lippi's *Death of Lucrezia* and Raphael's *Madonna dell'Impannata*, both in the **Sala di Ulisse**.

## The State Apartments

The right half of the Pitti also contains the **State Apartments** (*included as part of the visit to the Galleria Palatina*). These were last redone in the 19th century by the Dukes of Lorraine, with touches by the Kings of Savoy, who occupied them during Florence's interlude as national capital. Among the garish furnishings, there is a fine series of Gobelin tapestries ordered from Paris by Elisa Baciocchi.

## Galleria d'Arte Moderna

*Open 8.30–1.50, closed 2nd and 4th Sun and 1st, 3rd and 5th Mon of month; adm exp; tickets from main ticket office on ground floor.*

On the second floor above the Galleria Palatina has been installed Florence's modern – read late 18th- to 20th-century – art museum. Though the monumental stair may leave you breathless (the Medici negotiated it with sedan chairs and strong-shouldered servants), consider a visit for some sunny painting of the Italy of your great-grandparents.

The 'Splatterers' or *Macchiaioli* (Tuscan Impressionists) illuminate **Room 16** and the rest of the museum, forming an excellent introduction to the works by Silvestro Lega, Giovanni Fattori, Nicolo Cannicci, Francesco Gioli, Federigo Zandomeneghi and Telemaco Signorini, with an interval of enormous Risorgimento battle scenes. What comes as a shock, especially if you've been touring Florence for a while now, is that the marriage between painting and sculpture that characterizes most of Italian art history seems to have resulted in a nasty divorce in the late 1800s: while the canvases radiate light, statuary becomes disturbingly kitsch, obsessed with death and beauty, culminating on one level with the *Pregnant Nun* and the *Suicide* by Antonio Ciseri in Room 19.

The Galleria was reopened after a major reorganization in 1999 and now consists of over 30 rooms. The most recent paintings on display are those in the last rooms, which cover the years 1900–23. There are plans eventually to open 13 more rooms covering 1923–45.

## Museo degli Argenti

*Open daily 8.30–1.50; closed 2nd and 4th Sun and 1st, 3rd and 5th Mon of month; adm valid for Costume and Porcelain Museums.*

The ground floor on the left side of the Pitti was used as the Medici summer apartments and now contains the family's remarkable collection of jewellery, vases, trinkets and pricey curiosities. The Grand Duke's guests would be received in four of the most delightfully frescoed rooms to be found anywhere in Florence, beginning with the **Sala di Giovanni di San Giovanni**, which is named after the artist who painted it in the 1630s. The theme is the usual Medicean self-glorification – but nowhere does such dubious material achieve such flamboyant treatment. Here the Muses, chased from Paradise, find refuge with Lorenzo il Magnifico; Lorenzo smiles as he studies a bust of Pan by Michelangelo. His real passion, a collection of antique vases carved of semi-precious stones or crystal, is displayed in a room off to the left; the vases were dispersed with the rise of Savonarola, but Lorenzo's nephew Cardinal Giulio had no trouble in locating them, as Lorenzo had his initials LAUR.MED. deeply incised into each. The three **Reception rooms** were painted in shadowy blue trompe l'œil by two masterful Bolognese illusionists, Agostino Michele and Angelo Colonna.

The Grand Dukes' treasure hoard is up on the mezzanine. These golden toys are only a fraction of what the Medici had accumulated; despite the terms of Anna Maria's will, leaving everything to Florence, the Lorraines sold off the most valuable pieces and jewels to finance Austria's wars. Among the leftovers here, however, is a veritable apoplexy of fantastical bric-a-brac: jewelled bugs, cameos, sea monster pendants, interlaced ivory cubes, carved cherry pits, gilt nautilus shells, chalices made of ostrich eggs, enough ceramic plates to serve an army, a Mexican mitre made of feathers, intricate paper cut-outs, cups carved from buffalo horns, and 17th-century busts and figurines made of seashells that would not shame the souvenir stand of any seaside resort.

## More Pitti Museums

The **Museum of Costumes** (*open daily 8.15–1.50; closed 2nd and 4th Sun and 1st, 3rd and 5th Mon of month*) is housed on the second floor of the Palace, near to the Galleria d'Arte Moderna; which has the reconstructed dress Eleanor of Toledo was buried in – the same one that she wears in Bronzino's famous portrait. The **Porcelain Museum** (*open daily 9–1.30; closed 2nd and 4th Sun and 1st, 3rd and 5th Mon of month; adm inc. with Boboli ticket*) is housed in the casino of Cosimo III, out in the Giardino del Cavaliere in the Boboli Gardens (*follow the signs*). The **Museo delle Carrozze**, with a collection of Medici and Lorraine carriages and sedan chairs, has been closed for years.

## Boboli Gardens

*Open from 9am until one hour before sunset; adm; t 055 265 1838.*

Stretching back invitingly from the Pitti, the shady green of the Boboli Gardens, Florence's largest (and only) central public garden, is an irresistible oasis in the middle of a stone-hard city. Originally laid out by Buontalenti, the Boboli reigns as queen of all formal Tuscan gardens, the most elaborate and theatrical, a Mannerist-Baroque co-production of Nature and Artifice laid out over a steep hill, full of shady nooks and pretty walks and beautifully kept. The park is populated by a platoon of statuary, many of them Roman works, others absurd Mannerist pieces.

There are three entrances and exits: through the main courtyard of the Pitti Palace, from Via Romana and in Porta Romana. The main, route, from the Pitti Palace, starts at the **Amphitheatre**, which ascends in regular tiers from the palace, and was designed like a small Roman circus to hold Medici court spectacles. It has a genuine obelisk, of Rameses II from Heliopolis, snatched by the ancient Romans and shipped here by the Medici branch in Rome. The granite basin, large enough to submerge an elephant, came from the Roman Baths of Caracalla. Straight up the terrace is the **Neptune Fountain**; a signposted path leads from there to the pretty **Kaffeehaus**, a boat-like pavilion with a prow and deck offering a fine view of Florence and drinks in the summer. From here the path continues up to the **Belvedere Fort** (*currently under restoration, see* p.221). Other signs from the Neptune Fountain point the way up to the secluded **Giardino del Cavaliere**, located on a bastion on Michelangelo's fortifications. Cosimo III built the casino here to escape the heat in the Pitti Palace; the view over the ancient villas, vineyards and olives is pure Tuscan enchantment. The **Porcelain Museum** here (*open daily 9–1.30*) contains 18th- and 19th-century examples of china-work from Sèvres, Meissen and Vienna.

At the bottom right-hand corner of the garden lies the remarkable **Grotta di Buontalenti**, one of the architect's most imaginative works, anticipating Gaudí with his dripping, stalactite-like stone, from which fantastic limestone animals struggle to emerge. Casts of Michelangelo's *nonfiniti* slaves stand in the corners, replacing the originals put there by the Medici, while back in the shadowy depths stands a luscious statue of Venus coming from her bath by Giambologna. Just before the exit is the Mannerist statue of Cosimo I's court dwarf Morgante posing as a chubby Bacchus astride a turtle.

## Casa Guidi

In the old days the neighbourhood around the Pitti was a fashionable address, but during the 19th century rents for a furnished palace were incredibly low. Shortly after their secret marriage, the Brownings found one of these, the **Casa Guidi** at Piazza San Felice 8, the perfect place to settle; during their 13 years here they wrote their most famous poetry. The house is now owned by the Browning Institute, you can visit it at certain times (*open April–Nov Mon, Wed and Fri 3–6; closed Dec–Mar; donations expected*). Dostoevsky wrote *The Idiot* while living nearby, at No.21 Piazza Pitti. Note the doorbells at No.13, ten little wrought-iron gargoyles waiting to have their heads pulled.

## Stuffed Animals and Wax Cadavers

Past the Pitti on Via Romana 17, is one of Florence's great oddball attractions, the **La Specola** museum (*open Thurs–Tues 9–1; closed Wed; adm*). The **Zoological Section** has a charmingly old-fashioned collection of nearly everything that walks, flies or swims, from the humble sea worm to the rare Madagascar Aye-Aye or the swordfish, with an accessory case of different blades. The real horror show stuff, however, is kept hidden away in the **Museum of Waxes**. Dotty, prudish old Cosimo III was a hypochondriac and morbidly obsessed with diseases, which his favourite artist, a Sicilian priest named Gaetano Zumbo, was able to portray with revolting realism. His macabre anatomical models were one of the main sights for Grand Tourists in the 1700s.

## Santo Spirito

Piazza Santo Spirito, the centre of the Oltrarno, usually has a few market stalls in the morning under the plane trees as well as a quiet café or two. In the evening it changes face and the bars fill with people, who meet and chat in the piazza and on the church steps until the early hours. On one side, a plain 18th-century façade hides Brunelleschi's last, and perhaps greatest church. He designed Santo Spirito in 1440 and lived to see only one column erected, but subsequent architects were faithful to his elegant plan for the interior. This is done in the architect's favourite pale grey and *pietra serena* articulation, a rhythmic forest of columns with semicircular chapels is gracefully recessed into the transepts and the three arms of the crossing. The effect is somewhat spoiled by the ornate 17th-century *baldacchino*, which sits in this enchanted garden of architecture like a 19th-century bandstand.

The art in the chapels is meagre, as most of the good paintings were sold off over the years. The best include Filippino Lippi's beautiful, newly restored *Madonna and Saints* in the right transept and Verrocchio's jewel-like *St Monica and Nuns* in the opposite transept, an unusual composition and certainly one of the blackest paintings of the Renaissance, pervaded with a dusky, mysterious quality; Verrocchio, who taught both Leonardo and Botticelli, was a Hermetic alchemist on the side. The fine marble altarpiece and decoration in a nearby chapel is by Sansovino; the elaborate barrel-vaulted **Vestibule** and octagonal **Sacristy**, entered from the left aisle, are by Giuliano da Sangallo, inspired by Brunelleschi.

To the left of the church, in the **refectory** (*open 10–1.30, until 12.30 Sun and hols; closed Mon; adm*) of the vanished 14th-century convent, are the scanty remains of a *Last Supper* and a well-preserved, highly dramatic *Crucifixion* by Andrea Orcagna, in which Christ is seen alone against an enormous dark sky, with humanity ranged below and angels like white swallows swirling around in a cosmic whirlwind. The refectory also contains an interesting collection of Romanesque odds and ends, including 13th-century stone sea-lions from Naples.

## Santa Maria del Carmine and the Cappella Brancacci

*Open 10–5 (last adm 4.45), Sun and hols 1–5; closed Tues; adm; only 30 people are admitted at a time, for 15 minutes; you can usually avoid waiting if you go at lunchtime.*

There is little to say about the surroundings, the piazza-cum-car park, the rough stone façade, or the interior of the Oltrarno's other great church, Santa Maria del Carmine, which burned in 1771 and was reconstructed shortly after. Miraculously, the **Cappella Brancacci**, one of the landmarks in Florentine art, survived both the flames and attempts by the authorities to replace it with something more fashionable. Three artists worked on the Brancacci's frescoes: Masolino, who began them in 1425, and who designed the cycle; his pupil Masaccio, who worked on them alone for a year before following his master to Rome, where he died at the age of 27; and Filippino Lippi, who finished them 50 years later. Filippino took care to imitate Masaccio as closely as possible, and the frescoes have an appearance of stylistic unity. Between 1981 and 1988 they were subject to one of Italy's most publicized restorations, cleansed of 550 years of dirt and overpainting, enabling us to see what so thrilled the painters of the Renaissance.

Masaccio in his day was a revolution and a revelation in his solid, convincing naturalism; his figures stand in space, without any fussy ornamentation or Gothic grace, very much inspired by Donatello's sculptures. Masaccio conveyed emotion with broad, quick brush strokes and with his use of light, most obvious in the *Expulsion of Adam and Eve*, one of the most memorable and harrowing images created in the Renaissance. In the *Tribute Money*, the young artist displays his mastery of Brunelleschian artificial perspective and light effects. The three episodes in the fresco show an official demanding tribute from the city, St Peter fetching it on Christ's direction from the mouth of a fish, and lastly, his handing over of the money to the official.

Other works by 'Shabby Tom' include *St Peter Baptizing* on the upper register, and *St Peter Healing with his Shadow* and *St Peter Enthroned and Resurrecting the Son of the King of Antioch*, the right half of which was finished by Filippino Lippi. The elegant Masolino is responsible for the remainder, except for the lower register's *Release of St Peter from Prison*, *St Peter Crucified* and *St Paul Visiting St Peter in Prison*, all by Filippino Lippi, based on Masaccio's sketches.

Among the detached frescoes displayed in the cloister and refectory is a good one by Filippino's dad, Fra Filippo Lippi, who was born nearby in Via dell'Ardiglione.

## Around the Oltrarno

Stroll the streets of the Oltrarno and you discover one of the city's last real residential neighbourhoods, the streets lined with bakeries and barber shops instead of boutiques and restaurants. The westernmost quarter within the medieval walls, Borgo San Frediano, is known for its workshops and unpretentious antique dealers. The **Porta San Frediano**, its tall tower guarding the Pisa road, has its old wooden door and locks still in place. The domed 17th-century church of **San Frediano in Cestello**, with its blank poker face, is the landmark along this stretch of the Arno.

The neighbourhoods get trendier as you head east, especially along Via di Santo Spirito, lined with medieval palaces, its extension Borgo San Jacopo, and wide Via Maggio, leading inland from the Ponte Santa Trínita. All have fine palaces and medieval towers pruned by the Republic. Many great medieval bankers also erected their palaces in the Oltrarno. Several may still be seen along Via de' Bardi, east of the Ponte Vecchio, especially the 13th–14th-century **Palazzo dei Mozzi** in the piazza of the same name. At the time of writing it is being arranged as an extension of the **Museo Bardini**, also in the same piazza (*currently closed*), an eclectic collection of art and architectural fragments left to the city in 1922 by antiques dealer Stefano Bardini. Bardini built this lugubrious palace to incorporate the doorways, ceilings and stairs that he salvaged from the demolition of the Mercato Vecchio and other buildings in central Florence; he even installed a mock crypt to display his tombs and funereal altarpieces (there's an especially fine one by Andrea della Robbia). Also outstanding are Tino da Camaino's trecento *Charity*, a *Madonna* attributed to Donatello, a panel painting of *St Michael* by Antonio Pollaiuolo, and a magnificent set of Persian carpets, old musical instruments, furniture and armour. Near the museum, the nondescript postwar **Ponte alle Grazie** replaced a famous medieval bridge with seven chapels on it, home to seven nuns, who one imagines spent much of their time praying that the Arno wouldn't flood.

Further east, narrow Via di San Niccolò leads to **San Niccolò sopr'Arno**, a church rebuilt in the 14th century, with a lovely fresco in the sacristy of the *Madonna della Cintola* ('of the girdle') by Baldovinetti. The street ends with a bang at **Porta San Niccolò**, an impressively looming gate of 1340 that has recently been restored. A smaller gate just to the south, the **Porta San Miniato**, stands near the walkway up to San Miniato (see below).

# A City with a View

Great Aunt Florence, with her dour complexion and severe, lined face, never was much of a looker from street level, but improves with a bit of distance, either mental or from one of her hill-top balconies: the Belvedere Fort, San Miniato, Piazzale Michelangelo, Bellosguardo, Fiesole or Settignano. Few cities are so endowed with stunning vistas; and when you look down upon Florence's palaces and towers, her loping bridges and red tile roofs and famous churches, Brunelleschi's incomparable dome seems even more remarkable, hovering like a benediction over the city.

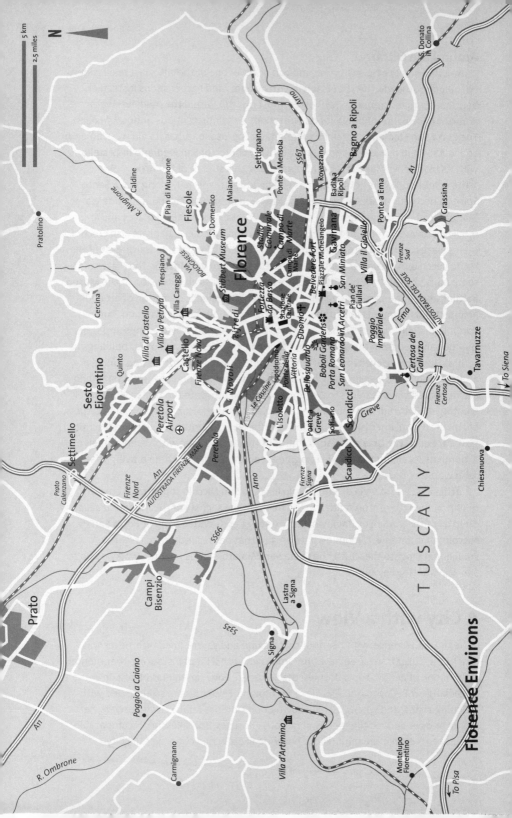

**Florence Environs**

T U S C A N Y

# Florence

5 km
2.5 miles
N

Prato
Settimello
Sesto Fiorentino
Peretola Airport
Quinto
Cercina
Pratolino
Caldine
Pian di Mugnone
Fiesole
S. Domenico
Maiano
Settignano
Ponte a Mensola
S. Donato in Collina
Bagno a Ripoli
Rovezzano
Grassina
Ponte a Ema
Badia a Ripoli
Firenze Sud
Gavinana
San Miniato
Villa il Gioiello
Pian de' Giullari
Poggio Imperiale
San Leonardo in Arcetri
Certosa del Galluzzo
Tavarnuzze
Chiesanuova
To Siena
Firenze Certosa
Ema
Greve
Scandicci
Soffiano
Ponte a Greve
L'Isolotto
Porta Romana
Boboli Gardens
Bellosguardo
Le Cascine
Ponte della Vittoria
Ippodromo
Novoli
Firenze Nova
Castello
Villa la Petraia
Villa di Castello
Villa Caregg̀i
Trespiano
Stibbert Museum
Rifredi
Stazione Centrale
Fortezza da Basso
Stadio Comunale
Campo di Marte
Belvedere Fort
Piazzale Michelangelo
San Miniato
Duomo
VIA BOLOGNESE
R. Mugnone
Arno
SS67
A1
AUTOSTRADA DEL SOLE
Firenze Signa
Signa
Lastra a Signa
Campi Bisenzio
Prato Calenzano
Settimello
Firenze Nord
A11
AUTOSTRADA FIRENZE MARE
Peretola
SS66
SS325
Arno
Poggio a Caiano
Carmignano
Montelupo Fiorentino
Villa d'Artimino
R. Ombrone
To Pisa

## Belvedere Fort and Arcetri

One of Florence's best and closest balconies is the rather run-down **Belvedere Fort** (*currently closed for what looks to be a long and indefinite bout of restoration*), a graceful, six-point star designed by Buontalenti and built in 1590–5, not so much for the sake of defence but to remind any remaining Florentine republicans who was boss. Since 1958, it has been used for special exhibitions, but you can usually enjoy unforgettable views of Florence and the surrounding countryside from its ramparts. Leading up to it is one of Florence's prettiest streets, **Costa San Giorgio**, which begins in Piazza Santa Felicità, just beyond the Ponte Vecchio. Costa San Giorgio winds up the hill, lined with old villas and walled gardens. The villa at No.19 was, from 1610 to 1631, the home of Galileo. At the top of the street stands the arch of the **Porta San Giorgio**, guarded by a 13th-century relief of St George and the dragon.

In this part of Florence, the countryside begins right at the city wall, a rolling landscape of villas and gardens, olives and cypresses. Via San Leonardo winds its way out towards Arcetri; a 10-minute walk will take you to the 11th-century **San Leonardo in Arcetri** (*usually open Sun am*). There is a wonderful 13th-century pulpit, originally built for San Pier Scheraggio, and a small rose window, made according to legend from a wheel of Fiesole's *carroccio*, captured by Florence in 1125. A half-kilometre further on, past the Viale Galileo crossroads, Via San Leonardo changes its name to Via Viviani, where it passes the **Astrophysical Observatory** and the **Torre del Gallo**. Another kilometre further on Via Viviani reaches the settlement of Pian de' Giullari, where Galileo spent the last years of his life, in the 16th-century **Villa il Gioiello**, virtually under house arrest after his encounter with the Inquisition in 1631, and where Milton is believed to have visited him.

## San Miniato

*Open daily summer 8–7.30; winter daily 8–12.30 and 2.30–7.30.*

From Porta San Miniato you can walk up to San Miniato church on the stepped Via di San Salvatore al Monte, complete with the Stations of the Cross, or take the less pious bus 13 up the scenic Viale dei Colli from the station or Via de Benci, near Ponte alle Grazie. High atop its monumental steps, San Miniato's beautiful, distinctive façade can be spotted from almost anywhere in the city, although relatively few visitors take the time actually to visit what is in fact one of the finest Romanesque churches in Italy.

San Miniato was built in 1015, over an earlier church that marked the spot where the head of St Minias, a 3rd-century Roman soldier, bounced when the Romans axed it off. Despite its distance from the centre San Miniato has always been one of the churches dearest to the Florentines' hearts. The remarkable geometric pattern of green, black and white marble that adorns its façade was begun in 1090, though funds only permitted the embellishment of the lower, simpler half of the front; the upper half, full of curious astrological symbolism (someone has written a whole book about it) was added in the 12th century, paid for by the Arte di Calimala, the guild that made a fortune buying bolts of fine wool, dyeing them a deep red or scarlet that no one else in Europe could imitate, then selling them back for twice the price; their proud gold eagle stands at the top of the roof. The glittering mosaic of Christ, the Virgin and St Minias, came slightly later.

The Calimala was also responsible for decorating the interior, an unusual design with a raised choir built over the crypt. As the Calimala became richer, so did the fittings; the delicate intarsia **marble floor** of animals and zodiac symbols dates from 1207. The lower walls were frescoed in the 14th and 15th centuries, including an enormous St Christopher. At the end of the nave stands Michelozzo's unique, free-standing **Cappella del Crocifisso**, built in 1448 to hold the crucifix that spoke to St John Gualberto (now in Santa Trínita); it is magnificently carved and adorned with terracottas by Luca della Robbia.

Off the left nave is one of Florence's Renaissance showcases, the **Chapel of the Cardinal of Portugal** (1461–6). The 25-year-old cardinal, a member of the Portuguese royal family, happened to die in Florence at an auspicious moment, when the Medici couldn't spend enough money on publicly prominent art, and when some of the greatest artists of the quattrocento were at the height of their careers. The chapel was designed by Manetti, Brunelleschi's pupil; the ceiling exquisitely decorated with enamelled terracotta and medallions by Luca della Robbia; the Cardinal's tomb beautifully carved by Antonio Rossellino; the frescoed *Annunciation* charmingly painted by Alesso Baldovinetti; the altarpiece *Three Saints* is a copy of the original by Piero Pollaiuolo.

Up the steps of the choir more treasures await. The marble transenna and pulpit were carved in 1207, with art and a touch of medieval humour. Playful geometric patterns frame the mosaic in the apse, *Christ between the Virgin and St Minias*, made in 1297 by artists imported from Ravenna, and later restored by Baldovinetti. The colourful **Sacristy** on the right was entirely frescoed by Spinello Aretino in 1387, but made rather flat by subsequent restoration. In the **Crypt** an 11th-century altar holds the relics of St Minias; the columns are topped by ancient capitals. The **cloister** has frescoes of the Holy Fathers by Paolo Uccello, remarkable works in painstaking and fantastical perspective, rediscovered in 1925. The monks sing Gregorian chant every afternoon at about 4pm – a magical experience.

The panorama of Florence from San Miniato is lovely to behold, but such thoughts were hardly foremost in Michelangelo's mind during the Siege of Florence. The hill was vulnerable, and to defend it he hastily erected the fortress (now surrounding the cemetery to the left of the church), placed cannons in the unfinished 16th-century campanile (built to replace one that toppled over), and shielded the tower from artillery with mattresses. He grew fond of the small church below San Miniato, **San Salvatore al Monte**, built by Cronaca in the late 1400s, which he called his 'pretty country lass'.

With these associations in mind, the city named the vast, square terrace car park below, **Piazzale Michelangelo**, the most popular viewpoint only because it is the only one capable of accommodating an unlimited number of tour buses (though now there are restrictions on the length of time buses are allowed to stop, the situation has improved a bit). On Sunday afternoons, crowds of Florentines habitually make a stop here during their afternoon *passeggiata*. Besides another copy of the *David* and a fun, tacky carnival atmosphere rampant with souvenirs, balloons and ice cream, the Piazzale offers views that can reach as far as Pistoia on a clear day.

## Bellosguardo

Many would argue that the finest view over Florence is from Bellosguardo, located almost straight up from Porta Romana at the end of the Boboli Gardens or Piazza Torquato Tasso. Non-mountaineers may want to take a taxi; the famous viewpoint, from where you can see every church façade in the city, is just before Piazza Bellosguardo. The area is a peaceful little oasis of superb villas and houses gathered round a square – there are no shops, bars or indeed anything commercial.

The grandest villa, Villa Bellosguardo, was built in 1780 for Marquis Orazio Pucci, ancestor of the late Florentine fashion designer Emilio Pucci. The great tenor Enrico Caruso bought the villa for his retirement, although he lived there for only three years before he died in 1921; he wanted his villa to become an academy of *bel canto*, and apparently he's about to get his wish (*t 055 872 1783 for details*).

# Fiesole

Florence liked to regard itself as the daughter of Rome, and in its fractious heyday explained its quarrelsome nature by the fact that its population from the beginning was of mixed race, of Romans and 'that ungrateful and malignant people who of old came down from Fiesole', according to Dante. First settled in the 2nd millennium BC, it became the most important Etruscan city in the region. Yet from the start Etruscan *Faesulae*'s relationship with Rome was rocky, especially after sheltering Catiline and his conspirators in 65 BC. Its lofty position made Fiesole too difficult to capture, so the Romans built a camp below on the Arno to cut off its supplies. Eventually Fiesole was taken, and it dwindled as the camp below grew into the city of Florence, growth the Romans encouraged to spite the old Etruscans on their hill. This easily defended hill, however, ensured Fiesole's survival in the Dark Ages. When times became safer, families began to move back down to the Arno to rebuild Florence. They returned to smash up most of Fiesole after defeating it in 1125; since then the little town has remained aloof, letting Florence dominate and choke in its own juices far, far below.

But ever since the days of the *Decameron*, whose storytellers retreated to its garden villas to escape the plague, Fiesole has played the role of Florence's aristocratic suburb; its cool breezes, beautiful landscapes and belvedere views make it the perfect refuge from the torrid Florentine summers. There's no escaping the tourists, however; we foreigners have been tramping up and down Fiesole's hill since the days of Shelley. A day trip has become an obligatory part of a stay in Florence, and although Fiesole has proudly retained its status as an independent *comune*, you can make the 20-minute trip up on Florence city bus 7 from the station or Piazza San Marco. If you have the time, walk up (or perhaps better, down) the old lanes bordered with villas and gardens to absorb some of the world's most civilized scenery.

## Around Piazza Mino

The long sloping stage of Piazza Mino is Fiesole's centre, with the bus stop, the local tourist office, the cafés and the **Palazzo Pretorio**, its loggia and façade emblazoned with coats of arms. The square is named after a favourite son, the quattrocento sculptor Mino da Fiesole, whom Ruskin preferred to all others. An example of his work may be seen in the **Duomo**, whose plain façade dominates the north side of the piazza. Built in 1028, it was the only building spared by the vindictive Florentines in 1125. It was subsequently enlarged and given a scouring 19th-century restoration, leaving the tall, crenellated campanile as its sole distinguishing feature. Still, the interior has an austere charm, with a raised choir over the crypt similar to San Miniato.

Up the steps to the right are two works by Mino da Fiesole: the *Tomb of Bishop Leonardo Salutati* and an altar front. The main altarpiece in the choir, of the Madonna and saints, is by Lorenzo di Bicci, from 1440. Note the two saints frescoed on the columns; it was a north Italian custom to paint holy people as if they were members of the congregation. The crypt, holding the remains of Fiesole's patron, St Romulus, is supported by columns bearing doves, spirals and other early Christian symbols.

Located on Via Dupré, the **Bandini Museum** (*open winter Wed–Mon 10–5; summer daily 10–7; closed Tues in winter; adm*) contains sacred works, including della Robbia terracottas and trecento paintings by Lorenzo Monaco, Neri di Bicci and Taddeo Gaddi.

## Archaeological Zone

Behind the cathedral and museum is the entrance to what remains of *Faesulae*. Because Fiesole avoided trouble in the Dark Ages, its Roman monuments have survived in much better shape than those of Florence; although hardly spectacular, the ruins are charmingly set amid olive groves and cypresses.

The small **Roman Theatre** (*open in summer Wed–Mon 9.30–7; in winter Wed–Mon 9.30–5; closed Tues; adm*) has survived well enough to host plays and concerts in the summer; Fiesole would like to remind you that in ancient times it had the theatre and plays while Florence had the amphitheatre and wild beast shows. Close by are the rather confusing remains of two superimposed temples, the baths and an impressive stretch of Etruscan walls (best seen from Via delle Mure Etrusche, below) that proved their worth against Hannibal's siege.

The **Archaeology Museum** (*opening hours as for Roman Theatre*), in a small 20th-century Ionic temple, displays early bronze figurines with flapper wing arms, Etruscan urns and stelae, including the interesting 'stele Fiesolana' with a banquet scene.

## Walking Around Fiesole

From Piazza Mino, Via S. Francesco ascends steeply (at first) to the hill that served as the Etruscan and Roman acropolis. Halfway up is a terrace with extraordinary views of Florence and the Arno sprawl, with a monument to the three *carabinieri* who gave themselves up to be shot by the Nazis in 1944 to prevent them from taking civilian reprisals. The church nearby, the **Basilica di Sant'Alessandro**, was constructed over an Etruscan/Roman temple in the 6th century, reusing its lovely *cipollino* (onion marble) columns and Ionic capitals, one still inscribed with an invocation to Venus. At the top of the hill, square on the ancient acropolis, stands the monastery of **San Francesco**, its church containing a famous early cinquecento *Annunciation* by Raffaellino del Garbo and an *Immaculate Conception* by Piero di Cosimo. A grab-bag of odds and ends collected from the four corners of the world, especially Egypt and China, is displayed in the quaint **Franciscan Missionary Museum** in the cloister (*open daily summer 10–12 and 3–6; winter 10–12 and 3–5*); it also has an Etruscan collection.

There are much longer walks to be had along the hill behind the Palazzo Pretorio. The panoramic Via Belvedere leads back to Via Adriano Mari, and in a couple of kilometres to the bucolic **Montecéceri**, a wooded park where Leonardo da Vinci performed his flight experiments, and where Florentine architects once quarried their dark *pietra serena* from quarries now abandoned but open for exploration.

In Borgunto, as this part of Fiesole is called, there are two 3rd-century BC **Etruscan tombs** on Via Bargellino; east of Borgunto scenic Via Francesco Ferrucci and Via di Vincigliata pass by Fiesole's castles, the **Castel di Poggio**, site of summer concerts, and the **Castel di Vincigliata**, dating back to 1031, while further down is American critic Bernard Berenson's famous **Villa I Tatti**, which he left, along with a collection of Florentine art, to Harvard University as the Centre of Italian Renaissance Studies. The road continues down towards Ponte a Mensola (six kilometres from Fiesole; *see* over) and Settignano, with buses back to Florence.

## San Domenico di Fiesole

Located between Fiesole and Florence, San Domenico is a pleasant walk from Fiesole towards Florence down Via Vecchia Fiesolana, a steep, narrow road that passes the **Villa Medici** (*free*), built by Michelozzo for Cosimo il Vecchio; Lorenzo and his friends of the Platonic Academy would come to escape the world within its lovely gardens; it was also Iris Origo's childhood home. San Domenico, at the bottom of the lane, is where Fra Angelico first entered his monkish world. The church of **San Domenico** (15th century) contains his *Madonna with Angels and Saints*, in a chapel on the left, and a photograph of his *Coronation of the Virgin*, which the French snapped up in 1809 and sent to the Louvre. Across the nave there's a *Crucifixion* by the school of Botticelli, an unusual composition of verticals highlighted by the cypresses in the background. In the chapterhouse of the monastery (*ring the bell at No.4*) Fra Angelico left a fine fresco *Crucifixion* and a *Madonna and Child*, which is shown with its sinopia, before moving down to Florence and San Marco.

### Badia Fiesolana

The lane in front of San Domenico leads to the Badia Fiesolana (*open only Sun am*), Fiesole's cathedral, built in the 9th century by Fiesole's bishop, an Irishman named Donatus, with a fine view over the rolling countryside and Florence beyond. Though later enlarged, perhaps by Brunelleschi, it preserves its original elegant façade, a charming example of the geometric black and white marble inlay decoration that characterizes Tuscan Romanesque churches, while the interior is adorned with *pietra serena* in the style of Brunelleschi. The ex-convent next door now houses the European University Institute.

# Settignano

The least touristic hill above Florence is under the village of Settignano (bus 10 from the station or Piazza San Marco). The road passes **Ponte a Mensola**, which was Boccaccio's childhood home; it is believed he set a number of scenes of the *Decameron* at the Villa Poggio Gherardo. A Scottish Benedictine named Andrew founded its church of **San Martino a Mensola** in the 9th century and was later canonized. The church was rebuilt in the 1400s and has three trecento works: Taddeo Gaddi's *Triptych*, his son Agnolo's paintings on St Andrew's casket, and high altar triptych by the school of Orcagna. A number of quattrocento works are also to be found here includiing Neri di Bicci's *Madonna and Saints* and an *Annunciation* by a follower of Beato Angelico.

Settignano is one of Tuscany's great cradles of sculptors, producing Desiderio da Settignano and Antonio and Bernardo Rossellino; Michelangelo too spent his childhood here, at Villa Buonarroti. Strangely, they left behind no work as a reminder; the good art in **Santa Maria** church is by Andrea della Robbia (an enamelled terracotta *Madonna and Child*) and Buontalenti (the pulpit). However, there are more splendid views from Piazza Desiderio, and a couple of places to quaff a glass of Chianti.

# Medici Villas

Like their Bourbon cousins in France, the Medici dukes liked to while their time away acquiring new palaces for themselves. In their case, however, the reason was less self-exaltation than simple property speculation; the Medici always thought several generations ahead. As a result the countryside around Florence is littered with Medici villas, most of them now privately owned, though some are at least partly open to the public.

## Villa Careggi

*Open Mon–Fri 9–6, Sat 9–12; but you can stroll through the grounds free.*

Perhaps the best-known of the Medici villas is Careggi (Viale Pieraccini 17, bus 14C from the station), originally a fortified farmhouse, but enlarged for Cosimo il Vecchio by Michelozzo in 1434. In the 1460s this villa became synonymous with the birth of humanism.

The greatest Latin and Greek scholars of the day, Ficino, Poliziano, Pico della Mirandola and Argyropoulos, would sometimes meet here with Lorenzo il Magnifico. The group met with the purpose of holding philosophical discussions in imitation of a Platonic symposium, calling their informal society the Platonic Academy. It fizzled out when Lorenzo died. Cosimo il Vecchio and Piero had both died at Careggi and, when he felt the end was near, Lorenzo had himself carried out to the villa, with Poliziano and Pico della Mirandola to bear him company. After Lorenzo died, the villa was burned by Florentine republicans, though Cosimo I later had it rebuilt, and Francis Sloane had it restored.

# Villa la Petraia

*Open 8.15–6; closed 2nd and 4th Mon of month; extended hours on summer eves; gardens open an hour later than villa; adm.*

Further east, amid the almost continuous conurbation of power lines and industrial landscapes that blight the Prato road, Villa la Petraia manages to remain Arcadian on its steeply sloping hill. It's very hard to reach on your own. If you don't have a car, it's best to take a taxi or, if you are adventurous, bus 28 from the station, and get off after the wastelands, by Via Reginaldo Giuliano. La Petraia was purchased by Grand Duke Ferdinando I in 1557 and rebuilt by Buontalenti, keeping the tower of the original castle intact.

Unfortunately Vittorio Emanuele II liked it as much as the Medici, and redesigned it to suit his relentlessly bad taste. Still, the interior is worthwhile for its ornate Baroque court, frescoed with a pastel history of the Medici by 17th-century masters Volterrano and Giovanni di San Giovanni; Vittorio Emanuele II added the glass roof in order to use the space as a ballroom. Of the remainder, you're most likely to remember the Chinese painting of Canton and the games room, with billiard tables as large as football fields and perhaps the world's first pinball machine, made of wood. A small room contains a most endearing statue by Giambologna, *Venus Wringing Water from Her Hair*. La Petraia's beautiful gardens and grounds, shaded by ancient cypresses, are open throughout the afternoon.

# Villa di Castello

*Garden open 8.15–6; closed 2nd and 4th Mon of month; extended hours on summer eves; adm.*

One of Tuscany's most famous gardens is just down the hill from La Petraia, at Villa di Castello (turn right at Via di Castello and walk 450 metres). The villa was bought in 1477 by Lorenzo di Pierfrancesco and Giovanni de' Medici, two cousins of Lorenzo il Magnifico who were Botticelli's best patrons, and they hung the walls of this villa with his great mythological paintings now in the Uffizi. The villa was sacked in the 1530 siege and then restored by Cosimo I; today it is the headquarters of the Accademia della Crusca, founded in 1582 and dedicated to the study of the Italian language. The garden was laid out for Cosimo I by Tribolo, who also designed the fountain in the centre, with a statue, *Hercules and Antenaeus*, by Ammannati.

Directly behind the fountain is the garden's main attraction, a fascinating example of the Medici penchant for the offbeat and excessive, an artificial cavern named the **Grotto degli Animali**, filled by Ammannati and Giambologna with marvellous, true-to-life statues of every creature known to man (some are copies of Giambologna's originals in the Bargello), and lined with mosaics of pebbles and shells. The terrace above offers the best view over the garden's geometric patterns; a large statue by Ammannati of January, or *Gennaio*, emerges shivering from a pool among the trees.

A 20-minute walk north from Villa di Castello to Quinto takes you to two unusual 7th-century BC **Etruscan tombs**. Neither has any art, but the chambers under their

25ft artificial hills bear an odd relationship to ancient cultures elsewhere in the Mediterranean – domed *tholos* tombs as in Mycenaean Greece, corbelled passages like the *navetas* of Majorca, and entrances that look like the sacred wells of Sardinia.

## Sesto Fiorentino

You can change gears again by heading out a little further in the sprawl to Sesto Fiorentino, a suburb that since 1954 has been home to the famous Richard-Ginori china and porcelain firm. Founded in Doccia in 1735, the firm has opened the **Doccia Museum** on Via Pratese 31 (*signposted*) to display a neat chronological exhibition of its production of Doccia ware, including many Medici commissions (a ceramic *Venus de' Medici*), fine painted porcelain, and some pretty Art Nouveau works (*open Tues, Thurs and Sat 9.30–1 and 3.30–6.30; closed Aug; adm*).

## Villa Demidoff at Pratolino

*Open April–Sept Thurs–Sun 10–8; Mar and Oct Sun 10–6;*
*closed Nov–Feb; adm. Take bus 25 which leaves about every 20 mins*
*from the station.*

The village of Pratolino lies 12 kilometres north of Florence along Via Bolognese and it was here that the infatuated Duke Francesco I bought a villa in the 1568 as a gift to his mistress, the Venetian Bianca Capello. Francesco commissioned Buontalenti – artist, architect, and hydraulics engineer, nicknamed 'delle Girandole' for the wind-up toys he made – to design the enormous gardens. He made Pratolino the marvel of its day, full of water tricks, ingenious automata and a famous menagerie.

Sadly, none of Buontalenti's marvels has survived, but the largest ever example of this play between art and environment has (perhaps because it is impossible to move) – Giambologna's massive *Apennino*, a giant rising from stone, part stalactite, part fountain himself, conquering the dragon, said to be symbolic of the Medici's origins in the Mugello just north of here. The rest of the park, made into an English garden by the Lorena family and named for Prince Paolo Demidoff who bought it in 1872 and restored Francesco's servants' quarters as his villa, is an invitingly cool refuge from a Florentine summer afternoon.

## Poggio a Caiano

*Open Nov–Feb 8.15–3.30; April, May and Sept 8.15–3.30; Mar and Oct 8.15–4.30;*
*June–Aug 8.15–6.30; adm. COPIT buses, t 800 277 825, go past every half-hour,*
*departing from in front of McDonald's on the north side of the station.*

Of all the Medici villas, Poggio a Caiano is the most evocative of the country idylls so delightfully described in the verses of Lorenzo il Magnifico; this was not only his favourite retreat, but is generally considered the very first Italian Renaissance villa. Lorenzo purchased a farmhouse here in 1480, and commissioned Giuliano da Sangallo to rebuild it in a classical style. It was Lorenzo's sole architectural commission, and its classicism matched the mythological nature poems he composed here, most famously 'L'Ambra', inspired by the stream Ombrone that flows nearby.

Sangallo designed the villa according to Alberti's description of the perfect country house in a style that presages Palladio, and added a classical frieze on the façade, sculpted with the assistance of Andrea Sansovino (now replaced with a copy). Some of the other features – the clock, the curved stair and central loggia – were later additions. In the **interior** Sangallo designed an airy, two-storey **Salone**, which the two Medici popes had frescoed by 16th-century masters Pontormo, Andrea del Sarto, Franciabigio and Allori. The subject, as usual, is Medici self-glorification, and depicts family members dressed as Romans in historical scenes that parallel events in their lives. In the right lunette, around a large circular window, Pontormo painted the lovely *Vertumnus and Pomona* (1521), a languid summer scene under a willow tree, beautifully coloured. In another room, Francesco I and Bianca Cappello his wife died in 1587, only 11 hours apart; Francesco was always messing with poisons but in fact a nasty virus is the probable killer.

In the **grounds** (*open Mon–Sat 9–6.30, Sun 9–12.30; winter Mon–Sat 9–4.30, Sun 9–12.30*) are fine old trees and a 19th-century statue celebrating Lorenzo's 'L'Ambra'.

## Carmignano and Villa Artimino

A local bus continues five kilometres southwest of Poggio a Caiano to the village of **Carmignano**, which possesses, in its church of **San Michele** (*open daily 7.30–5*), Pontormo's uncanny painting *The Visitation* (1530s), a masterpiece of Florentine Mannerism. There are no concessions to naturalism here – the four soulful, ethereal women, draped in Pontormo's accustomed startling colours, barely touch the ground, standing before a scene as substantial as a stage backdrop. The result is one of the most unforgettable images produced in the 16th century

Also to the south, at **Comeana** (3km, signposted), is the well-preserved Etruscan **Tomba di Montefortini**, a 7th-century BC burial mound, 35ft high and 260ft in diameter, covering two chambers. A long hall leads to the vestibule and tomb chamber, both covered with false vaulting; the latter preserves a shelf most probably used for gifts for the afterlife. Nearby, the equally impressive **Tomba dei Boschetti** was seriously damaged over centuries by local farmers (*both open Mon–Sat 8–2; closed Sun*).

The Etruscan city of Artimino, four kilometres to the west, was destroyed by the Romans and is now site of a small town and another Medici property, the **Villa Artimino** ('La Ferdinanda'), built as hunting lodge for Ferdinando I by Buontalenti. Its semi-fortified air with buttresses was aimed to fit its sporting purpose, but the total effect is simple and charming, with the long roofline punctuated by innumerable chimneys and a graceful stair, added in the 19th century from a drawing by the architect in the Uffizi.

There is an **Etruscan Archaeological Museum** in the basement, containing findings from the tombs; among them a unique censer with two basins and a boat, bronze vases, and a red figured krater painted with initiation scenes, found in a 3rd-century tomb (*villa open for guided tours only on Tues, t 055 875 1427; museum open Mon–Sat 9.30–1, Sun 9.30–12.30; closed Wed; adm*). There's a convenient place for lunch in the grounds. Also in Artimino is an attractive Romanesque church, **San Leonardo**, built of stones salvaged from earlier buildings.

## Poggio Imperiale and the Certosa del Galluzzo

One last villa open for visits, the **Villa di Poggio Imperiale** (*open Wed 10–12 by request, t 055 220 151*), lies south of Florence, at the summit of Viale del Poggio Imperiale, which leaves Porta Romana with a stately escort of cypress sentinels. Cosimo I grabbed this huge villa from the Salviati family in 1565, and it remained a ducal property until there were no longer any dukes to duke. Its neoclassical façade was added in 1808, and the audience chamber was decorated in the 17th century by the under-rated Rutilio Manetti and others. Much of the villa is now used as a girls' school.

The **Certosa del Galluzzo** (also known as the Certosa di Firenze) lies further south, scenically located on a hill off the Siena road (*open Tues–Sun 9–12 and 3–6; closed Mon; take bus 36 or 37 from the station*). Founded as a Carthusian monastery by 14th-century tycoon Niccolò Acciaiuoli, the monastery has been inhabited since 1958 by Cistercians; there are 12 now living there, one of whom takes visitors around.

The Certosa has a fine 16th-century courtyard and an uninteresting church, though the crypt-chapel of the lay choir contains some impressive tombs. The Chiostro Grande, surrounded by the monks' cells, is decorated with 66 majolica tondi of prophets and saints by Giovanni della Robbia and assistants; one cell is opened for visits, and it seems almost cosy. The Gothic Palazzo degli Studi, intended by the founder as a school, contains five lunettes by Pontormo, painted while he and his pupil Bronzino hid out here from the plague in 1522.

# Chianti and the Mugello

09

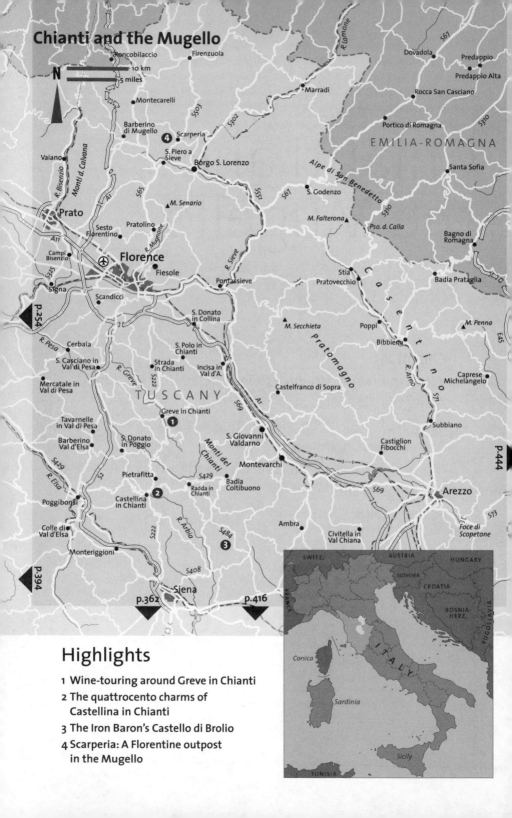

# Highlights

1 Wine-touring around Greve in Chianti
2 The quattrocento charms of
  Castellina in Chianti
3 The Iron Baron's Castello di Brolio
4 Scarperia: A Florentine outpost
  in the Mugello

These two regions, Chianti to the south and the Mugello to the north of Florence, one world-famous and one obscure, are delightfully rural and endowed with every Tuscan charm. No Brunelleschi could have designed the grand stone farmhouses that crown every hill, built with an intuitive aesthetic that rarely fails, each different, offering endless variations of arches, loggias and towers, set in an equally endless variety of rolling hills, vineyards, olives and cypresses. Towns are few, monuments scattered and of minor interest, paintings and sculpture very rare. But you'll find few places more enchanting to explore – by car, by bicycle, by foot – in a day or a lifetime.

# Chianti

*From good Chianti, an aged wine, majestic and*
*imperious, that passes through my heart and chases*
*away without trouble every worry and grief...*
Francesco Redi, Bacchus in Tuscany

In the 17th century, naturalist and poet Francesco Redi was the first to note the virtues of 'Florentine red' from Chianti, but since then the Italians have invested a lot of worry and grief into defining exactly what 'Chianti' means. The name apparently derives from an Etruscan family named Clanti; geographically it refers, roughly, to the hilly region between Florence and Siena, bordered by the Florence–Siena Superstrada del Palio and the A1 from Florence to Arezzo. The part within Siena province is known as *Chianti Storico* or *Chianti Geografico*, once the territories of the Lega del Chianti, a consortium of barons formed in 1385 to protect their interests (and their wine), who adopted a black cockerel as their emblem.

But Chianti is an oenological name as well as a geographical one, and as such first became official in 1716, when Grand Duke Cosimo III defined which parts of Tuscany could call their vintage Chianti, in effect making wine history – it was the first time that a wine had its production area delimited. The Lorraine grand dukes promoted advances in wine-making techniques and the export of Chianti. Yet the Chianti as we know it had yet to be developed, and it was largely the creation of one man – the 'Iron Baron', Bettino Ricasoli, briefly the second prime minister of unified Italy. The baron was very wealthy but not very good-looking, and Luigi Barzini, in *The Italians*, recounts how jealous he became when a young man asked his new bride to dance at a ball in Florence. Ricasoli at once ordered her into their carriage and gave the driver the address of the ancient family seat at Brolio in the Monti del Chianti – an isolated castle that the poor woman rarely left ever after.

To pass the time the baron began to experiment with different vines and processes, eventually hitting upon a pleasing mix of red Sangiovese and Canaiolo grapes, with a touch of white Malvasia, twice fermented in the old Tuscan manner. Meanwhile, the famous dark green flask was invented, the *strapeso*, with its straw covering woven by the local women. The end product took the Paris Exhibition of 1878 by storm; imitators soon appeared and, in 1924, the boundaries of Chianti Storico were more than doubled to create Chianti Classico, drawn by local producers to protect the wine's name, adopting the now familiar black cockerel as its symbol. In 1967 Chianti Classico, along with Tuscany's six other Chianti vinicultural zones, was given its *denominazione di origine* status, and production soared, but quality and sales declined. To improve it, the Chianti Classico Consortium was upscaled to a DOCG rating to guarantee that all wines bearing the black cockerel would be tested and approved by a panel of judges.

But it was tales of Elizabeth Barrett Browning quaffing Chianti and finding her inspiration in its ruby splendour, as well as the sunny rural elegance of the region, that attracted first the English and Dutch, then the Swiss, Americans, French and Germans, especially in the 1960s and 1970s; they form one of Italy's densest foreign colonies, wryly nicknamed 'Chianti-shire'. The newcomers brought more money than Chianti's mouldering barons and contessas had seen since the Renaissance; property prices shot to the moon. But the presence of so much money has begun to cast a shadow over the heart of this ancient, enchanting region; snobbery and pretensions threaten to poison the pleasurable plonk of yesteryear. Some vintners offer limited-edition numbered bottles; designer-label Chianti is upon us. The old vines, following the contours of the hills, are being pulled out to make room for specialized vines in geometric straight lines. And as any old-timer will tell you, the modern DOCG Chianti Classico sniffed and gurgled by wine professionals isn't anything like the joyous, spontaneous wine that made Chianti famous in the first place.

Some 800 farms and estates (only a selection of the most historic are listed below) produce wine in the 70,000 hectares of the Chianti Classico zone, and one of the chief pleasures is trying as many labels as possible – with the different mixtures of grapes, different soils and bottling methods, each should be, or at least strives to be, individual. Nor do estates limit themselves to Chianti; many produce *vinsanto*, a white wine called Bianca della Lega, and many reds, as well as Chianti's other speciality, a delicate *extra-vergine* olive oil. Before setting out, call to check hours.

# Western Chianti: Florence to Tavarnelle Val di Pesa

Chianti begins 10km south of Florence, but on the way you may want to follow the sign west off SS222 just past the *autostrada*, for **Ponte a Ema** and the prettily sited 14th-century chapel of the Alberti, **Santa Caterina dell'Antella**, with contemporary frescoes on St Catherine's life, one of Spinello Aretino's greatest works (*open Nov–Mar Sat 3–5.30pm and Sun 9.30–12; April–Oct Sat 4–6.30pm and Sun 9–12*). Further along, at Grassina, there's a turn-off to **Impruneta**, a large town on a plateau noted for its terracotta tiles (including those on Brunelleschi's dome) and pottery, very much on sale, especially during the enormous **St Luke's Horse and Mule Fair** in October. The fair takes place in the main piazza, in the shadow of Impruneta's pride and joy, the ancient **Collegiata**, built to house a miraculous icon of the *Madonna and Child* attributed to St Luke, dug up by a team of oxen in the 10th century. Bombed during the last war, restorers took the opportunity to bring the Collegiata back to its Renaissance appearance to match its two beautiful chapels, one housing the

Prato

Chianti

▲ *M. Senario*
Bivigliano

S95

Pratolino

*R. Mugnone*

Florence

*R. Sieve*
Rufina

Fiesole

Pontassieve

Pelago

Dicomano

*Pso. d. Consuma*

A1

A11

S325

Signa

Scandicci

Bagno a Ripoli

S. Donato
in Collina

Saltino

Vallombrosa
▲ *M. Secchieta*

Grassina

Rignano sull' Arno

Chiesanuova

Tavarnuzze

*R. Pesa*

Cerbaia

S. Andrea in
Percussina

Impruneta

S. Polo in Chianti

S. Casciano in Val di Pesa

*R. Greve*

Strada
in Chianti

Incisa in Val d'A.

Mercatale in
Val di Pesa

Cintoia

S222

Bargino

Vicchiomaggio

Figline Vald.

S69

A1

Montefiridolfi

Verrazzano

TUSCANY

Passignano

Greve in Chianti

Tavarnelle
in Val di Pesa

Vignamaggio

S. Giovanni
Valdarno

Conv. Montecarlo

Terranuova
Bracciolini

Barberino
Val d'Elsa

Montagliari

Panzano

Monti del
Chianti

Cavriglia

Montevarchi

S. Donato
in Poggio

S429

S2

Granaio

Pietrafitta

S429

Badia
Coltibuono

Rendola

Poggibonsi

*R. Elsa*

Castellina
in Chianti

Radda in
Chianti

Gaiole in Chianti

Meleto

Staggia

Colle di
Val d'Elsa

Monteriggioni

S222

*R. Arbia*

S484

Ambra

🏰 *Cast. di Brolio*

Quercegrossa

S541

S408

† *Osservanza*
Siena

Castelnuovo
Berardenga

Monteaperti

S73

*R. Ombrone*

N

Montecchio

S73

S223

S2

*R. Arbia*

Pievina

10 km
5 miles

# Getting Around

The two main north–south routes through Chianti, the old Roman Via Cassia (SS2) and the Chiantigiana (SS222), rival one another in beauty; an ideal motoring wine tour would take in the east–west SS429 between the Badia a Coltibuono and Castellina. Distances aren't great, though the single-lane winding routes make for leisurely travel.

Public transport is fairly easy in Chianti and all by **bus**, though you may not always find connections between two towns very commodious; from Florence SITA buses will take you to Greve (25km/45min), Gaiole (55km/1½hrs), Castellina in Chianti (44km/1hr), Mercatale, S. Casciano in Val di Pesa (17km/25min), Tavarnelle Val di Pesa (29km/40min), Panzano, Strada, and Radda (42km/1hr); CAP buses run frequently from Florence to Impruneta (14km/20min). From Siena TRA-IN buses go to Castellina (20km/25min), Radda (30km/40min), Tavarnelle (38km/50min) and S. Casciano (49km/1¼hrs), Tavarnuzze and Strada.

# Tourist Information

**Impruneta**: Piazza Buondelmonti 41, t/f 055 231 3729, *proimpruneta@rtd.it*,

*www.proimprunetartd.it. Open Nov–April Mon–Sat 9.30–12.30 and 3–6, Sun 10–1; May and Oct Mon–Sat 9.30–12.30 and 3.30–6.30, Sun 10–1; June–Sept Mon–Sat 9.30–12.30 and 2–7, Sun 10–1.*

**San Casciano in Val di Pesa**: Piazza della Repubblica, t/f 055 822 9558, *www. prosanca.supereva.it. Open Mon–Sat 9–1 and Mon 3.30–6, Tues, Thurs & Fri 3.30–7 and Sat 3.30–6.*

**Barberino Val D'Elsa**: Via Cassia 31a, t/f 055 807 5622, Nov–Mar t 055 805 2214, *comune@barberinovaldelsa.net, www.comune.baberinovaldelsa.net. Open April–Oct Mon–Sat 9–1 and 3–7.*

**Greve in Chianti**: Viale G. da Verrazzano 59, t 055 854 6287, f 055 854 4240. *Open Oct–May Mon–Sat 10.30–12.30 and 3–7, Sun 10.30–12.30; June–Sept Mon–Sat 10.30–1.30 and 5–8, Sun 10.30–1.30.*

**Castellina in Chianti**: Two agencies provide tourist leaflets: **Colline Verdi**, Via Della Rocca 12, t/f 057 774 0620; **Tuscan Enterprises**, Via delle Mura 22–24, t 057 774 0623, f 057 774 0950, *tuscan@si.tdnet.it, www.tuscanenterprise.it.*

**Radda**: Piazza Ferrucci 1, t/f 057 7738 494. *Open April–Oct, Mon–Sat 10–1 and 3–5, Sun 10–1; closed Nov–Mar.*

icon and the other a piece of the True Cross, both designed by Michelozzo and richly decorated with enamel terracottas by Luca della Robbia. In an adjacent chapel is a marble relief, the *Finding of the Icon*, by the school of Donatello; the bronze crucifix in the nave is attributed to Giambologna. The campanile survives from the 13th century, and the fine portico from 1634. Among the many terracotta shops, **Artenova** (*Via della Fonte 76, t 055 201 1060; open Mon–Fri 8–12.30 and 2–6.30, Sat 8–12*), has creative designs and a good selection of gifts.

## Macchiavelli in Exile

From the SS222 south of Florence, a byroad leads west from Tavarnuzze (8km) to **Sant'Andrea in Percussina**, long the country fief of the Macchiavelli. Here Niccolò spent his tedious exile, which he described in a letter as whiling away the day in the tavern 'playing at *cricca* and tric-trac, and this gave rise to a thousand arguments and endless exchanges of insults, most of the time there is a fight over a penny…and so surrounded by these lice, I blow the cobwebs from my brain and relieve the unkindness of my fate'. In the evening he would retire to work on *The Prince*.

## Where to Stay and Eat

In this section of Chianti, hotels tend to be small and usually annexed to restaurants, though note that many of the larger wine estates have a few rooms or apartments to let; call ahead to see what's available.

### Candeli ✉ 50100
*****Villa la Massa**, Via della Massa 24, t 055 6261, f 055 633 102, *info@villalamassa.com*, *www.villalamassa.com* (*luxury*). A large hotel, recently and spectacularly renovated, with a swimmimg pool and 39 rooms, all with bath and air-conditioning. *Closed Dec–Feb*

### Impruneta ✉ 50023
***La Vallombrosina**, Via Montebuoni 95, t 055 202 0491 (*expensive*). A comfortable roof over your head.
**Via Paolieri 26, t/f 055 231 2558**, *www.rtd.it/b&b* (*moderate*). A spacious, brand-new B&B just off the main piazza, with nicely furnished rooms and apartments, and lovely views of the hills.
**I Falciani**, Via Cassia 245, t 055 202 0091 (*inexpensive*). A rustic place full of locals, where you may dine with the TV for company on tasty Fiorentina beef steak.

### Bagno a Ripoli ✉ 50012
**Centanni**, Via Centanni 7, t 055 630 122 (*expensive*). Exceptionally pleasant, set among olive groves, where you can dine on a delicious array of *antipasti*, and Renaissance recipes like *brasata dei Medici*, a sweet and sour braised beef dish dating from the 17th century. *Closed lunch and Sun.*

### Località I Falciani ✉ 50029
**Antica Trattoria dei Cacciatori**, Via Chiantigiana 22, t 055 232 6327 (*moderate*). Offers sturdy dishes, such as *rognone al ginepro*, kidneys with juniper. *Closed Wed.*

### Tavarnuzze ✉ 50029
****Gli Scopeti**, Via Cassia 183, t 055 202 2008, f 055 237 3015 (*moderate*). A cheaper alternative.

### Sant'Andrea in Percussina ✉ 50029
**Albergaccio di Macchiavelli**, Via Scopechi 64, t 055 828 471 (*expensive*). Macchiavelli's old tavern, now owned by the Conti Serristori Wine Company, serves simple Tuscan meals – in summer, order the refreshing *panzanella* – and fine wines from the estate; you can also buy bottles to take home. *Closed Mon and Tues.*

His old tavern is still a tavern and his home, the **Albergaccio** (literally, 'nasty little inn'), contains a small museum devoted to his life. Near Chiesanuova, to the north, there's the 16th-century **Palazzo al Bosco**, attributed by some to Michelangelo, a villa built atop a 13th-century structure. The stately, theatrical 15th-century **Villa Tattoli** to the west (on the Chiesanuova–Cerbaia road) features two levels of arcades. Near Cerbaia itself, five kilometres from San Casciano, **Villa Talente** is the former property of the artists who built Orsanmichele in Florence (*offers Chianti, white wine and olive oil*).

# Along the Via Cassia (SS2)

Up-to-date **San Casciano in Val di Pesa**, 17km south of Florence, is the largest and busiest town in Chianti. Long an outpost of Florence, it suffered numerous vicissitudes until its **walls** were begun by the ill-fated Duke of Athens in 1342. Within these, near the gateway, the church of **Santa Maria del Prato** (1335) has retained its trecento interior and trecento art: a fine pulpit by Giovanni Balducci da Pisa, a pupil

# Where to Stay and Eat

Most of the district's lodgings are here, as well as some of Chianti's best restaurants.

### Cerbaia ✉ 50026
**La Tenda Rossa**, Piazza del Monumento 11, **t** 055 826 132 (*very expensive, but worth it*). A family-run abode of haute cuisine: pumpkin-filled *tortellini*, or perhaps lettuce crêpes filled with artichoke hearts for starters, followed by chicken breasts with grated *porcini* mushrooms, or duck's breast in balsamic vinegar. The challenge is trying to save room for one of the Red Tent's excellent, innovative desserts, all prepared with the lightest of touches. *Closed Mon lunch and Aug.*

### San Casciano ✉ 50026
***L'Antica Post**, Piazza Zannoni 1/3, **t** 055 822 313, **f** 055 822 278 (*moderate*). 10 comfortable rooms, all with bath, as well as a restaurant to rival La Tenda Rossa (*see* above), but with more Persian rugs and silver decorations; among the offerings are a risotto with artichokes and crayfish, *taglierini* with razor clams and asparagus, breast of pheasant flavoured with thyme, or rabbit in a sauce of creamed mussels; the wine list is superb. Reservations are obligatory. *Closed Tues.*
**Nello**, Via IV Novembre 64, **t** 055 820 163 (*moderate*). The menu features fresh fish, and a dish you don't find every day in Tuscany – pasta with *pesto alla genovese*;

wines include most Chianti labels. *Closed Wed eve, Thurs and 1 July–15 Aug.*

### Bardella ✉ 50024
**\*\*Minisoggiorno**, Via Leonardo da Vinci 5, **t** 055 820 732 (*cheap*). Several simple rooms.

### Bargino ✉ 50024
**\* Bargino**, Via Cassia 122, **t** 055 824 9055 (*cheap*). Seven rooms in a garden along the old Roman road, with an excellent fish restaurant, **La Trattoria del Pescea**.

### Mercatale ✉ 50026
**\*Soggiorno Paradiso**, Piazza V. Veneto 28, **t** 055 821 327, or 055 821 7784, **f** 055 821 281 (*cheap*).

### Tavarnelle ✉ 50028
**Youth Hostel**, Via Roma 137, **t** 055 807 7009, *www.franchostel.it (cheap)*. One of the pleasant Chianti hostels, with 60 beds. *Open all year.*

### Barberino Val d'Elsa ✉ 50021
**\*\*Primavera**, Via della Republicca 27, **t/f** 055 805 9223 (*cheap*). A pleasant, simple hotel.

### San Donato in Poggio ✉ 50028
**Villa Francesca**, Strada Monastero 12, **t** 055 807 2849 (*moderate*). Tasty roasts, risotto with porcini mushrooms and Florentine steaks. *Open April–Oct Wed–Sun; Nov–March Sat–Sun. Closed two central weeks in August.*

of Andrea Pisano, a crucifix attributed to Simone Martini, a triptych by Ugolino di Neri, and framed paintings on the pilasters by Giotto's pupil, Taddeo Gaddi. Try to make time for the recently opened **Museum of Sacred Art** (*open Sat 4.30–7, Sun 10–12.30 and 4–7*), which includes the *Madonna and Child*, considered to be the first work by Ambrogio Lorenzetti.

In the vicinity of San Casciano Florentine merchants and noblemen dotted the countryside with villas: the late Renaissance **Fattoria Le Corti**, 2km east on the Mercatale road, owned by the princely Corsini family for the past six centuries (*t 055 820 123; own Chianti on sale; open winter Tues 9–12.30, Wed–Sat 9–12.30 and 3–6; summer Tues–Sat 9–12.30 and 4–7; closed Sun and Mon*) and the 17th-century **Poggio Torselli**, just off the SS2, approached through a long avenue of cypresses and surrounded by a lovely garden.

## Mercatale, Bargino and Barberino Val d'Elsa

**Mercatale**, 5km east of San Casciano, grew up around its *mercato* (market), protected in the old days by the **Castle of the Florentine Bishops**, now a ruin fit only to protect the odd lizard. More muscular, just east on the road to Passo dei Pecorai, is the **Castello di Greve** (*t 055 821 101; tastings and lunches with advance notice, own Chianti, vinsanto and olive oil on sale*), bound by four round towers. The Bardi put it up in the 11th century, before they moved to Florence and founded the greatest pre-Medici bank. Other villas worth visiting near Mercatale are **Villa Caserotta**, once property of the Strozzi, and the fortified **Villa Palagio**, on the Mercatale–Campoli–Montefiridolfi road, adapted from a 14th-century castle. The Mercatale–Panzano road will bring you to **La Torre a Luciana**, an unspoiled medieval hamlet once belonging to the Pitti family.

The Via Cassia, between San Casciano and Bargino, passes by the ancient **Castle of Bibbione**, once residence of the Buondelmonte family, who owned much of the surrounding territory in the days when they were throwing fat on the Guelph and Ghibelline fires in Florence. Near **Bargino**, in the same bellicose spirit, is the impressive fortified hamlet of **Montefiridolfi**, just east of the Via Cassia. This road, meanwhile, rolls south through lovely hills towards **Tavarnelle Val di Pesa**, of mostly 19th-century origin, and medieval **Barberino Val d'Elsa**, with some Etruscan finds in the town hall and a good Romanesque church, the **Pieve di Sant'Appiano**, built in the 10th century. From here the Via Cassia continues to **Poggibonsi** (*see* pp.397–8), with a possible detour to **La Paneretta**, a sturdy 15th-century fort amid the olive groves, with Baroque frescoes inside.

# Central Chianti: Along the Chiantigiana (SS222)

From Florence the scenic Chiantigiana (SS222) passes the Ugolino Golf Course (*see* p.116) and offers its first tempting detour at Petigliolo: turn left after four kilometres for the ivy-covered **Santo Stefano a Tizzano**, a Romanesque church built by the Buondelmonti, not far from an 11th-century castle-villa, the **Castello di Tizzano** (*currently closed for restoration, due to re-open end 2002/early 2003; t 055 855 438; offers Chianti Riserva, Vinsanto Naturale and prize-winning olive oil* ). The same road continues for 2km to **San Polo in Chianti**, the centre of Tuscany's iris industry, celebrated in an **Iris Festival** (May). On a hill from San Polo you can see a lonely building once belonging to the Knights Templar; an equally ancient church, **San Miniato in Robbiana**, was reconsecrated in 1077 by the Bishop of Fiesole, according to a still legible inscription. San Polo's **Antico Toscano** is a wine shop with offerings from all over the region.

**Strada**, 14km from Florence along the Chiantigiana, is thought to take its odd name from an old Roman road. Just to the south, the road towards the Valdarno was protected in the Middle Ages by the **Castello di Mugano**, one of the best preserved in the region and polished up by a recent restoration. The rolling countryside is the

# Where to Stay

## Greve ✉ 50022

***Del Chianti**, Piazza Matteotti 86, t 055 853 763, f 055 853 764 (*moderate*). Pleasant and recently refurbished near the centre, with comfortable, stylish air-conditioned rooms, and a pool and garden in the back.

***Giovanni da Verrazzano**, Piazza Matteotti 28, t 055 853 189, f 055 853 648 (*moderate*). 11 elegant rooms in the middle of town.

**Villa Vignamaggio**, Via Petriolo 5, t 055 854 661, f 055 854 4468, *agriturismo@ vignamaggio.com, www.vignamaggio.com.* Situated about 5mins drive from Greve on the Panzano road, you can stay in one of many beautifully converted apartments in the villa and grounds, all with tennis and pool facilities.

## Panzano ✉ 50022

****Villa le Barone**, Via S. Leolino 19, t 055 852 621, f 055 852 277, *villalebarone@libero.it, www.villalebarone.it* (*expensive*). Just south of Greve is the 16th-century villa of the della Robbia family, who still own it: it's a lovely, intimate hotel, a great base for visiting the region, or for lounging in the pretty garden by the pool; bring the children. Many rooms are decorated in della Robbia blue and white. *Open April–Oct; min. stay 3 nights.*

## Monte S. Michele ✉ 50020

**Villa San Michele**, t 055 851 034 (*cheap*). The youth hostel, with beds for 60. *Open weekends only Nov–Dec; closed Jan–Feb.*

## Castellina ✉ 53011

****Tenuta di Ricavo**, t 0577 740 221, f 055 741 014 (*very expensive*). 3km north of Castellina, this is more than a hotel – it's an entire medieval hamlet of stone houses,

wonderfully isolated in the pines and with a large garden and pool. Many rooms are situated in the old houses, ideal for families. *Open April–Oct.*

*****Villa Casalecchi**, t 0577 740 240, f 0577 741 111 (*very expensive*). A comfortable old house, set among trees and vineyards on a slope, with some elegant rooms full of antiques and some not so elegant, but a big pool and enchanting views over the hills. *Open April–Oct.*

***Salivolpi**, Via Fiorentina 89, t 0577 740 484, f 055 740 998 (*moderate*). Two old farmhouses have recently been combined to create this smart establishment just outside Castellina; a garden and pool are added attractions.

# Eating Out

## San Polo

**Trattoria Merendero**, Via S. Lavagnini 14, t 055 855 019 (*moderate*). Out here in the open countryside you will find some tasty un-Tuscan surprises: fried stuffed olives (a speciality of the Marches) and *spaghetti al pesto*, as well as the region's old standbys.

## Greve

**Giovanni da Verrazzano**, Piazza Matteotti 28, t 055 853 189 (*expensive*). Of Greve's many options, one of the most charming here in the centre, furnished with 19th-century antiques and with a lovely terrace for summer dining, overlooking the piazza. The main meat dishes are especially good here – *nana in sugo* (duck in wine sauce), turkey with olives, and a varied mixed grill. *Closed Mon and 7 Jan–end Feb.*

**Bottega del Moro**, Piazza Trieste 14r, t 055 853 753 (*moderate*). Right in the heart of Greve,

dominant feature until **Vicchiomaggio**, with a distinctive castle that once hosted Leonardo da Vinci. This is now the British-run **Fattoria Castello di Vicchiomaggio** (*call t 055 854 079; offers own-label Chianti, vinsanto, olive oil and delicious honey*).

Nearby **Verrazzano** is a name most New Yorkers will recognize at once thanks to Giovanni da Verrazzano, not the usual Chianti landlubber but a captain who, in the service of François I of France, discovered New York Harbour and Manhattan island in 1524. The plucky explorer disappeared on his second voyage to Brazil, but surely

a simple *trattoria* where you can eat typical Tuscan dishes. *Closed Wed, Nov and first week in June.*

There are also a number of good places in the following villages, situated close to Greve.

## Montefioralle

**Taverna del Guerrino,** Via di Montefioralle 39, t 055 853 106 *(moderate).* A rustic place surrounded by a panoramic garden, offering good Tuscan home cooking, including *panzanella,* stuffed tomatoes, sausage and beans *all'uccelletto* and wines from the local *fattoria. Closed Feb; Mon–Wed from Nov–April; Mon from May–Oct.*

## Spedaluzzo

**La Cantinetta,** on the Chiantigiana 93, t 055 857 2000 *(moderate).* Good home-made pasta and country specialities like stuffed rabbit, pigeon, stuffed artichokes and grilled meats.

## Località Lucolena

**BorgoAntico,** t 055 851 024, *www.ilborgoantico.it (moderate).* Worth trying for tasty pasta with red peppers and cream sauce. *Closed Mon–Thurs in winter.*

## Panzano

**Montagliari,** Via di Montagliari 29, t 055 852 184 *(moderate).* Decorated in the style of an old Tuscan farmhouse, with tables in the panoramic garden. First courses include ravioli with walnut sauce or penne with raw tomatoes and basil; for seconds try the boar *alla cacciatora* or the *pollastro Montagliari al vino bianco* (chicken with white wine and black olives). *Booking recommended. Closed Mon and 10 Jan–7/8 Feb.*

## Castellina

**Antica Trattoria Le Torre,** Piazza del Comune 1, t 0577 740 236 *(moderate).* A popular, family-run place, with a cosy atmosphere and tasty dishes including *fagiano alla Torre,* prepared to an ancient Chianti recipe. *Closed Fri.*

**Albergaccio di Castellina,** Via Fiorentina 36, on the road to San Donato, t 0577 741 042 *(expensive).* On the outskirts of town, this serves fresh food, attractively presented, with a glass of *spumante* and free rolls with every meal. Excellent value. *Closed Sun, Wed & Thurs lunch and either Nov or Jan.*

**Pietrafitta Bar-ristorante,** Località Pietrafitta 41, t 0577 741 123 *(moderate).* This is slightly cheaper, owned by an Australian lady and run by English and New Zealanders, offering surprisingly good regional and international dishes. *Closed Tues.*

# Wine Tasting in and around Greve

**Bottega del Chianti Classico,** Via Cesare Battisti 4, t 055 853 631.

**Enoteca del Chianti Classico,** Piazzetta S. Croce 8, t 055 853 297. *Open Thurs–Tues 9.30–1 and 3.30–7.30.*

**Castello di Querceto,** just outside Greve on the Figline Val d'Arno road, t 055 859 21, f 055 859 2200, *querceto@castellodiquerceto.it, www.castello-querceto.it.* A lovely place offering a wide variety of wines, including Sangiovese aged in wooden *barriques,* and olive oil *(tastings with one week's notice).* Flats also available.

**Fontodi,** Via S. Leolino 89, oat Panzano in Chianti, t 055 852 005, *www.fontodi.com.* Also has wine aged in *barriques,* Chianti, Vin Santo, Flaccianello, Pinot Nero and olive oil *(tastings with one week's notice).*

smiles down from heaven on the bridge named in his honour, so many miles away from Chianti. His birthplace, the **Castello di Verrazzano** *(call t 055 854 243, tastings with a week's notice; can visit gardens and cellars by booking in advance),* offers a tasty range of wines and olive oils. Just east of the Chiantigiana, one and a half kilometres north of Greve, stands the fine **Castello di Uzzano,** built by the Bishop of Florence in the 13th century and then gradually converted into one of Chianti's most impressive villa estates.

## Greve in Chianti and Environs

The biggest **wine fair** in Chianti occurs every September in the medieval townlet of Greve (pop. 10,800), and as such it is seen as the region's capital. Located on the banks of the river, it is celebrated for its charming, arcaded, funnel-shaped **Piazza del Matteotti**, studded with a statue of Verrazzano. And that's about all – its castle was burned in 1387, and its Franciscan convent converted to a prison in the last century. However, in the parish church of **Santa Croce** there's a triptych by Lorenzo di Bicci and a painting by the 'Master of Greve'.

Greve is awash with wine, so it is well worth seeking out the specialized wine shops (*see* 'Wine Tasting in and around Greve', above). Meat-lovers from miles around, meanwhile, flock to the **Macelleria Falorni** (*Piazza Matteotti 69/71,* **t** *055 853 029; open Mon–Sat 8–1 and 3–7, Sun 10–1 and 3–7*), one of the region's most famous butchers, and justly acclaimed for its cured hams and *finocchiona* salamis, which are flavoured with fennel seeds.

In a nearby hamlet, **Cintoia**, east of Chiocchio, there is the little church of **Santa Maria a Cintoia** with a beautiful 15th-century panel attributed to Francesco Granacci.

A kilometre west of Greve is the ancient village and castle of **Montefioralle**, where the people of Greve lived in the bad old days. Recently restored, it is an interesting place to poke around in, with its octagonal walls intact, its old tower houses, and two Romanesque churches: **Santo Stefano**, housing early Florentine paintings, and the porticoed **Pieve di San Cresci a Montefioralle**, just outside the walls. A minor road to the west passes after one kilometre the ruined castle of **Montefili**, built in the 900s as the eastern outpost of one of Chianti's most powerful religious institutions, the **Badia a Passignano**, a fortified complex of ancient foundation, converted since into a villa. The old abbey church, **San Michele**, can be visited, and contains paintings by Ghirlandaio, Alessandro Allori and Domenico Cresti (better known as Passignano) and a bust of San Giovanni Gualberto, founder of the Vallombrosan Order, who arrived here preaching reform in the mid-11th century. Most buildings date from the 14th century, with a few remodellings in the 17th and 19th centuries.

Just east of Greve, **Vignamaggio** is the site of a beautiful old villa built by the Gherardini family, the most famous member of whom, Lisa, was born here, and later married Francesco del Giocondo before going on to pose for the world's most famous portrait. In 1992 it was used as the setting for Kenneth Branagh's film version of *Much Ado About Nothing*. **Panzano**, an important agricultural centre 6km south of Greve on the Chiantigiana, played an important role in the Florence–Siena squabbles, but retains only part of its medieval castle. Today it is best known for its embroidery, and visited for the **Pieve di San Leolino**, 1km south, with its pretty 16th-century portico on a 12th-century Romanesque structure; inside there's a triptych by Mariotto di Nardo. Another Romanesque church south of Panzano, **Sant'Eufrosino**, just off the SS222, enjoys especially fine views. Near Panzano is the **Fattoria Montagliari** (*Via di Montagliari 29,* **t/f** *055 852 014, info@montagliari.it, www.montagliari.it; sells a wide variety of its own wines, grappa, olive oil, cheese, salami, honey, etc.*). **Pietrafitta**, 9km further south and 4km from Castellina, is a lovely old hamlet hidden in the woods.

## Castellina in Chianti

One of Chianti's most charming hill-top villages, Castellina (pop. 2,700) was fortified by Florence as an outpost against Siena, and for centuries its fortunes depended on who was momentarily on top in their stupid, endless war. Most grievous to the Florentines was its loss to a combined Sienese-Aragonese siege in 1478, though after the fall of Siena itself in 1555 both cities lost interest in Castellina, and today it looks much as it did in the quattrocento: the old circuit of **walls** is almost intact, complete with houses built into and on top of them; the **Rocca**, or fortress, in the centre, its mighty *donjon* now home of the mayor; and the covered walkway, **Via delle Volte**, part of the 15th-century defensive works. Less historic but just as worth visiting is the **Bottega del Vino Gallo Nero**, Via della Rocca 10 (*sells wines and olive oils*). A kilometre from the centre, you can explore the **Ipogeo Etrusco di Montecalvario**, a 6th-century BC Etruscan tomb, recently restored. West of Castellina on the SS429, **Granaio** is synonymous with one of Chianti's most renowned wineries, the **Melini Wine House**, established in 1705, one of the big innovators in Chianti technology.

There are many splendid old farmhouses and villas around Castellina, nearly all formerly fortifications along Chianti's medieval Maginot line, like the **Villa La Leccia** just southwest of Castellina, and the **Castello di Campalli** near **Fonterutoli**, an ancient hamlet south on the Chiantigiana. In the 13th century Florence and Siena often met here trying to work out peace settlements, none of which endured very long. Peace, however, is the rule at the **Fattoria di Fonterutoli** (*t 0577 73571, f 0577 735 757, www.fonterutoli.com*) in the family since 1435, the *fattoria* produces wine in traditional oaken casks, including Chianti and Bianco della Lega, also honey, products made from lavender, and an *extra-vergine*, widely considered to be Tuscany's finest. Further south, **Quercegrossa**, 10km from Siena, but now practically a suburb of the city, and was the birthplace of quattrocento sculptor Jacopo della Quercia. A road forks northeast for Vagliagli, site of the medieval **Fattoria della Aiola** (*t 0577 322 615, f 0577 322 509; with wines, grappa, olive oil, honey and vinegar*).

## Monti del Chianti: Radda and Gaiole

East of Castellina lies the steeper, more rugged region of the Monti del Chianti. One of the higher hills supports the ancient capital of the Lega del Chianti, **Radda in Chianti** (pop. 1,650) where the streets have kept their medieval plan, radiating from the central piazza and its stately **Palazzo Comunale** (*t 0577 738 003*), encrusted with coats of arms and a 15th-century fresco in the atrium. Just outside the town is a pretty, porticoed Franciscan church, called the **Monastero**, dating from the 15th century. There are two resolutely medieval villages nearby: **Ama**, with its castle 8km to the south, near the attractive Romanesque church of **San Giusto**; and **Volpaia**, 7km to the north, with another ancient castle and walls, and an unexpected 'Brunelleschian' church, called **La Commenda**, in a doll-sized piazza. Also near Radda is the **Fattoria Vigna Vecchia** (*t 0577 738 090, f 0577 738 551; offers Chianti, grappa, vinsanto, olive oil and tastings with 3 days' notice*).

# Where to Stay

**Radda** ✉ 53017

**\*\*\*\*Relais Vignale**, Via Pianigiani 8, t 0577 738 300, f 0577 738 592 (*luxury–very expensive*). Thirty rooms in a charming old house, with some fine views and a pool for hotter days. *Open April–Oct.*

**\*Il Girarrosto**, Via Roma 41, t 0577 738 010 (*cheap*). Much simpler are the nine rooms annexed to this very popular restaurant in the village centre.

**Villa Miranda**, Villa a Radda t 0577 738 021, (*expensive*). An unlovely place which has occasioned more readers' letters to us than any other establishment in Italy; none were complimentary.

**Podue Terreno**, Via della Volpaia, t 0577 738 312 f 0577 738 400 (*moderate*). A working wine-producing farm and *agriturismo*, 5km north of Radda. Rooms are simple, the atmosphere relaxed, with meals served at a communal table in a cluttered living room. *Closed over Christmas.*

**Gaiole** ✉ 53013

**\*\*\*\*Park Hotel Cavarchione**, on the Vertine road, t 0577 749 550 (*expensive*). An imaginatively renovated farmhouse run by Germans, with only 11 rooms, and lovely views, a pool and garden. *Open mid-April–Oct.*

**\*\*\*\*Castello di Spaltenna**, t 0577 749 483, f 0577 749 269 (*luxury–very expensive*). Beautifully located in a proper old fortified monastery in Spaltenna, a hill just above Gaiole, with some theatrical medieval touches and delightful, comfortable bedrooms with stunning panoramic views over the valley or courtyard; 21 antique furnished rooms. *Closed 7 Jan–22 Mar.* The restaurant in the ancient castle refectory serves traditional and creative Tuscan dishes, such as steak of Chianino veal with beans in Chianti and olive oil.

**Castello di Brolio**, (*rented by Staglioni del Chianti*, t 0552 657 842, f 0552 645 184, *www.staglionidelchianti.com*). Three large apartments are available in the famous site, near to Gaiole. *Reserve far in advance.*

# Eating Out

## Radda

**Il Vignale**, Via XX Settembre 23, t 0577 738 094 (*expensive*). A family-run place belonging to the Fattoria Vignale, featuring refined Tuscan home cooking, very popular locally. *Closed Thurs.*

**Il Girarrosto** (*see* 'Where to Stay' above) (*moderate*). Ideal if you're in the mood for a roast meat and wine debauch. *Closed Wed.*

**Le Vigne**, along the S408, t 0577 738 640 (*moderate*). Here, dishes such as sage and butter ravioli and *pici* with aubergines and pecorino cheese are on offer out on a terrace which makes a perfect spot if the sun is shining. *Closed end Nov–early Mar.*

**Badia a Coltibuono**, closed for refurbishment until March 2002 next to the old abbey of the same name between Radda and Gaiole, t 0577 749 031 (*expensive*). Delicious tortelloni, guinea fowl and porcini mushroom terrine, meats roasted on a spit, and tempting desserts. *Closed Mon and 7 Jan–5 Mar.*

**Antica Trattoria Botteganova**, Via Chiantigiana 29, t 0577 284 230 (*expensive*). Well known for fish and meat in interesting combinations – tortelli with truffle and parmesan sauce, clams with aniseed, and sweet and sour pigeon. The desserts are wonderful – leave space. *Closed Mon.*

## Brolio

**Osteria del Castello**, t 0577 747 277 (*expensive*). Now transformed into a delightful restaurant, serving understated, elegant food in surroundings to match. *Closed Thurs and Nov–Mar.*

Gaiole, 10km east of Radda, is reached by way of the ancient **Badia a Coltibuono**, one of the gems of Chianti, a singular place set among centuries-old trees and gardens. The abbey is believed to have been founded in 770, but passed to the Vallombrosan Order in the 12th century. The Romanesque church of **San Lorenzo** dates from 1049,

## Fagioli Cotti nel Fiasco

The traditional way of cooking *fagioli* (white beans) was to put olive oil, herbs, beans and a little water inside an empty Chianti bottle (with the straw wrapping removed) and leave them to cook for several hours beside or above the embers of a charcoal fire. Aficionados will tell you it is the best way to cook beans – the bottle's small opening keeps in all the flavours and perfumes. However, Chianti bottles are no longer made of a glass resistant enough, so it is probably best to use a casserole. Cover and cook the beans (if using dried haricot beans, soak them first) in the above way, on a slow heat for several hours. Just before serving add more olive oil and garnish with tuna fish, herrings or anchovies; alternatively you can add more oil, some sage, garlic and chopped tomatoes and reheat the beans until the tomatoes have disintegrated.

while the monastery was converted into a splendid villa, owned in the 19th century by the Poniatowski, one of Poland's greatest noble families, and now occupied by a wine estate (P. Stucchi Prinetti) and restaurant (*see* 'Eating Out', opposite).

Gaiole in Chianti (pop. 4,780) was an ancient market town and these days is basically a modern one; the **Agricoltori Chianti Geografico** (*Via del Mulinaccio 10, t 0577 749 489; open Mon–Sat 9–1 and 2–6; closed Sun and public holidays; sells Chianti, Vernaccia di San Gimignano,* vinsanto *and olive oil* ) is the headquarters of a local cooperative; the **Enoteca Montagnani**, Via B. Bandinelli 9, specializes in Chianti Classico. Beside wine tasting Gaiole has little to offer, but serves as a starting point for visiting the impressive castles in this strategic area between the Arno and Siena. Just to the west are the walls and imposing donjon of the **Castello di Vertine**, a well-preserved slice of the 13th century and one of the most striking sights in all Chianti. To the east of Gaiole stands the ancient fortified village of **Barbischio**, and just 3km south on the SS408 is the impressive medieval **Castello di Meleto** with its sturdy cylindrical towers still intact. From here the road continues another 4.5km up to the mighty **Castello di Castagnoli**, guarding a fascinating little medieval town in a commanding position.

Most majestic of all is the Iron Baron's celebrated isolated **Castello di Brolio** (*open summer daily 9–12 and 3–sunset; winter Sun–Thurs 9–12 and 2–5*), some 10km south of Gaiole along the SS484, high on its own hill with views for miles around. First mentioned in 1009, when Matilda of Tuscany's father Bonifacio donated it to the monks of the Badia in Florence, it came into the possession of the Ricasoli in 1167. The castle was bombarded for weeks in 1478 by the Aragonese and Sienese, who later had it demolished, so the 'the walls levelled with the earth'. After the war, Florence rebuilt it, and in the mid-19th century Baron Ricasoli converted it into the splendid fortified residence while experimenting on the modern formula for Chianti; you can sample the famous wines and olive oil and visit the cellars 10km south at the **Cantine Barone Ricasoli** by phoning ahead (*t 0577 7301, www.ricasoli.it; open Nov–Mar Mon–Fri 8–12 and 1–5; April–Oct Mon–Fri 8am–7pm, Sat–Sun 11am–7pm*). The **Fattoria dei Pagliaresi** (*t 0577 359 070, offers older wines as well as new, and olive oil*) is located near Castelnuovo Berardenga, between S. Gusmé and Pianella. There are riding stables 5km east at the **Fattoria San Giusto**, at Monti, **t** 0577 363 011. To the south you come across **Castelnuovo Berardenga**, which is an agricultural centre with the remains of a 14th-century castle. From here it's 16km to **Monteaperti**, where Florence almost went down the tubes (to continue south, see 'Monte Oliveto Maggiore and Around', p.418).

# The Mugello

Over the years, as their ambitions became less discreet, the Medici concocted a pretty story of how they were descended from knights of Charlemagne. In truth they came down to Florence from the Mugello, the hilly region just to the north – as did Giotto and Fra Angelico. As far back as Boccaccio's time, the Mugello was considered the loveliest region of the Florentine *contada*, and its bluish-green hills are dotted with elegant weekend and summer retreats, rather smarter than the typical stone *fattorie* of the Chianti. The Florentines come here whenever they can, and if you find yourself stewing with them in the traffic gridlocks approaching Piazza della Libertà, know that all you have to do is turn up the Via Bologna or Via Faentina and in 10 minutes you'll be in a cool, enchanting world immersed in green.

North of Florence altitudes rise appreciably towards the central Appennine spine that divides Tuscany from Emilia-Romagna. Tucked in these hills lies the Mugello basin, a broad valley along the river Sieve and its tributaries, which, in the Miocene era, held a lake. Most of the towns of the Mugello are here, surrounded by a sea of vines; olive groves cover the slopes, but soon give way to deep forests of pines, chestnuts and oaks, cool and refreshing, dotted with small resorts. And like any fashion-conscious Florentine, the Mugello changes colours with the seasons, and is strikingly beautiful any time of year, a place to return to, again and again.

## The Original Medici Villa

Following Via Bologna (SS65) north, past the gardens of **Pratolino**, one of the last Medici villas (see **Florence**, 'Medici Villas', p.226), it's a panoramic and winding 30km to two of the very first. On the way, a slight detour to the east (from Pratolino or Vàglia) ascends to **Monte Senario** (2,680ft), where in 1233 seven wealthy noblemen from Florence founded the mendicant Servite Order, living in the grottoes and building simple cells in the woods, which you can still see. The Servites went on to build Santissima Annunziata in Florence, but their monastery here, rebuilt in the 16th century, is less striking than the remarkable views over the Arno valley and Mugello.

Further north, towards San Piero a Sieve, there's a turn-off to the west on an untarred road for the Medici **Castello di Trebbio**, an ancient family estate remodelled in 1461 by Michelozzo into a fortified villa with a tower. It has a formal Italian garden, which you can visit; the interior is open only on the first Tuesday of each month.

A bit further up looms the even grander **Villa Cafaggiolo**, which was much favoured by Cosimo il Vecchio and Lorenzo il Magnifico, who spent as much of the summer in its cool halls as possible. Cosimo had Michelozzo expand and transform this ancient family seat into an imposing castellated villa, its entrance protected by a bulging tower, adorned with an incongruous clock. There's no admittance to the villa, though you can walk through the grounds. To the east, a minor road leads up to the lovely wooded **Bosco ai Frati**, with a simple porticoed church also by Michelozzo; inside there's a fine crucifix by Donatello, and another attributed to Desiderio da Settignano.

## To the Passo della Futa

Just off the *autostrada*, the largest town on the western rim of the Mugello basin is **Barberino di Mugello**, a market town spread under the **Castello dei Cattani**. Barberino's 15th-century **Palazzo Pretorio**, like many in the region, is emblazoned with coats of arms; nearby stands yet another work by Michelozzo, the open **Loggie Medicee**. On SS65, 5km from Barberino at Colle Barucci, stands one of the grandest estates to be found in the Mugello, the **Villa delle Maschere** ('of the masks').

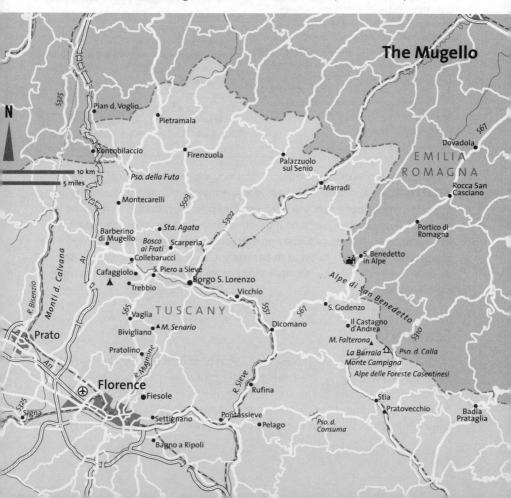

## Getting Around

The Mugello lies to the east of the A1 *autostrada* and north of Pontassieve. It has two exits off the A1: at Barberino (28km/ 20min from Florence) and Roncobilaccio (47km/35min) near the Passo della Futa (miss that one and you'll be in Bologna before you know what hit you).

The two principal roads north from Florence are the SS65 (Via Bologna) to the Medici Villas and Passo della Futa and the SS302 to Borgo San Lorenzo (28km/40min). Both of these make for a pretty drive. North of the river Sieve, though, winding mountain roads slow travelling times down considerably. You should count on at least two hours from Florence to Firenzuola (51km) and even more to Marradi (64km).

Although it's possible to make a loop by **train** through the Mugello from Florence, passing through Pontassieve, Dicomano, Vicchio, Borgo San Lorenzo (from where another line continues over the Apennines to Faenza, by way of Marradi), San Piero a Sieve, and Vàglia, SITA **buses** are more scenic and just as infrequent; check timetables before setting out (most pass through the junction at San Piero).

Better still, hire a car.

## Where to Stay and Eat

### Bivigliano ✉ 50030

The Mugello has quite a few hotels, most fairly pricy and nearly all located in the countryside, where you'll need a car to reach them. ★★★**Giotto Park Hotel/Giotto Park Hotel dipendenza**, Via Roma 11, **t** 055 406 608, **f** 055 406 730 (*expensive or moderate for the dipendenza, depending on the season; there are cheaper rooms, some without bath in the annexe*). In the resort of Bivigliano near Monte Senario, this small, newish but restful villa, along with the cheaper *dipendenza*, is the most comfortable option, set in a garden with a tennis court.

### Barberino di Mugello ✉ 50031

★★**Il Cavallo**, Viale della Repubblica 7, **t** 055 841 8144 (*moderate, cheaper without bath*). A posthouse dating from the early 19th century, Il Cavallo also has a good restaurant (*moderate*), with fresh seafood specialities including pasta with scampi and a delicious surf and turf (seafood and beef) grill. *Closed Wed and 23 Dec–6 Jan.*

### San Piero a Sieve ✉ 50037

★★★**Ebe**, Le Mozzette 1a, **t** 055 849 8333, **f** 055 848 567 (*moderate*). 25 pleasant rooms,

Continue 14km north for the truly breathtaking views to be had from the **Passo della Futa** (2,962ft), a pass on the principal Apennine watershed; below, the whole Mugello is spread out before you like a relief map. Not surprisingly, in 1944, the pass was the Germans' strong point on the Gothic Line – until the allies rendered it useless by capturing Firenzuola to the north. Beyond the pass the road winds under the craggy **Sasso di Castro** (4,185ft); at La Casetta you can turn off for Firenzuola (*see* p.250) or hotfoot it over the mountains in time for dinner in Bologna, the culinary capital of Italy.

## Scarperia

Standing at the major crossroads of the SS503 north and the SS551 along the Sieve, **San Piero a Sieve** is a busy little town defended by a mighty Medici citadel, the **Fortezza di San Martino**, designed by Buontalenti in 1571. Its Romanesque parish church, with a façade of 1776, contains a remarkable octagonal baptismal font in polychrome terracotta, by Luca della Robbia. From here it's 4km (30km from Florence)

attached to a fine restaurant (*cheap*) serving delicacies from nearby Emilia-Romagna such as tortellini with orange filling and various other delicious pasta dishes, as well as tender grilled meats. *Closed on Fri.*

**\*Ebe Dipendenza**, Via di Cafaggio 11 (*cheap*). Cheaper rooms, none of which have bath.

## Scarperia ✉ 50038

**\*\*Il Cantagallo**, Viale Kennedy 17, t 055 843 0442, f 055 843 0443 (*moderate*). A tidy little hotel overlooking a shady garden.

**Teatro dei Medici**, Via La Torre 12, t 055 845 9876 (*expensive*). Set in an old house that once belonged to the Medici, this is the place to go for Mugello cooking – and everyone does – so in summer it's worth booking ahead. Country *antipasti*, good pasta dishes and wild game in season. *Closed Sun eve, Mon in summer and 15 Aug– 1 Sept.*

## Firenzuola ✉ 50041

**\*\*\*Antica Casa Gualtieri**, Via Nazionale Pietramola 81, t 055 813 596, f 055 813 590 (*cheap*). In the mountains north of Firenzuola, at Pietramala, this has a restaurant (*moderate*) and is a charming place to help you beat the heat. *Closed Tues from Oct–April.*

## Vicchio ✉ 50039

**\*\*\*Villa Campestri**, Via de Campestri 19, t 055 849 0107, f 055 849 0108 (*very expensive*). On a hill south of Vicchio stands one of the most beautiful hotels in the region: an elegant Tuscan villa set in a 300-acre park, boasting a pool with a view, exquisitely furnished rooms and a good restaurant.

**La Casa di Caccia**, Roti Molezzano, Vicchio, t 055 840 7629 (*moderate*). An isolated old hunting lodge high in the hills, about 20mins north of Vicchio, with views across the valley. Game, home-made pasta, grilled meats. *Closed Tues and Feb.*

## Sagginale ✉ 50032

**Trattoria Sagginale**, Via Belvedere, t 055 849 0130, (*cheap*). Between Borgo San Lorenzo and Vicchio is this family-run restaurant serving rustic food in a simple setting – try the home-made ravioli (stuffed with ricotta and spinach or potato). *Closed Thurs.*

## Ponte a Vicchio ✉ 50032

**Casa del Prosciutto**, t 055 844 031 (*cheap*). Part-grocer, part-*trattoria*, specializing in local dishes including good char-grilled chicken and potato-stuffed tortelli (to take away as well). *Closed Mon, Tues afternoon, July and Jan; shop open 8–3.30 and 5–7.30.*

to **Scarperia**, the most charming little town in the Mugello, high on a shelf over the valley. Florence fortified it in 1306, and laid out its simple rectangular plan, with one long main street.

Scarperia's landmark is **Palazzo Pretorio** (*open summer Mon–Thurs 3–7, Fri 9.30–12.30, Sat 9.30–12.30, Sun 3–6.30; winter Sat, Sun and public holidays 10–12.30 and 3.30–7; adm can be combined with Museo deil Ferri Taglienti, below*), also called Palazzo dei Vicari and dating from 1306; it is so heavily coated with stone and ceramic coats of arms that it resembles a page from a postage stamp album; its atrium and upper halls have 14th- and 15th-century frescoes, the earliest ones by the school of Giotto; and the palace also includes the **Museo dei Ferri Taglienti** (*open summer Mon–Thurs 3–7, Fri 9.30–12.30, Sat 9.30–12.30, Sun 3–6.30; winter Sat, Sun and public holidays 10–1 and 3.30–7; adm*), a small museum dedicated to knife-making and cutting tools. The oratory of the **Madonna di Piazza** has an attractive Renaissance front and a cinquecento fresco of the Madonna and Child, attributed to Iacopo del Casentino; another church in Scarperia is dedicated to Our Lady of the Earthquakes with a fresco attributed by some to Filippo Lippi.

## Deluxe Virgins

One fine day, on a trip to one of the fancier Italian food shops, you may well pause near the section devoted to condiments and wonder at the beautiful display of bottles of unusually dark whiskies and wines, with corks and posh, elegant labels – why, some is even DOC, though much of it is far more costly than the usual DOC vintages. Take a closer look, however, and you'll notice that these precious bottles are full of nothing but olive oil. Admittedly *olio extra vergine di oliva* from Tuscany (as well as Umbria) makes a fine salad dressing – according to those in the know the oil of the Chianti brooks few rivals, Italian or otherwise. Its delicate, fruity fragrance derives from the excellent quality of the ripe olive and the low acidity extracted from the fruit without any refinements. The finest, Extra Virgin, must have less than 1 per cent acidity (the best has 0.5 per cent acidity). Other designations are Soprafino Virgin, Fine Virgin, and Virgin (each may have up to 4 per cent acidity) in descending order of quality. As any Italian will tell you, it's good for you – and it had better be, because Tuscan (and Umbrian) chefs put it in nearly every dish, as they have for centuries. The only difference is that it now comes in a fancy package for a fancy price, a victim of the Italian designer label syndrome and Tuscan preciosity. Not only does the olive oil have corks, but the trend in the early 1990s was for some of the smarter restaurants to offer an olive oil list similar to a wine list – one restaurant in Tuscany even had an oil sommelier. Many of these, perhaps fortunately, seem to have gone out of business.

From the 16th century, Scarperia had the monopoly on the manufacture of cutlery in Tuscany, and supplied the duchy not only with knives, forks and scissors, but daggers and even swords. At the turn of the century there were no fewer than 46 thriving firms, though machine-made competition has reduced this to a mere six who make shepherds' knives and other specialized tools. Efforts are being made by those who care about such things to revive the old craft and a week-long fair (the 'Mercato dei Ferri taglienti') celebrates the art in late August. Scarperia is better known these days, however, for the **Autodromo Internazionale del Mugello**, a 5km track built by Florence's Auto Club in 1976, which sounds ghastly but is fairly well hidden in the hills east of town.

Four kilometres north of Scarperia you can visit the Mugello's most fascinating historical relic, the parish church of **Sant'Agata a Fagna** (*open Mon–Fri 9–6, Sat 9–5, Sun 9–10 and 12–6*), constructed at the turn of the millennium and restored after an earthquake in 1919, with an unusual apse and a pulpit from 1175, decorated with white and green marble intarsia designs and animals. Refreshingly cool even in August, **Firenzuola** is 22km north of Scarperia. A small holiday resort, it was devastated in the Second World War and rebuilt along the lines of the original street plan, between the Porta di Bologna and the Porta di Firenze. West 4km in **Cornacchiaia** is a church believed to date back to Carolingian times.

# Borgo San Lorenzo and Vícchio

Borgo San Lorenzo (pop. 14,600) on the river Sieve is the boom town of the Mugello, and set to boom even more with the opening of a new fast-train rail link to Florence. It's surrounded by new residential neighbourhoods with gardens full of little chameleons; and indeed they are fond of animals here, as evidenced by the **Statue of Fido** in honour of man's best friend, in Piazza Dante. Otherwise, the main sights are two fine Romanesque churches: **San Lorenzo**, with an unusual hexagonal campanile built in 1263, and 3km north, the parish church of **San Giovanni Maggiore**, where the bell tower is square at the base but octagonal on top; here too is a lovely 12th-century pulpit in marble intarsia. To the north the road divides into the SS477 to **Palazzuolo sul Senio** and the SS302 to **Marradi**, also small resorts; in Palazzuolo you can visit a small, recently refurbished **Ethnographic Museum** (*t 0558 046 114, open Mar–June and Sept–Dec Sun only 3–7; Jul–Aug 3–7, Tues 8–11am; closed Jan, Feb, Mon in July–Aug*) in the 14th-century Palazzo dei Capitani.

Vícchio, east of San Lorenzo, is a sleepy little town that gave birth to the Blessed Fra Angelico (Giovanni da Fiesole, 1387–1455) and was often a home away from home for Benvenuto Cellini. The Palazzo Pretorio contains the **Museo Comunale Beato Angelico** (*open Sun 10–12 or by request; t 055 844 002*), with detached frescoes, Etruscan finds from nearby Poggio alla Colla, and a 13th-century holy water stoup.

Not to be outdone, the nearby and even more minute hamlet of **Vespignano** was the birthplace of Giotto di Bondone (1267–1337). The simple stone cottage where the father of Renaissance painting is said to have first seen the light of day has been carefully restored as the **Casa di Giotto** (*open summer Tues and Thurs 4–7, Sat–Sun 10–12 and 4–7; winter Tues and Thurs 3–5 and Sat–Sun 10–12 and 3–6; adm*). According to tradition, Cimabue discovered Giotto near the old (restored) bridge over the torrent Enza, where the young shepherd was sketching his sheep on a stone.

## The Valdisieve

The lower Sieve valley is mostly industrial: **Dicomano** can boast of an interesting fresco by the school of Piero della Francesca but little else besides the junction for the SS67, which climbs east into a pretty range of mountains called the Alpi di San Benedetto. San Godenzo, 10km up the SS67, is the largest village, site of an 11th-century **Benedictine abbey**; its plain church has a raised presbytery and a polyptych by the school of Giotto.

From San Godenzo a road continues up to the birthplace of Andrea del Castagno, now called **Il Castagno d'Andrea** ('Andrew's chestnut') (3,355ft), a small holiday village, or you can wind a further 18km up to **S. Benedetto in Alpe**, with a 9th-century Benedictine abbey that sheltered Dante (*Inferno*, Canto XVI, 94–105), where horses may be hired to visit the enchanting Valle dell'Arquacheta with its pretty waterfall. In the old town of **Portico di Romagna** 11km further north, the Portinari family, including the beautiful Beatrice, spent their summers – their house still stands in the main street. Deeper into Romagna lie the fascinating medieval town of **Brisighella**, the ceramic city of **Faenza**, and **Ravenna**, not only filled with ravishing Byzantine mosaics from the time of Justinian but also the site of Dante's real tomb.

There is little along the lower Sieve, though **Rufina**, 10km south of Dicomano, is dominated by the 16th-century **Villa Poggio Reale**, of interest to wine lovers for its production of *Chianti Putto* and *Pomino* wines. In Poggio Reale there's a small wine museum (*t 0558 397 932, open Sat–Sun 10–1 and 4–7 or call ahead for booking*). From **Pontassieve**, a large town at the confluence of the Sieve and the Arno, the scenic SS70 leads up to the dramatic **Passo della Consuma** (3,355ft) before descending into the Casentino (*see pp.449–52*).

# The Valdarno, Prato and Pistoia

10

# Valdarno, Prato and Pistoia

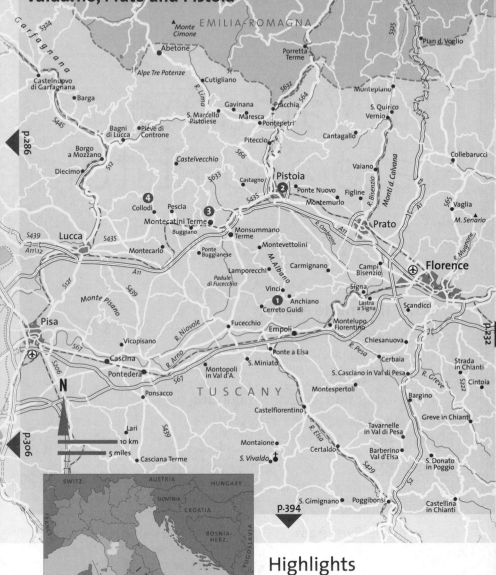

## Highlights

1 A museum of Leonardo's inventions, at Vinci

2 The tiger-striped medieval churches of Pistoia

3 Montecatini Terme, grandest of Italy's Belle Epoque spas

4 Ornate Baroque gardens and labyrinth at Castello Garzoni in Collodi

Whether you travel by car, bus or train, there are two routes between Florence and Pisa. The route along the Arno, often hemmed in by the hills, has always been historically and economically the least important and carries less traffic. The large cities of Prato, Pistoia and Lucca grew up in an arc north of the Monte Albano hills, where there's more fertile land and room to grow, and the route takes in the nearby Florentine towns of Vinci, Castelfiorentino and Certaldo.

# Down the Arno to Pisa

## Florence to Empoli

The old Florentine satellite town of **Scandicci** (6km west), once in the business of renting villas to foreigners like Dylan Thomas and D. H. Lawrence (who finished *Lady Chatterley's Lover* here), has since the war found more profit in industry. Most of the towns along the Arno specialize in certain products; in **Lastra a Signa** it's straw goods, sold in numerous village shops. Lastra retains its 14th-century walls and the **Loggia di Sant'Antonio**, all that survives of the hospital founded by Florence's Silk Guild in 1411; many believe Brunelleschi was the architect, and that the work was a prototype of Florence's Spedale degli Innocenti, which the same guild also funded. Just outside Lastra, the church of **San Martino a Gangalandi** contains a beautiful, semicircular apse with *pietra serena* articulation designed by Alberti. In **Signa**, the next village, the Romanesque church of **San Lorenzo** houses a remarkable 12th-century marble pulpit and trecento frescoes.

After Signa the road and river continue 12 kilometres through a gorge before **Montelupo Fiorentino**, celebrated for its terracottas and delicately painted ceramics since the Renaissance. The town hosts an important ceramics fair at the end of June, also including Renaissance music and costumes, demonstrations and exhibitions. The new **Museo Archeologico e della Ceramica**, Via Baccio Sinaldi 45 (*open Tues–Fri 9–12 and 2.30–7; t 0571 51352; adm*), has examples from nearly every period, and a display on the lower Valdarno's prehistory, while Montelupo's shops would be happy to sell you a more recent ceramic creation. The old **castle** here was built in 1203 by the Florentines, during the wars against Pisa; the church **San Giovanni Evangelista** contains a lovely *Madonna and Saints* by Botticelli and his assistants. On the outskirts of Montelupo, you can see Buontalenti's **Villa Ambrosiana** (1587) from the outside, though you'll probably want to avoid being invited in – it's a mental hospital. From Montelupo a road leads southeast 20 kilometres to the town of San Casciano in Val di Pesa, in Chianti (*see* p.237).

### Empoli

The modern market town of **Empoli**, 32 kilometres from Florence, was witness to one of the turning points in Tuscan history: in 1260, the Ghibellines of Siena, fresh from their great victory over Florence at Monteaperti, held a parliament in Empoli to

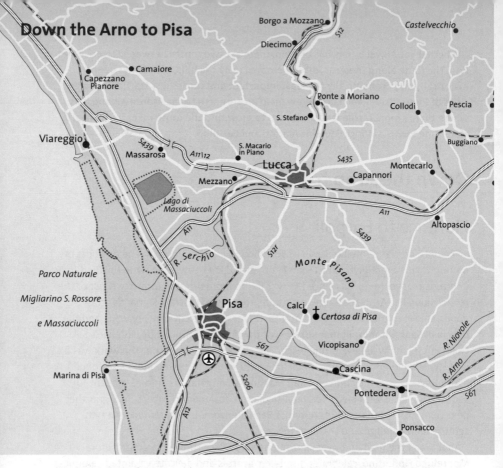

decide the fate of their arch enemy. Everyone was for razing Florence to the ground once and for all, and waited for the approval of their leader, Farinata degli Uberti.

The Uberti were Florentine gangster nobles famous for their hatred of their fellow citizens, but Farinata surprised all when he stood up and announced that, even if it meant standing alone, he would defend Florence for as long as he lived. The Sienese let their captain have his way, and lost their chance of ever becoming *numero uno* in Tuscany. The prosperous new Empoli (pop. 45,000) produces green glass and raincoats; you'll find little to recall the days of Farinata, until you reach the piazza named after him: here is the palace where the parliament convened, across from the gem of a Romanesque church, the **Collegiata Sant'Andrea**, with its green and white marble geometric façade in the style of Florence's San Miniato. The lower portion dates from 1093; the upper had to wait until the 18th century, but it harmonizes extremely well.

## Museo della Collegiata

Empoli has its share of 13th- and 14th-century Florentine art as well, much of it now in the small but choice **Museo della Collegiata** (*open Tues–Sun 9–12 and 4–7; closed Mon; adm*) in the Collegiata's cloister. The most celebrated work is Masolino's *Pietà* fresco, with its poignant faces; upstairs there's an elegant relief of the

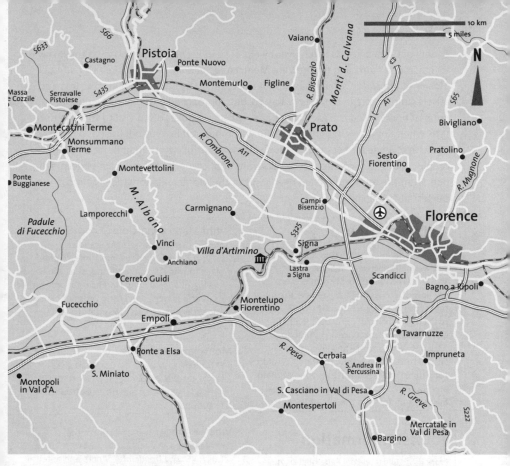

Madonna and Child by Mino da Fiesole and a painted tabernacle of St Sebastian by his brother Antonio. Lorenzo Monaco contributes a long-eyed *Madonna and Saints*; Lorenzo di Bicci's scene of San Nicola da Tolentino shielding Empoli from a rain of plague arrows is a quattrocento view of the city. There is a rare series of frescoes by Masolino's master, Starnina, as well as two saints by Pontormo, who was born nearby, and the fine *Tabernacle of the Holy Sacrament* by Francesco Botticini and his son Raffaello, with a good predella.

The upper Loggia has works by Andrea della Robbia, and the suspended wooden wings of the donkey that is made to fly down on a wire from the church tower on *Corpus Domine* (although a papier-mâché donkey has of late replaced the original one). Empoli's **Santo Stefano** church (*open Tues–Sun 9–12 by appt – enquire at the Museo della Collegiata; closed Mon*), restored after damage during the Second World War, has more beautiful frescoes by Masolino and a marble *Annunciation* by Bernardo Rossellini.

## Cerreto Guidi and Vinci

Northwest of Empoli, in the Monte Albano, you can find the old hill townlet of **Cerreto Guidi** (COPIT buses from Piazza Vittoria). This is the former property of the

Counts of Guidi and was taken over by Florence in 1237. It is mainly known these days for its *Chianti Putto*, and for the **Villa Medicea** (*open daily 9–6.30; closed 2nd and 3rd Mon of month; adm*), which was rebuilt for Cosimo I by Buontalenti in 1564. It is a relatively simple cottage as Medici villas go, but approached by a grandiose double ramp of bricks called the 'Medici bridges'. The grand dukes often visited the villa until 1576, when Cosimo I's daughter Isabella was murdered here by her husband Paolo Orsini in revenge for her infidelities; if you look carefully you can find the unhappy couple among the scores of Medici portraits that comprise the villa's chief decoration. From the terrace there are fine views of the Monte Albano, which is almost treeless at this point.

## Getting Around

If you're **driving**, persist: the Florentine sprawl finally gives way at Signa and after that the Arno road (SS67) becomes even scenic in stretches. LAZZI **buses** take the main route to Pisa; SITA goes directly from Florence to Castelfiorentino or Certaldo; for Vinci, COPIT. **Trains** at least once an hour follow the Arno between Florence and Pisa, and at Empoli turn off for Castelfiorentino, Certaldo, Poggibonsi and Siena. Note that San Miniato and Fucécchio share a railway station; local buses commute from there to both centres.

## Tourist Information

**Empoli**: Via Giuseppe del Papa 98, t 0571 76115.*Open Sept–July Mon–Fri 5–7pm.*
**Vinci**: Via della Torre 11, t 0571 568 012, f 0571 567 930. *Open Mar–Oct Mon–Sun 10–7; Nov–Feb Mon–Sat 10–1, Sun and holidays 10–6.*
**Castelfiorentino**: c/o the Station, Via Ridolfi, t/f 0571 629 049, *infocastello@libero.it. Open April–Oct Mon–Thurs 9.30–12.30 and 3.30–6.30, Fri–Sun 9–12.30 and 3.30–7.*
**San Miniato**: Piazza del Popolo 3, t/f 0571 42745, *www.cittadisanminiato.it. Open Mon–Sun 9.30–1 and 3.30–7.*

## Where to Stay and Eat

The lower Arno Valley isn't exactly awash in pleasure domes but there are a reasonable number of places to stay and more than a handful of decent restaurants; you won't have to sleep in the car or starve!

**Santa Maria a Marciola** ✉ 50018
**Fiore**, Via di Marciola 112, near Scandicci, t 055 768 678 (*expensive–moderate*). A good place to stop if it's time to eat just as you're leaving or approaching Florence, not only for its delicious crêpes and *fritto misto* of meats and greens, but for its lovely garden setting and pine-clad slopes. *Closed Wed.*

**Montelupo** ✉ 50056
★★★**Tonio**, Via 1 Maggio 23, t 0571 541 444, f 0571 541 436 (*moderate*). A pleasant place with a large garden and nice, cool rooms in summer.

**Vinci** ✉ 50059
★★★**Alexandra**, Via dei Martiri 36, t 0571 56224, f 0571 567 972 (*moderate*). Vinci's one hotel; quiet and comfortable.
As for restaurants, there isn't much choice.
**Da Pippo**, Via della Torre 19, t 0571 56100 (*moderate*). Near the Leonardo museum, this is flagrantly touristy and the fare is undistinguished, but there's a pretty view from the terrace.
**Bar Centrale**, Via Fucini 16, t 0571 56054 (*cheap*). You might do better with the simple, tasty meals served here.

**Empoli** ✉ 50053
Empoli isn't a posh town by any means, but it can be an agreeable place to stay over.
★★★**Sole**, Piazza Don Minzoni, t 0571 73779 (*moderate*). A good bargain, by the station. Neither will you have any difficulty finding a restaurant.
**La Panzanella**, Via dei Cappucini 10, t 0571 922 182 (*cheap–moderate*). An old-fashioned

From Cerreto it's five kilometres to **Vinci**, a tiny town among hills of olives and vines. It is, of course, most famous as the home of Leonardo, who was born in a humble house in Anchiano on 15 April 1452, the illegitimate son of the local notary and a peasant girl. In his honour, the town's landmark Conti Guidi Castle has been converted into the **Museo Leonardiano** (*open daily 9.30–6; in summer until 7; adm*), full of models of inventions he designed in his *Codex Atlanticus* notebooks, most of which this supreme 'Renaissance man' never had the time or attention span to build. The museum has kindly added descriptions in English of the 100 or so machines it houses, including some inspired by those invented by Brunelleschi to build Florence's cathedral dome. More speculative designs include a flying machine, a paddle boat, a

*trattoria*, also by the station, which does wonderful things with porcini mushrooms in season; sometimes snails, too. *Closed Sun.*
**Il Galeone**, Via Curtatone e Montanara 67, t 0571 72826 (*moderate*). Fresh fish dishes. *Closed Sun.*

### San Miniato ✉ 56027
**★★★Miravalle**, Piazza Castello 3, t 0571 418 075, f 0571 419 681 (*moderate*). Sleep in Frederick II's 12th-century imperial palace, near the top of town.
**Il Canapone**, Piazza Bonaparte 5, t 0571 418 121 (*moderate*). A simple place where you can try the local truffles on spaghetti, in risotto, or with veal *scaloppine*; in the spring there's rice with asparagus. *Closed Mon.*

### Certaldo ✉ 50052
**★★Il Castello**, Via della Rena 6, t/f 0571 668 250 (*moderate*). One of the more interesting of the three small hotels in town.
**★★★Osteria del Vicario**, Via Rivellino 3, t/f 0571 668 228 (*moderate*). A beautiful 12th-century ex-monastery with a garden surrounded by a Romanesque courtyard. Rooms are simple, with terracotta floors, and the restaurant (*expensive*) serves fresh local fare.
One place in Certaldo can satisfy all your little vices at once:
**Dolci Follie**, Piazza Boceccio (*cheap*). A fancy *pasticceria*, a wine bar and also a fine little restaurant, where the cuisine is more than a prelude to the exquisite desserts.

### Artimino ✉ 50040
**Paggeria Medicea**, t 055 871 8081, f 055 871 8080 (*expensive*). An interesting place,

located in the Medici Villa Artimino near Carmignano. A former country residence of the famous family, the stables have been converted into a very comfortable hotel with pool and tennis.
**Da Delfina**, t 055 871 8074 (*expensive*). This restaurant boasts a Michelin star and enjoys a well-deserved reputation. There's Tuscan food (ravioli stuffed with potato), and a terrace for dining out.

### Fucécchio ✉ 50054
**Le Vedute**, Via Romana-Lucchese 121, t 0571 297 498 (*expensive*). A good inland seafood restaurant pleasantly situated in the country, where in summer you can linger on the veranda over your favourite denizen of the deep – good meats as well, especially in autumn. *Closed Mon.*
**★★★La Campagnola**, Viale Colombo 144, t 0571 260 786, f 0571 261 781 (*moderate*). 25 air-conditioned rooms.

### Montópoli in Val d'Arno ✉ 56020
**★★★Quattro Gigli**, Piazza Michele 2, t 0571 466 878, f 0571 466 879, *www.quattrogigli.it.* (*moderate*). In this little place across the Arno, the old town hall has been converted into an inn with 28 rooms of varying quality. The restaurant (*moderate*), beyond the permanent display of Montópoli's painted ceramics, has a delightful terrace and features an imaginative menu, based on Tuscan dishes, with plenty of mushrooms, vegetables and salads depending on the season, and an Italian rarity – roast potatoes. The duck and game dishes are excellent. *Closed Sun eve and Mon.*

spring-driven mechanical car, an almost perfect modern bicycle, diving gear, a para-chute, and a device to walk on water. Also present are Leonardo's famous tank, machine gun and helicopter. This otherwise gentle fellow once said, 'I'll do anything for money', which must be one of the most startling quotes of the Renaissance. On the other hand, nothing could be more typical of the age than brilliance combined with utter immorality; while he often neglected his art, Leonardo was always happy to help the bellicose princes who employed him with their military problems. We should probably be thankful that these gadgets never escaped from his notebook. Leonardo was baptized in the font in **Santa Croce**, next door to the museum.

From Vinci it's a three kilometre walk (or drive) southeast to **Anchiano** (*open daily 9.30–6; in summer until 7; adm*), where the simple stone house where Leonardo was born has been restored. There are plans to restore the beautiful landscape between Vinci and Anchiano to its 16th-century appearance.

## San Miniato

Just southwest of Empoli, the river Elsa flows into the Arno near **San Miniato** (pop. 23,000), a refined old hill town that grew up at the crossroads of the Via Francigena (the main pilgrimage route from France to Rome) and the Florence–Pisa road; on a clear day the view takes in everything from Fiesole to the sea. Its defensi-bility and strategic location made it the Tuscan residence of the Emperors, from Otto IV to Frederick II; Matilda of Tuscany was born here in 1046, and in the 12th century it was an important imperial fortress.

Of the citadel, only two towers survive: the present campanile of the cathedral and the taller 'Torrione', in the shady Prato del Duomo that crowns San Miniato, with its peculiar chimney-like structures on top. It was from the top of this tower that Frederick II's secretary and court poet Pier della Vigna, falsely accused of treason, leapt to his death, to be discovered by Dante in the forest of suicides, as described in the *Inferno* XIII. Also in the Prato del Duomo stand the 12th-century **Palazzo dei Vicari dell'Imperatore** and the **Duomo** itself, with a Romanesque brick façade, incorporating pieces of sculpted marble and 13th-century majolica, which catch the light as the sun sets. Most of the art in the interior is Baroque, except for a fine 13th-century holy water stoup; most of the earlier artworks from the region have been placed in the **Museo Diocesano d'Arte Sacra**, to the left of the cathedral (*open summer Tues–Sun 9–12 and 3–5; closed Mon; winter Sat and Sun only 9–12 and 2.30–5; adm*). Among the prizes are the fresco of the *Maestà* by the 'Maestro degli Ordini' from Siena, a bust of Christ attributed to Verrocchio, Neri di Bicci's *Madonna con Bambino* and a *Crucifixion* by Filippo Lippi. Since 1968, the Prato del Duomo has also been the site of the **National Kite Flying Contest** (*1st Sun after Easter*).

More art awaits in the Piazza del Popolo's 14th-century church of **San Domenico** – including minor works by Masolino, Pisanello, the della Robbias, and Bernardo Rossellino, who carved the fine tomb of Giovanni Chiellini, the Florentine founder of San Miniato's Hospital of Poor Pilgrim Priests in the 15th century; the tomb is mod-elled after Rossellino's famous tomb of Leonardo Bruni in Florence's Santa Croce. The beautiful church of **San Francesco** has fresco remains by a follower of Masolino.

Kite contests aren't the only sideline to San Miniato – Napoleon paid a visit in 1797, not to revel in this old seat of emperors but to visit his relatives in the **Palazzo Bonaparte**. In the surrounding countryside are rich caches of white truffles, sought fervently in the autumn for the large market on the last Sunday in November; and many of what appear to be plain-looking Romanesque churches around San Miniato are actually tobacco-curing barns from the 1900s.

## Castelfiorentino and San Vivaldo

Some 12 kilometres south along the Valdelsa from San Miniato, **Castelfiorentino** (pop. 18,000) is another old hill town, though much rebuilt after damage in the Second World War. Castelfiorentino's church of **Santa Verdiana** dates from the 18th century and houses the **Pinacoteca** (*open June–April, Sat 4–7, Sun 10–12 and 4–7; May, daily but times vary; groups may also visit on request*), with some excellent trecento paintings, including a *Madonna* attributed to Duccio da Buoninsegna, another by Francesco Granacci, and a triptych by Taddeo Gaddi. The **Cappella della Visitazione**, Via Gozzoli 55, is covered with frescoes by Benozzo Gozzoli and his school.

One of the more unusual sights in Tuscany, the **Monastery of San Vivaldo**, lies in the rather empty zone to the southwest of Castelfiorentino, beyond the village of Montaione. Vivaldo was a hermit from San Gimignano who lived in a hollow chestnut tree and was found dead there in 1301, still in the attitude of prayer. A Franciscan community grew up in his footsteps, and in 1500, when the monastery was being rebuilt, one member, Fra Tommaso da Firenze, thought to take advantage of the monastery's wooded hills to build a 'New Jerusalem' with 34 chapels replicating the sites of Christ's Passion. To render the symbolic journey more realistic for pilgrims, the 34 chapels combined polychrome terracottas by Giovanni della Robbia and other artists, set in frescoes – Pope Leo X immediately granted a fat indulgence to anyone who did the whole route. Today only 17 of the chapels survive, set in lovely woods.

## Certaldo

**Certaldo** (pop. 16,000), former seat of Florence's deputy, or Vicarate of the Valdelsa, is synonymous with Giovanni Boccaccio, who spent the last 13 years of his life up in the old town, known as Castello Aldo, which could be a set for the *Decameron* itself (don't confuse it with the ugly sprawl of the new town at the bottom of the hill). Everything here is of good, honest brick, from the pavements to the palazzi, of which the most striking is the 14th-century castellated **Palazzo Pretorio**. Inside it has a beautiful courtyard and museum (*open summer 10–1 and 2.30–7.30; winter 10–1 and 3–5.30; adm*) containing Etruscan artefacts, detached frescoes and, in the annexed church and cloister, Gozzoli's *Tabernacle of the Punished*, not one of his more cheerful works. In the old jail the walls still bear the forlorn graffiti of past prisoners.

The house traditionally associated with Certaldo's great author is the **Casa di Boccaccio**, on Via Boccaccio 18, which has been restored and is now the seat of the International Centre of Boccaccio Studies (*open 10–12 and 3–6*). Boccaccio died here in 1375 and lies buried in **Santi Michele ed Iacopo**, under an epitaph he penned himself; a 16th-century monument erected in his honour was destroyed by prudes in

1783. Boccaccio himself, in his later years, regretted the racy frivolity of his most famous book, wishing he had spent his time on serious Latin works – not a regret too many people have ever shared. From Certaldo you can follow a pretty road to the south which leads to **San Gimignano** (*see* pp.398–402), about 13 kilometres away.

# Empoli to Pisa

There is no real reason to stop in the lower Valdarno unless you're low on petrol. If you're spending more time here, consider a visit to **Fucécchio** for its panoramic views, or better yet for the **Padule di Fucécchio** (*the Centro di Ricerca, Documentazione e Promozione del Padule di Fucécchio offers guided nature tours, t 0573 84540*), claimed to be Italy's biggest inland swamp and an excellent place for bird-watching.

Next comes **Montópoli in Val d'Arno**, a medieval town dating from the 11th century on the south bank. Further down-river lies industrial **Pontedera**, where the Piaggio Company produces most of Italy's motor scooters. Here you may detour south on the SS439 to Volterra (*see* pp.403–10), by way of **Ponsacco** and the four-towered **Villa di Camugliano**, built by Alessandro and Cosimo I. Between here and Volterra roll the Pisan Hills, some of the quietest, most rural countryside in Tuscany; the main attraction may be precisely its lack of art and history. Alternatively, from Ponsacco, you can head southwest to tiny **Lari**, with the remains of a Medici fortress, and if your rheumatism is acting up, to Casciana Terme, famous for its cures in Roman times, and rebuilt by the Pisans in the 14th century. The hamlet of **Rivalto**, six kilometres south of the spa, has almost perfectly preserved its medieval character.

**Vicopisano**, north of the Arno, defended the eastern frontier of Pisa from the ambitions of Lucca, and its impressive *castello* was remodelled by Brunelleschi after the Florentine conquest of Pisa; vineyards now surround its mighty walls and towers. Across the bridge, **Cascina** still has most of its medieval walls and Roman grid plan from its days as a military camp. It also has three churches that are worth a visit: **San Casciano**, an unusual 12th-century Romanesque church, with blind arches and some fine sculptural details; Romanesque **San Benedetto a Settimo**, adorned with a 14th-century alabaster altarpiece of Irish origin; and **San Giovanni Evangelista**, built by the Knights of St John, with trecento Sienese frescoes, recently restored after the church was used as a barn for several centuries. Further west lies the Certosa di Pisa (8km; *see* p.330) and Pisa itself (14km).

# Prato

**Prato** is only 18 kilometres from Florence but a world away in atmosphere; this is a city that works hard for its living. The population has doubled since the Second World War to 145,000, making it the third largest in Tuscany after Florence and Livorno. And a vibrantly, joyously proletarian city it is, fond of Henry Moore and comic books and avant-garde theatre and noisy heavy-metal bars that are full of people wanting you to sign petitions or buy encyclopaedias. All are proud to live in 'the

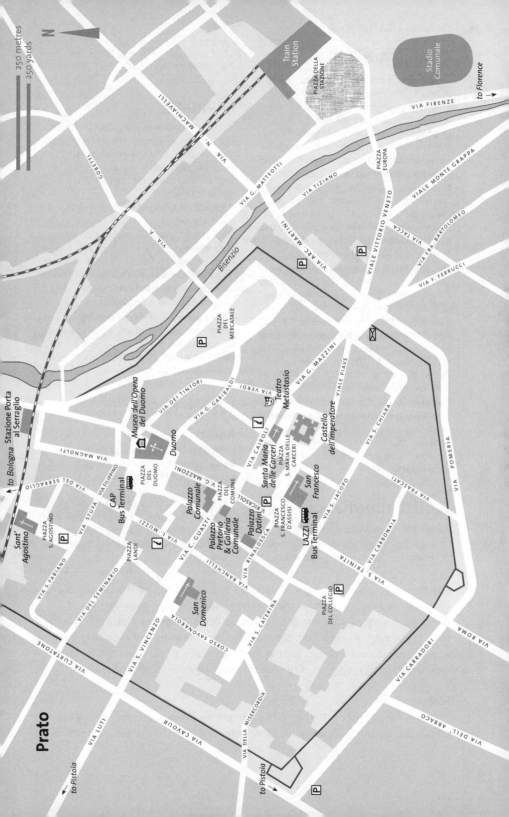

# Getting Around

Prato is easily reached by **train** from Florence (18km/25mins), Pistoia (17km/25mins) or Bologna (85km/55mins), and has two stations, the main Stazione Centrale, facing a pretty green square just on the other bank of Prato's river, the Bisenzio; and the Stazione Porta al Serraglio (not all trains stop), just north of the walls and closer to the centre, on the Florence–Pistoia line. This was one of Italy's first railways, built in 1848 for the Lorraine grand dukes by an Englishman named Ralph Bonfield, who so pleased the grand duke that he was made Count of St George of Prato. These days, the Prato tourist office is searching for his descendants, to claim the title and supply a likeness of Bonfield so they can erect a proper monument in his honour. All Bonfields take note!

**Buses** from Prato depart from Piazza Ciardi north of the Duomo or the Stazione Centrale; all pass through Piazza San Francesco (CAP or LAZZI buses, every half-hour to Florence with connections to the Mugello; also LAZZI buses to Pistoia, Montecatini, Lucca, Pisa and Viareggio).

Prato has two exits on the *autostrada* A11 between Florence and Pisa (from Florence get on at Peretola). Note that the centre is closed to traffic; Piazza Mercatale is a convenient place to park.

# Tourist Information

**Prato**: Piazza Santa Maria delle Carceri 15, t/f 0574 24112, *www.pratoturismo.toscana.it*. Open Easter–Oct Mon–Sat 9–1.30 and 2–7, Sun 10–1 and 2.30–6; Nov–Easter Mon–Sat 9–1.30 and 2–6.30.

# Shopping

Prato still makes its living from fine fabrics and clothing, and people from all over Tuscany come to visit the **factory outlets** where these are available at discount prices. One of the specialities is **cashmere**, produced in numerous spots.

**Ottomila**, Via Friuli Venezia Giulia 20, in suburban Macrolotto.

**Maglieria Artigiana G. Pierattini**, Via del Mandorlo 21.

**Tessiture Cecchi & Cecchi**, Via delle Calandre 53. Does covers, scarves and such in cashmere, wool and silk; located in the Calenzano *zona industriale*.

There are also some good **clothing** options.

**Enrico Pecci**, Via di Pantano 16, in Capalle.

**Gruppo Osvaldo Bruni**, Via Galcianese 67.

**Lanificio Cagnoli**, Via del Bisenzio a San Martino 6.

# Where to Stay

**Prato** ✉ 50047

Prato's hotels are mostly of the businessman variety, but can be a good bet in the summer when Florence tends to get packed to the gills.

**\*\*\*San Marco**, Piazza San Marco 48, t 0574 21321, f 0574 22378 (*moderate*). A pleasant place between the Stazione Centrale and the Castello, convenient if you arrive by train.

Manchester of Tuscany'. Living in Florence's shadow for the past thousand years has not dampened Prato's spirits as much as one might suppose; as in the days of Francesco di Marco Datini, immortalized in Iris Origo's book *The Merchant of Prato*, this city still earns its keep from the manufacture of textiles, and especially from the recycling of old wool and rags. During the Renaissance, it made enough from these rags to hire the great artists of the day to embellish its churches and palaces.

### History

Prato made its historical début in the 9th century, under the name of Borgo al Cornio; outside the town was a meadow, or *prato*, site of the market and fortifica-

***Villa Santa Cristina**, Via Poggio Secco 58, t 0574 595 951, f 0574 572 623 (*expensive*). A relaxing spot with a garden, pool and most other comforts, over the river in the hills to the east of Prato.

***Flora**, Via Cairoli 31, near S. Maria dei Carceri, t 0574 33521 f 0574 40289 (*expensive*). Good if you prefer modernity and air-conditioning.

****Villa Rucellai**, Via di Canneto 16,4km northeast of town, t 0574 460 392 (*moderate*). A delightful B&B in a Renaissance villa, with formal gardens and pool. What's more, it's excellent value.

****Toscana**, Piazza Ciardi 3, t 0574 28096, f 0574 25163 (*moderate*). More economical though still pleasant enough, the Toscana is on a quiet square on the far side of the Stazione Porta al Serraglio; some rooms have air-conditioning.

## Eating Out

One reason for staying in Prato is the quality of the food to be found here, especially if you like fish.

**Il Pirana**, Via Valentini 110, (south of Viale Vittorio Veneto, the main street between the central station and Piazza San Marco), t 0574 25746 (*expensive*). Maintains a justified reputation for some of the best seafood in inland Tuscany; try the scampi. *Closed Sat lunch and Sun.*

**Osvaldo Baroncelli**, Via Fra Bartolomeo 13, t 0574 23810 (*very expensive*). A small, unpretentious establishment opposite the Metastasio theatre, with an innovative chef who turns out dishes like tagliatelle with artichokes, veal *scaloppine* with truffles, duck stuffed with its own kidney or stuffed celery (a favourite Pratese dish), as well as more traditional Tuscan favourites. *Closed Sat lunch and Sun.*

**Enoteca Barni**, Via Ferucci 24, t 0574 607 845 (*expensive*). Boasts an excellent wine list, as the name would imply; the food is also good with simpler, cheaper lunchtime menus and more interesting but still good value choices in the evenings – asparagus soufflé with foie gras sauce, red mullet with basil, black olives and tomato, bean and cabbage soup with lobster, lasagne with pigeon, and a first-rate cheese board. *Closed Sat and Sun in Aug.*

**Trattoria Lapo**, Piazza del Mercatale 141, t 0574 23745 (*moderate*). Popular if unspectacular.

**Hotel Flora**, Via Cairoli, t 0574 33521 (*cheap–moderate*) Vegetarians will want to make a beeline for the lovely roof garden at this hotel in the centre, serving unusual salads, pâtés, quiches and organic wines, and with an excellent value set menu. *Closed lunch and all day Sun.*

**La Vecchia Cucina di Soldano**, Via Pomeri 23, t 0574 34665 (*cheap*). A very gratifying *trattoria* for something less elaborate, with a traditional menu cooked and served by the Mattei family that's full of *ribollita* and *pasta e fagioli*, stuffed celery and all the other old-fashioned soups and stews, including the house speciality, a hearty beef and onion stew known as *francesina*. *Closed Sun.*

**Nelson Pub**, Via M. Nistri 51. A favourite rendezvous for Prato's homesick Brits and anglophiles.

tions, which gradually became so important that the whole town took the name. It was first ruled by the Alberti, one of the region's more ambitious feudal families, who conquered lands from the Maremma to the Mugello. In 1107 Countess Matilda personally led a combined Tuscan army against Prato in order to humble the Alberti; then, in 1140, the Pratesi humbled their counts even more by ridding them of most of their power and running their city as a free *comune*. In 1193, at the height of the city's power, it even managed to snatch some of Florence's own *contado*. By this time Prato had also become one of Europe's most important manufacturers of woollen goods, so wealthy that the University of Paris created a special college for Pratesi students.

Florence, however, could not countenance so near and ambitious a rival, and in 1350, on charges of fomenting rebellion in the Valdelsa, Florence besieged Prato. An honourable peace was made; the next year Florence cemented its hold over its neighbour by purchasing it for the sum of 17,500 florins from its nominal overlord, the Angevin Queen of Naples.

Despite the ignominy of being bought, Prato functioned more as Florence's ally than its possession, retaining a certain amount of local autonomy. The late 14th century was the day of Francesco di Marco Datini, the Merchant of Prato, one of the richest men in Europe and history's first recorded workaholic businessman. However, although he built his palace in his home town of Prato, the big profits were to be had in Florence, and Datini spent most of his time there. Under the influence of Savonarola's preaching, Prato joined Florence in rebelling against Medici rule, but was soon to play the role of whipping boy, when the Spaniards, at the instigation of the Medici Pope Leo X, besieged and sacked the city with unheard-of brutality. Since that dark day, Prato's history has followed that of its imperious neighbour, until a few years ago, at least. You can't keep a good town down forever, and Prato and its hinterlands have finally wriggled out from Florentine control and become a province in their own right – one of Italy's newest, and smallest.

## Frederick's Castle

*Open June–end Sept Wed–Mon 9.10–6.30; Oct–May Wed–Sat and Mon 10–4, Sun 10–1; closed Tues.*

Most people, whether arriving by car, bus, or at the Stazione Centrale, approach the walled core of Prato through the Piazza San Marco, embellished with a white puffy sculpture by Henry Moore from 1974. Viale Piave continues to the defiantly Ghibelline swallowtail crenellations of the **Castello dell'Imperatore**. Built in 1237 by Frederick II, Holy Roman Emperor and heir to the Norman kingdom in southern Italy and Sicily, it marks a strange interlude in Prato's past. Frederick, unlike his grandfather Frederick Barbarossa, never spent much time in Tuscany, preferring his more civilized dominions in Apulia and Sicily, where he could discuss poetry, philosophy and falconry (in Arabic or Latin) with his court scholars. When he did come, it was in magnificent progress featuring dancing girls, elephants and the Muslim imperial bodyguard. His Tuscan taxpayers were not impressed; nor did they much appreciate Frederick's tolerant, syncretistic approach to religion. The popes excommunicated him twice. He built this castle here because he had to, not so much to defend Prato, but to defend his imperial *podestà* from the Pratesi, and perhaps impress the locals with its design – its clean lines must have seemed very sharp and modern in the 13th century.

Don't doubt for a minute that this castle is quite intentionally a work of art. The design, by a Sicilian named Riccardo da Lentini, is perfectly in tune with the south Italian works of the 'Hohenstaufen Renaissance' of Frederick's reign, a reminder of a rare age when artistically the south was keeping up with northern Italy, and often a little in advance. There isn't much inside the castle now, though the city often uses the space for special exhibitions. Usually it is possible to walk up along its walls for a bird's-eye view of Prato.

## Santa Maria delle Carceri

Next to the castle stands the unfinished black and white marble façade of **Santa Maria delle Carceri**, begun in 1485 by Giuliano da Sangallo. Brunelleschian architecture was always a fragile blossom, as is clearly shown by the failure of this sole serious attempt to transplant it outside the walls of Florence. Santa Maria always merits a mention in architectural histories. It was an audacious enterprise: Sangallo, a furiously diligent student of Vitruvius and Alberti, attempted to create a building based entirely on philosophical principles. Order, simplicity and correct proportion, as in Brunelleschi's churches, were to be manifest, with few frills allowed. Sangallo, the favourite of Lorenzo il Magnifico, unfortunately proved to be a better theorist than he was an architect. Santa Maria was a clumsy tombstone for the sort of theoretical architecture that was a fad in the 1400s, one more often expressed in paintings than actual buildings. The interior is better than the exterior; a plain Greek cross in the Brunelleschian manner with a decorative frieze and tondi of the four Evangelists by Andrea della Robbia. The church's name – *carceri* means prisons – refers to a local miracle, a speaking image of the Virgin painted on a nearby prison wall, that occasioned the building of the church. Behind the church is Prato's grand 1820's **Teatro Metastasio**, home to frequent concerts and some of the most innovative theatre in Italy.

## Piazza San Francesco and Datini

From Santa Maria delle Carceri you can see the apse of Prato's huge brick church of **San Francesco**, dating from the end of the 13th century, and embellished in front with white and green marble stripes. Inside, on the left wall is the Tomb of Gemignano Inghirami, one of Europe's crack lawyers of the quattrocento, the design attributed to Bernardo Rossellino (1460s); near the altar is the **tomb slab of Francesco di Marco Datini** (1330–1410) by Niccolò di Piero Lamberti. Off the elegant Renaissance cloister you'll find the entrance to the **Cappella Migliorati**, beautifully frescoed in 1395 by Niccolò di Pietro Gerini, one of the period's finest draughtsmen; here he depicts the Lives of Saints Anthony Abbot and Matthew.

Niccolò also frescoed the **Palazzo Datini** (nearby on Via Mazzei 33, *open Mon–Sat 9–12 and 4.30–7; closed Sun*), the showplace palace built in the 1390s by the Merchant of Prato. If there were an Accountants' Hall of Fame, Francesco di Marco Datini would surely be in it; he helped invent that dismal science. Nor did he ever let anyone throw anything away, leaving to posterity 150,000 documents, ledgers (all inscribed: 'For God and Profit') and private letters that are stored in the archives in this palace; these formed the basis for Iris Origo's fascinating account of his life and times. Datini left nearly all of his indecent fortune to the Ceppo, a Pratese charity he founded in 1410 and which now has its headquarters on the first floor of this palace; in gratitude the city had the façade frescoed with scenes of his life, unfortunately now much faded.

## Galleria Comunale

*Currently closed. Some of the works here and in the Museo di Pittura Murale may be temporarily on display in the Museo dell'Opera del Duomo (see opposite)*

Just north lies Prato's charming civic centre, the **Piazza del Comune**, decorated with a 19th-century **statue of Datini** with bronze reliefs of the merchant's life, and a pretty fountain by Tacca nicknamed 'Il Bacchino', or Little Bacchus (1659). The city's **Palazzo Comunale**, behind the portico, retains only traces of its medieval heritage; drop in to see its **Sala di Consiglio** with its coffered ceiling, two quattrocento frescoes and portraits of the grand dukes. The rugged **Palazzo Pretorio** is entirely medieval, a relic of the days when Prato governed itself without any help from the Medici; the stair on the façade leads up to the **Galleria Comunale** with a good collection of mostly Florentine art. There's a tabernacle by Filippino Lippi, painted for his mother and later restored after damage in the war; up in the grand **Salone Udienza** with the fine wood ceiling is Bernardo Daddi's *Story of the Holy Girdle*, a predella telling the tale of Prato's most famous relic, the Virgin Mary's belt. According to tradition she gave it to Doubting Thomas, from whom it was passed down until it became part of the dowry of a woman who married Michele, a knight from Prato during the First Crusade. Michele returned to Prato and hid the precious relic under his mattress; angels lifted him off, and the girdle was given into the care of the cathedral. In the same hall are fine 14th-century works by Giovanni di Milano, Michele di Firenze, Lorenzo Monaco, and a tondo attributed to Luca Signorelli. In an adjoining room, there is a curious work by Battistello, a follower of Caravaggio, whose unique *Noli me tangere* portrays Christ wearing a fedora at a rakish angle, doing a quick dance step to evade the Magdalene's touch.

Also on Piazza del Comune, Prato celebrates its medieval and modern textile industry in the **Museo del Tessuto** (*open daily Mon and Wed–Fri 10.30–6.30, Sat 10.30–2.30; adm*) with a unique collection of fabrics and looms dating back to the 5th century AD. The museum is only here temporarily; there are plans to expand it eventually into a new home in one of the city's old textile mills outside the walls.

## Cathedral of Santo Stefano

In the centre of Prato rises its cathedral, like a faded beauty who never recovered from the blow of a broken engagement. It was begun with great promise in the 13th century, and added to on and off for the next 200 years, with ever dwindling passion and money. The best features are an exotic, almost Moorish campanile, an Andrea della Robbia lunette of the *Madonna and St Stephen* over the door, a big clock on the half-striped façade that makes you smile when you notice it sitting where the rose window ought to be and, above all, the circular **Pulpit of the Sacred Girdle**, projecting from the corner of the façade. Perhaps no other church in Italy has such a perfectly felicitous ornament, something beautiful and special that the Pratesi look at every day as they walk through the piazza. Michelozzo designed it (1428) and Donatello added the delightful reliefs of dancing children and *putti* along the lines of his *cantoria* in Florence's cathedral museum (the bas reliefs are only casts, but you can see the originals in the Museo dell'Opera). The Holy Girdle is publicly displayed here five times a year on Easter Day, 1 May, 15 August, 8 September and Christmas Day.

The Duomo's interior continues the motif of green and white stripes in its Romanesque arcades and ribs of the vaulting. The **Chapel of the Sacred Girdle**, just to the left as you enter, is protected by a screen, and the inside is covered with frescoes by Agnolo Gaddi on the legend of the Girdle (*see* above), and adorned with a beautiful marble statue, the *Madonna and Child*, by Giovanni Pisano. In the left aisle there's a masterful **pulpit** carved by Mino da Fiesole and Antonio Rossellino, with harpies around the base. Have some small change to hand to illuminate Filippo Lippi's celebrated frescoes in the choir, on the Lives of Saints John the Baptist and Stephen (*recently restored*), the merry monk's first major work (1452–66). While painting them, Lippi fell in love with a brown-eyed novice, Lucrezia Buti, who according to tradition posed for his magnificent *Herod's Banquet*, either as the melancholy Salome herself or as the figure in the long white dress, second from the right; Fra Filippo placed himself among the mourners for St Stephen, third from right, in a red hat. The less lyrical frescoes in the next chapel (lit with the choir) are by Uccello and Andrea di Giusto. There's a lovely, almost Art Nouveau, candelabra on the high altar by Maso di Bartolomeo (1440s), closely related to his work in Pistoia cathedral.

The **Museo dell'Opera del Duomo** (*open Mon and Wed–Sat 9.30–12.30 and 3–6.30, Sun 9.30–12.30; closed Tues; adm*) is located next door in the cloister, one side of which retains its 12th-century geometric marble decorations and rambunctious capitals. The tragic star of the museum is the original pulpit of the Sacred Girdle, with Donatello's merry *putti* made lepers by car exhaust. Lippi's recently restored *Death of San Girolamo* was painted to prove to the bishop that he was the man to fresco the cathedral choir. Other works include his son Filippino's *St Lucy*, blissfully ignoring the knife in her throat, and another full-length portrait, of *Fra Jacopone di Todi*, believed to be an early work by Uccello. More dancing *putti* adorn the *Reliquary of the Sacred Girdle* (1446) by Maso di Bartolomeo, which was stolen but recovered at the Todi antique fair. Also worth seeing are the saccharine *Guardian Angel* by Carlo Dolci, a sophisticated *Madonna with Saints* by the quattrocento 'Master of the Nativity of Castello', and a strange reliquary that resembles a mushroom.

## Walking Through Prato

Most of Prato's old streets are anonymous, self-effacing Tuscan. Some areas suffered bomb damage in the war, notably the great pear-shaped **Piazza del Mercatale** on the banks of the Bisenzio. This was long the working core of the city, surrounded entirely by porticoes and workshops; it was and is the site of Prato's big market and fairs. A few faded, peeling, porticoed buildings remain, overlooking the river that has laundered the products of Prato's principal industry for eight centuries.

Sunday is a good day to visit sturdy brick **San Domenico** on the west side of town, a large Gothic church begun in 1283 and completed by Giovanni Pisano, one side of it lined with arcades. There's not much to see inside, but the adjacent convent, the home of painter Fra Bartolomeo and Pratese address of Savonarola, holds the **Museo**

**di Pittura Murale** (*open Mon and Wed–Sat 10–1 and 3.30–7, Sun 10–1 only; closed Tues; adm*), a collection of detached frescoes from surrounding churches, currently holding some of the works of Prato's other museums while they undergo some complicated reorganization. There are charming quattrocento graffiti court scenes from the Palazzo Vaj, a sinopia from the cathedral attributed to Uccello, and Niccolò di Piero Gerini's *Tabernacle of the Ceppo*. Filippo Lippi painted the *Madonna del Ceppo* for the Ceppo offices in the Palazzo Datini; it portrays the tycoon himself, with four fellow donors, who contributed less and thus get portrayed as midgets.

Just north of San Domenico, **San Fabiano**, Via del Seminario 30, has an enchanting pre-Romanesque mosaic pavement, depicting mermaids, birds and dragons biting their own tails; north of San Fabiano, 15th-century **Sant'Agostino** contains Prato's most ridiculous painting, the *Madonna della Consolazione* (attributed, naturally, to Vasari), who does her consoling by distributing belts from heaven.

Despite all its artistic treasures, Prato isn't about to sit on its Renaissance laurels. In 1988 the city opened the ambitious **Centro per L'Arte Contemporanea Luigi Pecci**, on Viale della Reppublica in the suburbs (*Wed–Mon 10–7; adm exp*), with a collection of modern works from artists around the world. Since the successful reception of Henry Moore's big lump by the train station in the 1970s, Prato has also accumulated out-door abstract sculpture in a big way. Two that stand out, if only for their breathtaking pretentiousness, are Barbara Krueger's billboard *Untitled* (Viale da Vinci), and Anne and Patrick Poirier's *Monumentum Aere Perennis*, in the grounds of Centro Luigi Pecci.

## North of Prato: the Val di Bisenzio

Prato's river begins some 40 kilometres up in the Apennines, and along its valley runs the SS325, a secondary highway towards Bologna. This valley was long the fief of the Alberti counts, whose fortifications dot its steep sides. **Vaiano**, the first town on the main route, has a Romanesque abbey church and green-striped campanile as its landmark; just beyond are the impressive ruins of the Alberti's **Rocca di Cerbaia** (12th century). The highway continues to **Vernio** and **San Quirico**, with another ruined Alberti castle up above.

From San Quirico's neighbour to the west, **Cantagallo** ('Cock's crow'), a path leads up to the **Piano della Rasa** in little over an hour, a panoramic valley with an alpine refuge (*open April–Oct*). Further north on the SS325, at the resort of **Montepiano**, the waters destined for the Tyrrhenian and Adriatic split. There is another abbey here, the Vallombrosan **Badia di Santa Maria**, with 13th- and 14th-century frescoes. From the abbey begins another path up to **Alpi di Cavarzano** (3,306ft), and from there, in another hour, up to the highest peak in the region, **Monte La Scoperta** (4,192ft).

## Figline and Montemurlo

The old road between Prato and Pistoia passes near **Figline di Prato**, a medieval village known for its terracotta vases. Figline has a 14th-century parish church with contemporary mural paintings, including a 'primitive' *Last Supper* and a *St Michael* with a finely detailed background; a small parish museum contains other 'primitives'. **Montemurlo**, on its hill over the plain of Prato, is also medieval; in 1537 its castle of the

Guidi counts was the Alamo for the anti-Medici republican oligarchs of Florence, led by Filippo Strozzi, who were defeated here once and for all by the troops of Cosimo I. The old walled town is interesting to explore, with an impressive and rather stylish **Rocca** for its crown, approached these days by a Mannerist ramp. The Romanesque church of 'Beheaded John' (**San Giovanni Decollato**) has a pretty campanile and some good art in its Baroqued interior, including a miraculous Byzantine crucifix and a 16th-century painting by Giovanni da Prato illustrating its story.

# Pistoia

You know **Pistoia** (pop. 94,000) is near when the road plunges into a Lilliputian forest of miniature umbrella pines and cypresses, all in tidy rows. These are Italy's most extensive ornamental nurseries, a gentle craft that thrives in the rich soil at the foot of the Apennines. But Pistoia wasn't always content to cultivate its own garden; this is the place, after all, that gave us the word 'pistol' – originally referring to the surgical knives made in the city, but later coming to mean daggers, and finally guns.

Today it specializes in light rail trains (the Breda works built the cars for the Washington DC metro), mattresses, cymbals and baby trees. Its notorious, dark past lingers only in the Florentine histories; modern Pistoiese laugh it off, and if you find the ghosts of its intrigues haunting the often grim, ancient lanes, there are plenty of lovely old churches where you can exorcize them. Although seldom sampled by the moveable feast of tourism, the historic centre of Pistoia is almost perfectly intact, and behind its medieval walls there is some fine art to be seen, part Pisan, part Florentine, reflecting its position between the two great rivals.

## History

*...Proud you are, envious, enemies of heaven,*
*Friends to your own harm and, to your own neighbour,*
*The simplest charity you find a labour.*
'Invective against the People of Pistoia', a sonnet by Michelangelo

Pistoia's fellow Tuscans have looked askance at her ever since Roman times, when the city was called *Pistoria* and saw the death struggle of the Catiline conspiracy, the famous attempted coup against the Roman Republic in 62 BC, which ended when the legions tracked down the escaped Catiline and his henchmen near Pistoia. Its position on the Via Cassia helped it prosper under the Lombards, who elevated it to a royal city. In 1158 Pistoia became a *comune*, and was seen as enough of a threat for Florence and Lucca to gang up against it twice. In the 13th century Pistoia's evil reputation gave it credit for having begun the bitter controversy between Black and White Guelphs that so obsessed Florence; Dante, himself a victim of that feud, made sure that in writing the *Divina Commedia* he never missed an opportunity to curse and condemn the fateful city. In 1306 Florence exacted revenge by capturing Pistoia, and as usual she adapted her politics to the nature of her conquest: Prato she made an ally, Pisa she

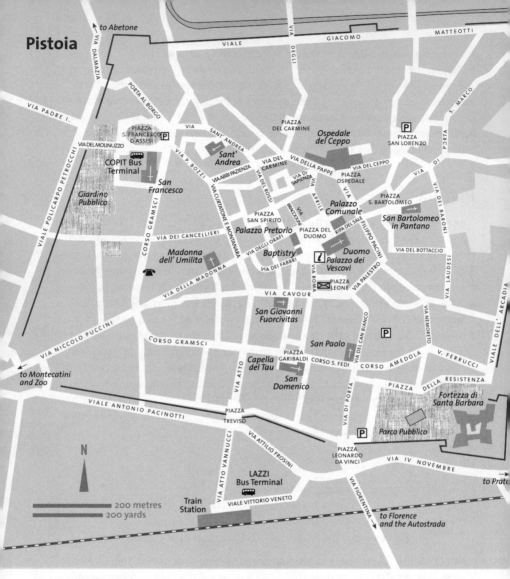

held with fortresses, but Pistoia she controlled with factions. The only interlude came between 1315 and 1328, when Lucca's Castruccio Castracani held Pistoia as part of his empire; it was a short-lived respite, however: after his fall the Florentines soon returned. Pistoia, preoccupied with its own quarrels, carried on happily ever after, making a good living from its old speciality, ironworking. It proudly supplied the conspirators of Europe with fine daggers, and later, keeping up with technological advances, with pistols.

## Piazza del Duomo

Pistol-Pistoia no longer packs any heat, but it packs in the heart of its 16th-century diamond-shaped walls one of the finest squares in Italy, a lesson in the subtle

# Getting Around

Pistoia lies along the A11, and at the foot of two important routes north over the Apennines, the SS64 towards Bologna and SS633 to Abetone. From the station, just south of the city walls at the end of Via XX Settembre, there are frequent **trains** along the main Florence–Lucca line. COPIT buses for Vinci and Empoli (37km/2hrs – a beautiful, twisting road over the Monte Albano), Cutigliano (37km/1hr 45min), Abetone (50km/2½hrs), the zoo, Montecatini (16km/30min), and other destinations in Pistoia's little province depart from Piazza San Francesco. LAZZI **buses** depart for Florence (35km/1hr), Prato, Lucca (43km/1½hrs), Montecatini, Viareggio and Pisa (65km/2hrs) from Viale Vittorio Veneto, near the train station. **Cars** are banned from most of the city centre (in theory, anyhow) but there's plenty of parking around the Fortezza di Santa Barbara in the southeast corner of the walls.

# Tourist Information

**Pistoia**: Piazza del Duomo, in the bishop's palace, t 0573 21622, f 057 334 327, *www.turismo.toscano.it.*
*Open Mon–Sat 9–1 and 3–6.*
**Post office**: Via Roma 5.

# Festivals

**Giostra dell'Orso** ('Joust of the Bear'), 25 *July.* The culmination of a month of concerts, fairs and exhibits. The Joust began in the 14th century, pitting 12 knights against a bear dressed in a checked cloak. The bear has been replaced by two wooden dummies, but the pageantry remains the same.

# Where to Stay

**Pistoia** ✉ 51110

Pistoia gives the impression that it's more accustomed to lodging and feeding business travellers than pleasure-seekers; all things considered it might be better to make this city a day trip, or alternatively, stay in nearby Montecatini Terme.

There are a couple of options if you travel a few kilometres outside town.

★★★**Il Convento**, Via S. Quirico 33, 5km east at Pontenuovo, t 0573 452 651, f 0573 453 578 (*moderate*). A former convent, preserving its exterior if not its interior. The setting is quiet, with views over Pistoia; one of the city's better restaurants.

**Villa Vannini**, about 6km north of town, t 0573 42031, f 0573 26331 (*moderate*). Delightful villa set amongst fir trees; excellent-value rooms, as well as a good restaurant.

There are a few reasonable options if you do need somewhwere in Pistoia itself.

★★★**Leon Bianco**, Via Panciatichi 2, t 0573 26675, f 0573 26704 (*moderate*). Older, but comfortable, with views over the campanile,

★★★**Piccolo Ritz**, Via Vannucci 67, t 0573 26775, f 0573 27798 (*moderate*). A newer place near the station – nice, but somewhat noisy.

★★**Firenze**, Via Curtatone e Montanara 42, t 0573 23141, f 0573 21660 (*moderate–cheap*). The closest thing to inexpensive accomodation, near Piazza del Duomo, but it's a bit woebegone.

★★**Il Boschetto**, Viale Adua 467, in Loc. Capostrada, t 0573 401 336 (*moderate*). Seven rooms and a restaurant (*moderate*) next door.

# Eating Out

Pistoia is known, not for its good restaurants, but for its lack of them. In the city itelf there are mostly simple *trattoria*s and pizzas.
**Valle del Vincio**, Via Vignano 1, t 0573 477 012 (*moderate*). Near the zoo; serves traditional dishes and lots of mushrooms.

Anything else worth seeking out tends to be outside the town itself.
**Rafanelli**, Via Sant'Agostino 47, Sant'Agostino, t 0573 532 046 (*moderate*). Tuscan home cooking, including *maccheroni* with duck, game dishes and lamb, served in a pretty country villa setting. *Closed Sun eve, Mon and Aug.*
**Locanda degli Elfi**, Via della Chiesa 3, Loc. San Felice, t 0573 416 770, 057 341 490 (*expensive–moderate*). A beautiful 18th-century villa, offering fish and local dishes. *Closed Mon lunch and Tues.*

medieval aesthetic of urban design, an art lost with the endless theorizing and compulsive regularity of the Renaissance. The arrangement of the buildings around the L-shaped **Piazza del Duomo** seems at first to be haphazard. The design is meant to be experienced from street level; if you try walking into the piazza from a few of its surrounding streets, you'll see how from each approach the monuments reveal themselves in a different order and pattern, like the shaking of a kaleidoscope; the windows of the Palazzo del Comune echo those on the Palazzo del Podestà, and the striped decoration of the baptistry is recalled in the campanile and Duomo. The piazza provides the perfect setting for Pistoia's great annual party, the colourful *Giostra dell'Orso* (*see* 'Festivals', p.273).

The **Duomo** (*t 057 325 095; open daily 8.30–12.30 and 3.30–7*), dedicated to San Zeno, dates from the 12th century; the Pisan arcades and stripes of its façade, combined over the geometric patterns of the Florentine Romanesque and polychrome terracotta **lunette** by Andrea della Robbia, strike an uneasy balance between the two architectural traditions. The outsize **Campanile**, originally a watchtower, tips the balance towards Pisa, with exotic, almost Moorish candy-striped arches at the top added in the 14th century when it was converted to church use – though you can still see the old Ghibelline crenellations on top. Inside the cathedral is a wealth of art – on the right a **Font** with quaint medieval heads, redesigned by Benedetto da Maiano, the **Tomb of Cino da Pistoia** (1337), a close friend of Dante, shown lecturing to a class of scholars, and a 13th-century painted crucifix by Coppo di Marcovaldo. The cathedral's most precious treasure is in the **chapel of St James** (*open daily 8–12 and 3.30–5.30; closed during Mass Mon–Sat 9.30–10, Sun 10 and 11.15; adm*): a fabulous altar made of nearly a ton of silver, comprising 628 figures, begun in 1287 and added to over the next two centuries; among the Pisan, Sienese and Florentine artists who contributed to this shining *tour de force* was Brunelleschi, who added the two half-figures on the left before he decided to devote all his talents to architecture. Some of the oldest art, fine medieval reliefs of the Last Supper and Gethsemane, have been relegated to the dim and ancient crypt. By the altar there's a fine painting by Caravaggio's pupil, Mattia Preti, and Maso di Bartolomeo's lovely bronze candelabra. On the left the **chapel of the Sacrament** contains a bust of a Medici archbishop attributed to Verrocchio, who also added the statues of Faith and Hope to the weeping angels on the **tomb of Cardinal Forteguerri** just left of the main entrance.

Next to the Duomo stands the partly striped, partly brick **Palazzo dei Vescovi**, mangled by remodellings over the centuries. The tourist information office is here, and the restorations undertaken to install it uncovered some Etruscan *cippi* (gravestones), not to mention the foundations of Pistoia's original cathedral. The Etruscan finds, along with relics of Roman Pistoia, have been arranged in an '**Archaeological Itinerary**' in the Palazzo's basement, and the old cathedral is now included in the **Museo San Zeno** (*t 0573 369 272, guided tours of both offered Tues, Thurs, Fri and 2nd and 4th Sun in the month 10–1 and 3–5; joint adm*), along with some paintings and a fine reliquary by Lorenzo Ghiberti.

Across from the Duomo stands Pistoia's octagonal zebra of a **baptistry** (*open Tues–Sat 9.30–12.30 and 3–6; Sun 9.30–12.30; closed Mon*), whose proper name is

San Giovanni in Corte. Built over the site of a Lombard-era royal palace (the *corte*), it was finished in 1359, to a design by Andrea Pisano. It is one of the few outstanding Gothic buildings in Tuscany, embellished with fine sculptural details on the outside. The interior has a remarkable conical ceiling of brick and a Gothic pulpit. Nearby is a medieval well, topped by a Florentine *Marzocco*.

## Museo Civico

*t 0573 371 296; open Tues–Sat 10–7; Sun 9.30–12.30; closed Mon; adm.*

The Piazza del Duomo's other two palaces are civic in nature. The 14th-century **Palazzo Pretorio** on the west side has a decorated courtyard and an old stone bench where the judges once sat and where they often condemned malefactors to a unique punishment – they were ennobled. Not that Pistoia wanted to reward them; rather, to become noble meant losing one's rights as a republican citizen. The tower near here is known as the tomb of Catiline, who according to tradition was secretly buried here. On the other side of the piazza stands the elegant **Palazzo Comunale**, begun in 1294, and prominently embellished with the usual Medici balls and the more unusual black marble head, believed to be that of a Moorish king captured by a captain from Pistoia on a freebooting expedition to Mallorca. Besides the town council and offices, the palazzo houses the **Museo Civico**, an excellent collection of great and odd paintings to suit even the most jaded of palates. Pistoiese patrons were uncommonly fond of 'Sacred Conversations' – group portraits of saints around the Madonna, and there are good ones by Mariotto de Nardo, Beccafumi, Lorenzo di Credi and Pistoia's own Gerino Gerini (1480–1529), a follower of Raphael. From the 15th-century 'Maestro delle Madonne di Marmo' there's a sweetly smiling marble relief of the Madonna and child; then two fancy St Sebastians with flowing curls, who precede the *Madonna della Pergola*, by local painter Bernardino di Antonio Detti (1498–1554), whose flaccid charwoman of a Madonna holds a child with a large housefly on his chubby arm before a crazy quilt of confusing iconography – children with dolls, the Judgement of Solomon, a child with a fruit-bowl, a floor littered with flowers, amulets, spoons and rags. On the mezzanine is the document centre of the great 20th-century Pistoiese architect Giovanni Michelucci; a comprehensive collection of models and drawings, as well as photos of his buildings and the media reaction to them. One example of his work is the large, angular Santa Maria Novella station in Florence, another is the restaurant in the Parco Collodi (*see* p.283).

Plod up another flight of stairs to see some screamingly lurid paintings from the 17th–19th centuries, with enough historical canvases of murder and mayhem to suggest the local taste for violence lingered at least within the confines of art. There are two mythological paintings swathed in Caravaggesque darkness by Cecco Bravo; a 17th-century *Young Woman with a Flower*, bathed in ghostly light; a sensuous, pouting St Sebastian, disdainfully plucking arrows from his chest; an absurd allegory of Medici rule in Pistoia, with *putti* scattering the family's lily symbol like flowers over the city; a Magdalene fondly patting a skull; as well as two rather nightmarish imaginary battle scenes by a 17th-century Neapolitan named Francesco Graziani.

Just off the Piazza del Duomo on Ripa del Sale, the 16th-century Palazzo Rospigliosi houses two small museums, the **Museo Rospigliosi**, with a collection of its original furniture and paintings *in situ*, the paintings mostly by a Pistoiese artist named Giacinto Gimignani, and the **Museo Diocesano** (*t 057 328 740; both open Tues, Thurs and Fri, 10–1 and 4–7; Wed and Sat 10–1; closed Sun and Mon; joint adm*), displaying crosses and reliquaries from the early Middle Ages.

## Ospedale del Ceppo and Sant'Andrea

*Opening times may vary – call the tourist office for details.*

In medieval Tuscany, it was customary to collect alms in a hollowed-out log (or *ceppo*) left in a public place, to be gathered and distributed to the poor at Christmastime. *Ceppo* became synonymous with the word charity, as in Datini's famous foundation in Prato, and even earlier here in Pistoia, when the **Ospedale del Ceppo** was founded in the 13th century. Still functioning at the same address (walk down Via Filippo Pacini from the Palazzo Comunale), the building was given a fine arcaded porch in the 1500s, in the style of famous Spedale degli Innocenti in Florence. And as in Florence, the della Robbias were called upon to provide the decoration, in this case the usually insipid Giovanni, who with the help of his workshop and other artists, created not only the typical della Robbian tondi, but a unique terracotta frieze that spans the entire loggia in resplendent Renaissance Technicolor, with scenes of the acts of mercy and theological virtues. Inside there's a small **Museo dei Ferri Chirurgici** (*t 0573 352 209, open by appointment only*) dedicated to Pistoia's old iron industry, especially surgical knives.

A short walk west of the hospital on Via Sant'Andrea is the 12th-century church of **Sant'Andrea** (*t 057 321 912; open daily 8–12.30 and 3.30–6*), with a Pisan façade and over the door, a charming bas-relief of the Journey of the Magi, dated 1166, and a pair of ghastly, leering lions. The real jewel is inside: Giovanni Pisano's hexagonal **pulpit** (1297), exquisitely carved in stirring high relief with scenes of the Nativity, Massacre of the Innocents, Adoration of the Magi, Crucifixion and Last Judgement, with sibyls in the corners and pedestals in the forms of the four Evangelists – one of the masterpieces of Italian Gothic. Sant'Andrea contains three other crucifixions: Giovanni Pisano's wooden crucifix in the right aisle, a medieval version over the main altar, portraying Christ crowned and dressed in a kingly robe, and in the right nave, a large, rather mysterious painting of the saint crucified on a tree.

## San Francesco and the Madonna dell'Umiltà

Pretty striped churches circle the centre of Pistoia like zebras on a merry-go-round. The two plain ponies in the lot lie to the west. The large **San Francesco al Prato** (*t 0573 368 096, open daily 7.30–12 and 4–7*) in Piazza San Francesco d'Assisi, plain and Gothic like most Franciscan churches, has some notable 14th-century frescoes, especially in the chapel to the left of the altar, with Sienese scenes portraying the Triumph of St Augustine. On the side of the church there's an ancient olive tree and a memorial to assassinated prime minister Aldo Moro, a stark contrast with the heroic Fascist-era war monument in the piazza itself. South along Corso Gramsci is Pistoia's main theatre, the 1694 **Teatro Manzoni**; further south, on Via della Madonna, towers Pistoia's great experiment in High Renaissance geometry, the octagonal, unstriped **Basilica della Madonna dell'Umilità** (*t 057 322 045; open winter daily 8–12 and 3.30–6; summer daily 8–12 and 4.30–6*) begun in 1518 by local architect and pupil of Bramante, Ventura Vitoni, who graced it with an imposing barrel-vault-ed vestibule. In the 1560s Giorgio Vasari was called upon to crown Vitoni's fine start; not content to limit his mischief to Florence, he added a dome so heavy that the basilica has been threatening to collapse ever since. More work to shore it up is currently under way.

## San Giovanni Fuoricivitas and San Domenico

To the south of the Piazza del Duomo (Via Roma to Via Cavour) lies the tiny **Piazza San Leone**, the ancient Lombard centre of Pistoia; its stubby tower once belonged to the nastiest Pistoian of them all, a 13th-century noble thug and church robber named Vanni Fucci whom Dante found in one of the lower circles of Hell, entwined in a serpent, cursing and making obscene gestures up at God. Around the corner of Via Cavour, the 12th-century **San Giovanni Fuorcivitas** (*t 057 324 784; open daily 8–12 and 4–6.30*) claims the honour of being the most striped church in all Christendom, its green and white flank an abstract pattern of lozenges and blind arches that out-Pisas anything in Pisa. The gloomy interior holds a dramatic pulpit (1270) by Fra Gugliemo da Pisa, a pupil of Nicola Pisano, a holy water stoup supported by caryatids by Giovanni Pisano and a white, glazed terracotta group of the Visitation by Luca or Andrea della Robbia.

Piazza Garibaldi, also to the south, is adorned with a good equestrian statue of Garibaldi, some florid street lamps, and **San Domenico** (*t 057 328 158; open Mon–Sat 7–11.50 and 4.30–6, Sun, 7–11.50 and 4.30–8*) begun in the late 13th century. In its spacious, airy interior, there's a splendid Baroque organ from 1617 and two Renaissance tombs: that of Filippo Lazzari, by the Rossellino brothers, portraying the deceased lecturing to his pupils (one of whom can't help yawning), and the other of Lorenzo da Ripafratta, with a fine effigy. In 1497, Benozzo Gozzoli died of the plague in Pistoia and is buried somewhere in the cloister of San Domenico; you can see a fresco he began of the Journey of the Magi nearby. Although the monastery is still in use, you can ring to see the frescoes in the chapter house, among them good Sienese works and a *Crucifixion* with its sinopia, dating back to the mid-13th century. Even more interesting are the frescoes across the street in the little **Cappella del Tau** (*t 057 332 204; open Mon–Sat 9–2*), so named after the blue T its priests wore on their vestments. The vividly coloured scenes of Adam and Eve and assorted saints are attributed in part to Masolino. The convent of the chapel has become the Marino Marini centre (*t 057 330 285; open Tues–Sat 9–1 and 3–7, Sun 9–12.30; closed Mon; adm*). The collection traces the career of this Pistoiese artist, who died in 1980, in both paint and sculpture; it includes the bronze *Young Girl* which recalls the antique tradition not only in her facial features but also her truncated arms. Next to it, at No.72, note the coat of arms over the pretty window of two dancing bears, recalling the Giostra dell'Orso. There's another good Gothic façade on **San Paolo** (*t 057 320 291, open daily 9–12 and 5–7*), a block to the east, with broader stripes and a statue of St James on the very top, attributed to Orcagna.

There are more old churches in central Pistoia, but only one other worth going out of your way to visit: **San Bartolomeo in Pantano** 'St Bart in the Bog' (*t 057 324 297, open daily 8.30–12 and 4–6*), on the east side of town, built on marshy land in the 8th century and sinking gently into the ground ever since. It has an attractive, partially completed façade, and contains a carved marble lectern of 1250 by Guido da Como.

### The Zoo, the Medici and some Iron

The newest stripes in Pistoia may well be on the zebras in the **Pistoia Zoo** (*Via Pieve a celle 160/A, t 0573 911 219; open daily summer 9–7; winter 9–5; adm exp*), 4km northwest of the city in Via Pieve a Celle. Though the Medici always kept big menageries, modern Italians don't usually care for zoos; this is one of the best in the country, even though it's only 20 years old. Polar bears, kangaroos, giant turtles, reptiles, and all the other zoo favourites are in attendance. Southeast 13 kilometres off the SS66 is yet another Medici villa, the **Villa della Magia in Quarrata** (*closed for refurbishment until 2003; for info call t 0573 771 213*), begun in 1318. Its grand hall has 18th-century frescoes, and in 1536 it was the meeting place of Charles V and Alessandro de' Medici. In Pistoia itself you can visit one of the city's wrought-iron 'laboratories', **Bartoletti** (*open Mon–Sat; t 0573 452 784*), in Via Sestini 110.

## The Mountains of Pistoia

North of Pistoia rises a fairly unspoiled stretch of the central Apennines, luxuriantly forested and endowed with some lovely mountain escape routes, deep green in the summer and ski white in the winter. Main routes include the beautiful Bologna road (SS64) known as the 'Porrettana' which follows the Bologna–Pistoia railway through the sparsely settled mountains, and the equally beautiful, parallel SS632, less encumbered with traffic. The main mountain resorts up to Abetone are along the SS66 and SS12, as easily reached from Lucca as from Pistoia.

Due north of Pistoia, 10 kilometres along a byroad towards Piteccio, is the ancient hamlet of **Castagno**, now converted into a unique open-air art gallery. Its lanes are embellished with 20th-century frescoes on the 12 months; modern statues pose in the nooks and crannies; and Castagno's ancient church and oratory dedicated to St Francis, both with interesting frescoes, have recently been restored. A four kilometre backtrack will take you to the main SS66; at Pontepetri (20km) the SS632 veers north to the formerly popular little mountain resort of **Pracchia**.

Most visitors these days continue along the SS66 for the newer summer-winter resorts by way of the lovely state forest of Teso, at the fine old villages of **Maresca** and **Gavinana**. The latter is notorious in the annals of Florentine history for the defeat of its army by the imperial forces of Charles V, a battle that cost the lives of both commanders. The Florentine leader, Francesco Ferrucci, was knifed in the back, and is

# Tourist Information

**San Marcello Pistoiese**: Via Villa Vittoria 1292 28, t 0573 630 145, f 0573 622 120, *apt12pistoia@tin.it*. *Open Mon–Fri 8–2 and 3–6, Sat 8–2*.
**Cutigliano**: Piazza Catilina 22, t 0573 68029, f 057 368 200, *apt12cutig@tin.it*. *Open Mon–Sun 9–1 and 3–6*
**Abetone**: Piazza Piramidi, t 0573 60231, f 057 360 232, *apt12pistoia@tin.it*. *Open Mon–Sun 9–1 and 3–6*.

# Where to Stay and Eat

There's nothing posh about this pretty but neglected corner of Tuscany – nearly all hotels are good bargains. In the mountains, many open only during the ski season and in July and August.

## San Marcello Pistoiese ✉ 50128

**★★★Il Cacciatore**, Via Marconi 87, t 0573 630 533, f 0573 630 134 (*cheap*). A pleasant hotel, green and quiet. *Open all year; half-board only in high season*.

## Cutigliano ✉ 50124

**★★★Rondò Priscilla**, Via della Libertà 2, t 0573 68148/9, f 0573 68513 (*moderate*). A small

hotel with a garden and pool, near the centre of the village. *Open all year*.
**Fagiolino**, Via Carega 1, t 0573 68014 (*moderate*). Offers traditional Tuscan mountain cuisine (*risotto ai funghi*, roast kid, raspberry torte) served on a panoramic veranda.

## Abetone ✉ 51021

Those who ski usually head to the resort of Abetone, which is somewhat fancier.
**★★★Regina**, Via Uccelleria 5, t 0573 60007, f 0573 60257 (*moderate*). On a quieter street. *Open July–mid-Sept and Dec–April*.
**Ostello Renzo Bizzari**, Via Brennero 157 at Cosuma, t 0573 60117, f 0573 606 656 (*cheap*). The youth hostel, with room for 92. *Open Dec–March and July–Aug*.

There are quite a few economical holiday villas near the towns and alpine refuges in the surrounding mountains; the tourist office has a complete list.
**La Casina**, Via Brennero 245, t 0573 60073 (*moderate*). This is the place for dinner if you are keen on mushrooms – you can get them not only on pasta and polenta, but with most of the *secondi* too.
**La Capannina**, Via Brennero 256, t 0573 60562 (*moderate*). Rustic décor and excellently prepared dishes, with *porcini* mushrooms, ravioli with walnut sauce, trout, pigeon, and wild berries for dessert, accompanied by a wide selection of wines.

remembered with his own little museum in the main piazza. The SS66 continues to **San Marcello Pistoiese**, 29 kilometres from Pistoia, the 'capital' of the mountains, in a lovely setting, where since 1854 the inhabitants have launched a hot-air balloon every 8th of September as a farewell to summer. All year round, however, you can walk over the 220m **suspension bridge of Mammiano**, which might look more at home in the Andes. **Cutigliano**, a growing winter resort seven kilometres north, has 27 kilometres of ski trails and a cable car up to its highest peak, Doganaccia (3,854ft). In the village itself, the **Palazzo Pretorio** fairly bristles with the coats of arms of its former governors.

Near the northern border of Tuscany, through a lush and ancient forest, lies **Abetone** (4,592ft), one of the most famous resorts in the central Apennines. Named after a huge fir tree, the town grew up in the late 18th century, when Grand Duke Pietro Leopoldo built the road to the Duchy of Modena, a road specially designed not to pass through the detested Papal States (the modern province of Bologna). Two milestones at Abetone mark the old boundary. The closest major ski resort to Florence, it is highly developed, with 30 kilometres of trails, four cable cars and other chairlifts; in the summer its cool altitude, swimming pools and other recreational facilities make it almost as popular, especially as a weekend retreat.

## Montecatini Terme

West of Pistoia lies the Valdinievole, the 'Valley of Mists'. This is a land that is obsessed with water, though mostly of the subterranean, curative variety, which is available in Italy's most glamorous thermal spa, **Montecatini** (pop. 21,500). Leonardo da Vinci's first known drawing was of a view towards Montecatini from Lamporecchio, near his home town of Vinci (see pp.259–60), and it is believed that his lifetime fascination with canals and locks and currents and dams and the misty, watery backgrounds of his most famous paintings come from a childhood spent in the Valdinievole. He even designed a fountain for the baths of Montecatini in one of his notebooks, which after 380 years is now being built of Carrara marble as his monument.

Even in these days of holistic medicine, preventive medicine, herbal cures and pharmaceutical paranoia, it is the great despair of the Montecatini tourist board that Anglo-Saxons from both sides of the Atlantic refuse to believe that soaking

## Getting Around

Montecatini is easily reached by **train** from Florence (51km/1½hrs), Pistoia (16km/25mins) and Lucca (27km/45mins). The station, t 0572 71347/78551, is on Via Toti, as is the LAZZI **bus** terminal, t 0572 911 781, with hourly connections (at least until evening) to Florence, Lucca, Pisa, Viareggio and Montecatini Alto; also to Collodi via Pescia (6 daily).

## Tourist Information

Montecatini: Viale G. Verdi 66–68, t/f 0572 772 244, apt@montecatini.turismo.toscana.it, www.regione.toscana.it. Open May–Oct 9–12.30 and 3–6, Sun and holidays 9–12; Nov–April Mon–Sat 9–12.30 and 3–6.

## Where to Stay

### Montecatini Terme ✉ 51016

Even if you don't care to take the waters, Montecatini's scores of hotels ensure that you can find a room. Italy's choicest spa has no fewer than six hotels that claim the title of 'Grand' and a half-dozen others that only

decline to for discretion's sake. **Full board**, not counting breakfast, is the rule in most places; outside of the high season they might not require it, but ring ahead to make sure. The **APIA hotel association** on Piazza Gramsci 10, t/f 0572 75661, helps with bookings.

★★★★★**Grand Hotel Bellavista**, Viale Fedeli 2, t 0572 78122, f 0572 73352, www.panciolihotels.it (luxury). Among the grandest, offering golf, tennis, indoor pool, luxurious rooms, sauna, health club, and an infinite number of chances for self-indulgence. Open April–Nov.

★★★★★**Grand Hotel & La Pace**, Corso Roma 12, t 0572 75801, f0572 78451, www.grandhotellaplace.it (very expensive). Renowned throughout Europe for genuine belle époque charm, this has similarly impressive luxuries; and the restaurant is unquestionably elegant, if expensive. Open April–Oct.

★★★★**Grand Hotel Plaza e Locanda Maggiore**, Piazza del Popolo 7, t 0572 75831, f 0572 767 985 (expensive). This was apparently Verdi's favourite; it has a pool and air-conditioned rooms. Open all year.

★★★**Belvedere**, Viale Fedeli 10, t 0572 70251, f 0572 70252 (expensive). One of the more charming choices and just next to the Parco

in or drinking mere water can do anything as beneficial for them as imbibing a pitcher of Chianti. Unlike so many continental enthusiasts, we defy the wisdom of the ancients – especially the Romans, who spent the plunder accumulated from conquering the world on ever more fabulous baths. But it is sometimes forgotten that taking the waters, no matter how hot, radioactive, or chock-full of minerals, is only half the cure; the other is simply relaxation; the chance to stroll through gardens, listen to a little music, linger in a café, to indulge in a bit of the old *dolce far niente*. In Montecatini you can do just that without touching a blessed, unfermented drop, surrounded by *belle époque* nostalgia from the days when the spa seethed with dukes, politicians, literati and actresses; you may recognize it from the film *Dark Eyes* (*Oci Ciornie*), starring Marcello Mastroianni.

## Parco delle Terme

*Baths open May–October, exc the Excelsior, which stays open all year. Tickets for a day or subscriptions are available from the central office in Via Verdi 41, t 0572 778 511, f 0572 778 444.*

A short stroll from the station, past Montecatini's trendy boutiques, cafés, cinemas and some of its 200 hotels up to Via Verdi, will take you to the town's mineral water

delle Terme. Sports fans will enjoy making use of the indoor pool and tennis courts. Friendly service, . *Open April–Oct.*

**★★★Corallo**, Viale Cavallotti 116, t 0572 78288, f 0572 79512 (*expensive*). Small but refined, with a pool and garden, on a quiet side street near the park. *Open all year.*

**★Belsoggiorno**, Viale Cavallotti 131, up in Montecatini Alto, t 0572 78859 (*cheap*). This is a fairly reasonable place to stay, with rooms overlooking the hotel's garden. *Open April–Oct.*

**Villa Pasquini**, in Massa e Cozile, 8km from Montecatini, t 0572 72205, f 0572 910 888 (*expensive*). At once charming, old-fashioned, and excellent value, this is set in lush gardens with rooms verging on the grand (some even have frescoes). There is a better than average restaurant, and friendly, welcoming service. *Open mid-Mar–early Nov.*

## Eating Out

**Montecatini Terme** ✉ 51016

Most guests dine in their hotels, but there are some places which are worth the effort of getting there.

**Enoteca da Giovanni**, Via Garibaldi 25, t 0572 71695 (*expensive*). Break loose at least once for the imaginative fare at this unique and much-honoured place, where game dishes – hare, venison, wild duck – turn into impeccably *haute cuisine* in the hands of a master chef. *Closed Mon.*

**Cucina da Giovanni**, Via Garibaldi. This is next door to the *enoteca*, offering simple fare at more modest prices (try the wonderful *antipasti* and fabulous *maccheronicini* with duck sauce).

**Gourmet**, Via Amendola 6, t 0572 771 012 (*expensive*). The Gourmet offers fancy dinners by candlelight for a touch of romance, with piano music to add to the ambience. *Closed Tues.*

**Ristorante il Cuco**, Via Salsero 3, t 0572 72765 (*expensive–moderate*). Elaborate Tuscan cooking at more reasonable prices.

When you get tired of immersing yourself in the health-giving waters, why not dip into the vintages at a wine bar instead? Either of the following should do the trick.

*enoteca*, Via Forini 13.

**Antinori 'Degustazione Vini'**, Via Verdi 35.

Elysium, the immaculately groomed **Parco delle Terme**, where the high temples of the cult dot the shaded lawn. The Lorraine grand dukes, spa-soaks like their Habsburg cousins, were behind the initial development of Montecatini's springs, and many of the baths, or *terme*, are neoclassical pavilions – monumental, classical and floral architecture that lent itself nicely to the later Liberty-style embellishments of the 1920s. You can take in some of these Art Nouveau fancies in Montecatini's Municipio, on Via Verdi opposite the park, or in the most sumptuous and ancient of its nine major bathing establishments, **Tettuccio**. In the 1370s a group of Florentines attempted to extract mineral salts from the spring and built a little roof (*tettuccio*) over it; and although they failed it was soon discovered that the water had a curative effect on rotten livers – one of the first to come here was Francesco Datini, the Merchant of Prato, in 1401. By the 18th century, Tettuccio was in a state of ruin, and Grand Duke Leopold I had it splendidly rebuilt. His façade remains, while the interior was redone by Montecatini's greatest architect, Ugo Giovanozzi, in the 1920s, and embellished with paintings by Italy's Art Nouveau master, Galileo Chini, and ceramic pictures by Cascella in the drinking gallery; there's an elegant café, fountains, a reflecting pool and rotunda, writing hall, music rooms, a little city within a city – all adorned with scenes from an aquatic Golden Age of languid nymphs – the perfect place to sip your morning glass of liver-flushing water.

Other establishments, each with their special virtues, are nearby – the Palladian-style arcade of the **Regina** spring; the **Terme Leopoldine**, another grand ducal estab-lishment, with mud baths housed in a temple-like building dedicated to Aesculapius, the god of health; the half-neo-Renaissance, half-modern **New Excelsior baths**; the pretty Tuscan rustic **Tamerici**, in its lush garden; the **Torretta**, with its phony medieval tower and afternoon concerts in the loggia.

## During Digestion

While the water works its way through your system, you can work your way through Montecatini's diversions. The **Art Academy** consists solely of donations from Montecatini's admirers – the piano Verdi used during his annual stays in the Locanda Maggiore, where he composed *Otello*, and art by Salvador Dali, Galileo Chini, Fattori and many others. There's another wooded park, just behind the Parco delle Terme, called **Le Panteraie** (with a swimming pool), where deer roam freely; you can sip an elegant coffee at the **Gran Caffè Gambrinus**, or perhaps play a round at the beautiful **Montecatini Golf Course** (t 0572 62218), set among olive groves and cypresses; alternatively, play a game of tennis at the courts in Via dei Bari (t 0572 767 587/5), or try to win back your hotel bill at the trotting races at the **Ippodromo**. The **Circolo dei Forestieri** (foreigners' club) and the **Kursaal** (with cinema, nightclub, games) are popular meeting places. One of the prettiest excursions is to take is to ride the funicular up to **Montecatini Alto**, the original old hill town, with breathtaking views over the Valley of Mists and a charming little piazza with a charming little theatre; nearby you can visit the stalactites in the **Grotta Maona** (*open April–Oct*).

## Around Montecatini Terme

### Monsummano and Serravalle

Lovely narrow lanes crisscross the Valdinievole landscape, offering the visitor tempting excursions further afield. Some five kilometres east of Montecatini is its sister spa, **Monsummano Terme**, which boasts vapour baths in natural grottoes. The first of these strange caves was discovered by accident in 1849, when the Giusti family moved a boulder and discovered the entrance to a stalactite cave, the **Grotta Giusti**, 100m deep, with three small lakes fed by hot springs. Sadly, the caves, including the steamy **Grotta Parlanti** (*open May–Oct; info* **t** *0572 953 071*), are only open to visitors seeking serious thermal treatment. Monsummano meanwhile hasn't rested on its vapours, but has transformed itself into one of Italy's biggest shoe-making towns; like Montecatini it has an old antecedent atop a hill, **Monsummano Alto**, today all but abandoned, but with a pretty Romanesque church, a romantically ruined castle and splendid views. Another panoramic view may be had from **Montevettolini**, four kilometres from Monsummano, site of a villa built by Ferdinando I in 1597.

If you prefer your castles more intact, then you can continue east to the old fortress at **Serravalle Pistoiese**, which, as its name translates, 'locks the valley' between the Apennines and Monte Albano. This is a castle that has lived some. Its old Lombard tower and 14th-century additions saw considerable action in Tuscany's days of inter-urban hooliganism.

## Where to Stay and Eat

**Monsummano Terme** ✉ 51015
★★★★**Grotta Giusti**, Via Grotta Giusti 171, **t** 0572 51165, **f** 0572 51269 (*expensive*). Near the vaporous grottoes, the villa of the family of the poet Giuseppe Giusti has been charmingly converted with frescoed ceilings and antiques. *Open Mar–Nov.*

**Montevettolini** ✉ 51015
**San Michele**, Piazza Bargellini 80, Monte-vettolini, **t** 0572 617 547 (*cheap*). Try this café-bar-*enoteca*-pizzeria-restaurant for a tempting array of *antipasti* (smoked Canadian salmon, caviar, carpaccio with truffles), followed by spaghetti with lobster, perhaps, and prawns. *Closed Mon.*

**Pescia** ✉ 51017
★★★**Villa delle Rose**, Via del Castellare 21, **t** 0572 451 301, **f** 0572 444 003 (*moderate*). Just outside Pescia, with a pleasant garden and pool and comfortable, modern rooms.

**Cecco**, Via Forli 84, **t** 0572 477 955 (*expensive–moderate*). Fine dining on seasonal dishes starring Pescia's famous asparagus, or wild mushrooms, truffles or zucchini flowers; among the desserts, there's *torta di Cecco*, prepared according to an ancient recipe. *Closed Mon.*
**La Buca**, Piazza Mazzini 4, **t** 0572 477 339 (*moderate*). Serves traditional Tuscan favourites like *pappa al pomodoro*, *panzanella* and fish grilled over coals.

**Collodi** ✉ 51014
**All'Osteria del Gambero Rosso**, Parco Collodi, **t** 0572 429 364 (*moderate*). Set in the grand Parco Collodi, the Osteria has made a name for its food as well as its attractive surroundings. The building was designed by Giovanni Michelucci, arguably one of Italy's greatest 20th-century architects. You needn't agree – nor will your nose grow longer if you do – just tuck into cannelloni, tagliolini with porcini mushrooms and prosciutto, and excellent crêpes stuffed with seafood or spinach. *Closed Mon eve and Tues.*

## Pescia

To the west of Montecatini, there's another attractive old hill town, **Buggiano Castello**, and for those who imagine that frescoes went out of fashion years ago, there's San Michele in nearby **Ponte Buggianese**, freshly frescoed in stark colours by Pietro Annigoni. The colours are even more dazzling in **Pescia** (pop. 20,000), Italy's capital of flowers, a title snatched from San Remo on the Riviera. Some three million cut flowers are sent off every summer's day from Pescia's giant market; besides the gladioli, it is celebrated by gourmets for its tender asparagus and *fagioli*.

Pescia has several interesting monuments, beginning with a 14th-century church of **San Francesco**, containing a portrait of St Francis with scenes from his life, painted in 1235 by Bonaventura Berlinghieri and considered to be one of the most authentic likenesses of the saint; also take a look at the *Crucifixion* by Puccio Capanna in the sacristy. The **Duomo** was rebuilt in the 1600s, but has a fine Romanesque campanile sporting a little cupola, and a late terracotta triptych by Luca della Robbia. On the long, narrow Piazza Mazzini stands the imposing **Palazzo del Vicario**, with the usual mishmash of stone escutcheons; in nearby **Sant'Antonio**, from the 1360s, look up the 'Ugly Saints', a 13th-century wooden *Deposition from the Cross*.

The green, hilly region of prosperous villages north of Pescia in the upper Valdinievole is fondly known as its 'Little Switzerland'. In its cheerful core, some 12 kilometres from Pescia, stands one of Italy's most bizarre churches, the 12th-century **Pieve di Castelvecchio**, decorated with frightening stone masks, grinning and grimacing, that would look more at home in *Heart of Darkness*.

## Collodi and Pinocchio

West of Pescia is the old town of **Collodi**, often visited by Florentine writer Carlo Lorenzo (1826–90) as a child, since his uncle was a factor at the local castle; Lorenzo was so fond of it that he took its name as his own when he published his *Adventures of Pinocchio*. In honour of the creator of the wooden puppet, Collodi has built the **Parco di Pinocchio** (*open 8.30–sunset; adm*), with a bronze statue of the character by Emilio Greco and a piazza of mosaics with scenes from the book by Venturino Venturi, as well as other figures, all very much in the angular style of the late 1950s and early 60s; there's a lawn maze, a museum dedicated to the book, a playground and other amusements for the kids. Adults, meanwhile, can try to work their way through a much older labyrinth in the magnificent hillside gardens of the **Castello Garzoni** (*gardens open 9–one hour before sunset; mid-Nov–mid-Mar Sun only; adm*), designed in the 17th century by Ottaviano Diodati of Lucca and considered one of the finest late Italian gardens, ornate with a labyrinth, fountains and statuary. The castle 'of a hundred windows' has a few grand rooms, and the kitchen where young Carlo sat and dreamed up Pinocchio.

# Lucca, the Garfagnana and Lunigiana

11

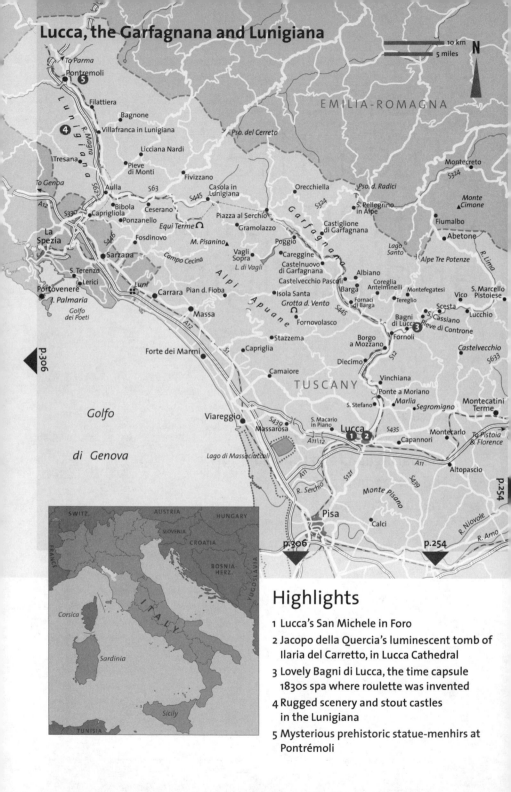

# Lucca, the Garfagnana and Lunigiana

10 km
5 miles
N

EMILIA-ROMAGNA

To Parma
Pontrémoli **5**
Filattiera
Bagnone
Villafranca in Lunigiana **4**
Tresana
Licciana Nardi
Pieve
di Monti
Fivizzano
To Genoa
Aulla
S63
Casola in
Lunigiana
Orecchiella
Pso. del Cerreto
Pso. d. Radici
S. Pellegrino
in Alpe
Montecreto
S324
Monte
Cimone
La
Spezia
Caprigliola
Bibola
Ponzanello
Ceserano
Piazza al Serchio
Gramolazzo
Castiglione
di Garfagnana
Fiumalbo
Abetone
S. Terenzo
Fosdinovo
M. Pisanino
Poggio
Lago
Santo
Alpe Tre Potenze
R. Lima
Lerici
Sarzana
Campo Cecina
Vagli
Sopra
L. di Vagli
Careggine
Castelnuovo
di Garfagnana
Albiano
Portovenere
I. Palmaria
Luni
Carrara
Pian d. Fioba
Castelvecchio Pascoli
Isola Santa
Grotta d. Vento
Barga
Coreglia
Antelminelli
Fornaci
di Barga
Montefegatesi
Tereglio
S. Marcello
Pistoiese
Vico
Lucchio
Golfo
dei Poeti
Massa
Fornovolasco
Bagni
di Lucca **3**
S. Cassiano
Pieve di Controne
Scesta
Castelvecchio
S633
Forte dei Marmi
Stazzema
Capriglia
Borgo
a Mozzano
Fornoli
Camaiore
Diecimo
Vinchiana
TUSCANY
S12
Viareggio
Massarosa
Lago di Massaciuccoli
S439
S. Macario
in Piano
A11/12
S. Stefano
Ponte a Moriano
Marlia
Segromigno
Montecatini
Terme
Lucca **1 2**
S435
Montecarlo
Capannori
To Pistoia
& Florence
A11
Altopascio
Golfo
di Genova
A11
S12r
Monte Pisano
S439
R. Serchio
Pisa
Calci
p.306
p.254
R. Niovole
R. Arno

SWITZ. AUSTRIA HUNGARY
SLOVENIA
FRANCE
CROATIA
Corsica
ITALY
BOSNIA-
HERZ.
YUGOSLAVIA
Sardinia
Sicily
TUNISIA

# Highlights

1 Lucca's San Michele in Foro
2 Jacopo della Quercia's luminescent tomb of
Ilaria del Carretto, in Lucca Cathedral
3 Lovely Bagni di Lucca, the time capsule
1830s spa where roulette was invented
4 Rugged scenery and stout castles
in the Lunigiana
5 Mysterious prehistoric statue-menhirs at
Pontrémoli

# Lucca

*Nowhere in Lucca
will you see the face of a Philistine.*
Heine, *Travels in Lucca*

Of all Tuscany's great cities, Lucca (pop. 92,500) is the most cosy, sane and domestic, a tidy gem of a town encased within its famous walls. Yet even these hardly seem formidable, more like garden walls than something that would keep the Florentines at bay. The old ramparts and surrounding areas, once the outworks of the fortifications, are now full of lawns and trees, forming a miniature green belt; on the walls, where the city's soldiers once patrolled, citizens ride their bicycles and walk their dogs, and often stop to admire the view.

Like paradise, Lucca is entered by way of St Peter's Gate. Once inside you'll find tidy, well-preserved Romanesque churches and medieval towers that destroyed Ruskin's romantic notion that a medieval building had to be half-ruined to be beautiful, a revelation that initiated his study of architecture. Nor do Lucca's numerous Liberty-style shop signs show any sign of rust; even the mandatory peeling ochre paint and green shutters of the houses seem part of some great municipal housekeeping plan. Bicycles have largely replaced cars within the walls. At first glance it seems too bijou, a good burgher's daydream. But after its long and brave history it has certainly earned the right to a little quiet. The annual hordes of tourists leave Lucca alone for the most part, though there seems to be a small number of discreet visitors, many of them German and Swedish, who come back every year. They don't spread the word, apparently trying to keep one of Italy's most beautiful cities to themselves.

## History

Lucca's rigid grid of streets betrays its Roman origins; it was founded as a colony in 180 BC as *Luca*, and in 56 BC entered the annals of history when Caesar, Pompey and Crassus met here to form the ill-fated First Triumvirate. It was converted to Christianity early on by St Peter's disciple Paulinus, who became first bishop of Lucca. The city did well in the Dark Ages; in late Roman times it was the administrative capital of Tuscany, and under the Goths managed to repulse the Lombards; its extensive archives were begun in the 8th century, and many of its churches were founded shortly after. By the 11th and 12th centuries Lucca emerged as one of the leading trading towns of Tuscany, specializing in the production of silk, sold by colonies of merchants in the East and West, who earned enough to make sizeable loans to Mediterranean potentates. A Lucchese school of painting developed and, influenced by nearby Pisa, Romanesque churches were erected. Ghibellines and Guelphs, and then Black and White Guelphs made nuisances of themselves and Lucca often found itself pressed to maintain its independence from Pisa and Florence.

In 1314, at the height of the city's wealth and power, the Pisans and Ghibellines finally managed to seize it. But Lucca had a trump card hidden up a secret sleeve: a remarkable adventurer named Castruccio Castracani. Castracani, an ambitious noble

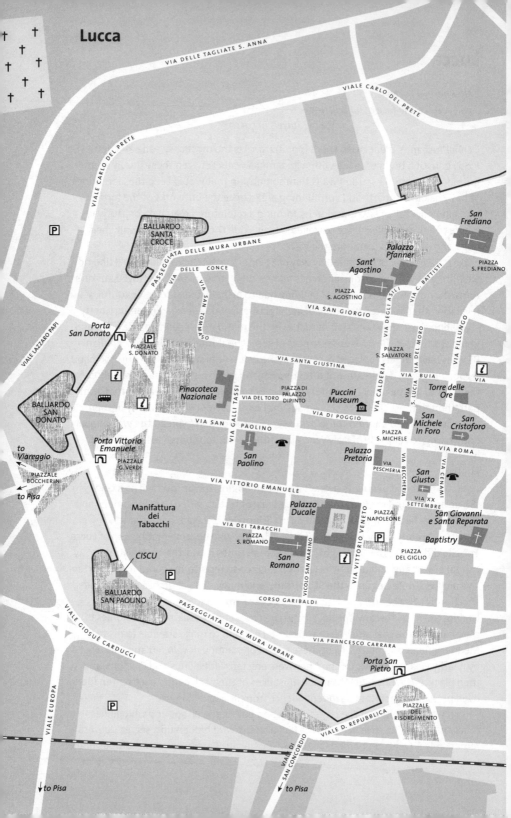

# Lucca

VIA DELLE TAGLIATE S. ANNA

VIALE CARLO DEL PRETE

VIALE CARLO DEL PRETE

VIALE LAZZARO PAPI

San Frediano

PIAZZA S. FREDIANO

Palazzo Pfanner

BALUARDO SANTA CROCE

PASSEGGIATA DELLE MURA URBANE

VIA DELLE CONCE

VIA SAN TOMMASO

Sant' Agostino

PIAZZA S. AGOSTINO

VIA SAN GIORGIO

VIA DEGLI ASILI

VIA C. BATTISTI

Porta San Donato

PIAZZALE S. DONATO

VIA SANTA GIUSTINA

PIAZZA S. SALVATORE

VIA S. LUCIA

VIA DEL MORO

VIA FILLUNGO

VIA BUIA

Torre delle Ore

VIA

BALUARDO SAN DONATO

to Viareggio

Pinacoteca Nazionale

VIA GALLI TASSI

VIA DEL TORO

PIAZZA DI PALAZZO DIPINTO

Puccini Museum

VIA CALDERIA

VIA DI POGGIO

VIA S. LUCIA

PIAZZA S. MICHELE

San Michele In Foro

San Cristoforo

Porta Vittorio Emanuele

PIAZZALE BOCCHERINI

to Pisa

PIAZZALE G. VERDI

VIA SAN PAOLINO

San Paolino

Palazzo Pretoria

VIA PESCHERIA

VIA BECCHERIA

VIA ROMA

San Giusto

VIA CENAMI

VIA VITTORIO EMANUELE

VIA XX SETTEMBRE

Manifattura dei Tabacchi

Palazzo Ducale

VIA DEI TABACCHI

PIAZZA S. ROMANO

PIAZZA NAPOLEONE

VICOLO SAN MARINO

VIA VITTORIO VENETO

San Giovanni e Santa Reparata

Baptistry

CISCU

San Romano

PIAZZA DEL GIGLIO

PIAZZA DEL GIGLIO

BALUARDO SAN PAOLINO

PASSEGGIATA DELLE MURA URBANE

CORSO GARIBALDI

VIALE GIOSUÈ CARDUCCI

VIA FRANCESCO CARRARA

Porta San Pietro

VIALE EUROPA

PIAZZALE DEL RISORGIMENTO

VIALE D. REPUBBLICA

VIALE DI SAN CONCORDIO

to Pisa

to Pisa

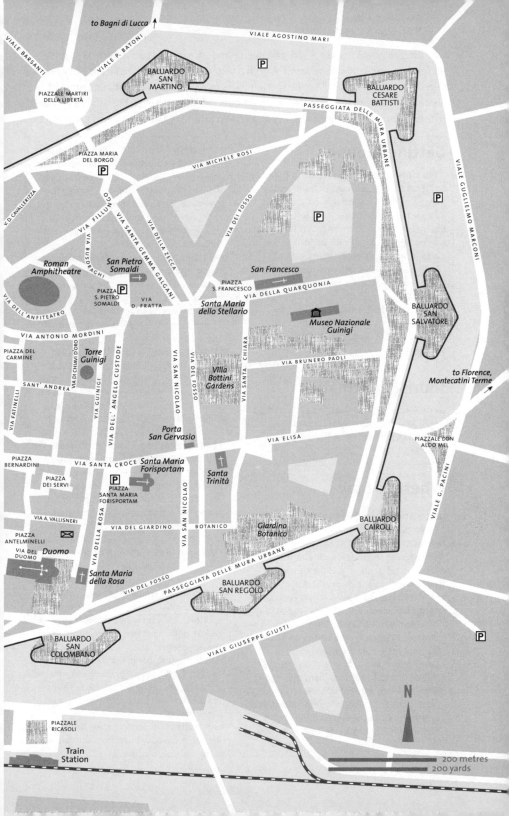

who lived for years in exile – part of it in England – heard the bad news and at once set forth to rescue his home town. Within a year he had chased the Pisans out and seized power for himself, leading Lucca into its most heroic age, capturing most of western Tuscany to form a little Luccan empire, subjugating even big fish like Pisa and Pistoia. After routing the Florentines at Altopascio in 1325, Castracani was planning to

# Getting Around

The **railway** station is just south of the walls on Piazza Ricasoli, with lots of trains on the Viareggio–Pisa–Florence line, t 848 888 088. **Buses** leave from Piazzale Verdi, just inside the walls on the western end: LAZZI buses to Florence, Pistoia, Pisa, Prato, Bagni di Lucca, Abetone, Montecatini and Viareggio, t 0853 584 876; and CLAP (that's right, CLAP) buses to towns within Lucca province, including Collodi, Marlia, and Segromigno, as well as the Serchio valley, t 0853 587 897. Get around Lucca itself like a Lucchese by hiring a **bicycle** from Comune Casermetta S. Donato, t 0583 515 064.

# Tourist Information

**Lucca**: Piazza Santa Maria 35, t 0583 419 689, f 0583 469 964, *www.lucca.turismo.toscana.it*. *Open Mar–Oct daily 9–7; Nov–Feb daily 9–1 and 3–7*.

# Where to Stay

## Lucca and Around ✉ 55100

Lucca can be less than charm city if you arrive without booking ahead; there simply aren't enough rooms (especially inexpensive ones) to meet demand, and the Lucchesi aren't in any hurry to do anything about it.

**\*\*\*\*\*Principessa Elisa**, Via Nuova Per Pisa, 1952, Massa Pisana, t 0583 379 737, f 0583 379 019, (*luxury*). Outside the city, you can bed down in Castruccio Castracani's own palace, built for the great Lucchese warlord in 1321. Often rebuilt since, it currently wears the façade of a stately rococo mansion, surrounded by acres of 18th-century gardens and a pool. Thoroughly modern inside, with amenities including air-conditioning, TVs and minibars in the rooms. *Open Mar–Nov*.

**\*\*\*Universo**, Piazza del Giglio, t 0583 493 678, f 0583 954 854 (*expensive, some rooms nicer than others*). Keeping within the walls, you won't do any better than this slightly frayed, green-shuttered and thoroughly delightful hotel, right in the centre; Ruskin slept here, paving the way for nearly everyone else who followed him to Lucca.

**\*\*\*La Luna**, Via Fillungo Corte Compagni 12, t 0583 493 634, f 0583 490 021 (*expensive–moderate*). A cosy place in a quiet part of the centre, with a private garage for your car.

**\*\*Ilaria**, Via del Fosso 20, t 0583 47558 (*cheap*). Fourteen sparkling rooms set right on Lucca's baby canal.

**\*\*Villa Casanova**, Via Casanova 1604, just outside the city at Balbano, t 0583 548 429, f 0583 368 955 (*moderate*). This has simple rooms but a pleasant garden, as well as tennis and a swimming pool to lounge by. *Closed 4 Nov–28–Dec and 5 Jan–28 Mar*.

**\*\*Diana** Via del Molinetto 11, t 0583 492 202, f 0583 467 795 (*moderate*). Situated near the cathedral, this is friendly and well run, offering some of the nicest cheaper rooms in Tuscany, some with bath. The Diana has recently opened a better equipped hotel (complete with marbled bathrooms, air conditioning and connections for modems) at Via Dogana 8 (*expensive*).

**\*\*Moderno**, Via V. Civitali 38, t 0583 55840, f 0583 53830 (*moderate*). Handy for the centre.

**Affittacamere S. Frediano**, Via degli Angeli 19, t 0583 469 630, f 0583 991 77 (*moderate*). Six spotless, nicely furnished rooms (not all with private bath) all at reasonable prices, near the Anfiteatro.

**Locanda Buatino**, Borgo Giannotti 508, t 0583 343 207, f 0583 343 298 (*cheap*). Just outside the city walls to the north, with five simple but welcoming rooms above a restaurant of the same name (*see* opposite).

**Youth Hostel**, 2km north of town on Via del Brennero, Salicchi (bus 6 from the station),

snatch Florence too, but died of malaria just before the siege was to begin – another example of Florence's good luck. Internal bickering between the powerful families soon put an end to Lucca's glory days, though in 1369 the city managed to convince Emperor Charles IV to grant it independence as a republic, albeit a republic ruled by oligarchs like Paolo Guinigi, the sole big boss between 1400 and 1430.

**t/f** 0583 341 811. Modern, comfortable and rarely crowded. *Open 10 Mar–10 Oct.*

## Eating Out

Within the walls:

**La Buca di Sant'Antonio**, Via della Cervia 3, **t** 0583 55881 (*expensive*). Has been an inn since 1782, offering old recipes like smoked herring and kid on a spit, and newer dishes like ravioli with ricotta and sage. *Closed Sun eve and Mon, two central weeks in Jan and first two weeks of July.*

**Il Giglio**, Piazza del Giglio 2, **t** 0583 494 058 (*moderate*). Lucca's best seafood place, in Hotel Universo – river trout is a speciality, or rabbit with polenta. *Closed Tues eve and Wed, first two weeks of Feb and last two weeks of July.*

**Da Giulio in Pelleria** Via Conce, **t** 0583 55948, (*moderate*). For something less expensive, head for the northwest corner within the walls, where you can enjoy some surprisingly sophisticated twists on 'peasant' fare. It's popular enough to warrant reservations. *Closed Sun and Mon.*

**Vecchia Trattoria Buralli**, Piazza S. Agostino 10, **t** 0583 950 611 (*cheap*). For a simple lunch, head around the corner from Sant'Agostino church for Lucchese home cooking on a good bargain buffet, or pay a bit more for house specialities like the beef 'tagliata' with rocket.

**Canuleia**, Via Canuleia 14, **t** 0583 467 470 (*moderate*). Situated near the amphitheatre in a medieval workshop, serving local food with some surprises such as aubergine soufflé and usually a choice of vegetarian dishes. *Closed Mon lunch and Sat.*

**Caffè di Sirio**, Via Fillungo. Come here for a drop of java in a classic turn-of-the-century *gran caffè*.

**Buatino**, Via Borgo Giannotti 508, **t** 0583 343207 (*cheap*). Here you can enjoy good value, excellent meals in lively surroundings: there's *zuppa di farro*, delicious roast pork, salt cod with leeks, and more. *Closed Sun and 15 July–15 Aug.*

Lucca's table service will be particularly memorable if you have the horsepower to reach its immediate surroundings.

**Solferino**, 6km west of Lucca in San Macario in Piano on the Viareggio road, **t** 0583 59118 (*expensive*). Duck with truffles, wild boar and grilled seafood are a just a few of the treats on the extensive menu at this restaurant, which has been run by the same family for four generations and remained famous throughout Tuscany for almost as long. Simple Tuscan country specialities are available too, but this is one place where you might want to splurge. *Closed Wed, and Thurs lunch.*

**La Mora**, Via Sesto di Moriano 1748, **t** 0583 406 402, **f** 0583 406 135, *www.ristorantelamora.it* (*expensive*). Another good choice, north of Lucca in Ponte a Moriano, located in an old posthouse. It has four cosy rooms inside and dining outside under a pergola in the summer; according to the season, you can choose delicious ravioli with asparagus or truffles, or roast pigeon.

**Vipore**, in nearby Via Pieve Santo Stefano 4469, **t** 0583 394 065 (*moderate*). Located in a 200-year-old farmhouse, with views over the fertile plain of Lucca. Top-quality prime ingredients go into the fresh pasta and meat dishes.

**Forassiepi**, Via della Contea, in Montecarlo, **t/f** 0583 229 475, *www.ristoranteforassiepi.it* (*expensive–moderate*). Here, a bottle of the local wine makes an excellent accompaniment to dishes such as truffle crêpes. The restaurant is housed in what was once an oil press, and from the terrace outside there are views stretching as far as Collodi and the Valdinievole. *Closed Tues, Wed lunch and 15 Jan–15 Feb.*

But Lucca continued to escape being gobbled up by its neighbours, functioning with enough tact and tenacity to survive even after the arrival of the Spaniards. Amazingly enough, after the Treaty of Câteau-Cambrésis, Lucca stood together with Venice as the only truly independent states in Italy. And, like Venice, the city was an island of relative tolerance and enlightenment during the Counter-Reformation, its garden walls in this case proving stout enough to deflect the viperous Inquisition. In 1805 Lucca's independence ended when Napoleon gave the republic to his sister Elisa Baciocchi, who ruled as its princess; it was given later to Marie Louise, Napoleon's widow, who governed well enough to become Lucca's favourite ruler and earn a statue in the main Piazza Napoleone. Her son sold it to Leopold II of Tuscany in 1847, just in time for it to join the Kingdom of Italy.

## The Walls

Lucca's bastions evoke images of the walled rose gardens of chivalric romance, enclosing a smaller, more perfect cosmos. They owe their charm to Renaissance advances in military technology. Prompted by the beginning of the Wars of Italy, Lucca began to construct the walls in 1500. The councillors wanted up-to-date fortifications to counter new advances in artillery, and their (unknown) architects gave them state-of-the-art examples. Being Renaissance Tuscans, the architects also gave them a little more elegance than was strictly necessary. The walls were never severely tested. Today, with the outer ravelins, fosses and salients cleared away (such earthworks usually took up as much space as the city itself), Lucca's walls are just for decoration; under the peace-loving Duchess Marie Louise they were planted with a double row of plane trees to create a splendid elevated garden boulevard that extends around the city for nearly four kilometres, offering a continuous bird's-eye view over Lucca. They are among the best preserved in Italy. Of the gates, the most elaborate is the 16th-century **St Peter's Gate**, near the station, its portcullis still intact, with Lucca's proud motto of independence, LIBERTAS, inscribed over the entrance.

## St Martin's Cathedral

*Open summer 7am–7pm; winter 7–5; no admittance during mass.*

Through St Peter's Gate (Porta San Pietro), and then to the right, Corso Garibaldi leads to Lucca's cathedral (Duomo), perhaps the most outstanding work of the Pisan style outside Pisa, begun in the 11th century and completed only in the 15th. Above the singular porch, with three different-sized arches, are stacked three levels of colonnades, while behind and on the arches are 12th- and 13th-century reliefs and sculpture – the best work Lucca has to offer. Look out for the works by Nicola Pisano displayed on the external facade, for the column carved with the Tree of Life, with Adam and Eve crouched at the bottom and Christ on top, and a host of fantastical animals and hunting scenes, the months and their occupations, mermaids and dragons (*see* Pienza, p.426), and a man embracing a bear, all by unknown masters. There is also a medieval maze on the right side of the portico, which you can trace with your finger. Walk round the back, where the splendidly ornate apse and transepts are set off by the green lawn. The crenellated **Campanile** dates from 1060 and 1261.

The dark interior of this cathedral offers an excellent introduction to the works of Lucca's one and only great artist, **Matteo Civitali** (1435–1501), who worked as a barber until his mid-30s, when he decided that he'd much rather be a sculptor. He deserves to be better known – but may never be since everything he made is still in Lucca. His most famous work is the octagonal **Tempietto** (1484), a marble tabernacle in the middle of the left aisle, containing Lucca's most precious holy relic, the world-weary *Volto Santo* ('Holy Image'), a cedar-wood crucifix said to be a true portrait of Jesus, which was sculpted by Nicodemus, an eyewitness to the crucifixion. Saved from the iconoclasts, it was set adrift in an empty boat and floated to Luni, where the bishop was instructed by an angel to place it in a cart drawn by two white oxen, and where the oxen should halt, there too should the image remain. They made a lumbering beeline for Lucca, where the *Volto Santo* has remained ever since. Its likeness appeared on the republic's coins, and there was a devoted cult of the image in medieval England; Lucca's merchant colony in London cared for a replica of the *Volto Santo* in old St Thomas's, and according to William of Malmesbury, King William Rufus always swore by it, '*per sanctum vultum de Lucca*'. Long an object of pilgrimage, the image goes out for a night on the town in a candlelight procession each 13 September.

Further up the left aisle a chapel contains Fra Bartolomeo's *Virgin and Child Enthroned*. Here, too, is an altarpiece by Giambologna, *Christ with SS Peter and Paul*. Civitali carved the cathedral's high altar, and also two expressive tombs in the south transept. A door from the right aisle leads to the sacristy, where you can see Lucca's real icon, the remarkable **Tomb of Ilaria del Carretto** (1408), perhaps Jacopo della Quercia's most beautiful work, a tender, tranquil effigy of the young bride of boss Paolo Guinigi, complete with the family dog at her feet, waiting for his mistress to awaken. Ilaria may not be here for long; they're contemplating moving her to the new cathedral museum, or somewhere else. In fact the city has always had a strange love-hate relationship with this lovely statue. Right after her husband was overthrown they hustled her out of the cathedral, and she didn't come back for centuries. Near the statue is a *Madonna Enthroned with Saints* by Domenico Ghirlandaio.

A side altar near the sacristy has a typically strange composition from the Venetian Tintoretto, a *Last Supper* with a nursing mother in the foreground and cherubs floating around Christ. In the centre, unfortunately often covered up, is a particularly fine section of the inlaid marble floor; on the entrance wall, a 13th-century sculpture of St Martin has been brought in from the façade.

An **Antiques Market** takes place in the cathedral's Piazza di San Martino the third Saturday and Sunday of each month. Next to the cathedral is the **Museo della Cattedrale** (*t 0583 490 530; open Apr–Oct daily 10–6; Nov–Mar Mon–Fri 10–3 and Sat–Sun 10–6; adm*), opened in 1992 and holding some of its treasures, including the crown and garments of the *Volto Santo*, some good 13th-century reliquaries and pyxes, tapestries and paintings from Lucca's ancient cathedral, San Giovanni, and della Quercia's *St John the Evangelist*. For all that, the best part of the museum may be the upstairs windows, affording a close-up view of some of the wonderful sculpture on the cathedral.

Across Piazza San Martino from the cathedral, **San Giovanni e Santa Reparata** was Lucca's original cathedral. The exterior has only parts of an 1187 portal to show for its old distinction, but inside there are some surprises (*open Apr–Oct daily 10–6; Nov–Mar Mon–Fri 10–3 and Sat–Sun 10–6; adm*). Excavations during the 1970s uncovered a series of buildings on this site that bring the city's history to life back to the earliest days. The church covers the site of a 5th-century basilica; adjacent to it stands the huge, square **baptistry** from the 1300s, and under this you can see the original Roman font – a walk-in model for total immersion baptisms – with bits of its mosaics, as well as later Romanesque pavements and a bishop's chair. San Giovanni also has a superb painted coffered ceiling and, above the main door, an attractive organ case. The organ is not playable as the pipes have been removed. Lucca was a city of organ builders in the old days, and many of the churches have beautifully crafted instruments with elaborate cases.

## Piazza Napoleone and Piazza San Michele

San Giovanni lies on the Via del Duomo between Piazza San Martino and Lucca's shady twin squares, **Piazza del Giglio** and **Piazza Napoleone**, the focus of the Lucchesi evening *passeggiata*. The architectural hodgepodge of a palace on Piazza Napoleone, formerly seat of the republican council, has been called the **Palazzo Ducale** ever since it was used by Lucca's queen for a day, Elisa Bonaparte Baciocchi. In the 16th century, Ammannati had a go at it, and the courtyard, at least, still preserves signs of his Mannerist handiwork. One of Matteo Civitali's most beautiful works, the tomb of San Romano, is in the rarely opened church of **San Romano**, behind the Palazzo.

Via Vittorio Veneto leads from Piazza Napoleone into Piazza San Michele, with a church many people mistake for Lucca's cathedral. Built about the same time, and with a similar Pisan façade, it is almost as impressive. The full name, **San Michele in Foro** (*open 7.40–12 and 3–6; no admittance during mass*), stems from its location on what was Roman Lucca's forum. The ambitious façade rises high above the level of the roof, to make the building look even grander. Every column in the Pisan arcading is different; some doubled, some twisted like corkscrews, inlaid with mosaic Cosmati work, or carved with myriad fanciful figures and beasts, exquisite work similar to the cathedral's, and recently completely restored. The whole is crowned by a giant statue of the Archangel – note the bracelet on his arm, set with real jewels. On the corner of the façade is a Madonna by Civitali; the graceful, rectangular campanile is Lucca's tallest and loveliest.

Inside, there's a glazed terracotta *Madonna and Child* attributed to Luca della Robbia, a striking 13th-century *Crucifixion* over the high altar and a painting of plague saints by Filippino Lippi. Giacomo Puccini began his musical career as a choirboy in San Michele (his father and grandfather had been organists in the cathedral) – he didn't have far to go, as he was born in Via di Poggio 30, just across the street. The house is now a little **Puccini Museum** (*t 0583 584 028; open winter Tues–Sun 10–1 and 3–6; summer daily 10–6; entrance in Corte San Lorenzo 9; adm*), with manuscripts, letters, mementos, the overcoat and odds and ends of the great composer, as well as the piano he used to compose *Turandot*.

## Pinacoteca Nazionale

The quarter west of San Michele is perfumed by the big state tobacco factory, a fine aroma that hides the fact that it produces Toscanelli cigars, the world's vilest smokes. Via San Paolino (the Roman *decumanus major*) leads shortly to the church of **San Paolino** where little Puccini played the organ to earn some pin-money. It contains two beautiful works: a 13th-century French *Madonna and Child* brought back by Lucchese merchants from Paris, and an anonymous quattrocento Florentine *Coronation of the Virgin*, with Mary hovering over a city of pink towers; she is crowned by God the Father instead of Christ, who usually does the honours.

The **Pinacoteca Nazionale** (*t 0583 55570; open Tues–Sat 9–7, Sun 9–2; closed Mon; adm*) is housed in the 17th-century Palazzo Mansi, in Via Galli Tassi. Most of the art, as well as the rich furnishings in certain rooms, dates from the 17th century; the few interesting portraits, by Pontormo and Bronzino, are found in the Prima Sala after the large hall. In the Salone hangs a dark, damaged Veronese, and a follower of Tintoretto's *Miracle of St Mark Freeing the Slave*, showing, with typical Tintorettian flamboyance, Venice's patron saint dive-bombing from heaven to save the day. There is also a set of neoclassical reliefs from the Palazzo Ducale of the *Triumphs of Duchess Maria Luisa*. The 1600s frescoes are more fun than the paintings, especially the *Judgement of Paris*, which Venus wins by showing a little leg. And one can't help but wonder what rococo dreams tickled the fancy of the occupants of the amazing bedroom.

## San Frediano and the Amphitheatre

East of San Michele, medieval **Via Fillungo** and its surrounding lanes make up the busy shopping district, a tidy nest of straight and narrow alleys where the contented cheerfulness that distinguishes Lucca from many of its neighbours seems somehow magnified. Along Via Fillungo you can trace the old loggias of 14th-century palaces, now bricked in, and the ancient **Torre delle Ore** 'tower of hours' (*open Nov–Feb 10–4.30; Mar–Sept 9–7.30; Oct 10–6; adm*), which since 1471 has striven to keep the Lucchesi on time, and perhaps now suggests that it's time for a coffee in Lucca's historic **Caffè di Simo** at Via Fillungo 58. At Via Fillungo's northern end stands the tall church and taller campanile of **San Frediano**, built in the early 1100s, and shimmering with the colours of the large mosaic on its upper façade, showing Christ and the Apostles in an elegant flowing style. The 11th-century bronze Arabian falcon at the top is a copy – the original is locked away in a safe.

The palatial interior houses Tuscany's most remarkable baptismal font, the 12th-century *Fontana lustrale* carved with reliefs, and behind it, an equally beautiful lunette of the *Annunciation* by Andrea della Robbia. On the left are several chapels, one containing frescoes by A. Aspertini with details of their restoration. In the last chapel on the left are an altarpiece and two tomb slabs by Jacopo della Quercia and his assistants. The bedecked mummy is St Zita, patroness of maids and ladies-in-waiting; even in England maids traditionally belonged to the Guild of St Zita. The Lucchesi are very fond of her, and on 26 April they bring her incorruptible body out to caress.

Next to San Frediano, on Via Degli Asili 33, the **Palazzo Pfanner** (*open Mar–mid-Nov daily 10–6; mid-Nov–Feb by appt only; adm*) has an 18th-century garden, a fine staircase, a collection of silks made in Lucca, and 17th–19th-century costumes. In the other direction, skirting Via Fillungo, narrow arches lead into something most visitors miss, the **Roman Amphitheatre**. Only outlines of its arches are still traceable in the outer walls, while within the inner ring only the form remains – the marble was probably carted off to build San Michele and the cathedral – but Lucca is a city that changes so gradually and organically that the outline has been perfectly preserved.

The foundations of the grandstands now support a perfect ellipse of medieval houses. Duchess Marie Louise cleared out the old buildings in the former arena, and now, where gladiators once slugged it out, boys play football and the less active while away the time in chi-chi cafés and shops around the piazza.

The streets in this quarter have scarcely changed in the past 500 years. Along Via Sant'Andrea and narrow Via Guinigi, you'll pass a number of resolutely medieval palaces, including that of the Guinigi family. Their lofty stronghold, the **Torre Guinigi** (*t 0583 48524; open Nov–Feb 10–4.30; Mar–Sept 9–7.30; Oct 10–6; adm*), stands next to their palace and is one of Lucca's landmarks, with a tree sprouting out of its top – the best example of that quaint Italian fancy. One of the most elaborate of medieval family fortresses, the tower has been restored; it's worth the stiff climb up for the view over the city and the Apuan Alps.

## The East Side

Roman Lucca ended near the Guinigi palace, and when a new church was built in the early 12th century it was outside the gate, hence the name of **Santa Maria Forisportam** in Via Santa Croce, a pretty church in the Pisan style with blind arcades. Inside, it not only looks but smells terribly old, and contains two paintings by the often esoteric Guercino. Beyond the church is the best-preserved gate of 1260, the **Porta San Gervasio** giving on to the former moat, now a picturesque little canal running along Via del Fosso. Just across the canal from the gate is **Santa Trinità** (*if closed, ask for the key in the convent next door*), home of Civitali's *Madonna della Tosse* (Our Lady of the Cough), a bit too syrupy sweet, but perhaps that helped the cure. Nearby on Via Elisa is the entrance to the **Villa Bottini gardens** (*t 0583 442140; open Mon–Sat 9–1, closed Sat; adm free*), one of the few green oases inside the city walls.

At the northern end of Via del Fosso stands a 17th-century column dedicated to another Madonna, and to the east, the church of **San Francesco**, a typical 13th-century Franciscan preaching church with the tombs of Castracani and Lucchese composer Luigi Boccherini (d. 1805) – he of the famous *minuet* – and some fine detached frescoes of the Florentine school. Beyond San Francesco stands the palatial brick Villa Guinigi, built in 1418 by the big boss Paolo Guinigi in his glory days. Now the **Museo Nazionale Guinigi** (*t 0583 496 033; open Tues–Sat 9–7, Sun 9–2; closed Mon; adm*), its ground floor houses an interesting collection of Romanesque reliefs, capitals and transennas, some of which are charmingly primitive – St Michael slaying the dragon, Samson killing the lion, a 9th-century transenna with birds and beasts, spirals and daggers. Upstairs, Room XI has a lovely *Annunciation* by Civitali. The painting gallery contains intarsia panels from the cathedral, each with scenes of Lucca as seen from town windows, some trecento works by the Lucca school and a charming quattrocento *Madonna and Child* by the 'Maestro della Vita di Maria'. Other rooms contain a miasma of oversized 16th-century canvases, some by Vasari.

## Villas around Lucca

In 16th-century Lucca, as elsewhere in Italy, trade began to flounder, and once-plucky, daring merchants, or at least those sufficiently well-upholstered, turned to the joys of property, where they could genteelly decline in a little country palace and garden. For the Lucchesi, the preferred site for such pleasure domes was in the soft, rolling country to the north and northeast of the city. Three of these villas or their grounds are open for visits. In Segromigno, 10 kilometres from Lucca towards Pescia, there's the charming, mid-16th-century but often modified **Villa Mansi** (*t 0583 920 234, 0583 920 096, f 0583 928 114; open Tues–Sun summer 10–12.30 and 3–7; winter 10–12.30 and 3–5; adm*), embellished with a half-Italian (i.e. geometric) and half-English (i.e. not geometric) garden laid out by the Sicilian architect Juvarra.

Nearby in Camigliano, the even more elaborate **Villa of Camigliano** (*t/f 0583 928 041; villa and park open March–Oct Wed–Mon 10–12.30 and 3–sunset; closed Tues; in winter call ahead t 0368 320 9614; adm exp*), also begun in the 16th century, was long celebrated for its fabulous parties and entertainments. Set in a lush park of pools and trees, it is furnished with 16th–18th-century furnishings. Elisa Bonaparte Baciocchi combined a villa and a summer palace to make her country retreat, now called the **Villa Pecci-Blunt ex-Villa Reale** in Marlia. Only the park and the Giardino Orsetti are open, but they are worth the trip (*guided tours by appt, t 0368 30108, f 0583 30009, March–Nov Tues–Sun at 10, 11, 12, 3, 4, 5 and 6; closed Mon; Dec–Feb, call in advance; adm*).

## The Lucchese Plain

East and west of Lucca, what was swampland in the Middle Ages has been reclaimed to form a rich agricultural plain. One of its features are its 'courts' – farm hamlets not constructed around a central piazza, but with houses in neat rows. At one time there were 1100 such 'courts' on the plain. Among the highlights of the area is curious **Castello di Nozzano** just to the west, built by Matilda of Tuscany on a hill, its pretty tower now incongruously topped by a large clock. To the east, one of the first villages, **Capannori**, is the head town of several 'courts' and has a couple of interesting Romanesque churches, especially the 13th-century **Pieve San Paolo**, around which a small village incorporated itself, using the campanile for defence. The most imposing monument nearby is the 19th-century **Acquedotto del Nottolini**, which is also visible from the *autostrada*. Just south is the pretty hill-top village of **Castelvecchio**, its tall houses forming an effective circular wall. **Altopàscio**, on the Lucca–Empoli road, was built around an 11th-century hospice run by an obscure chivalric order called the Hospitaller Knights of the Order of Altopàscio, who originally occupied themselves with rescuing travellers from the swamps. Only the campanile of their church remains in the village today. **Montecarlo** gives its name to a very good dry white wine produced in the immediate area.

# The Garfagnana and Lunigiana

The rugged northern finger of Tuscany encompasses the region's 'Alps', the tall and jagged **Alpi Apuane**, which like the real Alps wear brilliant white crowns, though not made of snow – that's marble up there, the 'tears of the stars', the purest and whitest in Italy. Historically the land is divided into two mini-regions: along the bank of the Serchio river, between the Apuan Alps and the Apennines, is the **Garfagnana**; while the region north of the village of Piazza al Serchio is the **Lunigiana**, former hinterland of the ancient Roman port of Luni. The Garfagnana and Lunigiana are relatively undiscovered, and threaten to dispel many people's typical image of Tuscany; the mountains are too high, the valleys are too narrow, and you're more likely to find yourself amidst pine forests than vineyards and olive groves.

# The Garfagnana

For many years the chief export of the Garfagnana has been Italians; the green hills and mountains, the narrow valley of the Serchio, between the Apennines and the Apuan Alps, the stone villages perched on slopes that look so picturesque on postcards were simply never generous enough to provide a sufficient livelihood for their inhabitants. The chief staple of the district until recently was flour made from chestnuts, and chestnut groves still cover much of the region.

## Lucca to Bagni di Lucca

North of Lucca, the first tempting detour off the SS12 is to one of the many Romanesque churches in the region, **San Giorgio di Brancoli**, near Vinchiana, as notable for its lovely setting as for its 12th-century pulpit. **Diécimo**, across the river, has a name that survives from Roman times – it lies 10 Roman miles (18km) from Lucca. The town's key landmark is the Romanesque campanile of the 13th-century church of **Santa Maria**, standing out starkly against the surrounding hills. **Borgo a Mozzano**, four kilometres upstream, is famous for its beautiful little hog-back bridge, with arches in five different shapes and sizes, which is dedicated to the Magdalene, or to the Devil. According to legend, he built it one dark and stormy night in exchange for the first soul to cross. The clever villagers outwitted him by sending a dog over in the morning. The real builder in this case was the slighty less lethal 11th-century Countess Matilda who, besides the bridge, endowed the villages around Borgo with a number of solid Romanesque parish churches.

To the north, just above the confluence of the Serchio river and the Torrente Lima lie the long and narrow riverside hamlets that make up **Bagni di Lucca**, Lucca's once-grand old spa. In the early 1800s, under the patronage of Elisa Bonaparte Baciocchi, it enjoyed a moment in high society's favour – long enough to build one of Europe's first official gambling casinos (1837; roulette was invented here), an Anglican church in an exotic Gothic Alhambra style, and an unusual 1840 suspension bridge (the **Ponte alle Catene**) – before sinking into obscurity. In Bagni's heyday, though, Byron, Browning,

# Getting Around

CLAP **buses** from Lucca connect the city to Bagni di Lucca (27km/40min), Barga (37km/1hr), and Castelnuovo di Garfagnana (50km/1½hrs); **trains** on the scenic Lucca–Aulla line go up the Serchio valley, though the stations for Bagni di Lucca and Barga are quite a distance from their centres and don't always have connecting buses; you'd be better off taking the bus to begin with. If you're **driving** from the south, the most convenient way into these mountains begins at Lucca; both the SS12 and SS445 routes follow the river Serchio.

# Tourist Information

**Bagni di Lucca**: Via Evangelina Whipple t 0583 805 745, f 0583 809 937. *Open 20 June–15 Sept Mon–Sat 9–1 and 3–7; 16 Sept–19 June Tues and Thurs 9–1 and 3–6, Wed, Fri and Sat 9–1.*
**Barga**: Piazza Angelio, t 0583 723 499.
**Castelnuovo di Garfagnana**:Via del Cavalier di Vittorio Veneto, t/f 0583 644 354/641 007, *info@corrieredigarfagnana.com, www.corrieredigarfagnana.com. Open Oct–Mar Mon–Sat 9.30–12 and 3.30–5; April–Sept Mon–Sat 9.30–12.30 and 3.30–7.* The Visitors Centre for the Parco Regionale delle Alpi Apuane is at Piazza delle Erbe 1, t 0583 644 242. *Open Oct–Mar Tues–Sun 9–1 and 3.30–5.30; April–May Mon–Sun 9–1 and 3.30–6.30; June–Sept Mon–Sun 9–1 and 3.30–7.30.*

# Where to Stay and Eat

There's nothing exceptional in the Garfagnana, but the Italians, at least, firmly believe the further north in Tuscany you go, the better the cooking; the pasta dishes in the region are especially good. Specialities include *torte di erbe* (vegetable pies), chestnut puddings and *pattona* (chestnut biscuits).

## Bagni di Lucca ✉ 55022

Bagni di Lucca is wonderfully genteel, with a score of quiet, modest Victorian hotels.
*\*Roma, Via Umberto I 110, t/f 0583 87278 (cheap).* Toscanini stayed here, a small place with a shady little garden at the back.
***Bridge**, Piazza Ponte a Serraglio 5a, t/f 0583 805 324 *(moderate).* In medieval Bagni.
**La Ruota**,Via Giovanni XXIII 29a, 3km outside town at Fornoli, t 0583 805 128 *(moderate–cheap).* Good Tuscan cooking. *Closed Mon eve and Tues.*
**Da Vinicio**, Via del Casino, t 0583 87250 *(moderate).* A chaotic and popular pizzeria a block west of Bagni's bridge..
**Circolo dei Forestieri**, Loc. Ville, t 0583 86038 *(moderate).* Slightly smarter, where you can eat *filetto al pepe verde* and *crêpes ai funghi. Closed Mon.*

## Barga ✉ 55051

****Il Ciocco in Castelvecchio**, 6km north at Pascoli, t 0583 7191, f 0583 723 197 *(expensive).* A huge resort hotel with tennis court, air-conditioning – in short, the works.
***Villa Libano**, Via del Sasso 6, t 0583 723 774, f 0583 724 185 *(cheap).* Set next to Barga's city park with a courtyard and a restaurant with tables out in the garden.
**Terrazza**, 5km north at Albiano, t 0583 766 155 *(cheap).* Again, the best restaurant is out of town, featuring the specialities of the region. *Closed Wed.*

## Castelnuovo di Garfagnana ✉ 55032

****Da Carlino**, Via Garibaldi 15, t 0583 644 270 *(cheap).* Travellers head for this old place with affection.
**Da Giacco** *(moderate).* If you take the route over the Apuan Alps, stop for lunch at Isola Santa. A quaint sort of roadside inn, with an owner who remembers a little tortuous English from his days in New Jersey. Roast trout, polenta with mushrooms, and a terrace overlooking the lake.

Shelley and Heine came to take the sulphur and saline waters, and perspire in a natural vapour bath. Heine was particularly enthusiastic:'A true and proper sylvan paradise. I have never found a valley more enchanting,' he wrote; even the mountains are 'nobly formed' and not 'bizarre and Gothic like those in Germany'. Little has changed, and these days Bagni di Lucca is a sleepy but charming little place, with some pretty villas, elegant thermal establishments that spring into action every summer, a miniature pantheon, and a fancy Circolo dei Forestieri, or foreigners' club (now a restaurant) on the river-front.

## Up the Lima Valley

From Bagni di Lucca, the SS12 leads towards San Marcello Pistoiese and the ski resort of Abetone (*see* p.279–80), following the lovely valley of the Lima. A byroad beginning at Bagni leads to picturesque, rugged stone hamlets like **Pieve di Controne** and **Montefegatesi** which only appear on the most detailed maps; from Montefegatesi, an unsealed road continues to the dramatic gorge of **Orrido di Botri** at the foot of the Alpe Tre Potenze (6,363ft). As the byroad winds back towards the SS12 at Scesta, it passes **San Cassiano**, site of a fine 13th-century Pisan-style church with a delicately carved façade; in its isolated setting few people ever see it.

## To Barga and the Cave of the Wind

The Garfagnana proper begins where the Lima flows into the river Serchio at Fornoli. In the 14th century this area was ruled by the kinsmen of Castruccio Castracani; one of their prettiest mountain hamlets is **Tereglio**, along the scenic northeast road to the **Alpe Tre Potenze**, before it meanders on to Abetone. The Castracani had their base at **Coreglia Antelminelli**, high above the Serchio and the main SS445 (turn off at Piano di Coreglia). Coreglia's church contains a magnificent 15th-century processional cross, and there's a **Museo della Figurina** (*open summer Mon–Sat 8–1, Sun 10–1 and 4–7; winter Mon–Sat 8–1; closed Sun; adm*) devoted to the Garfagnana's traditional manufacture of plaster figures. To the north, the hill town of **Barga** (pop. 11,000) stands above its modern offspring, Fornaci di Barga on the main SS445. Barga was astute enough to maintain its independence until 1341, when it decided to link its fortunes with Florence. At the very top of town stands Barga's chief monument, its **cathedral**, begun in the year 1000 on a terrace, with a panoramic view over the rooftops. Built of a blonde stone called *alberese di Barga*, its square façade is discreetly decorated with a shallow pattern, charming reliefs and two leering lions; on the side the campanile is incorporated into the church; over the portal, there's a relief of a feast scene with a king and dwarfs. There's yet another dwarf inside, supporting one of the red marble pillars of the **pulpit** by the idiosyncratic 13th-century Como sculptor, Guido Bigarelli. The other pillars required a pair of lions, one grinning over a conquered dragon, one being both stroked and stabbed by a man. Less mysterious are the naive reliefs around the pulpit itself, startlingly sophisticated versions of familiar scriptural scenes. In the choir note the venerable polychrome wood statue of St Christopher (early 1100s) and a choir screen with strange medieval carvings, including a mystic mermaid (*see* p.426). Around the back, the cathedral's garden has a magnificent Lebanon cedar. Next to the cathedral stands the **Palazzo Pretorio**, with a small **Museo Civico,** and 14th-century **Loggetta del Podestà**; if you go down the stairs towards the dungeon you can see Barga's old corn measures – a medieval Trading Standards Office.

The rest of Barga is a photogenic ensemble of archways and little palazzi piled on top of each other, with walls, gates and a ravine planted with kitchen gardens. Things get lively in July and August with the classes and performances of **Opera Barga** in the old Dei Differenti Theatre, founded in 1600. Between Barga and Fornaci di Barga, you can measure the showy success of the city's emigrants who returned to build modern palaces in the suburb of Giardino.

From Barga you can take a 17-kilometre potholing detour to Fornovalasco in the Apuan Alps to see Tuscany's best cave, the **Grotto del Vento** (*open daily all year; guided tours of one hour at 10, 11, 12, 2, 3, 4, 5 and 6pm, 3-hour tours for real cave fiends at 10 and 2pm; at certain times of year only part of cave is visited; adm exp; it's less crowded in the morning. The most comprehensive tours take place April–Sept; call t 0583 722 024, f 0583 722 053 for details*), a long cavern of fat stalactites, bottomless pits and abysses, and subterranean lakes and streams, set in a barren, eerie landscape.

## Castelnuovo di Garfagnana

Hanging over the Serchio, 11 kilometres north of Barga, is the lively **Castelnuovo di Garfagnana**, the region's 'capital', guarded by its **Rocca**, a castle decorated in the best 14th-century manner. Its most famous commander was Ludovico Ariosto, author of that great Renaissance epic poem of chivalry and fantasy, *Orlando Furioso*. Ariosto was employed by the Este Dukes of Ferrara to chase bandits and collect tolls here in the 1520s, but didn't take to it. 'I'm not a man to govern other men,' he wrote to his lover, 'I have too much pity, and can't deny the things they require me to deny.'

Northeast, past the small resort of **Castiglione di Garfagnana,** a tortuous mountain road continues through 16 kilometres of magnificent scenery to the **Foce delle Radici** (the pass into Emilia-Romagna) and **San Pellegrino in Alpe**, with magnificent views, an ancient monastery and a good little ethnographic museum, the **Museo della Campagna** (*open mid-June–mid-Sept 9.30–1 and 2.30–7; mid-Sept–Oct 9–12 and 2–5; at other times t 0583 649 072*). West of Castelnuovo a truly scenic road leads over the Apuan Alps to Carrara and the coast, through the desolate Turrite Secca, its sombre features relieved by the romantic oasis of **Isola Santa** (13km) – a tiny, slate-roofed village amid trees on a lake, once a hideout for medieval renegades.

North of Castelnuovo the road enters Garfagnana Alta, where Donatello and Piero della Francesca seem far away indeed. Just north of town, explorers wind their way to the **Parco Naturale dell'Orecchiella**, with eagles, mouflons, deer and a botanical garden, its mountains crisscrossed by paths; pick up a map at the visitor centre in Orecchiella. At Poggio, back on the Serchio, there's a turn-off for **Careggine**, a lofty old hamlet with commanding views, and the artificial **Lago di Vagli**. Creating this lake submerged the village of Fabbriche; the campanile may still be seen sticking stub-bornly out of the water. Above, there are more stunning views from **Vagli Sopra**, village of old marble quarries and an 18th-century road, deteriorated into a footpath, which leads into the Valle di Arnetola. Towering over all is **Monte Pisanino** (6,380ft), the tallest of the Apuan Alps; the road up to the summit and the alpine refuge of Donegani, passing by way of the lakelet of Gramolazzo, begins at **Piazza al Serchio**, leaving both the Serchio and the Garfagnana behind.

# The Lunigiana

Even less populous and less visited than the Garfagnana, the Lunigiana, separating Liguria and Emilia-Romagna from the rest of Tuscany, has traditionally been a tough nut for its would-be governors to crack. The Romans of Luni (founded in 180 BC to contain the fearsome Ligurians) found it a wild place; even in the 7th century, missionaries were still bashing revered ancient idols. This rugged territory of chestnut forests is crowded with the castles of would-be rulers and other toll-collecting gangsters. In the early 1900s the Lunigiana was a stronghold of rural anarchism, and in 1944 its partisans made it one of the bigger free zones in the north. Since then life has been fairly tranquil; rocky, forested landscapes, ruined castles (many bombed in the last war) and simple Romanesque churches form the main attractions.

## Piazza al Serchio to Aulla

Beyond **Piazza al Serchio**, the first town of consequence along the SS445 is fortified **Casola in Lunigiana** (20km); just beyond, a road veers south for the spa of **Equi Terme** in the mountains above. Equi is less known these days for its waters than for its cave, **La Buca del Cane**, or Dog's Hole, (*closed to visitors*) after its relics of prehistoric man's best friend. Our ancestors also apparently socialized with bears (or ate them), judging by the bones found here. **Fivizzano** to the north (on the SS63 or by road from Casola) belonged to the Malaspina of Massa until the Medici snatched it and fortified it as a grand ducal outpost. The main square, **Piazza Medicea**, has a grand fountain paid for by Cosimo III, a few Florentine-style palaces, and the 13th-century parish church. There are two interesting Romanesque chapels in the vicinity, **Santa Maria Assunta**, three kilometres towards Pognana, in a lovely isolated setting, and 12th-century **San Paolo a Vendaso** with carved capitals inside, on the SS63 towards the Passo di Cerreto.

From Ceserano, just south of the SS445, the SS446 heads southwest over the mountains to Sarzana, passing **Fosdinovo**, where the Malaspina castle that hosted Dante in 1306 is one of the most beautiful and majestic in the Lunigiana (*open Wed–Mon 9–1 and 3–6; closed Tues; guided tours Wed–Sat and Mon at 9, 10, 11, 4 and 5, Sun at 9, 10, 11, 3, 4, 5 and 6; adm*). Inside is a collection of arms and ornaments found in local tombs.

## Aulla

**Aulla** grew up at the Lunigiana's hotly contested crossroads, guarding access into the Magra valley. The powerful, 16th-century **Fortezza della Brunella** was built by the Genoese, who bought Aulla in 1543; Napoleon handed it over to his sister Elisa in Lucca; it now contains a museum of natural history (*open Tues–Sun 9–12 and 3–6; until 7 in summer; adm*). Nearby are the citadels of two other rivals who long fought for the town – the Bishop of Luni's **Caprigliola**, a fortified village still inaccessible to cars (six kilometres southwest on the SS62) and the Malaspinas' fortified hamlet of **Bibola** and their romantically ruined **Ponzanello**, both due south of Aulla. The Malaspina also fortified the strategic road to the pass, to the northeast at **Licciana Nardi** (surrounded by immensely thick 11th-century walls with only narrow passageways giving access to its centre), and especially at **Bastia**, four kilometres further on.

# Getting Around

If you're approaching from the north, **trains** and *autostrade* from Genoa (A12) and Parma (A15) merge near Aulla. From here there are frequent trains to Massa-Carrara, Viareggio and Pisa, Pontrémoli or Lucca. From Lucca, trains to Aulla take over 2hrs (85km) and to Pontrémoli 2½ hrs (108km). CAT buses serve the Lunigiana, with Aulla as the main depot; there are services to Massa and Carrara, and to Bagnone, Filattiera, Fivizzano, Fosdinovo, Licciana Nardi, Pontrémoli and Villafranca.

# Tourist Information

**Fivizzano**: Via Roma, t 0585 92017.
**Pontrémoli**: Piazza della Repubblica, t 0187 833 701.

# Where to Stay and Eat

## Equi Terme ✉ 54022

**\*La Posta in Via Provinciale**, t 0585 97937 (*cheap*). Here you will find a comfy bed, as well as a tasty meal (*moderate*); delicious *antipasti*. *Closed Jan–April*.

## Aulla ✉ 54011

**\*Alpi Apuane di Malatesta**, in Pallerone near Aulla, t 0187 418 045 (*cheap*). This old-fashioned former posthouse makes a good base for the region, though rooms are a sideline to the fine restaurant (*moderate–cheap*), very cosy in winter with its fireplace. Specialities include excellently prepared wildfowl – pheasant, duck and pigeon – and, for big appetites, kid with polenta.
**Da Fabio**, Via Matteotti 56, Tresana, t 0187 477 009 (*cheap*). A popular *trattoria* in a traditional 17th-century building that people drive out of their way to visit, in the mountains north of Aulla; the specialities are rustic, and the prices are good too. *Closed Fri.*

## Bagnone ✉ 54021

**I Fondi**, Via della Repubblica 26, t 0187 429 086 (*cheap*). Up in fortified Bagnone, you in turn can fortify yourself with good, solid country cooking – trout, mushroom dishes, rabbit, stuffed cabbage, venison with polenta – amid simple Italian elegance.

## Fivizzano ✉ 54013

**\*\*Il Giardinetto**, Via Roma 151, t 0585 92060 (*rooms cheap, food moderate*). A delightful place both to sleep and eat overlooking Piazza Medicea. Rooms are comfortable, and as the name implies, there's a little garden to lounge in. The *antipasti* are especially tempting, as well as the pasta and game; they also do a flan with spinach and cheese, made from a Renaissance recipe. *Closed Oct.*

## Pontrémoli ✉ 54027

Pontrémoli is rich in good restaurants, and has two smart hotels.
**\*\*\*Golf Hotel**, Via Pineta, t 0187 831 573, f 0187 831 591 (*moderate*). New to the scene, out of town in a pine wood, offering 90 very comfortable rooms, all with bath and TV.
**\*\*\*Hotel Napoleon**, Piazza Italia 2b, t/f 0187 830 544 (*moderate*). Modern, with a garage.
**Da Bussé**, Piazza del Duomo 31, t 0187 831 371 (*moderate*). An age-old restaurant featuring Pontrémoli's special *pasta testaroli*, roast meats, stuffed vegetables and other local dishes. *Open for lunch only Mon–Thurs, lunch and dinner Sat–Sun; closed Fri.*
**Da Ferdinando**, Via San Gimignano, t 0187 830 653 (*moderate–cheap*). Another good bet in the centre is this little bistro in a 17th-century building, where you can dine on *testaroli* with pesto or *boar alla cacciatora*. *Closed Mon.*
**Trattoria del Giardino da Bacciottini**, Via Ricci Armani 13, t 0187 830 120 (*moderate*). Over here in the old town you'll find *fritelle* of salt cod, marinated herrings and excellent *testaroli* with pesto and lamb.

From Aulla you can tuck down into Liguria and the **Italian Riviera** to visit the 'Gulf of the Poets' (or, more prosaically, the Gulf of La Spezia), named after Byron, who swam across it, and Shelley, whose last lived in San Terenzo near the Pisan town of **Lerici**. On the Gulf's western shore (in Liguria) lies enchanting old **Portovenere**, named after the goddess of love herself. Near Carrara are the excavations of ancient Luni (*see* p.309).

### Prehistoric Mysteries

Behind all these baubles, this hidden corner of Italy holds a genuine prehistoric mystery. To learn about it, climb up the narrow medieval lanes above Pontrémoli to the gloomy, 14th-century Castello del Piagnaro and its **Museo delle Statue-*stele* della Lunigiana** (*open Tues–Sun 9–12 and 3–6; closed Mon; adm*). It holds over a score of large, carved statue-*steles* of an unknown culture that flourished in the Lunigiana between the 3rd millennium BC and the 2nd century BC. The *steles*, rather like menhirs with personality, include stylized warriors with daggers or axes, and women with little knobbly breasts. The oldest (3000–2000 BC) have a U for a face and a head hardly distinguishable from the trunk; the middle period (20th–8th century BC) sport anvil heads and eyes; the last group (7th–2nd century BC) are mostly warriors, with a weapon in each hand, just as Virgil described the Gauls who invaded Lazio. They were often discovered near sources of water, and some scholars think they may have symbolized the heavens (the head), the earth (the arms and weapons) and the underworld (the lower third, buried in the ground). Similar statue-*steles* turn up in southern Corsica and other places around the Mediterranean. Some of the *steles* had their heads knocked off, a sure sign that the pope's missionaries in the 8th century were doing their job. Curiously, in the nearby hamlet of Vignola, a folk memory survives of the destruction of idols; during the patron saint's festival they make little wooden idols strangely similar to Pontrémoli's statue-*steles* and burn them to celebrate the triumph over the pagans.

North of Aulla is **Villafranca in Lunigiana**, along the Via Francigena, the pilgrimage route from France; here you can visit the 16th-century church of **San Francesco** and an **Ethnographic Museum** (*open Tues–Sun 9–12 and 3–6, in summer until 7; closed Mon; adm*) devoted to rural life in the Lunigiana, especially the chestnut industry. Yet another mighty castle beckons further up at **Bagnone**, five kilometres to the east.

### Pontrémoli

Long and low key, stretched lazily along the river Magra and the Torrente Verdi, is **Pontrémoli** (pop. 11,000), chief town of the Lunigiana and the northernmost in Tuscany. It wasn't always so peaceful: in 1322 Guelph and Ghibelline quarrels led Castruccio Castracani to build a fortress, called *Cacciaguerra* ('Drive-away war') in the town centre to keep the two parties apart until they made peace. Of this noble effort only the **Torre del Campanone** and what is now the campanile of the **Duomo** survive. The Duomo itself has a fine, ballroom interior, unusual for Tuscany. Over the Torrente Verdi, the church of **San Francesco** contains a lovely polychrome relief of the Madonna and Child attributed to Agostino di Duccio. Between the centre and the station the oval 18th-century church of **Nostra Donna** is a rare example of Tuscan rococo.

In 1471 the Virgin made an appearance a mile south of Pontrémoli, and to honour the spot the **church of Santissima Annunziata** was built with a lovely marble **Tempietto** by Jacopo Sansovino, a quattrocento fresco of the Annunciation by Luca Cambiaso, an elegant triptych of uncertain hand or date, and some fun trompe l'œil frescoes by a Baroque painter from Cremona named Natali.

# The Tuscan Coast

12

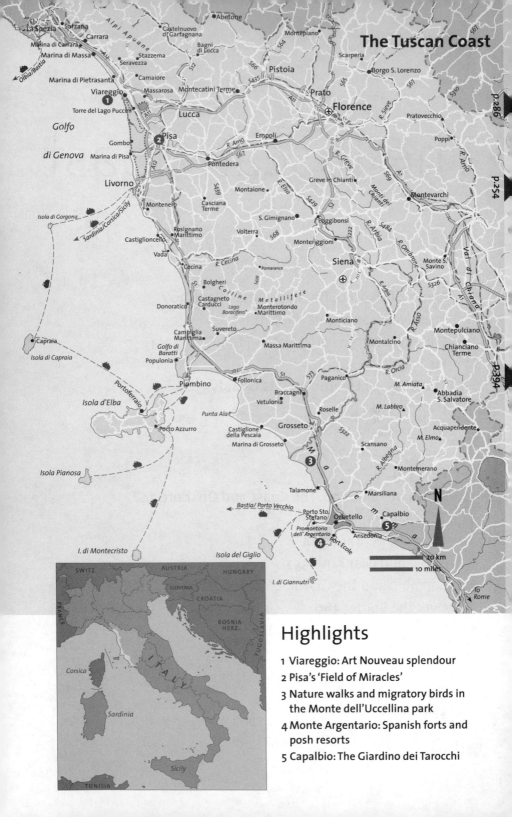

# The Tuscan Coast

## Highlights

1 Viareggio: Art Nouveau splendour
2 Pisa's 'Field of Miracles'
3 Nature walks and migratory birds in the Monte dell'Uccellina park
4 Monte Argentario: Spanish forts and posh resorts
5 Capalbio: The Giardino dei Tarocchi

The Etruscan Riviera, the Tyrrhenian shore, Tuscany by the sea – call it what you will, most of it is flat, straight, dull (apart from the incredible backdrop of marble mountains behind) and endowed with wide sandy beaches that are usually crowded. The sea isn't quite as clean as it might be, and the closer you get to the mouth of the Arno and Livorno, the less savoury it becomes. If you're intent on a spell on the beach, you may well find Tuscany's archipelago of seven islands more congenial – the sea is cleaner and the coast and beaches prettier.

But what is harder to escape, unless you go to the smallest islands, is Italian beach culture. Much of the shore is privately owned and you must pay for access to a veritable wall of deck chairs and beach umbrellas, packed as densely as possible; behind this there's inevitably a busy road, where the traffic is mainly vans with loudspeakers and motorcycles; behind the busy road is another wall of hotels, and perhaps a few pine woods. As always, you'll find an infinitely pleasanter, less frenzied Riviera if you visit outside July and August.

The most beautiful and fashionable section of the Tuscan coast is the Argentario, around Porto Santo Stefano, but it's also the most expensive. Elba, the largest island, is rugged and beautiful, but very busy as a Euro-holiday beacharama. Other places are an acquired taste: Viareggio, with more character than most, and the Puccini opera festival in nearby Camaiore, or Livorno, one of Italy's largest ports, famous for its seafood restaurants. The mellow old city of Pisa, an ancient maritime republic long ago silted up by the Arno, needs no introduction. In Carrara you can learn about marble in the Apuan Alps, in the Maremma you can learn about Italian cowboys and discover the lovely old town of Massa Marittima.

# North of Livorno: The Coast and Inland

## The Riviera della Versilia: Carrara to Viareggio

### Carrara

In the centre of the dynamic, up-to-date **Carrara** (pop. 69,000) there's a garden square called Piazza Gramsci with an unusual fountain, consisting of a large, snow-white sphere of marble that hypnotically revolves, glistening with water, while the Apuan Alps tower in the background, streaked with the white quarries from where the sphere was 'liberated'. Carrara means marble; its name is believed to come from 'kar', the Indo-European word for stone. The Romans were the first to extract it 2,000 years ago; they drove wooden wedges soaked in water into the natural cracks in the stone, and when the wedges swelled, the marble would break off, and was rolled away on iron balls and sent to Rome to become Trajan's column or Apollo Belvedere.

The same techniques were still being used when Carrara began its brilliant revival in 1502, when Pope Julius II sent Michelangelo to find the marble for his tomb. These mountains are haunted by the memory of the 'divine' sculptor, in his old clothes and smelly goatskin boots, taking his horse into the most inaccessible corners to discover new veins of perfect, white stone. Michelangelo thought quarrying just as serious an art as actual sculptural work; he loved to spend time here with his rock, and he claimed with his usual modesty to have 'introduced the art of quarrying' to Carrara. In some intangible way, marble has also made the Carraresi traditionally a breed apart – although their official past is dominated by the rule of godfatherish noble clans like the Malaspina and Cybo-Malaspina, the undercurrents were always fiercely independent, leaning strongly towards anarchism.

Some of Carrara's marble went into its one outstanding monument, the **cathedral**, a distinctive Romanesque church begun in the 11th century with marble stripes and an arch of marble animals, and later embellished with an exquisite 14th-century rose window made of marble lace, and marble art and statues inside, including a huge marble bowl in the baptistry. In the little piazza there's a bulky sculpture by the Florentine hack Bandinelli, generally known as the Giant, although it is supposed to

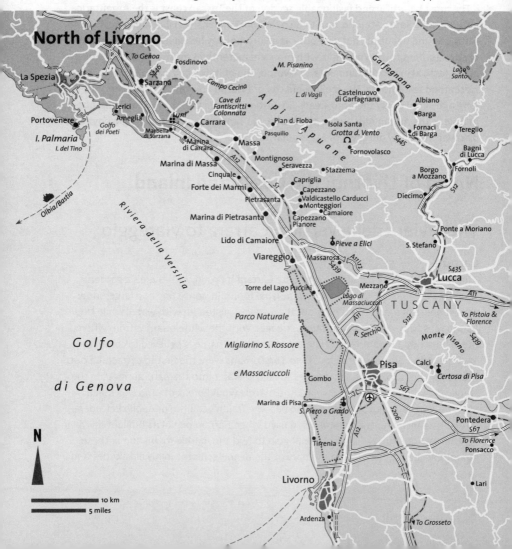

be *Andrea Doria in the Guise of Neptune*. Next to Piazza Gramsci, on Via Roma 1, is the **Accademia delle Belle Arti**, set in a medieval castle. It was converted into a palace in the 16th century by Alberico Cybo-Malaspina, the Marchese di Massa, whose descendants ruled Massa and Carrara until they died out in 1829, when the state joined the Duchy of Modena until unification. The courtyard contains sculptures from Luni and the *Edicola dei Fantescritti*, a Roman tabernacle from the Fantescritti quarry, with bas-reliefs of Jove, Hercules and Bacchus, arm-in-arm like old chums, surrounded by graffiti courtesy of Giambologna and other sculptors who visited the quarries.

## Marble Quarries and Roman Ruins

Even though Carrara exports half a million tons of different marbles a year, there is little danger of it running out soon; one wonders if they're joking when they gravely mention that there are only a few cubic kilometres of good stone left. Visiting one of the **quarries** surrounding Carrara is an unforgettable sight; usually they extend straight up to the sky, a blinding white scar down the mountain with a narrow access road zigzagging perpendicularly to the top. Signs from the centre of Carrara direct you to the quarries, or *Cave di Marmo* – **Colonnata** (8km, founded as a colony of Roman slaves), **Fantiscritti** (a Roman quarry still in use) and **Ravaccione** (with fine views over the mountains). Before leaving town stop by the **Museo Civico del Marmo** on Viale XX Settembre, the main road between Carrara and the train station (*open daily 8.30–1.30; adm*), which takes you through the history of marble with remarkable photographs of the marble-workers of a hundred years ago and the surreal world of the quarries; halls of polished slabs introduce the amazing variety of marbles and travertines from the area, and then from around the world; and there's marble art and a room of modern marble to prove it's no fuddy-duddy stone limited to churches and public buildings.

The proximity of the Apuan Alps, only a few kilometres from the sea, gives this stretch of coast a certain majesty. The beach at **Marina di Carrara** is divided in two by the marble port, from which the big blocks are sent all over the world; in July and August the port-resort puts on a big show of marble arts and crafts. Just to the north, on the border of Liguria near Marinella, you can visit the site of Roman **Luni**, a colony built as a bulwark against the fierce Ligurians. The city survived until the Middle Ages; the power-hungry Bishop of Luni survived even longer, until 1929, when the bishopric was combined with that of La Spezia. Excavations have brought to light a sizeable amphitheatre, forum, houses, temples, etc; on the site is the **Museo Nazionale di Luni** (*open Tues–Sun 9–7; closed Mon; adm*), with an interesting collection of marble statuary, coins, jewellery, portraits and so on, as well as a display of modern archaeological techniques used in the excavation of the site, which can be toured with a guide. To the east off the SS446, 20 kilometres up in the mountains, there is an extraordinary panoramic view over the marble quarries from **Campo Cecina**. The city of Carrara has an alpine refuge here, a good base for exploring the network of trails across the Apuan Alps (the tourist office can provide a map).

# Getting Around

Transport is very easy along the coast, by **train** or especially by **bus**, with three companies – CAT, CLAP and LAZZI – competing for your custom. CAT buses link the Marinas of the coast with Massa and Carrara, and the towns of the Lunigiana; CLAP links Forte dei Marmi and Viareggio with Lucca; LAZZI connects the coast with Lucca, Montecatini, Pistoia and Florence.

The coastal rail line hugs the shore everywhere, excepting the mouth of the Arno and the Maremma, and **trains** are usually very regular. Note that trains to Massa or Carrara leave you exactly between their beaches and their centres, but CAT bus connections to either are frequent.

By **car** you can whip through the dull stretches on the A12, or follow the Via Aurelia (SS1), the main Roman route, though both keep their distance from the sea.

# Tourist Information

**Marina di Carrara:** Viale Galileo Galilei, t 0585 632 519.
**Marina di Massa:** Viale Vespucci 24, t 0585 240 063, f 0585 869 015.

**Forte dei Marmi:** Via Franceschi 8b, t 0584 80091, f 0584 83214.
**Pietrasanta:** Piazza Duomo, t 0584 795 560.
**Marina di Pietrasanta:** Via Donizetti 14, t 0584 203 31.

# Where to Stay and Eat

**Carrara** ⊠ 54033
**\*\*\*Michelangelo**, Corso F. Rosselli 3, t 0585 777 161, f 0585 74545 (*moderate*). Considered the best hotel, with modern rooms and parking facilities.
**Ostello Apuano**, Viale delle Pinete 237, Marina di Massa e Carrara, t 0585 780 034, f 0585 74266 (*very cheap per head, price inc. breakfast*). The youth hostel, for anyone who's game. *Open mid-Mar–Sept.*

If you are planning a camping trip, choose one of many sites along the coast between the marinas of Massa and Carrara. This stretch of beach is also public. There are quite a few good restaurants – if you're lucky you may find a bottle of Candia, the white wine eked from Carrara's mountain terraces. Most of the good places to eat are outside town.

**Da Venanzio**, amid the quarries in Colonnata, t 0585 758 062 (*expensive*). Here you can try the local speciality, *lardo* – a delicately

## Massa

**Massa** (pop. 66,200), nearly the same size as Carrara and co-capital of the province, was the principal seat of the Cybo-Malaspina dukes. They were never great builders or patrons, except when it came to their own digs – their polychrome 17th-century **Palazzo Cybo-Malaspina**, on central Piazza degli Aranci, with its orange trees and obelisk, and their **Castello Malaspina** up the hill on Via della Rocca (*open Sat and Sun 9–12 and 3–5, but still partially closed for restoration; call t 0585 44774; adm*), an 11th-century castle with Renaissance additions, including a beautiful, ornate courtyard, loggias, and frescoed rooms. From Massa there are other marble quarries to visit, near **Pasquilio** 11 kilometres east, a balcony with views over the Gulf of La Spezia; in the same area, the **Pian della Fioba** has a botanical garden featuring the flora of the Apuan mountains, more stunning views, and another alpine refuge open all year.

**Marina di Massa**, on a marsh drained in the last century, is a lively proletarian resort with lots of pine trees; its neighbour, **Cinquale,** the 'Marina' of the old hill town of Montignoso, is smaller and prettier, and between it and Forte dei Marmi there's a long stretch of free beach. Near Montignoso stand the picturesque ruins of the **Castle of Aghinolfi,** a Lombard outpost built in AD 600 by King Agilufo.

flavoured pork fat lard preserved in salt and rosemary in large marble vats, or crêpes, delicious *tortelli*, pigeon in balsamic vinegar or even roast beef. *Closed Thurs, and Sun eve.*
**Locanda Apuane**, t 0585 768 003. A cheaper option, serving delicious and varied *antipasti* and excellent *tortelli* (meat, spinach and ricotta-filled ravioli).

If you do want something in the centre of town, here's one that won't disappoint:
**Roma**, Piazza Battisti, t 0585 70632 (*moderate–cheap*). A favourite for simple Tuscan cooking. *Closed Sat.*

### Forte dei Marmi ✉ 55042

Hotels here are more modern than in Viareggio, and the cruel rule of fashion is making prices higher all the time.
**★★★★Raffaeli Park**, Via Mazzini 37, t 0584 787 294, f 0585 787 418, *rafaelli@versilia. toscana.it* (*luxury*). The Park offers a stretch of private beach, a pool, tennis court and air-conditioned rooms, as does the more modest Villa Angela (*see below*).
**★★★Raffaeli Villa Angela**, Via Mazzini 64, t 0584 787 472, f 0585 787 115 (*very expensive*). The Park's less expensive companion.
**★★★Astoria Garden**, Via da Vinci 10, t 0584 787 054, f 0584 787 109 (*expensive*). This is set in

a park surrounded by woods, with a swimming pool. *Open May–mid-Sept.*
Less expensive places go for the same rates as in Viareggio, but there are fewer of these.
**Da Lorenzo**, Via Carducci 61, t 0585 84030 (*very expensive*). Dining is dealt a deft hand here; beautifully and imaginatively prepared seafood is their trump card. It's no secret though, so be sure to reserve. *Closed Mon.*
**La Barca**, Viale Italico 3, t 0585 89323 (*expensive*). Another good seafood place, offering more traditional Italian dishes. *Closed Tues.*

### Lido di Camaiore ✉ 55043

**Emilio e Bona**, Località Candalla, Via Lombrice 22, t 0585 989 289 (*expensive*). A restaurant just outside Camaiore, offering excellent fare; try their duck breast with herbs or steak with almonds. *Closed Mon.*
**Da Mario**, Via Colombo 102, t 0585 66096 (*moderate*). A large place, busy more often than not, serving a wide range of delicious fish dishes, including a warming seafood risotto. *Closed Mon.*
**Locanda delle Monache**, Piazza XXIX Maggio 36, t 0585 989 258 (*rooms and food both moderate*). An excellent hotel and restaurant housed in a former convent, located in the old part of Camaiore; clean and simple.

## Around Forte dei Marmi

**Forte dei Marmi** is one of the larger and, in recent years, smarter resorts on the coast. Founded in 1788, when Grand Duke Leopoldo constructed the fortress and sea-port to serve the marble quarried from Seravezza, its old loading pier is now used as a promenade. In the 1860s the first holiday villas were built, and today alongside the popular white sandy beach you'll find chi-chi designer boutiques and an excellent market on Piazza Marconi on Wednesday mornings. The public stretch is to the north of the town. **Marina di Pietrasanta** isn't quite so upmarket, but has in its **Parco della Versiliana** that last section of the primordial coastal forest, lush with parasol pines, holm oaks and myrtles. This was a favourite haunt of Gabriele D'Annunzio, and in the summer there are concerts, plays and ballets in its small outdoor theatre. **Lido di Camaiore**, the last resort before Viareggio, caters mainly to families, and differs from its neighbours in its elevated garden terrace along the beach front.

Inland from Forte dei Marmi is the important marble town of **Seravezza**, where Michelangelo lived in 1517 during one of his marble pilgrimages, this time to Monte Altissimo, rich in statue stone known as *statuario*. Not long afterwards, Duke Cosimo I commissioned Ammannati to build the **Villa Medicea** with its good Mannerist courtyard. The **cathedral** contains works by Florentine goldsmiths, including a crucifix attributed to one of the Pollaiuolo brothers; five kilometres away, the **Pieve alla Cappella** has a fine rose window nicknamed the 'Eye of Michelangelo'. Another pretty place is **Stazzema**, with a Romanesque church and more stunning views. The quarries nearby produce a blue and white streaked marble called 'flowered' that found its way into the Medicis' Princes' Chapel. Among the mountains is the curious Monte Forata (3,975ft), with a hole near its summit.

## Pietrasanta

**Pietrasanta**, near the coast, is a mellow old town rich in marbly traditions. These days Pietrasanta has a dual existence, as a chic resort patronized by well-heeled Italian holiday-makers, and as home to a permanent sub-culture of foreign artists, attracted by its proximity to one of the world's greatest sources of marble and by the facilities that have grown up around it, from marble studios to bronze foundries. Bottero, Henry Moore, Mitoraj – to name but a few – have all been temporary residents, using local craftsmen for their work. The town's walls date from 1255, though its regular quadrangle of streets suggests a Roman origin. Life centres around the large central Piazza del Duomo, with its Florentine *Marzocco* on a pillar (1514) and the **Duomo di San Martino**, begun in 1256 and restored in 1630 and 1824, with a rose window carved from a single block of marble and more marble inside, as well as a bronze crucifix by Tacca and a 13th-century fresco by the school of Giotto. Its Renaissance campanile looks half-finished. It shares the piazza with the **Palazzo Pretorio** and **Sant'Agostino** (14th century) with an attractive minimalist Pisan façade. From here a road leads up to the citadel, or **Rocca Arrighina**, built in the 1300s by Castruccio Castracani and lit up at night; it often hosted emperors on their way to Rome but all they left behind is the view. You can see what contemporary would-be Michelangelos are up to by calling Cosmave, t 0584 791 297, f 0584 790 885, who will give information about the work of local artists. Alternatively turn right from the main gate for the central market building, its parking area adorned with the world's most erotic market statue, of a woman *en déshabille* pulling a young bull after her. You can more or less count on finding a sculpture exhibition set up in the pretty piazza or the cloisters of Sant'Agostino.

## The Mountains Beyond Pietrasanta

From Pietrasanta a road heads inland towards **Valdicastello Carducci** (birthplace of the poet Giosuè Carducci) passing by way of the 9th-century **Pieve di Santi Giovanni e Felicità**, the oldest church in the Versilia, with 14th-century frescoes. There are lovely views stretching from La Spezia to Pisa from **Capezzano** and **Capriglia**, on the same road winding further up into the mountains.

**Camaiore** (from the Roman *Campus Major*, pop. 31,000) is an industrial town on the road to Lucca, of interest for its Romanesque churches – the **Collegiata, Santi Giovanni e Stefano** (with a stately bell tower and Roman sarcophagus for a font), and the 8th-century **Badia dei Santi Benedettini**, remodelled in the 11th century and adorned with a lovely portal. In Via IV Novembre, the little **Museo d'Arte Sacra** (*open*

*Thurs and Sat 4–6.30, Sun 10–12; summer Tues, Thurs and Sat 4–7.30, Sun 9–12*) contains some lovely Flemish tapestries. A panoramic road from Camaiore leads up to **Monteggiori**, with more fine views. Other destinations around Camaiore include the beautiful **Valle Freddana** and Monte Magno; and **Pieve a Elici**, near Massarosa, with another excellent Romanesque church, 12th-century **San Pantaleone**. From here a minor road continues up through majestic chestnut groves to **Montigiano**, one of the finest balconies in the Apuans.

# Viareggio to the Parco Naturale Migliarino

## Viareggio

Up until the 1820s **Viareggio** (pop. 59,000), Tuscany's biggest seaside resort, was little more than a fishing village, named after the medieval royal road, the 'Via Regia' that connected Migliarino and Pietrasanta. After the 14th-century battles with Pisa, Genoa and Florence, this little village was the republic of Lucca's sole access to the sea. Fortifications were built – Forte del Motrone (which it lost in 1441) and the Torre del Mare and Torre Matilde near the canal (open on request), which the Lucchesi managed to hold on to until the 19th century, although it was too marshy to do them much good. It was Lucca's beloved Duchess Maria Luisa who drained the swamps, developed the shipyards and fishing and resort industries, and laid out the neat grid of streets; by the 1860s the first cabanas and beach umbrellas had made their debut.

By the turn of the century Viareggio was booming, embellished with playful, intricate wooden Art Nouveau buildings that lined its celebrated seaside promenade, the Passeggiata Viale Regina Margherita. In 1917 a massive fire destroyed nearly all this, and when it was rebuilt in the 1920s, its most important buildings were designed by Galileo Chini and the eclectic Alfredo Belluomini. Chini (1873–1956) was one of the founders of Italian Art Nouveau, or the Liberty Style, which first caught the public's fancy in the 1902 *Esposizione Internazionale di Arti Decorative* in Turin. Chini was especially well known for florid ceramics, but he also designed stage sets for the New York Metropolitan Opera's premières of his friend Puccini's operas: *Turandot, Manon Lescaut* and *Gianni Scicchi*, as well as the throne room of the King of Siam (1911–14). In Viareggio he worked with Belluomini to produce what has become the symbol of Viareggio, the colourful, twin-towered **Gran Caffè Margherita**, in a kind of Liberty-Mannerism; as well as the **Bagna Balena** and what is now the Supercinema, all on the Passeggiata. You can compare their work with the 1900 **Negozio Martini**, the only wooden building to survive the 1917 fire. Chini and Belluomini also designed a number of hotels (*see* p.314) as well as Puccini's villa on Piazza Puccini and the buildings at Piazza D'Azeglio 15 and Viale Manin 20.

Even more colourful are the floats used in Viareggio's famous **Carnival**. It was begun in the 1890s but has grown to rival the much older carnivals of Rome and Venice, and in pure frivolity has surpassed them all. At the centre of the action are large, usually satirical papier-mâché floats. If you can't make the massive parade on *Martedì Grasso* (Shrove Tuesday) itself (also held on each of the four Sundays leading

# Tourist Information

**Viareggio**: Viale Carducci 10, t 0584 962 233, f 0585 47336, *aptversilia@versilia.turismo.toscana.it*, *www.versilia.turismo.toscana.it*. In season there is also an office in the train station. *Open June–Sept Mon–Sat 9–1 and 4–7, Sun 9.30–12.30, Oct–may Mon–Sat 9–1 and 3–6.*
**Torre del Lago**: Viale Kennedy, t/f 0584 359 893. *Open June–Aug Mon–Sat 9–12 and 4–7, Sept–May Mon–Sat 9–12.*

# Where to Stay

## Viareggio ✉ 55049

If you're Viareggio bound, why not experience a Chini-Belluomini confection?
***Grand Hotel Excelsior**, Viale Carducci 88, t 0584 50726, f 0584 50729 (*very expensive–expensive*). One of their most extravagant ventures to be found in the area, built in 1923. The public rooms preserve their original décor; all bedrooms have TV. *Open April–Oct.*
***Grand Hotel & Royal**, Viale Carducci 44, t 0584 45151, f 0584 31438 (*expensive, with an indoor pool and parking*). The Grand was built by Belluomini in a kind of neo-Renaissance eclectic style, with an impressive lobby. *Open April–Oct.*
***Liberty**, Lungomare Manin 18, t 0584 46247, f 0584 46249 (*moderate–cheap*). An ageing queen, by both men. *Open April–Oct.*

If none of the above take your fancy or are fully booked, there are scores of other hotels along the beach, especially in the mid–low section of the *cheap* bracket – it may not be special, but you won't have any problem finding a room.
***Da Antonio**, Via Puccini 260, t/f 0584 341 053. Pleasant enough and one of the cheaper places in Torre del Lago.

# Eating Out

The numerous good restaurants might lead you to suspect (and you're probably correct) that the hordes of Italians who descend on Viareggio do so mainly to eat.

## Expensive

**L'Oca Bianca**, Via Coppino 409, t 0584 388 477. Head of the list is south of the centre by the port; you can sample Mediterranean lobster (*aragosta*), all kinds of fish and other gourmet concoctions, elaborately prepared and served. For a special treat, why not try the *menu degustazione* (*very expensive*). *Closed Tues.*
**Romano**, Via Mazzini 122, t 0584 31382 (*very expensive*). This elegant restaurant, with its dining room and interior garden, is reputed to be the best; it's certainly very good and creative, serving delicious seafood *à la Toscana*. Make sure you reserve in advance. *Closed Mon.*

## Moderate

**Giorgio**, Via IV Novembre, t 0584 44493. This is a lively, welcoming seafood place, with fewer pretensions and lower prices than Romano, showcasing local artists' work. *Closed Wed.*
**Il Puntodivino**, Via Mazzini 229, t 0584 31046. A good place to go wine-tasting: the wines and champagnes come from all over Italy and France, even if the food is local – try the prawns with prosciutto, or if you're in a wild mood, anchovies with fennel. *Closed Mon.*
**Il Porto**, Via Coppino 319, t 0584 392 144. Famous for *antipasti* and pasta dishes (with clams, mixed seafood and crab). It's very popular, so be sure to book. *Closed Wed.*
**La Dorsena**, Via Virgilio 154, t 0584 392 785 (*cheap–moderate*). One of the great bargains of Viareggio is a tasty lunch at this simple *trattoria*, which is shared with workers from the local boatyards who flock here for incredible value *antipasti*, fabulous pastas or grilled and roast fish and crustaceans. It's more expensive in the evening. *Closed Sun.*

## Cheap

**Osteria Numero Uno**, Via Pisano 140, south of the harbour, t 0584 388 967. Thanks to this place, with a *menu fisso* for €8 at lunch, or more in the evenings for *cacciucco* or the more modest *baccalá*, you won't have to break the bank seeking out seafood in Viareggio. *Closed Wed.*

up to it), don't be too crestfallen – you can see the floats themselves being created in the huge **float hangars** along Viale Marco Polo and displayed in the **Hangar Carnivale** (*open daily 9–8*). Viareggio also has an open-air **flea market** around Piazza Manzoni on the fourth Saturday and Sunday of each month. These days some of the world's most luxurious yachts and gin palaces are built in its boatyards.

## Torre del Lago and Puccini

Puccini spent most of his later years in his villa at **Torre del Lago**, six kilometres south of Viareggio along Via dei Tigli (buses from Piazza D'Azeglio), a lovely road passing through an extensive pine wood. His villa, now the **Museo Pucciniano** (*open winter Tues–Sun 10–12.30 and 2.30–5.30; summer Tues–Sun 10–12 and 3–6.30; closed Mon; adm*), is on the banks of shallow Lake Massaciuccoli, where he could practise 'my second favourite instrument, my rifle' on passing coots. The villa contains its original furnishings, old photos, the piano on which Puccini composed many of his operas, his rifles and other mementos. The maestro, along with his wife and son, is buried in the adjacent chapel.

In July and August Torre del Lago holds a popular **opera festival** in its outdoor theatre, presenting both famous and more obscure works by the great composer. For a schedule and tickets contact the Festival Pucciniano, Piazzale Belvedere Puccini, Torre del Lago, **t** 0584 359 322.

Most of Lake Massaciuccoli and the marshlands, the *macchia*, and beaches to the south are part of the **Parco Naturale Migliarino San Rossore Massaciuccoli** (*open winter Sun and hols only 8–5.30; summer Sun and hols only 8–7.30; to visit Mon–Fri call t 050 539 111. Guided tours arranged from 8am to 2pm, call in advance, t 050 525 500*). You can explore some of these wetlands by catching one of the boats which run from Torre del Lago, or you can drive to the tiny village of Massaciuccoli. The wild beaches between Viareggio and Torre del Lago, with their low dunes and scrubby pine forest, are free and undeveloped. The forest of San Rossore, dating from Roman times, is today threatened by the spray blowing in from the polluted sea nearby; this is gradually killing the pines.

# Pisa

**Pisa** (pop. 104,000) is at once the best-known and the most mysterious of Tuscan cities. Its most celebrated attraction has become, along with the Colosseum, gondolas and spaghetti, a symbol for the entire Italian Republic; even the least informed recognize the 'Leaning Tower of Pizza' even if they've never heard of Florence or Siena. Tour buses disgorge thousands of people every day into the Field of Miracles; these tourists spend a couple of hours 'doing' the sights and then leave again for places that are more tangible, such as Florence, Elba or Rome. At night even the Pisani make a mass exodus into the suburbs, as if they sense that the city is too big for them, not physically, but in terms of unfulfilled ambitions, of past greatness nipped in the bud.

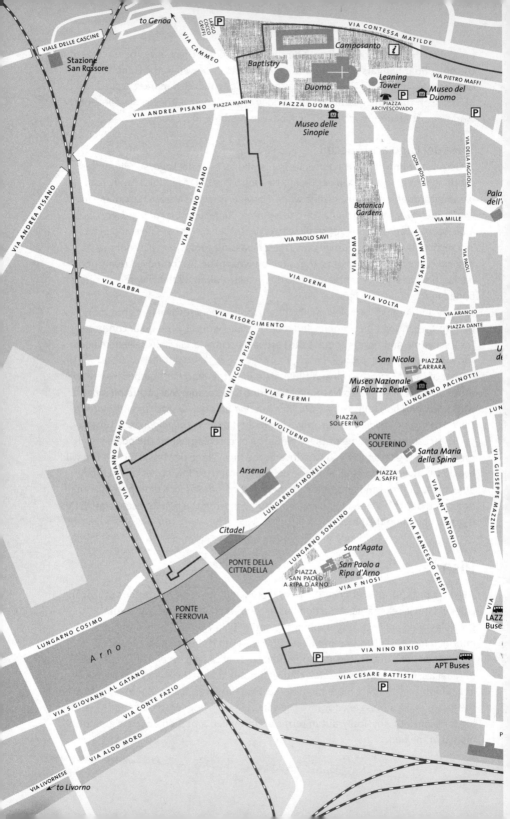

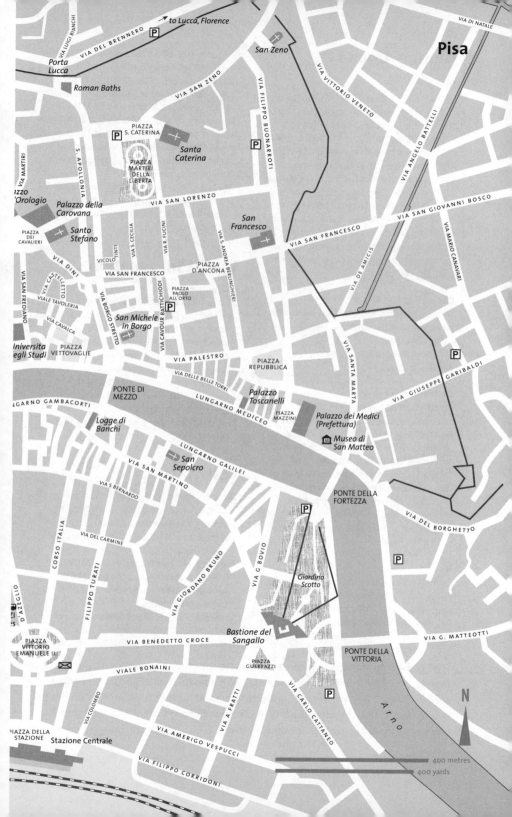

**Pisa**

to Lucca, Florence

VIA LUIGI BIANCHI

VIA DI NATALE

P

VIA DEL BRENNERO

Porta
Lucca

San Zeno

VIA VITTORIO VENETO

VIA ANGELO BATTELLI

Roman Baths

VIA SAN ZENO

VIA FILIPPO BUONARROTI

PIAZZA
S. CATERINA

P

Santa
Caterina

P

PIAZZA
MARTIRI
DELLA
LIBERTA

S. APOLLONIA

VIA MARTIRI

VIA SAN LORENZO

VIA SAN GIOVANNI BOSCO

azzo
l'Orologio

Palazzo della
Carovana

San
Francesco

VIA SAN FRANCESCO

VIA MARIO CANAVARI

PIAZZA
DEI
CAVALIERI

Santo
Stefano

VICOLO
TINTI

VIA S. CECILIA

VIA R. FUCINI

VIA S. ANDREA BERLINGHIERI

PIAZZA
D'ANCONA

VIA DE AMICIS

VIA DINI

VIA CASTELLETTO

VIALE TAVOLERIA

PIAZZA
PAOLO
ALL'ORTO

VIA SAN FREDIANO

VIA SAN FRANCESCO

VIA BORGO STRETTO

VIA CAVOUR BATTICHIODI

VIA CAVALCA

San Michele
in Borgo

P

Università
egli Studi

PIAZZA
VETTOVAGLIE

VIA PALESTRO

PIAZZA
REPUBBLICA

VIA SANTA MARTA

VIA GIUSEPPE GARIBALDI

VIA DELLE BELLE TORRI

PONTE DI
MEZZO

Palazzo
Toscanelli

LUNGARNO GAMBACORTI

LUNGARNO MEDICEO

PIAZZA
MAZZINI

Palazzo dei Medici
(Prefettura)

Logge di
Banchi

LUNGARNO GALILEI

Museo di
San Matteo

San
Sepolcro

VIA SAN MARTINO

PONTE DELLA
FORTEZZA

VIA S BERNARDO

VIA DEL BORGHETTO

CORSO ITALIA

VIA DEL CARMINE

VIA GIORDANO BRUNO

VIA G BOVIO

P

Giardino
Scotto

P

FILIPPO TURATI

D'AZEGLIO

PIAZZA
VITTORIO
EMANUELE II

VIA BENEDETTO CROCE

Bastione del
Sangallo

VIA G. MATTEOTTI

PONTE DELLA
VITTORIA

VIALE BONAINI

PIAZZA
GUERRAZZI

VIA COLOMBO

VIA A FRATTI

VIA CARLO CATTANEO

P

Arno

N

IAZZA DELLA
STAZIONE

Stazione Centrale

VIA AMERIGO VESPUCCI

400 metres

VIA FILIPPO CORRIDONI

400 yards

# Getting Around

## By Air

Pisa's international airport, Galileo Galilei, t 050 500 707, *www.pisa-airport.com*, 3km to the south, is linked to the city by bus no.3 which trundles into Piazza Stazione in front of the main station on the south side of the Arno – the airport and the station are only 10mins apart. The Pisa Aeroporto rail station also has a few trains daily that can take you to the centre as well as a special train service to Florence (1hr, every 1–2hrs daily). In addition, an off and on SITA bus service to Florence from the airport fills in the gaps in the train service. Information from the airport or on t 055 483 561.

## Car Hire at the Airport:

There are a number of options if you wish to pick up a car at the airport.
**Hertz, t** 050 49187.
**Maggiore-Budget, t** 050 42574.
**Avis, t** 050 42028.

## By Train

Note that Pisa has no fewer than three train stations: some coastal trains stop at **San Rossore**, close to the Campo dei Miracoli (visible from the window, as in the famous adverts Federico Fellini made for Pisa's Campari liquor). Some trains from Florence stop at **Pisa Aeroporto** (*see* above). Still you would be better off planning your trips through the **Stazione Centrale** south of the Arno, where all trains call: train information t 848 888 088.

## By Bus

All of Pisa's intercity buses depart from near Piazza Vittorio Emanuele II. This is the big roundabout just north of the central station: APT buses for Volterra, Livorno and the coastal resorts (to the left on Pza S. Antonio, t 050 505 511, f 050 884 284, open daily 7am–8.15pm) and LAZZI buses to Florence, Lucca, La Spezia (on Via Zandonai, t 050 46288, open Mon–Sat 6.40am–8pm, Sun 8.40am–8pm). Many of these buses also stop at Piazza D. Manin, just outside the walls of the cathedral. The Natural Park Migliarino San Rossore Massaciuccoli may be reached by city bus no.11 from Piazza Vittorio Emmanuele.

If you aren't afraid of juming into the saddle for a little energetic sightseeing, Pisa lends itself well to **bicycles**; you can hire one at Via Nino Bixio, near the station.

# Tourist Information

**Pisa**: Via Cammeo 2, near the Leaning Tower, t 050 560 464. With hotel booking service, t 050 830 253. *Open Mon–Sat 9–6, Sun 10.30–4.30.* Another tourist office can be found just outside the central station, t 050 42291, *iat.stazione@tiscalinet.it*. *Open Tues–sat 9–7 and Sun 9.30–3.30.*
**APT Pisa**, Via Pietro Nenni 24, t 050 929 777, f 050 929 764, *info@pisa.turismo.toscana.it*, *www.pisa.turismo.toscana.it*.
**Tourist office** at the airport, t 050 503 700. *Open daily 10.30–3.30 and 6.30–9.30.*

# Festivals

**Gioco del Ponte**, Ponte de Rezzo, *last Sun in June*. A tug-of-war dating from the 13th century and played out on the bridge, complete with costumes, processions and music (*see* p.328).
**Regatta and lights festival of San Ranieri**. An historic occasion, when the banks of the Arno glimmer magically with tens of thousands of bulbs.
**San Sisto**, *6 Aug*. Features folklore displays.

Yet go back to about 1100, when, according to the chroniclers, Pisa was 'the city of marvels', the 'city of ten thousand towers', with a population of 300,000 – or so it seemed to the awed writers of that century, who, at least outside Venice, had never before seen such a cosmopolitan city in Christian Europe since the fall of Rome. Pisan merchants made themselves at home all over the Mediterranean, bringing back new

Old Maritime Republics boat race (next one to be held in Pisa 2003). This is hotly contested each year between four old sea rivals: Pisa, Venice, Genoa and Amalfi; hosted by Pisa every four years.

## Shopping and Activities

Pisa is the best place in Tuscany to purchase tacky **souvenirs**, and the best selection is crowded around the Campo dei Miracoli. Light-up Leaning Towers in pink and yellow come in all sizes and are an amazingly good buy. There is a leaning tower to suit almost every taste. Some have pen and pencil sets attached for the scholar, or grinning plastic kittens for the kids' room, or naked ladies for your favourite uncle. Should these not appeal, the other specialities to be had are medieval weapons – crossbows, cudgels, maces, whips – and plastic skulls, reptiles and insects. If it is the boutiques you're after head down Via Oberdan and Corso Italia.

You can go **riding** at the Cooperativa Agrituristica in Via Tre Colli in Calci, **swim** in the pool in Via Andrea Pisano, or have a **drink** in Pisa's oldest coffee house, the Antico Caffè dell'Ussero, at Lungarno Pacinotti 27.

## Where to Stay

### Pisa ✉ 56100

As day-trip capital of the area, Pisa isn't known for fine hotels, but there's usually enough room for the relatively few visitors who elect to stay overnight.

****Grand Hotel Duomo**, Via S. Maria 94, **t** 050 561 894, **f** 050 560 418 (*very expensive*). The best, very close to the Campo dei Miracoli, is this modern though richly appointed luxury hotel with a roof garden and garage; all rooms are air-conditioned.

****Royal Victoria**, Lungarno Pacinotti 12, **t** 050 940 111, **f** 050 940 180 (*moderate*). Nothing if not long-established, this tasteful place has been managed by the same family since 1837; the building has been a hotel since the year 980.; its best features are rooms overlooking the Arno and its own garage; parking can be a problem in Pisa.

Many of the middle-range hotels are around the train station, south of the Arno.

*****D'Azeglio**, Piazza Vittorio Emanuele II 18b, **t** 050 500 310, **f** 050 28017 (*expensive*). Very convenient for both the buses and trains, this is a modern place offering comfortable, air-conditioned rooms.

****Terminus e Plaza**, Via Colombo 45, **t/f** 050 500 303 (*moderate*). Somewhat cheaper.

****Verdi**, Piazza Repubblica 5, **t** 050 598 947, **f** 050 598 944 (*moderate*). Another good choice in this price range, this time in the centre, set in a well-restored historic palace.

Inexpensive places are spread throughout town and are often full of students, particularly around the start of the university term; it's always best to call ahead, or else go up to the Campo dei Miracoli and try one of the following, all of which are relatively convivial and all situated within a few blocks of the cathedral.

***Gronchi**, in Piazza Arcivescovado 1, **t** 050 561 823 (*cheap*). The nicest of this group.

***Helvetia**, Via Don Boschi 31, **t** 050 553 084.

****Di Stefano**, Via Sant'Apollonia 35, **t** 050 553 559, **f** 050 556 038 (*moderate*). Central, this has recently been upgraded, with TVs in all the rooms.

***Giardino**, Piazza Manin, **t** 050 562 101, **f** 050 831 0392 (*moderate*). Just outside the walls.

**Youth hostel**, Via Pietrasantina 15, **t** 050 890 622 (*cheap*) (no.3 bus). As hostels go, this isn't far out: just 1km from the Campo dei Miracoli; it also provides cooking facilities if you fancy catering for yourself.

ideas and new styles in art in addition to their fat profit; Pisa contributed as much to the rebirth of Western culture as any city. Pisan Romanesque, with its stripes and blind arcades, which had such a wide influence in Tuscany, was inspired by the great Moorish architecture of Andalucía; Nicola Pisano, first of a long line of great sculptors, is as important to the renaissance of sculpture as Giotto is to painting.

# Eating Out

In Pisa you will find eating out difficult on a Sunday night. But come here during the rest of the week and walks on the wild side of the Tuscan kitchen seem more common than in other towns – you can find eels and squid, *baccalà*, tripe, wild mushrooms, 'twice-boiled soup' and dishes that waiters cannot satisfactorily explain.

**Ristoro dei Vecchi Macelli**, Via Volturno 49, t 050 20424 (*very expensive*). A gourmet stronghold on the north bank of the Arno, near Ponte Solferino, with highly imaginative dishes based on coastal Tuscan traditions. *Closed Wed and Sun lunch and 15–31 Aug.*

**Cagliostro**, Via del Castelletto 26–30, t 050 575 413 (*expensive*). It's hard to believe that you are in Italy at this extraordinary restaurant/*enoteca*/art gallery and general trendy hang-out; the cooking might be described as 'Tuscan Creative' but throws in other dishes from all over Italy. Lunch is a somewhat more modest (and cheaper) affair. *Closed Tues.*

**Da Bruno**, Via Luigi Bianchi 12, t 050 560 818, f 050 550 607 (*expensive–moderate*). Da Bruno is just outside the walls, a few blocks east of the Campo dei Miracoli, is another place to test how much you enjoy simple Pisan cooking – serving the likes of polenta with mushrooms and *baccalà* (dried cod). *Closed Mon eve and Tues.*

Pisa is well endowed with unpretentious *trattorias* popular with its students; many are located around the university.

**Osteria dei Cavalieri**, Via San Frediano 16, t 050 580 858 (*moderate*). Offers several fixed-price menus featuring seafood, meat and vegetarian dishes, and good game dishes such as rabbit with oregano. *Closed Sat at lunch and Sun, end July–end Aug and 27 Dec–7 Jan.*

**Osteria La Grotta**, Via San Francesco 103, t 050 578 105 (*moderate*). This is a cosy place with a simulated grotto and comforting, traditional dishes, imaginatively prepared and without pretensions. Meat-lovers are well catered for; try the *Gran Padellata del Maremmano*, a rich stew of three kinds of meat cooked with spicy sausage and vegetables. *Closed Sun.*

**Il Nuraghe**, Via Mazzini 58, t 050 443 68 (*moderate*). There is plenty to tempt the taste buds here including specialities such as ricotta ravioli. The chef is Sardinian, so Tuscan and Sarde specialities rub shoulders. *Closed Mon and 5–25 Aug.*

**Lo Schiaccianoci**, Via Vespucci 104, east of the station, t 050 21024 (*moderate*). Seafood delicacies hold pride of place in this pleasant restaurant. *Closed Sun.*

**Numero Undici**, Via Cavalca 11, t 050 544294 (*cheap*). A diminutive *trattoria* with no frills or graces; you order your food from the counter, and take your plate to the table. But it's worth it as prices are rock bottom and the limited menu delicious. *Closed Sat lunch and Sun.*

**Osteria dei Tinti**, Vicolo de Tinti 26, t 050 580 240 (*cheap*). Osteria dei Tinti is rather touristy and a bit hard to find (it's in an alley just off Via Oberdan), but the *primi* and *secondi* are fine and good value. *Closed Wed and Tues eve.*

**Re di Puglia**, Via Aurelia Sud 7, Loc. Mortellini, t 050 960 157 (*moderate*). Occupying a converted farmhouse, 1km from the Pisa Sud *autostrada* exit, this tends to use produce fresh from the farm. It's good, earthy cooking. Tuck into home-made pasta with mutton, rabbit or goat, followed by meat cooked on the huge grill. *Dinner only, also lunch on Sun. Closed Mon and Tues in winter and Mon in summer.*

Like a Middle Eastern city, Pisa has put all its efforts into one fabulous spiritual monument, while the rest of the city wears a decidedly undemonstrative, almost anonymous face, a little run-down. It is a subtle place, a little sad perhaps, but strangely seductive if you give it a chance. After all, one can't create a Field of Miracles in a void.

## History

Pisa used to like to claim that it began as a Greek city, founded by colonists from Elis. Most historians, however, won't accept anything earlier than around 100 BC, when a Roman veterans' colony was settled there. Records of what followed are scarce, but Pisa, like Amalfi and Venice, must have had an early start in building a navy and establishing trade connections. By the 11th century, the effort had blossomed into opulence; Pisa managed to build itself a small empire, including Corsica, Sardinia, and for a while the Balearics. Around 1060, work was begun on the great cathedral complex and many other buildings, inaugurating the Pisan Romanesque.

In 1135 Pisa captured and sacked its greatest rival in the western Mediterranean, Amalfi. The First Crusade, when Pisa's archbishop led the entire fleet in support of the Christian knights, turned out to be an economic windfall for the city. Unlike Amalfi, from the start Pisa had adopted a course of combat with the states of the Muslim world, less from religious bigotry than a clear eye on the main chance. When the Pisans weren't battling with the Muslims of Spain and Africa, they were learning from them. A steady exchange of ideas brought much of medieval Arab science, philosophy and architecture into Europe through Pisa's port. Pisa's architecture, the highest development of the Romanesque in Italy, saw its influence spread from Sardinia to Puglia in southern Italy; when Gothic arrived in Italy Pisa was one of the few cities to take it seriously, and the city's accomplishments in that style rank with Siena's. In science, Pisa contributed a great if shadowy figure, the mathematician Leonardo Fibonacci, who either rediscovered the principle of the Golden Section or learned it from the Arabs, and also introduced Arabic numerals to Europe. Pisa's long, scholarly tradition was crowned in the 1600s by its most famous son, Galileo Galilei.

Pisa was always a Ghibelline city, the greatest ally of the emperors in Tuscany if only for expediency's sake. When a real threat came, however, it was not from Florence or any of the other Tuscan cities, but from the rising mercantile port of Genoa. After years of constant warfare, the Genoese devastated the Pisan navy at the Battle of Meloria (an islet off Livorno) in 1284. It signalled the end of Pisan supremacy, but all chance of recovery was quashed by an even more implacable enemy: the Arno. Pisa's port was gradually silting up, and when the cost of dredging became greater than the traffic could bear, the city's fate was sealed. The Visconti of Milan seized the economically enfeebled city in 1396, and nine years later Florence snatched it from them.

Excepting the period 1494–1505, when the city rebelled and kept the Florentines out despite an almost constant siege of 15 years, Pisa's history as a key locale was ended. The Medici dukes did the city one big favour, in supporting the university and even removing Florence's own university to Pisa. In the last 500 years of Pisa's pleasant twilight, this institution has helped the city to remain alive and vital, and keep it in touch with the modern world; one of its students was the nuclear physicist Enrico Fermi.

# The Field of Miracles

*For the museums and monuments on the Field of Miracles,*
*you can save by getting the joint ticket.*

Almost from the time of its conception, this was the nickname given to medieval Italy's most ambitious building programme. As with Florence's cathedral, too many changes were made over two centuries of work to tell exactly what the original intentions were. But of all the unique things about this complex, the location is most striking. Whether their reasons had to do with aesthetics or land values – probably a little of both – the Pisans built their cathedral on a broad expanse of green lawn at the northern edge of town, just inside the walls. The cathedral was begun in 1063, the famous Leaning Tower and the baptistry in the middle 1100s, at the height of Pisa's fortunes, and the Campo Santo in 1278.

## The Baptistry

*Open winter daily 9–4.40; spring and autumn daily 9–5.40;*
*summer daily 8–7.40; adm (can be combined with a number of other*
*monuments in town).*

The biggest of its kind in Italy; those of many other cities would fit neatly inside. The original architect, who was blessed with the felicitous name of Master Diotisalvi ('God save you'), saw the lower half of the building done in the typical stripes-and-arcades Pisan style. A second colonnade was intended to go over the first, but as the Genoese gradually muscled Pisa out of trade routes, funds began to run short. In the 1260s, Nicola and Giovanni Pisano, members of that remarkable family of artists who did so much to re-establish sculpture in Italy, redesigned and completed the upper half in a harmonious Gothic crown of gables and pinnacles. The Pisanos also added the dome over Diotisalvi's original prismatic dome, still visible from the inside. Both domes were impressive for their time, among the largest attempted in the Middle Ages.

Inside, the austerity of the simple, striped walls and heavy columns of grey Elban granite is broken by two superb works of art. The great **baptismal font** is the work of Guido Bigarelli, the 13th-century Como sculptor who made the crazy pulpit in Barga. There is little figurative sculpture on it, but the 16 exquisite marble panels are finely carved in floral and geometrical patterns of inlaid stones, a northern, almost monochrome variant on the Cosmati work of medieval Rome and Campania. Nicola Pisano's **pulpit** (1260) was one of the first of that family's many masterpieces, and established the form for their later pulpits, the columns resting on fierce lions, the relief panels crowded with intricately carved figures in impassioned New Testament episodes, a style that seems to owe much to the reliefs on Roman triumphal arches and columns. The baptistry is famous for its uncanny acoustics; if you have it to yourself, try singing a few notes from as near the centre as they will allow you to go. If there's a crowd the guards will just be waiting for someone to bribe them to do it.

## The Cathedral

*Open winter Mon–Sat 10–12.45, Sun and hols 3–4.45; April–Oct Mon–Sat 10–7.40, Sun and hols 1–7.40; often closed to tourists for most of the day;adm.*

One of the first and finest works of the Pisan Romanesque, the cathedral façade, with four levels of colonnades, turned out to be a little more ornate than Buscheto, the architect, had planned back in 1063. These columns, with similar colonnades around the apse and the Gothic frills later added around the unique elliptical dome, are the only showy features on the calm, restrained exterior. On the south transept, the late 12th-century **Porte San Ranieri** has a fine pair of bronze doors by Bonanno, one of the architects of the Leaning Tower. The biblical scenes are enacted among real palms and acacia trees; naturally, the well-travelled Pisans would have known what such things looked like.

On the inside, little of the original art survived a fire in 1595. The roof went, as well as the Cosmati pavement, of which only a few patches remain. A coffered Baroque ceiling and some poor painting were contributed during the reconstruction, but some fine work survives nonetheless. The great mosaic of Christ Pantocrator in the apse is by Cimabue, and there are some portraits of the saints by Andrea del Sarto in the choir and his *Madonna della Grazia* in the right nave.

The **pulpit** (*c.* 1300), by Giovanni Pisano, is the acknowledged masterpiece of the family. The men of 1595 used the fire as an opportunity to get rid of this nasty old medieval relic, and the greatest achievement of Pisan sculpture sat disassembled in crates, quite forgotten until this century. Works of genuine inspiration often prove profoundly disturbing to ages of certainty and good taste. Pisano's pulpit is startling, mixing classical and Christian elements with a fluency never seen before his time. St Michael, as a telamon, shares the honour of supporting the pulpit with Hercules and the Fates, while prophets, saints and sibyls look on from their appointed places. The relief panels, jammed with expressive faces, diffuse an electric immediacy equal to the best work of the Renaissance. Notice particularly the Nativity, the Massacre of the Innocents, the Flight into Egypt, and the Last Judgement.

## The Leaning Tower

*Book through the Opera Primaziale Pisana, t 050 560 547, 050 561 820, priaziale@sirius.pisa.it; groups of 30 enter every 30mins by booking in advance.*

Re-opened on 15 December 2001 after major restoration work to secure the structure, Pisa's famous leaning tower is once again safe to visit. The stories claiming the tilt was accidental were most likely pure fabrications, desperate tales woven by the Pisans to account for what, before mass tourism, must have seemed a great civic embarrassment. The argument isn't very convincing. It seems hard to believe that the tower would start to lean when only 33ft tall; much of the weight would still be in the foundations. The argument then insists that the Pisans doggedly kept building it after the lean commenced. The architects who measured the stones in the last century to get to the bottom of the mystery concluded that the tower's odd state was absolutely intentional from the day it was begun in 1173. Mention this to a Pisan, and he will be as offended as if you had suggested lunacy is a problem in his family.

The leaning campanile is hardly the only strange thing in the Field of Miracles. The more time you spend here, the more you will notice: little monster-griffins, dragons and such, peeking out of every corner of the oldest sculptural work, skilfully hidden where you have to look twice to see them, or the big bronze griffin sitting on a column atop the cathedral apse (a copy) and a rhinoceros by the door, Muslim arabesques in the Campo Santo, perfectly classical Corinthian capitals in the cathedral nave and pagan images on the pulpit. The elliptical cathedral dome, in its time the only one in Europe, shows that the Pisans had not only the audacity but the mathematical skills to back it up. You may have noticed that the baptistry too is leaning – about 5ft, in the opposite direction. And the cathedral façade leans outwards about a foot, hard to notice but disconcerting if you see it from the right angle. This could hardly be accidental. So much in the Field of Miracles gives evidence of a very sophisticated, strangely modern taste for the outlandish. Perhaps the medieval master masons in charge here simply thought that plain perpendicular buildings were becoming just a little trite.

Whatever, the campanile is a beautiful building and something unique in the world – also a very expensive bit of whimsy, with some 190 marble and granite columns. At some 16½ft off perpendicular, the monument proved expensive for the local and national governments as they tried to shore up the lurching tower – $80 million since 1990, when rescue operations began. The first phase was completed a few years back, when counterweights (800 tonnes of lead ingots) were stacked at the base of the tower's leaning side, stopping the tilt. The next stage was trickier: replacing the lead ingots with an underground support, laying a ring of cement around the foundations, and anchoring it to 10 steel cables attached to the bedrock 164ft underground. But digging under the 14,000-tonne tower was perilous; in September 1995, while workers were freezing the ground to mute vibrations, they found a ring of cement from the last century, when suddenly to their horror the tower heaved a groan and tipped another tenth of an inch.

To prevent similar scares, in 1998 the tower was given a rather unsightly girdle of plastic-coated steel braces, attached by a pair of 72ft steel cables to a counterweight system hidden among the buildings on the north end of the Campo dei Miracoli, capable of increasing the tension to 100 tonnes if the tower started to sag again during digging. The most recent project involved removing soil from under the north, east and west sides of the tower from a depth of about six metres below ground level, thereby decreasing the difference in depth between the north and south side. This seemed to do the trick; the tower is not only stable but has actually righted itself several millimetres so far. Work was completed in 2001, and all went according to plan; the tower lost 10 per cent of its former lean (about 45cms) and was brought back to the angle it had 200 years ago. Struts were sunk into the ground to block this position. As the work drew to completion, the rumours proved to be true and the tower was once again open to visitors.

# The Campo Santo

*Open winter 9–4.40; spring and autumn 9–5.40; summer 8–7.40; adm.*

If an additional marvel in the Campo dei Miracoli is not excessive, there is this remarkable cloister, as unique in its way as the Leaning Tower. Basically, the cemetery is a rectangle of gleaming white marble, unadorned save for the blind arcading around the façade and the beautiful Gothic tabernacle of the enthroned Virgin Mary over the entrance. With its uncluttered, simple lines, the Campo Santo seems almost contemorary more like a work of our own century than one that was completed in the 1300s.

The cemetery began, according to legend, when the battling Archbishop Lanfranchi, who led the Pisan fleet into the Crusades, came back with boatloads of soil from the Holy Land for extra-blessed burials. Over the centuries an exceptional hoard of frescoes and sculpture accumulated here. Unfortunately, much of it went up in flames on a terrible night in July 1944, when an Allied incendiary bomb hit the roof and set it on fire. Many priceless works of art were destroyed and others, including most of the frescoes, were damaged beyond hope of ever being perfectly restored. The biggest loss, perhaps, was the set of frescoes by Benozzo Gozzoli – including the *Tower of Babylon, Solomon and Sheba, Life of Moses* and the *Grape Harvest*; in their original state they must have been as fresh and colourful as his famous frescoes in Florence's Medici Palace.

Even better known, and better preserved, are two 14th-century frescoes of the Triumph of Death and the Last Judgement by an unknown artist (perhaps Buffalmacco, who is described by Boccaccio in the *Decameron*) whose failure to sign his work unfortunately passed him down to posterity with the Hallowe'en name, 'Master of the Triumph of Death'. In this memento of the century of plagues and trouble, Death (in Italian, feminine: *La Morte*) swoops down on frolicking nobles, while in the *Last Judgement* (which has very little of heaven in it, but plenty of hell) the unfortunate damned are variously cooked, wrapped up in snakes, poked, disembowelled, banged up and chewed on; still, they are some of the best paintings of the *trecento*, and somehow seem less gruesome and paranoid than similar works of centuries to come (though good enough to have inspired that pop classic, Lizst's *Totentanz*).

Another curiosity is the *Theological Cosmography* of Piero di Puccio (*under restoration; call* **t** *050 560 547 for information*), a vertiginous diagram which depicts 22 spheres of the planets and stars, angels, archangels, thrones and dominations, cherubim and seraphim, etc; in the centre, the small circle trisected by a T-shape was a common medieval map pattern for the known earth. The three sides represent Asia, Europe and Africa, and the three lines the Mediterranean, the Black Sea and the Nile. Among the sculpture in the Campo Santo, there are sarcophagi and Roman bath tubs and, in the gallery of prewar photographs of the lost frescoes, a famous Hellenistic marble vase with bas-reliefs.

## The Museo delle Sinopie and Museo del Duomo

*Both open winter 9–4.40; spring and autumn 9–5.40 (Museo del Duomo 5.20); summer 8–7.40 (Museo del Duomo 7.20); adm.*

There are two museums surrounding the Campo dei Miracoli. Opposite the cathedral, the **Museo delle Sinopie** contains the pre-painting sketches on plaster of the frescoes lost in the Campo Santo fire. Many of these are works of art in their own right, which, though faint, help to give an idea of how the frescoes once looked. The **Museo del Duomo**, near the Leaning Tower in Piazza Arcivescovado, has been arranged in the old chapterhouse, with descriptions in English available for each room. The first rooms contain the oldest works – beautiful fragments from the cathedral façade and altar; two Islamic works, the very strange, original **Griffin** from the top of the cathedral, believed to have come from Egypt in the 11th century, and a 12th-century bronze basin with an intricate decoration. Statues by the Pisanos from the baptistry were brought in from the elements too late; worn and bleached, they resemble a convention of mummies.

Other sculptures in the next room survived better: Giovanni Pisano's grotesque faces, his gaunt but noble *St John the Baptist* and the lovely *Madonna del Colloquio*, so named because she speaks to her child with her eyes; and in the next room are fine works by Tino di Camaino, including the tomb of San Ranieri and his sculptures from the tomb of Emperor Henry VII, sitting among his court like some exotic oriental potentate. In Room 9 are works by Nino Pisano, and in Rooms 11–12, the Cathedral Treasure. Giovanni Pisano's lovely ivory *Madonna and Child* steals the show, curving to the shape of the elephant's tusk; there's an ivory coffer and the cross that led the Pisans on the First Crusade. Upstairs are some extremely large angels used as candlesticks, intarsia and two rare illuminated 12th- and 13th-century scrolls (called exultet rolls), perhaps the original visual aids; the deacon would unroll them from the pulpit as he read so the congregation could follow the story with the pictures. The remaining rooms have some Etruscan and Roman odds and ends (including a good bust of Caesar) and prints and engravings of the original Campo Santo frescoes made in the 19th century. The courtyard has a unique view of the Leaning Tower, which seems to be bending over to spy inside.

# North Pisa

With the cathedral on the very edge of town, Pisa has no real centre. Still, the Pisans are very conscious of the division made by the Arno; every year in June the neighbourhoods on either side of the river fight it out on the Ponte di Mezzo in the *Gioco del Ponte*, a medieval tug-of-war where the opponents try to push a big decorated cart over each other. From the Field of Miracles, Via Cardinale Pietro Maffi leads east to the ruins of some **Roman Baths** near the Lucca Gate; two interesting churches in the neighbourhood are **San Zeno**, in a corner of the walls, with some parts as old as the 5th century, and **Santa Caterina**, a Dominican church with a beautiful, typically Pisan façade. Inside there is an *Annunciation* and a sculpted Saltarelli tomb by Nino Pisano, and a large painting from the 1340s of the *Apotheosis of St Thomas Aquinas*, with Plato and Aristotle in attendance and defeated infidel philosopher Averroes below, attributed to Francesco Traini.

One long street near the Campo dei Miracoli begins as Via della Faggiola, leading into the **Piazza dei Cavalieri**. Duke Cosimo I started what was probably the last crusading order of knights, the Cavalieri di Santo Stefano, in 1562. The crusading urge had ended long before, but the duke found the knights a useful tool for placating the anachronistic fantasies of the Tuscan nobility – most of them newly titled bankers – and for licensing out freebooting expeditions against the Turks. Cosimo had Vasari build the **Palazzo della Carovana** for the order, conveniently demolishing the old Palazzo del Popolo, the symbol of Pisa's lost independence. Vasari gave the palace an outlandishly ornate *graffito* façade; the building now holds the Scuola Normale Superiore, founded by Napoleon in 1810. Next door, **Santo Stefano**, the order's church, is also by Vasari, though the façade was designed by a young Medici dilettante; inside are some war pennants which the order's pirates captured from the Muslims in North Africa. Also on the piazza, the **Palazzo dell'Orologio** was built around the 'Hunger Tower' (left of the big clock), famous from Dante's story in the *Inferno* of Ugolino della Gherardesca, the Pisan commander who was walled in here with his sons and grandsons after his fickle city began to suspect him of intrigues with the Genoese. The **University**, founded by his family in 1330 and still one of Italy's most important, is just south of here, while Via dei Mille leads west to the **Botanical Gardens**, created by Ferdinando I de Medici for the university in 1595; the institute, in the grounds, has an extraordinary façade entirely covered with shells and mother-of-pearl (*t 050 911 374, 050 560 045; open Nov–Feb Mon–Fri 8–5, Sat 8–1; Mar–Oct Mon–Fri 8–5.30, Sat 8–1; closed Sun*).

From Piazza dei Cavalieri, Via Dini takes you south into the twisting alleys of the lively market area, around **Piazza Vettovaglie** ('victuals square') where every morning except Sunday the city's ancient mercantile traditions are renewed. Tucked in the main street, old arcaded **Borgo Stretto**, you'll see one of the most gorgeous façades in the city, belonging to **San Michele in Borgo**, a 10th-century church redone in the 14th century, with three tiers of arcades. Much of the interior collapsed during the bombing raids of 1944. Off to the west, Via S. Francesco leads to the church of **San Francesco**: Gothic, with a plain marble façade, but containing some good paintings – a polyptych over the altar by Tommaso Pisano, frescoes by Taddeo Gaddi, Niccolò di Pietro Gerini (in the chapterhouse) and in the sacristy, *Stories of the Virgin* by Taddeo di Bartolo (1397). The unfortunate Count Ugo and sons are buried in a chapel near the altar.

## Museo di San Matteo

*t 050 541 865; open Tues–Sat 9–7, Sun 9–2; closed Mon; adm.*

On the Lungarno Mediceo, an old convent which also served as a prison now immures much of the best Pisan art from the Middle Ages and Renaissance. It has works by Giunta Pisano, believed to be the first artist ever to sign his work (early 1200s), and an excellent and well-arranged collection of 1300s paintings by Pisans and other schools gathered from the city's churches; a polyptych by Simone Martini, paintings by Francesco Traini, Taddeo di Bartolo, Agnolo Gaddi, Antonio Veneziano and Turino Vanni; some sculptures by the Pisanos (especially the *Madonna del Latte* by Andrea and Nino); and medieval ceramics from the Middle East, brought home by old Pisan sea dogs.

In Room 7, after all the trecento works, the Early Renaissance comes as a startling revelation, as it must have been for the people of the 15th century: here is Neri di Bicci's wonderfully festive *Coronation of St Catherine* bright with ribbons, a *Madonna* from the decorative Gentile da Fabriano, a sorrowful *St Paul* by Masaccio, with softly moulded features and draperies, an anonymous *Madonna with Angel Musicians*, and a beautifully coloured *Crucifixion* by Gozzoli, which looks more like a party than an execution. The last great work is Donatello's gilded bronze reliquary bust of *San Lussorio*, who could pass for Don Quixote.

## Along the Lungarno

Take time to head up the Lungarno Mediceo, where Pisa's **Prefettura** is housed in the lovely 13th-century stone, brick and marble Palazzo Medici. This was once a favoured residence of the magnificent Lorenzo. Nearby is the beautiful 16th-century **Palazzo Toscanelli** (which was once attributed to Michelangelo), where the English poet Lord Byron lived from 1821–2 and wrote six cantos of *Don Giovanni*. Behind it, picturesque **Via delle Belle Torri** is lined with houses from the 12th and 13th centuries, which rub shoulders with a lot of new constructions that fill in the gaps left by bombs.

Further down the Lungarno is the former Palazzo Reale, begun in 1559 by Cosimo I, which has recently found a new life as the **Museo Nazionale di Palazzo Reale** (*t 050 926 539; entrance at Lungarno Pacinotti 46; open Mon–Fri 9–2.30, Sat 9–1.30; adm*), an annexe to the Museo di San Matteo, housing a collection of old armour which gets dusted off every June for the *Gioco del Ponte*, as well as some 900 other pieces from the 15th–17th centuries. A new section concentrates on paintings, sculptures and collectables (mostly from the 15th–18th centuries) from the Medici and Lorraine archducal hoards.

Just behind the Palazzo Reale, look at Pisa's other famous bell tower, belonging to the 12th-century church of **San Nicola**: cylindrical at the bottom, octagonal in the middle, and hexagonal on top. Designed by Nicolò Pisano, it has exactly the same kind of tilt as the Leaning Tower itself, built to lean forward before curving back again towards the perpendicular. Ask the sacristan to show you the famous spiral stair inside, claimed by Vasari to have inspired Bramante's Belvedere stair in the Vatican. The church contains a fine *Madonna* by Traini, a wooden sculpture, also of the Madonna, by Nino Pisano, and a painting from the quattrocento of St Nicholas of Tolentino shielding Pisa from the plague (in the fourth chapel on the right).

# South of the Arno

After the Campo dei Miracoli, the thing that has most impressed Pisa's numerous visitors is its languidly curving stretch of the Arno. It is an exercise in Tuscan gravity, the river lined with two mirror-image lines of blank-faced yellow and tan buildings, all the same height, with no remarkable bridges or any of the picturesque quality of Florence. Its uncanny monotony is broken by only one landmark, but it is something special.

Opposite the Palazzo Reale, **Santa Maria della Spina** (*open Oct–Mar Tues–Sun 10–2; April, May and Sept Tues–Fri 10–1.30 and 2.30–7; June–Aug Tues–Fri 11–1.30 and 2.30–6, Sat and Sun 11–1.30 and 2.30–8; adm*) sits on the bank like a precious Gothic jewel box. Although its placement on the Lungarno Gambacorti is perfect, it was built at the mouth of the Arno, where it suffered so many floods that it was on the point of vanishing in 1871, when it was dismantled and rebuilt by the city on this new site. Although it's an outstanding achievement of Italian Gothic, it wasn't originally Gothic at all. Partially rebuilt in 1323, its new architect – perhaps one of the Pisanos – turned it into an extravaganza of pointed gables and blooming pinnacles. All of the sculptural work is first class, especially the figures of Christ and the Apostles in the 13 niches facing the streets.

The chapel takes its name from a thorn of Christ's crown of thorns, a relic brought back from the Crusades. Inside the luminous zebra interior, the statues of the Madonna and Child, St Peter and St John are by Andrea and Nino Pisano. A few blocks west, near the walls where the famous 'Golden Gate' – medieval Pisa's door to the sea – once stood, remains of the old brick Citadel and Arsenal are still visible across the river. Just down from Santa Maria della Spina, the church of **San Paolo a Ripa del Arno** has a beautiful 12th-century façade similar to that of the cathedral. San Paolo stands in a small park, and is believed to have been built over the site of Pisa's original cathedral; perhaps building cathedrals in open fields was an old custom. Behind it, the unusual and very small 12th-century chapel of **Sant'Agata** has eight sides and an eight-sided prismatic roof like an Ottoman tomb.

Down the Arno, the monotony is briefly broken again by the arches of the 17th-century **Logge di Banchi**, the old silk and wool market, at the Ponte di Mezzo and at the head of Pisa's main shopping street, the Corso Italia. A bit further down is another octagonal church, **San Sepolcro**, built for the Knights Templar by Diotisalvi.

Behind it, picturesque **Via San Martino** was Pisa's old casbah, the main street of the Chinizica, the medieval quarter of Arab and Turkish merchants. At No.19 a Roman relief was incorporated into the building, known since the Middle Ages as Kinzica, after a maiden who saved Pisa when the Saracens sailed up to the Golden Gate. At the east end of the Lungarno, there's a shady park, **Giardino Scotto**, in the former Bastion Sangallo. Shelley lived nearby, in the Palazzo Scotto (1820–22), where he wrote *Adonais* and *Epipsychidion*.

## Around Pisa

A couple of kilometres up river to the east stands 'Pisa's second leaning tower', the campanile of the Romanesque **San Michele dei Scalzi**. Under the slopes of Monte Pisano, **Calci** has a good 11th-century church and an eroded giant of a campanile; 11 kilometres from here, in a prominent site overlooking the Arno, is the ornate **Certosa di Pisa** (*t/f 050 938 430; guided tours Mon–Sat 9–7, Sun 9–1; closed Mon; adm*), founded in 1366, but then completely Baroqued in the 18th century, in a kind of 1920s Spanish-California exhibition style with three fine cloisters. There are some lavish pastel frescoes by Florentine Baroque artist Bernardo Poccetti and his school, and a giraffe skeleton, some stuffed penguins, Tuscan minerals, even wax intestines – all part of the university's **Natural History Collections**, founded originally by the Medici and housed in the Certosa since 1981 (*t 050 936 193; open mid-Sept–mid-June Tues–Sat 9–6, Sun and hols 10–7; mid-June–mid-Sept Tues–Fri 10–7, Sat, Sun and hols 4–midnight; adm*).

Towards the coast, six kilometres from Pisa, is the beautifully isolated basilica of **San Piero a Grado**. According to tradition it was founded in the first century by St Peter himself, and in the Middle Ages was a popular pilgrimage destination. Although first documented in the 8th century, the current buildings are 11th century, embellished with blind arcades and ceramic tondi. Like many early churches and basilicas, it has an apse on either end, though of different sizes; the columns were brought in from a variety of ancient buildings. The altar stone, believed to have been set there by St Peter, was found in recent excavations that uncovered the remains of several previous churches. Frescoes in the nave by a 14th-century Lucchese, Deodato Orlandi, tell the *Story of St Peter* with effigies of the popes up to the turn of the first millennium AD (John XVIII) and a view of heaven.

In 1822, a strange ceremony took place on the wide, sandy beach of **Gombo**, near the mouth of the Arno, described in morbid detail by Edward Trelawny: 'the brains literally seethed, bubbled, and boiled as in a cauldron, for a very long time. Byron could not face this scene, he withdrew to the beach and swam off to the *Bolivar*.' Such was Shelley's fiery end, after he drowned sailing from Livorno.

Gombo, and Pisa's other beaches, the **Marina di Pisa** and **Tirrenia**, are often plagued by pollution, although Marina di Pisa makes a pretty place to stroll, with its Liberty-style homes and pine forests.

# The Coast of Livorno and its Islands

## Livorno

*...There is plenty of space; it is a fully registered cemetery with an attendant keeper. So, if any of you have the intention of retiring to this very interesting part of Tuscany you will be well taken care of!*

Horace A. Hayward, on the British Cemetery in Livorno

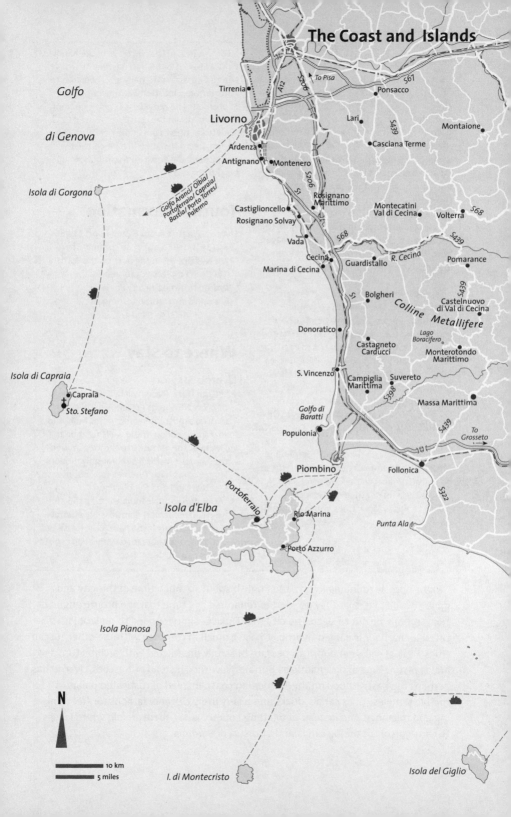

# The Coast and Islands

*Golfo*

*di Genova*

To Pisa →
Tirrenia
Ponsacco
S67

Livorno
Lari
S439
Montaione

Ardenza
Casciana Terme
Antignano
Montenero

*Isola di Gorgona*

Golfo Aranci/ Olbia/
Portoferraio/ Capraia/
Bastia/ Porto Torres/
Palermo

Rosignano
Marittimo
Montecatini
Val di Cecina
Volterra
S68

Castiglioncello
Rosignano Solvay

Vada
S68
R. Cecina
Pomarance

Cecina
Guardistallo

Marina di Cecina
Bolgheri
Castelnuovo
di Val di Cecina

*Colline*
Donoratico

*Isola di Capraia*
Castagneto
Carducci
Lago
Boracifero
Monterotondo
Marittimo

Capraia
S. Vincenzo
Campiglia
Marittima
Suvereto
*Sto. Stefano*

Massa Marittima
S398

*Golfo di*
*Baratti*

Populonia
To
Grosseto →
S439

*Portoferraio*
Piombino
Follonica

*Isola d'Elba*

*Rio Marina*

S322

*Punta Ala*

*Porto Azzurro*

**N**

*Isola Pianosa*

─── 10 km
─── 5 miles

*I. di Montecristo*
*Isola del Giglio*

# Getting Around

Livorno's **train** station is on the edge of the city, with plenty of trains to Pisa, Florence and any point along the Tyrrhenian coast. Some trains to Pisa go on to Lucca–Pistoia–Florence. There are some connections to Volterra, with a change down the coast at Cecina. The station is well over a mile from the city centre; take the no.1 bus (most other city buses also pass through the centre, though as one old Livornese put it, they make 'vicious circles' before getting there).

**Buses** for all villages in Livorno province (the strip of coast down as far as Follonica) leave from Piazza Grande. LAZZI buses for Florence depart from Scali A. Saffi, on the Fosse Reale, just off Piazza Cavour.

**Ferries:** Livorno is the main port for ferries to Corsica, with daily departures (Corsica Marittima line, t 0586 210 507, and Corsica Ferries, t 0586 881 380) from late March to early November; it's a 4-hour trip to Bastia, a very pleasant town, and some of the Corsica Ferries ships call at Porto Vecchio and Elba on the way.

Compagnia Sarda Navigazione/Linea dei Golfi, t 0586 409 925, has daily ferries to Olbia in Sardinia (a depressing town on a wonderful island) from April until September. There are other departures on the Sardinia Ferries line, t 0586 881 380, from Easter to October; these go to Golfo Aranci on the Costa Smeralda. A newcomer, with its striking, psychedelic-painted ships, is Moby Lines, which in summer take you to Bastia or Olbia; Via Veneto 24 in Livorno, t 0586 826 847.

For the Tuscan Islands, services are handled by TOREMAR, t 0586 896 113: they do a daily trip to Capraia, and a daily afternoon run to Portoferraio, Elba, from 16 June until 30 September. The main Elba services go from Piombino down the coast.

All ticket offices are in the port area. For departure information in a pinch, call the Capitaneria del Porto on this number: t 0586 893 362.

# Tourist Information

**Livorno:** Piazza Cavour 6 (2nd floor), t 0586 898 111, f 0586 896 173; in summer, there are two booths in the port, on the Porto Mediceo t 0586 895 320, *info@ livorno.turismo.toscana.it*, *www.livorno.turismo.toscana.it*. Open Mon–Fri 9–1 and 3–5, Sat 9–1.

# Where to Stay

**Livorno** ✉ 57100

**★★★Gran Duca**, Piazza Micheli 16, t 0586 891 024, f 0586 891 153 (*expensive*). This is Livorno's most interesting hotel, built into a surviving section of the walls right on the Piazza at the entrance to the area around the harbour. Inside it's thoroughly modern; some rooms have TV; some look out over the Quattro Mori and the busy port.

**★★★Gennarino**, Viale Italia 301, t/f 0586 803 109 (*moderate*). One possible alternative, particularly if you have a car, is to head out along the shore road, where you can stay in this neo-Gothic palace.

Right from its founding in 1577, the English spent so much time in this city and grew so fond of it, that they decided to rename it. It's time that the bizarre anglicization, *Leghorn*, be put to sleep. The city that Duke Cosimo founded to replace Pisa's silted-up harbour is named **Livorno**. It hasn't much in common with the other Tuscan cities – full of sailors and African pedlars, blissfully unafflicted with architecture and art, as picturesque and romantic as Buffalo, New York. Instead of frescoes, Livorno has perhaps the best seafood on the Tyrrhenian coast. Instead of rusticated palazzi and marble temples, it has canals, docks and a very lively citizenry famous for freethinking and tolerance. And instead of winding country lanes, there are big white ferries to carry you off to the Tuscan Islands, Corsica or Sardinia.

As it's a port town, visitors will find an abundance of inexpensive hotels. Many, though none especially distinguished, are across the piazza from the train station. Dozens more crowd the area around the port and Via Grande. Some are real dives, but Corso Mazzini, a few blocks south of the Fosso Reale, has some nice ones.

**★★Hotel Marina**, Corso Mazzini 148, t 0586 834 278, f 0586 834 135 (*cheap*). Old-fashioned, but pleasant.

**★Europa**, a block off Via Grande at Via dell'Angiolo 23, t 0586 888 581 (*moderate*). Clean, remodelled rooms, right in the centre.

**★★Giardino**, Piazza Mazzini 85, t/f 0586 806 330 (*moderate*). Near the port.

# Eating Out

The main purpose of a trip to Livorno is to eat seafood. The Livornese have their own ways of preparing it, now much copied throughout Tuscany, and restaurants usually prove easier on your budget than elsewhere. Besides lobster and grilled fish, pasta dishes with seafood figure on all the local menus, as does the Livornese dish, *cacciucco*, the famous fish stew that is to Livorno what the Leaning Tower is to Pisa.

After a rich meal, try a *bomba livornese* in place of a dessert. This is the local answer to Irish coffee and is made with equal quantities of coffee and rum served piping hot.

## Expensive

**La Chiave**, Scali della Cantine 52, t 0586 888 609. This is arguably Livorno's best restaurant, specializing, of course, in seafood; the menu changes often but do try one of the seafood pasta *primi*, such as the tagliolini with octopus. *Eves only.*

**La Barcarola**, Viale Carducci 63, t 0586 402 367. A big, noisy place towards the train station, serving up *zuppa di pesce*, penne with scampi, and everything else the Tyrrhenian has to offer, all in the old Livornese style. *Closed Sun and Aug.*

## Moderate

**L'Antico Moro**, Via Bertelloni 59, t 0586 884 659. This has been a local seafood favourite since the 1920s, near the city market. *Closed Wed.*

**Osteria del Mare**, Borgo dei Cappuccini 5, t 0586 881 027. A nice little place serving grilled fish, lobster and *spaghetti alle vongole*, near the mouth of the Fosso Reale. *Closed Thurs.*

**Cantina Nardi**, Via L. Cambini 6, t 0586 808 006. This wine bar comes as a pleasant surprise at lunchtime when a few tables are laid, surrounded by wine bottles – who could wish for better company? *Closed eves and Sun.*

Many of the best restaurants are to the south in the seaside suburb of Ardenza.

**Da Oscar**, Via Franchini 76, t 0586 501 258. This has been a favourite for decades, with a good selection of wines to accompany tempting linguini and clams, excellent risottos and grilled *triglie* and *orate*. *Closed Mon.*

**Trattoria Galileo**, Via della Campana 22, t 0586 889 009. A popular spot in the centre, north of Piazza Repubblica, with seafood among other dishes.

## History

The site had always been a safe harbour, and in the Middle Ages there was a small fortress to watch over it. It's odd no one thought of making a port here long before Cosimo. The Pisani considered it briefly in the 1300s, when it was becoming clear that Pisa's own port would ultimately fill up with the sands of the Arno. Eventually the fortress fell into the grasp of the Genoese, who sold it to Florence in 1421. Cosimo I, in his attempts to build Tuscany into a modern state, first saw the advantage of having a good port to avoid trading at the mercy of the Spaniards and Genoese. Cosimo expanded the fortress, but it was not until the reign of his successors, Francesco and Ferdinando, that Livorno got off the ground. The first stone was laid on 28 March 1577, and a regular gridiron city soon appeared, designed by Buontalenti, and surrounded by fortresses and canals.

Almost from the beginning there was an English connection. Sir Robert Dudley, illegitimate son of the Earl of Leicester – Queen Elizabeth's favourite – left England in 1605 after failing to prove his legitimacy in the Star Chamber court. (Perhaps he had other reasons; immediately upon arrival he converted to Catholicism and obtained a papal divorce from the wife he had abandoned back home.) Dudley built warships for the grand dukes, fortified the port of Livorno and drained the coastal swamps, making the region healthy and inhabitable for the first time.

In 1618, Livorno was declared a free port, free not only for trade but for the practice of any faith and for men of whatever nationality. It was a brilliant stroke, designed to fill out the population of this very rough and dangerous new town, and it is, to the eternal credit of the Medici dukes, an act of tolerance almost unthinkable in the Catholic Mediterranean of the 1600s. Before long, Livorno was full of persecuted Jews, Greeks, English Catholics, Spanish Muslims and loose ends from around Europe. As the only safe trading port in a sea full of Spaniards, the port acquired thriving communities of English and Dutch merchants. In the 1700s progressive, tolerant Livorno was a substantial city, a breath of fresh air in the decadent Mediterranean and a home away from home for British travellers. Shelley wrote *The Cenci* here, as well as 'To a Skylark'; he bought his fatal sailing boat in Livorno's port.

Livorno declined a little once the same low tariffs and trading advantages became available in other Mediterranean ports. The Austrian dukes, especially Leopold II, helped keep Livorno ahead of its rivals; nevertheless, true to its traditions, the city contributed greatly to the mid-century revolutionary movements and the wars of the Risorgimento. After unification it was still a lively place, full of men of many nations; it also began to make its first cultural contributions to the new Italy – the operatic composer Mascagni, the painter Modigliani, and several other artists of the Macchiaioli school. The Second World War and its bombers hit Livorno harder than anywhere in Tuscany, but the city rebuilt itself quickly. Long before other ports, Livorno realized the importance of container shipping. As the Mediterranean's first big container port, Livorno today has become the second city of Tuscany, and Italy's second-largest port after Genoa.

## Four Moors, Inigo Jones and the American Market

There isn't a lot to see in Livorno. You may enjoy the place and stay for a day or two, or you may be ready to bolt after five minutes. Though the streets are usually brimming, a combination of the prevailing north Tuscan austerity and an excess of dreary architecture make Livorno a disconcertingly anonymous city. It would have been a perfect setting for a German expressionist film of the 1920s; unfortunately, such cinematic possibilities have not so far been exploited. There's nothing disconcerting about the **port**, a busy, fascinating jumble of boats, cranes, docks and canals. Close to the port entrance on Piazza Micheli, the **Fortezza Vecchia** conceals the original Pisan fortress and an 11th-century tower built by the famous Countess Matilda. Piazza Micheli, Livorno's front door to the sea, is decorated with Livorno's only great work of art, the **Quattro Mori** by the Carraran sculptor Pietro Tacca (1623). The monument's original design became somewhat mangled, and Tacca's brilliant figures now sit in chains under a silly earlier statue of Duke Ferdinando I. The four Moors are a symbol of Sardinia, but the statue's original intent was to commemorate the successes of the great Tuscan pirates, the Order of Santo Stefano, against North African shipping.

From here, the arcaded **Via Grande** leads into the city centre; every original building on this street was destroyed in the bombings of 1944. **Piazza Grande**, the centre of Livorno, features the **cathedral**, designed on a bad day by Inigo Jones in 1605; the present building is a complete post-war reconstruction. Jones spent some time in Tuscany as a student of Buontalenti, and he took a little bit of Livorno home with him. His plan for Covent Garden (originally arcaded all round, without the market) is a simple copy of this piazza, with St Paul's in place of the cathedral. Via Grande continues on to **Piazza della Repubblica**, contender for the title of the most ghastly square in Italy. There are no trees on it, because the piazza is really a paved-over section of the **Fosso Reale**, the curving canal that surrounded the original city of Livorno. Just off to the north, the sprawling, brick **Fortezza Nuova** stands on an island in the canal, now landscaped as a park and a popular resort for the Livornese on Sundays. Nearby, on Via della Madonna, three adjacent churches (now recycled for other uses) make a fitting memorial of Livorno's career as a truly free city. The first is Greek Orthodox, the second Catholic, and the next Armenian. On the other side of Piazza della Repubblica, Piazza XX Settembre is the site of the Saturday **American Market**, so called for the vast stores of GI surplus sold here after the war, and still Livorno's street market for clothes and odd items.

## Little Venice and the Museo Civico

By now, you may be entirely despairing of finding anything really uplifting in Livorno. But just off Piazza della Repubblica is a neighbourhood unlike anything outside Venice. In fact, they call it 'Nuova Venezia', or 'Piccola Venezia', and for picturesque tranquillity it may outdo its famous precursor. **Little Venice** is a quarter only a few blocks square, laced with quiet canals that flow between the Fortezza Nuova and the port, lined with sun-bleached tenements hung with the week's wash. The pseudo-Baroque **Santa Caterina** church is typical of the ungainly, functional buildings of early Livorno. If you're here in late July or August you'll find a livelier Little Venice than usual as the restaurants stay open late for the *Effetto Venezia*, a 10-day summer festival featuring evening shows and concerts and foodstalls selling *cacciucco*, the hearty, locally made fish soup.

Leading out eastwards from the Piazza della Repubblica, Viale Carducci is Livorno's *grand boulevard*, heading towards the railway station. Along the way it passes the **Cisternone**, a neoclassical palace built to house the water works Leopold II constructed in the 1830s. Just next to this is the **Parterre**, a city park with a rather sad zoological garden.

Along the coast south of the centre, Viale Italia leads past the **Terrazza Mascagni**, a grandiose overlook on the sea. A few streets inland, in a park called the Villa Mimbelli, Livorno has just completed a new building for the **Museo Civico Giovanni**

**Fattori** (*open Tues–Sun 10–1 and 4–7; closed Mon; adm*). This contains a good collection of works by the Macchiaioli, Italy's late 19th-century Impressionists. The museum is on the third floor of the city library, housing a small collection that includes only one work by Modigliani, but a wealth of paintings that lead up to his art. The painters represented include Ulivi Liegi, Mario Puccini, that rare blossom Lodovico Tommasi and Livorno's own Giovanni Fattori, one of the leading figures of the Macchiaioli. Together, they make a natural progression from the Biedermeier art of the 1860s – including stirring scenes of Italian volunteers leaving for the front – to the sweet haziness of the *belle époque* 1890s.

South of Terrazza Mascagni, Viale Italia continues past the **Italian Naval Academy** (where you might just get a glimpse of one of the exquisite old sailing ships the Navy uses for training), and then through some neighbourhoods full of surprisingly blatant neo-Gothic and Art Nouveau villas dating from the 1890s, on the way to **Ardenza**, with its seafront park and marina.

### The English Cemeteries and Montenero

For a sentimental journey into Livorno's cosmopolitan past, pay a visit to the **English Cemeteries** on Via Pisa and Via Adua, situated next to the Anglican Church (*ask at Via Adua's Archiconfraternità della Misericordia*). Crotchety old Tobias Smollett, who never stopped crabbing about Italy and never quite got around to leaving it, is interred here, along with numerous members of the British trading community and quite a few Americans. Many of the tombs (dating back to 1670) are truly monumental, some with inscriptions from Scripture or Shakespeare; some are charmingly original. Many of those among the British community, including Byron and Shelley, chose to pass their time not in Livorno itself, but up on the suburban hill of **Montenero** to the south. Byron and Shelley spent six weeks in 1822 at Villa delle Rose (*open by request of the owner, Signor Varvaro di Valentina at No.57*), a fascinating romantic ruin of a place. There is a charming, old-fashioned funicular railway to take you to the top, where there has been a sanctuary and pilgrimage site since an apparition of the Virgin Mary there way back in the 1300s. The present church, full of ex votos, is the work of an 18th-century architect named Giovanni del Fantasia. In addition, there are also a small museum, an ancient pharmacy and a number of caves, the Grotte del Montenero.

## Tuscan Islands

The Tuscan Archipelago is a broad arch of islets stretching from Livorno to Monte Argentario and enclosing Elba, the only large and heavily populated member of the group. Fate has not usually been kind to these islands: what with deforestation, Saracen and Turkish pirates, and finally the Italian government, not much is left. Two of the islands are still prison camps, while another is a nature preserve where no one is allowed to stay overnight. Gorgona and Capraia get a daily boat from Livorno – and are in fact administratively part of Livorno. The others will be dealt with later:

Elba is most conveniently reached from Piombino, Giglio and Giannutri from Porto Santo Stefano.

## Gorgona

To see **Gorgona**, 37 kilometres from Livorno, you'll either have to get permission from the Ministero di Grazia e Giustizia in Rome (quite difficult) or else punch a *carabiniere*. Gorgona, a hilly, rectangular square mile, was first used as a prison by Pope Gregory the Great, 14 centuries ago. A later Carthusian monastery lasted until the new Italian state expropriated the entire island in 1869; in the beginning, it was to be a 'model prison' with workshops and vineyards, but it wasn't long before it deteriorated into just another lock-up. There's nothing to see on Gorgona, except maquis and a handful of olive trees, and you'll have to be content with the view from the boat, which stops daily on the way to Capraia to drop off new cons and supplies. Ambitious plans are afoot to close the prison and turn Gorgona into a wildlife preserve, but so far nothing has been decided.

## Capraia

**Capraia**, 65 kilometres from Livorno, is the third largest of the islands, after Elba and Giglio. It measures about 10 kilometres by five kilometres, and has some 400 inhabitants. Like Elba, it is mountainous, but has fewer trees; most of the island is covered with scrubby *macchia*.

## Tourist Information

**Isola Caprai**: Pro Loco, Via Assunzione 2, t 0586 905 138. *Open April–Sept 10–6*.
**Castiglioncello**: Via Aurelia 967, t 0586 752 291.
**San Vincenzo**: Via Aliata 2, t 0565 701 533, f 0565 706 914, *apt7svincenzo@tiscalinet.it, www.livarno.turismo.toscana.it. Open April–mid-Sept Mon–Sat 9–1 and 3.30–7, Sun 10–1; mid-Sept–Mar Mon, Wed and Fri 9–1 and 3.30–7, Tues, Thurs and Sat 9–1*.
**Piombino**: Loc. Fiorentina, t 0565 276 478. *Open summer only*.
**Suvereto**: Piazza dei Giudici 3, t 0565 829 304.

## Where to Stay and Eat

### San Vincenzo ✉ 57027

If the vast beaches of San Vincenzo fail to tempt you, then perhaps its seafood restaurants will.
**Gambero Rosso**, Piazza della Vittoria 13, t 0565 701 021 (*very expensive–expensive*). This is perhaps the most tantalizing, since it's widely considered to be one of Tuscany's top restaurants. It's earned its name not only for its fish, but also for serving devilishly perfect and delicate crustacea, pasta, pheasant and pigeon with foie gras; there's an equally thorough and tempting wine list. If by chance you can't decide what to pick then take the easy way out and order the *menu degustazione*; it's slightly cheaper than eating *à la carte*. *Closed Tues and Nov*.
**★★★Riva degli Etruschi**, Via della Principessa 120, t 0565 702 351, f 0565 704 011, *www.rivadeglietruschi.it* (*expensive*). One of the nicest hotels on this coast, where guests are accommodated in small cottages set in a forested park. And if your pockets aren't quite deep enough for the Gambero Rosso, the restaurant (*expensive*) also puts on an impressive seafood spread.

### Donoratico ✉ 57022

**Enoteca Maestrini**, Via Aurelia 1 (on the SS1), near Castagneto Carducci. A wine bar serving Tuscany's best, along with light dinners, local cheeses and home-made desserts. *Closed Mon and Sept*.

In Roman times Capraia seems to have been a private estate, and the ruins of an extensive villa can be seen. In the days of the Empire, the island was occupied by a colony of Christian monks. Such a setting was perfect for the Christian ideal of withdrawal and contemplation, but it also prevented the Church authorities from keeping a close watch on the colony, and the monks slipped into unorthodoxy and loose behaviour; an armed mission from Pope Gregory the Great was needed to force them back in line in the late 6th century.

When Saracen pirates began to infest the Tyrrhenian Sea, Capraia, like most of the group, became deserted. The Pisans thought it important enough to repopulate and fortify in the 11th century. Genoa eventually gained control, as she did in Corsica only 32 kilometres away. This proximity gave Capraia its one big moment in history; in 1767 the revolutionary forces of the Corsican nationalist leader, Pasquale Paoli, and the weakness of the Genoese, resulted in, of all things, an independent Capraia, which soon learned to support itself by piracy. French occupation put an end to that four years later.

Seven years ago tourist accommodation on Capraia consisted of one hotel and two tiny *pensioni*. Today, by a miracle of 20th-century Eurotourism, these have all grown into three-star hotels, and two more have sprouted to join them. It helps that Capraia is an island, and a pretty one, but its real attraction is its natural setting, its deep-sea diving and marine grottoes. In the last century the northern quarter of the island was put to use as an agricultural penal colony, which is what it is today. The civilian population is almost entirely concentrated in the port and only town, **Capraia Isola**.

The port is actually half a kilometre from the town, connected by the island's one and only tarmac road. In the town visitors can see the Baroque church and convent of **Sant'Antonio**. Used as a barracks in the last century, it is now crumbling and abandoned. On the outskirts are the ruins of the **Roman villa**, apocryphally the abode of Augustus' profligate daughter Julia, and an 11th-century Pisan chapel dedicated to the **Vergine Assunta**. Overlooking it all is the large and impressive fortress of **San Giorgio**, begun by the Pisans and completed by the Genoese. The well-preserved **watch-tower** at the port was built by the Genoese Bank of St George.

On the eastern side of town there is a beach under the cliffs with an interesting tower, built by the Pisans, and connected to the cliff by a natural bridge. A visiting Californian at the turn of the century was so struck by it that he built a copy of it on a beach near San Diego.

From Capraia Isola a road leads southwest across the island, passing another Pisan church, that of **Santo Stefano**, built on the ruins of a 5th-century church used by the early monks and destroyed by the Saracen pirates. Near Monte Pontica is a cave, the **Grotta di Parino**, a sacred spot used as a place of meditation by the monks. The road ends at a lighthouse on the western coast. Just south is a sea cave, the **Grotta della Foca**, where Mediterranean seals are still reported to live. At the southern tip of the island is another Genoese watchtower, the **Torre dello Zenobito**.

# Livorno's Coast

Livorno's clever tourist office has taken to calling this shore the 'Etruscan Riviera', conjuring up the irresistible idea of Etruscans lounging in beach chairs the way they do on their funerary urns. Beyond Antignano, the shoreline becomes jagged and twisting, dotted with beaches that are usually more than well exploited. **Castiglioncello** is a pretty corner of the coast, but the beaches are narrow and packed with Italians throughout the summer. Nearby **Rosignano** is a similar resort, graced with a gargantuan chemical plant. **Vada** and **Marina di Cecina** are a little better; both at least have stretches of free beach. Marina di Cecina, 36 kilometres from Livorno, is a suburb of Tuscany's newest city, **Cecina**, founded only a century ago, now an unkempt town populated by dissipated factory hands and motorcycle-heads. **San Vincenzo** is a booming, awful resort, but it has miles of good beaches on either side, perhaps your best chance on this strip of coast for a little seaside peace and quiet.

Next is the half-moon **Golfo di Baratti**, with more tranquil beaches and some Etruscan tombs from the once mighty town of **Populonia**. Modern Populonia has a small archaeological museum (ask there about visiting the ruins of the Etruscan city and tombs, which include a so-called 'arsenal' where the Etruscans turned Elban iron into armaments, **t** 0565 29338), as well as an impressive medieval castle. **Piombino**, at the tip of this stubby peninsula, is Tuscany's Steel City, mercilessly flattened during the war, and mercilessly rebuilt afterwards. The government might close the obsolete steelworks at any time, but Piombino will at least remain the major port for Elba. Towns of interest up in the hills include **Bolgheri**, near Cecina, centre of a DOC wine area (Bolgheri is a little-known dry white wine); **Castagneto Carducci**, a pretty town where strawberries are grown; and finally **Suvereto**, a seldom-visited medieval village with an arcaded Palazzo Comunale and the 12th-century Pisan church of San Giusto.

# Elba

When the government closed the steel mills on **Elba** after the war, the national and local governments sought to make up the lost income by promoting tourism on the island. They have been singularly successful: Elba has become one of Europe's most popular holiday playgrounds, and with tourists approaching some two million every year, prosperity has returned to its 30,000 inhabitants.

Tourist Elba, however, is no glamour-puss. It is a comfortable place attracting mainly families. Germans in particular are fond of the island; they have bought up most of the southern coast, and many of them return every year. There is no single big, crowded tourist ghetto, as on some other Mediterranean islands, but plenty of quiet, small resorts all around the coast. The lives of the Elbans themselves have adjusted to the cyclical rhythms of tourist migrations. In winter the island seems empty; much of the population stays only to work during the season. Other activities do exist to supplement tourism, such as fishing and mining, but the old iron mines, after thousands of years, have finally given out. The last of them closed in 1984.

In an unspectacular way, Elba is beautiful. Pink and green predominate – pink for the granite outcrops and houses, green because the island is heavily forested. Like its neighbour Corsica, it is a chain of mountains rising out of the sea, the tallest of which are to the west, grouped around Monte Capanne (3,546ft). For a mineralogist, Elba is a holiday dream – besides iron ore, dozens of common and rare minerals are found there, everything from andalusite to zircon. For most people, however, Elba's greatest attraction is its wealth of beaches and particularly mild climate – it hardly ever rains. The coastline, all bays and peninsulas, is over 150 kilometres in length, and there are beaches everywhere, large and small, sand or pebbles. Even in the crush of August, there's plenty of Elba-room for all, and if you look carefully, you just might find a beach that's not too crowded.

## History

*Able was I ere I saw Elba*
> The Napoleonic palindrome

Elba is close enough to the Italian mainland to have been inhabited from the earliest times. When Neanderthal Man was tramping through the neighbourhood about 50,000 years ago, Elba may still have been linked to the peninsula. Later peoples, a seemingly unending parade of them, colonized the island after 3000 BC, drawn by Elba's treasure hoard of metals. In the Copper Age they mined its copper; in the Bronze Age they alloyed the copper into bronze. The copper gave out just in time for the Iron Age, and Elba, conveniently, had vast deposits of this as well. Competition was fierce: Etruscans and Greeks fought over the island and established colonies of miners, but neither left any permanent settlements.

For Rome, which was expanding across the Italian peninsula in the 4th century BC, Elba was seen as an important prize. After its conquest at the end of the century, the Romans founded towns to consolidate their hold; thenceforth, whenever the

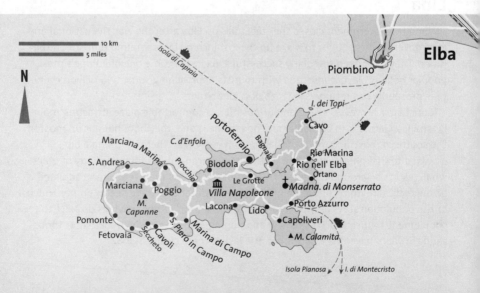

## Getting There and Around

You'll never have to wait long for a **ferry** to Elba, especially during the summer. Apart from the scant services from Livorno (*see* p.332), gritty Piombino is the point of departure. Any train going down the Tyrrhenian coast will take you as far as the station called Campiglia Marittima; from there the FS operates a regular shuttle train to Piombino (don't get off at the central station; the train has a short stop there and continues to the port). Three companies run services to Elba: TOREMAR (head office: Via Porto Mediceo, Livorno, **t** 0586 896 113; on Elba, Banchina dei Voltoni 4, Rio Marina, **t** 0565 962 073; Banchina IV Novembre 19 Porto Azzurro, **t** 0565 95004; Moby Lines (head office: Piazzale Premuda 13, Piombino, **t** 0565 221 212).

The most frequent passage is the 1-hour Piombino–Cavo–Portoferraio trip, and there are also TOREMAR hydrofoils that go from Piombino to Rio Marina and then to Porto Azzurro (2hrs). Services to Elba can be as frequent as every half-hour in July, down to two or three a day in winter. TOREMAR also has a daily Livorno–Portoferraio run (5hrs) by way of Gorgona and Capraia in the summer. To keep up with demand in the summer, Elba Ferries runs hydrofoils from Piombino to Portoferraio; these only take 25 minutes, but are more expensive.

Elba has just room enough for an **airport** (**t** 0565 976011), and there are plenty of flights in the summer – all to Germany, Switzerland and Austria, except for some infrequent services to Pisa, Florence and Milan.

Elba has an efficient **bus** service to every corner of the island, and buses depart with some frequency. Portoferraio is the hub of the system, with buses leaving and returning to the terminal by the Grattacielo, facing the harbour.

There are plenty of **car hire** agencies on the island, in all the principal towns; you can hire scooters and bicycles everywhere too (and the tourist office hands out itineraries for bike and mountain bike trips around the island.

## Tourist Information

**Elba**: Calata Italia 35, Portoferraio, across from the ferry dock, **t** 0565 914 671, **f** 0565 914 672, *www.aptlba.it. Open May–Sept 8am–8pm; Oct 8am–7.30pm.*

## Where to Stay

### Elba ✉ 57037

With more than 150 hotels around the island, Elba has something for everyone. The emphasis is on the not-too-expensive resort, attractive to family holiday-makers. Many hotels stay open all year, with substantial off-season discounts. Beware, however: Elba is a big package-tour destination, and despite its scores of lodgings, you'll need to book ahead to avoid disappointment.

**\*\*L'Ape Elbana**, Salità de' Medici 2, **t/f** 0565 914 245 (*moderate*). In Portoferraio, one interesting possibility is the 'Elban Bee', the oldest hotel on the island; it entertained Napoleon's guests. Half-board only in August.

**\*\*\*\*Villa Ottone**, at Ottone, **t** 0565 933 042 (*very expensive*). A little more up to date, in a 19th-century villa on the beach, with a shady garden and tennis court. *Open all year.*

**\*\*\*Villa Ombrosa**, Viale de Gasperi 3, **t** 0565 914 363 (*moderate*). Quite pleasant; one of several near Le Ghiaie beach and the park.

The resorts begin where Portoferraio's suburbs end. Some areas within a few kilometres offer good value in lovely settings.

**\*\*\*Mare**, at Magazzini, **t** 0565 933 069, **f** 0565 933 408 (*moderate*).

**\*\*Tirrena**, also at Magazzini, **t** 0565 933 002, **f** 0565 933 452 (*moderate*).

Roman legions ran their swords through Teutons, Persians, Gauls, Carthaginians or each other, they usually did it using Elban iron. The mines and forges, then as now, were concentrated on the eastern third of the island; anything else that was left became a holiday spot for the wealthy, as demonstrated by the remains of large villas discovered near Portoferraio.

At Cavo, on the east coast, prices tend to be slightly lower, and as Porto Azzurro can be crowded, there are plenty of campsites and holiday apartments there. The same is true of most beaches on the southeastern peninsula around Capoliveri.

**\*\*La Voce del Mare**, Naregno beach, t 0565 968 455 (*moderate*). One of many pleasant hotels right on the beach.

The best beach on Elba may be at Cavoli, west of Campo nell'Elba.

**\*\*La Conchiglia**, Cavoli, t 0565 987 010 (*moderate*). Small and air-conditioned.

Among the resorts to the west, there are some smart places near Prócchio, more modest hotels at Sant'Andrea and Pomonte, and a few that are blissfully out of the way. **\*\*Andreina**, at La Cala, t 0565 908 150 (*cheap*). One of the latter; west of Marciana Marina.

# Eating Out

In the long list of restaurants on the island, there are few that really stand out. What does stand out are Elba's DOC wines; both *Elba rosso* and *Elba bianco* can hold their own with any in Tuscany.

## Piombino (mainland) ✉ 57025
Ristorante Terrazza, Piazza Premuda, t 0565 226 135 (*moderate*). Somewhere to kill the hours while you wait for the ferry, above the bar in the port area, with delicious *spaghetti alle vongole* and a big picture window with a panoramic view of Piombino's steel mills.

## Portoferraio
La Ferrigna, Piazza della Repubblica 22, t 0565 914 129 (*expensive–moderate*). One of the most popular places in Portoferraio, offering some extravagant seafood *antipasti*, stuffed roast fish, and an Elban version of *Livornese cacciucco*; there are tables on the convivial piazza. *Closed Tues.*

La Barca, Via D. Guerrazzi, t 0565 918 036 (*expensive*). A good honest *trattoria* a few steps from Piazza della Repubblica, with all sorts of seafood *antipasti*, crab soup and fishy pastas galore. Friendly service.

For something really nice that doesn't cost a bomb, you'll have to go out to the suburbs. Ristorante Boris, Loc. Valdana, t 0565 940 018 (*moderate–cheap*). Not much fancy seafood beyond the *spaghetti vongole*, but the cooking is special. *Closed Tues in winter.*

## Porto Azzurro
Tavernetta, Lungomare Vitaliani 42, t 0565 95110 (*moderate*). One among many seafood restaurants on the beach in southern Elba, built over the sea for a fine view. *Closed Thurs.*

## Capoliveri
Chiasso, Via Nazario Sauro 20, t 0565 968 709 (*expensive*). Offers sole stuffed with shrimp and an Elban favourite that rarely travels to the mainland, *risotto al nero di seppia* (with cuttlefish in its own ink). *Closed Tues.*

Solemar, outside Capoliveri at Loc Lacona, t 0565 964 248 (*cheap*). A good, inexpensive *trattoria. Closed Mon in winter.*

## Póggio
Publius, Piazza XX Settembre 13, 0565 99208 (*expensive*). This place, situated 3km from Marciana, is as worth visiting for its lovely views as for its menu, with items you won't find elsewhere on the island: they serve *pappardelle* in boar sauce, *fagioli al fiasco* (traditional Tuscan beans), and game in season, as well as fish dishes. *Closed Mon.*

## Marciana Marina
Rendezvous, Piazza della Vittoria, t 0565 99251 (*expensive*). Famous for a curious dish of baked potato stuffed with seafood. *Closed Wed in winter.*

The fall of Rome brought invasions, disorder, depopulation and pirates to Elba; the Lombards in the 6th century, under the murderous Gummarith, subjugated the island with their usual bloodshed; Saracens and adventurous barons from Italy fought for the scraps. By the 11th century Pisa had assumed complete control, as the island lay across its most important trade route. It held Elba for almost 500 years, constructing fortresses at Luceri and Volterraio and exploiting the mineral resources. Then, the capital was called *Ferraia*, of which Portoferraio was only the port. Not a trace remains of the city (archaeologists are still trying to locate it).

From the 13th century on, Genoa contested Pisa's possession of the island. In the 16th century, Duke Cosimo I saw his opportunity and seized it for Florence. He built Portoferraio and the walls around it, but soon had to contend with the growing power of Spain in the western Mediterranean, and after some inconclusive skirmishes, Elba was partitioned between Tuscany and Spain. Spain built the town and fortress of Porto Azzurro as a counter to Portoferraio, an arrangement that lasted throughout the 18th century, despite French efforts to grab the island.

## Napoleon on Elba

During the Napoleonic wars, Elba was occupied for a time by the English, and Portoferraio was unsuccessfully besieged for over a year by Napoleon's troops in 1799. Napoleon finally annexed it in 1802, probably with no premonitions that the 1814 Treaty of Fontainebleau would put a temporary end to the First Empire and send him to Elba. After all these centuries, Elba suddenly found itself on the centre stage of world history.

Napoleon himself chose Elba, from the variety of small Mediterranean outposts offered him, for 'the gentleness of its climate and its inhabitants'. Also, perhaps because on clear days he could see his own island of Corsica. No one, however, seems to have consulted the Elbans themselves on the matter, and they can be excused for the cold indifference with which they received their new ruler.

On 4 May 1814, he arrived at Portoferraio with some 500 of his most loyal officers and soldiers and a British Commissioner charged with keeping an eye on him. But Napoleon soon won over the hearts of the Elbans by being the best governor they ever had. New systems of law and education were established, the last vestiges of feudalism abolished, and what would today be called economic planning was begun; he reorganized the iron mines and started work on Elba's modern network of roads.

Not that Napoleon ever really took his stewardship seriously. Remaking nations and institutions was a reflex by then, after doing it all across Europe for 20 years. It was the return to France that occupied his attention. The atmosphere was thick with intrigues and rumours, and secret communications flowed incessantly between Napoleon and his partisans on the Continent. On 20 February 1815, just nine months after his arrival, the Elbans and the embarrassed British watchdog awakened to find the emperor missing. The 'Hundred Days' had begun. Later, after Waterloo, a smaller, gloomier and more distant island would be found to keep Napoleon out of trouble.

Elba was returned to Tuscany, and soon after it joined the new Kingdom of Italy. It was hit hard by the Second World War; Portoferraio and environs were bombed in 1943–4, first by the Allies, and then by the Germans. In 1944, in one of the more disgraceful episodes of the war, Elba was 'liberated' by Free French and African troops, with more murder, pillage and rape than had been seen in the Mediterranean since the days of the pirates.

## Portoferraio

**Portoferraio**, with 11,000 souls, is the capital and only city of Elba. The massive walls built by Duke Cosimo remain, though Portoferraio has spilled out westwards along the bay. Here the ferries dock at the Calata Italia, where the visitor's introduction to Elba is the **Grattacielo** ('skyscraper'), a 10-storey pile of peeling paint built in the 1950s that is one of the most endearingly hideous buildings in the Mediterranean. It is also the most important building for tourists, since it contains the tourist information office, most of the ferry offices, and the Portoferraio bus terminal at the back, with connections to all Elba's towns and resorts.

Follow Calata Italia and its various pseudonyms under the walls, next to the old U-shaped harbour. On the far side rises the **Torre del Martello**, from which in the old days a chain was stretched across the harbour in times of danger. The main gate of the city is the **Porta a Mare** at the base of the U, over which can be seen the inscription of Duke Cosimo reminding us with the usual Medicean vanity how he built the whole town 'from the foundations upwards'; the new town had originally been dubbed Cosmopolis.

Directly inside the Porta a Mare is **Piazza Cavour**. Portoferraio is a big natural amphitheatre; from the piazza the town slopes upwards in all directions towards the walls on the high cliffs. North of the piazza, Via Garibaldi leads up to the main attraction, Napoleon's house, the **Villa dei Mulini** (*open Mon–Sat 9–7, Sun 9–1, in summer until 11.30 on Sat; joint adm with the Villa di San Martino*), yellowing, unloved, unchanged since Napoleon had it built according to his own simple tastes; inside you can see his furnishings, books and other paraphernalia, including the flag with three golden bees that he bestowed on the Elbans. It's well worth the trip if only to see the contemporary political cartoons mocking the emperor. The gardens are equally uncared for although they do offer fine views over the city walls. On either side you can see the two Medici fortresses dominating the highest points in the city: **Forte Falcone** to the west (*open daily Easter–Sept 9–6; July and Aug until midnight; adm*), which you can visit, and **Forte Stella** to the east, now used as housing.

On the way down Via Garibaldi, you may want to stop at one of the parish churches, the **Misericordia** (*open by appt only; t 0565 914 009*) or the **Holy Sacrament**, both of which have copies of Napoleon's death mask; on 5 May the Misericordia holds a procession to commemorate Napoleon's death, complete with a replica of his coffin. The **Town Hall**, which was originally a bakery for Cosimo's troops, was the boyhood home of Victor Hugo, whose father was the French military commander in Elba. There's a Roman altar displayed in the courtyard; inside, the **Biblioteca Foresiana** (*open Easter–June Mon–Fri 10–12, Tues and Thurs 3–7; adm*) has a collection of books about Elba and a small picture collection.

Two blocks west is the tiny but surprisingly grand **Teatro dei Vigilanti**, rebuilt by Napoleon from an abandoned church, while east of Via Garibaldi lies the **Piazza della Repubblica**, the throbbing heart of Portoferraio, with its crowded cafés, 18th-century **cathedral**, not really a cathedral at all these days, and the nearby market. Outside the walls, on the eastern side of the port, an old salt warehouse has been converted into the new **Museo Civico Archeologico** (*same hours as Biblioteca Foresiana; adm*), with items from the Roman patrician villas, one of which was discovered on this site.

## Around Portoferraio

Most of Portoferraio's hotels and restaurants are in the modern extension outside the city walls. There's a pebble beach, **Le Ghiaie**, on the north side, and another called **Le Viste** under the walls near Forte Falcone. One of the two roads from the capital leads along the northern coast to the small resorts of **Acquaviva** and **Viticcio**, and to **Capo d'Enfola**, a lovely headland rising sheer out of the sea, barely connected to the rest of the island.

The second road runs south to the junction of **Bivio Boni**, where it branches to the east and west. Nearby is a thermal spa at **San Giovanni**, and the ruins of a Roman villa at **Le Grotte**, on the south shore of the Gulf of Portoferraio, more interesting for its view than its scant remains. There are beaches here at Ottone, Magazzini and **Bagnaia**, the latter the site of the simple, beautiful 12th-century **church of Santo Stefano**, the best Pisan monument in the archipelago. At **Acquabona** you can shoot some bogeys at one of Elba's two golf courses (nine holes), or continue west from Bivio Boni to the resort at **Biodola Bay** and the **Villa Napoleone di San Martino** (*same hours as Villa dei Mulini in Portoferraio; joint adm*). The emperor soon tired of life in Portoferraio and built this house as his country retreat. In later years the husband of his niece (daughter of Jérome) purchased the place and added a pretentious neo-classical façade with big Ns pasted everywhere; it's now another Napoleonic museum, with a little art gallery including a *Galatea* by Canova.

## Eastern Elba

**Rio nell'Elba** is the old mining centre, though it's not at all what one would expect a mining town to look like – it's as pleasant and pastel as any other Elban town, set in the hills overlooking the eastern coast. Archaeological sites, the scanty remains of mines and Etruscan mining camps dot the neighbourhood. There are many undeveloped beaches on the western side of Rio's peninsula, including Nisporto and Nisportino. The road between Portoferraio and Rio passes the steep hill of **Volterraio**, where you can make the long climb to the 11th-century Pisan castle perched on the summit. **Rio Marina**, as its name implies, is the port for Rio nell'Elba. Here, the **Mineralogical Museum** (*open April–15 Oct Mon–Sat 9–1 and 3–6, Sun 9–12; adm*) in the Palazzo Comunale has displays of the island's unusual rocks and minerals – few places on earth have such a variety. Devoted rock hounds will continue on to the **Parco Minerario** (*closed; call* **t** *0565 962 009 for information*) in an old mine. Rio Marina has a busy harbour, its many small fishing boats under the vigilant eye of an octagonal Pisan watchtower. The eastern side of this peninsula, like the western side, has some fine beaches where you can sometimes escape the crowds – Ortano, Porticciolo, Barbarossa among others. On the northern tip stands **Cavo**, an older resort town on a tiny port.

## Porto Azzurro and Capoliveri

South of Rio, the road passes through some difficult terrain towards **Porto Azzurro**, built by the Spaniards and now a large holiday town. Until 1947 it was called *Porto Longone*. The fortress, built in 1603 to withstand the Austrians and French, was later converted into a famous Italian calaboose that hosted many political prisoners and criminal celebrities.

Besides the town beach, there are several others nearby, including a bizarre one at **Terrenere**, where a yellow-green sulphurous pond festers near the blue sea in a landscape of pebble beach and ancient mine debris – for those jaded travellers seeking something beyond Elba's mass tourism. During the season, day excursions run from Porto Azzurro to the island of Montecristo.

Just north of Porto Azzurro is the **Sanctuary of Monserrato**, a famous shrine with an icon known as the 'Black Madonna'. The Spanish governor built this here in 1606 because the mountain (Monte Castello) reminded him of the peculiar mountain of Monserrat near Barcelona. Similar Black Madonnas are revered from Portugal to Poland; over the centuries the oxidization of yellow paint has darkened them (just as it threatens Van Gogh's *Sunflowers*). South of Porto Azzurro is another Spanish fortress at **Capo Focardo**, on a large oval-shaped peninsula consisting of Monte Calamita and the rough hill country around it.

On this peninsula is **Capoliveri**, one of the oldest inhabited sites on the island. The town takes its name from the Roman *Caput Liberi*, which may refer either to the worship of Liber, an Italian equivalent of Dionysus (this has always been a winegrowing area) or to the free men (*liberi*) who lived there. In Roman times Capoliveri was an 'Alsatia', a refuge for any man who could escape to it. It has had a reputation for independence ever since, giving a bad time to the Pisans, the Spanish, and even Napoleon. Today it is a peaceful place, with fine views from its hill top over the surrounding countryside and sea. Although very scenic and laced with beaches, much of its coast is privately owned. South of Capoliveri, near the coast, is the **Sanctuary of the Madonna delle Grazie**, with a painting of the Madonna and Child by the school of Raphael, miraculously saved from a shipwreck. The coast west of Capoliveri is marked by two lovely broad gulfs, **Golfo Stella** and **Golfo di Lacona**, separated by a steep, narrow tongue of land. Both are developed resort areas, with centres at Lacona and Lido Margidore.

## Western Elba

Beyond Biodola, the scenic corniche road west from Portoferraio passes through the adjacent resorts of **Prócchio** and **Campo all'Aia**; the former is larger and one of the more expensive resorts on Elba. Seven kilometres west is **Marciana Marina**, another popular resort, with a 15th-century Pisan watchtower, the **Torre Saracena**. This is the port for **Marciana**, the oldest continuously inhabited town on Elba.

In the 14th and 15th centuries, when life near the coast wasn't safe, Marciana was the 'capital' of the feudal Appiani barons, the most powerful family on the island. Today, high in the forests on the slopes of Monte Capanne, it is surprisingly beautiful, characterized by narrow streets, stone stairs, archways and belvederes. Sections of the old city wall and gate are still intact, and the old Pisan **fortress** hangs over the town (*open June–Aug 'for a couple of hours' in morning and afternoon; t 0565 901 215*). The palace of the Appiani may be seen on a narrow *vicolo* in the oldest part of town. Marciana's **Archaeology Museum** (*closed for restoration*) has a small collection of prehistoric and Roman objects found in the area. In season, a cable lift (*departs daily April–Oct at 10, 12.15, 2.45 and 5.15; fare exp*) climbs to the summit of Elba's highest peak, 3,342ft **Monte Capanne**, with stupendous views over Corsica, the Tuscan archipelago and the mountains of Tuscany itself.

Three churches outside Marciana are of interest: the ruined Pisan **San Lorenzo**, the **Sanctuary of San Cerbone**, who escaped here from the troublesome Lombards (later his body was buried in a rainstorm, so they wouldn't see), and the **Sanctuary of the Madonna del Monte**, dating from the 11th century and one of the island's most important shrines, with a Madonna painted on a lump of granite. Pagan Elbans may have worshipped on this site as well, as did Napoleon for two weeks, after a fashion, with his Polish mistress, Maria Walewska. Another mountain village is **Póggio**, just to the east, with a natural spring where the Elbans bottle their *acqua minerale* – called Napoleone, of course. It's very good, but the Elbans keep it all to themselves.

On the rugged coast to the west and south of Marciana, there are yet more beaches and resorts: **Sant'Andrea**, **Patresi**, **Chiessi**, **Pomonte**, **Fetovaia** (a lovely stretch, protected by a rocky promontory), **Seccheto** and **Cavoli**. Seccheto has ancient granite quarries from which the stone was cut for the Pantheon in Rome.

Seven kilometres east of Marciana stretches Elba's pocket-sized plain, the **Campo nell'Elba**, extending from Prócchio to Marina di Campo, separating the western mountains from the central range. Elba's airport is here – the only place they could put it. Two old towns lie on the edge of the plain: **Sant'Ilario in Campo** and **San Piero in Campo**. San Piero's parish church of San Niccolò has interesting frescoes; it was built on the ruins of an ancient temple to Glaucus. Halfway between the towns are the ruins of the Pisan church of **San Giovanni**, along with a watchtower (*closed; may be viewed from outside*). On the coast is **Marina di Campo**, Elba's first, perhaps largest resort, with the largest beach. The harbour watchtower was built by the Medici.

# Pianosa and Montecristo

Two other members of the Tuscan archipelago are included in Livorno province: one you won't want to visit, and the other you usually can't. **Pianosa** is the black sheep of the chain. Its name, taken from the Roman *Planasia*, explains why – it's as flat as a pool table. Like Gorgona, Pianosa's unhappy fate is to serve as a prison island. There are some substantial ruins of a Roman villa, from the days when Pianosa was the playground of Cornelius Agrippa, Emperor Augustus' great general, but to see them you'll need special permission from the prison authorities in Rome.

Likewise, don't count on visiting **Montecristo**, 40 kilometres south of Elba. Once the hunting preserve of King Vittorio Emanuele III, the tiny island, in fact the tip of an ancient volcano, has now been declared a nature reserve. Private boats and day trips organized from Porto Azzurro on Elba may dock at Cala Maestra, but visitors are only allowed to stay on the cove and its beach; the mountain, ruins of a medieval monastery and royal villa (now the custodian's house) are out of bounds. In Roman times this was an important religious site, *Mons Jovis*, with a famous temple of Jupiter; not a trace remains. The early Church wasted no time Christianizing the place, renaming it Montecristo. The first monastic community was founded in the 6th century by San Mamiliano (*see* p.357), who reportedly killed a dragon upon arrival. None of the *The Count of Monte Cristo* is really set here; like the Count himself, seeing the place on a map is probably as close as Alexandre Dumas ever got.

# South of Piombino: The Coast and Offshore

## The Maremma

In a sense, this flat, lonely stretch of coast really belongs to Italy's south. As on the islands, history has been unkind to the Maremma, domain first of the Etruscans, later of the anopheles mosquito. Like many southern coastal regions, the Maremma was a prosperous agricultural region until Roman times. The Romans gave it its name: the 'maritime' zone (as recalled in town names such as Massa Marittima), gradually mangled into Maremma.

Historians sometimes give the Romans too much credit for capable governance; on the contrary, their grasping, bureaucratic state slowly corroded and eventually destroyed the Italian economy. Many centuries of Roman misgovernment – impossible taxes, cheap imported grain and especially, in this case, neglect of the Etruscans' system of drainage canals – doomed the Maremma to a slow death. When the drainage canals failed, much of the land was abandoned and reverted to swamps, breeding the malarial mosquitoes that made the Maremma of the Middle Ages a place of suffering and death, inhabitable only by the *butteri*, tough Tuscan cowboys that tended the herds in the abandoned marshy pastures. A considerable body of folklore has grown up around the *butteri*, and the Maremma's proudest moment came in the last century when some of them went to Rome and defeated Buffalo Bill and his travelling Wild West show in a test of cowboy know-how. The first work of reclamation began with the Austrian Grand Dukes. The Italian Kingdom that followed them forgot all about the Maremma, and it was not until after the Second World War that the task was completed. The Maremma today is back on its feet, a new region and a little rough around the edges, but prosperous once more.

### Follonica and Punta Ala

After Piombino, the coast bends eastwards into a broad arc, the Golfo di Follonica. Since the war, new resort towns have been popping up like toadstools all along the Tuscan coast. One of the biggest and least likeable is **Follonica**, 21 kilometres east of Piombino, partially redeemed by the long pine groves that follow its crowded

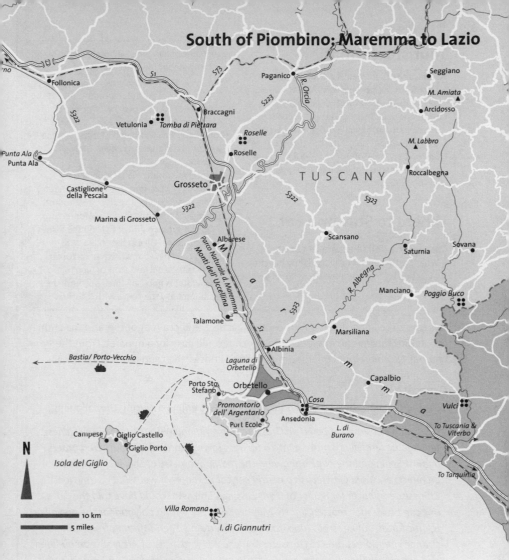

Follonica

Paganico

Seggiano

M. Amiata

Arcidosso

Braccagni

Vetulonia • Tomba di Pietrara

Roselle

M. Labbro

Punta Ala
Punta Ala

Castiglione
della Pescaia

Roselle

Roccalbegna

Grosseto

TUSCANY

Marina di Grosseto

Albarese

Scansano

Sovana

Saturnia

Parco Naturale d. Maremma
Monti dell' Uccellina

Talamone

Manciano

Poggio Buco

Bastia/ Porto-Vecchio

Marsiliana

Albinia

Laguna di
Orbetello

Capalbio

Porto Sto.
Stefano

Orbetello

Cosa

Vulci

Promontorio
dell' Argentario

Ansedonia

Port Ecole

Campese

Giglio Castello

Giglio Porto

L. di
Burano

To Tuscania &
Viterbo

Isola del Giglio

N

To Tarquinia

Villa Romana

10 km

5 miles

I. di Giannutri

beaches. Forget the beaches; Follonica has other enchantments, notably the **Museum of Iron and Cast Iron** (*open winter Tues–Sat am on request and 4–6; summer Tues–Sat 10–1 and 4–6; t 0566 40762*), in an old foundry of the 1830s where Elban iron was once smelted. On the promontory that closes the gulf, 14 kilometres to the south, **Punta Ala** is a new, entirely synthetic resort, built in the suburban style of the Costa Smeralda. It's an attractive location, with a fine sandy beach and views around the gulf, and it attracts a very well-heeled clientele with unusual (for Tuscany) diversions like golf (*at the Golf Hotel, Via del Gualdo*) and polo (*Polo Club*).

**Castiglione della Pescaia**, to the south, is just the opposite: much less exclusive, attached to an attractive, ancient fishing village. The beach isn't great, but the town on its hill, with trees and ivy-covered walls, is one of the more pleasant detours on

## Tourist Information

**Follonica**: Via Giacomelli II, t 0566 52012, f 0566 53833. *Open mid-July–Aug Mon–Sat 9–1 and 4.30–8, Sun and hols 10–12.*
**Castiglione della Pescaia**: Piazza Garibaldi 6, on the harbour, t 0564 933 678, f 0564 933 954, *www.provincia.grosseto.it/turismo. Open Easter–Oct Mon–Sat 9–1 and 4–8 Sun 10–1; Nov–Easter Mon–Sat 9–1 and 3.30–7.30, Sun 10–1.*

## Where to Stay and Eat

**Castiglione della Pescaia** ✉ 58043
What Castiglione lacks in appealing beaches, it makes up for in accommodation; it has a

wide range of inexpensive hotels, something of a rarity along this coastline.

★★**Rossella**, Via Fratelli Bandiera 18, t 0564 933 832 (*moderate*). At the reasonable end of the range and near the beaches. *Open late Mar–late Oct.*

★**Bologna**, Piazza Garibaldi 8, t 0564 933 746 (*cheap*). Basic and truly cheap, on the harbour.

★★★**Hotel Miramare**, Via Vittorio Veneto 27, t 0564 933 524 *miramare@tin.it* (*moderate*). Home to an excellent seafood restaurant. The dish to try is the *tesoro di Montecristo*, a delicious mixed grill of fish. All the dishes are innovative – like crêpes filled with prawns and baked *spaghetti al cartoccio*.
**La Fortezza**, Via del Recinto, t 0564 936 100 (*moderate*). A good, distinctively furnished restaurant; try the pasta with lobster.

this coast. The Spanish left a 16th-century castle, the Rocca Aragonese, and the church of San Giovanni has an interesting tower that could pass for a minaret. From the harbour, *Navimaremma* offers summer island cruises; the tourist office has details.

### Grosseto

For the original edition of this book, years ago, we enjoyed writing the following:

*When Duke Cosimo I gobbled up Grosseto in 1559, along with the rest of the Sienese republic, he resolved to make it into a fortress town, guarding his southern borders against Spain and the pope. Following the manic geometry of the age, Cosimo's architects enclosed Grosseto in a nearly perfect hexagon of walls. But as any good Chinese geomancer (or reader of Doris Lessing's* Shikasta*) could have told the Duke, one can't take such matters lightly. Maybe it was the wrong polygon for the prevailing telluric forces, but Grosseto (pop. 70,000) has certainly been suffering from some strange vibrations. Come to Grosseto, and you will find a city of Art Nouveau buildings and perverse teenagers, a city conducive to hallucinations, its streets alive with swirls of dust and flying plastic bags. Its citizens have a penchant for punk music and American football (the Grosseto 61ers), also, so they claim, the highest rate of drug addiction in Italy. It is the only city in Italy, outside Calabria, where you cannot buy a decent slice of pizza.*

God knows where the flying bags, the hallucinations and the 61ers have gone, and today the teenagers look no more perverse than anywhere else in Europe. Under the prevailing prosperity, the natural Tuscan sense of order and propriety has slowly been asserting itself here. Instead of punk music, there is a busy *assessorato della cultura* in the town hall laying on dance and chamber music concerts and scholarly conferences. Italy's Most Improved Town, always a likeable place, grows steadily more normal, even pleasant – though the *pizza a taglio* situation still needs some work.

## Around La Vasca

Via Carducci leads towards the fearful hexagon, passing Mussolini's contribution to the city, the circular Piazza Fratelli Rosselli that is really known to one and all as **La Vasca** (which can mean 'tub' or 'toilet bowl'); here the starring role is played by an exuberant Mussolini **post office**, with heroic statuary in travertine. The main gate is only a block away. Cosimo's walls are perfectly preserved, done in reddish brick festooned with Medici balls. Much of the old city looks very Spanish; the Art Nouveau pharmacies and shoe shops along the main street, Corso Carducci, contribute to the effect, as does the arcaded Piazza del Duomo, very like a Spanish *Plaza Mayor*. The **Duomo**, built 1190–1250, suffered from over-ambitious restoration in the 1840s; the façade looks more like a Hollywood prop than a cathedral. Have a look inside for Matteo di Giovanni's *Madonna delle Grazie* (1470). Around the side of the Duomo there is an interesting sundial, and in the piazza an allegorical monument to the Maremma's benefactor, the Lorraine Grand Duke Leopold II; the woman he is raising up represents the suffering Maremma, and the snake he's crushing is Malaria.

# Getting Around

**Trains** depart regularly for Siena, and travel via Roccastrada and Buonconvento (seven a day, some of which continue on to Florence), and on the coastal line for Livorno, or Orbetello and Rome. RAMA **buses** (t 0564 25215) have connections to Siena (nine a day) and every town in Grosseto province, including Massa Marittima (twice daily, *see* **Hill Towns West of Siena**, p.389), Arcidosso and Pitigliano (five daily, *see* **Southern Tuscany**, pp.414 and 418). A new bus station is under construction; until then, everything leaves from the train station.

# Tourist Information

**Grosseto**: Via Fucini 43c, t 0564 414 303, f 0564 454 606, *www.grosseto.turismo.toscana.it*, near the station. *Open Oct–April Mon–Fri 9–1 and 3.30–5.30, Sat 9–12; May–Sept Mon–Fri 9–1 and 4–6, Sat 9–12.*

# Where to Stay and Eat

**Grosseto** ✉ 58100

In the unlikely event that you can't find anywhere, the city's *Consorzio Albergatori* might be able to help: t 0564 415 446. Hotels here tend to be simple.

★★★★**Bastiani Grand Hotel**, Via Gioberti 64, t 0564 20047, f 0564 29321 (*luxury*). One exception to the rule is this city-centre hotel, housed in a gracious 1890s palazzo.

★★★**Leon d'Oro**, Via San Martino 46, t 0564 22128, f 0564 22578 (*moderate*). Offers double rooms with and without bath, and the restaurant's not bad either. *Closed Sun.*

★**Appennino**, Viale Mameli 1, t 0564 23009, f 0564 416 134 (*cheap*). Plain and well kept.

**Ristorante Claudio**, Via Manetti 1, t 0564 25142 (*moderate*). A new restaurant in an old setting, dug into the Medicean walls; they're already attracting attention for their pasta dishes and seafood. *Closed Sun.*

**Italiana**, Via P. Manescalchi 5, t 0564 22452 (*moderate*). Serving good, simple pasta and fish dishes.

**Danubo Blu**, Via Cavour (*cheap*). If you fancy a change from the norm, this is refreshingly eccentric, also inside the walls, with a menu including everything from goulash to paella. The town is full of English-style pubs, which are very popular with Grosseto's youth.

**Tredici Gobbi**, Via Mazzini 106. The best of the bunch, with large, wood-panelled rooms over two floors and a welcoming open fire. *Closed Tues.*

**La Taverna Etrusca**, Vetulonia (*cheap*). If you're going up to visit Vetulonia, try this good inexpensive *trattoria* at the top of town; it also has some reasonably priced rooms.

Around the corner in Piazza Baccarini, the **Archaeology Museum of the Maremma** (*recently reopened after restoration; t 0564 417 629 for new opening hours and info; closed Mon*) wants to show you something of life in this region before there ever was a Grosseto. Some parts of the this coastline just can't stand still. Thousands of years ago, Grosseto and most of its surrounding plain were under water; by the time of the Etruscans, the sea had receded, leaving a large lake on the plain. Two wealthy Etruscan cities, *Vetulonia* and *Roselle* (*see* below), stood on the hills above the lake, and they contributed most of the items here: cinerary urns with scenes from Homer, architectural fragments, and delicate terracottas, some preserving bits of their original paint. The collection is not a rich one, though well organized and relentlessly didactic. Up on the third floor, the city **Pinacoteca** has been closed for restoration for the last seven years. It houses some good Sienese art, including an amazing, very Byzantine *Last Judgement* by the 13th-century artist Guido da Siena.

Just north of the museum, San Francesco church has an early work of Duccio di Buoninsegna, the crucifix above the high altar, and some good 13th-century frescoes with haunting eyes. From here, you can start a walk around the Medicean walls. After Italian unification, the bastions were landscaped into beautiful semi-tropical gardens; some are still well kept, while others have decayed into spooky jungles. The liveliest parts of Grosseto are the shopping streets around Piazza del Mercato; near-by, just outside the walls, mornings see a large, almost picturesque street market.

## Roselle and Vetulonia

In fact, you can learn much more about these two Etruscan towns from the Grosseto museum than from actually visiting the ruins, although this can be fun. **Roselle**, seven kilometres north of the city, just off the main road to Siena, is the mother city of Grosseto. It survived Roman rule better than many other Etruscan cities, but writers of the 5th century report it being almost abandoned. Nevertheless, the bishops of Roselle hung on until 1178, when the seat was transferred to Grosseto.

Like so many other Etruscan towns, Roselle stands atop a high plateau and is surrounded by over three kilometres of walls. An ancient Roman road leads up to the complex where there are the foundations of a few buildings, remains of the baths, the imperial forum and the outline of the Roman amphitheatre, a medieval tower, and necropolises all around. To the north of the site are the ruins of a Roman villa (*open Nov–Feb daily 9–5.30; Mar–April daily 9–6.30; May–Aug daily 9–7.30; Sept–Oct daily 9–6.30; for guided tours call t 0564 402 403*) retaining parts of its original mosaic floor paving. Here, the archaeologists discovered that the last occupant was operating a forge to melt down bronze statues.

**Vetulonia**, 17 kilometres from Grosseto, above the Via Aurelia west of Braccagni, lives on in its worthy successor, Massa Marittima (*see* pp.411–3). On the site itself, a miniature hill town survives, set in rugged but lovely countryside with occasional views over the Tyrrhenian and the islands. Like Roselle, it lasted until the Middle Ages, and was probably destroyed in a 14th-century revolt against its Pisan overlords.

Bits of old Vetulonia can be seen in the **Aree Archeologiche** (signposted) and the nearby **museum** (*open daily 9–5, until 7.30 in summer; joint adm for both*). The scanty ruins are more Roman and medieval than Etruscan, but on the periphery are some interesting tombs (also signed): the massive **Tomba della Pietrera** and the unique **Il Diavolino** (7th century BC). Both of these consist of a long corridor leading under a tumulus, with an arched burial chamber in the centre; the Diavolino has an window to the sky.

## Monti dell'Uccellina: The Maremma Nature Park

*The visitors' centre is at Alberese, west of the coastal Via Aurelia/SS1; park open all year, but some sections can only be visited by guided tour; admissions limited daily; during busiest times – Easter, 29 April to 1 May, July and August – it's best to call ahead, t 0564 407 098; ask about guided tours in English during the summer; open daily from 8 until one hour before sunset; adm.*

One side effect of the Maremma's history of abandonment is a beautiful and unspoiled coastline. In the 1950s and 1960s developers followed the DDT wherever they could, but the government managed to set aside a few of the best parts. The **Monti dell'Uccellina**, a ragged chain of hills south of Grosseto, largely covered with umbrella pines, is a pit stop for migratory birds between Europe and Africa, hence the name.

The park has some pretty strict rules. Only 500 people a day, and no cars and no dogs, are allowed to enter. Nine walks have been laid out, lasting 2–6 hours, and visitors are expected to keep to them. Note that one of the walks begins from a separate park entrance at Talamone, further south, but it doesn't connect to the others. The visitors' centre recommends you bring good shoes and some water, and if you like they can book you an experienced guide for about €10 an hour.

For such a small area (*c.* 5x15km), the park has a lot to see: nine old defence towers, dozens of caves and the ruins of an 11th-century monastery, **San Rabano**, that belonged to the Knights of Malta. It retains its campanile and some early medieval stone-carving. Despite the park status, some people still make their living here, herding cattle, cutting cork oak, and gathering pine nuts for Italy's pastry cooks.

The park's landscape ranges from swamps to heather and scented *macchia* (mixed Mediterranean scrub) to pine groves, and includes among its fauna wild horses, deer and boar, along with the *uccellini* themselves – herons, eagles and falcons, ospreys and kingfishers, every sort of duck, and that most overdressed of all waterfowl, the *cavaliere d'Italia*. Some peripheral areas can be toured on horseback, and Il Rialto, t 0564 407 102, can fix you up with a steed; they also rent bikes and canoes.

### Talamone

The Sienese Republic never really had a port, gravely hampering its foreign trade. Now and then, it tried to make one out of **Talamone**, a fishing village at the tip of the Monti dell'Uccellina. Unfortunately, the little harbour couldn't be kept clear; even Dante dropped a jibe about foolishly 'hoping from Talamone'. Garibaldi had better luck: when in 1860 he and his 'Thousand' chose to stop here rather than Sardinia, they avoided the orders for their arrest that had been sent by the treacherous Count Cavour; Garibaldi also found a cache of weapons in Orbetello, which came in handy during the conquest of Sicily. Today the walled village on its rock has become a laid-back resort with a small marina. Above, a 16th-century Spanish castle sits like an abstract modern sculpture, set to house a museum devoted to nature in the area.

# Monte Argentario

In the last decade or so, this curiosity of the Tuscan coast has grown popular. It has much going for it: some attractive old towns, a genuine Mediterranean feeling and matching scenery, a noticeable attraction on the humdrum Tuscan coast. Once, long ago, Argentario was an island, the member of the Tuscan archipelago closest to the shore. No one seems able to explain how it happened, but the Tyrrhenian currents gradually built up two symmetrical sand bars, connecting the rugged, mountainous island to the mainland. In between, there was a peninsula with the Etruscan, then Roman city of Orbetello; the Romans built a causeway on to Argentario that split the natural lagoon in half. It is said that sailors named the Argentario in classical times, noticing the bright flashes of silver from the olive trees that still cover its slopes.

## Getting Around

Orbetello is the centre for public transport around the Argentario, with a bus station facing the northern lagoon, just off Piazza della Repubblica; **buses** leave regularly for Porto Ercole, Porto S. Stefano, Grosseto, and for the **railway station**, about 2km east of town, a stop on the Grosseto–Rome coastal line. There are also daily buses to Capalbio and Pitigliano.

## Tourist Information

**Orbetello**: Piazza della Repubblica 1, t/f 0564 860 447, *proorbet@ooverture.it. Open July–Aug Mon–Sun 10–12.30 and 4.30–8.30; Sept–June Mon–Sun 9–12.30 and 4–7.*
**Porto Santo Stefano**: Corso Umberto 55, t 0564 814 208, f 0564 814 052, *infs.stefano@gros-seto.turismo.toscana.it. Open mid-Nov–Easter Mon–Sat 9–1; Easter–mid-Nov Mon–Sat 9–1 and 4–6, Sun 9–1.*
**Capalbio**: Via Collacchioni 2, t 0564 896 611, f 0564 896 644, *capalbio@ouverture.it. Open 15 June–15 Oct 9–1 and 5.30–11.30.*

## Where to Stay and Eat

**Orbetello** ✉ 58035
*****Piccolo Parigi**,Corso Italia 169, t 0564 867 233 (*cheap*). Delightful, very friendly and very Mediterranean, in the middle of town, ideal if you're travelling on a budget and just want to pass through for a look at the Argentario.
******Verdeluna**, Via Banti just off the Corso, t 0564 860 410 (*moderate*). Newly opened and completely modern.
*****La Perla**, Via Volontari del Sangue 10, t 0564 863 546 (*cheap*). Another good, inexpensive choice.
**Osteria del Lupacante**, Corso Italia 103, t 0564 867 618 (*moderate*). Wonderful fresh seafood, from octopus and potato salad to spaghetti with sea urchin or courgette flowers stuffed with baby squid. *Closed Tues in winter.*

**Porto Ercole** ✉ 58018
********Il Pellicano**, Cala dei Santi, a cove near Porto Ercole, t 0564 858 111, f 0564 833 418, *www.pellicanohotel.com* (*luxury*). If you've bushels of money and like swilling gin with yachtsmen and Italian TV stars, this Relais et Châteaux hotel provides every imaginable

Most books that mention the Argentario describe Porto Santo Stefano and Porto Ercole as 'exclusive', even 'posh'. Not true. The Argentario attracts its share of the high life, but it's not necessarily pricier than other resorts. Nor has the peninsula become an overcrowded beach Babylon like Elba. The beaches are not special, and Tuscany's art and other attractions are far away, but on balance, if you're after the best place for a seaside holiday in the region, the Argentario presents a strong case.

## Orbetello

Go to the northern tip of **Orbetello**'s peninsula, near the causeway, and look over the water; below the modern breakwater, you can see bits of ancient wall in huge irregular blocks. These are the sole remnants of Etruscan Orbetello, probably the biggest port on the Etruscan coast, and defensible enough to give the city a minor historical role over the centuries. The Byzantines held out longer here than anywhere else on this coast; the city then fell into the hands of the Three Fountains Abbey in Rome, who handed it to the Pope – until 1980 the pope was also bishop of Orbetello. After the treaty of Câteau-Cambrésis in 1559, Orbetello became capital of a new province – the Spanish military *Presidio*, from which imperialist Spain could menace both Tuscany and the Pope, ruled by a viceroy directly responsible to the King.

amenity. There's a beach, a pool, windsurfing and every other watersport, as well as tennis – not to mention a first-class restaurant.
**★★★★Torre di Calapiccola**, t 0564 825 133, f 0564 825 235 (*very expensive*). An out-of-town apartment complex in a great setting, with a beach and plenty of activities, or equal doses of peace and quiet if that's what you're looking for, hidden away on the western tip of the peninsula.
**★★★Don Pedro**, Via Panoramica, t 0564 833 914, f 0564 833 129. A nice location, but some way off from the nearest beach. *Open April–Oct*
**★La Conchiglia**, Via della Marina, t 0564 833 134 (*cheap*). One of the few inexpensive places on Argentario proper.
**Gambero Rosso**, Lungomare Andrea Doria, t 0564 832 650 (*expensive*). Fancy seafood, such as spaghetti with lobster, at fancy prices; at weekends there's *zuppa di pesce*.
**La Grotta del Pescatore**, Via delle Fonti, t 0564 835 265 (*cheap*). A more moderate option, where you can try a bowl of steaming *zuppa di scampi con patate*, more stew than soup.

**Porto Santo Stefano** ✉ 58019
**★★★Filippo II**, t 0564 811 611 (*luxury*). Recently refurbished, this is doubtless the best in

town; it's air-conditioned and situated nice and close to the beaches at Poggio Calvella.
**★★★La Caletta**, Via Civinni 10, t 0564 812 939, f 0564 817 506 (*very expensive*). Pleasant rooms overlooking the sea. Minimum 7-night stay requested in August.
**★★Alfiero**, Via Cuniberti 12, t 0564 814 067 (*moderate*). A simple, less expensive hotel at the centre of the action around the harbour. Some of the places here are almost too swanky to be in such a little resort town.
**Dal Greco**, Via del Molo 1, t 0564 814 885 (*expensive*). Pricey, but still worth it, the chief offender is this impeccably elegant establishment on the yacht harbour. A *terrina di pesce* with vegetables is the star attraction, along with lobster and a wide choice of other dishes. *Closed Tues*.
**Il Delfino**, Piazzale Facchinetti, t 0564 818 394 (*expensive for full dinner, but it's also a pizzeria*). On the other harbour, with semi-outdoor dining; pleasant, but a little close to traffic. They pride themselves on inventive seafood concoctions and their home-made desserts and ice cream. *Closed Thurs*.
**Orlando**, Via Breschi 3, t 0564 812 788 (*moderate*). Popular and lively, this is one of the few genuine places left, specializing in grilled fish. *Closed Thurs in winter*.

The Spanish Presidio lasted only until 1707, but it had a strong impact on the area's buildings and its people. Orbetello was briefly something of a resort, but passed this role on to Porto Ercole and Porto Santo Stefano, and its most recent flash of glory came in the 1930s when Mussolini made it Italy's main seaplane base. Fascist hero Italo Balbo began his famous transatlantic flight from the lagoon in 1933, landing at the opening of the Chicago World's Fair.

Confined on its peninsula, with its palm trees and sun-bleached Spanish walls, Orbetello (pop. 13,500) is a charming town, where buses barely squeeze through the main gate. Viale Italia, the main street, runs down the centre of the peninsula; just north on Piazza della Repubblica, the **cathedral**'s façade has a sculpted portal and rose window from 1376 though its interior was rebuilt in the 1600s.

Orbetello's **lagoons**, on average about a yard deep, are partially used for fish farms, but most of the northern half has been declared a nature preserve, run by the World Wildlife Fund. Like the Monti dell'Uccellina, the area is a breeding ground for marine birds, and also storks and a species of eagle, not to mention the stilt plover, the bee-eater and the lesser hen harrier. Their nesting period lasts from April to October, and during part of this time, the reserve is closed to humans (*roughly mid-May–mid-July*). The visitors' centre is on the coast road between Orbetello and Albinia (*guided tours of the oasis leave mid-July–mid-May on Thurs, Sat and Sun at 10am and 2pm; for info call* **t** *0564 820 297; adm*).

## Porto Ercole and Porto Santo Stefano

Over the causeway from Orbetello on to Monte Argentario, you can go either north or south to begin the *gita panoramica*, the 24 kilometre road that makes a circle around the island (the road offers some exceptional views, but it's not paved the whole way and you won't get through unless you have a jeep). To the south, **Porto Ercole** wraps itself around a tiny fishing harbour, guarded on either side by Spanish fortresses. Forte Stella and Forte San Filippo were probably the last word in 16th-century military architecture, with low, sloping walls and pointed bastions draped over the cliffs; today they present an ominous, surreal sight. San Filippo is the most interesting, though you can't visit – it has been converted into holiday condominiums. Above the souvenir shops and seafood restaurants of the harbour, there is a fine old town, entered through a Gothic gate constructed by the Sienese. Little Piazza Santa Barbara is the centre, with the dignified 17th-century palace of the Spanish governor, and a view over the harbour below. Caravaggio was buried in the church of Sant'Erasmo in 1609 after dying of malaria in a tavern nearby; the artist was on his way back from Malta to Rome, where he had hoped the Pope would pardon him for a tennis-court murder committed years before. Beyond Porto Ercole, the coast road twists and turns under the slopes of Il Telegrafo, Argentario's highest peak (2,083ft). One feature of the *gita panoramica* is the many defence towers, some built by the Sienese, others by the Spaniards.

On the northern side of the Argentario, **Porto Santo Stefano** makes a matching bookend for Porto Ercole. A bit larger and trendier than its sister town, this one also began as a sleepy fishing village, though now the fishing boats are elbowed off to the side of the port by speedboats, big shiny yachts and the Giglio ferries, and the old town has become lost in the agglomeration of hotels and villas on the surrounding hills. There are really two harbours: the first, larger one has the ferries and the fish markets; the yachts – and some real dreadnoughts they are – call at the western harbour, at the other side of a small promontory.

# Giglio and Giannutri

Giglio is the largest of the Tuscan islands after Elba, measuring about 21 by eight kilometres. It is also second in population, with about 1,600 souls, almost all in its three little villages: Giglio Porto, Giglio Castello and Giglio Campese. Like many Italian islands, Giglio suffered grievously from deforestation and abandonment of the land in the last two centuries. Though much of it remains green and pretty, large expanses are now almost barren. Recently, however, a remarkable change in the Giglian environmental consciousness seems to have occurred; if the big signs all over the harbour are any indication, they've gone to the opposite extreme – no camping, no noise, no riding over the wild flowers (and no collecting rocks – they're part of the island too!).

The word *Giglio* means lily, and the lily has become the island's symbol, although it has in fact nothing to do with its name. The Romans called it *Aegilium* or *Gilium*. Under them, Giglio like most of the other Italian islands was a resort for the very wealthy. Pisa, Aragon and various feudal families held the island in the Middle Ages. Duke Cosimo seized it for Tuscany in the 16th century, but did little to protect it against its greatest danger, pirates. Fortunately, the Giglians had the holy right arm of San Mamiliano to protect them. This 6th-century Sicilian bishop, fleeing from the Arian heretics, became a hermit on Montecristo. When he died, a divine signal alerted fishermen from Elba, Giglio and even Genoa, who arrived at the same time and began to fight over the remains. In the true tradition of Christian brotherhood, they struck a deal and cut Mamiliano in three pieces. Giglio got the arm, which proved its worth by chasing away Turkish pirates in 1799. On other occasions it wasn't so helpful. The redoubtable pirate Barbarossa carried off most of the population in 1534, and his understudy Dragut came back for the rest in 1550.

## Giglio

**Giglio Porto**, the island's metropolis, is a colourful place, with red and green lighthouses to welcome the ferries, and pink and beige houses straggling up the hills. There are two beaches south of the town, at **Cala delle Canelle** and **Cala delle Caldane**, one to the north at **Punta Aranella**, all more or less developed, and in the town itself, the world's smallest beach, tucked behind the houses on the left side of the port. From Giglio Porto a difficult mountain road leads up to **Giglio Castello**, the only secure refuge in pirate days, and until recently the only real town. The fortress itself was begun by the Pisans and completed under the grand dukes. The

# Getting Around

Porto S. Stefano is the **port** for Giglio, a one-hour run; the ferry service is shared by the TOREMAR line, **t** 0564 810 803, and Mareciglio, **t** 0564 812 920, both in Porto S. Stefano; boats run at least twice daily, and more frequently in the summer.

The **railway station** for Porto S. Stefano, along the main Livorno–Rome line, is Orbetello Scalo; buses meet the trains to carry passengers to the port. Giannutri can be reached regularly only in July and August, on a daily boat from Porto S. Stefano. On Giglio, buses run fairly regularly from the ferry dock to Giglio Castello and Giglio Campese.

# Tourist Information

**Giglio Porto**: Via Umberto I 48, **t** 0564 809 400, *www.isoladelgiglio.artec.it. Open summer daily 9–1 and 4–8, winter 9–1.*

# Where to Stay and Eat

## Giglio ✉ 58012

The number of tourists, and hotels (12) on Giglio seems to have stabilized, leaving it not entirely overcrowded even in the summer.
**★★★Demo's**, Via Thaon De Revel, **t** 0564 809 235, **f** 0564 809 319 *(very expensive)*. Right in the port, and a little flash, in the 1960s Miami Beach style. *Open April–Oct.*
**★★La Pergola** next door, **t** 0564 809 051 *(moderate)*. Smaller and cosier.
**★★★Arenella**, Via Arenella 5, **t** 0564 809 340, **f** 0564 809 443 *(expensive)*. Persevere until you leave the Porto to enjoy something

rather more serene; this is near the beach, with a pretty garden and a good restaurant. If you really want to get away from it all, your best chance on the entire Tuscan coast is in Cala degli Alberi.
**★★Pardini's Hermitage**, Cala degli Alberi, **t** 0564 809 034, **f** 0564 809 177 *(very expensive)*. In its quiet cove, this can only be reached by boat (ask at the Giglio Sub shop on the port, but with only 11 rooms it's best to book). They'll arrange sports and nature activities if you want, or leave you to enjoy the sea and mountains by yourself. *Open 25 Mar–Dec.*

## Giglio Campese ✉ 58012

**★★★Campese**, Via della Torre 18, **t** 0564 804 003, **f** 0564 804 093, *www.hotelcampese.com (moderate)*. A good, modern beach hotel. *Open 9 April–28 Sept.*

## Giglio Porto ✉ 58013

La Margherita, **t** 0564 809 237 *(moderate)*. One of the most popular of the seafood restaurants dotted around the harbour; good fish and a terrace right on the beach.

## Giglio Castello ✉ 58012

Da Maria, Via Casamatta 3, **t** 0564 806 062 *(moderate)*. This is the real find on the island: not only does it have good seafood (like stuffed squid or lobster flambé) but also game dishes like the house speciality, wild rabbit *alla cacciatora. Closed Wed.*
Le Tamerici, Piazza Gloriosa 43, Giglio Castello, **t** 0564 806 266 *(moderate)*. A wide range of game and seafood, as well as such specialities as scampi with courgettes from Giglio and steamed fish with mayonnaise. Save room for their home-made desserts. *Closed Mon and winter.*

picturesque town inside, all medieval alleys and overhanging arches, has plenty of gulls and swallows, a few lazy German tourists, and a small Baroque church with an odd tower and the famous arm of San Mamiliano.

From Giglio Castello, a road leads southwards past **Poggio della Pagana**, the island's highest peak (1,633ft), through land largely reforested with pines to Punta del Capel Rosso, at the southern tip, then back along the coast to Giglio Porto. The main road from Giglio Castello continues on to **Giglio Campese**, a growing resort area with an old watchtower and a large sandy beach.

## Giannutri

**Giannutri**, the southernmost island of the Tuscan archipelago, is a rocky crescent about five kilometres long, with little water and no fertile ground, and little history to speak of. The ancient Greeks knew it as *Artemisia*, and the Romans as *Dianium*; perhaps the associations with the moon goddess came from the island's crescent shape. In Roman times it was an estate of the noble Ahenobarbus family, and substantial ruins of a **Roman Villa** (1st century AD) near Cala Maestra are visited by day-trippers from Porto Santo Stefano in the summer months. Though Giannutri has no permanent population, there is a tourist village and some holiday cottages near the well-protected bay, **Cala Spalmatoio**, on the eastern coast.

# Capalbio and the Giardino dei Tarocchi

Back on the coast south of Orbetello (8km), almost nothing is left of **Ansedonia**, destroyed by the Sienese in 1330. There's a beach, a few hotels, and an unusual Etruscan attempt to stop Cosa's harbour from silting up: deep channels hewn from the solid rock. For ruins you must climb up to **Cosa**, settled by Romans in the 3rd century BC to keep an eye on restless Etruscan cities – and maybe accelerate their decline by draining off trade. Cosa was sacked by Visigoths in the 5th century, but the ruins give a fair idea of the city: a typical rectangular circuit of walls with three gates, a strict street grid, a 'Capitoline' temple, and cisterns for rainwater. Remains of the port are visible from Ansedonia harbour and there is also a small museum on the site.

Before the Via Aurelia (SS1) passes from Tuscany into Lazio, it skirts another World Wildlife Fund project, a nature reserve at the **Lago di Burano** (*tours Sept–April Thurs and Sun at 10 and 2.30; in summer you can book, t 0564 898 829; adm*). Though small, the lagoon attracts all the same birds as the Monti dell'Uccellina and Orbetello lagoons; including, in summer, perhaps the only cranes left on the Italian mainland.

**Capalbio**, six kilometres inland, is one of the loveliest villages in southern Tuscany. It's a circular, hill-top enclave built around a castle, with a pretty 12th-century church. Head a few kilometres east, though, by the Lazio border, for a sneak preview of what may some day be one of Tuscany's best-known sights.

They don't want any publicity, and it isn't signed, but if you turn off the SS1 to Capalbio, and turn right just before the first petrol station, you'll get a surprise. The **Giardino dei Tarocchi** (*open mid-May–Oct Mon–Sat 2.30–7.30; in winter only on request by fax at f 0564 895 700; t 0564 895 122; adm*) is the project of French artist Niki de Saint-Phalle, known for her works at the Pompidou Centre and the Bastille Opera in Paris, and for the colossal, humorous figures she calls 'nanas' scattered over Europe. Someone is investing a lot into this place; the aim is to create a monumental sculpture representing each of the 22 key arcana of the Tarot deck, a sort of garden for abstruse meditation. Already over half are completed: mad, brilliant works in concrete, bright ceramics and mirrors that hark back to Antonio Gaudi. A few are over

50ft tall, glittering over the Maremma coast like some interplanetary Luna Park. Their symbolism is often obscure, but some, like the broken *Tower*, are unmistakable.

## Over the Border

If you're bound for Rome, there are a few attractions in Lazio to distract you along the way. The wealthiest Etruscan cities were here rather than Tuscany, and so the finest painted tombs are on the north Lazio coast at **Tarquinia** and **Cervetri**. Inland are the remains of the Etruscan town of **Vulci**, the fortress of Castello dell'Abbadia holds an Etruscan museum, and an Etruscan bridge spans the gorge. Not much has happened here since Etruscan times, but **Tuscania** has two extremely unusual early medieval churches in the style of medieval southern Italy. Further inland is a chain of lakes, including tranquil **Lake Vico**, and the city of **Viterbo**, once home to the popes.

# Siena

13

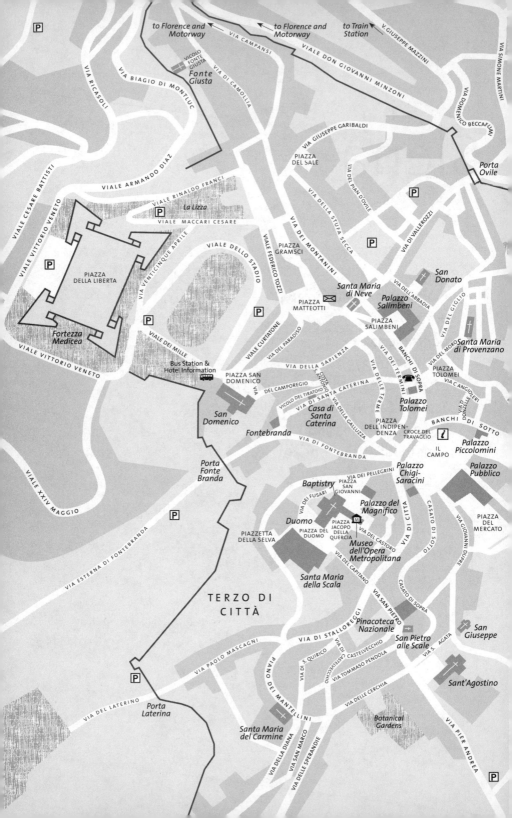

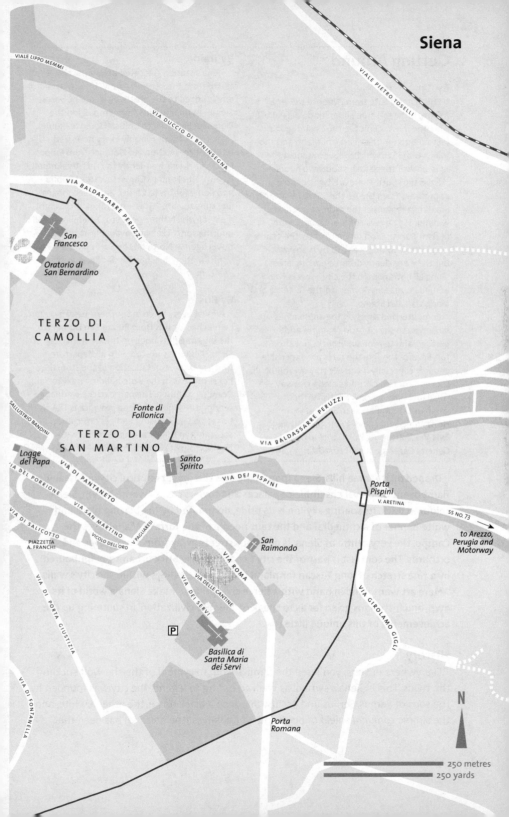

# Siena

VIALE LIPPO MEMMI

VIA DUCCIO DI BONINSEGNA

VIALE PIETRO TOSELLI

VIA BALDASSARRE PERUZZI

San Francesco

Oratorio di San Bernardino

**TERZO DI CAMOLLIA**

Fonte di Follonica

SALLUSTRIO BANDINI

**TERZO DI SAN MARTINO**

VIA BALDASSARRE PERUZZI

Logge del Papa

Santo Spirito

VIA DEI PISPINI

Porta Pispini

V. ARETINA

VIA DEL PORRIONE

VIA DI PANTANETO

SS NO. 73

VIA DI SALICOTTO

VIA SAN MARTINO

VICOLO DELL'ORO

V. PAGLIARESI

to Arezzo, Perugia and Motorway

PIAZZETTA A. FRANCHI

San Raimondo

VIA DI PORTA GIUSTIZIA

VIA DEI SERVI

VIA DELLE CANTINE

VIA ROMA

VIA GIROLAMO GIGLI

Ⓟ

Basilica di Santa Maria dei Servi

VIA DI FONTANELLA

Porta Romana

N

250 metres
250 yards

## Getting Around

### By Car

The fastest route from Florence to Siena (68km) is the toll-free Superstrada del Palio (1hr); the most scenic are the Chiantigiana (SS222) through the heart of Chianti and the Via Cassia (SS2), which weave amongst the hills. Both of these take about two hours.

From the south, there are two possible approaches from the A1: the SS326 by way of Sinalunga (50km) or the more scenic and winding SS73 by way of Monte Sansovino (44km). Cars are forbidden to enter the centre – and you wouldn't want to try it anyway – but there are clearly defined parking areas along all entrances to the city, especially around Piazza San Domenico, the Fortezza and along Viale del Stadio.

Computerized signs on the approaches direct you to the city-run car parks and garages, and tell you whether or not they're full. Beware though: the rates are expensive enough, especially if you are stay overnight. Look out for free car parks along the way – you'll just have to walk a little further.

Car rental companies in Sienna:

**Hertz**, Viale Sarde GNA 37 int.38, t 0577 45085
**Avis**, Via Martini 36, t 0577 270 305
**General Car**, Viale Toselli 20/26, t 0577 49518.

### By Train

Siena's station is located below the city, 1½km from the centre down Viale G. Mazzini, and is linked to the centre by frequent buses. Siena's main line runs from Empoli (on the Florence–Pisa line) to Chiusi (Florence–Rome).

There are trains roughly every hour, with frequent connections to Florence from Empoli (97km/1hr), less frequently to Pisa from Empoli (125km/2hrs) and to Chiusi towards Umbria and Rome (65km to Chiusi, 1hr). A secondary line runs towards Grosseto (70km/1hr) – eight a day, of which three go on to Orbetello. All rail information/tickets are available at the SETI travel agency, No.56 on the Campo.

Information line: t 848 888 088, *www.fs-on-line.com*

### By Bus

Almost every town in southern Tuscany can be reached by bus from **Piazza San Domenico**, the big transport node on the western edge of Siena. A board is posted with all departure times and the exact location of the stop; the ticket office is in the little building next to San Domenico church. The name of the company serving the whole of Siena province is TRA-IN, t 0577 204245, causing endless difficulties, according to the local tourist office, with English tourists looking for TRA-INs in the

---

Draped on its three hills, Siena (pop. 59,000) is the most beautiful city in Tuscany, a flamboyant medieval ensemble of palaces and towers cast in warm, brown, Siena-coloured brick. Its soaring skyline is its pride, dominated by the blazing black and white banner of a cathedral and the taut needle of the Torre di Mangia; yet the Campo, the very centre of Siena, is only four streets away from olive groves and orchards. The contrast is part of the city's charm: dense brick urbanity, neighboured by a fine stretch of long Tuscan farmland that fills the valleys within the city's walls.

Here art went hand in hand with a fierce civic pride to make Siena a world of its own, and historians go so far as to speak of 'Sienese civilization' in summing up the achievements of this unique little city.

## History

Everywhere in Siena you'll see the familiar Roman symbol of the she-wolf suckling the twins. This is Siena's symbol as well; according to legend, the city was founded by the sons of Remus, Senius and Ascius. One rode a black horse, the other a white, and the simple *comunal* shield of black and white halves (the *balzana*) has been the

train station; for some of the closer villages, look for TRA-INs on Viale F. Tozzi, just north of San Domenico.

Other companies depart for other cities like Florence (SITA, about once every hour, also to Rome, Perugia, Pisa, etc.), but all leave from San Domenico. Within the walls, there is now a bus service run by the TRA-IN, using what they call the *pollicini* or Tom Thumbs: little buses designed to get around narrow streets. Regular buses to the **train station** and everywhere else in the modern suburbs depart from **Piazza Matteotti** north of the Campo.

**Taxis**: Radio Taxi, **t** 0577 49222, 0577 289 350, 0577 44504.

## Tourist Information

**Siena**: Piazza del Campo 56, **t** 0577 280 551, **f** 0577 270 676, *aptsiena@siena.turismo.toscana.it*; *www.siena.turismo.toscana.it*. Open 15 Mar–Dec Mon–Sat 8.30am–7.30pm, Sun 9–3. **Post office**: Piazza Matteotti 1.

## Shopping

Siena is blissfully short of designer boutiques; even the usual tourist trinkets

seem to be lacking. Nevertheless, a thorough search of the back streets will turn up plenty of unpretentious artisan workshops – almost all of which are so unconcerned with the tourist industry that they don't even bother hanging out a sign. The following are just some examples.

**Stained glass**: Via Galuzza 5, just off Piazza Indipendenza. Creations (most of them portable) in a distinctive modern style.

**Ceramic**: Via di Città 94. Selling a range of interesting pieces.

**Libreria Senese**, Via di Città 62–64. Siena's best bookshop, just down the street.

**Antica Drogheria Manganelli**, Via di Città 71–73. One hundred-year-old original wooden shelving lines the walls of this gourmet's treasure trove, jammed full of delicious regional foods and wines.

**Pizzichieria**, Via di Città. The welcome you receive from the stuffed, bespectacled boar as you enter is just one of the more unusual aspects of this food shop. Inside you can buy delicious sandwiches made at your request, as well as wonderful local specialities like porcini mushrooms and truffles.

### Market Days

Held around the Fortezza and Via XXV Aprile. *Wed.*

other most enduring symbol of Siena over the centuries. It is most likely that somebody was living on these three hills long before this mythological pair. Excavations have found traces of Etruscan and even Celtic habitation. The almost impregnable site, dominating most of southern Tuscany, would always have been of interest. Roman-era *Sena Julia*, refounded by Augustus as a colony for his veterans, never achieved much importance, and we know little about the place until the early 12th century, when the emerging *comune* began keeping written records. In 1125, an increasingly independent Siena elected its first consuls. By 1169, the *comune* wrested political control away from the bishop, and some 10 years later Siena developed its own written constitution.

The political development of the city is complex, and with good reason. Twelfth-century Siena was a booming new city: having control over its rich countryside, supplying some of the best wool in Italy, helped start an important cloth industry, and a small silver mine, acquired from Volterra in the 1160s, provided seed capital for what was to become one of the leading banking towns of Europe. Like so many other Italian cities, Siena was able early on to force its troublesome rural nobles to

# Where to Stay

## Siena ✉ 53100

Many of Siena's finest hotels are outside the walls, in the countryside, or near the city gates. What's left, in the centre, is simple but comfortable enough. In the summer, rooms are in short supply so book ahead. If you come without a reservation try:

**Hotel Information Centre,** Piazza San Domenico 2, **t** 0577 288 084, **f** 0577 280 290, *info@hotelsiena.com, www.hotelsienna.com.* Make this your first stop. Run by the city's innkeepers, it's conveniently located at the terminus of all intercity bus routes. If you arrive by train, take the city bus up from the station to Piazza Matteotti, and walk a block down Via Curtatone. Even at the worst of times, they should be able to find you something – except during the Palio, of course, when you should make your booking several months in advance. *Open Mon–Sat 9–7, until 8 in summer.*

**Coptour,** Via Mattioli 9, **t** 0577 45900, **f** 0577 283 145. Also makes hotel bookings (for member hotels); located near the Campo car park. *Open summer Mon–Fri 9.30–7.30, Sat 10–7; winter Mon–Fri 9–7, Sat 9–1.*

## Luxury and Expensive

If you have a car, there are a number of hotels outside the walls which offer a rural Tuscan charm and views of the city that more than make up for the slight inconvenience of getting there.

**\*\*\*\*La Certosa di Maggiano,** 1km southeast of the city, near the Porta Romana, **t** 0577 288 180, **f** 0577 288 189. This must be one of the most remarkable establishments in Italy, set in a restored 14th-century Carthusian monastery. There are only 18 rooms; the luxuries include a heated pool, air-conditioning that works, a quiet chapel and a cloister, a salon where guests can play backgammon and chess, tennis courts, an excellent restaurant, and a library fit to feature in any antiquarian's dream. Needless to say, all this doesn't come cheap, but it is lovely. Half-board only

**\*\*\*\*Villa Scacciapensieri,** on Strada Scacciapensieri 10, 3km north of the city, **t** 0577 41441, **f** 0577 270 854. As a second choice, you can come here to marvel at glorious sunset views over Siena. This is a quiet country house divided into 28 spacious rooms; besides the view, it features a pool and a good restaurant with an outdoor terrace.

live within its walls, where they built scores of tall defence towers, fought pitched battles in the streets and usually kept the city divided into armed camps; in the narrowest part of the city, the *comune* once had to lay out new streets parallel to Via Camollia because of one particularly boisterous nobleman whose palace most Sienese were afraid to pass. Yet Siena was never completely able to bring its titled hoodlums under control. The businessmen made the money, and gradually formed their city into a sophisticated self-governing republic, but the nobles held on to many of their privileges for centuries, giving an anachronistically feudal tinge to Siena's life and art.

Like its brawling neighbours, medieval Siena enjoyed looking for trouble; in the endless wars of the 13th century they never had to look very far. Originally a Guelph town, Siena changed sides early to avoid being in the same camp with arch-rival Florence. Along with Pisa, Siena carried the Ghibelline banner through the Tuscan wars with varying fortunes. Its finest hour came in 1260, when a Florentine herald arrived with the arrogant demand that Siena demolish its walls and deliver up its large population of Ghibelline exiles from Florence. If not, the armies of Florence and the entire Guelph League – some 40,000 men – were waiting outside to raze the city

***Palazzo Ravizza**, Via Pian dei Mantellini 34, **t** 0577 280 462, **f** 0577 221 597. 30 rooms within an elegant old town house near the Porta Laterina, just inside the walls; the restaurant isn't anything special, but the rooms are cosy and there is a pretty terrace.

***Duomo**, Via Stalloreggi 38, **t** 0577 289 088, **f** 0577 43043. A comfortably old-fashioned place south of the Duomo.

***Garden**, Via Custoza 2, **t** 0577 47056, **f** 0577 46050. Boasts a swimming-pool.

### Moderate

Many of Siena's two- and three-star hotels cluster around the entrances to the city. However, there are also a number of options closer to the centre.

****Centrale**, Via Cecco Angolieri 26, **t** 0577 280 379, **f** 0577 42152. Just around the corner from the Duomo.

****Cannon d'Oro**, Via Montanini 28, **t** 0577 44321, **f** 0577 280 868. Located near the bus station, this is both well-run and a good bargain.

****Piccolo Hotel Etruria**, Via delle Donzelle 3, **t** 0577 283 685, **f** 0577 288 461. You won't do any better in location or amenities than the friendly, newly remodelled Etruria; it's just a stone's throw from the Campo, off Via Banchi di Sotto.

****Piccolo Hotel Il Palio**, Piazza del Sale 19, **t** 0577 281 131, **f** 0577 281 142. Slightly further from the centre, but enhanced by the very friendly and welcoming proprietress, who speaks English.

### Cheap

Inexpensive places can be hard to find – especially before term time when they're full of university students looking for a permanent place to live.

***Tre Donzelle**, Via delle Donzelle, **t** 0577 280 358. A few doors down, this is also good, though don't forget it has a midnight curfew.

****Il Giardino**, Via Baldassare Peruzzi 35, **t** 0577 285 290, **f** 0577 221 197. This hotel is near the Porta Pispini, with good views and a swimming-pool, and comes highly recommended in readers' letters.

***La Perla**, Villa delle Terme, **t** 0577 47144. Another affordable option close by.

**Ostello della Gioventù Guido Riccio**, Via Fiorentina 85, **t** 0577 52212, to book **f** 055 805 0618. The city runs its own youth hostel too, situated in Lo Stellino, 2km from the city (bus no.15 from Piazza Gramsci). No cards required; make sure you arrive early in July and August. *Closed Nov–Dec.*

to the ground. Despite the overwhelming odds, the Sienese determined to resist. They threw the keys of the city on the altar of the as yet unfinished new cathedral, dedicating Siena to the Virgin Mary (a custom they have repeated ever since when the city is endangered, most recently just before the battle for liberation in 1944). In the morning, they marched out to the **Battle of Montaperti** and beat the Florentines so badly that they captured their *carroccio*.

After the battle Siena had Florence entirely at her mercy and, naturally, was anxious to level the city and scatter the ground with salt. One of the famous episodes in the *Inferno* relates how the Florentine exiles, who made up a substantial part of the Sienese forces, refused to allow it. Unfortunately for Siena, within a few years Florence and the Tuscan Guelphs had the situation back under control and Siena was never again to come so close to dominating Tuscan affairs. Nevertheless the city would be a constant headache to Florence for the next three centuries.

When things were quiet at the front, the Sienese had to settle for bashing each other. The constant stream of anti-Siena propaganda in Dante isn't just Florentine bile; medieval Siena thoroughly earned its reputation for violence and contentiousness. The impressive forms and rituals of the Sienese Republic were merely a façade

# Eating Out

Sitting between three of Italy's greatest wine-producing areas, the Chianti, the Brunello of Montalcino and the Vino Nobile of Montepulciano, Siena always has something to wash down the simple dishes of the Sienese table. This city's real speciality is sweets, and a fair few visitors find they have no room for a meal after repeated visits to the pastry shops for slices of *panforte*, a heavy but indecently tasty cake laced with fruits, nuts, orange peel and secret Sienese ingredients, or *panpepato*, similar, but containing pepper.

They are all artists – shop windows flaunt gargantuan creations of cake and crystallized fruit, metres high and colourful as a Lorenzetti fresco, set out for all to admire before they are carted off to some wedding party.

The **Enoteca** inside the Medici fortress (*see* p.391) is another distraction; at times special tastings are organized, concentrating on a particular region of Italy.

As a university town, Siena is never short on snacks and fast food; try *cioccina*, their special variation on pizza; or *pici* (thick south Tuscan spaghetti) with a sauce prepared from ground pork, *pancetta*, sausages and chicken breasts, added to tomatoes cooked with Brunello wine, which is the city's favourite pasta dish.

## Very Expensive

**Da Enzo**, Via Camollia 49, t 0577 281 277. A traditional restaurant with a long and varied menu, offering plenty of choice between fish and meat. The spaghetti with baby clams (*vongole*) is good, and there is a roast fish of the day. *Closed Sun and last 2 weeks in July.*

**Cane e Gatto**, Via Pagliaresi 6, t 0577 287 545. Cane e Gatto is a creative and interesting little place near Porta Romana. For hearty appetites, the *menu degustazione* has some seven or eight courses and is good value. Alternatively, you can eat à-la-carte. *Dinner only, closed Thurs.*

**Antica Trattoria Botteganova**, Strada Chiantigiana 29, just outside Siena, on the road to Gaiole (SS408), t 0577 284 230, f 0577 271 519. This tempting *trattoria* produces earthy Sienese cooking, such as veal cooked in Chianti Classico, and creative fish dishes. *Closed Mon; booking recommended.*

**Osteria Le Logge**, Via del Porrione 33, off the Campo, t 0577 48013 (*expensive–moderate*). If you've survived the wine and the pastry shops, you'll appreciate the succulent risottos and pasta dishes here, with exotic second courses like stuffed guinea-fowl (*faraona*) and a fine wine list. *Closed Sun.*

concealing endless, pointless struggles between the various factions of the élite. Early on, Siena's merchants and nobles divided themselves into five *monti*, syndicates of self-interest that worked like political parties only without any pretence of principle. At one point, this Tuscan banana republic had 10 constitutions in 27 years, and more often than not its political affairs were settled in the streets. Before the Palio was invented, Siena's favourite civic sport was the *Gioco del Pugno*, a general, 300-a-side fist-fight in the Campo. Sometimes tempers flared, and the boys would bring out the axes and crossbows.

## Siena's Golden Age

The historical record leaves us with a glaring paradox. For all its troubles and bad intentions, Siena often managed to run city business disinterestedly and with intelligence. An intangible factor of civic pride always made the Sienese do the right thing when something important was at hand, like battling with the Florentines or selecting a new artist to work on the cathedral. The Battle of Monteaperti may have proved a disappointment in terms of territorial ambitions, but it inaugurated the most brilliant period of Sienese culture, and saw the transformation of the hilltop

## Moderate

**Al Marsili**, Via del Castoro 3, t 0577 47154. Just off the Piazza del Duomo is another of Siena's best offerings, in a singularly elegant setting. The menu could hardly be described as very traditional, with dishes like gnocchi in duck sauce, but it's hard to complain. *Closed Mon.*

**Taverna di Cecco**, Via Cecco Angioleri 19, t 0577 288 518. Specializes in pasta dishes, meats and almost everything else you can think of done up with either truffles or porcini mushrooms. *Closed Sun.*

**La Piana**, Via Camollia 122, t 0577 270 737. More memorable pasta is available here: try the *tagliata Piana I or II* (with fresh rocket). *Closed Sun.*

**Tullio ai Tre Cristi**, Vicolo di Provenzano 1/7, t 0577 280 608. This eaterie has been serving food since about 1830 and is perhaps the most authentic of all Sienese restaurants; the menu here includes things like *ribollita*, tripe with sausages, and roast boar from the Maremma region. Their *pici* is home-made. In the summer, you can enjoy all these *al fresco*, when they lay up tables outside. *Closed Wed.*

**Osteria Castelvecchio**, Via Castelvecchio 65, t 0577 49586. Osteria Castelvecchio provides an unusually creative menu with lots of vegetarian options for those that want them, located in a former stables near the Duomo. *Closed Tues.*

**Ristorante Il Duomo**, Via dei Fusari 19, hidden around the corner from Santa Maria della Scala, t 0577 287 556. A good, informal pizzeria, perfect for lunch after slogging through the Duomo. They also offer pasta and meat dishes such as wild boar. *Closed Wed.*

**La Torre**, Via Salicotto 7/9, t 0577 287 548. A fun, lively place; popular with students. *Closed Thurs.*

## Cheap

Less expensive places – and there are many – are often a little further from the Campo.

**Trattoria da Dino**, Casato di Sopra 71, t 0577 289 036. Makes a good *spiedini alle Senese*. *Closed Fri and last 2 weeks in July.*

**Il Cavallino Bianco**, Via di Città 20, t 0577 44258. Serves regional food and pizza, but its main bonus is that it stays open until late. *Closed Tues from Nov–Feb.*

**Osteria La Chiacchiera**, Costa di Sant' Antonio 4, t 0577 280 631. A small, packed-out rustic eatery near Casa di S. Caterina, serving *pici*, tripe, kidneys and other local specialities.

fortress-town into the beautiful city we see today. In 1287, under pressure from the Guelphs and their Angevin protectors, Siena actually allied itself with Florence and instituted a new form of government: the '**Council of the Nine**'. Excluding nobles from office, as Florence would do six years later, the rule of the Nine was to last until 1355, and it gave Siena a more stable regime than it knew at any other period.

Business was better than ever. The city's bankers came to rival Florence's, with offices in all the trading centres and capitals of Europe. A sustained peace, and increasing cultural contacts with France and Naples, brought new ideas and influences into Siena's art and architecture, just in time to embellish massive new building programmes like the **cathedral** (begun in 1186, but not substantially completed until the 1380s) and the **Palazzo Pubblico** (1295–1310). Beginning with Duccio di Buoninsegna (1260–1319), Sienese artists took the lead in exploring new concepts in painting and sculpture and throughout the 1300s they contributed as much as or more than the Florentines in laying the foundations for the Renaissance. Contemporary records betray an obsessive concern on the part of bankers and merchants for decorating Siena and impressing outsiders. At the height of its fortunes, in the early 14th century, Siena ruled most of southern Tuscany. Its bankers were known in London, in the Baltic and in Constantinople, and its reputation for beauty and culture was matched by few cities in Europe.

The very pinnacle of civic pride and ambition came in 1339, with the fantastical plan to expand the still-unfinished cathedral into the largest in all Christendom. The walls of that effort, a nave that would have been longer than St Peter's in Rome, stand today as a monument to the dramatic event that snapped off Siena's career in full bloom. The **Black Death** of 1348 carried off one-third of the population – a death toll perhaps no greater than in some other Italian cities, but it struck Siena at a moment when its economy was particularly vulnerable, and started a slow but irreversible decline that was to continue for centuries. Economic strife led to political instability, and in 1355 a revolt of the nobles, egged on by Emperor Charles IV who was then in Tuscany, overthrew the Council of the Nine. Then in 1371, seven years before the Ciompi revolt in Florence, the wool-workers staged a genuine revolution. Organized as a trade union of sorts, the **Compagnìa del Bruco**, they seized the Palazzo Pubblico and instituted a government with greater popular representation.

The decades that followed saw Siena devote more and more of its diminishing resources to buying off the marauding mercenary companies that infested much of

## Ancient Rivals

Few rivalries have been more enduring than that between Florence and Siena; to understand Tuscany, take a moment to compare the two. Long ago, while Florence was off at university busily studying her optics and geometry, Lady Siena spent her time dancing and dropping her scarf for knights at the tournament. Florence thought she had the last laugh in 1555, when Duke Cosimo and his black-hearted Spanish pals wiped out the Sienese Republic and put this proud maiden in chains. It's frustrating enough today, though, when Florence looks up in the hills and sees Siena, an unfaded beauty with a faraway smile, sitting in her tower like the Lady of Shalott.

For two towns built by bankers and wool tycoons, they could not have less in common. Siena may not possess an Uffizi or a David, but neither does it have to bear the marble antimacassars and general stuffiness of its sister on the Arno, nor her smog, traffic, tourist hordes and suburban squalor. Florence never goes over the top. Siena loves to, especially in the week around the race of the Palio, the wildest party in Tuscany, a worthy successor to the fabulous masques and carnivals, the bullfights and bloody free-for-alls of the Sienese Middle Ages. In fact, Florence has been clicking its tongue at Siena since the time of Dante, who refers sarcastically in his *Inferno* to a famous club called the *Brigata*, made up of 12 noble Sienese youths who put up 250,000 florins for a year of nightly feasting; every night they had three sumptuously laid tables, one for eating, one for drinking, and the third to throw out the window.

But there's more to Siena than that. This is a city with its own artistic tradition (*see* **Art and Architecture**, p.41); in the 1300s, Sienese painters were giving lessons to the Florentines. Always more decorative, less intellectual than Florence, Siena fell behind in the quattrocento. By then, fortunately, the greatest achievement of Sienese art was already nearing completion – Siena herself.

Italy at this time. By 1399 the city was in such straits that it surrendered its independence to **Giangaleazzo Visconti**, the tyrant of Milan, who was then attempting to surround and conquer Florence. After his death Siena reclaimed its freedom. Political confusion continued throughout the century, with only two periods of relative stability. One came with the pontificate (1458–63) of Pius II, the great Sienese scholar **Aeneas Silvius Piccolomini**, who exerted a dominating influence over his native city while he ruled at Rome. In 1487, a nobleman named **Pandolfo Petrucci** took over the government; as an honest broker, regulating the often murderous ambitions of the *monti*, he and his sons kept control of the republic until 1524.

## The Fall of the Republic

Florence was always waiting in the wings to swallow up Siena, and finally had its chance in the 1500s. The real villain of the piece, however, was not Florence but that most imperious Emperor, **Charles V**. After the fall of the Petrucci, the factional struggles resumed immediately, with frequent assassinations and riots, and constitutions changing with the spring fashions. Charles, who had bigger prey in his sights, cared little for the fate of the perverse little republic; he feared, though, that its disorders, religious toleration, and wretched financial condition were diseases that might spread beyond its borders. In 1530, he took advantage of riots in the city to install an imperial garrison. Yet even the emperor's representatives, usually Spaniards, could not keep Siena from sliding further into anarchy and bankruptcy on several occasions, largely thanks to Charles's war taxes. Cultural life was stifled as the Spaniards introduced the Inquisition and the Index. Scholars and artists fled, while poverty and political disruptions made Siena's once proud university cease to function.

In 1550, Charles announced that he was going to build a fortress within the city walls, for which the Sienese were going to pay. Realizing that the trifling liberty still left to them would soon be extinguished, the Sienese ruling class began intrigues with Charles' great enemy France. A French army, led by a Piccolomini, arrived in July 1552. Inside the walls the people revolted and locked the Spanish garrison up in its own new fortress. The empire was slow to react, but inevitably, in late 1554, a huge force of imperial troops, along with those of Florence, entered Sienese territory. The siege was prosecuted with remarkable brutality by Charles's commander, the **Marquis of Marignano**, who laid waste much of the Sienese countryside (which did not entirely recover until this century), tortured prisoners and even hired agents to start fires inside the walls. After a brave resistance, led by a republican Florentine exile named **Piero Strozzi** and assisted by France, Siena was starved into surrendering in April 1555. Two years later, Charles's son Philip II sold Siena to Duke Cosimo of Florence, and the republic was consumed by the new Grand Duchy of Tuscany.

If nothing else, Siena went out with a flourish. After the capture of the city, some 2,000 republican bitter-enders escaped to make a last stand at Montalcino. Declaring 'Where the *Comune* is, there is the City', they established what must be the world's first republican government-in-exile. With control over much of the old

Sienese territory, the '**Republic of Siena at Montalcino**' held out against the Medici for another four years.

With its independence lost and its economy irrevocably ruined, Siena withdrew into itself. For centuries there was to be no recovery, little art or scholarship, and no movements towards reform. The Sienese aristocracy, already decayed into a parasitic *rentier* class, made its peace with the Medici dukes early on; in return for their support, the Medici allowed them to keep much of their power and privileges. The once-great capital of trade and finance shrank rapidly into an overbuilt farmers' market, its population dropping from a 14th-century high of 60–80,000 to around a mere 15,000 by the year 1700. This explains largely why medieval and Renaissance Siena is so well preserved – for better or worse, nothing ever happened to change it.

By the 'Age of Enlightenment', with its disparaging of everything medieval, the Sienese seem to have quite forgotten their own history and art, so it is no surprise that the rest of Europe forgot them too. During the first years of the Grand Tour, no self-respecting northern European considered visiting Siena. Few had probably ever heard of it, and those who stopped overnight on the way to Rome were usually dismayed at the 'inelegance' of its medieval buildings and art.

It was not until the 1830s that Siena was rediscovered, with the help of *literati* like the Brownings, who spent several summers here, and later that truly Gothic American, Henry James. The Sienese were not far behind in rediscovering it themselves. The old civic pride that had lain dormant for centuries yawned and stretched like Sleeping Beauty and went diligently back to work.

Before the century was out, everything that could still be salvaged of the city's ancient glory was refurbished and restored. More than ever fascinated by its own image and eccentricities, and more than ever without any kind of an economic base, Siena was ready for its present career as a cultural attraction, a tourist town.

## Orientation: *Terzi* and the *Contrade*

The centre of Siena, the site of the Palio and, importantly to the Sienese, the 'farthest point from the world outside', is the piazza called **Il Campo**. The city unfolds from it like a three-petalled flower along three ridges. It has been a natural division since medieval times, with the oldest quarter, the **Terzo di Città**, to the southwest; the **Terzo di San Martino** to the southeast; and the **Terzo di Camollia** to the north.

Siena is tiny, barely over a square mile in size. The density, and especially the hills, make it seem much bigger when you're walking. There are no short cuts across the valleys between the three *terzi*. Although there are few cars in the centre, taxis and motorbikes will occasionally try to run you down.

### Contrade

The Sienese have taken the *contrade* for granted so long that their history is almost impossible to trace. Basically, the word denotes the 17 neighbourhoods into which Siena is divided. Like the *rioni* of Rome, they were once the original wards of the ancient city – not merely geographical boundaries, but self-governing entities; the

# The Palio

The thousands of tourists who come twice a year to see the Palio, Siena's famous horse race around the Campo, probably think the Sienese are doing it purely for their benefit. Yet, like the *contrade* which contest it, the Palio is an essential aspect of Sienese culture, as significant to the city today as it was centuries ago. Here are the plain facts on Italy's best-known annual festival.

The oldest recorded Palio was run in 1283, though no one knows how far the custom goes back. During the Middle Ages, besides the horse races there were violent street battles, bloody games of primeval rugby and even bullfights. (Bullfights were also common in Rome and there's an argument to be made that Italy is actually the place where the Spaniards got the idea, back in the 16th and 17th centuries when Spain's own medieval passion for such things was all but forgotten.) At present, the course comprises three laps around the periphery of the Campo, although in the past the race has been known to take in some of the city's main streets.

The *palio* (Latin *pallium*) is an embroidered banner, offered as a prize to the winning *contrade*. Two races are held each year, on 2 July and 16 August, and the *palio* of each one is decorated with an image of the Virgin Mary; after political violence the city's greatest passion has always been Mariolatry. The course has room for only 10 horses in each race, so some of the 17 *contrade* are chosen by lot each race to ensure that they all have a fair chance. The horses too are selected by lot, but the *contrade* are free to select their own jockeys.

Although the race itself lasts only a minute and a half, there's a good hour or two of pageantry preceding it; the famous flag-throwers or *alfieri* of each participating *contrada* put on a dazzling show, while the medieval *carroccio*, drawn by a yoke of white oxen, is pressed into service to circle the Campo, bearing the prized *palio* itself.

The Palio is no joke; baskets of money ride on each race, not to mention the sacred honour of the district. To obtain divine favour, each *contrada* brings its horse into its chapel on race morning for a special blessing (and if a little horse manure drops during the ceremony, it's taken as a sign of good luck). The only rule stipulates that you can't seize the reins of an opponent. There are no rules against bribing opposing jockeys, making alliances with other *contrade*, or ambushing jockeys before the race.

The course around the Campo has two right angles. Anything can happen; recent Palii have featured not only jockeys but *horses* flying through the air at the turns. The Sienese say no one has ever been killed at a Palio. There's no reason to believe them. They wouldn't believe it themselves, but it is an article of faith among the Sienese that fatalities are prevented by special intervention of the Virgin Mary. The post-Palio carousing, while not up to medieval standards, is still impressive; in the winning *contrada* the party might go on for days on end.

No event in Italy is as infectiously exhilarating as the Palio. There are two ways to see it, either from the centre of the Campo, packed tight and always very hot, or from an expensive seat in a viewing stand, but book well in advance if you want one of these. Several travel agencies offer special Palio tours (*see* **Travel**, pp.82–3); otherwise make sure you book by April.

ancients with their long racial memories often referred to them as the city's 'tribes'. In Siena, the *contrade* survived and prospered all through classical times and the Middle Ages. More than anything else, they maintained the city's traditions and sense of identity through the dark years after 1552. Incredibly enough, they're still there now, unique in Italy and perhaps all Europe. Once Siena counted over 60 *contrade*. Now there are 17, each with a sort of totem animal for its symbol:

*Aquila* (eagle), *Onda* (dolphin), *Tartaruga* (turtle), *Pantera* (panther), *Selva* (rhinoceros) and *Chiocciola* (snail): all southwest of the Campo in Terzo di Città.

*Leocorno* (unicorn), *Torre* (elephant), *Civetta* (owl), *Nicchio* (mussel shell) and *Valdimontone* (ram): in Terzo di San Martino southeast of the Campo.

*Oca* (goose), *Drago* (dragon), *Giraffa* (giraffe), *Lupa* (wolf), *Bruco* (caterpillar) and *Istrice* (porcupine): all in the north in the Terzo di Camollia.

Sienese and Italian law recognize each of these as legally chartered communities; today a *contrada* functions as a combination of social-and-dining club, neighbourhood improvement organization, religious confraternity and mutual assistance fund. Each elects its own officials annually in May. Each has its own chapel, museum and fountain, its own flag and colours, and its own patron saint who pulls all the strings he can in Heaven twice a year to help his beloved district win the Palio.

Sociologists, and not only in Italy, are becoming ever more intrigued with this ancient yet very useful system, with its built-in community solidarity and tacit social control. (Siena has almost no crime and no social problems, except of course for a lack of jobs.) The *contrade* probably function much as they did in Roman or medieval times, but it's surprising just what up-to-date, progressive and adaptable institutions they can be, and they are still changing today. Anyone born in a *contrada* area, for example, is automatically a member; besides their baptism into the Church, they also receive a sort of 'baptism' into the *contrada*. This ritual isn't very old, and it is conducted in the pretty new fountains the *contrade* have constructed all over Siena in recent years as centrepieces for their neighbourhoods.

To learn more about the *contrade*, the best place to go is one of the 17 little *contrada* museums. The tourist office can give you a list of addresses. One of the best is that of the Goose in the Terzo di Camollia. Though the caretakers usually live close by, most of them ask visitors to contact them a week in advance. The tourist office also has details on the dates of the annual *contrada* festivals, and the other shows and dinners they are wont to put on; visitors are always very welcome.

## Walking in Siena

If you keep your eyes open while walking the back streets of Siena you'll see the city's entire history laid out for you in signs, symbols and a hundred other clues. You usually won't have trouble guessing which *contrada* you're in. Little ceramic plaques with the *contrada* symbol appear on buildings and street corners, not to mention flags in the neighbourhood colours, bumper stickers on cars and the fountains, each with a modern sculptural work, usually representing the *contrada*'s animal.

Look for noblemen's coats of arms above the doorways; aristocratic, archaic Siena will show you more of these than almost any Italian city. In many cases they are still the homes of the original families, and often the same device is on a dozen houses on one block, a reminder of how medieval Siena was largely divided into separate compounds, each under the protection (or intimidation) of a noble family. One common symbol is formed from the letters IHS in a radiant sun. Siena's famous 15th-century preacher, San Bernardino, was always pestering the nobles to forget their contentiousness and enormous vanity; he proposed that they replace their heraldic symbols with the monogram of Christ. The limited success his idealism met with can be read on the buildings of Siena today.

They don't take down old signs in Siena. One, dated 1641, informs prostitutes that the Most Serene Prince Matthias (the Florentine governor) forbids them to live on his street (Via di Salicotto). Another, a huge 19th-century marble plaque on the Banchi di Sotto, reminds us that 'in this house, before modern restorations reclaimed it from squalidness, was born Giovanni Caselli, inventor of the pantograph'. A favourite, on Via del Giglio, announces a stroke of the rope and a 16-*lira* fine for anyone throwing trash in the street, with proceeds to go to the accuser.

# The Campo

There is no lovelier square in Tuscany, and none more beloved by its city. The Forum of ancient *Sena Julia* was on this spot, and in the Middle Ages it evolved into its present fan shape, rather like a scallop shell or classical theatre. The Campo was paved with brick as early as 1340; the nine sections into which the fan is divided are in honour of the Council of the Nine, rulers of the city at the time. Thousands crowd over the bricks every year to see the Palio run on the periphery

For a worthy embellishment to their Campo, the Sienese commissioned for its curved north end the **Fonte Gaia** from Jacopo della Quercia, their greatest sculptor, though what you see now is an uninspired copy from 1868. He worked on it from 1408 to 1419, creating the broad rectangle of marble with reliefs of Adam and Eve and allegorical virtues. It was to be the opening salvo of Siena's Renaissance, an answer to the baptistry doors of Ghiberti in Florence (for which della Quercia himself had been one of the contestants). Perhaps it was a poor choice of stone, but the years have been incredibly unkind to this fountain; the badly eroded remains of the original can be seen up on the loggia of the Palazzo Pubblico.

No one can spend much time in Siena without noticing its fountains. The republic always made sure each part of the city had access to good water; medieval Siena created the most elaborate engineering works since ancient Rome to bring the water in. Fonte Gaia, and others such as Fontebranda, are fed by underground aqueducts that stretch for miles across the Tuscan countryside. Charles V, when he visited the city, is reported to have said that Siena is 'even more marvellous underground than it is on the surface'. The original Fonte Gaia was completed in the early 1300s; there's a story that soon afterwards some citizens dug up a beautiful Greek statue of Venus signed by Praxiteles himself. The delighted Sienese carried it in procession through the city and installed it on top of their new fountain. With the devastation of the Black Death, however, the preachers were quick to blame God's wrath on the indecent pagan on the Fonte Gaia. Throughout history, the Sienese have always been ready to be shocked by their own sins; in this case, with their neighbours dropping like flies around them, they proved only too eager to make poor Venus the scapegoat. They chopped her into little bits, and a party of Sienese disguised as peasants smuggled the pieces over the border and buried them in Florentine territory to pass the bad luck on to their enemies.

## Palazzo Pubblico

If the Campo is like a Roman theatre, the main attraction on stage since 1310 has been this brick and stone palace, the enduring symbol of the Sienese Republic and still the town hall today. Its façade is the face of Siena's history, with the she-wolf of Senius and Ascanius, Medici balls, the IHS of San Bernardino, and squared Guelph crenellations, all in the shadow of the tremendous **Torre di Mangia** (*open Nov–mid-Mar daily 10–4; mid-Mar–Oct daily 10–7; July–Aug daily 10am–11pm; adm*), the graceful, needle-like tower that Henry James called 'Siena's Declaration of Independence'. At 332ft, the tower was the second-tallest ever raised in medieval Italy (only the campanile in Cremona beats it). At the time, the cathedral tower up on its hill completely dominated Siena's skyline; the Council of the Nine wouldn't accept that the symbol of religious authority or any of the nobility's fortress-skyscrapers should be taller than the symbol of the republic, so its Perugian architects, Muccio and Francesco di Rinaldo, made sure it would be hard to beat.

There was a practical side to it, too. At the top hung the *comune*'s great bell, which had to be heard in every corner of the city tolling the hours and announcing the curfew, or calling the citizens to assemble in case of war or emergency. One of the first men to hold the job of bell-ringer gave the tower its name, a fat, sleepy fellow named *Mangiaguadagni* ('eat the profits') or just Mangia for short; there is a statue of him in one of the courtyards. Climb the tower's endless staircase for the definitive view of Siena – on the clearest days you'll also be able to see about half of the medieval republic's territory, a view that is absolutely, positively worth the slight risk of cardiac arrest. At the foot of the tower, the marble **Cappella della Piazza**, with its graceful rounded arches, stands out clearly from the Gothic earnestness of the rest of the building. It was begun in 1352, in thanks for deliverance from the Black Death, but not completed until the mid-15th century.

Most of the Palazzo Pubblico's ground floor is still used for city offices, but the upper floors have been made into the city's **museum** (*open daily 10–7; adm*).

Here the main attraction is the series of state rooms done in frescoes, a sampling of the best of Sienese art throughout the centuries. First, though, come the historical frescoes in the **Sala del Risorgimento,** done by an artist named A.G. Cassioli in 1886: the meeting of Vittorio Emanuele II with Garibaldi, his coronation, portraits and epigrams of past patriots, and an 'allegory of Italian Liberty', all in a colourful and photographically precise style.

Next, on the same floor is the **Sala di Balia** with frescoes depicting the life of Alessandro VII and some vigorous battle scenes by the Sienese Spinello Aretino

(1300s) and the *Sixteen Virtues* by Martino di Bartolomeo. The adjoining **Anticamera del Concistoro** has a lovely *Madonna and Child* by Matteo di Giovanni. In the **Sala del Concistoro**, Gobelin tapestries adorn the walls while the great Sienese Mannerist Beccafumi contributed a ceiling of frescoès in the 1530s celebrating the political virtues of antiquity; that theme is continued in the **vestibule to the Chapel**, with portraits of ancient heroes from Cicero to Judas Maccabeus, all by Taddeo di Bartolo. These portrayals, along with more portraits of the classical gods and goddesses and an interesting view of ancient Rome, clearly show the extent of a real fascination with antiquity even in the 1300s.

Intruding among the classical crew, there's also a king-sized St Christopher covering an entire wall. Before setting out on a journey it was good luck to catch a glimpse of this saint, and in Italy and Spain he is often painted extra-large so you won't miss him. In a display case in the hall, some of the oldest treasures of the Sienese Republic are kept: the war helmet of the Captain of the People, and a delicate **golden rose**, a gift to the city from the Sienese Pope, Pius II.

The **chapel** (Cappella del Consiglio) is surrounded by a lovely wrought-iron grille designed by Jacopo della Quercia; when it is open you can see more frescoes by Taddeo di Bartolo, an altarpiece by Il Sodoma, and some exceptional carved wood seats, by Domenico di Nicolò (*c.* 1415–28). In the adjacent chamber (the **Sala del Mappamondo**), only the outline is left of Lorenzetti's cosmological fresco, a diagram of the universe including all the celestial and angelic spheres, much like the one in the Campo Santo at Pisa. Above it, there is a very famous fresco by Simone Martini (*c.* 1330), showing the redoubtable *condottiere* **Guidoriccio da Fogliano** on his way to attack the castle of Montemassi, during a revolt against Siena. Also by Martini is an enthroned Virgin, or *Maestà*, that is believed to be his earliest work (1315).

## The Allegories of Good and Bad Government

When you enter the **Sala dei Nove** (or Sala della Pace), meeting room of the Council of the Nine, you'll understand at a glance why they ruled Siena so well. Whenever one of the councillors had the temptation to skim some cream off the top, or pass a fat contract over to his brother-in-law the paving contractor, or tighten the screws on the poor by raising the salt tax, he had only to look up at Ambrogio Lorenzetti's great frescoes to really feel like a worm. There are two complementary sets, with scenes of Siena under good government and bad, and allegorical councils of virtues or vices for each. Enthroned Justice rules the good Siena, with such counsellors as Peace, Prudence and Magnanimity; bad Siena groans under the thumb of one nasty piece of work, sneering, fanged Tyranny, and his cronies: Pride, Vainglory, Avarice and Wrath, among others. The good Siena is a happy place, with buildings in good repair, well-dressed folk who are dancing in the streets, and well-stocked shops where the merchants appear to be making a nice profit. Bad Siena is almost a mirror image, only the effects of the Tyrant's rule are plain to see: urban blight, crime in broad daylight, buildings crumbling and abandoned, and business bad for everybody – a landscape which for many of us modern city dwellers will seem all too familiar.

Lorenzetti finished his work around 1338, probably the most ambitious secular painting ever attempted up to that time. The work has been recently cleaned and restored; fittingly, Good Government has survived more or less intact, while Bad Government has not aged so well and parts have been lost. In the next room is Guido da Siena's large *Madonna and Child* (mid-1200s), the earliest masterpiece of the Sienese school. If you're not up to climbing the tower, at least take the long, unmarked stairway by the Sala del Risorgimento, leading up to the **loggia**, with the second-best view over Siena and disassembled pieces of della Quercia's reliefs from the Fonte Gaia, not particularly impressive in their worn and damaged state.

### Around the Campo

Part of the Campo's beauty lies in the element of surprise; one usually enters from narrow arcades between the medieval palaces that give no hint of what lies on the other side. Two of Siena's three main streets form a graceful curve around the back of the Campo; where they meet the third, behind the Fonte Gaia, is the corner the Sienese call the **Croce del Travaglio** (a mysterious nickname: the 'cross of affliction').

Here, the three-arched **Loggia della Mercanzia**, in a sense Siena's Royal Exchange, was where the republic's merchants made their deals and settled their differences before the city's famed commercial tribunal. The Loggia marks the transition from Sienese-Gothic to early Renaissance style – begun in 1417, it was probably influenced by Florence's Loggia dei Lanzi. The five statues of saints on the columns are the work of Antonio Federighi and Vecchietta, the leading Sienese sculptor after della Quercia.

The three streets that meet here lead directly into the three *terzi* of Siena. All three are among the city's most beautiful, in particular the gracefully curving **Banchi di Sotto**, main artery of the Terzo di San Martino. Just beyond the Campo, this street passes Siena's most imposing *palazzo privato*, the **Palazzo Piccolomini** (*currently closed for restoration; call the tourist office for information*), done in the Florentine style by Rossellino in the 1460s. This palace now houses the old Sienese state archive (*reading hall open Mon and Fri 8–2, Tues, Wed and Thurs 8–5.30, Sat 8–1.45; closed Sun, public hols and first 2 weeks in Aug*) – not a place you might consider visiting but for the presence of the famous *Tavolette della Biccherna* (the account books of the *Biccherna*, or state treasury). Beginning in the 1200s, the republic's custom was to commission the best local artists to decorate the covers of the *tavolette*, portraying such prosaic subjects as medieval citizens coming to pay their taxes, city employees counting their pay and earnest monks trying to make the figures square – all are Cistercians from San Galgano (*see* pp.413–4), the only people medieval Siena trusted to do the job. Among other manuscripts and documents you'll find Boccaccio's will.

## Terzo di Città

Southwest from the Croce del Travaglio, Via di Città climbs up to the highest and oldest part of Siena, the natural fortress of the Terzo di Città. Among the palaces it passes is the grandiose **Palazzo Chigi-Saracini**, with a wretched old tree, barely surviving, hanging over the street from its stony courtyard. The palace contains an internationally important music school, the Accademia Musicale Chigiana, and a large collection of Sienese and Florentine art (*only open on request, t 0577 22 091*). Next door is yet another reminder of the Piccolomini, the **Palazzo delle Papesse** (*open daily 12noon–7;adm*). The family, along with the Colonna of Rome and the Correr of Venice, was one of the first to really exploit the fiscal possibilities of the papacy; Aeneas Silvius (Pius II) built this palace, also designed by Rossellino, for his sister, Caterina Piccolomini.

## The Duomo

All approaches from Via di Città to Siena's glorious **cathedral**, spilling over the highest point in the city, are somewhat oblique. Easiest, perhaps, is Via dei Pellegrini, which winds around the back, past the unusual crypt-baptistry tucked underneath (*see* pp.384–5), up the steps to the Piazza del Duomo, and through a portal in a huge, free-standing wall of striped marble arches, a memorial to that incredible ill-starred 1339 rebuilding plan confounded by the plague. The cathedral the Sienese had to settle for may not be a transcendent expression of faith, and it may not be an great landmark in architecture, but it is certainly one of the most delightful, decorative ornaments in Christendom.

Begun around 1200, one of the first Gothic cathedrals in central Italy, it started in the good medieval tradition as a communal effort, not really a project of the Church. There doesn't seem to have been much voluntary labour – even in the Middle Ages Italians were a little too blasé for that – but every citizen with a cart was expected to bring in two loads of marble from the quarries each year, earning him a special indulgence from the bishop. One load must have been white and the other black for, under the influence of Pisa, the Sienese built themselves one thoroughly striped cathedral – stripes darker and bolder than Pisa's or even Pistoia's. The campanile, with its distinctive fenestration, narrowing in size down six levels, rises over the city like a giant ice cream parfait. Most of the body of the church was finished by 1270, and 14 years later Giovanni Pisano was called in to create the sculpture for the lavish **façade**, with statues of biblical prophets and pagan philosophers. The upper half was not begun until the 1390s, and the glittering mosaics in the gables are, like Orvieto's, the work of Venetian artists of the late 19th century.

### The Cathedral Interior: the Marble Pavement

*Open Nov–mid-Mar Mon–Sat 7.30–1 and 2.30–5, Sun 2–5; mid-Mar–Oct Mon–Sat 7.30am–7.30pm, Sun 2–5.*

This is a virtual treasure-box, fit to keep a serious sightseer busy for an entire day. Upon entering the main portal, the ferociously striped pilasters and the Gothic vaulting, a blue firmament painted with golden stars, inevitably draw the eye upwards. The most spectacular feature, though, is at your feet – the marble pavement, where the first peculiar figure smiling up at you is **Hermes Trismegistus** (*see* p.382), the legendary Egyptian father of alchemy, depicted in elegant *sgraffito* work

Piazza San Giovanni

# Siena Cathedral

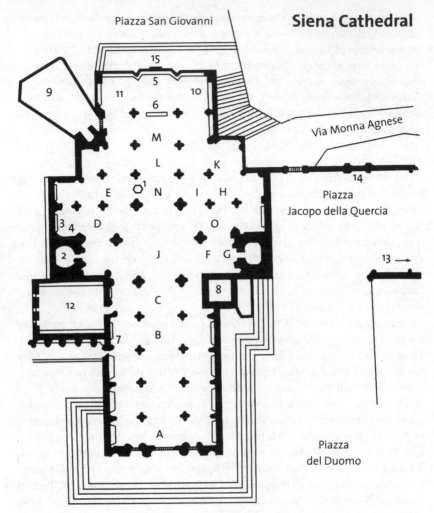

1 Pisano's Pulpit
2 Chapel of San Giovanni Battista
3 Tomb of Cardinal Pecci (Donatello)
4 Tomb of Cardinal Petroni (Tino da Camaino)
5 Stained Glass of Duccio
6 High Altar
7 Piccolomini Altar (della Quercia,
   Michelangelo)
8 Campanile
9 Sacristy
10 Cantorie
11 Choir
12 Piccolomini Library
13 To Cathedral Museum
14 Cathedral Extension
15 Bapistry (lower level)

A Hermes Trismegistus
B Allegory of Virtue
C Wheel of Fortune
D Massacre of the Innocents
E Judith Liberating Bethulia
F Seven Ages of Man
G Allegories of Faith, Hope and Charity
H Story of Absalom
I Emperor Sigismund on his Throne
J Sacrifice of Elias, Execution of the False Prophets
K Samson and the Philistines
L David the Psalmist
M Sacrifice of Abraham
N Moses Receives the Commandments
O Story of Jephta

of white and coloured marble. In fact, the entire floor of the cathedral is covered with almost 12,000 square metres of virtuoso *sgraffito* in 56 scenes, including portraits, mystical allegories and Old Testament scenes. Like the Biccherna covers in the Palazzo Piccolomini, they were a tradition carried on over centuries. Many of Siena's best artists worked on them, beginning in 1369 and continuing into the 1600s; Giorgio Vasari claimed that Duccio di Buoninsegna himself first worked in this medium, though he has none among the pictures here.

Even in a building with so many marvels – the Piccolomini Library, Nicola Pisano's pulpit, Duccio's stained glass, works by Donatello, della Quercia, Pinturicchio, Michelangelo, Bernini and many others – this pavement perhaps takes pride of place. The greatest limitation of Sienese art was always the conservatism of its patrons, accustomed to demanding the same old images in the same old styles. Commissions from the Office of Cathedral Works, controlled by the state, were usually more liberal, allowing the artists to create such unique, and in some cases startling images, one of the greatest achievements of Renaissance Siena.

The Hermes on the cathedral pavement, by Giovanni di Stefano, was completed in the 1480s, a decade after Ficino's translation; he is shown with Moses, holding a book with the inscription 'Take up thy letters and laws, O Egyptians'. On either side, all 10 prophetic *Sibyls*, done by various artists at the same time, decorate the aisles. Nor are Hermes and the sibyls the only peculiar thing on this floor. Directly behind him begins a series of large scenes, including a *Wheel of Fortune*, with men hanging on to it for dear life, another wheel of uncertain symbolism, and emblems of Siena and other Tuscan and Latin cities. Oddest of all is a work by Pinturicchio, variously titled the *Allegory of Virtue* or the *Allegory of Fortune*; on a rocky island full of serpents, a party of well-dressed people has just embarked, climbing to the summit where a figure of 'Socrates' accepts a pen from a seated female figure, and another, 'Crates', empties a basket of gold and jewels into the sea. Below, a naked woman with a gonfalon stands with one foot in a boat, and another on land.

Unfortunately, many of the best scenes, under the crossing and transepts, are covered to protect them. You'll need to come between 15 August and 15 September to see the visionary works of Alessandro Franchi – the *Triumph of Elias* and other events in that prophet's life – and Domenico Beccafumi's *Sacrifice of Elias* and the *Execution of the False Prophets of Baal*. Other works uncovered all year include *The Seven Ages of Man* by Antonio Federighi, *Scenes From the Life of Moses* by Beccafumi, Matteo di Giovanni's *Massacre of the Innocents* (always a favourite subject in Sienese art), and, best of all, the beautifully drawn *Judith Liberating the City of Bethulia*, a collaboration of Federighi, Matteo di Giovanni and Urbano da Cortona.

## Elsewhere in the Cathedral

Perhaps the greatest attraction above floor level is the great Carrara marble **pulpit** done by Nicola Pisano in the 1280s. Pisano started on it directly after finishing the one in Pisa; one of the assistants he brought here to help with the work was the young Arnolfo di Cambio. The typical Pisano conception is held up by allegorical figures of the seven liberal arts – more sibyls, prophets, Christian virtues and saints tucked away in the odd corners, and vigorous, crowded relief panels from the Passion as good as the ones in Pisa. Nearby, in the left transept, the **chapel of San Giovanni Battista** has frescoes by Pinturicchio and a bronze statue of St John the Baptist by Donatello, who also contributed the **Tomb of Giovanni Pecci**, a 1400s Sienese bishop. Another tomb worth a look is that of Cardinal Petroni, an influential early Renaissance design from 1310 by Tino di Camaino.

Some of the **stained glass** in the cathedral is excellent, especially the earliest windows, in the apse, designed by Duccio, and the rose window with its cornucopia. Over the high altar is a bronze **baldachin** by Vecchietta, and in the north aisle the **Piccolomini Altar** includes four early statues of saints by Michelangelo, and one by Torrigiano, the fellow who broke Michelangelo's nose and ended up in exile, working in Westminster Abbey. There is also a *Madonna* by Jacopo della Quercia. Throughout

## Hermes Trismegistus

Hermes Trismegistus is someone rarely seen in art, though he is a mysterious protagonist in a great undercurrent of Renaissance thought. 'Thrice-great Hermes', mythical author of a series of mystic philosophical dialogues from the 2nd century AD, had a profound influence on Greek and Arabic thought, gradually becoming associated (correctly or not) with the Egyptian god Thoth, inventor of writing and father of a deep mystical tradition that continues up to this day.

In the 1400s, the Hermetic writings were introduced in the west, thanks largely to the work of Greek scholars fleeing the Ottoman conquest of Constantinople and Trebizond. These writings made quite a splash, prompting a number of key figures to take action. So great was its impact that Marsilio Ficino, the Florentine Humanist and friend of Cosimo de' Medici, completed the first Latin translation of the Hermetic books in 1471 – Cosimo specifically asked him to put off his translations of Plato to get this more important work finished!

To the men of the Renaissance, Hermes was a real person, an Egyptian prophet, who lived in the time of Moses and may perhaps have been his teacher. They saw, revealed in the Hermetic books, an ancient, natural religion, prefiguring Christianity and complementary to it – and, in fact, much more fun than Christianity, for the magical elements in it were entirely to the taste of neo-Platonists like Ficino. From a contemporary point of view, the recovery of Hermes Trismegistus was one of the main intellectual events of the century, one that witnessed a tremendous revival of natural magic, alchemy and astrology.

The memorable Hermes in Siena is depicted surrounded by a bevy of ten Sibyls: those of Cumae and Tivoli (the Italian contingent), Delphi, Libya, the Hellespont, Phrygia and others. These ladies, part of a pan-Mediterranean religious tradition even older than Hermes Trismegistus, are far more common in Tuscan religious iconography (as seen in the Baptistry and Santa Trinita in Florence, or most famously, on Michelangelo's Sistine Chapel ceiling), for the belief that they all in some way foretold the birth of Christ.

the cathedral, as everywhere else in Siena, be sure to keep an eye out for details – little things like the tiny, exquisite heads of the popes that decorate the clerestory wall. The Office of Works never settled for anything less than the best, and even such trifles as the holy water fonts, the choir stalls, the iron grilles and the candlesticks are works of genuine artistic merit.

## Piccolomini Library

*Open Nov–mid-Mar Mon–Sat 10–1 and 2.30–5, Sun and public hols 2.30–5; mid-Mar–Oct Mon–Sat 9–7.30, Sun and public hols 2.30–5; adm.*

This is the room with the famous frescoes by Pinturicchio, built to hold the library of Aeneas Silvius, the greatest member of Siena's greatest noble family. The entrance is off the left aisle, near the Piccolomini Altar.

Aeneas Silvius Piccolomini, eventually to become Pope Pius II, was the very definition of a Renaissance man. He was probably the greatest geographer of his age: his works were studied closely by Columbus. Beyond that, and his activities as a poet, diplomat and historian, founder of Pienza and an important patron of artists and humanist scholars, he had, of course, a busy clerical-political career, working fitfully to reform the Church of Rome and the constitution of his native city. In 1495, 31 years after his death, Cardinal Francesco Piccolomini, the man who would become Pope Pius III, decided his celebrated uncle's life would make a fine subject for a series of frescoes. He gave the job to Pinturicchio, his last major commission; among his assistants was the young, still impressionable Raphael – anyone who knows his *Betrothal of the Virgin* will find these paintings eerily familiar.

The 10 scenes include Aeneas Silvius' attendance at the court of James I in Scotland – a Scotland with a Tuscan fantasy landscape – where he served with an embassy. Later he is shown accepting a poet laureate's crown from his friend Emperor Frederick III, and presiding over the meeting of Frederick and his bride-to-be, Eleanor of Aragon. Another fresco depicts him canonizing St Catherine of Siena. The last, poignant one portrays a view of Ancona, and its cathedral up on Monte Guasco, where Pius II went in 1464, planning a crusade against the Turks. While waiting for the help promised by the European powers, help that never came, he fell ill and died.

Art historians and critics, following the sniping biography of the artist by Vasari, are not always kind to Pinturicchio. As with Gozzoli's frescoes for the Medici Palace in Florence, the consensus seems to be that this is a less challenging sort of art, or perhaps just a very elevated approach to interior decoration. Certainly Pinturicchio seems extremely concerned with the latest styles in court dress and coiffure. However, the incandescent colour, fairy-tale backgrounds and beautifully drawn figures prove irresistible. These are among the brightest and best-preserved of all quattrocento frescoes; the total effect is that of a serenely confident art, concerned above all with beauty for beauty's sake, even when chronicling the life of a pope. Aeneas Silvius' books have all been carted away somewhere but one of his favourite things remains, a marble statue of the *Three Graces*, a copy of the work by Praxiteles that was much studied by the artists of the 1400s.

## Museo dell'Opera Metropolitana

*Open Nov–mid-Mar daily 9–1.30; mid-Mar–Sept daily 9–7.30; Oct daily 9–6; adm.*

Around the side of the cathedral, off the right transept, Piazza Jacopo della Quercia is the name the Sienese have given to the doomed nave of their 1330s **cathedral extension**. All around the square, the heroic pilasters and arches rise, some incorporated into the walls of later buildings. Beyond the big, blank façade, a little door on the right allows entrance to the **Museo Metropolitana**, built into what would have been one of the cathedral transepts. This is the place to go to inspect the cathedral façade at close range. Most of the statues on the façade today are modern copies, replacing the works of great sculptors like Nicola Pisano, Urbano da Cortona and Jacopo della Quercia. The originals have been moved to the museum for better preservation, and you can look the cathedral's marble saints right in the eye – if you care to; many of these remarkable statues, fairly alive with early Renaissance *prontezza* (alertness), seem ready to hop off their pedestals and start declaiming if they suspect for a minute you've been skipping Sunday mass.

Besides these, there are architectural fragments and leftover pinnacles, as well as some bits of the marble pavement that had to be replaced. On the first floor, a collection of Sienese paintings includes Duccio di Buoninsegna's masterpiece, the *Maestà* that hung behind the cathedral's high altar from 1311 until 1505. Painted on both sides, the main composition is a familiar Sienese favourite, the enthroned Virgin flanked by neat rows of adoring saints – expressive faces and fancy clothes with a glittering gold background. Among the other paintings and sculptures are works by Pietro and Ambrogio Lorenzetti, Simone Martini, Beccafumi and Vecchietta.

Among the works on the top floor is the *Madonna dagli Occhi Grossi* ('of the Big Eyes') by an anonymous artist of the 1210s, a landmark in the development of Sienese painting and the original cathedral altarpiece. There's a hoard of golden croziers, reliquaries and crucifixes from the cathedral treasure, including another lovely golden rose from the Vatican – probably a gift from Aeneas Silvius. A stairway from here leads up to the top of the **Facciatone**, the 'big façade' of the unfinished nave, where you can contemplate vain ambitions and enjoy a view over the city.

## Baptistry

*Open summer daily 9–7.30; Oct daily 9–6; winter daily 10–1 and 2.30–5; adm.*

Outside the unfinished cathedral nave, a long, steep set of stairs leads down around the back of the church to Piazza San Giovanni. In this lower but prominent setting the Office of Works architects squeezed in a baptistry, perhaps the only one in Italy situated directly under a cathedral apse. Behind its unfinished 1390s Gothic façade, this baptistry contains yet another impressive hoard of art. It's hard to see anything in this gloomy cellar, though; bring plenty of coins for the lighting machines. Frescoes by Vecchietta, restored to death in the 19th century, decorate much of the interior. The crown jewel, however, is the **baptismal font**, a king-sized work embellished with some of the finest sculpture of the quattrocento. Of the gilded reliefs around the sides, *Herod's Feast* is by Donatello, and the *Baptism of Christ* and *St John in Prison* by Ghiberti. The first relief, with the *Annunciation of the Baptist's Birth*, is the work of Jacopo della Quercia, who also added the five statues of prophets above. Two of the statues at the corners of the font, the ones representing the virtues Hope and Charity, are also by Donatello.

Just across the street from the baptistry, the Renaissance **Palazzo del Magnifico** was the family headquarters of the Petrucci, Sienese power-brokers (and perhaps would-be tyrants) in the late 15th and early 16th centuries.

## Santa Maria della Scala

*t 0577 224 811, www.santamaria/comune.siena.it; open Mar–Oct daily 10–6; Nov–Feb daily 10.30–4.30; 23 Dec–7 Jan daily 10–6; adm.*

Opposite the old cathedral façade, one entire side of the piazza is occupied by the great **Ospedale di Santa Maria della Scala**, believed to have been founded in the 9th century and for centuries one of the largest and finest hospitals in the world. According to legend, the hospital had its beginnings with a pious cobbler named Sorore, who opened a hostel and infirmary for pilgrims on their way to Rome. (Siena was an important stop on medieval Europe's busiest pilgrimage route, the Via Francigiana). Sorore's mother, it is said, later had a vision here – of babies ascending a ladder (*la scala*) into heaven, and being received into the arms of the Virgin Mary – and consequently a foundling hospital was soon added. A meticulous attention to the health of its citizens was always one of the most praiseworthy features of Siena; even in the decadence of the 1700s advances in such things as inoculation were being made here. In the 14th century it insisted on such revolutionary practices as the washing of hands by doctors and nurses, meals adapted to each patient's illness, and the use of iron beds (to prevent the spread of bed-bugs). To encourage donations, laws were passed allowing wealthy Sienese to deduct gifts from their taxes (remember, this was the 14th century) and not a few left huge sums in their wills; after the plague of 1348, the hospital was up to its ears in gold.

In recent years, the hospital functions have been gradually moved out to more accessible locations (one of the last to die here was novelist and folktale compiler Italo Calvino). As the place closed up, there was talk of converting it into a museum. Now they're doing it, and in a big way. The Sienese say that their new museum, dedicated to all the arts and the city's history, will be one of the largest in the world, with three times the exhibition space of the Pompidou Centre. Don't ask when it will be finished; the point of this innovative exercise is that it will *never* be finished. An international competition was held to plan the new complex; the winner, Professor Guido Canali of Parma, came up with the idea of a *cantiere didattico*, a kind of 'educational construction site', where the process of museum-building itself is part of the attraction. They should have many of the permanent exhibits in place in ten years or so, along with shops, temporary exhibits and restoration workshops. In a typical gesture of Sienese pride, the *comune* declined to ask for state help in completing this project; they mean to keep control by paying the whole bill themselves.

For now, it's definitely worth the price of admission just to see the big frescoes in the **Sala dei Pellegrini**, the hospital's main reception hall. Another pioneering fresco-cycle devoted to a secular subject, like those in the Palazzo Pubblico, this is a tribute to old Siena's advanced, humanistic outlook; all the scenes are devoted to the history of the hospital, including the vision of Sorore's mother, and everyday views of the hospital's activities. In the best of them, Domenico di Bartolo shows how Sienese art was still keeping up with the Florentines in 1441 with his *Reception, Education and Marriage of a Daughter of the Hospital*; care of abandoned children, the *getatelli* (literally, 'little ones thrown away'), was one of the hospital's important functions. Other frescoes, by different Sienese artists, portray in loving detail the caring for the sick, the distributon of alms to the poor, and the paying of the wet-nurses of the *getatelli*. All are lively, crowded scenes of life in a unique institution, and an insight into a side of old Siena you might not have thought existed.

Already, there is plenty to see, including a collection of precious golden reliquaries and other church paraphernalia, some of it from medieval Constantinople, in refur-bished chambers cheerfully marked *isolamento dei contagiosi*. Some other original features of the hospital include the **Cappella del Sacro Chiodo**, with damaged fres-coes by Vecchietta, the elaborate **Cappella SS. Annunziata**, and the thoroughly spooky **Cappella di Santa Caterina**, which begins with a leering skull and ends with an altarpiece by Taddeo di Bartolo. Old views and relics of the hospital are displayed in many of the long hallways; in some of the oldest, you can see how the façade was originally covered with frescoes (by Pietro and Ambrogio Lorenzeti), a colourful counterpoint to the cathedral façade across the way. Another part of the complex now houses the **Museo Archeologico** (*open Mar–Oct daily 10–6; Nov–Feb daily 10.30–4.30; 23 Dec–7 Jan daily 10–6; adm*) with an Etruscan and Roman collection.

## The Pinacoteca

The ancient quarter of steep narrow streets north of the cathedral is the *contrada* of the *Selva* (forest) – rhinoceros country. In its heart, Piazza della Selva, one of the most charming of the new *contrada* fountains has a bronze statue of the neighbour-hood's rhinoceros symbol. Leaving the cathedral in the opposite direction, south down Via del Capitano, will lead you into the haunts of the dolphin and turtle (*Onda* and *Tartaruga*). Where the street meets Via di Città, it changes its name to Via San Pietro, passing the 14th-century Palazzo Buonsignori, one of the most harmo-nious of the city's noble palaces, now restored as the home of the **Pinacoteca Nazionale** (*open Mon 8.30–1.30, Tues–Sat 8.15–7.15, Sun 8.15–1.15; adm*).

This is the temple of Sienese art, a representative sampling of this inimitable city's style; many of the works have been recently restored. The collection is arranged roughly chronologically, beginning on the top floor with Guido da Siena and his school in the mid-13th century (Room 2), continuing through an entire room of deli-cate, melancholy Virgins by Duccio and his followers, before reaching a climax with Duccio's luminous though damaged *Madonna dei Francescani* in Room 4. Madonnas and saints fill room after room, including important works by Siena's greatest 14th-century artists. One of the most famous is Simone Martini's *Madonna and Child*; the story goes that this Madonna was a great Palio fan. When everyone had gathered in the Campo for the event, she would wander out in the empty streets and tiptoe over for a look. One day, she lingered too long in the Campo and had to run back home, losing her veil in her haste. She has yet to find it, and according to the Sienese, she weeps sweetly during the Palio, probably because she can't get through the Pinacoteca's security system. Other Madonnas that stand out are those of Pietro and Ambrogio Lorenzetti (*Madonna Enthroned* and the *Annunciation*, both in Room 7) and Taddeo di Bartolo (*Triptych*, in Room 11) stand out, with their rosy blooming faces and brilliant colour, a remarkable counterpoint to the relative austerity of contemporary painting in Florence. One element that is clearly evident in many of these paintings is Sienese civic pride; the artists take obvious delight in including the city's skyline and landmarks in the background of their works – even in Nativities.

Sienese Renaissance painters are well represented, often betraying the essential conservatism of their art and resisting the new approaches of Florence: Domenico di Bartolo's 1433 *Madonna* in Room 9; Nerocchio and Matteo di Giovanni of the 1470s (Room 14); Sano di Pietro, the leading painter of the 1440s (Rooms 16–17). The first floor displays some of Il Sodoma's most important works, especially the great *Scourging of Christ* in Room 31 (1514); in Room 37 the *Descent into Hell* is one of the finest works by Siena's greatest Mannerist, Beccafumi.

## Around the Terzo di Città

Next to the Pinacoteca, the church of **San Pietro alle Scale** contains *The Flight into Egypt*, an altarpiece by Rutilio Manetti, the only significant Sienese painter of the Baroque era, a follower of Caravaggio. **San Giuseppe**, at the end of Via San Pietro, marks Siena's uneasy compromise with the new world of the 1600s. One of the city's first Baroque churches, it was nevertheless built not in Baroque marble or travertine but good Siena brown brick. This is the church of the *Onda* district; the *contrada*'s fountain is in front. Just around the corner, the gloomy bulk of **Sant'Agostino** (*open mid-Mar–Oct 10.30–1.30 and 3–7.30; adm*)conceals a happier rococo interior of the 1740s by Vanvitelli, the Dutchman (born Van Wittel) who was chief architect for the Kings of Naples. Most of the building dates back to the 13th century, however, and there are surviving bits of trecento frescoes and altarpieces all around. In the north aisle, the Piccolomini chapel (*usually shut*) has a fine painting by Il Sodoma, an *Epiphany*, and a *Massacre of the Innocents* by Matteo di Giovanni.

Via Piero Andrea Mattioli leads from here to the city walls and the Porta Tufi, passing along the way a path that leads to Siena's small **Botanical Gardens** (*open Mon–Fri 8–12.30 and 2.30–5.30, Sat 8–12; book in advance for guided tours, t 0577 232 874, www.unisi.it/ricercal/dip/dba/orto*). Further west, the *contrada* of the *Chiocciola* (snail) is centred on the church of **Santa Maria del Carmine**, a 14th-century church remodelled by Baldassare Peruzzi in 1517; inside there is a painting of *St Michael* by Beccafumi and a rather grimly Caravaggiesque *Last Judgement* by an anonymous 16th-century artist.

# Terzo di San Martino

Beginning again at the Croce del Travaglio and the Palazzo Piccolomini (*see* p.378), Banchi di Sotto leads into the quiet eastern third of the city, passing the **Loggia del Papa**, a Renaissance ornament given to Siena by Aeneas Silvius Piccolomini in 1462. The most intriguing parts of this neighbourhood are found on the hillside behind Piazza del Mercato, old streets on slopes and stairs in the *contrada* of the *Torre* – one of the 'unlucky' *contrade* that hasn't won a Palio in decades. Nevertheless they have a fine fountain with their elephant-and-tower emblem on pretty Piazzetta Franchi. One of the more characteristic streets in this part of town is **Via dell'Oro**, an alley of overhanging medieval houses, much like the ones in the Palazzo Pubblico's frescoes of Good and Bad Government (*see* p.377). For something different, **Via Porta Giustizia** will lead you on a country ramble within the city's walls, down the valley that separates Terzo San Martino and Terzo di Città.

Among the noteworthy churches in this Terzo are **Santo Spirito** on Via dei Pispini, with further frescoes by Il Sodoma in the first chapel on the right; and **Santa Maria dei Servi**, to the south on Via dei Servi in the *contrada* of *Valdimontone* (ram). Here, in the north transept, is one of the earliest and finest Sienese nativities, the altarpiece in the second north chapel, by Taddeo di Bartolo. Good paintings include a *Madonna* by Coppo di Marcovaldo and the *Madonna del Popolo* by Lippo Memmi. An interesting comparison can be made between two versions of that favourite Sienese subject, the *Massacre of the Innocents*: one from the early trecento by Pietro Lorenzetti, and another from 1491 by Matteo di Giovanni.

Nearby on Via Roma, the *Società Esecutori Pie Disposizioni* keeps an **oratory** and a small but good collection of Sienese art (*call ahead, t 0577 284 300; open Mon and Fri 9–12, Tues and Thurs 3–5; closed Sat and Sun*). This Terzo also has two of the best surviving city gates, the **Porta Romana** at the end of Via Roma, and the elegant **Porta Pispini** on the road to Perugia. The latter was once embellished with a *Nativity* by Sodoma, of which only traces are still visible.

# Terzo di Camollia

Leading north from the Campo, **Via Banchi di Sopra**, a most aristocratic thoroughfare, lined with the palaces of the medieval Sienese élite, forms the spine of this largest and most populous of the *terzi*. The first important palace is also one of the oldest, that of the Tolomei family, a proud clan of noble bankers who liked to trace their ancestry back to the Greek Ptolemies of Hellenistic-era Egypt. The **Palazzo Tolomei**, begun in 1208, is the very soul of Sienese Gothic; it gave its name to Piazza Tolomei in front, the space used by the republic for its assembly meetings before the construction of the Palazzo Pubblico. Just a few blocks down Banchi di Sopra, **Palazzo Salimbeni** on Piazza Salimbeni was the compound of the Tolomeis' mortal enemies; their centuries-long vendetta dragged Sienese politics into chaos on more than a few occasions. Together with the two adjacent palaces on the square, the

Salimbeni is now the home of the *Monte dei Paschi di Siena*, founded by the city as a pawnshop in 1472, now a remarkable savings bank with a medieval air about it that has a tremendous influence over everything that happens in southern Tuscany, and branches as far away as Australia – they also have a good art collection, sometimes open to the public along with special exhibitions. The national government is currently trying to privatize the Monte dei Paschi, which makes the Sienese hopping mad. A little further up the street, the plain brick **Oratory of Santa Maria di Nevi** is almost always locked up; if you should chance to see it open, stop in to see the altarpiece, the finest work of the late 1400s painter Matteo di Giovanni.

East of these palaces, in the neighbourhood of the *Giraffa* (giraffe), is one of the last important churches built in Siena, the proto-Baroque **Santa Maria di Provenzano (1594)**, at the end of Via del Moro. This particular Virgin Mary, a terracotta image said to have been left by St Catherine (*see* below), has had one of the most popular devotional cults in Siena since the 1590s; the annual Palio is in her honour. The quiet streets behind the church, Siena's red-light district in Renaissance times, lead to **San Francesco**, begun in 1326, one of the city's largest churches. It's a sad tale; after a big fire in the 17th century, this great Franciscan barn was used for centuries as a warehouse and barracks. Restorations began in the 1880s, and the 'medieval' brick façade was completed only in 1913. The interior is still one of the most impressive in Siena, a monolithic rectangle with vivid stained glass (especially in late afternoon) and good transept chapels in the Florentine manner. A little artwork has survived, including traces of frescoes by both the Lorenzettis in the north transept. To the right is the fine Renaissance cloister.

Next to San Francesco is the equally simple **Oratorio di San Bernardino** (*open mid-Mar–Oct daily 10.30–1.30 and 3–5.30; adm*), begun in the late 1400s in honour of Siena's famous preacher and graced with the preacher's heart. Its upper chapel, a monument of the Sienese Renaissance, contains frescoes by Beccafumi, Il Sodoma and the almost forgotten High Renaissance master Girolamo del Pacchia, few of whose works survive. The areas west of San Francesco, traditionally a solid working-class quarter, make up the *contrada* of *Bruco*, the caterpillar; their fountain is under the steps on Via dei Rossi. On the wall of the house opposite is a curious marble relief of a woman at a window peering at a pomegranate from behind half-closed curtains. Caterpillars are everywhere.

*Bruco*'s name recalls the Compagnia del Bruco, the trade union that initiated the revolt of 1371, temporarily reforming Siena's faction-ridden government. The workers paid a terrible price for it; while the revolution was under way, some young noble *provocateurs* started a fire that consumed almost the entire *contrada*. Today *Bruco* fares worst of the 'unlucky' neighbourhoods; it hasn't won a Palio since 1955.

## St Catherine, St Dominic and the Goose

Unlike the poor caterpillar, the equally proletarian *Oca* (goose) seems the best organized and most successful *contrada*. On occasion during the Napoleonic Wars, with Tuscan and city governments in disarray, the *Oca*'s men took charge of the city.

The goose's most famous daughter, Caterina Benincasa, was born here, on Vicolo del Tiratoio, in 1347. She was the last but one of twenty-five children born into the family of a wool-dyer. At an early age the visions started. By her teens she had turned her room at home into a cell and, while she never became a nun, she lived like a hermit, a solitary ascetic in her own house, sleeping with a stone for a pillow. After she received the stigmata, like St Francis, her reputation as a holy woman spread across Tuscany; popes and kings corresponded with her, and towns would send for her to settle their disputes. In 1378 Florence was under a papal interdict, and the city asked Catherine to plead its case at the papal court at Avignon. She went, but with an agenda of her own – convincing Pope Gregory XI to move the papacy back to Rome where it belonged. As a woman, and a holy woman to boot, she was able to tell the pope to his face what a corrupt and worldly Church he was running, without ending up dangling from the top of a palace wall.

Talking the pope (a French pope, mind you) into leaving the civilized life in Provence for turbulent, barbaric 14th-century Rome is only one of the miracles with which Catherine was credited. Political expediency probably helped more than divine intervention – much of Italy, including anathemized Florence, was in revolt against the absentee popes. She followed them back, and died in Rome in 1380, aged only 33.

Canonization came in 1460, and in our own century she has been declared co-patron of Italy (along with St Francis) and one of the Doctors of the Church. She and St Teresa of Avila are the only women to hold this honour; both for their inspired devotional writings and practical, incisive letters encouraging church reform.

The *contrada* of the Goose stretches down steeply from Banchi di Sopra to the western city walls. At its centre, on Vicolo di Tiratoio, St Catherine's house is preserved as a shrine; the **Santuario e Casa di Santa Caterina** (*Costa di S. Antonia; open winter daily 9–12.30 and 3.30–6; summer daily 9–12.30 and 2.30–6*) includes the whole of the Benincasa home and the dyer's workshop, each room converted into a chapel, many with frescoes by 15th- and 16th-century Sienese artists. The adjacent oratory is now the Oca's *contrada* chapel (take time to note the goose in the detail of the façade).

Via Santa Caterina, the main street of the Oca, slopes down towards the city walls and **Fontebranda**, a simple pointed-arched fountain of the 13th century. It doesn't seem much now, but medieval and Renaissance travellers always remarked on it, an important part of Siena's advanced system of fountains and aqueducts. The church of **San Domenico**, on the hill above Fontebranda, similarly fails to impress, at least when you see it close up from the bus depot on Piazza San Domenico. From Fontebranda, however, the bold Gothic lines of the apse and transepts give a great insight into the straightforward, strangely modern character of much Sienese religious architecture. It's a long climb up to the church from here. Inside, the church is as big and empty as San Francesco; among the relatively few works of art is the only portrait of St Catherine, on the west wall, done by her friend, the artist Andrea Vanni. In this church, scene of so many incidents from the saint's life, you can see her head in a golden reliquary, though the real attraction is the wonderfully hysterical set of murals by Il Sodoma in the **Cappella Santa Caterina**, representing the girl in various states of serious exaltation.

The open, relatively modern quarter around San Domenico offers a welcome change from the dark and treeless streets of this brick city, in a shady park called **La Lizza** and the green spaces around the **Fortezza Medicea**. Though the site is the same, this is not the hated fortress Charles V compelled the Sienese to build in 1552; as soon as the Sienese chased the imperial troops out, they razed it to the ground. Cosimo I forced its rebuilding after annexing Siena, but to make the bitter pill easier to swallow he employed a Sienese architect, Baldassare Lanci, and let him create what must be the most elegant and civilized, least threatening fortress in Italy. The Fortezza, a long, low rectangle of Siena brick profusely decorated with Medici balls, seems more like a setting for garden parties or summer opera than anything designed to intimidate a sullen populace.

The Sienese weren't completely won over; right after Italian reunification they renamed the central space of the fortress **Piazza della Libertà**. The grounds are now a city park, and the vaults of the munition cellars have become the **Enoteca Italiana** (*t 0577 288 497, f 0577 270 717, enoteca@enoteca-italiana.it; open Tues–Sat 12noon–1am, Mon 12noon–8; closed Sun*), the 'Permanent Exhibition of Italian Wines'. Almost every variety of wine Italy produces can be bought here, by the glass or by the bottle. The Enoteca's purpose is to promote Italian wines – it ships thousands of bottles overseas each year and hosts an annual *Settimana dei Vini* featuring regional wines in the first half of June.

East of the fortress, beyond the Lizza and the city stadium, lie the twin centres of modern Siena, **Piazza Gramsci**, terminus for most city bus lines, and **Piazza Matteotti**. Continuing northwards towards the Camollia gate, you pass the little Renaissance church of **Fonte Giusta**, just off Via di Camollia on Vicolo Fontegiusta. Designed in 1482 by Urbano da Cortona, this church contains a fresco by Peruzzi (another sibyl) and a magnificent tabernacle over the main altar; there is also a whalebone, left here, according to local legend, by Christopher Columbus. The **Porta Camollia**, in the northernmost corner of Siena, underwent the Baroque treatment in the 1600s. Here you will see the famous inscription 'Wider than her gates Siena opens her heart to you'. Old Siena was never that sentimental. The whole thing was added in 1604 – undoubtedly under the orders of the Florentine governor – to mark the visit of Grand Duke Francesco I, who wasn't really welcome at all.

# Peripheral Attractions

From Porta Camollia, Viale Vittorio Emanuele leads through some of the modern quarters outside the walls. Beyond the gate it passes a column commemorating the meeting of Emperor Frederick III and his bride-to-be Eleanor of Aragon in 1451 – the event captured in one of the Pinturicchio frescoes in the Piccolomini Library. Next looms a great defence tower, the **Antiporto**, erected just before the Siege of Siena, and rebuilt in 1675. Further down, the **Palazzo dei Diavoli** (1460) was the headquarters of the Marquis of Marignano during the siege.

There isn't much on the outskirts of the city – thanks largely to Marignano, who laid waste lovely and productive lands for miles around. Some two kilometres east (take Via Simone Martini from the Porta Ovile), in the hills above the railway station, the basilica and monastery of **L'Osservanza** (*open by request Mon–Sat 10–12 and 4–6, t 0577 332 444*) has been carefully restored after serious damage in the last war. Begun in 1422, a foundation of San Bernardino, the monastery retains much of its collection of 13th-and 14th-century Sienese art.

To the west of the city, the road to Massa Marittima passes through the hills of the Montagnola Sienese, an important centre of monasticism in the Middle Ages (*see* San Galgano, pp.391–2). Near **Montecchio** (6km), the hermitage of **Lecceto**, one of the oldest in Tuscany, has been much changed, but still has some Renaissance frescoes in the church and a 12th-century cloister; nearby, the hermitage of **San Leonardo al Lago** is mostly in ruins but the 14th-century church survives, with masterly frescoes (*c.* 1360) by Pietro Lorenzetti's star pupil, Lippo Vanni. Just outside the village of **Sovicille** (13km), there is a 12th-century Romanesque church, the **Pieve di Ponte alla Spina**.

The village of **Rosia** (17km) has another Romanesque church, and just south is the Vallombrosan **Abbey of Torri** (*open Mon–Fri 9–12*), with much from its original foundation in the 1200s; it has a rare three-storey cloister, with three types of columns.

# Hill Towns West of Siena

14

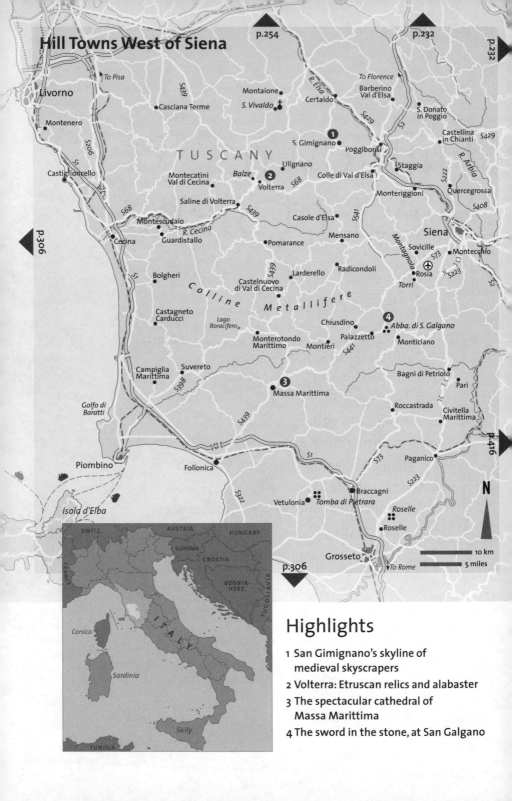

p.254

p.232

p.232

To Pisa

Livorno

To Florence

Montaione

S. Vivaldo ✝

Certaldo

Barberino
Val d'Elsa

Casciana Terme

Montenero

S. Donato
in Poggio

S439

S429

Castellina
in Chianti

S429

**①** S. Gimignano

Poggibonsi

TUSCANY

Castiglioncello

Ulignano

Staggia

Montecatini
Val di Cecina

Balze

**②**

Colle di Val d'Elsa

Volterra

Monteriggioni

Quercegrossa

S206

S1

S222

S408

Saline di Volterra

S439

S68

Casole d'Elsa

S541

Siena

Montescudaio

R. Cecina

Sovicille

Montecchio

Cecina

Guardistallo

Pomarance

Mensano

Montagnola

Rosia

Montecchio

S573

S68

S1

Bolgheri

Larderello

Radicondoli

Torri

S223

S2

Castelnuovo
di Val di Cecina

S439

*Colline   Metallifere*

Castagneto
Carducci

Lago
Boracifero

Chiusdino

**④** Abba. di S. Galgano

Monterotondo
Marittimo

Palazzetto

Monticiano

Montieri

S441

Campiglia
Marittima

Suvereto

Bagni di Petriolo

Pari

S398

**③** Massa Marittima

Roccastrada

Golfo di
Baratti

S439

Civitella
Marittima

p.306

p.416

Piombino

Follonica

Paganico

S1

S573

S223

Isola d'Elba

S322

Braccagni

Vetulonia

*Tomba di Pietrara*

Roselle

Roselle

**N**

Grosseto

To Rome

10 km

5 miles

SWITZ.   AUSTRIA   HUNGARY

FRANCE   SLOVENIA

CROATIA

*Corsica*

BOSNIA-
HERZ.

ITALY

YUGOSLAVIA

*Sardinia*

*Sicily*

TUNISIA

p.306

# Highlights

1 San Gimignano's skyline of
  medieval skyscrapers
2 Volterra: Etruscan relics and alabaster
3 The spectacular cathedral of
  Massa Marittima
4 The sword in the stone, at San Galgano

In the late Middle Ages, this dramatically diverse, often rugged countryside was a border region, both culturally and politically, its people alternately subject to the strong pull of Florence and Siena. Its towns do not have that much in common: Poggibonsi is almost all new, while Volterra goes back to the Etruscans. San Gimignano presents its famous skyline of medieval skyscrapers, while parts of the Metal Hills show outlandish silhouettes of cooling towers from the ubiquitous geo-thermal power plants. San Gimignano and Volterra are the main attractions, both beautiful cities containing some remarkable works of art. Massa Marittima, often overlooked, has one of the finest cathedrals in Italy. Beyond that there is a doll-sized walled city, bubbling sulphurous pits, alabaster souvenirs, a Roman theatre, lonely moors, and a sword in a stone (not King Arthur's but someone else's).

# Monteriggioni, Colle di Val d'Elsa and Poggibonsi

## Monteriggioni

Eleven kilometres north of Siena, the SS2 passes a genuine curiosity, the tiny fortified town of **Monteriggioni**. For much of Siena's history, this was its northern-most bastion, often in the front lines in the wars with Florence after its construction in 1219. Now it sits like a crown on its roundish hill, a neat circle of walls with 14 towers, with just enough room inside for two oversized piazzas, a few houses and their gardens. Some three kilometres further towards Colle di Val d'Elsa, there is a turn-off to the left for the 12th-century Abbey of Santi Salvatore and Cirino, better known as the **Abbadia dell'Isola**. The Cistercians began it in 1101 on an 'island' among the marshes, hence the name. Inside this stark Romanesque building is a restored fresco by Taddeo di Bartolo, and a Renaissance altarpiece.

## Colle di Val d'Elsa

**Colle di Val d'Elsa** (pop. 16,300), a striking, ancient town up on a steep hill, presents an impressive silhouette if you see it from the right angle – it's long enough but at most only three blocks wide. Colle first became prominent in the 12th century, a safe, fortified stronghold that attracted many migrants from the surrounding plains. Later, it was known for the manufacture of wool, paper and ceramics; today, Colle is Italy's largest producer of fine glass and crystal. The Collegiani will never allow the world to forget that their town was the birthplace of Arnolfo di Cambio, the great architect who built Florence's Palazzo Vecchio and began its cathedral.

Down on the plain below the citadel, the modern part of the town surrounds the arcaded **Piazza Arnolfo di Cambio**. Via Garibaldi or Via San Sebastiano will take you up to old Colle – but for a proper introduction you'll need to come on the road from Volterra, passing through a grim Renaissance bastion called the **Porta Nuova**, designed by Giuliano da Sangallo, and then across the medieval-Renaissance suburb known as the **Borgo**. Between the Borgo and the old town, called the **Castello**, there is a picturesque narrow bridge and the **Palazzo di Campana** (1539, by Giovanni di Baccio d'Agnolo); the arch in its centre is the elegant gateway to the town.

# Getting Around

The main routes between Florence and Siena – the Via Cassia (SS2) or the parallel Superstrada del Palio – have exits for Colle di Val d'Elsa (27km/35mins from Siena, 49km/1hr from Florence) and Poggibonsi, 7km further north on SS68.

Poggibonsi is a major **bus** junction in south Tuscany, with easy connections to Florence, Siena, San Gimignano, Volterra and Colle di Val d'Elsa (TRA-IN buses if you're coming from Siena, SITA from Florence). Poggibonsi is also on the Empoli–Siena **railway** line, with a branch or bus beyond to Colle in 15 mins.

# Tourist Information

**Castello di Monteriggioni**: Largo Fontebianda 5, t/f 0577 304 810.

**Colle di Val d'Elsa**: Via Campana 43, t 0577 922 791, f 0577 922 621, infocolle@tin.it. Open winter Mon–Sat 10–1 and 3.30–7.

# Where to Stay and Eat

## Monteriggioni ✉ 53035

If you're heading from Florence to Siena, or from Siena out to the west, try the little castle-village of Monteriggioni for lunch.

**Il Pozzo**, Piazza Roma 2, t 0577 304 127 (*expensive*). Here they do some of the simpler dishes very well but their real forte is fancy desserts (they even serve *crêpes Suzette*). *Closed Sun eve and Mon.*

**Hotel Monteriggioni**, t 0577 305 009, f 0577 305 011 (*very expensive*). If you want to keep within the walls, you can have a very comfortable stay at the Monteriggioni, made up of two old stone houses, which has a garden and even a tiny pool.

## Colle di Val d'Elsa ✉ 53034

**★★★Villa Belvedere**, Località Belvedere, t 0577 920 966, f 0577 924 128 (*expensive*). Located a kilometre or so east of the town, near the Siena highway, this pretty, old villa has a big garden, a restaurant (*moderate*) and 15 simple rooms. *Restaurant closed Wed, 1–15 Aug and 15 days in Jan or Feb.*

**★★★Arnolfo**, in the Borgo at Via Campana 8, t 0577 922 020, f 0577 92224, *www.arnolfo.com* (*moderate*). Simple and comfortable, in the town itself, with a popular restaurant (*see below*).

**Arnolfo restaurant**, Via XX Settembre 52, t 0577 920 549 (*very expensive*). Located just around the corner, this now occupies a Renaissance palace and makes the perfect setting for what is widely considered one of the top restaurants in Italy; menus change with the seasons, but you can always choose from two *menu degustazioni* – one 'traditional', one 'creative'. *Closed Tues, Wed, 1–10 Aug and 10 Jan–10 Feb.*

**Ristorante lo Sfizio**, Via Gracco del Secco 86, t 0577 922 115 (*expensive–moderate*). A good-value alternative; nearly as upmarket as Arnolfo. *Closed Fri.*

**Fattoria di Mugnano**, t 0577 959 023 (*cheap*). This was once an old farm and is now a thriving business, situated out among the olive groves in the nearby hamlet of Mugnano. The delightful restaurant offers local and Sicilian cuisine; they'll sell you some of the wine and olive oil they produce, or arrange horse-riding and tours of the countryside. *Closed Thurs and Jan.*

## Poggibonsi ✉ 53036

**★★★Alcide**, Viale Marconi 67a, t 0577 937 501, f 0577 981 729 (*moderate*). If you're spending time in Poggibonsi this offers doubles with air-conditioning. Their **restaurant** (*very expensive–expensive*) is one of the better places for seafood in this landlocked province, featuring dishes such as *caciucco* and linguine with European lobster. *Restaurant closed Sun eve, Mon, central 2 weeks in Jan and the 2 weeks after the Palio in July.*

Via del Castello runs straight up the centre, with narrow medieval alleys on both sides. Here you'll find the **cathedral**, built in 1603 (Colle only got its own bishop in 1592) with a Victorian-era façade, a few Renaissance palaces, and some little museums. Opposite the cathedral, in the Palazzo Pretorio, a small **Museo Archeologico** (*open Oct–Mar Tues–Fri 3.30–6, Sat, Sun and hols 10–12 and 3.30–5.30; April–Sept Tues–Fri 10–12 and 5–7, Sat, Sun and hols 10–11 and 4–7; closed Mon; adm*) displays Etruscan objects; there is a small picture collection in the nearby **Museo Civico** (*open Nov–Mar Sat, Sun and hols 10–12 and 3.30–6.30; April–Oct Tues–Sun 10–12 and 4–7; closed Mon; adm* ). The best of them all is the **Museo d'Arte Sacra** (*same hours as Museo Archeologico; adm*) in the old episcopal palace , with a few Sienese and Florentine paintings in addition to the frescoes commissioned by some jolly 14th-century bishop – scenes of the hunt and from the Crusades, believed to be the work of Ambrogio Lorenzetti.

Near the end of Via del Castello, the Collegiani claim an old tower-fortress as the **House of Arnolfo di Cambio**. Arnolfo's father, a gentleman and an architect, probably came to Colle di Val d'Elsa from Lombardy some time in the 1230s, bringing the great tradition of the Lombard master-masons into Tuscany. Arnolfo himself may have received his initiation into the new (for Italy) Gothic style from studying works in Siena or the new Cistercian abbey at San Galgano. He worked for Nicola Pisano on the Siena cathedral pulpit, and for Giovanni Pisano on the Fonte Maggiore in Perugia, and probably moved to Florence in the 1270s.

South of Colle, many of the villages in the hills retain their simple Romanesque churches from the 11th–12th centuries, beginning with the isolated **Badia à Coneo**, a Vallombrosan foundation of the 1120s (five kilometres from Colle, on an unpaved lane off the road to Casole). At **Casole d'Elsa** (15 kilometres south, local bus), a town that took hard knocks in the last war, there is an interesting **Collegiata** church begun in the 12th century, with Sienese frescoes, two fine, late 14th-century sepulchres by Gano da Siena, and terracottas by Giovanni della Robbia. Casole's Sienese **Rocca** held out into the 16th century, long after the rest of the Valdelsa flew the Florentine flag. South from Casole, the road winds through pleasant, green countryside leading up to the Colline Metallifere, the 'metal hills', and you can seek out more Romanesque churches in **Mensano** (7km) and **Radicondoli** (15km, the church of **San Simone**).

## Poggibonsi

If you spend enough time in Tuscany, sooner or later you are bound to pass through **Poggibonsi** (pop. 25,700), a major knot on the SS2, SS429 and Superstrada del Palio road links from Siena to Florence and Pisa. These days, residents of the pretty tourist towns of central Tuscany are not above having a laugh at the expense of this homely, industrial centre. Poor Poggibonsi! Founded only in 1156, the original *Poggiobonizzo* grew rapidly. By 1220, it was probably one of the largest cities in Tuscany; in that year, Emperor Frederick II declared it a 'Città Imperiale' with special rights. Ghibelline politics and its imperial favour, however, were to prove its undoing. In 1270, San Gimignano and Colle di Val d'Elsa, along with the Florentines and the troops of Charles of Anjou, besieged and conquered the city, then razed it to the ground. Most of its citizens migrated elsewhere, but a number of the poorer ones stayed behind, refounding the town as a modest market village on the plain. Poggibonsi was thoroughly wrecked again during the battles of 1944, but has grown tremendously since to become the biggest town between Florence and Siena.

There isn't much to see; the 14th-century Palazzo Pretorio and the collegiate church on the main street recall something of the appearance of pre-war Poggibonsi. Close by, the **Castello della Magione** is a small complex from the 1100s; the Romanesque chapel and outbuildings form a little closed square, a fortified pilgrims' hospice said to have been built by the Templars. Above the town, an unfinished fortress begun by Lorenzo de' Medici covers much of the original city of Poggiobonizzo.

Just two kilometres south of town near the SS2, the austerely Franciscan **Basilica of San Lucchese** occupies an attractive site in the hills; inside are some good frescoes, including works by Taddeo Gaddi and Bartolo di Fredi. Not surprisingly, this strategically important corner of Tuscany is scattered with castles, including the 13th-century **Castello della Rochetta**, once the home of the famous *condottiere* Sir John Hawkwood, and the romantically ruined **Rocca di Staggia** (five kilometres south of Poggibonsi on the SS2), built by the Florentines in the 1430s – a counterpart to Sienese Monteriggioni, just a few kilometres down the same road.

# San Gimignano

In the miniaturist landscape of this corner of Tuscany, **San Gimignano**, Italy's best-preserved medieval city, is an almost fantastic landmark. Seen from Poggibonsi or from the Volterra road its medieval towers, some of them over 50m tall, loom over the surrounding hills. Once, almost every city in central Italy looked like this; more than just defensive strongholds in the incessant family feuds, these towers served as status symbols both for the families and the cities themselves, a visible measure of a town's power and prosperity, even if it also betrayed the bitterness of its internal divisions. By the 16th century, most of Italy's towers had succumbed to age, decay and particularly to the efforts of the urban *comuni*, which pruned and destroyed these symbols of truculent nobility at every opportunity. For whatever reason, this did not happen in San Gimignano, famous even in the 1300s as the '*città delle belle torri*'. Originally there were at least 70 towers (in a town barely one-eighth of a square mile in size); now only 15 remain. Nevertheless, when taken alongside the beautiful streets, churches and public buildings, they are enough to give you the impression that the town has been hermetically sealed in a time-capsule from the Middle Ages.

## History

According to legend, the town was originally called Castel della Selva. When the Gothic army of Totila passed through in the 550s, the townsfolk for some reason chose to pray to an obscure saint named Gimignano, a martyred bishop of Modena, for their salvation from a near-guaranteed sacking. Gimignano came through in style, looming down from the clouds in golden armour to scare away the besiegers.

Although it must have been an important and prosperous place, San Gimignano does not cut much of a figure in the medieval chronicles. The city was an independent republic from the early 1100s until 1353, when it came under the rule of Florence. It certainly participated in the Guelph–Ghibelline strife, and in all the other troubles of the period, though today it is probably best remembered as the home town of that excellent poet, Folgore of San Gimignano (*c.* 1250), famous for his lovely sonnets to the months of the year. As in so many other medieval towns, San Gimignano has the air of a false start, a free *comune* that could build a wall and defend itself, yet lacked the will or the money to make itself into a Siena or a Florence. When it lost the wealth or the fierceness that briefly made it an important player on the Tuscan stage, the city crystallized into its medieval form, a perfect preparation for its role as a tourist town. Today San Gimignano has a population of some 7,700. On a good day in July or August it may see several times that in day-trippers. Even during the Renaissance the town seems to have been a resort for the Florentines; Dante, Machiavelli and Savonarola all spent time here, and artists like Ghirlandaio and Gozzoli were only too happy to come up for a small commission. Don't let the prospect of crowds keep you from visiting. San Gimignano handles them gracefully; its fine art, elegant medieval cityscapes and the verdant rolling countryside right outside its gates make this one of the smaller towns of Tuscany most worth seeing.

## Piazza del Duomo and the Palazzo del Popolo

From the southern gate, Porta San Giovanni, the street of the same name leads towards the town centre, passing the little churches of **San Giovanni**, built by the Knights Templar, and **San Francesco**, with a good Pisan-Romanesque façade, now deconsecrated and converted into a wine shop. Another ancient gate, the Arco dei Bacci, leads into the triangular **Piazza della Cisterna** and the adjacent **Piazza del Duomo** – a superbly beautiful example of asymmetrical, medieval town design, seemingly haphazard but really quite sophisticated. Piazza della Cisterna contains the town's well, whence the name, and some of its towers.

On Piazza del Duomo, two stout, Gothic public buildings with Guelph crenellations and lofty towers compete with the Collegiata church for your attention. The **Palazzo del Podestà**, with its vaulted *loggia*, was begun in the 1230s by Emperor Frederick II at the height of imperial power for his *podestà*. Above it stands the Torre della Rognosa, with a small cupola; at 167ft it once marked the height limit for private towers. Later, when the *comune* was able to wrest power from the emperors, it built an even taller tower for the **Palazzo del Popolo** across the piazza; the 177ft Torre Grossa was completed about 1300 and the rest of the Palazzo about 20 years later.

Underneath this tower, an archway leads into the charming, thoroughly medieval **Cortile**, or courtyard, with bits of frescoes (one by Il Sodoma) and the painted coats of arms of Florentine governors from after 1353. A stairway leads up to the **Museo Civico** (*open Nov–Feb 10–5.30; Mar–Oct 9.30–7.30; adm*), with an excellent collection of art from both Florentine and Sienese masters. One of the oldest works is a paint-ed crucifix by Coppo di Marcovaldo (*c.* 1270) that predates (and some might say sur-passes) the similar, more famous crucifixes of Giotto. The museum has two sweet Madonnas by Benozzo Gozzoli, a pair of tondi by Filippino Lippi portraying the Annunciation, and a big, colourful enthroned Virgin of Pinturicchio's that looks like it strayed here from that artist's Piccolomini chapel in Siena. Taddeo di Bartolo con-tributes paintings depicting the story of San Gimignano; he is pictured calming the

## Getting Around

The railway station is 11km away, an infrequent stop on the Empoli–Siena line. Buses to the town *usually* coincide with the **trains**, but from either Siena or Florence you'll be better off taking the bus, which leaves you right at the Porta San Giovanni, the main entrance to the town. TRA-IN **buses** from Siena (38km/ 45mins – the same bus that goes to Colle di Val d'Elsa) are very frequent, though for most you will need to change in Poggibonsi. Several daily SITA buses arrive from Florence (54km/1hr 15mins) and there are four buses a day to nearby Certaldo.

If you're **driving**, San Gimignano is 11km west of Poggibonsi, 13km south of Certaldo, or 14km from Colle di Val d'Elsa, each route more scenic than the last. Within the walls San Gimignano is usually closed to traffic; the main car park is outside Porta San Giovanni. Get a pass from the police to park at one of the hotels inside.

## Tourist Information

**San Gimignano**: Piazza del Duomo 1, t 0577 940 008, f 0577 940 903, *www.sangimignano.com. Open Mar–Oct Mon–Sun 9–1 and 3–7; Nov–Feb Mon–Sun 9–1 and 2–6.*

## Admission

If you plan to visit all the key sights it is worth buying the cheaper joint ticket (*biglietto comulativo*) which covers the four museums, the tower of Palazzo del Popolo and the Capella di Santa Fina.

## Shopping

There isn't any particular artisan tradition here, but so many tourists visit that enterprising shop owners have assembled a host of interesting things – the town hasn't quite turned into a great trinket bazaar, but it's getting there.

**Linea Oro**, Via San Giovanni. Among the good buys are pretty things in alabaster from nearby Volterra.

**Via San Matteo 85**, north of Piazza del Duomo. One of the best shops for alabaster is here.

**La Stamperia**, Via San Matteo 88. Sells original prints including views of Tuscan towns and countryside.

**Ceramics** are everywhere; some of the local work is quite good and inexpensive.

Just within Porta San Giovanni is a 13th-century church now converted to a shop for local wine, olive oil and other farm products.

San Gimignano's other specialities are a formidable white wine called *Vernaccia* (*see* p.402) and a sweet called *mandorlato*, very like the *panforte* of Siena. Many local vineyards would be glad to sell you a bottle of *Vernaccia*. One such is **Cantine Baroncini**, Casale, t 0577 940 600.

## Activities

If you want to explore the surrounding countryside on horseback, there is a riding centre close by.

**Agriturismo Il Vecchio Maneggio**, Sant'Andrea 22, on the road from San Gimignano to Ulignano, t 0577 950 232. Booking is advisable.

sea, exorcizing a devil who had been inhabiting the daughter of Emperor Jovian, and succumbing to the flesh while saying mass (he has to pee, but on sneaking out of the church a winged devil attacks him; fortunately he has a crucifix to hand).

To the San Gimignanese, the biggest attraction of the museum is the Sala del Consiglio, or **Sala di Dante**, where the poet spoke in 1299 as an ambassador of Florence, seeking to convince the *comune* to join the Guelph League. The frescoes on its walls include more works by Gozzoli, a glittering company of angels and saints in the *Maestà* of the Sienese artist Lippo Memmi, and some trecento scenes of hunting and tournaments. After this, contemplate a climb up the **Torre Grossa** (*same hours as Museo Civico; adm*) – several hundred steps, but the view is worth the effort.

# Where to Stay

## San Gimignano ✉ 53037

In the summer, you may want a hand finding a place to sleep.

**Hotel Association**, just inside the gate on Via S. Giovanni, **t/f** 0577 940 809, *www.sangimignano.com. Open Easter–Oct Mon–Sat 9.30–7 and Nov–Easter Mon–Sat 9.30–12.30 and 2.30–6.30.*

**★★★Leon Bianco, t** 0577 941 294, **f** 0577 942 123 (*moderate*). An excellent hotel, on Piazza della Cisterna, with modern rooms.

**★★★La Cisterna, t** 0577 940 328, **f** 0577 942 080 (*moderate*). If the Leon Bianco is full, this is located in the same square, and also comes highly recommended.

**Antico Pozzo**, Via San Matteo 87, **t** 0577 942 014, **f** 0577 942 117 (*expensive*). A stylish alternative, situated next to the main square. The building dates from the 1500s – several of the rooms even have delicately frescoed ceilings.

**★★★Le Renaie**, Loc. Pancole, about 7km towards Certaldo, **t** 0577 955 044, **f** 0577 955 126 (*expensive*). If you prefer the tranquillity of the very lovely Tuscan countryside hereabouts, head north of town to find this attractive modern building, with a garden, pool and tennis court.

All the hotels in San Gimignano are in the moderate range or higher, but the vacuum of low-cost accommodation has been filled by a score of San Gimignese who rent out rooms, usually at about €20–25.

**Il Pino** Restaurant (*see* 'Eating Out', right), Via San Matteo 102. This family provides doubles without bath. The tourist office can give you a list of the others.

# Eating Out

San Gimignano may entertain a good many visitors, but it makes a fine host.

**Dorando**, Vicolo del Oro 2, **t** 0577 941 862 (*expensive*). For the more adventurous, where the chef attempts to recreate authentic Etruscan cuisine – *cibreo* (a chicken liver pâté so rich Caterina de' Medici nearly died from a surfeit of it), *pici* served with mint-leaf pesto, crème caramel flavoured with coriander, and things stranger still. Readers have written to us highly praising this place. *Closed Mon.*

**Le Terrazze**, in Hotel La Cisterna (*see left*), **t** 0577 940 328 (*moderate*). One of the most popular places, as much for its panoramic views as for the cuisine. The *medaglione al vinsanto* is a surprise treat, or else the *osso buco 'alla Toscana'*, following old house specialities like *zuppa sangimignanese* and *pappardelle alla lepre* (wide noodles with hare sauce). *Closed Tues, and Wed lunch.*

**Il Pino**, Via San Matteo 102, **t** 0577 940 415, **f** 0577 942 225 (*moderate–cheap*). Situated at the opposite end of town, the main attraction to be savoured here is the inviting *antipasti*; but it can be pricier if you indulge in the dishes with truffles that are Il Pino's pride. *Closed Thurs.*

**Osteria delle Catene**, Via Mainardi 18, **t** 0577 941 966. Has good regional food at a moderate price; try their *ribollita alla sangimignanese. Closed Wed.*

**La Stella**, Via S. Matteo 75, **t** 0577 940 444 (*cheap*). Just a little way along from Il Pino but less extravagant, serving good *ribollita* and a succulent *stracotto alla Chianti. Closed Wed.*

## The Collegiata

The name Piazza del Duomo is a little misleading: San Gimignano doesn't have a cathedral any more, but a **Collegiata** (Basilica di Santa Maria Assunta), begun in the 12th century and enlarged in the 15th, which would make an impressive seat for any bishop. It turns a blank brick façade to the world, but the interior is a lavish imitation of Siena Cathedral, with its tiger-striped arches and vaults painted with a firmament of golden stars. Its walls, however, outshine the larger cathedral with first-class frescoes of the 14th and 15th centuries, mostly by artists from Siena.

In the north aisle, Bartolo di Fredi painted the Old Testament scenes in the 1360s. Note *Noah with the Animals*, and *The Torments of Job* (also how each scene is accompanied by a neat explanation in simple Italian, a fascinating example of the artists and the Church coming to terms with a newly literate public). Some of Bartolo's best work is in the lunettes off the north aisle: a medieval cosmography of the Creation, scenes of Adam naming the animals and a graphic view of the creation of Eve. New Testament pictures by Barna da Siena (about 1380) cover the south wall; his *Crucifixion* is an exceedingly fine work. On the west wall, over the entrance, is a well-punctured *Saint Sebastian* by Gozzoli and a real surprise, the most perverse *Last Judgement* in Italy. What moved Taddeo di Bartolo – a most serendipitous painter of rosy Sienese Virgins – to this madness isn't recorded. You may think you have seen the damned suffering interesting tortures and indignities before; Italy has plenty of such scenes. This is the first time, however, that delicacy forbids us to describe one. It's a little faded, unfortunately, but you'll find it near two wooden figures depicting an Annunciation, by Jacopo della Quercia.

Off the south aisle, the **Chapel of Santa Fina** (*open April–Oct Mon–Fri 9.30–7.30 and Sat 9.30–5, Sun and hols 1–5; Nov–Mar Mon–Sat 9.30–5, Sun and hols 1–5; adm*) offers a delightful introduction to one of the most irritating hagiographies in Christendom. Little Fina was going to the well for water, according to the story, when she accepted an orange from a young swain. Upon returning home, her mother told her how wicked she was to take it, whereupon the poor girl became so mortified over her great sin that she lay down on the kitchen table and prayed for forgiveness without ceasing for the next five years. Finally, St Anthony came down to call her soul up into heaven, and the kitchen table and all the towers of San Gimignano burst into bloom with violets. Domenico Ghirlandaio got the commission to paint all this; he pocketed the money and did a splendid job (1475) in the brightest springtime colours. In the last scene, note San Gimignano's famous towers in the background.

Just to the left of the Collegiata, there is a lovely small courtyard where musicians sometimes play on summer weekends. Here, on the wall of the baptistry, you will see another fine fresco by Ghirlandaio, an *Annunciation* that has survived reasonably well for being outside for 500 years. The **Museo Etrusco** has a small collection of local archaeological finds (*Via Folgore da San Gimignano; open 16 Jan–28 Feb Mon, Fri, Sat and Sun 11–6, Mar–Oct daily 11–6; Nov–Dec Sat–Thurs 11–6*). The **Museo d'Arte Sacra**, besides the usual ecclesiastical clutter, has some good painted wood statues from the late Middle Ages (*Piazza Pecori; open April–Oct 9.30–7.30; Nov–20 Jan and March 9.30–5; closed 20 Jan–end Feb; adm*).

## Local Wine

San Gimignano has its own wine, *La Vernaccia di San Gimignano* (makes one think of varnish), a dry, light yellow white, with a pungent bouquet and a slightly bitter aftertaste. It is generally drunk with fish dishes and as an apéritif, but it's also good to try with typical San Gimignano dishes such as liver, tripe, rabbit and *panzanella*.

The wine is made only from the hills around San Gimignano and has been around since antiquity. It gets a mention in Dante's *Purgatory*: Pope Martin IV apparently drowned eels in Vernaccia before roasting them over a charcoal fire. It has recently been awarded the DOCG.

## Around the Town

From Piazza del Duomo, it's not too difficult a climb up to the **Rocca**, a somewhat ruined fortress of the 1350s that offers one of the best views of this towered town. During the summer it's the site of an outdoor cinema. Down Via di Castello, in the eastern end of town, the **Oratory of San Lorenzo in Ponte**, now unused, has quattrocento Florentine frescoes and an exhibition of finds from a 16th- to 18th-century pharmacy that once functioned in the nearby Hospital of Santa Fina. The busiest and finest street of San Gimignano, however, leaves Piazza del Duomo towards the north: Via San Matteo, lined with shops and modest Renaissance palaces. It begins by passing the three truncated **Salvucci Towers**, once the fortified compound of one of San Gimignano's most powerful families (the Salvucci were Ghibellines; the towers of their mortal enemies, the Guelph Ardinghelli, are the ones on the west side of Piazza della Cisterna).

The day-trippers do not often venture into the quiet streets on the north side of town, and so usually miss the church of **Sant'Agostino**, famous for a series of frescoes by Gozzoli on the Life of St Augustine on the walls behind the high altar. The merriest of all Renaissance painters has a good time with this one; many of the frescoes are faded and damaged, but not the charming panel where the master of grammar comes to drag sullen little Augustine off to school. Another well-preserved scene shows Augustine in Rome, with most of the city's ancient landmarks visible in the background. Gozzoli also contributed the *St Sebastian* on the left aisle. There is a haunting altarpiece, done by Piero Pollaiuolo in 1483 with an anticipatory touch of the El Greco to it, and some good trecento Sienese painting in a chapel off to the right. Across the piazza from Sant'Agostino, the little church of **San Pietro** has more Sienese painting of that era. Via Folgore di San Gimignano leads off to the northeastern corner of the town; the church of **San Jacopo** stands under the town wall, another simple but interesting building left by the Templars.

Around much of San Gimignano, the countryside begins right outside the wall. Pleasant walks or picnics can be had in any direction, with a few landmarks to visit along the way: the **Fonti**, arched, medieval well-houses much like Siena's, are just outside the Porta dei Fonti, south of San Jacopo. Further from town, there is the **Pieve di Cellole,** a pretty 12th-century church in a peaceful setting, four kilometres west from the Porta San Matteo; its harmonious serenity amid the cypresses inspired Puccini's opera *Suor Angelica*. There are a number of ruined castles and monasteries around the town, each offering a different view of San Gimignano's remarkable skyline.

# Volterra and Around

How you see **Volterra** may well depend on the cast of the skies when you come. On a good day in spring or summer, the sunshine illuminates elegant streets and *piazze* full of Volterrans going about their business, and bouncing holiday-makers come to buy alabaster cups and lampshades. A cloudy, windy day may remind you of fate and

## Getting Around

Volterra lies 81km/2½hrs southwest of Florence by way of Colle di Val d'Elsa and the winding SS68; it's 50km/1½hrs west from Siena; and 61km/2hrs southeast of Pisa by way of Cascina and the SS439. It isn't the easiest town to reach if you don't have a car.

The only **train** service gets as far as Saline di Volterra, 10km southwest of the city. This is an infrequent branch line that goes to Cecina, 30km to the west on the coast south of Livorno. Some trains continue on from Cecina to Pisa. (It wasn't like this in the old days: as late as the 1920s, if old photographs are to be believed, a little steam train used to climb right up to the town.) Buses connect the Saline station with Volterra, but not always when you need them.

All **buses** leave from Piazza Martini della Libertà, just inside the walls. You can get information, timetables and buy tickets from the tourist office. There are plenty of buses which go direct to Pisa and Montecatini Terme, four a day to Florence and Siena via Colle Val d'Elsa, and a few to Poggibonsi and San Gimignano; three a day go to Livorno via Cecina; there are also two to Massa Marittima (you usually have to change at Monterotondo for these).

**Cars** aren't allowed within Volterra's walls, but lots of parking space is provided all around the walls and at the gates. Strangely enough there are also some street parking spaces inside, and you can usually sneak your car into one that's near your hotel in the evening; it's best to check out the situation on foot beforehand.

## Tourist Information

**Volterra**: Palazzo dei Priori, Via Turazza 2, t 0588 86150, f 0588 90350, *provolterra@libero.it, www.provolterra.it.* Open mid-Mar–Oct Mon–Sun 9–1 and 2.30–7; Nov–mid-Mar Mon–Sun 9–12.30 and 3–6.

## Alabaster-shopping

Archaeological evidence has the Villanovan culture in Tuscany finding creative uses for the *pietra candida*, alias $CaSO_4.2H_2O$, as early as 800 BC. The Etruscans made good use of this luminous, easily worked mineral in their funeral urns and everyday objects. It appears that the locals forgot all about it during the Dark Ages, though now and then some artist would turn a chunk into a vase or cup (the Medici, with their insatiable lust for dust magnets, bought quite a few). The craft of carving alabaster revived dramatically in the last two centuries. Volterra today is full of small workshops, and even a few large firms that turn the stone into vases, figurines, ashtrays and everything else that's serviceable or collectable.

Many of the alabaster-workers are genuine artists, turning out one-of-a-kind pieces at high prices; the city runs a contest each year for the best. Others produce vast numbers of attractive little baubles from a few euros up.

There are shops selling alabaster in every corner of Volterra; it's best to seek these out, and avoid the temptations of the big glossy establishments in the most prominent places.

**Via Porta all'Arco 45**. The shop of Paulo Sabatini, who has won several prizes in the annual competition, with some of the most original creations in town.

**Via Porta all'Arco 26**. Stocks some more unusual alabaster miniatures.

More can be found along Via di Sotto.

**Via di Sotto 2**. Simple, elegant vases and lamps.

**'Come una Volta'**, Via di Sotto 6.

**Via Antonio Gramsci** Nos.20 and 53. Two of the more interesting shops among many.

**Via Guarnacci 26**. More avant-garde, with some splashy modern work in coloured alabaster.

**City Artisans' Cooperative**, Piazza dei Priori 4–5, t 0588 87590, *www.italbusiness.it/volterrasalabaster*.

of the Etruscans, who arrived here some 2,700 years ago. Like so many of their other cities, the Etruscans founded Volterra on top of a steep hill with a flat top; from afar you see only a silhouette looming over an eerie, empty landscape. The soil around

Giuseppe Bessi, Via San Lino 52. Offers some conservative, well-crafted pieces. Via San Lino 46, just next door. Specializes in carved olive wood.

For really serious alabaster – say, complete bathrooms, or life-size copies of the Trevi Fountain – try the big shops with big car parks around the outskirts of town.

If Auro Bongini's workshop on Via Don Minzoni 54 is open, it's well worth taking a look. This craftsman makes doll's house furniture from local olive wood in 19th-century style. His exhibition work fills the small workshop, but there are also a few individual pieces for sale. If you are interested you can call in advance to make an appointment, t 0588 88040.

# Where to Stay and Eat

## Volterra ✉ 56048

Volterra does not see as many tourists as San Gimignano, but is nevertheless just as expensive – at least, inexpensive rooms are hard to find.

***Villa Nencini, Borgo S. Stefano, t 0588 86386, f 0588 80601 (moderate). A 16th-century house with beautiful views, located just north of the city centre.

***Nazionale, Via dei Marchesi 11, t 0588 86284, f 0588 84097 (moderate). A pleasant old hotel within the walls.

****San Lino, Via San Lino 26, near Porta San Francesco, t 0588 85250, f 0588 80620 (moderate). More upscale, with tastefully remodelled rooms in an old cloister, standing out only for being the only place with parking.

L'Etrusca, Via Porta all'Arco 37, t 0588 84073 (cheap). Has small apartments with kitchenettes just off Piazza del Popolo.

Ostello della Gioventù, Via Don Minzoni, t 0588 8557. Students aren't entirely out of luck: there's the hostel, providing an institutional atmosphere at rock-bottom rates.

Many restaurants in Volterra specialize in roast boar and the like, good medieval cuisine that is entirely in keeping with the spirit of the place.

Il Porcellino, Vicollo delle Prigioni 18, t 0588 86392 (moderate). The menu in this restaurant combines seafood and familiar Tuscan favourites with local treats like roast pigeon and boar with olives; a good bargain. Closed Oct–Mar.

Il Sacco Fiorentino (the name refers to Lorenzo de' Medici's massacre of the citizens of Volterra in 1472), Piazza XX Settembre 18, t 0588 88537 (expensive–moderate). Combines a vast assortment of crostini, wonderful gnocchi with baby vegetables, penne with Tuscan cheeses, roast pork with black olives, rabbit cooked in garlic and Vin Santo and lamb with mint and sultanas in an imaginative menu which changes with the seasons.

Tre Scimmie ('three monkeys'), Via dei Sarti, t 0588 86047 (moderate). Not too many tourists make it to this small, delightful bar. Closed Mon.

La Tavernetta, Via Guarnacci 14, t 0588 87630 (moderate). Offers Tuscan fare for the heartier appetite. Closed Tues and 2 weeks in Feb.

Sant' Elisa, about 2km away on the SS68, at KM 36500, t 0588 80034, f 0588 87284 (cheap). One of the restaurants most popular with the Volterrans is just outside town: the country setting is plain enough, but the simple, home-cooked food (mainly pizza and pasta dishes) is quite simply superb. The restaurant also serves lots of game, such as pappardelle with wild boar, or wild boar stew with black olives. Closed Mon.

Taverna dei Priori, Via G. Matteotti 19, t 0588 86180 (cheap). This little eaterie is ideal if you are after nothing more than a quick bite to eat: it's essentially a tavola calda, serving sandwiches, salads and cooked food. Closed Wed.

Volterra (pop. 12,796) is a thin clay, not much good for vines or olives. Few trees grow here. It makes good pasture land – not as barren as it looks, but disconcerting enough among the green woods and well-tended gardens of this part of Tuscany.

## History

Etruscan *Velathri*, one of the largest and most powerful cities of the Dodecapolis, grew up in the 9th or 8th century BC from an even earlier settlement of the Villanovan culture; it is undoubtedly one of Italy's oldest cities. The attraction that has kept this hill continuously occupied for so many centuries is easily explained – sulphur, alum, salt, alabaster, lead and tin; the town is at the centre of one of the richest mining regions in Italy. In Etruscan days there was iron, too, and the people of Velathri did a thriving trade with the Greeks and Carthaginians.

Velathri reached the height of its prosperity in the 5th and 4th centuries BC, leaving as testimony three great circuits of walls; the largest is over eight kilometres in length, enclosing an area three times the size of the present city. The Romans captured it sometime in the 3rd century, and Velathri began to decline. Along with most of Etruria, the city chose the populist side in the Social Wars, and was punished with a siege and sacking by Sulla in about 80 BC. Yet Roman *Velaterrae* remained an important town. It was the home of Saint Linus, successor to St Peter and the second pope. Even though many of the mines were giving out, Volterra survived the Dark Ages intact. The Lombards favoured it, and for a time it served as their capital. Medieval Volterra was ruled by its bishops, increasingly finding themselves in conflict with the rising middle class. An independent *comune* was established late in the 12th century, a good Ghibelline town that participated in most of the factional wars of the period, finally coming under the nominal control of Florence in 1361.

The Florentines were content with an annual tribute until the 'affair of the alum' in the 1470s, an Italian ruckus that caused Pope Sixtus IV to plot the murder of Lorenzo de' Medici, excommunicate him, and finally declare war on him. Lorenzo had taken over a syndicate to mine here for alum, a key material used in dyeing cloth, on which the popes had a monopoly. Besides alarming the pope, Lorenzo also caused the Volterrans to revolt when they realized that he wanted to keep production down and prices high without letting any profit trickle down to them (the Medici Bank, not surprisingly, also controlled the sale of the pope's alum). Lorenzo eluded the pope with some difficulty (*see* **Florence**, History, pp.141–2) and then hired the mercenary captain Federico da Montefeltro – none other than the famous broken-nosed Duke of Urbino, patron of artists and scholars – to subdue the Volterrans. This he did with a brutality quite unbecoming to the 'ideal Renaissance prince'. Lorenzo wept some crocodile tears over Volterra; after extinguishing the city's independence once and for all, he offered it the magnificent sum of 2,000 florins in damages.

Fortunately for the Volterrans, the mining business was picking up again. Between 1400 and 1800, many pits that had been abandoned since Roman times were reopened. In particular, Volterra became Europe's centre for the mining and working of alabaster, a craft tradition that is still the city's biggest business today.

## A Little Archaeology

Coming from Florence or Siena, the entrance to Volterra will be the eastern gate, the **Porta a Selci**, with a moving tribute to the *partigiani* of Volterra killed in 1944–5. Inside the gate, Via Don Minzoni leads towards the bus terminal at Piazza XX

Settembre, passing along the way at no.15 the **Museo Etrusco Guarnacci** (*t 0588 86347, open 16 March–2 Nov daily 9–7; 3 Nov–15 Mar daily 9–2; adm exp; a joint ticket covers Volterra's other museums*), the repository for finds from the Velathri necropolises. Over 600 sculpted alabaster, travertine or terracotta cinerary urns make up the core of the collection. Exhibits are arranged in chronological order, except for the original Guarnacci collection which is grouped by subject matter. These tend to be conventional – an Etruscan family would ask the artist for a scene from Greek mythology, from the Trojan War perhaps, or something like the death of Actaeon, or a daemon conducting the souls of the dead down to the underworld. Perhaps the artist already had one in stock. One rule of Etruscan art is its lack of rules. Expect anything: some of the reclining figures of the dead atop the urns are brilliant portraiture, while others could be the first attempts of a third-grade craft class. All, holding the little cups or dishes they carry down into Hades, look as serene and happy as only a defunct Etruscan can.

As always, the Etruscans do their best to make you laugh. One terracotta, the *Urna degli Sposi*, portrays a hilariously caricatured couple who look as if they are about to start arguing over whose turn it is to do the dishes. Another Etruscan joke is the *Ombra della Sera* (evening shadow), quite a celebrity around Volterra, a small, carefully detailed bronze of a man with a quizzical expression and spidery, grotesquely elongated arms and legs. There are also prehistoric finds, Roman mosaics from the baths, artefacts discovered in the theatre, and some Etruscan jewellery.

The museum lies a stone's throw from Piazza XX Settembre, the bus terminal; from here Via Gramsci leads towards the town centre. Climb any of the alleys to the south of the museum, however, and you'll reach Volterra's **Parco Archeologico** (*open 11–5*) just inside the walls. There isn't much that's archaeological about it – some Etruscan foundations and a huge ancient cistern called the *Piscina Romana* – but the park is a marvel, a lush English garden of manicured lawns and shady groves unlike anything else in Tuscany. Above the park stretches an exceptionally long and elegant castle, the **Fortezza Medicea**, begun in 1343 and completed by Lorenzo de' Medici in 1472. You can't get in; it has been a prison almost from the day it was built, perhaps the fanciest in this nation of fancy calabooses.

## Piazza dei Priori

This is a fine little republican piazza, surrounded by plain, erect *palazzi* that call your attention ever so discreetly to the sober dignity of the *comune*. The **Palazzo dei Priori**, of 1208, is said to be the oldest such building in Tuscany, the model for Florence's Palazzo Vecchio and a score of others. Its tower has long been closed to visitors, but if you ever find it reopened, climb up for a view that literally takes in all of Tuscany; on a clear day you'll see Monte Amiata, all the coast from La Spezia to the Argentario, and Corsica and Elba as well.

Across the square, the simple **Palazzo Pretorio** is almost as old; next to it, the rakishly leaning **Porcellino Tower** takes its name from the little pig sculpted in relief near the base, just barely visible after seven centuries.

## The Cathedral and the Etruscan Arch

Just to the right of the Palazzo dei Priori, a bit of green and white striped marble façade peeks out between the palaces. This is the back of the Archiepiscopal Palace, located around the corner in the **Piazza del Duomo**. Quiet and dowdy, the contrast of this square with the well-built Piazza dei Priori is striking. Its octagonal **baptistry**, begun in 1283, has its marble facing completed only on one side. Within, there is a fine baptismal font sculpted by Andrea Sansovino in the early 1500s, an altar by Mino da Fiesole, and a holy water dish carved out of an Etruscan boundary stone.

The plain **cathedral** façade has a good marble doorway. This was begun in the Pisan-Romanesque style in the 1200s, and worked on for the next two centuries. The campanile went up in 1493, and the interior was entirely redone in the 1580s when the blatant Medici coat of arms was placed over the high altar. Don't pass by; the works of art inside are few in number, but of an exceptionally high quality. Fittingly, as this is Volterra, some of the windows are made of thin-sliced alabaster, a stone that was also used in the intricate, Renaissance **tabernacle** by Mino da Fiesole over the high altar. The chapels on either side have excellent examples of Tuscan wood-carving: a 15th-century one attributed to a local artist named Francesco di Domenico Valdambrino off to the left, the *Madonna dei Chierici*, and to the right, a polychromed *Deposition* with five separate, full-sized figures, among the best of 13th-century Pisan sculpture, shining immaculately after a recent restoration. Another chapel off to the right contains fragments of unusually good anonymous trecento frescoes of the *Passion of Christ*, very much ahead of their time in composition, in the figures and the folds of the draperies – even Giorgio Vasari might have liked them.

In the left aisle, the **pergamo** (pulpit) is one of the lesser-known works of the Pisani, less spectacular than the ones in Pisa, Siena and Pistoia, but still showing something of the vividness and electric immediacy seen in the best Pisan sculpture. Guglielmo Pisano did the fine relief of the *Last Supper* (note the faces of the Apostles, and the sly metaphorical monster sneaking under the table). The pulpit's supporting columns rest on two lions, a bull and one unclassifiable beast, all by Bonamico Pisano. In the oratory, off the left aisle near the entrance, behind a 16th-century wooden statue group of the *Adoration of the Magi*, is a small fresco said to be by Benozzo Gozzoli, though perhaps because of its deterioration or early date, it lacks Gozzoli's usual charm.

Close by in the Archiepiscopal Palace, a small **Museo d'Arte Sacra** (*open 16 Mar–Oct daily 9–1 and 3–6; Nov–15 Mar daily 9–1 only; adm exp*) displays sculpture and architectural fragments, and a della Robbia terracotta of St Linus, Volterra's patron.

From the Duomo, if you retrace your steps back towards Piazza dei Priori and turn down Via Porta all'Arco, you'll find the quaintest old relic in Volterra, the **Arco Etrusco**. The Etruscans built the columns at least, though the arch above them was rebuilt in Roman times. Set into this arch are three primeval black basalt sculpted heads from the original gate, *c.* 600 BC, believed to represent the Etruscan gods Tinia (Jupiter), Uni (Juno) and Menvra (Minerva). Some of the features of Juno are barely traceable; 2,700 years of wind and rain have worn all three into great black knobs – carved out of the voussoirs, they resemble nothing so much as garden slugs.

# The Pinacoteca

*Palazzo Minucci Solaini, Via dei Sarti 1, t 0588 87580, open 16 Mar–2 Nov daily 9–7; 3 Nov–15 Mar 9–2; adm exp; a joint ticket covers Volterra's other museums.*

Just off Piazza dei Priori, the intersection of Via Roma and Via Buonparenti is one of the most picturesque corners of Volterra, with venerable stone arches and tower houses such as the 13th-century Casa Buonparenti. Via Buonparenti leads into Via dei Sarti; the elder Antonio da Sangallo's Palazzo Solaini (note the elegant arcaded courtyard) has been restored to hold Volterra's **Pinacoteca**, another small but choice collection. Trecento Sienese painting is well represented, including a glorious altar-piece of the *Madonna and Child* by Taddeo di Bartolo. To complement the remarkable 14th-century wood sculptures in the Duomo, the Pinacoteca has two figures portray-ing the *Annunciation* by Francesco di Valdambrino. Neri di Bicci was a quattrocento Florentine, but his *St Sebastian* here looks entirely Sienese – probably at the request of the customer. Among other Tuscan works, there is a shiny altarpiece by Ghirlandaio, and two by Luca Signorelli (or his workshop): a *Madonna and Saints* and an *Annunciation*. Only tantalizing fragments are left of another altarpiece by Giuliano Bugiardini (1475–1554), a little-known Florentine with a very distinctive style.

For all that, the prize of the collection is the Rosso Fiorentino *Deposition*, dated 1521 and perhaps his greatest work in all Italy. Even out in the boondocks of Volterra, it attracts considerable attention from the art scholars, being a seminal work and one of the thresholds from the Renaissance into Mannerism, with all the precision and clarity of the best quattrocento work, yet also possessing an intensity that few works had ever achieved. The *Descent from the Cross* is a starkly emotional subject; in Rosso's work it is terror and disarray, a greenish Christ and a small, nearly hysterical crowd dramatically illuminated against a darkening deep blue sky. You'll find little that this painting has in common with Rosso's contemporaries, not even with his fel-low madman Pontormo (who did his own, quite different, *Deposition* in Florence's Santa Felicità) – but oddly enough it could almost be mistaken for a work of Goya.

## San Francesco and the Roman Theatre

On the corner east of the Pinacoteca, the church of **San Michele** has a Pisan Romanesque façade. In the other direction, towards the Porta San Francesco on the western edge of town, you pass through back streets dusty with alabaster work-shops, before finally arriving at the church of **San Francesco** on Via San Lino. Here the attraction is off to the right of the altar, the **chapel of the Holy Cross**, completely frescoed in 1410 by a Florentine artist whose name seems to be Cenni di Francesco di Ser Cenni – a rare soul, indeed, with a sophisticated, wonderfully reactionary, medieval sense of composition and his own ideas about Christian iconography, done in a bold style. The *Legend of the Cross* frescoes generally follow those of Gaddi at Santa Croce in Florence (*see* pp. 205 and 208), and there are also scenes of *St Francis*, the *Passion*, and the *Massacre of the Innocents*. Note the *Dream of Constantine* (or of Heraclius), in his tent adorned with the imperial eagle; naturally the artist had never seen a Roman eagle, but he painted a very nice medieval German one instead.

Just to the right of San Francesco, a pedestrian passage under the walls takes you out to Viale Francesco Ferrucci, home to a lively outdoor **market** on Saturday mornings. Beneath the walls, ancient Velaterrae's large **Roman theatre** (*open 11–5*) has been excavated. Not much of the *cavea* is intact, but enough marble slabs and columns survived for the archaeologists to reconstruct part of the stage building, an impressive testimony to the past importance of the city. Behind the theatre are ruins of **baths** and a large rectangular **palaestra**, a yard for exercise and gymnastics.

## The *Balze*

Leaving Volterra from San Francesco gate, you pass the Borgo San Giusto and its ruins of the 12th-century Pisan-Romanesque church of **Santo Stefano**. The road to Pisa exits through the outer **Etruscan walls**; though barely more than foundations, they are traceable for most of their length around the city, and easily visible here.

Some two kilometres beyond, decorating the moors, are the *balze*; barren clay-walled gullies that may have begun as Etruscan mining cuts. They've a life of their own; medieval chronicles report them gobbling up farms and churches around the city, and no one has yet found a way to stop their inexorable growth. In the 1700s they tried to atone for their appetite, revealing some of the most important Etruscan necropolises yet discovered, and contributing urns to the Guarnacci Museum. Now even the necropolises are all but gone, though on the edge of one cliff you can see the **Badia**, an 11th-century Camaldolensian abbey, now half-devoured.

## The Val di Cecina and the Metal Hills

There are few attractions in the romantic emptiness of the Volterran hills. If you take the SS68 west from Volterra along the Cecina valley to Guardistallo, you reach a rolling valley with pines and cypresses in just the right places. **Montecatini Val di Cecina**, in the hills to the north, is quiet and medieval, with a 12th-century castle. Further west, a big wine area extends around **Montescudaio** (Montescudaio, red and white, is a distinguished though lesser-known dry variety with a DOC label).

The most unusual road from Volterra, the SS439, leads south over the Colline Metallifere towards Massa Marittima and the coast. These 'metal hills', along with the iron mines of Elba, did much to finance the gilded existence of the Etruscans. Several mines operate today, though driving through the hills you may see little but oak forests and olive groves. **Pomarance** holds few surprises, but wait for **Larderello**, the self-proclaimed 'World Centre of Geothermal Energy'. This is the north boundary of volcanic Italy; that extinct volcano, Monte Amiata, and the ancient crater lakes of Umbria and Lazio are not far away. This far north, the only manifestations of a subterranean nature are benign little geysers and gurgling pools of sulphurous mud. Larderello is a growing town; huge ugly cooling towers of the type that signify a nuclear power plant anywhere else can be spotted wherever there is a geothermal source worth tapping. Near the centre, there is a strange, postmodernist church designed in the 1950s by Michelucci, the architect of Florence's rail station, and the **Museo della Geotermia** (*t 0588 67724; open daily 9.30–12.30 and 1.30–5.30; closed Sat in winter*), which may explain something of this overheated little town's career.

After Larderello, and almost as far as Monterotondo, the landscape is downright uncanny. It smells bad too; geysers and steam vents (*soffioni*) whistle and puff by the roadside, while murky pits bubble up boric salts amidst yellow and grey slag piles. Follow the yellow signs of the *'itinerario dei soffioni'* to see the best of it. Despite the sulphur and borax, the cooling towers and occasional rusting hulks of old mining equipment, the Metal Hills are quite winsome, especially south of Larderello (still on the SS439) around the medieval village of Castelnuovo di Val di Cecina, surrounded by chestnuts and the Ala dei Diavoli ('Devils' Wing') pass at the crest of the hills. Monterotondo Marittimo, further south, has more than its fair share of sub-surface curiosities; nearby Lago Boracifero is Italy's centre for borax mining. In some places the ground is covered with strange webs of steam pipes, built since the *comune* discovered its unique resource could power almost everything in town for free.

# Massa Marittima

This lovely, rugged area is part of the coastal Maremma district only in name; even in Roman times it was considered part of the 'maritime' province. And for just as long, **Massa Marittima** has been making its living from the mines, though today its 10,000 people are not enough to fill the space within its medieval walls. Albeit small, its brief prosperity left it beautiful, and well worth visiting: firstly, to see the second city of the Sienese Republic, a lesson in urban refinement within a small place; and secondly, to see its exquisite cathedral: one of Tuscany's great medieval monuments.

This town appeared as a free *comune*, the *Repubblica Massetana*, around 1225, just coinciding with a dizzying period of prosperity owing to its discovery of new silver and copper deposits nearby. Unfortunately, this wealth proved fatally attractive to Massa's bigger neighbours. Pisa and Siena fought over it for a century, and it finally fell to the latter in 1337. Soon after, the mines gave out, putting Massa into centuries of decline. Malaria was a problem from the 1500s, and not until the Lorraine dukes drained the wet places and reopened some of the mines did things start looking up.

### The Duomo

It's quite a sight, rising incongruously on its pedestal, its effect heightened by its setting above and at an angle to Massa's **Piazza Garibaldi**, a true *tour de force* of medieval town design. Reconstruction of an earlier cathedral began around 1200 and finished in 1250, though some additions were made; note the contrast between the original Pisan-Romanesque style, with blind arches and lozenges, and the Sienese campanile, added about 1400. Its best features include Gothic windows, capitals and the carvings of animals protecting humans on the façade and the left side.

The interior, under massive columns with delicate capitals, each one different, has a few trecento and quattrocento frescoes, including one of St Julian tending the sick near the main entrance. On the left, there is a luminous *Madonna* by Duccio (1318) and unique reliefs from the original 11th-century church: staring priests and apostles in vigorous, cartoon-like style. On the right hangs the *Nativity of Mary* by that most

# Getting Around

Massa is only 22km off the coastal Via Aurelia at Follonica, absolutely worth the diversion if you are passing that way; direct from Siena it's a not particularly captivating 65km/1hr20mins drive on the SS73 (passing by San Galgano) and the SS441.

There are three or four **buses** a day from Volterra (change at Monterotondo), five to nearby Follonica, and frequent buses and **trains** from there to Grosseto (Massa is in Grosseto province); also two a day to Florence and Siena, and one direct to Grosseto.

Information and tickets are from *Agenzia Massa Veterensis* opposite the Duomo. Most buses stop on Via Corridoni, behind and a little downhill from the Duomo.

# Tourist Information

**Massa**: Via Parenti 22, **t** 0566 902 756, *stravin@cometanet.it. Open Oct–Mar Tues–Fri 9–12.30, Sat 9–12.30 and 3.30–6, Sun 10–12.30; 25 May–Sept Mon–Sat 9–12.30 and 4–7.30, Sun 10–1.*

# Where to Stay and Eat

**Massa** ✉ 58024

Massa becomes ever more popular, and its room capacity is often stretched to the limit.

★★**Duca del Mare**, Via D. Alighieri 1/2, **t** 0566 902 284, **f** 0566 901 905 *(moderate).* One of the town's three hotels, just below the town centre on the Via Massetana, in a lovely setting with a garden and views over the countryside (Massa lies on a rather steep hill); it's set in a modern building and has a simple *trattoria.*

★★**Girifalco**, Via Massentana, **t** 0566 902 177 *(cheap).* Nearly impossible to tell apart from Duca del Mare – both charge about the same price, offer the same amenities and the same views.

Dining in Massa is uncomplicated.
**Da Bracali**, Via di Perolla 2, Località Ghirlanda, **t** 0566 902 318 *(very expensive).* This fine restaurant offers haute cuisine variations on local dishes and a formidable wine list, in a very elegant setting. *Closed Mon and Tues, only Tues in summer, 1–15 Nov and mid-Jan–mid-Feb.*

**Taverna del Vecchio Borgo**, **t** 0566 903 950 *(moderate).* This too comes highly recommended, not only for its food – game dishes including pheasant, boar and venison – but for its extensive list of grappas. *Closed Sun eve and Mon.*

**Pizzeria Le Murol**, Via Norma Parenti (behind the Duomo), **t** 0566 940 055. Just down the road, this is somewhat less ambitious, serving good pizza or alternatively, affordable full dinners that might include grilled swordfish.

peculiar Sienese artist, Rutilio Manetti (d. 1639): woebegone ladies and a jellicle cat attend a pug-nosed, thumb-sucking, very un-beatific baby Mary. Nearby is a fine font with reliefs by Giraldo da Como (*c.* 1250) and a Renaissance tabernacle added in 1447. A wooden crucifix by Giovanni Pisano hangs over the high altar; in the Gothic apse is the *Ark of San Cerbone* with more reliefs (1324) on the life of Massa's patron saint.

### Up and Down Massa

Next to the cathedral on Piazza Garibaldi, the 1230 **Palazzo del Podestà** holds Massa's **Museo Civico** (*t 0566 902 289; open Oct–March Tues–Sun 10–12.30 and 3.30–5; Apr–Sept Tues–Sun 10–12.30 and 3.30–7; closed Mon; adm* ), with a well-organized if uninspiring archaeological collection – the Medici dukes carried the best finds to Florence. In the small Pinacoteca, the best work is a *Maestà* by Ambrogio Lorenzetti, aglow with rosy faces, flowers and golden trim. Note the angel with the distaff and spindle in the centre – a sure sign that the local wool-guild paid for the painting. Today the city offices are in the **Palazzo Comunale** across the square, a group of connected tower-houses from the 13th and 14th centuries. Note the inscription above the door of another old building there: MASSA VETERNENSIS CELEBRIS VETULONIA QUONDAM.

Just as Grosseto sees itself as successor to Etruscan *Roselle*, Massa is heir to lost *Vetulonia*, the once-great city of the Dodecapolis near the coast (*see* pp.352–3). Piazza Garibaldi is lively, often crowded with Teutons perching on the steps of the Duomo or swilling beer in the café-pizzerias. Via Libertà leads into the older quarter, a nest of arches and alleys barely changed over centuries. Like Siena, Massa is divided into three *terzi*; this is the *terzo* of Civitavecchia. Via Moncini climbs to the **Città Nuova**, a 14th-century suburb behind unusual Sienese fortifications; the street ends at Piazza Matteotti, with the 1330 **Torre del Candeliere** (Torre dell'Orologio), linked to the fortifications by the **Sienese Arch**, a slender walkway; it's a beautiful ensemble, more for show than any military consideration (*open Nov–March Tues–Sun 11–1 and 2.30–4.30; April–Oct Tues–Sun 11–1 and 3.30–7; closed Mon all year; t 0566 902 289 to visit; adm*). Up Corso Diaz, **Sant'Agostino** church (completed 1313), has works by Rutilio Manetti.

Finally, no visit to Massa is complete without a trip to a mining museum (ask politely at the city library and they may show you the city's treasure, the 1310 *Codice Minerario Massetano*, modern Europe's first code of laws concerning mining rights). The **Museo di Arte e di Storia della Miniera** on Piazza Matteotti (*t 0566 902 289; open April–14 July and Sept Tues–Sun 10–11 and 3.30–5; 15 July–31 Aug Tues–Sun 10–12 and 4–7; Oct–Mar by appointment only; closed Mon;adm*) is small but worth a visit.

### Pampered Tuscan Science Turtles

Once you've seen the mines, you can but head down to the coast to Follonica (SS438) and visit **CARAPAX** (*Loc. Vemelle, t 0566 940 083, www.carapax@novars.it, 0566 202 387; visiting times 21 Mar–31 May Sat, Sun and hols 9–12.30 and 2.30–6; June–Sept daily 9–12.30 and 4–7; Oct–20 Mar Sat, Sun and hols 9.30–12.30 and 2.30–5; feeding time 3pm in winter, 6pm in summer*), the European Centre for the Protection of Turtles and Tortoises, 15 kilometres away. No fooling. They study turtles, save endangered ones and reintroduce them into the wild. Visitors are welcome to look at the turtle clinic and nursery, and see exotic species from as far as the Amazon and the Sahel. The centre is also working to reintroduce the stork to Italy, and has a colony of them in Italy's biggest aviary.

# San Galgano and the Sword in the Stone

The SS73 east from Massa to Siena skirts the southern Colline Metallifere, through lands that saw a great medieval flowering of monasticism. The monks are mostly long gone, but they left one of the most unusual, least-visited sights in Tuscany, the ruined Cistercian **Abbey of San Galgano** (*open daily 8–12 and 2–sunset*), some two kilometres north of Palazzetto. In certain older paintings in Siena's Pinacoteca, you will see the oddly Arthurian figure of a man apparently drawing a sword from a stone. This is San Galgano and, in fact, he is putting the sword in.

Galgano Guidotti, from nearby Chiusdino, was a dissolute soldier who one day had a vision of St Michael on the slopes of Montesiepi, ordering him to change his ways. Thrusting his sword into a rock to symbolize his new life, Galgano became a holy hermit; an ensuing career of miracles ensured his rapid canonization in 1181.

Almost from the start, the community he founded here was associated with the Cistercian Order, attracting monks from France as well as from around Siena. For centuries they played a vital role in the community, draining swamps, building mills and starting up a small textile industry. The Republic of Siena found them indispensable as architects, administrators – and as accountants. Many of the *Biccherna* covers in the Siena archives show Cistercians puzzling over the books or handing out pay. With its immense wealth, and its French architects eager to initiate the backward Italians in the glories of the new Gothic style, the order began its great **Abbey Church** in 1218. The Cistercians were already in a bad way when the abbey was dissolved in 1600; soon after their departure the roof, the façade and the campanile collapsed, leaving the grandest French-Gothic building in Tuscany a ruin. Its beautiful travertine columns and pointed arches remain, with the sky as roof and green lawns as carpet. Parts of the monastery survive, now in the care of Olivetan nuns.

After Galgano's death, St Michael appeared again on a hill above the abbey to command his followers to build the **Cappella di Montesiepi** (*open 8–12 and 2–sunset*) over the sword in the stone. The curious round chapel, one of very few in Italy, was begun in 1185. The sword is still there, protruding from its rock right in the centre. As with all the sites associated with St Michael, it is a reminder of a branch of medieval mysticism that, while not entirely lost, is hardly well understood. It's a very curious place – during a recent visit, a beautiful woman in black entered, carrying a gleaming silver sword, and went off to a side room with the caretaker; we didn't ask. Note the pair of human hands in a glass box, with a card explaining how they were bitten off by wolves. The altar has a cross of the type often seen on buildings of the Knights Templar, and the ceiling dome, patterned in 22 concentric stripes, may be a representation of the heavenly spheres of medieval cosmology (as in the famous fresco in Pisa's Campo Santo). In a side chamber is a series of frescoes by Ambrogio Lorenzetti on the life of the saint, an *Annunciation* and a *Coronation of the Virgin*.

In the silent countryside around town, possible detours include **Chiusdino** (8km west), the dense, sleepy birthplace of San Galgano, or the aged **Monticiano**, south on the SS73, where a Romanesque church has trecento frescoes by Bartolo di Fredi.

## South Along Route 223

Possibly the least interesting route south from Siena leads to Grosseto, passing through the fertile, but nearly empty, valley of the River Merse. Once into Grosseto province it becomes even emptier, though there are a few towns worth a visit: old, walled **Bagni di Petriolo**, with thermal springs to relieve your gout; **Civitella Marittima**, a hill town with the Romanesque church of San Lorenzo al Lanzo, and **Pagánico**, a charming village retaining its Sienese walls. Its church, San Michele, has well-preserved frescoes by trecento and quattrocento Sienese artists.

# Southern Tuscany

15

# Highlights

1 Monte Oliveto Maggiore: Siena's élite Renaissance hermitage
2 Pienza: Pope Pius II's Renaissance city
3 Montepulciano: Vino Nobile and fine art
4 Chiusi: underground Etruscan mysteries

Not counting the coastal Maremma around Grosseto, the old territories of the Sienese Republic make a complete and coherent landscape, rolling hills mostly given over to serious farming and pastureland. It isn't as garden-like as some other parts of Tuscany, though tidy vineyards and avenues of cypresses are not lacking. Hill towns, ready landmarks, poke above the horizon – Montepulciano off to the east, Pienza a bit to the left, while that castle on the left of the road must be Castiglione d'Orcia. At times it seems the whole region is laid out before you, bounded on one side by the hills around Siena, on the other by the cones of Monte Amiata and Radicófani.

In the little tourist offices in these towns, they remark that not too many English or Americans pass through, which is a pity. It's beautiful countryside, the food and wine are among the best in Tuscany, and there are delightful towns with souvenirs from the Renaissance and Middle Ages.

## Asciano and the *Crete*

The SS326 from Siena heads east; its main purpose is to get you out to Cortona (*see* p.466–70) and then to Umbria. Before it leaves Siena province, the road passes the village of **Monteaperti**, where the Sienese won their famous victory over Florence in 1260, and **Rapolano Terme** (27km), a small spa that retains some of its medieval walls. Besides the hot springs there is a surplus of natural gas in the area, some of it pumped out from wells, and some just leaking out of the ground – don't drop any matches. **Asciano**, 10 kilometres south of Rapolano, has walls built by the Sienese in 1351, and a good collection of Sienese art in the **Museo d'Arte Sacra**, next to the Romanesque church of the Collegiata (*open by appt only, t 0577 718 207*). Finds from Etruscan necropolises in the area have been assembled in the church of San Bernardino, a modest **Museo Etrusco** (*Corso Matteotti 46; open mid-Sept–mid-June Tues–Sun 10–12.30; mid-June–mid-Sept Tues–Sun 10–12.30 and 4.30–6.30; closed Mon; adm*). In a house at Via del Canto 11, there are some recently discovered Roman mosaics; ask at the pharmacy on Corso Matteotti to arrange a visit.

Southeast of Siena, the valleys of the Ombrone and the Asso enclose the country of the *crete*. Like the *balze* of Volterra, these are uncanny monuments to the power of erosion. The countryside around Asciano is dotted with them, exposing chalk cliffs where the soil above has eroded; they often appear in the backgrounds of 14th- and 15th-century Sienese and Florentine paintings (similar eroded chalk hills are called *biancane*). This is sheep country, and it suffered a great deal after the Second World War, when many men went to seek work in the cities. Today, immigrants from Sardinia make up a sizeable minority of the population, born shepherds who are trying to get the business back on its feet. Old **Sinalunga**, up on its hill, is next (22 kilometres west), but offers little to detain you; the main square is named after Garibaldi, to commemorate his arrest here in 1867, on the orders of King Vittorio Emanuele, who was afraid his volunteers were about to attack Rome. **Torrita di Siena**, an old Sienese border fortress six kilometres southwest of the junction with the A1 from Florence to Rome, owes its name to the tall towers of its walls, some of which remain.

## Tourist Information

**Rapolano Terme**: Piazza Garibaldi,
t 0577 724 079, *inforapolano@inwind.it*.
*Open summer Tues–Sat 10–1 and 3.30–7, Sun
10–1; winter Tues–Fri 9–1 and 3–6, Sat 9–1 and
3–7*.
**Asciano**: Corso Matteotti 18, t/f 0577 719 510,
*www.cretesenesi.com. Open summer
Wed–Mon 9.30–12.30 and 2.30–6.30*.
**Buonconvento**: Via Soccini 32, t 0577 807 181,
t/f 0577 807 181. *Open 15 Mar–Oct Tues–Sun
10.30–1 and 3–7; Nov–14 Mar Sat and Sun
10–1 and 3–5*.
**San Giovanni d'Asso**: Via XX Settembre 15,
t 0577 803 203.

## Where to Stay and Eat

Accommodation isn't always all that easy to
find in this quiet corner of Tuscany. Villages
may only have one real hotel, or none.
However, there are plenty of rooms in the
various *agriturismo* farmhouses dotted
around; either follow signs on the road, or ask
at the local tourist office. Some restaurants
too have rooms to rent, and there are always a
few private homes with rooms to rent that
don't advertise. Don't be shy; ask around and
you'll find something.

### Asciano ☒ 53041

**Da Miretta**, near Asciano at Loc. La Pievina on
the Laurentana road, t 0577 718 368
(*moderate*). A very friendly, reasonably priced
place serving regional dishes and seafood –
save some room for the home-made
desserts. *Closed Mon and Tues*.

### Buonconvento ☒ 53022

**\*\*Albergo Ristorante Roma**, Via Soccini 14,
t 0577 806 021, f 0577 807 284 (*cheap*). The
closest rooms to Monte Oliveto Maggiore
are to be found in Buonconvento, on the
main street of the old town. Simple and old-
fashioned, the Roma also has a very good
*cheap* restaurant. After visiting Monte
Oliveto Maggiore, the restaurant in the
gatehouse is a nice place to have a snack if
you are feeling peckish.

### Sinalunga ☒ 53048

**\*\*\*\*Locanda dell'Amorosa**, 2km south of
Sinalunga at Locazione L'Amorosa,
t 0577 679 497, f 0577 678 216 (luxury–*very
expensive*). This is something really special,
though you need to reserve long in advance
since there are only seven rooms; more than
an inn, this is an entire medieval hamlet,
albeit a tiny one, complete with a manor
house and frescoed church. There are no
particular amenities to speak of, but it has
beautiful rooms in a memorable setting,
along with a prize-winning restaurant.
The menu follows the seasons, but usually
includes some freshwater fish dishes (Lake
Trasimeno isn't far away) such as the *ravioli
di pesce*; for seconds, try stuffed pigeon or
the big Florentine steaks. *Closed Mon lunch
and Tues*.

# Monte Oliveto Maggiore and Around

South of Siena, the SS2 wends towards Rome, roughly following the Roman *Via
Cassia* and the medieval pilgrims' path to Rome, the *Via Francigena*. Along the way, it
passes **Lucignano d'Arbia** (16km), a charming, tiny village with a medieval church, and
**Buonconvento** (27km), a gritty industrial town that hides a miniature walled medieval
centre – it would make a pretty hill town, if it only had a hill. The walls are no longer
either very proper or military and are peppered with windows of the houses that
have been built against them. There are two fine gates at either end of the main
street, and in the middle the 14th-century parish church with an altarpiece by Matteo
di Giovanni.

In the broken, jumbled hills south of Asciano, austere green meadows alternate with
ragged gullies and bare white cliffs. At the centre of these *crete*, in the bleakest and

most barren part, there is a grove of tall, black cypresses around the monastery of **Monte Oliveto Maggiore** (*open daily 9.15–12 and 3.15–5; until 5.45 in summer*), nine kilometres from Buonconvento on the SS451. Some of the great gentlemen of Siena's merchant élite founded Monte Oliveto, including Giovanni Tolomei and Ambrogio Piccolomini, both jaded merchants and sincere Christians who retired here in 1313 to escape the fatal sophistication of the medieval city. Their new Olivetan Order was approved by the pope only six years later. With such wealthy backers, the monastery became a sort of élite hermitage for central Tuscany. An ambitious building programme carried out throughout the 1400s made it a complete, though little-known, monument of quattrocento architecture and art. In its isolated setting, Monte Oliveto is a marvel of Renaissance clarity and rationality, expressed in simple structures and good Siena brick. The beautiful, asymmetrical **gatehouse**, decorated with a della Robbia terracotta, makes a fitting introduction to the complex. Inside, the well-proportioned brick **Abbey Church** (finished in 1417) has an exceptional set of wooden intarsia **choir-stalls** by the master of the genre, Fra Giovanni da Verona, among the best work of this kind in all Italy. Take time to admire the beautiful and unusual dome with an octagon of interlocking arches, an Islamic Andalucian design that made its way here via Spanish Christian churches and the chapel of the Castel Nuovo in Naples.

The monastery's greatest treasure, however, is the **Great Cloister**, embellished with 36 frescoes of scenes from the life of St Benedict (whose original rule Tolomei and the Olivetans were trying to restore). All 36 of these are currently undergoing a much-needed restoration; the first nine are by Luca Signorelli and depict formidable ladies and bulky, white-robed monks in the artist's distinctive balloonish forms and sparing use of colour. All the rest are the work of Il Sodoma (1505–8) – some of his best painting, and contain ethereal scenes of Pre-Raphaelite ladies and mandarin monks, with blue and purple backgrounds of ideal landscapes and cities.

If you are of the persuasion, popular enough a century or so ago, that it was with Raphael and Michelangelo that the Renaissance started to go wrong, you owe a visit here. Il Sodoma, not a Florentine nor really even a Sienese (he was from Vercelli in the north), wrote the last word to the mainstream tendency of Tuscan painting before the excesses of Mannerism. Mr Sodomite himself makes an appearance in the scene '*Come Benedetto risaldò lo capistero che era rotta*' ('How Benedict repaired the broken sieve'); he's the dissipated fellow on the left with the white gloves. Look carefully – not only did Sodoma paint himself in, but also his pet badgers, of which he was very fond. The badgers and others of Sodoma's many pets appear in various other frescoes.

Unlike so many great Tuscan art shrines, Monte Oliveto, isolated here in the Sienese hills, retains something of its original aloof dignity. Although Napoleon himself suppressed the monastery in 1810, a group of talented brothers still works here, specializing in the restoration of old books. They won't be telling you much about the place – they're vowed to silence – but there is a monkish gift shop outside with home-made wine and honey, and other products from monasteries around Tuscany.

In the *crete* around Monte Oliveto, the village of **San Giovanni d'Asso** (8km south-east) is built around a Sienese fortress; the church of San Pietro in Villore is from the 12th century, with an ambitious, unusual façade. From here, wandering unsignposted byroads lead east to **Montisi** (7km) and **Trequanda** (12km), two fine villages, seldom visited perhaps because they're so hard to find; the latter has a 13th-century castle and another Romanesque church. If you're lucky you might even find **Sant'Anna in Camprena**, between Montisi and Pienza, an ambitious medieval monastery complex that time forgot – until the location scouts from *The English Patient* arrived. The place is now being fitfully restored, and if you liked Sodoma's work in Monte Oliveto you can stop in here to see another of his frescoes, portraying Christ with children, small dogs and fantasy Roman monuments.

# Montalcino and Around

Situated on a lofty hill inhabited since Etruscan times, swathed in vineyards and olive groves, the walled village of **Montalcino** (pop. 5,400) dominates the serene countryside 14 kilometres south of Buonconvento. Its major attraction is liquid – Brunello di Montalcino, a dark pungent red proudly holding its own among Italy's finest wines.

Every year at the Palio in Siena, there is a procession of representatives from all the towns that once were part of the Republic. The honour of leading the parade belongs to Montalcino, for its loyalty and for the great service it rendered in 1555 after the fall of Siena (*see* **Siena**, History, p.371–2). During the siege, a band of diehard republicans escaped from Siena to the nearly impregnable fortress of Montalcino, where they and the local populace established the 'Republic of Siena at Montalcino', holding out against the Medici until 1559. Today, Montalcino tries hard to be up to date (it was the first town in Tuscany to declare itself a 'denuclearized zone'); in reality it's a friendly, resolutely sleepy town where people often forget to wind the clocks.

## Within the Walls

Right on Piazza Cavour is one of Montalcino's modest museums: the small **Archaeology Museum**, set in a former hospital pharmacy with detached frescoes by a student of Il Sodoma. Via Mazzini leads west to the Piazza del Popolo, and the attractive **Palazzo Comunale**, begun in the late 13th century, with a slender tower that apes the Torre di Mangia in Siena. Nearby, **Sant'Agostino** is a simple Sienese church, preserving some original frescoes from the 1300s. The **Diocesan and Civic Museum** around the corner, just reopened after restorations (*t 0577 846 014; open Jan–Mar Tues–Sun 10–1 and 2–5.30; April–Dec Tues–Sun 10–6; closed Mon; adm*), has a collection of Sienese painting and polychromed wood statues, including Madonnas by three great Sienese artists (Martini, Pietro Lorenzetti and Il Vecchietta), and some of the earliest successes of Sienese art, an illuminated Bible and painted crucifix, both from the 12th century. Besides some minor works of the 14th–15th-century Sienese masters, there is a collection of locally produced majolica from the same period.

# Getting Around

There are regular **buses** from Siena (41km/1hr), a few of which involve a change at Buonconvento, near the SS2 crossroads for Montalcino. Buses stop at Piazza Cavour at the eastern end of town; you can obtain tickets and (if you ask politely) information at the bar, which is on the piazza. Unfortunately there are no convenient buses to take you to Sant'Antimo.

# Tourist Information

**Montalcino**: Costa del Municipio 8, t/f 0577 849 331, *www.prolocomontalcino.it. Open Nov–Mar Tues–Sun 10–1 and 2–5.40; April–Oct daily 10–1 and 2–5.40.*

# Where to Stay and Eat

**Montalcino** ✉ 53024
★★★**Dei Capitani**, Via Lapini 6, t/f 0577 847 227 (*moderate*). The best bet for somewhere to stay in the area is this old palazzo in the centre, which enjoys wonderful views, a small pool and (a rarity here) a car park.

★★★**Il Giglio**, Via Soccorso Saloni 5, t 0577 848 167 (*moderate*). Reasonable hotel and similarly central.
★★**Giardino**, Via Cavour 4, t 0577 848 257 (*cheap, some rooms without bath*). The Giardino is handily positioned and right by the bus stop.
★★★**Al Brunello**, Loc. Bellaria, t 0577 849 304, f 0577 849 430 (*moderate*). This reasonably-priced hotel is situated in its own attractive garden.
**Locanda Sant'Antimo**, near the church in Sant'Antimo. Locanda Sant'Antimo is a good pizzeria which also has inexpensive rooms in case you want to stay.

As well as wine, Montalcino is justly famous for its delcious honey, which comes into its own in early September at Italy's **National Honey Fair**.

**Cucina di Edgardo**, Via S. Saloni 9, t 0577 848 232 (*expensive*). Some of the best and most creative *cucina nuova* this side of Siena; be sure to reserve. Some of Montalcino's famous honey laces the desserts.
**Il Pozzo**, Piazza del Pozzo, Loc. S. Angelo in Colle, t 0577 844 015 (*moderate*). Worth the detour for a cheap, full-blown traditional meal. *Closed Tues.*

Just down Via Ricasoli, at the east end of Montalcino, visitors can find the impressive 14th-century **Rocca** (*open April–Oct Tues–Sun 9–8; Nov–Mar Tues–Sun 9–6; closed Mon; free, but adm to go up on the walls*). This was the centre of the fortifications that kept the Spaniards and Florentines at bay. For Italian patriots this citadel is highly significant; it was the last stronghold not only of the Sienese, but symbolically of all the medieval freedoms of the Italian cities blotted out in the bloody, reactionary 1500s. Near the entrance there is a plaque with a little poem from the 'Piedmontese Volunteers of Liberty', extolling Montalcino's bravery in 'refusing the Medici thief'. Now a city park, with views that on a clear day stretch over half the province, the Rocca itself contains the last battle standard of the Sienese republic and an **Enoteca** where you can become better acquainted with Montalcino's venerable Brunello and other local wines such as Moscadello and Rosso di Montalcino.

Following the town walls on the north side, you pass through neighbourhoods that are largely made up of orchards and gardens – Montalcino isn't nearly as busy a place as it was in the 1400s. The **cathedral**, on Via Spagni, was mostly rebuilt in the 1700s. Follow that street past the Baroque church of the Madonna del Soccorso, and you come to the city park, the 'Balcony of Tuscany', with views over Siena and beyond.

## Sant'Antimo

*Open Mon–Sat 10.30–12.30 and 3–6.30; Sun 9.15–10.45 and 3–6.*

A few of the vineyards that produce the famous Brunello di Montalcino can be found on the road south for **Sant'Antimo**. The **Azienda Agricola Greppo** welcomes visitors (*make sure you call before visiting:* **t** *0577 849 421*). Sant'Antimo itself is only about 10 kilometres south of Montalcino and is worth the detour if you have the time. One of the finest Romanesque churches in the whole of Tuscany can be found here. This church originally formed part of a 9th-century Benedictine monastery founded, according to legend, by Charlemagne himself. The present building, which was begun in 1118, includes parts of the Carolingian works, including the crypt.

This half-ruined complex, reached by a long, winding avenue of cypresses, could easily serve as the set for *The Name of the Rose*. An important monastic community once flourished here, and there are still some monks about; they'll happily sell you a CD featuring their Gregorian chant. The church, though, is exquisite, with its elegant tower and rounded apse. Some of the stone inside, which is on the capitals and elsewhere, is made of luminous alabaster from Volterra. The sophistication of the architecture is impressive indeed – in particular the Byzantine-style women's gallery, and the ambulatory behind the apse with its radiating chapels.

# The Val d'Orcia

**San Quirico d'Orcia**, a humble little agricultural centre where the SS146 from Pienza joins the SS2, still has some of its medieval walls. Once on the pilgrim route of the Via Francigena, the town was endowed with hospices and hospitals built to accommodate pilgrims en route to Rome. The magnificent **Collegiata**, rebuilt in the 12th century over an earlier 8th-century church, has an exceptional façade built from local travertine, and three portals from the 1200s, sculpted with lions and telamons, the finest of their kind in the area. Just behind it is the newly-restored and somewhat forbidding 17th-century **Palazzo Chigi** – a surprisingly grand presence for such a tiny town. Since its restoration, the frescoed rooms are open to visitors for part of the year (*open on request, call* **t** *0577 898 247 for info*). There are a couple more attractive churches in the town: **Santa Maria di Vitaleta**, with a Gothic façade and an enamel Annunciation by Andrea della Robbia on the high altar, and the pretty little 11th-century **Santa Maria Assunta**. You can also visit a lovely Renaissance garden, the **Horti Leonini** (*open daily, dawn to sunset*), designed in the late 15th century by Diomede Lioni as a resting place for pilgrims.

There are a couple of points of interest nearby: **Ripa d'Orcia**, a hamlet with a stately castle of its own (*now a hotel residence, call* **t** *0577 89776, expensive*), seven kilometres to the south, and **Bagno Vignoni**, a spa town south off the SS2, where the piazza has a *'vasca termale'* built by Lorenzo de' Medici, who came for the waters. There used to be three of these pools – one for men, one for women and one for horses. The pools have long since closed, but if you long for a bathe, it is possible to buy day tickets for the hot springs at the Hotel Posta Marcucci (*see* 'Where to Stay', opposite).

# Tourist Information

**San Quirico:** Via Dante Aligheri 33, t 0577 897 211 f 0577 898 303, *info@parcodellavaldorcia.com*. *Open Mar–Oct and Dec Tues–Sun 10–1 and 3.30–6.30.*
**Castiglione d'Orcia:** Via G. Marconi, t 0577 887 363.
**Radicofani:** Via R. Magi 31, t 0578 55684.

# Festivals

'**Incontri in Terra di Siena':** t 0578 69101 for details, *July and Aug.* During the summer, a chamber music festival is based at *La Foce*, home of the writer Iris Origo, on the Monte Amiata road from Chianciano. Concerts are also held at Casteluccio, Pienza, Montalcino, Sarteano and Cetona.

# Where to Stay and Eat

**Bagno Vignoni** ✉ 53027
**Albergo Le Terme**, Bagno Vignoni, t 0577 887 150, f 0577 887 497 (*moderate*). Once the summer house of Pope Pio II Piccolomini. It is now a comfortable hotel that overlooks a basin filled with hot spring water.
**Hotel Posta Marcucci**, Via Ara Urcea, t 0577 887 112, f 0577 887 119 (*moderate; pool open to public exc. Thurs; adm*). If you want to take the waters the easy way, you can swim in the naturally heated pool at this nearby hotel.
**Osteria del Leone**, Via dei Mulini 4, t 0577 887 300 (*moderate*). Despite its diminutive size, Bagno has a very good restaurant to further enhance your stay. Specialities include traditional Tuscan *bruschetta, pici* and duck with grapes and fennel. *Closed Mon.*

**Radicófani** ✉ 53040
**La Palazzina**, Loc. Le Vigne, t 0578 55771, f 0578 53553 (*cheap*). La Palazzina is 200-year-old villa located just outside the village with a few rooms, a pool, and a restaurant (*moderate*) focusing on traditional local recipes – it offers home-made pasta as well as delicious home-grown vegetables. *Open Mar–Nov.*

Long before the modern SS2 was ever built, the old Via Francigena traversed the valley of the Orcia, passing a patch of castles and fortified towns that began in the early Middle Ages. **Castiglione d'Orcia** (nine kilometres south of San Quirico) is as medieval-looking a town as you could ever wish for (though its cobbled piazza and fountain are actually from the 1600s) with two parish churches. The ruined fortress, which overlooks the town, was built by the Aldobrandeschi family, who controlled much of southern Tuscany as late as the 1200s. If you're planning to spend some time around Castiglione, get in touch with the Centro Agriturismo 'I Lecci' on t 0577 887 287. They can arrange horses for tours of the countryside, hunting trips and nature excursions. Just outside to the north a pretty road winds up through olive groves to **Rocca d'Orcia**, another well-preserved medieval village clustered below its impressive castle, the **Rocca di Tentatenno**, which is open to visitors and used for art exhibitions.

Another 15 kilometres south of Castiglione is **Vivo d'Orcia**, which began as a Camaldolensian monastery in 1003; when the monastery withered the village grew instead, leaving only the pretty Romanesque **Cappella dell'Ermicciolo** in the woods above the town.

**Bagni San Filippo**, some eight kilometres east of Vivo, circling back towards the SS2, may go into the books as the world's smallest thermal spa – a telephone booth, a few old houses, and one small hotel. It takes its name from San Filippo Benizi, a holy hermit of the Middle Ages who hid here when he heard there was a movement to elect him pope. Gouty old Lorenzo il Magnifico used to come here too, though he didn't leave any embellishments like the piazza in Bagno Vignoni. You can stop here for a swim in the natural terraced pools of the **Fosso Bianco**, a glistening limestone formation – a sort of stone waterfall – created by the flowing sulphurous waters.

## Radicófani

Some wonderfully rugged countryside lies in the valley of the Orcia, east of this chain of villages, especially along the roads approaching **Radicófani**, a landmark of southern Tuscany, with its surreal, muffin-shaped hill topped by a lofty tower. The ruined fortress around it, originally built by Pope Adrian IV (the Englishman Nicholas Breakspear), served in the 1300s as headquarters for the legendary bandit Ghino di Tacco, solid citizen of Dante's *Inferno* and subject of a story in the *Decameron* (day 10, number 2), about how he imprisoned the Abbot of Cluny in this tower. The elegant loggias on the highway, just outside town, belong to the 17th-century Palazzo La Posta, once the only good hotel between Siena and Rome; most of the famous on the Grand Tour stopped on their way through.

# Pienza

Some 50 kilometres south of Siena on the SS2, you'll come across a perfect, tiny core of Renaissance order and urbanity, surrounded by a village of about 2,500 souls. **Pienza** is a delightful place, even if it does get more than its share of tourists. Like Monte Oliveto Maggiore, it is a small dose of the best of the Renaissance, a jewel set among some of the most glorious and archetypal of Tuscan landscapes.

During a period of political troubles, common enough in Renaissance Siena, the great family of the Piccolomini chose to exile itself temporarily in one of its possessions, the village of Corsignano. Aeneas Silvius Piccolomini (*see* p.383) was born there in 1405; later, as Pope Pius II, he became determined to raise his country birthplace into a city. No historian has ever discovered any compelling economic or military reason for a new town here. Architect Bernardo Rossellino designed it, with some help from Pius, the pennies of the faithful paid for it, and Pius named it after himself: Pienza. No one knows if Rossellino merely meant to build the pope a monument, or was consciously creating a model city of Renaissance town planning. Perhaps fortunately, after the first wave of papal patronage Pienza was nearly forgotten. The strict grid of streets that was to extend over the Tuscan hills never materialized, and only the central piazza with a new cathedral and a Piccolomini palace was ever completed – enough, at least, to reveal something of the original intention.

### Pienza's Piazza Pio II

Piazza Pio II, the heart of Rossellino's design scheme, is simple and decorous; it displays the chief buildings of the town without any of the monumental symmetry of the later Renaissance, seemingly relying on proportion alone to tie the ensemble together. Such a square shows how, despite all its paintings of ideal buildings and

# Tourist Information

**Pienza:** Pro Loco, Piazza Pio II, **t/f** 0578 749 071, *www.infinito.it/utenti/ufficio.turistico.* Offers occasional guided tours of town. *Open Mon–Sun 9.30–1 and 3–6.30.*

# Shopping

Corso Rossellino leads from the centre of the village to Porta Murello and the bus terminus, passing trendy artisan shops selling ceramics and leatherwork, antique shops and health food stores. Pienza for some reason has dozens of these, offering among other things the very good, locally made honey and preserves. And if Renaissance architecture leaves you cold, you can at least come for the sheep's cheese, maybe Italy's best. Pienza's variety of *cacio* is mild, even delicate in taste; this self-proclaimed 'capital of sheep's cheese' has been making it at least since the time of the Etruscans.

# Where to Stay and Eat

**Pienza** ✉ 53026

**★★★Il Chiostro**, Corso Il Rossellino 26, **t** 0578 748 400, **f** 0578 748 440 (*very expensive*). As the name implies this is an old cloister, in the centre just off Piazza Pio II; the modernized rooms have been stylishly restored with all the amenities on hand – beautiful gardens.

**★★★Corsignano**, Via della Madonnina 9, **t** 0578 748 501, **f** 0578 748 166 (*moderate*). Modern and comfortable.

**Ristorante del Falco**, Piazza Dante 3, **t** 0578 748 551 (*cheap*). If you're looking to economize, this offers a fair number of spartan rooms for rent, near the bus stop. *Closed Fri.*

**Il Prato**, Viale S. Caterina 1/3, **t** 0578 749 924 (*moderate*). The best place to stop for a bite to eat is across the piazza; there are tables outside in the little garden and a huge menu of simple local dishes to tempt the taste buds, featuring home-made *pici* (thick spaghetti) and crêpes filled with ricotta cheese, among others. *Closed Wed.*

**Latte di Luna**, Via S. Carlo 2/4, **t** 0578 748 606 (*moderate*). Popular with the locals, serving good home-made pasta with truffles, duck with olives, and grappa made in town. *Closed Tues.*

**Sperone Nudo**, Via G. Marconi, **t** 0578 748 641. Sperone Nudo is a great stop for lunch if you're sightseeing, where you can get a glass of wine and *bruschetta*, sandwiches or other snacks; it's nice and central too. *Closed Mon.*

**La Saracina**, about 7km from Pienza on the road to Montepulciano, **t** 0578 748 022 (*luxury*). Meanwhile, if you'd rather stay somewhere more rural, this has five suites and rooms in an old farmhouse with beautiful gardens, pool and tennis, out in the nearby countryside.

streetscapes, the Early Renaissance still followed the 'picturesque' urban design of the Middle Ages; Piazza Pio was made to be a stage set for daily life, or the background of a painting.

Rossellino designed a truly elegant façade for the **cathedral** (1462), capturing the spirit of the times by omission – there is no hint anywhere on this façade that it belongs to a Christian building, though the arms of the Piccolomini and the papal keys are prominently carved on the pediment (*open daily 8.30–1 and 2.30–7*). The interior, though equally elegant, is a surprise: it's done in a squarish, tamed Gothic – as if this bold Renaissance architect were a slightly embarrassed humanist who believed that only Gothic truly suited a church. Rossellino also carved a marble altar and baptismal font in the lower church; in addition, some of the leading Sienese artists contributed altarpieces: Sano di Pietro, Matteo di Giovanni, Vecchietta and Giovanni di Paolo. Nothing in this cathedral has been changed, or even moved, since the day it was completed; Pius' papal bull of 1462 expressly forbade it. See it while it lasts: the cathedral, built on the edge of a slight cliff, has been subsiding almost since it was built. Occasionally sulphurous fumes seep from the floor. If you walk around the left side of the building, there is a fine view over the countryside, and also a glimpse of the fearfully large cracks that have been developing in the apse. No one has yet discovered a way to shore it up permanently, and even though restoration work has been done it could still collapse, at least partially, at any time. The cathedral has a small **museum** in the adjacent Canon's House (*open Sat and Sun 10–1 and 3–6; adm*) with paintings from the Sienese school.

Next to the cathedral, the columned **well**, a favourite sort of Renaissance urban decoration, is also by Rossellino. So is the **Palazzo Piccolomini**, a rehash of the more famous Palazzo Rucellai in Florence, built by the architect after designs by Alberti. The best part of the design is at the rear, where a fine three-storey loggia overlooks a 'hanging garden' on the edge of the cliff. The interior of the palace and gardens are open to visitors (*t 0578 748 503; open Tues–Sun 10–12.30 and 4–7; adm*). Other buildings on the piazza include the **Archbishop's Palace** and the Gothic **Palazzo Comunale**. Behind the Palazzo Piccolomini, the church of **San Francesco** predates the founding of Pienza; there are some 14th–15th-century frescoes inside including one small work attributed to Luca Signorelli. Finally a new museum, the **Museo Diocesano di Pienza** (*t 0578 749 905; open 15 Mar–Oct Wed–Mon 10–1 and 3–6.30; Nov–14–Mar Sat, Sun and hols 10–1 and 3–6; adm*), has just opened in the sumptuously restored 15th-century Palazza Borgia in Corso Rossellino. Inside you'll find a collection of objects from surrounding churches and a number of paintings (including several by Signorelli), as well as Flemish tapestries.

Few people visit the 11th-century **Pieve** of old Corsignano, one kilometre west of the town (signposted from the car park/piazza at the entrance to the central pedestrian zone). This unusual church, where Aeneas Silvius was baptized, has some even more peculiar carvings over its entrance. Mermaids, or sirens, turn up with some frequency in Romanesque tympana and capitals, in Tuscany and Apulia especially, as well as many other places in Italy and France. Here there are several – one spreading its forked tail to display the entrance to the womb, flanked by others, and a dancer and a musician, with dragons whispering into their ears. Such symbols are steeped in medieval mysticism, not entirely inaccessible to the modern imagination. One scholar interprets this scene as a cosmic process: the sirens, representing desire, as the intermediary by which nature's energy and inspiration (the dragons) are conducted into the conscious world. It has been claimed that they betray the existence of an ecstatic cult, based on music and dance and descended from the ancient Dionysian rituals.

# Montepulciano

Another graceful hill town lingers south of Siena, also with a distinguished past and best known for wine. **Montepulciano** is larger (pop. 14,500) and livelier than Montalcino, with some fine buildings and works of art. Old Montalcino was a home from home for the Sienese, while Montepulciano usually allied itself with Florence.

This town's Vino Nobile di Montepulciano, while perhaps not as celebrated as Montalcino's Brunello, was being praised by connoisseurs over 200 years ago, and can certainly contend with Italy's best today.

Inhabitants of this town, which began as the Roman *Mons Politianus*, are called *Poliziani*, and that is the name by which its most famous son is known. Angelo Ambrogini, or Poliziano, scholar at the court of Lorenzo de' Medici and tutor to his children, was one of the first Renaissance Greek scholars, also an accomplished poet and critic. Botticelli's mythological paintings may have been inspired by his *Stanze per la Giostra*. Today's Poliziani are a genteel and cultured lot, still capable of poetic extemporization and singing. The town's biggest festival is the *Bruscello*, a partly improvised play on medieval and Renaissance themes in music and verse, acted by the townspeople in the Piazza Grande each August. A second August festival requires no poetry but plenty of sweat: the *Bravio delle Botti*, when teams from the various neighbourhoods race up the steep main street pushing huge barrels.

## Palazzi and Pulcinella

Entering the city through the **Porta al Prato**, visitors will first encounter a stone column bearing the *marzocco*, a symbol of Montepulciano's long attachment to Florence. Though nominally under Florentine control, the city was allowed a sort of independence up to the days of Cosimo I. The main street, called here Via di Gracciano del Corso, climbs and winds its way in a circle up to the top of the city (if you follow it all the way, you'll walk twice as far as you need to, and end up thinking Montepulciano is a major metropolis). This stretch is lined with noble palaces: those at No.91 and No.82 are both the work of the late Renaissance architect Vignola, famous for his Villa Giulia in Rome and the Farnese Palace in Caprarola (Lazio). Up at No.73, **Palazzo Bucelli** has the most unusual foundation in Italy – made almost entirely of Etruscan cinerary urns, filled with cement and stacked like bricks, many still retaining their sculpted reliefs. Montepulciano was once Etruscan, though the urns probably came from Chiusi.

Piazza Michelozzo, where the street begins to ascend, is named after the Florentine architect of **Sant'Agostino** church, which has an excellent, restrained Renaissance façade, similar to the cathedral in Pienza though more skilfully handled. Michelozzo also contributed the terracotta reliefs over the portal. Across the piazza, note the figure atop the old **Torre del Pulcinello**. To anyone familiar with Naples, the white *Commedia dell'Arte* clown banging the hours on the town bell will be an old friend. It is said that a Neapolitan bishop was once exiled here for indiscretions back home, and when he returned he left this bit of Parthenopean culture as a souvenir, to thank the Poliziani.

Continuing along the main street, you pass a dozen or so more palaces, reminders of what an aristocratic city this once was. There is one florid Baroque interior, in the **Gesù Church** by Andrea Pozzo. Further down, the street curves around the medieval **Fortezza**, now partially residential, within the oldest part of Montepulciano, a fascinating quarter of ancient alleys.

## Piazza Grande

These days, when even the stalwart citizens of hill towns are a little too spoiled to walk up hills, the old centres of towns sometimes become quiet and out-of-the-way. So it is in Montepulciano, where the **Piazza Grande** is city's highest point. On one side, Michelozzo added a rusticated stone front and tower (*open May–Oct Mon–Sun 10–6*) to the 13th-century **Palazzo Comunale** to create a lesser copy of Florence's Palazzo Vecchio. Opposite, a Renaissance well stands in front of the **Palazzo Contucci**, built by the elder Antonio da Sangallo. On the west side, a tremendous pile of bricks, a sort of tenement for pigeons, proclaims the agonizing unfinishability of the **cathedral** (*open 8–11 and 3–5 or 6 according to the season*), sad victim of a doomed rebuilding project begun in 1592. Like the toad, believed by medieval scholars to conceal a precious jewel in its brain, this preposterous building hides within its bulk a single transcendent work of art. Atop a marble Renaissance altar adorned with putti stands an *Assumption of the Virgin* by Taddeo di Bartolo, one of the greatest of all 14th-

## Getting There and Around

Montepulciano is situated 12½km/20mins east of Pienza on the SS146, 66km/1½hrs from Siena, and 16km/30mins west of the Chiusi exit on the A1.

Getting here by **train** is not, perhaps, the best option. The train station (Florence–Rome line) is way out in the countryside, irregularly served by buses to town, and it tends to be only local trains that stop; a better possibility is to use the station at Chiusi-Chianciano, which has bus connections up to Chiusi town, to Chianciano Terme, Montepulciano and occasionally Pienza.

The **bus** station in Montepulciano is just a short distance outside the Porta al Prato, which is the main gate into the city. There are very regular buses to Chianciano Terme–Chiusi–Chiusi station. There are slightly fewer to Pienza; one each in the morning and afternoon for Siena (via Pienza and San Quirico), also daily connections to Abbadia San Salvatore, Montalcino, Perugia and Arezzo. There is an LFI bus information booth inside the train station at Chiusi; outside, besides the buses mentioned above, there are rather infrequent LFI connections to Cortona, Arezzo, Perugia, Orvieto and Città della Pieve.

And if you aren't feeling up to climbing all the way up to the top of Montepulciano, the LFI runs a handy **minibus** service up the Corso to Piazza Grande.

## Tourist Information

**Montepulciano:** Via Gracciano del Corso 59a, off Piazza Grande, t/f 0578 757 341. *Open April–July and Sept Mon–Sun 9.30–2.30 and 3–8; Oct–Mar Mon–Sat 9.30–12.30 and 3–6, Sun 9.30–12.30.*

## Where to Stay and Eat

**Montepulciano** ✉ **53045**

Montepulciano is an hospitable place and puts out the welcome mat at a few very amiable hotels.

**★★★Marzocco**, Via G. Savonarola 18, t 0578 757 262, f 0578 757 530 (*moderate*). An airy, serendipitous establishment, family-run, and located, naturally, next to the *Marzocco* itself, just inside the main gate.

**★★★Borghetto**, Borgo Buio t 0578 757 535 (*moderate*). Just around the corner, with pleasant rooms, some of which have great views over the edge of the town.

**Il Riccio**, Via Talosa 21, t/f 0578 757 713 (*moderate*). Simple and very central, with a pleasant rooftop-terrace for catching the Tuscan sun.

If you can't find a room in the town, there are a plentiful supply of them just a few miles south at Chianciano Terme (*see p.432*) and if you go to Sant'Albano, 3km from Montepulciano, you'll find seven more hotels, all in the *cheap* range, stuck bizarrely in the

century Sienese paintings. Set in glowing, discordant colours – pink, orange, purple and gold – this is a very spiritual Madonna, attended by a court of angel musicians. Don't miss the predella panels beneath; each is a serious, inspired image from the Passion, including one panel of the *Resurrection* that can be compared to Piero della Francesca's more famous version in Sansepolcro.

The **Museo Civico**, holding the **Pinacoteca Crociani** just down Via Ricci (**t** 0578 713 300; *open summer Tues–Sun 10–7; winter Tues–Sun 10–1 and 3–6*), houses several collections under one roof. On the first and second floors are some della Robbia terracottas from the dissolved convent that was once downstairs, and the Crociani collection of paintings. The old collection, with a *Crucifixion* from Filippino Lippi's workshop, an *Assumption* by the Sienese Jacopo di Mino, an odd work by Girolamo di Benvenuto – baby Jesus as an *objet d'art* – and, even more peculiar, an inexplicable *Allegory of the Immaculate Conception* by one Giovanni Antonio Lappoli (d. 1552), has gained additions from other collections in Montepulciano. However, the key

---

middle of nowhere; presumably because there are more thermal baths nearby.

The best restaurants are outside town.

**La Chiusa**, Via Madonnina, Montefollonico, **t** 0578 669 668 (*very expensive*). Located in an old *frantoio* or olive press, in the village of Montefollonico, with panoramic views back towards Montepulciano. (Sadly the press was closed after a recent and particularly virulent frost killed off most of the trees in the area.) La Chiusa has been acclaimed as the best restaurant in southern Tuscany, and though its reputation has wobbled slightly in recent years, you're guaranteed at the very least an incredible seven-course *menu degustazione* and an exhaustive wine list. Above the restaurant itself there are some very luxurious suites and rooms. *Closed Tues.*

**Il Pulcino**, 3km down the road to Chianciano, **t/f** 0578 758 711 (*moderate*). Less extravagant, specializing in grilled meats and fish.

**La Grotta**, **t** 0578 757 607 (*expensive*). Right next to the dramatic San Biagio, serving traditional Tuscan dishes with a creative twist, with the likes of smoked goose breast, *pici* with duck sauce, pigeon stuffed with truffles or duck breast with juniper berries and orange peel. *Closed Wed.*

If you want to eat in Montepulciano itself, then there are a couple of reasonable choices to be found along the Corso.

**Osteria dell'Aquacheta**, Via del Teatro, about halfway up the Corso. An excellent-value

little *osteria* where you can have a tasty light lunch for very little – *crostate* or *bruschette* and a pasta dish.

**Caffé Poliziano**, also on the Corso. This is Montepulciano's old-fashioned *gran caffé*, where the same deal can be had for a little more money. It is well worth visiting, at least for a cup of coffee.

If you don't fancy eating in a restaurant, why not have a picnic? Stock up on some of the fine local products – honey and preserves, pecorino cheese, ham or boar salami and a case of Vino Nobile; any of the back roads off the SS146 will lead you at some point to an ideal spot.

## Monticchiello ✉ 53020

**L'Olmo**, **t** 0578 5133, **f** 0578 755 124 (*very expensive*). Just below Montichiello is an elegant guest house in a beautifully restored stone post-house, with gardens and a pool overlooking the Val d'Orcia. Bedrooms are supremely comfortable and decorated in sophisticated rustic style; dinner is available on request. *Closed in winter.*

**La Porta**, Via del Piano 3, **t** 0578 755 163. An excellent *osteria*/wine bar, with wonderful views over Pienza and the valley from its panoramic terrace. Here you can have anything from a sandwich or a plate of local cheeses with a glass of wine, to a pasta dish or a succulent *tagliata* of tender steak topped with rocket leaves. *Closed Thurs.*

## Vino Nobile and Other Delights

Montepulciano and its environs are full of delightful *cantine*, and each of these in their turn are packed full of people ready for long discussions on the virtues of this famous wine.

After two years, it carries the bouquet of unknown autumn blooms, a perfume that confounds melancholy; its colour is a mystery of faith. Certain writers are known to be very fond of it. A wine tour of Montepulciano should begin with the **Cantine Cantucci**, on the Piazza Grande, where they might show you the salon with frescoes by Baroque artist Andrea Pozzo. The **Cantina Gattavecchia**, next to the church of Santa Maria at the southern end of town, has a *cantina* dating back to the 1500s; don't neglect the venerable cellar built into the embankment beneath Piazza Grande, next to the Teatro Poliziano.

Vino Nobile isn't the only variety of wine made in these parts. There is a version of Chianti – *Chianti Colli Senesi*, a creditable white *Valdichiana* and a sweet dessert *Vinsanto*. And on those evenings when quantity means more than quality, try any of the mass-produced Montepulciano reds; more honourable plonk is hard to find.

Besides wine, Montepulciano has a number of other local surprises to offer. Among these are jams, preserves, honey and other farm specialities, which have all recently become prominent in this corner of Tuscany, where the ideology of natural food has become just as popular as in the trendiest neighbourhoods of New York. You'll find them in almost any grocer's.

Montepulciano has some very good antique stores on its back streets, and a sound crafts tradition, especially in woodcarving. On Piazza Grande, there is a School of Mosaics; take a peek at the mosaic fountain in the courtyard.

improvement is the archaeological section on ground level, now rearranged to include the contents of five locally discovered Etruscan tombs previously housed in the Uffizi. Artefacts include Bucchero ware, ceramics and bronzes dating from the 5th to the 2nd century BC.

If you continue down Via Ricci you will find the church of **Santa Lucia**, which has a small *Madonna* by Luca Signorelli in a chapel off to the right.

## Antonio da Sangallo's San Biagio

One of the principle set pieces of Renaissance architecture was the isolated temple. Renaissance builders looked upon such designs as a chance to create an ideal building in an uncluttered setting, often on the edge of a city. Giuliano da Sangallo's Santa Maria delle Carceri in Prato was the first and (for most people) the worst. It was followed by Bramante's San Pietro in Montorio in Rome and the Tempio della Consolazione in Todi (Umbria). Montepulciano's own example of this genre lies south of the city (it is a lengthy walk downhill, and back again, if you don't have a car) near the road junction for Chianciano; a stately avenue of cypresses, each over a small marker commemorating a local soldier who died in the First World War, leads to the site.

Antonio da Sangallo, long in the shadow of his less talented brother Giuliano, left his masterpiece here. **San Biagio** stands in a small park, a central, Greek-cross church of creamy travertine. As with so many other Renaissance churches, there is more architecture than Christianity in the design, a consciously classical composition, using not the Doric but an adaptation of the 'Tuscan' order on the ground level, then Ionic on the second and finally Corinthian on the upper storeys of the campanile, gracefully fitted into one of the corners of the Greek cross. The interior, finished in marble and other expensive stones, is equally symmetrical, rational and impressive, appealing to an entirely different side of the religious sensibility than the flowering Gothic churches or the soaring histrionics of the Baroque. Over the handsome altar, a Latin inscription proclaims *'Hinc deus homo et homo deus. Immensum Concepti – Aeternum Genuit'*. The beautiful **Canon's House**, with its double loggia, is also the work of Sangallo.

### Around Montepulciano

Among some beautiful villages on the hills around Montepulciano, **Montefollonico** (some eight kilometres northwest), has a frescoed church and Palazzo Comunale, both 13th-century. **Monticchiello,** which is seven kilometres southwest on a back road towards Pienza, hangs languorously on its hilltop; it too has a 13th-century church, with a rose window, an altarpiece by Pietro Lorenzetti and Sienese frescoes (late 14th century).

# Chianciano Terme

*'Chianciano – Fegato Sano'* – this is the slogan you see everywhere in **Chianciano Terme** (pop. 7,500): on the signs that welcome you, on the municipal buildings, even on the garbage trucks. It translates as 'Chianciano, for a healthy liver'. And after rotting yours on too much Montepulciano wine, it may be extremely convenient to have one of Italy's most attractive spas close at hand to flush it out and get it pumping again.

The healing waters here were known to the Etruscans, but have only been exploited in a big way over the last 50 years or so. There is an old walled town, Chianciano Vecchio, with a medieval clock tower and a Museo d'Arte Sacra; at the gate is the bus station and information booth. Just outside the old town, the **Museo Civico Archeologico delle Acque** (*t 0578 30471; open April–Oct and mid Dec–7 Jan 10–1 and 4–7; Nov–Mar Sat and Sun 10–1 and 4–7*) occupies an old granary, displaying mainly Etruscan and Roman exhibits excavated locally since 1986. Among the usual bronzes and ceramics are finds from Poggio Bacherina, an Etruscan farm uncovered between 1986 and 1989.

Beyond, modern Chianciano stretches for miles down Viale della Libertà, passing hundreds of hotels, gardens with clipped lawns, and bathhouses in a clean, modern style from the 1950s. Everything is just as pleasant as it could be, and, besides repairing your liver, Chianciano has mineral mud packs for your acne, hot aerosol

# Tourist Information

**Chianciano Terme**: Piazza Italia 67,
t 0578 63167.

# Where to Stay and Eat

## Chianciano Terme ✉ 53042

Whether or not you feel ready to entrust yourself to the thermal torture of the spa, Chianciano can be a usefu stop off in the summer months when hotels are booked solid everywhere else.

**Azienda Autondma di Cura**, Viale Roma 67. Offers help with accommodation.

Most of Chianciano's hotels were built in the last 30 years – none of them are particularly outstanding, but you will find a fair amount of choice within every price range. As in most spa towns, people tend to dine in their hotels, but a few restaurants have cropped up too.

**La Casanova**, Strada della Vittoria 10, t 0578 64837 (*moderate*). The menu here is fairly typical, but the cooking is good quality.

**La Foce**, Casella Postale 55, t 0578 69101, (*expensive–luxury*). Several of the farm-houses on the estate have been turned into upmarket self-catering apartments, sleeping 2–14 guests. The furnishings are elegant though rustic in style, and are adorned with plenty of antiques. Each house has use of a pool and a private garden. Meals available on request.

**L'Oasi**, Loc. La Foce, t 0578 755 077 (*moderate*). A useful stop-off just below La Foce on the road to Monte Amiata, this is a rustic, family-run bar/restaurant, serving *panini* with slabs of the local *pecorino* or heartier fare, such as *pici* and wild boar.

**La Rosa del Trinoro**, on the road between La Foce and Sarteano, at Castriglioncello del Trinoro, t 0578 265 529 (*moderate*). It's worth climbing the 11km of 'white road' from La Foce (turn left just after the villa towards Amiata) for the view alone, but also for the 'other worldliness' of this tiny hamlet. Enjoy generous portions of local dishes, such as *minestra di pane*, *pici* and grilled meats; there are also a few modest rooms.

douches and plenty of other medically respected treatments for your every ailment. They'll lock you in a room full of gas for a collective dry nebulization, throw you in the hydro-gaseous bath and then hand you over to the masseuses (this last is apparently meant as a curative for patients who are suffering from trauma), or put you face-to-face with the sulphurous sonic aerosol spray. Such rigourous treatments are not to everyone's taste and perhaps because of this Chianciano Terme is not a major tourist destination. 'Ah,' said the despairing Italians, 'the English never come. They simply do not understand the baths...'

## Around Chianciano: La Foce and Castelluccio

Southwest of Chianciano lies **La Foce**, a large estate on the hills overlooking the Val d'Orcia. Its strategic position on the Via Francigena has long attracted settlers; recent excavations brought to light a burial place from the 7th-century BC.

Antonio and Iris Origo bought the property in 1924 when it was barren and poverty-ridden and worked throughout their lives to regenerate the area. Their energy seemed almost boundless and together, they set up a school, a day clinic and a nursery. During the war the couple also founded and orphanage. Iris Origo's autobio-graphical books *Images and Shadows* and *War in the Val d'Orcia* make fascinating reading: the former covers the estate's development, while the latter focuses on the war years.

The villa itself was built in the late 15th century and was used as a hostel for pilgrims and merchants. It was estored by the Origos under the watchful eye of an

English landscape architect named Cecil Pinsent, who designed the delightful gardens (*t 0578 69101; tours on the hour: winter 3 and 4pm; summer 3, 4, 5 and 6pm*). Opposite the villa, on the road to Montepulciano, is the medieval **Castelluccio**, which is also part of the estate and open to visitors. As well as exhibitions, it holds concerts in the summer, as a venue for the **Incontri in Terra di Siena** music festival (*see* p.423).

# Chiusi and Around

If anyone ever read you Macaulay's rouser *Horatio at the Bridge*, you will remember the fateful Lars Porsena of Clusium, leading the Etruscan confederation and their Umbrian allies to attack Rome in brave days of old. Thanks to Horatio, Rome survived and made a name for itself; here you can see what happened to Clusium – or *Camars*, as the Etruscans called it. Most of its 9,500 citizens live in the new districts by the railway station, but the hill town on the site of Lars Porsena's capital still thrives.

## Archaeological Museum

*t 0578 20177; open daily 9–7.30; adm.*

From those brave days of old, Chiusi retains at least an excellent **Archaeological Museum**. As with so many Etruscan collections, the main attraction to be seen here is the large number of cinerary urns, and as usual the Etruscans are able to produce a bewildering variety of styles and themes. Large urns with thoughtful, reclining figures are fairly common, as are a number of mythological battle scenes with winged gods. Not all the tombs contained the well-known rectangular urns; some Etruscans chose to be buried in 'canopic' jars, which are surmounted by a terracotta bust of the deceased. In its day, Camars was a wealthy town, and the excavations at its necropolises unearthed a large amount of Greek pottery – note the urn with Achilles and Ajax playing at dice, and the Dionysiac scenes of revelry that include sexy maenads and leering satyrs. Many Etruscan imitation vases are on display; it's easy to believe the local talent could have done as well as the Greeks, had they only possessed thinner paintbrushes. To end the collection, there is a glittering hoard of nice barbaric trinkets from some 6th–7th-century Lombard tombs on the Arusa hill just outside town.

## Etruscan Tombs and Tunnels

If you're interested in seeing some of the Etruscan tombs (5th–3rd century BC) where these items were discovered, mention it to the museum guards, who arrange guided tours – in fact they'll probably ask you first. These are the only good painted tombs in Tuscany; the best of them, the **Tomba della Scimmia**, contains paintings of wrestlers and warriors, in addition to the monkey that gives the tomb its name. The Tomba della Pellegrina and the Tomba del Granduca are also interesting, as is the Tomba Bonci Casuccini, in a different necropolis east of town.

## Tourist Information

Chiusi: Pro Loco, Via Porsenna 67,
t 0578 227 667.

## Where to Stay and Eat

### Chiusi ✉ 53043

Most of the hotels are down by the railway station in Chiusi Scalo, and unremarkable.

**\*\*\*Centrale**, Piazza Dante 3, t 0578 20118 (*cheap*). A typical offering, with several modern rooms.

**Zaira**, Via Arunte 12, t 0578 20260 (*moderate*). Italians in the know make the detour off the Rome–Florence *autostrada* up to the oldest part of Chiusi, heading for this restaurant with its speculative 'Etruscan cuisine'. Surely the Etruscans, so often portrayed with plates of food on their funerary urns, had some tasty dishes, but every restaurant that tries to reconstruct an Etruscan menu comes up with something different. No matter; it's a harmless fancy, and with dishes such as *pasta del lucumone* (with ham and three different cheeses), duck cooked in Vino Nobile and pheasant *al cartoccio*, it's hard to complain. Zaira takes special pride in the wine list; having one of Tuscany's largest cellars. It's good value too. *Closed Mon.*

**La Solita Zuppa**, Via Porsenna 21, t 0578 21006 (*moderate*). The name is too modest by half – not really the 'same old soup', but their speciality: four or five different kinds on any given day, along with home-made *pici* and good meat dishes, in a warm, old-fashioned *osteria* atmosphere up in the old town. *Closed Tues.*

**Residenza Santa Chiara**, Piazza S. Chiara, t 0578 26512, f 0578 266 849, (*expensive*). A nice old building at the top of the town with a cool, shady garden, simple but perfectly adequate rooms, and a good restaurant.

**Da Gino**, Via Cabina Lago 42, t 0578 21408. Cheaper still. *Closed Wed.*

**Le Anfore**, Via Chiusi 30, t 0578 265 871. An attractive and beautifully restored farmhouse just outside town, providing good value family accommodation with pool, tennis and riding – there's even a restaurant.

If your car can't climb the hill up to Chiusi, take it out to Lago di Chiusi to the north.

**\*\*\*La Fattoria**, Conciarese al Lago, t 0578 21407 (*moderate*). An old farmhouse with views over the lake; there are eight nice rooms and a very good restaurant specializing in fresh fish from the lake, plus every sort of roast and pasta dish made with porcini mushrooms. *Closed Mon.*

## The Cathedral

Across the street from the museum, Chiusi's cathedral is the oldest in Tuscany. Only parts of it – the recycled Roman columns in the nave – go back to the original 6th-century building. The cathedral was rebuilt in the 12th century and again in the 19th. Have a look at the mosaics that cover the walls inside. At first glance they seem astounding, an unknown chapter in early Christian art. Then you'll notice they have a touch of Art Nouveau about them – and finally you realize they aren't mosaics at all, but skilfully sponged-on squares of paint, a crazy masterpiece of mimicry completed in 1915.

The small **cathedral museum** (*open June–Sept Mon–Fri 9.30–12.45 and 4–6; Oct–May 9.30–12.45 only; adm*) contains Roman fragments and a collection of beautiful 15th-century illuminated choir books. Far and away the best part, though, is that your admission includes a climb up the campanile, and a descent into the mysterious network of tunnels and galleries underlying the town, bits of which go back to the time of the Etruscans. Whatever their original purpose, some were converted into catacombs by early Christian communities; there's also an underground cistern from Roman times.

## Sarteano ✉ 53047

**La Giara**, Viale Europa 2 (6km southwest of Chiusi), t 0578 265 511 (*moderate*). Usually crowded with Sartanese, and with good reason, lured in by the home-made pasta, roast duck and lamb chops. *Closed Mon.*

**Osteria Da Giuliano**, Via Roma 5, t 0578 268 022. A simple *osteria* just down the road from the archaeological museum, with wooden tables and benches. Excellent local dishes include gnocchi (on Thursdays), tripe or *pecorino al forno*. *Closed Tues.*

## Cetona ✉ 53040

★★★★**La Frateria**, Convento di San Francesco, t 0578 238 015 (*very expensive*). The most unusual hotel in the area, situated in the buildings of a 13th-century monastery founded originally by St Francis. It's now run by a community of young people who have managed to preserve a feeling of peace and tranquillity in keeping with the setting, despite the lavish physical comforts on offer. Among the luxuries is an excellent, if somewhat overpriced, restaurant. *Closed Jan.*

## San Casciano dei Bagni ✉ 53040

**Fonteverde**, Loc. Terme 1, t 0578 58023, f 0578 58013 (*very expensive*). This is a new, luxury spa hotel built in and around a Medici villa with extensive gardens on the site of the thermal baths. Choose between B&B or a package including full-board and a huge range of beauty therapies and treatments.

**Sette Querce**, Viale Manciati 2, t 0578 58174, f 0578 58172 (*expensive–very expensive*). Step inside this delightful hotel and you'll find a riot of colour and bright, contemporary fabrics. The comfortable rooms have their own sitting area and some have kitchenette. Breakfast is served in your room, but other meals can be had at Da Daniela (*see below*).

**La Fontanella**, Via Roma 6, t 0578 58300, (*moderate*). This hotel is also new and though not too interesting from the outside, it is good value, and with an excellent restaurant (*moderate*).

**Da Daniela**, t 0578 58041. This restaurant is under the same ownership as Sette Querce, and serves interesting variations on local themes in a beautiful, brick-vaulted room. Sample bean soup, ravioli stuffed with pigeon, stuffed quail, fricassee of lamb with artichokes or rich, bubbling *pecorino* with truffles. Try to leave room for *mousse di marrons glacées* topped with forest fruits. *Closed Wed in winter.*

# Around Chiusi: Lakes, Sarteano and More *Crete*

Just northeast of Chiusi, the **Lago di Chiusi** and the **Lago di Montepulciano** are pretty patches of blue on the border between Tuscany and Umbria, smallest in the chain of lakes that begins with Lago Trasimeno. Lago di Chiusi, in particular, is nice for a picnic.

Nine kilometres south of Chianciano or Chiusi, **Sarteano** is a smaller resort-spa, attached to a fine old hill town with some Renaissance palaces, a squarish medieval fortress, and the church of **San Martino in Foro**, with an *Annunciation* that is one of the best works of the Sienese Mannerist Beccafumi. A small and delightful Etruscan museum – the **Museo Civico Archeologico** – has opened in the impressive Palazzo Gabrielli, containing some wonderful funerary accoutrements. Most striking of all are the magnificent urns containing bones and other anthropomorphic paraphernalia.

Another six kilometres south of Sarteano, off the ruggedly scenic SS321, lies **Cetona**, a small, untouristic gem, with a growing population of discerning foreign residents who have rejected Chianti country and all that it implies. The Palazzo Comunale has a **Museo Civico per la Preistoria del Monte Cetona**, documenting archaeological discoveries since the 1920s, including an enourmous bear some believe to be 50,000 years old.

Take the road to Sarteano, and after six kilometres or so you'll reach the **Parco Archeologico Naturalistico di Belvedere**, with remains from one of the most important Bronze Age sites in Italy. On the approach to Sarteano, you can visit the 14th-century ex-convent of Santa Maria a Belvedere, now inhabited by the same community who run the up-market Frateria di Padre Egidio (*see* 'Where to Stay' p.435), but also housing frescoes attributed to Petruccioli and Andrea di Giovanni.

The SS478 from Sarteano towards Monte Amiata passes one of the loneliest, most barren regions of *crete* en route to the Val d'Orcia (*see* p.422), while the road south from Cetona takes you on a beautiful, winding drive skirting Monte Cetona, punctuated with dramatic views as you pass through woods and olive groves towards **San Casciano dei Bagni**, a pretty spa town on the borders of Umbria and Lazio. There are a couple of ancient churches and a castle; the hot springs are just outside to the south. The resort's heyday was in the Renaissance, when Grand Duke Ferdinand built a villa there and developed the spa; the baths have been restored and the Medici villa transformed into a luxury hotel (*see* 'Where to Stay and Eat', p.435).

# Monte Amiata and Around

**Monte Amiata**, the rooftop of southern Tuscany, is an extinct volcanic massif with a central peak over a mile high (5,649ft). With no real competition close by, it has become a skiing and hiking centre – the closest to Rome, and as such popular in both summer and winter. The presence of Europe's second-largest mercury mine (a complex that has been putting dinner on the table for Abbadia San Salvatore since the Middle Ages) does not detract from area's natural beauty. The lower, unculitivated slopes are covered in chestnut and beech. Higher up, there are only beautiful mature forests, which catch the early frosts, and change colour marvellously in the autumn.

## Abbadia San Salvatore

A thousand years ago, you might have heard of this town, home of the most important monastic centre in Tuscany and a fair-sized city in its own right. History passed by **Abbadia San Salvatore** a long time ago; today it makes its living as a mountain resort. Abbadia (pop. 7,900) appears modern at first, but just behind Viale Roma a narrow gateway leads into the grey, quiet streets of the **medieval centre**. It isn't very large, and there are no buildings of particular interest, but it is as complete and unchanged as any medieval quarter in Tuscany. Note the symbols carved into many of the doorways: coats of arms, odd religious symbols (a snake, for example) or signs like a pair of scissors that declare the original owner was a tailor.

The **abbey church** is outside the centre, a few blocks north in Via del Monastero; in the Middle Ages it must have been open countryside. According to legend – there's even a document telling the story, dated the Ides of March, 742 – the Lombard King Rachis was on his way to attack Perugia when a vision of the Saviour appeared to him. Rachis not only founded the monastery, but retired to it as a monk. Historians consider the whole business a convenient fabrication, but by 1000 the abbey had

# Getting Around

Don't try to get to Amiata by **train**; there's a 'Monte Amiata station' on an infrequent branch line from Siena, but it's really some 40km on the northern side of the massif, near Castiglione d'Orcia. It's much easier to get a **bus** from Siena, Chiusi or Grosseto. Buses stop on Viale Roma in the centre of Abbadia S. Salvatore (tickets and timetables in the toy store behind the information booth); a few go daily to Buonconvento and Siena (79km/2½hrs), Montepulciano–Chiusi (48km/1½hrs); five a day go from Abbadia to Arcidosso (25km/1hr) and Castel del Piano on the western side of Amiata.

Note that Arcidosso and the other towns on the west slope are in Grosseto province; almost all the buses there go on to Grosseto. There are also at least two daily ACOTRAL or SIRA buses that run through Castel del Piano, Arcidosso and Abbadia S. Salvatore to Viterbo and on to Rome.

# Tourist Information

**Abbadia San Salvatore**: Via Adua 25,
t 0577 775 811, *info@amiata.turismo.
toscana.it. Open Mon–Sat 9–1 and 4–6.*
**Castel del Piano**: Via G. Marconi 9,
t 0564 955 323.
**Arcidosso**: Via Ricasoli 1, t 0564 966 083.

# Activities

As one of the few good **skiing** areas close to Rome, Monte Amiata can be a busy place when the snow flies. The pistes begin almost at the summit; there are two chair lifts and 15 ski lifts. The 15 runs (the longest is 1,500m) are connected by paths through the forest. There is also a ski school.

It's also the perfect landscape for **cross-country skiing** and **hiking**, also very popular here. A whole network of hiking trails have been marked, extending as far as Castiglione d'Orcia. The tourist offices can give you a map; ask for the *cartografia dei sentieri*.

For snow news and other information, call the tourist office in Abbadia San Salvatore, t 0577 775 811.

# Where to Stay and Eat

## Monte Amiata ✉ 53021

For skiing, there are pleasant facilities near the summit.

★★★**Rifugio Cantore**, at '*secondo rifugio 10*', along the road from Abbadia, t 0577 789 704 (*moderate*). Stays open all year to cater for summer mountaineering.

★★★**La Capannina**, Vette Amiata, t 0577 789 713, f 0577 789 777 (*moderate*). A cosy place a little further up. The hotel restaurant is probably the best in the area; lots of dishes with mushrooms (including polenta, that northern Italian alternative to pasta that is also popular around here); also stuffed pigeon. *Open 15 Dec–Easter, also June–Sept.*

## Abbadia San Salvatore ✉ 53021

Abbadia San Salvatore is popular, not just for winter skiing, but also as a cool summer retreat. There are a dozen or so hotels in town.

★★★**Adriana**, Via Serdini 76, t 0577 778 116, f 0577 777 177 (*moderate–cheap*). A few blocks north of the centre.

★★**San Marco**, Via Matteotti 19, t/f 0577 778 089 (*moderate*). Newer, this has a **ristorante-rosticceria** with a *menu fisso* (*cheap*).

## Arcidosso ✉ 58031

An excellent base for Amiata; there are several good modern hotels at bargain rates.

★★★**Aiole**, Loc. Aiole, t 0564 967 300. If you like mushrooms, stop for the restaurant, specializing in porcini mushroom soup, but also other sturdy dishes and excellent local cheeses. *Closed Mon in winter.*

★★**Gatto d'Oro**, Aia dei Venti, t 0564 967 074.

## Castel del Piano ✉ 58033

A few km from Arcidosso are a one or two further options.

★★★**Impero**, Via Roma 7, t 0564 955 337 (*moderate–cheap*). An old hotel, set in an attractive park.

★★★★**Contessa**, at Prato della Contessa, t 0564 959 000 (*moderate*). Benefits from its lovely setting above town on the slopes of Amiata, and an ambitious management that organizes nature walks, cultural tours and more. The restaurant is also good, laying on special seasonal menus.

achieved considerable wealth and influence, ruling over a large piece of territory and waging occasional wars with the Bishop of Chiusi. In 1036, the present church was begun, an excellent Romanesque work that may seem plain to us, but was undoubtedly one of the grandest sights in Tuscany when it was new.

Behind the twin-steepled façade, the church is surprisingly long; the eastern end consists of a raised chancel, leading to a series of arches over the altar and choir. Here, a series of quirky frescoes, by an early 1700s artist named Nasino, tells the story of King Rachis. His **crypt**, under the chancel, was the original 8th-century church. The proportions and even the shapes of the arches are thoroughly Byzantine, with stone vaulting and oddly carved columns and capitals, no two alike.

South of Abbadia San Salvatore, **Piancastagnaio** is a smaller mountain resort. It has a **castle** of the Aldobrandeschi, housing a small museum, a 17th-century palace and, as its name implies, lots of chestnut trees. Chestnuts and chestnut flour were once the staple food around Amiata; restaurants still occasionally offer chestnut polenta.

## Around Amiata

If you take the panoramic route around Amiata, you'll encounter **Seggiano**, 20 kilometres northwest of Abbadia, which has an unusual 16th-century church with a square cupola, the Madonna della Carità. Seven kilometres south of here is **Castel del Piano**, with an old centre, laid out in *belle époque* parks and boulevards. **Arcidosso**, another four kilometres south, is the largest town (pop. 4,500) on the Grosseto side of Amiata. It's been around for a long time; there's a stately Aldobrandeschi fortress, and one church outside the town, the triple-apsed Santa Maria in Lamula, begun in the 900s and redone in the 12th century.

The town is best known, however, for the strange career of David Lazzaretti, a millenarian prophet gunned down by the Carabinieri during a disturbance in 1878. People in this area still talk about Lazzaretti; his movement, combining reformed religion and plain rural socialism (in an age when land reform was Italy's biggest social issue), spread widely in southern Tuscany. Before Lazzaretti's murder, his followers had started a sort of commune on **Monte Labbro**, 10 kilometres to the south. The tower, bits of buildings and remains of the church they built on Monte Labbro still stand, and a few of the faithful occasionally hold 'Giurisdavidical' services there.

**Roccalbegna**, 20 kilometres south on the SS323, has another Aldobrandeschi castle, and a sampling of mostly Sienese art in its church of SS. Pietro e Paolo and the nearby Oratorio del Crocifisso. For a landmark Roccalbegna has one very conspicuous rock, a bizarre conical mass looming over the village called simply 'La Pietra'. The Aldobrandeschi also built at **Santa Fiora**, a pleasant town seven and a half kilometres south, with della Robbia terracottas in its three churches. Just south of Arcidosso, on the northern slopes of Monte Labbro, a large forested section has been made into a nature reserve, the **Parco Faunistico del Monte Amiata** (*open Tues–Sun dawn–sunset; closed Mon; t 0564 966 867*). Hiking trails have been laid out for visitors, offering a look at various kinds of deer, mountain goats, and maybe wolves – the park recently started a project to reintroduce these to the wild here.

Amiata's summit, decorated with the obligatory iron crucifix (made in the Victorian foundries of Follonica, like the bandstands and even some of the fountains you will see locally), lies about halfway between Abbadia and Arcidosso; roads reach almost to the top. The skiing area is here too, at the point called **Vetta Amiata**.

# The Lost Corner of Tuscany

Not many readers, we suspect, planned to spend their holiday in Saturnia or Pitigliano this year. Only a true connoisseur of regional obscurity would appreciate the inland reaches of Grosseto province, the largest stretch of territory in Italy north of the Abruzzo without a single well-known attraction. Once part of the Etruscan heartland, these towns have been poor and usually misgoverned ever since – by the Romans, the noble Aldobrandeschi, the popes and the Tuscan dukes. Some don't even consider the area part of Tuscany, and it's true that in many ways it has more in common with the haunted, empty expanses of northern Lazio across the border.

## Sorano

Southeast 20 kilometres from Santa Fiora, **Castell'Azzara** takes its name from a medieval game of dice (the word similar to our *hazard*); one of the Aldobrandeschi won it in a crap shoot. **Sorano**, a grim, grey town to the south, clings tenaciously to its rock, almost hidden between two deep and lovely wooded canyons. Bits of the town have been crumbling down into the surrounding valleys for centuries; after a recent landslide the town was declared uninhabitable and largely abandoned, though there have been efforts to restore it. Sorano is dominated by two equally grim castles; the larger is the 15th-century **Rocca degli Orsini**. Outside town on the road to Sovana is a strange natural rock formation called the **Mano di Orlando**, the 'Hand of Roland'.

## Sovana and the Vie Cave

**Sovana**, 10 kilometres to the west, with its population of about 190, is another medieval time capsule, a town almost perfectly preserved in its 13th- or 14th-century appearance. Sovana was an important Etruscan city, and in the 11th century it thrived as the family headquarters of the Aldobrandeschi. This powerful clan, controlling much of southern Tuscany and northern Lazio, had a political role on a European level. The zenith of its influence came with the election to the papacy of one of its members in 1073. Gregory VII (his common name *Hildebrand* betrays the Aldobrandeschis' Teutonic origins) made a great reforming pope, the man who defeated the emperors in the great struggle over investiture, but he also took care of the family interests.

On Sovana's humble main street, the Via di Mezzo, you can see the 13th-century Palazzo del Pretorio, with only a clock and bifore windows to betray its civic dignity. There is some interesting early Christian and medieval sculpture preserved in the 12th-century church of **Santa Maria** in the village centre, including a remarkable

# Tourist Information

**Sorano**: Piazza Busatti, t/f 0564 633 099.
*Open Nov–Feb Thurs–Tue 10–1 and 3–6.30
(closed Wed); Mar–Oct Mon–Sun 10–1 and
3–6.30.*
**Pitigliano**: Via Roma, off the main piazza,
t/f 0564 67111. The ground beneath
Pitigliano is laced with fascinating caves
and tunnels, and a local organization
offers tours of them; ask at the tourist office
for details.
**Saturnia**: in the old town, Piazza Vittorio
Veneto 8, t 0564 601 280, f 0564 601 257.
*Open April–Oct Mon–Sat 10.30–1 and 3–7;
Nov–Mar Mon–Sat 10.30–5.*
**Manciano**: Via Roma 2, t 0564 629 218.

# Where to Stay and Eat

Real pioneers will find a reasonable variety
of accommodation and good food
throughout. The region produces some good
but little-known wines, notably Morellino di
Scansano, a severe dry variety with a beautiful
deep red colour.

## Pitigliano ☑ 58017

**\*\*Corano**, Loc. Corano on the SS74,
t/f 0564 616 112 (*cheap*). Just outside
Pitigliano, with 35 modern rooms and a pool.
**\*\*Guastini** on Piazza Petruccioli 4,
t 0564 616 065, f 0564 616 652 (*moderate–
cheap*). Central, with a restaurant (*moderate*)
Guastini specializes in home-made pasta,
Bianco di Pitigliano wine, and 'Etruscan-
style' dishes like *biglione d'agnello*; well
worth the price.
**Trattoria dell'Orso**, Piazza San Gregorio.
Offers a broad range of the local *cucina
tipica*: tagliatelle with truffles, boar *alla
cacciatore*, and plenty of roast meats. The
price is right too; there's an excellent-value
menu, and it's well within the *cheap* range
for *à la carte*.
**Il Tufo Allegro**, Vicolo della Costituzione, t 0564
616 192 (*moderate–cheap*). The menu is
seasonal: in winter hearty dishes include
rabbit stewed in locally made Morellino, or
*pappardelle* with lamb and artichoke sauce;
in summer *tagliolini* with marinated vegetables. There's a good wine list too. *Closed Tues.*

## Sovana ☑ 58010

**\*\*\*Taverna Etrusca**, Piazza Pretorio,
t 0564 616 183, f 0564 614 193 (*moderate*).
Soak up the ambience of the Dark Ages in
this square. Roast boar and the other south
Tuscan favourites are on the menu while
pleasant, simple rooms are upstairs if you
want to stay (*also moderate*).
**\*Scila**, Via del Duomo 5, t 0564 616 531, f 0564
614 329. Inexpensive rooms and a nice
restaurant (*cheap*), serving a homely menu
(including spinach and ricotta soup) out on
the terrace, which is a great place to sit out
if the sun is shining. *Closed Tues.*

## Saturnia ☑ 58050

Saturnia, being a spa of sorts, has plenty of
accommodation.
**\*\*\*\*Hotel Terme di Saturnia**, Strada
Provinsiale della Follonato, t 0564 601 061,
f 0564 601 266 (*very expensive*). This hotel is
far and away the best to be found in the
town, though it's hard to imagine anyone
paying this much up here. However, the
restaurant (*moderate*) repays a visit with
fresh seafood, including a good *risotto
marinaro*, besides game dishes like quail
with olives.
**\*\*Saturnia**, Via Mazzini 4 in the old town,
t/f 0564 601 007 (*moderate–cheap*).
Infinitely more reasonable in terms of value
for money, particularly if you are just
passing through.
**Locanda Landomia**, Poderi di Montemerano,
7km south of Saturnia, t 0564 620 062,
f 0564 620 013 (*cheap*). Locanda Landomia
offers peace and quiet in the countryside,
with 12 pretty bedrooms, which all enjoy
lovely views. The hotel's restaurant is over
the road; ravioli and *aquacotta* (vegetable
soup) are very good.

## Montemerano ☑ 58050

**Caino**, Via Canonica 3, t 0564 602 817, f 0564
602 807 (*expensive*). This is a surprisingly
elegant restaurant for such a little hamlet
(just 600 inhabitants), where the
menu varies regularly according to the
availability of the fresh ingredients and
the delicacies arrive on silver platters.
*Closed Wed, and Thurs lunch in winter;
open daily in summer.*

9th-century ciborium in bold barbaric arabesques and floral motifs, along with Renaissance frescoes. The **Duomo**, just outside the village, has an octagonal dome from the 900s, a crypt 200 years older, and some sculptural work on the façade that may have been recycled from a pagan temple.

The **Vie Cave**, which you will see signposted all around this area, are sacred ways of the Etruscans, carved for part of their length out of the tufa and often lined with tombs. In many cases they follow modern roads, as with the pretty road from Sovana to Saturnia. Here you can stop to see the **Tomba della Sirena**, where the pediment is carved with a much-eroded fork-tailed mermaid – possibly the original of the mermaids on the Pieve di Corsignano and elsewhere around Tuscany.

Not far from here is the 3rd-century BC **Tomba Ildebranda**. This elaborate tomb once had the façade of a Greek temple, though little of the colonnade survives. It resembles the rock-cut tombs of the same era common in Lycia, on the south coast of Turkey, built by people who may have been the Etruscans' cultural cousins.

## Pitigliano

Just eight kilometres away is **Pitigliano**, another ominous-looking place that could be Sorano's twin. It makes a memorable sight, perched along the edges of the cliffs; underneath are countless holes in the cliff faces that were once Etruscan tombs, now used as stables or storehouses. Once inside, you'll find the hill town itself as attractive as any of the better-known ones further north. Piazza della Repubblica has a big fountain and the 14th-century **Fortezza Orsini**, stronghold of the powerful Roman family that aced the Aldobrandeschi out of many of their holdings in south Tuscany. The castle has a small **museum** of Etruscan finds, and an analemmic sundial with a Latin inscription reminding us the hours are 'for work, not for play'.

Pitigliano has a picturesque medieval centre, and a 16th-century **aqueduct**, running across Via Cavour. The alleys around Vicolo Manin, where parts of **synagogue** still stand, were once Pitigliano's Jewish ghetto (*open Sun 10–1, with a tour that takes in other Jewish relics of the town*); the centuries-old Jewish community was decimated in 1945. On the cliffs underneath the town, along the road for Sovana, is a Christian **cave chapel** (*c.* 400 AD). They claim it's the oldest in Italy.

## Saturnia

Little **Saturnia**, 25 kilometres west of Sovana, sits all alone above the Val d'Albegna. One of the most ancient centres in Italy, it claims, no less, to be the first city ever founded there – by the god Saturn himself, in fact, in the Golden Age. The present village, an attractive hill town, was originally Roman, but fragments of monolithic, pre-Etruscan walls can be seen, and aerial photography has discerned traces of an older city beneath the Roman level. There are hot sulphur springs in the neighbourhood, still in use as they were throughout antiquity; ruins are everywhere, including another Etruscan necropolis to the north. **Manciano**, 12km to the south, has a Sienese fortress and not much else. There is another Etruscan necropolis on the road to Pitigliano, called **Poggio Buco**.

To the west on SS323, the walled city of **Magliano in Toscana**, heir to the Etruscan town of Heba, has a Sienese-style Palazzo dei Priori, and the church of San Giovanni Battista, with a Renaissance façade. Its best-known attraction, though, is the **Ulivo della Strega** (the witches' olive), a gnarled tree over a thousand years old, said to be the site of ritual dances in pagan days, and still haunted today. The tree is just outside the Porta San Giovanni, near the Romanesque **Annunziata** church, containing Sienese frescoes. About two kilometres southeast, on the road for Marsiliana, are the ruins of the 12th-century abbey of **San Bruzio**.

# Arezzo and its Province

# Arezzo Province

Florence

**Santa Sofia**
Alpe di San Benedetto
S. Godenzo
M. Falterona
Pso. d. Calla

EMILIA ROMAGNA
Bagno di Romagna
Badia Prataglia

MARCHES

Stia
Pontassieve
Pratovecchio
Camaldoli
Alpe di Serra
Balze

Bagno a Ripoli
Vallombrosa
Rignano sull' Arno
Poppi
La Verna ②
Bibbiena
Badia Tedalda
Sestino

S. Donato in Collina
Reggello
Pieve Sto. Stefano
Alpe d. Luna
Mercatello s. Metauro

Incisa in Val d'A.
Caprese Michelangelo

Figline Vald.
Castelfranco di Sopra
Loro Ciuffenna
Talla
Sansepolcro

Greve in Chianti
S. Giovanni Valdarno
Subbiano

Castiglion Fibocchi
Anghiari

Cavriglia
Montevarchi
Citerha
Monterchi
Citta di Castello

Badia Coltibuono
Arezzo ③

TUSCANY

Castelnuovo Berardenga
Civitella in Val Chiana
Foce di Scopetone
Morra

Siena
Monte S. Savino
Castiglion Fiorentino

Marciano d. Chiana
Montecchio
Umbertide

Lucignano
Cortona ④

Foiano della Chiana
Ossaia
UMBRIA

Passignano s. Trasimeno

Lago Trasimeno
p.416

Perugia

To Orvieto

p.232

# Highlights

1 Medieval mountain villages of the Casentino
2 La Verna: St Francis' rugged hermitage
3 Piero della Francesca's masterpiece frescoes in San Francesco, Arezzo
4 The surprising Renaissance art town of Cortona

Between Florence and Umbria lies a lovely region of nature and art, most of which is included in the province of Arezzo. Watered by the newly born Arno and Tiber rivers (which at one point flow within a mere 15 kilometres of each other), it occupies a keystone position in Italy, not only geographically but as amazingly fertile ground for 'key' Italians: Masaccio and Cosimo il Vecchio's humanist Greek scholar and magician, Marsilio Ficino, were born in the Arno Valley; Petrarch, Michelangelo,

Piero della Francesca, Paolo Uccello, Luca Signorelli, Andrea Sansovino, Vasari, the great satirist Aretino, Guido Monaco (inventor of the musical scale), Pietro da Cortona and the Futurist Gino Severini were born in Arezzo or its province. Because of its strategic location battlefields and castles dot the countryside, yet here too is St Francis' holy mountain of La Verna, where he received the stigmata.

There are two possible routes between Florence and Arezzo: the quick one, following the trains and Autostrada del Sole down the Valdarno, or the scenic route, through the Passo della Consuma or Vallombrosa, taking in the beautifully forested areas of Pratomagno and the Casentino.

# The Valdarno and Casentino

## Florence to Arezzo

If a Tuscan caveman ever yearned for the ideal neolithic home, he would have wanted to live in what is now the Arno Valley. In the Pliocene Age the valley was a lake, a popular resort of ancient elephants, and farmers are not surprised when their ploughs collide with fossils. The typically Tuscan towns of the Valdarno, however, are hardly fossilized. On the contrary, it is a highly industrialized region: lignite and felt hats stand out in particular, but new factories and power-lines seem to be going up all the time.

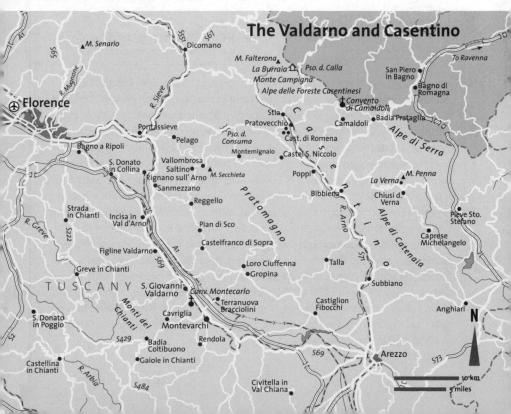

## Tourist Information

San Giovanni Valdarno: Palazzo d'Arnolfo, Piazza Cavour 1, t 055 559 054.

## Where to Stay and Eat

**Figline Valdarno** ✉ **50063**
**★★★Antica Taverna Casagrande**, t 055 954 4851, f 055 954 4322 (*expensive*). Thirteen rooms and a garden cater for a comfortable stay.

**San Giovanni Valdarno** ✉ **52027**
**★★★La Bianca**, Viale Don Minzoni 38, t 055 912 3402 (*moderate*). San Giovanni doesn't get many tourists, and accommodation is limited; however, this will provide an agreeable stay.
**Adriano**, in Piazza Masaccio 15, t 055 912 2470 (*moderate*). A tiny place where you can dine well on the local stew, called *stufato alla sangiovannese*, or home-grown roast chicken, home-made desserts, and wines from across Tuscany.
**Da Giovanni**, Piazza della Libertà 24, t 055 912 2726 (*cheap*). A family-run place with typical Tuscan fare. *Closed Wed.*
**Las Vegas**, Via Fratelli Cervi 3, t 055 912 2072. An institution of sorts overlooking the Arno, with two barn-size dining rooms, a pool,

hearty inexpensive fare, *focacce*, and two deft *pizzaiolos* making the most popular pies in the area, as well as beers from around the world.

**Montevarchi** ✉ **52025**
**★★★Delta**, Via Diaz 137, t 055 901 213, f 055 901 727 (*moderate*). The best that Montevarchi has to offer, complete with a garage, air-conditioning and TV in all the bedrooms.
**L'Osteria di Rendola**, Via di Rendola, t 055 970 7491 (*expensive*). A wonderful restaurant, serving creative Tuscan dishes such as chick-pea soup with lobster, beetroot soufflé, spaghetti with aubergines and octopus, and pigeon breast on braised cabbage, in addition to an interesting wine list. *Closed Wed.*

**Castelfranco di Sopra** ✉ **52020**
Vicolo del Contento, Loc. Mandri 38, t 055 914 9277 (*expensive*). The cuisine here matches the elegant décor: you can sample delicious ravioli filled with crab meat, well-prepared meat and fresh fish, followed, perhaps, by a slice of *pecorino* from Pienza. Fine Chianti and other wines. *Closed Mon and Tues.*
**Il Corvo**, Via Sette Ponti, t 055 914 9011 (*moderate*). Serves excellent fish.

Besides the *autostrada*, the main valley routes are the old SS69, and the beautiful 'Strada dei Sette Ponti', following the old Etruscan road of 'Seven Bridges' from Saltino by Vallombrosa to Castiglion Fibocchi, along what was once the upper shore of the ancient lake, between the Valdarno and the Pratomagno ridge. Along it are areas strikingly eroded into pyramids, around Pian di Scò and Castelfranco. By public transport the Valdarno's peripheral attractions are harder to reach; buses from Arezzo to Loro Ciuffenna and Castelfranco di Sopra take in much of the Strada dei Sette Ponti.

The most scenic route from Florence to the Valdarno follows the A1 down to Incisa (23km), although it's worth turning west at Torre a Cona for **Rignano sull'Arno**, with sculptures by Mino da Fiesole and Bernardino Rossellino in the church of San Clemente, and for **Sanmezzano** (two kilometres across the Arno). Here a medieval castle was converted into a Medici villa and in the 19th century purchased by the Ximenes d'Aragona family, who gave it a Spanish-Moorish fantasy face-lift. Down river, at **Incisa Valdarno**, cliffs and hills begin to squeeze the Arno; in the upper old town Petrarch spent his childhood. There's an old bridge off which, the Italians claim, Lucrezia Borgia jumped in 1529, fleeing the Prince of Orange, despite the fact that she had died in childbirth 10 years earlier.

Five kilometres south, **Figline Valdarno** (pop. 15,000) was, in 1439, the birthplace of Ficino, after whom the main piazza is named. The historic centre has preserved much of its character from Ficino's day: the loggia of the old Serristori Hospital, the Palazzo Pretorio, and the **Collegiata di Santa Maria**, containing among its works of art a beautiful painting of the *Madonna with Child and Angels* by the 14th-century 'Maestro di Figline', and a fresco by the school of Botticelli.

## San Giovanni Valdarno

If you're only planning to make one stop within the Valdarno, **San Giovanni** (pop. 19,500) is the logical choice: though it is one of the most industrial towns in the region, it's also one of the most interesting. The Florentines fortified it in the 13th century against the warlike Aretini and sent Arnolfo di Cambio, a jack of all trades like most artists of his day, to lay out the streets and fortifications, and to design the handsome arcaded **Palazzo Comunale**; its arches are echoed by the buildings giving on to the piazza, and are covered with a collage of escutcheons left by local Florentine governors.

The oft-restored **Basilica di Santa Maria delle Grazie** (1486) has a rich 17th-century interior, though most paintings have been removed to the adjacent **Museo della Basilica** (*open Tues–Fri 11–1 and 3–5, Sat 11–1 and 3–6, Sun 3–6; closed Mon; adm*): a *Madonna, Child and Four Saints*, long attributed to native son Masaccio (1401–28), an *Annunciation* by Jacopo di Sellaio, Baroque paintings by Giovanni di San Giovanni (also born here, 1592–1636), and an interesting fresco of a local miracle, in which a grandmother is suddenly able to give milk to her starving grandchild (14th century). Best of all is Fra Angelico's enchanting *Annunciation*, in deep, rich colours, seemingly a model for the *Annunciation* in Florence's San Marco, though here Adam and Eve can be seen off to the left, fleeing the Garden of Eden. Earlier frescoes adorn the Gothic church of **San Lorenzo**.

Some two and a half kilometres south of San Giovanni is the Renaissance **Convento di Montecarlo**. From here the road continues up to the Monti del Chianti by way of **Cavriglia**; the hills around are scarred with the amphitheatres of open lignite mines. Not all the earth is exploited, however: Cavriglia is also a natural park, where you can find modern deer and buffalo roaming along with other animals from around the world.

The Valdarno also offers a look at older species of animal, especially the large *elephas meridionalis* in the **Museo Paleontologico** (*open 9–12.30 and 4–6, Sun 10–12; closed Mon; adm*) in **Montevarchi**. Montevarchi is a major marketing centre of the region, famous for its hats and chickens; in its ancient core, you can trace the oval medieval street plan. In the centre stands the old **Collegiata di San Lorenzo**, which had a complete facelift in the 18th century. Within it is an unusual reliquary 'of the holy milk', brought from a cave in the Holy Land where the Holy Family is said to have rested and where a fountain of milky water flows; a small museum holds a quattrocento **Tempietto** covered inside and out with Andrea della Robbia's cherub friezes. Across the Arno, **Terranuova Bracciolini** is an old Aretine fortress town, its walls still standing.

## Along the Road of Seven Bridges

East of the Arno, the panoramic Strada dei Sette Ponti passes several medieval towns en route to Arezzo. **Reggello** (eight kilometres east of Sanmezzano) stands amid its famous olive groves in a beautiful setting; some streets retain their medieval arcades, and the 12th-century parish church of **San Pietro a Cascia** has good, early Romanesque columns with carved capitals depicting striking figures on horseback and other lively scenes. **Castelfranco di Sopra**, 12 kilometres south, was another Florentine military town laid out by Arnolfo di Cambio, with fine palaces, and to the north at **Pulicciano** you'll find a landscape eroded into pyramidical forms, or *balze*, more common around Volterra. Oddly named **Loro Ciuffenna** offers some picturesque medieval corners, a Romanesque bridge and tower, and a triptych by Lorenzo di Bicci in **Santa Maria Assunta**. Best of all is the tiny 12th-century parish church of **Grópina** (from the Etruscan *Kropina*), two kilometres away, an excellent example of rural Romanesque.

Although it was referred to in the 8th century, the current church was built in the early 1200s. Dominated by its huge campanile, the façade is simplicity itself, while the three naves and little semicircular apse have never been altered. The columns are carved with primitive tigers, eagles, etc., while the round marble **pulpit** is a bizarre relic of the Dark Ages, carved with archaic figures raising their arms over a marble knot; over them is a kind of totem pole, geometrical and floral decorations, and a sexy siren with a snake whispering sweet nothings in her ear. **Castiglion Fibocchi**, 13 kilometres from Arezzo, is another typical town where little has changed, except for the industry on its outskirts.

# The Pratomagno and Vallombrosa

The Strada dei Sette Ponti skirts the west rim of the **Pratomagno**, not a big meadow as its name suggests, but a wrinkled, forested mountain ridge. Its highest peak, Croce di Pratomagno (5,222ft), is due north of Loro Ciuffenna; winding roads from Loro go through tiny mountain hamlets, while the Loro–Talla route crosses over into the Casentino.

Other roads from the west into the Casentino are much further to the north. The two routes from Florence, both taking in fine, wooded scenery, are the SS70 over the **Passo della Consuma** (3,362ft), a favourite Italian rest stop, and the secondary route through **Vallombrosa** ('shady valley'), famous for its abbey founded by San Giovanni Gualberto of Florence, and still the headquarters of his Vallombrosan order. The abbey itself has undergone several remodellings in the 15th and 17th centuries and is mainly of interest for its splendid position, while **Saltino**, a kilometre away, is a small summer resort surrounded by firs, an excellent base for a walk or a drive. One of the most beautiful routes leads up to the Monte Secchieta (4,753ft), affording views over most of north-central Italy; in the winter the skiing facilities spring into action. For a longer outing, follow the **Panoramica del Pratomagno**, which crosses nearly the entire Pratomagno to join the Strada dei Sette Ponti near Castiglion Fibocchi.

# The Casentino: North to South

The Casentino's blue mountains, pastoral meadows and velvet valleys have long been Tuscany's spiritual refuge. Since the 18th century, travellers have trickled into the area, attracted initially by its famous monasteries, then charmed by one of the loveliest and most peaceful regions in Tuscany.

The Arno, such a turgid, unmannerly creature in its lower reaches ('the emblem of Despair', Norman Douglas once called it), is a fair, sparkling youth near its source at Monte Falterona (5,438ft); one of the classic excursions is to take the trail up and spend the night, to witness the sunset over the Tyrrhenian sea and dawn over the Adriatic. **Stia** (pop. 3,000), the first town the Arno meets, is pretty and medieval, centred about large porticoed Piazza Tanucci and **Santa Maria Assunta**. The 17th-century façade hides a fine Romanesque interior, with some curious primitive capitals, a triptych by Lorenzo di Bicci and a Madonna by Andrea della Robbia. Wool – the thick, heavy, brightly coloured *lana del Casentino* – is the main industry; in the

## Getting Around

As elsewhere in rural mountain Tuscany, a car is the best way to see the sights, but in the Casentino you might enjoy trying the LFI narrow-gauge **rail** line that passes through Stia, Poppi and Bibbiena on its way to Arezzo.

## Tourist Information

**Stia**: Pro Loco, Piazza Tanucci 65, t 0575 504 106.
**Badia Prataglia**: Piazza 13 Aprile, t 0575 559 054. *Open Wed–Sun 9–12.30, Sat 9–12 and 3.30–6.*
**Bibbiena**: Via Berni 25, t/f 0575 593 098. *Open Mon–Sat 9–1.*

## Where to Stay and Eat

**Stia** ✉ 52017
**★★La Foresta**, Via Roma 27, t 0575 504 650 (*cheap*). The only hotel in Stia; basic but comfortable.
**Falterona o Filetto**, Piazza Tanucci 85, f 0575 504982 (*cheap*). Nine newly renovated double and single rooms. Their restaurant is across the piazza at No. 28 (*see* below).
**Falterona o Filetto**, Piazza Tanucci 28, t 0575 504 569 (*moderate*). Linked to the hotel of the same name (*see* above), this offers *pappardelle* with wild boar.

**La Roma**, Località Tirasso, t 0575 582 226 (*moderate*). Pleasantly situated in a forest on the banks of the Arno, this is a family-run affair which specializes in choice home-produced charcuterie.

**Poppi** ✉ 52010
**★★Casentino**, Piazza Repubblica, t 0575 529 090 (*cheap*). A shady little *pensione* right opposite the castle – the only option in the old town.
**★★Campaldino**, Via Roma 95, t 0575 529 008, f 0575 529 032 (*moderate–cheap*). A little inn actually situated in the lower town at Ponte a Poppi. Established long ago in 1800, it offers 10 simple guest rooms; in the pretty, old-fashioned dining room upstairs (*moderate*) you can enjoy a meal of tasty local prosciutto, ravioli stuffed with a combination of vegetables and ricotta, or succulent lamb and chicken, and for dessert, *semifreddi* made *in casa*.
**★★★Il Rustichello**, Via del Corniolo 14, t/f 0575 556 046 (*moderate–cheap*). Just a couple of kilometres from the monastery at Camaldoli is this small but modern resort hotel, a great place to bring the kids; attractions include tennis, mini-golf and walks in the woods. The hotel's restaurant (*moderate*) is a good place to stop even if you're not staying, featuring great pasta dishes from nearby Emilia-Romagna, grilled meats, and Casentino cheeses.

old days Stia was the market for the Guidi counts, whose ruined **Castello di Porciano** (*open mid-May–mid-Oct Sun 10–12 and 4–7; call* **t** *0575 582 626 to visit out of season*) guarded the narrow Arno valley from the 10th century. Near this (four kilometres north of Stia) is the **Sanctuary of Santa Maria delle Grazie**, a 14th-century church containing frescoes, works attributed to Luca della Robbia, and a painting by Lorenzo di Niccolò Gerini. This road continues into the Mugello (*see* p.246), while the SS310 from Stia skirts Monte Falterona towards the **Passo la Calla** and Emilia-Romagna; near the pass, the Alpine pasture **Burraia** (15 kilometres from Stia) is an ideal spot for a cool summer picnic.

Down the Arno from Stia, **Pratovecchio** was the birthplace of Paolo Uccello in 1397, and chances are he'd still recognize its narrow, porticoed lanes. Just a couple of kilometres from the centre is the most beautiful Romanesque church of the Casentino, **Piero di Romena**, founded in 1152, which has retained its original lines in spite of several earthquakes and subsequent repairs. Although the façade is plain, the apse has two tiers of blind arcades, pierced by narrow windows. Inside, the well-preserved capitals are decorated with a medieval menagerie of people, animals and monsters. Among the works of art, dating back to the 1200s, is a Madonna by the Maestro di Varlungo. Nearby, the Guidis' **Castello di Romena** was one of the most powerful in the Casentino, with its three sets of walls and 14 towers (now reduced to three), and wide-ranging hilltop views. Dante mentioned it in the *Inferno*, as well as the **Fonte Branda**, the ruins of which are close by.

Dante knew this region well; at the age of 24 he fought with the Guelphs against the Ghibellines of Arezzo and their allies at the **Battle of Campaldino** (1289), which took place on a small plain just to the south of Pratovecchio. The victory was of paramount importance for Florence; it made her the leading power in Tuscany, and from there she went on to conquer Pisa and Arezzo. A column commemorating the battle was erected near the crossroads in 1921. At the head of the plain, just off the SS70, Countess Matilda's **Castel San Nicolò**, the wee medieval hamlet of **Strada** and its little Romanesque church form a picturesque ensemble in the wooded hills.

## Poppi and Camaldoli

Between 1000 and 1440 the Casentino was ruled by the Counts Guidi, who had their headquarters in the compact little bump of **Poppi** (pop. 5,700), set above a charming landscape of low rolling hills. From miles around you can see the Guidis' stalwart and erect **Castello** (*open Tues–Sun 9.30–12.30 and 2.30–5.30; closed Mon; adm*), modelled on the Palazzo Vecchio in Florence. The best-preserved medieval castle in the region, it has a magnificent courtyard, emblazoned with the coats of arms of every noble who ever visited the place, and stairs that zigzag to and fro with a touch of Piranesi. If you ask the custodian, he'll show you the grand hall with Florentine frescoes of the 1400s (more coats of arms), the frescoed chapel, and the commanding views from the tower.

The centre of Poppi is made up of ancient porticoed lanes, winding around a small domed chapel with a train station clock; at the end of the main street is the Romanesque church of **San Fedele**, with a 13th-century *Madonna and Child*. Shops selling locally made copperware line the main street of lower Poppi, and there's the little **Zoo Fauna Europea** for the kids.

A beautiful road leads northeast up to the ancient hermitage and monastery of **Camaldoli**, founded in 1012 by St Romualdo. Romualdo was a Benedictine monk who longed to found a community of hermits similar to those of the early Christians, and was given this forest by Count Maldolo (hence the name 'Camaldoli'). A conflict, however, arose even during Romualdo's lifetime, for the piety of the hermits soon attracted pilgrims and visitors who interfered with their solitary meditations. Romualdo's solution was ingenious: he founded another monastery lower down, with a more relaxed rule, whose sole purpose was to entertain visitors and care for the forest domains that belonged to the order. Perhaps of all monastic orders, the Camaldolese are the most ecologically minded – self-sufficient vegetarians whose rule orders them to plant at least 5,000 new trees every year. Little remains of San Romualdo's original foundation, except for portions of the 11th-century cloister, the rich library, and the 16th-century pharmacy, where the monks sell their balsams, herbal remedies and liqueurs. Some 300m further up, a beautiful hour's walk, is the **Eremo** (*only men are admitted past the gate*), with its 20 cottages set in an amphitheatre of pines, each with its own chapel and walled kitchen garden, where the hermits exist in silence and solitude, meeting only on certain feast days and in the church, which was decorated inside by Vasari and has two marble tabernacles by Desiderio da Settignano.

**Badia Prataglia**, 10 kilometres from Camaldoli, is the region's most popular secular retreat, a summer resort spread out among the trees and hills, with beautiful walks along streams and waterfalls leading off in all directions.

## Bibbiena and La Verna

As chief town of the modern Casentino, **Bibbiena** has been enveloped in sprawl and lacks Poppi's quaint charm, though in its heart it retains its old Tuscan feel. Few buildings stand out – a good Renaissance palace, **Palazzo Dovizi**, and the church of **San Lorenzo**, where there are some excellent polychrome terracottas by Andrea della Robbia. From Bibbiena, the S208 crosses east over into a range of hills bravely called the Alpe di Catenaia, which divides the Arno from the Tiber valley, to the famous Franciscan monastery of **La Verna**, high up on a bizarre rocky outcrop, which, according to one of St Francis's visions, had been rent and blasted into its wild shape at the moment of the Crucifixion. The land was given to Francis in 1213 by another pious nobleman, Count Orlando, and the saint at once built some mud huts here for a select group of his followers. He found La Verna a perfect spot for meditation, and came to his holy mountain on six different occasions. During the last, on 14 September 1224, he became the first person ever to receive the stigmata – an event pictured in the frescoes of Assisi and elsewhere – after which he could only walk in extreme pain.

The churches, chapels and convent at La Verna are simple and rustic, though the main church, the chapel of Stigmata and St Francis's tiny church of **Santa Maria degli Angeli** are decorated by the most transcendently beautiful blue, green and white terracottas Andrea della Robbia ever made, especially the *Annunciation* in the nave. You can also visit the **Sasso Spicco**, Francis's favourite retreat under a huge boulder, and **La Penna** (4,208ft), on a sheer precipice, with romantic views of the Arno and Tiber valleys. The nearby village of Chiusi della Verna is a small resort and there are many summer homes in the area.

# Arezzo

Strategically located on a hill at the convergence of the Valdarno, Casentino and the Valdichiana valleys, ancient **Arezzo** (pop. 92,000) was one of the richest cities of the Etruscan Dodecapolis. Nor is modern Arezzo a loser in the money game – it has one of the biggest jewellery industries in Europe, with hundreds of small firms stamping out gold chains and rings, and bank vaults full of ingots. Its second most notable industry, one that fills the shops around its main Piazza Grande, is furniture-making and marketing antiques; on the first weekend of each month the entire square becomes an enormous antique curiosity shop.

Arezzo is a bit of a curiosity shop itself. It had only a brief, though remarkable, bask in the Renaissance sunshine, although in the Middle Ages it was a typical free *comune*, a Ghibelline rival to Florence and a city of great cultural distinction. Around

the year 1000 it gave birth to Guido Monaco (or Guido d'Arezzo), inventor of musical notation and the musical scale; in the 13th century it produced Margarito, or Margaritone, an important painter in the transition from the Byzantine to the Italian styles. In 1304 Petrarch, the 'first modern man', was born here into a banished Florentine Black Guelph family; his Arezzo contemporary was Spinello Aretino, one of Tuscany's trecento masters. Arezzo was at its most powerful in the early 1300s, when it was ruled by a remarkable series of warrior bishops. One died in the Battle of Campaldino; another, the fierce Guido Tarlati, ruled the city from 1312 to 1327. He expanded its territory, built new walls, settled internal bickerings, renewed warfare with Florence and Siena, and was excommunicated. After Bishop Guido came the deluge – his brother sold the city for a brief period to Florence, family rivalries exploded, the plague carried away half the population and, to top it all, in 1384 the French troops of Louis d'Anjou sacked the city and brought it to its knees, refusing to move on until Arezzo paid 40,000 florins. Florence came up with the ransom money, and in effect purchased Arezzo's independence. Although henceforth an economic backwater, on the fringe of the Renaissance, it managed to produce two leading personalities: Giorgio Vasari and Pietro Aretino, the uninhibited writer and poet whose celebrated poison pen allowed him to make a fortune by *not* writing about contemporary princes and popes – the most genteel extortionist of all time.

## San Francesco

If you arrive by train or bus, Via Guido Monaco leads up to the old centre of Arezzo by way of a stern statue of musical monk Guido, and passes on the left one of Italy's prettiest post offices, with an ornate ceiling, before ending in Piazza San Francesco, site of **San Francesco** (*open Mon–Sun 8.30–12 and 2–7; entrance free but booking is essential to see the newly restored frescoes, call ticket office on* t *0575 352 727 for details; adm*). This dowdy barn of a Franciscan church contains Arezzo's star attraction: Piero della Francesca's frescoes on the popular pseudo-classical/Christian subject of the *Legend of the Cross* (*see* **Florence**, p.208), the most riveting cycle of frescoes of the 1400s and the gospel of Renaissance painting, the *ideal* – other works seem a mere commentary. Piero literally wrote the book on the new science of artificial perspective, and yet as strictly as these frescoes obey the dictates of the vanishing point they make no concessions to realism; simplified and drawn with geometrical perfection, Piero's beings are purely spiritual creatures. It is intriguing that Piero and Uccello, the two artists most obsessed with perspective and space, should have created the most transcendent art; few compositions are as haunting as Piero's *Dream of Constantine*, a virtuoso demonstration of lighting, colouring, and perspective, the angel swooping down from the upper left-front of the scene – and yet all is uncannily still, the scene of the dream itself like a dream; the soldiers stand guard, woodenly unaware; the sleeping emperor's attendant gazes out with a bored expression. Note too the rather uncanonical *Annunciation* in which Gabriel announces both the birth and death of her son to Mary.

The fact that the frescoes exist at all is nothing short of a miracle. The walls have been damaged by an earthquake, struck by lightning, burned twice, and shot at by

# Getting Around

From Florence (75km/1½hrs), Perugia (73km/1½hrs), and Cortona (32km/45mins), the **train** is the easiest way to reach Arezzo; the station is at the southern end of town, where Via Guido Monaco crosses Viale Piero della Francesca and the old city walls. The little LFI light-gauge rail line from Arezzo to the Casentino has reopened after a complete rebuilding, and is at your service for a picturesque ride up to Subbieno, Bibbiena, Poppi and Stia (about 12 daily); another LFI line heads south for Monte San Savino, Lucignano and Sinalunga, with connections to Chiusi and Siena.

**Buses** for Cortona and other towns in Arezzo province, as well as for Siena (five a day) and Florence (six a day), leave from the station directly opposite on Viale Piero della Francesca, **t** 0575 22663.

# Tourist Information

**Arezzo**: Piazza della Repubblica 28, in front of the train station, **t** 0575 377 678, **f** 0575 20839. *Open winter Mon–Sat 9.30–12.30 and 3.30–6; summer Mon–Sat 9.30–1 and*

*3.30–6.30, Sun 9.30–1.*
*info@arezzo.turismo.toscana.it.*

# Where to Stay

**Arezzo** ✉ 52100

No hotels in Arezzo really stand out, unlike some of Tuscany's art cities, the forces of tourism have yet to convert old villas into modern accommodation. What the city does have is clean, comfortable, and up-to-date, but nothing to tempt you into lingering.

★★★**Minerva**, Via Fiorentina 4, **t** 0575 370 390, **f** 0575 302 415 (*expensive*). This may be the most convenient if you're travelling by car; it's a few blocks west of the city walls, but besides pleasant rooms, TV and air-conditioning, it can offer you a parking place. It also has an excellent, unpretentious restaurant (*moderate*).

In town, most rooms are close to the station.

★★★**Continentale**, Piazza Guido Monaco 7, **t** 0575 20251, **f** 0575 350 485 (*moderate*). A fine, older hotel; you can enjoy contemplating the towers and red rooftops of town from the roof terrace.

★★★**Europa**, Via Spinello 43, **t** 0575 357 701, **f** 0575 357 703 (*moderate*). Continentale's

Napoleon's troops, who also scratched the eyes of the figures. To keep the church standing after so much abuse, the first restorers injected tons of cement into the walls, which, combined with humidity, nearly ruined the frescoes once and for all. Although the frescoes were cleaned in the 1960s, no attempt was made to protect them from further damage. Now, after 15 years of painstaking and complex work, they have at last been fully restored and, hopefully, saved. Various bits have been hidden away during work over the years; on April 7th 2000 three fully completed sides of the chapel opened to the public for the first time.

During the restoration, it was discovered that the 'night' the art historians always referred to in Piero's *Dream of Constantine* is not actually night after all. After removing layers of dirt and remnants of previous restoration, it became obvious the artist had in fact portrayed a magnificent dawn, the rising sun chasing away the last nocturnal stars. So much for the most famous night-time painting in the history of art.

## Piazza Grande

Few *piazze* in Italy have the eclectic charm of Arezzo's **Piazza Grande**, the perfect backdrop for both the *Giostra del Saracino* in early September and the monthly antiques fair. On this occasion, the town sports from the four quarters of Arezzo don

competitor, just across from the station; it's similarly modern and plain, but many rooms have air-con.

**Truciolini**, Via Pacinotti 6, t 0575 984 104, f 0575 984 137 (*moderate*). Less expensive, with parking and air-con.

Budget hotels do exist out of the centre. The following are near Porta San Lorentino.

**Toscana**, Via Pirennio 56, t 0575 21692 (*cheap*).

**Chimera**, Via V. Veneto 46, t 0575 902 494 (*cheap*).

**Ostello Villa Severi**, Via Francesco Redi 13, t 0575 299 047. The local youth hostel. *Open summer, Easter and Christmas hols only.*

## Eating Out

**Buca di San Francesco**, Via S. Francesco 1, t 0575 23271 (*expensive–moderate*). This is a tourist favourite, but it has an honest-to-goodness medieval atmosphere and tasty Tuscan fare, if adapted for the uninitiated. *Closed Mon eve and Tues, also July.*

**Le Tastevin**, Via de' Cenci 9, t 0575 28304 (*moderate*). One restaurant that tries hard (it even has a piano bar, which may seem a little incongruous after a day in medieval Arezzo). Enjoy carpaccio, good penne with

pepper sauce and a selection of wines from around the world.

**Il Saraceno**, Via Mazzini 6, t 0575 27644. For a moderately priced meal, head for Via Mazzini, just off the Corso; at this place you can find *pici* and polenta, and game in season including stewed boar and rabbit. *Closed Wed.*

**Agania**, Via Mazzini 10, t 0575 295 381 (*moderate*). Down the street, with slightly cheaper, solid conventional home cooking.

**Torre di Gnicchi**, Piaggia San Martino 8, near Piazza Grande, t 0575 352 035 (*cheap*). A wine bar with over 400 labels to suit all pockets with light suppers including a good onion soup and local specialities. *Closed Wed.*

**Osteria La Capannaccia**, Loc. Campriano 51c, t 0575 361 759 (*moderate*). One of the best, serving specialities of the Aretine countryside – simple *minestra di pane*, roast meats and Colli Aretini wines – at unpretentious prices. *Closed Sun eve and Mon.*

**Al Principe**, Piazza Giovi 25, t 0575 362 046 (*moderate*). Near the Arno, between Arezzo and Subbiano; fine traditional dishes include eels (once fished from the Arno) in *piccante* tomato sauce, home-made *pici*, *minestra di pane*, and good local wines. *Closed Mon and most of August.*

13th-century costume to re-enact an event first documented in 1593, a celebration of the feats of arms against Saracen pirates who menaced the Tyrrhenian coast, and penetrated inland even as far as Arezzo. Revived in 1932, the festival begins with a parade of costumes and flag-tossing by the *sbandieratori*, and is followed by a test of individual prowess between eight knights, two representing each quarter, who tilt against a wooden figure named 'Buratto, king of the Indies' for the prize of a golden lance. The *Fiera Antiquaria* is probably the biggest of its kind in Italy, attracting hundreds of vendors from all over the country – everything from Renaissance ceramics to 1950s junk; it takes place on the first Saturday and Sunday of each month (Sunday is the big day), but ring the tourist office in advance to make sure. On one side of the piazza is the **Loggia del Vasari**, a large building Vasari designed for his home town in 1573, with the idea of replicating a Greek stoa, with little shops and workshops under the portico. Vasari also designed the clock tower of the **Palazzetto della Fraternità dei Laici**, an old ornate building, half Gothic and half by Renaissance master Bernardo Rossellino. Although it looks like a town hall, the palazzo is really the home of a lay brotherhood founded in the 1200s. The old Palazzo del Popolo exists only in ruins, behind Vasari's loggia on Via dei Pileati. Like Pisa's, it was destroyed by the Florentines after they captured the city.

## Santa Maria della Pieve

Perhaps most impressive on Piazza Grande is the round, Romanesque arcaded apse of Arezzo's great 12th-century church of **Santa Maria della Pieve** (*t 0575 22629; open daily 8–12.30 and 3–6.30*). The church rather eccentrically turns its back on the piazza, while directing its unusual Pisan-Lucchese façade towards narrow Via dei Pileati, where it's hard to see well. Few things in Tuscany look as ancient as these four tiers of shallow arcades, rough-hewn and eroded like a vertical stone cliff. Each tier of arches is successively narrower, in a unique rustic style with no two columns or capitals alike (*covered for restoration at time of writing*). The campanile 'of a hundred holes' has so many neat rows of double-mullioned windows that it resembles a primitive skyscraper.

Under the arch of the front portal, note the interesting early medieval *Reliefs of the Twelve Months*: April with her flowers, February with his pruning hook, and the pagan two-headed god Janus for January. The dim interior has an early Romanesque relief of the *Three Magi* on the entrance wall and finely decorated capitals in the nave. Like many early churches, the presbytery is raised above the low crypt, the most ancient part of the church, with primitive capitals – human faces mingling with rams, bulls and dragons. On the left wall there's another primitive relief of the *Nativity* and *Christ's Baptism*, while above in the choir is a beautiful polyptych by Pietro Lorenzetti (1320), which has been recently restored to its glimmering original appearance, featuring the *Madonna and Saints* modelling the latest Tuscan fashions and fabrics.

Below Santa Maria descends Corso Italia, Arezzo's main evening parade, while above, Via dei Pileati continues into the oldest quarter of the city, passing by way of **Petrarch's House** (*open Mon–Fri 10–12 and 3–5; Sat 10–12; closed Sun*), a replacement for the original bombed in the last war; it stands near the picturesque 14th-century Palazzo del Pretorio, decked with coats of arms of imperial and Florentine governors.

## The Duomo

*Open daily 7–12 and 3–6.30.*

From the Piazza Grande, narrow streets lead up to the **Passeggio del Prato**, an English-style park with lawns, trees, a café, and a big white elephant of a Fascist monument to Petrarch. All of Arezzo slopes gradually upwards from the railway station, ending abruptly here; from the cliffs on the edge of the Prato there is a memorable view over the mountains, extending towards Florence and Urbino. Overlooking the park is a half-ruined Medici fortress of the 1500s and at the other end is the back of the **Duomo**, with a lovely Gothic bell tower – from the 19th century. The cathedral, built in bits and pieces over the centuries (1276–1510), has a nondescript façade but several great works of art in its sombre, dimly lit Gothic naves, not least its stained-glass **windows**, created by the greatest 16th-century master of the art, the Frenchman Guillaume de Marcillat, seeming almost like illuminated frescoes by a Gozzoli or a Luca Signorelli. The magnificent marble Gothic High Altar is dedicated to San Donato, and there are impressive tombs – the first is of Pope Gregory X

(1205–76) with a canopy and 4th-century sarcophagus, holding the mortal dust of the pope who holds the record for taking the longest to be elected; the enclave, in Viterbo, lasted from 1268 to 1271, and only ended when the Viterbans starved the cardinals into deciding. The second, even more impressive, is the 1327 **Tomb of Bishop Guido Tarlati**, a fascinating early predecessor of the heroic sculptural tombs of the Renaissance, perhaps designed by Giotto. The tomb is divided into three sections, with a relief resembling a miniature theatre and a Ghibelline eagle like a party badge on top; below lies the battling bishop's effigy; and below that, 16 fine relief panels that tell the story of his life, his battles and his good works. Near it is Piero della Francesca's fresco of the Magdalene holding a crystal pot of ointment. The **Museo del Duomo** (*t 0575 23991; open Thurs–Sat 10–12noon; adm*) contains detached frescoes by Spinello Aretino and his son Parri di Spinello, a terracotta depicting the Annunciation by Bernardo Rossellino, and paintings by 13th-century master Margarito d'Arezzo, Signorelli and Vasari.

## Museo d'Arte

*Open Mon–Sat 9–7; Sun 9–1; adm.*

Diagonally opposite the cathedral stands Arezzo's Ghibelline **Palazzo del Comune** with its distinctive tower; from here Via Ricasoli descends past the birthplace of Guido Monaco (with a plaque of Guido's do-re-mi), to the **Museo d'Arte Medioevale e Moderna** (*t 0575 409 050; open Tues–Sun 8.30–7.30; adm*) where you can get to know some local medieval and Renaissance artists not often seen elsewhere. The collection is housed in a medieval palace, remodelled in the Renaissance, perhaps by Bernardo Rossellino, and later used as a customs house. All is arranged chronologically: the attractive courtyard contains medieval columns and capitals, a fine sculpted horse's head and gargoyles, while the two rooms on the ground floor contain sculptural details from the cathedral façade and a fine 10th-century *pluteo* carved with peacocks.

Among the works on the first floor are a stylized Byzantine *St Francis* by Margarito d'Arezzo, painted just after the saint's death and an *Enthroned Virgin* by Guido da Siena, studded with chunky, plasticky gems. Next you'll find detached frescoes by Spinello Aretino, the city's greatest trecento artist, and by his son Parri di Spinello (1387–1453), whose ghostly battle scene *Sconfitta di Massenzio* was discovered in the Badia after the war; the museum also has one of his beautifully dressed Madonnas. Another native of Arezzo, Bartolomeo della Gatta, painted the plague saint Rocco praying to liberate the city from the Black Death. Also on the first floor is a fresco attributed to Signorelli; a huge busy canvas by Vasari of *Esther's Wedding Banquet* ; a collection of small Renaissance bronzes, including a bear with a monkey on his head; beautiful ceramics from Urbino, Deruta and Montelupo; and a plate by Master Giorgio of Gubbio with his secret red. On the second floor there's a strange painting by Angelo Cacoselli (d. 1652) called the *Maga*, of an enchantress with her animals, a small room of 18th-century Neapolitan *presepi* figurines, and some splashy Mannerist canvases by Vasari, Allori and the great Rosso Fiorentino.

## Vasari, Cimabue and More Vasari

Around the corner, at Via 20 Settembre 55, is the **Casa di Giorgio Vasari** (*t 0575 409 040; open Mon and Wed–Sat 8.30–7.30, Sun 8.30–1; closed Tues; adm*). Vasari was so fond of his own brand of spineless Mannerism that he wasn't about to leave it all for Duke Cosimo, but decorated his own house with the same fluff. Mediocrity attracts mediocrity; besides the frescoes there are several rooms of nondescript paintings, of which three stand out: the most repugnant St Sebastian ever committed to canvas, a terracotta portrait of Galba, one of Rome's ugliest mugs, by Sansovino, and a painting by a follower of Santi di Tito, of Christ and the Apostles dining in the 17th-century equivalent of a greasy spoon.

From Vasari's house, Via San Domenico will take you to the 13th-century church of **San Domenico** (*t 0575 22906; open daily 9–7*), with a simple asymmetrical exterior and a fine stone Gothic chapel (1360s) on the right wall, while the rest of the walls are covered with frescoes that overlap like pages on the bottom of a canary cage. The main altar has a crucifix by Cimabue (*c.* 1265); the chapel to the left contains a fine triptych of the Archangel Michael by the 'Maestro del Vescovado'.

Via Garibaldi from the art museum returns to the centre by way of **Santissima Annunziata**, Arezzo's late response to Brunelleschi, begun by Bartolomeo della Gatta in the 1490s and completed by Antonio da Sangallo; the fourth altar has a painting by Pietro da Cortona and in the choir there's a stained-glass window by Marcillat. Further up, off Via Porta Buia, stands **Santissime Flora e Lucilla in Badia** (*t 0575 356 612; open Mon–Sat 8–12 and 4–6.30, Sun 7–9 and 10.15–12.30*), a 13th-century church with an unusual interior remodelled by Vasari. He also designed the two-sided altar, with reliefs from the Gospel of St Matthew on the front and St George slaying the dragon on the back. Over the presbytery the impressive cupola is a masterful fake by 17th-century *trompe-l'œil* master Andrea Pozzo. At the entrance there's a good fresco of St Lawrence by della Gatta; the fine cloister is by Giuliano da Maiano, a student of Brunelleschi (entrance No.2, Piazza della Badia).

On the southern edge of Arezzo, near the station on Via Margaritone, the remains of a small **Roman amphitheatre** (*open summer 7am–8pm; winter 7.30am–6pm*) have become a quiet city park. The former Olivetan monastery, built on a curve over the amphitheatre's foundations, has been restored to house the **Museo Archeologico** (*open daily 8.30–7.30; adm*). Not much has survived of the thriving Etruscan and Roman city of *Arretium*, but there are some mosaics and sarcophagi, Etruscan urns and Greek vases, examples of the Roman-era red *corallino* vases and an excellent portrait of a rather jaded-looking middle-aged Roman, worked in gold.

## Santa Maria delle Grazie

*Open daily 8–12 and 4–6.30.*

Finally, you can take a 15-minute walk from Via le Mecenate out through Arezzo's auto-clogged southern suburbs to see a simple but exceptionally pretty Renaissance church, **Santa Maria delle Grazie**, finished in 1444 and given a jewel of a porch by Benedetto da Maiano, in 1482. With its subdued, delicate decoration, and round arches braced with slender iron bars, this could be the archetypal creation of early

Renaissance architecture – certainly it will call to mind the backgrounds of any number of Tuscan paintings. The interior has an early Renaissance delight to match, a
colourful terracotta altarpiece full of coloured fruit and *putti* by Andrea della Robbia,
surrounding Parri di Spinello's *Madonna della Misericordia* (1430).

# Along the Valtiberina and the Valdichiana

## The Valtiberina

The Valtiberina, or upper valley of the Tiber, is a luminous patchwork of glowing
pasturelands and pine and beech woodlands, birthplace of Michelangelo and
Piero della Francesca.

### Arezzo to Sansepolcro

Although Michelangelo took fresh air and stone-flavoured milk from his native
place, Piero della Francesca carried the light and luminous landscape along the
Tuscan-Umbrian frontier with him throughout his career, and left more behind in his
native haunts than Michelangelo. From Arezzo, it's a pretty 41-kilometre drive to
Sansepolcro, especially along the SS73, which ascends through the Foce di Scopetone
(with panoramic views back towards the city) then continues another 17 kilometres
to the short turn-off for **Monterchi**. Dedicated to Hercules in Roman times, the town
is a tiny medieval triangle; while strolling its lanes, don't miss the curious underground passageway around the apse of the parish church, dating back to the Middle
Ages but of uncertain purpose. Monterchi is most famous, however, for Piero della
Francesca's extraordinary fresco in the little chapel at the cemetery. The *Madonna del
Parto* (1445) is perhaps the first (and last?) portrayal of the Virgin in her ninth month,
a mystery revealed by twin angels who pull back the flaps of a tent, empty but for
Mary, weary and melancholy, one eyelid drooping, one hand on her hip, the other on
her swollen belly, almost painful to see. It is now housed in a former school building
on Via della Reglia, well signposted from all directions (*open Tues–Sun 9–1 and 2–6;
Jul–Aug also 9pm–midnight; closed Mon; adm*). Details of its restoration are exhibited
with the painting.

**Anghiari** (pop. 6,200), between Monterchi and Sansepolcro, is a fine old town
located on a balcony over the Valtiberina. Once a property of Camaldoli and later
of the Tarlati family, it was the site of a 1440 victory of the Florentines over the
Milanese, a decisive victory in corking up Visconti ambitions over Tuscany and the
rest of Italy – also a nearly bloodless one, the epitome of Renaissance Italy's civilized
chessboard wars; only one man died at Anghiari, and that was an accident. Leonardo
da Vinci chose it as his subject matter in the Battle of the Frescoes in Florence's
Palazzo Vecchio – one of the Renaissance's greatest un-happenings, though the
cartoons left behind by the master were often copied and became one of the inspi-
rations of Florentine Mannerism. In Anghiari's Renaissance Palazzo Taglieschi at Via
Mameli 16, the **Museo delle Arti e Tradizioni Popolari dell'Alta Valle del Tevere** (*open*

# The Valtiberina and Valdichiana

EMILIA-ROMAGNA

To Ravenna

S. Leo

Novafeltria

M o n t e f e l t r o

M. Falterona

La Burraia

Pso. d. Calla

Bagno di Romagna

Pennabilli

Montecopiolo

Stia

Camaldoli

Badia Prataglia

Monte Fumaiolo

M. Carpegna

Sassocorvaro

Pratovecchio

Balze

Carpegna

MARCHES

Castel S. Niccolo

M. Penna

R. Foglia

Piandimeleto

Poppi

La Verna

Badia Tedalda

Sestino

Bibbiena

Chiusi d. Verna

Pieve Sto. Stefano

S. Angelo in Vado

R. Metauro

Caprese Michelangelo

Mercatello s. Metauro

Talla

R. Candigliano

Subbiano

Sansepolcro

TUSCANY

Castiglion Fibocchi

Anghiari

To Florence

Arezzo

Monterchi

Citta di Castello

Civitella in Val Chiana

Foce di Scopetone

Monte Sta. Maria Tiberina

Morra

Gargonza

Castiglion Fiorentino

R. Nestore

Montone

Sta. Maria d. Vertighe

UMBRIA

Monte S. Savino

Montecchio

Marciano d. Chiana

Umbertide

Lucignano

le Celle

Camuccia

Cortona

Sta. Maria d. Calcinaio

Preggio

Antognola

Foiano della Chiana

Ossaia

Sinalunga

Tuoro sul Trasimeno

Castel Rigone

Petrignano di Lago

Lago Trasimeno

To Orvieto

To Perugia

10 km

5 miles

Mon–Fri 3–7; Sat–Sun 9–1 and 3–7; adm) has exhibits relating to traditional crafts of the Upper Tiber Valley. Just over one kilometre to the southwest, there's the pretty Romanesque **Pieve di Sovara**, and on the Sansepolcro road you can still make out the 8th-century Byzantine origins of **Santo Stefano**.

## Sansepolcro

**Sansepolcro** (pop. 15,500) is the largest town of the Valtiberina, famous for lace, pasta (the Buitoni spaghetti works are just outside the city), and Piero della Francesca. The painter was born here some time between 1410 and 1420, and given his mother's name as his father died before his birth. Although he worked in the Marches, Arezzo and Rome, he spent most of his life in Sansepolcro, painting and writing books on geometry and perspective until he went blind at the age of 60. Piero may have had a chance to discuss his theories with a younger son of Sansepolcro, the great mathematician Luca Pacioli (born 1440), who wrote his *Divina Proporzione* with some help from Leonardo da Vinci (he also gets credit for the first book on accounting).

Sansepolcro was founded around the year 1000, and like Anghiari belonged to the monks of Camaldoli until the 13th century. The historic centre, with its crew-cut

# Getting Around

CAT **buses** from Arezzo serve this area efficiently if not especially frequently. Sansepolcro is the terminus of Umbria's FCU light **rail** line, which takes you down to Città di Castello (16km/25mins), Umbertide, Perugia, Todi and Terni. Buses from Sansepolcro (station just outside the walls) go to Città di Castello, Caprese Michelangelo (26km/45mins), Arezzo (38km/1hr), Florence and Pieve Santo Stefano.

# Tourist Information

**Anghiari**: Corso Matteotti 103, t 0575 749 279. *Open daily 9–12.30 and 4–7.30.*
**Sansepolcro**: Piazza Garibaldi 2, t/f 0575 740 536. *Open daily Mon–Sun 9.30–1 and 3.30–6.30.*

# Where to Stay and Eat

## Anghiari ✉ 52031

**Locanda al Castello di Sorci**, near Anghiari at San Lorenzo, t 0575 789 066 (*cheap*). A country beanery located in a former tobacco barn: you can only eat a set menu, but it's good value and includes wine: the fare is simple, much of it (wine and meats) coming from the farm annexe. *Closed Mon.*

## Sansepolcro ✉ 52037

****La Balestra**, Via del Montefeltro 29, t 0575 735 151, f 0575 740 370 (*moderate*). A pleasant place with modern, comfortable rooms, parking and a good restaurant (*moderate*), with delicious home-made pasta; for seconds try the lamb chops with courgette flowers.

***Fiorentino**, Via L. Pacioli 60, t 0575 740 350, f 0575 740 370 (*moderate*). Situated near the main gate, this has been the town inn since the 1820s; the rooms provide all the basics, and there's a garage. The restaurant (*moderate*) is Sansepolcro's best; it's a good place to try Italian onion soup; other local specialities are especially well prepared, and there's a wide assortment of local cheese. *Closed Fri.*
**Orfeo**, Viale Diaz, t 0575 742 061 (*cheap*). Around the corner from the Fiorentino, this will do if the others are full.
**Paola e Marco Mercati dell'Oroscopo**, Loc. Pieve Vecchia, Piazza Togliatti 66, t 0575 734 875 (*moderate*). An unusual place mixing traditional fare with more creative cooking, such as flamed king prawns in garlic sauce and a delcious chocolate tart with *zabaglione* and mascarpone. *Dinner only, closed Sun.* They also have a small hotel (*cheap*) with 12 rooms.
**La Cisterna**, Via San Giovanni 32, called (*moderate*). A fine old-fashioned *trattoria* in the centre, serving home-made pasta and desserts, *fritelle*, and *saltimbocca alla Romana*, a rarity in these parts.

## Caprese Michelangelo ✉ 52033

***Il Faggeto**, t 0575 793 925 (*cheap*). Up in the Alpe Faggeto, above Caprese Michelangelo, is a pleasant little mountain hotel and restaurant, set in a lovely forested landscape. The hotel has simple rooms; its restaurant, the **Fonte Galletta** (*moderate*), uses the freshest local ingredients – chestnuts, wild mushrooms, truffles, game, mountain hams – to create tasty dishes. The pasta is excellent, as are the home-made *semifreddi. Open daily July–Aug.*

towers, has plenty of character, though it's a bit dusty and plain after several earth-quakes and rebuildings. It is enclosed within well-preserved walls, built by the Tarlati and given a Renaissance facelift by Giuliano da Sangallo. **Piazza Torre di Berta** is the centre of town, where on the second Sunday of September crossbow-men from Gubbio come to challenge the home archers in the *Palio della Balestra*, an ancient rivalry. Along Via Matteotti are many of the city's surviving 14th–16th-century palaces, most notably the Palazzo delle Laudi and the 14th-century palace housing the **Museo Civico** (*open daily 9.30–1 and 2.30–6; until 7.30 in summer; adm exp. The building suffered some damage in the 1997 earthquake, but most rooms are still open while they determine what restoration is needed*). Here you can see Piero della Francesca's masterpiece, the *Resurrection*, an intense, almost eerie depiction of the solemnly triumphant Christ stepping out of his tomb surrounded by sleeping soldiers and a sleeping land, more autumnal than springlike. It shares pride of place with two of Piero's early works, the *Misericordia Polyptych*, a gold-background altar-piece dominated by a serene, giant goddess of a Madonna, sheltering under her cloak members of the confraternity (note the black hood on one) who commissioned the picture, and a damaged fresco of San Giuliano.

Other works are by his greatest pupil, Luca Signorelli (a *Crucifixion* with two saints on the back), Pontormo (*Martyrdom of San Quintino*), Santi di Tito, Mannerist Raffaellino del Colle, and the 16th-century Giovanni de' Vecchi, also of Sansepolcro, whose *Presentation of the Virgin* is interesting for its unusual vertical rhythms. You can see a 16th-century scene of Sansepolcro in the *Pilgrimage of the Company of the Crucifix of Loreto*, a relic of the days of the Black Death, as are the wooden panels of *Death* (one showing a fine strutting skeleton). Downstairs, a room contains sculptural fragments gathered from the town, including a rather mysterious 12th-century frieze of knights; upstairs there's a collection of detached frescoes.

Sansepolcro also has a couple of pretty churches: near the museum is the Gothic church of **San Francesco**, with a fine rose window and portal. The **Duomo** is on Via Matteotti; it was built in the 11th century but has been much restored since. Among the art inside is a fresco by Bartolomeo della Gatta and a polyptych by Matteo di Giovanni; note the huge rose window, made of alabaster. Another church, **San Lorenzo**, has a *Deposizione* by Rosso Fiorentino.

## Up the Tiber: Caprese Michelangelo

Signor Buonarroti, a minor noble of Florence, was *podestà* in the tiny town of Caprese, 26 kilometres northwest of Sansepolcro, when his wife gave birth to little Michelangelo. As was the custom in those days, the baby was sent into the country-side to be nursed, in this case by the wife of a mason. 'If my brains are any good at all, it's because I was born in the pure air of your Arezzo countryside,' Michelangelo later told Vasari. 'Just as with my mother's milk I sucked in the hammer and chisels I use for my statues.' Although he only returned once to the Valtiberina, to select sturdy firs to float down the Tiber for the scaffolding in the Sistine Chapel, Caprese does not let any opportunity slip by to remind us of its most famous son, even changing its name to **Caprese Michelangelo**. The artist's purported birthplace, the

14th-century **Casa del Podestà** (*open summer Mon–Fri 9.30–6.30, Sat–Sun 9.30–7.30; winter Mon–Fri 10–5, Sat–Sun 10–6*), has been restored and now houses a museum in his honour, with photographs and reproductions of his works. Caprese's medieval castle contains questionable tributes from modern sculptors. From here it's only a few bumpy kilometres into the Alpe di Catenaia and La Verna (*see* p.451).

### Caprese to Sestino

East of Caprese the countryside is the biggest attraction; between **Pieve Santo Stefano** (Roman *Sulpitia*, mostly rebuilt after the Second World War) and **Badia Tedalda** (a small resort) lie the rolling Alpe della Luna, the Mountains of the Moon.

**Sestino** (from the Roman woodland god Sextius), Tuscany's easternmost *comune* on the border of the Marches, was ruled by the Montefeltro dukes of Urbino until 1516. It has been the agricultural centre for its area since antiquity and preserves many medieval buildings. Near its little Romanesque parish church, the **Antiquarium** (*to visit call in advance; t 0575 772 718*) will show you the headless *Venus of Sestino* and other local finds. The church, built in the 8th century, shows the influence of Ravenna, Byzantine capital of the west; its 13th-century altar sits on a Roman boundary stone. Sestino is Tuscany's eastermost village; if you like this part of the world you may wish to continue over the border into the Marches – specifically, into the lovely upland region called the Montefeltro, above the Renaissance city of Urbino.

# South of Arezzo: the Valdichiana

The flat Valdichiana south of Arezzo is the largest, broadest valley in the Apennines, rimmed by surrounding hills and old towns like a walled garden. The Etruscans, headquartered at Cortona, were the first to drain its marshlands, making it their bread-basket, so rich, it is said, that even after Hannibal's troops pillaged and burned on their way to Lake Trasimeno, there was still more than enough to feed the army and its elephants. By the Middle Ages, however, the valley had reverted to a swamp, forcing the inhabitants back into the hills. And so it stayed, until the beginning of the 19th century, when the Lorraine Grand Dukes initiated a major land reclamation scheme. Now, once again, prosperous farms are the main feature of the Valdichiana. The equally prosperous-looking cattle you may notice are a prized breed called the Chianina, named after the valley, and descendants of the primal herds whose fossils were discovered in the vicinity.

### Monte San Savino and Lucignano

But there is more to the Valdichiana than farms and *bistecca alla fiorentina* on the hoof. On both sides of the valley are some of the most beautiful villages in this part of Tuscany. Cortona is the most famous, but there are others, like **Monte San Savino** (21 kilometres from Arezzo, on the west side of the valley), the birthplace of Andrea Contucci, better known as Andrea Sansovino (1460–1529), artistic emissary of Lorenzo de' Medici to Portugal and one of the heralds of the High Renaissance; his

# Tourist Information

**Monte San Savino**: c/o Biblioteca, Piazza Gamurrini 2, t 0575 559 002.
**Castiglion Fiorentino**: Corso Italia 111, t 0575 658 713 (*in season only*).

# Where to Stay and Eat

## Monte San Savino ✉ 52048

****Castello dei Gargonza**, an entire walled village 8km from Monte San Savino, just off the SS73, t 0575 847 021, f 0575 847 054 (*moderate*). King of the Valdichiana for peace, quiet and medieval atmosphere, with 20 rooms in restored houses and a pool, all surrounded by forests; local specialities are served at the popular restaurant (*moderate*), boasting a choice wine list. *Closed Tues.*

***Sangallo**, Piazza Vittorio Veneto 16, t 0575 810 049, f 0575 810 220 (*moderate*). A fine provincial hotel, providing all you need, in the centre of town; there's no restaurant.

## Castiglion Fiorentino ✉ 52043

***Park**, on the main Via Umbro-Casentinese 88, t 0575 680 288, f 0575 680 008 (*moderate*). A big, modern hotel with a pool; not the most picturesque, but it's fine for a night or two.
**Antica Trattoria la Foce**, t 0575 658 187 (*moderate*). Situated just outside the centre at La Foce, this doesn't look particularly impressive, but it serves some of the most authentic food in the area. Choose from pasta dishes with boar, hare, duck or goose, and Valdichiana beef as a classic *secondo*; they also do a mean pizza. *Closed Mon and weekday lunchtimes.*

Florentine pupil Jacopo adopted his surname and went on to become chief sculptor and architect in Venice in its Golden Age. Monte San Savino, spread out on a low hill, is an attractive town with a *mélange* of late medieval and fine Renaissance palaces. Andrea Sansovino left several works to his home town: an attractive portal on the church of **San Giovanni**, terracottas (along with others by the della Robbias) in the little church of **Santa Chiara** in Piazza Jalta, and the lovely cloister of **Sant'Agostino** (13th-century, with a small rose window by Guillaume de Marcillat). Sansovino, or Antonio da Sangallo the Elder, designed the beautiful and harmonious **Loggia dei Mercanti**, with its grey Corinthian capitals in the early 1500s, while Antonio da Sangallo gets credit for the simple, partly rusticated **Palazzo Comunale**, originally the home of the Del Monte family, whose money paid for most of Monte San Savino's Renaissance ornaments. Foremost among the medieval monuments, the **Palazzo Pretorio** was built by the Perugians, while the city walls are the work of the Sienese.

On a cypress-clad hill two kilometres east, **Santa Maria della Vertighe** was built in the 12th century and restored in the 16th; it houses a rare 13th-century triptych by Margarito d'Arezzo and 14th-century works by Lorenzo Monaco. Some seven kilometres west there's the pretty **Gargonza**, with its mighty tower dominating a tight cluster of houses on a wart of a hill, the whole of which is now a hotel (*see* 'Where to Stay and Eat', above).

Best of all, perhaps, is cheerful little **Lucignano**, south of Monte San Savino, unique among Italian hill towns for its street plan – it will literally run you round in circles; Lucignano is laid out in four concentric ellipses, like a kind of maze, with four picturesque little *piazze* in the centre. One piazza is dominated by the Collegiata with a theatrical circular stair, another by the 14th-century **Palazzo Comunale**, now the Museo Civico, containing a good collection of 13th–15th-century Sienese works, a

Madonna by Signorelli, and, most famously, a 14th-century masterpiece of Aretine goldsmiths, the delicate reliquary *Albero di Lucignano*. There are more good Sienese paintings in the little tiger-striped church of **San Francesco**. Outside the centre there's a 16th-century Medici fortress, and the **Madonna delle Querce**, a Renaissance temple sometimes attributed to Vasari, with a fine Doric interior.

**Marciano della Chiana**, six kilometres northeast of Lucignano, is another old fortified village with an impressive main gate, which also does time as clock and bell tower. **Foiano della Chiana**, just to the south, is encompassed by newer buildings, but in its **Collegiata** has a good *Coronation of the Virgin* by Signorelli and a terracotta by Andrea della Robbia. Between Marciano and Foiano, keep an eye open for the curious octagonal church of **Santa Vittoria**, built by Ammannati for Cosimo I.

## Castiglion Fiorentino

To the east, piled on the last hill overlooking the Valdichiana plain, fortified **Castiglion Fiorentino** was known as Castiglion Aretino until the Florentines snatched it in 1384. Another age-old Etruscan settlement, with rather severe medieval streets, it nevertheless had more than a nodding acquaintance with the Renaissance. Like many a larger town (*see* Cortona, over), it built an ornamental geometric temple below the walls, the octagonal **Madonna della Consolazione**, untampered with since 1607. Then there's the 16th-century **Loggiato Vasariano**, overlooking the countryside from the old market square, and, opposite, the **Palazzo Comunale**. The 1860 plebiscite that brought Tuscany into the kingdom of Italy made a big impression here: the Palazzo Comunale has a marble plaque recording not only the precise vote, but the exact day, hour and minute of the count. The façade also fits in a computerized tourist information screen.

Just behind and above the Palazzo Comunale, Castiglion's ancient heart is known as the Càssero (from the Roman *castrum*): here you'll find a Palazzo Pretorio and the church of Sant'Angelo, the latter housing yet another small **Pinacoteca Civica** (*open Tues–Sun 10–12.30 and 4–6.30; closed Mon*). The prizes are a French Renaissance gilded silver reliquary bust of Sant'Orsola, a pair of 13th-century crucifixes, the *Stigmata of St Francis* by Bartolomeo della Gatta, a *portrait of St Francis* (1280) by the workshop of Margaritone di Arezzo, and the 15th-century *Probatica Piscina*, an uncommon subject (of Jerusalem's sheep pond, with curative waters) by Jacopo de Sellaio. The **Collegiata**, completely rebuilt in the 19th century, has kept its art: *Enthroned Madonnas* by Della Gatta, an *Adorazione* by Lorenzo di Credi and, in the adjacent Pieve Vecchia, Signorelli's fresco of the Deposition. Another church to aim for is Gothic 13th-century **San Francesco** with its cloister, some frescoes and a wooden *Crucifixion* sculpted by Giambologna.

Dilapidated castles from the bad old days are all around Castiglion, most impressively at **Montecchio**, four kilometres south, with its tall honey-coloured tower and walls, a landmark visible all over the Valdichiana. For a while in the 1400s it was the stronghold of the *condottiere* Sir John Hawkwood, he of the famous 'monument' by Uccello in Florence cathedral.

# Cortona

Floating high above the Valdichiana plain on terraced slopes of olives and vines, **Cortona** (pop. 27,000) figures among the crown jewels of Tuscan hill towns. Some 600m above sea level, sweeping down a spur of Monte Sant'Egidio, Cortona's crooked, cobblestone streets climb precipitously to the Medici fortress – even halfway up, between the houses, you can see Lake Trasimeno in Umbria and Mounts Amiata and Cetona near Siena. In Cortona, where babies are born with their heads in the clouds, three became celebrated artists: Luca Signorelli; Baroque painter Pietro Berrettini (1596–1669), better known as Pietro da Cortona, master of the rooms in the Pitti Palace; and Futurist-Impressionist-mosaicist Gino Severini (1883–1966), all of whom left works in their hometown.

Cortona's remarkable site brought it notoriety early on; according to Virgil and popular tradition, the city is nothing less than the 'Mother of Troy and Grandmother of

## Getting Around

Cortona is just off the main Florence–Arezzo–Rome **railway** line; the nearest station is Camucia, 5km west; if you're coming up from Umbria, the station is Teròntola, 10km south. Both stations have frequent LFI **buses** up to Cortona. There are also LFI train connections to Arezzo (34km/50mins), Castiglion Fiorentino, Foiano della Chiana, and Castiglione del Lago on Lake Trasimeno (22km/30mins); schedules for both buses and trains, and tickets for the former, are posted in the office in Via Nazionale, near the bus terminus and car park in panoramic Piazzale Garibaldi, or call t 0575 398 813.

## Tourist Information

Cortona: Via Nazionale 42, t 0575 630 352, f 0575 630 656. *Open winter Mon–Fri 9–1 and 3–6, Sat 9–1; summer Mon–Sat 9–1 and 3–7, Sun 9–1.*

## Events and Activities

**Antique furniture market**, *Aug–Sept*. Antiques are the big business in Cortona; besides the offerings in the town's shops, it hosts the national antique furniture market.
**Copperware show and market**, *April*. A showcase for another of the local handmade specialities.

**Umbria Jazz Festival**, *July*. Concerts are held thoroughout the month in the public gardens as part of the festival.
**Sagra di Bistecca** (festival of the beefsteak), *15 August*. Featuring a huge outdoor grilling of the Valdichiana's chief product.
**Swimming**: Just off the mountain road above Torreone, set amongst the chestnut woods at Tornia is a pool called the 'Priest's Hole', which is both prettier and more tranquil than the public pool at Il Sodo (no set fee, but they ask for a donation).
**Riding**: Horses can be hired from Unione Popolare Sport Equestre, loc. Ossaia, Montanino di Cortona, t 0575 67500.

## Where to Stay

**Cortona** ⊠ 52044
In Cortona, available lodgings have yet to catch up with demand, especially since the town is the site of both a language school and a University of Georgia art programme, operative beween June and October.
★★★**Oasi Neumann**, Via Contesse 1, t 0575 630 354, f 0575 630 354 (*expensive–moderate*). One of the nicest places to stay, with rooms in a fine old mansion, lovely gardens and a very warm welcome. *Open April–Oct.*
★★★**San Michele**, Via Guelfa 15, t 0575 604 348, f 0575 630 147 (*moderate*). Occupies a Renaissance palace, but has most mod-cons.

Rome' – founded by Dardanus, who according to legend was fighting against a neighbouring tribe when he lost his helmet (*corythos*) on the hill, thus giving the name *Corito* to the city that grew up on the spot. Dardanus later went on to Asia to found Troy and give his name to the Dardanelles. Like all myths, there may be a germ of truth in the story. The mysterious Etruscans themselves claimed to have come from Western Anatolia (perhaps around the year 900 BC), and inscriptions very similar to Etruscan have been found on the Greek island of Lemnos, near Troy; arte-facts from the Iron Age found in Anatolia and Tuscany suggest cultural affinities. Cortona was an important Etruscan city, one of the Dodecapolis and one of the largest in the north; ragged Etruscan stonework can still be seen in the foundations of its walls. These stretch over three kilometres of the perimeter, but still cover only two-thirds of the area of the original Etruscan fortifications; recent yields from Etruscan tumuli in the plain are certainly evocative of past grandeur.

**★★★San Luca**, Piazza Garibaldi 2, t 0575 630 460, f 0575 630 105 (*moderate*). Simple but comfortable; many of the rooms enjoy wonderful views.

**★Athens**, Via S. Antonio, t 0575 630 508. Named after Athens, Georgia, not Greece, this is a good budget choice (no rooms with en-suite) high up in the old town, with spacious rooms in an older building. *Open June–Nov.*

**Ostello San Marco**, Via Maffei 57, t 0575 601 392 (*cheap, with budget meals to match; IYHA card required*). One of Italy's more pleasant youth hostels, a 3km walk up from Piazza Garibaldi, and a viable option if all is full. *Open Mar–Oct.*

**Istituto Santa Margherita**, Via C. Battisti 15, t 0575 630 335/62162. Another cheap option, this has rooms with or without bath.

**★★★★Il Falconiere**, San Martino a Bocena, 3km away, t 0575 612 679, f 0575 612 927 (*luxury–expensive*). The local luxury choice is outside the centre; refined, frescoed and furnished with antiques and canopied beds, it also has a pool and a first class restaurant (*expensive*) serving delicious meat and fish dishes. *Closed Wed in winter.*

**★★★Portole**, Via Umbro Cortonese 39, in Portole, 9km from Cortona, t 0575 691 008, f 0575 691 035 (*moderate*). Further afield, this has pleasant rooms in a garden setting and good Valdichiana steaks in the restaurant. *Closed Fri, open April–Oct.*

# Eating Out

Cortona's restaurants are not fancy, but make a point of using local ingredients – home-made pasta, *salumeria* and beefsteaks from the Valdichiana, mushrooms and truffles in season, and the local white wines, called *bianchi vergini* (the white virgins).

**Tonino**, Piazza Garibaldi, t 0575 630 500 (*expensive*). Cortona's most elegant restau-rant, serving wonderful *antipasti*, followed by traditional pasta dishes and the tender beef. *Closed Mon eve and Tues.*

**Osteria del Teatro**, Via Maffei 5, t 0575 630 556. For half as many *lire*, this little place will fill you up with seasonal treats; in summer don't miss their ravioli with pumpkin flowers. *Closed Wed.*

**La Grotta**, Piazzetta Baldelli 3, t 0575 630 271 (*expensive–moderate*). Friendly but intimate restaurant that the Cortonese would like to keep secret. *Closed Tues.*

**Dardano**, Via Dardano 24, t 0575 601 944 (*moderate*). A simple *trattoria* with an elegant vaulted ceiling. It's popular with the locals, but the food is good. *Closed Wed.*

**Miravalle**, Frazione Torreone 6, t 0575 62232 (*moderate*). Situated on the edge of town, and aptly named, for its stunning views out over the valley. The food's not bad either; try their home-made tagliatelle.

**La Saletta**, Via Nazionale. If you feel thirsty rather than hungry, down some Tuscan wines with regional snacks at this little wine bar near the centre.

As a medieval *comune*, Cortona held its own against Perugia, Arezzo and Siena, while internally its Ghibellines and Guelphs battled until the Ghibellines won out, and when that fight was settled the ruling family, the Casali, spent the 14th century bumping each other off. This feast of self-destruction ended in 1409, when King Ladislas of Naples captured the city, selling it to Florence at a handsome profit.

## Palazzo Casali – Museo dell'Accademia Etrusca

*Open Tues–Sun 10–7; closed Mon; adm.*

The heart of Cortona, the **Piazza della Repubblica**, is a striking asymmetrical square, with lanes leading off in all directions. Dominant here is the **Palazzo Comunale** (13th-century), with a tower from 1503, its monumental steps a favourite place to dally away the early evening. Just behind is Cortona's most impressive medieval palace, the 13th-century **Palazzo Casali**, home of the city's murderous lordlings and now the seat of the Etruscan Academy, a cultural organization founded in the 17th century by the local nobility in search of Cortona's Etruscan roots.

Through the palazzo's attractive courtyard awaits the **Museo dell'Accademia Etrusca**, a fascinating collection begun by the Academy in 1727, encompassing a good set of Etruscan bronzes; Greek vases, attesting to the city's wealth and trading contacts of long ago; Egyptian mummies and a doll-like Egyptian funeral bark; and Cortona's most famous relic, an Etruscan bronze chandelier suspended in a little theft-proof gazebo, with 16 lamps dating back to the 5th century BC, found in a nearby field. Each of the lamps is a grotesque squatting figure, uncircling a ring of stylized waves and dolphins, and in the centre, an archaic gorgon. There is a fine collection of paintings, the oldest of which is a Roman portrait of the Muse Polyhymnia. Other works include paintings by Pietro da Cortona, *Two Saints* by Niccolò di Pietro Gerini, a 12th-century Tuscan mosaic of the Madonna, a fine polyptych by Bicci di Lorenzo, an incongruous self portrait by James Northcote, a Madonna by Pinturicchio, and another by Signorelli, who portrays her in the company of the saintly protectors of Cortona, with a nasty-looking devil squirming at their feet. One room is dedicated to Francesco Laperelli (1521–70) from Cortona, who built the walls of Valletta for the Knights of Malta; also ivories, globes of the earth and sky from 1714, costumes, the library founded by the Etruscan Academy in 1727, ceramics, and a fine Roman alabaster Hecate, the queen of the night. The latest permanent exhibition is the town's pride and joy: artefacts from and a re-creation of the inside of the Etruscan tumulus with the ripe name of the Secondo Melone di Sodo, excavated in 1991 (*see* p.470). Part of the tumulus' unique platform altar, sculpted with a man stabbing a lion while it bites off his head, is on display as well.

## Museo Diocesano

*Open April–Sept Tues–Sun 9.30–1 and 3.30–7; Oct–Mar Tues–Sun 10–1 and 3–5; closed Mon; adm.*

Behind the civic museum signs point the way back to the **Duomo**, an 11th-century church unimaginatively rebuilt in 1560, probably by Giuliano da Sangallo; inside there's a mosaic by Gino Severini. However, across the piazza in the deconsecrated church of Gesù there's the excellent **Museo Diocesano** with two masterpieces: Luca Signorelli's *Deposition*, with scenes of the Crucifixion and Resurrection (the latter composition inspired by his master Piero della Francesca) with an excellent *predella*, and a beautiful, luminous *Annunciation* by Beato Angelico, who came to Cortona to paint this solemn angel gently whispering his tremendous message; it has another exceptional *predella*. Note how the frame echoes the Corinthian columns of the loggia. Other works in the collection include a 14th-century crucifix by Pietro Lorenzetti, a triptych by Il Sassetta, a fine Sienese *Madonna* by the school of Duccio di Buoninsegna, and a 2nd-century AD Roman sarcophagus with reliefs of the Battle of Lapiths and Centaurs that was closely studied by Donatello and Brunelleschi. Don't miss the fine coffered wooden ceiling of the church itself. Below the Piazza del Duomo is one of Cortona's most picturesque lanes, the medieval Via Jannelli (or del Gesù), where some houses have *porte del morto* (doors of the dead), more common in medieval Umbria than in Tuscany. Other picturesque streets to look out for are Via Ghibellina, Via Guelfa and Via Maffei, with its town palaces.

## Up and Down Cortona

You'll need your climbing shoes to see the other monuments of Cortona, although **San Francesco** is only a short walk up from Piazza della Repubblica. St Francis's controversial lieutenant Brother Elias was a native of Cortona and founded this little church at an interesting angle in 1245; it still retains its original façade and one side. Both Brother Elias and Luca Signorelli are buried here, and on the left wall is a fine fresco of the *Annunciation*, the last work of Pietro da Cortona. On the high altar is a slice of the Holy Cross brought back from Constantinople by Brother Elias, housed in an ivory reliquary that Byzantine emperor Nicephoras Phocas carried into battle against the Saracens in the 960s, as described in the Greek inscription on the back. From here handsome Via Berrettini continues up to Piazza Pozzo and Piazza Pescaia and the medieval neighbourhood around **San Nicolò**. This handsome little Romanesque church, built by an anachronistic architect in the 1440s, was the seat of San Bernardino da Siena's Company of St Nicholas, for whom Luca Signorelli painted a magnificent standard of the *Deposition* still hanging by the altar.

You can reach the loftiest church of them all, the **Santuario di Santa Margherita**, from San Nicolò. The views become increasingly magnificent, until you reach the pretty 19th-century neo-Romanesque sanctuary. The original church was built by Santa Margherita (1247–97) a beautiful farmer's daughter and mistress of a young nobleman; upon his sudden death she got religion, became a Franciscan tertiary and founded a convent and hospital where she cared for the sick. Her remains are in a silver urn on the altar; her fine but empty Gothic sarcophagus on the left wall is by Angelo and Francesco di Pietro. To the right of the altar are standards and lanterns captured from the Turks in 18th-century sea battles, donated by a local commander. Just above, the overgrown **Medici Fortress** of 1556 occupies the site of the old Etruscan acropolis. Descend from Santa Margherita to the centre by way of Via Santa Margherita and the **Via Crucis**, made up of mosaic shrines by Gino Severini, commissioned in 1947 by the people of Cortona to thank their patron saint for sparing their city from the war.

As in many Etruscan and Roman towns, Cortona's gates are orientated to the four points of the compass. The northern **Porta Colonia** has an Etrusco-Roman arch and is near some well-preserved remains of the Etruscan walls; from here it's a 15-minute walk to the late, tall Renaissance church of **Santa Maria Nuova**, partly by Vasari and one of the more serene works to come out of the Counter-Reformation, designed in a Greek cross and crowned by a dome. Outside the southern **Porta Berarda**, at the end of Via Nazionale, the Gothic church of **San Domenico** has an elegant interior, presided over by a grand triptych by Lorenzo di Niccolò Gerini (1402) given to the Dominicans by Lorenzo de' Medici; and in the apse there's a *Madonna with Angels* by Signorelli. Nearby is a good stretch of Etruscan wall and the beginning of the Passeggiata Pubblica through Cortona's shady public gardens, the **Parterre**, with more grandstand views over the Valdichiana.

## Around Cortona

In the Renaissance it was fashionable in Tuscany and Umbria to decorate the outskirts of a town with a perfectly symmetrical church, exercises in geometry and divine order visible from all four sides – something, by the 16th century, impossible to do in the built-up town centres. Cortona has one of most graceful of these ornamental set pieces, **Santa Maria delle Grazie al Calcinaio**, isolated three kilometres down the road to Camucia. Built between 1485–1513 by Sienese architect Francesco di Giorgio Martini, this Latin cross topped with an octagonal drum has a harmonious interior, done in Brunelleschian dark and light accents, luminous and airy and pure, with accents in colour provided by fine stained glass by Guillaume de Marcillat. Unfortunately it's rarely open; ask at the tourist office.

Ancient tombs dot the plain below. One of the most evocative, the Hellenistic **Tanella di Pitagora**, is signposted from the crossroads near Santa Maria delle Grazie (*call ahead to visit,* **t** *0575 603 083*). Named after Pythagoras – apparently the ancients confused Cortona with Croton in Calabria, where the philosopher lived – the 3rd-century BC hypogeum is prettily surrounded by cypress trees and has an unusual vault over its rectangular funeral chamber. Northwest of Cortona, near the Camucia station, there's the 7th-century BC **Melone di Camucia**, an Etruscan tumulus containing two large chambers and corridors; and nearby, at Il Sodo ('the hard-boiled egg'), are two large 6th-century BC tumuli with massive walls, the **Meloni del Sodo** (*to visit tumulo I call one day in advance,* **t** *0575 630 415; guided tours available; adm*), 200m in perimeter. The keeper will take you around tumulo I; tumulo II, with its five mortuary chambers, yielded the treasures and altar in Cortona's museum and is still being excavated.

Beyond Santa Maria Nuova the road continues another three and a half kilometres along the slopes of Monte Sant'Egidio to the **Convento delle Celle**, founded by St Francis in 1211 in a beautiful setting. Little has changed; its simple rustic buildings have preserved their Franciscan spirit better than many others – the humble founder's cell retains the saint's stone bed.

# Glossary

**Acroterion**: decorative protrusion on the rooftop of an Etruscan, Greek or Roman temple. At the corners of the roof they are called *antefixes*.

**Ambones**: twin pulpits (singular: *ambo*), often elaborately decorated.

**Ambulatory**: an aisle around the apse of a church.

**Atrium**: entrance court of a Roman house or early church.

**Badia**: an abbey or abbey church also (*abbazia*).

**Baldacchino**: baldachin, a columned stone canopy above the altar of a church.

**Basilica**: a rectangular building, usually divided into three aisles by rows of columns. In Rome this was the common form for law courts and other public buildings, and Roman Christians adapted it for their early churches.

**Borgo**: from the Saxon *burh* of S. Spirito in Rome: a suburb or village.

**Bucchero ware**: black, delicately thin Etruscan ceramics, usually incised or painted.

**Calvary chapels**: a series of outdoor chapels, usually on a hillside, that commemorate the stages of the Passion of Christ.

**Campanile**: a bell tower.

**Campanilismo**: local patriotism; the Italians' own word for their historic tendency to be more faithful to their home towns than to the abstract idea of 'Italy'.

**Campo santo**: a cemetery.

**Cardo**: transverse street of a Roman *castrum*-shaped city.

**Carroccio**: a wagon carrying the banners of a medieval city and an altar; it served as the rallying point in battles.

**Cartoon**: the preliminary sketch for a fresco or tapestry.

**Caryatid**: supporting pillar or column carved into a standing female form; male versions are called *telamones*.

**Castrum**: a Roman military camp, always neatly rectangular, with straight streets and gates at the cardinal points. Later the Romans founded or refounded cities in this form, hundreds of which survive today (Lucca, Florence, Como, Brescia, Ascoli Piceno and Ancona are clear examples).

**Cavea**: the semicircle of seats in a classical theatre.

**Cenacolo**: fresco of the Last Supper, often on the wall of a monastery refectory.

**Chiaroscuro**: the arrangement or treatment of light and dark areas in a painting.

**Ciborium**: a tabernacle; the word is often used for large, free-standing tabernacles, or in the sense of a *baldacchino* (q.v.).

**Comune**: commune, or commonwealth, referring to the governments of the free cities of the Middle Ages. Today it denotes any local government, from the Comune di Roma down to the smallest village.

**Condottiere**: the leader of a band of mercenaries in late medieval and Renaissance times.

**Confraternity**: a religious lay brotherhood, often serving as a neighbourhood mutual-aid and burial society, or following some specific charitable work (Michelangelo, for example, belonged to one that cared for condemned prisoners in Rome).

**Contrapposto**: the dramatic, but rather unnatural twist in a statue, especially in a Mannerist or Baroque work, derived from Hellenistic and Roman art.

**Convento**: a convent or monastery

**Cosmati work**: or *Cosmatesque*: referring to a distinctive style of inlaid marble or enamel chips used in architectural decoration (pavements, pulpits, paschal candlesticks, etc.) in medieval Italy. The Cosmati family of Rome were its greatest practitioners.

**Crete**: in the pasturelands of southern Tuscany, chalky cliffs caused by erosion. Similar phenomena are the *biancane*, small chalk outcrops, and *balze*, deep eroded ravines around Volterra.

**Cupola**: a dome.

**Decumanus**: street of a Roman *castrum*-shaped city parallel to the longer axis, the central, main avenue called the Decumanus Major.

**Dodecapolis**: the federation of the twelve largest and strongest Etruscan city-states (*see* **History**, p.xx).

**Duomo**: cathedral.

**Ex voto**: an offering (a terracotta figurine, painting, medallion, silver bauble, or whatever) made in thanksgiving to a god or Christian saint; the practice has always been present in Italy.

**Forum**: the central square of a Roman town, with its most important temples and public buildings. The word means 'outside', as the original Roman Forum was outside the first city walls.

**Fresco**: wall painting, the most important Italian medium of art since Etruscan times. It isn't easy. First the artist draws the *sinopia* (q.v.) on the wall, then this is covered with plaster, but only a little at a time, as the paint must be on the plaster before it dries. Leonardo da Vinci's endless attempts to find clever short-cuts ensured that little of his work would survive.

**Ghibellines**: one of the two great medieval parties, the supporters of the Holy Roman Emperors.

**Gonfalon**: the banner of a medieval free city; the *gonfaloniere*, or flag-bearer, was often the most important public official.

**Graffito**: originally, incised decoration on buildings, walls, etc; only lately has it come to mean casually-scribbled messages in public places.

**Greek cross**: in the floor plans of churches, a cross with equal arms. The more familiar plan, with one arm extended to form a nave, is called a *Latin Cross*.

**Grisaille**: painting or fresco in monochrome.

**Grotesques**: carved or painted faces used in Etruscan and later Roman decoration; Raphael and other artists rediscovered them in the 'grotto' of Nero's Golden House in Rome.

**Guelphs** (*see Ghibellines*): the other great political faction of medieval Italy, supporters of the Pope.

**Intarsia**: decorative inlaid wood or marble.

**Loggia**: an open-sided gallery or arcade.

**Lozenge**: the diamond shape—these and stripes are trademarks of Pisan architecture.

**Lunette**: semicircular space on a wall, above a door or under vaulting, either filled by a window or a mural painting.

**Martroneum**: the elevated women's gallery around the nave of an early church, a custom adopted from the Byzantines in the 6th and 7th centuries.

**Narthex**: the enclosed porch of a church.

**Naumachia**: mock naval battles, like those staged in the Colosseum.

**Opus Reticulatum**: Roman masonry consisting of diamond-shaped blocks.

**Palazzo**: not just a palace, but any large, important building (though the word comes from the Imperial *palatium* on Rome's Palatine Hill).

**Palio**: a banner, and the horse race in which city neighbourhoods contend for it in their annual festivals. The most famous is at Siena.

**Pantocrator**: Christ 'ruler of all', a common subject for apse paintings and mosaics in areas influenced by Byzantine art.

**Pietra dura**: rich inlay work using semi-precious stones, perfected in post-Renaissance Florence.

**Pieve**: a parish church.

**Pluteo**: screen, usually of marble, between two columns, often highly decorated.

**Podestà**: in medieval cities, an official sent by the Holy Roman Emperors to take charge; their power, or lack of it, depended on the strength of the *comune*.

**Predella**: smaller paintings on panels below the main subject of a painted altarpiece.

**Presepio**: a Christmas crib.

**Putti**: flocks of plaster cherubs with rosy cheeks and bums that infested much of Italy in the Baroque era.

**Quattrocento**: the 1400s—the Italian way of referring to centuries (*duecento, trecento, quattrocento, cinquecento*, etc.).

**Sbandieratore**: flag-thrower in medieval costume at an Italian festival; sometimes called an *alfiere*.

**Sinopia**: the layout of a fresco (q.v.), etched by the artist on the wall before the plaster is applied. Often these are works of art in their own right.

**Stele**: a vertical funeral stone.

**Stigmata**: a miraculous simulation of the bleeding wounds of Christ, appearing in holy men like St Francis in the 12th century, and Padre Pio of Apulia in our own time.

**Telamon**: see *caryatid*.

**Thermae**: Roman baths.

**Tondo**: round relief, painting or terracotta.

**Transenna**: marble screen separating the altar area from the rest of an early Christian church.

**Travertine**: hard, light-coloured stone, sometimes flecked or pitted with black,

sometimes perfect. The most widely used material in ancient and modern Rome.

**Triptych**: a painting, especially an altarpiece, in three sections.

**Trompe l'œil**: art that uses perspective effects to deceive the eye—for example, to create the illusion of depth on a flat surface, or to make columns and arches painted on a wall seem real.

**Tympanum**: the semicircular space, often bearing a painting or relief, above the portal of a church.

**Voussoir**: one of the stones of an arch.

# Language

The fathers of modern Italian were Dante, Manzoni and television. Each played its part in creating a national language from an infinity of regional and local dialects; the Florentine Dante, the first to write in the vernacular, did much to put the Tuscan dialect into the foreground of Italian literature. Manzoni's revolutionary novel, *I Promessi Sposi*, heightened national consciousness by using an everyday language all could understand in the 19th century. Television in the last few decades has performed an even more spectacular linguistic unification; although many Italians still speak a dialect at home, school and work, their TV idols insist on proper Italian.

Italians are not especially apt at learning other languages. English lessons, however, have been the rage for years, and at most hotels and restaurants there will be someone who speaks some English. In small towns and out-of-the-way places, finding an Anglophone may prove more difficult. The words and phrases below should help you out in most situations, but the ideal way to come to Italy is with some Italian under your belt; your visit will be richer, and you're much more likely to make some Italian friends.

## Pronunciation

Italian words are pronounced phonetically. Every vowel and consonant except 'h' is sounded. Consonants are the same as in English, with the following exceptions.

The *c*, when followed by an 'e' or 'i', is pronounced like the English 'ch' (*cinque* thus becomes cheenquay). Italian *g* is also soft before 'i' or 'e' as in *gira*, or jee-rah. *Z* is pronounced like 'ts'. The consonants *sc* before the vowels 'i' or 'e' become like the English 'sh', as in sci, pronounced 'shee'. The combination *ch* is pronouced like a 'k', as in *Chianti*, 'kee-an-tee'. The combination *gn is pronounced* as 'nya' (thus *bagno* is pronounced ban-yo). The

combination *gli* is pronounced like the middle of the word million (so *Castiglione* is pronounced Ca-steel-yoh-nay).

Vowel pronunciation is as follows. *A* is as in English *father*. *E* when unstressed is pronounced like 'a' in *fate* (as in *mele*); when stressed it can be the same or like the 'e' in *pet* (*bello*). *I* is like the 'i' in *machine*. *O*, like 'e', has two sounds, 'o' as in *hope* when unstressed (*tacchino*), and usually 'o' as in *rock* when stressed (*morte*). *U* is pronounced like the 'u' in *June*.

The stress usually (but not always!) falls on the penultimate syllable. Accents indicate if it falls elsewhere (as in *città*). Also note that in the big northern cities, the informal way of addressing someone as you, *tu*, is widely used; the more formal *lei* or *voi* is commonly used in provincial districts, *voi* more in the south.

## Useful Words and Phrases

**yes/no/maybe** *si/no/forse*
**I don't know** *Non (lo) so*
**I don't understand (Italian)** *Non capisco (l'italiano)*
**Does someone here speak English?** *C'è qualcuno qui che parla inglese?*
**Speak slowly** *Parla lentamente*
**Could you assist me?** *Potrebbe aiutarmi?*
**Help!** *Aiuto!*
**Please** *Per favore*
**Thank you (very much)** *Grazie molte/mille*
**You're welcome** *Prego*
**It doesn't matter** *Non importa*
**All right** *Va bene*
**Excuse me/I'm sorry** *Permesso/Mi scusi/ Mi dispiace*
**Be careful!** *Attenzione!/Attento!*
**Nothing** *Niente*
**It is urgent!** *È urgente!*
**How are you?** *Come sta?*
**Well, and you?** *Bene, e Lei?/e tu?*

What is your name? *Come si chiama?/Come ti chiami*
Hello *Salve or ciao (both informal)*
Good morning *Buongiorno (formal hello)*
Good afternoon, evening *Buonasera*
Good night *Buona notte*
Goodbye *ArrivederLa (formal), Arrivederci/Ciao, (informal)*
What do you call this in Italian? *Come si chiama questo in italiano?*
What?/Who?/Where? *Che?/Chi?/Dove?*
When?/Why? *Quando?/Perché?*
How? *Come?*
How much (does it cost? *Quanto (costa)?*
I am lost *Mi sono perso*
I am hungry/thirsty/sleepy *Ho fame/sete/sonno*
I am sorry *Mi dispiace*
I am tired *Sono stanco*
I feel unwell *Mi sento male*
Leave me alone *Lasciami in pace*
good/bad *buono/cattivo*
well/badly *bene/male*
hot/cold *caldo/freddo*
slow/fast *lento/rapido*
up/down *su/giù*
big/small *grande/piccolo*
here/there *qui/lì*

## Days

Monday *lunedì*
Tuesday *martedì*
Wednesday *mercoledì*
Thursday *giovedì*
Friday *venerdì*
Saturday *sabato*
Sunday *domenica*
holidays *festivi*
weekdays *feriali*

## Numbers

one *uno/una*
two/three/four *due/tre/quattro*
five/six/seven *cinque/sei/sette*
eight/nine/ten *otto/nove/dieci*
eleven/twelve *undici/dodici*
thirteen/fourteen *tredici/quattordici*
fifteen/sixteen *quindici/sedici*
seventeen/eighteen *diciassette/diciotto*
nineteen *diciannove*
twenty *venti*
twenty-one/twenty-two *ventuno/ventidue*
thirty *trenta*
forty *quaranta*
fifty *cinquanta*
sixty *sessanta*
seventy *settanta*
eighty *ottanta*
ninety *novanta*
hundred *cento*
one hundred and one *centouno*
two hundred *duecento*
one thousand *mille*
two thousand *duemila*
million *un milione*

## Time

What time is it? *Che ore sono?*
day/week *giorno/settimana*
month *mese*
morning/afternoon *mattina/pomeriggio*
evening *sera*
yesterday *ieri*
today *oggi*
tomorrow *domani*
soon *fra poco*
later *dopo/più tardi*
It is too early/late *È troppo presto/tardi*

## Public Transport

airport *aeroporto*
bus stop *fermata*
bus/coach *autobus*
railway station *stazione ferroviaria*
train *treno*
platform *binario*
taxi *tassì/taxi*
ticket *biglietto*
customs *dogana*
seat (reserved) *posto (prenotato)*

## Travel Directions

One (two) ticket(s) to xxx, please *Un biglietto (due biglietti) per xxx, per favore*
one way *semplice/andata*
return *andata e ritorno*
first/second class *Prima/seconda classe*
I want to go to... *Desidero andare a...*

How can I get to...? *Come posso andare a...?*
Do you stop at...? *Si ferma a...?*
Where is...? *Dov'è...?*
How far is it to...? *Quanto è lontano...?*
What is the name of this station? *Come si chiama questa stazione?*
When does the next ... leave? *Quando parte il prossimo...?*
From where does it leave? *Da dove parte?*
How much is the fare? *Quant'è il biglietto?*
Have a good trip *Buon viaggio!*

# Driving

near/far *vicino/lontano*
left/right *sinistra/destra*
straight ahead *sempre diritto*
forward/backwards *avanti/indietro*
north/south *nord/sud*
east *est/oriente*
west *ovest/occidente*
crossroads *bivio*
street/road *strada/via*
square *piazza*
car hire *autonoleggio*
motorbike/scooter/moped *motocicletta/Vespa/motorino*
bicycle *bicicletta*
petrol/diesel *benzina/gasolio*
garage *garage*
This doesn't work *Questo non funziona*
mechanic *meccanico*
map/town plan *carta/pianta*
Where is the road to...? *Dov'è la strada per...?*
breakdown *guasto*
driving licence *patente di guida*
driver *guidatore*
speed *velocità*
danger *pericolo*
parking *parcheggio*
no parking *sosta vietata*
narrow *stretto*
bridge *ponte*
toll *pedaggio*
slow down *rallentare*

# Shopping, Services, Sightseeing

I would like... *Vorrei...*
Where is/are... *Dov'è/Dove sono...*

How much is it? *Quanto costa?*
open/closed *aperto/chiuso*
cheap/expensive *a buon prezzo/caro*
bank *banca*
beach *spiaggia*
bed *letto*
church *chiesa*
entrance/exit *ingresso/uscita*
hospital *ospedale*
money *soldi*
newspaper *giornale*
pharmacy *farmacia*
police station *commissariato*
policeman *poliziotto*
post office *ufficio postale*
sea *mare*
shop *negozio*
room *camera*
tobacco shop *tabaccaio*
WC *toilette/bagno/servizi*
men *Signori/Uomini*
women *Signore/Donne*

# Useful Hotel Vocabulary

I'd like a double room please *Vorrei una camera doppia (matrimoniale), per favore*
I'd like a single room please *Vorrei una camera singola, per favore*
with/without bath *con/senza bagno*
for two nights *per due notti*
We are leaving tomorrow morning *Partiamo domani mattina*
May I see the room, please? *Posso vedere la camera, per cortesia?*
Is there a room with a balcony? *C'è una camera con balcone?*
There isn't (aren't) any hot water, soap, *Manca/Mancano acqua calda, sapone,*
...light, toilet paper, towels *...luce, carta igienica, asciugamani*
May I pay by credit card? *Posso pagare con carta di credito?*
May I see another room please? *Per favore, potrei vedere un'altra camera?*
Fine, I'll take it *Bene, la prendo*
Is breakfast included? *E' compresa la prima colazione?*
What time do you serve breakfast? *A che ora è la colazione?*
How do I get to the town centre? *Come posso raggiungere il centro città?*

# Further Reading

## General

**Bentley, James and Palmer, Hugh,** *The Most Beautiful Villages of Tuscany* (Thames & Hudson, 1997). Lavish photos of 37 gems.

**Carmichael, Montgomery,** *In Tuscany* (Burns & Oates, 1910).

**Goethe, J.W.,** *Italian Journey* (Penguin Classics, 1982). An excellent example of a genius turned to mush by Italy; good insights, but big, big mistakes.

**Hutton, Edward,** *Florence and Assisi, in Unknown Tuscany,* and *Siena and Southern Tuscany* (Hollis & Carter). Modern travel classics.

**McCarthy, Mary,** *The Stones of Florence and Venice Observed* (Penguin, 1986). Brilliant evocation of Italy's two great art cities, with an understanding that makes many other works on the subject seem sluggish and pedantic; don't visit Florence without it.

**Mayes, Frances,** *Under the Tuscan Sun* and *Bella Tuscany* (Broadway Books). The best-selling Peter Mayle-style reads, about life as an expat in Tuscany.

**Morton, H.V.,** *A Traveller in Italy* (Methuen & Co., 1964). Among the most readable and delightful accounts of Italy in print. Morton is a sincere scholar and a true gentleman.

**Raison, Laura** (ed), *Tuscany: An Anthology* (Cadogan, 1983). An excellent selection of the best by Tuscans and Tuscany-watchers.

**Romer, Elizabeth,** *The Tuscan Year: Life and Food in an Italian Valley* (North Point, 1996). Daily life in a Tuscan village, as seen through foods, the seasons and harvests.

**Spender, Matthew,** *Within Tuscany* (Viking, 1992). Poet Stephen Spender's son, on everything from porcupines to Pontormo's bowel movements.

**Williams, Egerton R.,** *Hill Towns of Italy* (Smith, Elder, 1904). An Englishman goes exploring in Tuscany and Umbria.

## Art and Literature

**Boccaccio, Giovanni,** *The Decameron* (Penguin, 1972). The ever-young classic by one of the fathers of Italian literature. Its irreverent worldliness still provides a salutary antidote to whatever dubious ideas persist in your mental baggage.

**Burckhardt, Jacob,** *The Civilization of the Renaissance in Italy* (Harper & Row, 1975). The classic on the subject (first published in 1860), the mark against which scholars still level their poison pens of revisionism.

**Castiglione, Baldassare,** *The Courtier* (Penguin)

**Cellini, B.,** *Autobiography of Benvenuto Cellini* (Penguin, trans. by George Bull). Fun reading about the vicious competition of the Florentine art world by a swashbuckling braggart and world-class liar.

**Clark, Kenneth,** *Leonardo da Vinci* (Penguin).

**Dante, Alighieri,** *The Divine Comedy* (plenty of good translations). By far the greatest work of Dante, few poems have ever had such a mythical significance for a nation. Anyone serious about understanding Tuscany, Italy, the Italian language and the Italian's world view will need more than a passing acquaintance with Dante.

**Gardner, Edmund G.,** *The Story of Florence, The Story of Siena;* also Gordon, Lina Duff, *The Story of Assisi* and *The Story of Perugia* and Ross, Janet, *The Story of Pisa* (J.M. Dent, 1900s). All in the excellent and highly readable Medieval Towns series.

**Ghibert/Linscott,** *Complete Poems and Selected Letters of Michelangelo* (Princeton Press, 1984).

**Hale, J.R.,** editor, *A Concise Encyclopaedia of the Italian Renaissance* (Thames and Hudson, 1981). An excellent reference guide, with many concise, well-written essays. Also *Florence and the Medici: The Pattern of Control* (1977) which describes just how the Medici did it.

**Hibbert, Christopher,** *Rise and Fall of the House of Medici* (Penguin, 1965). One of the classics – compulsive reading.

**Hook, Judith,** *Siena* (Hamish Hamilton, 1979). A little weak on art, good on everything else.

**Leonardo da Vinci,** *Notebooks* (Oxford, 1983).

**Levey, Michael,** *Early Renaissance* (1967) and *High Renaissance* (both Penguin). Old-fashioned accounts of the period, with a breathless reverence for the 1500s – but still full of intriguing interpretations.

**Masson, Georgina,** *Frederick II of Hohenstaufen* (London, 1957).

**Murray, Linda,** *The High Renaissance* and *The Late Renaissance and Mannerism* (Thames and Hudson, 1977). Excellent introduction to the period; also Peter and Linda Murray, *The Art of the Renaissance* (1963).

**Origo, Iris,** *The Merchant of Prato* (Penguin, 1963). Everyday life in 14th-century Tuscany with the father of modern accounting, Francesco di Marco Datini. Also *Images and Shadows; War in the Val d'Orcia*, about a Tuscan childhood and life during the war.

**Petrarch, Francesco,** *Canzionere and Other Works* (Oxford, 1985). The most famous poems by the 'First Modern Man'.

**Procacci, Giuliano,** *History of the Italian People* (Penguin, 1973). An in-depth view from the year 1000 to the present – also an introduction to the wit and subtlety of the best Italian scholarship.

**Richards, Charles,** *The New Italians* (Penguin, 1995). An observant and amusing study of life in Italy during and since the political upheaval and the financial scandels in the early 1990s.

**Symonds, John Addington,** *A Short History of the Renaissance in Italy* (Smith, Elder, 1893). A condensed version of the authority of a hundred years ago, but still fascinating today.

**Vasari, Giorgio,** *Lives of the Painters, Sculptors and Architects* (Everyman, 1996). Readable, anecdotal accounts of the Renaissance greats by the father of modern art history.

# Index

Main page references are in **bold**. Page references to maps are in *italics*.

**Answers to 'A Florentine Puzzle' (see Topics, p.60)**
1 Façade to **San Miniato**
2 **Baptistry**, interior apse
3 Windows at the rear of **San Iacopo sopr'Arno**, visible from Santa Trínita
4 Windows, **Orsanmichele**
5 Façade, **Santa Croce** (inspired by Orcagna's tabernacle in Orsanmichele)
6 Baptistry doors (Pisano's and Ghiberti's first set); portico of the Bigallo, interior apse, **Santa Croce**
7 **Loggia dei Lanzi**
8 Rucellai Chapel, **San Pancrazio**

**PARIS**
Dana Facaros & Michael Pauls

**ROME**
Dana Facaros & Michael Pauls

CADOGANguides

CADOGANguides

**BRUSSELS**
Antony Mason

CADOGANguides

**Available Feb 2002**
Amsterdam
Barcelona
Brussels
Madrid
Paris
Rome

**Available June 2002**
Bruges
Florence
London
Prague
Sydney

Cadogan City Guides...
the life and soul
of the city

**CADOGAN**guides
well travelled well read

# Also available from Cadogan Guides in our European series...

## Italy

Italy
Italy: The Bay of Naples and Southern Italy
Italy: Lombardy and the Italian Lakes
Italy: Tuscany, Umbria and the Marches
Italy: Tuscany
Italy: Umbria
Italy: Northeast Italy
Italy: Italian Riviera
Italy: Bologna and Emilia Romagna
Italy: Rome and the Heart of Italy
Sardinia
Sicily
Rome, Florence, Venice
Florence, Siena, Pisa & Lucca
Venice

## Spain

Spain
Spain: Andalucía
Spain: Northern Spain
Spain: Bilbao and the Basque Lands
Granada, Seville, Cordoba
Madrid, Barcelona, Seville

## Greece

Greece: The Peloponnese
Greek Islands
Greek Islands By Air
Corfu & the Ionian Islands
Mykonos, Santorini & the Cyclades
Rhodes & the Dodecanese
Crete

## France

France
France: Dordogne & the Lot
France: Gascony & the Pyrenees
France: Brittany
France: Loire

France: The South of France
France: Provence
France: Côte d'Azur
Corsica
Short Breaks in Northern France

## The UK and Ireland

London–Amsterdam
London–Edinburgh
London–Paris
London–Brussels

Scotland
Scotland: Highlands and Islands
Edinburgh

Ireland
Ireland: Southwest Ireland
Ireland: Northern Ireland

## Other Europe

Portugal
Portugal: The Algarve
Madeira & Porto Santo

Malta
Germany: Bavaria
Holland

## The City Guide Series

Amsterdam
Brussels
Paris
Rome
Barcelona
Madrid
London
Florence
Prague
Bruges
Sydney

Cadogan Guides are available from good bookshops, or via **Grantham Book Services,** Isaac Newton Way, Alma Park Industrial Estate, Grantham NG31 9SD, **t** (01476) 541 080, **f** (01476) 541 061; and **The Globe Pequot Press,** 246 Goose Lane, PO Box 480, Guilford, Connecticut 06437–0480, **t** (800) 458 4500/**f** (203) 458 4500, **t** (203) 458 4603.

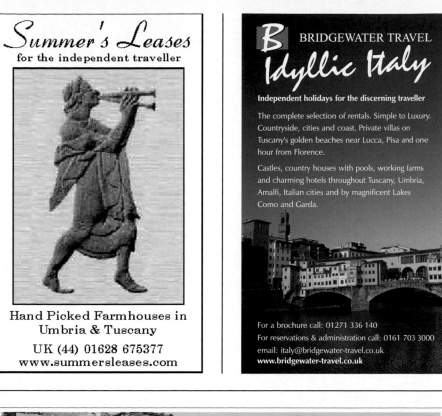

# CASTELLO DI RESCHIO - UMBRIA / TUSCANY BORDERS

'More than a house - a countinuous service' - *Egon Ronay, London*

Castello di Reschio is a unique 2,000-acre estate dating back to medieval times and preserving some 30 ancient farmhouses scattered across protected land. Purchasers enjoy custom-renovated homes designed with Italian gardens and interiors to highest standards. The state-of-the-art maintenance, security, letting and full concierge services, as well as sports and leisure facilities combined with a professional purchase process contribute to Reschio's seven years of proven success. In the cultural heart of Italy Count Antonio Bolza and his family have created and continue to provide the perfect hideaway for the most exclusive international clientele.

**Contact: Count Benedikt Bolza** CdR s.r.l.
TEL.: +39-075-844362  FAX: +39-075-844363
info@castellodireschio.com / www.castellodireschio.com

CHRISTIE'S
GREAT ESTATES

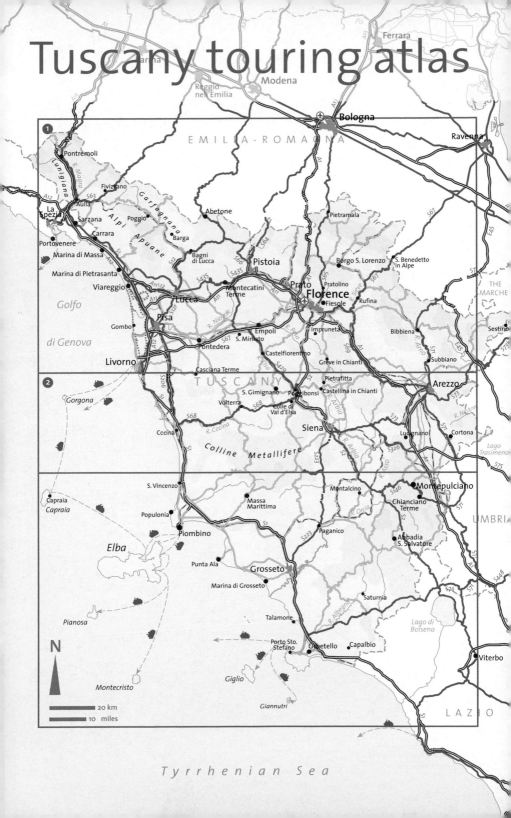
# Tuscany touring atlas

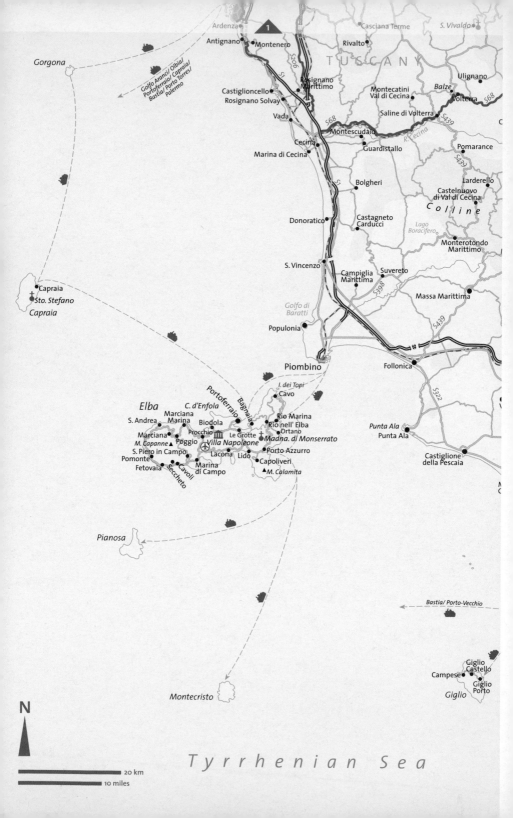

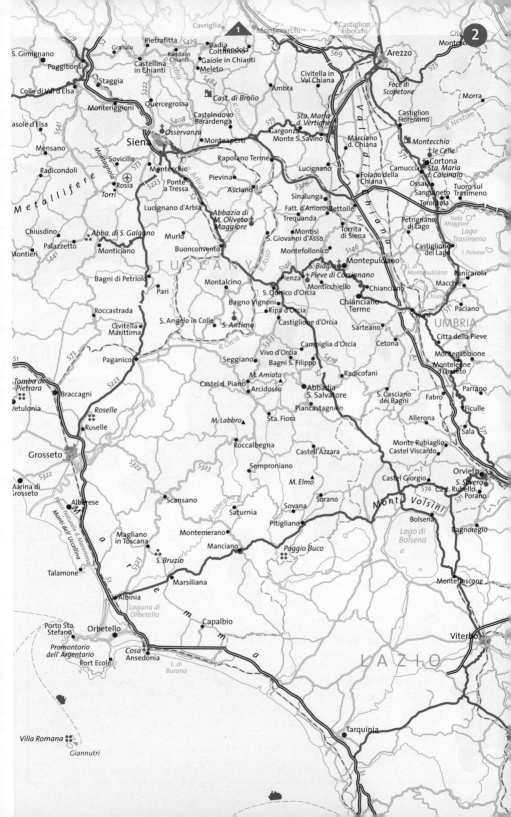

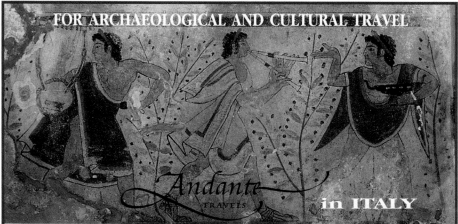

regional social institutions on organizational structures and strategies in an era of globalization.

**Andrew Parker** is Lecturer in Sociology/CEDAR at the University of Warwick. He was previously a Senior Lecturer in the School of Behavioural Studies at Nene University College, Northampton. He has written about the construction of masculinity in various educational and sporting locales.

**Ray Pawson** is a Reader in the School of Sociology and Social Policy at the University of Leeds. His main interest is research methodology and he has published widely on the principles and practice of research, covering methods – qualitative and quantitative, pure and applied, contemporaneous and historical. He is author of *A Measure for Measures: A Manifesto for Empirical Sociology* (Routledge, 1989) and (with N. Tilley) *Realistic Evaluation* (Sage, 1997). He is currently president of the Committee on Logic and Methodology of the International Sociological Association. He has recently served much time in prison (for research purposes), being the UK director of the International Forum on the Study of Education in Penal Systems.

**Leslie Sklair** is Reader in Sociology at the London School of Economics. He is on the Editorial Advisory Boards of the *Review of International Political Economy* and *Chinese Social Sciences Quarterly* and has served as a consultant to several United Nations bodies.

He has lectured at universities and at conferences all over the world. His publications include *Sociology of the Global System* (1995, translated into Portuguese, Japanese and Persian), *Assembling for Development: The Maquila Industry in Mexico and the United States* (1993) and he edited *Capitalism and Development* (1994). His paper, 'The transnational capitalist class and global capitalism: the case of the tobacco industry' appears in the journal *Politcal Power and Social Theory* (1998).

**Stephen Small** is Assistant Professor in the Department of African American Studies at the University of California, Berkeley. He is writing a book – *Black People of Mixed Origins in Jamaica and Georgia During Slavery: A Structural Analysis* – that entails an analysis of material inequalities, institutional practice and ideological articulations of 'race mixture'. His most recent book is *Racialised Barriers: The Black Experience in the United States and England in the 1980s* (Routledge, 1994).

**Alan Swingewood** is Senior Lecturer in Sociology at the London School of Economics. His main interests are sociological theory and the sociology of literature and culture. He has published widely in these areas and his books include *A Short History of Sociological Thought* (Macmillan, 1994) and *Cultural Theory and the Problem of Modernity* (Macmillan, 1998). His current research is a sociological and historical analysis of modern English culture focusing on music and modernist fiction.

**Steve Taylor** teaches medical sociology part time at the London School of Economics and Coventry University. He has undertaken research on suicide and self-harm, child care and medical law and his books include *Durkheim and the Study of Suicide* (Macmillan, 1982), *Suicide* (Longman, 1988), *Sociology of Health and Health Care* with D. Field (Blackwell, 1997) and *Sociological Perspectives on Health, Illness and Health Care*, edited with D. Field (Blackwell, 1998). He is a qualified lawyer and his current research is on the socio-legal aspects of changing attitudes to death. He is also the author of three sociology videos, the latest of which is on postmodernity.

# Preface

The motivation for this book came a few years ago when, having taken on the first year sociology course at the LSE, I was wading through the available introductory sociology textbooks. I found there wasn't one I could recommend with any enthusiasm. Too many corners had been cut, too many tired old ideas recirculated and too many new ones omitted. Instead of being immersed in their topics, the writers often gave the impression that they were peering rather vaguely at them from a distance. In my view this was not the fault of the authors; indeed, it seemed to me most of them had done a pretty good job in the circumstances. It was just that 'the circumstances' seemed insurmountable. Sociology has become such a massive and diverse enterprise that the task of mastering the range of material now available is simply beyond a single author, or even a small team of authors.

*Sociology: Issues and Debates* is based on the very different idea of producing a *general* sociology text that makes use of *specialist* knowledge by having each chapter written by authors with established records of writing and research in the area. However, the contributors were chosen not only for their specific expertise, but also for their ability to write in a clear and accessible way and every effort has been made in this book to keep complex sociological terminology to a minimum. Terms of central importance, such as methodology, theory and the various dimensions of power, are all explained in the relevant chapters and a glossary of other key concepts is provided at the back of the book.

To try to ensure consistency, each chapter is structured around the origins, key ideas, development and current concerns of sociological work in the areas that have been examined. However, in a book with so many contributors, it is inevitable that there are some variations in style and emphasis. In my view, these variations are less a reflection of individual preferences and idiosyncrasies than of the different ways in which the specialist areas of sociology have developed. Two key differences can be identified in this context. First, while some areas in sociology have been driven primarily by theoretical developments, others, such as the sociology of health and medicine, are predominantly empirically orientated. Second, while some areas of research seem to be characterized by a sense of uncertainty, as if sociologists working within them recognize they are trying to construct a jigsaw puzzle where most of the pieces are missing, in other areas most sociologists do not seem greatly troubled by any sense of doubt, the picture is clear and sociology is about helping to right the wrongs it clearly reveals. My own position on this latter issue, for what it is worth, is that sociology sometimes has to be a little more robust in its assertion and defence of its capacity to provide specialist knowledge of human societies. However, at the same time, the exercise of justifying our claims to special knowledge lead us to recognize that the limitations of sociological theories and methods simply do not allow us to be *that* certain about anything. However, this book is not about my views, it is about how the key areas of sociology are seen by those with expert knowledge of them.

I would like to express my gratitude to all the contributors not only for their excellent work but also for their patience and co-operation with my various editorial requests. I should also like to thank Alf Barrett, David Field, Rosie Gosling, Tony Lawson, Andrew Pilkington, Jo Roberts, Keith Sharp and Nick Tilley for their help with various chapters; thanks also to Sue Taylor for her editorial help with all the chapters and, finally, to Catherine Gray of Macmillan for helpful and perceptive advice throughout this project.

STEVE TAYLOR

# 1

# Introduction

## *Steve Taylor*

---

Sociology is the most ambitious of all the social sciences. It is concerned with all that happens to people in terms of their relations with each other and the scope of its inquiries can range from things such as the mass movement of populations over centuries to two commuters catching each other's eye on the morning train to work. The key idea of sociology is that the lives of individuals cannot be understood apart from the social contexts in which they live. This chapter aims to introduce readers to the idea of 'sociological thinking', illustrate the importance of theory for all sociological research and outline the key areas of applied sociological research around which this book is organized. It should help you understand:

- The key questions sociologists ask about human societies

- Why all social research is theory dependent

- What the central areas of applied sociological research are

- The relationship of sociology to modernity

---

### CONCEPTS

social order ■ socialization ■ objective knowledge
theory dependence ■ social structure ■ social action ■ life chances
social institutions ■ modernity ■ postmodernity

# What is Sociology?

The simplest definition of sociology is that it is the study of human societies. It stresses the *interdependence* of different parts of societies and attempts to go beyond the description of specific events by establishing *generalizations*. For example, we all know that there are hundreds of different occupations but rather than trying to classify them all, some sociologists have argued that groups of people who do much the same type of job and earn roughly the same amounts of money may be generalized as constituting distinct 'social classes'. Sociologists also attempt to be systematic in the ways they study societies. Rather than just snatching at 'facts' which happen to support a particular point of view, they try to collect evidence in a more consistent way. For example, sociologists interested in health and illness could look at rates of illness between different social classes and this may then allow them to make further generalizations about the relationship between health and society.

However, defining sociology as the systematic study of societies does not take us far enough, because there are other academic subjects – anthropology, economics, politics and psychology for example – which also attempt to make systematic generalizations about social behaviour. So, as sociology cannot be defined either in terms of *what* it studies (people living in families, going to work, getting ill and so on) or in terms of *how* it studies them (making generalizations, interpreting statistics, asking questions and so on), how is it distinguishable from the other social sciences? The answer to this is to be found in the *questions* that sociologists ask about social life. Sociology begins by asking how societies are possible. The fact that social life is a problem to be explained rather than a natural condition makes sociology *the* social science. It is first and foremost a particular way of thinking about societies. It involves being curious about the very fact of social order, about how it changes and, above all, about how our lives as individuals are shaped by the societies in which we live. I shall now consider each of these questions in a little more detail.

## *The Order of Social Life*

Walk out into the street and just watch for a few minutes. There is social order all around you – people walking in an orderly way, queuing in line at bus stops, stopping their cars at red lights and so on. This is a taken for granted order and it is likely that the only time most people are aware of it is when someone breaks the rules, for example by moving straight to the front of the queue or not stopping the car at a red light. It seems as if there are sets of rules to social life which most people play by most of the time. Of course, we do not need sociologists to tell us that there are rules to social life. We know ourselves as members of society that we must not drive through red lights and that if we miss sociology classes and do not read the books, we will probably fail the course.

However, if we dig a little deeper we find more evidence of these regularities. For example, in a contemporary society roughly the same number of people are born each year, get married, get divorced, commit crimes or kill themselves. It seems as if there are other, underlying sets of rules by which people are unconsciously playing and which can, literally, affect their lives. For example, in developed societies, year in and year out, the death rates of people from the manual, or working, classes are consistently higher than those of the professional and managerial classes. Similarly, adults with few close social ties to other people have rates of illness which are more than double those with strong social ties.

Sociologists are interested in documenting and trying to explain these regularities of social life. They are interested in the unusual – things like mass suicides in religious cults, bizarre crimes and revolutions – but their starting point is a curiosity about the taken for granted world of order and regularity that is all around us. However, a problem for the sociologist is that, unlike the objects studied by most scientists, societies do not stand still, but are constantly changing.

## Social Change and Narrative

Sociology began in nineteenth-century western Europe at a time of unprecedented and rapid social upheaval. There was a mass movement of population from the countryside to towns and cities, as an economic system based predominantly on agricultural production and craft industries gave way to a new industrial-capitalist economic order built around machine technology, organized labour and the systematic pursuit of profit. Localized personal authority, based on inheritance and aristocratic privilege, declined and political power became increasingly centralized in bureaucratic nation states. Culturally, traditional and customary ways of doing things were replaced by rational planning and bureaucratic regulations. Religious institutions increasingly lost power and authority, and religious interpretations of the world gave way to scientific and rational explanations. These changes are generally referred to as the transition from *traditional* to *modern* society.

The fact that societies could be transformed so dramatically and in such a comparatively short space of time led to an increasing curiosity about the nature of social order and social change. The subject that became sociology was born out of this curiosity. Some of the earliest sociologists such as Auguste Comte (1798–1857), who coined the term sociology, and Karl Marx (1818–93) tried to make sense of this new present by *comparing* it with what had come before. They tried to describe the main characteristics of this new industrial order and explain why western societies had developed this way. They also believed there was a purpose to these changes and that history was a progressive movement to 'higher' forms of social order. They were confident that careful application of scientific methods to the study of societies would reveal the sources of this change and that understanding the 'laws of historical progress' gave the power to anticipate and influence the future.

Today, most sociologists are much less optimistic about the societies they study and they talk about them changing rather than progressing. They are also rather less ambitious for sociology. Few believe that societies can be understood in the same way as the natural world; most of them talk about trends rather than laws and few attempt to predict the future. However, in some ways they are still like the early sociologists. They are trying to make sense of the present, but looking only at the present is a bit like coming into a film halfway through. To have any idea of what the film is about, you have to try to work out what has already happened. It is the same for sociologists. They can only make sense of the present by comparing it with what has just ceased to be. Sociology, then, involves a sense of narrative and a sense of history. As the chapters in the book will show, thinking sociologically means developing ideas which help us to understand societies, or aspects of them, as continually changing social processes.

## The Individual and Society

Most people assume, and many social scientists argue, that as societies are clearly created by individuals, it is the study of the individual (through psychology and socio-biology for example) that provides the best way to understand societies. For example, in all human societies, most of which developed independently of each other, the fact that women have taken responsibility for things like nurturing the young and caring for the sick, while men have fought wars and run political institutions, could be explained in terms of the differences in 'natural' female and male instincts.

In questioning the idea that social behaviour can be reduced to the study of the individual, sociologists are not, as is sometimes claimed, rejecting the study of the individual in favour of the 'group'. Indeed, a great deal of sociological research involves talking to and observing individuals. It is rather that thinking sociologically involves seeing the relationship between the individual and society as a two-way, rather than a one-way, street. Individuals obviously create societies by their actions but, less obviously, individuals are also created by societies. But how can this happen?

As social life evolves from its most basic forms, certain types of behaviour and belief, such as religious practices or tribal customs, become reproduced by successive generations as 'accepted' ways of doing things. In sociological terms they become *institutionalized*. Language is a good example of a social institution. People learn their language and use it for their own purposes, but none of them created it and it will be there after they have gone. Many key areas in sociology, such as the family, education, work and religion, are defined around the study of distinct social institutions. The values and beliefs surrounding the institutional practices of a society or social group comprise its *culture*. The various ways in which this culture is transmitted to people, which begins from the time they are born and goes on throughout their lives, is called *socialization*. The pressures placed directly and indirectly on people to conform to the values and practices of a society is called *social control*. Of course, as people we are not simply passive recipients of socialization. We have various ways of responding to the expectations social institutions place on us: some may conform willingly, others reluctantly, while some may resist. However, even those who resist and try to behave in a very different way are still confronted by the pressure of social expectations. For example, if I refuse to speak in my native language and insist on speaking in some other way, I am still confronted by the institutional expectation to speak in a certain way. People may refuse, or find it impossible, to communicate with me; I may be refused work or perhaps treated as insane and locked up.

To return to the earlier example of differences in the behaviour of males and females. Sociologists, without necessarily rejecting biological explanations, have shown that there is still a tendency for different expectations to be placed on boys and girls. For example aggressive, boisterous behaviour is more acceptable in boys, while girls are expected to take on more domestic chores and help with younger siblings. Thus, to some extent, boys and girls learn to take on 'masculine' and 'feminine' roles: becoming a man or a woman is not simply a product of biology, it is also a process of socialization. These processes of socialization and social control are not confined to childhood. In Chapter 6 Mary Maynard shows how relations between women and men are structured and shaped by institutional practices, such as the sexual division of domestic labour, the law and the state, which act as sources of social control on women.

So far I have been looking at what sociology is in terms of the questions that sociologists ask about societies. However, to justify investment in sociological research, sociology departments in schools and universities (to say nothing of your investment in this book), sociology has to do rather more than ask interesting questions. It has to come up with a few answers. Furthermore, it has to validate these answers, that is, show that they are something more than opinion or common sense. To begin to understand how sociologists go about doing this and some of the problems they face, we have to know something about theory and method in sociology.

## Theory and Method

It sometimes a source of annoyance to those involved in 'real' research that some of the most famous sociologists just write about theory. However, there are good reasons for sociologists' preoccupation with theory. Put simply, theory is unavoidable. First, all research findings are *dependent* on some form of theory. Second, it is only through theories that sociologists can hope to make sense of their data. Although these points are linked, I shall take each in turn.

Supposing I say that I am not interested in all this theorizing and that I just want to get on and do a piece of 'real' research, and uncover 'the facts' about the relationship between social class and illness. However, this ambition is just not tenable, because the very act of doing a piece of research *necessarily* involves making certain unproven – that is, *theoretical* – assumptions about the nature of the social world and how it is to be studied. Why is this so?

Before I can start my research I have to have a definition of social class and, as you will see in Chapter 5, sociologists have some very different ideas about what social class is. Thus I have to select, or construct for myself, what I think is the most appropriate idea of class. This is then a *theoretical* definition. Similarly, although it may seem obvious whether or not person is ill, I have to define what I mean by illness. For example, do I use a *subjective* definition of whether or not people *feel* ill and simply ask them, or do I use some more *objective* definition, such as whether or not a doctor has diagnosed them as ill? If I use the latter do I count all illnesses (in which case having a cold and having cancer would count in the same figure) or do I just count 'serious' illnesses and leave others out? The permutations are endless, but the point is that to do my research, I *have* to use theoretical notions of 'social class' and 'illness'. These ideas will then shape the 'facts' I come up with. Different theoretical ideas may well produce very different 'facts'. Research is thus dependent on theory. Rather than pretend otherwise, as sociologists are sometimes tempted to do when they are putting forward a favoured case, it is important to remember that data are not self-evident 'facts', but reflections of the theoretical ideas in terms of which they are collected. Thus, in assessing a piece of sociological research, it not just a question of what sociologists are telling us, but also a question of *how* they found out, how they can validate what they are telling us. This is where *methodology* comes in. It is the study of how sociologists find out.

In Chapter 2, Ray Pawson identifies the main principles of social research and illustrates some of the different strategies sociologists use to study the social world. Although there is considerable debate between the proponents of these different approaches all of them are confronted with the questions of how their research is validated. For many sociologists the aim of sociological research is to produce *objective* knowledge of societies – that is, knowledge which is free from bias and prejudice. They argue that the best way to achieve this is by following, as far as possible, the methods of the natural sciences, for example, by using clearly defined concepts that produce data that can be measured, compared and checked by other researchers. Other sociologists argue that the theory-dependent nature of research data and the fact that the same piece of data is open to different interpretations, means that sociology has to abandon its quest for objectivity. Sociological accounts are therefore validated not by any claims of scientific truth, but by the rich and authentic data they produce. However, if this view is taken it then becomes difficult to establish whether one account is better than any other. Sociology simply offers different interpretations and this view is called relativism.

In his chapter Pawson argues that for a long time discussion of methodology became trapped into a position of mutual hostility between these two approaches with the assumption that sociologists were obliged to choose one way or the other. However, contemporary thinking on methodology is moving on from this 'war'. For example, developing his position from more recent 'realist' philosophies of science and social science which attempt to reconcile the goal of objectivity with the theory-dependent nature of all data, Pawson argues that the purpose of empirical research is not to test whether a theory is 'true' or not, but rather to identify the competing theories and generate data which help the researcher to choose between them. This point of view means recognizing that, while sociological research can never be proved to be universally 'true', neither can we lapse into a relativism where one account is as good as any other. Research can show that one theory is better than another in given circumstances. Although complete objectivity is impossible in practice, it can still serve as a goal to which good research should aspire.

The second point is that theory is not just essential to the generation of data, it is also crucial to their interpretation and to the direction of further research. Suppose I have done my research on class and health. To try to make sense of this mass of data without theory would be rather like arriving late at night in a foreign city without a map. To pluck a statistic here, an interview extract there without the guidance of some theory would have no more purpose than wandering aimlessly from street to street with no idea where I was, where I had come from, or where I was going.

Of course, sociologists do not wander aimlessly through their data. Their research has a sense of direction and this comes from theory. For example, I might want to see if the relationship between health and class is influenced more by 'material' factors, such as type of housing, or lifestyle choices, such as diet. This would then guide me to construct research that might throw some light on this question. I might also want to relate my specific research on class and health to wider social contexts in which case I need some more general theory of how societies work and change. In short, theoretical ideas guide the research and give it a sense of purpose. They shape how it is structured, how the data are interpreted and how specific research data are related to other aspects of society.

Sociological theories, then, are kinds of 'sociological maps' that help researchers find their way around the mass of data available to them. Of course, just because we have a map does not solve all the problems. It is very easy to get lost! Sociological maps are always incomplete and are sometimes very sketchy. For some sociologists committed to a particular point of view they consist of little more than a single street. There is also the problem that sociologists working in the same area may be using very different maps! To understand where sociologists are taking us we need to know something about the maps they are using. This is where sociological theorists come in. They are the sociological cartographers. They examine the maps, compare them, identify in what ways they are different and where they are similar. They raise questions, such as whether the maps can be made clearer, extended, combined, updated and made relevant to new social developments.

Many of the earliest social theorists like Karl Marx and Emile Durkheim (1858–1917) developed theoretical maps which were rather like street plans of the whole city, looking at how the different parts were linked together. Theories which look at societies as a whole are called *structural* and the focus of research is on *macro-society;* that is, large-scale organizations and widespread social processes such as the distribution of resources within societies. However, Max Weber (1864–1920), another of the classical theorists, took a different approach. He argued that such large-scale maps tell us very little about the day-to-day lives of the people living in these streets. Individuals do not just react to social conditions but consciously act in certain directions. Thus, for Weber, sociological theory should be about what is called *social action.* It has to incorporate understanding of the meanings that individuals give to their action and what motivates them to act in certain ways. From this point of view, social research tends to focus on the *micro-dimensions* of social life, that is, detailed study of small-scale social processes.

The linking of macro- and micro-social processes is a major problem in sociology and it is the focal point of Alan Swingewood's chapter (3). He begins with the work of the classical sociologists and then examines the contribution of the major perspectives of 'modern' social theory, function-alism and interactionism. Structural functionalist theory, which tries to combine Durkheim's notion of structure with Weber's idea of action, starts with the idea of societies as systems into which individuals are socialized. Interactionism, in contrast, begins with the problem of how individuals make sense of the situations in which they find themselves and focuses on the importance of language in linking the micro with the macro. The final part of Swingewood's chapter looks at some of the more recent attempts in social theory to synthesize the macro- and micro-aspects of society, including those of three of the most famous theorists in contemporary sociology: Habermas, Giddens and Bourdieu.

Power is another central issue for sociological theory as the relations between individuals and institutions studied by sociologists necessarily involve questions of authority, control and actual (and potential) conflicts of interest. But what do sociologists mean by power and how is it used in sociological analysis? These questions are addressed in Chapter 4 by Chris-tine Helliwell and Barry Hindess. They identify the three meanings of power most commonly used in sociology. The first of these is power as 'control or command over others', a capacity to get people to do what you want even if they do not want to. From this point of view, sociologists have been interested in identifying which social groups have power (and which do not) and the social conditions under which it is produced. For example, the famous American sociologist C. Wright Mills (1916–62) argued that political power in America was concentrated in a comparatively small 'élite', whose power stemmed from their control of the major institutions of industry, government and military.

The second meaning of power considered by Helliwell and Hindess is the legal ability or authority to act; for example, the legal right of governments to pass laws and collect taxes. While some sociologists, such as Weber, have merely concerned themselves with how legitimacy is established, most of them have taken a more *critical* stance and questioned whether or not such legitimacy is justified. For example, Mills argued that what he called the American 'power élite' were more concerned with their own interests rather than those of the majority of the population and, as they often used secret and 'undemocratic' means to pursue these ends, their authority was not legitimate as the people were not in a position to give true consent. However, as Helliwell and Hindess observe, the lack of any clear criteria for deciding whether or not true consent has been given, leads to sociologists passing judgement on the basis of their own preferences and commitments.

The third much more general meaning of power identified by Helliwell and Hindess is simply the ability to do or affect anything. From this point of view, power is not a 'resource' which some groups have more or less of, but simply an inevitable feature of everyday life. Contemporary social theory has become increasingly influenced by the development of this view in the work of the French social theorist, Michel Foucault (1926–84). Foucault's approach directs attention away from measuring power and debating its legitimacy towards trying to understand its effects. For example, Foucault and those influenced by him have shown how in modern societies government does not only come directly from the state (through laws and so on) but also indirectly from institutions such as education and medicine that also help to regulate citizens' conduct. For followers, the advantages of Foucault's approach is that sociology does not become trapped in intractable debates about who does or does not have power and whether or not it is legitimate.

Just as there can be no sociological research without theory, there is little point in developing theory for theory's sake in sociology. Theoretical ideas are only relevant to the extent that they inform research. Ideas have to be put into action to illuminate aspects of social life. The following section outlines the main areas of applied sociological research around which this book is organized.

# Key Areas of Sociological Research

## Social Divisions

Most sociologists are not concerned simply with how societies work and change, they are also interested in how they might be improved. A long-standing concern in this context has been with questions of various forms of social inequality. For many sociologists, the obvious inequalities of wealth, opportunity and status we see all around us are neither inevitable nor merely the result of differences of individual talent and effort. Rather, they are the consequence of institutional arrangements in societies that give rise to systematic differences in the 'life chances' of different social groups. From this point of view societies are not characterized by a consensus of common interests, but by conflicts of interest (acknowledged or not) between different social groups.

Of the classical sociologists, Marx was the most strident advocate of a conflict view. He argued that all societies were divided into a ruling class and subordinate classes. The ruling class owed its dominance to its ownership and control of the means of producing economic wealth. Modern industrial societies were dominated by the capitalist class which owned the factories and financial institutions. However, Marx did not see this inequality as permanent. He argued that class conflict in modern societies would lead to a new type of 'classless' socialist society, where the means of production would be collectively owned. Marx's predictions have not been realized, but the idea of social class – that is, a group of people sharing a similar economic position – continues to be seen by many sociologists as one of the most important, if not the most important, division in contemporary societies.

In Chapter 5 Rosemary Crompton begins by looking at the origins of the concept of social class in the classical sociology of Marx and Weber. She then looks at some of the key issues in the contemporary study of social class; the techniques of and problems involved in measuring class, the impact of recent social changes on class formation and the question of whether or not it still makes sense to talk of social classes in an increasingly fluid and individualized social world.

While the study of class has a long history, the sociological study of gender and gender relations is comparatively recent. As Mary Maynard observes in Chapter 6, there was little systematic study of gender and women prior to 1970. Maynard begins by illustrating how increased interest in gender has not only opened many new areas of study pertaining to women's experiences, but also led to new feminist ways of thinking sociologically. She then looks at the sexual division of labour in households, sexuality and violence and the law and state as examples of institutional arrangements which have functioned to reinforce existing patterns of gender relations and, in particular, the subordination of women to men. However, as Maynard notes, conventional ideas of gender and gender relations (like class relations) have recently been subjected to some critical scrutiny. In an increasingly diverse and rapidly changing world, it is becoming more difficult to conceptualize women and men as clearly identifiable social groups and some recent research has been concerned not simply with differences *between* women and men, but also with differences *within* these categories.

A third area of social division studied by sociologists focuses on 'racial' and ethnic inequalities. The word 'race' is invariably placed in quotation marks because it occupies an apparently paradoxical position in social research. While most sociologists (and scientists) reject the idea of naturally occurring 'racial' groups with fixed biological and mental attributes, they remain interested in the ways in which *ideas* of 'race' and 'race relations' contribute to discrimination and inequalities in societies.

Robert Miles and Stephen Small begin Chapter 7 with discussion of this problem, arguing that sociological explanations of 'racial' and ethnic inequalities have to be focused on economic, political and institutional processes that operate to create and sustain them. In this context, they put forward the key concept of *racialization*, which refers to processes whereby certain groups come to be *thought of* as constituting distinct biological races. Processes of racialization are independent of any specific physical attributes, such as skin colour. While in contemporary European societies most people are familiar with the racialization of diverse ethnic groups from Africa, the Caribbean and Asia, there have been many instances of the racialization of Europeans by other Europeans. For example, the Irish have been racialized by the British and the racialization of the Jews in Germany was a prelude to their mass slaughter by the Nazis. In the second part of the chapter Miles and Small compare the idea of racialization with more traditional sociological approaches based on the centrality of race, while the final section looks at patterns of racialized inequality in Britain.

## Social Institutions

In spite of the rapidly changing nature of contemporary societies, most people living in them still grow up in families, spend many years in full-time education and the majority go to work in organizations of one sort or another. Sociologists have had a longstanding interest in the key social institutions of family, education and work; in particular, how they change, their relationship to each other and to other institutional processes, and how their organization and structure affects individuals' lives.

Traditionally, the sociology of 'the family' was primarily concerned with the relationship between different types of family life and wider society; for example, the changes to the family brought about by industrialization.

Sociologists tended to assume that experiences of family life were by and large positive and that problems were brought about by 'external' factors, such as poverty or war. However, as Stevi Jackson observes in Chapter 8, more recent research has tended to undermine these old sociological certainties about the family. First, the increasing instability and diversity of patterns of domestic life has led some sociologists to question whether it still makes any sociological sense to talk about the family. Second, many sociologists – and feminist sociologists in particular – have become increasingly sceptical about family life, arguing that families *themselves* can both reflect and reinforce patterns of inequality between women and men and adults and children.

Jackson argues that in spite of their increasing diversity, there remain regularities of family life which generate systematic economic and emotional inequalities between women and men; not only do women on average contribute more labour than men to the running of families, they also put in more emotional labour to child care and to the marriage itself. The chapter concludes by looking at relationships between adults and children and some of the current issues facing the sociology of the family.

Most of the early sociological work on education, like that on the family, was concerned with the macro-issue of the relationship of educational institutions (mainly schools) to wider institutional processes. For example, Durkheim argued that schools had an integrative function; first, by helping to socialize children into social values and second, by providing them with the opportunity to develop their skills and talents. An alternative macro-approach, developed more from Marxist ideas, argued that rather than creating equality of opportunity, education systems served to reproduce existing divisions of class and status. The extent to which education does, or does not, provide some form of equality of opportunity has been a recurring theme in educational studies and Robert Burgess and Andrew Parker begin Chapter 9 by looking at the evidence from Britain on education, social class and social mobility.

The second part of the chapter looks at sociological research within schools. From the 1960s there was a shift in emphasis in the sociology of education. Instead of just asking how schools fitted into society, sociologists became increasingly interested in finding out how teachers and pupils fitted into the school. There are obvious similarities here with the work of those sociologists who were trying to find out what was going on inside families. However, as family life is more or less impossible to observe directly, sociologists were largely dependent on what they were told second hand in interviews. Educational sociologists, in contrast, had the methodological advantage of being able to go into schools to observe what was going on for themselves. As Burgess and Parker observe, while questions of inequality (of gender and ethnicity as well as class) remained important, other issues general to education, such as the ways in which teachers established rules and how they were negotiated by teachers and pupils, were highlighted. The final part of the chapter examines educational policy and, in particular, the effects of reorientating education to the demands of an increasingly market-driven economy and the effects of greater accountability on teachers' working lives.

The study of work and organizations occupied a central place in the work of many of the classical sociologists who, as I observed earlier, were trying to make sense of the changes brought about in the nineteenth century by a transition from an agricultural to an industrial order. In the contemporary world, with new technologies and the development of a world economy bringing about another fundamental social transition, the sociology of work and organizations is back in the centre of the sociological stage. Glenn Morgan begins Chapter 10 by examining three key issues raised by classical sociologists' analysis of work and organizations in modern societies: an increasingly specialized division of labour, the emergence of new forms of power and inequality and the capacity of the free market to transform existing patterns of social order. The second part of the chapter looks at the development of these processes in the era of mass industrial production in developed societies, known as 'Fordism'. The following section looks at the disruption of this order since the 1970s with a new series of changes in work and organizations brought about by new forms of technology and the establishment of global markets. The chapter concludes by outlining a new economic sociology needed to make sense of these changes and their impact on people's daily lives.

## *Order, Deviance and Sickness*

As I observed in the first section, in any society, or social situation, there are necessarily expectations as to how people should behave. Sociologists use the term *deviance* to describe behaviour which departs significantly from these expectations. Although criminal, delinquent and other forms of deviance are, by definition, breaking the rules of a society, they are not random acts but – like all forms of social action – have their own 'rules' and regularities which make them open to sociological explanation.

David Downes begins Chapter 11 by outlining some of these regularities, such as the fact that, in spite of the increasing prosperity of developed societies, crime rates continue to increase, some social groups consistently commit more crime than others and severity of punishment has little influence on crime. The second part of the chapter examines the four major theoretical explanations of crime: strain theories focus on social integration, interactionist theories are more concerned with the societal reaction to crime and its effects, radical theories relate crime to the political economy of capitalism and control theory, more pragmatically, focuses on the significance of various controls against deviance. The chapter concludes by outlining some of the current issues in the area.

The sociological study of health and illness has much in common with the study of deviance and some of its key ideas, such as labelling, illness and identity and illness career were adapted from the interactionist approach to deviance. Chapter 12 is structured around three distinct lines of sociological inquiry, each of which questions the dominant biological approach to health. First, sociologists have demonstrated that diseases have social as well as biological origins by documenting the relationship between health and social variables, such as class and integration. Second, sociological research has shown that becoming ill or disabled involves a series of social as well as biological changes, as people's experiences of illness are shaped by the reactions of others. Third, sociologists have explored the extent to which ideas about illnesses and their treatment are shaped by social and cultural influences.

A key distinction between crime and illness has long been that the former is intentional and usually results in punishment, while the latter is unintentional and results in treatment. However, in contemporary societies these boundaries are starting to become blurred. There are some doctors who now insist that many violent criminals should not be punished but treated, as they suffer from a genetic predisposition to violence, while other doctors are refusing some people treatment for their illness on the grounds that they are responsible for their condition by, for example, poor diet or smoking.

## Culture and Globalization

Sociologists use the term *culture* to describe the beliefs, customs and way of life of a society or social group. Culture provides systems of meaning which people draw on to make sense of the world and for most of human history this has been provided by organized religion. But what exactly is religion and what part does it play in contemporary societies? These are the questions tackled by Grace Davie in Chapter 13. She begins by distinguishing between contrasting sociological definitions of religion which give rise to different questions. *Substantive* definitions focus on what religion is, while *functional* definitions focus on what it does. The second part of the chapter outlines the development of the sociology of religion from its classical origins, while the third section examines some of the major themes in the contemporary study of religion, such as the debate about whether or not organized religion is losing its influence, the rise of new religious movements and emergence of religious fundamentalism. The chapter concludes with a brief section on current dilemmas in the sociology of religion.

In the modern world cultural ideas are increasingly transmitted by the mass media, that is, means of communication such as radio, film and TV which reach mass audiences. Sociologists have very different interpretations of the role of the media. Some are pessimistic, arguing that the mass media are mechanisms by which the ideas and interests of the dominant groups are spread throughout societies. However, others are more optimistic, arguing that the media give people more access to information and help to promote social integration. However, as Natalie Fenton observes in Chapter 14, students of the media all believe that, in one way or another, the media have implications for freedom and control which are crucial to sociology's quest to understand societies.

Fenton begins by looking at the questions raised by the study of the mass media, especially the question of whether the media reflect or create cultural ideas. The second part of the chapter examines the sociology of media production, which covers both ownership and control and professional practices. The next two sections examine some of the ways in which sociologists study media content and how it is received by audiences; for example, are audiences relatively powerless or powerful consumers? The final section outlines some contemporary issues in media research, the most significant of which is the role of mass communications in helping to create a global culture in which western ideas, such as the ideology of consumerism, have spread across the world often supplementing, or replacing, local cultures. Some sociologists argue that the population of the world is now becoming bonded into a single, global society and new sociological ideas are required to understand it. The theme of globalization is the topic of the final chapter.

While most pieces of sociological research are restricted to one society, or comparisons between different societies, global theorists focus on processes – such as the activities of transnational corporations – which transcend national boundaries. So how have sociologists tried to explain these processes and what issues do they study? Leslie Sklair addresses these issues in Chapter 15. He begins by identifying four main theoretical approaches to globalization: world systems, global culture, world society and global capitalism models. He then examines some of the most important concrete issues studied by global theorists, such as environmental change, gender relations, global urbanization and the links between global and regional processes. The chapter then explores the relationship between globalization and everyday life, and some of the ways it has been resisted by new social movements. Although there is, as yet, no unified global theory and some sociologists remain sceptical of the idea, as Sklair observes, issues of globalization are now very much on the sociological agenda.

## Modernity and Postmodernity

As I observed earlier, sociology emerged as an attempt to make sense of the transition from a 'traditional' to a 'modern' social order. However, this process of modernization was more than a series of economic and structural changes. It was also characterized by the consolidation of a distinctly modern way of thinking, the most important aspect of which was the replacement of faith in

God and divine Providence by a new faith in the power of human *reason* (manifested most clearly in the achievements of science) not only to understand how the world works but to improve it for the greater good of humanity. Sociology was a product of this modern way of thinking and it remains fundamentally 'modernist' today with the continuing ambition of most sociologists to explain how aspects of societies work and change in the hope of contributing, in some way or other, to their improvement.

However, in the last two decades in particular, there has been a mounting challenge – or, more precisely, series of challenges – to this 'modernist' way of thinking by a diverse group of writers loosely labelled 'postmodernists'. Postmodern ideas began in the arts and architecture, spread to the study of popular culture and were developed most fully in philosophy, but they are now becoming increasingly influential in the social sciences, particularly in sociology. Postmodernists argue first, that we are in another period of intense social change in which modernity is dissolving and being replaced by a new form of *post*-modern social order. Second, they reject the 'modernist' idea that it is possible (even in principle) to obtain some form of objective understanding of this world, which could then be used (in theory) for the betterment of the human condition.

A great deal of postmodern theory in sociology (and popular culture) is an attempt to come to terms with some of the effects of living in a media-saturated society. Postmodernists argue, contrary to some sociological theories, that a result of the 'information explosion' of the last two or three decades has been to offer people more choice and greater possibility of changing their lives. The postmodern condition has been described as a time of incessant choosing, where many established conventions and old certainties are called into question.

A consequence of this, postmodernists argue, is that the institutional orders sociologists call societies, or social structures, have become increasingly diverse and the 'divisions' between different social groups, such as class, gender and ethnic groupings, have fragmented. Thus the *generalizations* sociologists typically make about the relationship between social institutions and individual behaviour and the *comparisons* they make between different social groups have become increasingly difficult to sustain.

A second issue concerns the ideas sociologists use to try to understand this changing world. The discussion of methodology showed that sociologists differ about the best ways of trying to produce valid sociological knowledge. However, postmodernists would not be interested in such a debate because they reject what they see as the 'modernist' idea of valid social knowledge. They argue that in a fluid, fragmented social world, where even apparently hard scientific truths are called into question, there are no longer any clear criteria for determining whether one theory, or one piece of research, is any better than any other. For postmodernists, theories are evaluated not in terms of some abstract idea of 'truth', but simply in terms of their utility; how useful or helpful people find them. Postmodernists argue that sociologists have to recognize the diversity of the social world and develop their ideas accordingly. They are particularly critical of general sociological theories, such as Marxism and some feminisms, which they describe as grand narratives (big stories). What is called research in these theories is simply selectively accumulated data aimed only at convincing people of the 'truth' of the story.

Most sociologists are sceptical and even hostile to postmodernist ideas. First, critics have highlighted the inconsistencies in the postmodern position. They point out that, by suggesting that there has been a transition from one era to another and bringing in evidence to support their claims, postmodernists are exhibiting some strongly modernist tendencies.

Second, sociologists argue that postmodernist claims of a transition to a new social order are exaggerated as so many features of modernity – such as a tightly organized division of labour, rational calculation and the continuing dominance of science and technology – remain intact.

Nonetheless, postmodern theory should not be dismissed from the sociological agenda. It has made valuable contributions to the study of culture and media in particular and, by drawing attention to the increasingly diverse nature of contemporary societies, it has raised important questions for sociology and forced a re-examination of some key ideas. The chapters on methodology, theory, class, gender, education and media in this book, for example, all contain discussion of the postmodern point of view. Postmodern ideas also serve as a useful corrective for those sociologists, or schools of sociological thought, which tend to be intolerant of their key ideas being questioned. Postmodernism reminds us that there is no one right way of thinking about human societies. The diverse nature of social life and the precarious authority of sociological knowledge mean that sociologists can never be certain about any aspect of social life. If research discussed here, or in any other sociology book you read, seems to be preaching at you, giving you one point of view, then it is important to question it yourself and ask what other explanations are possible. Sociology offers interpretations of the world, not uncontested truths.

# Further Reading

Bauman, Z. *Thinking Sociologically*, Oxford, Blackwell, 1990. A readable collection of essays from a leading sociologist using everyday examples to illustrate what it means to think sociologically.

Bourdieu, P. *Sociology in Question*, London, Sage, 1993. A collection of interviews, talks and question and answer sessions exploring some central issues in sociology.

Giddens, A. *Sociology: A Brief but Critical Introduction*, 2nd edn, Basingstoke, Macmillan, 1986. An accessible introduction to the origins of sociology and some of its key themes.

Mills, C. *The Sociological Imagination,* London, Penguin, 1959. One of the classic statements of sociology's quest to link the individual and the social.

# Resources

## *Videos*

*Theory and Method in Sociology,* a 45-minute video using case study examples and interview extracts from leading sociologists to explain the relationship between theories of knowledge and sociological research.

*Making Sense of Sociological Theory,* a 60-minute video explaining the major theoretical perspectives in sociology and linking them to case study examples.

*Postmodernity*, a 45-minute video examining modernity, the suggested transition to postmodernity and the implications for sociology.

Videos available from Halo Vine Video, PO Box 104, Leicestershire LE10 2WW.

## *Journals*

*Sociology Review,* a journal aimed at sociology students with articles of key areas of sociological research, published four times a year.

Available from Philip Allan Publishers, Market Place, Deddington, Oxfordshire OX15 0SE.

*S* magazine, a quarterly magazine focusing on topical issues of sociological interest.

Available from Updates, PO Box 6, Denbeigh LL16 3WG.

# 2
# Methodology

*Ray Pawson*

Methodology is the study of how sociological claims to specialized knowledge of societies are validated. Methodological issues are thus fundamental to all the areas of sociology covered in this book. The aim of this chapter is to examine and illustrate some of the major technical and theoretical issues involved in gathering and interpreting data. It should help you to understand and illustrate:

- What is meant by methodology and the importance of epistemological, ontological and technical questions in social research

- The key strategies of social research and the myth of quantitative versus qualitative research

- Why there is a discrepancy between the ideal and actual in the process of doing social research

- The distinction between 'realism' and 'relativism'

---

### CONCEPTS

epistemology ▦ ontology ▦ paradigms ▦ positivism
phenomenology ▦ hypothesis testing
interviews: structured and unstructured
realism ▦ relativism

---

# Introduction

The purpose of this chapter is to help the beginner reflect upon the justification for sociology's claim to specialist knowledge of human societies. The high ambitions of sociology need to be grounded in real substance. The fine words need to be matched with deeds. Sociologists know best, or at least like to think they do. But what is the basis for sociological knowledge? How do sociologists know that they are correct? How do they respond when challenged with alternative views? This chapter will attempt to chart some answers to these huge, age-old questions.

The great claim for sociological expertise goes by the name of *methodology*. As well as developing specialists in all the substantive areas covered in this book, such as gender relations, work, deviance and so on, sociology has always generated scholars (methodologists) whose task is to inspect and evaluate this research output in an attempt to improve the basic modes of investigation of the discipline. The assertion that sociological research provides an authoritative understanding of the workings of the social world is thus based on claims about the usage of some *special tools of inquiry*.

## *The Methodological Task: Principles and Practice*

We have already achieved a pocket definition of 'methodology' as the 'tools of inquiry of a discipline'. As with any statement of such brevity, this is both helpful and misleading. Thinking about tools and toolboxes may lead one to ponder that carpenters use hammers, dentists use drills, scientists use microscopes and that, by extension, sociological methodology is thus about interviews, questionnaires and such like. This is true enough, but only *part* of the methodological story. We can get to the whole of the story by thinking about the tools of inquiry used in other disciplines like mathematics or philosophy. Mathematicians and philosophers, self-evidently, do research. But there are, self-evidently, no mathematical hammers, no philosophical drills, no algebraic microscopes, no metaphysical questionnaires to be seen. The tools of inquiry in such cases are thus not 'practical' skills but 'thinking' skills. Mathematical and philosophical inquiry are thus governed by the basic laws of number, arithmetic, proof, logic and reasoning. Inquiry, in such instances, is superintended by a set of 'agreed principles'.

Most disciplines, in fact, require a *blend* of thinking skills and practical skills. And thus sociological methodology can be said to have the task of *developing and amalgamating the principles and practice of social research*. A first attempt at describing these basic ingredients is made in Figure 2.1 in which a further important distinction is made. We expand the notion that 'methodology' = 'principles' + 'practice' by subdividing the middle term into two further categories drawn from the philosophical literature, namely 'epistemology' and 'ontology'.

> METHODOLOGY = EPISTEMOLOGY + ONTOLOGY + METHOD
>
> Epistemology = Guiding principles of inquiry
>
> Ontology = Essential nature of the (social) world
>
> Method = Practical techniques of research

**Figure 2.1** The basic ingredients of research methodology

*Epistemology* establishes the guiding principles or rules of inquiry. 'An epistemology is a theory of knowledge: it presents a view and a justification for what can be regarded as knowledge – what can be known, and what criteria knowledge must satisfy in order to be called knowledge rather than beliefs' (Blaikie, 1993: 7). For instance, of much concern for the epistemologist is the traditional question about whether sociology can be a *science* and thus follow the latter's methods of experimentation and measurement. This, in turn, generates other questions about whether sociology has *laws* in the same way that physics has laws, or whether the *causes* of social action can be understood in the same way as the causes of physical phenomenon. A quite different kind of epistemological question concerns the *subject/object* dilemma. People are the objects of sociological inquiry, but (until proof to contrary is available!) we assume that sociologists are people too. This has led to a debate about whether 'involvement' or 'detachment' is the best vantage point from which to understand the social world. Some epistemologists in the former camp, for instance, argue that to understand properly the 'subjugation of women' or the 'oppression of the working class', it is necessary to be a member of those groups. Others take the view that requiring every researcher to have a 'standpoint' will result in the total fragmentation of knowledge, so that only women will be said to understand women, only the working class will comprehend the working classes, only lesbians will follow lesbians, only Ford workers will fathom Ford workers and so on. No attempt is made to answer such *huge* questions here, my purpose here is simply to introduce the scope of epistemology by noting the adjective.

*Ontology* establishes some first principles about the essential nature of the world we are studying. 'Ontology refers to the claims or assumptions... about the nature of social reality – claims about what exists, what it looks like, what units make it up and how these units interact with each other' (Blaikie, 1993: 6). More *huge* questions are on the agenda here. Given the considerable scope of sociological explanation, there is a variety of claims made about what constitutes the core activities under study. These range from whole societies and cultures and their histories to the actions, biographies, meanings and motivations of individuals. Not only is there debate about the 'stuff' of sociology, there are also ontological questions to be raised about how these basic components 'work'. For example, those favouring structural explanation perceive that human actions are shaped by institutions and ideologies, while those favouring 'human agency' stress the choice and reasoning lying behind our every action (see Chapter 3). The former camp has difficulty explaining why, if action is determined, people have changed history, and the latter has trouble with the fact that the exercise of free will appears to generate a world that is remarkably orderly.

'*Methods* of research are the actual techniques or procedures used to gather and analyse the data related to some research questions or hypothesis' (Blaikie, 1993: 7). There are dozens and dozens of techniques and procedures which make up the sociological toolbox. Some of these methods are extremely well known and used well beyond the sociological domain. Thanks to opinion polling and market research, most members of the general public will have a fair conception of what is involved in an 'interview' or 'question-naire', as well as some clue about what goes on and what can go wrong in 'sampling'. Next, but known more out of fear than familiarity, is the host of 'statistical' and 'computational' methods associated with data analysis. Beyond this there are methods of 'direct observation' and 'document analysis' imported from other disciplines such as social anthropology and history. Reaching still further, we come to the linguistic-based techniques where sociologists make detailed analysis of everyday conversations, and the methods of 'content analysis' used in media research (see Chapter 14). This list could go on and on, as can the permutation and combination of procedures, a situation which has led to the analogy being made between research techniques and recipes, and thus the need for rather massive methods 'cookbooks' to demonstrate and teach them all (for example Babbie, 1989).

Clearly, there is much ground to cover in becoming a social researcher. There is a need to master both philosophy *and* craft. Social investigation is always a case of knowing *and* doing. The previous three paragraphs should be regarded as an 'invitation' to the daunting and complex territory of sociological methodology. Their purpose is simply to establish that, from the outset, researchers must have clear answers to some very basic questions:

- How do I know that my research provides answers which are valid?
- What is the nature of the social reality I have chosen to investigate?
- Why have I selected a particular technique as the best tool for the job?

## The Scope of Sociological Research: Chalk and Cheese

Simply put questions like these often generate complex answers, and the first thing that I should make clear is that the methodological jury is still out, struggling to come to terms with these basic issues. There is, and never will be, complete agreement on the epistemological, ontological and technical foundations of the discipline as a whole. What I can report however is much localized progress and the fact that it is possible to distinguish several 'families' of social research which operate with close agreement on the hows, whats and whys of research methodology.

There is, then, a series of identifiable *research strategies* in sociology, each operating with a distinct *set* of interrelated epistemological, ontological and practical foundations. There are many reasons for this diversity of approach, the principal one being the 'life, universe, everything' explanatory ambitions of the discipline. If one is prepared to tackle questions such as 'why did capitalism follow feudalism in world history?' on one hand, and 'what does it feel like to be an assembly-line worker?' on the other, then it is hardly surprising that one formulates quite different strategies to answer them.

I shall return shortly to the pros and cons of having *rival* dynasties of research in the *same* discipline. For the present, I want to accomplish the three tasks of identifying the principal research strategies of sociology, showing how each blends together distinctive bodies of principle and practice, and providing a well-known exemplar of each approach in action. In Figure 2.2 and the paragraphs that follow, I distinguish *four* key families of social research. Let the reader beware – this is a textbook simplification! No one can say definitively whether there are two, three, four, seven, seventeen or 700 'types' of sociological research. The following typology will, therefore, do damage to some researchers' sensibilities about their own specialisms and it will ignore yet further permutations created by investigators who have attempted to combine facets of different approaches. The point, however, is simply to show that sociological researchers are not all the same.

## Family I – The Ethnographers

These are also known as 'participant observers', 'field researchers', 'phenemenologists', 'qualitative researchers'. They are, incidentally, probably the biggest family active in empirical sociology in the UK at the present time. The family gets its identity from a crucial *ontological* belief that all social action is intentional. Understanding social behaviour is therefore a matter of deciphering the reasoning that underlies action. Social life revolves around shared meanings which are created in processes of social interaction. These fundamentals place immediate requirements on *method*. In order to understand how people behave, research has to imitate real life and become involved in those interactions which create the everyday meanings. Hence the basic research technique involves participating with the group under study over a length of time, observing and sharing their everyday activities, and asking them to explain their reasoning and choices. Analysis follows these same themes, thus the ethnographic report attempts to explain by reproducing the 'lived experience'

| RESEARCH STRATEGY | EPISTEMOLOGY | ONTOLOGY | METHODS |
|---|---|---|---|
| Ethnography *a.k.a.* participant observation and field research | Reality is grounded in the beliefs and interpretations of particular groups. The primary task of social explanation is to 'reproduce' those meanings as accurately as possible. | The social world is a human creation. Social life is constituted in the reasoning and everyday meanings which people create in mundane, routine social interaction. | Methods imitate 'folk' reasoning: fieldwork, participation, introspection, observation, narrative building, respondent validation and so on. |
| Survey research including measurement and statistical research | The primary task of social explanation is the discovery of societal regularities. Research is based on distinguishing the key variables and their interrelationship which express the social order. | The social world is ordered. While there is much local and immediate change in attitudes and behaviours, these actions underlie gross regularities and patterned outcomes at the societal level. | Variable analysis methods: sampling, questionnaires, measurement, indicator selection, cocing, correlation and multivariate analysis and so on. |
| Comparative, historical and cross-cultural research | There is a pattern to societal evolution. The primary task of social explanation is to treat each nation as a case and to classify it according to patterns of similarities and differences. | The social world is an historical process. Societies evolve in the way that they do because they already possess configurations of properties which channel potential future possibilities. | Historical records are combed to identify countries with different configurational profiles. Data are created via a secondary analysis of existing historical reportage. |
| Applied, policy and evaluation research | The primary task of social explanation is to create experimental conditions so that the causes of change can be discerned. Research is thus based on manipulation, control and measurement of planned social change. | The social world is open to change via policies and programmes. Social reality is complex with other factors also producing change, making it difficult to discern whether a programme is the crucial agent of transformation. | Experimental and quasi-experimental designs. Random allocation of subjects to experimental and control groups. Pre- and post-programme measurement. |

**Figure 2.2**  The principal research strategies of sociology

of the particular group. A narrative is produced which contains a series of crucial incidents and typical group behaviour in order to show how these are embedded in a common set of beliefs. The authenticity of the account is checked by such means as 'respondent validation' which involves putting the interpretations of the ethnographer back to the group for further comment and clarification. This devotion to the subject's point of view is further expressed in terms of an *epistemological* principle, known as Thomas' Dictum (1976), which posits that if 'people define situations as real they are real in their consequences'. Since the world is experienced as a reality by those who comprise it, participant observation is done on the basis that it gets closer to *the* lived reality of those being studied.

*Example.* For over twenty years, Willis' *Learning to Labour* (1977) has been cited as a major contribution to ethnography. The study followed twelve working-class boys in their final year at school. Willis attended their classes and career interviews, participated in their break-time conversations and after-school leisure activities, creating a mass of information by means of group discussions, tape recordings, diaries and self-reports. The study is saluted for its 'feel' of the thoughts, words and deeds of the 'lads'. These are reproduced in passage after passage of dialogue from the fieldwork, which for illustration's sake I boil down to a single utterance from 'Joey': 'I think... laffing is the most important thing in... everything.' To find out what makes Joey 'laff', you will need to go to page 29 of *Learning to Labour* and find his tale of 'coppin' it' in a fight which is told with a degree of realism yet to be achieved in a 1000 episodes of school-based soaps. Willis perceives the 'lads' laugh as a crucial symbol of their counter-school culture which centres on a loathing of 'pen-pushing' teachers and 'ear 'ole' conformist pupils. For Willis, the key aspect of the lads' culture is that it is born out of choice; they know that not everyone can succeed, they know that individual effort will not get them out of the pack, they know they are destined for manual work. Life is made more tolerable if it is laughed at in the face and this becomes their motto to prepare for life on the shopfloor.

## Family II – The Surveyors

These are also known as 'quantitative researchers', 'variable analysts', and 'social statisticians' (and, by the unkind, as 'number crunchers'). There are family differences on, for instance, the best time-frame of the survey work and the particular techniques of statistical analysis to be preferred. What holds the dynasty together is the *epistemological* principle that explanation consists of uncovering the statistical 'regularities', 'tendencies', 'patterns', 'orderly outcomes' which constitute social life. For instance, inequalities of social condition (class, race, gender and so on) are common to most societies and remain in place over considerable time. This gives survey research the task of identifying the important regularities, specifying their scope (time and place), and explaining them. The *methods* of survey research consist of a well-rehearsed sequence of steps. The unit of analysis is established, usually at the 'societal' level, giving inquiry the task of establishing regularities which pertain across a whole nation or region or institution. A representative sample of that target population is obtained. Information is sought from them (usually by questionnaire) on a whole array of measures or 'variables'. Data analysis then takes place which seeks to establish regularities and patterns, known as 'correlations' between these variables (social group A does better than group B; the more of C one has, the more likely one is to have D; Es get X while Fs get Y). These patterns are further established by 'multivariate' analysis in which the relative influence of a number of variables (K, L, M, N, and so on) on a particular outcome (O) are deciphered. Theories are developed to explain the social processes which lead to these dominant patterns.

*Example.* Marshall *et al.*'s *Social Class in Modern Britain* (1988) provides a good example of survey research. Their task was to discover whether social class is still crucial in structuring economic, political and social life. They took a random sample of 1315 adults in the UK and asked questions to determine their social class and their attitudes and behaviour across a wide spectrum of other activities. The authors conclude that the influence of social class has not withered away and their data demonstrate a series of clear correlations between people's class position and how they vote, their housing tenure, their parent's class position, their membership of unions, and their support for a range of policies on such matters as 'taxation', 'wage restraint', 'positive discrimination' and so on. They show the quantitative tradition's concern for rigour in measurement by comparing the rival class definitions of Goldthorpe (1980) and Wright (1985) in order to discover which is better able to predict this range of behaviour (see Chapter 5). One of their particular interests is to engage with arguments suggesting that concerns other than class now lie at the root of political beliefs, as for instance the claim that housing tenure (owner-occupation or renting) is more significant than class position in determining voting patterns. They engage in multivariate analysis which shows that while the upper- and lower-class vote remains stable regardless of housing tenure, the vote of the intermediate classes changes significantly according to whether they own (Tory) or rent (Labour) their home.

## Family III – The Comparative Researchers

These are also known as 'cross-cultural researchers' and, since the comparisons often feature very broad time-frames, strategies of 'historical sociology' are also kindred. We face a significant shift in scope here, for *whole nations* are often the unit of analysis and the strategy is aimed at explaining why nations have their particular characteristics (for example why did Britain industrialize early?) The crucial *ontological* principle is revealed in the way such a question is answered in terms of a *configuration* of other characteristics which give rise to the feature in question (for example Britain industrializes early because of technological advance, population pressure, weak aristocracy, emerging middle class, colonial empire to exploit and so on). It is the 'combination', the 'juxtaposition', the 'joining together' of all these other factors which is said to generate the crucial outcome. The big *epistemological* idea is that the crucial explanatory configurations are best uncovered by searching for *similarities and differences* between cases. The nation is thus treated as one of a number of *cases* featuring one outcome (say, early industrialization) and compared with cases with a different outcome (say, late industrialization). The *method* of comparative research is thus to search the historical records of different cases (nations) trying to find what is common in countries which have evolved the key characteristic in question and what differentiates those countries which have experienced an alternative development. The practical work of gathering information on what features are present and absent in each country's historical profile gets done in the form of *secondary analysis* of historical writing and other documents such as public records.

*Example*. Moore's *Social Origins of Dictatorship and Democracy* (1966) is a classic work of comparative historical sociology and is responsible for establishing much of the thinking behind the last strategy. He sought to explain the development of seven major agrarian states (England, France, the United States, Germany, Japan, China, Russia) and, in particular, why they had travelled along one of three roads – to democracy, fascist dictatorship or communist dictatorship. His answer involves studying each country with respect to the strength of the commercial middle classes in relation to landowners, the modes of agricultural commercialization, the rebellious potential and type of leadership of the peasantry, and the strength of the peasantry in relation to landlords. He argues, on the basis of available historical evidence, that it is the precise configuration of these factors which determines the path that will be followed. Each route contains two or three nations and Moore demonstrates that the nature and combination of these factors is highly similar *within* each pair or triple. For instance, in communist dictatorships (China and Russia), the commercializing tendencies are very weak, there is a rebellious peasant solidarity, and landowners have lacked absolute control over agricultural production. By contrast, substantial differences in these configurations are revealed as he makes comparisons *between* the growth of democratic, communist and fascist states.

## *Family IV – Evaluation Researchers*

These researchers pursue a much more policy-orientated research task and their aim is to examine social programmes (educational schemes, crime-reduction initiatives, health-promotion interventions and so on) in order to see if they 'work'. The basic research strategy can be described as one of 'trial and error'. More formally, we can locate the *epistemological* loyalties in terms of experimental science notions of 'manipulation and control'. A laboratory scientist might apply heat (manipulation) to a metal rod, while keeping every other condition in the laboratory stable (control), and therefore be sure it is the heat which causes expansion. It is much more difficult to establish the link between social programmes and their effects because of the *ontological* reality that the complexity of the social world renders it much more difficult to control. For instance, if we introduce a neighbourhood watch scheme into a locality and find crime goes down, this may have been the result of other, unforeseen and uncontrolled activities, such as a change in police tactics, rather than the activities of the neighbours. This brings us to *method*, the primary task of which is to bring additional control to 'field settings'. The basic idea, as illustrated in Figure 2.3, is to split the recipients of a programme into two groups known as the 'experimental' and 'control' groups. Assignment to these groups is random, ensuring that the two groups are initially 'matched' or 'balanced' in their background characteristics. The programme (X) is then applied to the experimental group but not to the other. Changes are monitored by measuring the behaviour of both groups prior to ($O_1$) and after ($O_2$) the programme period. The explanatory logic is thus in place – being identical to begin with the only difference between the groups is the application of the programme, so if there is change, it must be the programme which is responsible.

*Example.* Because evaluation research is aimed at policy makers rather than an academic audience, there are no 'classics' of evaluation research in the same way as the other paradigms. I thus choose as illustration an example in which the programme may be well known, if not the research. *Sesame Street* played a key part in the US educational policy called 'head-start'. The guiding notion is that there is far more cognitive development going on in our heads between the ages of two and five than at any other interval in the lifespan. Educational disadvantage at this stage will thus prove harder to overcome. One fruit of such thinking was an educational television series, which was very serious about its playful approach to learning. Of particular note was the use of black and Hispanic presenters, a feature designed to attract members of those minority groups who were traditionally disadvantaged at school. Two types of field experiments were carried out – 'kindergarten' and 'at-home' evaluations (Bogatz and Ball, 1971). In the first, nursery classes in a particular area were randomly assigned to groups which were given facilities to view the programmes and those who were not. In the at-home version, households were randomly assigned to conditions in which the experimentees were canvassed, given publicity materials and visited by educational staff. The control groups received none of the material. 'Before and after' testing featured in both versions of the evaluation and took the form of simple reading and reasoning tests repeated at the obvious intervals. The results? As with so many other evaluations, these turned out to be complex and controversial (Pawson and Tilley, 1997). The very first trial with the scheme was pronounced a success, with the 'Sesame Street kids' significantly outperforming the controls in reading and reasoning by the end of the scheme. Successive follow-ups with the original groups, however, showed that these initial gains soon dissipated. Later trials in other localities resulted in smaller differences between experimentees and controls. Other data analysis also suggests that white, middle-class groups gained more advantage from the programmes than did blacks and Hispanics.

|  | Pre-test | Programme | Post-test |
|---|---|---|---|
| Experimental group | $O_1$ | X | $O_2$ |
| Control group | $O_1$ |  | $O_2$ |

**Figure 2.3**   The basic experimental design

## *Paradigms: Heroes and Villains*

I have introduced the diverse strategies of sociological research via the eminently sensible idea that one will need a different investigatory tack according to what it is one is investigating. At one level this is all perfectly satisfactory and straightforward. Most people would recognize this as the sheer commonsense notion of 'horses for courses'. Just as you hire a plumber to fix a leak and an electrician to mend the wiring, it is fairly obvious that the small-scale, unobtrusive, respondent-orientated style of ethnography suits the investigation of tight-knit, local communities, whereas skills in tracking documentary sources, cross-cultural sensitivity and experience in secondary analysis are the requirement for historical and comparative research. Not surprisingly, this idea that different-substantive-fields-of-enquiry-will-fetch-up-different-investigatory-strategies has pride of place in the canons of sociology research and has become known as the *principle of methodological pluralism*.

Alas, a notion which appears so balanced, uncontentious and fair minded, has, in fact, unleashed a torrent of bile, prejudice and polemic into the methodological literature. To understand why this has occurred, we need to go back to the original 'role' of methodology which was raised at the beginning of this discussion. For every social problem, there lurk scores of pundits and dogmatists waiting to express their own opinions and to deliver their own verdicts. Through its methodology, sociology aspires to go beyond spleen venting and axe grinding in order to deliver some expert and authenticated body of knowledge. Hence followed decades of careful and deliberate laying down of the basic principles and practice outlined in the previous section.

But what has been the result of these Herculean labours? Well, we have not seen the development of one unified and coherent set of sociological principles and practices. Neither have we seen a genteel, pluralist democracy in which epistemological chalk gives way gracefully to ontological cheese according to the research topic under study. Rather, according to many observers, the development of sociological methodology is a history of 'rift' and 'schism'. On this view, the research strategies depicted in the preceding section (and the summary in Figure 2.2) are not just 'different methodologies' but 'contradictory paradigms'. The term *paradigm* was introduced into the philosophical literature by Kuhn (1970) and by it, he intends to convey the idea that research gets organized not just through the rational adoption of particular strategies and methodologies, but rather that all the contributory ideas get wrapped up into an overall 'vision' or 'creed' or 'doctrine' about the correct way to do research. Thus methodology, Kuhn points out, can itself become a kind of dogmatism which *includes* by identifying good practice and thereby *excludes* by vilifying alternative approaches as misguided, wrong headed, dim witted and so on.

This rather combative language serves as my introduction to what have become known as *the paradigm wars*. What struck a whole generation of sociologists about the families of ontology-epistemology-method is that they are not only different but they, in fact, involve downright contradiction. Thus much methodological writing from the early 1960s to the early 1990s portrayed two camps of basically opposite persuasion gathering and glaring at each other in mutual hostility. And the name of that 30-year encounter was *Positivism versus Phenomenology*.

Each of these schools of thought pays homage to a contrasting set of first principles. The positivists believe that social research can be accomplished according to the same set of guidelines which direct natural science inquiry. Consequently, they place their faith in the detached measurement and quantification of the subject's behaviour in carefully sampled and controlled conditions in the belief that social research will uncover a single reality revealing the laws of social order and organization. The phenomenologists are committed to a more humanist vision of the sociological enterprise born principally out of the belief that all social actions are intentional. Accordingly, they place their faith in close, empathetic relationships with their subjects in order to discover the processes of understanding and meaning which underlie social action in the belief that social research produces authentic qualitative descriptions of the multiple social realities which constitute social life. These two traditions are in a state of permanent warfare with positivist research instruments being accused of insensitivity in the face of the richness, mutability and adaptability of human thought and language, and phenomenological method being accused of unbridled subjectivity and thus reducing sociology to 1000 travellers' tales.

The whole of the above paragraph has been placed in a box, not for its wisdom but for its superficiality, and not because it is a methodological maxim but because it is a *methodological myth*. I occupy valuable space here in discussing a myth because *positivism versus phenomenology* and *qualitative versus quantitative* have been the standard formats of many introductory texts on methods. Exaggeration and simplification are inevitable features of all introductory treatments but I think in the case of methodology, this style has had the damaging consequence in that beginners, having sensed a battle, are keen to get on the winning side. Thus, perhaps inadvertently, perhaps surreptitiously, perhaps conspiratorially, a 'victor' has been allowed to emerge in many depictions of the paradigm wars. 'Since the sixties, a story has got about that no good sociologist should get his hands dirty with numbers... a generation of young researchers have been thrown out into a sceptical world with their heads full of the standard critiques of positivism but often empty of ideas about how to match exciting theories with rigorous research designs' (Silverman, 1985).

One purpose of this chapter is thus to insist that no good sociologist should get his or her hands dirty with the paradigm wars. I will make this case in detail in the following sections on data collection and data analysis, where I show that both qualitative and quantitative approaches face *identical* problems and need to adopt *common* solutions. In addition I can cite briefly three further problematics which also demonstrate that the war is over. The first is that so much of the sociological research agenda lies *outside* the 'positivism versus phenomenology' agenda. For instance, if one goes back to the domain of historical sociology and a typical task, for instance, of trying to compare the causes of the Russian and Chinese revolutions, it is not going to be a great deal of help to ponder a period of fieldwork and empathetic understanding, or to hit the research trail looking for samples, variables and correlations. Second is the fact that there exists so much social inquiry which has employed a *combination* of qualitative and quantitative methods – apparently without the researcher suffering signs of schizophrenia (Brannen, 1992). Third is the point that the bitterest methodological disputes are likely to occur, these days, *within* rather than between paradigms with, for instance, ethnographers being less sure whether their efforts end up 'reproducing' or 'constructing' reality. Recall that the original foundation for participant observation was the attempt to get closer to *the* lived reality of those being studied. Nowadays there is a family feud with many ethnographers conceding that there are *multiple* realities and their accounts are but one version among many (Hammersley, 1992). To be sure then, while we have not finished with methodological disputes, there is little more to said about 'that one'.

## The Research Process: The Ideal and the Real

Having introduced some of the basic ingredients and strategies of methodology, it is time to press further into the tale and show how all the various parts are welded together into an activity which is known as the 'research process'. What I am describing here is the assembly line of sociological research, the actual process in which the sociological work gets done.

Research, of course, is always inspired by a 'problem'. The puzzles facing sociology, as I have already pointed out, are legion, and their variety is well represented by the issues tackled in the exemplars discussed earlier. It is questions such as these which start the production line of sociological knowledge. The first point of note about this particular assembly line is that it goes back and forth. This is illustrated in Figure 2.4a in which we see directional arrows leading to and fro between the sociologist's ideas (labelled 'theory') and the social behaviour of those under study (labelled 'subject'). In between comes 'method' and it is through method that sociological explanations get developed and refined. The figure illustrates a four-step process of inquiry which can be spelled out in a rather abstract way as follows. Research begins with a theory which is developed in the form of 'hypothesis making' which involves putting forward tentative ideas to solve the problem under study. These hypotheses suggest that particular forms of data on particular issues will shed light on the research problem and so 'data-collection' instruments are devised which extract the vital evidence from the appropriate people and places. There follows a phase of 'data analysis' in which all the material is collected together in order to see if the initial hunches of the researcher are borne out. This inspection of the data provides for 'hypothesis testing' – if the results of the investigation square with the researcher's initial ideas then the theory is said to be 'verified', and if these first hunches turn out to be wrong the theory is 'falsified'. There is little chance that the sociologist's initial stab at explanation will be correct first time and in all respects, and so the expectation is that the initial hypotheses may need a little refinement which will set in place a further sequence of hypotheses making, data collection, data analysis and testing. Further investigators join the fray and the process shunts back and forth between theory and evidence until the sociological community is satisfied that firm conclusions are being reached.

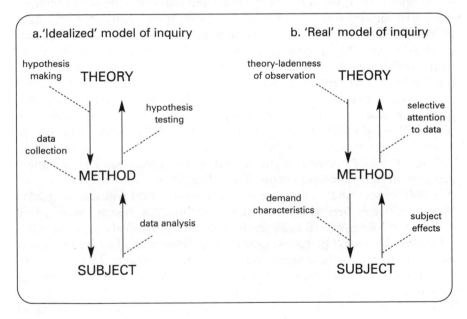

**Figure 2.4**    The research process

Figure 2.4a has labelled this process an 'ideal'. This is not simply a matter of the compression involved in my over-simple, single-paragraph, one-idea-at-a-time illustration. The 'real' picture is portrayed in Figure 2.4b. What this shows is that the move from theory to evidence is never straightforward and that all the processes of hypothesis making, data collection, data analysis and hypothesis testing are in fact *contested*. These problems and pitfalls are described in 2.4b using an alternative set of descriptors for the four legs of the journey. The overall dilemma being described here can be captured in the sentence – *evidence does not speak for itself*. What this means, as we observed in Chaper 1, is that we have to abandon the simplistic notion that social researchers are mere 'fact gatherers'. There is no such thing as 'raw data', 'out there', which we can observe 'directly' and use to 'prove' theories. Rather, it is the *process* of going back and forth between ideas and evidence which advances knowledge.

When encountered for the first time, such ideas can seem rather unsettling, particularly for those brought up on the notion that science *is* the business of gathering facts. It is necessary, therefore, to advance this alternative understanding of the nature of investigation by stages. The key idea is introduced by that mouthful of a phrase, the *theory-ladenness of observation*. This notion came to prominence with some famous experiments in the psychology of perception. Best known is the Dunker 'dot and frame' illusion which involves the use of subjects sitting in front of an oblong frame with a dot set within it. These objects are the only things illuminated in an otherwise completely darkened room. The experimenter then moves the frame in one direction (say, to the right) and asks subjects what they have seen. Invariably, they report that the dot has moved in the opposite direction (left). What is the reason for the misperception? Being in the dark and lacking any other fixed reference points for gauging movement, the subjects rely on the learned expectation (gained, perhaps, from watching too much TV!) that frames tend not to move, whereas objects within them might do so.

Now, if something as straightforward as the perception of movement depends on prior assumptions (or, if you like, 'theories'), then it is obvious that observations of a vastly more complex social world will also be guided by theories. From here, it is a short step to the idea that researchers may well pick and choose empirical evidence to suit their theoretical tastes. By this I refer to the likelihood that a researcher's commitment to a favoured idea (pet theory) will lead to the search for self-confirming evidence (pet data). For instance, in the sociology of religion, the 'secularization thesis' about the decline in religious belief in modern society is much debated. If the researcher is committed to this thesis, she might monitor the decline in church attendance over the decades in order to 'verify' it. If the researcher, however, is opposed the thesis, he might attempt to 'falsify' it by gathering evidence on the apparent rise in what is often called 'common religion', which refers to people's belief in magic, luck, superstition, cults, alternative lifestyles and so forth.

In Figure 2.4a, 'hypothesis making' is the prelude to 'hypothesis testing', and in Figure 2.4b the fact that 'all observation is theory-laden' has a counterpoint in the notion of 'selective attention to data'. This refers to the fact that evidence, once collected, does not speak for itself but will automatically enter a further round of interpretation and reinterpretation. For instance, let us consider one of the most famous bits of quantitative data in sociology, reproduced in almost every introductory textbook, showing that over the century there has been a steady decline in the proportion of the national wealth held by the richest one/five/ten per cent of the population. This is often taken at 'face value' to indicate that Marxian prediction about the increasing stranglehold of the capitalist class has proven woefully mistaken. Marxists, however, do not see it this way. They would ask, for instance: from whence does this evidence come? (answer – Inland Revenue Statistics based on death duties); who provides the initial information? (answer – accountants of the wealthy); in whose interests do these agents act? (answer – self-evident). The 'redistribution' of wealth, in this view, is thus seen as an accountancy ploy, and the 'real' evidence of the stranglehold of the capitalist class is sought elsewhere in terms of information on, say, 'interlocking' directorships and shareholdings in the major global conglomerates.

In utilizing these examples, I am not attempting to give succour to proponents or opponents of the secularization or polarization theses, merely to show that the very idea of 'proving' a theory is much more complex than the ideal model allows. I shall return to a more 'realistic' theory of theory testing later, but for now we turn to another mighty conundrum for the standard conception of the research process.

Figure 2.4a presents the idealized conceptualization of data collection and analysis. This is the point of interface between sociologists and their subjects. On the basis of their theoretical deliberations, researchers arrive at a body of information they require from respondents and this is translated into a range of questions, tests, scales and so on. Subjects attune themselves to these inquiries and return the requisite information to be processed in data analysis and provide a test of the original conjecture. So the story goes. Figure 2.4b presents the alternative picture. Its basic assumption is that human subjects are not passive respondents, so that retrieving information from the (wo)man on the street presents rather different problems from exploring the leaf on the tree or the specimen under the microscope.

Figure 2.4b thus describes the flow of information between the researcher and the researched with two different terms, *demand characteristics* and *subject effects*. The basic idea of the former is that the research act in sociology is invariably a meeting between people, and so is itself a social situation. In such a meeting, it is incredibly difficult to isolate the particular questions, variables and measures in which the sociologists are interested from the totality of other influences present. For instance, confront any normal living, breathing subject with a stranger asking questions and he or she will be thinking, 'who is this person?', 'why does she want to know this stuff?', 'what is she doing it for?', 'who is she doing it for?', 'why have I been selected?', 'am I getting anything out of this?', 'do I really want to tell her this?' and so on. In the face of all this, there is little wonder that the original intentions of the researcher may get distorted and the meaning of that apparently simple questionnaire item may get mangled. This *totality* of cues and concerns which confront the research subject are known as 'demand characteristics'.

The reverse side of the same coin consists of 'subject effects'. During the course of the research act, subjects will make up their mind in respect of some of their own anxieties and queries. Thus, what the researcher gets back from the subject are not mere 'responses' but a mixed bag of intuition, helpfulness, courtesy, curiosity, guesswork, vigilance, guardedness, pluck and bloody-mindedness. Subject effects are encountered in all research strategies. Picking out representative examples is difficult but probably the most (in)famous arise during the questionnaire and experimental approaches. According to the topics they raise, some questionnaire items can be seen by the subject as a 'threat'. Accordingly, a *social desirability effect* comes into play in which respondents are, for instance, likely to *over-report* 'voting', 'giving to charity', 'knowing the issues', 'participating in education', 'being employed' and so on, but *under-report* 'illness', 'disability', 'alcohol consumption', 'savings', 'being unemployed' and so on (Foddy, 1993: Ch. 9). Another admirable tendency in the majority of questionnaire respondents is *yea-saying*. Because most people are just so nice, they prefer on balance to 'acquiesce', and so answers labelled 'agree' rather than 'disagree', or 'satisfied' rather than 'dissatisfied' have a small but significant head-start when it comes to analysis (Foddy, 1993: Ch. 11). The grandfather of all subject effects is the *Hawthorne Effect* (Roethliberger and Dickson, 1939). This was one of the first examples of 'work study' which sought to discover the optimum conditions to maximize productivity at the Western Electric Works in Chicago. Researchers created workteams little and large, lighting levels subdued and bright, break patterns intermittent and absent, and to their surprise found productivity under the different conditions just kept on improving. Labour thus triumphs over logic, the scrupulous attention given to the workforce via the research being said to have been more significant that the actual work conditions.

Most researchers have their favourite example of subject effects and this is my opportunity to present mine. The research, conducted in a prison, was intended to evaluate whether a higher education course offered by the local university contributed towards rehabilitation. Recall that one of the standard ways to measure the effect of programme is to conduct some before-and-after measurement of attitudes, beliefs, behaviours, and so at the very start of the initiative, your intrepid researcher entered the prison classroom armed with a battery of questionnaires and attitude tests. There is a bit of prison folklore, which the reader should know and which I knew well enough at the time, that inmates like to retain control of the one thing they can control in an otherwise totally superintended world, namely – what goes on inside their own heads. The 'demand characteristic' thus loomed large that I was a Home Office spy, or (worse still) a psychologist, rather than a docile sociologist. I hoped to get by with charm, grace, humility, docility, and besides, the questionnaire was a compulsory part of the course! So how did it go?

Well, in fact all the questionnaires got completed, but in a way which led me directly back to the methodological drawing board. The expected grilling I received about the purpose of the questions including the unexpected thoughts of one prisoner, which you could actually see dawning on his face, 'you'll do these again at the end of the course to see if we have changed, eh?' The idea that subjects will try to figure out the ideas of the researcher is known as 'hypothesis-seeking behaviour' – this is a sophisticated example of 'methodology-seeking behaviour'. Another classic example of the subject effect is 'faking-good' and this tactic of sticking to socially desirable was also taken to new heights in the prison. One of the attitude tests used a fixed answer boxes for all items as follows:

| Strongly agree | Generally agree | Somewhat agree | Somewhat disagree | Generally disagree | Strongly disagree |
|---|---|---|---|---|---|
| 0 | 1 | 2 | 3 | 4 | 5 |

This was deliberately designed without a 'neutral point', but so keen was another of the respondents to appear as 'Mr Average', he went through and recorded most of the items as a 2.

We return to the respondents-from-hell later in this chapter. Here, I simply affirm to newcomers to social inquiry the sheer significance of the quartet of ideas introduced in this section. The 'theory-ladenness of observation', 'selective attention to data', 'demand characteristics' and 'subject effects' constitute an immense battery of difficulties. It is not resorting to hyperbole to say that the battle for rigour in sociological research is the battle to confront these problems. It is of particular interest to note that this family of processes casts its uncertainties well beyond the particular cases I have illustrated and, in fact, afflicts all four strategies of research introduced in an earlier section. It is also true to say that it yields to no quick fix, indeed it is precisely these problems which have led some sociologists to wring their hands and declare that we should abandon the search for clear methodological principles and recognize that research is necessarily subjective and relativistic. Doughtier souls should, however, stay on board. While there is no instant dissolution of these problems, it is true to say that resolution begins with a proper recognition of the task in hand, and we now move on to describe some strategies developed with such a goal in mind.

## Data Collection: Structured and Unstructured

The fact that 'talk is cheap' has propelled social researchers galore into using the interview as *the* tool for data collective. Yet, these artificial, unrehearsed encounters between strangers remain an enigma, leaving researchers at loggerheads on how to harness the flow of information that emerges from them. I refer, once again, to the paradigm wars and one particular battle which has developed during the conflict in respect of a preference for 'structured' versus 'unstructured' interviewing. My purpose here is to re-examine this old debate in order to transcend it. I want to show, first, that the investigatory goals of social research are so diverse that we need a variety of interview techniques at our disposal. Second, I want to show that these supposedly opposing methods have common failings and that all interviewing techniques share common priorities if they are to be improved.

Figure 2.5 represents the flow of information in the more formal, structured approaches to interviewing. The researcher begins with a theory which indicates the information (variables) required from the subject; these are then operationalized into set questions and fixed response categories; respondents answer by saying which of the categories applies to them; and finally responses are analysed to gain an overall picture of the population studied. The rationale is to provide a simple, neutral stimulus in order to tap the true 'responses' or true 'values' of individual subjects. Questions are asked in the simplest possible form which will nevertheless remain faithful to the conceptual intentions of the researcher. To these ends the major effort of this school can be summarized in the oft-stated goals that the interview schedule be clear, precise, unambiguous, intelligible and so on, yet *not* leading, hypothetical, embarrassing, memory defeating and so forth. Great care is also taken over question form, dealing with such matters as to whether to word questions negatively or positively, whether to include 'don't know' response categories, how to arrange the sequence of questions and so on. Since it is understood that 'who asks' can be as influential as 'what is asked', much effort is also made to neutralize and standardize personal factors which may influence the subjects. In short, the use of an identical stimulus and set responses categories with all subjects is said to allow for proper comparison to be made across the entire field of potential viewpoints.

Figure 2.6 represents the flow of information in the informal, unstructured interview. Since proponents of this view assume that the basis of all human action lies in the intelligibility of the social world to subjects, steps are taken to ensure that the research act is intelligible to them. There is thus no truck with question–response logic, it is assumed that even identical, plain words delivered by identical and plain interviewers can still mean different things to different people. There is no place for detachment and neutrality; what is required from the interviewer is 'involvement' and 'responsiveness'.

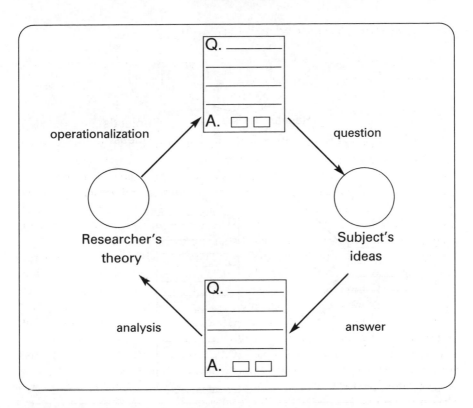

**Figure 2.5** The structured interview

Data collection thus has the task of creating a conversational setting in which the information provided is faithful to the frame of reference of the respondent. The investigator offers minimal steerage of the research topics within broad areas of discussion as they seem appropriate to each respondent. The idea is that mutual understanding emerges via the in-depth exchange of ideas. The researcher then selects for report those extracts from the total dialogue which most thoroughly crystallize the perspective of the subject. Analysis then consists of a descriptive narrative, bringing together the key statements voiced by the respondents.

Readers will see at glance that there is little by the way of sweetness and light between these views and indeed there was a period when methodological writing on the interview was all bile and rancour. The classic contribution to this was Oakley's famous (1981) paper entitled, 'Interviewing women: a contradiction in terms'. She added a feminist twist to these antagonisms by advocating that the traditional textbook advice on the formal interview is written by powerful male academics who try to gain scientific respectability for their views by their stress on neutrality and objectivity. She makes her case

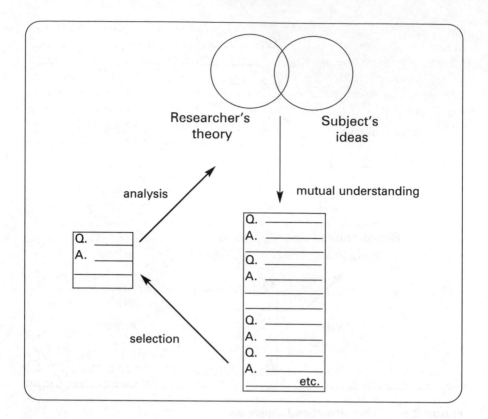

**Figure 2.6**    The unstructured interview

by quoting at length from some of the preposterous advice given to new researchers in some of the classic US 'methods' textbooks, with the following tips (on what the interviewer should do if the interviewee actually begins to speak up) taking the biscuit:

> Suppose the interviewee does answer the question but then asks for the opinion of the interviewer... In most cases the rule remains that he is there to obtain information, and to focus on the respondent not himself. Usually a few simple phrases will shift the emphasis back on the respondent. Some which have been fairly successful are 'I guess I haven't thought enough about it to give a good answer right now' [and] 'Well, right now, your answers are more important than mine'... Sometimes the diversion can be accompanied by a headshaking gesture which suggests 'That's a hard one!' while continuing with the interview. (Goode and Hatt, 1952)

At this point in my lectures on this topic, I usually stop and ask the students to try the 'head-shaking gesture'. For some reason, it usually seems to come out 'That's what it feels like to be a prat', rather than 'That's a hard one'. Meanwhile, back at the debate, Oakley continues to attempt to rip asunder the structured (male) model. She does this via an account of her own research on childbearing and motherhood which involved long periods of extensive interviews-cum-conversations. The argument is that the structured approach would just not work, and that before any genuine information of a worthwhile nature would flow on the private experience of becoming a mother, there had to be a 'transition to friendship'. All of this is evoked in the famous, final sentence of her paper:

> The mythology of 'hygienic' research with its accompanying mystification of the researched and the researcher as objective instruments of data production [must] be replaced by a recognition that *personal involvement* is more than a dangerous bias – it is the condition under which people come to know each other and admit each other to their lives. (Oakley, 1981, my emphasis)

You will find no finer thumping of the tub in the literature – alas, it does not make for a honing of the methodology. An alternative picture is drawn by Malseed (1987) in a paper arguing that the conventional wisdom on interviewing, even in the ancient US cookbooks, does not really consist of the wooden detachment illustrated in the first quotation from Oakley. The basic ethos, according to Malseed, is a pluralist one – different research topics call for different interviewing styles. If, for instance, one was interviewing for the census or an opinion poll and the information sought was, 'how many toilets are there in your home?' or 'how will you vote in the next election?', it is tough to see the 'contradiction' involved which means that for half the sample a 'transition to friendship' would be required to extract the data. Conversely, if the researcher was involved in an in-depth inquiry into personal issues, he would indeed feel like a lemon, shaking his head to indicate 'that's a hard one', because it would have been he who was responsible for raising just that matter. Oakley, in short, can be said to have created a 'strawman' in her notion of the all-pervasive, all-powerful formal interview.

There is worse to come for die-hards of structured/unstructured battle. In their struggle over the *form* of the interview (neutrality versus detachment), both perspectives can be criticized for having a deficient understanding of the *role* of the interview (Pawson, 1996). In concentrating on their very different ways of posing questions, both can be accused of ignoring the issue of *why* questions are put. Both can be accused of forgetting the proper function of the interview in the production and testing of sociological explanation. Recall the basic idea of Figure 2.4a which shows that the task of data collection is to produce evidence which will help verify or falsify the researcher's theory. 'Hypotheses' rather than 'respondents' should be considered as the subject matter of research. In this light, both interviewing methods have been accused of common error, known as the *imposition problem*. Instead of being a test of the researcher's theory, that theory is said often to be 'invisible' to the respondent, being 'smuggled in' only in the wake of data collection. Let us follow this argument through in both interviewing styles.

In the formal style the researcher's conceptual system is *imposed* wholesale upon the flow of information. The researcher determines the range of questions to be asked and also the range of answers which are appropriate for each question. The subject's response is limited to ticking boxes, agreeing, disagreeing and so on. Set questions and predetermined response categories offer little opportunity to question, or even understand, the researcher's theoretical framework. The end result is that the evidence is necessarily couched in the concepts and variables chosen by the researcher, with the result that only a selection of the subject's own ideas may get across. For instance, recalling a previous example, Marshall *et al.* (1988) have been accused of the methodological 'imposition' of their view that social class remains a central feature of everyday experience via the use of a questionnaire which is dominated by items on social class (Emmison and Western, 1990).

The informal approach takes the form of a conversation and so its data are diverse and discursive and thus hard to compare from respondent to respondent. Researches are sometimes accused of *selecting* small fragments of the respondent's utterances into their own preferred explanatory framework. While the data are supposed to emerge in 'mutual' understanding, the researcher's theory may not be clearly on view to the subject, and only show its face after the event in the research report. The end result is that only a selection of the respondent's own ideas may get across. For instance, Oakley in her research on becoming a mother could be accused of 'imposition', by favouring those epidural-fearing, consultant-wary, control-seeking views which resemble her own.

In the face of this common problem, it might be that a rather different model of the interview is to be preferred. Rather than the interviewer only telling the researcher about themselves (through tick boxes or anecdotes), it may be preferable to think of the subject as an 'informant', passing judgement through their own eyes on the researcher's theory. I return to my respondents-with-attitude (or to be precise, 'with jail sentences') for an example. Recall that the research sought to discover whether education could play a significant role in their rehabilitation. I have already described how they reduced to tatters my first attempts to record their opinions through a formal, structured questionnaire. I should add that this was followed by several months of gathering informal tales about their lives and times, which taught me a lot about their lives and times, but little about whether education might change them.

What did the trick was actually a combination of the structured and unstructured approaches. I compiled a long list of formal statements, derived from the theoretical literature, about how education might be said to change a prisoner. These were asked in tick-box format to find out if the men strongly agreed, agreed, disagreed and so on with each item. Later each man was interviewed informally with the idea of getting them to explain the basis for each of their answers. These sessions brought forth a torrent of reflection about how the inmates were making use of their classroom experiences. Interestingly, the most acute observations often came in respect of initial questions which they deemed 'patronizing' or 'stupid'. These evoked important conceptual distinctions about how education had not change them directly but deepened their own *capacity* for change (for details, see Pawson, 1996). For the first time they talked about *their* world in *my* language. What we have here, in short, is not 'hygienic research', nor a 'transition to friendship', but a research relationship which allows respondents to think, 'well, that's your theory but in my experience it happens like this'. It is another important item for the interview toolkit.

## Data Analysis: Qualitative and Quantitative

We now put the assembly line into reverse and follow through the issue of how to analyse the data in order to examine if the original hypotheses have been fruitful. Data arrive back at the social researcher's office in all shapes and sizes – from disks packed full of coded survey responses, to scratchy tapes of patchy conversations, to scribbled fieldnotes from frazzled fieldworkers, to unfileable heaps of newspaper clippings, to highlighted portions of illuminating manuscripts. Clearly, I am not about to work through the sometimes fearsome technical details of how all these materials get processed. I will tackle, instead, what is often considered to be the basic divide, that between the use of 'verbal' and 'numerical' data. Again, we are in the territory of the qualitative versus the quantitative and, once again, I want to attempt to break the mould and argue – same problem, same solution.

### Numerical data

I take as my example the 'mobility matrix' from the famous Nuffield Survey into social class mobility (Goldthorpe, 1980). Mobility, in the sense used here, refers to the movement in social class position between generations. The question posed is as follows: are class boundaries 'rigid' and do people tend to stay in the class into which they were born; or is the class structure 'fluid' and is there a considerable shift in people's life chances? The answer to this question is to be found in the data in Table 2.1.

*Sociology*

**Table 2.1** Class composition by class of father (percentage by column)

| | | Respondent's class | | | | | | | |
|---|---|---|---|---|---|---|---|---|---|
| | | 1 | 2 | 3 | 4 | 5 | 6 | 7 | Total |
| *Father's class* | 1 | 25.3 | 12.4 | 9.6 | 6.7 | 3.2 | 2.0 | 6.5 | 680 |
| | 2 | 13.1 | 12.2 | 8.0 | 4.8 | 5.2 | 3.1 | 2.5 | 547 |
| | 3 | 10.4 | 10.4 | 10.8 | 7.4 | 8.7 | 5.7 | 6.0 | 687 |
| | 4 | 10.1 | 12.2 | 9.8 | 27.2 | 8.6 | 7.1 | 7.7 | 886 |
| | 5 | 12.5 | 14.0 | 13.2 | 12.1 | 16.6 | 12.2 | 9.6 | 1072 |
| | 6 | 16.4 | 21.7 | 26.1 | 24.0 | 31.0 | 41.8 | 35.2 | 2577 |
| | 7 | 12.1 | 17.1 | 22.6 | 17.8 | 26.7 | 28.0 | 36.6 | 2126 |
| | Total | 1230 | 1050 | 827 | 687 | 1026 | 1883 | 1872 | 8575 |

**Key**

1  Higher professional, higher administrators, senior managers, large proprietors

2  Lower grade professional, administration and managers, high-grade technicians and supervisors

3  Routine non-manual – mainly clerical and sales personnel

4  Small proprietors and self-employed artisans

5  Lower grade technical and supervisors

6  Skilled manual workers

7  Semi-skilled and unskilled manual workers

*Source*: Adapted from Goldthorpe, 1980

Part of a training in research methods is to learn how to 'read' such information and so I proceed with a one-paragraph lesson. The basic idea is to follow one generation to the next in terms of their class position. The baseline measure of social class is an occupational schema reproduced at the foot of the table which breaks the population down into seven classes. A random sample of male respondents was selected and two pieces of information were sought from them: their occupation and their father's occupation. This gives every family unit a place on the grid in Table 2.1. For instance, I am an academic (classified class 1 by Goldthorpe, 1980), my father was a grocer (class 4). Thus on the table, we would appear in column one, row four. The sample of 8575 father/son pairs are assigned to the various cells in the same fashion. The other significant feature of the table is given in the heading which explains that the data are presented as a 'percentage by column'. So, for example, if we look down column 1, this gives us a picture of the 'inflow' into that particular class. Starting at the top and reading down, the evidence reveals the following picture: *of respondents in class 1*, 25.3 per cent of their fathers were also in class 1, 13.1 per cent had class 2 fathers, 10.4 per cent came from class 3, 10.1 per cent had class 4 origins, 12.5 per cent were born into class 5, 16.4 per cent had skilled manual fathers, and 12.1 per cent had leapt all the way from the bottom of the occupational structure.

Having established the nature of the data, let us now see how they are put to work in analysis. Goldthorpe used the data to test a variety of hypotheses, one of which is referred to as the 'closure thesis' (1980: Ch. 2). This is a Marxist-inspired idea which argues that the élite class has an obvious interest in maintaining its position down the generations, and has sufficient clout to ensure that its own offspring retain their position while also making it difficult for other classes to enter this topmost group. It suggests, in short, that there will be a high degree of 'self-recruitment' to class 1, and relatively little upward mobility from below, especially from the ranks of the working classes. So what is the verdict on the closure thesis? We have already examined the crucial bit of evidence, namely the inflow into class 1. A quarter (25.3 per cent) of the class 1 respondents in the Nuffield Survey do indeed come from that background, but the other three-quarters have origins elsewhere in the class structure and, moreover, the upward march seems remarkably well distributed all the way through that class structure. Indeed, respondents from manual working backgrounds make up over a quarter (16.4 per cent + 12.1 per cent) of the élite positions. On first sight, we seem to have here a ringing denunciation of the closure thesis and a picture of significant fluidity within the British class system.

We now reach the methodological point I wish to make – which is that data analysis requires second sight! Put more formally, the lesson is that data never speak for themselves and that hypotheses get tested only by taking into account rival ideas and further evidence. For instance, an alternative hypothesis accounting for the upward swell of folks into class 1 is the so-called 'room-at-the-top' thesis. This argues that there has been a significant change in the occupational structure in 'late' industrial society and that the production process has changed in a way that creates more managers, professional, clerical and service-sector workers and which destroys traditional manual work. It could be this shift in the workforce needs, rather than the efforts of individuals, which are causing the high levels of mobility. Evidence for this alternative thesis can be seen instantly in Table 2.1. If we look at the sum total of respondents in class 1 (bottom of the column), we see that there are 1230 of them. Compare this with the 680 fathers who had class 1 position (end of column one) to get a clear picture of the vacuum created by the expansion of top positions which may well have had the effect of sucking up recruits from below.

Another rival hypothesis argues that the closure thesis still holds – but was intended for a much more narrowly defined élite class than that defined in

Goldthorpe's class 1. No self-respecting Marxist, for instance, would include academics and production managers as part of the self-perpetuating élite but, as we have seen, they fall within this initial test of the thesis. Such arguments led another member of the Nuffield team to re-examine the data and look at upward mobility into the component sectors of class 1. Heath (1981) thus discovers that the 25.3 per cent rate of recruitment into class 1 from class 1, shoots up to 40.2 per cent and 44.2 per cent in turn, if one narrows down the definition of that class to 'self-employed professionals' and 'large proprietors' respectively.

We are beginning to get a picture of how data analysis and hypothesis testing actually work. The key is to identify and choose between rival theories. Thus our example started with one regularity – considerable upward mobility into the élite class. This datum could be explained in (at least) three ways:

1. the class structure is fluid
2. the workforce has transformed
3. some parts of the 'élite' are open and some closed.

Good research has the patience to hold back on affirming the former before the others get checked out. The 'closure thesis' quickly becomes the 'closure theses' as it is interrogated by different facets of the data. One idea spins off another and the spotlight falls on one part of the data matrix then another. The result is that it takes Goldthorpe 310 pages to complete an analysis of the social processes that produce Table 2.1, and this is not to mention the volumes of critique and counter-critique which followed (Pawson, 1993). Analysis is not a terminus but a process.

*Verbal data*

Most data analysis in the qualitative traditions takes the form of the presentation of transcripts of dialogues taken from the group under study which are then put into context and 'explained' by the researcher. I take as my example a typical and highly respected piece of ethnographic analysis, Pollert's (1981) *Girls, Wives, Factory Lives* and also draw on a critique of her research contained in Hammersley (1990: Ch. 4). We join the analysis with Pollert explaining the daily grind of factory life:

> 'Cutting off', or separating the 'inner self' from what is objectively happening on the 'outside' is one of the sorry 'skills' we are forced into, in an existence dominated by alienated relations of production. It is otherwise know as 'wishing one's life away'. Some girls actually pride themselves in the art of switching off, pitying those who were bad at it, and thinking themselves to be very lucky to be working at all:

*Racquel*: Yes you get bored sitting up here, very bored... You gets used to it though. I think that it's imagination a lot of the time. I get fed up sometimes, but I don't really get that fed up, because I haven't really got anything to be fed up about.

*Anna* (the researcher): What do you think about?

*Racquel*: Nothing, really. I can sit up here a whole day without really speaking. (Pollert, 1981)

Hammersley's point is that in such analysis it is vital to inspect closely the relationship between the evidence and claims, as they to do not always match. In this particular extract he perceives that Pollert makes at least three claims:

1. that the workers cut themselves off or switch off from their work
2. that they refer to this as wishing one's life away; and that it is a 'sorry' skill produced by alienating relations of production
3. that some of the women prided themselves on their ability to switch off and pitied those who were bad at it judging themselves to be lucky to be working.

His judgement is that the evidence (the dialogue between Racquel and Anna) justifies only the first of these propositions and that the other two remain unsupported. The point here is not to take sides between Pollert and Hammersley but rather to show that in qualitative analysis the data will usually allow for alternative explanations to be made. Indeed, authors of qualitative research know full well the possibility that their accounts can be challenged. It is this knowledge that differentiates them from story-tellers. Thus it is for the good researcher, as part of the analysis, to take into account potential rival theories and bring forth further evidence which will help the reader in coming to a preference for one particular 'reading'. The best qualitative analysis, therefore, takes the form of a *pattern-making exercise* (Diesing, 1971) in which particular claims are buttressed and counter-claims anticipated and rebutted by a whole patchwork of evidence.

Let me now pull together some conclusions from both the quantitative and qualitative examples. *Rule one* is a negative. Do not be misled into thinking that it is the data themselves which provide analytical power. So it is not 'hard data', 'number crunching' or 'statistical power' which gives quantitative analysis its clout. Nor is it 'rich data', 'a good story', or 'empathetic ability' which makes qualitative analysis convincing. *Rule two* is a positive. Data analysis and hypothesis testing are two sides of the same coin. One will need several hypotheses to make sense of any datum and one will need much data to make sense of any hypotheses. Data analysis, whether quantitative or qualitative, is about *utilizing evidence to discern and choose between theories*. The principal skill of data analysis is the refinement of theory.

## Conclusion: The Realists and the Relativists

I began this chapter by drawing attention to a basic conundrum about the sociologist's expertise. Every explanation that the sociologist comes up with implies an act of faith. How do they know they are correct and how does anyone else know that they are correct? An obvious danger is lurking. The world is full of so-called 'experts'. Soothsayers come and go. Priests and politicians, agony aunts and commercial consultants, indeed anyone with a couple of beers down their throat is prepared to act as an instant pundit on the social world and its problems. Making claims for sociological wisdom thus requires a leap of imagination. Is this sheer bravado, mere conceit or is there some basis for this 'special knowledge'?

As we have seen, this 'quest for certainty' goes by the name of 'methodology'. Coming to grips with 'research methods' thus presents something of a challenge to the beginning student. 'Methods' is the hard bit. 'Methods' is the bit that slows down the imagination. It is the bit that is supposed to turn the pontification into justification. I have introduced the methodological domain via a series of dichotomies between principle and practice, pure and applied, structured and unstructured, qualitative and quantitative, and so on and so forth. We now reach the *big dualism*. After the effort expended on methodological strategies and tactics, do we end up with objectivity or subjectivity? Is it all truth or merely opinion?

In academic terms, we are discussing the opposition between 'realism' and 'relativism' in social research methodology. Realism is founded on the belief that the social world is real and external to our senses. It assumes that people have power and individuals have intentions, and these things are just as real as horses having hooves and water having wetness. Relativists do not believe that it is possible to know about the world in a way which is independent of the knower. They believe that beauty is in the eye of the beholder and, so too, is our understanding of good and bad, right and wrong and, of course, power and intentions. While it is clearly an oversimplification to imagine that every piece of research is either a search for objective fact or a crusade on behalf of subjective opinion, sociology has suffered tremendous mood swings in relation to these poles.

If I can give a personal view, the answer to the big question lies in the small detail of the dilemmas, problems and disputes already covered in previous sections of this chapter. It will not surprise the reader, therefore, to discover that my inclination on 'realism versus relativism' is that, for practical purposes, it is a phoney opposition in exactly the same way as were many of the detailed 'debates' already covered. That is to say, it is as plain as day that researchers do *not* have to choose between starting their investigations under the assumption that they have automatic access to the facts, nor that their findings will turn out to be only as good as any other viewpoint.

So, I come down on the side of the truth – knowing that the truths of sociological research will always be partial and provisional and never uniform and universal. I figure that certainty requires humility – and that research can only help us in choosing between theories rather than proving one. I rest content that good-quality research comes with qualifications – our hypothesis will work only for certain people in certain circumstances at certain times.

'Truth' and 'objectivity' thus remain the *goals* and *ambitions* of sociological research, and I can do no better than to conclude with Gordon's brilliant quip for preserving them:

> That these ideals cannot be attained is not a reason for disregarding them. Perfect cleanliness is also impossible but it does not serve as a warrant for not washing, much less for rolling about in a manure pile. (Gordon, 1992)

Be careful where you tread. There's a lot of it about.

## Further Reading

Babbie, E. *The Practice of Social Research,* 5th edn, Belmont, Wadsworth, 1989. The best traditional 'cookbook' introduction to methods of inquiry.

Blaikie, N. *Approaches to Social Inquiry,* London, Polity, 1993. Provides a good introduction to a range of research strategies.

Hammersley, M. *Reading Ethnographic Research,* Harlow, Longman, 1990. A clear introduction to ethnographic research methods.

Pawson, R. and Tilley, N. *Realistic Evaluation,* London, Sage, 1997. An introduction, with case study examples, to the comparatively new area of evaluation methodology.

deVaus, D. *Surveys in Social Research,* 4th edn, London, University College Press, 1996. The standard text on the survey method.

Williams, M. and May, T. *Introduction to the Philosophy of Social Research,* London, University College Press, 1996. A good introduction to epistemology, ontology and matters philosophical.

# 3

# Sociological Theory

## *Alan Swingewood*

The aim of this chapter is to provide an introduction to some of the major theories and theoretical perspectives that have been developed by sociologists to help explain the key 'sociological questions' of social order, social change and the relationship between the individual and society. This chapter examines some of the most important contributions to these questions made by classical, modern and contemporary social theoriests. It should help you begin to understand:

■ The origins of sociological theory in the 'classical' theories of Durkheim, Marx and Weber

■ 'Modern' structural functional, symbolic interactionist, ethnomethodological and Marxist theories

■ The significance of the macro-micro distinction in social theory

■ Giddens' theory of the structuration and Bourdieu's theory of fields

■ The postmodern critique of meta-narratives

---

### CONCEPTS

macro- and micro-theory ■ social integration ■ ideology
materialism and idealism ■ methodological individualism ■ agency
hegemony ■ culture industries ■ meta-narratives

---

# Introduction

While the previous chapter on methodology examined theoretical issues concerned with the *production* of sociological knowledge, this chapter is concerned with *substantive* sociological theory. Substantive theories are the 'sociological maps' identified in Chapter 1 that sociologists use to help them explain what societies are and how they work and change. Substantive theories attempt to organize the apparently random nature of social life into coherent social knowledge and, at the same time, raise new questions for social research on the relations between different parts of society, such as how they are constituted and survive as permanent structures and how they affect individual actions. The central problem for sociological theory in this context, and the problem on which this chapter will focus, is the nature of the relationship between large-scale institutions, such as bureaucracies or religious organizations (the macro-dimension), and patterns of face-to-face interactions between individuals in everyday life (the micro-dimension).

Sociological theories are not developed in a vacuum, they are *ideas* which invariably arise from theorists' attempts to develop, refine, criticize or replace existing theories. There is thus a tradition, or legacy, of sociological theory, and many theoretical ideas from the 'classical sociology' of the nineteenth and early twentieth century continue to influence contemporary theory. Consequently, this chapter begins with a discussion of the legacy of the classical theories of Durkheim, Marx and Weber. It then looks at the major perspectives of 'modern' social theory; the macro-approach of structural functionalism and the micro-sociology of interactionism and ethnomethodology. It goes on to examine some of the most important attempts in sociological theory to synthesize the macro and the micro in sociology and concludes with a brief discussion of the challenge of postmodern theory.

# Classical Social Theory

## *Durkheim*

Emile Durkheim (1858–1917), the first professor of sociology, probably did more than anyone to establish sociology as an independent academic subject. He was particularly influenced by the work of Auguste Comte (1798–1857). Comte argued that, to make sense of societies, sociology had to adopt the methods of the natural sciences, especially biology, as the basis for a positivist social science. However, while sociological analysis must be based on careful observation, these observations only make sense when interpreted by theory. The idea that no real observation is possible unless it is first directed, and finally interpreted by some theory, was developed by Durkheim and is one of the valuable legacies of Comte's early sociological positivism (Comte, 1896).

Second, Comte defined society *holistically*, that is, as a system which exists *independently* of individuals and determines their actions in ways which can be understood scientifically. Durkheim followed Comte in seeing the focus of sociological inquiry being on *social structures* rather than on the *individuals* who comprised them. However, unlike Comte, he argued that, although sociology dealt with objective facts which could be observed and measured, these 'social facts' were not mere objective *things* but external, collective phenomena which were general through society, such as law and religion, and which constrained individual action but which were not reducible to being explained in 'individual' terms. As things like moral codes and language were social facts so, less obviously, were invisible moral currents generated by collective social life. One of Durkheim's most striking demonstrations of this theory is found in his major study, *Suicide* (1897/1952). Statistics from European countries showed not only that there were significant variations in the suicide rates of different countries, and social groups within these countries, but that these variations were remarkably consistent over time. For Durkheim, the stability of the suicide rates was a collective phenomenon which could only be explained in relation to other social facts. He argued that the major cause of variations in the suicide rate was the degree of social integration (or social solidarity) existing in specific social groups. For example, he explained the consistently lower suicide rates of Catholic communities compared to Protestant communities in terms of the fact that Catholic society binds the believer more effectively than Protestant society into an established set of shared beliefs and ritualized practices common to all the faithful. Protestant communities are thus less integrating and, in times of crisis, Protestants were more likely to be thrown back onto their own resources and were thus more vulnerable to suicide. The greater protection from suicide for Catholics came not from their religion as such, but from the more intense and integrating quality of their social life. By relating the suicide rate to social solidarity, Durkheim raised important questions about the ways individuals internalize the culture of a specific group and thus regulate their behaviour from within. Durkheim's concept of culture as the mechanism of social integration was to exert a great influence in the subsequent development of sociology.

Another of Durkheim's concepts in his analysis of suicide was anomie, a condition of normlessness, a breakdown in the internalizing of values and the strong social bonds generated by social solidarity. Durkheim's substantive theory focused on the disintegration of social order brought about by rapid social change and the subsequent erosion of traditional institutions and values. He argued that modern societies would not work through external compulsion but only through people internalizing values and acting through their beliefs. A mechanistic, purely external concept of society eliminates its 'soul which is the composition of collective ideals' (Durkheim, 1964: 312).

What Durkheim suggested is that social life contains social facts that function as collective symbols (for example religious rites and national flags) through which society becomes 'conscious of itself'. He defined these forms as 'collective representations', the embodiment of ideals which constitute a *symbolic* order, a universe of shared meanings. The soldier who dies for his country thus dies for the flag, a sign with no value in itself but a collective representation signifying a specific reality which succeeds in motivating action.

Thus culture and symbolic representations can strengthen social solidarity and work against the anomic tendencies of advanced industrial society. Durkheim developed a more complex notion of social facts, involving the internalizing of values and the possibility of action through beliefs. Thus, societies were *both* physical and mental entities. However, in spite of valuable insights of this idea critics argue that Durkheim did not link it with the *active* part individuals play in the 'making' of the social world. In Durkheim's theory, individuals execute their beliefs and values, but are not involved in *changing* ideas and symbols through collective action. Durkheim's theory does not really explain which social groups produce specific values. Preoccupied with the problem of social order and the concept of society as an organism Durkheim did not really address questions of power, conflict and change.

## Marx

Unlike sociological positivism, Marxism identified social theory with the interests of a specific social class, the industrial working class, and defined capitalism as the inevitable prelude to the penultimate stage of social development, socialism. While Marx's first writings were largely philosophical, concerned with abstract questions of freedom, it was with *The German Ideology* (Marx and Engels, 1845) that he established the framework for what he termed 'the materialist conception of history'. In this text he defines society in terms of its forms of economic production, its structure of property, the division of labour, class structure and class struggles. Society is conceived as historical and *relational*: 'Society does not consist of individuals; it expresses the sum of connections and relationships in which individuals find themselves' (Marx, 1971). Society exists through its 'material infrastructure'; that is, the forces of production (tools, machinery) and highly organized forms of collective social labour (wage labour in capitalism). For Marx, it is this material 'base' that generates the 'superstructure' of ideas, religion, education, political systems and so on. Hence the real foundations of any society are the forces of production and those who own and control the forces of production are the ruling class. Ideas reflect class interests: 'The ruling ideas of each epoch are those of the ruling class' (Marx and Engels, 1845/1964: 37–8). Thus, free-market economics reflected the ideological values and interests of the ruling capitalist class, the bourgeoisie, and helped legitimize its domination.

Marx believed, like Comte, that human society develops through the workings of certain laws, which he argued were specific to a particular mode of production. However, unlike Comte and Durkheim who regarded conflict as 'pathological', he argued that social and historical development occur through contradictions and conflict. For Marx, the source of change was a contradiction between the technological forces of production and the relations of production, that is, the way production is organized socially. For example, within the feudal mode of production a fundamental contradiction develops between the burgeoning capitalist classes' 'need' for markets, the free exchange of commodities and a mobile labour force, and the economically static and restrictive nature of feudal economic institutions where land, for example, could not be bought, only inherited.

Thus in Marx's theory of social change, different stages in historical development were defined in terms of their mode of production, with each containing elements within it that point the way to 'higher', more advanced and complex forms of social organization. Thus industrial capitalist production involves the concentration of masses of workers in close proximity. Herded together in towns and factories, Marx believed the working class will become increasingly aware of common interests and how these interests are in conflict with those of the owning class. This will lead to political awareness and increasing conflict over the ownership of the forces of production. Marx predicted that as capitalism will not be able to resolve its internal contradictions, it is a social system historically doomed with the bourgeois class acting as the 'gravediggers' of their own economic and social order.

Marx's model of society, then, is a system built around the primacy of economic processes and laws of production which assumes a deterministic relationship between the forces and relations of production, between base and superstructure. Hence his statement 'the handmill gives you society with the feudal lord; the steam mill society with the industrial capitalist' (Marx, 1962: 109). Although Marx has been criticized for producing an 'economically determined' model of society, he was aware – like Durkheim – of the critical role played by ideas in the constitution of society and he frequently argued that in particular contexts ideas can play a decisive role in shaping social institutions and social change. In his major work, *Capital* (1957), he noted, almost in anticipation of Weber's thesis on the link between ascetic religion and modern capitalism, that 'Protestantism, by changing all the traditional holidays into work days, plays an important part in the genesis of capital' (Marx, 1957: 276). In the same text he notes that at the end of every labour process, we get a result that already existed in the imagination of the labourer before commencement' (ibid.: 174). Thus the concept of production itself is not crudely materialistic: for production always involves knowledge, imagination, skills, reflexivity. Although culture and ideas may reflect specific social conditions, like the reflexive nature of the architect, they contribute actively to its further development. Marx thus allows space for social action. Collective agents, in the form of social classes, become aware of their position in class society, their relations with other classes and develop institutions for consolidating and furthering their interests.

How does this recognition of the importance of ideas fit in with Marx's concept of system and laws of development? Society is defined as a hierarchically organized structure involving social struggles between different groups and classes. In contrast to Durkheim, Marx emphasizes the violent and abrupt nature of social change generated through conflict and contradictions. This is change at the system level but it also takes place through collective action. If Marx's work held to a rigidly deterministic theory of iron laws and inevitable historical change (as with Comte), there is no scope for either collective or individual action. However, as I have suggested, Marx's model does provide for knowledgeable collective agents to act in pursuit of goals given their consciousness of interests and the fluid, dynamic structure of modern capitalism (Sztompka, 1994). One of Marx's most important insights, which continues to influence sociological theory, was his grasp of the revolutionary nature of modern capitalism, a system constantly undergoing rapid change, dynamically transforming both the economic structure as well as all social relations, culture and ideas. The broad, macro-historical process in which collective human action takes place is never at rest but, through the workings of social struggles and contradictions, permanently challenges all traditions and fixed notions. Thus Marx's concept of modern societies, or modernity, is one in which 'all that is solid melts into air' (Marx and Engels, 1962).

## Weber: Social Action and Social Change

While Marx emphasized that history was the product of economic change and collective action, Weber (1864–1920) opposed this macro-theory and advanced a theory of 'methodological individualism' rather than Marx's 'methodological collectivism'. Weber was especially critical of the concept of objectively determining laws with the assumption that culture existed merely as a passive reflection of material forces. He believed that Marx's emphasis on systems and laws diminished the active role of the individual, known in sociology as agency or action. In contrast to the rather deterministic view of the individual reacting to structural arrangements put forward by positivism and Marxism, Weber argued that society should be conceived primarily in terms of the *meaningful* social action of people. Collectivities such as classes, bureaucracies and states do not determine behaviour, but rather exist as modes of 'actual or possible social actions of individual persons' (Weber, 1978: 14). Weber argued that, rather than trying to analyse human action from the 'outside', sociology has to be based on the interpretative understanding (*verstehen*) of the meanings that people give to their actions. People are motivated to act because they believe in the reality of certain ideas.

Weber applied his methodological individualism in his study of the relation between the rise of capitalism and the Protestant religion. Capitalism was not simply the inevitable product of objective economic laws but was also the result of a pattern of motivation engendered by Protestant culture with its rejection of worldly pleasures and the promotion of the values of a disciplined work ethic, investing rather than consuming and seeking salvation through a specific course of action (doing good works) in this world. These values were internalized and translated into economic and social principles which rejected luxury, immediate gratification and the avoidance of all spontaneous enjoyment of life. Individuals were self-controlled and disciplined in relation to pleasure and use of time. Rather than a passive reflection of class interests, ideas such as these, which helped bring about a distinct and disciplined 'work ethic' conducive to the development of modern capitalism, constituted active material forces. As Weber expressed it:

> Material and ideal interests directly govern men's conduct. Yet very frequently the 'world images' that have been created by 'ideas' have, like switchmen, determined the tracks along which action has been pushed by the dynamic of interest. (Weber, 1948b: 280)

Protestantism, especially the Calvinist sects, linked material economic needs closely with ideal interests in salvation. Martin Luther's concept of the 'calling', fulfilling one's duty to God, helped to promote disciplined action, while Calvin's doctrine of predestination – with its claim that God had chosen few believers for eternal grace and no one knew who they were – produced an anxiety which could be offset to some extent by economic success in this world as a sign of God's favour. Through useful activity, self-control, commitment to the ideal of work as an end in itself, Protestants could hope for salvation. This 'ethic' was an important part of the 'spirit' of capitalism.

For Weber, then, the springs of action and hence of social change were psychological. While India and China developed markets, division of labour, money economy and trade routes, it was in western Europe that these material conditions linked up with a particular *culture* to produce a highly rationalized form of capitalism, one based on the principles of systematic and impersonal rules, calculation and predictability.

Weber's theory of social action thus linked the micro-level of everyday social action with the macro-level of large-scale historical transformation in a way that avoided a determinism based on laws of development. In short, Weber's methodological individualism attempts to integrate a broad historical sociology with a concept of action. Weber's critique of Marx was that social change is always 'open ended', based as it is on the unpredictability of human action. The impossibility of predicting how people will act in any given context means that sociology will always lack the predictability of action conditioned by laws. It cannot offer a vision of the future.

# Modern Social Theory

## Functionalism and its Critics

Marxism, the sociological positivism of Comte and Durkheim and social action constituted the three major classical sociologies which continued to influence the post-classical phase of sociology. As sociology grew and developed into a professional academic subject, it continued to lack a unified social theory, although for a time structural functionalism became the most widely accepted general theory in sociology.

Structural functionalism had its origins in positivism with its concept of society as an organism in which the various component parts contribute to the integration of the whole. In his *Rules of Sociological Method* (1895/1982), Durkheim distinguished functional from causal explanation, arguing that the causes of social facts must be investigated separately from the function they fulfil socially. Causes refer to origins, functions to intrinsic properties: hence the causes of the division of labour must be sought in preceding social facts, such as changes in population and urbanism, while its function is to generate reciprocity of services and thus produce social solidarity. However, examining functions in this way fails to resolve the problem of the making of institutions and the role agents play in their everyday functions. This issue is particularly marked in the work of Parsons (1902–79) who laid out the basic principles of modern functionalism in painstaking and elaborate detail notably in works such as *The Social System* (1951) and *Toward A General Theory of Action* (Parsons and Shils, 1962).

While classical sociology integrated theoretical analysis and empirical research, Parson's work reflects an emerging trend within sociology towards the 'autonomy of theory'. Parsons described himself as 'an incurable theorist' and although his work examined many empirical and historical issues – fascism, family and socialization, social evolution, education and medicine – it was at an extremely abstract level of pure theory which at times seemed to have lost contact with social and historical reality. For example, his view of society as a social system was defined in terms of 'needs' or 'functional prerequisites', the generalized conditions essential for survival including provision for an adequate relationship of the individual with the environment, differentiation of roles, communication, shared goals, socialization and the social control of deviant behaviour. These prerequisites are grouped under four headings: adaptation (activities by which a system adapts to its environment modifying and controlling it in terms of system needs); goal attainment (mobilizing resources for specific goals); integration (the solidarity of the system, its survival as a cohesive whole); and finally, latency (accumulation and distribution of energy in the form of motivation). This was popularly known as the AGIL schema (Parsons, 1967).

A system is further held together by three sub-systems including the personality sub-system (motivation, values), the cultural (action orientated to symbolic forms, beliefs, ideas) and finally, the social sub-system (interaction between actors sharing common understandings and stable roles). Although many of these formulations approximate to commonsense propositions, the broad tendency of Parsons' conceptual framework lies in its emphasis on the degree of functional integration of a system: actors successfully internalize values to maintain the persistence of the system itself. Parsons' functionalist model takes little account of the possibility that motivation and the internalization of values may produce conflict and struggle. For example, values can be divisive, working to exclude rather than include specific groups into the system. There is also the question of *whose* values prevail in given situations.

Effectively, a functionalist model of society removes contradiction; the system functions behind the backs of its agents producing a huge moving equilibrium, integrated through a central value system, 'a set of normative judgements held by members of society who define... what to them is a good society' which becomes institutionalized into normative expectations and internalized 'need dispositions' (Parsons and Shils, 1962: 225–7). Parsons' functionalism thus assumes a neatly ordered, closed social world, a vast filing cabinet consisting of systems and sub-systems, multiple divisions and subdivisions, endless classifications with the most tenuous relation to historically produced societies, a theoretical framework in which questions of who makes values, and why and how, have been systematically removed. Moreover, system changes occur not through social struggles over resources and ideology but through modes of internal disequilibrium and re-equilibrium. Parsons' concept of actor is also too one-dimensional, too easily conforming to the existing norms and values, lacking a many-sided and reflexive self capable of engaging in the strategies and practices linked to social change and to the broader issues of power.

Critics of functionalism have frequently pointed to its apparent failure to provide an adequate explanation of social change and the related issues of conflict and social struggle. Some functionalists, however, have integrated the concept of conflict within the model by arguing that it functions as 'a safety mechanism', producing an equilibrating and stabilising impact' (Coser, 1967). However, this is to define conflict in terms of system needs and fails to address the problem Marx raised of conflict playing a productive and constituting role in the making of institutions and values. The concept of system needs removes the actor as an active force from the structure so that 'conflict' is divorced from action. Thus the functionalist analysis of education, for example, points to its role in allocating individuals to specific occupations. However, it fails to address the conflict that can develop *within* the educational system. For example, as we saw in Chapter 2, Willis' (1977) research highlighted the conflicts between working-class children and the formal structure of the school, which resulted in anti-educational sub-cultures with their own specific values.

The concept of system needs seemingly reinforces the general criticism of Parsonian functionalism as based in an 'oversocialized' notion of the individual, a cultural dope with no apparent autonomy. Parsons has always rejected this criticism pointing to his concept of 'pattern variables' for providing actors with some autonomy and choice. Pattern variables structure modes of action, by providing the actor with choices over pairs or dichotomies of values, options which decide their relations with others. They include particularism/universalism (relating to others on the basis of gender or class and so on, or as a human being); affectivity/affective neutrality (choosing emotional involvement in relations, or as a business arrangement); specifity/diffuseness (relations defined in terms of role, lawyer, teacher, or more broadly through marriage and family; quality/performance (choosing relations through persons or through ends). Action is a mixture of the pattern variables but it remains limited and formal. Thus, in one of his own examples, Parsons' argues that the doctor/patient relationship involves universalism, specificity and affective neutrality. While this has been seen as a major theoretical contribution to the sociology of sickness (see Chapter 12), it has been criticized for failing to account for the fact that doctors are increasingly treating patients as sources of income in a competitive capitalist culture, striving for status and power within a hierarchically organized medical profession and sometimes 'medicalizing' areas of life for their own interests. Such action is difficult to accommodate to Parsons' abstract categories.

## Action and Interaction: Problems of the Macro-micro Link

As a macro-sociological theory, functionalism conceived society as an external system structured in equilibrium and self-regulation, a whole superior to its constituent parts, in which the active human agent exercised little significant role in constituting and transforming institutions, structures and ideas. Although Parsons refers to his concept of system as 'a system of action', it is hard to find links between action and structure other than the concept of the actor assimilating cultural values which then become institutionalized components of the system itself and regulate the scope of action.

Micro-sociology is an attempt to resolve this problem by developing a distinctive sociological concept of the active, human self. The major contribution to sociology's concept of the self came from Mead (1863–1931). Mead emphasized the fluid and open nature of social order and the capacity of individuals to create new roles and meanings. For Mead, communication is effected through 'significant gestures', self-conscious acts which distinguish human from non-human behaviour. Animals do not communicate through universal symbols such as language, but react and adjust to situations. In contrast, humans interpret the *meaning* of other people's actions; language gives them the unique capacity to 'take the role of others' and see themselves from the point of view of others. The self is thus developed through its reciprocal relation with others and the wider community, both as a subject and an object. Mead theorized the self in terms of an 'I' and a 'Me'. The 'I' is the subject which thinks and acts, while the 'Me' is a consequence of the individual's awareness of self as object existing for others. It is the 'I' that has ideas, drives, impulses (such as the desire to walk out of a very boring class) while the 'Me' takes into account the reactions of others (that wouldn't look good, the tutor has to mark your examination paper). The 'I' is a combination of biological drives and social experiences, while the 'Me' arises almost entirely from communication through language. The self is thus a 'social structure' developing through patterns of interaction with itself, with others and with the community or social group. Hence the individual player within a football team must take account of the role and structure of the whole team. The self arises by taking into account the attitude of others and assimilating the group's 'social habits', values and goals. Mead suggests that it is shortly after childhood that the individual internalizes roles, especially the collective role of the group, which he called the 'generalized other' (Mead, 1934).

Mead regarded his work as social psychological rather than strictly sociological. It was Blumer who, in 1937, extended Mead's ideas to the field of social structure, coining the term 'symbolic interactionism', to refer to those modes of action whereby individuals 'negotiate' the different social situations encountered in everyday life to produce new meanings (Blumer, 1967). What is striking in Blumer's work is the emphasis on reciprocity, that social action occurs only through the self taking account of others – their values, ideas, definition of the situation – within a fluid and open structure, where relations are never fixed and rigidly stabilized.

While this approach focuses on the 'voluteristic' nature of social life, interactionism has been criticized for avoiding institutional analysis and macro-sociological issues of social class and power. In this context the work of Goffman (1922–82) is especially important for attempting to define interactionism more precisely and for taking up the problems of the micro-macro-link. In his late essay, 'The interaction order' (1983), Goffman argued that face-to-face interaction constitutes a *specific* order defined by its own distinctive internal properties (language, symbols, rules and moral obligations) and clear boundaries. The interaction order is not a mere reflection of the macro-institutional order but exists in its own right. Goffman's (1991) early work on mental hospitals had shown how, in the face of a depersonalizing social order where patients are classified by the institution as if they were objects and divested of any moral responsibility, there nevertheless develops an informal interaction order which enables them to sustain a sense of identity and engage in morally responsible social action.

Goffman's point is that the interaction order always involves a moral dimension, trust and tact in encounters with others and a commitment to sustain the order itself. For Goffman, the queue is perhaps the best example of the working of the interaction order as external influences (such as class or status) are usually blocked, with individuals accepting the inherent orderliness of the first-come-first-served basis.

But how is this interaction order linked with the macro-order? Goffman suggests that society exists and is integrated loosely through talk, with everyday conversation acting as a ritual affirmation of a commonly shared reality. Talk plays a key symbolic role in defining, strengthening and maintaining the structure of social groups and patterns of interaction. Through talk a world of other participants is created in everyday conversation, in pubs and work, and in public ceremonies, university seminars and learned societies, each one 'a little social system with its own boundary maintaining tendencies' (Goffman, 1972: 113). Goffman's point is that while the self develops only in relation to its social context, it is constituted at the macro-level by symbolic forms and shared meanings common to the micro-level of talk. Everyday conversation, for example, is usually sustained through the symbolic and ritual elements of politeness, with its respect for the other participants that is similar to the conception of the individual in religious institutions. Thus the institutional and interaction orders are 'loosely connected' through their common basis in symbolic and ritual forms that define the individual as embodying sacred and moral value (ibid.: 73, 95).

While this example of the 'loose coupling' of the micro- and macro-orders is ingenious, it has been criticized for failing to deal sufficiently with interaction within the institutional order itself. In common with many other micro-sociologists, Goffman focuses on interaction *only* at the micro-level. However, many other sociologists argue that all interaction is hierarchically structured. Within bureaucracies, for example, administrators and managers will generate their own distinctive interaction order producing meanings and new ideas that will affect the everyday life of those in subordinate positions, in the micro-contexts of the shopfloor, hospital wards, supermarkets. In 'The interaction order' Goffman suggested that in everyday interaction individuals draw on resources from institutional contexts, those relating to class and ethnic relations for example, to sustain them in encounters with others. However, class and ethnicity play important roles in constituting the interaction orders of both macro- and micro-contexts. And, while both orders can be empirically distinguished, it is rather a question of a tight, not a loose, coupling.

Goffman's micro-sociology has also been criticized from an action point of view for its conceptualization of the reflexive nature of the self. He argued that individuals do not have a unified self but, rather, have multiple selves in their everyday lives as they constantly move in and out of varied social and linguistic contexts. However, in stressing that the self is always 'embedded' and thus conditioned by a specific context, Goffman tends to minimize the cognitive and reflexive elements that constitute the self and its actions. He examines neither the sources of motivation (the Weber problem), nor how individuals come to believe in certain values while rejecting others and how they act with others on the basis of such beliefs.

It is ethnomethodology, perhaps the most radical of micro-sociologies, that represents the most strenuous attempt to deal with the question of motivation. Developed by Garfinkel during the 1960s, ethnomethodology (*ethno* referring to the observational study of the stock of commonsense knowledge available to individuals, while *method* refers to the strategies individuals employ to make sense of the social world and communicate meaning) was concerned with 'common sense knowledge of social structures as an object of theoretical interest' (Garfinkel, 1984: 77).

Ethnomethodology was influenced by the work of Schutz (1899–1959). Schutz agreed with Weber that sociological explanation should be based on the meanings that individuals give to their actions, but he argued that Weber had ignored an important problem:

> [Weber's] concept of the meaningful act of the individual – the key idea of interpretive sociology – by no means defines a primitive, as he thinks it does. It is, on the contrary, a mere label for a highly complex and ramified area that calls for much further study. (1972: 7–8)

This 'further study' involves the attempt to explain the ways in which people actually 'accomplish' social interaction. Reciprocity of perspectives cannot be assumed – it has to be explained. From this basis, Schutz developed the concept of the life world, the everyday world of experience, 'an inter-subjective world of culture' (Schutz, 1974: 134–5). Within this world of everyday experience, meaning is constantly produced by individuals who share in a common culture and a commonsense knowledge of how the elements of the everyday world work. This emphasis on knowledge, understanding, shared meanings and inter-subjective relationships contrast with Parsons' stress on the external and constraining role of norms in the socialization of individuals and their embodiment in the personality system.

Garfinkel, following Schutz, argued that social life is an 'accomplishment' of 'the organised artful practices of everyday life' (ibid.: 11). When agents choose particular goals they do so in terms of the taken-for-granted, mundane knowledge that is available in any given situation. A sociological theory of action must not only include the agent's own account of that action, but also examine how agents draw on commonsense knowledge and the *unstated* rules and assumptions of everyday life. It is through a process of practical social reasoning that individuals come to understand and grasp the rules that govern everyday social action. Although we may believe that our activities are shaped by clearly understood rules, this is not the case. The order around us is fragile. To illustrate this Garfinkel conducted a series of 'breaching experiments' in which individuals were faced with the breakdown of their expectations. For example, he encouraged his students to act as if they were lodgers within their own homes, thus disrupting the taken-for-granted routines of everyday life bringing to light its basis in commonsense assumptions. This disrupted situation caused anger and confusion, as individuals strove to re-establish the rules of everyday life. Hence Garfinkel's view, contrary to Parsons, that social order is not the result of the workings of system imperatives, or a common culture, but the practical accomplishments of highly reflexive agents as they make and remake meanings within everyday social interaction.

However, while ethnomethodology addresses the problem of motivation by positing a knowledgeable, imaginative and reflexive self, it tends to over-emphasize this voluntarism (agents vary in their capacity for reflexivity) and to place sociological analysis too narrowly within the micro-contexts of everyday social interaction. Ethnomethodology 'resolves' the agency structure problem by dissolving the latter. Such an approach thus ignores the possibility that individuals may be *unaware* of the ways in which social structural elements, external to their immediate situation, may shape their understanding and action: class position, ideology, power relations may influence educational, religious or political values and play a key role in determining the individual's attitude to others and to society. It is this exclusion of the macro-dimension which limits ethnomethodology as a sociological theory, for interaction occurs at both the macro- and micro-level. It is the complex relation of these two dimensions of social life which constitutes one of the major problems of sociological theory. The following sections examine attempts to develop concepts and substantive theory which might link the macro- and micro-dimensions in Marxism, structuration and field theory.

# Attempts at Theoretical Synthesis

## *Marxism: From Gramsci to Habermas*

Although Marx had noted the reflexive nature of human agents and argued for the role of collective agents (social classes) in social change, his work largely concentrated on the macro-economic and social processes. Few Marxists developed concepts which could link the macro- and micro-dimensions of the social formation. An important exception was Gramsci (1891–1937) who was one of the first major Marxist theorists to address this issue by analysing the workings of the cultural superstructure. He argued that socio-historical change was not the product of impersonal laws but the result of collective human will organized in collective social institutions, such as trade unions and political parties, involving both struggles over material resources as well as ideas. Gramsci used the concept of *hegemony* (derived from a Greek word meaning the leadership of one state over another) to describe a process whereby those social groups and classes aspiring to political and economic domination must develop both narrow 'corporate' interests, such as control over economic resources, *and* broader intellectual and moral leadership, including cultural, ethical, political ideas and values. Gramsci's thesis was that while 'corporate' interests are specific to a class, hegemonic interests are general to the whole society. He cites the case of the French Revolution where the revolutionary Jacobins developed from a class which initially functioned to organize a bourgeois mode of production to a class which represented all the popular social forces, such as the middle classes, working class and peasants, in opposing the old, aristocratic feudal regime. As a concept, hegemony elucidates the ways 'rising' classes seek to dominate not merely through the use of force and coercion but through *consent*, through generating ideas which command the support of subordinate classes, such as universal suffrage, expansion of education and the legal system. In modern societies individuals actively internalize the cultural values of a dominant or rising class ('the moment of hegemony') and this points to a voluntarist element in political domination with agents consenting and thus legitimating class rule. In modern society no one class can dominate 'from above' by excluding and ignoring other groups and classes. A dominant class must listen to the voices of subordinate classes thus producing a balance or 'equilibrium'.

Force and coercion belong to the state, while hegemony belongs to what Gramsci called 'civil society' (institutions such as the family, church, trade unions which are partly independent from the state). In this sense Gramsci conceives modern society as pluralist, a balance of forces between state and civil society, although one structured in class struggles. Within this context hegemony works at both the macro- and micro-levels. For example, during the nineteenth century Alpine mountaineering clubs became very popular in Britain, especially after 1850, bringing together different 'factions', of the upper and middle classes: the landed aristocracy, industrial bourgeoisie, old and new professions and intellectuals all united around an ideology which emphasized masculine, romantic and individual values. At this micro-level the values reflected the competitive individualism of the 'rising' capitalist class. It is through these specific values that the macro- and micro-levels can be linked in a tight coupling which focuses both on class and power as well as Goffman's interaction order (Robbins, 1987).

Hegemony thus points both to macro- and micro-processes involving agents seeking to establish new values. Although the concept of internalizing values brings Gramsci close to Parsons, the theory of hegemony is anti-functionalist, for the internalization of culture leads to a critical and cognitive awareness of existing values and the possibilities for opposition and change. Within Gramsci's model, then, there is no sense of a process of total incorporation of the individual into an integrated social whole.

Another Marxist perspective, equally concerned with the problem of social integration is the Frankfurt School. Its leading theorists, Adorno, Horkheimer and Marcuse abandoned the idea of working-class revolution, arguing that modern capitalism had developed into a highly centralized economic and political system dominated by the mass production of commodities, an increasingly atomized social structure and a passive, consumerist population. Capitalism had become a 'mass society' in which the principle socializing agencies were no longer those of class and family but the newly emerging mass media or 'culture industries'. The classical Marxist theory of capitalism was no longer relevant and, in Frankfurt School theory, the concept of mass culture replaced the concept of mode of production. Culture was the new mechanism of social order.

The conceptual framework employed by the Frankfurt School was derived less from Marx than from Weber, with culture industry (films, radio, television and so on) built on the basis of formal or *instrumental rationality*, which is largely concerned with the efficient functioning of the existing society and with narrowly defined goals, as distinct from *substantive rationality,* which is concerned with 'ultimate questions' such as freedom, justice, equality. Through the culture industries, organized entirely to make profits, culture becomes commodified, marketed as efficiently as possible to entertain and socialize individuals into a state of uncritical acceptance of society as it is.

Describing their approach as critical theory, in contrast to positivism which they termed 'traditional theory', the Frankfurt School analysed the processes whereby the institutions, culture and social consciousness of modern mass society had become one dimensional. Individuals were becoming less and less autonomous and increasingly incapable of critical thought and reflexive action. Thus their conclusions were bleakly pessimistic: the culture industry worked like an 'apparatus' socializing individuals into mass conformity. Unlike Gramsci, the Frankfurt School theorized social integration as indoctrination. Their substantive theory went on to postulate the questionable proposition that all forms of industrial society (capitalist, communist, fascist) were broadly similar in structure, integrated around a centralized, cultural apparatus.

Habermas, the leading figure of the second generation of critical theorists, rejected the Frankfurt School's concept of an inert, alienated mass and attempted to develop a more rounded, comprehensive theory. He argued that Marxism must be reformulated by integrating it with systems theory (especially Parsons) and with action theory (especially Weber, Mead and Schutz). Habermas agreed with Parsons about the importance of sociology explaining how consensus is achieved in societies. For Habermas, a major problem with Marx's model of the base and superstructure is that it lacked a concept of communicative interaction;

that is, it said little about how action is orientated towards establishing mutual agreement and understanding and a consensus governed by shared norms. Habermas' concept of communicative action follows Mead in arguing that it is through 'linguistically mediated interaction' that individuals achieve understanding and co-operation with others. In contrast to Marxism, which ignored the role of language in social evolution defining society in terms of a 'productivist model' based in collective social labour, Habermas argues that society consists of 'networks of communicative actions' which involve speaking as well as tool-making agents (Habermas, 1989).

Habermas makes a key distinction between the life world and the system. Following Schutz, the life world refers to the everyday world of active subjects trying to understand each other. In this context, Habermas follows the ethnomethodologists in highlighting the ways in which people draw on a stock of taken-for-granted assumptions to order their interactions. The life world is the sphere of active subjects trying to understand each other. However, society consists of both a life world and a system. The latter refers to things which are not linked by communicative action, such as state bureaucracy and capitalist economics. Here money and power rule and it functions through purposive, instrumental action. The system works through efficiency and profit, imposing its norms and constraining discourse. Action is orientated to the specific goals of the system and the most efficient means for realizing them. These are the system imperatives such as the maximization of profit irrespective of consequences for the quality of life within the life world. In contrast, communicative action is orientated to raising issues over the quality of life and engaging in open dialogue with others.

While the life world and system are separated in modern society, there is always a tension, especially acute in contemporary capitalist societies, between them. Habermas argues that there has been colonization of the life world by the system as more areas of life become subject to the imperatives of money and power. For example, culture and education have become commodities to be organized for profit rather than developed for mutual understanding. The result is the development of 'distorted' forms of communication based on force and coercion limiting the potential for rational communicative action. However, Habermas is not as pessimistic as Weber or the generation of Frankfurt School sociologists who preceded him. He argues that system elements could be forced out of the life world to create a more rational and egalitarian society. Habermas argues that this will come not from organized working-class resistance in the classical Marxist sense, but from 'new political movements', based on things like environmental concerns and the rights of various minority groups, which seek to reclaim aspects of the life world from the colonization of the system.

By positing a tension between system and life world, and emphasizing everyday face-to-face interaction, Habermas achieved a dynamism missing from Parsonian functionalism and the theory of culture industry. However, the role given to the impersonal logic of system imperatives – money and power – in the colonization of the life world suggests an absence of voluntarist social action which, to critics, seems uncomfortably close to a reassertion of functionalist systems theory. Society is integrated behind the backs of agents even though Habermas allows for social struggles in the life world.

Two more recent attempts to resolve the fundamental dualisms of sociological theory are Giddens' theory of structuration and Bourdieu's theory of habitus and field. Unlike Habermas, both reject Parsonian systems theory, arguing for a sociology built around the notion of reflexivity.

## Structuration

Giddens first announced his theory of structuration in *New Rules of Sociological Method* (1976) developing it further in a series of publications culminating in *The Constitution of Society* (1984). Structuration theory seeks to unify sociological theory through the concept of the *duality* of structure through which it becomes possible to analyse human practices as both action and structure. The focus is on the making of structures, social life as 'the production of active subjects' (Giddens, 1976: 120–1). Society is not an external, constraining system but the result of skilled, knowledgeable and reflexive agents whose actions occur within specific social contexts. Giddens is not suggesting that the agent is the sole source of society, but rather, that all so-called objective structures are substantiated in practice as agents produce and reproduce the structures which underpin and enable action to take place. Thus structure is not theorized as a fixed and inert property of a social system but is 'carried' in reproduced practices embedded in time and space: it is *both* the medium for, and outcome of, social action. This is close to Weber's concept of social action, that social institutions and structure have no existence apart from the actions they embody. For Giddens, the focus for sociological analysis is not on an objectively existing system, nor the experiences of individuals, but 'social practices ordered across space and time' (Giddens, 1984: 170–1).

Giddens defines his concepts of structure and practices in terms of 'rules' and 'resources'. Rules provide the basis for an ordered and stable social life. They can be formal and public, such as those governing elections and teaching practices, and informal, governing the varied encounters of everyday life. Rules operate on two levels of consciousness: first, a discursive level in which agents have a tacit or theoretical grasp of the rules involved in the reproduction of social practices thus enabling them to understand and give reasons for action; and second, on a practical level, an awareness of the skills and knowledge which enable agents to carry out forms of action. Resources are those elements which agents incorporate into 'the production and reproduction of social practices' such as education, knowledge, skills which enable people to interact with others and transform relations. Resources, in short, are employed to 'make things happen' within specific social contexts. Through rules and resources social life is not intentionally realized by agents but 'recursively' structured. By this term Giddens means that while social practices change a situation, they simultaneously reproduce the social order on which the rules governing action depend. This is the key to understanding Giddens' argument that structure is both the *medium* and the *outcome* of social action (ibid.: 181).

Structuration theory, unlike Parsonian functionalism and Habermasian systems theory, is built around the concept of reflexive agents capable of monitoring their actions through practical and discursive consciousness. Agents, then, are not over-socialized and passive but knowledgeable, creative and active. While Giddens is right to stress the making of structures, the problem is that structure is collapsed into agency. For structures do not exist simply as practices, but both pre-exist and endure beyond individual and collective action. In many modern European societies, for example, compulsory military service, administered through military and political institutions, exerts an external, constraining influence on specific individuals; it acts on them as a structure limiting their choices and freedom to act. This suggests a dualism rather than a duality of structure, that is, structures *can* exist independently and objectively of individuals and constrain their action rather than necessarily being bound together with action (Mouzelis, 1991: Ch. 2).

## Theory of Fields

Bourdieu's reflexive sociology, in contrast with Giddens, provides a body of concepts and substantive theory which link social practices and objective structures theoretically and empirically. Bourdieu (1990) conceives society as a network of specific 'fields', or 'social spaces', characterized by complex internal differentiation and hierarchical structures. Modern society comprises many different fields (education, religion, economic, cultural, political) each with its own specific institutions, rules and practices. In all fields those agents occupying dominant positions adopt defensive 'conservation strategies' to preserve their position and status, while newcomers develop 'subversion strategies' aiming to overthrow the governing rules and establish new ones. For example, within the cultural field there are struggles taking place over the concept of art, between conceptual painters and more traditional artists, with each group seeking to control the networks of galleries, art magazines and media journalism.

While fields are objective structures they are made through human action. Bourdieu makes the important point that this process of making is only possible because agents become socialized in ways which enable them to participate in the field itself. They do so by internalizing the social structure of the field, the hierarchy of positions, its history, its traditions and institutions. This is the 'habitus', a set of acquired and durable dispositions enabling agents to understand, interpret rules and act within a field. To participate in the educational field, for example, agents must acquire specific dispositions enabling them to understand relations between students and teachers, rules governing class discussion, tutorials and relations with others. Agents are thus not adapting passively to a pre-given social world but, through the creative and imaginative use of knowledge and skills, participate and enhance their position within a field (Bourdieu, 1990).

Habitus is grounded in practical knowledge and, although it can be modified by later experiences, it becomes ingrained, internalized as second nature. Thus within the field of diplomacy the dispositions linked to an upper-class family background and prestigious education enable individuals to move with confidence and style in the highly formalized social world of official ceremonies and pomp. Bourdieu has advanced a sociological explanation for the historical development of fields and the role of agents in their structure and transformation and, while marking an advance on the work of Parsons, Habermas and Giddens, it is not without its problems. The concept of habitus suggests a rather rigid social self based almost exclusively on self-interest and egoism, concerned only with pursuing goals that enhance status and position within a field. Action seems only to be instrumental in enabling agents to maintain or increase their assets and not bound up in any kind of fundamental belief in things such as politics, economics or art. Nevertheless, Bourdieu has made a major contribution to resolving many of the dualisms within sociological theory and has reunited theoretical analysis with the empirical research, something which constituted the hallmark of classical sociology.

# Conclusion: Postmodernity and Social Theory

If the history of sociological theory can be understood in terms of attempts to reconcile the fact that societies are collectivities (structures) which are produced by the intentional actions of individuals (action), then postmodern social theory represents a decisive break with that tradition. While it is possible to categorize previous contributions to sociological theory in terms of the degree to which they emphasize the determining effects of structures, or the relative independence of human agency, it is not possible to categorize postmodern theory in this way. Postmodernism falls outside these traditional categories of sociological theory.

The starting point for postmodernists, as we saw in Chapter 1, is that we are now living in an altered postmodern condition of increasing diversity and fragmentation, where many of the divisions that characterized modern societies have collapsed. However, for postmodernists, it is not enough to reflect on these changes, the form and content of sociological ideas must themselves be *deconstructed* (Derrida, 1982). Deconstruction is a specifically postmodern idea, developed from literary criticism, that involves taking apart the internal characteristics of an approach rather than trying to supplement it with an alternative set of 'better' ideas. Postmodernists deconstruct the central idea of sociology, that there are ordered and related phenomena called 'societies' which can be understood by specialist concepts and methods. As McLennan puts it, the postmodernist asks:

> What gives us the right to see society as a totality, as a unified and coherent being? Why isn't it just a motley collection of bits and pieces? And how can we ever tell if our concepts genuinely do 'grasp' or 'reflect' this thing called society accurately? Indeed, who is to say what knowledge of society really amounts to? (1992: 329)

The postmodern critique can be seen most clearly in relation to structural theories, such as Marxism and structural functionalism, which purport to incorporate all aspects of social life into a set of universal structural principles. Postmodernists are sceptical of such theories because they represent grand narratives, or 'meta-narratives'; that is, single, overarching explanations which claim a superior grasp of truth over all others. For Marx, social phenomena could ultimately be explained in terms of the economic base, while for Parsons, it was the functional prerequisites which hold the key. Lyotard (1984), one of the most influential voices of postmodernism, argued that such meta-narratives reflect an arrogant and outdated modernist assumption that it is possible to have objective knowledge based on scientifically established truths. Postmodernists thus reject not only the substance of structural sociological theories, but also the very assumption that there can ever be a single valid account of society.

While the relationship between postmodernism and social action theories is undoubtedly more complex, the same basic objections that have been raised against structural theories still apply. This is because, even though social action theorists like Goffman and Garfinkel propose very different models of society from those advanced by structural theorists, they share the same desire to produce some form of authoritative account of social life. For example, Garfinkel's ethnomethodological account of social order is proposed in opposition to, and as superior to, the model of normative order proposed by Parsons. Even though social action theorists do not appeal to scientific truth to validate their accounts, from the postmodernist point of view, they are still locked into the modernist idea of producing some form of true, or better, accounts of society. These truths may be different – here actors are seen as rational, self-motivated and artful, whereas in structural theories they tend to be passive recipients of external forces – but they are presented as truths all the same.

Postmodern social theorists, in contrast, argue for the co-existence of a range of competing and incommensurable theoretical approaches, with no overarching set of principles by which to choose between them. While this position is no doubt useful as a corrective to some of the more ambitious grand theories which have emerged in sociology, it does nevertheless pose some real difficulties. The first is the tendency towards *relativism*, which seems inherent in postmodern theorising. Relativism, as we saw in Chapter 2, is the idea that no one theory can in principle be judged superior to any other. It is problematic because if we cannot judge any theory superior to any other, neither can there be any rational grounds to reject weak or incorrect theories. Thus Weber's account of the origins of capitalism must be regarded as just as valid as Marx's or, for the matter, as the incoherent ravings of a lunatic. Taking the postmodern critique to its logical – or rather illogical – conclusions, if no account can, in principle, be judged superior to any other, then we might as well question whether there is any purpose in doing sociological research in the first place.

Second, the extent to which to which postmodernists adhere to their own principles has been questioned. For example, Baudrillard (1983) has argued that contemporary societies are characterized by the endless consumption of signs and symbols generated by the electronic media. It is no longer a question of whether or not the media reflect reality, they have *become* reality. Consequently, we are living in a state of unreality, or *hyperreality* (see Chapter 14 for further discussion of the postmodern view of the media). Whatever the merits of this theory, it is a theory nonetheless, and one which Baudrillard supports with evidence and examples. It is thus difficult to see how postmodern theorists can express their own ideas without at the same time undermining them.

Third, postmodernism has been criticized by writers like Habermas for being inherently 'conservative'. If there are no criteria for judging one point of view better than any other, then it follows that there can be no valid, or authoritative, criticism of the ways in which societies are organized for the benefit of some groups at the expense of others. However, Foucault, whose work had a great influence on the postmodern movement, counters this by arguing that Habermas' work is naive and utopian. The idea that there are some fundamental 'truths' to be uncovered about social life is one of the myths of modernity. Foucault argues that critical theory's analysis of power and inequality, although claiming some sort of objective status, simply involves contrasting one set of value judgements with another. This debate reflects a more general question in sociology. Much of the credibility of sociologists' critical analyses of social arrangements rests on their conceptualizations of power and how it operates in societies. So what is power and how have sociologists tried to explain it? This is the subject of the following chapter.

# Further Reading

Giddens, A. and Turner, J. (eds) *Social Theory Today*, Cambridge, Polity Press, 1987. A series of informed essays on some of the major trends in social theory.

Layder, D. *Understanding Social Theory*, London, Sage, 1994. An excellent, clear introduction, organised around the macro-micro dilemma in social theory.

Mouzelis, N. *Sociological Theory: What Went Wrong?*, London, Routledge, 1995. Advances a distinctive critical position, emphasizing the need for conceptual and substantive rigour.

Swingewood, A. *A Short History of Sociological Theory*, 2nd edn, Basingstoke, Macmillan, 1991. A discussion of the origins and development of sociological theory.

# 4

# Power

## *Christine Helliwell and Barry Hindess*

The concept of power is central to many areas covered elsewhere in this volume: from the organization of work to class and stratification, from the family to gender relations, from religion to crime and deviance. Yet the concept itself is subject to considerable confusion. The aim of this chapter is to clarify some of these confusions by exploring three different understandings of power and the divergent sociological approaches they generate. It should help you understand:

■ The fact that power has different meanings which give rise to different sociological questions

■ Theories of the distribution and production of power

■ Theories of the legitimacy and effectiveness of power

■ Theories which focus on how the effects of power are produced

■ The importance of looking for the theories of power which underlie different sociological perspectives and research studies

---

**CONCEPTS**

false consciousness ■ zero-sum view of power ■ coercion

legitimacy ■ power élite ■ government ■ liberalism

---

# Introduction

The *Oxford English Dictionary* (OED) provides several different meanings of the word 'power'. Of these, three are used in discussions of social life. Accordingly, this chapter is divided into three main parts, each of which deals with one of these meanings.

The first part explores the understandings and assumptions encapsulated in the *OED* definition of power as 'possession of control or command over others'. This is what most sociologists mean, most of the time, when they talk about power: the capacity to get others to do what we want them to do. In this sense, teachers have power over pupils, presidents over populations and parents over children. This conception of power as some kind of *capacity* is intimately linked to a view of power as *quantifiable*.

The second part examines the understandings and assumptions encapsulated in the *OED* definition of power as 'legal ability, capacity or authority to act; especially delegated authority'. Power here refers to the legal authority or *right* that some people have to get others to do what they want them to do. In this sense, as well, teachers have power over pupils and presidents over populations; in addition, police have power over citizens and, until very recently, husbands had power over wives. While this view of power as *right* has been less widely accepted among sociologists than that of power as capacity, its advocacy in the work of certain key thinkers has rendered it extremely influential.

While these first two meanings of power are those used in most sociological discussions on the subject, there is a third, more general and much older, meaning which has recently begun to garner support in contemporary sociology as a result of its elaboration by the French theorist Michel Foucault. The third part of the chapter explores this conception of power, focusing primarily on its use in Foucault's work. This is the conception encapsulated in the *OED* definition of power as the 'ability to do or affect something or anything'. Power, in this sense, relates to human *agency*; that is, to one's ability to 'make a difference' in the world. On this definition, all human beings have power, in that we all have the ability to alter some pre-existing situations, no matter how trivial. Students have the power, for example, to disrupt a lecture or a tutorial class; a population has the power to resist the actions of its president.

It is easy to see that the three meanings of power given above overlap with one another. In the case of the first two, one's *capacity* to exercise control or command over others (power in the first sense) can often be seen as resulting, at least in part, from one's legal *right*, or authority, to do so (power in the second sense): the power of teachers over pupils, or police over citizens, being obvious examples. In the case of the first and third meaning, anyone's capacity to control or command others (that is, one's power in the first sense) is frequently understood as being a product of their more general ability to affect things – to make things happen in the world at large (power in the third sense).

Yet, while there are obvious congruencies between these three meanings, it is nevertheless important to keep them conceptually distinct. Hindess (1995) argues that the tendency to conflate the different meanings of power (which he sees as endemic to contemporary social and political theory) has had adverse consequences for the ability of social scientists and others to understand social and political life.

# Power as Quantitative Capacity

One of the assumptions that pervades sociological discussions of power is that power is some kind of quantitative entity, like wealth: something that one can have 'more of' or 'less of'. This is the understanding set out in Weber's famous definition of power as 'the chance of a man or a number of men to realise their own will even against the resistance of others' (Weber, trans. 1978: 926). Weber is suggesting here that everyone has some chance of realizing their own will (or of 'getting their own way', as we might now say), but that some have a greater chance of doing so than others. In this understanding, power is usually seen as a *capacity* – the capacity to get one's own way – with some individuals or groups understood as having more of this capacity and others as having less. Most sociological writing on power has focused on questions to do with its *distribution* – who has it and who does not, and how much different parties have relative to one another – and/or its *production* – under what conditions greater or lesser amounts of it are created. The appeal, for many social scientists, of this conception of power as quantitative capacity is that it suggests that the study of power is a straightforward empirical matter: a matter simply of measuring and comparing. In practice, as we shall see shortly, it is less straightforward than it seems.

## *The Distribution of Power*

Most sociologists who hold to a quantitative view of power – indeed, most sociologists writing about power – have been primarily concerned with its *distribution*: with which members of a society have more of it, and which have less. This, in turn, allows them to ask questions about what happens when parties with different *quantities* of power at their disposal come into conflict, and how power operates to enable those who have more of it to exercise their will over those who have less. For example, how is it that oil barons and newspaper tycoons seem so readily to get their way with governments, even when their wishes are opposed by the majority of the population? These kinds of questions require that the different quantities of power held by different parties can be measured and compared with one another, so that it becomes possible to state definitively that some parties have more than others. Since, as we have seen, the conventional sociological understanding of power is that it is what allows one party to command or control, or to impose their own will over others, then it follows that the outcome of social interactions will accord with the wishes and interests of those with more power. All one has to do in order to predict such outcomes, then, is to measure who has the most power and find out what their wishes and interests are.

The distribution of power, in this respect, suggests an obvious analogy with wealth. However, while it is possible to establish the overall quantities of wealth which someone holds in terms of money, it is much more difficult to establish the quantities of power which different parties hold, since there is no equivalent unit in terms of which power may be measured. As a result, the question of how the power holdings of different individuals or groups within a society are to be identified and compared with each other has been a matter of considerable debate among sociologists and others.

Lukes (1974) still provides one of the most useful introductions to the issues in dispute here. His discussion takes the form of an extended commentary on the 'community power debates', a series of famous debates about the nature and location of political power in the United States which took place among American sociologists and political scientists in the 1960s and 70s. Reflecting on these debates, Lukes argues first, that power has three aspects or dimensions, all of which must be considered in any serious analysis of the distribution of power. These three dimensions are:

1. the dimension which operates to determine the outcome of direct conflict
2. the dimension which operates behind the scenes so as to exclude certain interests from direct public conflict in the first place
3. the dimension which operates on people's thoughts and desires.

Lukes attributes the first two of these views to two sets of antagonists in the community power debates; the third view is his own.

The simplest and, on Lukes' account, the least satisfactory of these three views is the 'one-dimensional' or 'liberal' view of power, which he attributes to thinkers such as Dahl (1957, 1958, 1961) and Polsby (1963, 1980). Those who hold such a one-dimensional view focus exclusively on the first dimension of power: on that dimension which operates to determine the outcome of direct conflict. Methodologically, then, we can be certain that one party has more power than another only if we have evidence to show that that party has, in fact, been able to prevail on some occasion in the face of the other's opposition. During the community power debates, Dahl and Polsby argued, against Mills (1959) and others, that one cannot determine who has power in American society simply by establishing who is the 'ruling élite' (that is, by establishing who controls or commands 'major institutions' such as business, government and the military); one must also provide clear evidence that the members of this supposed élite can indeed impose their wishes against majority opposition.

In contrast, those who adopt a 'two-dimensional' or 'reformist' view of power regard as profoundly simplistic the 'one-dimensional' stress on power as largely manifest in contexts of direct, overt conflict. For reformists such as Bachrach and Baratz (1969) power is often also exercised in such a way as to *prevent* certain conflicts of interest from coming into public play in the first place. The approach adopted by thinkers such as Dahl and Polsby, they suggest, focuses only on the 'public' face of power, thereby ignoring the manner in which certain interests are excluded from consideration in council chambers, parliamentary assemblies and other venues in which major decisions affecting the community are taken. Thus, any study focusing exclusively on who prevails in cases of overt conflict is likely to obscure an important dimension of the actual exercise of power in any society.

Lukes describes this two-dimensional view as 'reformist' because it insists not only that the interests of certain individuals and groups are not represented in political debate, but also that the exclusion of those views is illegitimate. It suggests, in other words, that political and other institutions are in need of substantial reform. Thus, on Lukes' account of the dispute between supporters of the one-dimensional and the two-dimensional views of power during the community power debates, what is at issue between them is a matter not only of method (how to identify who has power and who has not) but also of values (how power should be distributed in society).

Lukes argues, however, that both views, at least as he describes them, treat power as enabling some parties to prevail over others in conditions where there are clear differences between what each regard as their respective interests. Lukes himself believes that it is necessary to go even further. He suggests that while there are certainly cases in which power works in the relatively straightforward ways which are the concern of the one- and two-dimensional views, there are also important cases in which it does not, such as when those who suffer from the workings of power are prevented from recognizing that their interests are at risk. Some of the most influential forms of the exercise of power in the modern world, in his view, work by manipulating the thoughts of those whose interests are adversely affected. Indeed, he asks:

> Is it not the supreme exercise of power to get another or others to have the desires you want them to have – that is, to secure their compliance by controlling their thoughts and desires? (Lukes, 1974: 23)

This is the basis of Lukes' own 'three-dimensional' or 'radical' view of power.

The attempt to influence the thoughts and desires of others is a feature of most social interaction, and the individuals concerned often have a fair idea of what is being done to them. What Lukes has in mind is something less obviously mundane, in which the victims of power are unaware of its action on them. The most significant of these kinds of cases are those in which power is not exercised over individuals in any direct fashion, but operates instead via 'socially structured and culturally patterned behaviour' (1974: 22). In other words, Lukes is suggesting that *socialization* processes themselves are part of the exercise of power in any society. In such cases the exercise of power will generally go unrecognized by those whose interests are injured by its effects: it influences the thoughts and desires of its victims, but it does so largely through the workings of 'collective forces and social arrangements' (ibid.). According to Lukes, it is possible for the social scientist to work out which members of society are the victims of power, through imagining how an autonomous life – a life unconstrained and unshaped by the exercise of power over it – would be lived. Those whose lives deviate from this autonomous ideal – those who are constrained in the pursuit of their autonomous interests – are those over whom power is being exercised by others.

Lukes' 'three-dimensional' view rests on the twin understandings that not only do all individuals have the potential to achieve true autonomy if they are free from the constraining and distorting effects of power, but also that it is possible to have a society in which the third dimension of power plays no significant part. In the next section of the chapter we shall see that these two understandings are central to an extremely influential body of analysis which focuses primarily on power not as a capacity, but as a *right*, and which is thus primarily concerned with issues of consent and legitimacy.

In addition, Lukes' analysis requires that we regard all social interaction as a potential conduit for the workings of an insidious form of power. This involves two assumptions which are fundamentally Marxist in origin. First, that society can be understood as an arena of conflict between overarching social forces which themselves represent the interests of particular social groups. Second, that the institutions of capitalist society operate in such a way as to impose a distorting *ideology* or a *false consciousness* on the masses of the population, that is, to prevent them from recognizing either the true character of their position in society (for example, the fact that they are oppressed or exploited by a small minority) or the interests which arise from that position. These same two assumptions underlie the argument of the influential Italian Marxist, Gramsci, that as we saw in Chapter 3, the rule of the bourgeoisie in advanced capitalist societies is based on both coercion and consent, and that the latter is made possible by the fact that members of the subordinated classes are not aware of their interests in the overthrow of capitalist domination (Gramsci, 1971). Lukes' view is radical because, like Gramsci and other Marxist scholars such as Marcuse and Habermas, he argues that contemporary social institutions must be completely transformed if those who are the victims of social and political power are ever to free themselves of its effects.

The three approaches to the study of power delineated by Lukes all treat power as a quantifiable capacity – usually as a capacity to command or control others, that is, to impose one's will over others – and they are also concerned primarily with the *distribution* of this quantifiable entity – with who has more of it, and who less. However, each of these views differs markedly over how power should be measured, and how its distribution should thus be ascertained. Ironically, then, while the conception of power as quantitative capacity appears to promise that its distribution can, like wealth, be unambiguously determined through simple techniques of measuring and counting, it has in fact given rise to intractable dispute – as exemplified in the community power debates and Lukes' later intervention in them – over exactly how those techniques should be applied.

## The Production of Power

While most sociological writing on power has focused primarily on its distribution, a number of very significant discussions have been concerned largely with questions to do with its *production*. Those writing on production also invariably assume that power is a quantifiable capacity whose possession determines the outcome of social interactions. However, their primary concern has been with the social conditions that explain why some parties have been able to have more power than others. This focus on the 'why' questions has meant that these analyses are in certain respects more sophisticated than those which focus only on the simple 'who/where' questions of the distribution of power.

We have already noted that the understanding of power as a quantitative phenomenon suggests an analogy with money or wealth. One of the most significant and forceful elaborations of this analogy is Parsons' critique of what he calls the 'zero-sum' conception of power which, in his view, informs much of the academic discussion of the distribution of power in American society (Parsons, 1969a, 1969b). 'Zero-sum' is a technical term taken from game theory. It is used to characterize a distinctive feature of competitive games, such as poker, in which a fixed quantity of assets is at stake. Because the stake is fixed, there are only a finite number of ways in which it can be distributed among the players, and so only a finite number of possible outcomes to any particular game. For those playing the game, the exclusive concern is with the distribution of the stake and, specifically, with how to maximize one's own share of it. Similarly, Parsons argues, according to the zero-sum conception of power there is only a fixed quantity of the stuff to go around, and the most important issues to be raised in any investigation of power are thus concerned with its distribution: who has it and who has not?

Parsons' central point is that it is a mistake to treat power in this 'zero-sum' way: as a fixed quantity. Doing this, he implies, is like analysing economic activity by focusing only on the circulation of money and wealth in market exchanges. Such an analysis would ignore, in particular, the *production* of goods and services. Economic commentators commonly argue that we should not allow our concern with matters of equity in the distribution of income and wealth to obscure the importance of the production of wealth. They have observed that some societies have considerably more wealth than others, and that the condition of a poor individual in a wealthy society may be superior to that of a wealthy individual in a poor one. For this reason, many sociologists of development have suggested that, in most 'undeveloped' societies, what is needed to improve the condition of the poor is economic growth – the *production* of new wealth – rather than a different *distribution* of existing wealth.

Similarly, Parsons and others argue that power is something that is not simply distributed in societies, but is also produced there: the quantity of power potentially available to any society is thus not fixed. In particular, they have observed that, even allowing for differences in population size, some societies have been able to generate considerably more power than others. Like wealth, power will often be used in pursuit of sectional interests but much of it will also be available for the benefit of society as a whole. Continuing the analogy between power and wealth, they have gone on to argue that the production of power is at least as important an issue for our understanding of modern societies as is its distribution.

Parsons argues that power is produced by the particular set of social conditions found in any society. In particular, he suggests that the amount of power in a society will depend on the extent to which it is possible to generate and to sustain the belief among the population at large that the actions and instructions of those in positions of authority are indeed legitimate. This belief by a population that those in positions of authority have the *right* to exercise power (in the first sense of control or command) over them – that their power is, in other words, legitimate – is usually referred to by sociologists (and by social and political theorists in general) as a belief in the *legitimacy* of that power or, indeed, of the ruling élite itself. In fact, the notion of legitimacy often involves rather more than this, as we shall see in the following section of the chapter. For now, however, we need to note that just as, in extreme cases of inflation, loss of confidence in money can inhibit the production of wealth and encourage increasing resort to barter, so, in Parsons' view, can a loss of belief in legitimacy inhibit the production of power and encourage the use of coercion.

Returning to the three definitions of power with which we began this chapter, we can see that Parsons' use of the term combines the first and second of these: power as control over others and as legal capacity or authority to act. Power in the sense of capacity to control or command others Parsons describes not as power, but as *coercion*, unless it occurs in combination with power in the second sense; unless, that is, it is legally authorized or 'legitimate'. A belief by the members of society at large in the legitimacy of those wielding power over them, then, is integral for Parsons to the constitution of power – to its very production – in the first place. Without such a belief there is not power; there is simply coercion.

Like Parsons, Weber sees the continuing power to control or command others as a product of social conditions or social arrangements; he stresses that it is dependent on both organization (the presence of a chief and administrative staff – and therefore some system of hierarchy – as well as a relatively complex system of administration) and compliance or co-operation on the part of those over whom the power is exercised. He goes on to argue that compliance is unlikely to survive for long unless it is accompanied by a belief in the legitimacy of the leader's power. Thus, while Parsons sees legitimacy as essential for the *production* of power in the first place, Weber sees it as necessary only for the *continuation* of certain kinds of power.

A more recent, influential approach to the study of the production of power is developed by Mann (1986). He identifies power in general as 'the ability to pursue and attain goals' (1986: 6) – that is, in the third sense identified at the beginning of the chapter. He then goes on to define *social* power – the power pertaining to relationships between people – as involving two distinct aspects: first, the power which one individual or group exerts over others and, second, the power produced by a number of people engaged in collective action, whereby their co-operation allows them 'to enhance their joint power over third parties or over nature' (ibid.). Mann's point, with respect to this second aspect, is that a group of individuals co-operating is able to produce far greater power than any individual can produce on their own. Like Weber, he stresses the importance of *organization* for the production and maintenance of social power: individuals must be organized relatively efficiently if they are to co-operate to the degree necessary for the production of significant amounts of social power. Mann suggests that in most significant forms of social power both of these aspects are present: people usually co-operate with one another to produce larger amounts of power because of the power exerted over them by others (because they are commanded to, or required to, by others). As with Weber, the production of power thus requires both hierarchy and co-operation. Mann distinguishes four types of social power – economic, ideological, military and political – which correspond, in his view, to the four fundamental spheres of organized social life. While these are different from one another in certain important respects, they nevertheless all involve the two aspects of social power outlined earlier.

Parsons, Weber and Mann all provide analyses of power which are rather different in orientation from those which focus only on questions of its distribution. Nevertheless, there is a sense in which their arguments continue to rest on the quantitative conception of power outlined at the beginning of this section. In particular, as we have seen, all are concerned with the social conditions under which 'more' power may be produced, with Parsons stressing the role of legitimacy in this respect, and Weber and Mann emphasizing also the significance of organization and co-operation. While Parsons' analogy between power and wealth makes explicit this conception of power as a quantifiable entity, so too does Mann's claim that those with 'more' economic, ideological, military or political power commonly prevail over those with less power of the same kind. We find here the conventional sociological assumption that the outcome of social interactions or disputes is determined by the quantities of power available to different parties, with those with more able to impose their own will onto those with less.

The conception of power as some kind of quantitative entity is thus pervasive throughout sociology and, indeed, throughout the social sciences in general. Yet, there are problems with this conception, and its widespread acceptance has hampered attempts by sociologists and others to come to terms with what we mean by power. The first concerns the notion of power as some kind of homogeneous essential substance – a notion which is invariably accepted by those who wish to compare quantities of power as distributed within a society or, indeed, as produced under different social conditions. Those sociologists and others engaging in such comparative/quantitative work have little choice but to accept an essentialist notion of power as something which remains unchanged across the many diverse contexts in which it comes into play. This is because without such a notion the comparative enterprise would become untenable: how does one compare quantities of one 'kind' of power obtaining in certain specified social contexts with quantities of a different 'kind' of power obtaining in others? In order to make such comparisons and so to assess who has more and who less power in society at large, or what kinds of overall societies produce greater amounts of power than others, sociologists must be able to regard all of these potentially different 'kinds' of power as equivalent in some sense – as able to be compared in a meaningful way. They do this by treating power as if it involved some kind of common substance: as if it has the same fixed, fundamental character regardless of the context in which it occurs or how it is used.

As a result, sociologists often draw a distinction between power *itself* (which remains unchanged in its essential character from one social context to another) and the *means* by which that power is exercised (which varies from one context to another). Giddens, for example, stresses the need to distinguish between power and 'resources': 'the media through which power is exercised' (1984: 16). The latter include material conditions of various kinds (land, machines, weapons) as well as what he calls 'authoritative resources' related to patterns of social organization and legitimacy. Giddens' point in stressing this distinction is that while these 'resources' may vary from context to context, the underlying power which they have in common remains the same.

While this distinction, between on the one hand, the essential, unchanging substance power and, on the other, the diverse, changing resources through which that power is exercised, is necessary to most quantitative analyses of power, it is, nevertheless, deeply problematic. In practice, the 'quantity' of power which any party is able to exercise on any particular occasion cannot so easily be separated from the resources through which it is exercised. To take a straightforward example: a would-be rapist has a much higher chance of imposing his will onto his victims if he threatens them with a weapon such as a knife or a gun than if he merely engages in verbal abuse to get his way. In other words, the quantity of power which he is able to exercise over them is directly related to the use of certain kinds of resources. In fact, a number of those analysts who hold to a quantitative understanding of power are aware of this problem, and have attempted to circumvent it. It is partly in order to do this that Mann, for instance, distinguishes (as we have seen) between political, economic and other kinds of powers; he thus avoids essentializing power and so is able to link it more closely to the particular contexts in which it operates.

The second (closely related) problem is a much more profound one, and concerns the most fundamental assumption underlying the understanding of power in quantitative terms: viz, that it is a *difference* in power which allows one party to impose its own will over others, even against the wishes of those others. Quite apart from the fact that it is much more difficult than it appears at first sight, as we have seen, to work out which party has more power in any social situation, there is a deeper problem with this assumption. This is that it is by no means always the case that the relative quantities of power (however these might be measured) held by different parties allow us to determine the outcome of any conflict between them. No doubt there will be cases in which the power available to one party is so outweighed by that available to another that the outcome of any conflict between them could hardly be in doubt. However, the experience of the USA in Vietnam or of Russia in Chechnya suggests that such cases are fewer than one might imagine. In other words, the outcome of interactions or disputes between contending parties is influenced by much more than simply how much power in the abstract is available to each: it is also influenced by such things as the tactics which each employs to achieve its goals, how they make use of the resources at their disposal and so on. The notion that the shape of social life is determined entirely by the sheer quantities of power available to different parties is clearly oversimplified.

# Power as Right

While, as we have seen, almost all sociological accounts of power have been concerned with it as the quantitative *capacity* of one party to command or control, or to impose its will on others, many of these have also been concerned with power in the second of those senses: as a *right* which some parties have to command or control others. In contemporary western societies this right is generally recognized as such by those over whom it is exercised, with the result that they are willing to *consent* to being commanded or controlled. To take some obvious examples, we all consent to pay our taxes, or to drive according to the rules of the road, because we accept the *right* of our leaders to demand these things from us; they can thus be described as having the 'power' to tax us, or the 'power' to demand that we abide by the road rules. Central, then, to most modern discussions of power as right are questions to do with *consent*, and specifically with whether or not the fact that we accord power as right to certain authorities (such as the power/right of the government to tax us) means that we can genuinely be said to have consented to that power being exercised over us. At issue here is the notion of *legitimacy* which, as we have already noted, is at the core of many discussions of power.

It is helpful to distinguish between two rather different approaches to the study of legitimacy and power as right. The first of these is that taken by Weber and Parsons, in which the focus is on how a population's belief in the legitimacy of the power exercised over it is produced and sustained. In this approach, little attention is paid to the question of whether this belief is itself well founded or 'true'. Rather, what is of concern to these thinkers is the simple fact that such a belief *does* exist, and how it came into being. Weber notes, for example, that in modern democratic societies 'the chief and his administrative staff often appear formally as servants or agents of those they rule', and he adds that this fact 'does nothing whatever to disprove the quality of dominance' (1978: 215). However, what matters for Weber's analysis of political power in democratic societies is the existence of this belief and its consequences for political organization, not the fact (as he sees it) that it is based on a misapprehension about the nature of political power. Parsons takes a similar view. Rather than presenting democracy as a system in which the people rule, he treats it instead as one which promotes a pervasive feeling of obligation among the people with respect to the commands of those able to exercise power as right (that is, those in legitimate positions of authority) He suggests democracy is more effective in this respect than any other form of rule yet seen; it is partly for this reason that he regards democratic societies as having reached the highest known stage in his scheme of societal evolution (Parsons, 1971).

However, for many sociologists, the Weber/Parsons stress on the *effectiveness* of power smacks of moral bankruptcy. They are also interested in whether a population's belief in the right of their rulers to exercise power over them – and their consequent consent to that power – is well founded, or justifiable. At issue for these thinkers, in other words, is not *belief* in the legitimacy of power, but rather legitimacy itself. If, for instance, people consent to power being exercised over them because they are unaware of the real character and effects of that power, can they truly be said to have *consented* to its use, and is the power in question truly legitimate? To take a straightforward example: if the populations of the USA, Australia and New Zealand 'consented' to the sending of troops to fight in Vietnam on the basis of deliberately distorted information about the situation in that country, can we describe this as 'true' consent, and can we describe the governments of those countries as having a 'true' right to send the troops? Many members of the populations of the USA,

Australia and New Zealand clearly thought that the answer to all these questions was no, resulting in outbreaks of civil disobedience which occurred in all three countries for the duration of the war.

This notion of power as right has appeared in many sociological discussions, especially those dealing with political power as it operates in modern democracies, most particularly in the United States. These studies are concerned, in particular, with the question of whether the belief of the American people at large that their government has the right to exercise power over them necessarily renders this power right, or legitimate. In the previous section we looked at the 'community power debates' of the 1960s and 70s, in the context of Lukes' discussion of what he called the one-, two- and three-dimensional approaches to the study of power. While we focused there on the differences between the protagonists concerning questions to do with the *distribution* of power (concerning who has it, and how we can measure it), in fact, for those involved, these questions were simply a means to answering a much more important set of questions: those concerning the *legitimacy*, or the *right*, of political power in the United States. The differences between the protagonists regarding questions of the distribution of power in fact prefigured the differences between them regarding whether the widespread consent to the exercise of power by the ruling élite was justified, and whether that power could therefore be said to be legitimate.

The community power debates were sparked off by Mills' condemnation of the American power élite for operating a system of rule which he describes as one of 'organised irresponsibility' (1959: 361). In Mills' view, the 'ruling élite' – those in charge of major institutions such as business, government and the military – is concerned with the pursuit of its own interests at the expense of those of the people, and is not truly accountable to the people. He argues, then, that American democracy is not, in reality, operating in the ways in which most Americans believe it to be operating; the people thus give their consent to their rulers under false pretences. For Mills, this renders illegitimate the power exercised by those rulers.

In opposing this view, Dahl (1961) acknowledges, in his study of politics in the American city of New Haven, that the conduct of political life in America does not conform to received understandings of democracy. However, in his view, this shows that these understandings should be modified to take account of the complexity of twentieth-century democratic societies, rather than that such societies are not democratic. As he puts it: New Haven 'is a republic of unequal citizens – but for all that a republic' (Dahl, 1961: 86). In other words, while America may be a long way from the democratic goal of political equality, it is nevertheless a society in which the people rule. At the most fundamental level then, according to Dahl, the system operates in the way in which its citizens believe that it does. Their consent to that system is thus justified, and the power exercised over them by their rulers thus legitimate, or 'right'.

Bachrach and Baratz (1969) argue, in turn, that Dahl's conclusion rests on a failure to recognize that power itself may be used, covertly, to exclude the interests of those who are not well served by the American political system.

Lukes, and other adherents to the 'radical' view of power, go one step further. They suggest that in contemporary western democracies not only are the interests of many people excluded by the covert use of power but, in addition, this power operates in such a way as to mislead *those people themselves* concerning where their real needs or interests lie. Another celebrated example of this kind of argument is found in Marcuse's *One-Dimensional Man*, where he argues that liberty, in contemporary democratic societies, has been made 'into a powerful instrument of domination' (Marcuse, 1972: 21). Marcuse is, in effect, claiming that the fact that people have been misled into believing that they are free in those societies, leads them to consent to a system which is, in fact, profoundly unfree.

We can see that the concepts of *false consciousness* and *ideology*, which we discussed in the previous section, are central to this kind of argument: people consent to power being exercised over them because they have been socialized into believing that society is operating differently (more in line with their interests) from how it actually is operating. Lukes, Marcuse and like-minded thinkers argue that under such conditions, the 'consent' of the members of these societies to the power in question serves simply to perpetuate the very exercise of power which works against their own needs and interests. This is why, of course, many of those who have adopted this kind of position – most particularly Marxist scholars – have advocated civil disobedience, or even revolution, seeing this as a 'legitimate', or morally justifiable, response to such an illegitimate use of power.

A central difficulty with all of these discussions which take the second approach to the study of power as right, is that there is no straightforward basis on which we can decide, in any particular case, whether or not 'true' consent has been given by people to the exercise of power over them, and whether that power is therefore legitimate. Because there is no systematic basis for agreement between them, different scholars decide these questions, and pass judgement on any particular case, according to their own political understandings and commitments. In the community power debates for example, as we have already seen, some scholars (Dahl, Polsby) claim that the exercise of political power in the USA *is* based on the people's consent and is therefore legitimate, while others (Mills, Bachrach and Baratz, and later, Lukes) argue equally vehemently that it is neither of these things. The lack of any objective basis on which to make such judgements suggests in fact that such disputes are, ultimately, irresolvable.

There is an additional, related, problem with the 'radical' view adopted by Lukes, Marcuse and others. According to this view, the consent that matters for our evaluation of the legitimacy of political power is the consent that people would give under conditions in which their thoughts and desires were not affected by the impact of power. For example, if we wished to evaluate whether or not the consent of Australians to the exercise of power by their government in sending troops to Vietnam was 'true' consent, we would need to imagine whether they would have consented to this action were they members of a society in which Lukes' 'insidious' power was not influencing their thoughts and actions. The difficulty here is that we can identify the effects of such an insidious power only through *imagining* what a society without such an insidious power might be like. We are back in the terrain of contentious ethical and political judgements and, consequently, interminable dispute.

We have already noted that most sociological work concerned with power as quantitative capacity has focused around apparently 'empirical' questions such as who has power, who has not, and how it is produced. Furthermore, the study of power as right raises 'political' or 'ethical' questions to do with whether or not those who exercise power over others have the *right* to do so. In practice of course, as we noted at the start of the chapter, many thinkers tend to run these two senses of power together, with the result that 'empirical' and 'political' questions become entangled. Consequently, academic debates about power in the sense of quantitative capacity have usually been animated by broader political concerns, especially those to do with the legitimacy of government and the defence of individual autonomy.

To take the latter as an example, *quantitative* studies of who has 'more' and who 'less' power in a society – such as those occurring as part of the community power debates – are frequently motivated by the *political/ethical* assumption that substantial inequity in the distribution of power in society is a 'bad' thing. Such inequity is believed to be 'bad' because it enables some parties to influence profoundly the behaviour of others, or to 'get their own way' even against the wishes of others. In western societies, where an extremely high value is placed on individual autonomy, or individual freedom, this is seen by most scholars as highly undesirable.

Partly for this reason, power over others is often represented in *negative* terms in sociological and other kinds of discussion, as an imposition or constraint on the autonomy of those over whom it is exercised. The power of the modern state is regarded as being particularly important in this respect, since it is seen as constraining the liberty or autonomy of all of its subjects. In this view, power is invariably negative in its effects when exercised over people: it is seen as *taking something from* people, rather than as giving something to them. This 'negative' view of power – the notion of power as *constraint* or *imposition* – underlies the disputes over legitimacy which we considered earlier: the political power of the state is seen as legitimate if its capacity to constrain or impose on the liberty of its subjects is based on their consent, and illegitimate if it is not. Indeed, in Lukes' version of this argument, power can even be used to prevent its victims from thinking what they otherwise would have thought and so to elicit from them a consent which they otherwise would not have given. However, as we will see in the following section of the chapter, sociologists do not necessarily have to understand power in negative terms.

## Power as Acting on the Actions of Others

If the study of power as quantifiable capacity is invariably caught up with broader political and ethical concerns, then criticism of that understanding of power can be expected to have widespread ramifications for social and political theory in general and, more particularly, for the issues considered in earlier sections of this chapter. This point brings us to the work of Foucault, which offers a radical alternative both to conventional understandings of power and to the alternative views offered by thinkers such as Lukes.

Foucault understands power as the ability of individuals or groups to act on the actions of others or, in other words, to act in such a way as to affect the actions of others. Giddens has a related understanding in mind when he insists that action:

> Depends upon the capability of the individual to 'make a difference' to a pre-existing state of affairs or course of events. An agent ceases to be such if he or she loses the capability to 'make a difference', that is, to exercise some sort of power. (Giddens, 1984: 14)

For Foucault, however – unlike for most other thinkers who make use of this conception of power – the ability to *act* on the actions of others is not the same as the ability to *control* or *command* the actions of others, which Foucault (1988) calls domination. Thus, in contrast to most other thinkers, Foucault is not running together the first and third meanings of power provided at the start of the chapter; in his view, people can affect or influence the actions of others without controlling those actions. Power is, here, an inescapable feature of all human interaction.

This view of power as *action* (and, specifically, as acting on the actions of others) has a number of radical implications for the study of power by sociologists and others. First, it suggests that power cannot be understood (and hence analysed) in quantitative terms. Foucault describes power as the 'total structure of actions' (Foucault, 1982: 220) that one brings to bear on the actions of others: in other words, power simply *is* (it is all of one's actions directed at other people), rather than something that one can have more or less of. A crucial point to note here is that for Foucault power *is* action, rather than something which animates – or underlies – action, as it is for many other thinkers. We have seen, for example, that Giddens distinguishes between particular resources 'through which power is exercised', and the underlying capacity – power itself – which those resources represent.

Foucault's view, on the contrary, is that power in the sense of such an under-lying capacity simply 'does not exist' (1982: 217).

Second, and following on from this, the view of power as *action* renders irrelevant questions about whether a population's belief in the right of their rulers to exercise power over them is 'truly' legitimate or right. As we have seen, these questions are a central focus for most sociologists – and most other scholars – concerned with power. But if, as in Foucault's view, power is everywhere, and is an inescapable component of all social relationships, then these kinds of questions are of little value. This is not to say that Foucault is not concerned with the *belief* in legitimacy: the fact that people obey commands because they *believe* that others have the right to issue them. In this respect *belief* in legitimacy plays a similar role in Foucault's analysis to that of Parsons and Weber: the concern is with how that belief is produced and sustained and what its effects are, rather than with whether or not it is 'true' or well founded.

In Foucault's view, then, the focus on legitimacy in most writings on power is misplaced and we need 'a political philosophy that isn't erected around the problem of sovereignty' (Foucault, 1980: 121). Just as Foucault does not conflate the first and the third of the meanings of power provided at the beginning of the chapter, neither does he conflate the second and third. In adopting a notion of power as to do with human agency, he is not assuming that it automatically follows from this that power concerns the ability to exer-cise control over others, and that it therefore necessarily involves questions to do with legitimacy or 'right'.

The radical significance of Foucault's analysis of power, then, lies not in suggesting a new set of answers to questions about how power is distributed and produced, and on what basis it can be said to be 'legitimate' or 'right'. Rather, the significance of Foucault's contribution lies precisely in his *displace-ment* of these issues from the centre of discussions about power: in effect, the most radical implication of his view of power as a ubiquitous, inescapable feature of all human interaction is that there is little of value to be said about power itself. We all act on the actions of others, but our actions in this respect (our 'powers') have nothing in common with each other: end of story. Foucault's analysis then, leads us away from the study of power *per se*, and into quite different areas of inquiry.

We can illustrate this point by reference to Foucault's discussions of the relations between power and autonomy. We have seen that the understanding of power as quantifiable capacity suggests that the power of others should be seen as an actual or potential constraint or imposition on one's autonomy, or freedom, and that this view of power as constraint or imposition – as *nega-tive* in its effects – is assumed in most discussions on power. Autonomy, in this view, is a matter of not being subject to the power of another. But if we accept Foucault's account of power as a matter of acting on the actions of others, then autonomy in this sense is illusory: we are always subject to the power of others, just as others are subject to our power.

However, while for Foucault the ideal of 'true' autonomy (and, hence, true 'consent') is an illusion (since others are always acting on our actions), this does not mean that he sees individual behaviour or conduct as *determined* by the actions – by the power – of others. On the contrary, in his view, people are always able to choose, to some degree, how they will conduct themselves in any situation. Indeed, for Foucault, the effective exercise of power *requires* that individuals possess a significant degree of freedom. This is because for people to be able to act on the actions of others – that is, to exercise power over others – those others must themselves be able to act and, indeed, to reciprocate that exercise of power. In fact, as Foucault argues in *Discipline and Punish* (1979), power often has the effect of *enhancing* the capacities of those over whom it is exercised. The exercise of discipline, for example, can provide individuals with new skills and attributes, help them to control their own behaviour in trying conditions, and promote their ability to follow commands and to act in concert with others. Foucault's concept of power, then, is profoundly radical in a further sense: it construes power as most usually *productive* in its effects, as *adding to* the capacities and abilities of individuals. This is in marked contrast to conventional depictions of power which, as we have seen, almost invariably assume it to be *negative* in its effects: to *take away from* – to constrain and distort – people's 'true' capabilities. Moreover, while questions of *production* are important in Foucault's analysis, the focus is on how the *effects* of power are produced. In this respect, his work differs also from that of other thinkers for whom the issue of production is important – such as Weber, Parsons and Mann – where the focus is on the production of *power itself*.

The fact that power depends on the freedom of its subjects means, in Foucault's view, that where there are relations of power there is also the possibility of resistance. Nevertheless, in marked contrast to Lukes' notion that we can judge the effects of power on people's thoughts and desires by imagining a world in which those effects are not present, Foucault's understanding of power appears to invoke no such utopian possibilities. Indeed, his work has often been criticized on precisely these grounds (for example Taylor, 1986; Fraser, 1989; McCarthy, 1992). However, the difference between these two positions is less clear-cut than it might seem. Thus, while he insists that power depends on the freedom of those on whom it is exercised, Foucault also recognizes that conditions will often be such that those who are subject to the effects of power will find that their 'margin of liberty is extremely limited' (Foucault, 1988: 12). This is what Foucault calls 'domination', using that term to designate 'what we ordinarily call power' (ibid.: 19) – that is, the capacity of one or more persons to impose their will even, in Weber's words, 'against the resistance of others who are participating in the action' (1978: 926).

While Foucault makes no secret of his hostility to states of domination, his own later studies of power are more concerned with an asymmetrical relationship of another kind, that is, with *government*. Foucault (1991) uses the term 'government' in a very general sense to refer not only to the regulation of the population and the territory of a state by a legally constituted authority – that is, by *the* government – but also to the regulation of oneself, of a household or organization, or even of a collectivity such as the poor, the sick or the unemployed. Rather than operating in the manner of domination to determine directly the behaviour of individuals, government, in Foucault's view, aims to affect their behaviour *indirectly* by influencing the manner in which they regulate their own behaviour. A change in interest rates, for example, or in the tax regime, can have a substantial impact on the conduct of numerous individuals without any of them being told directly what to do.

While this overarching concern with the regulation of conduct is central to all of his discussions on government, Foucault pays particular attention to the predominant modern understanding of government as identified with the state. His aim here is to distinguish this form of government both from the other forms which coexist with it in the contemporary era (government of oneself, of one or more others, and of a household or organization) and from the forms of government which existed in earlier times (for example, the rule of the prince, feudal magnate, church or emperor over the populations of late medieval Europe). In this context, Foucault is more concerned with the different *effects* of each of these forms of government, and with how these are produced, than he is with those questions of the *legitimacy* of governmental power which have so preoccupied other scholars. For this reason, his discussions of government have focused especially on the different *rationalities* associated with different forms of government. By rationalities he means the ways of thinking about the nature of government and its objectives, about the character of the population to be governed and the organizations and collectivities that exist within it, and about the knowledge and practical resources that government can draw upon and the obstacles that stand in its way.

Particularly important here is Foucault's treatment of liberalism, since he sees liberalism as the most influential of all rationalities of government in contemporary western societies (Foucault, 1997: 73–9). Liberalism is a way of thinking about government which is distinguished by its emphasis on individual liberty. Conventional academic accounts of liberalism treat its overarching commitment to liberty as a matter of principle: frequently debating whether such a commitment can be justified and whether the forms of government to which it gives rise can therefore be regarded as legitimate. In addition, most such accounts treat the stress on individual liberty as implying that liberal forms of government will be characterized by a strictly *limited* interference in, and regulation of, the lives of citizens.

Foucault's account of liberalism as rationality of government presents a very different view of the role of liberty in liberal government. The stress on individual liberty is seen here, not as a philosophical/ethical stance giving rise to certain forms of government, but rather as a *means* by which government itself can be effected. Liberal ideas are thus understood in this model as representing less a political/ethical commitment than a body of knowledge concerning how the citizens of modern states can most effectively be governed. The importance of liberalism, for Foucault, lies not in questions of the legitimacy of liberal government but rather in its *effectiveness* as a practical means of governing modern populations, that is, to regulating the conduct of individuals. In this view, liberal government is characterized not so much by the *restriction* of government in the name of liberty, as by the *exercise* of government via that same stress on liberty (Rose, 1995, 1996; Hindess, 1996).

Thus, where liberal government is conventionally understood as concerned with minimizing the impact of state activities on the pre-existing freedom of individuals, the Foucauldian view understands it both as actively *producing* certain forms of freedom and as using them for its own purposes. This is what Rose and Miller have in mind when they describe liberal government as a matter of 'governing at a distance' (Rose and Miller, 1992: 173), that is, as a matter of producing certain kinds of 'free' individuals who are thus able to regulate or govern their own behaviour in line with governmental norms. Foucault's treatment of liberalism in these terms has been taken up and developed by a number of contemporary sociologists and others concerned with investigating the role of government (in its broadest sense) in contemporary western societies. Rabinow (1989), for instance, has argued that the development of urban planning in nineteenth-century France is linked to this kind of 'government at a distance': thus public spaces and buildings were designed in such a way as to instil in individuals a sense of constantly being watched (and judged) by others and so, in turn, to induce a process of self-monitoring and self-regulation, or self-government, in those individuals. Likewise, Hunter's studies of the development of systems of mass compulsory education in contemporary democratic states such as Britain and Australia have emphasized the governmental concern with ensuring that individuals acquire appropriate means of analysing their own behaviour and the behaviour of others (Hunter, 1988, 1994). Here, education is seen as a matter not only of academic and vocational training, but also of forming individuals whose capacities and habits of thought are such that they normally can be relied upon to govern themselves. Dean (1998) has suggested that many welfare programmes can be seen not only as delivering various benefits to the members of groups such as the unemployed and the aged, but also as shaping the desires and aspirations of those people by attributing to them particular statuses, rights and obligations. In his view, even the 'free' decisions of the unemployed have been turned into components of government labour market programmes, that is, into means whereby the unemployed themselves may be governed.

These brief and schematic remarks on government seem to have taken us a long way from the study of power as such. This is because those sociologists and others who have followed Foucault's lead in this area have shown little interest in the kinds of questions more conventionally associated with the study of power: questions to do with its distribution and production or with its legitimacy. Foucault's discussion of power allows us to recognize that ways of acting on the actions of others are, first, considerably more diverse and, second, frequently far more complex and sophisticated than can be accounted for by a focus on power as either a capacity or a right. As we have seen here, a Foucauldian focus on how the effects of power are produced – rather than on power itself as the explanation for such effects – enables those who adopt this kind of approach to avoid many of the problems associated with an understanding of power as either capacity or right, and so to break away from the intractable disputes concerning how we should identify and measure power, and how we should determine its legitimacy.

Nevertheless, we should note that Foucault himself (and many who write in a Foucauldian vein) fall back into using, on occasion, something that looks very like the conventional conception of power that his work elsewhere so trenchantly critiques. Thus, we have already noted that he uses the term 'domination' to mean almost exactly what other thinkers refer to as power in the sense of capacity: it is presumed in his use of this term that some parties are able to exercise power more effectively than others (and so to reduce their margin of liberty). This returns us to the familiar problems outlined earlier for the view of power as quantitative capacity: how do we decide in any context who is suffering from such effects of power or, in Foucault's terms, from 'domination'?

We have also seen that, just as Lukes and others offer the utopian prospect of social relations in which the distorting effects of power are not present, so Foucault imagines the possibility of social relations in which the effects of domination are reduced to an absolute minimum (Foucault, 1988: 18–20). This, of course, raises the question of what, if any, relations of domination could be seen as legitimate or as unavoidable. Foucault does not deny the legitimacy, for example, of hierarchical relations of the kind that appear in many teaching situations, provided that the pupils are not subjected to 'the arbitrary and useless authority of a teacher' (ibid: 18). But the problem here, as many pupils will have discovered for themselves, is that the difference between an exercise of authority which can be justified on pedagogic grounds, and one which is 'arbitrary or useless', is a much more difficult one to draw than it appears at first sight and must inevitably depend on personal evaluation. We are back in the familiar terrain of ethical and political judgements and consequent intractable dispute. It seems that in spite of his wish to leave behind conventional notions of power, Foucault is unable to relinquish them entirely, smuggling them into his model under a different name.

# Conclusion

The concept of power as used by sociologists is far less clear-cut than most of us imagine it to be. As we have seen, sociologists can mean three rather different things by the term, each of which gives rise to a distinctive kind of analysis. For example, in analysing class, gender and 'race' – the next three topics discussed in this book – sociologists will inevitably use one or more of the three understandings of power discussed in this chapter. Those who see power as the quantifiable capacity of one party to get others to do what they want them to will generally be concerned with questions such as whether we can speak of members of the upper class, men or 'racial' majorities as a 'dominant' social group and working-class people, women or 'racial' minorties as a 'subordinate' social group. Those who assume some notion of power as the right of one party to get others to do what they want might focus on questions such as how societies operate to instil into working-class people, women or ethnic minorities a sense that the statuses they fill are the right and 'natural' ones. In fact, many analyses in these areas will use power in both of these senses, sometimes without any acknowledged awareness of the differences between them and the different assumptions which each involves. Significantly, analyses based on either or both of these understandings will often see power purely in negative terms, as an undesirable aspect of social relations that enables one social group to reduce the scope of action of another.

Students who understand power in a Foucauldian sense will tend to question the categories of class, gender and 'race'. On this view, categories such as 'the poor', 'the unemployed', 'blacks', 'whites', 'Asians', 'men', 'women', 'transvestites' are means by which the members of contemporary societies are governed. Analyses of these types will see power largely in productive terms: as promoting individual dispositions, ways of thinking and patterns of behaviour identified with each of these categories. As we have seen, for Foucault, the fact that power is productive in its effects is not to say that it is necessarily positive or good. In particular, when power veers towards domination, then it may well be resisted by the dominated groups.

This brings us to the final point of this chapter. While Foucault's view of power as an inescapable element of all human action appears to release sociologists from intractable disputes about power as capacity and right, it still retains conceptions of power in these terms under the different name of domination. It is tempting to conclude from this that conventional conceptions of power as capacity and right may be unavoidable simply because they accord with the harsh empirical reality that, whether we like it or not, some people are always going to dominate others. On this view, if Foucauldians are going to use the term 'power' to mean something different, they must find a new name for this reality. However, there is an alternative explanation for Foucault's resurrection of the conventional conceptions of power, one to which we have alluded in our discussion of power as right. On this view, the conceptions of power as capacity and as right reflect the high value placed on individual autonomy in modern societies. As such, they are so deeply implicated in contemporary western ways of understanding and organizing social relations that no matter how hard we try, we can never quite free ourselves from them.

## Further Reading

Hindess, B. *Discourses of Power: From Hobbes to Foucault*, Oxford, Blackwell, 1995. Offers a critical examination of the treatment of power in western political thought and an extended discussion of Foucault's radical alternative to conventional approaches to the study of power.

Lukes, S. (ed.) *Power*, Oxford, Blackwell, 1986. An excellent edited collection which brings together a range of different accounts of power, including Lukes' own reflections on the argument of his 1974 book.

Wartenberg, T. *The Forms of Power: From Domination to Transformation*, Philadelphia, Temple University Press, 1990. Combines a useful account of the historical development of the concept of power with a critical discussion of its main contemporary interpretations.

Wrong, D. *Power: Its Forms, Bases and Uses*, 2nd edn, Chicago, University of Chicago Press, 1988. Still the most useful survey of mainstream sociological understandings of power.

# 5

# Class and Stratification

## *Rosemary Crompton*

Social classes are groups of people sharing a broadly similar market, or economic, situation. Class is one of the most fundamental concepts used in sociology to explain differing life chances. The idea had its origins in the classical sociology of Marx and Weber, examined in Chapter 3, and continues to be particularly relevant to areas of research considered later in the book, such as education, work and organizations, crime and deviance and health. This chapter aims to explain theories of class, the major strategies for measuring class inequalities and the debates surrounding the relevance of class in contemporary societies. It should provide understanding of:

■ Marxian and Weberian theories of class and their legacy in modern sociology

■ How sociologists go about measuring class inequalities and criticisms of these methodologies

■ Changes in the class processes of modern societies

■ Some of the major issues surrounding the 'end of class' debate

■ Changing patterns of inequality in contemporary societies

---

### CONCEPTS

social stratification ■ class conflict ■ status ■ class consciousness
lifestyles ■ deskilling ■ social mobility ■ polarization

# Introduction

'Class' is a word which has a number of different meanings in sociology as well as in everyday life. Beyond a fairly basic level of complexity, all known societies are stratified – that is, differentiated according to one or more principles of classification, which is usually hierarchical. These principles have included age, ritual purity (as in the Hindu caste system), citizenship and the division of labour, and religious and military hierarchies. Thus the term 'class' is often used to describe the ranking of a group in a formal hierarchical order – for example the 'class' of plebeians in ancient Rome. These hierarchies were woven into the fabric of society and carried with them legal and quasi-legal rights and obligations (relating, for example, to the right to practice a particular occupation). The linkage of 'class' with hierarchy persists today, in that class is a term which is widely used to describe unequally rewarded groups, such as the Registrar General's 'social classes' in Britain. These are employment aggregates corresponding to broad divisions within the occupational order – manual workers, white-collar workers, managers and professionals, and so on. In contemporary societies, however, such groupings are not characterized by any formal, legal distinctions, rather, they summarize the outcome, in material terms, of the competition for material resources in market capitalism. This chapter begins by discussing concepts of class. It then examines the measurement of 'class' inequalities and recent changes which have affected class processes. The next section considers the recurring question of the 'end of class' and the chapter concludes with discussion of the 'underclass' and the deepening inequalities in Britain over the past two decades.

# Concepts and Definitions

Marx saw 'class' categories as relating to the ownership of property, and production relationships. However, as we saw in Chapter 3, Marx argued that 'classes' were not mere social categories, but also transforming social forces and 'all history was the history of class conflict'. Marx saw all complex societies as characterized by the relationship between antagonistic classes. Out of these conflicts came major social changes culminating in changes in production and property relationships. In feudal Europe, for example, the Church and feudal lords, who controlled access to land and property, exploited the major producers, the peasantry, through the direct appropriation of a portion of that which they produced either directly, in the form of produce, or through taxes. The antagonistic relationship between lord and peasant was intermittently expressed through wars and peasant revolt but, in Marx's analysis, the revolutionary (that is, epoch-changing) class of the feudal era was the rising bourgeoisie, the merchants and nascent capitalist manufacturers, who sought to remove the restrictions on production and the market (such as restrictions on the movement of labour and capital), which maintained the feudal order (Marx and Engels, 1962). Thus they struggled for a fundamental transformation of society from feudalism to market capitalism.

A significant element of Marx's conceptualization of class was that classes were identified according to their relationships in production – owner and non-owner of the means of production such as land and property, controller and non-controller of labour power. Thus 'classes' for Marx are identified not simply according to the extent that they possess a particular attribute – such as money or social honour – but rather, in terms of their *relationship* to other classes. This 'relational' conceptualization may be distinguished from a 'graduational' view of class which Wright argues merely describes. Although the groupings identified by Marx are characterized by material inequalities, classes were for Marx defined primarily by their relationship to other classes rather than the extent of their material and/or social inqualilty relative to other classes (Wright, 1980, 1997).

The concept of 'class', therefore, may be used to describe hierarchical groupings characterized by material and social inequalities, prestige rankings, and actual social forces with the capacity to transform societies. There is no 'correct' definition of the term although it is, of course, legitimate to debate the correct interpretation of a particular social theorist's use of the concept. Theoretical debates about the use of the concept of class have sometimes been very prominent in sociology, particularly during the 1970s and 80s. In the context of these theoretical debates, a contrast was often drawn between 'class' in particular and the more general concept of 'stratification', which, as we have seen, describes the general principles according to which societies are differentiated. This was often associated with the attempt to isolate the impact of 'class' – understood broadly to refer to groups emerging from the patterning of property, production and market relationships – from other stratification principles such as prestige (status), ethnicity, gender and age – and indeed, 'class' was sometimes seen as the ultimate determinant of these other axes of differentiation (see discussion in Bradley, 1996). In practice, of course, the complex nature of modern societies is reflected in the complexity of their systems of stratification, which are invariably multi-stranded.

## Classical Theories

In sociology, Marx and Weber have had the major impact upon theoretical approaches to class, and sociological debates still reflect the contrast between these two. Both were concerned with the transition from pre-capitalist to modern industrial capitalist societies, and the consequences of this transition for social organization and institutions. Marx was an active revolutionary, and his analyses of the class structure were undertaken as part of the development of a political agenda. He developed a distinctive materialist theory of history which, as we have seen, argued that the ownership and control of the material means of production (for example, land in feudal societies, factories in industrialism) was associated with distinctive societal types and class-related patterns of exploitation and inequality. Modern capitalism was a particularly dynamic type of society, in which the 'two great classes' were the bourgeoisie (the private owners and controllers of the material means of production), and the proletariat (those who, having no ownership or rights in the means of production, are dependent upon the sale of their labour power in order to survive).

However, capitalism is not just a 'two-class' society, as there are other classes besides the bourgeoisie and proletariat, including the petty bourgeoisie (small employers, often of family labour), the small peasantry and the lumpenproletariat (people without regular employment existing on the fringes of capital). Capital itself is divided between industrial capitalists, financial capitalists, and landowners (Marx, 1962). Nevertheless, Marx believed that it would be the conflict between the bourgeoisie and the proletariat which would bring about the transition to the next historical stage of society; first to socialism, then to true communism. This conflict would come about because of the inherent contradiction between the forces and relations of production in capitalism – that is, between the increasingly social nature of the production process and the private ownership of the means of production. In this conflict, the proletariat would be the revolutionary class, whose conscious endeavours, like those of the bourgeoisie during the feudal era, would eventually bring about a new stage of societal development.

Weber, as we saw in Chapter 3, was critical of this exclusively materialist view, arguing that influential ideas and social movements can also be sources of important historical changes. In a similar vein, he argued that although 'classes' were defined largely in material terms, societal *ideas* about 'better' and 'worse', 'higher' and 'lower', were also significant factors in social stratification. Here the concept of 'status' was central to his thinking. He used it to describe:

1. social honour or prestige
2. an associational group or 'consciousness community'
3. non-market claims to material resources.

Thus for Weber, the feudal estates just described, whose claims rested upon tradition and customary rights rather than 'market forces' as such, represented status groups rather than, as they did for Marx, classes. Indeed, Weber considered that classes – groups characterized by their differential access to the property and labour markets – were characteristic only of capitalist societies. Unlike Marx, Weber saw the development of class consciousness as essentially contingent – that is, consciousness might or might not develop depending upon circumstances. However, classes and status groups were very likely to come into conflict with each other, as the pretensions of status honour (and claims to privileged positions) would be offended by the bargaining which accompanied market (that is, class) situations.

In summary, theories of class and stratification have long been regarded as central sociological concepts. Because the class concept is flexible and has a number of different meanings, a number of different, if related, topics are involved. In the most general stratification terms, at the macro-level the concepts are seen by some sociologists to capture the transition from systems of inequality characterized largely by ascription (status) to achievement (class) (Parsons, 1954). In the 1960s and 70s, such optimistic arguments were associated with the notion that a true (and essentially 'fair') meritocracy was in the process of being created (Kerr *et al.*, 1973). In opposition to these arguments, Marxist-influenced writers have found the value of the class concept in both explaining the broad contours of social change and indicating how societies might develop in the future. At a more micro-level, however, class and stratification theories have been used in order to identify actual and potential sources of social conflict and to explain why some social groups have been more or less successful than others. This latter dimension lies at the root of the inescapable association of class and inequality, and the capacity of stratification concepts to describe and explain inequalities of power, ownership, and control, and access to scarce goods and resources. Not surprisingly, therefore, class and stratification concepts have always been associated with the measurement of material and social inequalities and it is to this dimension that we now turn.

## Measuring 'Class'

Classes are made up of individual human beings, who must therefore be allocated to a class according to some kind of principle or other. Many theorists working in the area of class analysis would argue that the question of how to allocate individuals and thus measure and describe 'social classes' cannot be separated from the question of class consciousness – that is, the extent to which individuals in the same class situation share a sense of their common interests, and thus think or behave in a similar manner.

As has already been noted with reference to the discussion of Marx and Weber's work, one major difference between modern industrial and pre-industrial societies is that the majority of the population are directly or indirectly dependent upon paid employment in order to survive. Access to positions in the labour market and employment are closely related to levels of material inequality, and class relationships – of ownership and non-ownership, power and control – are obviously reflected in work and employment relationships. Therefore, employment position has been widely used in order to allocate individuals to 'classes', and the structure of employment has been divided up in various ways in order to generate them (Marsh, 1986). We may describe this as the *employment aggregate* approach to class analysis.

A number of different class schemes are available. In Britain, the Office of Population Censuses and Surveys (OPCS) currently supports two occupational classifications: Registrar General's Social Class (RGSC), as well as a more detailed Socio-Economic Grouping (SEG). (The Office of National Statistics is currently undertaking a review of social classifications, and they will be revised in the 2001 census.) Other nation states also have their own versions – for example, the Nordic Occupational scheme, used in the Scandinavian countries. The RGSC has six categories, ranging from higher professional and managerial through to unskilled manual workers, which represent, in broad outline, the hierarchy of occupational advantage and disadvantage in Britain. The OPCS schemes have been widely used in social policy applications. Another scheme, which is widely used in advertising and market research, is Social Grade (A, B, C1, C2 and D). This scheme is maintained by the advertising industry, and includes an assessment of 'lifestyle' as well as a separate categories for the self-employed and unemployed. Both the OPCS schemes and Social Grade have been devised with practical applications in mind – to chart social inequalities, to monitor the spending and reading habits of individuals and families.

Sociologists have also constructed class schemes for their own purposes. In Britain, probably the best-known practitioner of 'employment aggregate' class analysis is Goldthorpe, who devised his scheme as part of his work on social mobility. Employment status (whether employed or self-employed) is a key category of the Goldthorpe scheme. In his early work, Goldthorpe was closely associated with the theoretical approach that had been developed by Lockwood (Lockwood, 1958; Goldthorpe *et al.*, 1969). Lockwood had identified the Weberian category of 'market' situation (together with 'work' situation) as key factors in locating occupations within 'classes'. Goldthorpe's *original* formulation of his class scheme carried over this 'Weberian' aspect of Lockwood's approach.

This neo-Weberian characterization was thrown into sharp relief with the development of an explicitly Marxist programme of employment aggregate class analysis by Wright (1976). Wright's explicit aim has been to develop the empirical investigation of a number of Marxist-derived theories – for example, the 'proletarianization' of the labour force. In British sociology, Wright's approach was incorporated into a major empirical investigation of the 'class' (that is, employment) structure carried out in the 1980s (Marshall *et al.*, 1988). Marshall and his colleagues used the same data set to compare outcomes using the Registrar General's 'common sense' class scheme, Goldthorpe's neo-Weberian class scheme, and Wright's Marxist class scheme. They not only found a number of apparent anomalies in Wright's scheme (Wright's 'autonomous worker' category, for example, grouped together lawyers and forklift truck drivers), but also that Goldthorpe's scheme corresponded most closely to political preferences and voting intentions. Goldthorpe's 'Weberian' scheme, therefore, was declared the 'winner'. The presentation of evidence of Marshall *et al.* may be read as an empirical evaluation of three different class schemes: Goldthorpe's, Wright's, and the Registrar General's, within the employment aggregate approach to 'class analysis' (see Marshall, 1988). However, as the three schemes were designed for different purposes (and it is certain the RGSC was not designed with reference to sociological understandings) it is not surprising that the outcomes of the schemes should vary. Recently, however, Goldthorpe and Marshall (1992) have asserted that the Goldthorpe scheme is not characterized by any particular 'theory' of class. Rather, they now assert that it focuses upon *employment relations,* as it combines employment status (whether employer, self-employed or employee) together with the employee relationship – that is, whether the employee has a 'service' or 'labour' contract of employment. In particular they reject any notion that work tasks and roles play any part in the construction of the scheme. Goldthorpe has modified his scheme over the years, largely as a consequence of practical requirements (such as the separate identification of agricultural and farming occupations) in order to achieve cross-national comparability in his comparative study of social mobility (Erikson and Goldthorpe, 1992).

In practice, although Goldthorpe and Wright are frequently presented as representing different theoretical traditions (Weber and Marx), the methodological assumptions underlying their empirical approach – that is, the comparative analysis of national, large-scale, sample surveys – are in fact very similar. Over the years this has resulted in a considerable convergence in these apparently conflicting approaches to employment aggregate 'class analysis'. Despite their being constructed according to different principles, the 'Marxist' class scheme of Wright and the (Weberian) class scheme of Goldthorpe in fact give very similar measures of the same phenomena (Emmison, 1991). Indeed, as Wright has recently argued: 'as a practical set of operational categories, the ("Marxist") class structure matrix... does not dramatically differ from the class typology used by Goldthorpe' (Wright, 1997: 37).

The 'employment aggregate' approach to class analysis has been useful in identifying the contours of major inequalities – for example, in health, and access to educational opportunities – and describing attitudinal and behavioural differences such as political affiliation and voting patterns. However, it should not be taken to represent 'class analysis' as a whole as there are a number of empirical and theoretical problems associated with this approach.

The first difficulty with the aggregate employment approach is that the focus upon employment means that some very significant class categories are inadequately considered – in particular, major owners of capital (Westergaard, 1995). The number of such major owners in the population is too small for them ever to be counted in sufficiently large numbers within a sample survey. However, the impact of this class is out of all proportion to its numerical significance, and the study of large capital holders should obviously be incorporated into the field of 'class analysis'. Second, there is the problem of gender. Given the persistence of occupational segregation by sex, then the 'class structure' as revealed by an employment aggregate class scheme is very different for women and men. Men tend to predominate in skilled manual and higher professional and managerial occupations, women in lower professional and white-collar occupations. However, it may be argued (as Goldthorpe has done) that, although the 'class' (that is, occupational) structure is different for men and women, the class differences for women in 'women's' jobs and men in 'men's' jobs are of a similar order – that is, 'service-class' women differ from 'working-class' women in the same way that 'service-class' men differ from 'working-class' men – even though there may be differences between 'service-class' men and 'service-class' women. More intractable problems, however, are presented by the growth of long-term unemployment. Individuals who have never held a permanent, full-time job, as well as households headed by individuals who are long-term unemployed, are difficult to classify using the 'employment aggregate' approach. Thus many commercial agencies, for example, prefer to use a measure such as social grade (rather than sociological class measures) as this scheme allows for the identification of those on state benefits.

Another problem is caused by changes in the occupational structure itself. This may lead to the reclassification of certain key occupations – for example, the Registrar General once placed clerks in Social Class II but they have been moved to III – as well as the problem of allocating new occupations to an appropriate category. Even more problematically, the criteria by which occupations are allocated to categories may themselves change over time. For example, as we have seen, a crucial element of the Goldthorpe class scheme is employment relations, in which the presence or absence of job security and, above all, a career is central. Goldthorpe regards the career as an attribute of the job, rather than the individual: 'It is not so much that reward is being offered in return for work done, but... "compensation"... in return for the acceptance of an obligation to discharge trust "faithfully"' (1982: 169). Once on the career escalator, it is assumed that individuals did not get pushed off it as long as they abided by the rules – although some might move to faster tracks. However the last fifteen years have seen a transformation of the 'service' relationship which breaks with many of the assumptions central to Goldthorpe's definition. The growth of self-employment and short-term contracting, together with individualized and performance-related pay systems, serves to make individual 'employability' potentially more significant than the job-related employment conditions (see Chapter 10 for further discussion).

There is, therefore, a range of problems associated with the employment aggregate approach, which stem from the difficulties of devising a reliable measure of a rapidly changing and developing employment structure. However, it has been more generally argued that changes in the relative significance of 'work' as employment may be undermining the utility of the 'class' concept in sociology – and indeed, the project of class analysis as a whole. Authors such as Pahl (1989) and Saunders (1987) have argued that 'work' as employment, and thus 'class', is declining in its significance at the end of the twentieth century. The shift to the service sector and the development of new production systems is leading to an erosion of work hierarchies and the decline of work-centred social identities (Clark and Lipset, 1991; Beck, 1992). More particularly, it is argued that consumption and 'lifestyles' are becoming more central to people's lives than 'class'. Thus whereas class might have been an appropriate concept for the analysis of industrial societies in the late nineteenth and first half of the twentieth century, this is no longer the case in the era of increasingly individualized contemporary society.

## Class Processes: Recent Developments

Foremost among those who criticized the impetus towards classification in (structural) sociological approaches to 'class' was the historian E.P. Thompson (1968). In the 1960s, sociologists such as Parsons (1954) and Dahrendorf (1969) had described the 'class structure' as corresponding to an abstract structure of social roles and positions. In contrast, Thompson argued: 'I do not see class as a "structure", nor even as a "category", but as something which in fact happens' (1968: 9). For Thompson, 'structure' and 'action' could not be separated: 'Classes do not struggle because they exist, but exist because they struggle' (Joyce, 1995: 127). Thus his major work is on the *making* of the English working class; the 'class' does not exist outside its making.

Social history in Britain has been enormously influenced by Thompson, even though recent discussions have gone beyond his (contested) materialism to embrace the 'linguistic turn' in which 'class' is defined largely in relation to experience and consciousness, and indeed, the notion of structure disappears altogether. Not surprisingly, however, there developed an affinity between historical approaches stressing the unity of structure and action, and sociological commentaries on class with a similar emphasis. Giddens (1973, 1981) examined the processes whereby classes become stable and enduring social aggregates by reproducing themselves intergenerationally. Giddens has not carried out any subsequent work in the field (Giddens, 1990: 298). The significance of Giddens work on 'class', therefore, lies largely in its emphasis upon the sociological study of class *processes*. This position was rather different from the focus on the *measurement* of social class, and class-related attributes, which was a major feature of the employment aggregate approach of authors such as Goldthorpe.

At the time, however, Giddens' work was seen as making a contribution to the theoretical elaboration of the class concept and, in particular, the growing debate between sociological 'Marxist' and 'Weberian' approaches to class (see Crompton and Gubbay, 1977). The 1970s were characterized by a surge of interest in Marx's work, including both French structural Marxism (as represented by the work of Althusser and Poulantzas), as well as a more culturalist version influenced by the Gramscian notion of 'hegemony' described in Chapter 3. Marxist accounts of the class structure were complemented by a renewed interest in the labour process stimulated by Braverman's work (1974). Braverman's account of the 'deskilling' or 'proletarianization' of the contemporary labour force seemed to offer an avenue whereby relations in production might be mapped onto the job structure – a strategy which, as we have seen in the previous section, was taken up by Wright. The revival of interest in Marx meant that the 'Marx vs Weber' debate assumed a high profile and came to represent *the* major polarity within class analysis.

However, more important was the (largely unacknowledged) split within the sociology of 'class analysis' between, on the one hand, employment aggregate practitioners concerned mainly with the analysis of national data sets, and, on the other, socio-historical and other case studies focusing largely upon the processes of class formation, emergence, and consciousness. The latter were particularly concerned with the impact of major social changes which had occurred very recently – for example, the increasing employment of married women, economic decline and rising unemployment, deindustrialization and the shift to the service sector, and the corresponding growth of 'middle-class' occupations. Within this approach the emphasis was above all on *change* (see for example Lash and Urry, 1987), whereas within the employment aggregate approach (particularly as represented in the work of Goldthorpe and his associates), there developed what appeared to be a contrary emphasis upon *stability*, rather than change.

The view is taken here that the field of 'class analysis' as a whole must incorporate both change and continuity, as well as a range of methodologies including large-scale surveys and case studies as well as socio-historical and contemporary research (Crompton, 1993). The remainder of this section, therefore, will explore the impact of changes in the organization of productive activity and in the labour market which have had important impacts on the 'class structure'. These include the expansion of the middle class and the decline of the working class, together with an associated increase in social mobility and the increasing employment of women.

## The Decline of the 'Working Class'

As we have seen in the previous section, the strategy of using the employment structure as a proxy for the class structure is a longstanding convention. Changes in class structuring are indeed reflected in labour markets and the occupational structure, and one of the most notable of these changes since the end of the Second World War has been the decline of manual work in manufacturing which has been long associated with the idea of the 'proletariat' or 'working' class, together with an increase in service-related employment of all kinds (in education, health, financial services, leisure, and so on). In Britain, using the Registrar General's measure, the 'working class' (skilled and unskilled manual workers) has declined from 64 per cent to 42 per cent of the employed population since the Second World War. Since the end of the 1970s, deindustrialization has resulted in the further decline of manufacturing industry, and between 1971 and 1993, employment in manufacturing declined from 36.4 per cent to 20.4 per cent, while employment in services grew from 52.6 per cent to 72.8 per cent.

Economic and political change, therefore, has brought with it the proportional and numerical decline of the 'working class'. The shrinking of the working class over the last twenty years has effectively eclipsed a topic which flourished during the Marxist revival of the 1970s – the apparent failure of this class, in the advanced industrial societies, to develop a consciousness of its revolutionary political role and act accordingly. As Savage (1996) has argued, the 'working class' has been the reference point against which other classes have been identified, and its apparent decline came to be associated with notions of the 'end of class' itself. More particularly, the working class was the main focus of arguments relating to 'class dealignment' – that is, the apparent decline of the link between class and voting behaviour (the working class being more likely to vote for socialist parties, the middle and upper classes to vote for right-wing parties). In Britain, the failure of the Labour Party to be elected during the 1980s and early 1990s was seen as being a consequence of a shift in the allegiance of the skilled working class in particular. As a consequence, the 'end' of class politics was widely heralded. In fact, the data suggest that there has been a 'trendless fluctuation' in the working-class vote, rather than any permanent shift in voting behaviour (Heath *et al.*, 1991). Nevertheless, as we have seen in recent years, the changes in the occupational structure brought about by economic and industrial restructuring have been reflected in the strategies of both of the major political parties – both of whom seem to be largely preoccupied with gaining the middle-class vote.

The increased employment of married women, as well as the enhanced participation of women in the labour force more generally, has also affected approaches to 'class analysis'. As feminists have argued, a whole range of concepts in the social sciences – and class analysis in particular – were developed so as to incorporate the assumptions of the 'male breadwinner' model of the gender division of labour, in which men were held to be responsible for market work and the public sphere, whereas women were located in the domestic sphere. This convention had been incorporated into the employment aggregate approach via the collection of 'men only' samples in empirical investigations of class and stratification during the 1960s and 70s, as well as the designation of the male breadwinner as the 'head of household', 'even when the female partner was in employment'.

Besides the problems associated with this practice, the growth in women's employment from the 1960s also served to undermine other assumptions relating to 'class'. Chief among these was the question of causal primacy in respect of the major determinants of material inequalities and associated structures of stratification. To put this argument crudely, did 'class' also determine the shape and extent of other major inequalities such as gender and ethnicity, or should these attributes and their social structuring be regarded as independent dimensions of stratification? Marxist theory had provided a set of arguments to the effect that the subordination of women was, indeed, largely to be seen as a consequence of successive types of class domination (Engels, 1940) and, following this view, in the 'state socialist' countries the 'liberation' of women had been officially announced following their incorporation into the paid labour force (Buckley, 1989). This approach to the 'woman problem' took no account of the domestic division of labour, as feminists argued. Besides the lack of any substantial change in the domestic division of labour, the increasing employment of women in the 'public' sphere also served to highlight the extent to which women had been excluded from better paid and higher level jobs, as well as the way in which 'women's' work had been devalued (Cockburn, 1983; Walby, 1986). Increasingly, it was argued that women's subordination was largely a consequence of patriarchal, rather than class, processes (for further discussion, see Chapter 6). A parallel set of arguments has been developed in respect of 'race' (Anthias and Yuval-Davis, 1992). 'Class analysis' came increasingly to be regarded in some quarters as an over-deterministic mono-theory, in which the multiple sources of social inequality had been reduced to the simplicities of 'class'.

Parallel with this emphasis upon alternative sources of social inequality, it was also increasingly argued that 'class' had lost its salience as a source of individual and social *identity*:

> In the traditional models, people were socialised into worlds of home and work in which they 'knew their place'. They joined a class, learned its values, developed its attitudes and behaved accordingly – again throughout their lifetimes. These fairly rigid boundaries have now gone. (Thrift and Johnston, 1993: 84, cited in Savage, 1996)

Rather than 'class', it was argued, other sources of identity, such as those of 'race', lifestyle, age and gender, were becoming more significant. The loss of class identity was explicitly linked to political developments including the supposed decline of class politics. Political life, it was argued, was becoming increasingly concerned with specific issues (for example, the environment, 'race'), rather than class, and these politics were organized and pursued by new 'social movements', rather than class-political parties (Offe, 1985). However, it may be suggested that what they are describing is a society shaped by a relatively stable *status* order, and that there are rather more grounds for arguing for the contemporary decline of the status, rather than the class, order.

The linked social processes of the erosion of the traditional working class, the apparent decline of class voting, the increase in women's employment and the growing emphasis upon other sources of inequality and identity have all served to contribute to the growing tide of arguments relating to the 'end of class' (Hall and Jaques, 1989), which will be considered in the next section. For the moment, I shall briefly examine a further important outcome of the process of class restructuring – the expansion of the 'middle classes'.

## The 'Middle Classes'

The decline of manufacturing and the corresponding increase in service-sector employment brought with it a growth not just in routine clerical work, but also in administrative and managerial, technical and professional occupations. The 'middle classes' have always been regarded as somewhat problematic from within a Marxist framework. Do their interests lie with those of the working class, or with those of the bourgeoisie? These debates have not just been couched at an abstract level (see Poulantzas, 1975), but have also focused upon the type and nature of these expanding 'middle-class' occupations. It was argued that much of the growth in middle-class occupations was in fact more apparent than real as those at the lower level were deskilled and routinized. Indeed, it was suggested that this process of 'proletarianization' was in fact extending beyond lower level white-collar workers to include managerial occupations (Braverman, 1974; Crompton and Jones, 1984). Contrary to some of the more apocalyptic earlier predictions, it would seem that a widespread process of 'deskilling' has not in fact taken place, although many white-collar jobs in retail and other services *are* extremely routine, poorly paid, and insecure and would nowadays be located in the 'working' or lower levels of most class schemes. There still remains, however, the wider problem of the societal consequences of middle-class expansion.

Goldthorpe has argued that the expansion of the 'service' (that is, middle) class is a source of social stability, largely because service-class families will seek to secure and pass on their advantages to future generations (Goldthorpe, 1987; Erikson and Goldthorpe, 1992). In contrast, others have argued that the extent of internal differentiation within the middle classes is such that such cohesion cannot be reliably anticipated (Lash and Urry, 1987; Savage *et al*., 1992; Butler and Savage, 1996). Goldthorpe has argued that besides status in employment (that is, whether employed, self-employed or an employee), the crucial differentiating feature of the 'class structure' is whether the employee is in a 'service' or a 'labour contract only' employment relationship. The 'service' relationship, as we have seen, is held to be an attribute of the job, rather than the individual, or of the kind of work they do. Thus the service relationship encompasses a heterogeneous range of occupations. It is a feature of the service relationship that it contains important prospective elements, including salary increments, security of employment, and 'above all, well-defined career opportunities' (Goldthorpe, 1996: 315). Labour contracts, by implication, carry with them no such advantages.

Savage and his colleagues have in contrast argued for an 'asset-based' approach which identifies considerable diversity within the middle classes. Three different types of asset are identified: property, cultural capital (a concept Savage takes from Bourdieu and which mainly includes formal qualifications) and organizational assets or 'property in positions'. He argues that these assets give rise to different patterns of interests and thus the possibility of intra-class conflict, rather than homogeneity and stability (see also Urry, 1996).

In this section, we have moved from considerations relating to the measurement of social class towards greater emphasis on the processes of class formation and structuring, focusing in particular on the impact of recent changes in work and employment. However, questions of measurement, location, and labelling cannot be avoided, even by those emphasizing the 'processual' approach to class analysis. Thus we have come full circle back to a major question which occupied us in the second section – that is, how do individuals get allocated to social classes? This suggests that common threads run through different approaches to class and stratification.

## The 'End of Class'

The 'end of class' has been a recurring theme of post-war sociology. In the 1950s and 60s, academic sociology in Britain was engaged in debates with the normative functionalism of US sociology, as well as a critique of 'industrialization theory' – that is, the argument that all 'industrial' societies were moving along a similar path towards a destination in which class conflict would be a thing of the past (Kerr *et al.*, 1973). During the late 1980s and early 1990s, however, 'class' seems to have become 'decentred' as a focus of sociological debate and, at worst, treated as an irrelevance.

When people like the ex-Prime Minister, John Major, asserted that Britain has become (or is becoming) a 'classless' society, what they usually mean is that 'social background' is becoming less important to individual success and that societies like Britain are becoming more meritocratic. This kind of argument hails back to the debates about the increasing 'openness' of 'industrial societies' in the 1960s and 70s, in which it was argued that individual effort, rather than inheritance or nepotism, was becoming increasingly more important as far as eventual social destination was concerned (Blau and Duncan, 1967).

Considerable 'long-range' mobility is indeed possible in contemporary societies. Nevertheless, surveys of individuals in top positions regularly reveal that
by far the majority originate from privileged backgrounds (Scott, 1991). For
example, an analysis of the 100 top people in Britain revealed that 66 went
to public school, and 54 to Oxbridge. Moreover, these figures had changed
very little since a similar sample was investigated in 1972 (*The Economist*,
1992). Changes in the occupational structure – in particular, the growth of
administrative, managerial and professional occupations – mean that there has
been a considerable increase in upward occupational mobility so that, overall,
many people will have moved into jobs where their rewards are better than
those of their parents. However, a series of empirical investigations has
demonstrated that, whereas absolute rates might have increased, *relative*
mobility rates – that is, individual chances of upward mobility relative to
social origin – have not changed (Goldthorpe, 1987). Thus mobility chances
are unevenly distributed through the employment class structure, and those of
people in the lower classes are worse than those of those in the higher.

Another factor which has contributed to the perception of a more open
society is the continuing decline of the traditional status order. Institutions
such as the established church, and the monarchy, are no longer treated with
the automatic deference which once prevailed. Even though Britain may not
be a meritocracy, meritocratic *ideas* have been very influential. On the whole,
it is no longer acceptable for elevated positions to be acquired on the basis of
birth or breeding alone. This tendency is reflected in the survey of 'top people'
described above, in which twice as many had received higher education than
in 1972. Reflecting this trend, *The Economist* (1992: 21) commented: 'Fewer
dumb aristocrats have got to top jobs on the basis of little education and
much family influence.'

It has been argued that changes in production and markets, which have seen
both the decline of old classes and the rise of new ones, means that this
emerging structure cannot be conceptualized using class concepts which were
developed with reference to nineteenth-century industrialism. This is not just
a problem for the class schemes of the employment aggregate approach, as the
'processual' approach to class analysis is also concerned with the identification
or class character of newly emerging groups. The decline of class politics,
together with the proliferation of issue politics and the coming to the fore of
new 'identities', such as those associated with sexualities, gender and ethnicity,
have all been used to argue that 'class' is no longer important. Contemporary
societies, it is argued, are characterized by an increasing 'individuation'
(Giddens, 1991b; Beck, 1992), in which the collectivities of 'class' have been
left behind and 'old' class and stratification patterns and their associated ideologies have no place in increasingly fluid, late modern, or 'postmodern', societies.

It may be suggested that much of the debate relating to class and stratification reflects broader themes within sociological theory – in particular, the
structure/action debate discussed in Chapter 3. In rather different ways, both

Marx and Weber used the class concept to link structure and action, and to match patterns of power, control, and material production to the propensities for collective action. However, Hindess (1987) and Pahl (1989) have criticized 'class analysis' for its failure to link structure and action theoretically and empirically. Thus Pahl, for example, argues that the class concept has ceased to 'do any useful work' for sociology and should be abandoned because the structure → consciousness → action (SCA) chain had not been 'adequately theorised' or demonstrated. Indeed, he argues, 'lifestyles', are more important determinants of attitudes and behaviour than 'class', and changes in production processes are making the development of class consciousness extremely unlikely. Thus non-'class' indicators such as age or income might be more useful as far as social policy is concerned.

Much of the thrust of Pahl's argument, it may be suggested, in fact concerns the usefulness of employment-derived class schemes as social indicators and/or indexes of attitudes and behaviour. Similarly, for Clark and Lipset (1991), the shift to the service sector, the increased proportion of managerial and technical occupations, as well the decline in class-related voting and the growing significance of 'lifestyle' issues, suggest that where class theories may once have mapped onto the employment structure in a fairly satisfactory manner, it is doubtful if this is still the case given recent changes. If this is so, is 'class' any more a useful concept?

These critiques have generated substantial debate (see *International Sociology*, 1993; Goldthorpe and Marshall, 1992). Criticisms relating to the failure of class consciousness and action to materialize relate largely to orthodox Marxist accounts of class. Here, as Pakulski (1993) has suggested in the context of Clarke and Lipset's arguments, we may in fact be witnessing the 'failure' of a particular version of Marxist class analysis, rather than of the sociology of class and stratification as such, while Mullins (1991) has argued the 'failure' to link structure and action is not peculiar to class analysis, but rather, reflects underlying problems in social theory. In fact, it may be argued that recent sociological criticisms, such as those of Pahl, and Clark and Lipset, derive from an overly narrow perception of class analysis. In particular, these critics have failed to make a distinction, between 'employment aggregate' and 'processual' approaches to the investigation of class and stratification (Crompton, 1993, 1996, 1998).

# The Underclass

The deindustrialization and economic restructuring of many contemporary societies have resulted in a substantial rise in the level of unemployment, as well as the proliferation of self-employment, temporay contracts and casual working. The growth in the numbers of the severely disadvantaged has been followed by arguments to the effect that this disadvantage is a consequence of their own actions – or rather, lack of them. The 'underclass', it is argued, has had its capacities eroded by state benefits to such an extent that it no longer wishes to work or support itself, and a life of indolence, petty crime, and single parenthood is a much more attractive option as far as it is concerned. Such people have become apathetic, fatalistic and rejective of the values of the wider society (Murray, 1990).

Sociologists in Britain and America have responded to these arguments by exploring the structural *processes* of 'underclass' development. At the macro-level, Wilson (1987) argued that, in the United States, the loss of manufacturing employment, together with the exit from the ghettos of the urban black middle classes, had contributed to the formation of the black 'underclass'. As Wilson argues, what differentiates the very poor of today from the very poor of a previous era is the dual problem of marginal economic position, together with social isolation in highly concentrated areas of poverty. Thus studies of underclass formation have increasingly focused upon the meso-level of the locality (Wilson, 1993). In Britain, Morris' (1995) study of Hartlepool, for example, carefully explores the intertwining of employment opportunities, social networks, and households which structure patterns of advantage and disadvantage in the search for employment at the local level. Her research reveals a complex picture of unemployment and insecure employment, no-earner and two-earner households and different patterns of household budgeting, which belies the homogeneity of the 'underclass' label.

Much systematic empirical research on the 'underclass', therefore, has taken the form of case studies which have served to reveal the structural processes resulting in increased social polarization. This approach may seem very different from the statistical manipulations of 'employment aggregate' practitioners. Nevertheless, large-scale survey analysis has also made an important contribution to the 'underclass' debate. Gallie (1994) and Marshall *et al.* (1996) have suggested that the long-term unemployed are no less committed to the idea of employment than those in employment, that the attitudes of the very disadvantaged are not more 'fatalistic' than the better off, nor are they socially marginalized on a range of attitudes relating to authority, attitudes to economic success, and so on. This kind of evidence presents a direct challenge to those such as Murray who have characterized disadvantaged groups as existing 'outside of' society.

The underclass debate, therefore, may be used as an example of the need to draw upon a range of sociological approaches to class and stratification in order to explore the different dimensions of the debate. It may also be used as evidence of the continuing relevance of 'class thinking' for the understanding of contemporary social divisions. This does not mean that individual identities are not significant, nor that individuals will not consciously seek to develop and make sense of them, but it should always be recognized that they invariably do so within a socially structured context.

# Conclusion: Deepening Inequalities

From the end of the 1970s, inequalities in many developed societies have widened considerably. Technological innovation has meant that fewer people are required in order to achieve a rising level of manufacturing output. In Britain, for example, the low level service jobs which have been a major source of occupational expansions over the last two decades are on the whole low paid, part time and often temporary.

Women's employment has become increasingly important in maintaining household living standards. However, the increasing number of women moving into higher level and well-paid jobs means that the positive impact of women's employment is much greater in some households than others. Thus there has been a widening gulf between households in which there are two earners, and households in which there is none. Households without a full-time earner have lower average incomes, in real terms, than in 1979. In respect of male, full-time wages, the Rowntree Report has shown that:

> Between 1966 and 1977 all wages grew at much the same rate. After 1978, the experiences of the three parts of the distribution diverged: wages for the lowest paid hardly changed, and by 1992 were lower in real terms than in 1975; median wages grew by 35 per cent; but high wages grew by 50 per cent. (Joseph Rowntree Foundation, 1995: 20)

Over the last fifteen years, therefore, the material impact of occupational success or failure has become increasingly important, as the gap between the lowest and highest paid has widened. One consequence has been that educational credentials have become ever more important in the labour market. The Rowntree Report (1995: 20) argues that the 'stakes have become higher for young people entering the labour market, with greater differences between those who do well (linked to high educational levels) and those who do not than there were twenty, or even ten, years ago'.

While the recent increase in social inequality could be seen as a 'natural' development arising from social changes and the declining demand for unskilled labour in manufacturing industry, there can be little doubt that government policies aimed at increasing marketization have also increased levels of inequality. Indeed, it could be argued that one major reason for the persistence of the perpetually criticized structure → consciousness → action links in the sociological class analysis chain is that the capitalist class *does* manifest all the signs of being both conscious of its material interests and capable of protecting them. Capitalist interests are not difficult to identify, and the legitimacy of this interest (enterprise success and profitability) is widely accepted in society and supported by the state. Not all capitalists need to be organized in order to represent the interests of the whole, and short-term conflicts of interest may be accommodated. In contrast, oppositional forms of organization do not possess the same 'taken-for-granted' legitimacy. Workers have to be persuaded that their interests have to be articulated (and are distinct from those of the capitalists), and organization is rarely successful unless all workers are involved.

In Britain in the 1980s, legislation was introduced which facilitated the payment of lower wages to workers who were often poorly paid in the first place. They included the removal of rights granted by the Employment Protection Act of the mid-1970s; the privatization of public-sector services, as a consequence of which those workers who did not lose their jobs were often rehired at lower rates of pay, subsidies to encourage low wage rates for young workers and the removal of wages council protection in low-paid industries. At the same time, the abandonment of wage and salary controls allowed the incomes of the very highest earners to spiral up to previously unheard-of levels. Sustained high levels of unemployment, together with legislation against trade union strategies such as picketing and the closed shop, have further eroded the basis of collective action and thus the capacity to protect wage levels. By 1988 trade union membership in the United Kingdom had declined by fully 24 per cent from its peak level of 13.3 million members in 1979 to just over 10 million.

During the same period, direct tax cuts disproportionately benefited the better off. Between 1979 and 1986, it has been calculated that out of the £8.1 billion in tax cuts, nearly half went to the richest 10 per cent and almost two-thirds went to the richest 20 per cent. Rising unemployment, declining wage levels, and demographic changes mean that the increase in households headed by single parents, and the proportion of households dependent on social security benefits has risen – social security payments accounted for a fifth of all income in 1992 and 1993 (Goodman *et al.*, 1997). Since 1980, social security benefits have been indexed to prices, rather than wages. As wages (except those of the lowest paid) have risen faster than prices, then the value of benefits, in relative terms, has been declining.

The restructuring of other institutions has increased inequality by opening up opportunities to 'earn' very high incomes. Among the most important examples here are deregulation of the financial sector in 1986, together with the selling off of state-owned utilities. Financial deregulation resulted in an explosion of finance-related jobs, some of them very highly paid indeed. The 1996 annual report of KPMG, one of the 'Big Six' accountancy firms, revealed that the earnings of their 586 partners ranged from £123,000 to £740,000 a year (Adonis and Pollard, 1997: 87). For the very highest of flyers in the financial sector, yearly bonuses can run into millions of pounds. The directors of privatized industries found themselves able to award themselves huge salaries.

Increasing social polarization over the last two decades, therefore, has a number of different sources. In part, the morphology of inequality has changed – women's earnings, for example, have become much more important than they once were. Class processes remain crucial to the maintenance of educational advantage and, given that educational qualifications have become more important in getting a good (that is, secure and well-paid) job, then this aspect of class inequality has become more important. In addition, the institutional filters of class in Britain have been adjusted so as to increase levels of inequality and benefit the better off, that is, in the interests of capital, rather than labour. It could well be that all of these trends suggest, as Westergaard (1995) has argued, a hardening of class inequalities rather than the 'death of class'. At the very least, it seems that the questions that class analysis was designed to address remain as important as ever.

# Further Reading

Bradley, H. *Fractured Identities*, Cambridge, Polity, 1996. A wide-ranging attempt to synthesize the inequalities of class, gender, 'race' and age.

Butler, T. and Savage, M. (eds) *Social Change and the Middle Classes*, London, UCL Press, 1996. A range of papers focusing on different aspects of the continuing expansion of the 'middle classes'.

Crompton, R. *Class and Stratification*, 2nd edn, Cambridge, Polity, 1998. A revised and updated edition of the 1993 textbook, covering the different theoretical and methodological approaches to the study of class.

Lee, D. and Turner, B. *Conflicts over Class,* London, Longman, 1996. Organized around the debate relating to the 'death of class'.

Scott, J. *Stratification and Power*, Cambridge, Polity, 1997. A contemporary version of the 'Weberian' approach to class analysis by an author who has carried out extensive research on the 'ruling class'.

# 6
# Gender Relations
## *Mary Maynard*

The study of women and of gender relations has been a major growth area in sociology over the past three decades, influencing sociological theory and methods as well as many core areas of sociological research, such as family, education, work, health and the media. The aim of this chapter is to examine the ways in which gender has been conceptualized in sociology and illustrate the part played by social institutions in the construction of gender relations. It should help you to understand:

- The importance of including a gender perspective in sociology and some of the different ways in which gender has been theorized

- The significance of the sexual division of labour in shaping the life chances of women and men

- Feminist arguments concerning sex and violence as gendered social control

- How the state, the law and citizenship construct men and women differently

- The limitations of the 'traditional' division between radical, socialist and liberal feminism

---

### CONCEPTS

feminism ■ gender blindness ■ patriarchy ■ sex and gender
sexual division of labour ■ domestic labour ■ sexual harassment
welfare state ■ citizenship ■ post-structuralism

# Introduction

It is salutary to remember that for most of its history sociology has been gender blind (Abbott and Wallace, 1996). There has been little recognition that differences in the experiences of women and men, together with changes in the relationship between them, could have profound and significant implications for the ways in which social phenomena are conceptualized and investigated. For instance, as the example of class considered in the previous chapter illustrates – prior to the 1970s much empirical sociology focused on men and boys as its subjects. Areas researched tended to concentrate on the so-called public spheres of life, those existing outside the private sphere of the home, such as the workplace and the school. It was assumed either that the experiences of women could be simply inferred from those of men or that men had the normal or customary kinds of lives, with those of women being treated as unusual and deviant. Such narrowness, which effectively excluded one half of the population from investigation, also had implications for the formulation and development of important sociological ideas. For example, concepts such as social class, alienation, work and citizenship, along with others that have been central to sociological theory, were all drawn from male perceptions and understandings about the essential features of social life. Overall, then, for the first 100 or so years of its existence sociology was largely written from the standpoint of men.

The situation began to change with the resurgence of organized feminism in the late 1960s. The women's movement had a more immediate influence on sociology than on other academic disciplines, both because much of its subject matter is concerned with everyday life and because it has always been a particularly popular area of study for women. In a relatively short period of time the study of women began to develop from a peripheral minority interest into a major area of activity and debate. This has had implications at all levels of sociology, from topics chosen for research, to theoretical perspectives, to methods used for investigation.

This chapter examines some of the insights to be gained in understanding contemporary western societies when gender relations are taken into account. It first considers the kinds of criticisms which have been made of mainstream sociology by beginning with an overview of the recent history of the sociological study of women, men and gender relations. This will examine why a feminist intervention was required, what this might be said to have achieved and debates as to how gender itself is conceptualized. The chapter then considers the issue of power and gender inequality. In this, it will focus on three particularly important areas which have been researched: life chances and the sexual division of labour; sexuality and violence; and the law, citizenship and the state. These areas have been chosen both for their topicality and for their ability to highlight the gendered nature of social life. Finally, the chapter examines some of the current issues which promise to mould the future of gender research in the twenty-first century.

# Why Study Women and Men?

Criticisms of the gender blindness of sociology have taken three forms, which have elicited three responses (Maynard, 1990). The first of these addressed the *invisibility* of women in most sociological work. Here the emphasis was on the extent to which sociology's focus on men's lives and experiences led to the neglect of women and the production of biased and one-sided knowledge. The aim was to undertake studies of women in areas where they had been previously ignored. This 'additive' approach, which characterized the early stages of the development of gender awareness in sociology, involved studying women in most of the sub-areas taken to be constitutive of the discipline. So, for example, work was produced on women's education, paid employment, health and illness, deviancy, youth culture and their relationship to social policy and the state. The approach was 'additive' because it simply added extra research about women onto that which already existed about men. It has been criticized subsequently for failing sufficiently to challenge sociology's basic assumptions and concepts, with women being tagged on rather as an afterthought. However, such arguments tend to play down the important role played by such studies in raising the profile of women in sociology, thereby ignoring the significant impact that they had at the time.

The second kind of criticism of sociology's gender blindness arose from the first. As research on women began to proliferate, it became clear that simply adding women into the subject would not suffice. There were whole areas of women's experiences which they did not share with men and concerning which sociology remained silent. It also became apparent that many of the perspectives and concepts at the very heart of sociology required substantial revision or transformation if they were to be applied in any meaningful way to the lives of women. So, new aspects of social experience and activity, alongside new ways of thinking sociologically had to be introduced (Maynard, 1990). For example, new themes addressed ranged from housework, motherhood and childbirth to sexuality, pornography and male violence. The inclusion of such areas of social life radically extended the parameters of the sociology of gender, as well as increasing the scope of sociology overall.

In addition, some ideas and terms had to be revised. For instance, the meaning of 'work' had to be extended to include both unpaid as well as paid labour. Leisure, previously regarded as activity carried out away from paid employment, had to be redefined to include housewives and those with a 'dual burden' of both labour market and domestic commitments. Some now refer to the family as the 'household' in order to take account of single people, single parents, those living together in unmarried relationships and others who do not conform to stereotypical notions of the nuclear family. In these ways, taking account of gender has involved challenging previous taken-for-granted assumptions about what counts as the 'proper' subject matter for sociological discussion. The terms and topics which structured the practice of the discipline have been re-evaluated and some have had to be redesigned.

A third way in which the gender blindness of sociology has been tackled focuses on the theoretical and methodological perspectives which have been central to the discipline. In terms of theory, for example, previous insistence on the precedence of social class in understanding inequality has been challenged (Walby, 1990). Instead, feminists have focused on women's unequal relationship to men and the resulting patterning of inequality which constructs men as the dominant group and women as subordinate. Feminist theorists are particularly concerned with the power relations between men and women (Davis *et al.*, 1991). They have adopted the concept 'patriarchy' through which to analyse the depth, pervasiveness and interconnectedness of different aspects of women's subordination (Walby, 1990). Although there are many kinds of feminist theory, emphasizing different aspects of patriarchy and the reasons for women's unequal positioning *vis à vis* men, all are concerned to explicate the mechanisms through which women are controlled, together with the circumstances under which resistance might also be possible. Thus, a rich and wide-ranging literature has been established, presenting an important challenge to the established ungendered orthodoxy in sociological theory.

Feminists have also been responsible for generating some heated debates about sociological research practice (Stanley and Wise, 1990). Many have argued, for instance, that qualitative rather than quantitative methods, and especially the in-depth interview, are more appropriate when studying women. This is because they facilitate the collection of rich and detailed material, as opposed to the limited data obtained via less intrusive methods, and encourage the participation of those being researched in the research process itself. Feminists have also expressed concern about the relationship between the researcher and the research participant. As we saw in Chapter 2, some have been critical of textbook guidelines which recommend that social distance be maintained between them, pointing out that this gives the researcher untold power to exploit subjects with a view to extorting as much information from them as possible. Feminists have contributed to the argument that the act of researching is as much a social process as are the experiences of the people sociologists study. It is, therefore, important to acknowledge and take account of this fact, rather than pretending that research proceeds as an unsullied and value-neutral activity.

## The Concept of Gender

So far this chapter has used the term gender in an unproblematic way. However, the meaning of the concept is contested. The most usual sociological formulation distinguishes gender from sex. Whereas sex is taken to denote the anatomical and physiological differences which define biological femaleness and maleness, gender refers to the social construction of femininity and masculinity. Further, gender is not regarded as being a direct product of biological sex. Rather, gender roles, behaviour and identities are seen as being differently created and interpreted by particular cultures and in particular periods of historical time. In other words, what it means to be feminine or masculine is not fixed but changes. It is subject to a variety of cultural definitions and understandings.

This sociological conception of sex and gender, however, is not without its critics. For example, some feminists have questioned the assumption that gender is culturally constructed, while sex is still seen as having an innate biological basis (Ramazanoglu, 1995). Such an approach is essentialist because it implies that how we interpret and give meaning to biological phenomena is unproblematic, inherent and independent of cultural discourses and practices. Further, this way of thinking perpetuates the opposition between nature and culture which permeates western societies. It precludes the possibility of analysing the various ways in which bodily functions and processes (for instance, pain or pleasure) may influence the gendered experience of social life. Ramazanoglu (1995), for example, argues that ideas about the body are social, although not entirely independent of biology. It is important to take account of people's bodily existence (for women, such things as menstruation and childbirth), without assuming that this determines their behaviour.

Other feminists have questioned the very existence of gender and the categories 'women' and 'men'. Jackson (1998) has suggested that there are two main ways in which this has occurred, through materialist and postmodern feminisms. Materialist feminists focus on social structural relations between women and men (Delphy and Leonard, 1992). Following Marx, these are conceptualized as a class-like relationship in which women are unequal and exploited. Instead of seeing men and women as two natural biological groupings with relatively inevitable unequal social positions, the sexes are regarded as being socially distinguishable only because one dominates the other. Anatomical distinctions between the sexes have been made socially relevant because of, and as a justification for, unequal gender relations. It is the inequality of gender which gives salience to the otherwise socially insignificant differences of biology.

In contrast, postmodern feminists concentrate on the ways in which the categories 'men' and 'women' are culturally constructed through discourse. Butler (1990), for example, deconstructs our understandings of both sex and gender. She argues that if gender is not inherently linked to physiology and anatomical bodies, there is no reason to believe there are only two genders and that this binary opposition is based on a heterosexist world-view. Bodies become gendered through being socially classified as biologically different and through the continual process of people acting in gendered ways. For Butler, gender has no pre-given essential existence. Femininity only exists to the extent that it continues to be performed. It is, thereby, rendered diverse, fluctuating and volatile, rather than a stable and relatively homogeneous identity. Because performing gender brings gender itself into being, Butler regards the latter as being much less stable than is usually accepted. Gender does not have an existence outside the performance. By focusing on its ambiguities, her intention is to signal the possibility of new forms of non-hierarchical relationships. However, along with other postmodern feminists, she has been criticized for her portrayal of 'women' as a construct with no existence or unity prior to discourse (Jackson, 1998).

Other commentators have also been concerned with gender and diversity but in a rather different way. For example, black and Third World women have criticized early work on gender for focusing on the concerns of white, middle-class, educated, western women, thereby neglecting the experiences of women from other backgrounds, countries and cultures (Ramazanoglu, 1989; Collins, 1990). They argued that the significance of race and racism in their lives qualitatively effected their experiences of being women and, thus, needed to be taken into account during any analysis concerning gender. Similar concerns were also voiced by other groups of women, indicating that factors such as age, sexual orientation, disability and socio-economic status were also important in structuring the experience of being a woman. Thus gender inequality and women's subordination are no longer regarded as relatively straightforward and uncontradictory. Some women may be able to exert power over others by virtue of their race, sexuality or wealth and some may even be able to exercise power over some men. Analyses which unproblematically supposed a unified notion of gender oppression have been deconstructed and critiqued.

Another new development in the sociology of gender has been to focus on men and masculinity. It may seem strange to describe this as a 'new' area of study, particularly when the current interest in gender arose largely in response to the fact that sociology had previously been concerned almost exclusively with men. Yet, although it is the case that men historically have been the main subjects of empirical and theoretical work, they were studied in a purely genderless sense. There was little direct focus on the social construction of 'men', being male or having masculine characteristics and behaviour. For these reasons, it has been argued that, in focusing on men and masculinity, researchers are paying attention to an area of study which is long overdue. Now that the significance of gender for women has been subject to scrutiny, it is time to repeat a similar kind of exercise for men.

The critical study of men and of masculinities is currently a major area of growth in the sociology of gender (Hearn, 1992; Connell, 1995). Concern has been expressed that such work detracts from the many projects on women which still need to be undertaken, that it involves providing sociological justifications for unacceptable male behaviour and that it is an attempt by men to 'muscle in' on the study of gender, by intruding on women's hard fought for and jealously guarded space (Hanmer, 1990). Yet, the best work in the field raises a variety of problems of how men are, how they behave, how they should behave, why men have power, how that power is socially structured, what different kinds of men and masculinities there are, and how current arrangements can be changed (Hearn, 1996). Its significance for sociology is, therefore, immense.

# Life Chances and the Sexual Division of Labour

The previous sections have considered some of the reasons why it is important to include a gender perspective within sociology, along with conceptual debates to which these give rise. One significant factor is that gender plays a major part in structuring the opportunities which are available to social groups, the kinds of experiences they are likely to have and the ways in which they are represented in a range of societal institutions, from the mass media to the welfare state and social policy. Despite widespread rhetoric about equal opportunities policies and legislation, major inequalities between women and men still remain in western societies, as the following sections illustrate.

## Gender Inequalities in Education and Employment

Historically, sociologists have always emphasized material factors in the analysis of inequality, focusing on such issues as pay and the kinds of employment undertaken, relationship to the means of production, educational opportunities, and access to resources such as money, housing and consumer goods (Brannen and Wilson, 1987; Rees, 1992; Drew *et al.*, 1998). Feminists have argued that all these aspects of social life have a gendered, as well as a class and race, dimension. However, the evidence indicates that the picture is neither static nor uncontradictory. For instance, early work in the area of schooling showed girls generally performing better than boys at the beginning of their school career, a situation which was reversed during its later stages (Acker, 1994; Skelton, 1997). For older school students, research focused on such topics as girls' under-achievement in science and technology subjects, the ways in which boys command more of a teacher's time in the classroom and the comparative lack of strong role models for girls (Skelton, 1993; Acker, 1994). The overall picture of girls' education emerged as one of under-achievement and lack of confidence in the face of boys' bravado and domination in the classroom.

The gendered educational experience which girls received has also been linked to the gendered nature of their future position in the labour market. More women than ever before are working in paid jobs and they are doing so for longer, less intermittent periods of time, due to the trend to return to work between the births of children (Rees, 1992; Drew *et al.*, 1998). Yet they still appear to fare less well than men in terms of such factors as hours worked, pay received and the kinds of jobs they undertake. This is partly because many women work part time. In Britain, for example, 28 per cent of all those at work did so in 1995, although there are important ethnic differences between women, with fewer Asian and Afro-Caribbean women thus employed (Witz, 1997). It is also the case that the labour market remains gender segregated, both horizontally and vertically. Not only are women and men employed in different occupations and industries, women are concentrated in a much smaller number of jobs, particularly those in catering, retail, banking and other services, than are men (Rees, 1992; Witz, 1997). Further, the existence of a 'glass ceiling', whereby men continue to dominate in management, especially senior management, means that even when women increase their presence in a particular occupation, they may still fail to achieve their full potential within it. The existence of these forms of gender segregation are regarded, by feminist sociologists and policy makers alike, to be the single most important reason for the persistence of gender inequalities, particularly wage differentials, in the labour market (Witz, 1997).

Recently, however, the situation with regard to women's and men's position in education and the labour market appears to have been changing, although the implications of these changes are still not entirely clear. One aspect of this, which has caused much public comment, is girls' educational performance. In Britain, this is because they have been achieving an increasing number of good passes in public examinations, now surpassing the boys, although there are still fewer of them doing physics and chemistry (Walby, 1997). As a result, concern has switched from that about girls and science to one about boys' more general under-achievement and especially their relatively poor performance in linguistic and verbal skills.

Changes in the nature of the labour market also have a gendered aspect. For example, the manual occupations in which men have been traditionally over-represented, such as manufacturing and construction, have generally collapsed (Rees, 1992). By contrast, part-time work in shops, offices and other kinds of so-called 'women's work' has increased. Taken together, these educational and employment trends have raised the spectre of a potentially increasing number of unemployed, and unemployable, young men, mainly those who are from working-class backgrounds. Commentators have talked about a 'crisis of masculinity', created, in part, by the dismantling of the traditional male breadwinner image and the notion of 'jobs for life'. Under such circumstances, it is feared that those young men who are particularly disadvantaged will increasingly resort to lives of crime and violence (MacDonald, 1997). Such concerns underline the importance of sociologists including studies of men and masculinity, as well as women, in their gender analyses. However, caution needs to be exercised, lest the impression be given that, overall, women are no longer disadvantaged in relation to men. The significance of this is affected by class and race, as well as by gender factors.

## Gender Inequalities in Family/Household

One area which emphasizes the nature of women's disadvantage, and on which feminists have done a lot of work, is that of the family/household. In this, they have focused on the notion of 'reproduction', using this as the central organizing concept through which women's material position within the household is to be understood, in a way analogous to the sociological use of 'production' to analyse capitalistic relations at work (Jackson, 1997). For feminist sociologists studying gender, the idea of reproduction has three meanings. The first refers to women's childbearing and mothering capacities. The second relates to the ways in which women's domestic servicing makes it possible both for the current generation of workers (husbands/partners) to work and looks after, nurtures and cares for the next generation of workers (their children). The third connotation of the term reproduction is concerned with how women's roles and expected activities within the household serve to make them subordinate both to their own husbands and partners and to men more generally. In other words, women's unequal situation within the household helps to make them also unequal outside it.

Part of the reasoning to support these arguments rests on the distribution of, and time spent on, domestic tasks within the home. Extensive research has shown that the majority of women still undertake the bulk of household jobs compared to men, even when they are themselves in full-time employment (Morris, 1990; Robertson Elliot, 1996; Drew *et al.*, 1998). Another aspect of gender inequality in the family/household relates to the unequal ways in which resources are managed, controlled and distributed. For instance, whatever mechanisms are adopted for money management, men usually have more personal spending money, while women generally keep little money for themselves (Pahl, 1989). Since husbands generally earn considerably more than their wives, they have potentially greater power in determining how any income should be spent and subsequent purchases used. In this context, studies have focused on the use and ownership of computer and video technology within the home, the amounts and types of food consumed and allocation of time for leisure and other pursuits. Men have been found to exercise a major amount of control in all these areas (Gray, 1992; Morgan, 1996). Why should this be the case?

Feminist sociologists have argued that the key to this question lies in the unpaid nature of the housework women undertake (Jackson, 1997). This is socially beneficial in several related senses. It benefits men who are able to exploit women's labour power and keep women dependent on them, by receiving services for which they do not have to pay, apart from contributing to their wives' maintenance. Further, the work that women do in the home creates men's leisure; it constrains their own free time while also making that of others possible. Women's unpaid domestic work, it is argued, also benefits capitalist employers in the labour market. This is because, if men had to pay for these services they would expect to be compensated by a rise in wages. In fact, it is only when such work is performed within households that domestic tasks are unpaid. Outside the home these can be undertaken as paid jobs and the services provided purchased on the market.

This section has focused on education, employment and the household and the ways in which one's gender can bestow both material benefit and constraint. Indeed, gender is an important influence on access to opportunities and resources, throughout the life course (Arber and Ginn, 1995). However, more attention needs to be paid in this area to some of the differences which exist between women, as well as the things they are likely to share. For instance, Afro-American and Afro-Caribbean women have been critical of some aspects of sociologists' preoccupation with the family, particularly when their analyses suggest that it is the basis of women's oppression (Collins, 1990). This is because families can provide protection from and resistance to racism. There are also important ethnic differences between women with regard to employment. For example, in Britain, Afro-Caribbean women are much less likely to be working part time than white women (Witz, 1997). Further, whereas for white women, pay and conditions of work vary greatly between full- and part-time employment, the same is not true for Afro-Caribbean women. Thus, the picture often presented concerning the material aspects of women's lives frequently fails to tell the whole story.

## Sexuality and Violence Towards Women

The issues of sexuality and of violence towards women are examples of two interrelated areas which have been introduced into sociological analysis as a direct result of a feminist concern with gender. Previously, sexuality was commonly regarded as a private and personal matter and largely ignored by sociologists. Because it was treated as something innate or natural, sexuality was not seen as a legitimate topic for sociological investigation, being, at best, a subject for biologists or psychologists (Dobash and Dobash, 1980). Similarly, men's violence towards women tended to be explained away as the acts of a few 'sick' or psychologically deranged individuals, who had probably been provoked by women's provocative and inciteful behaviour. It was implied that such violence was a relatively rare occurrence and that it was perpetrated outside the home by abusers who were unlikely to be known to their victims.

### Violence Towards Women

Sociological work on violence to women arose as a direct result of the contradictions faced by those who were both politically active in the women's movement in the 1970s and involved in feminist academic work at the same time. As the significance of violence in women's lives started to emerge at a grassroots level, support networks and groups began to be established for them (Dobash and Dobash, 1992). Yet, the extent of the violence that women appeared to be experiencing in everyday life did not appear to be mirrored in the appropriate official statistics, which recorded relatively small numbers of incidents (Maynard and Winn, 1997). It is now widely accepted that such figures significantly under-estimate the amount of violence that actually occurs. This is because many women do not report their attacks to the police, especially if their attacker is known to them, as is frequently the case. In addition, police have often been reluctant to intervene in those cases they define as 'domestics'. Evidence from Australia, Britain, Canada and the United States indicates their unwillingness to get involved if an incident takes place in the private setting of a woman's home because of a tendency to regard it as simply 'trouble' in a personal relationship (Hanmer *et al.*, 1989).

By contrast, feminist sociologists have been able to uncover the extent to which violence against women is hidden, by using female interviewers and adopting more sensitive research techniques. For instance, early quantitative work by Russell in the US found that 44 per cent of a random sample of 930 women had been the subject of rape or attempted rape during their lifetime; 21 per cent of those who had been married had been beaten by their husbands at some time; and 16 per cent had experienced incestuous abuse before the age of 18 (Russell, 1982, 1984). Kelly's (1988) in-depth interviews with 60 women found that the majority had experienced violence, the threat of violence, sexual harassment or pressure to have sex. These studies, along with similar research, suggest that violence towards women is far more extensive than official figures might lead us to believe. They demonstrate that, whereas sexual violence is often trivialized or treated as insignificant, it represents an important, complex and ever-present part of gender inequality in many women's lives (Hester *et al.*, 1996; Kennedy Bergen, 1998).

## Sexual Violence

The term 'sexual violence' is used in feminist analyses for very specific theoretical reasons. It represents an attempt to link together a number of different forms of violence and the ways in which they occur and are experienced. Thus 'sexual violence' refers to acts which are directed at women because their bodies are socially regarded as sexual. Kelly defines sexual violence to include: 'Any physical, visual or sexual act that is experienced by the woman or girl, at the time or later, as a threat, invasion or assault, that has the effect of hurting her or degrading her and/or takes away her ability to control intimate contact' (1988: 41).

This widely used definition, which feminists have based on the accounts and experiences which women themselves have offered during the course of research, encompasses a wide spectrum of behaviour including the threat or fear of force, as well as its physical use, together with emotional abuse. It includes rape, sexual assault, woman beating, sexual harassment, incest, child sexual abuse and pornography. They are linked by virtue of the fact that they are overwhelmingly *male* acts of aggression against women and girls, often use *sex* as a means of exercising power and domination, and their effect is to intrude upon and curtail women's activities. They all, therefore, compel or constrain women to behave or not to behave in certain ways. In other words, both the reality and the threat of violence act as a form of gendered social control.

For example, for feminist sociologists, sexual harassment involves a variety of behaviours, some involving physical contact, some of a verbal or psychological kind, ranging from suggestive remarks, looks or joking to unwanted touching or patting, to direct sexual propositioning. What distinguishes sexual harassment from friendly banter or flirtation is that 'it is not mutual; it is not welcome; it offends; it threatens' (Halson, 1989: 132). It may even lead a girl or woman to alter her activities by taking a different route to school or changing her job.

Pornography is also included by some feminists in their definition of violence. Dworkin (1981), for instance, is famous for her arguments that pornography is at the heart of male supremacy. It portrays women's bodies as belonging to men and presents women's sexuality in an objectified, debasing and humiliating way. Dworkin sees this as constituting the foundation of women's oppression, because it legitimates women as the property of men and as subordinate to them. It is a violation of women as human beings and an encouragement to men to treat women as inferior and in abusive ways. For Dworkin, then, it is not just a question of whether pornography contains or causes violence towards women (although she argues both to be the case). Rather, she claims that pornography is itself violence to women and that it pervades and distorts every aspect of western culture.

It is only recently that researchers on violence have begun to address the issue of race. Mama (1992) points out that, in Britain, due to racism, ethnic minority women are very reluctant to call the police, even when serious or life-threatening crimes are being directed against them When the police are present, they tend to avoid enforcing the law and there is evidence to suggest that the police themselves perpetrate crimes, particularly against Afro-Caribbean people (Maynard and Winn, 1997). This means that ethnic minority women suffer a lack of protection within the community and can be particularly isolated if they live in white areas. However, although much progress has been made in highlighting the extent and severity of male violence, a great deal still remains to be done in terms of how it is treated and dealt with (Elman, 1996; Maynard and Winn, 1997; Jasinski *et al.*, 1998). Most material is still overwhelmingly about male violence towards white, apparently heterosexual women, thus ignoring issues of racism and heterosexism in its findings. It is, therefore, important that the parameters of research are broadened in the future in order to be able to investigate any factors which may effect women's differing experience of violence.

# The Law, Citizenship and the State

The idea of the state refers to the mechanisms for government exercised over a particular population of people. These are usually defined territorially and nationally, although the definition of where the boundaries lie may shift and change over time. Hence, the state has been defined as a body of institutions centrally organized to distribute and redistribute resources and as a form of control (Anthias and Yuval-Davis, 1989; Randall and Waylen, 1998). As such, it has a variety of tools for enforcement at its disposal. For example, both the military and the police have access to the physical means of social control. The state also operates through the more subtle means of ideological persuasion, particularly because it can use institutions, such as the education system and the media.

As the state in so-called democratic countries is said to have legitimate authority over its citizens, it has been seen as important to investigate the extent to which this is equal for men and women. Three linked and significant areas have been given particular investigation. The first looks at the operation of welfare states, particularly in the context of a growing sense of their power since the 1980s to regulate, define, provide for and monitor individuals' lives (Sainsbury, 1994). The second area has been concerned with the law, how it tends to ignore women's experiences and views, thereby disempowering them. Drawing on arguments from the previous two, the third area focuses on the notion of citizenship in liberal democratic countries, how far it constructs men and women differently and the consequences of this for women.

## *Welfare and Social Policy*

A welfare state is a system under which the state more generally undertakes to protect the health and well-being of its citizens, especially those in financial need, by means of the provision of services, grants, pensions and so on. Since the mid-1970s, sociologists and social policy analysts have become increasingly interested the ways in which welfare states function and who their most likely beneficiaries are. Feminist work on social policy and welfare states has sought to bring women and gender to the centre of this analysis. The work has had two particular emphases. First, it has documented the inequalities between women and men as recipients of welfare benefits, for example in pensions and unemployment provision (Sainsbury, 1994). It has highlighted the role of familial and gender ideologies in influencing state provision of benefits and services. The tendency to treat the household as an undifferentiated unit, thereby assuming that any resources will be distributed equally within it, has been especially criticized, as has the assumption that women are largely dependent on men who are willing to support them. By examining the nature of informal care and care in the community, feminists have also shown how this is mainly undertaken by women, is unpaid and reinforces a sexual division of labour which increasingly absolves the state from obligations towards the elderly, sick and disabled (Ungerson and Kember, 1997; Sevenhuijsen, 1998). Their work on lone mothers has also highlighted the plight of women and their children, who are inadequately provided for by the state (Duncan and Edwards, 1997). All this work has broadened the analytical focus of welfare state research in comparison to mainstream analysis.

Second, feminist work on welfare and social policy has also studied the historical assumptions built into the structures of various welfare states, which remain largely intact today (Sainsbury, 1994). These tend to be based upon the expectation of full male employment, that the majority of married/co-habiting women would abandon paid work to be financially supported by a male breadwinner, and stable and intact families (Lister, 1998). But, of course, these sorts of conditions are less fulfilled today than in previous decades. In the 1990s, a significant level of unemployment is the norm, more married women than ever have employment and extra-marital births, and both cohabitation and divorce are substantially on the increase. This means that the assumptions on which welfare entitlements are based tend to be outmoded. As a consequence, many women who rely on such entitlements live in poverty. The central cause of this is the devaluing of women's caring and domestic work in the family, together with the assumption that women are, and should be, financially dependent on men. It is only by adopting a gendered approach to welfare analysis that the particular difficulties which women face on this score come into view. However, much still needs to be done to integrate feminist findings into current policy provision.

## Women and the Legal System

The state has also been slow to respond to the wealth of evidence, now amassed, concerning violence towards women. Feminist researchers' claims that the violence which they were beginning to uncover was but the tip of an iceberg were dismissed, amidst accusations of exaggeration, provocation and lying on the part of women (Maynard and Winn, 1997). Subsequently, the feminist contentions have been upheld, with the seriousness of rape, domestic violence and child sexual abuse being more recognized. Yet, although violence towards women has received an increasingly high public profile, the practical response of state agencies has been very patchy. It even appears that the very laws passed with the precise aim of assisting women in their fight against male violence have been relatively ineffective (Maynard and Winn, 1997). Research on domestic violence legislation describes how reactionary interpretations of such legislation in courts of law have limited what can be achieved. This is because of the unsympathetic attitudes towards women held by the courts and by the police who are the gatekeepers to the legislation. Thus, although domestic violence legislation has undoubtedly improved the formal legal rights of battered women, the real improvement in their position is substantially less (Hester *et al.*, 1996).

There are also other problems with the ways in which the legal system deals with violence against women. For instance, researchers have referred to the police and courts of law as a rape victim's 'second assailant', where the women themselves are put on trial. Women, it has been found are reluctant to report rape because of the ways in which questioning and medical examinations are carried out (Lees, 1997). In court they have to give details of the whole process of the rape, talking intimately and publicly about parts of their body. Their accusations of rape may well be dismissed if there is no sign of bruising or struggle, even though resistance may put a woman's life in jeopardy. Attempts are made by those defending the accused to establish that a woman consented to intercourse, that even when she said 'no' she meant 'yes' and that she dressed provocatively to encourage sexual attention. In other words, women may be treated as unreliable witnesses (Lees, 1997).

This is also largely the case with the way in which courts treat children who have been sexually abused. Some sociological research has suggested that there is a common belief that children lie about sexual abuse and that they are likely to make false accusations (Smart, 1989a). Consequently, the child does not enter the witness box on neutral terms, but has been partly disqualified in terms of the perceived legitimacy of its evidence. Commentators argue that the way in which the procedures of the court operate in child sexual abuse cases, as in those of rape, are precisely designed to find ambiguities and flaws in the victim's story (Smart, 1989). Further, as in rape trials, the child's evidence must be corroborated by independent evidence, from doctors, social workers or witnesses, which is often impossible, before a conviction can be secured. For the courts, when it comes to the question of the violence committed against them, the word of the woman or child alone is not sufficient.

## Citizenship

The issues raised in relation to the state, social policy, legislation and the operation of courts of law, alongside those previously considered concerning women's material circumstances and the violence committed towards them, all have implications for current debates about the gendered nature of citizenship. The concept of citizenship is important because it suggests that individuals can claim certain rights from the state which, in turn, has obligations towards them. Much of the recent social science discussion on the subject, as is so often the case, is concerned with class and omits gender. Most commentators draw on the work of Marshall (1950), who distinguished between three elements of citizenship – the civil or legal, the political and the social. Each is associated with a set of rights guaranteed for the individual by the state and made available through its judicial, political and welfare institutions. However, those researching gender point out, not only have women been slower in attaining many aspects of citizenship, some of them still do not apply to women at all (Walby, 1997). Women still tend to be an under-represented group in mainstream political processes and government (Walby, 1997). They may have the right to own property and make contracts along with men, but do they have liberty of the person and the right to justice? (Walby, 1997; Lister, 1998). If we return to some of the sociological evidence already cited in this chapter, it appears they do not. Not only may the widespread existence of sexual violence and abuse, rape and the extensive availability of pornography be regarded as infringements of women's personal liberty but, as has been seen, the courts and other institutions of the state scarcely provide adequate protection of women's rights in this area. What kind of citizenship rights do women have when they are regularly warned not to dress too eye-catchingly or walk alone at night for fear of provoking male attack? (Lees, 1997). Gender research shows, therefore, that the benefits supposedly bestowed by citizenship are not as available to women as they are to men.

There is also a tension between social citizenship for women and their location in the family as primary carers. One of the problems is that social citizenship often depends on being fully employed for access to rights. Those who do not contribute via employment can fall back on only very meagre levels of support. With regard to pensions, for example, women who work part time or spend long periods caring for children, husbands or elderly relatives may not have direct access to the same level of pensions as do men. It is for such reasons that Lister (1998) argues that women's financial dependency on men is an obstacle to their social citizenship. She shows how governments, when discussing the 'problem of dependency', consider only the public form of dependency on the state and neglect the extent of their private dependency in the family. Yet, it is the latter which leads to gender inequalities in welfare payments. Arguing that those women who care for elderly and disabled people at home might be regarded as the ideal model of the modern active citizen, Lister bemoans the fact that this seems to be the very opposite of the case (Lister, 1998). Further, excessive demands on women's time to undertake unpaid work in the household not only undermines their citizenship in a social sense, they also limit the extent to which women can participate fully in political life.

## Current Concerns

The previous discussions have illustrated some of the ways in which adopting a gender approach in sociological analysis can help in understanding important aspects of contemporary society. In particular, focusing on the different life experiences of women and men is a way of highlighting both the nature of and the degree to which inequalities exist between them. As has been acknowledged, however, it is also necessary to take account of the fact that there are also differences and inequalities within the categories of women and men. One current and major concern within the sociology of gender is to pay more attention to this issue of difference on both an empirical and a theoretical level. This will involve becoming more sensitive to dimensions of things like 'race', ethnicity, sexuality and disability, and the ways in which they interlink with questions of gender.

Other matters are also at the forefront of sociological concerns about gender at the start of a new century. Although there are many which could have been chosen for discussion, three have been selected, in particular, both for their potential to influence the sociology of gender itself and for their likely impact on the gendered nature of society. They relate to gender and sociological theory, ageing and ageism, and the impact of the new information technologies on women.

With regard to theory, it was customary, until recently, to analyse and explain women's subordinate social situation in terms of three major perspectives, each with their own historical tradition and legacy. The first of these, liberal feminism, is depicted as focusing on individual rights and on the concepts of equality, justice and equal opportunities. In this, women are presented as being prevented from achieving equality with men by certain social barriers. It is, therefore, argued that specific legal and social policy changes are the necessary tools for rectifying women's inferior position. The second position, that of Marxist feminism, is identified by a concern with women's oppression as it is tied to forms of capitalist exploitation of labour. Here women's paid and unpaid work are each analysed in relation to their function within the capitalist economy. Third, radical feminism is 'radical' because, unlike the previous two, it challenges existing theoretical frameworks and attempts to formulate new ways of theorizing women's relationship to men. In particular, men's social control of women through various mechanisms of patriarchy is emphasized, especially violence, heterosexuality and reproduction, where men as a group are seen as responsible for maintaining women's oppression.

It is now recognized, however, that this perspectival approach is far too simple and that it is increasingly difficult to categorize feminist thought in this way. Different ways of thinking have developed, for example black, materialist, lesbian and eco-feminisms. Further, adoption of new theoretical frameworks means that it is more appropriate to view feminist theorizing about gender as a complex, dynamic and evolving process, rather than in terms of static stereotypes (Maynard, 1995). The emphasis now is much more on theory as an active process of understanding and less on the 'mugging up' of pre-given ideas.

Two general theoretical trends, those of psychoanalysis, particularly the thinking of Lacan, and post-structuralism, through the ideas of Foucault, have been especially influential in this process. Together, they have led to an increasing emphasis on language, culture and discourse. As a consequence, explorations of the meanings of 'difference' for women have begun to involve not just a concern for diversity of experience but also a postmodern emphasis on diversity within the individual. This involves the deconstruction of an individual's subjectivity. One's 'self' is no longer presented as rational and unified, so that what constitutes womanhood is seen as fragmented, pluralistic and continually changing (Butler, 1990; Maynard, 1995). In terms of gender theory, this has involved rejecting any claim that there can be *a* specific *cause* of women's oppression (be this male violence, capitalism's need for a docile workforce or discriminatory laws). Instead, arguments are made about the unevenness of power and relationships between men and women being far from the same and uniform (Ramazanoglu, 1989). Not all of women's experiences are negative, neither are they always and necessarily those of being oppressed. Developments such as these are indicative of considerable changes taking place in what constitutes feminist theory, when compared to the earlier 'perspectives' approach.

The other current interests must be dealt with rather more briefly. There has been a call for a focus on age and ageism, amidst concern that older women have been ignored and marginalized in gender analysis (Arber and Ginn, 1995). Despite much room for further improvement, more attention has been paid to differences in gender experiences related to such factors as race and sexuality, than has been given to ageing. Feminists have mainly studied younger women and those in their child bearing and child rearing years. Their virtual silence concerning those in older age groups has contributed to the negative stereotyping of the latter as 'past it' and as constituting continual social problems due to their lack of money, poor housing and ill-health. Little is known about the 'normal' experience of ageing for women (or men), since most research only concentrates on the difficulties they cause. Yet, most western countries have an increasingly ageing population. Further, a high proportion of the older population is female, due to a longer life expectancy and a tendency to outlive male partners (Arber and Ginn, 1995). Many of these women live an active life and contribute to society, certainly until their mid-70s. Gender relations are clearly not static throughout their life course and a great deal more research is needed to explain how the lives of older women in society are both experienced and constructed.

Finally, the analysis of gender must not be immune to the changes currently being wrought by the information revolution (Spender, 1995). Whether directly or indirectly, large-scale electronics communications media are changing both leisure and working lives. The pace of work, its location and distribution, alongside the nature of free time (from what is done to with whom) is being transformed, whether one is concerned about electronic banking or virtual sex (Star, 1996). While there has been much debate about the benefits or otherwise of this new technology, little of this has been gender sensitive. Yet, there are, arguably, two areas of immediate concern to women, which necessitate research. The first is the extent to which many women are excluded from and silenced within electronic networks and other technological work (Star, 1996). This occurs because, within the home, boys have more access to, and are more likely to be socialized into, new technology than girls, and because they receive more training at school and at work. Women's marginalization also occurs as a result of the reproduction of violence towards women, where fantasy games which may involve rape and pornography are readily available electronically. The technology, then, ceases to be gender neutral and becomes suffused with masculine values and culture.

A second concern is the extent to which the new technologies are entering the work environment. It is now perfectly possible, and increasingly likely, for some jobs to be done from terminals or computers at home (Star, 1996). Further high-tech developments have aided the generation of a global economy in which both production and services are increasingly moved from the 'first' world to vulnerable and impoverished workers in the 'third' (Mitter, 1991). The possible implications of this for women cannot be overlooked. In less developed nations it is likely to mean sweatshop labour in appalling conditions of work (for further discussion of gender and global changes, see Chapter 15). In the more developed ones it could lead to women's increased isolation into 'homeworking', in which they are expected to combine with child care and which remains outside health, safety and other labour regulations. This is an area which clearly requires further research.

## Conclusion

This chapter has explored some of the sociological insights to be gained from taking account of gender. Clearly, much progress has been made and a new and thriving sub-area of the discipline has been established in little over twenty years. However, it is important that sociologists do not simply confine their gender awareness to a separate and specific field of study. For it is obvious, from the material and arguments covered here, that gender permeates and has repercussions for every aspect of social life. Thus a concern for gender relations needs to be included in every aspect of sociologists' work. While the in-depth work conducted by gender researchers is significant in its own terms, this has fundamental and far-reaching implications for the whole of sociology.

# Further Reading

Abbott, P. and Wallace, C. *An Introduction to Sociology: Feminist Perspectives*, 2nd edn, London, Routledge, 1996. An introduction to feminist perspectives in sociology, demonstrating how conventions are challenged when gender is taken into account: covers education, the household, health, work, crime and politics, theory and method.

Hallett, C. (ed.) *Women and Social Policy*, London, Prentice Hall/Harvester Wheatsheaf, 1996. An introduction to the key topics and issues in social policy as they affect women, both as users and as providers of welfare services, including employment, poverty, housing, education, health care, community care and male violence.

James, S. and Busia, A. (eds) *Theorizing Black Feminisms*, London, Routledge, 1993. A collection of essays providing an overview of 'black' women's thinking about feminism.

Robinson, V. and Richardson, D. (eds) *Introducing Women's Studies*, London, Macmillan, 1997. A comprehensive overview of a range of important issues relating to women and gender; focuses, among other topics, on sexuality, the family and marriage, work, race, history, violence, reproduction and motherhood, methodology and language and literature.

Walby, S. *Gender Transformations*, London, Routledge, 1997. Examines how increased opportunities for women in Europe and America have been accompanied by new forms of inequality.

# 7
# Racism and Ethnicity

*Robert Miles and Stephen Small*

While sociologists reject the idea of naturally occurring biological races, they are interested in the ways in which ideas and beliefs about 'race' are important sources of inequality and identity. The aims of this chapter are to question the concepts of 'race' and 'race relations' and explain and illustrate the concept of 'racialization' and 'racialized' inequalities. It also considers how 'racial' inequalities relate to inequalities of class and gender considered in the previous chapters. This chapter should help you understand:

■ The distinctions between 'race' and ethnicity and 'race relations' and 'racialized relations'

■ What sociologists mean by racism and new racism

■ Some of the major theoretical approaches that have been developed to examine 'race' and ethnicity

■ How the idea of racialized inequality can be applied to the example of Britain

---

**CONCEPTS**

ethnicity ■ 'race relations' ■ ideology ■ new racism
nationality ■ colonialism ■ discrimination

---

# Introduction

If asked to identify the most important problems of the day, a large proportion of the populations of developed countries would include in their list the
problem of racism and the disadvantage that results from it. They may also
make a reference to immigration and to the need for 'strict immigration
control'. In this chapter we use the example of Britain to show how sociologists analyse these concerns. In Britain, there has been a long tradition of
politicians, journalists and the 'ordinary man and woman in the street'
claiming that 'immigrants' create social problems such as crime and violence,
deteriorating housing conditions and housing shortages. The objection to
'immigrants' is not just about material concerns. They are blamed for simply
being here, for challenging the 'British way of life' by refusing to adapt to
'British culture' expressed in terms of language, law, religion, dress, food and
moral values. The argument may be given a further twist by claiming that
these same 'immigrants' are living in Britain illegally, and that there are many
millions more seeking to enter Britain illegally for the sole purpose of
enjoying the benefits of the National Health Service, schooling or housing
available in Britain. Generally, the central claim is that 'immigrants' (identified
as the Other) create problems for 'decent citizens' (that is, Us).

These arguments may be accompanied by the statement that British people
are neither 'prejudiced' nor 'racist'. Rather, it will be suggested that they have
always been, and remain, tolerant of 'immigrants'. But, so the argument
continues, their tolerance has a limit. That limit is reached when 'too many
immigrants' are admitted to Britain and when 'they' fail to 'adjust' to the
'British way of life'. Then, it is 'natural' for 'our own people' (Us) to become
hostile to 'immigration' and to the 'immigrant presence' (the Other). Such
hostility is not racism, it will be said. Rather, it is an inevitable human reaction to being 'overrun', to the destruction of 'our way of life'.

While these views no longer attract widespread public support to the same
degree as in the past, they continue to shape opinion, especially when 'immigration' becomes the focus of political attention. Moreover, historically, there
is little new in these claims. As social historians have demonstrated (Fryer,
1984; Holmes, 1988) a review of the press and of political debate in Britain
in the nineteenth century or in the 1930s reveals similar arguments. What
differs is the group that is identified by the term 'immigrant': in the mid-
nineteenth century it was 'the Irish', in the late nineteenth century it was
Russian and Polish 'Jews' and in the 1930s it was German 'Jews'. Other
groups have become stigmatized in this way at specific moments, including
Germans and Italians. Since the mid-1950s, any reference to 'immigrants' in
Britain has been understood to refer to 'coloured people', to those migrating
to Britain from the Caribbean, Africa and the Indian sub-continent. Yet,
while there is diversity in terms of the group signified as a problematic presence, to varying degrees each has also been identified as a distinct 'race'. This

language of 'race' has had a particular resonance and significance with respect to post-1945 migration to Britain because of the way in which the immigrant presence has been signified by reference to human physical features such as skin colour, but all these earlier migrant populations were similarly labelled as 'races'.

Over the last four decades, it has come to be seen as self-evident that Britain has a 'race relations' problem as a result of the fact that 'coloured immigrants' are resident in very large numbers. It is thus suggested that 'race relations' are the 'natural' outcome of different 'races' living together in Britain. Underlying this suggestion is the subsidiary assumption that 'race relations' are the inevitable outcome of the 'natural' differences between different 'races' in terms of their mental and biological constitution, and the cultural practices, institutions and behaviour that are believed to follow from this. Hence, it is concluded that Britain's 'race relations' problem results from immigration: and if 'we' had not allowed 'them' into 'our country', we would not have such a problem.

Students approaching an analysis of 'race relations' by accepting these assumptions are building their conceptual foundation on shifting sands and risk legitimating dominant (and in some instances racist) discourses and the practices that derive from them. Many sociologists believe that it is preferable to commence the analysis of 'race relations' by questioning the language of 'race relations' and the assumptions which underlie such language (for example Miles, 1982; Miles and Torres, 1996). Many of the words just used are based on misleading claims and assumptions. Rather than accept them at face value, these sociologists urge students to challenge them in order to expose their unquestioned assumptions. Doing this raises questions about the motivations and intentions of those in positions of power who use them so uncritically. Accordingly, this chapter will begin by providing some definitions of the key concepts that will be used. It will then look at some of the major theoretical approaches to the study of 'race' The following sections look at patterns of racialized inequality in Britain and issues of immigration and citizenship.

# Concepts

## *'Race' and Ethnicity*

Words like 'race relations', 'race' and 'racial' in have been placed in quotation marks because these are commonsense words whose meaning and significance are hotly contested. For many sociologists, these words, and the assumptions underlying them, create problems of understanding and analysis. The words 'race' and 'racial' presume the existence of discrete biological 'races', and imply that anything which is 'racial' results primarily from, and is explained by, this supposed fact. For example, the idea of 'racial conflict' suggests conflict results primarily, even inevitably, from contact between 'races' in and of themselves, rather than because of factors such as economic and political competition. However, the vast majority of scientists, genetic and social, agree that discrete biological 'races' do not exist (Hannaford, 1996). That is to say, most scientists do not believe that the human population is divided into a number of distinct types of species in such a way that evident physical characteristics or even hidden genetic characteristics correlate in a determined way with social, psychological and cultural characteristics. They also agree that the physical distinctiveness that does exist across human populations bears little relationship to the racialized identities of communities scattered across the world today.

Even though they are regarded as synonymous in much commonsense discussion, most sociologists are agreed that the terms 'race' and ethnicity should be clearly distinguished for analytical purposes. Use of the idea of 'race' usually indicates a belief in the existence of naturally occurring groups, each exhibiting real and imagined biological and mental attributes and characteristics which are regarded as fixed. While the idea of 'race' necessarily both self-identifies and other-identifies (to identify the Other as a distinct 'race' entails simultaneously identifying Us as another 'race'), a great deal of academic work has focused upon the ways in which it has tended to be imposed upon populations as part of a process of subordination, rather than being sought after and embraced. Research on the ways in which Africans have been regarded as the 'black race', and as biologically and culturally inferior, illustrates this process (Miles, 1982). More recently, interest has been shown in the ways in which self-identified, superior 'race' identities have been constructed and sustained (for example Roediger, 1996).

The concept of ethnicity refers to specific social and cultural attributes (such as language, religion, dress, food, music, beliefs of origin and genesis) and to the social and cultural (and negotiable) boundary between two or more self-identifying collectivities who claim a historical existence by reference to such attributes. Hence, ethnic groups are identified by a pattern of cultural signifiers which sustains claims of difference and distinctiveness through historical time: in some instances, the claims of distinctiveness may be supported by beliefs about natural difference (that is, by a belief in the existence of 'races'). Ethnicity tends to be embraced rather than imposed and is fluid and flexible because the identifying social and cultural attributes can and do change through time. Most of what was called 'race' in the past is now usually referred to as ethnic or ethnic relations: the description of 'racial group' is replaced by that of ethnic group (and 'race relations' by ethnic relations).

Given the limitations of the idea of 'race' as an analytical category, this development has significant advantages. This is because the conceptual language no longer reproduces an echo of a racialized discourse in such a way that commonsense beliefs in the existence of 'races' are implicitly or explicitly legitimated. Yet it needs to be recognized that beliefs about 'race' are still employed in self- and other-identification: members of a group may simultaneously self-identify in relation to some combination of, for example, religious belief, language, cuisine and dress *and* the imagination of itself as a 'race'. And, of course, ideas of 'race' are still often central to negative other-identification: for example, people of Irish origin resident in Britain distinguish themselves and are distinguished by others by reference to a range of cultural attributes but they are also other-identified negatively by a belief in their existence as a distinct 'race' as evidenced by their supposed mental inferiority. What is sociologically significant is not only the variation in what is signified but also the economic, political and ideological forces that shape these variations.

## 'Race Relations' and Racialized Relations

Close to the idea of 'race' is the notion of 'race relations'. This notion often leads to an oversimplified focus on 'race' by positing the existence of a distinct category of social relations (that is, relations between supposedly distinct 'races') while ignoring the relevance of economic and political processes and the consequences of the routine operation of key institutions in contemporary life. Many sociologists now reject the term 'race relations' because there are no 'races' and so there cannot be any social relations between them. But if 'race relations' are not the relationship between biologically different 'races', why are certain types of social relation defined as such? In order to answer this question, it is necessary to turn our attention to economic and political processes and to the ways in which structures, images and ideologies operate to sustain inequality. Additionally, we need to consider the impact of the ideological dimension of resistance to such inequality. In this kind of analysis there is no presumption that 'race' is a variable in and for itself. Rather, it is argued that ideas and beliefs about 'race' have shaped these relationships, alongside the impact of, for example, class and gender.

This approach is usually described as the *racialization problematic* (or framework). This framework is a set of assumptions and concepts which explore the multiple factors that shape what has previously been described as 'race relations'. Some of these factors entail explicit reference to 'race', for example, beliefs about the existence of 'races', and discrimination based on such beliefs. But other factors – such as competition for economic and political resources (education, jobs, housing, elected office) – may seem to have no 'racial' reference. The racialization problematic enables us to draw out the relationship between these seemingly unrelated variables, and to assess the significance of each of them. What this conceptual approach requires, rather than presumes, is that there is a need to question and explain the social and cultural boundaries and identities by which groups called 'races' have been, and continue to be, defined. We believe a historical and comparative approach is the best way to do this.

The key concept within the racialization problematic is the process of *racialization* (and hence the notion of racialized social relations) which has been defined in a number of ways (see Small, 1994 for an overview). We use it to refer to a historically specific ideological process, and to the accompanying structures, that results in certain social collectivities being thought of as constituting naturally (often biologically) distinct groups, each possessing certain ineradicable features. The groups racialized in this way vary. The example with which most people are familiar with is the racialization of diverse ethnic groups from the Caribbean, Asia and Africa in order to constitute a 'black race' which stands in contrast (even in conflict with) the 'white race'. This particular instance of racialization is founded in part on colonization and imperial conquest. It also refers to the associated institutional arrangements: the legal system (in slavery, and post slave societies, including legislation on immigration), the economic system (the plantation economy, and the distribution of jobs), as well as housing (with, for example, African-Caribbeans, Pakistanis and Bangladeshis generally confined to inferior housing).

People of African and Asian origin are not the only populations to be racialized by Europeans (who simultaneously racialized themselves). There have been many instances of racialization of Europeans by other Europeans (Miles, 1993: 80–104). During the nineteenth century, the Irish were widely racialized by the British while, during the twentieth century, the racialization of Jews was a prelude to the Holocaust. Moreover, the laws and policies introduced to promote equal opportunities and multiculturalism sustain the process of racialization even though their objectives are clearly very different: for example, the very title of the legislation legitimates the ideas of 'race' and 'race relations' while the content of the legislation includes a legal definition of a 'race'.

The concrete examples elaborated in the following text demonstrate that this is not simply a matter of changing the words, or playing semantics; rather it is a matter of challenging the assumptions, and of improving the analysis, by identifying as central a number of variables that are usually neglected or obscured. It is useful to distinguish several aspects of this process of racialization. Racialized structures are the institutional pillars of society. They are the routine, recurrent and organized features of contemporary life. The idea of racialized structures has two key components.

First, it refers to the distribution of valuable resources such as political power, employment, education and housing. Primarily this aspect involves who owns what, works and lives where, and has good health. Second, it refers to the normal, recurrent and routinized procedures of institutions that shape and constrain our daily lives, from politics (voting and political representatives), economics (businesses, employment), education (universities, schools), health (hospitals) and other spheres of social life (family, media, music, sport). These behaviours and actions sustain the distribution of resources. The practices of key institutions in contemporary societies shape and determine who succeeds and who fails, who is rewarded and who is punished.

Ideologies are systematic statements about the way in which society is organized, or ought to be organized, if it is to function well. Ideologies are racialized in several ways. Ideologies that make explicit reference to 'race' are the most obvious examples of racialized ideologies, closely followed by those in which 'race' is indirectly referred to, or implied. But all ideologies are racialized in that they have differential consequences for populations labelled for example as 'black', Asian and 'white'. For example, the 'Keep Britain White' slogan is an explicit expression of a racialized ideology, asserting as it does a racialized conception of Britishness and of immigration control. Not far away from such ideologies are those in which the policies of multiculturalism, anti-discrimination and equal opportunities are blamed for deteriorating 'race relations'. Here it is suggested, or stated, that such policies favour 'black' people who are thereby privileged illegitimately.

There are also less explicit racialized ideologies, for example, those with a coded racialized reference. In these ideologies, while no reference is made to 'race', the words themselves are heavily saturated with such meanings and interests as the result of a specific history in the course of which a particular social group is attributed with a fixed nature and/or whose presence is associated with a set of (usually undesirable) social consequences. When people refer to crime in the 'inner city', the 'immigration problem' or to 'reverse racism', and when they claim that multiculturalism devalues their culture, these all have a 'racialized' reference.

There are also ideologies without any racialized reference, but in which we can identify the hostile intentions of those advocating them, or the likely adverse consequences of the ideology for 'blacks' and/or Asians. Some policies around policing exemplify this type of ideology. For example, the practice of 'Stop and Search', which gives the police to stop and search persons suspected of crimes on rather slender suspicion, is defended by arguments about the need to act directly to deal with street crime. This policy – and the one which preceded it (the 'Sus law)' – has been enforced with disproportionate impact on young black men of Caribbean origin (Smith and Gray, 1987).

Racialized identities are the collective identities embraced by people previously and contemporarily described as 'races'. As Europeans created for themselves the idea that they are a 'white race', they also created the idea of the 'black race' which categorized and controlled people originating from Africa, or the Asian race for those from the Indian sub-continent and the surrounding region. In some contexts, the category of 'black' or 'coloured' has been used to refer to all those considered to be 'not-white' while in other contexts these groups have been subdivided, as with distinctions by nation, for example, 'Indians' or the 'brown race'. The racialized identity of whiteness serves as a platform on which to organize; and so, too, does the racialized identity of blackness. These identities serve to defend and promote the interests of those people labelled by them, and/or embracing them. Hence, social movements of 'blacks' or 'Asians' have emerged expressing their collective strategies of resistance around racialized identities and many continue to do so. In this regard, they fulfil a number of group interests. However, they also mask the very real differences within these groups, along lines of class and gender differentiation, religion, language or political interests.

These various aspects of racialization interact in ways that shape one another. Racialized structures shape representations and ideologies. Poverty causes material hardship for 'blacks' and 'Asians' and media institutions have employed images of such people in poverty and on welfare dependency. Control of government institutions affect the policies that prevail, just as control of businesses hinders or helps opportunities. These same institutions are positioned so as to restrict or expand the incidence of racialized discrimination. In African-Caribbean communities, the never-employed, the unemployed, the unskilled and the skilled continue to face hostility. Similarly, racialized images and ideologies can influence social structure: African-Caribbean and Asian communities continue to be the subject of negative media images which can increase hostility not only from 'white' people but also from some sections of African-Caribbean and Asian communities towards each other (for some examples, see Gabriel, 1994). The psychological consequences are immense. At the same time, ideologies of 'colour-blindness' create the appearance of equality and fairness, while hiding practices of discrimination.

## Racism, New Racism and Racisms

The concept of racism is especially problematic for a number of reasons (cf. Miles, 1989, 1993). First, despite the fact that it is now widely used as if it had a universal existence and reference, the word 'racism' was created in the 1930s. Precursors such as 'race prejudice' embody a similar meaning but the specific origin of the word 'racism' has had implications for its use and meaning in later historical periods. Given that the word was created to refer to the scientifically justified belief in the existence of an ordered hierarchy of biologically distinct 'races' that was used to legitimate fascism in Germany during the 1930s, some sociologists have argued that, in so far as such a belief is in decline, then racism is in decline. Moreover, if the meaning of the concept is so firmly grounded in its immediate referent, then it cannot have an object in earlier historical periods: simply stated, there cannot have been racism before the rise of science as a form of human knowledge in Europe.

Second, in the light of what is now widely known to have been done in the name of racism in earlier historical periods (the events of European colonization and of the Holocaust are especially significant), the ideology of racism is widely discredited. As a result, the concept of racism has taken on a very negative connotation and the accusation that someone is a racist is extremely condemnatory. Thus, explicit references to an alleged 'racial inferiority' of the

Other are rare in the formal, public arena and, when they are made, they attract widespread media attention and censure.

In the light of these historical developments, there are two main sociological approaches to the scope of the concept of racism. On the one hand, there are those who, in effect, sustain the original definition of the concept which refers to the ideology that the world is divided into a number of separate 'races' (for example, Europeans, Africans and Asians) who are endowed with different physical and mental attributes, that 'race' determines culture, and that Europeans are superior both mentally and culturally. On the other hand, there are those who revise or extend the definition in various ways. They claim that the original referent is only one specific form of racism, this being identified as biological or scientific racism.

The revision has taken two main forms. First, there are those who retain the idea that the concept refers to a specific form of ideology and who argue that there are a variety of historically specific racisms which refract the particular context in which they are formed and expressed. Second, there are those who extend the definition in such a way as to include both beliefs and practices which lead to the subordination of specific racialized groups. In some versions of this argument, evidence of the existence of racism is found in the comparative material disadvantage of, for example, 'black people' or 'Asians' irrespective of any beliefs held about the group.

The debate concerning the scope of the concept of racism has been particularly lively over the past two decades. The concept of a *new racism*, formulated initially by Barker (1981), has been especially influential. The emergence of this concept is grounded in the previously mentioned declining expression of biological or scientific racism, at least in the formal spheres of social life. It is argued that this 'old racism' has been superseded by a new racism which is characterized by an assertion of the naturalness of both a desire to live among 'one's own people' (Us) and hostility towards a culturally distinct immigrant presence (the Other) that threatens the existence of 'our way of life'. This concept was incorporated into the influential analysis of the Centre for Contemporary Cultural Studies (1982). Gilroy argues (1987) that hostility to people of African Caribbean and Asian origin in Britain in the 1980s was dominated by hostility to their religion, family values and language, rather than to their skin colour. A similar emphasis upon cultural signifiers is found in Modood's claim that there is less discrimination against people of African and African-Caribbean origin because their cultures are closer to that of 'white' Britons, and more against British Muslims in particular and British Asians in general because their cultures are seen as being more 'alien' (Modood, 1992). While retaining the essence of the idea of a new racism, a rather different emphasis is found in the assertion that hostility is dominated by a concern with profit and prosperity in the context of a 'new world order' of global capitalism: 'Racism is no longer about racial or cultural superiority... Racism is about prosperity, and pros-

perity is white, Western, European' (Fekete and Webber, 1994). One can conclude from this that there are many different racisms which differ in motivation, content and outcome.

It is important to recognize that contemporary social reality is complex. For example, it is problematic to say that a person who opposes equal opportunities policies for people of African-Caribbean origin or who is in favour of tighter immigration control is necessarily articulating racism because these views may be grounded in a variety of beliefs and assumptions. For example, the former may be motivated by a genuine belief in treating all individuals equally without regard to ethnicity or 'race'. But neither can we say that a person who expresses support for 'colour blind' policies is necessarily 'anti-racist' or 'non-racist'. The intentions people have, and what they actually do, can be markedly different from what they say they will do. In so far as the concept of racism is used to refer to a particular ideology, this complexity creates particular difficulties for the sociologist when seeking to determine whether any particular set of assertions warrant description as an instance of racism.

Because of this difficulty, our preference is to use the concept of racism to refer to a specific kind of ideology: this at least avoids the problem of reading intentions and beliefs from actions and outcomes. But we also criticize those writers who have used the concept of racisms without also attempting to specify what each specific instance of racism has in common with all other instances to warrant description as a racism. Put another away, if historically there are many different racisms, each instance must express a set of core characteristics that allow it to be described as a racism. Thus, elsewhere, one of the current authors has proposed the following definition (Miles, 1993: 99, but see also pp. 100–2):

> Racism is a form of ideological signification which constructs a social collectivity as a discrete and distinct, self-reproducing population by reference to certain (real or imagined) biological characteristics which are purported to be inherent, and which additional attributes the collectivity with other negatively evaluated (biological and/or cultural) characteristics. Racism, therefore, attributes meaning to the human body, either somatically or genetically, in order to construct an Other which reproduces itself through historical time and space.

Moreover, an analysis of racism which is grounded in this kind of definition will need to identify not only the features that an ideology must exhibit in order that it may be identified as an instance of racism but also the wider historical and structural factors that shape its existence. An analysis of this kind will therefore seek out the links between racism as ideology, and broader economic and political structures. This will have a historical dimension because we have inherited a system of beliefs about 'race' and mental and physical abilities, and a commonsense language which we use to describe present differences between racialized populations.

Yet understanding racism is not simply a matter of looking at beliefs inherited from the past. Current beliefs and ideologies are shaped by past beliefs but also by current social arrangements, especially economic and political structures. Social structure is important, because racism (in the past and at present) has been a moment in the reproduction of economic, political and social structures which continue to shape our attitudes and behaviour, with significant consequences. For example, ideas of 'race' helped channel and shape patterns of colonization and conquest, the various systems of slavery instituted across the Americas, as well as the circumstances and conditions surrounding the independence of countries like India and Pakistan, Ghana and Nigeria, and Jamaica, not to mention the mass murder of Jews in Europe prior to and during the Second World War. In all these different situations, the ideology of racism was used by the dominant groups to identify other populations as naturally inferior and therefore deserving of domination and exploitation.

Contemporary racisms are also shaped by the division of the world into distinct nation states and by the ideology of nationalism (Anderson, 1983; Balibar and Wallerstein, 1991; Miles, 1993). Once again, there is a historical dimension to this relationship. Commencing in the late eighteenth century in western Europe, the rise of a new ruling class, the bourgeoisie, was accompanied by an appeal to the 'common people' to see themselves as members of a single nation with common interests. This process of nation state formation was legitimated by the belief that (as with supposed 'races') nations too were naturally occurring populations. The languages of 'race' and nation were thereby closely intertwined, and supported by a binary opposition between Us and Other. As populations were persuaded to think of themselves as unitary, homogeneous nations, a process that was accompanied by a significant degree of real cultural change (regional languages were, for example, eliminated), rights of political participation and of eligibility for welfare benefits were gradually granted to most members of the nation.

Post-1945 migrations have highlighted the significance of these arrangements: should the new arrivals have equal access to these rights and resources reserved for members of the nation? In the case of Britain, as we shall see shortly, many of the migrants were British subjects who did therefore have the right to work, political participation and access to welfare benefits. But racism was used to identify them as illegitimate competitors: the language of 'our own people' became simultaneously a nationalist and a racist discourse, defining the nationalized Us by reference to 'whiteness'. In this instance, racism and nationalism articulated to identify a racialized Other whose presence marked the necessity of redrawing the boundary of who belonged and who should not belong to the nation. The relationship between racism and nationalism, and its structural consequences, should therefore be viewed as historically contingent: the precise interrelationship between these two ideologies varies from one set of circumstances to another.

# Theories

Sociological debate is shaped by the emergence and decline of different theorietical approaches which themselves express changing social conditions. In British sociology, for example, the origin of theoretical discussion about 'race' can be traced back to the late 1960s when 'race' and 'immigration' were becoming identified as major social problems. Two texts expressed the emergence of the *sociology of 'race relations'*: Banton (1967) and Rex (1970). While the underlying presuppositions of these two texts differed in significant respects, they shared the objective of defining 'race relations' as a legitimate object of sociological investigation and explanation. Moreover, both sought to understand the British situation through frameworks that were historical and comparative: British 'race relations' were thereby compared with 'race relations' in the USA and South Africa. The crucial difference between the two texts lay in their understanding of the nature of racism: Banton argued that the ideology of racism was no longer widely expressed while Rex argued that it was a defining feature of a 'race relations' situation and that it continued to be a major ideological force in Britain, even if its form and content had changed.

As we saw in Chapter 5, during the late 1960s and early 1970s, British sociology was shaped by a renewal of interest in Marxist theory and in the interconnections between the centre and periphery of the world capitalist economy. Out of these developments emerged other theoretical perspectives which came to constitute specific challenges to the sociology of 'race relations' during the late 1970s and 1980s. These can be described collectively as *Marxist theories of 'race'*: because the Marxist tradition itself encompasses a variety of perspectives, these were reflected in different analyses of the British 'race' problem, but they were agreed that:

1. 'race' was the object of analysis
2. understanding the relationship between class and 'race' was the central theoretical and empirical priority
3. racism remained a central determinant of inequality in contemporary capitalist societies.

Their concern to explain the disadvantage and discrimination arising from racism within the broader framework of Marxist theory distinguished these writers from both Rex and Banton.

In the light of the influence of political movements in the USA, this theoretical development was divided into 'black' and 'white' sub-sections, the former arguing that 'black people' needed to assert political (and therefore theoretical) autonomy in order to overcome the legacy of colonialism. References to 'white sociology' and 'black Marxism' became commonplace for a time, reflecting the influence of these different perspectives. Examples of contributions to Marxist theories of 'race' include the writings of the Centre for Contemporary Cultural Studies (1982) and Ben-Tovim *et al.* (1986).

What can be called the *theory of racialization* emerged during the 1980s (Miles, 1982, 1989) out of a critique of what (despite their fundamental differences on many other matters) the sociology of 'race relations' and the Marxist theory of 'race' were agreed on, namely that 'race' was the object of study. The main features and themes of this theory have been outlined in preceding sections. But it was not the only theoretical development of this decade: there were three others.

First, the sociology of 'race relations' gave birth to the *sociology of ethnic relations*. This reflected in part the influence of the academic discipline of anthropology, grounded in the ethnographic study of colonized people, many of whom had migrated from periphery to centre of the world economy. Studies of the culture and way of life of African-Caribbean and Asian migrants during the 1970s revealed them as social groups embodying distinct histories and cultural traditions and therefore not just the victims of racism and discrimination (for example Watson, 1977). The concepts of ethnicity and ethnic group entered the theoretical language, stimulating a debate about the distinction and relationship between 'race relations' and ethnic relations (Banton, 1983; Anthias and Yuval-Davis, 1992). Moreover, the exploration of the production and transformation of cultural traditions (and their simultaneous maintenance across time and space following migration) has highlighted the distinctiveness of ethnic groups resident in Britain following the colonial migrations of the 1950s and 60s. As a result, not only is the idea of a single 'black community' unified by the collective experience of racism now undermined by a distinction between African-Caribbean and Asian ethnic groups, but this dichotomy is itself fractured by the revelation of the significance of, for example, religious belief and practice to those whose migrant origin lies in the Indian sub-continent (Modood, 1992).

The second development arose from the growth of feminist theory within the social sciences. The sociology of 'race relations' and Marxist theories of 'race' were not immune from the silence about gender that characterized much of the academic discipline of sociology. The key theoretical developments took place in relation to Marxist theories of 'race', concerned as it already was with the articulation between the social divisions of class and 'race': it was but a small step to add gender to this articulation. But what we might describe as the *theory of class, 'race' and gender* was far from being a unitary theory.

The political division between 'white' and 'black' feminists was reflected in the debates of the 1980s and early 1990s: 'race' was conceived as fragmenting gender as much as it was conceived as dividing class (for example Centre for Contemporary Cultural Studies, 1982; Bryan *et al.*, 1985). The idea of triple oppression along with that of simultaneous articulation or intersectionality shaped these expressions of the relationship between 'race', class and gender (Centre for Contemporary Cultural Studies, 1982; Cheney, 1996). Whereas the first concept assumed men and women who were 'black' or 'Asian' experienced a similar racism, and all women experienced a similar sexism, intersectionality rejected this as an oversimplified accumulation. Instead it was argued that 'black' and 'Asian' women's experience of racism was uniquely gendered, their experience of sexism uniquely racialized. One example of this is the primary purpose rule in immigration law which required 'black' and 'Asian' women to demonstrate that their primary purpose in getting married to a UK citizen was not for purposes of immigration. Both triple oppression and intersectionality continue to be stated, or suggested, in works that explore patterns of dominance against 'black' and 'Asian' women, as well as women from other ethnic minorities (Brah, 1996).

The third development arose out of the theoretical critique of Marxism itself. A number of sociologists (for example Touraine, 1981; Gorz, 1982) had argued, long before the collapse of communist states in central and eastern Europe forced a wider critique of Marxist theory, that class relations were no longer the key force shaping historical development. Such an argument had a particular attraction to self-identified 'black' sociologists who were asserting that 'race' was an autonomous social force, reflected in the existence of a 'black' community shaped by a distinct historical experience and culture (for example Gilroy, 1987). The arena of cultural studies provided fertile ground for the development of the *theory of the autonomy of 'race'*.

Focusing as it does on cultural production and consumption in everyday life, cultural studies has facilitated the analysis of the production of collective identities through adherence to a specific lifestyle (expressed in dress, language, religion, music): 'race' is theorized as one social division which sustains such a collective identity by means of both a resistance to exclusion and marginalization determined by racism, as well as the celebration of a positive cultural tradition. Such a perspective has merged with certain of the theoretical currents that have been labelled as postmodernism (Hall and du Gay, 1996).

Most attempts to classify races gloss over, even obscure, connections and overlaps between categories or groups which are presented as absolutely separate and distinct: the preceding distinctions between different theories is no exception. In particular, the theoretical developments of the 1980s are closely linked. Some postmodernist perspectives have adopted the concepts of identity and ethnicity, even if they have been employed in a distinctive manner (Rattansi and Westwood, 1994; Hall and du Gay, 1996). There is no fundamental obstacle to the integration of a racialization perspective with one which highlights the interrelationship between class and gender inequalities (Anthias and Yuval-Davis, 1992; Brah, 1996; Sudbury, 1997).

Those writers who reject theories which take 'race' as their point of origin and as an explanatory concept do so because they doubt that such a theory can offer a satisfactory explanation of the structures and patterns of social relations described in this chapter. They argue that any explanation of these structures and patterns must relate the unfolding of social practices and beliefs associated with the idea of 'race' to associated patterns of economic and political power, and gender differences, nationally and internationally. Even though there are many individual, and indeed collective, examples of people acting on the basis of a belief in the existence of 'races' without regard to economic or political consequences, the broad contours of racialized structures, processes and ideologies are best explained in relation to these broad patterns (for example Small, 1994).

## Racialized Inequality in Britain

At the turn of the century, British African-Caribbeans and British Asians find themselves collectively at a significant disadvantage, as compared with British 'whites', deprived of many basic resources and facing racist hostility. Racialized inequality is revealed in the differences in the share of, and access to, valued resources. However, an overview of racialized inequality is not straightforward, given the many differences *within* the various racialized groups in Britain. Although commonsense discussions argue that British African-Caribbeans are not doing as well as British 'whites', or that British Asians are doing better than both, the evidence reveals a more complex picture. There are major differences within these broadly defined groups (for example, between British Asians who originate from the different countries of the Indian sub-continent and between British Africans and African-Caribbeans). While these differences are clearly real, collectively all negatively racialized groups face some institutional discrimination.

British African-Caribbeans and Asians are more likely to be unemployed, under-employed (that is, to have more qualifications than their job merits), to receive low pay, and/or Social Security benefits. They have comparatively worse jobs, worse work conditions (shifts, night work, part-time work) and less pay and security (Jones, 1993). In the 1980s, African-Caribbean and Asian males earned 10–15 per cent less than 'whites'; and almost twice as many African-Caribbean and Asians, as compared with 'white', households were likely to be reliant on child benefits (Brown, 1984: 242). Compared to 'white' people, African-Caribbeans are less likely to be self-employed, and more likely to be in manual and lower paid jobs while 'white' men are more likely to be employed as corporate managers and in skilled and semi-skilled jobs. For example, Brown reported that, while 19 per cent of 'whites' were found in the top socio-economic group, only 5 per cent of African-Caribbeans were. And the proportion of 'whites' in other 'non-manual' jobs was double that for African-Caribbeans (Brown, 1992: 157). This is true despite the fact that more African-Caribbeans were economically active in the late 1980s. While they are more likely to be unemployed, African Caribbeans and Asians are less likely than 'whites' to claim unemployment benefits (Jones, 1993: 119).

British African-Caribbean and Asian people are overwhelmingly an English urban population where they are more likely to live in sections of the inner city, and to be residentially segregated from 'whites'. Five English metropolitan areas – London, West Midlands, the North West, Yorkshire and Humberside – account for more than 90 per cent of all African-Caribbean people in Britain. Similarly high numbers of Asians live in these conurbations. Compared to British African-Caribbeans, and to Pakistanis and Bangladeshis, British 'whites' are more likely to live in owner-occupied housing (66 per cent of the latter own their own homes compared to 42.3 per cent of the former) (Owen, 1994: 6). African-Caribbean, Pakistani and Bangladeshi households are more likely to be over-crowded and to share a bathroom, and less likely to own cars. The evidence on educational performance displays considerable racialized disparities, with African-Caribbeans, Pakistanis and Bangladeshis generally less likely to receive qualifications.

But not all British African-Caribbeans and Asians experience this pattern of disadvantage: there is clear evidence of class, occupational and educational differences among these populations. Surveys in the 1990s have found that British African Asians and Indians, as well as Africans, reveal greater levels of educational and economic success than do African Caribbeans, Pakistanis and Bangladeshis (Jones, 1993). Those who are financially better off include business owners and managers, the self-employed, professionals (such as academics, doctors and social workers), local and central government workers, civil servants and politicians. There is also a small but highly visible number of wealthy individuals such as sports personalities, television celebrities and musicians. In part, this reveals the higher class origins of these immigrants in the countries from which they migrated. This being said, the absolute number of those experiencing these materially privileged circumstances is tiny, and when compared to the rest of the British population, the relative number is even smaller. For women the number is smaller still.

While the explanation for this pattern of inequality cannot be reduced to a single factor, racialized discrimination is certainly a determinant. Racialized discrimination is widespread, and continues to constrain the aspirations of African-Caribbean and Asian people, at all class positions, and both genders. This includes violence and physical attacks, verbal abuse and exclusion. A series of studies carried out since the mid-1960s shows that racialized discrimination in employment, housing and education persists at high levels (described in Brown and Gay, 1985). This is despite three Race Relations Acts (passed in 1965, 1968 and 1976) which have made such discrimination illegal and provided institutions (for example the Commission for Racial Equality) and procedures to identify and prevent it, and have also sought to encourage a wider social commitment to multiculturalism and to equal opportunity policies, particularly in the area of employment. Both government and private employers publicly and officially support equal opportunities policies but, by postponement and prevarication, they ensure that they are not fully or effectively implemented (McCruddon *et al.*, 1991).

While racialized discrimination is widespread, the forms that it takes are far more diverse than in the past. Patterns of direct individual and institutional racialized hostility are accompanied by indirect and furtive forms. This means overall a continued move from direct, overt and conspicuous racialized discrimination in which it is relatively easy to identify motives predicated on racialized beliefs (for example, immigration legislation or violence accompanied by racist abuse) to indirect, covert and inconspicuous discrimination in which motives and intentions are less obvious. Those who harbour hatred and hostility employ code words and double meanings to camouflage the vehemence and virulence of their attitudes and actions: apparently neutral language such as 'our own kind' and 'British people', appeal to a racialized nationalism (according to which 'whiteness' is a precondition of being considered British), while a greater emphasis on networks, word of mouth, internal adverts, and 'acceptability' criteria for recruitment in employment can be highly effective in excluding racialized minorities. The pursuit of their distinctive cultural practices, including language, religion, dress, music (sometimes in resistance against racialized hostility) is labelled culturally myopic and anti-British.

While all racialized groups face some common restraints, different groups have been targeted for attack or victimization of various sorts. Asians are more likely to be targeted for violence by neo-fascist groups such as the National Front while young African-Caribbean men have a greater likelihood of experiencing police violence. Murders of African-Caribbeans have continued as have violence and abuse, with the latter too frequently finding themselves and their properties attacked (Hesse *et al.*, 1992). One of the most widely publicized recent deaths was that of Stephen Lawrence, savagely murdered at a bus stop. This particular case became well known because it led to a high profile campaign for justice by the African-Caribbean and Asian communities. There is also a high level of accusations of racialized intimidation by the police and a number of deaths of young African and African-Caribbean men in police custody, many of them in suspicious circumstances (*The Voice*, 1995).

In the face of these patterns of disadvantage and discrimination, African-Caribbean people continue to resist in various ways (Sivanandan, 1990). This resistance entails collective and individual strategies, as well as physical and ideological strategies, many of which are articulated around the organizations and institutions of the African-Caribbean communities and the cultural patterns prevalent within them. The various forms of resistance present today reflect, in part, traditions of resistance by African Caribbeans and Asians to European conquest and colonization, but also their relationship to British political structures and traditions of resistance.

Various goals and strategies are articulated at both local and national levels. In education, health and welfare, the criminal justice system and housing, various groups fight poor facilities, inadequate finances and homelessness, and establish alternative community-based services (Sivanandan, 1990; Solomos and Back, 1995). Some groups seek integration and incorporation in the present system while focusing on overcoming discrimination and injustice; others seek a fundamental change in the organization of society, expressing socialist or communist aspirations; still others see the way forward in developing distinctive racialized institutions and communities (Small, 1994; Brah, 1996). Strategies also vary: some seek broad alliances with 'white' people, as in the Anti-Racist Alliance; others call for the consolidation and expansion of 'black' organizations and the regeneration of self-reliance and self-dependence, as in the case of Southall Black Sisters or the National Black Caucus.

The contribution of women has differed from those of men, as have their modes of organization, because of their experience of gendered and racialized inequality and exclusion. They have been involved in industrial and workplace struggles, in immigration and legal defence campaigns and they have mobilized to combat male violence within their own communities (Brah, 1996). While ethnic minority men have faced racialized and class hostility, ethnic minority women have also faced sexism from most men and racism (much of it from 'white' women). Social analyses have also tended to ignore or understate their unique position. For example, by saying that the inequality between 'white' women and ethnic minority women is less than that between 'white' men and ethnic minority men, one gains the impression that ethnic minority women are doing well (Jones, 1993: 70). In fact, the average earnings of women are lower than that of men. In this way ethnic minority women occupy a position at a unique intersection of hostilities, and the strategies they have developed have varied accordingly.

## Immigration, Nationality and Citizenship

British immigration legislation is thoroughly racialized: the passport held by British citizens corresponds to a significant extent to skin colour. Until the early 1960s, one passport was held by all citizens of the United Kingdom and Colonies, regardless of origin and skin colour, and its possession guaranteed, at least in principle, identical rights, privileges and obligations. Today there are three different passports: British Citizen, British Overseas Citizen and British Dependent Territories Citizen. Only those holding the first category of passport have the right to enter and work in Britain. These passport holders are overwhelmingly 'white'. Holders of the second and third type of passport – who are overwhelmingly of ethnic minority origin – have no rights to enter or work in Britain. Over a period of little more than ten years, successive British governments deprived millions of people of British citizenship. These measures have largely stopped the migration and settlement of South Asian and African-Caribbean people in Britain.

Between 1880 and the beginning of the Second World War, immigrants to Britain were mainly of European origin: with the exception of Irish migrants, these immigrants were legally aliens (Holmes, 1978, 1988). A large proportion of these immigrants originated from Ireland, which was a British colony until the 1920s, but there were significant minorities from central and eastern Europe, Italy and Germany. After the Second World War, and in the light of the urgent demand for labour to rebuild and restructure the British economy, attention focused initially on these 'traditional' sources of labour. While Ireland once again supplied such labour, the countries of north-west Europe were unable to do so, and attention turned to a variety of refugee and displaced populations. These included, for example, members of the Polish Army that had fled to Britain during the war, and male and female refugees from various central and eastern European countries who were living in British-maintained refugee camps in Germany and Austria. The latter constituted the source for the European Volunteer Worker Scheme which was set up by the post-war Labour government (Kay and Miles, 1992).

But while considerable energy was invested in a variety of labour recruitment schemes orientated towards aliens from Europe, a small number of (mainly male) migrants from the Caribbean arrived in Britain largely as the result of their own initiative. These included men who had worked in Britain or had served in the British armed forces during the Second World War. In common with the population of all British colonies and of those ex-colonies that gained political independence but became members of the British Commonwealth, citizens of the British islands in the Caribbean were legally British subjects. As such, they had the right to enter, live and work in Britain. Yet, despite the existing labour shortage, there was considerable panic within the British state concerning their arrival and a secret Cabinet committee was set up in 1950 to investigate the possibility of controlling the entry of 'coloured people' into Britain. The underlying concern was that such immigration would create a 'race relations' problem in Britain. While no legislation was passed at this point in time, a variety of administrative and bureaucratic devices were used to limit the migration not only from the Caribbean but also from India and Pakistan (Miles and Phizacklea, 1984).

Migration from the Caribbean and the Indian sub-continent continued throughout the 1950s, encouraged by British employers, including the National Health Service and London Transport. The evidence shows that this migration was shaped by the level of labour demand in the British economy (Peach, 1968), and facilitated not only by the legal status of the migrants as British subjects but also by the relatively poor economic circumstances in the countries of origin. The resulting settlement in the major urban conurbations of England, and to a much lesser extent Wales and Scotland, provoked an increasingly active and hostile political response as the decade proceeded, stimulated by racism and by conflicts over access to housing and welfare benefits. A small number of politicians, as well as right-wing groups of various kinds, played an active role in this process, alongside, in some instances, members of the trade union movement.

By the early 1960s, 'immigration' had become defined as a national problem requiring political action: the claim was that 'immigration' had created a 'race relations' problem in Britain which could be solved only by the introduction of controls (Miles and Phizacklea, 1984). In practice, what was being demanded was a discriminatory system of control. The discourse of 'race relations' entailed a coded reference to 'coloured immigrants', with the result that the demand was not for immigration control in general (and anyway there was already a system of control in place to regulate the entry of aliens into Britain) but rather for control over the entry of British citizens from the Caribbean and the Indian sub-continent. Thus, when legislation was passed in 1962, it specifically excluded from its terms of reference citizens of the Irish Republic who had retained the right of entry into Britain since 1945. Further legislation, accompanied by administrative action, followed during the 1960s, the most important being the Commonwealth Immigrants Act 1968. Its objective was simultaneously to remove the right of entry into Britain of UK passport holders who did not also have a parent or grandparent born in Britain while ensuring that citizens of independent Commonwealth states such as Canada, Australia and New Zealand who did have a parent or grandparent born in Britain retained the right of entry.

The legislation of the 1960s was consolidated and further 'rationalized' by the 1971 Immigration Act. It also anticipated the consequences of Britain's entry into what has since become the European Union. British entry meant that citizens of other member states had the right to live and work in Britain, and this entailed removing the restrictions that applied to citizens of the relevant European nation states (other than the Republic of Ireland) who, in terms of British law, were aliens. Put another way, while the 1971 Act reinforced the controls over 'coloured' British citizens, it also removed controls over the entry of citizens of France, Germany, the Netherlands and so on. The racialized preference for European and 'white' immigration was therefore reinforced. Yet, while legislation by the late 1960s had effectively ended the entry of 'coloured people' seeking work, the spouses and children of earlier migrants from the Caribbean and the Indian sub-continent had not been formally banned from joining family members now effectively settled in Britain. This continuing migration flow became the object of political agitation during the 1970s and 80s which was expressed in very similar terms to those that dominated the agitation during the 1960s (for example the idea that 'immigration control is necessary to maintain good race relations'). As a result, the 'immigration problem' remained high on the political agenda, and further restrictions were imposed on this particular group of migrants with the intention of limiting the categories of people eligible to enter Britain, and discouraging by a variety of bureaucratic mechanisms the arrival of those who retained the right.

During the 1980s the old theme was given a new dimension as a result of the increasing flow of refugees into Europe caused by a variety of political and economic crises in Africa and the Indian sub-continent (Joly and Cohen, 1989). Individuals seeking asylum have a particular status in international law, mirroring a parallel status in humanitarian considerations. But the latter was not recognized in the reaction of the British state. Rather, those entering Britain seeking refugee status were identified as yet another group of 'coloured immigrants' who, in this instance, were pretending to be refugees but who were 'really' 'economic migrants'. They were therefore identified as being guilty of subterfuge, their presence denoting illegality: the language of 'bogus refugee' came to be widely used. A variety of legal and administrative changes (including the withdrawal of all forms of social security in certain circumstances) in the early 1990s were intended actively to discourage those seeking asylum from entering Britain.

During the 1980s, the British state's continued identification of 'strict immigration control' as a major political priority meshed with a wider debate about immigration and immigration control within the European Union. In accordance with the principles embodied in the Treaty of Rome (1957), some member states of the European Union sought to remove the existing restrictions on the movement of people across the internal borders of the EU in order to ensure that people moved as freely as capital and commodities. This proved difficult to achieve within the political structures of the EU, with the result that the states committed to this objective initiated negotiations between themselves following an initial meeting at the small town of Schengen. The so-called Schengen group eventually negotiated the Schengen Treaty in 1990, to which a majority of EU member states are now signatories, although effective implementation of the commitments remains uneven (Miles and Thranhardt, 1995).

The central objectives of the Treaty are to remove all controls on the movement of people across the internal borders of the signatory states, to increase the controls on movement across their external borders, and to increase surveillance to identify illegal migrants within the territories of the signatory states. This initiative has been widely described as the creation of a 'Fortress Europe' (Sivanandan, 1990), a description that is not entirely appropriate (Miles, 1993: 194–216). British governments have been consistent in their opposition to the Schengen group and its objectives, claiming that it is essential to sustain 'strict immigration controls', even on its borders with other EU member states. Thus, the intensely racialized debate in Britain about the need for 'strict immigration control' has been reinforced by the need to take a position with respect to this particular dimension of the evolution of European integration, ensuring that the issue of immigration remains high on the political agenda.

# Conclusion

It has been argued in this chapter that the usual starting point for an analysis of 'race relations' is seriously flawed, because it starts with a set of 'common-sense' ideas and beliefs about 'race'and 'immigration' which cannot withstand close scrutiny. Hence, it has been suggested that the language, concepts and theories used in debates of 'race relations' should be questioned rigorously and that there is no place in sociological analysis for the use of the idea of 'race' as an analytical concept. Such an approach will lead to a more complex analysis of the structures, processes and ideologies in play in what are popularly called 'race relations' situations and, in particular, to an understanding of the relationships between those variables which appear to be explicitly 'racialized' (for example racist beliefs, prejudice, cultural differences) and others which appear to have no explicit racialized content (for example, economics, politics and power relations). This mode of analysis will help us understand the motivations and benefits of the key institutions involved in shaping patterns of racialized social relationships, as well as private employers, and the media.

In a world of increasing interdependence and competition – and a dizzying array of factors that shape racialized and ethnic relations – international factors can only become more important. While 'race relations' are experienced, interpreted and often described at the local level, the latter is increasingly being shaped by national and especially international factors. However, while it is indispensable to have an understanding of the historical unfolding of these processes, it has been argued here that the legacy of the earlier conceptual framework of 'race relations'should be transcended. Rather than seeking to understand 'race relations' it is better to conceptualize social relations which have been racialized, and to understand the factors that shape such processes locally, nationally and globally.

# Further Reading

Anthias, F. and Yuval-Davis, N. *Racialized Boundaries,* London, Routledge, 1992. A good example of the use of the racialization framework to analyse the interrelationship between different modes of exclusion.

Brah, A. *Cartographies of Diaspora, Contesting Identities,* London and New York, Routledge, 1996. An excellent example of a recent attempt to draw upon postmodern themes and preoccupations to analyse racism and ethnic relations in Britain.

Miles, R. *Racism After 'Race Relations',* London, Routledge, 1993. A series of essays which explore the way in which the concept of racism can be used to analyse British and European history.

Small, S. *Racialised Barriers: The Black Experience in the United States and England,* New York and London, Routledge, 1994. A comparative analysis of experiences of racism.

# 8

# Families, Households and Domestic Life

*Stevi Jackson*

While families seem to be a taken-for-granted part of everyday life for most people, the change and diversity of patterns of domestic life in contemporary societies has resulted in the concept of 'the family' being called into question by some sociologists. This chapter aims to examine contemporary debates about the 'family' and domestic life. While the sociology of class examines inequalities between families, sociological studies of families and households are also interested in inequalities within them. Like the sociology of gender relations, contemporary studies of family are strongly influenced by feminist theories; the influence of families also plays an important part in other areas of sociological research, such as education, work, deviance and health. This chapter should help you understand:

■ The changing, and increasingly critical, orientation of the sociology of the family and domestic life

■ Challenges to the concept of the family

■ Inequalities within families generated by the economics of domestic life

■ Sociological interpretations of marriage, parenthood and childhood

---

**CONCEPTS**

nuclear family ■ symmetrical family ■ household ■ marriage
domestic labour ■ domestic violence ■ childhood

---

# Introduction

From the standpoint of everyday life families are taken for granted as part of the social landscape. After all, most of us have direct experience of family relationships and have spent at least part of our lives living with those we count as 'family'. Yet 'the family' is also the focus of a great deal of public concern and political debate, frequently represented as a cherished but endangered institution, threatened by changes in the moral climate, high rates of divorce and single parenthood. Here, as elsewhere, sociology fosters a degree of scepticism about commonsense views of the world and offers fresh insights into public issues. Sometimes the questions sociologists raise are disquieting, for they invite us to look critically at valued personal relationships; to consider, for example, sources of power and inequality within families. We might ask whether the popular image of the 'normal family' corresponds with empirical reality: indeed the concept of 'the family' itself is now being called into question, and there is an increasing tendency to talk of households or families rather than 'the family' in the singular.

Some of the difficulties presented by the concept of 'the family' are obvious once we reflect on the multiple meanings which the term has in our everyday language. When someone says that they like 'all the family' to sit down together for the main meal of the day, they usually mean those family members who live together. When we say that 'the whole family' attended a wedding or funeral, usually this implies a wider group of relatives – uncles, aunts, cousins and so on. When we say that a treasured possession has been 'in the family' for generations we are speaking of the family through time, tracing relationships back to our forebears. When a couple talk of 'starting a family' they usually mean having children, implying that a couple on their own are not a family, but with children they become one. We also recognize different types of families such as lone parent or lesbian and gay families – but the two parent, heterosexual family remains the dominant, normative ideal.

While the meaning of 'family' varies, this does not usually cause us problems in our daily lives; we usually understand what is meant from the context in which the word is used. Sociologists, however, have developed a more precise vocabulary to define different senses of the lay concept of 'family' or to describe different family forms. The term *kin* is used to mean relatives and *kinship* is usually thought of in terms of networks of people related to each other. Those who can trace their descent back to a common ancestor collectively form a *lineage*. A heterosexual couple with children is a *nuclear* or *conjugal* family while an *extended family* includes additional kin. Those who live together and in some way recognize their home as a shared space entailing some degree of collective responsibility and housekeeping are a *household*. Family members who live together constitute a household as well as a family, but not all households are based on families.

The existence of this sociological lexicon does not entirely dispel the ambiguity surrounding the concept of 'the family' itself; it remains a protean term covering a complex array of relationships and practices. This ambiguity goes some way towards explaining why many sociologists are wary of the concept of 'the family'. However, recent challenges to the concept are more fundamental, a result of radical shifts in sociological perspectives on family life over the last three decades of the twentieth century. During this period there have been changes in the way family life is lived, and also in the way sociologists conceptualize it. There is no longer a clearly defined field of study describable as 'the sociology of the family', despite continued socio-logical interest in family relationships and domestic life. In what follows, I shall consider how the old sociological certainties about the family came to be undermined before evaluating the current debate about 'the family'. Data about changing patterns of family life will be introduced along the way. I shall then examine aspects of current research and thinking on families and households in more detail, concentrating on economic relationships, marriage, parenthood and childhood.

## Whatever Happened to the Sociology of the Family?

During the 1950s and 60s, sociologists assumed that the family was a key social institution, a fundamental element of social structure. It was taken, for example, as the basic unit of stratification in studies of class and social mobility, as a central agency of socialization, and as a mechanism by which individuals were integrated into wider ties of community and society. Until the early 1970s, at least in the USA, the dominant perspective on the family was functionalism, associated in particular with the work of Parsons. While some of these theorists argued that the family performed similar functions in all societies and throughout history, Parsons was more interested in demon-strating that the nuclear family was functional for advanced industrial society (Parsons and Bales, 1956).

According to Parsons, the modern family has shed some functions – such as productive work – and become more specialized, concentrating on the socialization of children and the 'stabilization of adult personalities'. The nuclear family had also become relatively isolated from wider kinship ties, thus adapting to the instrumental (pragmatic and goal-orientated) ethos of industrial society, with its emphasis on individual achievement. These values conflict with the 'affective' (emotional) bonds, and more collective orienta-tion which govern relations among kin. The potential strain between these two sets of values is minimized by loosening wider kin ties and by a special-ization of functions within families: husbands, who work in the outside world, take on instrumental roles while wives, who stay at home, specialize in affective roles.

This picture of emotional housebound women and rational male bread-winners now looks hopelessly sexist and outmoded, but Parsons' analysis may be more understandable in its historical context. In the period following the Second World War there had been a reassertion of women's supposedly 'traditional' domestic role. Most women gave up paid work to rear children and, since this was a time of full employment, most married men expected to earn enough to support their families. Even then, however, not all families conformed to the model. What Parsons was describing was the white middle-class suburban family. Other forms of family tended to be ignored or dismissed as deviant 'problem families'. Yet there were already changes taking place. In particular, in many western countries the proportion of married women in the labour market was increasing, despite the ideal of domesticated femininity. For example, British women's labour force participation rates rose from 21.74 per cent in 1951 to 38.8 per cent in 1966. A few sociologists began to pay attention to women's dual commitments to home and employment (see Myrdal and Klein, 1956), but such issues remained peripheral to the sociology of the family.

British sociologists were often sceptical of the functionalist orthodoxy and inclined towards empirical studies, often locating families within wider communities (see Morgan, 1996). Yet even here the issues studied sometimes related to the Parsonian agenda, such as research on the relative isolation of the nuclear family and the degree to which wider kin networks were maintained (Young and Wilmott, 1962; Bott, 1971). Although there was some discussion about the extent to which patterns of family life were class related, it was widely assumed that there was a trend towards looser kin ties and a more privatized style of family life accompanied by more egalitarian, companionate marital relationships. This, according to Young and Wilmott (1973), heralded the arrival of the symmetrical family. While inequalities between husbands and wives were recognized in some studies, it was assumed that they were disappearing.

The idea of egalitarian marriage also featured in one of the major American challenges to functionalism in this period. Berger and Kellner (1964) argued, from a phenomenological perspective, that rather than marital roles being pre-defined, marriage was an arena in which individuals could construct their own social reality. They suggested that husbands and wives experience their marriage as their joint creation in which they inhabit 'a fully shared world of meaning' (1964, 1971: 18). Where Parsons had at least recognized that women's experience of family life differed from that of men, Berger and Kellner theorized any such differences out of existence. What they shared with functionalism, and with British empirical sociologists, was an assumption that marriage and the family 'worked'. The picture of family life painted by most sociologists prior to 1970 was a rosy one.

## Challenges for the Sociology of the Family

By the 1960s, however, there were already dissident voices. In the USA the feminist writer Friedan (1965) identified 'the problem with no name': the discontent of suburban housewives, the boredom and emptiness of their lives. Komarovsky's (1962) study of blue-collar couples revealed divergences between husbands' and wives' expectations and experiences, with many wives unhappy with the lack of emotional intimacy and companionship in their marriages. In Britain, Gavron (1966) considered the plight of 'the captive wife', trapped into social isolation by her domestic and maternal responsibilities. Studies such as these presaged the sustained feminist critique of the family which was to emerge in the 1970s. By the time Bernard published *The Future of Marriage* in 1972, there was sufficient evidence for her to argue that in any marital union there were two marriages – 'his' and 'hers' and that his was considerably better than hers.

Feminist research and theory was to have a major impact on the way in which sociologists thought about family life, but others were also contributing to the critique. Far from being a cosy domestic haven, the privatized nuclear family was seen as stultifying and damaging. In his 1967 Reith Lecture, Leach announced that 'the family with its petty privacy and tawdry secrets is the source of all our discontents'. Anti-psychiatrists such as Laing (1971) saw the close confines of the family life as giving rise to highly charged, disturbed and disturbing interpersonal relationships. Marxists saw the retreat to the family as symptomatic of the alienation characteristic of capitalist society, and argued that the family could not possibly satisfy all our emotional and social needs (Zaretsky, 1976).

Most of these critics still took it for granted that the typical modern family was the isolated nuclear family. It was widely believed that extended families had been the normal living arrangement prior to industrialization, an assumption which underpinned the idea of a functional fit between industrial society (or, for Marxists, capitalism) and the nuclear family. In the 1970s and 80s new historical research began to cast doubt on this assumption, revealing that households based on extended families had not been common in pre-industrial western Europe. This does not mean, however, that nothing changed as a result of the rise of industrial capitalism. It has become clear that the history of family life is much more complex than was once thought (see Anderson, 1980).

The meaning of the 'family' has itself changed – for much of our pre-industrial history it was used to refer to all those living under one roof under the authority of the head of household, whether or not they were related. Most productive work, prior to the rise of industrial capitalism, was centred on such 'families' engaged in farming or craft production. Men, women and children all contributed to household production. Families often contained unrelated employees (known as 'servants'), usually young people. These servants worked, lived and ate alongside other family members. Households varied greatly in size – more prosperous families with many servants could be very large, while the poorest were small. Demographic factors, such as the prevalence of remarriage after all too common widowhood, also produced diversity in family forms. Moreover, historians became aware of the ways in which household composition varied as a result of local economic conditions and changed over the life course. Surveying these data, Anderson (1980) concluded that there has never been a single family form in western society.

Historians also began to think of family members as participants in economic and social processes, engaged in the active pursuit of strategies which enabled them to survive in changing times. Hence it became possible to think of family organization having an effect on social change rather than simply being affected by it. Feminists, and those influenced by them, suggested that pre-existing patriarchal relations helped shape the form of industrial capitalism – as did the tactics men used to retain their privileges under changed conditions (Hartmann, 1976; Walby, 1986). Older forms of patriarchal control based on control of family production and labour were eroded, but were ultimately replaced by new forms based on the ideal of the male breadwinner and dependent, domesticated wife.

Industrialization created a split between family life and commercial enterprise. Among the bourgeoisie in the early nineteenth century women withdrew from active participation in the family business and a new 'domestic ideology' defined the home as women's 'natural' sphere (Hall, 1992). A version of this ideology was subsequently adopted by sections of the working class who fought to establish the principle of the male breadwinner earning a family wage (Walby, 1986; Jackson, 1992). However, women were never entirely excluded from paid work and the direction and pace of change was uneven, with class and regional variations in the organization of domestic life. Nonetheless there were patterns beneath these variations, in particular persistent inequalities between men and women.

Such inequalities also emerged in research on contemporary families as sociologists began to pay more attention to what went on within families. As new critical perspectives emerged, sociologists found themselves investigating an institution which was itself changing. The increasing participation of married women in the labour market, along with much higher rates of unemployment than were prevalent in the 1950s and 60s, has eroded the norm of families dependent on a sole, male breadwinner. Over 70 per cent of all women of working age were economically active in 1996, including about half of those with pre-school children. The isolated housewife is now much rarer than the woman struggling to cope with the double shift of paid and domestic work. Moreover, perhaps because of these changing employment patterns, people are now marrying and having children later than they did two or three decades ago.

From the early 1950s until the early 1970s there was a trend towards early marriage and parenthood; since then, this trend has been reversed. In 1971, 87 per cent of British women were married before they were 30 and the median age of marriage for women was 21.4; 78.5 per cent of babies born in that year had mothers under 30 (figures from Coleman, 1988; Kiernan and Wicks, 1990; Central Statistical Office, 1993). By 1994 the average age at first marriage was 28 for men and 25.8 for women. More women now delay childbearing until they are in their thirties and more are apparently choosing not to have children. Cohabitation prior to or instead of formal marriage has become common: between 1981 and 1995 the proportion of women under 50 cohabiting doubled to 9 per cent of all women and 25 per cent of non-married women. Divorce rates rose swiftly in the 1970s, and subsequently more slowly, stabilizing at rates much higher than those of the 1950s and 60s Whereas there were only 2 divorces per 1,000 of the married population in 1961, there were over 13 in 1995. On current trends as many as two in five marriages are likely to end in divorce. High rates of divorce have swelled the ranks of one parent families – and also step-families, since most of those who divorce subsequently remarry or cohabit. Moreover, more children are now born to unmarried parents, over one-third in 1995. As a result of these trends, 20 per cent of children live with a lone parent and a further 7.9 per cent live in step families (figures from Office for National Statistics, 1997). While these figures are British, the trends they record are not specific to any one country, but are observable in most other contemporary societies.

One effect of all these changes has been to increase the variability of family forms. Britain has also become ethnically more heterogeneous and patterns of family life differ from one ethnic group to another. The diversity of family life has become a central issue in sociological analysis, and a major basis for problematizing the concept of 'the family'. In the next section I will explain why 'the family' has been called into question and consider whether these doubts are sufficient to justify the abandonment of the idea of the family as a social institution.

## The Trouble with 'the Family'

Since the 1980s, many sociologists have suggested that the 'the family' is a term which represents an abstract idea, an ideological construct, rather than the way people actually live (Barrett and McIntosh, 1982; Bernardes, 1997). Some wish to retain the concept of the family (see, for example Delphy and Leonard, 1992), but even those who still define the family as an institution nonetheless conceptualize it very differently from earlier generations of sociologists. Three main objections to 'the family' have been raised:

- the term is essentialist, as it presupposes an essential basic unit discernible in all cultures at all times
- it treats as a unity something which is in fact internally differentiated, thus concealing inequalities within it
- it masks the diversity of family forms existing in society today.

I will deal with each of these in turn, but it is the third of these – diversity – which is most often taken to signal the demise of the family as a useful conceptual tool.

## The Charge of Essentialism

If used incautiously, especially in cross-cultural and historical analysis, the term 'the family' can imply a universal phenomenon. Asking whether the family is universal or, how it has changed since pre-industrial times, effectively decides the issue in advance: that even if it varies in form there is still some essential entity identifiable as the family which exists across time and in all societies. The commonly used terms 'nuclear' and 'extended' family also suggest a basic nucleus which is, under some circumstances, extended to a wider orbit of kin. This essentialist view has often entailed treating 'the family' as a clearly bounded unit set apart from wider society, something which is affected by differing or changing social structures but which has no effects beyond its own boundaries. This is why sociologists in the past talked of the effects of industrialization on 'the family' without considering that family relations might affect wider social relations.

As we have seen, the term 'family' has not had the same meaning throughout history; household and family relations have not always intersected in the ways they do today. Cross-culturally, there is even greater variability. Anthropological evidence suggests that here is no simple, single entity that can be defined as 'the family' and compared across cultures. What we are dealing with is not a fixed structure but a complex set of relationships and practices – who counts as kin, who lives with whom, who can or should marry whom, who should perform which activities inside the domestic unit – all of which vary cross-culturally (see, for example Edholm, 1982; Harris, 1990). This suggests that the concept of 'the family' as we understand it is historically and culturally specific and should be used, if at all, only in the context of contemporary society.

## Differences within Families

If families are constituted through a complex of relationships and practices, it follows that individuals are differently located within families and not all members of the same family experience it in the same way. In particular, families are differentiated by gender and generation. The term 'the family' can often mask these differences. We should not, for example, speak of the effects of poverty on 'the family', without considering that these effects might not be felt equally by all family members family. Nor should we assume that 'the family' or even 'a family' acts collectively. Even when family members do something together, they may not be engaged in exactly the same activities in precisely the same ways. To take one example, Morley's (1986) study of families watching television revealed distinct gender differences in viewing practices. Men generally controlled the remote control device and gave the television their full attention while women often combined viewing with domestic chores, such as ironing. This example suggests that work and leisure are unequally distributed within families and that families are also sites of power relations: Morley sees the remote control device as a symbol of power, rather like a medieval mace, which sits 'on the arm of Daddy's chair' (Morley, 1986: 148).

Differences within families, however, do not provide grounds for denying that the family is an institution. After all, most social institutions are internally differentiated. Moreover, we are not dealing here with accidental differences, but with regular, patterned gender and generational hierarchies, as will become clear later in the chapter. Family relationships appear to be structured, institutionalized relationships despite the diversity of domestic arrangements existing in society today.

## The Problem of Diversity

It is certainly the case that the abstract idea of 'the family' does not correspond with the lived reality of family life. In one sense 'the family' is an ideological construct, and one with considerable emotional appeal – which is why it is often invoked by politicians to win us to their cause and by advertisers to encourage us to buy their products. Clearly the advertiser's image of comfortable, middle-class, two parent, two child families does not reflect reality. But this ideal does have real effects; it encourages to look to the family to meet our personal, social and emotional needs; it serves as a perpetual excuse for the paucity of public services; it encourages us to blame ourselves or our partners if our own family life does not live up to expectations. In a sense, then, this representation of 'the family' is 'anti-social' (Barrett and McIntosh, 1982).

Moreover, the popular image of the family is an ethnocentric one, based on 'white' families, which obscures ethnic differences in patterns of family life. Such differences have long been evident in countries such as the USA and are are now coming to be recognized as an important source of family diversity in Britain. Here South Asian households are more likely to contain more than one family with children than either Afro-Caribbean or white households. However, the proportion of nuclear family households among South Asians is also high – more than double that found among the white population. African-Caribbean women are more likely to head single parent households than white or South Asian women. In 1989–91, nearly half Afro-Caribbean mothers were lone mothers, compared with around 15 per cent of 'white' mothers and less than 10 per cent of those of South Asian descent (Central Statistical Office, 1993, 1994, 1995). Conceptualizing 'the family' from a 'white' perspective can easily lead to a failure to appreciate cultural differences and to branding 'black' families as deviant.

The main reason for the disjunction between the ideal of 'the family' and lived experience, or so it is argued, is that there is no normal or typical family but rather a diverse and shifting array of different forms of household (Barrett and McIntosh, 1982; Bernardes, 1997). The most telling evidence for this point of view is that only a minority of households today are inhabited by nuclear families of two parents and dependent children, and the proportion of such households is declining. In 1996 such households comprised only 23 per cent of all British households and accounted for 40 per cent of the total population (Office for National Statistics, 1997). These figures might suggest that the family is in terminal decline and is becoming a minority lifestyle. But is it?

Such a view can only be sustained if we view this statistical snap-shot as the full picture and if we define the family in very narrow terms. Families are not static entities, but dynamic ones, changing over the life course as people marry, rear children and see their children leave home – or as couples divorce or remarry or one of them dies. Even if there were no divorce or untimely death, each individual would live in a nuclear family only at certain stages of the life course. Most households are, in fact, based on family ties, on marriage or parenthood: in 1996, 70 per cent of all households, contained 85 per cent of the population (Office for National Statistics, 1997). Most of the remaining 30 per cent of households are accounted for by people living alone; over half of these individuals are over the age of retirement, and most of them will at one time have married and reared children. The 13 per cent of households inhabited by single people under retirement age are a much more mixed group. They will include those who have chosen a single life and those who are single by default, young people who will marry and have children in the future and older people who have married and parented at some stage in their lives. Only 2 per cent of households are lived in by two or more unrelated adults, and again their composition is very diverse. They might include, for example, lesbian or gay couples, those who choose a communal way of life and young people flat-sharing as a relatively transitory arrangement.

Looked at this way, we gain a rather different picture of family life: it is certainly shifting and dynamic, but most of the population live in households based on family relationships for much of their lives. Moreover, if we look only at households, we forget that family ties persist after family households have broken up. For example, my mother, my sister and I all live in separate households in different cities, but we still count each other as family. We should not conflate families with family-based households: significant family relationships, carrying with them all manner of social expectations and oblig- ations, exist across the boundaries of households as well as within them (Finch and Mason, 1993). Nuclear family households may be a minority, but most of us have families.

Focusing only on households rather than families can be used to downplay the importance of family relationships. Delphy and Leonard argue that this strategy gives the misleading impression that 'households are only sometimes, contingently, or as a matter of choice, based on family relationships' (1992: 5). The idea of family diversity thus conceals the regularities of family life and can also divert attention from the structural inequalities, the hierarchies of gender and generation within families. Even if we are wary of the concept of 'the family' *per se*, it must be accepted that the most crucial elements of family life, the bonds of marriage and parenthood are *institutionalized* through social expectations and legal regulation.

These debates around the concept of the family have made sociologists much more aware of the complexity of family life, of the interplay between family, household and kinship networks. Sociologists have become much more sensitive to differentiation and inequality within families. Morgan uses the apt analogy of the kaleidoscope to capture this complexity:

> With one turn we see a blending of the distinctions between home and work, family and economy, and the idea of the household comes into focus. With another turn, the apparently solid boundaries of the household dissolve and we see family and kinship, and possibly other, relationships spreading out across these fainter bound- aries. With each twist of the kaleidoscope we see that these patterns are differently coloured according to gender, age and generation and other social divisions. (Morgan, 1996: 33)

The effect of this can be dizzying, and also makes it difficult, if not impos- sible, to summarize the full range of sociological work on family life. In order to simplify matters I will concentrate here on the key relationships through which families are constituted: those between husbands and wives and between parents and children. I will start, however, with the economics of domestic life – an area once largely ignored by sociologists but which is now recognized as vitally important.

# The Economics of Domestic Life

Family ties entail economic co-operation, support and dependency, but also inequality and exploitation. Economic obligations often extend beyond family-based households and include wider kin, but here, and for the remainder of the chapter, I shall concentrate on family-based households, those founded on heterosexual couples and/or parent–child relationships. In exploring these economic relations I begin by looking at the income coming into families and how it is allocated.

Most married women now have paid work, although there are ethnic differences here: in Britain 71.9 per cent of 'white' women were defined as economically active in 1993, compared with 66 per cent of women of African and African Caribbean descent, 61.4 per cent of those of Indian descent and 24.8 per cent of those of Pakistani or Bangladeshi descent (Central Statistical Office, 1995). For most women, total dependence on a male worker is now unusual and women's earnings make a vital contribution to household finances. However, women's jobs are generally lower paid than men's, and many women, especially those with young children, are employed part time. Because men usually earn 'full' wages while women often earn only a 'component wage', one insufficient to run a household, most married women are at least partly financially dependent on their husbands (Siltanen, 1994). A number of studies have found that even where women make a substantial contribution to household income, the importance of their earnings may be played down so that the man is still defined as *the* breadwinner. Women's wages, however essential, are often seen as covering 'extras' (Mansfield and Collard, 1988; Pahl, 1989; Brannen and Moss, 1991).

Recent research has challenged the assumption that families are units in which all resources are distributed equally (Brannen and Wilson, 1987; Jackson and Moores, 1995). There is growing evidence that 'while sharing a common address, family members do not necessarily share a common standard of living' (Graham, 1987a: 221). Since husbands generally earn more than their wives, they tend to have more power over the disposal of family income – although the degree to which men exercise direct control over domestic expenditure varies depending on the strategy couples adopt for apportioning money. Whether women control the bulk of domestic finances, have housekeeping allowances, draw from a common pool, or cover certain costs from their own wages, they usually spend little on themselves. Men, by the same token, almost always have greater access to personal spending money. The 'extras' women spend their earnings on are usually for their children or the family as a whole rather than for themselves. Hence women often contribute a higher proportion of their wages to housekeeping than do men (Pahl, 1989).

During the 1980s researchers in the UK uncovered considerable evidence of hidden poverty in families dependent on men. One telling indicator of this is that some studies found that a substantial proportion, sometimes as many as half, of previously married single mothers felt that they were as well off or better off financially than they were when with their partners (Graham, 1987a). This is surprising given that, during this period, two out of three lone mothers lived on state benefits and that households headed by lone mothers were three times more likely to be poor than two parent households. It was not only men's spending on personal consumption that accounted for this, but also the greater degree of control lone mothers had over the total family budget. They could plan their expenditure, decide their priorities and make economies in the interests of their children and themselves without having to take a man's desires and demands into account. In part this represented a freedom to go without, since women were often prepared to make personal sacrifices in order to provide more for their children, but lone mothers sometimes found that exercising their own preferences led to a more economical lifestyle (Graham, 1987).

The domestic distribution of money is unlikely to have changed substantially in the 1990s and serves to demonstrate a more general point, backed by a range of research, that consumption within families rarely takes place on the basis of fair shares for all (see Jackson and Moores, 1995). The same can also be said of patterns of work and leisure. Families are often seen as sites of leisure but, for women, home is also a place of work.

## Work within Families

Men's participation in routine housework has increased slightly since the early 1980s but, as we saw in Chapter 6 on gender relations, women still carry most of the burden of domestic labour, whether or not they are in waged work. Men may help more around the house, but the domestic division of labour in both Britain and the USA remains largely unaltered (Mansfield and Collard, 1988; Hochschild, 1989; Brannen and Moss, 1991). Women have less free time than men and are more likely to spend it at home so that they are constantly 'on call' even when not actually working, resulting in fragmented, interrupted periods of leisure (Chambers, 1986; Sullivan, 1997). Men have greater freedom to enjoy leisure since they do not have to consider who is taking care of the children or whether there are clean clothes ready for the next day. Someone else is doing the work and taking the responsibility.

It is only since the 1970s, as a result of feminist critique, that sociologists began to take housework seriously and to investigate women's experience of it. British studies carried out in the 1970s and 80s revealed that women's feelings about housework were profoundly ambivalent. Women commonly expressed dissatisfaction with this work, finding it monotonous, repetitive, isolating, tiring and never-ending. They were often well aware that they carried an unfair burden, especially when they also had paid jobs. However, in stating these grievances, women usually stopped short of an overall critique of their situation; they rarely dismissed housework as a whole as unrewarding, and were even less likely to challenge the sexual division of labour which made housework their responsibility (Oakley, 1984; Westwood, 1984). The work itself may be the focus of declared dissatisfactions, but women value the ideals of caring for others and creating a home. In her study of women factory workers, Westwood heard all the usual complaints about housework. Yet the women also saw it as 'their *proper* work' which was invested with meaning and status because it was 'work done for love' which demonstrated their commitment to their families. Thus boring, routine work was 'transformed into satisfying, caring work' (Westwood, 1984: 170).

It has been suggested that only 'white' middle-class women dislike housework. The research I have cited shows that there is little class difference in women's feelings about the work itself and, in the case of Westwood's research, little difference between 'white' and Asian women. Thorogood (1987) found a high degree of dissatisfaction with domestic chores among Afro-Caribbean women, and those of them living independently of men felt a major advantage of this arrangement was that it reduced the amount of housework they had to do. More recently, Brah found that many young Pakistani women in Birmingham (both married and single) felt over-burdened with domestic work. As wives or daughters they were often caring for large households which, because of poverty, lacked the domestic appliances more privileged women take for granted (Brah, 1994). While 'black' women may find family life a welcome refuge from a racist society (Collins, 1990), this does not mean that they escape from an inequitable division of domestic labour or that they like housework itself any more than 'white' women.

Housework has also been the object of much theoretical interest, especially in the 1970s. Marxists and Marxist feminists were primarily interested in the contribution housework made to capitalism through the reproduction of labour power – servicing the existing labour force and rearing the next generation of workers. A major limitation of this approach was that it concentrated on the contribution of domestic labour to capitalism and did not consider the extent to which men benefit from it. Other theorists, notably Delphy and Leonard (1992) and Walby (1986) have argued that housework takes place within patriarchal relations in which men exploit women's labour. Marxist feminists objected to the idea that men benefited sufficiently from women's work to justify the term exploitation (see, for example Barrett, 1980). More recently, however, some neo-Marxists have argued that household labour does involve exploitative relations (see Gibson-Graham, 1996). The empirical evidence suggests that men gain a great deal from women's household labour. Men do not simply evade their share of housework, they have their share done for them.

Most recent work on the distribution of domestic labour is less concerned with grand theory and more focused on specific situations and the effects of changes and variations in working practices. There is less emphasis on women's experience of housework *per se* and more on the continued inequities imposed by the 'double shift' (Hochschild, 1989; Brannen and Moss, 1991). Among the well-paid professional classes, women's increased labour market participation has led to the re-emergence of paid domestic labour, the employment of nannies and cleaners (Gregson and Lowe, 1994). Some attention has also been paid to those who are in some way resisting male-dominated patterns of domestic organisation. In a study of heterosexuals committed to anti-sexist living arrangements, Van Every (1995) found that the traditional division of labour was avoided in a number of ways: individuals doing chores such as washing and ironing only for themselves; sharing cooking and cleaning; buying in domestic help or services. The strategies used, however, were constrained by income, by the differential earning capacities of men and women, and also by the expectations of others outside the household. There has also been a little research on lesbian and gay couples and families suggesting a more equitable division of labour than is typical in heterosexual partnerships (Dunne, 1997; Heaphy *et al.*, 1997).

Work within families is not always confined to domestic labour. Small businesses are now part of the social landscape and are often based on families. There is a particularly strong tradition of family-based enterprise among Asian communities in Britain. Of those in employment in 1994 over 20 per cent of Pakistani and Bangladeshi people and around 18 per cent of Indian people are self-employed, and most of these are men (Central Statistical Office, 1995). Here family obligations can mean wives and daughters working for little or no remuneration within family enterprises (Westwood and Bhachu, 1988; Afshar, 1989). This is not a situation peculiar to Asian women. In general, the wives of self-employed men, from plumbers to accountants, may provide free labour to their husbands' businesses – and three-quarters of the self-employed are men.

There are also grey areas where housework shades into work connected to a husband's business or employment such as entertaining his colleagues or clients and taking telephone messages. A woman may thus find herself married to her husband's job (Finch, 1983). Since patterns of paid work affect the performance of unpaid domestic work, another area of investigation is the practice of homeworking. Twenty-nine per cent of employed men and 24 per cent of employed women work from home at least some of the time (Office for National Statistics, 1997). For women homeworking is usually poorly paid and is a means of combining domestic responsibilities with earning a small wage (Phizacklea and Wolkowitz, 1995). Men who work at home are often in professional and managerial occupations and it seems unlikely that they are taking on extra housework as a result. Given Finch's (1983) observations on the ways in which men call on their wives' labour in carrying out their paid work, it is more probable that these male homeworkers are increasing their wives' workload. However, this has yet to be researched.

## Children as Economic Actors

Research on the economics of family life has generally focused on husbands and wives, but it has recently been recognized that children and young people are also economic actors located within family divisions of labour. Children may perform domestic labour (Brannen, 1995), help out in family businesses (Song, 1966) or be earning their own pocket money outside the home (Morrow, 1994). However, the situation of most children is that of economic dependants within families. As such, they have things bought for them rather than buying them for themselves and exercise consumer choice only if their parents allow them to. Gifts of money and pocket money are given at adults' discretion and adults may seek to influence how it is spent. Adult-mediated consumption is one facet of parents' power over children (Leonard, 1990). Hence independent employment can be attractive to children themselves, although often seen as a problem by adult society. I shall return to the position of children in families later, but first I shall survey some of the research on the more personal aspects of married life.

# Marriage as a Personal Relationship

The changes in patterns of marriage discussed earlier in the chapter do not indicate a wholesale flight from matrimony. Cohabitation may now be common, but most of those who cohabit later marry and cohabitation, in any case, is not so very different from formal marriage. Despite increasing numbers opting to delay or eschew marriage, most young people still expect to marry. The majority of British marriages still involve a bride and groom who are both under the age of 30, and the traditional pattern of women marrying men older than themselves persists (Office for National Statistics, 1997).

The 'normality' of marriage is central to the maintenance of 'compulsory heterosexuality' (Rich, 1980), making lesbian and gay relationships appear to be a deviant and unnatural choice. Some gay rights organizations are campaigning for the right to marry, although others see this demand as a capitulation to the heterosexual norm (see Rahman and Jackson, 1997). It may also be the case that, among the heterosexual population, expectations about marriage are changing. Giddens (1992) has suggested that we are witnessing a move away from marriage as life-long commitment to an idea of the 'pure relationship' – a more provisional, contingent form of intimacy in which relationships last only as long as they fulfil individual desires. While high divorce rates may be an indicator of this, there is no evidence that individuals *entering* marriage treat it as provisional: most expect and want it to last. Giddens may, however, be correct in noting a trend in aspirations, led by women, towards a more egalitarian ideal. Recent research suggests that young women now hope for greater equality and autonomy in their marriages (Sharpe, 1994).

Although the decision to marry is in part a pragmatic one, within the western cultural tradition being 'in love' is seen as an essential precondition for marriage. Marrying other than on the basis of free choice and romantic love, particularly the practice of arranged marriage within Asian communities, may be judged very negatively from the standpoint of the dominant white culture. Yet Asian parents usually select their children's spouses with considerable care, and young people have varying degrees of choice in the matter (Westwood, 1984; Afshar, 1989; Sharpe, 1994). The ideal is that love should develop within marriage. While the reality does not always match the ideal, this is equally true of marriage founded on romantic love.

Research on 'white' couples suggests that romantic love does not deliver what it promises. 'Togetherness' is central to the modern western ideal of marriage, but it is often one-sided; the disjunction between 'his' and 'her' marriage (Bernard, 1972) persists. Mansfield and Collard's study of newly weds, carried out in the 1980s, found that husbands and wives defined the ideal of 'togetherness' differently. The men wanted a home and a wife, a secure physical and emotional base, something and someone to come home to. The women desired 'a close exchange of intimacy which would make them feel valued as a person and not just as a wife'. They 'expected more of their husbands emotionally than these men were prepared, or felt able, to give' (Mansfield and Collard, 1988: 179, 192). These findings are not unique: similar patterns emerged from a number of British and North American studies in the 1980s, while more recent studies suggest that women put a great deal of emotional labour, as well as domestic labour, into maintaining marital relationships. Here, as well as in the economic aspects of marriage, they give more than they receive (Duncombe and Marsden, 1993; Langford, 1998).

These emotional imbalances, along with economic inequities, suggest that marriage is a power relationship. Traditional sociological approaches to marriage either ignored this issue or considered it only in terms of decision making and weighted wives' decisions over choice of food purchases as equal to husbands' decisions about relocating the family home (see, for example Blood and Woolfe, 1960). Research over the last three decades has suggested that power in marriage is complex and multi-dimensional and that it is rooted in the structural relations of male domination (Bell and Newby, 1976; Edgell, 1980; Komter, 1989). It is not, however, always subtle and can be brutal. Violence against wives is by no means a modern phenomenon, but it has only recently been recognized as a widespread social problem.

Even as late as the 1960s and 70s, many social scientists considered wife abuse to be the result of individual male inadequacy or provocation from nagging wives. The first in-depth British sociological study on marital violence (Dobash and Dobash, 1979) challenged this view, revealing a pattern that was to become very familiar in subsequent research: violence was used systematically by men to keep women under control; it occurred across the full range of the class spectrum; it often entailed serious injury and it was very difficult to escape from. Some recent research has suggested that men and women are equally likely to resort to violence in marital disputes (for example Berliner, 1990). Such studies, relying on quantitative methods, 'counting' violent incidents without considering their context, severity or effect, are seriously methodologically flawed (Nazroo, 1995). Women may hit men and throw things at men, may fight back in self-defence when attacked, but most evidence indicates that domestic violence is primarily male violence. It is estimated that between 80 and 90 per cent of domestic assaults are perpetrated by men on women (see Maynard and Winn, 1997).

One indicator of women's refusal to accept maltreatment, as well as emotional and economic deprivation, is that almost three-quarters of British divorces are initiated by women (Office for National Statistics, 1997). This may reflect women's greater need to formalise financial and child custody arrangements once a marriage has broken down (Delphy and Leonard, 1992), as well as their greater marital unhappiness. Divorce, however, only ends a particular marital relationship. It does not necessarily undermine the institution of marriage itself. Most of those who divorce subsequently remarry, or enter into heterosexual cohabitation – many only to separate or divorce again. Discontent with marriage seems to be experienced as disillusionment with a particular relationship, rather than with the institution.

## Parenthood and Childhood

Earlier sociologists tended to follow lay assumptions in regarding parenthood as the logical outcome of marriage and treated both parenthood and childhood as relatively unproblematic. The gender differentiation of parenting was largely taken for granted and the status of children within families was rarely questioned. This has now changed, with far greater critical attention being given to the social construction of motherhood, fatherhood and childhood.

It is perhaps self-evident that parenthood is differentiated by gender. Consider the meanings of the phrases 'to mother a child' and 'to father a child', where mothering implies nurturing and fathering no more than the act of conception. Transforming fathering into fatherhood – a relationship with the child – requires an ongoing relationship with the child's mother. Hence sociologists have long held that fatherhood is a social institution whereas motherhood was, in the past, often taken for granted as the natural outcome of bearing a child. Both motherhood and fatherhood, however, are fully social and given form and meaning by the culturally and historically specific situations in which they are practised. Since women carry more of the burden of child care, it is not surprising that there has been more research on motherhood than on fatherhood. However, there has recently been some investigation into the social meanings and experiences of fatherhood.

While becoming a mother has traditionally been seen as the fulfilment of women's 'natural destiny', not all women are seen as fit mothers. Although there is now less stigma attached to unmarried motherhood, there is still a tendency to scapegoat lone mothers, especially if they are young (Phoenix, 1990; Laws, 1994; Millar, 1994). This is evident, for example, in the way in which teenage pregnancy continues to be defined as a major social problem, even though its incidence has declined steadily over the last two decades (Office of National Statistics, 1997). Young motherhood is thought of as an accident resulting from ignorance rather than a rational choice or, if seen as a choice, is deemed to be motivated by a desire to scrounge from the state or jump housing queues. The recent availability of forms of assisted conception have raised new questions about who should be allowed to bear a child. For example, in Britain in 1991 the use of artificial insemination by lesbians provoked a mini moral panic around 'virgin births', with subsequent calls for restrictions on the availability of other reproductive technologies.

Sociological investigations into motherhood have revealed a gap between the ideal of motherhood as something which comes naturally to women and the actuality of motherhood as it is experienced (see Richardson, 1993). First-time mothers often feel ill-prepared for the realities of looking after a child, do not automatically experience a surge of maternal feeling and often find that the positive aspects of motherhood are undercut by sleepless nights, the constant demands of a needy infant and social isolation. Even as children grow, women many continue to experience a loss of identity: they have ceased to be recognized as individuals and have become, instead, someone's mother. There are also contradictions within the idea of motherhood: it is supposed to be natural and yet there is a long tradition of advice from experts telling women how to be mothers. This advice changes over time, as views on children's needs change; motherhood is never defined in its own right, but always in response to children's perceived needs.

Fatherhood, like motherhood, has been redefined over time in relation to changing ideas on childhood. Until the early nineteenth century the emphasis was on children's duty to their parents rather than parental responsibilities to them. It was the father, as familial patriarch, who was held to be the parent to whom children 'naturally' belonged. Gradually, with the emergence of the modern idea of children as a category of people with specific psychological needs, mothers came to be regarded as more important to children's well-being and women gradually gained more rights in relation to their children and were increasingly awarded custody of them in the event of divorce. Women only gained full legal equality as parents in 1973 and their rights have always been conditional on being seen as a good mother. Those deemed unfit, and hence at risk of losing their children, were often those who flouted patriarchal convention: in the 1950s the adulterous wife, more recently, the lesbian (Smart, 1989a). Since the 1980s, however, there has been a move in the direction of reinstating paternal rights and responsibilities which has been reflected in legal decisions and policy changes.

The 1989 Children Act enshrined the idea of joint parenthood after divorce, on the assumption that children need social contact with their fathers. Here fatherhood is constructed as a caring relationship. The 1991 Child Support Act, however, was targeted at purportedly 'feckless' fathers who abdicated their financial responsibilities for their children. In obliging absent fathers to provide financial support for their children, it represented fatherhood as an economic obligation. The different assumptions underpinning these two pieces of legislation may reflect a wider uncertainty about the role of fathers in contemporary families and contradictory trends in patterns of fatherhood today. On the one hand, many absent fathers have little or no contact with their children; on the other some evidence suggests that fathers are becoming more involved in child care (see, for example, Smith, 1995). We should be wary, however, of accepting uncritically the idea of the 'new father'. It may now be routine for fathers to attend the birth of their child and to participate in caring for them, but the primary responsibility remains with mothers. When men are at work, they are often working long hours and may have little opportunity to care for their children (Lewis, 1995). When mothers return to full-time work after maternity leave it is they, rather than fathers, who take responsibility for alternative child care arrangements (Brannen and Moss, 1991). Moreover, those fathers who are keen to claim residence or contact with their children after divorce have not necessarily taken much part in caring for them before the divorce; sometimes they are building a new post-divorce relationship with their children on the basis of little prior involvement with their day-to-day care (Neale and Smart, 1997).

Not surprisingly, many feminists are sceptical about reinstating fathers' rights while women still bear most of the burden of caring for children. Other feminists, while sharing these concerns, are wary of asserting that mothers' rights over children should automatically take precedence over those of fathers. Delphy, for example, argues that this might reinforce the traditional view that child care is women's business and thus undermine demands for equality. Moreover, she suggests that mothers' rights can easily become rights *over* another category of people – children – with children becoming a commodity to be fought over (Delphy, 1994).

## Children in Families

It is only recently that sociologists have given attention to children and childhood other than from an adult-centred perspective. Within the traditional socialisation paradigm children were thought of as incomplete adults whose experiences were not worth investigating in their own right, but only insofar as they constituted learning for adulthood (Thorne, 1987). Thinking of childhood as a developmental stage and psychological state masks the fact that it is still a social status, that children are neither citizens nor legal subjects but are under the jurisdiction of their parents. It may be that parents today have less power and autonomy than in the past because child rearing is regulated by experts and state agencies. Nonetheless, parents retain a great deal of latitude to rear their children as they wish, to set acceptable standards of behaviour, to decide what their children should eat and wear and how they should be educated and disciplined. Others' interference in these matters is regarded as violation of family privacy and an assault on parents' rights; public regulation generally only intrudes where parents are deemed to have abused their power or not exercised it effectively enough – where children are 'at risk' or delinquent.

Modern families are often described as child centred. Certainly children's needs are given a high priority, but these are defined for them by adults. This is in part tied to the responsibility placed on parents to raise children 'properly'. This responsibility is far reaching and is heightened by increased public concern about risks to children. Often such concerns reflect risk anxiety as much as actual dangers – for example widely expressed fears of sexual assault and murder by strangers, despite the lack of evidence that risks to children come primarily from this quarter (see Scott *et al.*, 1998). Risk anxiety, however, does have material effects in that parental fears can lead to further limits on children's autonomy. In 1971, 80 per cent of British seven and eight year olds went to school on their own; by 1990 only 7 per cent were doing so (Hillman *et al.*, 1990). Other factors, such as increased car ownership may contribute to this trend, but parental fears about safety figure significantly in decisions on where children are able to go without adult supervision.

Home and family life is frequently thought of as a place of safety for children, but this is not always so. Children suffer many serious accidents in the home, especially where housing conditions are poor. Moreover children are far more likely to be assaulted and sexually abused within the family circle than outside it. Although this is widely known, it is still the shadowy figure of the 'pedophile' which haunts the popular imagination. There is now a large and growing body of research on child abuse, especially sexual abuse, which suggests that it is men children know who are more likely to abuse them. Like violence against wives, this can be seen as a result of the power structure and privacy of family life which can effectively place children entirely at the mercy of violent men.

## Conclusion

I have not attempted to cover the whole field of sociological work on family life, but the research which I have reported challenges the cosy image of the family as a haven of harmony and security. Sociologists have demonstrated that family life is organized hierarchically, with men having power over women and adults of both sexes having power over children. We now know a great deal about the ways in which this situation is experienced by women, but rather less about men's understanding of their position in the family and less still about children's perspective. There has recently, however, been a move towards considering the world from children's own point of view (see, for example, Brannen and O'Brien, 1994). Ongoing research in this area is likely to offer us a new point of view on family life.

There are other areas which require further investigation. Despite the recent emphasis on diversity in family life, there is still little work on sources of variation other than demographic ones. Most existing research concentrates on white families, so that much remains to be done on the specific, and changing, forms of domestic organization found among Britain's diverse ethnic minority populations. We are also only just beginning to address issues raised by alternative forms of family life, such as lesbian and gay families and those consciously seeking to build anti-sexist living arrangements (Weston, 1991; Van Every, 1995). Sociologists are still finding aspects of family life which are so taken for granted that they are only now being subjected to critical scrutiny, such as the institutionalization of heterosexuality (Richardson, 1996). New issues are also being raised by wider social change – for example the implications of assisted conception for the ways in which we understand parenthood and kinship (Stacey, 1992; Strathern, 1992). The field of family studies is continually evolving to take up new issues. Meanwhile, family life will continue to change, as it always has, throwing up new challenges for sociologists seeking to understand the shifting kaleidoscope of household, family and kinship.

# Further Reading

Bernardes, J. *Family Studies: An Introduction*, London, Routledge, 1997. A basic text emphasizing the diversity of family forms and questioning monolithic conceptualisations of the family.

Gittins, D. *The Family In Question*, 2nd edition, London, Macmillan, 1993. An accessible, introductory overview of debates and research on family life from a feminist perspective.

Jackson, S. and Moores, S. (eds) *The Politics of Domestic Consumption: Critical Readings*, Hemel Hempstead, Prentice Hall/Harvester Wheatsheaf, 1995. A reader bringing together critical work on the everyday practices of domestic consumption: includes readings on money, food, leisure, the media, domestic technologies, and the cultural construction of home.

Jamieson, L. *Intimacy*, Cambridge: Polity, 1998. An interesting new perspective on familial relationships focusing, as the title suggests, on the quality of personal relationships and how patterns of intimacy may be changing.

Morgan, D. *Family Connections: An Introduction to Family Studies*, Cambridge, Polity, 1996. An interesting and readable overview of sociological research on family life over the last two decades, showing how it intersects with wider sociological concerns.

# 9

# Education

## *Robert G. Burgess and Andrew Parker*

Education is a distinct form of 'secondary socialization'. Educational institutions are specifically created and legally sanctioned to transmit knowledge, skills and values; they also play an important part in determining people's position in society. Although most contemporary societies place great stress on equality of opportunity, a great deal of sociological work has suggested that education not only reflects, but also helps to reproduce, inequalities of class, gender and 'race' discussed in earlier chapters. This chapter aims to illustrate how sociologists have examined how schools work and their relationship to wider society. It should help you understand:

- The significance of functionalist, interactionist and Marxist theories to the development of the sociology of education

- The relationship between education, social class and social mobility in post-war Britain

- Ethnographic studies of stratification within schools and the influence of class, gender and 'race' on classroom interaction

- Sociological analyses of the effects of increasing marketization, competition and accountability in contemporary education

---

### CONCEPTS

consensus and conflict models ■ post-structuralism
postmodernism ■ social mobility ■ culture of deprivation
cultural reproduction ■ social policy ■ marketization
'New Right' ■ post-Fordism ■ surveillance

---

# Introduction

Most of us know something about education as a consequence of our exposure to it as pupils in school, and as students in college or university. Education is a 'commonsense' part of our society; a built-in set of expectations which we are all obliged to fulfil at specific points in time; a process whereby certain 'types' of knowledge are legitimized and mediated via teacher/instructor–student/pupil relations. These expectations are largely determined by statutory government guidelines and/or 'orders' which, in turn, structure institutional policy and practice. The sociology of education has attempted to analyse and explain the role of education within our society, to examine how it works, what it achieves and who benefits from its provision.

Education is one of the major institutions of modern societies, but what kind of questions have been asked by educational sociologists? First, at the structural level, sociologists have been interested in asking questions about the relationship between education and other major institutions such as family, class and work. For example, how do things like class and ethnic background influence educational attainment? What is the relationship between people's education and the jobs they end up doing? Second, sociologists have looked behind the statistics and wider social processes to examine the day-to-day practice of education. How do schools and classrooms 'work'? How, for example, do the attitudes of teachers and pupils influence each other? Third, sociologists have examined the influence on educational institutions of the social and political contexts in which they are located. For example, to what extent do centralized educational systems (such as those of France, Germany and Japan for example) and decentralized systems (such as those of England and Wales) result in different educational processes (Archer, 1979)? In the last two decades there have been vast amounts of legislation concerned with educational change worldwide. In England and Wales, for example, the Education Reform Act 1988 brought about changes in curriculum, assessment and testing. Sociologists of education have been interested in exploring the nature and effects of these developments. For example, how have policies aimed at making schools more 'efficient' and 'accountable' affected educational practices?

This chapter is organized around the questions raised above by providing specific illustrations of these general themes. It begins by introducing some of the major theoretical approaches in the sociology of education. It then looks at the relationship between education, inequality and social mobility and goes on to examine sociological research into what actually happens in educational settings and how this gives rise to further questions about different experiences of education. The chapter concludes by examining the changing context of educational policy, and how this affects the processes and practices of schooling.

# Theoretical Perspectives in the Sociology of Education

The sociology of education has been influenced by a number of theoretical standpoints offering different explanations of what education is and how it operates. Three major theoretical perspectives can be identified as central to the way in which sociologists have analysed educational systems and their related contexts: functionalist (or consensus) theory, social action theory and Marxist (or conflict) theory. Feminist and multicultural theories have been influential in studies of educational experiences in the last 20 years and more recent commentaries on educational issues have alluded to aspects of post-modern thought.

In investigating education, the questions sociologists ask and the ways in which evidence is interpreted are necessarily influenced by their underlying theoretical perspectives. Functionalists, for example, have been keen to analyse the school as a social system; to establish the relationship between the structure of society as a whole and education as part of that structure, and to examine the effectiveness of education as an agent of socialisation. Durkheim was the first major theorist to make a thorough examination of the role of education within contemporary society. For Durkheim, as well as teaching specific skills, education is the central means by which society perpetually recreates the conditions of its existence by a systematic socialization of a younger generation:

> Education is the influence exercised by adult generations on those that are not yet ready for social life. Its object is to arouse and to develop in the child a certain number of physical, intellectual and moral states which are demanded of it by both the political society as a whole and the special milieu for which it is specifically destined. (1956: 71)

Education thus provides an important link between the individual and society. An appreciation of history, for example, helps children to see society as something 'larger' than themselves. Durkheim argued that this moral education was becoming more important in an increasingly individualized, competitive and secular modern world. The idea that schools play an important role in transmitting cultural values has been a theme of continuing importance in the sociology of education.

Like Durkheim, Parsons (1961) sought to identify education in terms of the societal function it serves, depicting it as a context in which individuals are taught the fundamental rules and values of society thereby facilitating the maintenance of moral order and consensus. For example, in order to prepare children for the orientations of society at large, schools promote the value of achievement and success, with responsibility for development in these areas being primarily located with children themselves. In turn, schools also function to select people for work roles which are appropriate to their abilities.

Functionalism has been widely criticised for presenting an essentially 'conservative' and uncritical view of education. However, this is not a *necessary* consequence of the functionalist approach. For example, Durkheim was insistent that for education to be an effective source of socialization it had to provide *real* equality of opportunity. As we shall see in the following section, within this tradition a great deal of work has been directed towards documenting and explaining the structural causes of education's failure to achieve these ideals.

Social action theorists, on the other hand, have adopted a more 'interpretive' approach towards educational practice. They have looked closely at the ways in which educational institutions are organized and structured; how those who work within them interpret, negotiate and carry out their roles, and how the resulting web of interrelationships impacts upon processes of teaching and learning. This approach has been most strongly influenced by symbolic interactionism which, presenting clear challenges to the work of functionalists, focuses on the subjective meaning of individual action rather than issues relating to societal structures and systems. These contentions reflect an ongoing structure/agency debate in sociological theory which was discussed in some detail in Chapter 3. A major focus within the social action approach has been to explore the relationship between educational processes and children's identities. For example, once a child has been identified as a 'troublemaker', 'clown' or 'high-flyer', is there then a tendency for their actions to be interpreted in terms of this label? Interactionists also consider the extent to which such labels might then be internalized and become the basis for the way in which children think about themselves and the social world.

While functionalist and social action theorists have adopted the notion of 'social inequality', particularly equality of opportunity, as a key feature of their work, Marxist (or conflict) theorists have traditionally presented a more radical analysis of educational institutions and systems, highlighting issues of social class, power relations and inequality, locating schooling as a process of unequal distribution of societal resources and opportunities. As a result the school system has been portrayed by some as part of a state machine eager to allocate pupils from specific social class backgrounds into certain roles within society, particularly within the world of work. Althusser (1972) provides an example of this approach by locating education as the central component of state policy with regard to ideological dominance of the masses in mature capitalist societies. For Althusser, education has taken the place of religion (the Church) as the key ideological focus of such societies and, in so doing, serves as the primary method by which the relations of capitalist production (capitalist relations of exploitation) are reproduced:

No other ideological State apparatus has the obligatory (and not least, free) audience of the totality of the children in the capitalist social formation, eight hours a day for five or six days a week out of seven. But it is by an apprenticeship in a variety of 'know-how' wrapped up in the massive inculcation of the ideology of the ruling class that the *relations of production* in a capitalist social formation... are reproduced. The mechanisms which produce this vital result for the capitalist regime are naturally covered up and concealed by a universally reigning ideology of the school, universally reigning because it is one of the essential forms of the ruling bourgeois ideology. (1972: 261)

Such analyses have attracted a good deal of criticism as a consequence of the way in which individual action is portrayed as being constrained by the economic logic of capitalism and its inherent structures. However, this has not deterred sociologists from utilising Marxist theory to explain the inner workings of educational systems. In their book, *Schooling in Capitalist America,* Bowles and Gintis (1976) offer a strong critique of the way in which the bureaucratic and hierarchically ordered format of schools resembles that already established within the workplace and how socialization is necessarily carried out in an institutional atmosphere of subordination and domination. Outlining a clear relationship between the economy and education Bowles and Gintis go on to advocate that pupils in school learn to be workers via a 'correspondence' between the social relations of production and the social relations of education.

Critical perspectives have also been adopted by feminist researchers to investigate patterns of inequality on the grounds of gender (see Riley, 1994; Weiner, 1994; Arnot *et al.*, 1996), and by those exploring issues of 'race', racism and ethnicity to evaluate the impact of multiculturalism within and upon the educational system (see Mac an Ghaill, 1988; Gillborn, 1990; Foster *et al.*, 1996). While vestiges of functionalist, social action and Marxist 'theoretical' approaches remain apparent within contemporary studies of schools, it is evident that there has been a shift away from fundamental questions concerning selection, socialization, social class and social mobility to those dealing with broader and more complex notions of educational process, policy and practice. In this sense, contentions and concerns over issues of social class, gender and 'race' and ethnicity are still high on the sociological agenda within the context of education, yet in more recent years these issues (and indeed, a host of others) have come under increasingly critical scrutiny by sociologists who have begun to cite instances of cultural and educational fragmentation and diversity as a clear indication that we now live in a postmodern age requiring different forms of sociological analysis.

Such developments are evident in contemporary analyses of educational settings and the kinds of theoretical perspectives being utilized. The work of Foucault, for example, has been adopted by a number of sociologists in order to present post-structuralist accounts of educational experience. In particular, Foucault's assertions regarding the 'geneology of power/knowledge' and the emergence of powerful societal *discourses* (bodies of ideas, concepts and theories which define social phenomena) have proved influential in this respect (cf. Foucault, 1979, 1986; Sarup, 1993). Drawing on the work of Nietzsche,

Foucault's 'genealogical' analysis emphasizes the relationship between knowledge and power and how this relationship manifests itself by way of *discourses* or *discursive formations* through which particular modes of thought are rendered legitimate and others denied (see Storey, 1993; Hall, 1997). While the term 'discourse' is commonly associated with language and linguistics, for Foucault it additionally encompasses notions of *practice*:

> Discourse, Foucault argues, constructs the topic. It defines and produces the objects of our knowledge. It governs the way that a topic can be meaningfully talked about and reasoned about. It also influences how ideas are put into practice and used to regulate the conduct of others. Just as discourse 'rules in' certain ways of talking about a topic, defining an acceptable and intelligible way to talk, write or conduct oneself, so also, by definition, it 'rules out', limits and restricts other ways of talking, of conducting ourselves in relation to the topic or constructing knowledge about it. (Hall, 1997: 44)

Ball (1994) utilizes a post-structuralist approach (in conjunction with critical policy analysis and critical ethnography) to evaluate the impact of the 1988 Education Reform Act on the UK education system, and more specifically on classroom practice and teachers' lives. Pinpointing at the outset of his work how he intends 'to examine some of the "power networks", discourses and technologies which run through the social body of education: the local state, educational organisations and classrooms', Ball's (1994) explicit aim is 'to theorize educational reform and thereby achieve an unmasking of power for the benefit of those who suffer it'. In considering 'policy as *discourse*', Ball attempts to uncover the way that a 'free-market' ethos has been legitimised within the context of educational provision, the consequences of which have ultimately come to shape the organizational *practices* of modern-day schools.

In their analysis of gender relations within schools, Weiner *et al*. provide a more detailed explanation of how the notion of *discourse* might serve to provide sociologists with a kind of analytical framework. For them, Foucault

> uses discourse to explain ways of thinking about the world that are so deeply embedded in practice that we are unconscious of their existence. Discourses are structuring mechanisms for social institutions (such as schools), modes of thought, and individual subjectivities... Further, Foucault's understanding of power–knowledge relations allows for the relationship to be established between knowledge (say, relating to the curriculum, policy and so on) and power (who creates, controls, receives specific knowledges). (1997: 621)

There is an affinity between post-structural and postmodern theory and, indeed, the two are sometimes used interchangeably. However, postmodernism is a much more difficult term to pin down. There is debate in sociology about whether it is a 'movement', 'condition' or a 'system of ideas', and also whether or not contemporary society has in fact witnessed a dissolution of those social forms associated with modernity bringing about a postmodern or post-industrial phase (see Sarup, 1993). For those who advocate this position, postmodernism appears to represent key changes concerning the way in which we think about society and the events and occurrences which go on within it. First, as we saw in Chapter 3, postmodernists refute the existence of any overarching theoretical explanation, grand theory or meta-narrative (particularly Marxism) about how society has developed and proffer radical scepticism about the philosophical basis of knowledge. Second, it is argued that changes such as the development of a global economy, the emergence of flexible and highly responsive service industries, faster modes of travel and communication (the evolution of the information super-highway) and the subsequent breakdown of old state/relational 'boundaries' have transformed the condition of modernity.

While education has remained largely divorced from this overall debate there is evidence to suggest that it too is 'going through profound change in terms of purposes, content and methods' which seemingly exhibit features of postmodernity (Usher and Edwards, 1994: 3). Many of these changes can be compared to those taking place within broader industrial contexts in terms of their impact on institutional relations and workplace practices (see Ball, 1990, 1994) Analysing such changes within the context of Canadian schools, for example, Hargreaves (1994: 3) suggests that the contemporary crisis of schooling and teaching can essentially be defined in terms of the contradictions posed by the experiences of teachers who, on the one hand, inhabit an occupational world dominated by the intensities, diversities, complexities and uncertainties of post-industrialism, while, on the other hand, working in and around 'a modernistic and monolithic school system that continues to pursue deeply anachronistic purposes within opaque and inflexible structures'. The following sections explore some of the research carried out within the theoretical perspectives outlined, starting with the sociology of education's long-standing interest in the relationship between education, social class and equality of opportunity.

## Education, Social Class and Social Mobility

The relationship between social class, social mobility and education has always been of interest to sociologists of education. Social mobility refers to the movement of people between social class categories and rates of social mobility are often taken as 'indicators' or 'measures' of the degree of fluidity and openness in societies. The idea of creating greater equality of opportunity in Britain, for example, was embodied in the 1944 Education Act. This made education compulsory up until the age of 15, guaranteed all children a place in secondary school, with access to the more academic grammar schools being determined by the results of a national 11+ examination which children took in their final year of primary education. The hope was that better schools and more equality of opportunity in education would lead to greater social mobility by identifying talent and enabling it to flourish irrespective of social origin. A major focus of sociological studies was to examine the impact of these reforms, particularly their impact on social mobility.

Early work in the 'political arithmetic' tradition by sociologists at the London School of Economics suggested that there was comparatively little upward social mobility from the lower parts of society to the top (Glass, 1954). The more recent and more sophisticated research of Goldthorpe *et al.* (1980) – using the employment-aggregate class scheme described in Chapter 5 – suggests a rather more complex picture. Goldthorpe and his associates found that there had been a significant increase in *absolute* social mobility. However, this was largely due to an increase in professional and managerial occupations 'sucking up' more people from the lower classes which, in effect, meant that there had been little change in the *relative* mobility of people from different socio-economic origins. The work of Halsey *et al.* (1980), which compared cohorts of men educated before and since the educational reforms, found that although educational opportunities had improved for all classes, the differentials between classes had hardly changed. For example, although the rate of university entrance was 3.5 times higher for upper and lower classes, the chances of the sons of 'service-class' fathers (Classes I and II) going to university remained over seven times greater than that of the working-class boys (Classes VI to VII) (see also Heath and Clifford, 1996).

In more recent years class has lost its central place in the sociology of education and, according to Mortimore and Whitty, 'teachers who dared to mention the subject have been branded as defeatist or patronising for even considering that class can make a difference' (1997: 1). However, data from the 1980s and 90s continue to suggest a systematic relationship between low social class and comparatively poor examination performance (see for example, Denscombe, 1993). In this context sociologists are still suggesting, as they have done for the last 30 years, that improvements *within* schools to increase educational attainment will only be partially successful if carried out in isolation. Whitty argues that 'where schools have seemed to make progress, the *relative* performance of the disadvantaged groups has often remained similar or worsened even when the absolute performance of such groups has improved' (1998: 4). For Mortimore and Whitty, 'the priority of any government must be to implement strategies to deal with poverty and associated disadvantage: schools cannot go it alone' (1997: 12).

Education is crucially important within the context of social inequality and social mobility as formal qualifications (or the lack of them) have come to be key determinants of an individual's position in the occupational structure. In general, the higher people's level of qualifications, the higher their income. For example, data from the General Household Survey of 1991, showed that the average earnings of men and women with degrees was double that of

*Sociology*

those with no qualifications (Table 9.1). However, despite formal equality of opportunity access to education, levels of educational attainment continue to be *systematically* linked to socio-economic background. For example, over half of those with Social Class I backgrounds obtained a degree or similar qualification compared to just 8 per cent from Social Class VI (Figure 9.1). Similarly, those with no educational qualifications increased from 7 per cent in Social Class I to 60 per cent in Social Class V.

**Table 9.1**   Median weekly earnings (£) by holders of given qualifications, by sex, Great Britain 1991

| Qualifications | Male | Female |
|---|---|---|
| Degree (or equivalent) | 440 | 332 |
| Other higher education | 330 | 296 |
| GCSE A–C grades (or equivalent) | 252 | 193 |
| No qualifications | 220 | 193 |

*Source:* General Household Survey (1991).

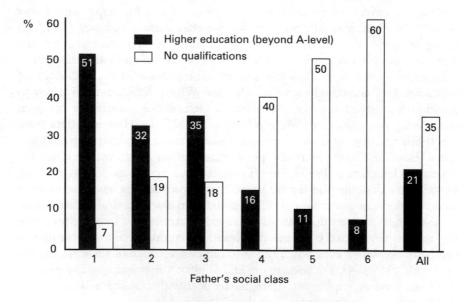

**Figure 9.1**   Percentage of persons with higher or no educational qualifications, by father's social class, Great Britain, 1990–91 (General Household Survey, 1991)

Early sociological explanations of the relationship between educational performance and socio-economic background focused not on the school but on factors in wider society, particularly the working-class home (see Foster *et al.*, 1996). Material deprivation, such as sub-standard housing, lack of resources, and the comparatively poorer health of working-class children, were seen as particularly important influences. Douglas (1964), in a major longtitudinal study which followed 5000 children from primary to secondary school, found clear links between reduced educational performances and 'unsatisfactory' living conditions. However, while material deprivation was seen as an important influence, many felt that it could not explain the whole problem. For some theorists, another important part of the answer was to be found in the comparative deprivations of working-class culture, particularly the different expectations, values and child rearing practices of middle-class and working-class parents. Douglas' research found that middle-class parents showed more interest in their children's education, were more likely to visit the school, and placed greater emphasis on educational attainment. The idea of cultural deprivation was reinforced by research suggesting that working-class forms or 'codes' of speech (which tended to be more restricted and context-tied than middle-class patterns) were less compatible with the demands of educational institutions (see Bernstein, 1975). Halsey *et al.* (1980) attempted, as far as possible, to separate out material and cultural influences. They found that cultural influences, especially parental attitudes, were the principal determinant of a boy's progress up until the age of 11 (when selection was made) but that after that material circumstances became an increasingly important determinant of school-leaving age and the qualifications obtained.

One of the earliest accounts of the way in which working-class children used a grammar school education to be upwardly mobile was reported in a classic study by Jackson and Marsden (1962). This study, based on 88 children from a town in the north of England, focused on one question: what occurred within the school to perpetuate social class differences in achievements among children of similar ability? The study charted the way in which children from working-class backgrounds experienced the educational system. It demonstrated how talented working-class children who passed the 11+ examination at the end of primary school and went into the selective grammar schools under-achieved by leaving school early and not proceeding into higher education. It showed that mobility from the working to the middle classes carried with it social isolation. The relationship between home and school was an 'us versus them' phenomenon, whereby the working-class child did not make the transition between the culture of the working-class community and the middle-class school which was experienced as an alien world in which they felt they did not belong. The grammar school system thus helped to reproduce social class divisions. The study raised important questions, such as the relationship between social class background and academic performance, the content of the school curriculum, the quality of teacher/pupil interaction and the ways in which assessments were made of pupils, that were subsequently investigated by sociologists of education. The study was seen as something of a landmark, not just in the sociology of education but in sociology generally, linking back to class analysis on the one hand and forward to ethnographic studies of schools.

## Studies of Schools

Prior to the 1960s it was rare for sociologists to engage in any small-scale studies of schools and the ways in which they operated. However, in the early 1960s sociologists and social anthropologists developed a series of studies in which the methods of investigation that had been used to study small-scale societies, social situations and social events were used to examine the dynamics of schooling. A programme, directed by Gluckman at the University of Manchester, used techniques of observation and participant observation, in-depth interviewing and documentary analysis to develop detailed studies of schools. These were the precursors of a number of ethnographic studies in schools that were to be conducted over the next 30 years. Gluckman's programme looked at patterns of school organization by focusing on a boys' grammar school (Lacey, 1970), a boys' secondary modern school (Hargreaves, 1967) and a girls' grammar school (Lambert, 1976). A major theoretical influence was the interactionist approach, which focuses attention on the ways individuals' perceptions of themselves are shaped by the expectations of others. The studies focused on the internal organization of these schools, especially the impact of stratification within schools – that is, streaming groups in terms of different ability – on pupils' identities, behaviour and achievement. These were the themes associated particularly with the 'classical' accounts of Hargreaves and Lacey.

   Lacey (1970) identified social processes associated with streaming and developed a model of 'differentiation' and 'polarisation'. The former referred to the way in which pupils were separated and ranked according to specific academic criteria within the school, while the latter indicated the way in which pupil anti-school sub-cultures might develop in response and opposition to the academic value structures in place. This model of differentiation and polarization was central to Lacey's study: those who conformed to teacher expectations and demands and who valued academic success were rewarded, while those who did not were perceived by their teachers in increasingly negative terms. As these processes were linked to streaming, Lacey was able to associate differentiation and polarization with the streams to which pupils were allocated. Hargreaves (1967) reported a process of sub-cultural differentiation in 'Lumley' School, whereby the higher the stream in which pupils were allocated, the better their behaviour, while the 'anti-school' culture was manifest in the lower streams. Like Lacey, Hargreaves proposed a model of the way in which the sub-culture of the school operated. The dominant values of the A and B streams of 'Lumley' were said to be 'academic', while those of the C and D streams were predominantly 'delinquescent', that is based on rule breaking and lack of interest in academic work. The study demonstrates how the A and D streams become the poles of differentiation. In the former there was a *correspondence* between school and peer group values, while in the latter they were in *opposition*, with disruptive behaviour being associated with high peer group status.

The clear emergence of the theme of differentiation and polarization in the studies by Lacey and Hargreaves influenced further research into the fundamental processes that occurred in schools and the social implications of their internal academic organization. In a later study Ball (1981) examined the organization of 'Beachside', a comprehensive school where entry was non-selective. In 'Beachside' new pupils were placed in one of three ability bands, band 1 being high and band 3 being low. Although allocation to bands was supposed to be based entirely on 'academic' criteria, like Jackson and Marsden 20 years earlier, Ball found that a significantly higher proportion of working-class children were allocated to the lower ability bands.

While the majority of pupils were conformist and co-operative when they first came to 'Beachside', Ball found a clear divergence in the behaviour of children in the different bands developed. The banding system had the effect of separating pupils into a number of groups who had access to different kinds of subject knowledge, different teaching methods and had different kinds of relationships with their teachers. Pupils were found to make relationships within their own bands and Ball suggested that an anti-school culture, similar to that which had been found by Hargreaves and Lacey, was prevalent among band 2 pupils, who were regarded by teachers as behaviourally problematic, in contrast to band 1 pupils, who fulfilled the ideal pupil role and band 3, who were expected to have learning problems but not create difficulties. However, these processes of differentiation could not be explained entirely by banding. During Ball's research, 'Beachside' changed its system of banding to mixed-ability teaching. While pupil behaviour improved, teachers continued to make clear distinctions between 'bright' and 'dull' pupils, thus reproducing the 'stratification' of banding in a mixed-ability context of the classroom. For example, while the 'brighter' children were encouraged to enter for national exams, some of the less able were 'cooled out' and advised to set their sights lower.

In another celebrated ethnographic study of a comprehensive school, Keddie (1971) examined pupil–teacher interaction in humanities subjects where the same syllabus was taught across different streams. She argued that teachers would change the content of the 'same' lesson, 'withholding' some of the more complex material from C stream children. They were also less responsive to questions from children in the low streams, thus differentiating in their teaching methods on the basis of their preconceived assumptions of the 'given' abilities of children in different streams. Keddie gives a number of examples to illustrate this process. For example, in one lesson, children in one of the C streams were discussing the solitary confinement of the 'wolf child':

| | |
|---|---|
| *Teacher*: | The interesting thing is the boy was fostered out. He was illegitimate you see. If you think about it he must have had the beginnings of speech – so what do you think happened? |
| *Boy*: | The woman who put him in a chicken coop made him go backwards. |
| *Teacher*: | Very good... |
| *Boy 2*: | Well done. |
| *Boy*: | How do you unlearn? |
| *Teacher*: | Well you simply forget – in school – tests show that. |
| *Boy*: | (Makes some untranscribable objection.) |
| *Teacher*: | You need to keep practising skills. |

A noticeable feature of this sequence is that the teacher's response renders the question unproblematic: 'Well you simply forget'. (Keddie, 1971: 153)

For Keddie, the curriculum is not a 'given'; rather it is socially constructed in different ways according to teachers' preconceived assumptions about the abilities of children in different streams. The consequence of this is that children in the lower streams have restricted opportunities to access knowledge which may have been crucial to their educational success.

While ethnographic studies of schools have made an important contribution to understanding educational processes, it is important to recall the observations made in Chapter 2 about ethnographic methods. Pawson illustrates how qualitative data are usually also open to interpretations other than the one being put forward by the researcher. In the context of Keddie's work, McNamara (1980), for example, complains that while Keddie's interpretation is plausible, the teacher may have simply wanted to keep the lesson moving, been running out of time, or the topic may have been the subject of next week's lesson. This observation does not, of course, detract from the value of ethnographic studies, of schools or anything else, but it does direct attention to the way in which the researcher deals with alternative interpretations

While studies of the internal organization of schools still dominated the sociology of education in the 1970s and early 1980s, other ethnographies emerged, offering a variation in theoretical approach. The first, signalling an increasing interest in cultural production, was influenced by Willis' *Learning to Labour* (1977), which adopted a more radical perspective towards education, working-class youth and cultural reproduction. It drew on both Marxist and interepretive theory to address the central question of how and why working-class 'kids' get working-class jobs. The study's ethnographic methods – discussed in Chapter 2 – documented the school and post-school experiences of a small group of adolescent males in an industrial city in England. Willis' findings mapped out the detailed construction of sub-cultural masculinity in and around these working-class locales, the stark realities of which allowed him to conclude that issues of social class and social mobility were as much to do with structural constraint and sub-cultural determinism as they were to do with education *per se*. The 'lads' Willis studied developed a counter-culture of resistance to the school which rejected education, teachers and conforming pupils. Willis found that the strategies the lads had used for coping with the authority and boredom of school, such as insubordination, time wasting, having a laugh and distinguishing between 'us' and 'them', were also serving them in the repetitive and supervised world of manual labour. There is thus a correspondence between school and work. However, this process did not come from the school socializing them into obedient, compliant pupils as suggested by Bowles and Gintis (1976). Paradoxically, it was the *rejection* of the school and the *active* development of an oppositional counter-culture that had prepared them for the demands of unskilled labour. Willis has been criticised for drawing his conclusions from such a small and unrepresentative sample and for not taking into account a much wider range of responses to school (Brown, 1989). However, with its emphasis on culture and resistance and recognition of the importance of both agency and structure, Willis' study was an important development in the sociology of education, providing a theoretical model which influenced other 'culturist' research studies.

It is interesting to compare the work of Willis with that of Hargreaves from the previous decade. Both consider the plight of working-class pupils in the lower 'streams' of secondary schooling and both uncover the existence of a delinquent, anti-counter-school sub-culture among their respondents. While Hargreaves sees the development of disaffected sub-cultural attitudes as a response to individual and collective notions of institutional 'failure', Willis regards them as a proactive form of pupil resistance whereby the anti-academic nuances of working-class culture fight against the school's imposition of middle-class values and belief systems. The differences between these studies are not only indicative of theoretical bias but also of a broader disciplinary shift in the early 1970s which came to be known as the 'new sociology of education' (cf. Young, 1971). Moving away from a preoccupation with notions of educational access and organization and what needed to be done to allow working-class children to benefit from the opportunities on offer, this shift marked the point at which education itself came under scrutiny in terms of the kinds of *knowledge* it promoted. In this respect, the 'new' sociologists:

> Began to challenge the whole nature of the education provided in schools. This was itself now seen as a barrier to the achievement of educational (and social) equality. One aspect of this was the argument that the knowledge and skills purveyed, or at least those accorded high status, stem[med] from the culture of dominant social groups. In other words, the very knowledge schools offer[ed] reflect[ed] the unequal social structure of the wider society. (Foster *et al.*, 1996: 10)

Thus, the 'new sociology of education' heralded the point at which sociologists switched emphasis away from the individual circumstances and backgrounds of pupils, towards issues concerning the inequality of power between the social classes and how this power was used to define the constituent elements of 'education'.

Another development, indicative of broader sociological concerns, was that educational sociologists became increasingly interested in issues of gender and 'race'. Indeed, while social differentiation and inequality had been key themes from the early post-war period up until the 1970s, in practice the majority of studies had focused upon specific groups of white, working-class anti-school boys, a pattern which, as Mac an Ghaill (1996) points out, was something of an anathema to the arguments put forward by a fast growing feminist and anti-racist lobby. As a consequence, the 1970s and 80s saw the sociology of education shift its focus away from issues of social class to explore what Mac an Ghaill (1996: 167) describes as 'the differentiated schooling experiences of girls and of Asian and Afro-Caribbean students' (see also Weiner, 1994). Without doubt, such initiatives located issues of gender and 'race' at the centre rather than the periphery of educational debate, but as Mac an Ghaill (1996) stresses there is a sense in which a subsequent preoccupation with issues pertaining to gender and 'race' then served to displace notions of social class to the extent that theorists were distracted from the development of a more holistic analytical framework involving the complex 'articulation' of all three themes. Nevertheless, these advances in the investigative remit did constitute a clear change for sociologists working within education. What they also provided were the grounds on which some understanding might be gained of what actually went on in classrooms. What they also provided were the grounds on which some understanding might be gained of what actually went on in classrooms, and it was this influence that dominated the 1980s.

## Sociologists 'inside' Classrooms

Up until the 1980s many sociological studies focused on how schools functioned and operated as a whole. However, many later studies examined some of the taken-for-granted routines of the classroom, redering them 'strange' in order to understand them. Delamont (1981), for example, argued that there were specific strategies that could be used to help understand teacher–pupil interaction. She suggested the placement of these strategies into four categories. First, different kinds of classrooms should be examined in which different subjects are taught. This has resulted in sociologists studying classroom activities, not only in schools, but also in higher education institutions and also in different subject areas. Second, comparative studies can provide a stimulus for looking at familiar classroom settings – too few cross-cultural studies have been conducted, especially between Britain and Europe (see Burgess, 1998). Third, non-educational settings can be compared with educational settings, as in studies of youth training where classroom learning is compared with work-based learning (see Banks *et al.*, 1992). Fourth, the familiar aspects of schooling, such as the way gender is used to organize classroom activities, should not be taken for granted but used as a basis for questioning routine procedures in schools and classrooms – a theme that has been taken up in several studies (see Riddell, 1992; Weiner, 1994).

Such strategies have been useful in helping sociologists understand the process of schooling. For example, many researchers have examined initial encounters and routines in classrooms in order to find out how teachers attempt to organize and determine pupil behaviour. Measor and Woods (1984), in their study of pupils transferring from primary to secondary school, reported that the pupils went through a honeymoon period with teachers, whereby each presented their best fronts to each other before 'coming out' by probing, testing and negotiating rules. These phenomena were explored in several studies where sociologists examined how teachers established routines in the classroom and how pupils 'tested out' teachers (see also Beynon, 1985). Another major study by Galton and Delamont (1980) followed pupils who were transferring from first to middle schools. Using ethnographic studies in classrooms, they examined the ways in which teachers went about establishing rules in initial lessons with classes, thus providing further evidence on some of the fundamental processes identified by Measor and Woods in their school transfer study.

Of course, not all classroom interaction results in pupil conformity. In a study of a secondary school in South Wales, for example, Beynon and Atkinson (1984) report on ways in which pupils challenged the authority of women teachers. Similarly, a number of sociologists have looked at the ways in which such situations are used by pupils to disrupt classroom activity, where 'mucking about', 'doing nothing' and 'having a laugh' are cited as ways in which pupils develop subversive behaviour in classrooms to challenge teacher authority and control (see Corrigan, 1979).

Many of these themes have persisted throughout the 1980s and 90s with sociologists not only exploring fundamental processes of education, but also the ways in which gender and sexuality and 'race' influence schooling (cf. Epstein, 1994; Foster *et al.*, 1996; Haywood and Mac an Ghaill, 1996; Parker, 1996).

## Gender

Gender has been a systematic source of inequality in education. Until recently, girls fell behind boys in secondary education despite outperforming them in primary education. Research in classrooms has suggested that, in addition to institutional disadvantages (discussed in Chapter 6) which have contributed to women's subordinate position in society, girls were also disadvantaged in patterns of classroom interaction in mixed schools. Spender (1983) found from tape recordings of lessons that not only did boys typically dominate classroom interactions with girls, they also received more attention from teachers, their contributions were generally taken more seriously and their work judged more favourably.

Stanworth (1983) also looked at the way in which boys and girls were treated differently by teachers in lessons. She found that both male and female pupils indicated that boys received more teacher attention in terms of being asked questions and being praised in the classroom. She argued that such teacher actions resulted in discrimination between boys and girls and the way in which pupils evaluated themselves and how pupils and teachers evaluated each other. The effect of this was to reinforce existing patterns of gender inequality by girls leaving school with an implicit understanding of their place in the world as second-class citizens. These uncompromising critiques of the consistently gendered nature of classroom interaction have themselves been subject to critical evaluation. Stanworth's conclusions have been criticized for being based entirely on secondary interview data, while Spender did not specify most of her methods, making evaluation and replication impossible (Delamont, 1986). A subsequent study by Randall (1987) failed to find the same gender bias from teachers, with girls receiving the same, and sometimes more, attention than boys.

A recent development now interesting educationalists is why girls have not only caught up with boys but seem to be overtaking them academically in many subjects. This appears to be a global trend. Research in the Caribbean, for example, found that girls were outperforming boys in most subject areas (Parry, 1996). Recent research exploring the 'problem' of boys' under-achievement has suggested that some of the factors previously believed to favour boys, such as teachers' greater tolerance and boys' overconfidence in their own abilities, may in fact be working to their detriment.

However, the position is rather more complex than the simple statement 'girls are now outperforming boys' suggests. For example, in Britain in 1995, girls outperformed boys at all Key Stages for Reading/English; however, results for Mathematics were broadly similar and boys did slightly better in Science at Key Stages 2 and 3 (Arnot et al., 1998: 4–7). The results of national examinations at 16 (GCSEs) must also be carefully unpicked. In the decade prior to 1995, boys actually improved their overall exam performance (measured by number of A*–C passes), but the increase was not at the same rate as it was for girls (Arnot et al., 1998). At this point an important caveat must be inserted. Preliminary research by Stobart et al. (1992) suggested that tiered entry for GCSE Mathematics masks some interesting gender biases. Girls may be entered for 'intermediate' maths, where they can gain no more than a C grade, rather than 'higher' maths which is aimed at students who

Have been moves to disempower centralised educational bureaucracies, and to create in their place devolved systems of schooling entailing significant degrees of institutional autonomy and a variety of forms of school-based management and administration. (1997a: 299)

Similar changes were occurring within other western (post-) industrial societies, particularly the USA (see David, 1991). Moreover, there is evidence to suggest that since the late 1980s other nations such as Australia (Kenway, 1993), New Zealand (Grace, 1991), the Netherlands (Sleegers and Wesselingh, 1993), Spain (Bonal, 1995) and Canada (Elliott and Maclennan, 1994) have experienced some form of educational upheaval on a national scale in line with 'free market' economic forces.

In the case of Britain the consequence of such change, Brown *et al.* (1997) suggest, is that a devolution of financial staffing and policy issues has been carried out with regard to individual institutions (that is, schools), where assumptions have been made about the potential of educational establishments to 'compete' irrespective of their intake and the added pressure of 'parental choice' (see also Brown and Lauder, 1991). To this end, teachers have experienced considerable change, not only in the content of their work but also in relation to their occupational role. For example, schooling has become the subject of league tables in national newspapers with the result that teachers and schools are able to compare their position with national trends. Whereas at one time pupil assessment was simply structured around issues of 'certification' and 'selection' (Broadfoot, 1996), now such procedures are utilized to monitor school effectiveness and performance, as Torrance points out:

> The government's basic position seems to be that improving educational standards is of paramount importance in improving economic competitiveness within an increasingly competitive global economy, and that a new national assessment framework will help to raise standards by setting publicly accessible targets; measuring whether or not they have been met; encouraging schools to compete with each other by publishing the results; and allowing parents to choose their children's schools and tying finance in part to students numbers. (1997: 320)

An example of how this practice works is provided in Table 9.2, taken from recent report from the National Commission on Education (1996), where Jobson *et al.* (1996) comment on the work of Crowcroft Park Primary School in Manchester in terms of results in standard attainment tasks. The results give an indication of the way in which a school can compare itself to national results in Reading, Mathematics and Science.

For postmodernists (and post-structuralists), simply trying to compare the experiences of black, Asian and white students, for example, is fundamentally misconceived. Not only do such crude categories ignore many other minority groups, but also the differences that lie *within* these categories (Brah, 1992). In this context Gilroy (1992) has argued that anti-racist strategies, which focus exclusively on the dichotomy of 'black' and 'white', should be replaced by a cultural politics of difference; that is, recognizing and attempting to understand the diversity of cultural identities in contemporary societies. Postmodernists are similarly critical of studies which compare the experiences of 'girls' and 'boys' as if they were homogeneous categories. Rather, research should take into account the plurality and diversity which exists in contemporary classrooms and examine, for example, the *different* ways in which girls are defined and positioned in classroom interaction (Jones, 1993). This is but one aspect of a much wider critique of 'modernist sociology' by postmodernists who argue that the increasingly fluid and diverse nature of contemporary societies makes attempts to explain education (or anything else) in terms of blanket categories, such as class, gender or 'race', increasingly difficult to sustain.

## From Policy to Practice

While studies of schools have contributed greatly to understanding routine educational processes and, in particular, the ways in which inequalities of class, gender, 'race' and culture may be reproduced, it is also important for sociologists to examine the changing contexts in which schools and other educational institutions exist. The policies of the state which shape the conditions under which pupils and teachers interact are particularly important in this context. The systematic sociological study of education in Britain began by investigating the effects of the major policy reforms brought about by the Education Act of 1944, aimed at providing greater equality of opportunity and access to education. In many contemporary western societies there has been another important shift in educational policies over the past couple of decades and it is to this issue that the chapter now turns.

The whole infrastructure of education, like many other institutions and organizations in contemporary society, has undergone a period of intense modification over the past decade with issues of marketization, competition and accountability coming to the fore. Sociologists are interested in examining how these policies develop, the processes of restructuring arising from them and their impact on the practice of education.

In Britain many of these changes were embodied in the Education Reform Act 1988 (ERA) which introduced a national curriculum (bringing the UK in line with most other European societies), standardized attainment tests, school governance and the establishment of city technology

these beliefs did not then determine their attitudes to education in the manner assumed in labelling theory. Like Willis, Mac an Ghaill's study emphasized resistance to the culture of the school through the development of a distinct sub-culture. Resistance was, therefore, the main theme within their schooling. This did not necessarily manifest in anti-education attitudes. Some students developed strategies to reconcile their resistance to the culture of the college and the content of much of the curriculum while maintaining their educational aspirations by playing the game. Fuller (1983) also gave examples of groups of female Afro-Caribbean students who found ways of resisting many of the institutional demands of the school, and what they believed to be a racist curriculum, while remaining committed to the value of education itself and the importance of obtaining academic qualifications. A more recent ethnographic study by Sewell (1997) came to very similar conclusions to Mac an Ghaill and Fuller. He found that students were 'positive about education but many rejected the schooling process' (1997: 102). However, although students adopted a number of coping strategies, Sewell maintains that, unlike the females in Fuller's study, some male students found it impossible to operate within the school system and confrontation with teachers became inevitable.

Some writers, such as Troyna, have adopted a fervently anti-racist stance towards issues of theory and practice within educational contexts and in doing so contested the way in which 'multicultural' policy has been traditionally structured (see Troyna and Hatcher, 1992; Troyna, 1993). For Troyna, the idea of attempting to modify individual attitudes towards issues of multiculturalism and developing a climate of cultural awareness in schools is merely a form of curricular 'benevolence'. Instead he advocates the implementation of anti-racist educational policies which directly address and contest issues of societal racism. According to Troyna, such policies should constitute a form of political education which highlights issues of racism.

However, this critique of the inherently racist character of schools and classroom interaction has itself been criticised on both empirical and theoretical grounds. Foster *et al.* (1996) argue that there is currently no convincing evidence by which discrimination against black students can be established. They argue that ethnographic studies alleging racist attitudes are subject to the selective interpretation discussed earlier in relation to Keddie's research. That is, evidence is filtered through a preconceived assumption that schools are racist. For example, an incident involving censure of a black child is put forward as evidence of racial discrimination when other explanations might be possible. In fact Foster (1992) has argued that teachers' views of students owe rather less to cultural stereotypes and rather more to the behaviour and abilities of students in the classroom. However, this in turn has to be balanced against research by Mac an Ghail (1988) and others that did find evidence of cultural stereotyping on the part of teachers.

colleges and grant-maintained schools, (neither of which would be under the control of local education authorities in England). Much of this legislation involved reducing the power and status of local authorities while re-orientating education towards a market-driven economy of greater diversity and consumer choice.

Although the full impact of the ERA 1988 on schools has only recently become apparent, the changes it has brought can be more fully understood when viewed within the context of economic development in Britain over the past two decades. For example, one of the main features of the Act is the way in which, since the late 1970s, state educational policy has become more prescriptive in accordance with the increasing demands of economic productivity. While at first glance notions of 'education' and 'economy' may appear unrelated, clear and established links exist between these two entities which have been ever-present since the 1940s and 50s when, as both functionalist and Marxist theories articulated, education was explicitly located as a central instrument of post-war reconstruction. The general impetus here centred around the dissolution of previously pervasive class-based notions of an 'academic' versus 'vocational' split in schools with the intention of promoting egalitarian practices of educational 'equality' (see Floud and Halsey, 1961). However, more recent manoeuvres to rekindle the education–economy relationship have come about as a consequence of broader political and economic changes in society and, in particular, the emergent demands of a global economic culture. The commercialization and marketization of education, with schools and colleges being reorganized more like businesses, reflect this pressure.

## Education, Marketisation and the 'New Right'

Often cited as a stimulus for such change in Britain was the wave of economic and cultural renewal which came about as a consequence of the election of the Conservative government of the late 1970s, whose processes of policy implementation and economic practice were guided by what has come to be known as the 'New Right' (see Brown, *et al.*, 1997; Whitty, 1997a). The explicit aim of the 'New Right' was to create an atmosphere of 'incentive' and 'enterprise' among individuals within society in order to engender a competitive market ethos, whereby people would strive to better themselves financially and alleviate notions of state dependency – the idea being to place the onus on individuals and individual institutions to become more responsible and accountable for their own livelihood without relying too heavily on financial support from public sources. Like a host of other institutions, education was part of this overall plan. It too would have to 'market' itself, 'compete' for clients and thereby gain state funding according to the levels of success incurred. Central to this restructuring process, Whitty argues:

Have been moves to disempower centralised educational bureaucracies, and to create in their place devolved systems of schooling entailing significant degrees of institutional autonomy and a variety of forms of school-based management and administration. (1997a: 299)

Similar changes were occurring within other western (post-) industrial societies, particularly the USA (see David, 1991). Moreover, there is evidence to suggest that since the late 1980s other nations such as Australia (Kenway, 1993), New Zealand (Grace, 1991), the Netherlands (Sleegers and Wesselingh, 1993), Spain (Bonal, 1995) and Canada (Elliott and Maclennan, 1994) have experienced some form of educational upheaval on a national scale in line with 'free market' economic forces.

   In the case of Britain the consequence of such change, Brown *et al*. (1997) suggest, is that a devolution of financial staffing and policy issues has been carried out with regard to individual institutions (that is, schools), where assumptions have been made about the potential of educational establishments to 'compete' irrespective of their intake and the added pressure of 'parental choice' (see also Brown and Lauder, 1991). To this end, teachers have experienced considerable change, not only in the content of their work but also in relation to their occupational role. For example, schooling has become the subject of league tables in national newspapers with the result that teachers and schools are able to compare their position with national trends. Whereas at one time pupil assessment was simply structured around issues of 'certification' and 'selection' (Broadfoot, 1996), now such procedures are utilized to monitor school effectiveness and performance, as Torrance points out:

> The government's basic position seems to be that improving educational standards is of paramount importance in improving economic competitiveness within an increasingly competitive global economy, and that a new national assessment framework will help to raise standards by setting publicly accessible targets; measuring whether or not they have been met; encouraging schools to compete with each other by publishing the results; and allowing parents to choose their children's schools and tying finance in part to students numbers. (1997: 320)

An example of how this practice works is provided in Table 9.2, taken from recent report from the National Commission on Education (1996), where Jobson *et al*. (1996) comment on the work of Crowcroft Park Primary School in Manchester in terms of results in standard attainment tasks. The results give an indication of the way in which a school can compare itself to national results in Reading, Mathematics and Science.

**Table 9.2** Crowcroft Park Primary School

| | Teacher Assessment Year 2 (percentage) | | | | | | | |
|---|---|---|---|---|---|---|---|---|
| | Level 1 | | Level 2 | | Level 3 | | Level 4 | |
| | 1993 | 1994 | 1993 | 1994 | 1993 | 1994 | 1993 | 1994 |
| Reading national results | 18 | | 51 | | 28 | | 0 | |
| Crowcroft Park | 14 | 13 | 43 | 60 | 29 | 13 | 14 | 13 |
| Maths national results | 17 | | 70 | | 11 | | 0 | |
| Crowcroft Park | 11 | 0 | 50 | 39 | 70 | 30 | 0 | 0 |
| Science national results | 12 | | 70 | | 14 | | 0 | |
| Crowcroft Park | 0 | | 63 | | 37 | | 0 | |

*Source:* Jobson *et al.* (1996), p. 49.

Sociologists have viewed the impact of educational change on policy and practice in terms of wider social processes. Some, for example, have suggested that such changes are confirmation of the fact that society has entered a post-industrial and/or post-Fordist age as a specific result of the revolutionary forces at work in the fields of technology and communication and the implications these have cumulatively posed for each nation state in terms of economic control (Menter *et al.*, 1997; Whitty, 1997b). In attempting to locate the nuances of the Australian education system within the context of this 'new-look' post-industrial scenario, Kenway succinctly maps out the broader consequences of 'market' ideology:

> As states struggle to transform their national economies and as they direct their resources accordingly, what we see is a shedding of welfare responsibilities. In the case of education... what we see is a transfer of certain responsibilities and costs away from the state to civil society. Accompanying this shift is an organisational and psychological reorientation of the education community within the state, encouraging a market/consumer orientation which feeds into the state sponsored privatisation momentum. ...What also becomes evident is that information and communications technologies and scientific discourses are deployed to promote and legitimate such adjustments. Policy making becomes increasingly caught up in the marketing and policing of images... Indeed, images and meaning have been generated which not only attract and attach people to this market discourse but which also persuade them that it is working in the interests of all. (1993: 114)

The terms post-Fordist and post-industrial are notoriously contentious, and remain open to a range of interpretations and will be discussed in more detail in the following chapter. However, in general terms, they refer to the way in which contemporary society and the institutions within it appear to have broken away from the highly stringent and routinized 'working' practices characteristic of earlier decades (Whitty, 1997b). In applying this kind of analysis to educational contexts, Ball (1990) argues that schools themselves have become post-Fordist in the sense that they have moved away from the narrow mind-set of previous years in terms of the mass production of single-skilled 'workers' and look instead towards the production of innovative, multi-skilled individuals whose diversity equips them to cope more readily with the 'flexible' demands of the global economy (see also Kenway, 1993). In turn, what a number of commentators have intimated is that the restructuring of educational bureaucracies has, to some degree, allowed the promotion of cultural differentiation to take place whereby different types of schools (that is, city technology colleges, maintained schools, non-maintained schools), accommodate the differing needs of various communities and interest groups, thereby demonstrating choice and diversity in accordance with post-industrial expectation.

## Accountability, Control and Teachers' Lives

The restructuring of education in England and Wales might represent something of a contradiction with regard to notions of decentralisation. Indeed, as we have noted, the national curriculum itself constitutes a highly prescriptive educational format which, in terms of teacher autonomy and professionalization, may be viewed as much for its contribution to state control and surveillance as it is for its perceived educational benefits (see Whitty, 1997a). Sociologists are interested in exploring how these changes get implemented in schools and what effect they have on teachers' working lives.

Ball (1990) focused on the ways in which senior civil servants, inspectors of schools and Secretaries of State for Education moulded the ERA 1988, the aim of which was to reconstitute education under the 'twin bases' of increased central state control on the one hand and 'free market' parental choice on the other. Subsequent research set out to chart the impact of such measures on everyday educational practice. Bowe and Ball (1992), for example, identified ways in which clear managerial tensions emerged in some schools as a direct consequence of New Right policy changes, many of which were centred around notions of fragmentation within the context of teacher/senior manager relations and the development of an 'us and them' institutional sub-culture on the part of teachers (see also Ball, 1994). In this sense, the implementation of the ERA 1988 has meant that teaching as a profession has undergone a number of fundamental changes which collectively, Ball claims, have asserted 'a massive and complex technology of control over teachers' work in all its aspects' (1994: 12). These changes have, as Whitty points out, brought with them a host of new demands, pressures and responsibilities:

Classroom teachers face a number of new pressures – increased workloads, attempts to use them more flexibly to counter the effects of budget restrictions, performance-related pay and the substitution of full-time, permanent, qualified staff by part-time, temporary, less-qualified and less-experienced (and therefore less-expensive) alternatives. (1997a: 305)

Some of these concerns were explicitly born out in the feelings of the 88 teachers interviewed during a research project set up by Pollard and his associates (1994) which was designed to examine the impact of the ERA at Key Stage 1 in infant schools in England and Wales where the national curriculum was first implemented. The overall findings of this project suggested that the teachers concerned sensed a severe lack of autonomy and certainty with regard to the implementation of educational reform. Pollard and his colleagues asked about how teachers occupational roles had changed as a result of the national curriculum and assessment. Many of those interviewed felt very negative about their experiences of educational change, as the following quotation indicates:

I'm just more stressed now. I feel pulled in different directions and I feel the need to fulfil attainment targets and to cover the core subjects as a constant unspoken pressure. The relaxed atmosphere I used to have in my class has gone. I can't spend so much time with individual children and I don't feel able to respond in a spontaneous way to some initiative introduced by the children. I no longer have the luxury of being responsive and creative. (Pollard *et al.*, 1994: 85)

While some teachers felt more secure in the knowledge that a standardised curriculum format was in place as a consequence of the ERA (1988), such views were in a minority with many regarding the national curriculum as something which promoted feelings of professional loss in terms of autonomy in pedagogic (teaching) decision making (see also Whitty, 1997a). The different responses of teachers to the greater surveillance and examination of their working lives were brought together using five concepts: compliance, incorporation, mediation, resistance and retreatism. These were defined as follows:

● *Compliance*: acceptance of the imposed changes and adjustment of teachers' professional ideology accordingly so that greater control is perceived as acceptable, or even desirable
● *Incorporation*: appearing to accept the imposed changes but incorporating them into existing modes of working, so that existing methods are adapted rather than changed and the effect of change is considerably different from that intended
● *Mediation*: taking active control of the changes and responding to them in a creative, possibly selective, way

- *Retreatism*: submission to the imposed changes without any change from professional ideology, leading to deep-rooted feelings of resentment, demoralisation and alienation
- *Resistance*: resistance to the imposed changes in the hope that the sanctions available to enforce them will not be sufficiently powerful to make this impossible (Pollard *et al.*, 1994: 100).

While some teachers acted as mediators by taking ownership and control of innovations and trying to use them to develop new forms of practice in pedagogy and assessment, others were involved in retreatism by taking early retirement or some other action, the most common response being 'incorporation'. In spite of the negative feelings aired, resistance, in the form of refusal to implement the national curriculum or assessment, was found to be virtually non-existent. Such evidence clearly illustrates the difficulty with which some teachers in England and Wales have adapted to the demands of the ERA (1988) and its aftermath. This situation has been exacerbated by the fact that schools have also had to contend with continued policy modifications along the way, some of which have come about as a consequence of governmental change.

The lasting impact of the 1988 reforms can be seen in the fact that Labour politicians abandoned their previous policy of developing a common, comprehensive education for everyone and adopted the 'New Right' language of testing, educational standards and parental involvement. More recent educational initiatives from Labour politicians have, for example, stipulated a rationalization of the national curriculum to facilitate improved numeracy and literacy standards (Qualifications and Curriculum Authority, 1998). Likewise, a more prescriptive curricular format has been put forward for the training of teachers in order to raise pupil performance in schools with early dismissals for failing teachers (DfE, 1998). While these changes may be viewed in terms of the ongoing battle to socialize and educate children on egalitarian grounds, they might also be interpreted as a further contradiction to the deregulation rhetoric emanating from state agencies in Britain. Such instances of contradiction are not confined to the implementation of policy or the practicalities of educational delivery. They also exist in and around current theoretical interpretations of the changes, particularly the debate about modernity and postmodernity. On the one hand, images of diversity, choice, fragmentation and plurality appear to favour a postmodern interpretation, displacing what Whitty (1997b: 123) has termed the 'oppressive uniformity' of modernist thinking within educational spheres. On the other hand, they can be seen as a further twist in the longstanding 'modernist' tale of class, deprivation and educational disadvantage. As Whitty observes:

> Rather than benefiting the urban poor, as many of the advocates of quasi-market systems of public education claim... the emphasis on parental choice and school

autonomy in recent reforms seems to be further disadvantaging the disadvantaged. It is certainly increasing the differences between popular and less popular schools on a linear scale – reinforcing a vertical hierarchy of schooling types rather than providing the promised horizontal diversity. (1997b: 124)

Of course, in reality, it will be some time before such theoretical postulations can be confirmed or dismissed by sociologists of education, and a number of years before the consequences of more recent educational policy measures can be fully observed and interpreted. Needless to say, it will be issues like these which will dominate sociological analyses of educational developments into the new millennium.

# Further Reading

Ball, S.J. *Policy Making and Education*, London, Routledge, 1990. A major study in the tradition of 'policy sociology' which raises key issues in terms of the impact of the ERA (1988).

Halsey, A.H., Lauder, H., Brown, P. and Stuart Wells, A. *Education: Culture, Economy, Society*, Oxford, Oxford University Press, 1997. This text provides an up-to-date and global compilation of various themes and perspectives within the sociology of education.

Mac an Ghaill, M. *The Making of Men: Masculinities, Sexualities and Schooling*, Buckingham, Open University Press, 1994. An engaging account of the complexities of male identities and the role schools play in the transformation of boys to men.

Foster, P., Gomm, P. and Hammersley, M. *Constructing Educational Inequality*, London, Falmer Press, 1996. A challenging and critical review of much of the research carried out in the sociology of education in the past half century.

Usher, R. and Edwards, R. *Postmodernism and Education*, London, Routledge, 1994. An accessible text which attempts to describe, explain and analyse education in relation to postmodern thought.

# 10

# Work and Organizations

## *Glenn Morgan*

Contemporary societies are dominated by the twin imperatives of work and organization. Our social and economic system revolves around the production of goods and services within organizations. This chapter aims to examine the relationship between work and organizations and social transformation, from classical sociologists' attempts to understand the impact of industrialization to contemporary sociologists' analyses of the effects of new technological developments and the opening of global markets. Changes in work and organization have important implications for power relations, patterns of inequality and the question of globalization. This chapter should help you understand:

- The centrality of changes in work and organizations in the transition from traditional to modern society.

- Classical sociologists' interpretation of industrialization and social change

- What is meant by Fordism and sociological interpretations of the 'Fordist era'

- The changes in contemporary societies giving rise to 'post-Fordism'

- Recent developments in economic sociology

---

### CONCEPTS

industrialism ■ industrialization ■ division of labour ■ bureaucracy

feudal society ■ markets ■ the 'affluent society' ■ Fordism and

post-Fordism ■ global commodity chain

---

# Introduction

As consumers and citizens, we rely on private and public sector organizations to provide us with material goods such as food, clothing and housing as well as services such as education, leisure, health care, credit, and protection from crime. As workers, we rely on the existence of organizations to provide us with the income that will enable us to pay for goods and services. For people living in industrialized and urbanized societies, their lives consist of inter-acting continuously with organizations in order to sustain their identities as workers, citizens, consumers, parents, students and so on.

It does not take a great deal of historical understanding or sociological imagination to realize that the world was not always like this, and indeed, that many parts of the world still do not match this model. Education, the subject of the previous chapter, can provide an example of this change. In Britain, over 30 per cent of the age cohort now attend university and most people stay in some form of education until they are 18. Sixty years ago, the standard age of leaving school was 13 and the numbers who continued through to university were nearer 3 per cent. One hundred and sixty years ago, there was very little schooling of any sort for the majority of the popu-lation, most of whom would be working in factories, mines or agriculture by the time they were 7 or 8 years old. For the great majority of the population, there were no special organizations known as schools, colleges or universities. What they learnt, they learnt from their families and friends in the local settings where they lived and worked. These conditions still exist in parts of Africa, Asia and Latin America. Education to university level is confined to the élite and wealthy, while the majority receive only basic instruction, gaining most of their knowledge and understanding of the world from friends and families passing on oral traditions.

The world in which we live has been transformed by the growth of formal organizations. If we are to understand that world, we need to be able to analyse the roles which organizations play, how they are structured and how that affects the ways in which people live and work. These issues were central to the concerns of the early sociologists as they sought to define the nature of the new societies which were emerging from the impact of industrialism, urbanism and the ideas of the Enlightenment. Their writings show a commit-ment to the integrated analysis of social change in which work and organiza-tions are a central element. This approach has been developed further through the twentieth century as societies and economies have undergone further changes. The chapter is designed to introduce students to these issues. In the first section, I discuss how the classical sociologists conceptualized work and organizations in the context of social transformation. I then describe how these ideas were further developed in the 1950s and 60s as sociologists sought to understand how western societies appeared to have overcome the class conflicts and social instabilities which seemed endemic in earlier periods of industrialization. However, the relative stability of these years was over-taken again from the 1970s onwards with what appeared to be a new set of changes and uncertainties in the world of work and organizations. The final section examines the changing theoretical framework which is now evolving to take account of this process.

# The Rise of Industrial Societies: Work and Organization in the Classical Sociologists

Changes in work and organizations were central to the transformation of western European societies over the course of the nineteenth century. At the start of the century, most of the population were working on the land and living in small rural communities. The notion of work as a distinct sphere of activity which took place outside the home and in a social context distinctive from that of family was only just beginning to emerge in both country and town (see Laslett, 1965; Pahl, 1988). By the end of the century, there had been a major shift away from the land and the country to the factory and the town. This shift involved not just the development of manufacturing and the emergence of an industrial working class but also the emergence of new functions for the state, such as education, the maintenance of professional armies, the collection of taxes and customs duties and the regulation of conditions in workplaces and public spaces (Mann, 1993). Although these shifts proceeded at a different pace and in a different manner in different European societies, there was a common sense of transformation in Europe that was affecting all the great powers from Britain in the west to Imperial Russia in the east. This sense of a set of forces overwhelming national differences was frequently conceptualized in dualistic terms as a shift from one set of social principles to another; for Marx, it was from feudalism to capitalism; for Durkheim, it was from a mechanical solidarity of similarity to an organic solidarity of interdependence; and for Weber it was from traditional authority structures to bureaucratic structures geared around the efficient pursuit of organizational goals.

These dualisms and the way in which they were conceptualized by the classical sociologists captured distinctive aspects in the process of industrialization and its impact on work and organizations (Giddens, 1971). Three aspects were of crucial importance: the division of labour, new forms of power and inequality and the dynamics of modern markets. This section will consider each of them.

## *The Division of Labour*

The classical sociologists were concerned with how the social transformations they observed affected the division of labour; that is, the differentiation of tasks involved in the production of goods and services. In pre-modern societies, the division of labour tended to be limited. Within peasant economies, most aspects of social life were co-ordinated through the co-operative activity of the family members. Family relations also permeated the political order in such systems and ties based upon family or 'proto-family' clientelistic relationships constituted key principles of political ordering. Modern societies are characterized by a vast extension in the division of labour which generally separates the informal processes of household work from the processes of the formal economy where wages are earned (Rattansi, 1982). As well as the process of economic reproduction being taken out of the household, functions such as education, health care, welfare and leisure become separated from the family and concentrated in specialized organizations.

The differentiation of social functions leads to more specialized organizations which require specialist workers. Specialization within the organization can have two distinct effects. It can be a mechanism for creating highly skilled employees for whom specialization requires a high level of knowledge and understanding of the work context. It can also be a mechanism for creating extremely fragmented tasks that require only unskilled workers to fill them. Specialization and differentiation inevitably lead to increased problems of integration and co-ordination both within the organization and across society as a whole. This in turn leads to a further extension in the role of bureaucracy and management as a central means for controlling and co-ordinating the disintegrating effects of complexity and differentiation. Thus, as Durkheim (1893/1984) recognized, the enhanced division of labour potentially creates greater interdependence among people while also creating greater individualization and therefore fragmentation.

Technology is an essential element in this process. Technology embodies human knowledge and human intentions adapted to what it is possible to think and do in certain periods of time. Once certain forms of technology become established, they create trajectories of development which encourage the refinement and improvement of practices and processes around the basic model. The classical sociologists saw that technology was changing the limits of what it was possible for societies to produce. However, they also realized that this implied changes in the nature of social relationships between owners, managers and workers as well as between different groups in the workforce. The increasing importance of specialized organizations, the potential fragmentation of tasks within organizations, the necessity for processes of co-ordination and control through management and bureaucracy and the impact of technology were essential parts of the changing social division of labour in the nineteenth century.

## Power and Inequality

The second set of key issues revolves around power and inequality in the division of labour. For the classical sociologists, these processes involved conflicts and tensions as different groups within society sought to adapt and respond to industrialism. The types of inequality between the various ranks in feudal society were transformed as societies industrialized. The main routes to power and prestige were increasingly determined by the dynamics of the industrial and financial sectors of the economy. The new division of labour was necessarily shaping a more complex structure of power and inequality. In the nineteenth century, the classical sociologists saw mostly deepening and increasingly visible divisions within society. In the new urban areas, those dependent on paid employment were crowded together in unhealthy and insanitary conditions. The sort of employment which they could get was often short term, casual, poorly paid and frequently dangerous. The struggle to overcome these effects was often led by male trade unionists from the skilled crafts and middle-class reformers for whom a decent standard of living also implied adherence to a model of family life in which the woman stayed at home and the man worked in the paid sector of employment. Although many women continued to take on paid employment, this often remained casual and poorly paid and their dependence and subordination to men was institutionalized within the emergent industrial system. Even for male workers outside the skilled crafts or those sectors such as mining, dockwork (where spatial proximity helped induce collective consciousness), trade unionism was not well developed in most countries until the twentieth century. Thus inequalities within the working class, that is, between male workers in different sectors of the economy and between male and female workers as a whole were significant and continuously militated against collective political or social action. The broader inequalities which existed between the entirety of this class and the other groups in society were often less significant than these intra-class differences.

Industrialization generally involved a transformation in the nature of the rich, from a group predominantly based on landed power to one based on ownership and control of industrial and financial resources (Scott, 1982). Whereas feudal society was theoretically based on a system of reciprocal obligations and duties, industrialism tended to release the rich from this sense of obligation in the name of the market and individual responsibility. Thus at the same time as the differences between rich and poor became clearer, so the willingness of the rich to recognize any obligations to the poor tended to decrease (although the extent and nature of employer paternalism varied across and within European societies with important implications for the nature of the social order, see for example Bendix, 1956; Moore, 1966). Maintaining social order in the factory and in the cities in the light of the changing nature of inequality led to a range of responses from states and employers.

The classical sociologists took different attitudes towards these processes and their long-term impact. The depth and visibility of inequality in industrial systems gave Marx cause for optimism that this would lead to working-class political action and the eventual overthrow of capitalism. For Durkheim, inequality was the impetus for social reform led by the state and professional groups in order to create a greater organic solidarity. Weber had a darker and more complex vision in which the quest for amelioration of inequality through socialism would not necessarily lead to greater freedom but rather accelerate the trend towards the 'iron cage of bureaucracy' trapping individuals more tightly in its grasp. While they might differ about diagnosis and prognosis, the classical sociologists shared a concern with understanding how power and inequality were being reshaped under industrialism.

## The Market

Central to the dynamic changes in the division of labour and structures of power and inequality was the role of the market; that is, an arena where people freely exchange commodities usually for money. The classical sociologists recognized that market relations embodied complex and sometimes contradictory forces. On the one hand, markets operate on the basis of individual choice – the freedom to buy and sell goods, services, land, labour power. On the other hand, people may lose freedom in the sense that markets cannot work unless there is a category of the population who have no choice other than to sell their labour power. This means that they must have been stripped of the ability to produce their own means of subsistence, for example by maintaining a plot of land, and forced to enter the money economy. Nor can markets work if there are traditional or legally based restrictions on what can be bought on the market, how goods and services may be produced and how they may be priced. Traditional societies have often involved a range of proscriptions over market-type relations. For example, the idea that one's labour belonged to oneself and could therefore be sold voluntarily on the market only established itself gradually from the sixteenth century onwards. In feudal systems, the serf was the property of the lord who had first call on the labour of his vassal. The right of the serf to move parishes was severely proscribed and considered a crime. There was no right to sell one's labour to another since it belonged not to the serf but to the lord. Selling it to another was therefore selling something one did not own and equivalent to stealing. Even the right to consume was not based simply on money. Sumptuary laws were common in feudal societies. These laws stated who could and could not wear certain types of clothing, usually furs and other signs of rank and status.

Market societies are based on the formal abolition of these restrictions. Property becomes defined from the point of view of the individual owner who can sell land, labour and other goods under market conditions and not subject to traditional proscriptions. Similarly, in formal terms, it is possible to buy anything legal on the market without any restrictions. The idea that anything can in theory be traded on the market becomes corrosive of traditional social relationships. What and how it is actually 'morally' acceptable to buy and sell is rather different from the theory. Even advanced capitalist societies possess diffuse and complex forms of social relationship which define what it is morally acceptable to sell (Thompson, 1968; Zelizer, 1994), leading to frequent agonized debates either about particular issues, such as whether or not it is right that people should be able to buy private health care or education? The formal abolition of these restrictions does not mean that the expectations or obligations disappear as easily. Even in the sphere of wage labour, debate continues as to what is being sold. The argument about how much effort and commitment is purchased by the employer in return for the wage continues to rage (see for example Kunda, 1992). Workers and managers often seek to create obligations and duties about who can do what task (Bendix, 1956; Fox, 1985).

Nevertheless, markets introduced a dynamism into social and economic relations that had not been there previously. Marx referred to the bourgeoisie as the most revolutionary class in history because in spreading market relations, it undermined all traditional systems of social order. Durkheim viewed the market and individualism as closely interlinked. The decline of traditional societies wiped away the limited horizons which people previously had, leaving them with no clear sense of their identity. The sense of meaningless which Durkheim described as 'anomie', or over-developed individualism, undermined stable social order. He therefore looked for ways in which new codes could be created to settle people in their social position and avoid conflict and disorder. Weber, in contrast, feared a society in which market rationality increasingly took over and left no room for individuals.

## Social Transformations, Work and Organizations in the Classical Sociologists

In summary, the classical sociologists looked at work and organizations through the lens of their interest in the broader process of social transformation that was occurring in nineteenth-century Europe. This led them to identify aspects of the new order which were common and shared across Europe. The extension of the social division of labour and its embodiment in new forms of organization and technology, the struggle over power and inequality played out within the work setting and the dynamics of the market distinguished nineteenth-century Europe from its predecessors. Yet these authors were also convinced that they were living through a process that had not by any means reached its end-point. For Marx, this was only a stage en route to proletarian revolution, the overthrow of capitalism and the establishment of socialism. In Weber, the advance of the 'iron cage' of industrial bureaucratic rationality was likely, but not inevitable. There may be new social movements based on inspirational charismatic leadership where old ideals may be reborn, or society may solidify into 'mechanised petrifaction'. In Durkheim, the transition from mechanical to organic solidarity was in danger of creating anomie, a situation where individuals were left without values and meaning. Societies needed to develop intermediary institutions that would provide this framework, thereby allowing individualism to flourish without becoming self-destructive egoism.

For these authors, the study of work and organizations was part of their wider understanding of how societies were being transformed. It was therefore concerned essentially with processes of change and how processes inside the organization interacted, reproduced and changed the wider social context. As a result, they sought to identify the essential elements of this transformation in the division of labour, power and inequality and market dynamics. In doing so, they tended to emphasize the homogeneity of the processes which they identified. National contexts might speed up or slow down these processes but this was of marginal interest compared to the sense that this was going to happen everywhere eventually. 'De te fabula narratur' ('About you, the story is told') Marx wrote in the Preface to the first German edition of *Capital*, warning the rest of the world that his account of the dynamics of capitalism in Britain described what was going to happen to them in the future – 'the country that is more developed industrially only shows to the less developed, the image of its own future' (Marx, 1970: 9).

## Approaches to Work and Organizations in the Fordist Era

By the middle decades of the twentieth century, industrial capitalism had been established for over 100 years across most of western Europe and the USA. War and economic depression had dominated the politics of the twentieth century up to the 1950s, reinforcing some of the warnings of the classical sociologists about the divisive impact of industrialism. However, during the 1950s, it appeared as if the system was at last achieving some sort of stability. Real incomes began to rise in the western economies, unemployment fell, the scope of welfare services, such as health and education, as well as unemployment and pension benefits were widened. Commentators began to refer to the 'affluent society', the 'welfare state' and 'the end of ideology'.

Sociologists at the time responded in a variety of ways to these changes. In the USA, which was by far the most successful of the capitalist economies, there was a widespread sense that the conflicts of the past had been overcome and society was now entering a phase of relative industrial peace. The sociological theory of structural functionalism, described in Chapter 3, was a product of this way of thinking with its emphasis on stability and consensual values. The idea of 'industrialism' as a system of production which relied on large firms using increasingly advanced technologies with a workforce which was generally well paid and co-operative was propounded, as we saw in Chapter 5, as representing the end of class-based politics. The authors of one of the most famous texts of the era even went so far as to suggest that industrialism would force a convergence in political and social structures across not only western societies but also those in the Soviet bloc (Kerr *et al.*, 1973).

Other authors were more sceptical. Marxists continued to argue that there remained fundamental class conflicts in capitalist societies. While some argued that what had occurred was an ideological blinkering of the working class, others challenged the actual premises of the argument. They noted that there remained high levels of industrial conflict, sometimes visible and formal (in strikes and other types of dispute) and sometimes invisible in absenteeism and 'industrial sabotage' (Hyman, 1975). Weberian sociologists, however, tended to be more cautious about what was happening; in the most widely quoted study of the period in Britain, 'The Affluent Worker' project, Goldthorpe and colleagues argued that workers had made a pragmatic adjustment to the realities of the assembly line (Goldthorpe *et al.*, 1968). In return for relatively high wages, they would co-operate up to a point with management. However, they maintained the right to argue about what were acceptable conditions of work in the light of the wages which they were offered. Their pragmatic acceptance was also dependent on continued high wages. It was therefore a conditional acceptance of the system for as long as it gave them the resources and time to pursue their interests outside work.

This era was described as *Fordism,* taking its name from the American car manufacturer, Henry Ford, who had developed the world's first mass production car plant. The key characteristics of Fordism revolved around the way in which it resolved the problems of order and control in an unequal society both at the workplace level and more generally in society. At the level of the production system, managerial control was high and workers were relatively deskilled. To make this work, employers had to be able to pay these workers high wages. High wages were viable where firms were making high profits. Firms achieved this in a number of ways. One way was by growing big and using economies of scale to reduce costs. Another was to co-operate with other firms on the limits to competition; in other words, to operate informal price setting cartels. All of this required governments which were willing to co-operate with business by stimulating mass market demand. Trade unions were brought into this process at various levels. Within the firm, they negotiated wages and control. Within the broader social context, they were 'social partners' in varying forms of corporatism (that is, high level agreements between employers, government and the trade unions to compromise over their conflicting demands). Essential to most versions of this corporatism was the creation of a welfare state which offered access to health, education, pensions and other benefits. The expansion of the state sector and state services relied on the maintenance of a taxation base which could supply the revenue. The tax base and the actual material benefits of the system varied across different countries although the basic structure remained similar.

The Fordist structure did not resolve questions of inequality and power in society or in the workplace. Instead, it tended to displace their effects on to either excluded groups or on to society more widely. For example, the Fordist system was built on the model of the male breadwinner dominant within the patriarchal family. Large manufacturing firms employed mainly men in their more well-paid manual jobs. Women found work in part-time or casual employment, while retaining the primary responsibility for children and the home more generally. The welfare state reinforced this by also being built on the presuppositions of the male breadwinner model; most unemployment insurance and pension systems provided few benefits to the pattern of labour market participation experienced by women. Furthermore, the sort of conditions which enabled the Fordist compromises were not possible in many more competitive sectors of the economy, such as small manufacturing firms, the retail and personal service sectors where wages and benefits tended to be low and work was often part time and temporary. As well as women workers (and some white male workers), migrants from South East Asia, the Caribbean, eastern Europe and Africa tended to congregate in these jobs. This reflected a broader process within the Fordist system which was the dependence on cheap raw materials (most obviously oil) and food from the non-developed part of the world. Fordism's expansion was on the basis of the subordination of most of the rest of the world to its requirements. This went along with a total disregard for the ecological consequences of the mass production system.

## Post-Fordism and the End of Organized Capitalism?

From the 1970s onwards economic crises in the west, new technologies and the opening of world markets made it increasingly difficult to sustain the foundations of Fordism, giving rise to an emerging model of work and organizations described somewhat unoriginally as post-Fordism (Lash and Urry, 1987). In order to understand this, we can return to the previous themes of the classical sociologists.

### The Division of Labour

The transformation of the 1980s and 90s have been centrally about the division of labour both within and across firms and across societies. Research has identified a number of important changes in the nature of work. First, the application of new information technology to manufacturing and service processes has changed the distribution of labour within organizations. Large numbers of routine manual, clerical and managerial jobs have been lost as control and co-ordination functions have been embedded in technology. The result has been reductions in the number of managerial levels and increases in the amount of skill required by key workers. This process has also led to a growing differentiation between the core workers within the firm and the peripheral workers. The latter may be on short-term, part-time or temporary contracts. As Castells says:

> The traditional form of work, based on full-time employment, clear-cut occupational assignments and a career pattern over the lifecycle is being slowly but surely eroded away. (Castells, 1996: 268)

These changes are associated with an increased technological flexibility in the production process which enables more rapid changes in products and processes in response to market pressures.

**Table 10.1**    Characteristics of Fordism

| Level of analysis | Key features |
| --- | --- |
| Labour process | Mass production: assembly lines: semi-skilled workers |
| Mode of macro-economic growth | Based on economies of scale and investment in mass production systems: rising wages and increased mass demand |
| Social mode of economic regulation | State involvement in (a) managing conflicts between labour and capital (b) managing economic growth through Keynesianism (c) maintaining welfare system |
| General pattern of social organization | Based on consumption of standardized products: predicated on stable nuclear families with male heads of household; social order managed by centralized bureaucratic state. |

*Source*: Adapted from Jessop 1994.

The restructuring process within the firm has led to changes in the relationships between firms. In the Fordist era, large firms tended to do everything in-house. However, as the pressure has increased on firms to cut costs, there has been a tendency to buy goods and services in from the outside. Outside contractors can be squeezed by their dependence on the large firm and thereby forced to hold down wages or reduce employment benefits. This process may occur in relatively low skilled areas such as catering and cleaning as well as in the production of components for manufacturing systems. It may also have a spatial dimension with firms purchasing from overseas where wages are low and controls on work conditions non-existent.

These processes are subject to diverse interpretations of their significance. On the one hand, some authors argue that these changes represent the end of mass production and, with it, the end of the oppressive conditions of large-scale hierarchical organizations peopled by semi-skilled workers subjected to close supervision and control. In this context, the changing nature of work and organizations is also perceived to open up new possibilities for political and social movements which will reduce inequalities inside and outside the workplace. This is generally associated with those approaches that emphasize the growing importance of co-operative networks for economic production.

The changing division of labour between firms has reflected a growing interest in patterns of co-operation between firms and their implications for social and political order and competition. Sabel and Zeitlin (1997) have argued that there are two broad types of industrial production which have co-existed for some time. The first is the Fordist mass production system based on big firms, high differentiation between managers and workers accompanied by high levels of inequality and detailed control systems over workers. The second is the form which arises from pre-industrial traditions of craft work. This is generally based on small and medium-sized firms, with low levels of differentiation and inequality between managers and workers. This tradition relies on high levels of skilled worker input to the production process in order to develop high-quality outputs. It is usually locally based with high levels of co-operation between local governmental institutions (for example training) and firms, as well as high levels of co-operation between firms. This latter model which is referred to as 'flexible specialization' can be identified in various specific locations, usually described as 'industrial districts' to reflect their specialization in a particular sector of industry. For example, in Italy, particular towns and regions specialize in specific sectors such as ceramics in Sassuolo, knitwear in Modena, wool textiles in Prato. Within these local networks, close inter-firm relations interact with high levels of specialization and skill to produce a pressure towards continuous process and product innovation (Langlois and Robertson, 1995) that is particularly important in current competitive conditions. This leads some authors to suggest that as economic competition favours industrial districts and their ability to produce high-quality outputs, flexible specialization as a mode of organizing production will become common (see Piore and Sabel, 1984; Sabel and Zeitlin, 1997), thus in practice leading to a reduction in inequalities and a greater emphasis on co-operation within and between firms. From this perspective, industrial districts and the networks of co-operation within them give rise to higher levels of social co-operation, less use of centralized authority structures and narrower spreads of inequality in wealth and income. They are generally based on strong local political institutions which take an active role in shaping economic life. This approach offers an optimistic view of the future for organizations and work, based on the gradual decline of hierarchy, control and inequality.

An alternative approach argues that the localism of industrial districts and firms is embedded within a larger structure, dominated by multinational corporations. From this perspective, the outputs of industrial districts are generally merely inputs to a more complex chain of production organized by multinationals. Multinational corporations are the main mechanism through which this is achieved as they increasingly locate production facilities around the world according to calculations about advantages deriving from labour costs, labour discipline, labour skills, access to local markets, provision of tax breaks and incentives, and access to locally specific knowledge and networks. Multinational economic co-ordination also occurs through what Gereffi has termed 'global commodity chains' (Gereffi and Korzeniewicz, 1994; Gereffi, 1995; see also Dicken, 1998). This concept describes how firms produce goods and services by co-ordinating the provision of the various elements that go to make up the product from conception and design through to manufacture to distribution and sale. Each of these elements may be produced in-house or purchased from outside. In either case, the elements may come from the home base or from another part of the world. As Gereffi and others have shown, more and more industries are now operating and controlling commodity chains which are global in their scope and orientation (see the articles in Gereffi and Korzeniewicz, 1994; also Dicken, 1998, Chs. 9–12). What this results in is a system where rich western consumers purchase from their high-street stores such as Gap, Toys R Us and Sportshoes Unlimited products such as clothes, toys, and trainers, which are produced in countries such as China, Vietnam and India with low wages, child labour, no trade union rights, and poorly monitored health and safety or welfare systems. From this perspective, therefore, multinationals reproduce and reinforce global inequalities. Their actions may be influenced by public opinion or state regulation but their ability to shift production around the world makes this influence limited. The result is that key economic decisions are being made further and further away from the people most directly affected. Even democratic nation states find it hard to influence the decisions of these multinationals which are basically reached behind closed doors according to a logic of capital accumulation that has little to do with social welfare and are characterized by high levels of inequality between their top directors and workers in far-flung subsidiaries. They are also not tied to local political systems and move their investment according to a logic of capital accumulation that has little to do with social welfare.

It has been argued that while these alternative models are useful for high-lighting the issues, they do not grasp the complexity of the different forms of production, work and organization that exist in practice. In this context Boyer and Durand (1997) propose a more complex typology which identifies a number of different routes out of Fordism which have distinct implications for work, organizations and patterns of social and economic inequality.

## Flexible specialization

Workers exert control over machines and potential compromises between capital and labour occur at the level of the company or the local labour market (for example the industrial district).

## Toyotaism

This 'reorganises production, maintenance and management tasks so that operators are responsible for controlling production equipment, rather than the reverse, with a tight set of incentives at the company level inducing worker commitment'.

## Uddevallaism

This is named after the Swedish car factory which rejected the traditional Fordist assembly line and became a symbol of the Scandinavian 'work humanisation' movement; it 'combines the most radical reorganisation of the division of labour (elimination of the assembly line, fixed station assembly and greatly extended cycle times) with a capital–labour compromise situated at the national level (centralized negotiations over wages, training and work time)'.

## Market-pushed neo-Fordism

Based on the introduction of new technologies to impose more control by machines of workers – workers are forced to accept changes for fear of unemployment.

## Corporate-pushed neo-Fordism

Similar to the previous model but based on compromise between capital and labour within the company or sector.

## Social democratic neo-Fordism

Based on a nationwide compromise between capital and labour which provides the framework within which new technologies and restructuring at the firm level is implemented.

Within this framework, particular national contexts have evolved specific forms of Fordism. While the crisis of this production model is general, the nature of the changes and the trajectories after Fordism will differ. There is a path dependence created by national institutional features which limits the opportunities available to particular countries (see for example the country studies in Whitley, 1992; Crouch and Streeck, 1997; also Hollingsworth and Boyer, 1997). This also implies that the impact on inequality of these various routes will also be different. Thus Boyer and Durand are implicitly criticizing those authors who believe that globalization undermines the capacity of national governments or social actors to take decisions which will affect the nature and distribution of inequality in a society (see also Weiss, 1998).

**Table 10.2**    Routes out of Fordism

| Types of post-Fordism | Control of technology at firm level | Role of the market |
|---|---|---|
| *Flexible Specialization* | High level of control by skilled workers | Mediated at local level by collective institutions e.g. for training |
| *Toyotaism* (from the Japanese model) | Operators responsible for continuous production improvement | Mediated by long-term and close linkages with suppliers |
| *Uddevallism* (from the Swedish model) | Job rotation and teamwork | Bargaining over wages and conditions conducted at national level |
| *Social Democratic Fordism* | Management control of technology and work process but role of trade unions accepted | State continues to provide benefits to workers to mediate market pressures |
| *Corporate-pushed Fordism* | Management control of technology but recognition of importance of core workers | Core workers in firms protected from market pressures |
| *Market-pushed neo-Fordism* | Replacement of labour by technology predominant thrust | Unrestricted market forces |

*Source*: Adapted from Boyer and Durand 1997.

## Power and Inequality

The second main theme identified in the classical sociologists was the inter-relationship between work and organizations and structures of power and inequality. In the modern transformation which has been described, the impact on power and inequality is also of central significance. I will examine this in four contexts; within firms, between firms, between those in employment and those out of employment and finally between societies as a whole (the international dimension of inequality).

First, the changing nature of work and organizations is impacting on power and inequality within firms. The basic distinction which has already been described is between those employees who constitute the core workforce and those who constitute peripheral workers. The core workforce are those with high levels of managerial, professional and technical skills whose continued commitment to the organization is necessary for its success. This group will generally receive high levels of material rewards, such as income and fringe benefits linked to performance outcomes. Organizations have reduced the absolute numbers of their employees which can be counted as core as they have got rid of layers of management and administration. Core employees are often rewarded through performance-related pay and share options. The distribution of these rewards tends to be increasingly skewed with senior management in particular benefiting, thus increasing levels of inequality within the firm, even within the core workforce. Castells notes US research which indicates that while the 'median wage for men working full-time has fallen from \$34,048 in 1973 to \$30,407 in 1993, the earnings of the top 20 per cent grew steadily and real per capita GDP rose 29 per cent' (Castells, 1996: 275).

There is a great deal of evidence that shows that this division between core and peripheral workers reinforces and reproduces existing social divisions. Women are far more likely than men to be in part-time employment or on short-term contracts and constitute the great bulk of the peripheral work-force. In the UK, the 1993 Labour Force Survey found that 85 per cent of part-time workers were women. The young and the elderly also find it more difficult to gain positions in the core workforce as do members of ethnic minorities. The core workforce within organizations is still predominantly white and male at all levels.

Second, the distinction between core and periphery is also reproduced between certain sorts of firms. As previously noted, large firms often use small firms as mechanisms for retaining flexibility. When orders are high, large firms may subcontract out to small firms more of their production. When orders are low, subcontractors may find themselves without business. Large firms with networks of suppliers can use their position to squeeze down contract prices and in so doing, force small firms to reduce wages and employment conditions. Subcontracting also reduces the strength and power of trade unions by splitting potential members into smaller units which are geograph-ically and organizationally distinct, thus making union organization and collective bargaining less likely. Thus within the one location, firms which are interdependent in the production chain may be characterized by very different workforces with different wages and employment conditions.

Where subcontracting also crosses national boundaries, as is often the case, the result may be that wages and employment conditions are forced down even further by the use of young female labour and, in some cases, even child labour. As cross-national global commodity chains become more common, differences between levels of wages and rewards within the one commodity chain become dramatic.

Third, the process of restructuring has led to a stripping out of manage-ment and bureaucratic levels as well as a reduction in the number of employees involved in manufacturing and services. As well as specific redun-dancies, entry points into employment have reduced. Young people tend to spend longer in training and searching for paid employment than previously, often going through extended periods of part-time and casual employment before settling into a career position. Women who may have left the labour market in order to have children find it difficult to return to work other than through forms of part-time and temporary employment. Men and women who have been made redundant from declining industries find that they cannot get back into similar types of employment; some may have to face retirement in their early fifties. The restructuring of work reinforces other tendencies of social exclusion, creating an underclass of under-employed people who shift in and out of precarious positions on the periphery of the labour market. Furthermore, as societies seek to reduce welfare expenditure, many of those not in formal employment are pushed back to reliance on either family networks of support or the informal, black economy which may in certain cases shade into illegal activity.

Fourth, the restructuring of work and the development of global commodity chains has complex effects on inequality at the global level. The first basic distinction is between those areas of the world which are integrated within global commodity chains and those which are not. In the main, exclusion from these chains tends to mean exclusion from any access to even a small amount of the benefits of trade and development as well as aid funds. Countries in Africa and Asia which have nothing to sell on world markets are of little interest to governments, international agencies or funding sources until war, terrorism or famine forces them on to the international news agenda. They become trapped in a spiral of decline, unable to access any modern technologies either for production purposes or for health care – Castells refers to these as 'the Black Holes of Informational Capitalism' (Castells, 1998).

Where multinational companies have an interest in a particular area because of its natural resources, its labour or its markets, then there is the potential for a transfer of financial resources, in terms of either cash or production facilities. This transfer has a complex impact on societies (Dicken, 1998). In some societies, this transfer is effectively placed in the hands of a small and corrupt élite which siphons off a substantial share for luxury consumption while maintaining low wages, poor working conditions and high levels of labour discipline. In these circumstances, inequalities within the receiving society tend to increase. As some of the east Asian countries such as the Philippines (during the era of the Marcos presidency) and Indonesia (under Suharto) have found, there is a limit to people's willingness to accept these conditions. Given certain sorts of compromises within the élite of such societies, however, (and, in particular, social constraints on corruption) this transfer may become the basis for a sustained process of development. East Asian societies such as Singapore, Taiwan and Hong Kong show how it is possible to take advantage of these transfers and move from low-skilled assembly work for others up to constructing the whole product and even branding and selling it on one's own behalf (Wade, 1990; Gereffi, 1995; Weiss and Hobson, 1995; Castells, 1998). In these circumstances, there tends to be a wider spreading of the benefits of wealth and the creation of a substantial middle class which helps consolidate the home market. However, this process is frequently accompanied by increased commercial pressure on urban and rural communities, with the consequent deterioration in infrastructures and damage to the ecology of whole areas in the rush to industrialization (see Castells, 1997, for a discussion of these trends and emerging forms of resistance) as well as an over-expansion of lending and investment that can lead to the crisis which hit many east Asian economies in the late 1990s.

The divisions between societies are also powerful motors for the extension of international labour migration. Workers from the developing countries have moved into Europe and North America, through both legal and illegal means. Remittances from these migrants (that is, funds either sent or taken back by workers from their host state) to their home country are massive. Harris notes a number of estimates of the scale of these remittances from a World Bank figure in 1989 of $66 billion to an IMF estimate for 1990 at $33.8 billion. He estimates an average annual remittance of between $700–$1000 per year which for many less-developed countries is a major contributor to foreign exchange and therefore to the purchase of imports (Harris, 1996: 142). These remittances mitigate to a small degree the absolute inequalities between societies but at the expense of both breaking families apart and increasing inequalities within the receiving society. Migrant workers from the developing world generally move into the occupational structure in positions which the indigenous population has rejected although Cohen points out that there are different sorts of what he terms 'diaspora' with different consequences for the inequality and power (R. Cohen, 1997). For example, many east Asian migrants (from China and Korea) into the USA have had sufficient capital to set up small businesses in inner urban areas. Similar processes have occurred among some east Asian communities in the UK.

This restructuring process has seen an increased differentiation in the world division of labour. Patterns of power and inequality across societies have been affected by the actions of multinationals and global economic co-ordination. Divisions between the poorest and the richest societies have increased, as have divisions within some of the poorer societies as the benefits of industrialization are unevenly distributed.

## Markets

The opening up of world markets has had a major influence on the processes just described. The Fordist system was based on the ability of the *governments* of nation states to manage demand within their own borders. The sale and purchase of goods across national boundaries was limited by the way in which national governments manipulated tariff barriers and the availability of currencies. Balance of payments crises for individual states arose where purchases from abroad exceeded overseas sales. Governments could respond by reducing internal demand. Where this still failed to work, then the currency could be devalued, discouraging imports and increasing the competitiveness of exports (Van der Wee, 1991; Foreman-Peck, 1995; Panic, 1995). Within national contexts, markets for goods and services could be regulated to achieve broader social and political objectives such as the maintenance of employment and social stability.

Once governments could no longer control their markets in this way, the edifice began to collapse. The impetus to open up national borders came from the desire first to purchase goods at the cheapest price available on the world market and second the desire to borrow capital in larger amounts and at cheaper rates than national financial systems were providing. However, these benefits were at a price, in particular the threat to home industry of loss of markets and the potential instability of currencies, capital flows and investment arising from integration into the world system (see for example Strange, 1986, 1995; also Kapstein, 1994; Stubbs and Underhill, 1994; Morgan, 1997; Underhill, 1997). This also contributed to the crisis of the welfare state as 'the price of welfare' (that is, how much it cost in terms of taxes) became incorporated into the price of commodities. Countries with higher levels of welfare faced the problem of their products being more expensive than those with minimal welfare systems. This has led to efforts at restructuring the welfare state and shifting its focus away from redistribution towards an emphasis on training and what is known as work-fare (that is, making benefits conditional on willingness to participate in training and other job schemes) (Jessop, 1994; Esping-Andersen, 1997).

The ability of governments to control markets has therefore reduced. It has become more difficult to sustain industrial sectors such as mining or agriculture because of their social function. If they cannot adapt to the market, they will go out of existence and the people who work for them will be made dependent on states where welfare budgets are shrinking. The state sector itself is also under threat. Privatization has left most western societies with a vastly reduced public sector and that which is left has often been subjected to 'market testing'. Whole societies have been forced to open their boundaries by the power of international institutions such as the IMF and the World Bank to dictate the terms on which loans can be made available. The consequences of marketization have been dramatic in countries such as Russia where unemployment and the destruction of formal systems of welfare (and even wage payments) have led in many areas to a return to a barter economy and rising mortality and disease levels among the population.

However, there remain differences in how individual countries respond to this process. Boyer's emphasis on the national specificities of production systems discussed earlier (Boyer and Durand, 1997) reflects the concerns of a number of other authors in identifying 'national business systems' (Whitley, 1992) or 'social systems of production' (Hollingsworth and Boyer, 1997). The capacities and capabilities of organizations are shaped by their institutional context. Thus global market pressures are always adapted within local contexts. For example, societies with highly developed capital market systems on the Anglo-American model are more open to global competition than societies based on what is termed 'alliance capitalism' (that is, where ownership is concentrated in interlinked banks and firms who hold shares long term rather than trading them frequently for short-term profit gains; Whitley, 1992; Orru *et al.*, 1997; Scott, 1997). Alliance capitalisms are also usually able to achieve levels of co-operation between firms and the state in terms of running down declining areas of production or developing new capacities (Wade, 1990; Streeck, 1992). For example, in Japan, the Ministry of International Trade and Industry (MITI) has been instrumental in helping and persuading firms to move out of declining industries such as textiles and shipbuilding and into expanding ones such as electronics and computers (see Johnson, 1982). Similarly, some societies have developed work systems that are based on a highly skilled workforce supported by the education and training system (see Lane, 1989; Streeck, 1992; Sako and Sato, 1997; Storey *et al.*, 1997); such systems seem more capable of adapting to market change and higher consumer expectations than systems based on mass production and Fordism. Thus the ability of Japanese and German car firms to respond to changing consumer tastes (such as for higher quality products, safer cars with lower petrol consumption) in the late 1970s was at least partially due to the fact that workers in these firms were highly trained and skilled in resetting production systems. By contrast, British and US firms took much longer to adapt, partly because workers were less skilled and levels of conflict with management were higher, leading to resistance to change.

# Towards the New Economic Sociology

What sort of theory is required to make sense of these changes in work and organizations? There are at least three main ways in which the approach described here differs from that of the classical sociologists and the traditions developed from their work.

## Nations, Globalization and Change

The classical sociologists described the nineteenth-century transformation without much acknowledgement that this process could only be enacted through specific national contexts which in turn would shape the outcome.

The sort of dualistic thinking which the classical sociologists used (for example the contrast between feudalism and capitalism in Marx, between mechanical and organic solidarity in Durkheim, between traditional and bureaucratic authority in Weber) tended to conceal the issue of *national* differences. However, many sociologists place these national differences at the centre of analysis. It is precisely in the strength of the empirical research which can now connect national systems of organization and work to deeply embedded aspects of the institutional order that most progress is being made within this new economic sociology (Whitley and Kristensen, 1996, 1997; Boyer and Durand, 1997; Crouch and Streeck, 1997; Hollingsworth and Boyer, 1997).

Even when the degree of inter-connection within nation states and across them increases as it has done over the last twenty years, the process of glob-alization which occurs is not an abolition of the significance of space and territory but its incorporation into a broader set of social relationships (Amin and Thrift, 1995). Smith and Meiskins (1995) identify this in terms of a triple effect. There is the national context of organizations, there is the context of the international capitalist system and the role of particular firms and terri-tories within that context and finally there is the overall global political order in which certain nation states are dominant and set rules for others to follow either through the use of explicit military force or through informal economic power (for a discussion of globalization see Chapter 15). The new economic sociology is concerned with understanding the interaction between these national and international forces (Dicken, 1998). In this respect, it goes beyond the classical sociologists.

## Markets as Social Constructs

The classical sociologists tended to assume that there were certain economic processes which could be defined as beyond and outside human intentionality which acted as determinants of social action. In this respect, they under-estimated the importance of social processes in determining the nature and extent of the economy. The new economic sociology is not simply concerned to show how institutions 'affect' economic processes but rather how the two are integrally connected. For example, there has traditionally been a tendency to treat economic performance as a given, while the internal aspects of the organization can be considered as social processes, the consequences of those actions become goods and services on markets where outcomes are determined by relative efficiencies. However, markets themselves are socially constructed in many different ways. We can observe this for example in the way in which the public sector has been reconstructed over the last two decades. For example, in Britain under successive Conservative governments, an 'internal market' was constructed in the National Health Service, whereby hospitals and doctors were given budgets to buy and sell treatments which previously were provided as of right (see Ferlie *et al.*, 1996 for a discussion of these changes). The 'rules' of this market have been constructed by politicians and others seeking to implement policy objectives through creating a market which works in a particular sort of way (see Morgan and Engwall, 1999 for further examples). Even within what are seen as the traditional competitive industries, there are rules which determine who can compete and what they are trying to achieve. Smith's (1990) analysis of auctions shows how what appears to be a pure market process is in fact constructed through participants' use of shared understandings and rules of behaviour about who can bid what in particular contexts. In traditional economic analysis, the market acts as a self-regulating process, rewarding the efficient and deselecting the inefficient. Increasingly, sociologists are revealing how these processes have to be enacted by social actors, which in turn opens up the market as an arena of power and conflict in which groups struggle to impose their definition of how it should work, who should be considered winners and losers and how participants should benefit from their roles in the market (see Swedberg, 1994; Quack *et al.*, 1999).

## Action and Structure

Finally, the new economic sociology is entangled within the preoccupations of sociological theory with the relationship between action and structure which was discussed in Chapter 3. Only Weber of the classical sociologists really explored the ways in which actors shaped structure rather than being shaped by it. In the current period, this is a major preoccupation that defines a range of positions. At one extreme, there are those who emphasize the 'systemic' nature of institutions and organizations which means that it is extremely difficult for actors to influence outcomes. At the other, there are those who point to the ways in which the co-ordinated effort of key groups in a society can lead to change and development. For example, the efforts of certain key nobles to industrialize countries like Japan and Germany in the late nineteenth century were successful because in those societies there was still a great deal of power centralized in and exercised by the landholding aristocracy around the court. Similarly, the industrialization strategies led by the state in South Korea, Taiwan and Singapore worked because these states (for different reasons) were extremely powerful and not subject to significant resistance. Under certain circumstances, élite groups have been able to take control of the state and use its powers to reshape the basic institutions of society towards a new structure. Moreover, this may often relate to the broader international environment in which states are located. The support of the USA in the form of cheap credits, access to open markets without demanding reciprocity, and technology transfer to Japan, South Korea and Taiwan during the Cold War was crucial in enabling them to develop their industrial structure further.

# Conclusion

In this chapter, I have argued that the sociology of work and organizations is an integral part of understanding how societies work. In the writings of the classical sociologists, the understanding of work and organizations was part of an attempt to understand how life was being transformed through industrialization. These changes were related to changes in the division of labour, changes in power and inequality and changes in markets. As a result of these changes, new structures of work and organizations were emerging and giving rise to new forms of social order. In this perspective, the sociology of work and organizations is part of the broader sociological agenda about how societies are changing and adapting to processes of industrialization.

This tradition has been re-awakened in part by the sense that the world is currently undergoing a transformation of equivalent significance to that of the nineteenth century. This new set of transformations, which has to do with the establishment of global markets, new forms of technology, the incorporation into the world economy of new areas and the increasing competitiveness of firms within and across nations, is impacting and overturning existing patterns of the division of labour, power and inequality and markets. Yet the response to these upheavals clearly varies across countries. National business contexts create a form of path dependency for institutions and organizations. The aim of research is to understand more about how these dependencies constrain action or encourage it. This approach builds on the classical sociological accounts of transformation in the nineteenth century but with a new appreciation for national and territorial distinctiveness, the social basis of markets and the interaction between action and structure. Much of its research and its theorizing is essential to broader concerns about the nature of social change into the next millennium, and it is impossible to understand issues like class, power, inequality and globalization without referring to the growing literature within the sociology of work and organizations.

# Further Reading

Amin, A. (ed.) *Post-Fordism*, Oxford, Blackwell, 1994. An examination of the changing nature of work and organization placed in the context of new forms of politics and culture.
Dicken, P. *Global Shift: Transforming the World Economy*, 3rd edn, London, Chapman, 1998. An examination of how networks, multinational corporations and the state link together in particular industries.
Morgan, G. *Organisations in Society*, London, Macmillan, 1990. A review of the main theories of organization and their links with classical sociological theories and themes.
Thompson, P. and McHugh, D. *Work Organisations: A Critical Introduction*, 2nd edn, London, Macmillan, 1995. A thorough account of the changing geographical and organizational structure of production.

# 11

# Crime and Deviance

## *David Downes*

While criminology is confined to violations of the criminal law, the sociology of deviance has a much wider focus, examining any behaviour perceived as breaking the rules of a social group. Sociologists are not only interested in explaining why deviance occurs, but also why and how some actions are defined as deviant and why and how sanctions are applied to offenders. In this undertaking they draw on a wide range of theoretical perspectives including some of those examined in Chapter 3, such as functionalism, interactionism and Marxism. This chapter aims to explain and illustrate the development of the major sociological approaches to crime and delinquency. It should help you understand:

■ The distinction between the sociology of deviance and criminology

■ The development of strain theories from the work of Durkheim to the study of delinquent sub-cultures

■ Interactionist theory and the focus on social definitions of deviance

■ 'Social' and 'situational' control theories and their implications for crime prevention

■ Radical deviance theory

---

### CONCEPTS

victim survey ■ anomie ■ delinquent sub-culture ■ moral panic
primary and secondary deviance ■ critical criminology

---

# Introduction

The term 'deviance' covers the spectrum of socially proscribed behaviour: any form of conduct which elicits social sanctions that may range from mild censure to capital punishment. The attempt to explain and understand not only the 'bad' but the 'mad' and the 'odd' and how they are so designated and controlled constitute the field. Students of deviance have regarded blindness (Scott, 1969), stuttering (Lemert, 1967) and nudity (Douglas, 1977) as within their intellectual domain, although crimes, delinquencies and mental illness are the usual topics of theory and research.

The scope of deviance is thus far wider than that of crime and, as a result, the sociology of deviance differs in several ways from criminology. Most importantly, its subject matter is not defined by what happens to be sanctioned by the criminal law at any time or place. Although all societies prohibit theft and non-governmentally sanctioned violence, there are immense differences between societies, and within the same society over time, in the legal status of forms of sexual conduct, drug use and freedom of expression for example. It is thus analytically preferable to build the realities of flux, diversity and ambiguity into the subject, rather than to opt for the illusion that the criminal law provides the entire basis for inquiry. The criminal law is an essential part of the field, not its foundation. It is social definitions and controls which form the basic unit of analysis in the sociology of deviance, and they are only given legal form under certain conditions.

In practice, the fields of criminology and the sociology of deviance have much in common, and they have often worked to their mutual benefit. For example, victim surveys were originated by criminologists in the 1960s, and became firmly established in the 1980s, as a way of supplementing and testing trends in crime based on the official criminal statistics supplied by the police. They were motivated in part by the claims of some sociologists of deviance that rises in crime based on the police figures were unduly inflated, or even spurious, due to changes in reporting and recording processes. Victim survey data showed, as expected, that much very petty and some quite serious crime went unreported; the upward direction of the trends in the official figures was also confirmed, although at a lesser annual rate of increase (Maguire *et al.*, 1997).

However, despite such overlap, the two approaches remain distinct in principle. Criminologists are mainly preoccupied with highly focused inquiries into particular forms and trends of crime and its control. Sociologists of deviance not only cast their net more widely, but also pursue issues such as how the media selectively portray and convey images of deviance, the connections that may exist between crime, deviance and the political economy and the changing landscape of punishment in institutions and in the community (Cohen, 1985; Garland, 1990).

Sumner (1994) argues that the sociology of deviance came into being to challenge the grounds on which deviance was attributed to some groups rather than others, especially political deviants and other outsiders such as drugtakers. He claims that since that challenge has now been abandoned, the subject can no longer be said to exist. However, this assertion is groundless. The intellectual radicalism of the sociology of deviance resided in asking two sets of questions. First, how are some *behaviours*, and not others, defined as deviant? Second, given those definitions, why and how are some *persons* and not others processed as deviant, and with what consequences? On those two basic issues is built the entire edifice of the field. Since these two fundamental questions remain – and it is difficult to see how they can ever vanish – the sociology of deviance in some form or other will survive and even flourish.

This chapter will focus on how the sociology of deviance has evolved an array of theories to account for crime and delinquency. As these theories stem from intellectual roots which involve conflicting views about human nature and society, it is difficult to see how they can be fused into some overall synthesis. Moreover, 'crime' and 'delinquency' are terms that encompass a vast diversity of behaviours, united only by the common denominator that they are infractions of the criminal law. No one theory can begin to encompass them all. Nevertheless, the justification for attempting to theorize at all is that crime and delinquency are not utterly random and entirely unpredictable phenomena. Insofar as they display certain discernible patterns and forms, they are amenable – at least in principle – to causal explanation and the possibility of understanding the meanings and motivations of those engaged in them. The first section looks at some of these regularities, the following sections look at the main theoretical approaches to deviance and the final section outlines some of the current issues in the field.

# Some Regularities That Any Theory Must Fit

1. Crime rates have risen strikingly since the mid-1950s in virtually all societies. In Britain, there has been a tenfold increase in the crime rates over the past 40 years, although they levelled out in the 1980s, and fell in the USA in the 1990s. After 1981 victim surveys also showed a lesser but still marked rate of increase. This rise and rise of crime has not only presented the criminal justice system with immense logistical problems, it also confounded the simple belief that greater prosperity and welfare provision would *reduce* crime, which social reformers had argued was mainly due to mass poverty.

2. Offending behaviour is far more common among some groups than others. Males commit several times more crime than females and the young more than the old. Socio-economic deprivation is also an important risk factor for offending and anti-social behaviour. However, low family income, poor housing and large family size are better measures and

produce more reliable results than low occupational prestige (Farrington, 1997). As a result, offending is heavily skewed, some 6–7 per cent of males committing 60–70 per cent of officially recorded offences. Victimization is also heavily skewed, with 1 per cent of the population suffering some 25–40 per cent of household property crimes. Crime is a form of regressive taxation levied disproportionately, although not exclusively, by the poor on the poor.

3. Much crime is relatively hidden – being generally unreported and therefore unrecorded and investigated by the police – and its exposure would modify standard images of deviance. Domestic violence is also regressive but occupational crimes by employees and employers, and corporate crime by companies and businesses redress the balance. Poor people are hardly in a position to commit major frauds, insider dealing on the Stock Exchange or compel employees to work in dangerous conditions. However, the general fear of crime is greatest in relation to the non-hidden offences of burglary, robbery, crimes of violence and car-related crime.

4. Only a relatively small proportion of offences, perhaps as low as 2 per cent a year, result in the conviction of offenders. If the hidden volume of offending was added to the total which we know about from police figures and victim surveys, that percentage would shrink to even more negligible proportions. Yet – except in the worst-hit communities – crime remains a manageable problem. Some people, especially among the better off, sail through life without ever being victimized. The dynamics of crime seem to differ from those of punishment. Texas imprisons ten times as many offenders as Britain, but its murder rate remains several times higher (Hood, 1996). If the prospect of imprisonment as a fearsome deterrent was the main reason for keeping within the law, the situation should be the reverse. This suggests that social, cultural and economic factors are far more important in explaining crime than the severity of punishments. It also suggests that, although the situation may be steadily worsening, powerful constraints do operate in society to keep crime in check. The fact that the formal control system captures so few, although in the longer run an appreciable chance of conviction rises, points to *informal* social controls as immensely potent.

# Sociological Approaches to Crime and Delinquency

Social theories of crime have proliferated greatly over the past century. No one theory or approach has 'won out' over this period, and no 'knock out blow' has been delivered which would allow us to consign some of them to the sidelines. Nor did they emerge in neat chronological succession, although

some are more prominent at some period̸
adapted, extended, revised and renamed, ̸
made to blend two or more into a mo̸
master key to making sense of this pr̸
differentiate them into:

1. *Strain theories*, which stress the malint̸
   giving rise to deviant *motivations* on the part ̸
2. *Interactionist theories,* which stress the socially cons̸
   tity, and the consequent importance of *labelling* processes ̸
   and groups becoming deviant.
3. *Control theories*, which stress the significance of controls against dev̸
   Control theories have tended to divide into those which primarily stress
   *social* controls and those which emphasize *situational* factors.
4. *Radical* theories, which stress the fundamentally crime-generating nature of
   *capitalist* political economy.

## Strain Theories

The progenitor of strain theories was Durkheim, whose work was a major
influence on what came to be known as functionalism (for further discussion
of functionalism see Chapter 3). For Durkheim (1895/1982), the assignment
of functionality to an institution involved two criteria. First, was an institution widely prevalent, or even ubiquitous, in human societies? If so, the
sociologist was alerted to its likely functionality, since it would be unlikely that
an institution, such as the family and kinship, would survive unless it
promoted some fundamental social end. Second, however, it was essential to
ask the question: in what ways does the institution function to enhance the
conditions of social cohesion and group life? Only if the second criterion
could be fulfilled could functionality be inferred.

Durkheim's (1893/1984) most surprising demonstration of his claims for
the method concerned the functions of deviance. Crime, he argued, is normal,
and attempts to extirpate it altogether were doomed not only to failure but to
making things worse. His reasons were that crime functions to elicit responses
which arouse collective sentiments and mobilize upright consciences, the
result of which is to reinforce and clarify the most significant norms and values
in society. To eradicate crime, so signal a process of mobilizing consciousness
against the most trivial act of deviation would be needed that social stagnation
would result from all behaviour becoming excessively over-regulated. Thus, it
is a sign of social pathology if the crime rate falls too low just as when it rises
too high. Durkheim's theory was considered immoral in its day and in some
ways would elicit a similar reaction today. It would take a brave sociologist to
endorse the approach to an audience of parents of the children who were

heir school in Dunblane in Scotland. Not that such endorse-
be called for: Durkheim would have no doubt regarded such an
ological. For while it is clear that he regarded a crime-free society
adiction in terms, a sociological impossibility; what remains unclear
levels of crime are normal, and what are pathological. The only clue
Durkheim gave is that the norm is set by the average rate in societies of
parable development and type. But what if conditions are universally
sent to produce an unduly high crime rate globally?

That state of affairs is more or less theorized by Durkheim as existing in the transitional stage at which most societies stand in the evolution from mechanical to some future, somewhat utopian organic solidarity. In such societies, the free-market economy produces a predatory, highly competitive war of all against all, a dog-eat-dog world in which greed is good and the strain to anomie is ever present. Economic materialism has outstripped the capacity for moral regulation. In his celebrated study of *Suicide* (1897/1952) Durkheim introduced a major source of variation in suicide rates as stemming from economic boom and slump. In both extreme situations, the suicide rate rises, which he explained as due to the weakening of moral regulation under circumstances of rapid change. Here Durkheim relied on a view of human nature as innately liable to the malady of infinite aspirations. Lacking a moral order which alone can restrain them, people's aspirations rapidly overshoot any possible fulfilment, leading to a state of chronic frustration, bitterness and anger capable of driving them to such ultimate acts as suicide or homicide. In sum, a certain amount of crime is normal in any society, but crime and deviance assume pathological proportions in a state of anomie brought about by unduly turbulent economic change. Intervention in the economy to moderate such extremes was logically called for as a remedy.

Merton (1968, 1938/1993) reformulated Durkheim's theory of anomie in four crucial respects. First, he saw the capacity to aspire 'infinitely' not as a natural human trait but as a propensity which had to be *culturally* nurtured. The unique egalitarianism of the American 'way of life', in which everyone was led to accept the belief that anyone could make it from 'log cabin to White House', and in which advertising matched mass production with mass consumption, was the precursor of a global 'revolution of rising expectations'. Second, the strain to anomie was not, as in Durkheim, released only in exceptional circumstances, but became a routine feature of American life. Third, the causal sequence was reversed: for Durkheim, deregulation led to infinite aspirations; for Merton, infinite aspirations led to deregulation. The end result, however, was in each case the same: high rates of deviation. Fourth, for Durkheim, the strain to anomie was at its height in the upper reaches of society. For Merton, the disparity between aspirations and rewards was at its greatest in the lower depths. As a result, higher rates of crime and deviance were to be expected the lower the position in the social class hierarchy.

In some respects, Merton took not Durkheim but Marx as his inspiration. The most powerful element in Merton's theory is his emphasis on what Marx saw as the engine of capitalism: the fostering of the propensity to consume. Left to themselves, people do not necessarily want super-abundance: but they are goaded into ever-expanding realms of consumption by ceaseless advertising. The capitalist show can only be kept on the road by 'institutionalized dissatisfaction'. The result is at best 'mild economic anomie', the feeling that one has never quite made it until one buys the bigger car, the better holiday, the brighter washing powder. At worst, anomie becomes chronic, or long term, and deviant ways of adapting to it institutionalized: crime organized, fraud rampant, theft routinized and violence normal. Both Durkheim and Merton, in different ways, do address the central criminological problem of the twentieth century: how to explain the rise and rise of crime in the context of rising prosperity. It is not, in their view, prosperity as such which causes rising crime, but the disruptive effects of unplanned economic growth (in Durkheim's case) or the perpetuation of inequalities in the context of rising expectations (in Merton's), which leads to the experience of *relative* deprivation.

Fresh developments in strain theory arose in the attempt to explain the specific phenomenon of gang delinquency. In the post-war period of rising prosperity and limited welfare provision, it had been expected that crime and delinquency would gradually subside. In fact, the reverse occurred, with crime and delinquency both rising and assuming even more florid forms, first becoming manifest in the USA. Youth gangs, of the sort romanticized in the musical *West Side Story*, flourished, yet their bitter 'turf wars' and high death toll did not seem well accounted for by Merton's celebrated but rather mechanistic typology of 'deviant aspirations' to inequality. The goal of 'money-success' which he had taken as the acme of mass American culture, was difficult to link with delinquency which was primarily *expressive* rather than instrumental. They were far more likely to vandalize their school than to rob a bank.

Cohen (1955) argued that gang delinquency amounted to a way of life which was:

1. non-utilitarian, that is, not mainly concerned with economic gain
2. negativistic, in the sense that a certain malice entered into the defiance of authority
3. not simply at odds with respectable society, but lived by rules which ran counter to it
4. celebrated 'short-run hedonism', not only living for the moment, but actively resisting any attempt to plan for the future, was versatile rather than specialized in its delinquency and owed allegiance to the gang alone.

Such a way of life was concentrated in a small section of society, among some male, urban, working-class adolescents. In accounting for this behaviour, Cohen elaborated a theory of *sub-cultures,* that is, cultures within cultures. Sub-cultures emerge when people confront problems which they simply cannot avoid or solve, because they are set up by the way society is structured. In this case, the problem arises precisely because American egalitarianism, operating through the schools, insists upon high levels of achievement and ambition from allcomers. Yet the odds are stacked against working-class children from the outset. School failure therefore presents large numbers of working-class children, boys in particular, with a real problem which Cohen argued they resolve by creating a counter-framework within which they *can* succeed: the delinquent gang. The gang gives them status, a sense of achievement, and a way of hitting back at the system that has labelled them failures. Cloward and Ohlin (1960) supported the concept of the 'delinquent sub-culture' but argued against Cohen that at least three kinds could be distinguished: criminal (for gain); conflict (for turf); and retreatist (for drugs), depending on the character of adult crime. In neighbourhoods where adult rackets were prevalent gang delinquency serves as a kind of apprenticeship for recruitment to the mob. In areas so disorganized that even the rackets avoid them, the conflict gang prevails. Where 'double failure' occurs – the world of crime being no easier to succeed in than the 'straight' world – the retreatist pattern of drug use is likely to be chosen. Moreover, in all this swirl of activity, the school is of no account to downtown boys. What inspires their sense of alienation is not school failure but lack of material success. Well-paid jobs are their goal rather than status in school. Cloward and Ohlin predicted the crisis that would occur when de-industrialization led to the large-scale disappearance of secure and well-paid manual jobs, a development documented vividly by Wilson (1996).

Matza (1969) took a different tack, arguing that the idea of 'delinquent sub-cultures' conjured up a mythical picture of lower-class youth committed to incessant warfare against middle-class adult institutions. In reality, most delinquency was petty and intermittent. By over-predicting delinquency, these theories could not account for its decline in adulthood, nor for the 'techniques of neutralization' deployed in explanation by the young people involved (Sykes and Matza, 1957). Phrases such as 'I didn't mean to do it'; 'They had it coming to them'; 'Everybody does it'; are not just rationalizations but attempts to neutralize a sense of guilt which, if the offenders were so righteously indignant about their social situation, they would not even feel. So what makes delinquency attractive in the first place? Here the stress is placed on what delinquents have in common with the rest of society, rather than on what sets them apart.

They are seen as sharing adherence to 'subterranean values' (Matza and Sykes, 1961) such as the equation of toughness with masculinity, the search for excitement and a disdain for routine work. These are the values of gentlemen of leisure as well as delinquents: delinquents differ, however, in acting them out without respect for time and place. Their accentuation makes for a 'sub-culture of delinquency', in which law breaking is an option not a necessity. Youths may drift into delinquency by a temporary loosening of controls rather than through commitment to a delinquent way of life (Matza, 1964). The more extreme forms of delinquency arise from desperation or 'compulsive' behaviour. In correcting for what he saw as positive defects (the scientific search for causes which override free will), Matza may have under-predicted delinquency yet been obliged to retain a positivist model for its most extreme forms.

How well did these largely American theories, fashioned to account for gang delinquency in the USA, transplant to Britain? (See Tierney, 1996, for an unusually full account of these approaches.) Mays (1954) argued that 'growing up in the city' involved working-class boys almost inevitably in traditions of fighting to display toughness and vandalism and rowdiness to show daring. They would normally grow out of this phase, given decent jobs and education. Mays was also a pioneer of more robust forms of youth work and adventure playgrounds to divert youthful energies from law breaking (Mays, 1959). Morris (1958), in a study of suburban London, found that social planning and public housing recreated problems in certain areas which American sociologists had seen as peculiar to the inner city. Cramming the most turbulent families into a few neighbourhoods intensified their problems, a theme taken up later by Gill (1977) in Liverpool and in Sheffield by Bottoms and Xanthos (1989).

These approaches dealt well with the persistence but not the rise in rates of delinquency in the second half of the twentieth century. Applying sub-cultural theories to delinquency in East London, I inclined to Matza's approach as best capturing the impulse to delinquency in the search for excitement (Downes, 1966). However, Matza played down the class aspects of leisure, into which working-class boys and young men channelled their energies most potently. Out of the expanse of boredom that met rising expectations in the mid-twentieth century came both the creative format of British youth culture and the new styles of delinquency of the Teds and the Mods and Rockers. In these tentative beginnings, the American theories were borne out quite well by the mildness of delinquency in Britain, given the strength of working-class community, full employment and realistically low job aspirations. However, they also pointed to the ways in which this situation might change drastically if those structural guarantees changed.

## Interactionist Theories

Interactionist theories raise a fundamentally different set of questions about deviance. Instead of taking conformity for granted, and deviance as so odd that distinct motivations had to be sought to account for it, interactionists asked why some behaviour was defined as deviant in the first place, and why only some groups, and not others, became so labelled. Cohen (1980), in a book which added the phrase 'moral panic' to the English language, was not so interested in why the Mods and Rockers had running fights on the beaches of English seaside towns in the mid-1960s, but why the social reaction to them was so excessive. Youth 'letting off steam' was nothing new, but the media coverage invoked unprecedented forms of youthful deviance. Cohen went on to argue that not only was the reaction wildly exaggerated, it also had the ironical effect of making things worse. Alerted by saturation media coverage to these dramatic events, far more were recruited to the Mods and Rockers ranks than would otherwise have been the case. Labelling such groups as drastically deviant created a 'deviation amplification spiral', in which an ever-hardening minority of deviants increasingly resisted the imposition of authority. Eventually, the deviants may be dragooned back into conformity by the forces of law and order, but only after a bloody, protracted and largely unnecessary sequence of law enforcement.

The seminal work in this approach is Becker's *Outsiders* (1963). Indeed, it was Becker's achievement to recast what had been the 'sociology of social problems', 'social pathology' or criminology into the distinctive shape of the sociology of deviance. He did so by exploring, more purposefully than earlier theorists, the full implications of its social character:

> Social groups create deviance by making the rules whose infraction constitutes deviance, and by applying those rules to particular people and labelling them as outsiders. From this point of view, deviance is not a quality of the act the person commits, but rather a consequence of the application by others of rules and sanctions to an 'offender'. The deviant is one to whom that label has successfully been applied; deviant behaviour is behaviour that people so label. (1963: 9)

Becker's work is exemplified by the skill with which he demonstrated its relevance to an understanding of marihuana use. To Becker, marihuana use is actively learnt behaviour, to be understood only if the sequence of stages through which the learner must pass is grasped. It is not a sudden leap into the unknown, sparked off by social deprivation or anti-social character traits. Moreover, the very status of marihuana use as deviant is problematic originating, in Becker's view, from the 'moral entrepreneurship' of the Federal Bureau of Narcotics, whose case was more of a moral crusade than a scientific demonstration that the drug was more dangerous than alcohol or tobacco. *Outsiders* triggered a momentous chain reaction in the sociology of crime and delinquency. It brought into play as variables the very processes of defining behaviour as deviant, and of labelling some people but not others in that way, which had previously been ignored. Before Becker, the social and legal responses to crime had been little studied, assumed to be a constant, background element in processing offenders through the criminal justice system. Now that system became part of the picture, not simply its frame. Law making, prosecution, policing and sentencing were to be as intensively studied over the next few decades as offending behaviour itself. Moreover, the interaction between the two was now a central concern.

Labelling theory developed from the work of Mead which was discussed in some detail in Chapter 3. For Mead, the self is partly a compound of the social roles we learn to play (both within the family and in the larger worlds of neighbourhood, school and work), which he termed the 'me'; and partly an active, observing 'I', the unique source of one's identity. The result is a 'vital division within consciousness' (Downes and Rock, 1988: 192) which allows for the self-questioning, self-doubting aspects of the self. To a formidable extent, our sense of self is socially derived and sustained, which is not to say that it collapses with the absence or removal of our socially 'significant' others. Once formed, the self may still transform but it may also display astonishing resilience.

The implications of taking this approach seriously proved momentous for theory, method and policy making. If people are taken to retain the capacity for change throughout life, if they are taken to be sensitive to the definitions others make about their conduct and themselves and if they are active agents, rather than passive receptors, in the process, then character and motivation are not to be simply inferred from such attributes as gender, age, ethnicity, class and nationality, or from their wealth, income and education, but can only be known by direct observation. The main implications of the approach theoretically were that if social definitions are consequential for people's sense of self-worth and identity, then formal definitions are of particular significance. They flow from authorities with the power to impose definitions and enforce sanctions that may have enduring implications for those labelled deviant.

Lemert (1967) distinguished between 'primary' and 'secondary' deviation. Primary deviation abounds: many people, perhaps the majority, steal at some time or other. Secondary deviation is where 'the original 'causes' of the (primary) deviation recede and give way to the central importance of the disapproving, degradational, and isolating reactions of society' (Lemert, 1967: 81): a minority become processed as 'thieves', 'thugs', 'perverts' and so on. Lemert argued that research into secondary deviation is in many respects more pertinent, since the symbolic attachment of deviance to persons may fundamentally reconstitute their moral character, whether in the eyes of the wider society, their local networks, family intimates, themselves or a combination of all four. These ideas have also had a powerful influence on sociological explanations of sickness (see Chapter 12). In the work of Goffman (1991), for example, the 'moral career' of the mental patient was analysed in terms of such self-redefinition, and the asylum was seen as a prolonged assault on the psyches of those labelled 'mad'.

Out of this perspective was to come a welter of concern that the stigma-tizing social reactions to deviance were more to do with the public reconsti-tution of moral character than the prevention of crime or the rehabilitation of the mentally ill. Strong policy directions flow from this work: decriminaliza-tion should be preferred wherever possible to the imposition of the criminal sanction; destigmatization should be pursued, for example, in the form of diversion from court proceedings to some pre-trial alternatives: ultimately, decarceration should be prioritized, since imprisonment and mental hospital-ization are profoundly damaging to the self, and in ways which make subse-quent offending or illness more likely. Alternative community sanctions should be preferred wherever possible.

Criticisms of the approach include the view that it is a pendulum swung too far. Social reactions to deviance, and their implications for future deviance, may have been overly neglected in the past, but there are severe limits to decriminalization and diversion. Victims demand redress, or may 'take the law into their own hands', and even 'crimes without victims' may not be perceived that way as, for example, in hostile community responses to drug trafficking and prostitution.

Nevertheless, interactionist insights continue to influence the subject, most recently in the form of 'social constructionist' approaches to the study of the claims and counter-claims that enter into the processes of the making of 'social problems' (Hester and Elgin, 1992).

## Control Theories

Control theories come closer to commonsense views of crime and deviance than other approaches. In a sense, we are giving practical expression to control theories of a *social* kind whenever we accompany young children to school or keep tabs on who they are playing with, and of a *situational* kind whenever we lock our doors at night. The nub of control theories is the central importance given to variations in control as the key to trends in crime and deviance. It is a somewhat secondary matter for them to seek to understand what motivates offenders, who are presumed to be rational actors seeking to maximize their pleasures and minimize their pains. Far from looking for some special set of motives to account for crime, or some adverse effect of labelling, they assume we would all be deviant if we dared. What stops most of us most of the time are the losses we would incur if we are caught, and the investment we have made in good reputation that we value highly.

Such notions are not only widely held but have long been so. The idea that each fresh generation is somehow more lacking in discipline than one's own recurs regularly across the centuries (Pearson, 1983). It may be partly for that reason that sociologists were disinclined to take them seriously until recently: theorists tend to abhor the obvious. However, a more likely reason is that such views have tended to be associated with psychological approaches which focused on the individual in the family setting rather than the wider community and society. More tellingly still, the absence or weakness of control was seen as a poor basis for explaining the often non-utilitarian character of deviance. Why should anyone, left to their own devices, want to beat another up or wreck the local youth club?

The first formal attempt to theorize along these lines came from Hirschi (1969). He analysed the social bond linking individuals to society as composed of four main elements: attachment, commitment, involvement and belief. Effective social bonds attach people to key social institutions – the family, school, work – and the stronger their attachments, the more they develop commitments to those concerned – parents, teachers, employers. Such bonding entails involvement in conforming activities: family life, learning, earning, a 'virtuous circle' which encourages belief in abiding by the rules. None of us is immune from deviance, but the stronger our attachments, commitments and so on, the more we will choose to resist its temptations. We simply have too much 'stake in conformity' to risk losing the good opinion others hold of us and our family by violating the law. We have, as it were, built up a certain 'social capital' and become wary of losing it by offending. Hirschi backed up his theory by evidence from a self-report study of delinquency on over 4000 students in California. The variations in self-reported delinquency did not correlate much with differences of class, ethnicity or income – factors stressed heavily by strain and labelling theories – but did match with those associated with social control: for example, children scoring highly on measures of communication and identification with their parents were signally less involved in delinquency than those who scored less well in these respects. Two decades later, Hirschi felt sure enough of this approach to present it, with Gottfredson, as a general theory of crime (Gottfredson and Hirschi, 1990). Low self-control stemming from poor socialization in families and schools – and inconsistent monitoring and punishing of deviance – is viewed as the main common denominator in offending behaviour.

Wilson (1980) and Wilson and Herbert (1978), in a broadly similar study in England, developed a concept of 'chaperonage' to explain differences in delinquency between children from much the same background. In a carefully chosen sample of 56 socially deprived families, all of whom were poor, overcrowded and similarly circumstanced, striking differences in the delinquency of their children correlated strongly with the extent to which the parents monitored their behaviour as, for example, in accompanying them to and from school, setting play and bed times, and vetting children as companions. 'I blame the parents' was not, however, her conclusion, since the emotional costs involved in such chaperonage were too severe. She emphasized instead the priority of ending social deprivation. However, parental supervision, at least of young children, was seen as a 'neglected feature' of delinquency control.

Control theory also emerged well from an important study on the gender gap in offending behaviour. Hagan *et al.* (1979) used Hirschi's methods in Toronto to explore what they termed the 'sexual stratification of social control'. Boys and girls reported strikingly different experiences of parental supervision, encouragement to take risks and involvement in delinquency. In brief, boys were encouraged to take risks far more than girls and were more subject to lax parental controls. They were also far more likely to be involved in delinquency than girls. But these links held *within* as well as *between* genders, suggesting the causal significance of socialization for delinquency regardless of gender. Nevertheless, the major finding was that the informal social control of girls is far more intensive and extensive than that of boys, who as a result are more subject to formal social control by the police and the courts. These findings also confirm the importance of cultural definitions of masculinity in delinquency, which field studies have shown to be most power-fully associated with *machismo*, the overriding stress on the tough, arrogant, combative image of the male. An obvious inference from such findings is that placing delinquent boys and men in prisons, which are veritable *machismo* factories, is somewhat self-defeating.

Another theory in this vein links crime with changes in 'routine activities' (Felson, 1994). Opportunities for 'motivated offenders' to commit crime consist of 'suitable targets' and the absence of 'capable guardians', and the commonplace structures of social life can multiply such opportunities in unforeseen ways. For example, the huge increase in car ownership not only creates millions of fresh opportunities for car-related crime, but also makes it far easier for motivated offenders to travel rapidly and anonymously: the 'quick getaway' on a mass scale. Similarly, the growth of single person house-holds and women working part time expands targets for residential burglary denuded of capable guardians. Such trends arguably increase the supply of motivated offenders, because rational offending is enhanced by easier gains for less risk. The work of Newman (1972) was similarly based on the ways in which mass housing served to reduce informal social control. In such projects, it was often the case that surveillance and monitoring of local space which, as we saw in Chapter 4, leads to greater self-regulation of behaviour, were effectively 'designed out' by their architecture. Lacking 'defensible space', people withdrew into the confines of their own apartments, ignoring what went on outside by way of noise or disturbance, fearful of the empty lift and the deserted stairwell. Over the past decade, a great deal of crime preven-tion has focused on the need to redesign such projects to enhance a sense of symbolic ownership by providing electronic locks for access doors to blocks, for example – and by redesigning estates to provide better sight-lines over neighbouring properties.

Stress on the 'situational' in crime prevention gained prominence in England chiefly through the work of Clarke (1980, 1992) and his colleagues at the Home Office Research and Planning Unit. Clarke argued that criminology had for centuries sought the explanation for crime in 'dispositional' theories of social, psychological or even biological and genetic kinds. Not only had these proved less than adequate as explanations: they also had the drawback of proffering improbable strategies for prevention, notably social or psychological changes of a fundamental character, for example revolution or psychic cure. In all this root-cause explanation, Clarke argued, we have lost sight of the most obvious point of intervention: the crime situation itself. Most offending is opportunistic, and the scope for prevention is greatest at that point: either by 'target hardening' or enhanced surveillance or both. A good example of this is the unanticipated plummeting of the rate of motor-cycle theft after the introduction (for reasons of road safety) of compulsory safety helmets: bike thieves either had to walk around with helmets or drive without helmets and risk arrest. Situational control theorists could cite many examples of successful prevention by such means: rates of phone kiosk vandalism fell with the installation of tougher coin boxes; car thefts in Germany fell after steering locks were made compulsory, rates of domestic burglary halved following the removal of coin slot meters for gas and the 'cocooning' of burglary victims (Forrester *et al.*, 1988). 'Cocooning' meant the heightening of neighbours' awareness by police and agency workers that a particular household had been victimized by burglary, and encouragement for them to be vigilant over the next two weeks – the period of maximum risk of revictimization. Control theorists accept that professional criminals will not be deterred by such measures, but most crime is not committed by sophisticated professionals but by relatively disorganized opportunists.

Support for this approach stems from perhaps the most influential single article on crime prevention ever written: the Wilson and Kelling (1982) theory of 'broken windows', the inspiration for what is now termed (often misleadingly) 'zero-tolerance' policing. The root idea of 'broken windows' is that crime and disorder are intimately connected. Leaving 'broken windows' unrepaired signals community apathy and police indifference to 'incivilities', acts which are not in themselves crimes but which signify something awry about a neighbourhood. Without remedial action, graffiti proliferates, noise levels rise, vandalism burgeons and more windows get broken. The result is to tip a neighbourhood into decline: property values fall, insurance costs rise, respectable families move out (if they can), and deviants – petty criminals, the mentally ill, beggars – move in. The theory recommends repairing the first broken window, if the cycle of deterioration is to be halted: 'zero-tolerance' policing reverses decades of prioritizing only serious crimes and turning a blind eye to petty crime and disorderly behaviour. The results in New York have been claimed to verge on the momentous (Kelling and Coles, 1997). Beginning with a crackdown on subway disorders – 'aggressive' begging and fare dodging – William Britton, the NYPD Chief – extended the strategy to precincts across New York. In a few years, from 1993–96, the crime rate fell not only for standard crimes but for homicide too: a drop of

50 per cent, from some 1927 to 986 murders. Not surprisingly, the results have attracted global attention, and several police forces have adopted comparable methods in Britain. Few theories have seemingly received such dramatic confirmation in hard practice. The view that policing and criminal justice processes make little difference to crime trends – which are mainly responsive to social, economic and cultural causes – finds its credibility at stake in the wake of such developments.

Without belittling what may turn out to be a watershed in policing, some attempt must be made to put such trends and claims into context. First, even at what for New York is a very low figure, 986 murders in that city is still more than the total for the whole of England and Wales, and remains several times higher than the rate for London. *That* major difference still has to be accounted for. The huge disparity in handgun ownership is part of the story, but even the non-gun murder rate is markedly higher in the USA than in the UK. Second, the fall in overall crime in the USA over the past five years as measured by victim surveys is to a lesser extent also the case for Canada, where zero-tolerance policing has not been so intensively pursued. In contrast, crime rates in England, measured by victim surveys, rose steadily over that period, despite major investments in situational crime prevention such as closed circuit television (CCTV). Third, the USA has, over the past 20 years, become the most punitive nation, at least in the western world, with a prison population quadrupling from 400,000 in the mid-1970s to some 1,600,000 today. In some cities, one in three of the most at risk of offending groups, especially young black and hispanic males, is either in prison or under penal disciplines such as probation or parole. It would be surprising if such high levels of incapacitation had no effect on crime rates: but the gains are bought at a terrible price, both economically and socially. Fourth, situational crime prevention differs from social crime control in one key respect. In unashamedly tackling symptoms not causes, it risks displacing or deflecting offences from one site or type to another: the offender deterred from burglary by better security devices may turn to robbery; the offender may avoid well protected areas (the rise of 'gated' communities in the USA is another reflection of the fear of crime there) but home in on poorer and less defended areas: displacement can be by offence, victim, time, place or method. By contrast, insofar as they address the causes appropriately, social forms of crime prevention run no such risk. The bored teenager who steals cars for kicks may be content with a number of schemes for car racing laid on by community youth teams. Employment and training schemes around the country work surprisingly well for some young offenders who lacked elementary skills which denied them even routine work (Downes, 1993). The best crime prevention schemes combine both elements in an overall strategy.

## Radical Theories

Radical theories link crime to the political economy of capitalism. Taylor *et al.* (1973), drawing on the insights of the 'New Left' in Britain, applied two master concepts to existing theories. First, how 'fully social' a picture of deviance did they project? Second, how well did they analyse the political economy of crime? Measured against these criteria, all existing theories were found wanting. Labelling theory, although an advance of sorts on previous theories, still pictured the deviant as passive victim, while Marxism still gave too materialistic an image of deviance for a fully social, essentially human agency to be envisaged. However, by wedding the more constructive aspects of prior theories to a neo-Marxist analysis of political economy, a 'new' and 'critical' criminology could be developed. On that basis criminologists could work towards the overthrow of the capitalist system, in alliance with deviants victimized by the capitalist state, with the eventual aim of constructing a crime-free society based on 'social diversity' – a clean break with orthodoxy was envisaged.

A good example of this approach is *Policing the Crisis* (Hall *et al.*, 1978). Their starting point was the length of sentences passed against three youths who had 'mugged' a man for a paltry sum in 1973. The offenders had returned two hours after the attack to inflict further injury, and this in part explained the severe penalties of 20 and 10 years' imprisonment. However, these were exemplary sentences, imposed by the judiciary when the threat of a certain type of offence had reached epidemic proportions. Hall *et al.* argue that a 'moral panic' about robbery had been caused, not by a real increase, but by media reportage, the recent adoption of the term 'mugging' from the USA and a police-led campaign against 'black' muggers in particular. In this case, one youth was half West Indian, another of Cypriot background – the link with race was central to its media coverage. Unlike Cohen, who invented the term, Hall and his colleagues were disinclined to see 'moral panics' as simply arising 'from time to time': more fundamental interests are usually at stake when large investments of media resources become taken up with particular issues, in this case the threat to the capitalist state from the successful sequence of strikes, especially the miners.

In this 'crisis of legitimation' for the British state, the moral panic over 'mugging', especially of whites by blacks, became both a potent symbol of growing lawlessness and disorder and a convenient means for converting the crisis confronting the state at the point of production into a 'war against crime'. Hence, 'policing the crisis' is a metaphor for how the capitalist state was shielded from popular awareness of its critical condition by the deflection of attention to an essentially marginal issue – policing black muggers. The originality in this approach lay in applying neo-Marxist methods to the analysis of deviance, linking its diverse manifestations to the dynamics of capitalist political economy in Britain. In the USA, radical criminologists such as Chambliss (1978) and Platt (1978) had linked capitalism with organized crime and with street crime, but in a sweeping fashion which made little sense of changes over time or differences between societies which shared a capitalist economy.

Cohen (1972) provided a much more sophisticated method for explaining changes in deviance in the light of the dynamics of political economy. He linked the notion that sub-cultures are evolved by some groups to solve problems that the larger culture lands them with to the contradictions of post-war capitalist development. As a result of increasingly right-wing political and economic policies in many developed societies over the last two decades, people are now much more familiar with what such contradictions look like than they were in the early 1970s, for example the tendency of capitalist interests to ride roughshod over the needs of communities if they happen to stand in the way of making profits. Profits come first, unless governments dictate otherwise – and governments have shown an increasing tendency not to do so. However, the main object of Cohen's work was to account for the bewildering proliferation of youthful styles that were created in post-war Britain, styles which were deviant, not illegal, but which became strongly associated with delinquency. The Teddy Boys, the Mods and Rockers, the Skinheads and later the Punks were seen as attempts to resolve, albeit 'magically', a set of contradictions facing working-class youth; in particular the loss of community, family tensions, the breakdown of class solidarity and the failure to gain access to power in a newly 'affluent society'. In this impasse, working-class youth could revolt culturally if not politically. Thus, for example, the Mod style could be seen as an attempt to realize, in an imaginary way, the conditions of existence of the socially mobile white-collar worker (Cohen, 1972). The Mod office boy might be low in power and status but he could out-dress and out-talk the managing director. The Skinhead style symbolized the hard masculinity associated with traditional manual labour under threat from technological change. However, sartorial fashion is not structural change: these were revolts of the powerless, and they ultimately led nowhere. Hence the rise and fall of successive styles, resisting but never capable of resolving structural contradictions. Cohen provided a template that could be applied to diverse movements.

Such movements are a constant reminder that growing up in a class society stifles a huge creative potential which will seek expression in deviant form if conventional outlets are blocked or resented as patronage. As we saw in Chapter 9, Willis (1977) documented the process whereby working-class boys take on working-class jobs, not by forced labour, but by self-schooling into a subordinate culture of masculinity which idealizes physical strength, sexual prowess and verbal wit above educational achievement. The price is high: sexism and racism. But the pay-off for society is a willing cohort of manual labourers, ironically now consigned to the dole since the work for which they have been socialized over the generations has now largely vanished (Wilson, 1996). McRobbie and Garber (1976) similarly argued that 'the lads'... peer group consciousness and pleasure frequently seem to hinge on a collective disregard for women and sexual exploitation of girls'. As a result, 'girls tend to be pushed to the periphery of social activities and much "girl culture" becomes a culture of the bedroom rather than the street' (Newburn, 1997: 621). However, girls' insubordination is just as anti-school as that of boys and 'is as crucial in preparing them for the realities of the labour market as are Willis' lads in pre-shop floor collaboration' (Hobbs, 1997: 811). *Resistance Through Rituals* (Hall and Jefferson 1976) is the common thread linking diverse forms of youthful deviance.

Critics of the radical approach (Smart, 1976; Downes, 1979; Rock, 1979; Cohen, 1980) focused on the dangers of romanticizing motives and the unacceptability for victims, especially women, of impugning authoritative action against crime; on the vagueness of the socialist alternatives on offer; and on the extent to which the imaginative readings of deviance may also be imaginary. The force of such criticisms, some arising from the radicals themselves, led to a split in the approach, some retaining a strong neo-Marxist method, others developing what Young termed 'Left Realism' (Lea and Young, 1984; Matthews and Young, 1986). Its starting point was the reality of the pains of criminal victimization (never in doubt for many outside the Left), especially for working-class communities, and from street crime. They did much to document the extent and character of victimization in the worst-hit areas by pioneering local victim surveys (see Kinsey, 1984; Jones *et al.*, 1986). Their main explanation for rising crime is relative deprivation and social injustice, basically a return to the root-cause approach of strain theories. However, the approach is given a radical inflection by, for example, their emphasis on crimes of the powerful, on political as well as material and status deprivation and marginalization, and by their concern to bring policing more in line with people's needs at the very local level.

## Conclusion

The deviance perspective is now integral to sociological theory and is likely to remain so, largely because it provides a framework for the analysis of diverse social problems which are commonly linked by their social definition as warranting social control. The four main approaches to the explanation of distinct forms of crime and delinquency all have their strengths and weaknesses. Strain theories cope quite well with accounting for the 'rise and rise' of crime over the past four decades, largely because the combination of rising expectations in the context of persistent inequalities is central to the approach (for a recent and broader analysis of contemporary ills along similar lines, which also draws heavily on psychological evidence, see James, 1997). They also address the problem of motivation far more directly than other approaches, although they tend to 'over-predict' the scale of deviance in the process, a problem also for control and radical theories. Labelling theory alone lends itself to discounting much of the so-called rise in crime, seeing processes of redefinition as crucially involved. The virtues of labelling theory lie not so much in explaining trends as in questioning the definitions underlying them. As the approaches differ in key respects, for example in their views of the nature of society and the social bond, or of the importance of motivation compared with opportunity, no ready synthesis is likely. It is, of course, eminently possible to clump them together, seeing crime as increasingly due to growing social strains, more punitive labelling, weakening social controls and a context of capitalist greed careering out of control. Such an approach over-predicts the problem far more than any one approach taken alone, as well as glossing over the fundamental conflicts between them philosophically. However, although a neat consensus is not foreseeable, theoretical debate is immensely fruitful, not only for better theory but also for better informed method and policy making. It is as a result of informed uncertainty, rather than any spurious unison, that we have learnt as much as we have about deviance compared with our relative ignorance in the past.

# Current Issues

There is no neat list of issues which cover current debates, but the four that follow have immense implications for research and policy making. Discussion of these issues should be linked with the relevant parts of the chapter.

## *Crime and Inequality*

Many developed societies have experienced massive de-industrialization, particularly over the last two decades of the twentieth century, which has been combined with widening inequalities, growing poverty and increasing levels of male unemployment. However, the conclusion that the doubling of the crime rate and the re-emergence of urban riots in Britain, for example, were in any way due to these trends was denied by the government and some criminologists. They could point to counter-instances to refute the critics, such as the far lower crime rates in the 1930s, when the slump had led to even greater unemployment, and the 1960s, when crime rates rose annually despite full employment. In the 1980s, the USA experienced the same trends – vanishing work and growing inequality – but the crime rate hardly changed. In response, it can be said that *relative deprivation* is the key factor: that rising expectations, driven by the consumer society, make people ever more resistant to, and embittered by, joblessness and impoverization.

As for the USA, rates of criminal violence, especially homicide, remain far higher than in Europe, despite the far higher levels of imprisonment, which may have held property crime levels down to some extent, but at a huge cost socially and economically. What kinds of research would assist in clarifying this issue, which is of immense importance if we are to make informed polit-ical and policy choices?

## Restorative versus Punitive Justice

Politicians often make political capital for themselves by promising to get tough on crime and promising something closer to a US-style punitive sentencing system. Against that view, penal reformers increasingly argue for what has come to be called 'restorative justice', which emphasizes community-based sanctions, such as as probation, community service orders and mediation between victim and offender. These are intended to give offenders greater insight into their offending behaviour and its effects on the victim, and to jolt them into an awareness of the true causes and costs of their crime. Braithwaite (1989) boosted this approach by arguing that societies which practised inclusionary shaming, such as Japan, enjoyed far lower crime (and imprisonment) rates than those which practised punitive, exclusionary policies, such as the USA. Just how far and in which ways such forms of 'restorative' justice may be effectively used is a key question for criminal justice policy making.

## Situational versus Social Crime Prevention

The attraction of purely situational measures for governments and citizens is that they can be implemented piecemeal and very quickly without any need to address the underlying causes of crime. For example, CCTV monitoring, the electronic tagging of offenders, 'gated' communities and endless varia-tions on target hardening, such as satellite car tracking (top end of the market) or Rottweiler in the back of the van (bottom end) do not depend on elaborate theories of motivation and meaning. Yet the scope for ever more widespread and sophisticated forms of situational prevention holds the danger that, over time, they lead to a 'fortress' mentality, an increasingly constrained and yet still fearful society, where only designated persons can enter designated zones for designated purposes. It is already the case that in Los Angeles only those holding the right swipe-card can enter the business centre. By contrast, social forms of crime prevention carry no implications of repressive side-effects on the freedom of the streets or civil liberties.

*Drug-related Crime*

This term encompasses violations of the laws governing illegal substances, that is, their use, possession, production or distribution, and crimes committed as a consequence, such as burglaries to finance an addiction and violence to enforce payment for supply. The whole issue is especially germane for the sociology of deviance, because the criminal definition of certain substances is the key pre-condition for drug-related crime. This has led to arguments for the decriminalization, if not outright legalization, of some 'soft' drugs, especially cannabis, and for the return to a medical model of treatment for heroin addiction to cut out the 'black market' and its organized crime bases. On the other hand, few have argued for the legalization of cocaine which, in the form of 'crack', provides an unusually rapid route to an intense form of addiction. At present, all but a few governments have refused even to discuss the possibility of even very limited forms of decriminalization. The Dutch government is under intense international pressure to end its long-standing policy of limited tolerance of cannabis use in licensed venues. Yet the levels of cannabis and heroin use in the Netherlands are no higher and often lower than in other countries. The Prohibition era in the United States led to the explosive growth of organized crime there. The prohibition of illicit drugs globally seems to be leading to the same result worldwide. Is it possible to devise forms of regulation which neither criminalize nor lead to a commercial 'free-for-all'; which take account of the particular properties of each drug, and which are workable internationally?

# Further Reading

Davies, N. *Dark Heart,* London, Chatto & Windus, 1997. An account of an investigative journalist's close-up of some of the most damaging forms of deviance.

Downes, D. and Rock, P. *Understanding Deviance,* 3rd edn, Oxford, Oxford University Press, 1998. Provides detailed coverage of the major theories of deviance.

Maguire, M., Morgan, R. and Reiner, R. (eds) *The Oxford Handbook of Criminology,* 2nd edn, Oxford, Clarendon Press, 1997. A key reference book, containing informative articles on most key topics in the fields of crime, deviance and social control.

Tierney, J. *Criminology: Theory and Context,* London, Prentice Hall/Harvester Wheatsheaf, 1996. Provides a clear and detailed explanation of the history of criminology and its major theories.

# 12

# Health, Illness and Medicine

## *Steve Taylor*

The sociological study of health and illness has much in common with the study of deviance as illness is also a form of unintentional 'rule breaking'. Sociologists have examined both the social causes of diseases and also how the meanings of 'health' and 'illness' are constructed in social processes. There are also connections between the sociological study of medicine and religion. Some sociologists have argued that medicine has taken over some of the social control functions that have traditionally been associated with established religion and that in contemporary societies the religious distinction between good and evil is being increasingly replaced by the medical distinction between healthy and unhealthy. This chapter aims to illustrate how sociologists have examined the social origins of disease and the processes that shape both people's experiences of illness and disability and the medical knowledge and practices around which health care is organized. It should help you to understand:

- What is meant by the biomedical model of health and how it has been questioned in recent years

- How sociologists have tried to measure and explain health inequalities

- The relationship between stress, social support and health

- What is meant by the sick role and how sociologists have tried to illuminate people's experiences of sickness and disability

- How sociologists have explained ideas about health, illness and the human body as social constructions

---

### CONCEPTS

epidemiology ■ longitudinal study ■ materialist and lifestyle theories
stress ■ social support ■ illness behaviour ■ stigma
iatrogenic disease ■ holistic medicine

---

# Introduction

At first sight a *sociology* of health, illness and medicine appears something of a contradiction in terms. After all, in modern societies the study of health and disease and treatment of the sick has been dominated by the biological sciences and, for most of the twentieth century, it has been generally assumed that the battle against disease will be won in the laboratory and the treatment room. In this *biomedical model of health* disease can be defined objectively in terms of recognized symptoms and health is simply the absence of these symptoms. The body is likened to a machine to be restored to health by treatments of one sort or another. The biomedical approach still dominates the training of health professionals, the allocation of resources, and those at the top of health care's pyramid of power have traditionally been the experts in curative treatments.

In modern and modernizing societies health policies are still organized predominantly around the assumption that improvements in health will come largely from new and improved treatments and from the greater availability of medical resources. However, in the last two decades in particular, this view has been increasingly called into question. First, despite some spectacular medical advances in certain areas, the major diseases of modern societies, such as arthritis, cancer and heart disease have for the most part remained stubbornly resistant to effective medical treatment and cure, and the attentions of more health professionals and policy makers has switched to the environmental causes of disease. Second, modern medicine has been criticized for its detached and mechanistic approach to illness, where patients are seen as collections of symptoms rather than people. As the burden of disease in contemporary societies moves increasingly from acute (life threatening) to chronic (long-term) illness and disability, critics argue that more attention should be given to the social and psychological and, more recently, political consequences of illness and disability. Third, modern medicine's claim to be a beneficent and value-free science has been increasingly challenged in a more consumer-orientated and sceptical late modern world.

Sociologists of health and medicine have made significant contributions to each of these debates and this chapter is organized around these issues. The first section examines the social influences on health, the second looks at how people's experiences of illness are shaped by social contexts and the chapter concludes by considering the relationship between medical knowledge and practice and wider social influences.

# The Social Bases of Health

Most research within the biomedical model of health involves trying to identify the origins of specific diseases under controlled laboratory conditions with the aim of developing effective treatments which are usually adminis-tered in the form of personalized medical care. An alternative *epidemiological* approach involves trying to identify the environmental influences on health by examining their distribution in *populations* over time. This approach has shown that diseases do not strike randomly but are consistently linked to various environmental influences, including social variables, such as region, ethnicity, class, gender, age and culture. This section will illustrate the social influences on health by looking at two of the most important sociological variables, social deprivation and social integration.

## Socio-economic Factors and Health

Links between comparative economic deprivation and poor health have been reported in most developed countries, although international comparisons are difficult because so many different measures, or indicators, of socio-economic position have been used. These links are usually measured by calculating stan-dardized mortality and morbidity (that is, illness) rates for different socio-economic groups. A number of studies in Britain, for example, have found a persistent relationship between occupational class and rates of mortality and morbidity (Townsend *et al.*, 1988; Benzeval *et al.*, 1995) (Table 12.1). Four-fifths of all officially recorded causes of death, including heart disease, which is commonly thought to be predominantly a disease of the over-stressed high achieving executive classes, are more prevalent among the manual working classes. It has been estimated that if the death rate of manual workers was the same as that for non-manual, there would be 42,000 fewer deaths each year (Benzeval *et al.*, 1995). The result of this is that people from the manual working classes are more than twice as likely to die before retirement age than people from the professional class and are twice as likely to be suffering from a longstanding illness.

Social class also affects the health of children. Working-class mothers are more likely than middle-class mothers to have complications during preg-nancy and have low weight babies. Rates of infant mortality, that is babies dying in the first year of life, also vary between the social classes. On average, for every baby born to professional parents who dies, two die born to skilled manual workers and three die from unskilled manual back-grounds. These inequalities persist into childhood and the mortality rate of children from manual working-class backgrounds is double that of the children of Class I parents.

There has been a great deal of controversy and debate among sociologists and others about the interpretation of the statistics on class and health. One major source of debate concerns whether the statistics provide a comparatively reliable and valid measure of health inequality. Official statistics are not self-evident 'facts' simply waiting to be explained by sociologists. They are socially produced and necessarily reflect the conceptual categories and bureaucratic

*Sociology*

**Table 12.1** Occupational class and standardized mortality ratios for men aged 16–64, 1981–89: for all men and for unemployed men seeking work

|  | *All men* | *Unemployed men seeking work* |
| --- | --- | --- |
| Social class I | 60 | 73 |
| Social class II | 80 | 104 |
| Social class IIIN | 90 | 110 |
| Social class IIIM | 97 | 114 |
| Social class IV | 109 | 136 |
| Social class V | 134 | 172 |
| All men aged 16–64 | 100 | 125 |
| Ratio V/I | 2.2 | 2.4 |

Standardized mortality ratios represent the mortality of sub-groups within a population as a percentage of the mortality of the population as a whole.
*Source*: OPCS Longitudinal Survey, reported in Benthume, A. (1996) 'Economic activity and mortality of the 1981 Census Cohort in the OPCS Longitudinal Survey, *Population Trends*, **83**: 37–42.

procedures in terms of which they are compiled. In this context, a number of critics have argued that many of the difficulties of 'measuring' social class, discussed in Chapter 5, apply to research into socio-economic status and health.

First, there have been significant changes in the composition of the respective occupational classes in most developed societies. In Britain, since the Second World War, Class I has doubled while Class V has halved to around only 6 per cent of the working population. Thus Illsley (1986), for example, has argued that drawing general conclusions about the persistence (and sometimes even the worsening) of health inequalities simply by comparing the health of those in Class I with those in Class V, as many studies have done, is bound to distort and almost certainly exaggerate the extent of the problem. Second, the long established method of classifying women in terms of their husbands' occupation not only makes the statistics to some extent 'gender blind' (Arber, 1990), but also fails to take into account the significant differences between single and dual earner households. Third, using occupation as an indicator of socio-economic position is becoming increasingly limited in an ageing society where most people are living well beyond retirement age (Klein, 1988).

Some critics argued that the methodological problems just outlined mean that the existence of widespread (and possibly worsening) health inequality remains unproven and its persistence in the literature owes more to the political rhetoric of sociologists than established empirical evidence (Green, 1988). However, most academics working in the area do not take such a dismissive view of the problem. First, they argue that, in spite of acknowledged deficiencies, the data on occupational class do provide a useful outline of the problem. Second, they argue that some of the criticisms have been answered to some extent by studies using alternative techniques of 'measurement'. For example, an OPCS longitudinal study following a 1 per cent sample of the population using much more comprehensive data from the 1971 Census found that health inequalities persist after retirement age (Fox *et al.*, 1986). Other studies have used more specific indicators of comparative deprivation. For example, studies of different grades of employment within particular occupations and industries have found consistently higher levels of morbidity and mortality among the lower grades (Marmot, 1978; Davey Smith *et al.*, 1994), while specific indicators of material deprivation have been positively linked to poor health (Townsend *et al.*, 1988; Davey Smith *et al.*, 1991).

A second major debate concerns the alleged causes of health inequality. For most sociologists, the major explanations are located in terms of material factors associated with comparative poverty, such as low income, poor housing, the nature of manual work and the lack of it. For example, poor housing can affect health directly by making respiratory and parasitic diseases and childhood accidents more likely and, indirectly, by contributing to stress which can lead to conditions such as anxiety and depression (Eames *et al.*, 1993). It has been estimated that around 2 million people a year suffer from work-related illness. People in manual occupations run a far greater risk than people in non-manual occupations not only from industrial accidents, but also from the greater likelihood of contracting cancer and respiratory disorders. The repetitive nature of industrial work with its close supervision and lack of autonomy also makes the likelihood of stress-related disorders more likely. One study estimated that 20 per cent of the class variation in cancer mortality is due to hazards at work (Fox and Adelstein, 1978). More recently, emerging evidence of the long-term influences on health has led researchers to develop longitudinal models which explore the cumulative influences on health over people's life course. While some early influences on health in later life are probably programmed biologically, it is also likely that they are influenced socially, and sociologists have began to explore the cumulative influences of social disadvantages on health (Bartley *et al.*, 1994). For example, the socio-economic environment of a child's home is likely to influence their attitudes and educational attainments which will then become a determinant of their labour market position which will influence their economic position in middle and old age (Davey Smith *et al.*, 1997). In general, for most researchers, health inequality is to be explained in terms of material influences which are largely outside most people's direct control.

However some critics claim that the materialist theories tend to depict working-class people as essentially passive victims, condemned to comparatively poor health simply by their class position. They argue that such a view negates the importance of human agency; that is, it reduces people to mere puppets of the class system and fails to take into account the choices that people make in how they live their lives. In this context it is argued that a great deal of behaviour commonly known to produce increased risk of ill-health is class related. For example, smoking is one of the major preventable causes of ill-health and premature death, contributing to 100,000 deaths a year and a third of all cancers. However, on average, working-class people have been less receptive to warnings about the dangers of smoking and the proportion of smokers in Social Class V is two and half times that of Social Class I (Office of Population, Censuses and Surveys, 1996) (Table 12.2). Similarly, other well-known health risks such as sedentary lifestyle, high alcohol consumption and a poor diet of refined convenience foods all appear to be more prevalent among the working classes. Some theorists put forward the idea of a sub-culture of ill-health, where poor 'health behaviour' is passed down through the generations. From this point of view health inequality is less an automatic product of material deprivation and more a consequence of lifestyle and behavioural choices and, therefore, policy solutions are seen more in terms of health education rather than economic redistribution favoured by advocates of materialist theories.

**Table 12.2**   Cigarette smoking by sex and socio-economic group of head of household, persons aged 16 and over, Great Britain, 1974 and 1994 (%)

|                                                      | 1974 | | 1994 | |
| ---------------------------------------------------- | ---- | ------ | ---- | ------ |
|                                                      | *Male* | *Female* | *Male* | *Female* |
| Professional                                         | 29   | 25     | 16   | 12     |
| Employers and managers                               | 46   | 38     | 20   | 20     |
| Intermediate and junior non-manual                   | 45   | 38     | 24   | 23     |
| Skilled manual and own account non-professional      | 56   | 46     | 33   | 29     |
| Semi-skilled manual and personal service             | 56   | 43     | 38   | 32     |
| Unskilled manual                                     | 61   | 43     | 40   | 34     |
| Total non-manual                                     | 45   | 38     | 21   | 21     |
| Total manual                                         | 56   | 45     | 35   | 31     |
| All                                                  | 51   | 41     | 28   | 26     |

*Source*: OPCS/ONS (Office of Population, Censuses and Surveys, now Office for National Statistics) (1996): adapted from Table 4.9.

Some sociologists have argued that 'lifestyle' choices cannot be divorced from the material contexts in which they are made. For example, in her work on women and smoking Graham (1987b, 1994) has argued that the higher rates of smoking among working-class women with children, while reflecting 'free' choices, are still influenced by material factors. Caring for small children in difficult circumstances produced high levels of stress for some women, and smoking was a part of a strategy they used to take some 'time out' for themselves. Smoking thus occupied a paradoxical position in these women's lives. On the one hand it was an increased health risk for them and their children, on the other hand a part of a strategy for coping in deprived circumstances. A major task facing sociological research in this context is developing models which combine inherited lifestyle and material influences (Figure 12.1).

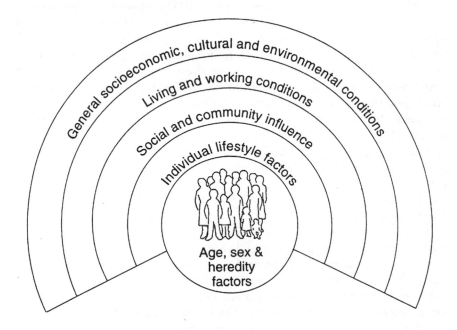

**Figure 12.1**    The Whitehead/Dahlgren model (Dahlgren and Whitehead, 1991, *Policies and Strategies to Promote Social Equity in Health*, Stockholm, Institue for Future Studies)

## Social Integration and Health

An allied approach to the social origins of disease has focused on the relationship between stress, social integration and health. Since the 1960s a number of studies have shown that exposure to stressful life events, such as bereavement, divorce, occupation change, unemployment, migration and social problems, can make people more vulnerable to disease and premature death (Williams and House, 1991).

Researchers are not entirely sure how people's life experiences influence their physical health but there is increasing evidence from the biological sciences that prolonged exposure to events which disrupt people's normal patterns of behaviour and cause psychological stress, such as worry or great sadness, can result in biochemical changes in the body which make the immune system (that is, the body's natural defences) less efficient, leaving the individual more vulnerable to 'non-specific' diseases (Kaplan, 1991). However, while stressful life events are associated with the higher risk of disease, they do not *necessarily* cause it and there has been a great deal of research, particularly in biology and psychology, into factors (such as genetic predisposition or personality type) which influence people's ability to adapt to stress.

Although sociological contributions to this problem are comparatively recent, one of their key ideas had its origins a century ago in the work of Durkheim. In his study of suicide Durkheim (1897/1952) argued that the variations between the suicide rates of different social groups and their consistency over time was a 'social fact' to be explained sociologically. For example, the statistics showed that Catholic areas had consistently lower suicide rates than Protestant areas, people who were married with children had lower suicide rates than the unmarried and childless and societies' suicide rates fell in times of war or political unrest. Durkheim argued that the underlying cause of these variations was the extent to which individuals are integrated, or bonded, into the social groups around them. In modern 'individualized' societies, the more people are integrated into society the more protected they appear to be from suicide. Durkheim's study of suicide has been widely criticized for its theoretical inconsistency and dependence on official suicide rates, but the concept of social integration has become one of the central ideas in sociology and, in the last two decades in particular, has been applied to the study of the relationship between stress and health. Sociologists have also used the concept of social support which refers to the extent and quality of a person's social relationships (Eurelings-Bontekoe *et al.*, 1995). Social integration and social support are clearly closely related and, while the terms are sometimes used interchangeably, social integration is usually used to refer to a characteristic of *populations*, while social support usually means a resource of *individuals* (Figure 12.2).

Studies of social support tend to use the longitudinal method of studying groups of individuals over time. For example, in one of the best-known studies, Berkman and Syme (1979) 'followed' a sample of 5000 adults aged 30–70 over a nine-year period. A social network score was calculated for each person using the indictors of marriage, regular contact with friends, church membership and membership of voluntary organizations. After controlling for health status and health behaviour the authors found that the mortality rates of those with low

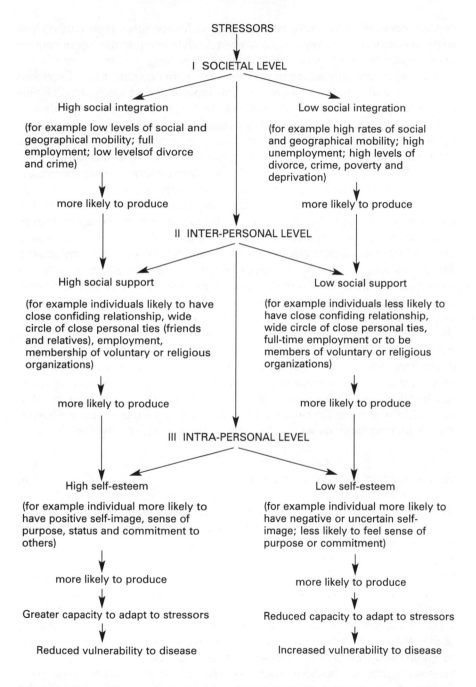

STRESSORS

I SOCIETAL LEVEL

High social integration

(for example low levels of social and geographical mobility; full employment; low levelsof divorce and crime)

more likely to produce

Low social integration

(for example high rates of social and geographical mobility; high unemployment; high levels of divorce, crime, poverty and deprivation)

more likely to produce

II INTER-PERSONAL LEVEL

High social support

(for example individuals likely to have close confiding relationship, wide circle of close personal ties (friends and relatives), employment, membership of voluntary or religious organizations)

more likely to produce

Low social support

(for example individuals less likely to have close confiding relationship, wide circle of close personal ties, full-time employment or to be members of voluntary or religious organizations)

more likely to produce

III INTRA-PERSONAL LEVEL

High self-esteem

(for example individual more likely to have positive self-image, sense of purpose, status and commitment to others)

more likely to produce

Greater capacity to adapt to stressors

Reduced vulnerability to disease

Low self-esteem

(for example individual more likely to have negative or uncertain self-image; less likely to feel sense of purpose or commitment)

more likely to produce

Reduced capacity to adapt to stressors

Increased vulnerability to disease

**Figure 12.2** The social context of stress and health (Taylor S., 1997, 'Social Integration, Social Support and Health' in Taylor S. and Field D. eds *Sociology of Health and Health Care*, 2nd edn, Oxford, Blackwell)

support network scores were between two and three times higher than those with high support networks. While some researchers argue that social support is of general benefit in promoting health, others suggest that its value is as a 'buffer', helping people adjust to stressful life experiences, including illnesses. A number of studies have also shown the importance of social support in helping people adapt to a range of diseases including various cancers, heart disease, stroke and depression (Ell, 1996). For example, in a study of 44 patients recovering from a first stroke, Glass and Maddox (1992) found positive correlations between high levels of support and good recovery, while Fitzpatrick *et al*. (1991) found higher levels of psychological deterioration among rheumatoid arthritis sufferers who had lower levels of social support.

The study of social support and health has become one of the most productive areas in sociology, linking social with biological and psychological factors, but it has also been subject to criticism. First, reflecting a more general critique of positivist methods in sociology, some sociologists have argued that life events and social support cannot simply be 'measured' through survey analysis, as the same life 'event', divorce for example, can have different meanings for different people (for further discussion of the general methodological implications of this issue, see Chapter 2). Second, the assumption made in most of the 'support literature' that social support is *necessarily* a 'good thing' has also been questioned. For example, caring for a sick person may well be supportive to the sufferer but stressful to the carer and, in some cases, support may have unintended negative consequences (Ell, 1996). These critiques do not invalidate the findings on health and social support, but they do point to the need for more in-depth evaluations of stress and support that go beyond the positivistic methods which characterize the majority of studies.

## Social Support and Material Factors

There are significant links between stress, social support and the material factors considered in the study of health inequalities. First, stressful life events such as unemployment, marital difficulties and bereavement are more common among the more disadvantaged socio-economic groups. Second, lower socio-economic status is associated with lower levels of social support. (Whelan, 1993). Third, the potential of social support to buffer people from the effects of stressful life events is influenced by material factors. For example, a family's ability to provide support for a sick person is also influenced by its ability to obtain external support from social services (Ell, 1996). A good example of the relationship between stressful life events, social support and class is provided by the classic study of Brown and Harris (1978) on the social origins of depression in women. Brown and Harris found a clear relationship between adverse life events, which were subjectively perceived by the women in the sample to have long-term implications, and the onset of depression.

However, whether the women then became depressed was influenced by four vulnerability factors: lack of paid employment outside the home, having three or more dependent children living at home, loss of the mother before the age of 11 and, most important, lack of close confiding relationship. The greater the number of vulnerability factors the greater the likelihood of depression. Working-class women were more vulnerable to depression than middle-class women because they were more likely to experience both stressful life events and greater vulnerability factors. As these precipitating factors arose out of social situations, Brown and Harris argued that although depression is a biological condition, its origins are essentially social.

## Sociological Approaches to Sickness and Disability

As societies modernize, and more people reach middle and old age, the proportion of the population suffering from chronic, or long-term, illnesses increases. While medicine is able to treat more of these conditions, such as heart disease and arthritis, it cannot cure most of them and thus living with illness becomes a way of life for an increasing number of people. It has now become common in the sociology of sickness to distinguish between impairment and disability. *Impairment* refers to some abnormality in the structure and function of the body, through disease or injury, while *disability* refers to restrictions of activities of daily living which may result directly from impairment but may also be social, such as negative reactions from others, lack of resources and restricted opportunities in work and leisure.

Estimates of the prevalence of disability vary due to the different 'measures' that have been used. In Britain, for example, a number of surveys carried out by the Office of Population, Censuses and Surveys between 1985 and 1988 – combining the judgements of researchers, professionals and people with disabilities – estimated that there were around 6 million adults with disabilities in Britain, almost 70 per cent of whom were over 60, with women outnumbering men (Martin *et al.*, 1988). Sociologists have been interested in examining the social consequences of illness and disability as well as its distribution. They have theorized about the relationship between sickness and social structures and explored people's experiences of illness and disability, particularly how their 'disruptive' effects are 'managed' in daily social life.

### Sick Role and Social Structure

Parsons (1951) was one of the first sociologists to conceptualize sickness as a social state. For Parsons, sickness was a form of deviance which posed a threat to the functioning of the social system as people were not complying with the work-orientated norms of modern industrial societies. Allocating people a distinct sick role helped the social system manage the potential threat posed by sickness to social and moral order.

The sick role consists of privileges and obligations. Sick people are exempted from their normal social roles and from responsibility for their illness. However, they are expected to be motivated to get better and they must seek professional medical help and comply with medical advice in the treatment of their illness. Failure to comply with the obligations may result in a loss of the privileges. Parsons also identified a corresponding medical role of privileges and obligations. While doctors had privileged access to the patient's body and confidential information, they were obligated to adhere to professional standards, remain objective, confine their interest to the patient's condition, and always act in the best interests of the patient. For Parsons, doctors not only served the interests of their individual patients, they also served the interests of wider society by acting as gatekeepers of the sick role in defining who was (and was not) legitimately sick.

Parsons did very little empirical research on illness himself but the concept of the sick role – with its recognition of sickness as a change in *social,* as well as biological, status – opened the door to a range of sociological questions about professional power, social control and the ways in which meanings are attributed to physical states. The concept can still provide insight into a number of contemporary issues, such as the distinction health professionals sometimes make between 'deserving' and 'undeserving' patients. Jeffrey (1979) found that casualty staff distinguish between 'good cases', such as head injuries or cardiac arrests, and what they called the 'rubbish', such as drunks and repeated overdosers. What characterized the 'rubbish' was that, like the unrepentant smokers who are pushed to the back of the waiting lists for cardiac surgery, they were seen to have been largely responsible for their condition and therefore not 'legitimately' sick.

The concept of the sick role has been subjected to a battery of empirical criticisms. First, it has been widely argued that Parsons' model cannot be applied to many chronic illnesses, such as arthritic conditions, where the patient cannot get better and leave the sick role. However, Gerhardt (1987) has argued that this critique is the result of 'a too literal reading of Parsons' and, as Parsons (1978) himself observed on a number of occasions, sometimes using the example of his own diabetes, people with chronic illness are still expected to comply with medical advice to control and minimize symptoms in a way that mirrors recovery in acute illnesses.

Second, it has been shown that access to the sick role is rather more problematic than Parsons' model assumes. Studies of illness behaviour, that is, the processes by which people come to define themselves as ill, have shown that only a minority of symptoms are brought to medical attention (Scambler *et al.*, 1984) and that a decision to consult a doctor is often the result of a long process of help seeking, influenced by a range of social and cultural factors. In this context it is argued that what Parsons is really talking about is a *patient role* rather than a sick role (Turner, 1995). A third criticism of the sick role focuses on the consensus it assumes in the doctor–patient relationship. A number of sociological studies of doctor–patient interaction have shown that consultations were rarely as smooth as Parsons' model supposes and that there was frequent negotiation and sometimes conflict over diagnosis and treatment (Tuckett *et al.*, 1985).

General criticisms of Parsons' structural functionalist theory for its overemphasis on both consensus and structure (see Chapter 3) are also reflected in specific critiques of the sick role. Like Parsons, Marxists also see medicine's management of the sick role in terms of social control. However, while Parsons saw this control being exercised for the benefit of the social system, or society as a whole, Marxists argue that it operates largely in the interests of the ruling class (Navarro, 1978). By conceiving sickness in 'individualistic' terms, as the result of biological predisposition or unhealthy lifestyle for example, medicine is performing an important ideological function by 'de-politicizing' the effects of capitalism and deflecting attention from the environmental and predominantly economic origins of disease. It has also been suggested that capitalism's preoccupation with production, profitability and 'materialist' values contributes to a process of excluding and devaluing people who are not 'productive', such as the mentally ill (Scull, 1993), elderly (Phillipson, 1982) and long-term sick and disabled (Oliver, 1996). The recent tendency for health economists and policy makers to talk grimly about the 'costs', and even the 'burden', of continuing to provide health and social care for the increasing number of elderly and long-term sick into the next century suggests that this idea is not without some foundation.

For social action theorists a major shortcoming of Parsons' formulation of the sick role is that it conceives sickness only in terms of its relationship to social structures. In contrast to Parsons, action theorists have developed concepts which help to illuminate the micro-social contexts of sickness, in particular the relationship between individuals' experiences of sickness and disability and the specific organizational contexts that shape those experiences.

## Experiences of Sickness and Disability

Despite the valid critique of Parsons' sick role, it is generally seen as a seminal contribution to the sociology of health and illness for its recognition that sickness is a social state where the sick person is surrounded by a new set of social and cultural expectations. Sociologists have been particularly interested in exploring how these expectations impute meaning to sickness and disability and shape people's experiences of them (Gerhardt, 1989). A great deal of this work has been influenced by symbolic interactionist theory developed from the work of Mead, Becker's (1963) ideas on social groups creating deviance by labelling some people as outsiders and Goffman's (1969) work on the presentation and protection of the self in everyday life. Like Parsons, the interactionist approach sees sickness and disability in terms of deviance. However, whereas Parsons is asking how the social system copes with sickness, interactionists are more interested in how sick and disabled individuals cope with society. In this context the distinction made by Lemert between primary and secondary deviance, described in the previous chapter, has been particularly helpful. The labelling of a person as sick or disabled constitutes a form of primary deviance, while secondary deviance refers to the adaptations a person makes in response to such labelling. In their analysis of sickness, interactionists have been interested in both the characteristics of societal reactions to sickness and their consequences for individuals.

Sickness labels can easily become a dominant status; that is, the impairment (especially if it is easily visible) comes to be seen by others (and sometimes by the person themselves) as a major source of identity, even if the person has a high profile in other areas they may still be seen as a *disabled* writer or a *diabetic* footballer for example. There is also a tendency to interpret a person's behaviour (past as well as present) in terms of the sickness label. For example, in his classic study of an American mental hospital Goffman (1991) observed how patients' resistance to their diagnosis would be interpreted by staff as further confirmation of their 'illness'.

Sickness and disabling conditions are often stigmatizing. People are socially stigmatized when they are seen to be in some way unacceptable or inferior and are thus denied full social acceptance (Goffman, 1968). There is thus a discrepancy between what Goffman calls their 'virtual social identity (the way they should be if they were 'normal') and the 'actual social identity' (the way they are). Those who are stigmatized are confronted with a series of decisions about the management of spoiled identity both in terms of their interaction with others and their own self-concept. People are more likely to experience stigmatized reaction from others when their impairment is highly visible. In Goffman's terms, they are 'discredited' and this may lead to a greater withdrawal from social participation, especially in public areas. When the condition is not visible, as in epilepsy or HIV for example, and the person is potentially 'discreditable', they have to decide whether to be open about their condition or try to 'pass' as 'normal'. Thus the implications of stigma go beyond public reaction. For example, Scambler and Hopkins (1986) found that comparatively few of the epileptics they interviewed had actually experienced a stigmatizing reaction from others (enacted stigma). However, the shame of being epileptic (felt stigma) led most of them to conceal their condition even from those close to them. For example, two-thirds of those experiencing epilepsy at the time of their marriage concealed it from their partners, while three-quarters had not disclosed their condition to their employers. The authors found that, paradoxically, felt stigma was more disruptive to people's lives than enacted stigma.

However, being officially diagnosed and labelled as sick is not *necessarily* stigmatizing in itself. Sometimes it can have the opposite effect. For example, some illnesses such as Parkinson's disease and multiple sclerosis can develop very slowly and there may be a long time between initial experiences of symptoms and medical diagnosis. In such circumstances diagnosis can be a relief in that it both legitimizes the patient's complaints and confirms the reality of their symptoms (Robinson, 1988), while the failure to obtain a diagnostic label can be stigmatizing. In her study of myalgic encephalomyelitis (ME) Cooper (1997) found a great deal of conflict between patients who felt ill and their doctors who could find no evidence of disease. Consequently, many were not allowed access to the sick role and, as result, 'their social position was to some extent eroded, their social identity devalued and stigmatised, and they found it difficult to obtain legitimate absence from work or disability benefit' (1997: 203).

Interactionists' interest in people's capacity to 'take the role of the other' and see themselves as they believe others see them has led them to explore the effects of societal reaction to sickness and disability for the individual's self-concept. A number of the earlier studies focused on the effects of the 'crisis' brought about by a person's comparatively sudden status transition from 'health' to 'sickness'. Some of these studies have gone as far as suggesting that the societal reaction creates the conditions of a self-fulfilling prophecy where, through a process of socialization, the person's identity comes to correspond with the images *others* have of the condition.

A good example of this approach is Scott's (1969) classical study of blindness. Scott argues that there is nothing in the condition of blindness itself which produces the stereotyped view of the 'blind personality' as passive, docile and compliant. From his observations of interaction between experts and their newly blind clients, Scott argues that the blind personality is a product of a process of socialization in which experts emphasize to clients the importance of coming to terms with blindness by defining themselves as blind. These expectations constitute a 'putative identity' which is gradually internalized by the clients as a basis for their own identity. Thus Scott argues that blindness is 'a learned social role' whereby the blind agencies create for blind people the experience of being blind.

Higgins (1980) presented a rather different view of socialization in his study of the long-term deaf. Although the deaf people he studied were 'discredited' in wider society and were vulnerable to public stereotypes of deaf people as slow and dim witted, these reactions did not tend to form part of their self-concept. They were confronted with spoiled *interaction* rather than spoiled identity. Higgins argues that this was because a major source of socialization for the deaf he studied – most of whom had been deaf since childhood – came largely from the deaf community which acted as an alternative sub-culture within which members felt no stigma. Although they may play the deaf role in public, sometimes mockingly or for strategic reasons, they were usually able to distance themselves from it subjectively.

Labelling theory is taken a stage further in studies of mental illness. Whereas studies of physical disabilities examine the way in which meanings are imputed to various conditions through societal reactions, some interactionists have argued that mental illnesses are *entirely* a product of societal reaction. In the best known of these studies Scheff (1966) argued that unusual, crazy or bizarre behaviour is widespread in society. It is only when this behaviour can no longer be accommodated within the individual's social situation that psychiatric intervention is sought. Thus it is the societal reaction rather than any objective clinical evidence that determines whether or not a person becomes the subject of psychiatric intervention. However, once a person is defined as 'mentally ill' – a definition which can, if necessary, be enforced with legal powers of detention and compulsory treatment – there is then pressure on the person to play the stereotyped 'mentally ill role'. In mental hospitals, for example, patients are socialized into their role by being rewarded for conforming to staff views and punished for deviating from them (Goffman, 1991).

The labelling theory of mental illness has been criticized for its failure to explain primary deviance and for its assertion, rather than its demonstration, of the effects of labelling. Pilgrim and Rogers (1993) suggest that the labelling theory of mental illness 'has now fallen out fashion'. However, such an obituary is rather premature as some of its key ideas, admittedly developed in a more sophisticated way, continue to influence contemporary work. For example, Prior (1998) has shown that the definition of certain behaviour as a 'psychiatric case' is determined by organizational requirements rather than 'intrinsic' evidence of psychiatric symptoms.

In more recent interactionist work on sickness and disability the focus has moved from 'crisis' to looking at illness more in terms of a series of gradual transformations of identity and experience. This shift in emphasis arose partly from a dissatisfaction with the rather mechanistic approach of the 'crisis model' and partly from sociologists' increased interest in chronic illness. Many chronic illnesses, such as arthritis, multiple sclerosis and Parkinson's disease are not characterized by a sudden 'event' which precipitates the individual into the sick role or a 'deviant identity'. On the contrary, they usually develop slowly and often inconsistently and, for many people, becoming ill is experienced as a series of status transitions. New ways of life and changes of self-concept have to be negotiated and re-negotiated as the disease progresses and sufferers reorientate their relationship to things like work, leisure and personal commitments. Thus illness is seen as 'adaptation rather than adoption of a deviant identity' (Bury, 1997).

Adaptations to illness, even the 'same' illness, can take a number of different forms. For example, in his study of colitis, Kelly (1992) has shown that some people adapt much more easily than others to the potentially stigmatizing consequences of the disease. While some are prepared to incorporate the condition into their self-concept, others make a rigid distinction between self and disease. However, underlying particular adaptations to illness is the recurring theme of people struggling to maintain a sense of order and coherence in the face of the difficulties brought about by illness. Adaptation involves managing both physical and biographical processes (Corbin and Strauss, 1991). The management of physical processes often involves the development of new skills, such as operating machinery, administering medication and building it into daily routines. People suffering from the disfiguring skin condition of psoriasis, for example, have to conform to a strict programme of bathing, scrubbing, putting on oils and creams which may take several hours a day (Jobling, 1988). Sufferers from physically debilitating conditions, such as respiratory disorders, have to learn very quickly what can be achieved in the day before chronic fatigue sets in and plan their days accordingly (Williams, 1993). The management of physical symptoms tends to be public in character and, rather like Parsons' sick role, often contains an element of 'performance', of being seen to be conforming to the 'obligations' involved in being ill.

Biographical adaptation, in contrast, tends to be more private and subjective and refers to the ways in which people with chronic illnesses try to make sense of what Bury (1982) has called the 'biographical disruption' to their lives and identities caused by illness. Part of this process involves developing 'explanations' for the illness and its progression. Williams (1984) and Williams *et al.* (1996) observed how many people with rheumatoid arthritis engage in a process of 'narrative reconstruction' in which their biography is reorganized in order to make sense of the onset of the illness. Similarly, people may construct narratives to explain the uncertainty and sudden fluctuations in symptoms that characterize many chronic illnesses in terms of preceding events, such as 'overdoing it' the day before or going out in the cold (Locker, 1983). While these 'lay theories' may have little clinical validity they are crucial in helping people try to restore some sense of order and meaning to their lives. In recent years, as a result of sociological work, health professionals have become more interested in lay theories of illness as they give important insight into the world of patients and can act as a bridge to aid professional–patient communication.

Like all approaches in sociology, interpretive studies of experiences of illness and disability have their limitations. One of the most important of these, reflecting a more general debate in sociology between macro- and micro-sociology described in Chapter 3, concerns the comparative lack of attention to the relationship between individual experiences of illness and social institutions. While many studies make vague references to 'wider society', its nature is rarely explored and, as such, it remains elusive and ephemeral, little more than a blank canvass on which micro-social contexts are etched.

A second issue involves relating people's experiences of illness to the changing, and increasingly fragmented, nature of late or postmodern, societies. In this context Kelly and Field (1998) have questioned sociologists' conceptualizations of illness and disability as processes necessarily involving the disruption of normality and consequent re-establishment of certainty with the development of illness identities. Not only is the 'normality' from which illness is a supposed 'deviation' increasingly difficult to identify with any certainty, but the idea of illness as a 'dominant and all-pervasive identity' is open to question as it implies a stability in the world of sickness which is less and less apparent elsewhere. Kelly and Field suggest that new conceptualizations of illness may be required which take account of the more fragmented and 'open' structuring of everyday life and the greater variety of ways in which chronic illness may be experienced. It may be that chronic illness is 'just one more uncertainty in a continually changing and uncertain world' (Kelly and Field, 1998: 15).

# Medicine and Society

Increasing interest in the social aspects of health and sickness in the last quarter of the twentieth century has been accompanied by a growing scepticism of modern medicine. Not only has medicine failed to find a cure for most of the major diseases of contemporary society, but research has also suggested that improvements in health in the past probably owed far more to social and behavioural changes than to clinical intervention (McKeown, 1979). Sociologists have contributed to this scepticism with their examination of the social nature of medicine, particularly the ways in which medical knowledge and practices both reinforce and reflect the social orders from they emerge. This section illustrates this general theme by looking first, at sociological interpretations of the consequences of medical intervention, particularly increasing medical intervention, in people's lives, and second, at the ways in which modern medical knowledge is shaped by social and cultural influences.

## *Medicalization*

Parsons (1951) argued that doctors perform an important social control function for society as a whole by restricting access to the sick role and by regulating the conduct of the sick. However, a later generation of sociologists went further, arguing that the medical profession does more than define *who* is (and is not) legitimately sick. It also has the power to decide *what* sickness is and has used this power to extend its professional dominance by bringing more areas of life under medical authority (Freidson, 1970). From the 1970s sociologists became increasingly critical of what was described as the 'medicalization' of modern societies; that is, the processes where experiences once seen as 'normal', such as pregnancy, childbirth, misbehaviour, feeling unhappy, growing old and dying, become seen as 'illnesses' requiring medical supervision and control.

Illich (1976) claimed that 'medical colonization' of societies has produced a dependency on medical expertise and treatment that is taking from people their capacity to cope with the pain and suffering that are an inevitable part of the human condition. He argued that medicine's monopolistic domination over health needs to be broken and that people should be encouraged to take more responsibility for their own lives rather than demanding a pill for every ill. 'Medicalization', for Illich, is just one aspect of a more general process in modern societies by which individual autonomy is crushed by the control of scientific and bureaucratic élites and, in this sense, it has similarities to Weber's pessimism about the 'iron cage' of industrialism.

For Navarro (1975), adopting a Marxist perspective, the explanation of medicalization is to be found not in industrialism as such, but in the political economy of industrial capitalism. It is the transnational pharmaceutical companies, the manufacturers of medical equipment and private hospital complexes that have most to gain from persuading doctors that medical treatments can be applied to an ever widening area of social life. Navarro disagrees with Illich's view that the medical profession causes medicalization; rather it merely administers it on behalf of capitalist organizations who gain from it directly in terms of greater profits and, indirectly, from extending control over the work force.

Feminists have argued that the medicine has had a powerful influence in defining femininity and legitimizing patriarchal control over women. Medieval systems of medical knowledge, derived from the 'classical medicine' of ancient Greece, tended to depict women as both biologically and morally inferior to men (James, 1994). Some feminists have argued that the medicalization of modern societies has reinforced patriarchal control. Medicalization of pregnancy and childbirth, for example, gave a predominantly male medical profession the power, once exercised by organized religion, to regulate women's bodies by controlling their sexuality and reproductive capacity (Oakley, 1984). The supervision of contraception, ante-natal care, delivery and abortion by medicine also plays an important part in defining and reinforcing women's sense of dependence on 'masculine' science and technology.

The medicalization thesis, although remaining popular, has been increasingly questioned in contemporary sociology. Empirically, it has been argued that the extent of medicalization has been exaggerated, and people's capacity to resist medical control underestimated (Williams and Calnan, 1996). There is also evidence of some 'demedicalization' in contemporary societies; for example in pregnancy and childbirth and mental health problems. Ethically, it has been argued that the effects of medicalization are not *necessarily* as negative as critics like Illich suggest. For example, the recognition of things such as battle fatigue, addiction and nervous shock as illnesses can be experienced by people as welcome relief from personal blame and possible punishment

(Seale, 1994). Theoretically, while the medicalization thesis is very critical of the *consequences* of some forms of medical intervention, especially those that produce *iatrogenic* (that is, doctor caused) complications, it does not challenge the *idea* of objective medical knowledge. Indeed, one of the most common criticisms of labelling things like life problems, deviance, eating and alcohol problems as 'diseases' is that these conditions do not meet the *objective* criteria needed for defining something as a disease. Thus the critical thrust of the medicalization thesis comes from comparing the 'illegitimate' with the 'legitimate' application of disease labels and ironically reinforces, rather than undermines, the ontological status of 'real' medical knowledge. For this reason it should be distinguished theoretically from an alternative *social constructionist* approach to medicine which questions the idea of *any* objective medical knowledge and any criteria for establishing its effectiveness. This approach is grounded in a radical philosophical idealism which holds that all knowledge, including scientific medical knowledge, cannot be divorced from the varying cultural contexts that produce it.

## Social Constructionism

The theoretical ideas underlying social constructionism are almost the opposite of the empiricist ideas that inform most medical sociology. In empiricism, a real world is described with theoretical (that is, fictional) concepts. For example, real inequalities in health are described through concepts such as 'class' or 'deprivation'. However, social constructionists argue that there are no 'real facts' which exist independently of systems of ideas or discourses. From this point of view nature is collapsed into culture. For example, the body and bodily processes are not natural phenomena whose reality has been uncovered by the progress of medical science. Rather they are cultural constructions that have no meaning outside the ideas and practices that surround them. Social constructionists put questions of the progress and benefits (or otherwise) of medical science to one side and focus instead on how some systems of knowledge and practice come to dominate health care at particular times.

For example, the emergence of the dominant modern biomedical views of the body and disease coincided with the growth and reorganization of hospitals in western Europe, especially Paris, towards the end of the eighteenth century. The new hospitals became centres for medical training and, for the first time, the bodies of a large number of relatively compliant and defenceless patients were brought under the inquiring eye of doctors and this changed the focus of medical knowledge. Whereas most doctors in the eighteenth century had taken a more holistic approach, seeing diseases in very general terms as symptoms of some disturbance within the whole *person*, the observation, dissection and systematic classification of patients gave rise to a new form of clinical medicine where diseases were located in specific parts of the human *anatomy,* such as the heart or liver. For social constructionists, this development was not the result of some progressive enlightenment, where the truth about the body was 'revealed' through clinical examination, but simply a different way of constructing, or 'reading', the body. As Armstrong, one of the leading social constructionists, puts it:

> The fact that the body became legible does not imply that some invariant biological reality was finally revealed to medical inquiry. The body was only legible in that there existed in the new clinical techniques a language by which it could be read. (1983: 2)

For Foucault (1973), the modern hospitals and the new anatomy that developed within them were manifestations of wider social and political changes, especially changes in the way in which power is exercised over citizens. He argued that in modern societies 'governmental' power is characterized less by visible demonstrations of physical force and more by invisible observation of people's actions, which has the effect of producing self-discipline in those observed. This disciplinary power was not just evident in the hospital, where bodies were laid open for inspection, but in the school, the asylum, army barracks and in punishment where surveillance of criminals increasingly replaced more public forms of punishment, such as pillorying and public floggings (Foucault, 1979). It was only when the body came to be seen as something essentially docile which could be surveilled, transformed and improved that a new medical approach, focused on the inspection of the body, could develop and flourish.

Foucault has been the major influence on social constructionism. Medical sociologists have used a Foucauldian approach to examine not only the consolidation of the biomedical model, but also new developments in health care arising largely from critiques of biomedicine. For example, in the later part of the twentieth century health professionals have become interested once more in the environmental causes of disease. The focus of their inquiries now extends beyond the sick to the monitoring of entire populations for evidence of risk of disease and this has resulted in mass screenings and programmes of health education and health promotion. Another comparatively recent development in medicine and medical education has been to encourage doctors and nurses to adopt a more holistic approach, taking notes on their patients' lives as well as their symptoms (Armstrong, 1995).

For social constructionists, these developments are not so much 'progress' towards creating a more socially conscious and person-centred medical profession but rather, an extension of disciplinary power where people are encouraged to be sentries of own bodies. As a major policy document outlining government strategy for health in England put it:

The way in which people live and the lifestyles they adopt can have profound effects on subsequent health. Health education initiatives should continue to ensure that individuals are able to exercise informed choice when selecting the lifestyles which they adopt. An increasing number of screening programmes are being implemented, such as those for breast and cervical cancer. The promotion of high uptake rates through effective health education is essential to the success of these programmes. (HMSO, 1992: 11)

From a Foucauldian perspective, this preventative strategy is a good example of what Helliwell and Hindess in their discussion of power in Chapter 4 called 'government at a distance', where free individuals regulate their behaviour in line with government norms.

Social constructionism has become one of the most creative and productive approaches in medical sociology. One of its major contributions has been to make problematic things sociology has tended to take for granted. For example, prior to social constructionism, most sociologists merely assumed that the human body was a given; a comparatively unchanging entity which was galvanized into action by relatively autonomous agents and constrained by social structures. Social constructionists, in contrast, have shown that medicine came before 'the body'; that is, the very idea of the body as an invariant *biological* structure which can become diseased and cured, is a product of medical discourses.

However, certainly in its more radical forms, social constructionists have suggested that the body is nothing *other* than a social construction (Lupton, 1994). There is thus nothing to be said about the body other than the systems of ideas that surround it. As Armstrong explains:

> To answer a question about the nature of the body with reference to what is seen simply sidesteps the problem because seeing is a form of perception. The body is what it is perceived to be; it could be otherwise if perception were different. The question is not therefore concerned with the nature of the body but with the perceiving process which allows the body's nature to be apprehended. (1987: 66)

Much of the plausibility of this kind of *relativist* stance comes from simply contrasting it with a crude *realism* where 'facts' – in this case 'facts' about the body – are assumed to 'speak for themselves'. As Pawson showed in his discussion of methodology in Chapter 2, the sociologist does not have to take one or other of these options. The fact that knowledge is culturally constructed need not rule out objective knowledge. The purpose of generating data in research, as Pawson argued, is to evaluate theories and help choose between them. Thus the fact that the modern treatment of prescribing penicillin for meningitis is a product of culturally relative medical discourses would not necessarily prevent even the most radical of social constructionists from taking the tablets if they contracted the disease, as available evidence has shown that, at present, this treatment represents the best hope for survival.

It seems that in quite rightly criticizing sociologists' long acceptance of a view of the body that reduces it to its biological components, social constructionists have substituted a view that reduces it to the cultural ideas in terms of which it is described. As Bury observes in his critique of the latter position:

> If the body is to be invoked in sociological inquiry, and especially in medical sociology, then the place of the biological sciences... have to be more clearly appreciated. (1997: 199)

It seems that the major task facing the emerging sociology of the body is synthesis of the biological and the cultural rather than giving precedence to one and eliminating the other (Osborne, 1997).

# Conclusion

It has become a topic of concern to a growing number of sociologists that many of the concepts which have long been cornerstones of sociological inquiry, such as class, gender and ethnicity, are becoming increasingly less stable bases of identity and behaviour. Some of the same concerns are beginning to be felt in medical sociology. As we have seen, a great deal of sociological work in this area – quite properly – involves making *comparisons* in one way or another between states of health and states of illness. For example, why does one social group stay healthier longer than another? Or, how do social contexts shape people's transition from health to sickness. However, a problem for sociologists is that these states of 'health' and 'illness' and the boundaries between them are becoming more difficult to identify. A consequence of changing cultural expectations and medical establishments now monitoring whole populations for risk factors is that symptoms are inevitably discovered everywhere and good health recedes. In a humorous article, Meador argues that well people are disappearing:

> I began to realise what was happening a year ago, at a dinner party. Everyone there had something. Several had high cholesterol levels. One had 'borderline' anaemia. Another had a suspicious Pap smear. Two others had abnormal treadmill-test results, and several were concerned about co-dependency. There were no well people. (1994, cited in Davey *et al.*, 1995: 423)

Of course, such developments are of little concern to the advocates of various branches of *relativism* in the sociology of health and medicine, such as social constructionists and postmodernists, whose aim is simply to explore varying discourses about 'health' and 'illness'. However, those sociologists who still wish to follow 'modernist' ambitions, such as exploring things like social influences on disease or people's experiences of illness, and engage in critical analysis, are faced with the challenge of securing the ontological reality of their key concepts, such as health, disease and sickness, in an increasingly fluid and fragmented social world.

## Further Reading

Bury, M. *Health and Illness in a Changing Society,* London, Routledge, 1997. An excellent, well-balanced general text which focuses on the impact of social change on experiences of health and illness.

Field , D. and Taylor, S. (eds) *Sociological Perspectives on Health, Illness and Health Care,* Oxford, Blackwell Science, 1998. A collection of original essays by leading medical sociologists on researching the sociology of health, social divisions and health and the provision of health care.

Taylor, S. and Field, D. *Sociology of Health and Health Care,* 2nd edn, Oxford, Blackwell Science, 1997. A clear introductory text for those new to the area.

Turner, B. *Medical Power and Social Knowledge,* 2nd edn, London, Sage, 1995. A general text which focuses on different theoretical explanations of health, disease and medical practice.

# 13

# Religion

*Grace Davie*

---

The sociological study of religion is about furthering the understanding of the role of religion in society, analysing its significance in human history and understanding the social influences that in turn shape religion. The key assumption is that the sociologist is interested in the relationship between religion and its social context. This chapter aims to explore some of the ways in which classical and contemporary sociologists have approached these questions. It should help you to understand:

- The different ways in which sociologists have defined religion and theorized its relation to wider society

- What is meant by secularization and the concept of a civil religion

- Sociological interest in new religious movements

- The difficulties of defining religious fundamentalism and explaining the rise of fundamentalist religious movements in contemporary societies

- The continuing significance of religion in everyday life

---

### CONCEPTS

alienation ■ sacred ■ cult ■ sect
new religious movements ■ ideal type

---

# Introduction

The principle task of the sociologist of religion concerns the subtle and elusive connections between religion and wider society (Hamilton, 1994). It is this relational quality that distinguishes the sociological approach from a variety of other disciplines that have interests in the area. However, the field remains a wide one, for both religions and societies vary enormously. Two preliminary points are important in this connection. The first is methodological and reflects the role of sociologists. Whatever their views in terms of their commitment (or otherwise) to religious belief and practice, as sociologists, they must remain agnostic. It is not sociologists' task to evaluate the relative truth claims of the religions that form the focus of their inquiry. The second point is substantive and opens up the question of definition, for it is by no means self-evident what should or should not be included within the category of religion. Decisions in this area are, moreover, of crucial significance, for once made they will lead the writer forward in a particular direction. Ultimately, therefore, choices about definition have theoretical as well as substantive importance.

This chapter starts by considering sociological definitions of religion and looking at the development of sociological understanding in the field of religion, from the earliest days of sociology onwards. It then examines a range of contemporary debates, and concludes by presenting some of the current dilemmas facing those working in this area. An important thread runs through all the sections. Sociologists of religion work in very varied contexts; their frames of reference are – at least in part – conditioned by the surrounding circumstances, whether these be defined in economic, social, intellectual or religious terms. It follows that debates that resonate in one part of the world may not resonate in another, a point that becomes increasingly significant as global, rather than western, perspectives begin to dominate the sociological agenda.

# Definitions of Religion

There are two ways of defining religion in terms of its relationship to society. The first is *substantive:* it is concerned with what religion *is*. Religion involves beliefs and practices which assume the existence of supernatural beings. The second approach is *functional:* it is concerned with what religion *does* and how it affects the society of which it is part. For example, religion offers answers to otherwise unanswerable questions (what happens when we die), or it binds people together in distinctive forms of collective action. The tension between the two types of definition has existed from the first days of sociology. As we shall see in the following section, Weber worked from a substantive point of view, while Durkheim developed a functional perspective.

Each standpoint has advantages and disadvantages. Substantive definitions limit the field to beliefs or activities which involve supernatural entities or beings. Such a limitation is helpful in that the boundaries are easier to discern, but even a preliminary survey will reveal the amazing diversity of forms that the supernatural can take in human society. More particularly, non-western forms of the supernatural often sit uneasily within frames of reference which derive from western culture. These are practical difficulties. The sharpest critique of substantive definitions comes, however, from those sociologists who maintain that the presence of the supernatural (however described) should not be the defining feature of religion. Such an emphasis is likely to exclude a whole range of activities or behaviour which – to the participants at least – take on the character of 'sacred' even if the supernatural as such is not involved. Any ideology, for instance, which addresses the ultimate problems of existence, such as an ecological or green movement, could be thought of as a religion, whether or not it makes reference to the supernatural. Also included should be certain forms of nationalism which undoubtedly provide collective frames of meaning and powerful inspiration for the populations involved, even if the goals remain firmly of this world rather than the next.

Where, though, can the line be drawn once the need for a supernatural element within the definition of religion has been discarded? This is the crucial problem with functional definitions and it remains for the most part unresolved. Once the gold standard, in the form of the supernatural, has been abandoned, it is very difficult to draw any precise or undisputed boundary about what should or should not be included in the sociological study of religion.

# Sociological Approaches

## *Beginnings*

The sociology of religion is inseparable from the beginnings of sociology as a distinctive discipline. Its early and distinguished practitioners were the founders of sociology itself: Marx, Weber and Durkheim. It is important to contextualize the writing of these scholars. As we have seen in earlier chapters, each of them was reacting to the economic and social upheavals of the late nineteenth and early twentieth century, prompted more often than not by the devastating consequences that rapid industrialization had inflicted on the populations of which they were part. The study of religion could hardly be avoided in this framework for religion was seen as an integral part of the society that appeared to be mutating beyond recognition.

There are two essential elements in the Marxist perspective on religion: the first is descriptive, the second evaluative. Marx *described* religion as a dependent variable; in other words its form and nature were dependent on social and above all economic relations. It was the economic order and the most fundamental relationship of all, that of the capitalist or worker to the means of production, that formed the bedrock of human society. The second aspect of Marxist thinking about religion pursues this line of thinking but contains an additional, *evaluative* element. Religion is a form of alienation; it is a symptom of social malformation which disguises the exploitative nature of capitalist society. The point is nicely illustrated in the lines of the Victorian hymn:

> The rich man in his castle, the poor man at his gate
> He made them high and lowly, each in their own estate.

Religion persuaded people that such relationships were natural and, therefore, acceptable. The real causes of social distress could not be tackled until the religious element in society had been stripped away to reveal the injustices of the capitalist system; everything else was a distraction.

Subsequent debates concerning Marx's approach to religion have to be approached with care. It has become increasingly difficult to distinguish between:

- Marx's own analysis of religious phenomena
- a subsequent school of Marxism as a form of sociological thinking
- what has occurred in the twentieth century in the name of Marxism as a political ideology.

The essential and enduring point to grasp from Marx himself is that religion cannot be understood apart from the world of which it is part. However, this crucial sociological insight needs to be distinguished from an over-deterministic interpretation of Marx which postulates the dependence of religion on economic forces in mechanical terms. The final point is more political. Marx was correct to point out that one function of religion is to mitigate the very evident hardships of this world and so disguise them. Nowhere, however, does Marx legitimate the destructive doctrines of those 'Marxist' regimes which maintained that the only way to reveal the true injustices of society was to destroy – sometimes with hideous consequences – the religious element of society. Marx himself took a longer-term view, claiming that religion would disappear of its own accord given the advent of the classless society: quite simply it would no longer be necessary.

Weber's contribution to the sociology of religion spread into every corner of the discipline. Central to his understanding is the conviction that religion can be constituted as something other than, or separate from, society. Three points follow from this (Beckford, 1989: 32). First, the relationship between religion and 'the world' is contingent and variable; how a particular religion relates to the surrounding context will vary over time and in different places. Second, this relationship can only be examined in its historical and cultural specificity. Documenting the details of these relationships becomes, therefore, the central task of the sociologist of religion. Third, the relationship tends to develop in a determinate direction; a statement which indicates that the distance between the two spheres, religion and society, is being steadily eroded in modern societies. This erosion, to the point where the religious factor ceases to be an effective force in society, lies at the heart of the process known as secularization.

These three assumptions underpin Weber's *magnum opus* in the field, *The Sociology of Religion* (Weber, 1922/1963), his comparative study of the major world faiths and their impact on everyday behaviour in different parts of the world. Everyday behaviour, moreover, becomes cumulative as people adapt and change their lifestyles; hence the social consequences of religious decisions. It is at this point that the question of definition begins to resonate, for it is clear that, *de facto* at least, Weber is working with a substantive definition of religion. He is concerned with the way that the *content* (or substance) of a particular religion, or more precisely religious ethic, influences the way that people behave. In other words different types of belief have different outcomes. Weber goes on to elaborate this theme: the relationship between ethic and behaviour not only exists, it is socially patterned and contextually varied. Central to his understanding in this respect is the complex relationship between a set of religious beliefs and the particular social stratum which becomes the principal carrier of such beliefs in any given society. Not everyone has to be convinced by the content of religious teaching for the influence of the associated ethic to be widespread. The sociologist's task is to use comparative analysis to identify the crucial social stratum at the key moment in history.

The questions, moreover, can be posed in ways that are pertinent to contemporary societies. For example, why is it that women seem to be more preoccupied by religion than men? Will the disproportionate influence of women as the principal carriers of the religious tradition in modern western societies have an effect on the content of the tradition itself, or will a male view continue to dominate despite the preponderance of women in our churches? What is the relationship between lifestyle and belief in such societies when the roles of men and women are mutating so rapidly? Such questions are just a beginning, but they build on the work of Weber; the approach, once established, can be taken in any number of directions. Inquiries could also be made, for example, about minority groups, especially in societies which are both racially and religiously diverse; for example, it is likely that majorities and minorities will maintain their traditions in different ways?

Durkheim began from a very different position. Working outwards from his study of totemic religion among Australian Aborigines, he became convinced above all of the binding qualities of religion: 'religion celebrates, and thereby reinforces, the fact that people can form societies' (Beckford, 1989: 25). In other words, his perspective is a functional one. Durkheim is concerned above all with what religion does: it binds people together. As we saw in Chapter 3, Durkheim was interested in what would happen when time-honoured forms of society begin to mutate so rapidly that traditional forms of religion inevitably collapse. How will the essential functions of religion be fulfilled? Durkheim responded as follows: the religious aspects of society should be allowed to evolve alongside everything else, in order that the symbols of solidarity appropriate to the developing social order (in this case incipient industrial society) may emerge. The theoretical position follows on: religion as such will always be present for it performs a necessary *function*. However, the precise nature of that religion will differ between one society and another and between different periods of time in order to achieve an appropriate 'fit' between religion and the prevailing social order.

Of the early sociologists, Durkheim was the only one to provide his own definition of religion. It has two elements:

> A religion is a unified system of beliefs and practices relative to sacred things, that is to say, things which are set apart and forbidden – beliefs and practices which unite into one single moral community called a Church, all those who adhere to them. (Durkheim, 1976: 47)

First, there is the celebrated distinction between the sacred (the set apart) and the profane (everything else) which includes an element of substantive definition. The sacred, however, possesses a *functional* quality not possessed by the profane; by its very nature it has the capacity to bind, for it unites the collectivity in a set of beliefs and practices which are focused on the sacred object. Acting collectively in a moral community, following Durkheim, is of greater sociological importance than the object of such actions.

## Subsequent Developments: the United States and Europe

What happened next in the sociology of religion depends very largely on where you look, for developments of each side of the Atlantic were very different. Each situation, moreover, reflects the prevalent cultural influences. In the United States where religious institutions remained relatively buoyant and where religious practice continued to grow, sociologists of religion in the early twentieth century were, very largely, motivated by and concerned with the social gospel. Christianity, rather like sociology itself, could be harnessed for the good of society. A second, rather less positive, theme ran parallel; one in which religion became increasingly associated with the social divisions of American society and their relationship to denominational boundaries (Demerath, 1965).

By the mid-1950s and 1960s, however, the principal focus of American sociology lay in the normative functionalism of Parsons, who stressed above everything the integrative role of religion (once again what religion does). Religion, a functional prerequisite (a necessary part of society), was central to the complex models of social systems and social action elaborated by Parsons and discussed in Chapter 3. His influence was lasting; it can be seen in the work of subsequent generations of scholars, both in America (Bellah, 1967 – see later) and elsewhere. The relationship with American society is also important. The functionalism of Parsons emerged from a social order entirely different from the turbulence that motivated the thinking of the early Europeans. Post-war America symbolized a settled period of industrialism in which consensus appeared not only desirable but possible. The assumption that religious (indeed Christian) values provided the natural underpinning of the social order was widespread.

Such optimism did not last. As the 1960s gave way to a far less confident decade, American sociology of religion shifted once again, this time to the social construction of meaning systems epitomized by the work of Berger and Luckmann (1967). Here the Parsonian model is inverted; social order (or social structure) indeed exists but it is constructed from below, not imposed from above. It is the product rather than the cause of social interaction and derives from the cumulative effect of individual actors or agents. The earlier consensus did not return: the later 1970s merge into the contemporary period, a world in which religion has become increasingly contentious. Conflict, including religious conflict, rather than consensus dominates the sociological agenda.

The sociology of religion had already taken a rather different turn in western Europe. Religious institutions on the European side of the Atlantic, unlike their American equivalents, were far from buoyant, and a growing group within French Catholicism were increasingly worried by the weakening position of the Catholic Church in French society (Godin and Daniel, 1943). Anxiety proved, however, a powerful motivator. In order that the situation might be remedied, accurate information was essential. A series of empirical inquiries were carried out under the direction of Gabriel Le Bras with the intention of discovering what exactly characterized the religion of the French people, or 'lived religion' as it became known.

# Themes and Perspectives

## Secularization

Secularization involves the assumption, now increasingly challenged, that religion is necessarily losing its significance in modern societies. With this in mind, it is hardly surprising that the debate about secularization and its relationship to other social processes dominates a large section of the literature within the sociology of religion. Wallis and Bruce (1989), for example, use this theme as a pivot for their review of the British contribution to the field. The first point to grasp is the close links between definitions of religion and the ongoing debate about secularization. Those who see religion primarily in substantive terms are more likely to argue that western society is becoming increasingly secular, for what they perceive as religion is diminishing in a way that can be convincingly measured (for example in the marked decline in regular churchgoing in almost all western European countries in the post-war period). Dobbelaere (1981), Wilson (1982) and Bruce (1996) are persuasive exponents of this approach. Those who see religion in functional terms, however, will be less convinced, for they will want to include within the definition a set of phenomena that at the very least meet the Durkheimian description of the sacred. These are phenomena which show considerable persistence even in contemporary societies.

Hervieu-Léger (1986, 1993) has generated an alternative approach to the secularization debate that steers between the extremes on either side. It is true that modern societies are destructive of certain forms of religious life (regular attendance at Mass, for example, or the unquestioning acceptance of Christian teaching), but it is also the case that modern societies create their own need for and forms of religion. Twentieth-century individuals are encouraged to seek answers, to find solutions, to make progress and to move forwards and, as contemporary societies evolve, such aspirations become an increasingly normal part of the human experience. Their realization, however, is – and must remain – problematic, for the goal will always recede. There is a permanent gap between the experiences of everyday life and the expectations that lie on or beyond the horizon. It is this utopian space that generates the need for the religious in Hervieu-Léger's analysis, but in forms compatible with modernity. The process of secularization becomes, therefore, not so much the disappearance of religion altogether, but an ongoing process of reorganization in the nature and forms of religion into configurations which are compatible with modern living. The two examples cited by Hervieu-Léger are the supportive emotional communities that can be discovered both inside and outside the mainline churches of western society (these are frequently charismatic in nature) and the types of religion which provide firm indicators of identity (both ethnic and doctrinal) in the flux of modern life. This point connects with the discussion of fundamentalism examined later in this chapter.

Another innovative contribution in the ongoing debate about secularization can be found in the work of Casanova (1994). Casanova builds on the work of Martin (1978) who has always been more ambivalent about the concept of secularization than many of his contemporaries (Martin, 1991). For Martin, using a Weberian framework, secularization may or may not occur and, if it does, the process will always be influenced by a wide range of contingent variables. Careful comparative analysis is necessary to discern both the nature of such influences and their effects. What emerges in Martin's work is a typology of possibilities in which different countries, or groups of countries, provide different 'versions' of secularization, or different versions of resistance. One of the most obvious contrasts lies in the opposing patterns of Europe and the United States. Why is it that the country with the most advanced economy in the world, a country which possesses a carefully worded constitution eliminating religion from privilege within the public sphere, turns out to be one of the most religiously active societies in the western world?

Casanova, to some extent following Dobbelaere (1981) in discerning different dimensions of religiosity, develops this theme by separating out three distinct strands within the concept of secularization:

> Secularization as differentiation of the secular spheres from religious institutions and norms, secularization as decline of religious beliefs and practices, and secularization as marginalization of religion to a privatized sphere... the fruitless secularization debate can end only when sociologists of religion begin to examine and test the validity of each of the three propositions independently of each other. (1994: 211)

The comparison between Europe and the United States illustrates this point very clearly.

American society has a strict separation of spheres but a high level of religious activity. European societies, with certain important exceptions, reveal closer connections between church and state and markedly lower levels of religious activity. The innovative emphasis in the work of Casanova lies, however, in the third strand within the concept of secularization. It is simply not the case, he argues, that privatization of religion is a modern structural trend. Privatization may well have occurred in some western societies – usually in those which display a parallel degree of religious decline – but this is a historical option, not a necessary feature of modern society. A glance at global politics at the turn of the millennium indicates that Casanova is right: whether we look at the New World (North and South America), the Pacific Rim or the rapidly modernizing societies in parts of the Islamic world, religion is playing an major part in the formation of both *social* structure and *public* policy.

A further point follows on: the secularization debate as it has been traditionally conceived is essentially a western, if not a European, debate. It has frequently embodied the crucial but dangerous assumption that what western Europeans do today in terms of their religious life, the rest of the world will do tomorrow. Secularization is seen as a necessary part of industrialization and as the world industrializes, it will secularize. This is simply not the case. Sociologists of religion must catch up with events. Martin (1996), for example – building on to his studies of Pentecostalism in Latin America (Martin, 1990) – is beginning to rethink the argument:

Initially, about a quarter of a century ago, I asked myself why the voluntary denominations of Anglo-American culture had not taken off in Latin America as they had
in the USA, and concluded that Latin America must be too similar to Latin Europe
for that to happen. But now I am inclined to reverse the question and ask why the
burgeoning denominations of Latin America have not taken off in Latin Europe.
(1996: 41; citation taken from the English original)

The essence of Martin's argument lies in the observation that the factors that
encouraged European secularization in the first place – a fortress Catholicism, buttressed by political power, and opposed by militant secularity – are
themselves beginning to erode. There is no reason, therefore, why the
patterns of the New World (based on voluntary membership rather than a
state church) should not transplant to the Old. It follows that the moderately
advanced secularization of western Europe, explainable by contingent and
time-limited features, may in the long term turn out to be the exception
rather than the rule.

In western Europe itself, the discussion relating to the dimensions of religiosity takes a slightly different form. Here the principal features of the late
twentieth century are the persistence of the softer indicators of religious life
(that is, those concerned with feelings, experience and the less specific religious beliefs) alongside the undeniable and at times dramatic drop in the hard
indicators (those which measure religious orthodoxy, ritual participation and
institutional attachment). These are the findings of the European Values
Study, an invaluable source of empirical information for a growing number of
European (and other) societies (Barker *et al.*, 1993). Bearing this perspective
in mind, sociologists vary in their interpretations of Britain as one illustration
of a European society. Bruce (1995), for example, sees Britain as a secular
society in which religion plays its part, but in forms – notably the denomina-
tion and the cult – which are compatible with modernization and rationalization (for Bruce the two are necessarily linked). Davie (1994), in contrast,
pays considerably more attention to the persistence of belief in modern
Britain despite the undeniable fall in religious practice since 1945. British
society is characterized by the phrase 'believing without belonging'; it is a
society in which belief has drifted away from the norms of Christian orthodoxy but has by no means disappeared.

Both the process of secularization itself and the debate that surrounds it are
far from straightforward. The impact of modernization is neither clear cut nor
consistent and it influences different societies in different ways. What has
happened in western Europe (that is, a marked decline in religious practice
and in some aspects of religious belief) has not happened elsewhere in the
world and, even in western Europe, religion remains a significant, if somewhat altered, feature of post-industrial life.

## Civil Religion

Another way into the comparative debate is through the concept of 'civil religion', a term associated above all with the work of Bellah, whose 'Civil religion in America' (1967) became a seminal article in the literature, drawing attention to the peculiar mix of transcendental religion and national preoccupations that characterized the belief systems of modern Americans. We have already seen that religion is eliminated from the public sphere of American society in terms of institutional privilege or church/state connections. Other forms of religion and religious language are nonetheless pervasive. Their nature can be summarized as follows:

> The widespread acceptance by a people of perceived religio-political traits regarding their nation's history and destiny. It relates their society to the realm of absolute meaning, enables them to look at their political community in a special sense, and provides the vision which ties the nation together as an integrated whole. (Piérard and Linder, 1988: 22–3)

Americans have evolved a whole series of rituals associated with the machinery of state, with the school system (swearing allegiance to the American flag) and with public holidays (Memorial Day, Thanksgiving and so on). American presidents reinforce the connections using carefully chosen vocabulary in high-profile speeches. There is considerable empirical evidence for the concept of civil religion in its American forms.

However, the concept of civil religion can be adapted to other contexts. The British equivalent is well described by Wolffe (1993). It is epitomized first of all in the sacredness that surrounds the royal family in Britain and the rituals associated with the monarch as head of state. The most obvious examples can be found in the coronation ceremony and associated jubilee celebrations, but powerful echoes exist in royal weddings, services of remembrance and national thanksgivings (in which the royal family plays – and is expected to play – a major role). Royal divorces are, however, more problematic and there can be little doubt that the sacredness evoked in the immediate post-war period (notably by the coronation) has become more than a little tarnished by the activities of the younger royals in recent years. There is an additional problem in the case of Britain or, to be more accurate, the United Kingdom. Strictly speaking, not one but four distinct civil religions co-exist within the United Kingdom as each national identity in the Union asserts its specificity. Up to a point, the royal family works to overcome these differences (the Celtic countries are carefully included in the titles, activities and venues of the royal family), but the position of the Church of England (with the monarch as Supreme Governor) does not. The Church of England is just what its name implies: it is the privileged church of one part of the United Kingdom only.

Its privileged constitutional status cannot, in many ways, be anything but excluding to the Scots, Welsh and the Northern Irish.

The debate about 'establishment' (the legal connection between the Church of England and the state) raises other issues in a society in which fewer and fewer British people attend their churches with any regularity, and only a minority of these attend the Church of England itself. Such issues are compounded by the arrival of numerically small, yet sociologically significant, other faith communities into Britain in the post-war period. The debate, however, is complex, for there is a considerable body of opinion within the other faith communities which supports the privileged position of the Church of England. It is regarded as an institution which protects the interests of anyone in the population who takes faith seriously, whether that faith be Anglican, other Christian or non-Christian (Modood, 1994). It seems that a numerically weak and relatively marginalized established church can operate as an *inclusive* institution, in a way that its historically stronger, somewhat intolerant, antecedents could not.

A third form of civil religion can be found in France. Here a coherent secular world-view or ideology has replaced the transcendent element still to be found in the United States and in Britain. Public life in twentieth-century France is dominated by the concept of *laïcité*, an idea best described as the creation of *neutral* space in public life. This is an areligious space in which no religion is privileged and all religions compete as equals. The transfer of power from one French president to another, for example, is a strictly godless ceremony. The tomb of the unknown warrior in Paris lies under the Arc de Triomphe, not in consecrated ground, while the British equivalent, in contrast, can be found just inside the door of Westminster Abbey. Unlike most European countries, the teaching of religion in state schools is not permitted in France; suggestions that this might change arouse extremely strong reactions.

An interesting development within the field of civil religion can be found in the debates surrounding the evolution of European identity. If the European Union is to function effectively, it will – it can be argued – require its own civil religion, complete with flag, anthem and belief system. Conversely the fact that such symbols of commonality have barely emerged since the early days of the European Community, and that attempts to create them resonate so little in popular consciousness may indicate the lack of viability in the idea of Europe as a socio-political entity. Only time will tell. Bearing this in mind, it is all the more paradoxical that a continent which has, very largely, ceased to practise its historic faith appeals so frequently to its Christian heritage in order to define and protect its borders.

## New Religious Movements and the New Age

There remains a persistent paradox within the material available to the sociology of religion. We know, sociologically at least, considerably more about new religious movements than we do about the beliefs and practices of the great majority within many western populations. Or to put the same point in a more positive way, there is an important and growing body of sociological material on sects, cults and new religious movements, which has been carried out by some of the most distinguished scholars in the field. Writers such as Barker, Beckford, Dobbelaere, Richardson, Wallis and Wilson have contributed substantially to our knowledge in this area.

What, then, is covered by the term 'new religious movement'? The best introduction to this field in the British context can be found in Barker's (1995) *New Religious Movements: A Practical Introduction,* which provides in a readily accessible form a large amount of practical as well as sociological material in this area. Included in the text is an extensive glossary of the new religious movements most likely to be encountered in Britain, giving a pen portrait of the group's history together with its principal beliefs. These range from the London Church of Christ (with beliefs that are relatively close to conservative evangelicals), through the groups that were especially well known in the 1960s and 70s (such as ISKCON or the Unification Church) to movements which are less easily assumed within the category 'religious' (such as the Human Potential Movements or Scientology). Indeed the first point to grasp is that new religious movements cannot just be lumped together as they are enormously varied both in their structures and in their belief systems. However, it *is* possible to establish categories – those for example of world-affirming or world-rejecting movements, plus those in-between which accommodate and adapt to the surrounding society – but such typologies are essentially heuristic devices (they help us to see patterns and contrasts), they are not absolute terms.

Bearing such diversity in mind, Barker (1995) suggests that some hundreds of thousands of British people may have had passing contact with new religious movements in the past 25 years. *Very* few of these, however, will have developed any sustained commitment to the groups in question. The main reason for new religious movements catching the attention of sociologists lies elsewhere, that is, in what they tell us about the nature of contemporary society. By looking at new religious movements and the controversies that they generate, we can discover a great deal about ourselves. What, for example, is regarded as normal or abnormal, as acceptable or unacceptable, as tolerable or intolerable in the name of religion and how does this vary from place to place or time to time? The answer lies in careful empirical analysis, which includes a comparative element. A good example can be found in the work of Richardson (1995) who looks at the workings of the emergent pan-European institutions with respect to minority religions and basic human rights in the European Union. This is an excellent study of social change. Change in this context should be understood in two ways: first in terms of institutions as a pan-European socio-legal framework begins to emerge and second, in terms of religious evolution as the notion of 'European religion' gives way to an increasing diversity of religions in Europe. New religious movements are one element in this diversity, the growing other faith communities are another. The legal aspect of this study gives it an admirably specific focus.

One form of new religious life at the turn of the millennium has acquired the title New Age. New Age religion (Heelas, 1996) is even harder to define than new religious movements, for it constitutes a rich amalgam of philosophies and practice from both eastern and western traditions. Like new religious movements, it can take myriad forms and can be discovered in a diversity of social contexts. Its influence can be felt, for example, in alternative medicine (in healing therapies), in the ecological debate (the Gaia principle), in the publishing world (scores of titles are published in this area every year) and in the world of management science. The overlap between the New Age and new forms of capitalism provides much food for thought for the sociologist. Is this a form of religion particularly suited to late capitalist development? Heelas (1996) explores this theme in some detail, looking at the New Age from two contrasting angles. At one and the same time the New Age is both a continuation of the key aspects of capitalism (global communication being an obvious illustration), and a rejection of these (preferring, for example, an altogether simpler and more human scale of living). In some ways it affirms the cultural trends of modernity, appealing more often than not to the successful or professional classes; in other ways it retains a counter-cultural element, a more or less explicit rejection of the societal aspirations, epitomized in the middle-class lifestyle. Broadly speaking, however, the real significance of the New Age in modern western societies lies in its affirmation of the sacred but in far from conventional forms. Whether or not it endures in the new millennium, the New Age itself remains a question for the next generation of sociological enquiry.

## Fundamentalisms in the Contemporary World

The emergence of fundamentalisms worldwide has, quite rightly, demanded both public and sociological attention. The general public was bewildered by the vehemence of religious expression in, for example, the Iranian Revolution and its repercussions in Britain at the time over Rushdie's *Satanic Verses*. Many Europeans feel equally uneasy about the televangelism in Northern America. Sociologists, however, were also ill-prepared for such a phenomenon: the appearance on a large scale and across several continents of the type of religion normally associated with the word 'fundamentalist' was not anticipated as the twentieth century came to a end. It upset established patterns. One commentator puts this as follows:

> Around 1975 the whole process went into reverse. A new religious approach took shape, aimed no longer at adapting to secular values but at recovering a sacred foundation for the organisation of society – by changing society if necessary. Expressed in a multitude of ways, this approach advocated moving on from a modernism that had failed, attributing its setbacks and dead ends to separation from God. The theme was no longer aggiornamento but a 'second evangelisation of Europe': the aim was no longer to modernise Islam but to 'Islamicise modernity'. Since that date, the phenomenon has spread all over the world. (Kepel, 1994: 2)

It is this phenomenon which is known by the term fundamentalism; its rise has both astonished and bewildered its observers.

It is, however, a term which is notoriously difficult to define. The following offers a starting point: 'Fundamentalism can be described as a world-view that highlights specific essential "truths" of traditional faiths and applies them with earnestness and fervour to twentieth-century realities' (Kaplan, 1988: 5). Two crucial points are present: the existence of essential truths and their application to twentieth-century realities. Both elements need to be there, for the word fundamentalism should not normally be used to describe the traditional elements of religion that have been left undisturbed by the modern world, nor does it mean the creation of new ideas. It evokes, in contrast, the reaffirming of essential truths within a situation that has been profoundly disturbed by the pressures of an expanding global economy and the effects that this has had on social, political or ideological life.

The word 'fundamentalist' itself emerges from the debates among American Protestants in the years immediately following the First World War. The focus lay on re-establishing what were felt to be the traditional truths of Protestant teaching; beliefs that had been threatened by more liberal interpretations of scripture. The 'fundamentals' were set down once and for all and included a strong emphasis on the literal truth of the Bible. An important question follows from this: is it possible to transfer this kind of thinking – developed in a markedly western, not to say Protestant culture – to other world faiths which embody entirely different thought processes? Answers to this question vary but, whatever the case, the study of fundamentalisms requires understanding and empathy from the sociologist: what does it feel like to be in a situation in which patterns of belief and practice established for centuries are under attack? It demands in addition considerable sensitivity to and empathy with world-views that may be very different from the sociologist's own.

One of the most constructive ways forward has been to make use of an ideal-type analysis – that is a 'pure' type of fundamentalism is constructed against which empirical examples can be measured. There are various examples of this kind of approach (Caplan, 1987; Marty, 1989; Hunter, 1991) and the introductions to the enormous volumes produced by the Fundamentalist Project, directed by Marty and Appleby in the University of Chicago. (The sheer scale of this project gives some indication of the seriousness with which American academics regard this question. Five volumes now cover not only diverse aspects of fundamentalism itself, but detailed empirical studies from every world faith and almost every corner of the globe.) The ideal type elaborated in the following paragraph is also by Marty (1988) and is entitled, aptly enough, the 'Fundamentals of Fundamentalism':

> Fundamentalisms usually occur on the soil of traditional cultures which have been relatively protected from disturbance either from within or from outside. The seeds of fundamentalism are sown when such a situation is challenged or disturbed. A vague sense of threat, however, requires articulation; hence the crucial importance of the leader in the emergent fundamentalist group. From which situation the *reac*tion begins to set in: *reaction, counter*action or *revanchist* action – these are the characteristics of fundamentalisms. They almost always make use of selective retrieval from the past, for which particular authority is sought. Such authority is very often discovered in the form of a sacred text or book. Subsequent actions aim to draw attention to the group in question. They are, quite frequently, aggressive actions, calculated to shock and indeed to intimidate. The 'us and them' mentality which emerges supplies a further characteristic of fundamentalisms; it is constructed quite deliberately to create and to maintain an impenetrable boundary between the group in question and the surrounding context.

A further point is crucial. In order to achieve such aims, fundamentalists make maximum use of modern technology. Hence the paradox in which groups that perceive themselves very largely as resistors to modernity, however this is experienced in each individual case, make optimal use of the products of the system which they regard as threatening to their very existence. The final step of the argument follows naturally enough: that fundamentalisms are themselves products of modernity in that they are born out of the clash between modernity and traditional cultures. Such a statement needs immediate qualification for not all such encounters end in a fundamentalist reaction; they seem, nonetheless, to constitute a necessary, if not sufficient, condition for the emergence of fundamentalist groups.

An important question concludes this section: should the word 'fundamentalism' be used in the singular or the plural? Is it possible, in other words, to find sufficient common elements between a wide diversity of movements to regard each of them as variations on a single theme? Commentators vary. It is probably more accurate to use the word in the plural, indicating a greater emphasis on difference rather than commonality; the ideal-type approach, in contrast, implies at least a degree of common themes or a family resemblance to use a different metaphor. Whatever the case, this is an additional area where careful comparative analysis is essential to the successful sociological task.

## Religion and the Everyday: Aspects of Embodiment

An alternative and more recent focus draws from a different line of socio-logical thinking. It concerns the significance of religion in everyday life, not least its impact on the basics of human existence and the relationships of humanity to the environment. All religions have something to say about the body and about nature: diet, sex, sexuality, health, healing, death, even martyrdom (to name but some features of this debate) all lie within the remit of religious control and religious teaching. It should be remembered, however, that social anthropologists have never stopped making connections between the everyday and religion. The work of Mary Douglas on purity and pollution, for example, is required reading for sociologists in this area (Douglas, 1973, 1978).

An interesting sub-theme within this section concerns the relationship between religion and gender (Walter and Davie, 1998). In modern western societies it is almost always the case that women are more religious than men: they practise more, they believe more and what they believe in is noticeably different from their male counterparts. Why should this be so? This is a ques-tion that opens up the debate between nature and nurture. One school of thought finds the explanation primarily in the roles that women have been, and to some extent still are, obliged to fulfil in western societies. It follows that as these roles gradually evolve to become more like those of men (in terms, that is, of entry into the labour market and increasingly shared family commitments) so, too, will the religious predilections of women alter. This view is well documented in the work of Steggarda (1993). An alternative argument, however, emphasizes the physiological differences between men and women and the implications of such differences for the most sacred moments in life: those of birth and death. This school of thought argues that it is women that give birth and this experience leads them to see 'life' differ-ently from men. Despite the very evident changes in the medical conditions in which most women give birth, this experience remains a pivotal moment in the lives of most women. It is also the case that women tend, even in late modern societies, to be closer to death than men; the caring roles are more often ascribed to women (even within institutions) and women frequently outlive their partners.

Indeed a second illustration of religion and the everyday can be found in the burgeoning studies of death in modern societies. After decades of silence, comparable to the Victorian distaste for talking about sex, both society and sociologists have become increasingly preoccupied with the greatest mystery of all: what happens to us when we die. Offering solutions to this mystery is, undoubtedly, one of the traditional functions of religion. What happens then when the time-honoured explanations are no longer considered valid but death remains as unavoidable as ever. All that can be said about modern societies is that death can be put off for longer and that we die in greater comfort than in previous generations, but we still die.

The work of Walter (1990, 1994, 1996) is central in this area. He describes the evolution of death from traditional, through modern to neo-modern societies. Parts of the story are by now commonplace: death has evolved from being primarily a public event embedded in community, to being a private affair discussed in medical rather than religious terms. Antibiotics are of greater use for most of our ailments than cycles of prayer. This is not the end of the story, however. As dissatisfaction with the modern way of death increases, there is pressure for further change. Following Walter (1994) there are two possibilities. On the one hand, 'late-modern' revivalists assert the right of individuals to know that they are dying and to express how they feel, insisting (perhaps too strongly) that there is a need for such expressiveness. The 'postmodern' revivalist, on the other hand, is both more radical and more conservative. Individuals must be allowed to choose: to know that they are dying, or not to know; to grieve in an expressive manner, or not to do so. Whatever works for the individual in question is right.

Beneath these questions, however, lies a powerful subtext: both the dying and the grieving individual must be considered as a person, not simply a bundle of symptoms or sorrows. Walter drives the argument to a provocative conclusion: he maintains that holistic care has entered the mainstream of medicine largely as a response to the needs of dying people. The issues that he raises go, therefore, far beyond the immediate subject matter of his book. Among other things, they challenge very directly both the institutional arrangements of modern societies and the theoretical implications of some aspects of the secularization theory. Increasing specialization – an essential tenet of this theory – is obliged to give way, as 'holy' and 'whole' re-acquire their common root. The set apart, or the sacred, becomes once again integral to the well-being of both individual and collective life. Religion is rediscovered in the everyday.

# Current Dilemmas

## *Imbalances*

Imbalances prosper within the sociology of religion. Sociologists know far more about the exotic edges of religious life than they do about the beliefs of ordinary people. Or to put the same point in a different way, the edges of the religious jigsaw are far more adequately explored than the middle, which remains – at times – alarmingly blurred. Nobody would deny that the edges throw up interesting questions, maybe the most interesting, but the lack of information about the centre is hardly reassuring. Explanations for this lack derive, at least in part, from a preoccupation with secularization. Sociologists have assumed that the picture in the middle is blurred because it is fading away. It is true that certain aspects of religious life show a marked decline in western societies and we need to know why this is so. However other aspects do not, and why not is an equally important question. Non-western societies, moreover, demonstrate markedly different religious evolutions.

The imbalance needs, therefore, to be tackled in two ways. On the one hand, there is a need to refocus attention on the middle of the western picture: on the beliefs and practices of ordinary people and the effects that these do, or do not, have on everyday behaviour. On the other hand, the sub-discipline needs to escape from the assumption that the west – and more particularly western Europe – is necessarily leading the way. Martin's studies of Pentecostalism in Latin America, for example, suggest that new spaces are being cleared in European societies which may permit forms of religion that come from the New World into the Old, rather than the other way round.

## *Isolation and Insulation from Mainstream Sociology*

Beckford (1989) has underlined both the insulation and the isolation of the sociology of religion from the parent discipline of sociology as it is tradition-ally conceived. This has proved a persistent weakness. For decades sociologists of religion have pursued their own interests, using their own frameworks of understanding, with relatively little reference to what has been going on else-where in sociology. Both partners have been impoverished as a result. The sociology of religion has lost the stimulus of theoretical developments within sociology itself; mainline (more especially European) sociologists continue to assume that religion is of marginal interest in contemporary society. Is it possible to escape from this dilemma? The following are tentative sugges-tions, which draw on the themes and perspectives of previous sections.

First, the sociology of religion – and especially the discussion about secu-larization – needs to escape from the discussions which concern the shift from pre-industrial to post-industrial societies (the shift which stimulated the early sociologists). The debate needs to move on if it is to get to grips with the characteristics of late-modern societies. Hervieu-Léger (1986) has made a significant start in this area, recognizing that the nature and forms of religion at the turn of a new century depend significantly on the nature of modern societies themselves. Contemporary religion is a product of, not a reaction to, modernity. At the same time Casanova has encouraged us to recognize the *public* nature of religion in the modern world; he does this by exploring case studies on both sides of the Atlantic.

A third possibility pursues an idea suggested by Beckford himself (1989): the proposition that religion should be seen as a cultural resource rather than a social institution, a focus that reflects a shift from structure to culture within sociology itself. Beckford sees the deregulation of religion as an unintended consequence of the secularization process. As religion frees itself from institutional control it changes its nature. It does not, however, disappear. Following Beckford, religion can become a highly significant cultural resource for a whole range of groups and individuals anxious to legitimate their point of view in an increasingly complex, and at times bewildering, society.

Finally, it is important to relate the evolutions in religious life to the changes taking place in secular society. It is true that religious institutions have declined since the Second World War and especially in western Europe. However, and the point cannot be emphasised too strongly, there have been similar changes in secular institutions; in, for example, political parties, trades unions and a wide range of leisure activities. To be more precise, the divergence between believing and belonging (already recognized in religious activities) can be seen in economic, political and cultural life as well (Davie, 1994 especially Chapter 10). Bearing this in mind, might it not be the case that explanations for at least some of these mutations lie in societal evolutions rather than religious ones? Or, to put the same point more provocatively, other areas of society appear to have been subject to some aspects of the process known as secularization.

Whatever the case, a demanding agenda awaits the sociologist of religion as the twentieth century gives way to the twenty-first. They must rise to the challenge, and religion must become once more an integral part of the discipline of sociology.

# Further Reading

Barker, E. *New Religious Movements: A Practical Introduction,* London, HMSO, 1995. An excellent introduction to new religious movements.

Bruce, S. *Religion in the Modern World: from Cathedrals to Cults,* Oxford, Oxford University Press, 1996. A robust defence of the secularization thesis.

Davie, G. *Religion in Britain Since 1945,* Oxford, Blackwell, 1994, and Bruce, S. *Religion in Modern Britain,* Oxford, Oxford University Press, 1995. Both offer empirical material and contrasting perspectives on the evolution of religion in modern Britain.

Hamilton, M. *The Sociology of Religion,* London, Routledge, 1994. A useful and accessible introductory text to the sociology of religion.

Heelas, P. *The New Age Movement,* Oxford, Blackwell, 1996. A comprehensive introduction to New Age movements.

# 14

# Mass Media

## *Natalie Fenton*

The mass media refers to institutions concerned with the large-scale production and diffusion of communication. In contemporary societies most of the information through which we understand the world around us is constructed from media images of one sort or another. The media are thus relevant to all areas of social research and media saturation of societies raises important issues for the key sociological questions of social order, social change and the relationship between the individual and society. The information explosion is also central to questions of globalization which are examined in the last chapter. This chapter aims to introduce you to some of the ways in which sociologists have examined the production, content and effects of media representations. It should help you to understand:

■ Issues surrounding the relationship between the media and dominant ideologies

■ The significance of ownership and control and professional practices in the production of media representations

■ The interpretations of media texts provided by semiology, content analysis and postmodernism

■ Differing sociological views on how media representations are understood by audiences

■ The importance of linking the analysis of production, texts, and audience reception in understanding media

---

### CONCEPTS

culture industry ■ ideology ■ hegemony
discourses hyperreality ■ text ■ genre ■ code

---

# Introduction: Why Study the Media?

The mass media are part of the 'cultural industries'. These industries contain public communications systems that differ from other areas of production by virtue of the goods they manufacture – newspapers, television programmes, advertisements, films and so on that play a pivotal role in organizing the images and discourses through which people make sense of the world. The ability of the media to construct meaning is debated widely. Do the mass media tell us how to think or do people create their own meanings through their experiences of life outside of the media? Does the type of media, whether it is radio, television, newspapers and so on effect the meaning we take from it? Does the context of reception matter; that is, where we happen to be, who we are with and the social and cultural issues that may arise from a viewing, listening or reading situation? How does the economic organization of these industries impinge on the production and circulation of meaning? These questions and others like them indicate that there are many different approaches to studying the mass media. However, their reasons for attending to the area of the mass media are remarkably similar – they all believe that mass communication has implications for freedom and control, consensus and the power structure of society. These issues are fundamental to sociology's quest to understand society.

A sociological approach to the media does not start with the media and say what they do to us. Rather it looks at the media as part of a set of institutions interconnected to other institutions within the wider context of society. Within this societal context it takes into account the production processes (standardized, routinized, controlled) and economic base of the media industries (types of ownership and uniform type), the content itself (narrative structure, genre), the audience (dependent, passive, organized, small, large) and what the sum effect of all this may be. This chapter gives a brief introduction to the study of media production, media content and media reception which is then situated in wider recent debates concerning globalization and new communication technologies.

# The Media and Ideology

Access to a full range of debate, ideas, political policies and the like gives us the possibility of making informed choices about how society is run and to pass judgement on events and their causes. These choices are controlled and limited by the array of information the mass media choose to represent. With the majority of mass media being market led; that is, operating for profit rather than the public good, it is argued that the choice available to the general public is constrained largely to that which is both popular and cheap. Hence the predominance of quiz shows, soap operas and chat shows.

This is only one way in which the ongoing manipulation of public information and imagery takes place. It is useful to think of this as macro-manipulation via global political economic systems that limit the range of media products available to us. Such control over cultural production is said to construct an ideology which, it is argued, helps to sustain the material and cultural interests of its creators. An ideology is a system of ideas about society which has normally been simplified and manipulated in order to obtain popular support for certain actions. The mass media have established a leadership in the production and transmission of a particular type of culture in contemporary society. Fabricators of such dominant ideologies become 'information elites'. Their power or dominance stems directly from their ability publicly to articulate their preferred ideas. Socio-economic élites are able to saturate society with their preferred ideological agenda because they control the institutions that disseminate symbolic forms of communication such as the mass media. Viewed in this way it is easy to understand why Gerbner (1969) said that the ultimate purpose of the study of mass communication is to 'illuminate the complex web of power roles that govern the collective image making of a culture'. This perspective is born of classical Marxist theory that stresses economic position as the strongest predictor of social differences.

Economic disparities still underlie and help reproduce social inequalities in industrialized societies. Technological developments in the twentieth century have made the manner of social domination more and more complex. Social class differences in today's world are not determined solely or directly by economic factors. Ideological influence is crucial in the exercise of power. As we saw in Chapter 3, Gramsci – to whom the term hegemony is attributed – broadened Marxist theory of the dominant ideology. Gramsci emphasized society's 'super structure', its ideology producing institutions, which were in constant struggles over meaning and power (for example Gramsci, 1971, 1978). A shift in critical theory was thus made away from a preoccupation with capitalist society's 'base' (its economic foundation) and towards its dominant dispensaries of ideas (Lull, 1995). Attention was given to the structuring of authority and dependence in symbolic environments that correspond to, but are not the same as, economically determined class-based structures and processes of industrial production. According to Gramsci's theory of ideological hegemony, mass media are tools that ruling élites use to perpetuate their power, wealth and status by popularizing their own philosophy, culture and morality. The mass media uniquely 'introduce elements into individual consciousness that would not otherwise appear there, but will not be rejected by consciousness because they are so commonly shared in the cultural community' (Nordenstreng, 1977: 226).

Elliot suggested that the most potent effect of mass media is how they subtly influence their audiences to perceive social roles and routine personal activities; the controlling economic forces in society use the mass media to provide 'a rhetoric [through] which these [concepts] are labelled, evaluated and explained' (1974: 262). Television commercials for example, encourage audiences to think of themselves as 'markets rather than as a public, as consumers rather than as citizens' (Gitlin, 1979: 255). Hegemony implies a willing agreement by people to be governed by principles, rules and laws they believe operate in their best interests, even though in actual practice they may not. So, control is exercised by social consent and not by coercion. The study of mass communications is an attempt to uncover and unravel the complex mechanisms by which the production, distribution and consumption of ideological content is managed without recourse to the coercive use of state power in capitalist society.

In reality, dominant ideologies are not unified codes. Media imagery contains variety and contradiction. Furthermore, the effects of ideological representation and technological mediations cannot be easily predicted. There is no uniform social response to the perspectives put forward by the mass media. While dominant ideologies are cultivated hegemonically and contribute to the formation of mainstream consciousness, human beings – as individuals, family members, workers, students and so on – interpret and use mass media in ways that do not always coincide with the message senders' intentions. Hegemony is fragile. It requires renewal and modification through the assertion and reassertion of power. Hegemony has to be actively won and secured in a process that often involves struggles over meaning and conflict of views. The concept of hegemony allows for social change originating both from those who hold power in society and also from those who do not, because, crucially, hegemonic struggles can be lost (Hall, 1977).

This struggle over meaning takes place between the process of production and the act of reception, both of which are determined by their place in a wider social, political, economic and cultural context. Both are subject to constraints. Choices made by the audience must be looked at within the social context of their daily life and the content itself must be interpreted according to the social and political circumstances of its production. So, rather than just looking at how the mass media may exert an ideological effect on the behaviour and attitudes of individuals, it is crucial to consider the functioning of the mass media within the larger sociological perspective of culture, social structure and social groups. To understand the role of the mass media in society we need to consider it in its social entirety from inception to reception. No one part is distinct from the other; neither is the making of meaning a straightforward linear process. Nonetheless, we still need a detailed understanding of the parts to appreciate the whole – and so to media production.

# Media Production – Encoding Meaning

The study of media production has developed in two main directions (Deacon *et al.*, 1999). The first considers how political and economic forces structurally delimit news production. This has focused largely on patterns of ownership in media industries and state regulation and the subsequent control exerted over the news creation process (for example Golding and Murdock, 1991). The second is more related to mainstream sociology with the study of media organizations and the sociology of occupations, the impact of professional practices, occupational routines and cultural values of journalists (for example Tunstall, 1971). Unlike the standard political economy perspective it takes the central problem for understanding journalism in liberal societies to be the journalists' professed autonomy and decision making power. The tensions between the traditions rest on the differing emphasis each gives to internal and external factors as the main determinants of news production.

## *Ownership and Control*

Ownership of private media is now largely in the hands of multinational corporations (Golding and Murdock, 1991). The power conferred by ownership to influence the ethos, editorial direction and market definition of commercial media – principally through the hiring and firing of staff, the setting of organizational policy and the allocation of rewards within media organizations – is mostly vested in one corporate sector. The increasing amount of cultural production accounted for by large corporations has long been a source of concern to theorists of democracy. These theorists saw a fundamental contradiction between the ideal that public media should operate largely in the public interest and the reality of concentrated private ownership. They feared that proprietors would use their property rights to restrict the flow of information and debate on which the vitality of democracy depended. These fears were fuelled by the rise of the great press barons at the turn of the century who had no qualms about using their large circulations to promote their pet political causes or to denigrate people they disagreed with. Since then, we are faced with multimedia conglomerates with significant stakes across a range of central communications sectors. The most well-known example is Rupert Murdoch's media empire (Figure 14.1).

| Place | Media ownership |
|-------|-----------------|
| London | News International ( *The Times*, the *Sun*, *Today*, *News of the World*, *The Sunday Times*), BSkyB (with over 20 satellite channels reaching over 4 million homes), HarperCollins UK, News Datacom |
| Hong Kong | Star TV and related satellite services |
| Australia | News Corporation, related newspaper interests, airlines |
| Germany | 50 per cent interest in Vox |
| South America | An interest in Canal Fox, joint ventures with the Globo organization |
| United States | Newspaper and magazine interests as well as control of Fox Television Stations |

**Figure 14.1**    Rupert Murdoch's global media empire

The rise of communications conglomerates facilitated by privatization, deregulation and the vast development of global media markets adds a new element to an old debate about potential abuses of owner power. Not only are there problems of proprietor power influencing editorials and the firing of staff who do not share their political philosophies, but different parts of the media industry have come together in support of each other to exploit the overlaps between the company's different media interests. The company's newspapers may give free publicity to their television stations or the record and book divisions may launch products related to a new movie released by the film division. The effect is to reduce the diversity of cultural goods in circulation. Growing concentration of ownership has increased the potential for centralized control over the media. Its dangers were illustrated in Italy's 1994 election when the Fininvest TV channel (with a 40 per cent market share) gave ill-disguised support to its controller and right-wing businessman, Silvio Berlusconi, who was thrust into the premiership without ever having held office before (Curran, 1996).

The production of communications, however, is not merely a reflection of the controlling interests of those who own or control the broad range of capital and equipment which make up the means by which cultural goods are made and distributed. It is also subject to those who produce the words and images on a daily basis – the media professionals.

## Professional Practices: the Sociology of News Production

News is the product of organizational processes and human interaction. It is shaped by the methods used in the news-gathering process which is in turn affected by the information sources available, and the organizational requirements, resources and policies of particular institutions. For example, the need of news organizations to secure regular and usable copy means that certain journalists are assigned to specific beats – such as Westminster or the law courts. This encourages fuller reporting of these areas. It also places journalists close to key sources where information is often traded for publicity (Gandy, 1982). With several newspapers covering the same beats, it has also been said to encourage a pack mentality in which journalists on the same beat form collective news judgements (Tunstall, 1971).

News relies on the sources journalists feed on for information. Sources can be anyone who can provide information of any sort, from the person in the street to a government minister or an 'expert'. The role of sources and their relationship to journalists and the production of news has contributed to a more recent third approach to the study of news production, which McNair (1994) labels the 'culturalist approach'. It differs from other approaches in its insistence that the production of news 'is not simply a function of ownership, nor of journalistic practices and rituals, but of the interaction between news organisations, the sources of their output, and other social institutions' (McNair, 1994: 48, cited in Deacon, 1996: 174). News creation is seen as a constant struggle between different players, each attempting to present their own version of reality. However, opportunities to access the news-making process are not the same for all. Those in positions of power are given the added advantage of speaking as an authority on a topic and asserting the primary definition of an issue to which all other interpretations must respond. This focus on news sources rather than the media organization *per se* has generated more interest in the specific dynamics of news creation. It has also led to criticisms of earlier accounts of news production for being excessively deterministic, and for exaggerating the ability of social and political élites to manage hegemonic power via the mass media.

On the whole the news may work hegemonically to reflect prevailing views, opinions, and values, but this hegemony is neither faultless nor all encompassing. Not all reporters support the dominant ideology in their writing. Rather, news reflects a continual struggle for renewal and renegotiation for a ruling bloc to maintain its position (Fenton *et al.*, 1995). From this perspective, the power of 'primary definition' (the initial interpretation of reality by those in positions of authority) is not a precise expression of the social structure, but an achievement gained through successful strategic action (Schlesinger, 1990). Although agencies of the state and other powerful élites enjoy many advantages in getting their messages across, their ability to define the news is not absolute. Tensions within political systems, investigative journalism, inter-governmental conflict, and political interventions by non-official sources who have gained credibility within the media, can and do open up media debate on certain issues (Deacon and Golding, 1994).

Approaching news production from the position of news sources brings social action and agency to the fore and dismisses earlier research based on reproductionist accounts of ideology. 'The concept of active production challenges the view that the media are just a passive conduit by which the powerful instruct the powerless what to think and feel. However, at the same time, most proponents... are sensitive to the dangers of overstating the diversity and plurality that this resistance is capable of creating' (Deacon *et al.*, 1999). The autonomy of the moments of production must also take account of the limits to this freedom.

One way of analysing how the media may present limitations to freedom is to look at the output of the cultural industries to gauge the type of imagery and information in circulation that we take for granted.

# Media Content

In a society saturated with mass media the images they produce are ever more responsible for the construction and consumption of social knowledge and represent a bank of available meanings which people draw on in their attempts to make sense of their situation and find ways of acting within and against it. The media select items for attention and provide rankings of what is and is not important – they set an agenda for public opinion. The way the media choose themes, structure dialogue and control debate is a crucial consideration in any discussion on representations.

Representations should be viewed as just that – accounts of the world that are incomplete interpretations rather than unmediated descriptions of the 'really real' (Rakow, 1992). Reality cannot be assimilated unproblematically into a representation that is merely descriptive because representation also entails delegation and construction.

## Semiology

One way of studying media representation is through semiology. Semiology is the study of signification, or meaning production. It treats language as a system of codes and signs which construct meaning. Semiology argues that material reality can never be taken for granted, imposing its meanings upon human beings. Reality is always constructed and made intelligible by culturally specific systems of meaning. This meaning is never innocent but rather has a particular purpose behind it which semiology can uncover. In Barthes (1957/1973) seminal work, *Mythologies*, he suggested that meanings are produced through the codes at work in representations, and that while meanings might appear to be natural and obvious they are in fact constructed. To enable us to understand this constructedness Barthes treated each sign as a combination of thing (material object) and interpretation (concept).

In semiology a sign is anything that stands for something else. For example, a bunch of red roses stands for passion. Signs also acquire meaning from the things that they fail to stand for – we know that it is a bunch of red roses because it is not a bunch of weeds – as well as from their position in social myths and conventions which shape the way we perceive ourselves; in our particular culture red roses may stand for passion, in another culture they may mean something entirely different. A bunch of red roses is in essence a load of flowers which have no significant meaning outside the systems of rules and conventions which constituted it as signifying passion. Barthes breaks the bunch of roses down analytically into a signifier, the roses (or form), a signified, passion (or concept), with the combination of the signified and the signifier together making the sign (the act of signification). This attribution of meaning – that the roses signify passion and not anger – cannot be understood simply in terms of the system of signs, but must be located in the context of social relationships in which the meaning making occurs.

The ideas of semiology go further than signifier+signified=sign to consider the concept of myth. The use of the mythic dimension in the analysis of texts allows us to pass from semiology to ideology. In Barthes' words the principle of myth 'transforms history into nature':

> What allows the reader to consume myth innocently is that he does not see it as a semiological system but as an inductive one... the signifier and the signified have, in his eyes, a natural relationship... any semiological system is a system of values; now the myth-consumer takes the signification for a system of facts: myth is read as a factual system, whereas it is but a semiological system. (Barthes, 1953/1967: 142)

An example given by Barthes is that the presentation of women in many media texts makes the role of women as mothers appear natural and inevitable. In his later work Barthes introduces two new concepts of denotation and connotation. Denotation is the literal, taken-for-granted meaning, a bunch of red roses, a white dress, a pair of running shoes. But the task of semiology is to go beyond these denotations to get at the connotations of the sign – respectively passion, purity and fitness. This reveals how myth works through particular signs. In this way the constructed, manufactured and historical location of the myth can be discovered. This may appear to be a bunch of roses but it connotes passion; this may appear to be just a picture of a woman in a white dress but it connotes purity and so on. Thus the methods of semiology reveal the ideologies contained in cultural myths (Strinati, 1995). Connotation or 'second order signification' concerns the latent cultural beliefs and values expressed by a sign or a sign system. A recognition and understanding of the various codes and conventions underlying the particular articulation of signs is necessary for second order signification to work; that is, one needs to have a thorough knowledge of the culture a sign system originates from.

A much-quoted semiological study of a girls' magazine called *Jackie* was undertaken by McRobbie in 1982. *Jackie* is conceived of as system of signs that work to 'position' the female readers for their later roles as wives and mothers by means of the ideology of teenage femininity it cultivates. The magazine addresses a young female audience on the basis of a consumerism and culture which defines female adolescence and which hides differences such as race or class. McRobbie uses semiology to reveal the codes which form the ideology of adolescent femininity. This methodology allows McRobbie to uncover the 'culture of femininity' which, as 'part of the dominant ideology', 'has saturated' the lives of the young girls, 'colouring the way they dress, the way they act and the way they talk to each other' (McRobbie, 1991: 93). Semiological analysis is used to discover codes in *Jackie* which define its ideology of teenage femininity, which McRobbie then argues acts as a powerful force on the lives of its readers. The main codes include the code of romance, which involves searching for (heterosexual) romance, finding the right boy and thus placing yourself in a competitive relationship with your girl friends; the code of personal life, which includes personal difficulties and concerns usually raised in the problem pages with the replies reinforcing the ideology of adolescent femininity found elsewhere in the magazine; the code of fashion and beauty which instructs readers on how to dress and look in order to be able to meet the demands of this ideology; and finally the code of pop music that involves stars and fans. Her analysis of these codes leads McRobbie to the following conclusion:

> *Jackie* sets up, defines and focuses exclusively on the 'personal', locating it as the sphere of prime importance to the teenage girl. This world of the personal and of the emotions is an all-embracing totality, and by implication all else is of secondary interest. Romance, problems, fashion, beauty and pop all mark out the limits of the girl's feminine sphere. Jackie presents 'romantic individualism' as the ethos *par excellence* of the teenage girl... This is a double edged kind of individualism since in relation to her boyfriend... she has to be willing to give in to his demands, including his plans for the evening, and by implication, his plans for the rest of their lives. (McRobbie, 1991: 131)

The main criticism of semiological analyses is that ultimately the conclusions it reaches are arbitrary. Depending on the views and opinions of the researchers the analysis of the representation will change. The 'meanings' taken from the text are implied meanings that rest on connotative interpretation. Semiological analysis is based on three main assumptions: first, that in the process of analysis the researcher can uncover the latent meaning that will match the understanding of every reader; second, that covert meanings have more impact on one's consciousness than overt or denotative meanings; and third, that the researcher is able to resist all manner of ideological influence.

## Content Analysis

Not all research on media texts has drawn on semiotic analysis – much of it has turned to content analysis. Content analysis is often used to assess the dominant characteristics of large quantities of media output. Content analysis is defined as 'a research technique for the objective, systematic and quantitative description of the manifest content of communication' (Berelson, 1952). Simplified greatly, the basic premise of content analysis is to count things like the amount of women characters, the roles they are presented in and the themes that accompany their representation. Studies that adopt this methodology have discovered that males greatly outnumber females in prime-time TV, in advertisements women stereotypically clean, launder and cook while men give the orders and eat the meals (Tuchman *et al.*, 1978; van Zoonen, 1994). This methodology has the advantage of being able to handle large quantities of data, such as months of newspaper coverage or broadcast material and offer an audit of the types of information and entertainment available to us. It has been criticized because it does not go beyond the manifest content and delve into the deeper connotative or latent meanings in a text. This limitation can be construed as an advantage, since it enables a methodology that fulfils traditional scientific requirements of objectivity with results that are reliable and able to be tested statistically for their significance. A focus on manifest content should ensure that a replication of the same project will produce roughly similar results. In practice the more sophisticated content analysis that accounts for thematic prevalence does demand some degree of qualitative evaluation. In these cases definitions of categories must be as tight as possible to ensure continuity and validity of the final figures.

## Putting Postmodernism in the Picture

Since the mid-1980s an approach which has been labelled 'postmodernism' has emerged that has impacted on the way we think about media content. Postmodern thinking has abandoned traditional sociological reasoning based on determinist models of social structure replacing it with how discourses comprising words and statements and other representational forms actively produce social realities as we know them. The term 'discourse' refers to specific meanings and values which are articulated in language in specific ways describing and delimiting what it is possible to say and not to say.

Those who go under the banner of postmodernism approach society as an ensemble of fragmented individual consumers swimming in a sea of images, from which they construct their own meanings about the world. There are no overarching narratives about how the world works. Reality is fragmented. The consequences of this are to conceptualize power as highly dispersed rather than concentrated in identifiable places or groups. In media studies this shift has been seen in a move away from the political economy of cultural production to a concern with words, texts and representations (or discursive constructions).

Postmodern theorists claim that contemporary communication practices are non-representational and non-referential. In other words, they have no purchase outside the text, they have no separate external domain. Rather, they are self-reflexive and self-referential. Contemporary culture becomes no more than a constant recycling of images previously created by the media. The recognition of media implosion has caused many postmodern theorists to question the practices of mass communication in terms of the relationship of an event and its media representation. It is claimed that the proliferation of new media technologies makes it difficult, if not impossible, to discern the difference between images and reality. Moreover, postmodernists point out that many media images are hyperreal; that is, more real than real. As Poster (1990: 63) explains, 'a communication is enacted... which is not found in the context of daily life. An unreal is made real... The end result is a sensational image that is more real than real and has no referent in reality.' Thus the notion of representation becomes problematic. Contemporary media do not represent reality, they constitute it.

Postmodernism asserts that popular culture signs and media images increasingly dominate our sense of reality, and the way we define ourselves and the world around us. In a media-saturated society it is no longer a question of the media distorting reality, rather the media have become reality – the only reality we have (Strinati, 1995). So, there is little point in studying the content of the mass media to see how they may affect our everyday lives; little point in counting instances of racism or sexism and arguing against them; little point even in studying how people understand the media since 'one interpretation is not by definition better or more valid than another' (van Zoonen, 1996: 48). There is little point because the media are reality, are inescapable. As McRobbie says:

> We do not exist in social unreality while we watch TV or read the newspaper nor are we transported back to reality when we turn the TV off to wash the dishes or discard the paper and go to bed. Indeed perhaps there is no pure social reality outside the world of representation. Reality is relayed to us through the world of language, communication and imagery. Social meanings are inevitably representations and selections. Thus when the sociologists calls for an account which tells how life really is, and which deals with the real issues rather than the spectacular and

exaggerated ones which then contribute to the moral panic, the point is that their account of reality would also be a representation, a set of meanings about what they perceive as the real issues. (1994: 217)

The idea that the mass media take over reality has been criticized for exaggerating their importance. The notion that reality has imploded inside the media such that they can only be defined by the media has also been questioned. Most people would probably still be able to distinguish between the reality created by the media and that which exists elsewhere. As Strinati (1995: 239) states, if reality has really imploded into the media how would we know it has happened? The only response is that we know it has happened because there are those who are all knowing and have seen it.

The world according to postmodernists is a world of surface appearances. No one experiences anything directly, there is only mediated reality resulting in a complete absence of lived experience. Issues of truth are treated as out of date in favour of speculation about the possible meanings of texts. However, whereas we may recognize the description of reality as disorderly and fragmented it also shows patterns of inequality. If the media are literally our reality we effectively deny that material inequalities do exist. This is insulting to all who suffer them. As Kitzinger and Kitzinger argue:

Feminists struggled for decades to name 'sexism' and 'anti-lesbianism'. We said that particular images of women – bound and gagged in pornography magazines, draped over cars in advertisements, caricatured as mothers-in-law or nagging wives in sitcoms – were oppressive and degrading. The deconstructionist insistence that texts have no inherent meanings, leaves us unable to make such claims. This denial of oppressive meanings is, in effect, a refusal to engage with the conditions under which texts are produced, and the uses to which they are put in the dominant culture. (1993: 15)

Ultimately, any work that focuses on texts, form and images alone at the expense of power and the structural constraints of class, income, culture and history is limiting and partial. For example, when studying gender in the media, an exploration of the concept of power in relation to female authority, influence, coercion, and manipulation inside media organizations as well as the public performance and record of high visibility women in economic and political élites is crucial to communications research on imaging and empowerment.

Similarly, any work that dismisses the role of the audience in the process of mass communication cannot account for differences or similarities in interpretation and runs the risk of reductionism whereby we all become either enslaved by ideology or free-floating discourses. In recognition of this, research has emerged that prioritizes the role of the audience in meaning making rather than seeing the audience as constructed or subsumed by the text:

If we are concerned with the meaning and significance of popular culture in contemporary society, and how cultural forms work ideologically or politically, then we need to understand cultural products as they are understood by audiences. (Lewis, 1991: 47)

# Media Reception – Decoding Meaning

The role of the audience, or consumer, in the construction of meaning has been subject to differing analytical perspectives. Each tackles in its own way the tension between audiences' constructive capabilities and the constraining potential of culture and ideology (expressed through the mass media). Media theorists in this area agree on the importance of media in our daily lives. Yet the majority disagree on most of the major dimensions of audience analysis: in their conception of the audience (is it active or passive, vulnerable or resistant?); of the programme (as a resource for diverse motivations or a normative pressure on all of us, as comprised of literal or hidden meanings); of the processes of effects (either by audience selectivity or by media imposition); of the nature of effects (ideological, symbolic, belief-based or behavioural); of the level of effects (individual, familial, social mainstreaming or political); and of the appropriate methods for study (ethnography, survey, experiment, text analysis, or social commentary) (Livingstone, 1991).

For the sake of simplicity, two intertwined strands can be distinguished. The first emphasizes the capacity of texts to position readers, thus ensuring that the limitations of response are provided by the texts themselves. Readers are thus 'held in ideology' (Tudor, 1995) by their textual placement. This audience positioning has led to texts being described as having 'inscribed readers'. The main thrust of this analysis was to see texts as instruments of ideology primarily in their capacity to situate the reader. The second strand shifts emphasis from the power of texts to confer meaning to the interpretative power of the audience.

## *Media Effects – The Audience as Powerless*

Media effects research has most commonly been associated with a stimulus–response learning theory. This suggests that mass media texts are very powerful and that their messages are more or less irresistible; the media are seen to behave like a hypodermic needle, injecting audiences with their messages. Throughout the 1950s and 60s this perspective recurred around two themes – could violence in the mass media induce violent behaviour in the audience; and what effect did the mass media have on people's political attitudes? In the case of media and violence many proponents of early effects studies argued that horrible images on the media will make us horrible, not horrified; that terrifying things will make us terrifying, not terrified; and to see something aggressive makes us feel aggressive, not aggressed against (Barker and Petley, 1997).

Media effects theory was widely criticized as textual determinism which robbed readers of their social context and critical agency leaving no room for interpretative manoeuvre. In the extreme this translated the audience into cultural dupes, blank slates waiting to be written on. Media effects research is also criticized for only studying one type of effect – that which is more or less immediate, behavioural and measurable. The effects measured are confined to those intended by the sender thus lacking a critique of the production of messages from within the power relations of society. Media effects research is said to take messages as neutral and non-problematic givens and to be overly simplistic in dimensions of messages selected for study. Ironically media effects research is criticized most of all for being unable to understand the effects of the mass media because it fails to take account of cumulative, delayed, long-term and unintended effects including those which stabilize the status quo (Golding and Murdock, 1978). For example, political coverage in the mass media may not change the way we actually vote, but it may influence the way we think politically. Similarly, the fact that violence in the media does not appear to generate homicidal tendencies in most who consume it does not mean that it is of no consequence (Lewis, 1991).

The downfall of 'effects' research lead theories of communication away from sender–receiver objectivist models to subjectivist theories which start from the premise that reality is socially constructed. In other words, theorists rejected the idea that 'reality' somehow exists 'out there' and all that the media do is act as a mirror to reflect it; to a more sophisticated understanding of 'reality' as something that is constantly changing, constructed and manipulated by all social players. The notion of a reality that the media pass on more or less truthfully and unproblematically is far too simplistic: media production is not just a matter of reflection but entails a complex process of negotiation, processing and reconstruction; media audiences do not simply take in or reject media messages, but use and interpret them according to their own social, cultural and individual circumstances – the audience is involved in making sense of the images they see; media are not only authorized to reflect reality but to represent our collective hopes, fears and fantasies (for example, in films which seek to challenge sexual stereotyping) – the message does not have the total monopoly on meaning. Of course, the power to set the media agenda may not be evenly spread as already discussed; neither may the ability to manipulate and interpret information be equal for everyone.

## *Media Reception – The Audience as Powerful*

As an antidote to a life condemned to ideological slavery came the second analytic strand – the active audience. Active audience theorists have stressed that audiences are capable of arriving at their own decisions about the meaning of a media text and that the text themselves were *polysemic* (for example Radway, 1984; Ang, 1985). Polysemy refers to the potential for multiple meanings to be taken from one text, thus allowing ambiguity and interpretative freedom.

Active audience research is most often associated with the work of the Centre for Contemporary Cultural Studies (CCCS) at the University of Birmingham from the late 1970s onwards. Hall (1980) the director of the centre argued that a text contains a 'preferred reading' – the meaning intended by the person who produced it – but that reading may be undermined when it is 'decoded' by the audience. A 'negotiated reading' may be generated in which audiences modify the text's meaning in the context of their own experiences, or an 'oppositional reading' may occur in which the meaning of the text is undermined by the audience.

Early empirical support for these ideas came in the form of research on audience interpretations of *Nationwide,* an early evening news programme in Britain in the 1970s. Morley (1980) showed recordings of the programme to groups which were made up of students, trade unionists, managers or apprentices. He found that managers and apprentices were most likely to interpret the texts in ways that were consistent with the preferred readings; teacher training and art students were most likely to construct negotiated readings; and groups of trade unionists tended to come up with oppositional readings. This research was seen to offer confirmation of the ability of certain segments of the audience to interpret certain texts differently from the meaning intended by the author or producer and from other audience groups. This stimulated further examinations of the role of the active audience in relation to (among others) television programmes (Ang, 1985; Corner *et al.*, 1990), romantic fiction (Radway, 1984) and comics (Barker, 1993). It also stimulated a tradition of what is often called 'ethnographic' research on audiences in which members are either interviewed about a text or invited to write about their consumption. The audience was no longer conceptualized as a collection of passive spectators but as a group of individuals who can see the hidden text of a cultural product for what it is and is not. The corollary of this was that as individuals have the capacity to undermine the intended meaning of texts, they can therefore subvert the relations of power within which they are located (Fenton *et al.*, 1998).

Postmodernism takes this theorizing one step further, insisting that we are all forever actively resisting that which is reality. We do this, it is claimed, through our knowledge of images and their construction. In other words we know we cannot escape mainstream imaging, we know that it is as real as our material existence but we also know that it is constructed and that we can play a part in the meanings given to it. The idea is that we play with the notion of constructedness and take what we want from the bits and pieces at our disposal. In most of this work audiences are seen as actively constructing meaning so that texts which appear on the face of it to be reactionary can be subverted. The subversion comes through the pleasures that are gained from it. For example, following postmodern ideas Ang argues that the world of fantasy is the 'place of excess where the unimaginable can be imagined' (1996: 106) and this is interpreted by Ang as liberatory. Based on the assumption that discourse is reality and there are always multiple discourses to choose from the individual becomes a self-made jigsaw of bits and pieces who recognizes, enjoys and plays with the constructedness of their own existence. This ignores the fact that someone made the jigsaw pieces in the first place, drew particular configurations on them and gave them to us in particular packaging designed to appeal and to sell. Postmodern perspectives suffer from an under-theorizing of the social conditions and foundations for creating meaning and communication or what Jameson (1991) has called a lack of historicity: they fail to situate their analyses within larger historical and structural contexts. There is also a huge contradiction in postmodernism which asserts both that representation constitutes reality and that the audience is powerful and able to resist media messages. Put simply, if the media are everywhere, inescapable, reality itself, then how can we resist them, avoid them, see through them and recognize their constructedness?

If the active audience theories are taken to the extreme they translate into an interpretative free-for-all in which the audience possesses an unlimited potential to read any meaning at will from a given text. There are many problems with studies that adopt such an extreme approach. Morley has criticized the neglect in most active audience research of 'the economic, political and ideological forces acting on the construction of texts' (1993: 15). By drawing attention away from the media and texts generally as instruments of power, they have been accused of a lack of appreciation of wider political factors and hence of political quietism (Corner, 1991) and ideological desertion. The same criticism can be directed at postmodern accounts.

The very notion of 'active' has been equated with powerful. This has caused several critics to question the extent to which audiences genuinely exert power over the text. Condit (1989), for example, argued that the common finding that audiences derive their own pleasures from texts should not be taken to imply that they are in fact deriving their own interpretation and therefore undermining the inscribed messages of those texts. She suggests through an examination of points made by two people about an episode of *Cagney and Lacey*, an American detective show, that 'they shared a basic construction of the denotations of the text' (1989: 107), in spite of holding very different views about the central focus of the episode (abortion). Thus, while audiences are active in their consumption of texts they are not necessarily critical of its denotation; nor do they derive alternative views about it (Fenton *et al.*, 1998). A further criticism is that the active audience approach fails to give adequate recognition to the fact that authors of texts are able to frame issues and messages. They do this through what is actually present in the text and through what is absent – the silences in texts are just as significant as the messages within the texts themselves in terms of the capacity of audiences to derive alternative interpretations (Bryman, 1995).

What is clear is that how we think about the audience depends on our theoretical framework. As a result of a growing awareness of the framing power of texts and an understanding that the text must be viewed in relation to hegemonic culture, more circumscribed accounts of audience activity have emerged. As the earlier example illustrates, these tend to recognize that differently located audiences may derive particular interpretations of texts, but that the text itself is rarely subverted. In other words, the essential power of authors to frame audience reception is accepted; audiences do engage in interpretation but that interpretation is marginal to the denotative structure of the text. In this manner ideology remains a crucial reference point. Examples of research which reveals this orientation include Kitzinger's (1993) research on AIDS in the media, Corner *et al.*'s (1990) study of the representation of the nuclear energy industry and Fenton *et al.*'s (1998) study of the representation of social science in the media. In the latter, the researchers analysed responses to newspaper, television and radio news reports of social scientific research to reveal a marked consistency between intended meaning at the point of production and audience understanding and interpretation of the text. This is not to say that audience members passively deferred to the text – on the contrary, they found substantial evidence of independent thought and scepticism. However, the 'distinctiveness of decoding' occurred when evaluating the text rather than at the point of interpretation. Resistance to the message did not lead to a renegotiation of it. It was interrogated but not expanded. Two reasons are given for this interpretative closure. The first relates to the genre of the text being analysed. Hard news reporting is governed by a range of mechanistic, narrative conventions that are intended to generate a denotative transparency to inhibit potential readings. For example, it is a genre where prominence and frequency of appearance are reliable indications of significance *and* signification. Most news consumers are conversant with the rules of this presentational game and construct their readings according to them. As such news is a peculiarly 'closed' form of actuality, coverage whose polysemic potential is circumscribed. There is none of the *interpretative* room to manoeuvre that is such an evident and essential facet of other forms of fictional and factual genres.

The second reason for this interpretative closure relates to the nature of the subject matter being reported. For example, one of the news reports under study is about a remote and esoteric issue (false memory) which, although its broader implications resonate with the audience, remains beyond their direct personal and professional experiences. This, it is argued, is a situation where we find the most acceptance of media definitions and the power of the audience is at its most limited (Fenton *et al.*, 1998).

In these analyses the reader can effect the reading process, can resist the 'preferred reading' (that is, that which appears dominant in the text) up to a point and to that end is an active agent. Yet agency is limited by structure. As Tudor (1995: 104) says:

> The remarkable capacity of human beings to construct diverse meanings and take a variety of pleasures from texts is matched only by the equally remarkable degree to which those meanings and pleasures are common to large numbers of people.

## Understanding the Mass Media

What this holistic approach to the sociology of the mass media reveals is that when we think about the role of the media in society we must include the location of the medium in economic structures (commercial or public media), their specific characteristics (print or broadcast), the particular genres (news or soap opera and so on), and the audiences they appeal to. Individually the elements of production, texts and reception of media make no sense; they are intrinsically linked in the process of meaning production (van Zoonen, 1994). The production of media texts is full of tensions and contradictions resulting from conflicting organizational and professional discourses. As a result of the tensions in the production or 'encoding' process (Hall, 1980), media texts do not constitute a closed ideological system, but reflect the contradictions of production. In this way media texts carry multiple meanings and are open to a range of interpretations. However, the range of meanings a text offers is not infinite. The encoded structures of meaning are brought back into the practices of audiences by their decoding process.

These largely theoretical debates on the mass media in society can be related to almost any development in the mass cultural industries. The processes of mass communication from production, text, to reception are fundamental to all forms of media. However, every so often new forms of media are developed that force us to reconsider the way we look at mass media and society. New communication technologies have resulted in a shrinking of time and space. Think of the birth of television that enabled us to watch images of starving children in another continent as we eat our evening meal; that enabled people all over the world simultaneously to watch live sporting events or worldwide fundraising initiatives. New communication technologies such as the video recorder and the portable video camera have also increased the potential for official and unofficial surveillance. For example, hand-held video footage of a racial assault by police on an Afro-Caribbean man, Rodney King, was filmed by a bystander and shown on television prompting outrage in the Los Angeles community that led to social unrest; in the UK surveillance cameras filmed a child, Jamie Bulger, with two young boys who were then accused and later found guilty of his murder. Most recently, the information superhighway, otherwise known as the Internet, has opened up debates on the democratic potential of communication technologies to provide everyone with access to a full range of information. Alongside and directly related to the development of new communication technologies the globalization of the cultural industries has taken place. Any sociology of the mass media must locate itself within this changing political economic context – it is to these two contemporary issues that this chapter now briefly turns.

# Contemporary Issues

## *Globalization*

Many media groups are increasingly operating internationally or globally. The term 'globalization', discussed in more detail in Chapter 15, refers to 'the intensification of worldwide social relations which link distant locations in such ways that local happenings are shaped by events occurring many miles away and vice versa' (Giddens, 1991a: 64). The increasing trend towards globalization of the mass media can be divided into three main areas. First, as noted earlier, the media industries are part of communication conglomerates which are increasingly transnational in terms of the range of their operations and activities. This is a process that has been spurred on by large-scale mergers and take-overs among the communication conglomerates. One example among many is the Japanese electronics giant Sony's take-over of the US-based CBS record label in 1987; the international record industry is now largely owned by five labels – Sony-CBS, RCA, Warner, Thorn-EMI and Poly-gram – each of which is owned by a multinational corporation. Another obvious example is Rupert Murdoch's media empire (Figure 14.1) with control over media industries around the world.

The second aspect of globalization refers to the increasing role of exports and the production of media goods for an international market. In the case of television the sale of programmes in foreign markets is becoming an important source of revenue. The BBC now sells it programmes to over 100 countries (Thompson, 1990). Programme producers, advertising agencies, as well as the companies that manufacture consumer products are owned in advanced capitalist societies. International film and television sales are largely dominated by American companies. In 1981 American films accounted for 94 per cent of foreign films broadcast on British television, 80 per cent of those broadcast on French television and 54 per cent of those broadcast on West German television. In western Europe as a whole in 1983 approximately 30 per cent of television broadcasting time was filled with imported programmes; American imports representing 75 per cent of all imports. The share represented by US-originated programming in other parts of the world is even greater. These media products depict western (often idealized) lifestyles. This *cultural imperialism* is transnational. More recently, there is some debate about whether US dominance is slipping in world television markets. American television programmes are facing increased competition at regional, national and local levels. However, what has happened to replace American programming in a number of countries is a local adaptation of the American commercial model and American television programme formats. In the process the American model has been generalized and adapted in a global model for commercial media (Straubhaar, 1997). This development illustrates that the process of globalization is not complete and those who argue the all-pervasive threat of globalization should also bear in mind:

> The slippery nature of the linguistic terms used in international communications analysis: that 'global' rarely means 'universal' and often implies only the actors of the North; that 'local' is often really 'national' which can be oppressive of the 'local'; that 'indigenous' culture is often already 'contaminated' through older cultural contacts and exists as a political claim rather than a clear analytic construct. (Sreberny-Mohammadi, 1991: 134)

A third aspect of globalization stems from the deployment of new communication technologies. We now have a mass media system that can dissolve and permeate boundaries between localities and between political entities allowing the transmission of cultural products to take place at an increasingly rapid rate.

Partly as a response to the changing technological make-up of the media industries, many western governments have sought to deregulate the activities of media organizations and to remove legislation that was perceived as restrictive. The trend towards deregulation has been particularly pronounced in the field of broadcasting. With the deployment of cable and satellite systems of transmission, the traditional arguments about the limited number of channels or restriction to a single-state organization on the basis that this would preserve the public interest and prevent commercialism and the potentially harmful and disruptive consequences of uncontrolled broadcasting began to appear less plausible. While deregulation (the removal of legislation that restricted unduly the pursuit of commercial interests) was welcomed by many as a necessary antidote to an overly regulated media sector, it has been criticized by others as an avenue for the acceleration of concentration in the media industries. This, it is argued, increases the dominant role of the conglomerates in the new global economy of information and communication.

## New Communication Technologies and the Social Order

The development of new communication technology is linked directly to glob-alization. New communication technologies have profoundly affected the activ-ities of the media industries from newspaper printing and desk-top publishing to the reproduction of music on tape and compact disc, from computerized systems of information recall to digital broadcasting. The more developed nations have been able to use modern communications technology to conduct business and represent their economic interests and cultural values worldwide. Schiller claims that 'what is now happening is the creation and global extension of a near total corporate informational-cultural environment' (1989: 128). As the United States still authors most internationally consumed messages, Amer-ican cultural commodities have 'overwhelmed a good part of the world' by 'smothering the senses' with a 'consumerist virus' (Schiller, 1991).

However, this media/cultural imperialism thesis assumes that institutional infrastructure and technology work together in a uniform way to benefit only their owners and managers. In reality mass media institutions and technology often do the opposite; they stimulate ideological and cultural diversity, some-times precisely by contradicting their owners and managers intentions. It is important to remember lessons learnt from political economic studies of the media that have gone before and even studies of media reception that intro-duced the active audience – institutions are constituted by human beings and whatever ideological preferences institutions confer they are neither static nor automatically perceived according to authorial intentions.

Worldwide hegemony of corporate ideology, speech and activity is, according to Schiller and his sympathisers, made possible by communications technology interacting with the enormous expansion of scientific and tech-nical information, computerization and the pre-eminence of the transnational corporation. The immediate benefactors of new communication technologies are those who can gain the most materially by an increased capacity to gather, store, manage and send information. Transnational corporations quickly took control of everything from satellite channels and multimedia configurations to car phones and voice mail systems. Capitalizing on communications also falls not only to rich countries but to rich individuals and rich people in poor countries who enjoy far greater access to technology allowing them to watch international television via satellite or conduct business with a cellular phone.

One example brings these debates into sharp focus – the information super-highway. The information superhighway or Internet is an international network of direct links between computers. The Internet is global in its reach but not total in its coverage. In 1995 Waters stated that the Internet had 15 million users, growing at a rate of 20–30 per cent every three months. Hyper-media software such as World Wide Web and Global Network Navigator act as agents for the user, independently searching the network, finding bits of information, combining them and presenting them back to the user. As with the introduction of other new communication technologies the Internet has been claimed to offer radical potential for increased democracy by providing open access to a wide range of information. There have been claims that the information superhighway will connect people to people and people to information giving everyone access to the information they need when and where they want it – at an affordable price.

However, the historical development of new communication technologies is determined by social and political factors. In the rich industrialized countries new communication technologies are central to the integration of business activities as well as to the production of commercial culture. Their increased use and development depends largely on private investment and competition. These rarely go hand in hand with open access and universal service. In 1984 the rich industrialized countries (US, Canada, western Europe, Japan and Australia) owned 96 per cent of the world's computer hardware; of the world's 700 million telephones, 75 per cent can be found in the 9 richest countries; in 39 countries there are no newspapers, while in 30 others there is only 1, Japan has 125 dailies and the US has 168; the world average for television set ownership is 137 per 1000 – in rich countries this is 447 per 1000, in poor countries this drops dramatically to 36 per 1000 (UNESCO, 1989). Inequalities also exist within countries: in the UK in the mid-1990s 52 per cent of professional households had a home computer and 98 per cent had a telephone – compared to 21 per cent of unskilled households with a computer and 73 per cent with a telephone. Similarly a much higher proportion of professionals than the most unskilled owned more advanced new communication technologies such as a CD-ROM, Internet link, mobile phone, or satellite or cable link (Office of Science and Technology, 1995).

The free flow of information and communications is essential to a democratic society and requires that powerful instruments of information and communication be accessible to all. Without a free flow of information, citizens cannot be adequately informed and without access to forums of public discussion and debate they are excluded from that which enables them to participate in society. In general there is a growing gap between the potential of new technology to give people better control over their lives and the drive by others to use it for profit and centralizing control. It is difficult to conclude that the introduction of such technology into a consumerist world controlled by capital can result in progress.

## Conclusion

This chapter began by asserting that the questions about who controls the media and debates over the public's access to media, media accountability and responsibility, media funding and regulation, and implications for individual freedom, democracy and collective well-being have been central to media sociologists over the years. If we believe that the mass media has implications for the reorganization of life on all its levels – from the economic to the experiential, from world trade to cognition then these questions will become ever more vital in the future. As Kellner has said 'the proliferation of media culture and technologies focuses attention on the importance of media politics and the need for public intervention in debates over the future of media culture and communications in the information highways and entertainment byways of the future' (Kellner, 1995: 337). Without an understanding of how the larger social forces, such as the nature of the mass cultural industries, pervade and create changes in culture, leisure activity and everyday life it is difficult to envisage how such a public intervention will take place. Without an understanding of the processes of production and reception and the nature of media output we will never know what shape such an intervention could take.

# Further Reading

Ang, I. *Living Room Wars: Rethinking Media Audiences for a Post-modern World,* London, Routledge, 1996. An analysis of contemporary debates around the audience.

Golding, P. *Beyond Cultural Imperialism: Globalization, Communication and the New International Order,* London, Sage, 1996. Discusses the implications for inequality, power and control of global media culture and politics.

McQuail, D. *Mass Communication Theory: An Introduction,* 2nd edn, London, Sage, 1994. A non-technical introduction to the range of approaches to understanding mass commuications related to the understanding of society as a whole.

Strinati, D. *An Introduction to Theories of Popular Culture,* London, Routledge, 1995. A clear and accessible guide to major theories of popular culture.

# 15

# Globalization

## *Leslie Sklair*

Globalization refers to the growing interdependence of different parts of the world. Globalization theories involve looking beyond nation states and the relations between them to social processes which result from social interaction on a world scale, such as the development of an increasingly integrated global economy and the explosion of worldwide telecommunications. The aim of this chapter is to explain some of the different ways in which sociologists have approached globalization and illustrate some of the major topics in globalization research. It should help you to understand:

- What sociologists mean by globalization

- What is meant by world-systems theory

- The ideas of a global culture and a global society

- The contribution of global capitalism theory

- Some of the main issues in globalization research

---

**CONCEPTS**

nation state ■ transnational corporations
newly industrializing countries ■ 'Third World' ■ global village
reflexive modernization ■ consumerism
export-processing enclaves ■ feminization of poverty
human development index

---

# Introduction

Globalization is a relatively new idea in the social sciences although people who work in and write about the mass media, transnational corporations and international business have been using it for some time. Jacques Maison-rouge, former President of IBM World Trade, was an early exponent of the view that the future lies with global corporations which operate as if the world had no real borders rather than organizations tied to a particular country. The influential US magazine, *Business Week* (May, 1990) summed this view up in the evocative phrase: 'The Stateless Corporation'.

The central feature of the idea of globalization is that many contemporary social issues cannot be adequately studied at the level of nation states; that is, in terms of each country and its inter-national relations, but need to be seen in terms of transnational processes, beyond the level of particular countries. Some globalists have even gone so far as to predict that global forces, by which they usually mean global economic institutions, global culture or globalizing belief systems/ideologies of various types are becoming so powerful that the continuing existence of the nation state is in serious doubt (Ohmae, 1990). This is not a necessary consequence of most theories of globalization, although many argue that the significance of the nation state is declining (even if the ideology of nationalism is still strong in some places). This chapter will begin by looking at what sociologists mean by globalization; it will then look at some of the main approaches that sociologists have adopted to study globalization and some of the problem areas that have attracted special attention in the globalization literature; the chapter concludes by looking at globalization and everyday life and resistances to globalization.

# Globalization

There is no single agreed definition of globalization and some argue that its significance has been much exaggerated but, as the ever-increasing number of books and articles discussing different aspects of it suggests, it appears to be an idea whose time has come in sociology in particular and in the social sciences in general (Robertson, 1992; Waters, 1995; Albrow, 1996). Globalization is important for sociology precisely because it challenges established ideas of society and nation state that are the basis of the theories and research of most contemporary writers (Holton, 1998). Most sociological research is rather narrow in focus and most research projects are restricted to one country, usually understood as a single society. Globalization theorists argue that more and more social relations and social structures can only be explained by looking beyond the boundaries of a single country, or society, as an increasing number of forces influencing social relations and moulding social structures are now global. These global forces are not bound to a single place, but are detached from what we normally understand by national origins and local culture.

This idea is very difficult for many people to accept, although the founders of sociology put forward ideas that have been developed in a global direction. Marx's analysis of capitalism has had an important influence on many ideas about the global economy and the forces that have dominated it for centuries (see Frobel *et al.*, 1980; Chase-Dunn, 1989; Ross and Trachte, 1990; Sklair, 1995), while Weber's influence has been most marked on those who have tried to analyse the idea of cultural globalization (see Robertson, 1992; Albrow, 1996).

One problem in understanding much of the globalization literature is that not all those who use the term distinguish it clearly enough from internationalization, and some writers appear to use the two terms interchangeably. In this chapter a clear distinction will be drawn between the inter-national and the global. The hyphen in inter-national is to signify that this conception of globalization is founded on the existing – even if changing – system of nation states, while the global signifies the emergence of processes and a system of social relations not founded on the system of nation states.

This difficulty is compounded by the fact that most theory and research in sociology is based on concepts of society that identify the unit of analysis with a particular country, sub-systems within countries or comparisons between single countries and groups of them. For example, the data on patterns of health inequalities discussed in Chapter 12 are based on national data sets and explanations developed in terms of factors *within* those societies, such as income distribution and lifestyle choices. This general approach, usually called state-centrism, is still useful in many respects and there are clearly good reasons for it, particularly the fact that most historical and contemporary sociological data sets have been collected on particular countries. However, most globalization theorists argue that the nation state is no longer the only important unit of analysis and some argue that it is now less important in some fundamental respects than global forces, such as the mass media and the corporations that own and control them, transnational corporations (some of which are richer than the majority of nation states in the world today) and social movements that spread ideas such as universal human rights, global environmental responsibility and the worldwide call for democracy and human dignity.

Yearley (1996) identifies two main obstacles to making sociological sense of globalization: first, 'the tight connection between the discipline of sociology and the nation state' (1995: 9) and second, the fact that countries differ significantly in their geographies. Despite these difficulties, he argues that the increasing focus on the environment encourages us to 'work down to the global' (1995: 17) from the universal, a necessary corrective to state-centrist conceptions which work up to the global from the nation state or even, as we shall see, from individualistic notions of 'global consciousness'. The point of this distinction is that 'the global' is a distinctive level of analysis, separate from universal (values or biological characteristics, for example), international (relations between states) and individual phenomena (like people's awareness of the global). For this to make sense, sociologists have to be able to identify and study *global* forces and institutions as I attempt to do in a later section, for example, when discussing my own contribution to globalization theory and research – the global capitalism approach.

The study of globalization in sociology revolves primarily around two main classes of phenomena which have become increasingly significant in the last few decades. These are the emergence of a *globalized economy* which, as we saw in Chapter 10, is based on new systems of production, finance and consumption, and the idea of *'global culture'*. While not all globalization researchers entirely accept the existence of a global economy or a global culture, most accept that local, national and regional economies are undergoing important changes as a result of processes of globalization (Scott, 1997). In this context, researchers on globalization have focused on two phenomena which have become increasingly significant in the last few decades. First, they have looked at the ways in which transnational corporations (TNCs) have facilitated the globalization of capital and production (Dunning, 1993; Barnet and Cavanagh, 1994; Dicken, 1998). Second, they have been interested in transformations in the global scope of particular types of TNCs, those who own and control the mass media, notably television channels and the transnational advertising agencies. This is often connected with the spread of particular patterns of consumption and a culture and ideology of consumerism at the global level, which will be discussed below (Featherstone, 1990; Sklair, 1995).

Transnational corporations are firms that have operations outside their countries of origin. They range from a small company that has one factory across the border in the next country to massive corporations that operate all over the world, such as Unilever, Mitsubishi or General Motors. The largest TNCs have assets and annual sales far in excess of the gross national products of most of the countries in the world. The World Bank annual publication *World Development Report* for 1996 reports that only about 70 countries out a total of around 200 for which there is data had GNPs of more than ten billion US dollars. By contrast, the 1996 *Fortune Global 500* list of the biggest TNCs by turnover reports that over 400 TNCs had annual sales greater than $10 billion. Thus, in this important sense, such well-known names as General Motors, Shell, Toyota, Unilever, Volkswagen, Nestlé, Sony, Pepsico, Coca-Cola, Kodak, Xerox and the huge Japanese trading houses have more economic power at their disposal than the majority of the countries in the world. These figures indicate the *gigantism* of TNCs relative to most countries. Figure 15.1 is a graphic illustration of these comparisons.

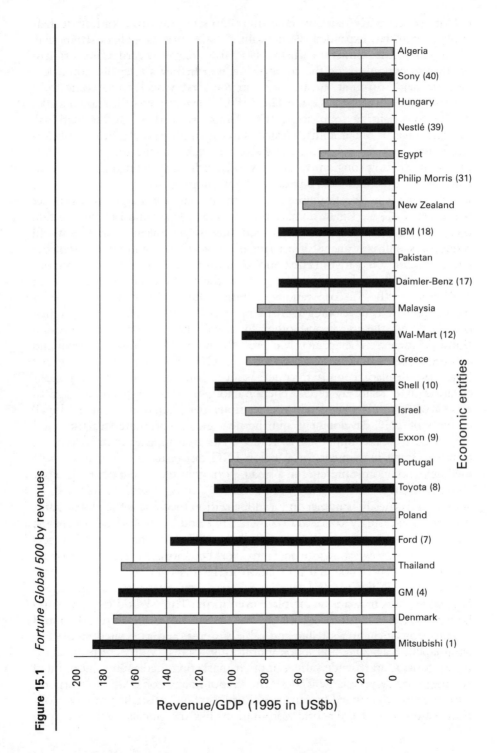

**Figure 15.1** *Fortune Global 500* by revenues

Not only have TNCs grown enormously in size in recent decades but their 'global reach' has expanded dramatically. TNCs such as Colgate–Palmolive, IBM, Nestlé, ICI, Unilever and Dow Chemicals regularly earn more than half of their revenues outside the countries in which they are legally domiciled. Not all major corporations are based in the First World, some come from what is conventionally called the Third World or that part of it known as the newly industrializing countries (NICs). Examples of these are the 'national' oil companies of Brazil, India, Mexico, Taiwan and Venezuela, banks in Brazil and China, an automobile company from Turkey, and the Korean manufacturing and trading conglomerates, a few of which have attained global brand-name status (for example, Hyundai and Samsung).

Writers who are sceptical about economic globalization argue that the fact that most TNCs are legally domiciled in the USA, Japan and Europe and that they trade and invest mainly between themselves means that the world economy is still best analysed in terms of *national* corporations and that the global economy is a myth (Hirst and Thompson, 1996). However, to globalization theorists, this deduction ignores the well-established fact that an increasing number of corporations operating outside their 'home' countries see themselves as developing global strategies. It cannot simply be assumed that all 'US', 'Japanese' and other 'national' TNCs somehow express a 'national interest'. They primarily express the interests of those who own and control them, even if historical patterns of TNC development have differed from place to place, country to country and region to region. Analysing globalization as a relatively recent phenomenon, originating from the 1960s, allows us to see more clearly the tensions between traditional 'national' patterns of TNC development and the new global corporate structures and dynamics. It is also important to realize that, even in state-centrist terms, a relatively small investment for a major TNC can result in a relatively large measure of economic presence in a small, poor country or in a poor region or community of a larger and less poor country.

A second crucial phenomenon for globalization theorists is the global diffusion and increasingly concentrated ownership and control of the electronic mass media, particularly television (Barker, 1997). The number of TV sets per capita has grown so rapidly in Third World countries in recent years (from fewer than 10 per thousand population in 1970 to 60 per 1,000 in 1993, according to UNESCO) that many researchers argue that a 'globalizing effect' due to the mass media is taking place even in the Third World (Sussman and Lent, 1991; Sklair, 1995). As we saw in Chapter 14, ownership and control of television, including satellite and cable systems, and associated media like newspaper, magazine and book publishing, films, video, records/tapes/compact discs, and a wide variety of other marketing media, are concentrated in relatively few very large TNCs. The predominance of US-based corporations is being challenged by Japanese, European and Australian groups globally, and even by 'Third World' corporations like the Brazilian media empire of TV Globo (Nordenstreng and Schiller, 1993). The following section examines some of the different ways in which sociologists have tried to make sense of globalization.

## Main Approaches to Globalization

There are several ways to categorize theory and research on globalization. One approach is to compare mono-causal with multi-causal explanations of the phenomenon (see McGrew, 1992). This is a useful way of looking at the problem, but it can end up putting thinkers with entirely different types of explanations, for example those who see globalization as a consequence of *material-technological* forces and those who see it as a consequence of *ideological and/or cultural* forces, in the same bag. A second approach is to compare the disciplinary focus of globalization studies. This is certainly an interesting and fruitful avenue to explore: contributions from anthropology, geography and international political economy are commonly borrowed by sociologists of globalization, and vice versa, and this will be reflected in my own categorization.

I have chosen to categorize globalization in sociology on the basis of four theory and research clusters in which groups of scholars are working on similar research problems, either in direct contact with each other or, more commonly, in rather indirect contact. Accordingly, I identify the following four sources of globalization research in contemporary sociology which cover what is currently being produced in the field:

- the world-systems approach
- the global culture approach
- the global society approach
- the global capitalism approach.

### World-systems Model

World systems as a model in social science research, inspired by the work of Wallerstein, has been developed in a large and continually expanding body of literature since the 1970s (see Wallerstein, 1979 and Shannon, 1989 for a good overview). The world-systems approach is not only a collection of academic writings but, like the Frankfurt School discussed in Chapter 3, it is also a highly institutionalized academic enterprise, based at the Braudel Center for the Study of Economies, Historical Systems and Civilization at the State University of New York, where Wallerstein has been Director since its foundation. Although the work of the world-systems theorists cannot be said to be fully part of the globalization literature as such (see King, 1991), it undoubtedly prepared the ground for globalization in the social sciences.

The world-systems approach is based on the distinction between core, semi-peripheral and peripheral countries in terms of their changing roles in the international division of labour dominated by the capitalist world system. The central idea is that the 'core' capitalist countries, like those of western Europe and the USA, have historically exploited the poor 'peripheral' countries of Africa, Asia and Latin America by extracting their raw materials cheaply and turning them into much more expensive manufactured goods, some of which they sell back to people in these poor countries. When manufacturing wages rise in the core countries, capitalists move some of their factories to the 'semi-periphery' countries in Latin America and east Asia for example, and people in these countries, while still being exploited, do better than raw material producers in the periphery. In their turn, when wages rise in the semi-periphery, some factories are shifted to countries in the periphery.

In some senses, Wallerstein and his school could rightly claim to have been 'global' all along – after all, what could be more global than the 'world system'? However, there is no specific concept of the 'global' in most world-systems literature. Reference to the 'global' comes mainly from critics who, reflecting a more general criticism of theories in sociology which give the 'economic' precedence over the 'cultural', argue that there is a world system of 'global culture' (see later) which cannot be 'reduced' to the economic processes of capitalism (see Featherstone, 1990). Chase-Dunn (1989) does try to take the argument a stage further by arguing for a dual-logic approach to economy and polity. At the economic level, he argues, a global logic of the world economy prevails whereas at the level of politics a state-centred logic of the world-system prevails. However, as the world economy is basically still explicable only in terms of national economies (countries of the core, semi-periphery and periphery), Chase-Dunn's formulation largely reproduces the problems of Wallerstein's state-centrist analysis.

There is, therefore, no distinctively 'global' dimension in the world-systems model apart from the international focus that it has always emphasized. Wallerstein himself rarely if ever uses the word 'globalization'. For him, the *economics* of the model rests on the international division of labour that distinguishes core, semi-periphery and periphery countries. The *politics* are mostly bound up with anti-systemic movements and 'superpower struggles' and the *cultural*, insofar as it is dealt with at all, covers debates about the 'national' and the 'universal' and the concept of 'civilization(s)' in the social sciences. Many critics are not convinced that the world-systems model, usually considered to be 'economistic' (that is, locked into economic factors), can deal with cultural issues adequately. Wolff tellingly comments on the way in which the concept of 'culture' has been inserted into Wallerstein's world-system model: 'An economism which gallantly switches its attentions to the operations of culture is still economism' (in King, 1991: 168). Wallerstein's attempts to theorize 'race', nationality and ethnicity in terms of what he refers to as different types of 'peoplehood' in the world system (Wallerstein, 1991) might be seen as a move in the right direction but few would argue that cultural factors are an important part of the analysis.

## Global Culture Model

A second model of globalization derives specifically from research on the 'globalization of culture'. The global culture approach focuses on the problems that a homogenizing mass media-based culture poses for national identities. As we shall see later, this is complementary to the global society approach, which focuses more on ideas of an emerging global consciousness and their implications for global community, governance and security. Although global culture researchers cannot be identified as a school in the same way as world-system researchers, their works do constitute a relatively coherent whole (see Featherstone, 1990). First, they tend to prioritize the cultural over the political and/or the economic. Second, there is a common interest in the question of how individual and/or national identity can survive in the face of an emerging 'global culture'.

A distinctive feature of this model is that it poses the existence of 'global culture' as a reality, a possibility or a fantasy. A major influence on the idea of a global culture is the very rapid growth that has taken place over the last few decades in the scale of the mass media of communication and the emergence of what McLuhan (1964) famously called 'the global village'. The basic idea is that the spread of the mass media, especially television, means that everyone in the world can be exposed to the same images, almost instantaneously. This, the argument goes, turns the whole world into a sort of 'global village'.

While globalization has brought about an increased cultural homogeneity where people all across the world can drink Coca-Cola, eat McDonald's and watch the same Hollywood films, it has also produced increasing differentiation. Increasingly different cultural traditions exist alongside each, other competing for people's attention. For postmodernists, such as Baudrillard (1988), the explosion of information technologies has produced cultural diversity and fragmentation rather than unity. As we saw in Chapter 14, Baudrillard and other postmodernists argue the 'electronic reality' created by the media has produced a state of hyperreality, where the distinction between the 'real' world and the media image is eroded. He argues that the hyperreal is becoming a condition of the whole of the contemporary world: reality is broken down and people's identities and lifestyles are no longer anchored in social structures but are rather constructed through the mass of media images of the lifestyle options available to them. In many cases old identities have been replaced by 'hybrid' identities (Hall *et al.*, 1992: 310).

An apparently paradoxical consequence of globalization has been to make people more aware of cultural and national differences. There has been an upsurge of regionalism and nationalism, particularly among groups which have been incorporated into larger units, such as those which once formed part of the former Soviet Union. In this context Friedman, a Swedish anthropologist, has argued that:

> Ethnic and cultural fragmentation and modernist homogenization are not two arguments, two opposing views of what is happening in the world today, but two constitutive trends of global reality. The dualist centralised world of the double East–West hegemony is fragmenting, politically, and culturally, but the homogeneity of capitalism remains as intact and a systematic as ever'. (Friedman, 1990: 311)

While not all would agree either that capitalism remains intact and systematic or that it is, in fact, the framework of globalization, the fragmentation of the control once exercised by eastern and western power blocs is beyond doubt. With the collapse of the Soviet Union and the declining influence of the hegemony of the United States, many old national and ethnic loyalties have reasserted themselves, sometimes resulting in political instability and war.

In this context a compilation of articles by edited by Albrow and King (1990) raises several central issues relevant to the ideas of global sociology, global society and globalization as new problem areas in the social sciences. One important emphasis has been the 'globalization' of sociology itself as a discipline; that is, the extent to which each society, or community, requires its own sociology. While the classical sociological theorists, notably Marx, Weber and Durkheim, all tried to generalize about how societies changed and tried to establish some universal features of social organization, none of them saw the need to theorize on the global level. This connects in some important ways with the debate about the integrity of national cultures in a globalizing world, and particularly the influence of 'western' economic, political, military and cultural forms on non-western societies. For example, there is a tendency to reduce globalization to 'westernization', or even 'Americanization', but this can distort the nature of genuinely global forces and mystify the relationship between globalization and capitalism. The more 'global' and less 'nationalistic' sociology becomes, the less likely this is to happen.

Globalization is not simply about the 'disembedding' of the 'local' by the 'global', it is rather about the creation of a new global–local nexus, about exploring the new relations between global and local spaces. These questions have been explored most fully in a sub-set of the global culture approach, known as *globo-localism*. Writers such as Alger (1988) and Mlinar (1992) have focused on the question of what happens to *territorial identities* (within and across countries) in a globalizing world. The apparent contradiction between globalization as a force for homogenization, and the disintegration of countries in central and eastern Europe, for example the former Yugoslavia, and in other parts of the world (notably Africa), and the so-called revival of nationalisms do present challenges to the more extreme versions of globalization.

The main research question in this context is the autonomy of local cultures in the face of an advancing 'global culture'. Competing claims of local cultures against the forces of 'globalization' have forced themselves onto the sociological, cultural and political agendas all over the world. This is largely continuous with the focus of the third globalization model, based on the idea of global society, which focuses more on ideas of emerging global consciousness and their implications for global community, governance and security.

## Global Society Models

Inspiration for this general conception of globalization is often located in the pictures of planet earth sent back by space explorers. A classic statement of this was the report of Apollo XIV astronaut Edgar Mitchell in 1971:

> It was a beautiful, harmonious, peaceful-looking planet, blue with white clouds, and one that gave you a deep sense... of home, of being, of identity. It is what I prefer to call instant global consciousness.

Had astronaut Mitchell penetrated a little through the clouds he would also have seen horrific wars in Vietnam and other parts of Asia, bloody repression by various dictatorial regimes in Africa and Latin America, dead and maimed bodies as a result of sectarian terrorism in Britain and Ireland, as well as a terrible toll of human misery from hunger, disease, drug abuse and carnage on roads all round the world as automobile cultures intensified their own peculiar structures of globalization.

Nevertheless, some leading globalization theorists, for example Giddens (1991) and Robertson (1992), do attribute great significance to ideas such as 'global awareness' and 'planetary consciousness'. Global society theorists argue that the concept of world, or global, society has become a believable idea only in the modern age and, in particular, science, technology, industry and universal values are increasingly creating a contemporary world that is different from any past age. The globalization literature is full of discussions of the decreasing power and significance of the nation state and the increasing significance (if not actually power) of supra-national and global institutions and systems of belief.

Globalization brings some of the 'foundational concepts' of sociology, such as nation state and society, into question (McGrew, 1992: 64). As we have seen from the previous chapters of this book, most empirical research in sociology is focused on a particular society, which is usually a nation state and its citizens. Global sociologists argue that this view is increasingly difficult to sustain as relations between individuals, institutions and states are being transformed by social processes which are worldwide. Global transportation and communications allow more and more people to overcome what used to be seen as insurmountable boundaries of time and space. Harvey (1989: 241) uses the term time–space compression to describe how processes of globalization compress, stretch and deepen space time for people all over the world thus creating the conditions for a global society.

Giddens (1991), in particular, has developed these themes in his analysis of the relations between globalization and modernity. He defines globalization in terms of four dimensions, the nation state system, the world military order, the international division of labour and the world capitalist economy, and explains it as a consequence of modernity itself. He characterizes the transformation of key social relations in terms of the relation between *globalizing tendencies* of modernity and *localized events* in daily life. More and more people live in circumstances where their relationships with others and with social institutions have become 'disembedded' from their local contexts. For Giddens, globalization is best conceptualized as 'reflexive modernization', by which he means that 'social practices are constantly examined and reformed in the light of incoming information about those very practices, thus constitutively altering their character' (Giddens, 1990b: 38). The global society thrust of Giddens' concept of globalization is clear from his reference to 'emergent forms of world interdependence and planetary consciousness'.

Spybey (1996) contrasts Giddens' view that 'modernity is inherently globalizing (1991: 63) with Robertson's (1992) view that globalization predates modernity with aspects going back 2,000 years. There is thus a debate in sociology about whether globalization is a new name for a relatively old phenomenon (which appears to be the argument of Robertson), or whether it is relatively new, a largely twentieth-century phenomenon (the argument of Giddens), or whether it is very new and primarily a consequence of post-1960s' capitalism (the argument of Sklair, discussed later in this chapter). Why does this matter? It matters because if we want to understand our own lives and the lives of those around us, in our families, communities, local regions, countries, supra-national regions and, ultimately how we relate to the global, then it is absolutely fundamental that we are clear about the extent to which the many different structures within which we live are much the same as they have been or are different.

The idea of globalization is itself a contested concept. Hirst and Thompson, in their attempt to demonstrate that globalization is a myth because the global economy does not really exist, argue that there is 'no fundamental difference between the international submarine telegraph cable method of financial transactions [of the early twentieth century] and contemporary electronic systems' (Hirst and Thompson, 1996: 197). However, to globalization theorists, the fundamental difference is, precisely, in the way that the electronics revolution (a post-1960s phenomenon) has transformed the quantitative possibilities of transferring cash and money capital into qualitatively new forms of corporate and personal financing, entrepreneurship and, crucially, the system of credit on which the global culture and ideology of consumerism largely rests. Some globalization theorists argue forcefully that these phenomena are all new and fundamental for understanding not only what is happening in the rich countries, but in social groups anywhere who have a part to play in this global system. In this sense, the idea of a global society is a very provocative one but, as I shall go on to discuss in the section 'Globalization in Everyday Life', while it is relatively easy to establish empirically the objective dimensions of globalization as they involve the large majority of the world's population, the idea of a global society based on *subjective* relationships to globalization, planetary consciousness and the like remains highly speculative.

For many writers the possibility of a global society is an important idea. As McGrew (1992) shows, this theme is elaborated by scholars grappling with the apparent contradictions between globalization and local disruption and strife based on ethnic and other particularistic loyalties. Perlmutter (1991), for example, argues that humankind is on 'the rocky road to the first global civilization' and, while others are more sceptical of the progress that we have made to this goal, it is safe to predict that the idea of a global society will be increasingly discussed in the social sciences. It is in this type of approach, in particular, that a growing appreciation of the ethical problems of globalization is to be found. The reason for this is simple: now that humankind has the capacity to destroy itself through war and toxic accidents of various types, a democratic and just human society on the global level, however utopian, seems to be the best long-term guarantee of the continued survival of humanity (Held, 1995).

## Global Capitalism Model

A fourth model of globalization locates the dominant global forces in the structures of an ever-more globalizing capitalism (for example, Ross and Trachte, 1990; Sklair, 1995; McMichael, 1996; Robinson, 1998). While all of these writers and others who could be identified with this approach develop their own specific analyses of globalization, they all strive towards a concept of the 'global' that involves more than the relations between nation states and state-centrist explanations of national economies competing against each other.

Ross and Trachte (1990) focus specifically on capitalism as a social system which is best analysed on three levels: the level of the internal logic of the system, that is, theories of how capitalism works (inspired by Marx and Adam Smith), how it changes over time and how capitalist societies differ from each other. They explain both the deindustrialization of some of the heartland regions of capitalism, for example the decline in the automobile industry around Detroit in the USA, and the transformations of what we still call the

'Third World', for example the rise of substantial manufacturing industries such as textiles, footwear and shipbuilding in these terms. They argue that the globalization of the capitalist system is deeply connected to the capitalist crises in the 1970s, brought about by rising oil prices, increasing unemployment and growing insecurity as the rich countries experienced problems in paying for their welfare states. This leads them to conclude that: 'We are only at the beginning of the global era' (Ross and Trachte, 1990: 230). Capitalism has not stopped changing and its future, in global perspective, will undoubtedly continue to hold surprises, such as the unexpected crisis in Asian economies in the late 1990s.

Sklair (1991) proposes a more explicit model of the global system based on the concept of *transnational practices*, practices that originate with non-state actors and cross state borders. They are analytically distinguished in three spheres: economic, political and cultural-ideological. Each of these practices is primarily, but not exclusively, characterized by a major institution. The *transnational corporation* (TNC) is the most important institution for economic transnational practices; the *transnational capitalist class* (TCC) for political transnational practices; and the *culture ideology of consumerism* for transnational cultural-ideological practices (Sklair, 1995). The research agenda of this theory is concerned with how TNCs, transnational capitalist classes and the culture ideology of consumerism operate to transform the world in terms of the global capitalist project.

This approach is really an attempt to limit the scope of globalization by focusing on the extent to which capitalism has been successful in extending its reach globally. The point here is that as globalization can cover so many things in the social world, the focus on the global *capitalist* system restricts the scope of application of the concept to its most characteristic economic institution (the TNC), its most characteristic political institution (the TCC) and its most characteristic cultural-ideological driving force (consumerism). This focus, however, should not lead to the conclusion that capitalism is the only global force even if, in the view of many theorists, it is the dominant force in the contemporary world.

The massive presence of transnational corporations has already been discussed. The transnational capitalist class is made up of four groups: those who own and control these corporations, their allies in the state (globalizing bureaucrats) and in political parties and professions (globalizing politicians and professionals) and consumerist élites. While this approach is developed from Marx's analysis of the revolutionary nature of modern capitalism, it differs from Marxism in several ways. First, it does not restrict membership of the capitalist class exclusively to those who own the means of production but extends it to those who directly serve the interests of capital. Second, it argues that the relative autonomy of the state to dominate the capitalist class is much reduced in global capitalism and that globalizing bureaucrats are the main representatives of the state in the interests of capital. Third, it explains how the system works in terms of the intimate connections between the TNCs, transnational capitalist class and the culture ideology of consumerism, the rationale of the system. While, as Scott (1997: 312) argues, there is little evidence as yet to establish firmly the existence of an 'integrated global capitalist class', there are indications that such a class is emerging. Table 15.1 suggests the structure (economic base, political organization and culture ideology) of the four groups in the transnational capitalist class and how their material, political and cultural interests interlock.

**Table 15.1** The global ruling class

| Transnational practices | Leading institutions | Integrating agents |
|---|---|---|
| *Economic sphere* | *Economic forces* | Global business élite |
| Transnational capital | Global TNCs | |
| International capital | World Bank, IMF, BIS | |
| State capital | State TNCs | |
| | | |
| *Political sphere* | *Political forces* | Global political élite |
| TNC executives | Global business organization | |
| Globalizing bureaucrats | Open-door agencies, WTO, | |
| Politicians and professionals | parties and lobbies | |
| Regional blocs | EU, NAFTA, ASEAN | |
| Emerging transnational states | UN, NGOs | |
| | | |
| *Culture-ideology sphere* | *Culture-ideology forces* | Global cultural élite |
| Consumerism | Shops, media | |
| Transnational | Think tanks, élite social | |
| Neo-liberalism | movements | |

The culture ideology of consumerism prioritizes the exceptional place of consumption and consumerism in contemporary capitalism, increasing consumption expectations and aspirations without necessarily ensuring the income to buy. The extent to which economic and environmental constraints on the private accumulation of capital challenge the global capitalist project in general and its culture ideology of consumerism in particular is a central issue for the global capitalist system approach (Sklair, 1994b; see also Durning, 1992).

McMichael (1996) focuses on the issue of Third World development and provides both theoretical and empirical support for the thesis that globalization is a qualitatively new phenomenon and not simply a quantitative expansion of older trends. He contrasts two periods. First, the 'Development Project' (late 1940s to early 1970s), when all countries tried to develop their national economies with the help of international development agencies and institutions. The second period he labels the 'Globalization Project' (1980s onwards), when development is pursued through attempts to integrate economies into a globalized world market, and the process is directed by a public–private coalition of 'Global Managers'. He explains:

> As parts of national economies became embedded more deeply in global enterprise through commodity chains, they weakened as national units and strengthened the reach of the global economy. This situation was not unique to the 1980s, but the mechanisms of the debt regime institutionalised the power and authority of global management within states' very organisation and procedures. This was the turning point in the story of development. (McMichael, 1996: 135)

To these writers on globalization and capitalism we can add other Marxist and Marx-inspired scholars who see capitalism as a global system, but do not have any specific concepts of globalization. The most important of these is the geographer, Harvey, whose Marxist analysis of modernity and post-modernity is significant for the attempt to build a bridge between the debates around economic and cultural globalization. For Harvey (1989), the shrinking of space, brought about by global capitalism that brings diverse communities into competition with each other, can lead to an increased awareness of locality and the development of specialized areas of production, such as the ceramics, knitwear and textile regions in Italy which were described in Chapter 10. This rehabilitation of locality and specialization is very different from the uniformity and economies of scale typically associated with global capitalism and is celebrated as further evidence of cultural diversity by postmodernists. However, for Harvey, this interpretation misses the underlying forces that lie behind this process; local self-assertion remains tied to globalism, particularly the requirements of a more developed, global capitalism.

## Summing-up the Approaches

Each of the four approaches to globalization has its own distinctive strengths and weaknesses. The world-system model tends to be economistic (minimizing the importance of political and cultural factors) but, as globalization is often interpreted in terms of economic actors and economic institutions, it still seems the most realistic approach to many. The globalization of culture model, on the other hand, tends to be culturalist (minimizing economic factors) but, as much of the criticism of globalization comes from those who focus on the negative effects of homogenizing mass media and marketing on local and indigenous cultures, the culturalist approach has many adherents. The world society model tends to be both optimistic and all-inclusive, an excellent combination for the production of world-views, but less satisfactory for social science research programmes. Finally, the global capitalism model, by prioritizing the global capitalist system and paying less attention to other global forces, runs the risk of appearing one-sided. However, the question remains: how important is that 'one side' (global capitalism)?

# Concrete Problems in Globalization Research

Among the most important substantive issues, widely discussed by globalization researchers inside and outside the four approaches discussed in the previous section, are global environmental change, gender and globalization, global cities, globalization and regionalization. Some of the main dimensions of these problems will now be outlined.

## Global Environmental Change

While the literature on all aspects of globalization has been expanding very rapidly in the last decade, it is probably no exaggeration to say that the literature on global environmental change has led the way. This is due to:

1. The enormous political, academic and popular interest in a series of high-profile international meetings throughout the 1970s and 80s, culminating in the United Nations Conference on Environment and Development in Rio in 1992.
2. Growing disquiet about daily environmental degradation (notably the destruction of the ozone layer, the greenhouse effect, decreasing bio-diversity, worsening land, air and water pollution in many places) and sudden environmental catastrophes such as the disaster at Chernobyl where a nuclear reactor exploded in 1986.
3. The rise of the global environmental movement.

These three forces have combined to provide a framework for the study of global environmental change in the context of 'sustainable development' (see World Resources Institute, 1994). Under this rubric the United Nations has established several bodies to manage environmental change at the global level and while many well-informed scientists and activists fear a variety of existing environmental crises and predict others, some notable advances have been made, for example in the control of CFC gases and the stewardship of the atmosphere, the oceans, forests, and other natural resources, the so-called 'global commons' (Yearley, 1996).

While many TNCs (some of the largest Fortune 500 companies as well as smaller consumer-sensitive companies) have begun to institutionalize in-house mechanisms for dealing with resource and pollution issues, of contin-uing concern is the laxity of other TNCs, their subcontracting partners and local firms in observing environmental good practice in production and waste disposal, even where required to do so by law. More generally, the role of the TNCs in promoting unsustainable patterns of consumption with little thought for the environmental consequences has been critically scrutinized (Durning, 1992; Sklair, 1994a). This latter issue raises fundamental questions about the capitalist global project and the central place of consumption for both economic growth and ideological credibility. While environmental concerns move up and down the agendas of social groups, the media, and governments all over the world, it is likely that they will continue to be one of the main areas of globalization theory and research for the foreseeable future. Yearley (1996: 24) is correct in his assertion that very few globaliza-tion theorists have grappled with the environment as a research site, but his work and that of others (see Redclift and Benton, 1994) should show more of them what a rich site it is.

## Gender and Globalization

Gender plays a particularly important role for many writers on globalization for two main reasons. First, much of the debate about globalization origi-nates from the version of the new international division of labour (NIDL) – formulated by Frobel *et al.* (1980) to describe the relocation of TNCs to Third World countries with low labour costs – particularly research that emphasized the role of young women working for TNCs in export-processing enclaves of various types (Nash and Fernandez-Kelly, 1983; Mitter, 1986). While many have questioned the economic significance of these new patterns of employment, there is no doubt as to their symbolic importance in publicizing, not only in academic circles but also through the mass media, the changing patterns of the global economy and their social, political and cultural consequences.

Second, the 'feminization of poverty' thesis (see Tinker, 1990) has drawn attention to the adverse consequences for both urban and rural women and their families of the process of development in general, and global structural adjustment policies in particular, in the 1980s and 90s. These policies have been imposed by transnational financial and aid institutions through national governments in many poor countries. This is one sphere in which the local consequences of global economic and social policies have been comprehensively researched and there appears to be a growing consensus that the processes of globalization may affect men and women differently. In addition, an increasing body of evidence suggests that such programmes tend to create more burdens for women and more opportunities for men (Beneria and Feldman, 1992). Mies (1998) argues that the position of women in the new international division of labour can be theoretically linked with the feminization of poverty. 'Women, defined as housewives and sex objects, are the optimal labour force for global capital' (Mies, 1994: 113). While not a direct contribution to the globalization literature, Mies provides both empirical evidence and conceptual insights of relevance for research in gender and globalization.

## Global Cities

With the tremendous growth of urbanization in the last few decades, particularly in the Third World, many scholars have begun to study the global as well as the national significance of cities, leading to the idea of world or global cities which are largely independent of national control. In the most influential formulation of this idea, Friedmann (1995) maintained that these can be identified in terms of the extent to which a city is a major financial centre, has global or regional TNCs and international institution headquarters, has rapid growth of business services, is an important manufacturing centre and is a major transport node. On the basis of these criteria, Friedmann constructs a 'world-city hierarchy' with primary and secondary cities in the core and semi-periphery countries. His formulation has been criticized on several counts, mainly because it appears to reproduce the problems of world-system analysis, but it remains an excellent starting point for this aspect of global studies. Subsequent research on global cities focuses on the global role of particular cities (London, New York, Los Angeles and Tokyo having attracted most attention), and the interconnections between the global economy, regions, cities and communities (Sassen, 1994).

'Global cities', however, are not located exclusively in the First World of rich countries. Processes of globalization have also been identified in the rapid growth of what have been conveniently if sometimes misleadingly labelled 'Third World' cities. Many researchers have noted the paradoxical phenomenon of cities like Kuala Lumpur, Manila, Bangkok, Calcutta and Shanghai in Asia; Mexico City and Buenos Aires in Latin America; Nairobi and Lagos in Africa; Cairo and Amman in the Middle East; and many others where world-class telecommunications and the skyscrapers that accommodate the global or regional headquarters of TNCs are in close proximity to shanty towns lacking basic amenities of sewerage, clean running water and a dependable electricity supply, not to speak of adequate schools and medical services (for data, see World Resources Institute, 1994). Globalization in the form of the increased coverage of the mass media, particularly access to television, is widely held to have added to the longstanding magnetic pull of the cities for the poorer strata of rural dwellers, many of whose livelihoods have been threatened or actually destroyed by global agribusiness (McMichael, 1996).

The sectoral composition of the labour force has not changed a great deal in many poor countries, particularly those with large populations, mainly because the absolute numbers of village dwellers tends to hide large increases in absolute numbers of industrial and service workers in the cities. Despite this, in more or less every country, the proportion of service workers in the labour force has increased in the last few decades (service workers include police and armed forces). Many of these service workers labour in the 'informal' sector, defined as all those people not in the formal waged economy. As we saw in Chapter 10, looking at inequalities in the contemporary world, a considerable literature has grown on the subject of such workers, and how they interact with those in the 'formal' economy in the local context and relate to the global economy. There are many conflicting interpretations of the informal sector, but the structural approach is of most interest to globalization theorists. Structuralists see the informal sector as an integral part of the capitalist economy, locally and globally, in the First World as well as the Third World. So the informal sector is theorized not as a more 'primitive form' of economic life, but as that part of a capitalist economy unregulated by the state, with its own structures of wealth and exploitation (see Portes and Castells, 1989). TNCs, for example, commonly use 'informal' (unregulated) producers and service-providers as part of their direct and indirect global production and distribution chains.

## Globalization and Regionalization

Many scholars who accept the declining significance of the nation state, particularly in economic affairs and mass culture, are uncertain about the existence of a truly global system. For them regionalization, that is, the comparison between different geographical zones, appears to be a more satisfactory answer than globalization to the 'sociological question' of social change. This thinking is clearly linked to ideas about the hegemony of the superpowers which have dominated analysis of the international system for centuries. In the 1970s there emerged a rather new mode of thinking which has come to be known as 'Trilateralism'; this is the view that the anti-communist powers, the USA, western Europe and Japan, each have their own 'natural spheres of interest' and that world peace and prosperity depended on these three regional powers being able to work out their differences peacefully and, eventually, destroy the global advance of communism. Since the demise of the Soviet empire and the 'opening up' of China, the trilateralism argument has been developed in a variety of directions. 'Regional responses' to globalization are, by the nature of the case, very varied. Most commentators argue that while much of western Europe, Japan and East Asia and North America has been able to take advantage of globalization and increase prosperity, most of the rest of the world has not been able to do so and that many communities have suffered from globalization. Brecher and Costello (1994) put forward the radical argument that globalization involves a 'race to the bottom' as corporations and governments scramble to reduce living standards for vulnerable groups of workers and citizens in order to compete 'successfully' in the global economy.

However, while much of the research on the relationship between the global and the regional provides very useful empirical examples and counter-examples for sociologists to consider, it remains difficult to conceptualize and research empirically global forces that drive certain kinds of development. Part of the problem is that regionalization itself relies on data in terms of national economies and societies (an idea that is very difficult to abandon but sometimes misleading when you want to study globalization). A global sociology requires more research comparisons between communities, cities, industrial districts, sub-national and supra-national regions to be made.

The little data on such comparisons that do exist yield quite surprising results. For example, the United Nations Development Programme (UNDP) *Human Development Report* (1993), although largely based on country-by-country rankings on a human development index (HDI), has started to disaggregate some of its findings. This reveals that the HDI for whites in the USA is slightly above the average for people in Japan as a whole, while the HDI for blacks in the USA is about the same as for people in Trinidad and Tobago. For hispanics in the USA the average is even lower, about the same as the average for the population of Estonia. Disaggregating on gender reveals similarly striking results. White females in the USA rank higher than any other group, anywhere, while black females rank well below, about the same as the Greek average. Black males in the USA rank slightly above the Bulgarian average (UNDP, 1993: 18). So, while country-level data will obviously continue to be usefully collected for the foreseeable future, it is just as obvious that such disaggregated data comparing the conditions of groups on other criteria across national borders are necessary if theories of globalization are to have adequate empirical foundations.

## Globalization and Everyday Life

The study of globalization appears much more abstract and much less obviously part of our daily lives than the other substantive topics considered in this book, such as gender, education or work. This is not surprising and, indeed, is a fundamental part of the problem and salience of globalization for an understanding of some of the determining circumstances under which we live out our daily lives. This is the reason why it is important to think about both the subjective, as well as the objective, side of globalization. These are not two separate issues, but merely two ways of looking at the same phenomenon. The subjective side looks at globalization from the point of view of the individual whose life is affected by globalization and whose own decisions (for example, media use, job preferences, voting behaviour, consumption choices) in their turn play a part in affecting the structures of globalization. The objective side starts from the forces of globalization themselves (mass media corporations, global economic forces, institutions that structure politics, global marketing) and how they create and condition opportunities for individual choices for different groups of people. Theories of globalization obviously have to consider both. However, as we saw in Chapter 3, linking structure and action raises a number of theoretical issues in sociology in general and which apply to globalization research in particular.

Many people who are sympathetic to the idea of globalization find most accounts of it excessively structuralist and abstract, focusing on impersonal global forces against which the individual has no say. This is exemplified in the declining influence of Wallerstein's world-system theory, with its obvious 'globalizing' tendencies from the outside, and the current popularity of more reflexive approaches to globalization, encapsulated in the idea of globalization as 'reflexive modernity'. However, Giddens' (1991: 175) view of globalization involving 'emergent forms of world interdependence and planetary consciousness' is misconceived for most of the world's people. Watching CNN or *Friends* or the World Cup on TV in a village, shanty town or global city does not necessarily mean that all viewers share the same experience let alone planetary consciousness, whatever that is (Dowmunt, 1993). What it does mean, however, is that if and when the viewer actually starts to become conscious of and to desire the global prestige of the lifestyles these products embody and eventually buys the products, then an objective relationship to the global corporations whose existence depends on the profits from these purchases is established. Whether or not any given individual or group has planetary consciousness, or consciousness of the global whole, is an open *empirical* question, although not one which any theorist of globalization has actually studied empirically, so far. The findings of studies on this question would help to evaluate the validity of the culturalist approach discussed earlier. Perhaps some people would recognize and confirm such consciousness in some contexts and on some occasions (perhaps when the media are full of some 'global' issue) but not in other contexts and at other times. This would be very interesting to research and would, of course, tell us much about the subjective side of globalization. But we cannot assume the existence of such consciousness and we certainly cannot assume it exists just because millions of people watch similar TV programmes and adverts, idealize the same stars and buy the same products all over the world. These 'objective' facts on media use, name recognition of celebrities and global sales are in the public record. These are what the objective side of globalization is about, and they do not depend for their validity on anyone's 'global consciousness'.

## Resistances to Globalization

Globalization is often seen in terms of impersonal forces wreaking havoc on the lives of ordinary defenceless people and communities. It is not coincidental that interest in globalization over the last two decades has been accompanied by an upsurge in what has come to be known as New Social Movements (NSM) research (Ray, 1993; Spybey, 1996). NSM theorists, despite their substantial differences, argue that the traditional response of the labour movement to global capitalism, based on class politics, has generally failed and that a new analysis based on identity politics (notably of gender, sexuality, ethnicity, age, community, belief systems) is necessary to mount effective resistance to sexism, racism, environmental damage, warmongering, capitalist exploitation and other forms of injustice.

The globalization of identity politics involves the establishment of global networks of people – made easier by the development of new means of communication such as the Internet – with similar identities and interests outside the control of international, state and local authorities. There is a substantial volume of research and documentation on such developments in the women's, peace and environmental movements, some of it in direct response to governmental initiatives, but most theorists and activists tend to operate under the slogan: think global, act local (Ekins, 1992).

The main challenges to global capitalism in the economic sphere have also come from those who 'think global and act local'. This normally involves disrupting the capacity of TNCs and global financial institutions to accumulate private profits at the expense of their workforces, their consumers and the communities which are affected by their activities. An important part of economic globalization today is the increasing dispersal of the manufacturing process into many discrete phases carried out in many different places. Being no longer so dependent on the production of one factory and one workforce gives capital a distinct advantage, particularly against the strike weapon which once gave tremendous negative power to the working class. Global production chains can be disrupted by strategically planned stoppages, but this generally acts more as inconveniences than as real weapons of labour against capital. The international division of labour builds flexibility into the system so that not only can capital migrate anywhere in the world to find the cheapest reliable productive sources of labour but also few workforces can any longer decisively 'hold capital to ransom' by withdrawing their labour. At the level of the production process globalizing capital has all but defeated labour. In this respect, the global organization of the TNCs and allied institutions like globalizing government agencies and the World Bank have, so far, proved too powerful for the local organization of labour and communities.

Nevertheless, the global capitalists, if we are to believe their own propaganda, are continuously beset by opposition, boycott, legal challenge and moral outrage from the consumers of their products and by disruptions from their workers. There are also many ways to be ambivalent or hostile about cultures and ideologies of consumerism, some of which the 'Green' movement has successfully exploited (see Mander and Goldsmith, 1996).

The issue of democracy is central to the advance of the forces of globalization and the practices and the prospects of social movements that oppose them, local and global. The rule of law, freedom of association and expression, freely contested elections, as minimum conditions and however imperfectly sustained, are as necessary in the long run for mass market-based global consumerist capitalism as they are for alternative social systems.

## Conclusion

This account of globalization has focused on what distinguishes *global* (transnational) from *inter-national* forces, processes and institutions and some of the models which have been developed to explain it. It is based almost exclusively on the European and North American literature, but this does not preclude the possibility of other and quite different conceptions of globalization being developed elsewhere. Despite the view, particularly evident in the accounts of 'global culture' theorists that globalization is more or less the same as westernization or Americanization or McDonaldization (Ritzer, 1995), more critics, especially from Africa and Asia, are beginning to question this one-way traffic bias in the globalization literature (see Albrow and King, 1990; Sklair, 1994b; Jameson and Miyoshi, 1998). It is very likely that an introduction to the sociology of globalization written ten years from now will reflect non-western perspectives much more strongly. Nevertheless, although of quite recent vintage, it is undeniable that globalization as a theoretical issue and an object of research, is now firmly on the agenda of the social sciences.

## Further Reading

Albrow, M. *The Global Age,* Cambridge, Polity Press, 1996. A 'Weberian' attempt to interpret globalization in terms of the transition to the global age.

McMichael, P. *Development and Social Change: A Global Perspective,* Thousand Oaks, Pine Forge Press, 1996. The first sociology of development textbook written from an explicitly global perspective.

Sklair, L. *Sociology of the Global System,* 2nd edn, Baltimore, Johns Hopkins University Press, 1995. A critical discussion of how global capitalism structures the world in terms of the transnational practices of transnational corporations, the transnational capitalist class and the culture ideology of consumerism.

Yearly, S. *Sociology, Environmentalism, Globalization: Reinventing the Globe,* London, Sage, 1996. One of the few books on environmental sociology that assesses issues of globalization.

# Glossary

**Agency** In sociology the term agent is sometimes simply used to mean individual. However, agency does have a rather more specific meaning. It refers to *purposeful* human action, that is, the choices people make to act in certain ways. There is a long-standing debate in sociology (and other social sciences) about the extent to which people are 'free agents'. Some theoretical perspectives, such as interactionism and ethnomethodology, place great stress on human agency. Others, such as Marxism and structural functionalism, focus more on the ways in which people's behaviour is influenced by processes in wider society.

**Alienation** This means estrangement or separation. Marx argued that the organization of production for private profit meant that most workers were denied the opportunity to realise their inherent creative capacities and were thus alienated from their true, or essential, selves. For Marx, religious belief was simply an expression of this alienation.

**Anomie** Literally a state of normlessness where the rules structuring social interaction have broken down or become meaningless to the individual. Durkheim linked anomie to a condition of **modernity** where the institutionalization of socially approved dissatisfaction was producing a situation where more individuals experienced an imbalance between their wants and the means of achieving them, making them vulnerable to, among other things, suicidal impulses.

**Bureaucracy** A system of administration associated with the complex organizations of modern societies based on formal rules, specialized occupational tasks, hierarchical structures and impersonality. For Weber, the growth of bureaucratic organizations was an inevitable consequence of the increasing rationality of modern societies, where calculation and efficiency replaced sentiment and tradition. However, sociologists have also documented the inefficiencies and irrationalities of bureaucracy.

**Childhood** The development of childhood as a distinct social category separate from adults began to develop in European societies with the children of the nobility and spread throughout *modern* societies in the nineteenth century with the passing of legislation to protect children from exploitation in the work place and make some education compulsory. This process was developed in the twentieth century with the extension of compulsory education, the development of 'child specialisms' such as child health, and legislation and services to try to protect children from harm in their own domestic environments.

**Citizenship** The political and economic rights entailed in being a member of a political community. The extension of the principle of citizenship from a narrow élite to the majority of the population is seen as one of the defining characteristics of the process of **modernization**.

**Class conflict** Political action arising from recognition of the different interests of social classes. Marx believed that class conflict would lead to the overthrow of the capitalist system and its replacement by socialism. Some sociologists writing in the middle years of the twentieth century, such as Dahrendorf, argued that **class consciousness** had become 'institutionalized in western societies; that is, rather than seeking to overthrow capitalism, working-class organizations and political parties pursued their interests within the capitalist system. In contemporary societies manifestations of class consciousness are much less apparent and the idea of class itself has become a contested concept.

**Class consciousness** Processes by which members of a social class become increasingly aware of their common interests. Marx predicted that working-class consciousness would grow under capitalism. However, this would not happen 'automatically'. Working-class sense of injustice had to be channelled into appropriate political action. Some sociologists argued that the growth of **culture industries** played a major part in inhibiting working-class consciousness, others point to the increasing diversity and fragmentation of the relatively homogenous working class of early capitalism.

**Code** This means the rules that govern a system of signs.

**Coercion** This usually describes situations where people feel compelled to do something through force, or threat of force, when they do not recognise the **legitimacy** of the controlling agency to have power over them.

**Colonialism** A process by which a nation state imposes its control over other territories. Colonialism usually refers to rule by western states over distant territories involving longstanding patterns of settlement and the separation of foreign and indigenous populations.

**Consensus and conflict** Consensus theories argue that the basis of **social order** in any society comes from people's common interests and shared values. Comte, Durkheim and Parsons tended to take this view. In Parsons' structural functionalist theory, for example, social stability is seen as the 'normal' condition of society, while conflict is 'pathological', rather like a disease in a part of the body. Consensus theorists are interested in questions of power and social control but, as Helliwell and Hindess argue in Chapter 4, they see them as general resources in society which are exercised by some, like the government and police for example, for the benefit of society as a whole. Conflict theorists, in contrast, take the view that all societies are divided into groups which are in competition over scarce resources, power and opportunity. They argue that social order is the result of some groups holding power over others. Marxists, for example, argue that there is always a conflict of interest between those who own the means of economic production (ruling class) and those who have only their labour power to sell (subordinate classes). Feminist sociologists also see societies in terms of conflicts of interest between women and men.

**Critical criminology** Theoretical approaches which attempt to locate the origins of crime and the societal reaction to it in terms of a critical analysis of the political economy of capitalism.

**Cult** A term loosely applied to religious organizations and groups whose practices and beliefs are seen to be individualistic, esoteric and somewhat divorced from the cultural traditions of the society in which they are practised. However, globalization and the fragmentation of cultural boundaries are making such a distinction difficult to establish empirically.

**Cultural reproduction** The processes by which the values of the dominant culture are explicitly and implicitly reproduced in educational institutions.

**Culture/culture industries** In everyday language, culture is usually used to refer to 'highbrow' things, such as classical music, art or literature. However, in sociology, culture has a much wider meaning and describes the ideas, values and customs of a social group. There is a debate in sociology about the relationship between culture and other aspects of society. **Materialist** theories argue that culture is shaped largely by the productive forces of society, while **idealist** theories argue that culture exerts an independent influence on societies. **Postmodern theory** takes this argument much further, arguing that, in the media saturated contemporary world, society has become 'collapsed' into culture; that is, there is no independent standpoint outside media images of one sort or another. Culture industry refers to institutions and organizations that produce and disseminate 'popular culture', through newspapers, magazines and television for example. Criticism of culture industries is associated with, but not confined to, Marxist theory. While Marx himself and most Marxist writers have adopted an essentially **materialist** view of society, other Marxists adopted a more idealist view. Writers of the Frankfurt School, Adorno and Marcuse for example, argued that culture industries played an important and independent role in maintaining capitalism by helping to produce a largely passive, uncritical, consumer-orientated public. Other sociologists have criticised this view, arguing that it underestimates the importance of human **agency**. People are not simply the 'passive' recipients of culture industries, but rather 'actively' select and interpret what they want from it.

**Culture of deprivation** The idea that aspects of working-class disadvantage, such as the comparatively poor educational performance of working-class children and the relatively poor health of working-class people, can be explained to some extent by the fact that the working-class home and neighbourhood provide less motivation and linguistic skills and a more fatalistic attitude to life.

**De-skilling** Processes by which occupations become downgraded. In the 1970s Braverman argued that many manual and white-collar occupations were becoming de-skilled. In opposition to this view, it has been argued that technical developments in production and an increase in service occupations has generally produced higher and more flexible levels of skill in the working population. Debates about de-skilling are complicated by problems in defining and 'measuring' skill levels and the fact that contradictory processes may be operating. For example, an occupation may be officially upgraded yet be less demanding in practice. Alternatively, an occupation may require more technical skills but may be undertaken under conditions of increased supervision and control. For example, teaching has become more demanding but, as Burgess and Parker show in Chapter 9, it is now carried out under much greater **surveillance** which reduces teachers scope for autonomous decision making.

**Delinquent sub-cultures** Social groups – usually, but not necessarily, comprised of young males – organized around practices and values which, in some respects, are opposed to dominant social norms and values.

**Discourses** Systems of language, ideas and practices around which the understanding of some aspect of social reality is established. The analysis of discourses is associated most commonly with post-structural theories. Foucault, for example, analysed the ways in which the control of madness had been informed by a number of different discourses.

**Discrimination** Practices of individuals and groups that systematically and adversely effect the **life chances** of others. Discrimination may arise from prejudice and active hostility to others, but it may also occur unintentionally even when people may be actively trying not to be prejudiced.

**Division of labour** The process of increasing specialization of production which can be used at the societal level to describe increased differentiation of sectors and functions and at the level of organizations to describe the specialization and fragmentation of occupational tasks. The division of labour is generally seen as an essential element in the process of industrialization and central to the increased productive capacity of modern societies.

**Domestic labour** The work involved in running a household, such as cleaning, shopping and child care, which is undertaken largely by women without remuneration.

**Domestic violence** Violent conduct perpetrated by one member of household against another.

**Epidemiology** The study of the distribution of health and disease in populations.

**Epistemology** Epistemological questions in philosophy are concerned with theories of knowledge, or *how* questions: how do we know something is true? In sociology, epistemological questions are related to methodological issues: how is the information the sociologist is putting forward justified?

**Ethnicity** An awareness of belonging to a social group sharing a common cultural identity and heritage.

**False consciousness** In its most general sense this term simply means an individual or social group having a distorted view of the 'truth'. It is most specifically associated with Marxist theory's description of the *working-class* people's continued compliance with the capitalist system instead of pursuing their own 'true' interests.

**Gender blind** Theories and research studies that fail to take into account gender differences.

**Genre** A text whose content is structured around a distinct and recognizable form such as 'sitcom', 'soap opera' or 'thriller'.

**Global commodity chain** This refers to the sequence of activities a commodity passes through before it is sold on the **market**. Commodity chain analysis looks particularly at two elements: first, how it is co-ordinated and second, the spacial distribution of the transformation. Commodity chain analysis is used increasingly to understand how transnational (or multinational) corporations organize their global production systems.

**Government** This describes the processes by which a society is regulated by some legally constituted authority. For many sociologists government not only involves the 'visible' exercise of authority, such as elections or the passing of laws, it also involves the 'invisible' authority where people are indirectly influenced to behave in various ways. From this perspective, educational, health and welfare organizations, for example, act as instruments of government.

**Hegemony** This word was originally used to describe the domination of one state by another. Gramsci adapted this idea to explain the continuing dominance of the ruling class in capitalist society through political and *ideological* dominance (Chapter 4). He argued that the ruling class did not, and could not, simply control society through active force but had actively to obtain the consent of the subordinate classes. In this context he was particularly interested in the role of cultural institutions, such as family, education and media, in helping to obtain this consent.

**Holistic medicine** Medical practices based on the idea that disease, rather than being localised in a specific part of the body, such as the heart or the liver, is a symptom of a disturbance of the whole person.

**Household** An individual, or group of people, sharing the same accommodation for a period of time. Many sociologists now use the term household in preference to 'the family' because they feel that the former, with its assumption of a married couple and children, fails to reflect the diversity of domestic arrangements in contemporary societies.

**Hyperreality** An idea advanced by some *postmodern* theorists, particularly Baudrillard, claiming that the media-saturated contemporary world increasingly involves the consumption of images that have no purchase in 'reality'; thus the boundaries between what is 'real' and what is 'illusory' become increasingly blurred.

**Hypothesis** This refers to an idea or a theory which has been developed in such a way that it can be 'tested' with relevant evidence.

**Iatrogenic disease** Disease resulting from medical treatment.

**Ideal type** A model describing the essential characteristics of an organization, institution or pattern of behaviour.

**Ideology** The concept of ideology is widely used in a number of different ways in sociology. In its most general sense ideology refers to the shared ideas, beliefs and values which are held by social groups and justify their action. Sociologists tend to see ideologies negatively and are particularly interested in the ways in which they help to justify social inequalities and reinforce the power of dominant groups in societies. For example, Marxists argue that the class that rules economically has the power to disseminate ideologies throughout society legitimizing its control. Similarly, feminists have examined the part played by **patriarchal** ideologies in the subordination of women. Some sociologists have argued that ideologies can create a **'false consciousness'** of conformity among the oppressed who remain unaware of their 'real' interests. However, this raises the question of defining what those 'real' interests are, which can lead to the circularity of comparing ideological beliefs and preferences (see Chapter 4).

**Industrialization** The development of mechanized technology and large-scale productive processes, seen most clearly in the factory system. Industrialization was a major source of the transformation of pre-modern to modern society. Sociology began as an attempt to make sense of industrial society.

**Interviews: structured and unstructured** In the structured, or 'closed', interview, respondents are asked a set of identical questions in more or less the same way and choose from a limited range of answers. Structured interviews enable the researcher to collect a large amount of data in a relatively short time and the results can be quantified. In the unstructured, or 'open', interview there is no set format and the interview is more like a conversation. There is comparatively little input from the researcher and respondents answer in their own words. Unstructured interviews tend to give richer, more detailed data. Although this technique appears to be giving the interviewee's 'own story', the researcher's subjective, or value, judgements play an important part in determining what is selected and reproduced in the final research report. While some sociologists prefer one technique or the other, for others the choice of method depends on the problem being studied.

**Kinship** Social relations deriving from blood ties. As societies modernise kinship becomes a less important basis for both social organization and determining an individual's position within institutions and organizations.

**Legitimacy** The belief of people that the power exercised over them is just because, for example, a leader was born to rule or a government has been democratically elected. While some sociologists, following Weber, have simply focused on *how* legitimacy is established, others, following Marx, have adopted a more critical stance by questioning *whether* or not belief in legitimacy is justified. However, as Helliwell and Hindess observe in Chapter 4, this latter approach can result in comparing one set of value judgements with another.

**Liberalism** A political doctrine which stresses the importance of the state guaranteeing the rights of free individuals by, for example, being freely elected, accountable and acting within the law. Liberalism is associated with modern western societies and the liberal tradition is usually compared favourably with other forms of **government**, such as traditional authority or the totalitarian **government** of the former Soviet Union. However, many sociologists have criticized western liberal democracies for the economic inequalities they produce, both within and between societies, and for failing to attain their democratic **ideology** in practice. Other sociologists have been more interested in exploring how liberal democracies work. For Foucault, as Helliwell and Hindess explain in Chapter 4, liberalism is a means by which **government** can be effected in increasingly complex and diverse societies.

**Life chances** The idea that an individual's prospects of attaining material rewards and high **status** in a society are profoundly influenced by *'structural* factors', such as their class position, gender or ethnic group.

**Lifestyles** Differences in the patterns of consumption of goods, services and culture which have been explained largely as a reflection of different class positions. In British sociology, in particular, there was a long-running debate focusing on the consequences of increasing numbers of more affluent working-class people adopting 'middle-class' lifestyles. For many sociologists, particularly those who argue that we are now living in a **postmodern** society, people's sense of identity is shaped more by what they consume than what they produce.

**Longitudinal study** Obtaining data from the same sample at regular intervals over a long period of time.

**Macro- and micro-theories** Macro-theories focus on larger social changes, such as broad historical changes and comparisons between societies and social institutions, and are usually associated with structural theories in sociology. Micro-theories are more likely to focus on face-to-face interactions of relatively small numbers of people and are usually associated with **social action theories**. While many studies in sociology are either macro or micro, others try to combine aspects of both. For example, in *Learning to Labour*, which is cited in several chapters in this book, Willis linked a detailed micro-analysis of the experiences of a small group of boys to macro-educational and industrial processes.

**Markets** Arenas within which buyers and sellers meet in order to exchange goods and money. In economics, the price of goods emerge from this interaction as expressions of the aggregated results of the preferences of individuals. This then feeds into production and consumption decisions. **Liberalism** holds that the market is the foundation of freedom in modern societies as it is based on choice, while Marxists argue that as people enter the market unequal it merely reproduces inequality. Economic sociologists are increasingly interested in how markets are socially constructed both inside and outside the exchange process.

**Marketization** The spread of market economics, especially in institutions concerned with things like education and health care which had largely been taken out of the market place by the expansion of social welfare policies.

**Marriage** A *social institution* which legally sanctions the union of partners. In the later part of the twentieth century marriage has become less important with an increasing proportion of the population choosing to cohabit outside marriage.

**Materialism and idealism** Materialism describes theories, such as Marxism, which hold that economic institutions are the major influence on how societies work and change. Idealist theories, in contrast, place more emphasis on the part played by culture, values and ideas.

**Materialist and lifestyle theories** Examining health inequalities, materialist theories argue that people's health is influenced primarily by their economic circumstances while lifestyle theories focus more on the choices people make, such as whether or not to smoke. Some sociologists have tried to synthesize the theories by exploring the extent to which people's lifestyle 'choices' are shaped by their material circumstances.

**Meta-narratives** This term, which is sometimes used interchangeably with grand narratives, describes general, encompassing ideas and beliefs about how the world works, such as religious or scientific doctrines. In sociology, general sociological perspectives, such as Marxism, functionalism or feminism, are sometimes described as meta-narratives, or grand-narratives. Postmodernists, in particular, are critical of meta, or grand, narratives for failing to recognize the diversity of the social world and for trying to tell people *how* they should think about the world.

**Methodological individualism** The view that sociological explanation has to be based on individual characteristics of one sort or another. Society should not be theorized as something 'over and above' individuals as such abstraction is not justified.

**Modernity** This is a very general descriptive term which is usually taken to mean two things. First, it refers to the emergence of modern societies based around things such as industrial production, urban living, science, technology, political democracy, rational planning and the growth of the state. Second, modernity is characterized by a particular outlook on the world which sets itself against tradition, superstition and religious interpretations. It celebrates the power of rational understanding, and science in particular, to understand how the world works. Sociology is closely tied to modernity. Not only did it begin in the nineteenth century as an attempt to understand the 'new' modern societies that were developing in western Europe, it was itself a product of modernity. That is, the idea of understanding how societies work with a view to improving them is a distinctly modern idea. Some theorists now argue that the modern era is ending and we are now moving to a new form of *postmodern* society.

**Moral panic** A term used to describe a media-fuelled over-reaction to a social group, form of behaviour or social problem. A characteristic of moral panic is that the specific issue is depicted as a symptom of a much more general breakdown of **social order** and values.

**Nationalism** An **ideology** founded on the belief that people living in the same national community share common interests that separate them from other nations.

**New racism** Racist **ideologies** based on cultural and religious identities rather than supposed biological differences.

**New religious movements** A term used to describe the growth of unorthodox religious beliefs and practices in contemporary societies.

**New Right** This loosely describes political and economic theories developed in the 1970s and 80s which celebrated the liberal tradition of free-market economies and opposed the continued expansion of welfare states on economic and moral grounds. New Right ideas were associated with the governmental policies of Margaret Thatcher in Britain and Ronald Regan in the USA in the 1980s.

**Nuclear family** A husband, wife and dependent children living in the same household. The term was used to contrast the smaller and relatively more isolated families of modern societies with what were taken to be the much larger extended families of pre-industrial societies. However, more recent research has suggested that such a distinction is oversimplified as extended family structures were not characteristics of all pre-modern societies and persist to some extent in modern societies.

**Objective knowledge** This is knowledge which is supposed to be free from bias, opinion, personal values and prejudices and is most commonly associated with scientific data that is generated under experimental conditions. While some sociologists argue that sociology is about producing objective knowledge of societies, others argue that this is an impossible ambition as the researchers' own subjective ideas and values will necessarily influence what is discovered and presented to others. Another point of view, put forward by Pawson in Chapter 2, is that sociologists should strive towards *greater* objectivity even though *total* objectivity is impossible in practice.

**Ontology** Ontological questions in philosophy are concerned with the nature of the things: *what* they are. In sociology, ontological questions are about what societies are. For example, are societies best conceptualised as interdependent institutions shaping individual lives (**structural theory**) or as the outcome of individual actions (**action theory**)?

**Paradigm** This describes a set of general ideas and practices around which specific areas of research are organised. In sociology there are several different paradigms, with their own theories and research strategies, and there are disputes between them about the 'right' way to do sociological research.

**Patriarchy** This originally means the rule of the father. Feminist sociologists use it much more generally to describe the *ideological* and *material* structures of power by which men dominate and control women.

**Phenomenology** Phenomenological sociology tries to avoid making preconceived judgements and hypotheses and focuses instead on people's subjective understanding of everyday life. Phenomenologists are critical of the idea of a 'scientific' sociology which tries to attribute causality to social phenomena. For example, a great deal of sociological research has tried to uncover some of the social causes of things like crime, suicide and educational failure. For phenomenologists, the fluctuating and subjective nature of social life makes this ambition impossible, the most sociology can do is employ in-depth, qualitative methods to explore how certain things come to be 'seen' by people as 'crimes', 'suicides' or 'educational failure'. Phenomenology has been very influential in sociology, but has been widely criticized for being both trivial and neglecting the importance of wider social influences on people's lives. Some sociologists, such as Weber, have adopted a neo-phenomenological approach by combining phenomenology's stress on subjectivity while retaining a notion of causality.

**Polarization** A concept used by Marx to describe a hardening of the divisions between the capitalist and working classes.

**Positivism** A philosophical doctrine holding that scientific knowledge can only deal with observable entities which then prove, or disprove, theories. In sociology positivism is associated with the idea that sociology should follow the principles of the natural sciences and produce objective knowledge through methods of research which are reliable, quantifiable and value neutral. Positivism has been heavily criticized in social theory by those, such as **realists**, who have different views of what science is, and by those, such as **phenomenologists**, who argue that scientific methods cannot be applied to the study of societies.

**Post-Fordism** A very general and contested term used to describe a transition from mass industrial production epitomised by the factory production line developed by Henry Ford's motor company, to more diverse and flexible systems of production, associated with information technology enterprises, for example. The term has also been used more generally to describe a transition from 'organised' state regulated capitalism to a more 'disorganised' and less regulated capitalism.

**Postmodernity and Postmodernism** These are very general terms which are sometimes used in a different ways by different writers. Postmodernity is usually used to describe a situation where developments such as de-industrialization, globalization of the economy, media saturation of societies and the collapse of grand ideologies, such as communism and socialism, are bringing about a new social condition which is different from *modernity*. Postmodernism usually describes a set of social and cultural beliefs, values and ways of behaving which result from living in modernity. Some sociologists, such as Lyotard and Baudrillard, argue that a consequence of these changes has been to fragment what sociologists previously understood as 'society', and that a new postmodern sociology is now needed to make sense of these developments. Others, such as Bauman, argue for a sociology *of* postmodernity while others, such as Giddens, believe that these radical changes have simply transformed, rather than ended, modernity.

**Post-structuralism** This describes a form of analysis which has much in common with **postmodern** theory. Post-structuralists argue that as social reality is only made intelligible through language, the focus of social inquiry should be on the various lilnguistic forms, or **texts**, through which the world is described. Texts can only be compared to each other as there is no independent 'reality' against which they can be evaluated. Post-structuralists are thus **relativists**.

**Power élite** Elites are groups who have power, influence and high *social status* in societies or social organizations. In sociology, 'élite theorists' have argued that both Marxist hopes for a 'classless society' and western notions of *liberal democracies* are impossible in practice as the major institutions of societies would always be controlled by élites who would inevitably use the power they hold over others for their own interests. Most famously, C. Wright Mills argued that despite its **ideology** of being open, accountable and democratic **government**, the United States was ruled by a relatively *integrated* and perpetuating power élite who controlled its political, economic and military institutions.

**'Race relations'** The study of racist ideologies, the structures that give rise to them and the consequences for people's **life chances**.

**Realism** In its most general sense realism means that societies are real in the sense of having certain invariant properties which then allow generalizations to be made. More specifically, realism describes a philosophical approach which argues, in opposition to positivism, that scientific, and social scientific, explanations involve uncovering the unobservable, but real, mechanisms that generate relations between observable phenomena. In the last twenty years 'new realism' has become increasingly influential in sociology. However, elements of social realism can be found much earlier in the work of Marx and Durkheim, for example. In his realist theory of suicide, Durkheim attempted to demonstrate that consistent relationships between suicide and other social factors, such as religion and family, were generated by invisible but real moral forces which had their origins in collective social life.

**Relativism** Relativists argue that as the knowledge that sociologists use to develop and test their theories is necessarily 'constructed' in terms of ideas and values which are variable and constantly changing, there are no independent and fixed criteria by which they can be evaluated. Therefore, sociological explanation cannot transcend the particular and offers only partial and temporary interpretations rather than general truths. *Phenomenological theory* (see Chapter 2), interactionist theories of deviance (see Chapter 11) and social constructionist approaches to medicine and the body (see Chapter 12) are all examples of relativist approaches in sociology.

**Sacred** That which is special, awe inspiring and set apart from the ordinary and everyday. The distinction between the sacred and the profane was the cornerstone of Durkheim's definition of religion.

**Secondary deviance** Behaviour which follows being identified and labelled as deviant which may, or may not include further rule breaking.

**Sect** A religious group which is formed by breaking away from an established religious organization.

**Sex and gender** Sex differences are typically seen as natural and biological while gender divisions are shaped by social values and vary between societies and within societies over time. However some sociologists dispute this distinction, arguing that even the apparently 'fixed' and stable anatomical reality of the human body is a cultural construction the meaning of which is given by social values and practices (see Chapter 12).

**Sexual harassment** Sexual advances by one person to another, or others, which persist in spite of the recipient making it clear that they are not welcome.

**Social action theory** Social action theories in sociology start from the idea that human behaviour has meaning and intention; that is people do not just respond to things, they actively interpret the world around them and have reasons for what they do. Action theorists usually begin by exploring how individuals interpret the situations in which they find themselves. Action theories are often contrasted to **structural** theories which focus more on wider social and organizational processes. A major question for action theory is how, if individuals are 'free', creative agents, do we explain **social order**? The relationship between action and structure is examined in Chapter 3.

**Social integration** A concept which describes the different ways in which people are tied, or bonded, to each other through joint membership of social institutions, such as the family, work and religious organizations. It was used most famously by Durkheim in his study of suicide, in which he argued that the more people in modern societies were integrated into *social institutions*, the less vulnerable they were to suicide. However, it has been widely developed in more contemporary sociology. For example, a great deal of research has shown that levels of social integration can profoundly influence people's mental and physical health.

**Social mobility** This describes the movement of people between social positions – usually occupational, or class categories. Intragenerational mobility compares an individual's position over a lifetime, while intergenerational mobility compares a person's present position with that of their origin. Rates of social mobility are often taken as indicators of the openness, or fairness, of a society.

**Social order** The description and explanation of social order is one of the key problems of sociological theory. Structural theorists tend to conceptualize order arising from the ways in which individuals' behaviour is constrained by the institutional organization of societies. Action theorists, in contrast, focus on the ways in which social order is produced from agents' identification and realization of goals.

**Social stratification** The hierarchical ranking of different social groups in terms of unequal access to wealth, income, **status** and power. For most sociologists, social stratification is structured, that is, it is a consequence of forms of social organization that produce systematic differences in the **life chances** of members of different social groups. For example, the average educational attainment of children from professional backgrounds is consistently higher than that of children from manual working-class backgrounds.

**Social structure** The idea of social structure is one of the ways in which sociologists have tried to conceptualize the relationship between the individual and society. It focuses on societies as enduring systems of organization which are larger than the individual and shape the individual's life in various ways. Sociologists have different interpretations of social structure. For some, such as Marx, societies are defined in terms of their economic structure, that is, the ways in which the production of goods and services is organised. For others, such as Durkheim, social structures are defined more in terms of the cultural ideas that help bind individuals to social groups. A common criticism of all 'structural' theories is that they do not attach enough importance to the part individuals play in actively shaping their own lives. Sociologists attempts to bring together ideas of social structure and individual actions are discussed at some length by Swingewood in Chapter 3.

**Socialization** A term used to describe the processes by which people become aware of social norms and values and learn what is expected of them in given situations. Socialization begins in infancy but continues through adult life and sociologists have used the concept to explore how people 'learn' gender, occupational or deviant roles, for example.

**Status** This describes the social standing or prestige of an individual or group with a society or social organization. Many sociologists have followed Weber in seeing status differences, arising from religion or **ethnicity** for example, as distinct sources of inequality which are in important respects independent of class or economic position. Status groups are often characterised by distinct **lifestyles** and values and can act an important source of identity for individuals.

**Stigma** People are socially stigmatized when they are discredited in some way and denied full social acceptance. Sociologists are interested in the processes by which individuals and groups become stigmatized and the effects this has on their identities and social behaviour.

**Stress** A theoretical concept used to describe the relationship of an organism to its environment; an organism is said to be stressed when the demands placed on it tax its adaptive capabilities. Sociologists and psychologists of health are interested in the ways in which 'stressful' life experiences which people find difficult to cope with make disease more likely.

**Surveillance** This means monitoring people's behaviour. Some sociologists describe the contemporary world as the surveillance society since people's behaviour is increasing being surveilled, directly by things such as security cameras and indirectly by the amount of information about them that is now stored by public and private institutions.

**Symmetrical family** This describes an idea that in late modern societies the domestic division of labour is becoming more flexible, with women taking on more paid employment outside the home and men becoming more involved in household responsibilities. While there is a great deal of evidence of the former, there is little to support the latter.

**Text** In its most general sense a text is a written or visual document. However, in **post-structural** analysis, it is used more specifically to refer to the ideas through which the world is made intelligible. Social analysis is the analysis of texts.

**Theory-dependence** Doing social research necessarily involves using general, or theoretical, ideas through which the information, or data, is gathered and interpreted. The data are thus shaped by the theory and there is no such thing as 'pure' knowledge. Facts never speak for themselves.

**Victim survey** Victim surveys attempt to get round the official underreporting of crime by interviewing representative samples of the general population to find out how many of them have been victims of crime in a given period.

**Welfare state** State provision of a range of services and economic benefits, such as education and pensions, to try and guarantee basic living standards for all citizens.

**Zero sum view of power** The view that there is only so much power in a given social situation and that one group therefore holds it at the expense of others.

# References

Abbott, P. and Wallace, C. (1996) *An Introduction to Sociology: Feminist Perspectives,* 2nd edn, London, Routledge

Abraham, J. (1995) *Divide and School: Gender and Class Dynamics in Comprehensive Education,* London, Falmer Press

Acker, S. (1994) *Gendered Education,* Buckingham, Open University Press

Adonis, A. and Pollard, S. (1997) *A Class Act,* London, Hamish Hamilton

Afshar, H. (1989) 'Gender roles and the "moral economy of kin" among Pakistani women in West Yorkshire', *New Community,* **15**(2): 211–25

*Agenda for Action,* London, King's Fund

Albrow, M. (1996) *The Global Age,* Cambridge, Polity

Albrow, M. and King, E. (eds) (1990) *Globalization, Knowledge and Society,* London, Sage

Alger, C. (1988) 'Perceiving, analysing and coping with the local-global nexus', *International Social Science Journal,* **117**: 321–40

Althusser, L. (1972) 'Ideology and ideological state apparatus: notes towards an investigation', in B. Cosin (ed.) *Education, Structure and Society,* Penguin/Open University Press, Harmondsworth

Amin, A. (1994) *Post-Fordism,* Oxford, Blackwell

Amin, A. and Thrift, N. (1995) *Globalization, Institutions and Regional Development in Europe,* Oxford, Oxford University Press

Anderson, B. (1983) *Imagined Communities: Reflections on the Origin and Spread of Nationalism,* London, Verso

Anderson, M. (1980) *Approaches to the History of the Western Family 1500–1914,* London, Macmillan

Ang, I. (1985) *Watching Dallas: Soap Opera and the Melodramatic Imagination,* London, Methuen

Ang, I. (1996) *Living Room Wars: Rethinking Media Audiences for a Post-modern World,* London, Routledge

Anthias, F. and Yuval-Davis, N. (1989) 'Introduction', in N. Yuval-Davis and F. Anthias (eds), *Woman-Nation-State,* London, Macmillan

Anthias, F. and Yuval-Davis, N. (1992) *Racialized Boundaries,* London, Routledge

Arber, S. (1990) 'Opening the black box: inequalities in women's health', in P. Abbott and G. Payne (eds) *New Directions in the Sociology of Health,* Basingstoke, Falmer

Arber, S. and Ginn, J. (eds) (1995) *Connecting Gender and Ageing,* Buckingham, Open University Press

Archer, M. (1979) *The Social Origins of Educational Systems,* London, Sage

Armstrong, D. (1983) *The Political Anatomy of the Body,* Cambridge, Cambridge University Press

Armstrong, D. (1987) 'Bodies of knowledge: Foucault and the problem of human anatomy', in G. Scambler (ed.) *Sociological Theory and Medical Sociology,* London, Tavistock

Armstrong, D. (1995) 'The problem of the whole person in holistic medicine', in B. Davey, A. Gray and C. Seale (eds) *Health and Disease: A Reader,* Buckingham, Open University Press

Arnot, M., David, M. and Weiner, G. (1996) *Educational Reforms and Gender Equality in Schools,* Manchester, Equal Opportunities Commission

Arnot M., Gray J., James M., Rudduck J. with Dunveen, G. (1998) *Recent Research on Gender and Educational Performance*, OFSTED

Babbie, E. (1989) *The Practice of Social Research*, 5th edn, Belmont, Wadsworth

Bachrach, P. and Baratz, M.S. (1969) 'Two faces of power' and 'Decisions and nondecisions', in R. Bell *et al.* (eds), *Political Power: A Reader in Theory and Research*, pp. 94–9, New York, Free Press

Balibar, E. and Wallerstein, I. (1991) *Race, Nation and Class: Ambiguous Identities*, London, Verso

Ball, S. J .(1981) *Beachside Comprehensive*, Cambridge, Cambridge University Press

Ball, S. J. (1990) *Politics and Policy-Making in Education*, London, Routledge

Ball, S. J. (1994) *Educational Reform: A Critical and Post-structural Approach*, Buckingham, Open University Press

Banks, M., Bates, I., Breakwell, G. *et al.* (1992) *Careers and Identities*, Milton Keynes, Open University Press

Banton, M. (1967) *Race Relations,* London, Tavistock

Banton, M. (1983) *Racial and Ethnic Competition*, Cambridge, Cambridge University Press

Barker, C. (1997) *Global Television*, Oxford, Blackwell

Barker, D., Halman, L. and Vloet, A. (1993) *The European Values Study 1981–1990. Summary Report*, London/Tilburg, European Values Study

Barker, E. (1995) *New Religious Movements: A Practical Introduction*, London, HMSO

Barker, M. (1981) *The New Racism*, London, Junction Books

Barker, M. (1993) 'Seeing how far you can see: on being a fan of *2000 AD*', in D. Buckingham (ed.), *Reading Audiences: Young People and the Media*, Manchester, University of Manchester Press

Barker, M. and Petley, J. (eds) (1997) *Ill Effects: the Media /Violence Debate*, London, Routledge

Barker, M. and Petley, J. (eds) (1998) *Ill Effects: the Media /Violence Debate*, 2nd edn, London, Routledge

Barnet, R. and Cavanagh, J. (1994) *Global Dreams*, New York, Simon & Schuster

Barrett, M. (1980/1988) *Women's Oppression Today,* London, Verso

Barrett, M. and McIntosh, M. (1982) *The Anti-Social Family*, London, Verso

Barthes, R. (1953/1967) *Writing Degree Zero*, London, Cape

Barthes, R. (1957/1973) *Mythologies*, London, Paladin

Bartley, M., Power, C., Blane, D., Davey-Smith, G. and Shipley, M. (1994) 'Birth weight and later socio-economic disadvantage: evidence from the 1958 British cohort study', *British Medical Journal*, **309**: 1475–8

Baudrillard, J. (1983) *Simulations,* New York, Semiotext

Baudrillard, J. (1988) *Selected Writings* (M. Poster, ed.), Cambridge, Polity

Bauman, Z. (1992) *Intimations of Postmodernity,* London, Routledge

Beck, U. (1992) *Risk Society*, London, Sage

Becker, H. (1963) *Outsiders: Studies in The Sociology of Deviance,* Basingstoke, Macmillan

Beckford, J. (1985) *Cult Controversies*, London, Tavistock

Beckford, J. (1989) *Religion and Advanced Industrial Society*, London, Unwin Hyman

Bell, C. and Newby, H. (1976) 'Husbands and wives: the dynamics of the deferential dialectic', in D. Leonard Barker and S. Allen (eds), *Dependence and Exploitation in Work and Marriage,* London, Hutchinson

Bellah, R. (1967) 'Civil religion in America', *Daedalus*, **96**: 1–21

Beneria, L. and Feldman, S. (eds) (1992) *Unequal Burden*, Boulder, CO, Westview

Ben-Tovim, G., Gabriel, J., Law, I. and Stredder, K. (1986) *The Local Politics of Race*, London, Macmillan

Bendix, R. (1956) *Work and Authority in Industry,* New York, Wiley & Sons

Bendix, R. and Lipset, S.M. (1967) 'Karl Marx's theory of social classes', in R. Bendix and S. Lipset (eds), *Class, Status and Power*, London, Routledge

Benzeval, M., Judge, K. and Whitehead, M. (eds) (1995) *Tackling Inequalities in Health: An Agenda for Action*, London, King's Fund

Berelson, B. (1952) *Content Analysis in Communication Research*, New York, Free Press

Berger, P. and Kellner, H. (1964) 'Marriage and the construction of reality', *Diogenes*, **46**(1): 1–23; reprinted in B. Cosin *et al.* (1971), *School and Society*, Open University Course Reader, London, Routledge & Kegan Paul

Berger, P. and Luckman, T (1967) *The Social Construction of Reality*, London, Penguin

Berkman, L. and Syme, S. (1979) 'Social networks and host resistance and mortality: a nine year follow-up of Almeda residents', *American Journal of Epidemiology*, **109**: 186–204

Berliner, L. (1990) 'Domestic violence: a humanist or feminist issue?', *Journal of Interpersonal Violence*, **50**: 128–9

Bernard, J. (1972) *The Future of Marriage*, Harmondsworth: Penguin

Bernard, J. (1982) *The Future of Marriage*, 2nd edn, Newhaven, CN, Yale University Press

Bernardes, J. (1997) *Family Studies: An Introduction*, London, Routledge

Bernstein, B. (1975) *Class, Codes and Control*, Vols 1–3, London, Routledge

Beynon, J. (1985) *Initial Encounters in the Secondary School*, London, Falmer Press

Beynon, J. and Atkinson, P. (1984) 'Pupils as data gatherers: mucking and sussing' in S. Delamont (ed.) *Readings on Interaction in the Classroom*, pp. 255–72, London, Methuen

Blaikie, N. (1993) *Approaches to Social Inquiry*, London, Polity

Blau, P. and Duncan, O. (1967) *The American Occupational Structure*, New York, Wiley

Blood, R. and Woolfe, D. (1960) *Husbands and Wives*, New York, Free Press

Blumer, H. (1967) *Symbolic Interactionism*, New York, Prentice Hall

Bogatz, G. and Ball, S. (1971) *The Second Year of Sesame Street: A Continuing Evaluation*, Princeton, Educational Testing Service

Bonal, X. (1995) 'Curriculum change as a form of educational policy legitimation: the case of Spain: international studies in sociology of education', **5**(2): 203–20

Bott, E. (1971) *Family and Social Network*, London, Tavistock

Bottoms, A. and Xanthos, P. (1989) 'A tale of two estates', in D. Downes (ed.), *Crime and the City*, London, Macmillan

Bourdieu, P. (1990) *In Other Words*, Cambridge, Polity

Bowe, R. and Ball, S. with Gold, A. (1992) *Reforming Education and Changing Schools*, London, Routledge

Bowles, S. and Gintis, H. (1976) *Schooling in Capitalist America*, London, Routledge & Kegan Paul

Boyer, R. and Drache, D. (1996) *States Against Markets*, London, Routledge

Boyer, R. and Durand, J. (1997) *After Fordism*, London, Macmillan

Bradley, H. (1996) *Fractured Identities*, Cambridge, Polity

Brah, A. (1992) 'Difference, diversity and differentiation' in J. Donald and A. Rattansi (eds) *Culture and Difference*, London, Sage

Brah, A. (1994) '"Race" and "culture" in the gendering of labour markets: South Asian young women and the labour market', in H. Afshar and M. Maynard (eds), *The Dynamics of Race and Gender: Some Feminist Implications*, London, Taylor & Francis

Brah, A. (1996) *Cartographies of Diaspora, Contesting Identities*, London and New York, Routledge

Braithwaite, J. (1989) *Crime, Shame and Integration*, Cambridge, Cambridge University Press

Brannen, J. (1995) 'Young people and their contribution to household work', *Sociology*, **29**(2): 317–38

Brannen, J. (ed.) (1992) *Mixing Methods: Qualitative and Quantitative Research*, Aldershot, Gower

Brannen, J. and Moss, P. (1991) *Managing Mothers.* London, Unwin Hyman

Brannen, J. and O'Brien, M. (eds) (1994) *Children in Families*, London, Falmer

Brannen, J. and Wilson, G. (eds) (1987) *Give and Take in Families: Studies in Resource Distribution*, London, Allen & Unwin

Braverman, H. (1974) *Labor and Monopoly Capital*, New York, Monthly Review Press

Brecher, J. and Costello, T. (1994) *Global Village or Global Pillage: Economic Reconstruction from the Bottom Up*, Boston, South End Press

Broadfoot, P. (1996) *Education, Assessment and Society*, Buckingham, Open University Press

Brown, C. (1984) *Black and White Britain. The Third PSI Survey*, London, Heinemann Educational

Brown, C. (1992) '"Same difference": the persistence of racial disadvantage in the British employment market', in P. Braham, A. Rattansi and R. Skellington (eds), *Racism and Antiracism. Inequalities, Opportunities and Policies*, pp. 46–63, London and Newbury Park, Sage

Brown, C. and Gay, P. (1985) *Racial Discrimination: 17 Years After the Act*, London, Policy Studies Institute

Brown, G. and Harris, T. (1978) *The Social Origins of Depression*, London, Tavistock

Brown, P. (1989) 'Schooling for inequality', in B. Cosin, M. Flude and M. Hales (eds) *School, Work and Equality*, London, Hodder & Stoughton

Brown, P. and Lauder, H. (1991) 'Education, economy and social change', *International Studies in Sociology of Education*, 1: 3–23

Brown, P., Halsey, A., Lauder, H. and Stuart-Wells, A. (1997) 'The transformation of education and society: an introduction', in A. Halsey, H. Lauder, P. Brown and A. Stuart-Wells (eds) *Education: Culture, Economy, Society*, pp. 1–44, Oxford, Oxford University Press

Bruce, S. (1995) *Religion in Modern Britain*, Oxford, Oxford University Press

Bruce, S. (1996) *Religion in the Modern World: From Cathedrals to Cults*, Oxford, Oxford University Press

Bryan, B., Dadzie, S. and Scafe, S. (1985) *The Heart of the Race*, London: Virago

Bryman, A. (1995) *Disney and His Worlds*, London, Routledge

Buckley, M. (1989) *Women and Ideology in the Soviet Union*, Hemel Hempstead, Harvester Wheatsheaf

Burgess, R. (1998) Postgraduate education in Europe, Special Issue, *European Journal of Education*, (June)

Bury, M. (1982) 'Chronic illness as biographical disruption', *Sociology of Health and Illness*, 4: 167–82

Bury, M. (1997) *Health and Illness in a Changing Society*, London, Routledge

Butler, J. (1990) *Gender Trouble: Feminism and the Subversion of Identity*, London, Routledge

Butler, T. and Savage, M. (eds) (1996) *Social Change and the Middle Classes*, London, University College London Press

Calnan, M. and Williams, S. (1992) 'Images of scientific medicine', *Sociology of Health and Illness*, 14: 233–54

Caplan, L. (ed.) (1987) *Studies in Religious Fundamentalism*, London, Macmillan

Casanova, J. (1994) *Public Religions in the Modern World*, Chicago, University of Chicago Press

Castells, M. (1996) *The Rise of Network Society*, Oxford, Blackwell

Castells, M. (1997) *The Power of Identity*, Oxford, Blackwell

Castells, M. (1998) *End of the Millennium*, Oxford, Blackwell

Central Statistical Office (1993) *Social Trends*, **23**, London, HMSO

Central Statistical Office (1994) *Social Focus on Children*, London, HMSO
Central Statistical Office (1995) *Social Trends*, **25**, London, HMSO
Centre for Contemporary Cultural Studies (1982) *The Empire Strikes Back. Race and Racism in 70s' Britain*, London, Hutchinson
Chambers, D. (1986) 'The constraints of work and domestic schedules on women's leisure', *Leisure Studies*, **5**: 309–25
Chambliss, W. (1978) *On the Take: From Petty Crooks to Presidents*, Bloomington, Indiana University Press
Chase-Dunn, C. (1989) *Global Formation*, Oxford, Blackwell
Cheney, D. (1996) 'Those whom the immigration law has kept apart – let no one join together: a view on immigration incantation', in D. Jarrett-Macauley (ed.), *Reconstructing Womanhood, Reconstructing Feminism*, London and New York, Routledge
Clark, T. and Lipset, S. (1991) 'Are social classes dying?', *International Sociology*, **6**(4): 397–410
Clarke, R. (1980) 'Situational crime prevention: theory and practice', *British Journal of Criminology*, **20**(2): 136–47
Clarke, R. (1992) *Situational Crime Prevention: Successful Case Studies*, New York, Harvard & Heston
Cloward, R. and Ohlin, L. (1960) *Delinquency and Opportunity*, London, Collier Macmillan
Cockburn, C. (1983) *Brothers: Male Dominance and Technological Change*, London, Pluto Press
Cohen, A. (1955) *Delinquent Boys*, London, Free Press
Cohen, P. (1972) 'Subcultural conflict in working class community', *Working Papers in Cultural Studies* No. 2, Centre for Contemporary Cultural Studies, University of Birmingham
Cohen, P. (1997) *Rethinking the Youth Question*, Basingstoke, Macmillan
Cohen, R. (1997) *Global Diasporas*, London, UCL Press
Cohen, S. (1980) *Folk Devils and Moral Panics*, 2nd edn, Oxford, Martin Robertson
Cohen, S. (1985) *Visions of Social Control*, Cambridge, Polity
Coleman, D. (1988) 'Population', in A.H. Halsey (ed.), *British Social Trends Since 1900*, Basingstoke, Macmillan
Collins, P. (1990) *Black Feminist Thought*, London, Routledge
Comte, A. (1896) *The Positive Philosophy*, London, Bell and Sons
Condit, C. (1989) 'The rhetorical limits of polysemy', *Critical Studies in Mass Communications*, **6**: 103–22
Connell, R. (1995) *Masculinities*, Cambridge, Polity
Cooper, L. (1997) 'Myalgic encephalomyelitis and the medical encounter', *Sociology of Health and Illness*, **19**: 186–207
Corbin, J. and Strauss, A. (1991) 'Comeback; the process of overcoming disability', in G. Albrecht and J. Levy (eds), *Advances in Medical Sociology*, Vol. 2, Greenwich, JAI Press
Corbridge, S., Thrift, N. and Martin, R. (eds) (1995) *Money, Space, Power*, Oxford, Blackwell
Corner, J. (1991) 'Meaning, genre, context: the problematics of public knowledge in the new audience studies', in J. Curran and M. Gurevitch (eds), *Mass Media and Society*, London, Edward Arnold
Corner, J., Richardson, K. and Fenton, N. (1990) *Nuclear Reactions: Form and Response in Public Issue Television*, London, John Libbey
Corrigan, P. (1979) *Schooling the Smash Street Kids*, London, Macmillan
Coser, L. (1967) *Continuities in the Study of Social Conflict*, New York, Free Press
Crompton, R. (1993/1998) *Class and Stratification*, Cambridge, Polity

Crompton, R. (1996) ' The fragmentation of class analysis', *British Journal of Sociology*, **47**(1): 56–67

Crompton, R. and Gubbay, J. (1977) *Economy and Class Structure*, Basingstoke, Macmillan

Crompton, R. and Jones, G. (1984) *White-Collar Proletariat: Deskilling and Gender in the Clerical Labour Process*, Basingstoke, Macmillan

Crompton, R., Gallie, D. and Purcell, K. (eds) (1996) *Changing Forms of Employment*, London, Routledge

Crouch, C. and Streeck, W. (eds) (1997) *Political Economy of Modern Capitalism*, London, Sage

Curran, J. (1996) 'Rethinking mass communications', in J. Curran, D. Morley and V. Walkerdine (eds), *Cultural Studies and Communications*, London, Arnold

Dahl, R. (1957) 'The concept of power', *Behavioural Scientist*, **2**: 201–5

Dahl, R. (1958) 'A critique of the ruling élite model', *American Political Science Review*, **52**: 463–9

Dahl, R. (1961) *Who Governs? Democracy and Power in an American City*, New Haven and London, Yale University Press

Dahrendorf, R. (1969) *Class and Class Conflict in the Industrial Societies*, London, Routledge

Davey, B., Gray, A. and Seale, C. (eds) (1995) *Health and Disease: A Reader*, Buckingham, Open University Press

Davey Smith, G., Bartely, M. and Blane, D. (1991) 'Black on class and health: a reply to Strong', *Journal of Health and Medicine*, **13**: 350–57

Davey Smith, G., Blane, D. and Bartley, M. (1994) 'Explanations for socio-economic differentials in mortality; evidence from Britain and elsewhere', *European Journal of Public Health*, **4**: 131–44

Davey Smith, G., Hart C., Blane D. and Hawthorne, V. (1997) 'Lifetime socioeconomic position and mortality: prospective observational study', *British Medical Journal*, **314**: 547–52

David, M. (1991) 'Comparisons of "educational reform" in Britain and the USA: a new era?', *International Studies in Sociology of Education*, **1**: 87–109

Davie, G. (1994) *Religion in Britain Since 1945*, Oxford, Blackwell

Davie, G. (1995) 'Competing fundamentalisms', *Sociology Review*, **4**(4)

Davie, G. (1996) 'Religion and modernity: the work of Danièle Hervieu-Léger', in K. Flanagan and P. Jupp (eds), *Postmodernity, Sociology and Religion*, pp. 101–17, London, Macmillan

Davis, K., Leijenaar, M. and Oldersma, J. (eds) (1991) *The Gender of Power*, London, Sage

Deacon, D. (1996) 'Voluntary activity in a changing communication environment', *European Journal of Communication*, **11**(2): 173–98

Deacon, D., Fenton, N. and Bryman, A. (1999) 'From inception to reception: the natural history of a news item', *Media, Culture and Society*, **21**(1): 5–31

Deacon, D. and Golding, P. (1994) *Taxation and Representation: The Media, Political Communication and the Poll Tax*, London, John Libbey

Dean, M. (1998) 'Administering asceticism: reworking the ethical life of the unemployed citizen', in M. Dean and B. Hindess (eds), *Governing Australia. Studies in Contemporary Rationalities of Government*, pp. 87–107, Cambridge and Melbourne, Cambridge University Press

Delamont, S. (1981) 'All too familiar? A decade of classroom research', *Educational Analysis*, **3**(1): 69–83

Delamont, S. (1986) 'Beyond Flanders: the relationship of subject matter and individuality to classroom style', in M. Stubbs and S. Delamont (eds) *Explorations in Classroom Observation*, Chichester, Wiley

Delphy, C. (1994) 'Changing women in a changing Europe: is "difference" the future for feminism?', *Women's Studies International Forum*, **17**(2/3): 187–201

Delphy, C. and Leonard, D. (1992) *Familiar Exploitation: A New Analysis of Marriage in Contemporary Western Societies*, Oxford, Polity

Demerath, N. (1965) *Social Class in American Protestantism*, Chicago, Rand-McNally

Denscombe, M. (1994) *Sociology Update 1994*, Leicester, Olympus Books

Derrida, J. (1982) *Margins of Philosophy*, Chicago, University of Chicago Press

DfEE (1997) *DfEE News*, 26 June, London, DfEE

DfEE (1998) *Teaching: High Status, High Standards*, London, DfEE

Dicken, P. (1998) *Global Shift: Transforming the World Economy*, 3rd edn, London, Paul Chapman

Diesing, P. (1971) *Patterns of Discovery in the Social Sciences*, London, Routledge

Dobash, R. and Dobash, R. (1980) *Violence Against Wives*, Shepton Mallet, Open Books

Dobash, R.and Dobash, R. (1992) *Women, Violence and Social Change*, London, Routledge

Dobbelaere, K. (1981) 'Secularization: a multi-dimensional concept', *Current Sociology*, **29**(2)

Douglas, J. (1964) *The Home and the School*, London, MacGibbon & Kee

Douglas, J. (1977) *The Nude Beach*, Beverley Hills, Sage

Douglas, M. (1973) *Natural Symbols*, London, Barrie & Jenkins

Douglas, M. (1978) *Purity and Danger*, London, Routledge & Kegan Paul

Dowmunt, T. (ed.) (1993) *Channels of Resistance: Global Television and Local Empowerment*, BFI/Channel Four

Downes, D. (1966) *The Delinquent Solution*, London, Routledge & Kegan Paul

Downes, D. (1979) 'Praxis makes perfect: a critique of radical criminology', in D. Downes and P. Rock (eds), *Deviant Interpretations*, Oxford, Martin Robertson

Downes, D. (1993) *Employment Opportunities for Offenders*, London, Home Office

Downes, D. and Rock, P. (1988) *Understanding Deviance*, 2nd edn, Oxford, Oxford University Press

Drew, E., Emerek, R. and Mahon, E. (eds) (1998) *Women, Work and the Family in Europe*, London, Routledge

Duncan, S. and Edwards, R. (eds) (1997) *Single Mothers in an International Context: Mothers or Workers?* London, UCL Press

Duncombe, J. and Marsden, D. (1993) 'Love and intimacy: the gender division of emotion and "emotion work"', *Sociology*, **27**(2): 221–41

Dunne, G. (1997) 'Women are doing it for themselves: new models for the organization of work in partnerships'. Paper presented to the British Sociological Association Annual Conference, University of York

Dunning, J. (1993) *Multinational Enterprises and the Global Economy*, Wokingham, Addison-Wesley

Durkheim, E. (1893/1984) *The Division of Labour in Society*, Basingstoke, Macmillan

Durkheim, E. (1895/1982) *The Rules of Sociological Method*, Basingstoke, Macmillan

Durkheim, E. (1897/1952) *Suicide: A Study in Sociology*, London, Routledge & Kegan Paul

Durkheim, E. (1912/1976) *The Elementary Forms of Religious Life*, London, Allen & Unwin

Durkheim, E. (1956) *Education and Sociology*, New York, Free Press

Durning, A. (1992) *How Much is Enough?*, London, Earthscan

Dworkin, A. (1981) *Pornography*, London, Women's Press

Eames, N., Ben-Shlomo, Y. and Marmot, M. (1993) 'Social deprivation and premature mortality: regional comparison across England', *British Medical Journal*, **307**: 1097–102

*Economist* (1992) 19 December: 21–2

Edgell, S. (1980) *Middle Class Couples*, London, Allen & Unwin

Edgell, S. and Duke, V. (1991) *A Measure of Thatcherism*, London, HarperCollins Academic

Edholm, F. (1982) 'The unnatural family', in E. Whitelegg, M. Arnot, E. Bartels, V. Beechey and L. Birke (eds), *The Changing Experience of Women*, Oxford, Martin Robertson

Edwards, R. (1993) 'The inevitable future: post-Fordism in work and learning', in R. Edwards, S. Sieminski and D. Zeldin (eds) *Adult Learners, Education and Training*, Buckingham, Open University Press

Ekins, P. (1992) *A New World Order: Grassroots Movements for Global Change*, London, Routledge

Ell, K. (1996) 'Social networks, social support and coping with serious illness: the family connection', *Social Science and Medicine,* **42**: 173–83

Elliott, B. and Maclennan, D. (1994) 'Education, modernity and neo-conservative school reform in Canada, Britain and the US', *British Journal of Sociology of Education*, **15**(2): 165–85

Elliott, P. (1974) 'Uses and gratifications research: a critique and a sociological alternative', in J. Blumler and E. Katz (eds), *The Uses of Mass Communications: Current Perspectives on Gratifications Research*, London, Sage

Elman, R. (ed.) (1996) *Sexual Politics and the European Union*, Ford, Berghahn Books

Emmison, M. (1991) 'Wright and Goldthorpe: Constructing the agenda of class analysis', in J. Baxter, M. Emmison and J. Western, *Class Analysis and Contemporary Australia*, Basingstoke and Sydney, Macmillan

Emmison, M. and Western, M. (1990) 'Social class and social identity', *Sociology,* **24**: 241–54

Engels, F. (1940) *The Origins of the Family, Private Property, and the State,* London, Lawrence & Wishart

Epstein, D. (ed) (1994) *Challenging Gay and Lesbian Inequalities In Education,* Buckingham, Open University Press

Erikson, R. and Goldthorpe, J. (1988) 'Women at class crossroads', *Sociology,* **22**: 545–53

Erikson, R. and Goldthorpe, J. (1992) *The Constant Flux,* Oxford, Clarendon Press

Esping-Andersen, G. (ed.) (1997) *Welfare States in Transition,* London, Sage

Eurelings-Bontekoe, E., Diekstra, R. and Verschuur, M. (1995) 'Psychological distress, social support and support seeking: a prospective study among primary mental health care patients', *Social Science and Medicine,* **40**:1083–9

Farrington, D. (1997) 'Human development and criminal careers', in M. Maguire, R. Morgan and R. Reiner (eds), *The Oxford Handbook of Criminology*, 2nd edn, pp. 361–408, Oxford, Clarendon Press

Featherstone, M. (ed.) (1990) *Global Culture: Nationalism, Globalization and Identity*, London, Sage

Fekete, L. and Webber, F. (1994) *Inside Racist Europe,* London, Institute of Race Relations

Felson, M. (1994) *Crimes and Everyday Life,* Thousand Oaks, Pine Forge

Fenton, N., Bryman, A. and Deacon, D. with Birmingham, P. (1998) *Mediating Social Science*, London, Sage

Fenton, N., Deacon, D., Bryman, A. and Birmingham, P. (1995) *Social Science the Media and the Public Sphere*. Paper presented at the European Sociological Association Conference, Budapest

Ferlie, E., Ashburner, L., Fitzgerald, L. and Pettigrew, A. (1996) *The New Public Management in Action,* Oxford, Oxford University Press

Finch, J. (1983) *Married to the Job: Wives' Incorporation into Men's Work*, London, George Allen & Unwin

Finch, J. and Mason, J. (1993) *Negotiating Family Responsibilities*, London, Routledge

Fiske, J. and Hartley, J. (1978) *Reading Television*, London, Methuen

Fitzpatrick, R., Newman, S., Archer, R. and Shipley, M. (1991) 'Social support, disability and depression: a longitudinal study of rheumatoid arthritis', *Social Science and Medicine*, **33**: 605–11

Floud, J. and Halsey, A. (1961) *Education, Economy and Society: A Reader in the Sociology of Education*, Milton Keynes, Open University Press

Foddy, W. (1993) *Constructing Questions for Interviews and Questionnaires*, Cambridge, Cambridge University Press.

Foreman-Peck, J. (1995) *A History of the World Economy: International Economic Relations since 1850*, 2nd edn, London, Harvester Wheatsheaf

Forrester, D., Chatterton, M. and Pease, K. (1988) *The Kirkholt Burglary Prevention Demonstration Project*, London, Home Office

Foster, P. (1992) 'Teacher attitudes and Afro/Caribbean educational attainment', *Oxford Review of Education*, **8**(3)

Foster, P., Gomm, R. and Hammersley, M. (1996) *Constructing Educational Inequality*, London, Falmer Press

Foucault, M. (1973) *The Birth of the Clinic*, London, Tavistock

Foucault, M. (1979) *Discipline and Punish*, Harmondsworth, Penguin

Foucault, M. (1980) *Power/Knowledge*, Brighton, Harvester

Foucault, M. (1982) 'The subject and power', in H. Dreyfus and P. Rabinow (eds), *Michel Foucault: Beyond Structuralism and Hermeneutics*, pp. 208–26, Brighton, Harvester

Foucault, M. (1984) *The Foucault Reader* (P. Rabinow, ed.), London, Penguin

Foucault, M. (1986) *The Birth of the Clinic*, London, Routledge

Foucault, M. (1988) 'The ethic of care for the self as a practice of freedom', in J. Bernauer and D. Rasmussen (eds), *The Final Foucault*, pp. 1–20, Boston, MA, MIT Press

Foucault, M. (1991) 'Governmentality', in G. Burchell, C. Gordon and P. Miller (eds), *The Foucault Effect*, pp. 87–104, Hemel Hempstead, Harvester Wheatsheaf

Foucault, M. (1997) *Ethics: Subjectivity and Truth*, (P. Rabinow, ed.), New York, New Press

Fox, A. (1985) *History and Heritage: The Social Origins of the British Industrial Relations System*, London, Allen & Unwin

Fox, A. and Adelstein, A. (1978) 'Occupational mortality: work or way of life?', *Journal of Epidemiology and Community Health*, **32**: 73–8

Fox, A., Goldblatt, P. and Jones, D. (1986) 'Social class mortality differentials: artefact, selection or life circumstances', in R. Wilkinson (ed.), *Class and Health: Research and Longitudinal Data*, London, Tavistock

Fraser, N. (1989) 'Foucault on modern power: empirical insights and normative confusions', in N. Fraser, *Unruly Practices: Power, Discourse and Gender in Contemporary Social Theory*, pp. 17–34, Cambridge, Polity

Freidson, E. (1970) *Profession of Medicine: A Study of the Sociology of Applied Knowledge*, Chicago, University of Chicago Press

Friedan, B. (1965) *The Feminine Mystique*, Harmondsworth, Penguin

Friedman, J. (1990) 'Being in the world: globalization and localization.' in M. Featherstone (ed.) op. cit.: 311–28

Friedman, J. (1995) 'Where we stand: a decade of world city research' in P. Knox and P. Taylor (eds) *World Cities in A World System*, Cambridge, Cambridge University Press

Frobel, F., Heinrichs, J. and Kreye, O. (1980) *The New International Division of Labour*, Cambridge, Cambridge University Press

Fryer, P. (1984) *Staying Power: The History of Black People in Britain*, London, Pluto

Fuller, M. (1983) 'Qualified criticism, critical qualifications', in L. Barton and S. Walker (eds) *Race, Class and Education*, Beckenham, Croom Helm

Gabriel, J. (1994) *Racism, Culture, Markets,* London and New York, Routledge

Gallie, D. (1994) 'Are the unemployed an underclass?', *Sociology,* **26**: 737–57

Galton, M. and Delamont, S. (1980) 'The first weeks of middle school', in A. Hargreaves and L. Tickle (eds) *Middle Schools: Origins, Ideology and Practice*, pp. 207–27, London, Harper & Row

Gandy, O. (1982) *Beyond Agenda Setting: Information Subsidies and Public Policy*, Norwood, NJ, Ablex

Garfinkel, H. (1984) *Studies in Ethnomethodology,* Cambridge, Polity

Garland, D. (1990) *Punishment and Modern Society: A Study in Social Theory,* Oxford, Oxford University Press

Gavron, H. (1966) *The Captive Wife*, Harmondsworth, Penguin

Gerbner, G. (1969) 'Toward "cultural indicators": the analysis of mass mediated public message systems', W.H. Allen (ed.), *AV Communication Review,* **17**(2): 137–48

Gereffi, G. (1995) 'Global production systems and Third World development', in B. Stallings (ed.), *Global Change, Regional Response*, pp. 100–42, Cambridge, Cambridge University Press

Gereffi, G. and Korzeniewicz, M. (eds) (1994) *Commodity Chains and Global Capitalism,* Westport, CT: Praeger

Gerhardt, U. (1987) 'Parsons, role theory and health interaction', in G. Scambler (ed.), *Sociological Theory and Medical Sociology,* London, Tavistock

Gerhardt, U. (1989) *Ideas about Illness,* Basingstoke, Macmillan

Gibson-Graham, J. (1996) *The End of Capitalism (as we knew it): A Feminist Critique of Political Economy*, Oxford, Blackwell

Giddens, A. (1971) *Capitalism and Modern Social Theory,* Cambridge, Cambridge University Press

Giddens, A. (1973/1981) *The Class Structure of the Advanced Societies,* London, Hutchinson

Giddens, A. (1976) *New Rules of Sociological Method*, London, Hutchinson

Giddens, A. (1984) *The Constitution of Society,* Cambridge, Polity

Giddens, A. (1990a) 'Structuration theory and social analysis', in J. Clark, C. Mogdil and S. Mogdil (eds), *Anthony Giddens: Consensus and Controversy*, Basingstoke, Falmer

Giddens, A. (1990b) *The Consequences of Modernity*, Cambridge, Polity

Giddens, A. (1991a) 'Structuration theory: past, present and future', in G. Bryant, G. Jary and D. Jary (eds), *Giddens' Theory of Structuration*, London, Routledge

Giddens, A. (1991b) *Modernity and Self Identity: Self and Society in the Late Modern Age*, Cambridge, Polity

Giddens, A. (1992) *The Transformation of Intimacy*, Cambridge, Polity

Giddens, A. and Turner, J. (eds) (1987) *Social Theory Today,* Cambridge, Polity

Gill, O. (1977) *Luke Street: Housing Policy, Conflict and the Creation of Deliquent Areas,* London, Macmillan

Gillborn, D. (1990) *'Race', Ethnicity and Education*, London, Unwin Hyman

Gilroy, P. (1987) *There Ain't No Black In the Union Jack. The Cultural Politics of Race and Nation*, London, Hutchinson

Gilroy, P. (1992) 'The end of antiracism', in J. Donald and A. Rattansi (eds) *Race, Culture and Difference*, London, Sage

Gitlin, T. (1979) 'Prime-time ideology: the hegemonic process in television entertainment', *Social Problems*, **26**: 251–66

Glass, D. (ed) (1954) *Social Mobility in Britain*, London, Routledge & Kegan Paul

Glass, T. and Maddox, G. (1992) 'The quality and quantity of social support: stroke recovery as a psycho-social transition', *Social Science and Medicine,* **34:** 1249–61

Godin, H. and Daniel, Y. (1943) *La France, Pays de Mission,* Paris, Cerf

Goffman, E. (1968) *Stigma: Notes on the Management of Spoiled Identity,* London, Penguin

Goffman, E. (1969) *The Presentation of the Self in Everyday Life,* London, Penguin

Goffman, E. (1972) *Interaction Ritual,* London, Penguin

Goffman, E. (1983) 'The interaction order', *American Sociological Review,* **48**

Goffman, E. (1991) *Asylums: Essays on the Social Situation of Mental Patients and Other Inmates,* London, Penguin

Golding, P. and Murdock, G. (1978) 'Theories of communication and theories of society', *Communication Research,* **5**(3): 390–456

Golding, P. and Murdock, G. (1991) 'Culture, communications and political economy', in J. Curran and M. Gurevitch (eds), *Mass Media and Society,* London, Edward Arnold

Goldthorpe, J. (1982) 'On the service class: its formation and future', in *Classes and the Division of Labour*, A. Giddens and G. Mackenzie (eds), Cambridge, Cambridge University Press

Goldthorpe, J. (1983) 'Women and class analysis: in defence of the conventional view', *Sociology,* **17**(4): 465–78

Goldthorpe, J. (1987) *Social Mobility and Class Structure in Modern Britain,* 2nd edn, Oxford, Clarendon Press

Goldthorpe, J. (1996) 'The service class revisited', in T. Butler and M. Savage (eds), *Social Change and the Middle Classes,* London, University College London Press

Goldthorpe, J. and Marshall, G. (1992) 'The promising future of class analysis', *Sociology,* **26**(3): 381–400

Goldthorpe, J., Lockwood, D., Bechhofer, F. and Platt, J. (1968) *The Affluent Worker: Industrial Attitudes and Behaviour,* Cambridge, Cambridge University Press

Goldthorpe, J., Lockwood, D., Bechhofer, F. and Platt, J. (1969) *The Affluent Worker in the Class Structure,* Cambridge, Cambridge University Press

Goldthorpe, J. with Llewellyn, C. and Payne, C. (1980/1987) *Social Mobility and Class Structure in Great Britain,* Oxford, Clarendon Press

Goode, W. and Hatt, P. (1952) *Methods in Social Research*, New York, McGraw-Hill

Goodman, A., Johnson, P. and Webb, S. (1997) *Inequality in the UK*, Oxford, Oxford University Press

Gordon, S. (1992) *History and Philosophy of Social Science,* London, Routledge

Gorz, A. (1982) *Farewell to the Working Class,* London, Pluto

Gottfredson, M. and Hirschi, T. (1990) *A General Theory of Crime,* Stamford, Stamford University Press

Grace, G. (1991) 'Welfare Labourism versus the New Right: the struggle in New Zealand's education policy', *International Studies in Sociology of Education,* **1**: 25–41

Graham, H. (1987a) 'Women's poverty and caring', in C. Glendinning and J. Millar (eds), *Women and Poverty in Britain*, Brighton, Wheatsheaf

Graham, H. (1987b) 'Women's smoking and family health', *Social Science and Medicine,* **25**: 47–57

Graham, H. (1994) 'Gender and class as dimensions of smoking behaviour in Britain: insights from a survey of mothers', *Social Science and Medicine,* **38**: 691–8

Gramsci, A. (1971) *Selections from the Prison Notebooks,* London, Lawrence & Wishart

Gramsci, A. (1978) *Selections from Cultural Writings*, Cambridge, MA, Harvard University Press

Gray, A. (1992) *Video Playtime,* London, Routledge

Green, A. (1997) 'Educational achievement in centralised and decentralised systems' in A. Halsey, H. Lauder, P. Brown and A. Stuart-Wells (eds) *Education: Culture, Economy, Society*, pp. 283–98, Oxford, Oxford University Press

Green, D. (ed.) (1988) *Acceptable Inequalities? Essays on the Pursuit of Equality*, London, Institute of Economic Affairs

Gregson, N. and Lowe, M. (1994) 'Waged domestic labour and the renegotiation of the domestic division of labour within dual career households', *Sociology*, **28**(1): 55–78

Habermas, J. (1989) *The Theory of Communicative Action:* Volume 2, Cambridge, Polity

Hagan, J., Simpson, J. and Gillis, A. (1979) 'The sexual stratification of social control: a gender based perspective on crime and delinquency', *British Journal of Criminology*, **30**

Hall, C. (1992) *White, Male and Middle Class: Explorations in Feminism and History*, Oxford, Polity

Hall, S. (1997) 'The work of representation' in S. Hall (ed.) *Representation: Cultural Representations and Signifying Practices*, London, Sage/Open University

Hall, S., Critcher, C., Jefferson, T., Clarke, J. and Roberts, B. (1978) *Policing the Crisis: Mugging, The State and Law and Order*, London, Hutchinson

Hall, S. (1977) 'Culture, media and the "ideological effect"', in J. Curran, M. Gurevitch and J. Woolacott (eds), *Mass Communication and Society*, London, Edward Arnold

Hall, S. (1980) 'Encoding/decoding', in S. Hall, D. Hobson, A. Lowe, and P. Willis (eds), *Culture, Media, Language*, London, Hutchinson

Hall, S. and du Gay, P. (eds) (1996) *Questions of Cultural Identity*, London, Sage

Hall, S., Held, D. and McGrew, T. (eds) (1992) *Modernity and its Futures*, Cambridge, Polity

Hall, S. and Jaques, M. (eds) (1989) *New Times*, London, Lawrence & Wishart

Hall, S. and Jefferson, T. (eds) (1976) *Resistance Through Rituals: Youth Subcultures in Post-war Britain*, London, Hutchinson

Halsey, A. (1977) 'Towards meritocracy? The case of Britain', in J. Karabel and A. Halsey (eds), *Power and Ideology in Education*, New York, Oxford University Press

Halsey, A., Health, A. and Ridge, J. (1980) *Origins and Destinations: Family, Class and Education in Modern Britain*, Oxford, Clarendon Press

Halsey, A., Lauder, H., Brown, P. and Stuart-Wells, A. (eds) (1997) *Education: Culture, Economy, Society*, Oxford, Oxford University Press

Halson, J. (1989) 'The sexual harassment of young women', in L. Holly (ed.), *Girls and Sexuality*, Milton Keynes, Open University Press

Hamilton, M. (1994) *The Sociology of Religion*, London, Routledge

Hammersley, M. (1990) *Reading Ethnographic Research*, Harlow, Longman

Hammersley, M. (1992) *What's Wrong With Ethnography?* London, Routledge

Hanmer, J. (1990) 'Men, power and the exploitation of women', in J. Hearn and D. Morgan (eds), *Men, Masculinities and Social Theory*, London, Unwin Hyman

Hanmer, J., Radford, J. and Stanko, E. (eds) (1989) *Women, Policing and Male Violence*, London, Routledge

Hannaford, I. (1996) *Race. The History of an Idea in the West*, Baltimore and London, The Johns Hopkins University Press

Hargreaves, A. (1994) *Changing Teachers, Changing Times: Teachers' Work and Culture in the Postmodern Age*, London, Cassell

Hargreaves, D. (1967) *Social Relations in a Secondary School*, London, Routledge & Kegan Paul

Harris, C. (1990) *Kinship*, London, Routledge

Harris, N. (1996) *The New Untouchables: Immigration and the New World Worker*, London, Penguin

Hartmann, H. (1976) 'Capitalism, patriarchy and job segregation by sex', *Signs*, **1**: 137–68

Hartmann, P. and Husband, C. (1973) 'The mass media and racial conflict', in S. Cohen and J. Young (eds), *The Manufacture of News*, London, Constable

Harvey, D. (1989) *The Condition of Postmodernity*, Oxford, Blackwell

Haywood, C. and Mac an Ghaill, M. (1996) 'Schooling masculinities', in M. Mac an Ghaill (ed.) *Understanding Masculinities: Social Relations and Cultural Arenas*, pp. 50–60, Buckingham, Open University Press

Heaphy, B., Donovan, C. and Weeks, J. (1997) 'Sex, money and the kitchen sink: power in same sex couple relationships'. Paper presented to the British Sociological Association Annual Conference, University of York

Hearn, J. (1992) *Men in the Public Eye,* London, Routledge

Hearn, J. (1996) 'Men's violence to known women: men's accounts and men's policy developments', in B. Fawcett, B. Featherstone, J. Hearn and C. Toft (eds), *Violence and Gender Relations,* London, Sage

Heath, A. (1981) *Social Mobility*, London, Fontana

Heath, A. and Britten, N. (1984) 'Women's jobs do make a difference', *Sociology,* 18(4): 475–90

Heath, A. and Clifford, P. (1996) 'Class inequalities and educational reform in twentieth-century Britain', in D. Lee and B. Turner (eds) *Conflict about Class: Debating Inequality in Late Industrialism*, pp. 209–24, London, Longman

Heath, A., Curtice, J., Jowell, R., Evans, G., Field, J. and Witherspoon, S. (1991) *Understanding Political Change,* Oxford, Pergamon

Heelas, P. (1996) *The New Age Movement*, Oxford, Blackwell

Held, D. (1995) 'Democracy, the nation state and the global system' in D. Held (ed.) *Political Theory Today*, Cambridge, Polity

Herman, E. and Chesney, R. (1997) *The Global Media: The New Missionaries of Corporate Capitalism*, London, Cassell

Hervieu-Léger, D. (1986) *Vers un Nouveau Christianisme*. Paris, Cerf

Hervieu-Léger, D. (1993) *La Religion pour Mémoire*, Paris, Cerf

Hesse, B., Rai, D., Bennett, C. and McGilchrist, P. (1992) *Beneath the Surface: Racial Harassment,* Aldershot, Avebury

Hester, M., Kelly, L. and Radford, J. (eds) (1996) *Women, Violence and Male Power,* Buckingham, Open University Press

Hester, S. and Elgin, P. (1992) *A Sociology of Crime*, London, Routledge

Higgins, P. (1980) *Outsiders in a Hearing World: A Sociology of Deafness,* London, Sage

Hillman, M., Adams, J. and Whitelegg, J. (1990) *One False Move: A Study of Children's Independent Mobility,* London, Policy Studies Institute

Hindess, B. (1987) *Politics and Class Analysis,* Oxford, Blackwell

Hindess, B. (1995) *Discourses of Power: From Hobbes to Foucault*, Oxford, Blackwell

Hindess, B. (1996), 'Liberalism, socialism and democracy: variations on a governmental theme', in A. Barry, T. Osborne and N. Rose (eds), *Foucault and Political Reason: Liberalism, New-liberalism and Rationalities of Government*, pp. 65–80, London, University College London Press

Hirschi, T. (1969) *Causes of Delinquency,* Berkley, University of California Press

Hirst, P. and Thompson, G. (1996) *Globalization in Question: The International Economy and the Possibilities of Governance*, Cambridge, Polity

Hobbs, D. (1997) 'Criminal collaboration', in M. Maguire, R. Morgan and R. Reiner (eds), *The Oxford Handbook of Criminology,* Oxford, Clarendon Press

Hochschild, A. (1989) *The Second Shift*, London, Piatkus

Hollingsworth, J. and Boyer, R. (1997) *Contemporary Capitalism: The Embeddedness of Institutions,* Cambridge, Cambridge University Press

Holmes, C. (1988) *John Bull's Island: Immigration and British Society,* London, Macmillan

Holmes, C. (ed.) (1978) *Immigrants and Minorities in British Society*, London, Allen & Unwin

Holton, R. (1998) *Globalization and the Nation State*, London, Mcmillan

Hood, R. (1996) *The Death Penalty,* 2nd edn, Oxford, Oxford University Press

Hovland, C. (1959) 'Reconciling conflicting results derived from experimental and survey studies of attitude change', *The American Psychologist*, **14**

Hunter, I. (1988) *Culture and Government. The Emergence of Literary Education*, Basingstoke, Macmillan

Hunter, I. (1994) *Rethinking the School*, Sydney, Allen & Unwin

Hunter, J. (1991) 'Fundamentalism and social science', *Religion and Social Order*, **1**: 149–63

Hyman, R. (1975) *Industrial Relations: A Marxist Introduction*, London, Macmillan

Illich, I. (1976) *Limits to Medicine: Medical Nemesis: the Expropriation of Health*, London, Calder & Boyars

Illsley, R. (1986) 'Occupational class, selection and the production of inequalities in health', *Quarterly Journal of Social Affairs*, **2**: 151–65

*International Sociology* (1993) *The Debate on Class*, 8(3): 1

Jackson, B. and Marsden, D. (1962) *Education and the Working Class*, London, Routledge & Kegan Paul

Jackson, S. (1992) 'Towards a historical sociology of housework: a materialist feminist analysis', *Women's Studies International Forum*, **15**(2): 153–72

Jackson, S. (1997) 'Women and the family', in D. Richardson and V. Robinson (eds), *Introducing Women's Studies*, 2nd edn, London, Macmillan

Jackson, S. (1998) 'Theorizing gender and sexuality', in S. Jackson and J. Jones (eds), *Contemporary Feminist Theories*, Edinburgh, Edinburgh University Press

Jackson, S. and Moores, S. (eds) (1995) *The Politics of Domestic Consumption: Critical Readings*, Hemel Hempstead, Prentice Hall/Harvester Wheatsheaf

James, M. (1994) 'Hysteria', in C. Seale and S. Pattison (eds) *Medical Knowledge: Doubt and Certainty*, Buckingham, Open University Press

James, O. (1997) *Britain on the Couch*, London, Hutchinson

Jameson, F. (1991) *Postmodernism, or, the Cultural Logic of Late Capitalism*, London, Verso

Jameson, F. and Miyoshi, M. (eds) (1998) *The Cultures of Globalization*, Durham, Duke University Press

Jasinski, J., Williams, L. and Finkelhor, D. (eds) (1998) *Partner Violence. A Comprehensive Review of 20 Years of Research*, London, Sage

Jeffrey, R. (1979) 'Normal rubbish: deviant patients in casualty departments', *Sociology of Health and Illness*, **1**: 90–108

Jensen, K. (1990) 'The politics of polysemy: television news, everyday consciousness and political action', *Media, Culture and Society*, **12**: 57–77

Jessop, B. (1994) 'Post-Fordism and the state', in A. Amin (ed.) *Post-Fordism*, pp. 251–79, Oxford, Blackwell

Jobling, R. (1988) 'The experience of psoriasis under treatment', in M. Bury and R. Anderson (eds), *Living with Chronic Illness: the Experience of Patients and their Families*, London, Unwin Hyman

Jobson, R., Bingham, G., Whitehouse, J. *et al.* (1996) 'Crowcroft Park Primary School' in National Commission on Education (eds) *Success Against the Odds*, pp. 43–68, London, Routledge

Johnson, C. (1982) *MITI and the Japanese Miracle*, Stanford, Stanford University Press

Joly, D. and Cohen, R. (eds) (1989) *Reluctant Hosts: Europe and its Refugees*, Aldershot, Avebury

Jones, A. (1993) 'Becoming a "girl": post-structuralist suggestions for educational research', *Gender and Education*, **5**(2)

Jones, T. (1993) *Britain's Ethnic Minorities*, London, Policy Studies Institute

Jones, T., Maclean, B. and Young, J. (1986) *The Islington Crime Survey*, Aldershot, Gower

Joseph Rowntree Foundation (1995) *Income and Wealth: Report of the Joseph Rowntree Foundation Inquiry Group*, Vol. 1 and 2, York, Joseph Rowntree Foundation

Joyce, P. (ed.) (1995) *Class*, Oxford, Oxford University Press

Kaplan, H. (1991) 'Social psychology of the immune system: a conceptual framework and review of the literature', *Social Science and Medicine*, **33**: 909–23

Kaplan, L. (ed.) (1988) *Fundamentalism in a Comparative Perspective*, Amherst, University of Massachusetts Press

Kapstein, E. (1994) *Governing the Global Economy*, Cambridge, MA, Harvard University Press

Kay, D. and Miles, R. (1992) *Refugees or Migrant Workers? The Recruitment of Displaced Persons for British Industry, 1946–1951*, London, Routledge

Keddie, N. (1971) 'Classroom knowledge', in M. Young (ed.) *Knowledge and Control*, London, Collier Macmillan

Kelling, G. and Coles, C. (1997) *Fixing Broken Windows*, New York, Free Press

Kellner, D. (1995) *Media Culture*, London, Routledge

Kelly, L. (1988) *Surviving Sexual Violence*, Oxford, Polity

Kelly, M. (1992) *Colitis*, London, Tavistock/Routledge

Kelly, M. and Field, D. (1998) 'Conceptualising chronic illness', in D. Field and S. Taylor (eds), *Sociological Perspectives on Health, Illness and Health Care*, Oxford, Blackwell Science

Kennedy Bergen, R. (ed.) (1998) *Issues in Intimate Violence*, London, Sage

Kenway, J. (1993) 'Marketing education in the postmodern age', *Journal of Education Policy*, **8**(2): 105–22

Kepel, G. (1994) *The Revenge of God*, Cambridge, Polity

Kerr, C., Dunlop, J., Harbison, G. and Myers, C. (1973) *Industrialism and Industrial Man*, London, Penguin

Kiernan, K. and Wicks, M. (1990) *Family Change and Future Policy*, London, Family Policy Studies Centre

King, A. (ed.) (1991) *Culture, Globalization and the World-System*, London, Macmillan

Kinsey, R. (1984) *The Merseyside Crime Survey: First Report*, Liverpool, Merseyside County Council

Kitzinger, J. (1993) 'Understanding AIDS: researching audience perceptions of Acquired Immune Deficiency Syndrome', in J. Eldridge (ed.), *Getting the Message: News, Truth and Power*, London, Routledge

Kitzinger, J. and Kitzinger, C. (1993) ' "Doing it": representations of lesbian sex', in G. Griffin (ed.), *Outwrite: Lesbianism and Popular Culture*, London, Pluto

Klein, R. (1988) 'Acceptable inequalities?', in D. Green (ed.), *Acceptable Inequalities? Essays on the Pursuit of Equality*, London, Institute of Economic Affairs

Komarovsky, M. (1962) *Blue-Collar Marriage*, New York, Random House

Komter, A. (1989) 'Hidden power in marriage', *Gender and Society*, **3**(2): 187–216

Kuhn, T. (1970) *The Structure of Scientific Revolutions*, Chicago, Chicago University Press

Kunda, G. (1992) *Engineering Culture: Control and Commitment in a High-Tech Corporation*, Philadelphia, Temple University Press

Lacey, C. (1970) *Hightown Grammar*, Manchester, Manchester University Press

Laing, R. (1971) *The Politics of the Family and Other Essays*, London, Tavistock

Lambert, A. (1976) 'The sisterhood', in M. Hammersley and P. Woods (eds) *The Process of Schooling*, pp. 152–9, London, Routledge & Kegan Paul

Lane, C. (1989) *Management and Labour in Europe*, Aldershot, Edward Elgar

Langford, W. (1998) *The Subject of Love*, London, Routledge

Langlois, R. and Robertson, P. (1995) *Firms, Markets and Economic Change*, London, Routledge

Lash, S. and Urry, J. (1987) *The End of Organized Capitalism*, Cambridge, Polity

Laslett, P. (1965) *The World We Have Lost*, London, Methuen

Laws, S. (1994) 'Undervalued families: standing up for single mothers', *Trouble and Strife*, **28**: 5–11

Layder, D. (1994) *Understanding Social Theory,* London, Sage

Lea, J. and Young, J. (1984) *What Is To Be Done About Law and Order?,* London, Penguin

Leach, E. (1967) *A Runaway World?,* London, BBC Publications

Lee, D. and Turner, B. (1996) *Conflicts over Class,* London, Longman

Lees, S. (1997) *Ruling Passions,* Buckingham, Open University Press

Lemert, E. (1961) *Social Pathology,* New York, McGraw-Hill

Lemert, E. (1967) *Human Deviance: Social Problems and Social Control,* Englewood Cliffs, Prentice Hall

Leonard, D. (1990) 'Persons in their own right: children and sociology in the UK', in L. Chisholm, P. Buchner, H.-H. Kruger and P. Brown (eds), *Childhood, Youth and Social Change: A Comparative Perspective*, London, Falmer

Lepkowska, D. (1999) 'Extra prep for boys who cannot write', Daily Express, 13 February

Lewis, C. (1995) 'What opportunities are open to fathers?', in P. Moss (ed.), *Father Figures: Fathers in the Families of the 1990s,* London, HMSO

Lewis, J. (1991) *The Ideological Octopus: An Exploration of Television and its Audience*, London, Routledge

Lister, R. (1998) *Citizenship. Feminist Perspectives*, London, Macmillan

Livingstone, S. (1991) 'Audience reception: the role of the viewer in retelling romantic drama', in J. Curran and M. Gurevitch (eds), *Mass Media and Society*, London, Edward Arnold

Locker, D. (1983) *Disability and Disadvantage,* London, Tavistock

Lockwood, D. (1956) 'Some remarks on "the social system"', *British Journal of Sociology,* 7(2): 134–46

Lockwood, D. (1958/1989) *The Black Coated Worker,* London, Allen & Unwin, Oxford, Oxford University Press

Lockwood, D. (1988) 'The weakest link in the chain', in D. Rose (ed.), *Social Stratification and Economic Change,* London, Unwin Hyman

Lukes, S. (1973) *Emile Durkheim: His Life and Work,* London, Penguin

Lukes, S. (1974) *Power: A Radical View,* London, Macmillan

Lukes, S. (ed.) (1986) *Power,* Oxford, Blackwell

Lull, J.(1995) *Media, Communication, Culture: A Global Approach*, Cambridge, Polity

Lupton, D. (1994) *Medicine as Culture,* London, Sage

Lyotard, J. (1984) *The Postmodern Condition,* Minneapolis, University of Minnesota Press

Mac an Ghaill, M. (1988) *Young, Gifted and Black*, Milton Keynes, Open University Press

Mac an Ghaill, M. (1994) *The Making of Men: Masculinities, Sexualities and Schooling*, Buckingham, Open University Press

Mac an Ghaill, M. (1996) 'Sociology of education, state schooling and social class: beyond critiques of the new right hegemony', *British Journal of Sociology of Education*, 17(2): 163–76

McCarthy, T. (1992), 'The critique of impure reason: Foucault and the Frankfurt School', in T. Wartenberg (ed.), *Rethinking Power*, pp. 121–48, Albany, State University of New York Press

McCruddon, C., Smith, D. and Brown, C. (1991) *Racial Justice at Work,* London, Policy Studies Institute

MacDonald, R. (ed.) (1997) *Youth, the 'Underclass' and Social Exclusion,* London, Routledge

McGrew, T. (1992) 'A global society?', in S. Hall, *et al.* (eds) op. cit.: Chapter 2

McKeown, T. (1979) *The Role of Medicine,* Oxford, Blackwell

McLennan, G. (1992) 'The Enlightenment project re-visited', in S. Hall, D. Held and T. McGrew (eds), *Modernity and Its Futures,* Cambridge, Polity

Mcleod, J., Kosicki, G. and Pan, Z. (1991) 'On understanding and misunderstanding media effects', in J. Curran and M. Gurevitch (eds), *Mass Media and Society*, London, Edward Arnold

McLuhan, M. (1964) *Understanding Media*, London, Routledge & Kegan Paul

McMichael, P. (1996) *Development and Social Change: A Global Perspective*, Thousand Oaks, Pine Forge Press

McNair, B. (1994) *News and Journalism in the UK*, London, Routledge

McNamara, D. (1980) 'The outsider's arrogance: the failure of participant observation to understand classroom events', *British Education Research Journal*, 6: 113–25

McRobbie, A. (1982) 'Jackie: an ideology of adolescent femininity', in B. Waites, T. Bennet and G. Martin (eds), *Popular Culture: Past and Present*, London, Croom Helm

McRobbie, A. (1991) *Feminism and Youth Culture*, Basingstoke, Macmillan

McRobbie, A. (1994) *Postmodernism and Popular Culture*, London, Routledge

McRobbie, A. and Garber, J. (1976) 'Girls and subcultures: an exploration', in S. Hall and T. Jefferson (eds), *Resistance Through Rituals*, London, Hutchinson

Malseed, J. (1987) 'Straw-men: a note on Ann Oakley's treatment of text-book prescriptions for interviewing', *Sociology*, 21: 99–108

Mama, A. (1992) 'Black women and the British state: race, class and gender analysis for the 1990s', in P. Braham, A. Rattansi and R. Skellington (eds), *Racism and Anti-Racism*, Buckingham, Open University Press

Mander, J. and Goldsmith, E. (eds) (1996) *The Case Against the Global Economy*, San Francisco, Sierra Club Books

Mann, M. (1986), *The Sources of Social Power. Vol. 1. A History of Power to A.D. 1760*, Cambridge, Cambridge University Press

Mann, M. (1993) *The Sources of Social Power. Vol. II. The Rise of Classes and Nation-States, 1760–1914*, Cambridge, Cambridge University Press

Mansfield, P. and Collard, J. (1988) *The Beginning of the Rest of Your Life: A Portrait of Newly-Wed Marriage*, London, Macmillan

Marcuse, H. (1972) *One Dimensional Man*, London, Abacus

Marmot, M., Rose, G., Shipley, M. and Hamilton, P. (1978) 'Employment grade and coronary heart disease in British civil servants', *Journal of Epidemiology and Community Health*, 32: 659–74

Marsh, C. (1986) 'Social class and occupation', in R. Burgess (ed.), *Key Variables in Social Investigation*, London, Routledge

Marshall, G. (1988a) 'Classes in Britain', *European Sociological Review*, 4: 141–54

Marshall, G. (1988b) 'Some remarks on the study of working-class consciousness', in D. Rose (ed.), *Social Stratification and Economic Change*, London, Unwin Hyman

Marshall, G., Newby, H., Rose, D. and Vogler, C. (1988) *Social Class in Modern Britain*, London, Hutchinson

Marshall, G., Roberts, R. and Burgoyne, C. (1996) 'Social class and underclass in Britain and the USA', *British Journal of Sociology*, 47(1): 22–67

Marshall, G., Swift, A. and Roberts, S. (1997) *Against the Odds?*, Oxford, Clarendon Press

Marshall, T. (1950) *Citizenship and Social Class*, Cambridge, Cambridge University Press

Martin, D. (1978) *A General Theory of Secularization*, Oxford, Blackwell

Martin, D. (1990) *Tongues of Fire*, Oxford, Blackwell

Martin, D. (1991) 'The secularization issue. Prospect and retrospect', *British Journal of Sociology*, 42(3): 465–74

Martin, D. (1996) 'Remise en question de la théorie de la sécularisation', in G. Davie and D. Hervieu-Léger, *Identités Religieuses en Europe*, Paris, La Découverte

Martin, J., Meltzer, H. and Elliott, D. (1988) *The Prevalence of Disability Among Adults*, London, HMSO

Marty, M. (1988) 'Fundamentals of Fundamentalism', in L. Kaplan (ed.), *Fundamentalism in a Comparative Perspective*, Amherst, University of Massachussetts Press

Marty, M. (1989) 'Fundamentalisms compared', *The Charles Strong Memorial Lecture 1989*, published for the Charles Strong Trust by the Australian Association for the Study of Religion

Marx, K. (1957/1970) *Capital*. Vol. 1, London, Lawrence & Wishart

Marx, K. (1962) 'The 18th Brumaire of Louis Bonaparte' in K. Marx and F. Engels *Selected Works*, Moscow, Foreign Languages Publishing House

Marx, K. (1971) *A Contribution to a Critique of Political Economy*, London, Lawrence & Wishart

Marx, K. and Engels, F. (1962a) *Manifesto of the Communist Party in Selected Works,* Vol. 1, Moscow, Foreign Languages Publishing House

Marx, K. and Engels, F. (1962b) *Selected Works*. Vol. 1, London, Lawrence & Wishart

Marx, K. and Engels, F. (1964) *The German Ideology,* London, Lawrence & Wishart

Matthews, R. and Young, J. (eds) (1986) *Confronting Crime*, London, Sage

Matza, D. (1964) *Delinquency and Drift,* New York, Wiley

Matza, D. (1969) *Becoming Deviant,* Englewood Cliffs, Prentice Hall

Matza, D. and Sykes, G. (1961) 'Juvenile delinquency and subterranean values', *American Sociological Review,* 26: 712–19

Maynard, M. (1990) 'The re-shaping of sociology? Trends in the study of gender', *Sociology*, 24(2): 269–90

Maynard, M. (1995) 'Beyond the "Big Three": the development of feminist theory into the 1990s', *Women's History Review,* 4(30): 259–82

Maynard, M. and Winn, J. (1997) 'Women, violence and male power', in D. Richardson and V. Robinson (eds), *Introducing Women's Studies*, 2nd edn, London, Macmillan

Mays, J. (1954) *Growing Up in the City,* Liverpool, Liverpool University Press

Mays, J. (1959) *On the Threshold of Delinquency,* Liverpool, Liverpool University Press

Mead, H. (1934) *Mind, Self and Society,* Chicago, University of Chicago Press

Meador, C. (1994) 'The last well person', *The New England Journal of Medicine,* 330: 440–1

Measor, L. and Woods, P. (1984) *Changing Schools: Pupil Perspectives on Transfer to a Comprehensive*, Milton Keynes, Open University Press

Menter, I., Muschamp, Y., Nicholls, P., Ozga, J. and Pollard, A. (1997) *Work and Identity in the Primary School: A Post-Fordist Analysis*, Buckingham, Open University Press

Merton, R. (1938/1993) 'Social structure and anomie', in C. Lemert (ed.), *Social Theory: The Multicultural Readings,* Boulder, Westview Press

Merton, R. (1968) *Social Theory and Social Structure,* New York, Free Press

Meyer, M. (1984) 'Measuring performance in economic organizations', in N. Smelser and R. Swedberg (eds), *The Handbook of Economic Sociology*, pp. 556–78, Princeton, NJ, Princeton University Press

Michie, J. and Smith, J. (eds) (1995) *Managing the Global Economy,* Oxford, Oxford University Press

Mies, M. (1998) *Patriarchy and Accumulation on a World Scale: Women in the International Division of Labour*, London, Zed Press

Mies, M. (1994) ' "Gender" and global capitalism', in L. Sklair (ed.) *Capitalism and Development*, Chapter 6, London, Routledge

Miles, R. (1982) *Racism and Migrant Labour: A Critical Text*, London, Routledge

Miles, R. (1987) *Capitalism and Unfree Labour: Anomaly or Necessity?,* London, Tavistock

Miles, R. (1989) *Racism*, London and New York, Routledge

Miles, R. (1993) *Racism After 'Race Relations'*, London, Routledge

Miles, R. and Phizacklea, A. (1984) *White Man's Country: Racism in British Politics,* London, Pluto Press

Miles, R. and Thranhardt, D. (eds) (1995) *Migration and European Integration: the Dynamics of Inclusion and Exclusion,* London, Pinter

Miles, R. and Torres, R. (1996) 'Does "race" matter? Transatlantic perspectives on racism after "race relations"', in V. Amit-Talai and C. Knowles (eds), *Re-Situating Identities: The Politics of Race, Ethnicity and Culture,* Peterborough, Broadview Press

Miles, S. and Middleton, S.(1988) 'Girls education in the balance', in M. Flude and M. Hammer (eds) *The Education Reform Act: Its Origins and Destinations,* London, Falmer Press

Millar, J. (1994) 'State, family and personal responsibility: the changing balance for lone mothers in the United Kingdom', *Feminist Review,* **48**: 24–39

Mills, C. (1959) *The Power Elite,* New York, Oxford University Press

Mitter, S. (1986) *Common Fate, Common Bond,* London, Pluto Press

Mitter, S. (1991) 'Computer-aided manufacturing and women's employment: a global critique of post-Fordism', in I. Eriksson, B. Kitchenham and K. Tijdens (eds), *Women, Work and Computerization,* Amsterdam, North Holland

Mlinar, Z. (ed.) (1992) *Globalization and Territorial Identities,* Aldershot, Avebury

Modood, T. (1992) *Not Easy Being British: Colour, Culture and Citizenship,* London, Runneymede Trust and Trentham Books

Modood, T. (1994) 'Ethno-religious minorities, secularism and the British state', *British Political Quarterly,* **65**: 53–73

Moore, B. (1966) *The Social Origins of Dictatorship and Democracy* London: Penguin

Moores, S. (1990) 'Texts, readers and contexts of reading: developments in the study of media audiences', *Media, Culture and Society,* **12**(1): 9–30

Morgan, D. (1996) *Family Connections: An Introduction to Family Studies,* Cambridge, Polity

Morgan, G. (1997) 'The global context of financial services: national systems and the international political economy', in G. Morgan and D. Knights, *Regulation and Deregulation in European Financial Services,* pp. 14–51, London, Macmillan

Morgan, G. and Engwall, L. (eds) (1999) *Regulation and Organizations,* London, Routledge

Morgan, G. and Knights, D. (eds) (1997) *Regulation and Deregulation in European Financial Services,* London, Macmillan

Morgan, G. and Quack, S. (1999) 'Confidence and confidentiality: the social construction of performance standards in German and British banking', in S. Quack, G. Morgan and R. Whitley (eds), *National Capitalisms, Global Competition and Economic Performance,* Berlin, De Gruyter

Morley, D. (1980) *The Nationwide Audience: Structure and Decoding,* London, British Film Institute

Morley, D. (1986) *Family Television,* London, Comedia/Routledge

Morley, D. (1993) 'Active audience theory: pendulums and pitfalls', *Journal of Communication,* **43**: 13–19

Morris, L. (1990) *The Workings of the Household,* Cambridge, Polity

Morris, L. (1995) *Social Divisions,* London, University College London Press

Morris, T. (1957) *The Criminal Area: A Study in Social Ecology,* London, Routledge & Kegan Paul

Morrow, V. (1994) 'Responsible children? Aspects of children's work and employment ourside school in contemporary UK', in B. Mayal (ed.), *Children's Childhoods: Observed and Experienced,* London, Falmer

Mortimore, P. and Whitty, G. (1997) 'Can school improvement overcome the effects of disadvantage?' Institute of Education

Mouzelis, N. (1991) *Back to Sociological Theory,* Basingstoke, Macmillan

Mouzelis, N. (1995) *Sociological Theory: What Went Wrong?*, London, Routledge

Mullins, P. (1991) 'The identification of social forces in development', *International Journal of Urban and Regional Research,* **15**(1): 119–26

Murray, C. (1990) *The Emerging British Underclass*, London, IEA Health and Welfare Unit

Myrdal, A. and Klein, V. (1956) *Women's Two Roles: Home and Work*, London, Routledge & Kegan Paul

Nash, J. and Fernandez-Kelly, M. (eds) (1983) *Women, Men, and the International Division of Labor*, Albany, NY: SUNY Press

National Commission on Education (eds) (1996) *Success Against the Odds*, London, Routledge

Navarro, V. (1975) 'The industrialisation of fetishism and the fetishism of industrialisation: a critique of Ivan Illich', *International Journal of Health Services,* **5**: 351–71

Navarro, V. (1978) *Class Struggle, the State and Medicine: An Historical and Contemporary Analysis of the Medical Sector in Great Britain*, London, Martin Robertson

Nazroo, J. (1995) 'Uncovering gender differences in the use of marital violence: the effects of methodology', *Sociology,* **29**(3): 475–94

Neale, B. and Smart, C. (1997) 'Experiments with parenthood?', *Sociology,* **31**(2): 201–20

Negrine, R. (1996) *The Communication of Politics*, London, Sage

Newburn, T. (1997) 'Youth, crime and justice', in R. Maguire, R. Morgan and R. Reiner (eds), *The Oxford Handbook of Criminology*, Oxford, Clarendon

Newman, O. (1972) *Defensible Space*, London, Architectural Press

Niebuhr, R. and Linder, R. (1988) *Civil Religion and the Presidency*, Grand Rapids, Zondervan

Nordenstreng, K. (1977) 'From mass media to mass consciousness', in G. Gerbner (ed.), *Mass Media Policies in Changing Cultures*, New York, Wiley

Nordenstreng, K. and Schiller, H. (eds) (1993) *Beyond National Sovereignty: International Communications in the 1990s*, Norwood, Ablex

Oakley, A. (1974) *The Sociology of Housework*, Oxford, Martin Robertson

Oakley, A. (1981) 'Interviewing women: a contradiction in terms', in H. Roberts (ed.), *Doing Feminist Research,* London, Routledge

Oakley, A. (1984) *The Sociology of Housework*, 2nd edn, Oxford, Blackwell

Oakley, A. (1984) *The Captured Womb: A History of the Medical Care of Pregnant Women*, Oxford, Blackwell

Offe, C. (1985) 'Work – a central sociological category?', in C. Offe (ed.), *Disorganized Capitalism*, Cambridge, Polity

Office for National Statistics (1997) *Social Trends,* **27**, London, The Stationery Office

Office of Population, Censuses and Surveys (1996) *Living in Britain: Results from the General Household Survey,* London, HMSO

Office of Science and Technology (1995) *Technology Foresight Panel 14: Progress through Partnership – Leisure and Learning*, London, HMSO

Oliver, M. (1996) *Understanding Disability: From Theory to Practice*, London, Macmillan

Orru, M., Biggart, N. and Hamilton, G. (1997) *The Economic Organisation of East Asian Capitalism*, London, Sage

Osborne, T. (1997) 'Medicine and the body', in D. Owen (ed.) *Sociology after Postmodernism*, London, Sage

Owen, D. (1994) 'Black people in Great Britain: social and economic circumstances', *National Ethnic Minority Data Archive*, Centre for Research in Ethnic Relations, 1

Pahl, J. (1989) *Money and Marriage,* London, Macmillan

Pahl, R. (1989) 'Is the Emperor naked?', *International Journal of Urban and Regional Research,* **13**(4): 711–20

Pahl, R. (ed.) (1988) *On Work: Historical, Comparative and Theoretical Approaches,* Oxford, Blackwell

Pakulski, J. (1993) 'The dying of class or of Marxist class theory?', *International Sociology,* **8**(3): 279–92

Panic, M. (1995) 'The Bretton Woods system: concept and practice', in J. Michie and J. Smith (eds), *Managing the Global Economy*, pp. 37–54, Oxford, Oxford University Press

Parker, A. (1996) 'The construction of masculinity within boys' physical education', *Gender and Education,* **8**(2): 141–57

Parker, H. (1974) *The View From The Boys,* Newton Abbott, David & Charles

Parry, O. (1996) 'Equality, gender and the Caribbean classroom', *21st Century Policy Review Special Issue: Institutional Development in the Caribbean*

Parsons, T. (1951) *The Social System,* New York, Free Press

Parsons, T. (1954) 'Social classes and class conflict in the light of recent sociological theory', in T. Parsons, (ed.), *Essays in Sociological Theory,* New York, Free Press

Parsons, T. (1961) 'The school class as a social system: some of its functions in American society', in A. Halsey, P. Broadfoot, P. Croll, M. Osborn and D. Abbott (eds) *Education, Economy, and Society*, pp. 434–55, London, Collier Macmillan

Parsons, T. (1967) *Sociological Theory and Modern Society,* New York, Free Press

Parsons, T. (1969a) 'The distribution of power in American society', in T. Parsons (ed.), *Politics and Social Structure*, pp. 185–203, New York, The Free Press

Parsons, T. (1969b) 'On the concept of political power', in T. Parsons (ed.), *Politics and Social Structure*, pp. 352–404, New York, The Free Press

Parsons, T. (1971) *The System of Modern Societies,* New York, Prentice Hall

Parsons, T. (1978) 'The sick role and the role of the physician reconsidered', in T. Parsons (ed.), *Action Theory and the Human Condition,* New York, Free Press

Parsons, T. and Bales, R. (1956) *Family: Socialization and Interaction Process,* London, Routledge & Kegan Paul

Parsons, T. and Shils, E. (1962) *Towards a General Theory of Action,* New York, Harper & Row

Pawson, R. (1993) 'Social mobility', in D. Morgan and L. Stanley (eds), *Debates in Sociology*, Manchester, Manchester University Press

Pawson, R. (1996) 'Theorizing the interview', *British Journal of Sociology*, **47**: 295–314

Pawson, R. and Tilley, N. (1996) *Realistic Evaluation,* London, Sage

Peach, C. (1968) 'West Indian migration to Britain: the economic factor', *Race,* **7**(1): 31–47

Pearson, G. (1983) *Hooligan: A History of Respectable Fears,* Basingstoke, Macmillan

Perlmutter, H. (1991) 'On the rocky road to the first gloabl civilization', *Human Relations*, **44**(9): 897–1010

Phillipson, C. (1982) *Capitalism and the Construction of Old Age,* London, Methuin

Phizacklea, A. and Wolkowitz, C. (1995) *Homeworking Women*, London, Sage

Phoenix, A. (1990) *Young Mothers?,* Cambridge, Polity

Piérard, R. and Linder, R. (1988) *Civil Religion and the Presidency*, Grand Rapids, Zondervan

Pilgrim, A. and Rogers, A. (1993) *A Sociology of Mental Health and Illness,* Buckingham, Open University Press

Piore, M. and Sabel, C. (1984) *The Second Industrial Divide,* New York, Basic Books

Platt, A. (1978) 'Street crime: a view from the left', *Crime and Social Justice,* **9**

Pollard, A., Broadfoot, P., Croll, P., Osborn, M. and Abbott, D. (1994) *Changing English Primary Schools,* London, Cassell

Pollert, A. (1981) *Girls, Wives, Factory Lives,* London, Macmillan

Polsby, N. (1963) *Community Power and Political Theory*, New Haven and London, Yale University Press

Polsby, N. (1980) *Community Power and Political Theory: A Further Look at Problems of Evidence and Inference*, New Haven and London, Yale University Press

Portes, A. and Castells, M. (eds) (1989) *The Informal Sector*, Baltimore, Johns Hopkins University Press

Poster, M. (1990) *The Mode of Information: Poststructuralism and Social Context*, Chicago, University of Chicago Press

Poulantzas, N. (1975) *Classes in Contemporary Capitalism*, London, New Left Books

Prior, L. (1998) 'The identification of cases in psychiatry', in D. Field and S. Taylor, *Sociological Perspectives on Health, Illness and Health Care*, Oxford, Blackwell Science

Qualifications and Curriculum Authority (1998) *Maintaining Breadth and Balance at Key Stages 1 and 2*, London, QCA

Quack, S., Morgan G. and Whitley, R. (eds) (1999) *National Capitalisms, Global Competition and Economic Performance*, Berlin, De Gruyter

Rabinow, P. (1989) *French Modern: Norms and Forms of the Social Environment*, Cambridge, MA, MIT Press

Radway, J. (1984) *Reading the Romance: Women, Patriarchy and Popular Literature*, Chapel Hill, University of North Carolina Press

Rahman, M. and Jackson, S. (1997) 'Liberty, equality and sexuality: essentialism and the discourse of rights', *Journal of Gender Studies*, **6**(2): 117–29

Rakow, L. (ed.) (1992) *Women Making Meaning: New Feminist Directions In Communication*, London, Routledge

Ramazanoglu, C. (1989) *Feminism and the Contradictions of Oppression*, London, Routledge

Ramazanoglu, C. (1995) 'Back to basics: heterosexuality, biology and why men stay on top', in M. Maynard and J. Purvis (eds), *(Hetero)sexual Politics*, London, Taylor & Francis

Randall, G. (1987) 'Gender differences in pupil–teacher interaction in workshops and laboratories', in G. Weiner and M. Arnot (eds) *Gender and the Politics of Schooling*, London, Hutchinson

Randall, V. and Waylen, G. (eds) (1998) *Gender, Politics and the State*, London, Routledge

Rattansi, A. (1982) *Marx and the Division of Labour*, London, Macmillan

Rattansi, A. and Westwood, S. (eds) (1994) *Racism, Modernity and Identity on the Western Front*, Cambridge, Polity

Ray, L. (1993) *Rethinking Critical Theory: Emancipation in the Age of Global Social Movements*, London, Sage

Redclift, M. and Benton, T. (eds) (1994) *Social Theory and the Global Environment*, London, Routledge

Rees, T. (1992) *Women and the Labour Market*, London, Routledge

Rees, T. (1998) *Mainstreaming Equality in the European Union*, London, Routledge

Rex, J. (1970) *Race Relations in Sociological Theory*, London, Weidenfeld & Nicolson

Rich, A. (1980) 'Compulsory heterosexuality and lesbian existence', *Signs*, **5**(4), 631–60

Richardson, D. (1993) *Women, Motherhood and Childrearing*, Basingstoke, Macmillan

Richardson, D. (ed.) (1996) *Theorising Heterosexuality: Telling it Straight*, Buckingham, Open University Press

Richardson, J. (1995) 'Minority religions, religious freedom and the new Pan-European political and judicial institutions', *Journal of Church and State*, **37**(1): 40–59

Riddell, S. (1992) *Gender and the Politics of the Curriculum*, London, Routledge

Riley, K. (1994) *Quality and Equality: Promoting Opportunities in Schools*, London, Cassell

Ritzer, G. (1995) *The McDonaldization of Society*, 2nd edn, Thousand Oaks, Pine Forge Press

Robbins, D. (1987) 'Sport, hegemony and the middle class', *Theory, Culture and Society,* **4**(4): 579–602

Robertson Elliot, F. (1996) *Gender, Family and Society,* London, Macmillan

Robertson, R. (1992) *Globalization: Social Theory and Global Culture*, London, Sage

Robinson, I. (1988) 'Reconstructing lives: negotiating the meaning of multiple sclerosis', in M. Bury and R. Anderson (eds), *Living with Chronic Illness: The Experiences of Patients and Their Families,* London, Unwin Hyman

Robinson, W. (1996) 'Globalisation: nine theses on our epoch', *Race and Class* **38**(2): 13–31

Robinson, W. (1998) '(Mal)development in Central America: globalization and social change' *Development and Change,* **29**: 467–97

Rock, P. (1979) 'The sociology of crime, symbolic interactionism and some problematic qualities of radical criminology', in D. Downes and P. Rock (eds), *Deviant Interpretations,* Oxford, Martin Robertson

Rock, P. (1990) *Helping Victims of Crime,* Oxford, Clarendon Press

Roediger, D. (1996) *Towards the Abolition of Whiteness,* London, Verso

Roethliberger, F. and Dickson, W. (1939) *Management and the Worker,* Cambridge, Harvard University Press

Rose, N. (1990) *Governing the Soul: the Shaping of the Private Self,* London, Routledge

Rose, N. (1995) 'Towards a critical sociology of freedom', in P. Joyce (ed.), *Class,* pp. 213–24, Oxford, Oxford University Press

Rose, N. (1996) 'Governing "advanced" liberal democracies', in A. Barry, T. Osborne and N. Rose (eds), *Foucault and Political Reason. Liberalism, Neo-liberalism and Rationalities of Government*, pp. 37–64, Chicago, University of Chicago Press

Rose, N. and Miller, P. (1992) 'Political power beyond the State: problematics of government', *British Journal of Sociology,* **43**(2): 173–205

Ross, R. and Trachte, K. (1990) *Global Capitalism: The New Leviathan*, Albany, NY, State University of New York Press

Ruigrok, W. and Van Tulder, R. (1995) *The Logic of International Restructuring,* London, Routledge

Russell, D. (1982) *Rape in Marriage,* New York, Macmillan

Russell, D. (1984) *Sexual Exploitation,* Newbury Park, Sage

Sabel, C. and Zeitlin, J. (1997) *Worlds of Possibility: Flexibility and Mass Production in Western Industrialization,* Cambridge, Cambridge University Press

Sainsbury, D. (ed.) (1994) *Gendering Welfare States,* London, Sage

Sako, M. and Sato, H. (eds) (1997) *Japanese Labour and Management in Transition,* London, Routledge

Sarup, M. (1993) *An Introductory Guide to Post-Structuralism and Postmodernism,* London, Harvester/Wheatsheaf

Sassen, S. (1994) *Cities in a World Economy*, Thousand Oaks, CA, Pine Forge Press

Saunders, P. (1987) *Social Theory and the Urban Question,* London, Unwin Hyman

Savage, M. (1996) 'Class analysis and social research', in T. Butler and M. Savage (eds), *Social Change and the Middle Classes,* London, UCL Press

Savage, M., Barlow, J., Dickens, A. and Fielding, T. (1992) *Property, Bureaucracy, and Culture,* London, Routledge

Scambler, G. and Hopkins, A. (1986) 'Being epileptic: coming to terms with illness', *Sociology of Health and Illness,* **8**: 26–43

Scambler, G., Scambler, A. and Craig, D. (1984) 'Kinship and friendship networks and women's demand for primary care', *Journal of the Royal College of General Practitioners,* **26**: 746–50

Scheff, T. (1966) *Being Mentally Ill: A Sociological Theory,* Chicago, Aldine

Schiller, H. (1989) *Culture Inc.: The Corporate Takeover of Public Expression*, London, Oxford University Press

Schiller, H. (1991) 'Not yet the post-imperialist era', *Critical Studies in Mass Communication*, **8**: 13–28

Schlesinger, P. (1990) 'Rethinking the sociology of journalism: source strategies and the limits of media centrism', in M. Ferguson (ed.), *Public Communication: The New Imperatives – Future Directions for Media Research*, pp. 84–100, London, Sage

Schutz, A. (1972) *Phenomenology of the Social World*, London, Heinemann

Schutz, A. and Luckmann, T. (1974) *The Structures of the Life World,* London, Heinemann

Scott, A. (ed.) (1997) *The Limits of Globalization*, London, Routledge

Scott, J. (1982) *The Upper Classes,* Cambridge, Polity

Scott, J. (1991) *Who Rules Britain?,* Cambridge, Polity

Scott, J. (1995) *Sociological Theory: Contemporary Debates,* London, Edward Elgar

Scott, J. (1997) *Corporate Business and Capitalist Classes,* Oxford, Oxford University Press

Scott, J. and Morris, L. (1996) 'The attenuation of class analysis', *British Journal of Sociology,* **7**(2): 134–46

Scott, R. (1969) *The Making of Blind Men,* Hartford, Russell Sage

Scott, S., Jackson, S. and Backett-Milburn, K. (1998) 'Swings and roundabouts: risk, anxiety and the everyday worlds of children', *Sociology,* **32**(4)

Scull, A. (1993) *The Most Solitary of Afflictions: Madness and Society in Britain, 1700–1900,* New Haven, Yale University Press

Seale, C. (1994) 'Medicalisation and surveillance', in C. Seale and S. Pattinson (eds), *Medical Knowledge: Doubt and Certainty,* Buckingham, Open University Press

Secretary of State for Health and Social Services (1992) *The Health of The Nation: A Strategy for Health in England,* London, HMSO

Sevenhuijsen, S. (1998) *Citizenship and the Ethics of Care,* London, Routledge

Sewell, T. (1997) *Black Masculinities and Schooling: How Black Boys Survive Modern Schooling,* Stoke-on-Trent, Trentham Books

Shannon, T. (1989) *An Introduction to the World-System Perspective*, Boulder, Westview

Sharpe, S. (1994) *'Just Like a Girl'. How Girls Learn to be Women: From the Seventies to the Nineties,* London, Penguin

Siltanen, J. (1994) *Locating Gender: Occupational Segregation, Wages and Domestic Responsibilities*, London, UCL Press

Silverman, D. (1985) *Qualitative Method and Sociology*, Aldershot, Gower

Sivanandan, A. (1990) *Communities of Resistance. Writings on Black Struggles for Socialism*, London and New York, Verso

Skelton, C. (1997) 'Women and education', in D. Richardson and V. Robinson (eds), *Introducing Women's Studies*, 2nd edn, London, Macmillan

Sklair, L. (1991) *Sociology of the Global System*, London, Harvester/Wheatsheaf

Sklair, L. (1994a) 'Global sociology and global environmental change', in M. Redclift and T. Benton, op. cit., Chapter 10

Sklair, L. (ed.) (1994b) *Capitalism and Development*, London, Routledge

Sklair, L. (1995) *Sociology of the Global System*, 2nd edn, Prentice Hall and Baltimore, Johns Hopkins University Press

Sleegers, P. and Wesselingh, A. (1993) 'Decentralisation in education: a Dutch study', *International Studies in Sociology of Education*, **3**(1): 49–67

Small, S. (1994) *Racialised Barriers: The Black Experience in the United States and England,* New York and London, Routledge

Smart, C. (1976) *Women, Crime and Criminology: A Feminist Critique,* London, Routledge & Kegan Paul

Smart, C. (1989a) 'Power and the politics of child custody', in C. Smart and S. Sevenhuijsen, *Child Custody and the Politics of Gender*, London, Routledge

Smart, C. (1989b) *Feminism and the Power of the Law,* London, Routledge

Smelser, N. and Swedberg, R. (eds) (1994) *The Handbook of Economic Sociology*, Princeton, NJ, Princeton University Press

Smith, C. (1990) *Auctions: The Social Construction of Value*, Berkeley, University of California Press

Smith, C. and Meiskins, P. (1995) 'System, society and dominance effects in cross-national organizational analysis', *Work, Employment and Society*, 9(2): 241–67

Smith, D. and Gray, J. (1987) *Police and People in London*, Aldershot, Gower

Smith, J. (1995) 'The first intruder: fatherhood, a historical perspective', in P. Moss (ed.), *Father Figures: Fathers in the Families of the 1990s*, London, HMSO

Solomos, J. and Back, L. (1995) *Race, Politics and Social Change*, London and New York, Routledge

Song, M. (1996) '"Helping out": children's participation in Chinese take-away businesses in Britain', in J. Brannen and M. O'Brien (eds), *Children in Families*, London, Falmer

Spender, D. (1983) *Invisible Women: the Schooling Scandle*, London, Women's Press

Spender, D. (1995) *Nattering on the Net: Women, Power and Cyberspace*, Melbourne, Spinifex

Spybey, T. (1996) *Globalization and World Society*, Cambridge, Polity

Sreberny-Mohammadi, A. (1991) 'The global and the local in international communications', in J. Curran and M. Gurevitch (eds), *Mass Media and Society*, London, Edward Arnold

Stacey, M. (ed.) (1992) *Changing Human Reproduction*, London, Sage

Stallings, B. (ed.) (1995) *Global Change, Regional Response*, Cambridge, Cambridge University Press

Stanley, L. and Wise, S. (1990) 'Method, methodology and epistemology in feminist research', in L. Stanley (ed.), *Feminist Praxis*, London, Routledge

Stanworth, M. (1983) *Gender and Schooling*, London, Hutchinson

Stanworth, M. (1984) 'Women and class analysis', *Sociology*, 18(2): 159–70

Star, S. (1996) 'From Hestia to home page: feminism and the concept of home in cyberspace', in N. Lykke and R. Braidotti (eds), *Between Monsters, Goddesses and Cyborgs: Feminist Confrontations With Science, Medicine and Cyberspace*, London, Zed

Steggarda (1993) 'Religion and the social positions of women and men', *Social Compass*, 40(1): 65–73

Stobart, G., Elwood J. and Quinlan M. (1992) 'Gender bias in exams: how equal are the opportunities?', *British Education Research Journal*, 18( 3): 261–76

Storey, J. (1993) *An Introductory Guide to Cultural Theory and Popular Culture*, London, Wheatsheaf

Storey, J., Edwards, P. and Sisson, K. (1997) *Managers in the Making: Careers, Development and Control in Corporate Britain and Japan*, London, Sage

Strange, S. (1986) *Casino Capitalism*, Oxford, Blackwell

Strange, S. (1995) 'From Bretton Woods to the Casino Economy', in S. Corbridge, N. Thrift and R. Martin (eds), *Money, Space, Power*, pp. 49–62, Oxford, Blackwell

Strathern, M. (1992) *Reproducing the Future: Anthropology, Kinship and the New Reproductive Technologies*, Manchester, Manchester University Press

Straubhaar, J. (1997) 'Distinguishing the global, regional and national levels of world television', in A. Sreberny-Mohammadi, D. Winseck, J. McKenna and O. Boyd-Barrett (eds), *Media in Global Context: A Reader*, London, Arnold

Streeck, W. (1992) *Social Institutions and Economic Performance*, London, Sage

Strinati, D. (1995) *An Introduction to Theories of Popular Culture*, London, Routledge

Stubbs, R. and Underhill, G. (eds) (1994) *Political Economy and the Changing Global Order*, London, Macmillan

Sudbury, J. (1997) Other Kinds of Dreams: Black Women's Organisations and the Politics of Transformation. Unpublished PhD in Sociology, University of Warwick

Sullivan, O. (1997) 'Time waits for no (wo)man: an investigation into the gendered experience of domestic time', *Sociology*, **31**(2): 221–40

Sumner, C. (1994) *The Sociology of Deviance: An Obituary*, Buckingham, Open University Press

Sussman, G. and Lent, J. (eds) (1991) *Transnational Communications: Wiring the Third World*, London, Sage

Swatos, W. (ed.) (1993) *A Future for Religion*, London, Sage

Swedberg, R. (1994) 'Markets as social structures', in N. Smelser and R. Swedberg (eds), *The Handbook of Economic Sociology*, pp. 255–82, Princeton, NJ, Princeton University Press

Sykes, G. and Matza, D. (1957) 'Techniques of neutralisation: a theory of delinquency', *American Sociological Review*, **22**: 664–70

Sztompka, P. (1994) *The Sociology of Social Change*, Oxford, Blackwell

Taylor, C. (1986) 'Foucault on freedom and truth', in D. Hoy (ed.), *Foucault: a Critical Reader*, pp. 69–102, Oxford, Blackwell

Taylor, I., Walton P. and Young, J. (1973) *The New Criminology: For a Social Theory of Deviance*, London, Routledge & Kegan Paul

Thomas, W. (1976) 'The definition of the situation', in L. Coser and B. Rosenberg, *Sociological Theory*, 4th edn, New York, Macmillan

Thompson, E. (1968) *The Making of the English Working Class*, London, Penguin

Thompson, J. (1990) *Ideology and Modern Culture*, Cambridge, Polity

Thorne, B. (1987) 'Revisioning women and social change: where are the children?' *Gender and Society*, **1**(1): 85–109

Thorogood, N. (1987) 'Race, class and gender: the politics of housework', in J. Brannen and G. Wilson (eds), *Give and Take in Families: Studies in Resource Distribution*, London, Allen & Unwin

Tinker, I. (ed.) (1990) *Persistent Inequalities: Women and World Development*, New York, Oxford University Press

Torrance, H. (1997) 'Assessment, accountability and standards: using assessment to control the reform of schooling', in A. Halsey, H. Lauder, P. Brown. and A. Stuart-Wells (eds) *Education: Culture, Economy, Society*, pp. 320–31, Oxford, Oxford University Press

Touraine, A. (1981) *The Voice and the Eye: An Analysis of Social Movements*, Cambridge, Cambridge University Press

Townsend, P., Davidson, N. and Whitehead, M. (1988) *Inequalities in Health: The Black Report/The Health Divide*, London, Penguin

Townsend, P., Phillimore, P. and Beattie, A. (1988) *Health and Deprivation: Inequality and the North*, London, Croom Helm

Troyna, B. (1993) *Racism and Education*, Buckingham, Open University Press

Troyna, B. and Hatcher, R. (1992) *Racism in Children's Lives: A Study of Mainly-white Primary Schools*, London, Routledge

Tuchman, G., Kaplan Daniels, A. and Benet, J. (1978) *Hearth and Home: Images of Women and the Media*, Oxford, Oxford University Press

Tuckett, D., Boulton, M., Olson, C. and Williams, A. (1985) *Meetings Between Experts*, London, Tavistock

Tudor, A. (1995) 'Culture, mass communication and social agency', *Theory, Culture and Society*, **12**: 81–107

Tunstall, J. (1971) *Journalists at Work*, London, Constable

Turner, B. (1995) *Medical Power and Social Knowledge*, 2nd edn, London, Sage

Underhill, G. (ed.) (1997) *The New World Order in International Finance,* London, Macmillan

UNESCO (1989) *World Communication Report*, Paris, UNESCO

Ungerson, C. and Kember, M. (eds) (1997) *Women and Social Policy*, 2nd edn, London, Macmillan

United Nations (1993) *World Investment Report*, New York, UNCTAD

United Nations Development Programme (1993) *Human Development Report 1993*, Oxford, Oxford University Press

Urry, J. (1996) 'A middle-class countryside?', in T. Butler and M. Savage (eds), *Social Change and the Middle Classes*, London, University College London Press

Usher, R. and Edwards, R. (1994) *Postmodernism and Education*, London, Routledge

Van der Wee, H. (1991) *Prosperity and Upheaval in the World Economy 1945–1980*, London, Penguin

Van Every, J. (1995) *Heterosexual Women Changing the Family: Refusing to be a 'Wife'!*, London, Taylor & Francis

van Zoonen, L. (1994) *Feminist Media Studies*, London, Sage

van Zoonen L. (1996) 'Feminist perspectives on the media', in J. Curran and M. Gurevitch (eds), *Mass Media and Society*, London, Arnold

Wade, R. (1990) *Governing the Market*, Princeton, NJ, Princeton University Press

Walby, S. (1986) *Patriarchy at Work*, Cambridge, Polity

Walby, S. (1990) *Theorizing Patriarchy*, Oxford, Blackwell

Walby, S. (1997) *Gendered Transformations*, London, Routledge

Wallerstein, I. (1979) *The Capitalist World-Economy*, Cambridge, Cambridge University Press

Wallerstein, I. (1991) 'The construction of peoplehood: racism, nationalism, ethnicity', in E. Balibar and I. Wallerstein (eds) *'Race', Nation, Class*, London, Verso

Wallis, R. and Bruce, S. (1989) 'Religion: the British contribution', *British Journal of Sociology*, **40**(3): 439–519

Walter, A. (1990) *Funerals and How to Improve Them*, London, Hodder & Stoughton

Walter, A. (1994) *The Revival of Death*, London, Routledge

Walter, A. (1996) *The Eclipse of Eternity*, London, Macmillan

Walter, A. and Davie, G. (1998) 'The religiosity of women in the modern West', *British Journal of Sociology*, **49**(4): 640–60

Walton, A. (1994) *The Revival of Death*, London, Routledge

Walton, A. (1995) *The Eclipse of Eternity*, London, Macmillan

Wartenberg, T.E. (1990) *The Forms of Power: From Domination to Transformation*, Philadelphia, Temple University Press

Waters, M. (1995) *Globalization*, London, Routledge

Watson, J. (ed.) (1977) *Between Two Cultures*, Oxford, Basil Blackwell

Weber, M. (1922/1963) *The Sociology of Religion*, London, Beacon Press

Weber, M. (1948a) 'Class, status and party', in H. Gerth and C. Mills (eds), *From Max Weber: Essays in Sociology*, London, Routledge & Kegan Paul

Weber, M. (1948b) 'The social psychology of the world religions', in H. Gerth and C. Wright Mills, *Essays from Max Weber*, London, Routledge & Kegan Paul

Weber, M. (1948c) *From Max Weber*, in C. Mills (ed.), London, Routledge

Weber, M. (1976) *The Protestant Ethic and the Spirit of Capitalism*, (Talcott Parsons tr.), London, Allen & Unwin

Weber, M. (1978) *Economy and Society. An Outline of Interpretive Sociology*, Berkeley, University of California Press

Weiner, G. (1994) *Feminism in Education: An Introduction*, Buckingham, Open University Press

Weiner, G. *et al.* (1997) 'Is the future female? Success, male disadvantage, and changing gender patterns in education', in A. Halsey, H. Lauder, P. Brown and A. Stuart-Wells (eds) *Education: Culture, Economy, Society*, pp. 620–30, Oxford, Oxford University Press

Weiss, L. (1998) *The Myth of the Powerless State,* Oxford, Polity

Weiss, L. and Hobson, J. (1995) *States and Economic Development,* Oxford, Polity

Westergaard, J. (1995) *Who Gets What? The Hardening of Class Inequality in the Late Twentieth Century,* Cambridge, Polity

Weston, K. (1991) *Families We Choose: Lesbians, Gays, Kinship*, New York, Columbia University Press

Westwood, S. (1984) *All Day Every Day: Factory and Family in Women's Lives,* London, Pluto Press

Westwood, S. and Bhachu, P. (eds) (1988) *Enterprising Women: Ethnicity, Economy and Gender Relations*, London, Routledge

Whelan, C. (1993) 'The role of social support in mediating the psychological consequences of economic stress', *Sociology of Health and Illness,* 15: 86–101

Whitley, R. (1992) *East Asian Business Systems,* London, Sage

Whitley, R. and Kristensen, P. (eds) (1996) *The Changing European Firm,* London, Routledge

Whitley, R. and Kristensen, P. (eds) (1997) *Governance at Work,* Oxford, Oxford University Press

Whitty, G. (1997a) 'Marketisation, the state, and the re-formation of the teaching profession', in A. Halsey, H. Lauder, P. Brown and A. Stuart-Wells (eds) *Education: Culture, Economy, Society*, pp. 299–310, Oxford, Oxford University Press

Whitty, G. (1997b) 'Education policy and the sociology of education', *International Studies in Sociology of Education*, 7(2): 121–35

Willaime, J.-P. (1995) *Sociologie des Religions,* Paris, Presses Universitaires de France

Williams, G. (1984) 'The genesis of chronic illness: narrative reconstruction', *Sociology of Health and Illness* 6: 175–200

Williams, D. and House, J. (1991) 'Stress, social support, control and coping: an epidemiological view', in B. Badura and I. Kickbusch, *Health Promotion Research,* Copenhagen, World Health Organisation

Williams, G., Fitzpatrick, R., MacGregor, A. and Rigby, A. (1996) 'Rheumatoid arthritis', in B. Dave and C. Seale (eds), *Experiencing and Explaining Disease,* Buckingham, Open University Press

Williams, S. (1993) *Chronic Respiratory Disorder,* London, Routledge

Williams, S. and Calnan, M. (1996) 'The "limits" of demedicalisation: modern medicine and the lay populace in "late" modernity', *Social Science and Medicine*, 42: 1609–20

Willis, P. (1977) *Learning to Labour,* London, Sage

Wilson, B. (1982) *Religion in Sociological Perspective*, Oxford, Oxford University Press

Wilson, H. (1980) 'Parental supervision: a neglected aspect of delinquency', *British Journal of Criminology,* 20: 203–35

Wilson, H. and Herbert, G. (1978) *Parents, Children and the Inner City,* London, Routledge & Kegan Paul

Wilson, J. (1975) *Thinking About Crime,* New York, Vintage

Wilson, J. (1987) *The Truly Disadvantaged,* Chicago, University of Chicago Press

Wilson, J. (1993) *The Ghetto Underclass*, London, Sage

Wilson, J. and Kelling, G. (1982) 'Broken windows', *The Atlantic Monthly,* March, 29–38

Wilson, W. (1996) *When Work Disappears,* New York, Knopf

Witz, A. (1997) 'Women at work', in D. Richardson and V. Robinson (eds), *Introducing Women's Studies*, 2nd edn, London, Macmillan

Wolffe, J. (1993) 'The religions of the silent majority', in G. Parsons (ed.), *The Growth of Religious Diversity*, Vol. 1, *Traditions*, London, Routledge

World Bank (1996) *World Development Report*, Oxford, Oxford University Press

World Resources Institute (1994) *World Resources 1992–93: A Guide to the Global Environment*, New York, Oxford University Press

Wright, C. (1986) 'School processes: an ethnographic study', in J. Eggleston, D. Dunn and M. Anjali (eds) *Education for Some*, Stoke-on-Trent, Trentham Books

Wright, C. (1992) 'Early education: multi-racial primary school classrooms', in D. Gill, B. Mayor and M. Blair (eds) *Racism and Education*, London, Sage

Wright, E. (1976) 'Class boundaries in advanced capitalist societies', *New Left Review*, **98**

Wright, E. (1980) 'Class and occupation', *Theory and Society*, 9(1): 177–214

Wright, E. (1985) *Classes*, London, Verso

Wright, E. (ed.) (1989) *The Debate on Classes*, London, Verso

Wright, E. (1997) *Class Counts*, Cambridge, Cambridge University Press

Wrong, D. (1988) *Power: Its Forms, Bases and Uses*, 2nd edn, Chicago, University of Chicago Press

Yearley, S. (1996) *Sociology, Environmentalism, Globalization: Reinventing the Globe*, London, Sage

Young, M. and Wilmott, P. (1962) *Family and Kinship in East London*, Harmondsworth, Penguin

Young, M. (ed.) (1971) *Knowledge and Control*, London, Collier Macmillan

Young, M. and Wilmott, P. (1973) *The Symmetrical Family*, Harmondsworth, Penguin

Zaretsky, E. (1976) *Capitalism, The Family and Personal Life*, London, Pluto Press

Zelizer, V. (1994) *The Social Meaning of Money*, New York, Basic Books

# Index